T0189558

Lecture Notes in Computer Science 12253

More information about this series at http://www.springer.com/series/7407

Osvaldo Gervasi · Beniamino Murgante ·
Sanjay Misra · Chiara Garau ·
Ivan Blečić · David Taniar ·
Bernady O. Apduhan · Ana Maria A. C. Rocha ·
Eufemia Tarantino · Carmelo Maria Torre ·
Yeliz Karaca (Eds.)

Computational Science and Its Applications – ICCSA 2020

20th International Conference
Cagliari, Italy, July 1–4, 2020
Proceedings, Part V

Editors
Osvaldo Gervasi
University of Perugia
Perugia, Italy

Sanjay Misra
Chair- Center of ICT/ICE
Covenant University
Ota, Nigeria

Ivan Blečić
University of Cagliari
Cagliari, Italy

Bernady O. Apduhan
Department of Information Science
Kyushu Sangyo University
Fukuoka, Japan

Eufemia Tarantino
Polytechnic University of Bari
Bari, Italy

Yeliz Karaca
Department of Neurology
University of Massachusetts
Medical School
Worcester, MA, USA

Beniamino Murgante
University of Basilicata
Potenza, Potenza, Italy

Chiara Garau
University of Cagliari
Cagliari, Italy

David Taniar
Clayton School of Information Technology
Monash University
Clayton, VIC, Australia

Ana Maria A. C. Rocha
University of Minho
Braga, Portugal

Carmelo Maria Torre
Polytechnic University of Bari
Bari, Italy

ISSN 0302-9743 ISSN 1611-3349 (electronic)
Lecture Notes in Computer Science
ISBN 978-3-030-58813-7 ISBN 978-3-030-58814-4 (eBook)
https://doi.org/10.1007/978-3-030-58814-4

LNCS Sublibrary: SL1 – Theoretical Computer Science and General Issues

This Springer imprint is published by the registered company Springer Nature Switzerland AG
The registered company address is: Gewerbestrasse 11, 6330 Cham, Switzerland

Preface

These seven volumes (LNCS volumes 12249–12255) consist of the peer-reviewed papers from the International Conference on Computational Science and Its Applications (ICCSA 2020) which took place from July 1–4, 2020. Initially the conference was planned to be held in Cagliari, Italy, in collaboration with the University of Cagliari, but due to the COVID-19 pandemic it was organized as an online event.

ICCSA 2020 was a successful event in the conference series, previously held in Saint Petersburg, Russia (2019), Melbourne, Australia (2018), Trieste, Italy (2017), Beijing, China (2016), Banff, Canada (2015), Guimaraes, Portugal (2014), Ho Chi Minh City, Vietnam (2013), Salvador, Brazil (2012), Santander, Spain (2011), Fukuoka, Japan (2010), Suwon, South Korea (2009), Perugia, Italy (2008), Kuala Lumpur, Malaysia (2007), Glasgow, UK (2006), Singapore (2005), Assisi, Italy (2004), Montreal, Canada (2003), and (as ICCS) Amsterdam, The Netherlands (2002) and San Francisco, USA (2001).

Computational science is the main pillar of most of the present research, industrial and commercial applications, and plays a unique role in exploiting ICT innovative technologies. The ICCSA conference series has provided a venue for researchers and industry practitioners to discuss new ideas, to share complex problems and their solutions, and to shape new trends in computational science.

Apart from the general track, ICCSA 2020 also included 52 workshops in various areas of computational science, ranging from computational science technologies to specific areas of computational science, such as software engineering, security, machine learning and artificial intelligence, blockchain technologies, and of applications in many fields. We accepted 498 papers, distributed among 6 conference main tracks, which included 52 in workshops and 32 short papers. We would like to express our appreciation to the workshops chairs and co-chairs for their hard work and dedication.

The success of the ICCSA conference series in general, and of ICCSA 2020 in particular, vitaly depends on the support from many people: authors, presenters, participants, keynote speakers, workshop chairs, session chairs, Organizing Committee members, student volunteers, Program Committee members, Advisory Committee members, international liaison chairs, reviewers, and others in various roles. We take this opportunity to wholeheartedly thank them all.

We also wish to thank our publisher, Springer, for their acceptance to publish the proceedings, for sponsoring part of the Best Papers Awards, and for their kind assistance and cooperation during the editing process.

We cordially invite you to visit the ICCSA website http://www.iccsa.org where you can find all the relevant information about this interesting and exciting event.

July 2020

Osvaldo Gervasi
Beniamino Murgante
Sanjay Misra

Welcome to the Online Conference

The COVID-19 pandemic disrupted our plans for ICCSA 2020, as was the case for the scientific community around the world. Hence, we had to promptly regroup and rush to set in place the organization and the underlying infrastructure of the online event.

We chose to build the technological infrastructure using only open source software. In particular, we used Jitsi (`jitsi.org`) for the videoconferencing, Riot (`riot.im`) together with Matrix (`matrix.org`) for chat and asynchronous communication, and Jibri (`github.com/jitsi/jibri`) for live streaming sessions on YouTube.

Six Jitsi servers were set up, one for each parallel session. The participants of the sessions were helped and assisted by eight volunteer students (from the Universities of Cagliari, Florence, Perugia, and Bari), who assured technical support and smooth running of the conference proceedings.

The implementation of the software infrastructure and the technical coordination of the volunteers was carried out by Damiano Perri and Marco Simonetti.

Our warmest thanks go to all the volunteering students, to the technical coordinators, and to the development communities of Jitsi, Jibri, Riot, and Matrix, who made their terrific platforms available as open source software.

Our heartfelt thanks go to the keynote speakers: Yaneer Bar-Yam, Cecilia Ceccarelli, and Vincenzo Piuri and to the guests of the closing keynote panel: Mike Batty, Denise Pumain, and Alexis Tsoukiàs.

A big thank you goes to all the 454 speakers, many of whom showed an enormous collaborative spirit, sometimes participating and presenting in almost prohibitive times of the day, given that the participants of this year's conference come from 52 countries scattered over many time zones of the globe.

Finally, we would like to thank Google for letting us livestream all the events via YouTube. In addition to lightening the load of our Jitsi servers, that will allow us to keep memory and to be able to review the most exciting moments of the conference.

We all hope to meet in our beautiful Cagliari next year, safe from COVID-19, and finally free to meet in person and enjoy the beauty of the ICCSA community in the enchanting Sardinia.

July 2020

Ivan Blečić
Chiara Garau

Organization

ICCSA 2020 was organized by the University of Cagliari (Italy), University of Perugia (Italy), University of Basilicata (Italy), Monash University (Australia), Kyushu Sangyo University (Japan), and University of Minho (Portugal).

Honorary General Chairs

Antonio Laganà	Master-UP, Italy
Norio Shiratori	Chuo University, Japan
Kenneth C. J. Tan	Sardina Systems, UK
Corrado Zoppi	University of Cagliari, Italy

General Chairs

Osvaldo Gervasi	University of Perugia, Italy
Ivan Blečić	University of Cagliari, Italy
David Taniar	Monash University, Australia

Program Committee Chairs

Beniamino Murgante	University of Basilicata, Italy
Bernady O. Apduhan	Kyushu Sangyo University, Japan
Chiara Garau	University of Cagliari, Italy
Ana Maria A. C. Rocha	University of Minho, Portugal

International Advisory Committee

Jemal Abawajy	Deakin University, Australia
Dharma P. Agarwal	University of Cincinnati, USA
Rajkumar Buyya	The University of Melbourne, Australia
Claudia Bauzer Medeiros	University of Campinas, Brazil
Manfred M. Fisher	Vienna University of Economics and Business, Austria
Marina L. Gavrilova	University of Calgary, Canada
Yee Leung	Chinese University of Hong Kong, China

International Liaison Chairs

Giuseppe Borruso	University of Trieste, Italy
Elise De Donker	Western Michigan University, USA
Maria Irene Falcão	University of Minho, Portugal
Robert C. H. Hsu	Chung Hua University, Taiwan

Tai-Hoon Kim	Beijing Jaotong University, China
Vladimir Korkhov	Saint Petersburg University, Russia
Sanjay Misra	Covenant University, Nigeria
Takashi Naka	Kyushu Sangyo University, Japan
Rafael D. C. Santos	National Institute for Space Research, Brazil
Maribel Yasmina Santos	University of Minho, Portugal
Elena Stankova	Saint Petersburg University, Russia

Workshop and Session Organizing Chairs

Beniamino Murgante	University of Basilicata, Italy
Sanjay Misra	Covenant University, Nigeria
Jorge Gustavo Rocha	University of Minho, Portugal

Award Chair

Wenny Rahayu	La Trobe University, Australia

Publicity Committee Chairs

Elmer Dadios	De La Salle University, Philippines
Nataliia Kulabukhova	Saint Petersburg University, Russia
Daisuke Takahashi	Tsukuba University, Japan
Shangwang Wang	Beijing University of Posts and Telecommunications, China

Technology Chairs

Damiano Perri	University of Florence, Italy
Marco Simonetti	University of Florence, Italy

Local Arrangement Chairs

Ivan Blečić	University of Cagliari, Italy
Chiara Garau	University of Cagliari, Italy
Ginevra Balletto	University of Cagliari, Italy
Giuseppe Borruso	University of Trieste, Italy
Michele Campagna	University of Cagliari, Italy
Mauro Coni	University of Cagliari, Italy
Anna Maria Colavitti	University of Cagliari, Italy
Giulia Desogus	University of Cagliari, Italy
Sabrina Lai	University of Cagliari, Italy
Francesca Maltinti	University of Cagliari, Italy
Pasquale Mistretta	University of Cagliari, Italy
Augusto Montisci	University of Cagliari, Italy
Francesco Pinna	University of Cagliari, Italy

Davide Spano	University of Cagliari, Italy
Roberto Tonelli	University of Cagliari, Italy
Giuseppe A. Trunfio	University of Sassari, Italy
Corrado Zoppi	University of Cagliari, Italy

Program Committee

Vera Afreixo	University of Aveiro, Portugal
Filipe Alvelos	University of Minho, Portugal
Hartmut Asche	University of Potsdam, Germany
Ginevra Balletto	University of Cagliari, Italy
Michela Bertolotto	University College Dublin, Ireland
Sandro Bimonte	CEMAGREF, TSCF, France
Rod Blais	University of Calgary, Canada
Ivan Blečić	University of Sassari, Italy
Giuseppe Borruso	University of Trieste, Italy
Ana Cristina Braga	University of Minho, Portugal
Massimo Cafaro	University of Salento, Italy
Yves Caniou	Lyon University, France
José A. Cardoso e Cunha	Universidade Nova de Lisboa, Portugal
Rui Cardoso	University of Beira Interior, Portugal
Leocadio G. Casado	University of Almeria, Spain
Carlo Cattani	University of Salerno, Italy
Mete Celik	Erciyes University, Turkey
Hyunseung Choo	Sungkyunkwan University, South Korea
Min Young Chung	Sungkyunkwan University, South Korea
Florbela Maria da Cruz Domingues Correia	Polytechnic Institute of Viana do Castelo, Portugal
Gilberto Corso Pereira	Federal University of Bahia, Brazil
Alessandro Costantini	INFN, Italy
Carla Dal Sasso Freitas	Universidade Federal do Rio Grande do Sul, Brazil
Pradesh Debba	The Council for Scientific and Industrial Research (CSIR), South Africa
Hendrik Decker	Instituto Tecnológico de Informática, Spain
Frank Devai	London South Bank University, UK
Rodolphe Devillers	Memorial University of Newfoundland, Canada
Joana Matos Dias	University of Coimbra, Portugal
Paolino Di Felice	University of L'Aquila, Italy
Prabu Dorairaj	NetApp, India/USA
M. Irene Falcao	University of Minho, Portugal
Cherry Liu Fang	U.S. DOE Ames Laboratory, USA
Florbela P. Fernandes	Polytechnic Institute of Bragança, Portugal
Jose-Jesus Fernandez	National Centre for Biotechnology, CSIS, Spain
Paula Odete Fernandes	Polytechnic Institute of Bragança, Portugal
Adelaide de Fátima Baptista Valente Freitas	University of Aveiro, Portugal

Manuel Carlos Figueiredo	University of Minho, Portugal
Maria Celia Furtado Rocha	PRODEB–PósCultura, UFBA, Brazil
Chiara Garau	University of Cagliari, Italy
Paulino Jose Garcia Nieto	University of Oviedo, Spain
Jerome Gensel	LSR-IMAG, France
Maria Giaoutzi	National Technical University of Athens, Greece
Arminda Manuela Andrade Pereira Gonçalves	University of Minho, Portugal
Andrzej M. Goscinski	Deakin University, Australia
Sevin Gümgüm	Izmir University of Economics, Turkey
Alex Hagen-Zanker	University of Cambridge, UK
Shanmugasundaram Hariharan	B.S. Abdur Rahman University, India
Eligius M. T. Hendrix	University of Malaga, Spain, and Wageningen University, The Netherlands
Hisamoto Hiyoshi	Gunma University, Japan
Mustafa Inceoglu	EGE University, Turkey
Peter Jimack	University of Leeds, UK
Qun Jin	Waseda University, Japan
Farid Karimipour	Vienna University of Technology, Austria
Baris Kazar	Oracle Corp., USA
Maulana Adhinugraha Kiki	Telkom University, Indonesia
DongSeong Kim	University of Canterbury, New Zealand
Taihoon Kim	Hannam University, South Korea
Ivana Kolingerova	University of West Bohemia, Czech Republic
Nataliia Kulabukhova	Saint Petersburg University, Russia
Vladimir Korkhov	Saint Petersburg University, Russia
Rosa Lasaponara	CNR, Italy
Maurizio Lazzari	CNR, Italy
Cheng Siong Lee	Monash University, Australia
Sangyoun Lee	Yonsei University, South Korea
Jongchan Lee	Kunsan National University, South Korea
Chendong Li	University of Connecticut, USA
Gang Li	Deakin University, Australia
Fang Liu	AMES Laboratories, USA
Xin Liu	University of Calgary, Canada
Andrea Lombardi	University of Perugia, Italy
Savino Longo	University of Bari, Italy
Tinghuai Ma	Nanjing University of Information Science and Technology, China
Ernesto Marcheggiani	Katholieke Universiteit Leuven, Belgium
Antonino Marvuglia	Research Centre Henri Tudor, Luxembourg
Nicola Masini	CNR, Italy
Ilaria Matteucci	CNR, Italy
Eric Medvet	University of Trieste, Italy
Nirvana Meratnia	University of Twente, The Netherlands

Noelia Faginas Lago	University of Perugia, Italy
Giuseppe Modica	University of Reggio Calabria, Italy
Josè Luis Montaña	University of Cantabria, Spain
Maria Filipa Mourão	IP from Viana do Castelo, Portugal
Louiza de Macedo Mourelle	State University of Rio de Janeiro, Brazil
Nadia Nedjah	State University of Rio de Janeiro, Brazil
Laszlo Neumann	University of Girona, Spain
Kok-Leong Ong	Deakin University, Australia
Belen Palop	Universidad de Valladolid, Spain
Marcin Paprzycki	Polish Academy of Sciences, Poland
Eric Pardede	La Trobe University, Australia
Kwangjin Park	Wonkwang University, South Korea
Ana Isabel Pereira	Polytechnic Institute of Bragança, Portugal
Massimiliano Petri	University of Pisa, Italy
Maurizio Pollino	Italian National Agency for New Technologies, Energy and Sustainable Economic Development, Italy
Alenka Poplin	University of Hamburg, Germany
Vidyasagar Potdar	Curtin University of Technology, Australia
David C. Prosperi	Florida Atlantic University, USA
Wenny Rahayu	La Trobe University, Australia
Jerzy Respondek	Silesian University of Technology, Poland
Humberto Rocha	INESC-Coimbra, Portugal
Jon Rokne	University of Calgary, Canada
Octavio Roncero	CSIC, Spain
Maytham Safar	Kuwait University, Kuwait
Francesco Santini	University of Perugia, Italy
Chiara Saracino	A.O. Ospedale Niguarda Ca' Granda, Italy
Haiduke Sarafian	Penn State University, USA
Marco Paulo Seabra dos Reis	University of Coimbra, Portugal
Jie Shen	University of Michigan, USA
Qi Shi	Liverpool John Moores University, UK
Dale Shires	U.S. Army Research Laboratory, USA
Inês Soares	University of Coimbra, Portugal
Elena Stankova	Saint Petersburg University, Russia
Takuo Suganuma	Tohoku University, Japan
Eufemia Tarantino	Polytechnic University of Bari, Italy
Sergio Tasso	University of Perugia, Italy
Ana Paula Teixeira	University of Trás-os-Montes and Alto Douro, Portugal
Senhorinha Teixeira	University of Minho, Portugal
M. Filomena Teodoro	Portuguese Naval Academy, University of Lisbon, Portugal
Parimala Thulasiraman	University of Manitoba, Canada
Carmelo Torre	Polytechnic University of Bari, Italy
Javier Martinez Torres	Centro Universitario de la Defensa Zaragoza, Spain
Giuseppe A. Trunfio	University of Sassari, Italy

Pablo Vanegas	University of Cuenca, Ecuador
Marco Vizzari	University of Perugia, Italy
Varun Vohra	Merck Inc., USA
Koichi Wada	University of Tsukuba, Japan
Krzysztof Walkowiak	Wroclaw University of Technology, Poland
Zequn Wang	Intelligent Automation Inc., USA
Robert Weibel	University of Zurich, Switzerland
Frank Westad	Norwegian University of Science and Technology, Norway
Roland Wismüller	Universität Siegen, Germany
Mudasser Wyne	SOET National University, USA
Chung-Huang Yang	National Kaohsiung Normal University, Taiwan
Xin-She Yang	National Physical Laboratory, UK
Salim Zabir	France Telecom Japan Co., Japan
Haifeng Zhao	University of California, Davis, USA
Fabiana Zollo	University of Venice, Italy
Albert Y. Zomaya	The University of Sydney, Australia

Workshop Organizers

Advanced Transport Tools and Methods (A2TM 2020)

Massimiliano Petri	University of Pisa, Italy
Antonio Pratelli	University of Pisa, Italy

Advances in Artificial Intelligence Learning Technologies: Blended Learning, STEM, Computational Thinking and Coding (AAILT 2020)

Valentina Franzoni	University of Perugia, Italy
Alfredo Milani	University of Perugia, Italy
Sergio Tasso	University of Perugia, Italy

Workshop on Advancements in Applied Machine Learning and Data Analytics (AAMDA 2020)

Alessandro Costantini	INFN, Italy
Daniele Cesini	INFN, Italy
Davide Salomoni	INFN, Italy
Doina Cristina Duma	INFN, Italy

Advanced Computational Approaches in Artificial Intelligence and Complex Systems Applications (ACAC 2020)

Yeliz Karaca	University of Massachusetts Medical School, USA
Dumitru Baleanu	Çankaya University, Turkey, and Institute of Space Sciences, Romania
Majaz Moonis	University of Massachusetts Medical School, USA
Yu-Dong Zhang	University of Leicester, UK

Affective Computing and Emotion Recognition (ACER-EMORE 2020)

Valentina Franzoni	University of Perugia, Italy
Alfredo Milani	University of Perugia, Italy
Giulio Biondi	University of Florence, Italy

AI Factory and Smart Manufacturing (AIFACTORY 2020)

Jongpil Jeong	Sungkyunkwan University, South Korea

Air Quality Monitoring and Citizen Science for Smart Urban Management. State of the Art And Perspectives (AirQ&CScience 2020)

Grazie Fattoruso	ENEA CR Portici, Italy
Maurizio Pollino	ENEA CR Casaccia, Italy
Saverio De Vito	ENEA CR Portici, Italy

Automatic Landform Classification: Spatial Methods and Applications (ALCSMA 2020)

Maria Danese	CNR-ISPC, Italy
Dario Gioia	CNR-ISPC, Italy

Advances of Modelling Micromobility in Urban Spaces (AMMUS 2020)

Tiziana Campisi	University of Enna KORE, Italy
Giovanni Tesoriere	University of Enna KORE, Italy
Ioannis Politis	Aristotle University of Thessaloniki, Greece
Socrates Basbas	Aristotle University of Thessaloniki, Greece
Sanja Surdonja	University of Rijeka, Croatia
Marko Rencelj	University of Maribor, Slovenia

Advances in Information Systems and Technologies for Emergency Management, Risk Assessment and Mitigation Based on the Resilience Concepts (ASTER 2020)

Maurizio Pollino	ENEA, Italy
Marco Vona	University of Basilicata, Italy
Amedeo Flora	University of Basilicata, Italy
Chiara Iacovino	University of Basilicata, Italy
Beniamino Murgante	University of Basilicata, Italy

Advances in Web Based Learning (AWBL 2020)

Birol Ciloglugil	Ege University, Turkey
Mustafa Murat Inceoglu	Ege University, Turkey

Blockchain and Distributed Ledgers: Technologies and Applications (BDLTA 2020)

Vladimir Korkhov	Saint Petersburg University, Russia
Elena Stankova	Saint Petersburg University, Russia
Nataliia Kulabukhova	Saint Petersburg University, Russia

Bio and Neuro Inspired Computing and Applications (BIONCA 2020)

Nadia Nedjah	State University of Rio de Janeiro, Brazil
Luiza De Macedo Mourelle	State University of Rio de Janeiro, Brazil

Computer Aided Modeling, Simulation and Analysis (CAMSA 2020)

Jie Shen	University of Michigan, USA

Computational and Applied Statistics (CAS 2020)

Ana Cristina Braga	University of Minho, Portugal

Computerized Evidence Based Decision Making (CEBDEM 2020)

Clarice Bleil de Souza	Cardiff University, UK
Valerio Cuttini	University of Pisa, Italy
Federico Cerutti	Cardiff University, UK
Camilla Pezzica	Cardiff University, UK

Computational Geometry and Applications (CGA 2020)

Marina Gavrilova	University of Calgary, Canada

Computational Mathematics, Statistics and Information Management (CMSIM 2020)

Maria Filomena Teodoro	Portuguese Naval Academy, University of Lisbon, Portugal

Computational Optimization and Applications (COA 2020)

Ana Rocha	University of Minho, Portugal
Humberto Rocha	University of Coimbra, Portugal

Computational Astrochemistry (CompAstro 2020)

Marzio Rosi	University of Perugia, Italy
Cecilia Ceccarelli	University of Grenoble, France
Stefano Falcinelli	University of Perugia, Italy
Dimitrios Skouteris	Master-UP, Italy

Cities, Technologies and Planning (CTP 2020)

Beniamino Murgante	University of Basilicata, Italy
Ljiljana Zivkovic	Ministry of Construction, Transport and Infrastructure and Institute of Architecture and Urban & Spatial Planning of Serbia, Serbia
Giuseppe Borruso	University of Trieste, Italy
Malgorzata Hanzl	University of Łódź, Poland

Data Stream Processing and Applications (DASPA 2020)

Raja Chiky	ISEP, France
Rosanna VERDE	University of Campania, Italy
Marcilio De Souto	Orleans University, France

Data Science for Cyber Security (DS4Cyber 2020)

Hongmei Chi	Florida A&M University, USA

Econometric and Multidimensional Evaluation in Urban Environment (EMEUE 2020)

Carmelo Maria Torre	Polytechnic University of Bari, Italy
Pierluigi Morano	Polytechnic University of Bari, Italy
Maria Cerreta	University of Naples, Italy
Paola Perchinunno	University of Bari, Italy
Francesco Tajani	University of Rome, Italy
Simona Panaro	University of Portsmouth, UK
Francesco Scorza	University of Basilicata, Italy

Frontiers in Machine Learning (FIML 2020)

Massimo Bilancia	University of Bari, Italy
Paola Perchinunno	University of Bari, Italy
Pasquale Lops	University of Bari, Italy
Danilo Di Bona	University of Bari, Italy

Future Computing System Technologies and Applications (FiSTA 2020)

Bernady Apduhan	Kyushu Sangyo University, Japan
Rafael Santos	Brazilian National Institute for Space Research, Brazil

Geodesign in Decision Making: Meta Planning and Collaborative Design for Sustainable and Inclusive Development (GDM 2020)

Francesco Scorza	University of Basilicata, Italy
Michele Campagna	University of Cagliari, Italy
Ana Clara Mourao Moura	Federal University of Minas Gerais, Brazil

Geomatics in Forestry and Agriculture: New Advances and Perspectives (GeoForAgr 2020)

Maurizio Pollino	ENEA, Italy
Giuseppe Modica	University of Reggio Calabria, Italy
Marco Vizzari	University of Perugia, Italy

Geographical Analysis, Urban Modeling, Spatial Statistics (GEOG-AND-MOD 2020)

Beniamino Murgante	University of Basilicata, Italy
Giuseppe Borruso	University of Trieste, Italy
Hartmut Asche	University of Potsdam, Germany

Geomatics for Resource Monitoring and Management (GRMM 2020)

Eufemia Tarantino	Polytechnic University of Bari, Italy
Enrico Borgogno Mondino	University of Torino, Italy
Marco Scaioni	Polytechnic University of Milan, Italy
Alessandra Capolupo	Polytechnic University of Bari, Italy

Software Quality (ISSQ 2020)

Sanjay Misra	Covenant University, Nigeria

Collective, Massive and Evolutionary Systems (IWCES 2020)

Alfredo Milani	University of Perugia, Italy
Rajdeep Niyogi	Indian Institute of Technology, Roorkee, India
Alina Elena Baia	University of Florence, Italy

Large Scale Computational Science (LSCS 2020)

Elise De Doncker	Western Michigan University, USA
Fukuko Yuasa	High Energy Accelerator Research Organization (KEK), Japan
Hideo Matsufuru	High Energy Accelerator Research Organization (KEK), Japan

Land Use Monitoring for Sustainability (LUMS 2020)

Carmelo Maria Torre	Polytechnic University of Bari, Italy
Alessandro Bonifazi	Polytechnic University of Bari, Italy
Pasquale Balena	Polytechnic University of Bari, Italy
Massimiliano Bencardino	University of Salerno, Italy
Francesco Tajani	University of Rome, Italy
Pierluigi Morano	Polytechnic University of Bari, Italy
Maria Cerreta	University of Naples, Italy
Giuliano Poli	University of Naples, Italy

Machine Learning for Space and Earth Observation Data (MALSEOD 2020)

Rafael Santos	INPE, Brazil
Karine Ferreira	INPE, Brazil

Building Multi-dimensional Models for Assessing Complex Environmental Systems (MES 2020)

Marta Dell'Ovo	Polytechnic University of Milan, Italy
Vanessa Assumma	Polytechnic University of Torino, Italy
Caterina Caprioli	Polytechnic University of Torino, Italy
Giulia Datola	Polytechnic University of Torino, Italy
Federico dell'Anna	Polytechnic University of Torino, Italy

Ecosystem Services: Nature's Contribution to People in Practice. Assessment Frameworks, Models, Mapping, and Implications (NC2P 2020)

Francesco Scorza	University of Basilicata, Italy
David Cabana	International Marine Center, Italy
Sabrina Lai	University of Cagliari, Italy
Ana Clara Mourao Moura	Federal University of Minas Gerais, Brazil
Corrado Zoppi	University of Cagliari, Italy

Open Knowledge for Socio-economic Development (OKSED 2020)

Luigi Mundula	University of Cagliari, Italy
Flavia Marzano	Link Campus University, Italy
Maria Paradiso	University of Milan, Italy

Scientific Computing Infrastructure (SCI 2020)

Elena Stankova	Saint Petersburg State University, Russia
Vladimir Korkhov	Saint Petersburg State University, Russia
Natalia Kulabukhova	Saint Petersburg State University, Russia

Computational Studies for Energy and Comfort in Buildings (SECoB 2020)

Senhorinha Teixeira	University of Minho, Portugal
Luís Martins	University of Minho, Portugal
Ana Maria Rocha	University of Minho, Portugal

Software Engineering Processes and Applications (SEPA 2020)

Sanjay Misra	Covenant University, Nigeria

Smart Ports - Technologies and Challenges (SmartPorts 2020)

Gianfranco Fancello	University of Cagliari, Italy
Patrizia Serra	University of Cagliari, Italy
Marco Mazzarino	University of Venice, Italy
Luigi Mundula	University of Cagliari, Italy

Ginevra Balletto	University of Cagliari, Italy
Giuseppe Borruso	University of Trieste, Italy

Sustainability Performance Assessment: Models, Approaches and Applications Toward Interdisciplinary and Integrated Solutions (SPA 2020)

Francesco Scorza	University of Basilicata, Italy
Valentin Grecu	Lucian Blaga University, Romania
Jolanta Dvarioniene	Kaunas University of Technology, Lithuania
Sabrina Lai	University of Cagliari, Italy
Iole Cerminara	University of Basilicata, Italy
Corrado Zoppi	University of Cagliari, Italy

Smart and Sustainable Island Communities (SSIC 2020)

Chiara Garau	University of Cagliari, Italy
Anastasia Stratigea	National Technical University of Athens, Greece
Paola Zamperlin	University of Pisa, Italy
Francesco Scorza	University of Basilicata, Italy

Science, Technologies and Policies to Innovate Spatial Planning (STP4P 2020)

Chiara Garau	University of Cagliari, Italy
Daniele La Rosa	University of Catania, Italy
Francesco Scorza	University of Basilicata, Italy
Anna Maria Colavitti	University of Cagliari, Italy
Beniamino Murgante	University of Basilicata, Italy
Paolo La Greca	University of Catania, Italy

New Frontiers for Strategic Urban Planning (StrategicUP 2020)

Luigi Mundula	University of Cagliari, Italy
Ginevra Balletto	University of Cagliari, Italy
Giuseppe Borruso	University of Trieste, Italy
Michele Campagna	University of Cagliari, Italy
Beniamino Murgante	University of Basilicata, Italy

Theoretical and Computational Chemistry and its Applications (TCCMA 2020)

Noelia Faginas-Lago	University of Perugia, Italy
Andrea Lombardi	University of Perugia, Italy

Tools and Techniques in Software Development Process (TTSDP 2020)

Sanjay Misra	Covenant University, Nigeria

Urban Form Studies (UForm 2020)

Malgorzata Hanzl	Łódź University of Technology, Poland

Urban Space Extended Accessibility (USEaccessibility 2020)

Chiara Garau	University of Cagliari, Italy
Francesco Pinna	University of Cagliari, Italy
Beniamino Murgante	University of Basilicata, Italy
Mauro Coni	University of Cagliari, Italy
Francesca Maltinti	University of Cagliari, Italy
Vincenza Torrisi	University of Catania, Italy
Matteo Ignaccolo	University of Catania, Italy

Virtual and Augmented Reality and Applications (VRA 2020)

Osvaldo Gervasi	University of Perugia, Italy
Damiano Perri	University of Perugia, Italy
Marco Simonetti	University of Perugia, Italy
Sergio Tasso	University of Perugia, Italy

Workshop on Advanced and Computational Methods for Earth Science Applications (WACM4ES 2020)

Luca Piroddi	University of Cagliari, Italy
Laura Foddis	University of Cagliari, Italy
Gian Piero Deidda	University of Cagliari, Italy
Augusto Montisci	University of Cagliari, Italy
Gabriele Uras	University of Cagliari, Italy
Giulio Vignoli	University of Cagliari, Italy

Sponsoring Organizations

ICCSA 2020 would not have been possible without tremendous support of many organizations and institutions, for which all organizers and participants of ICCSA 2020 express their sincere gratitude:

Springer International Publishing AG, Germany (https://www.springer.com)

Computers Open Access Journal (https://www.mdpi.com/journal/computers)

IEEE Italy Section, Italy (https://italy.ieeer8.org/)

Centre-North Italy Chapter IEEE GRSS, Italy
(https://cispio.diet.uniroma1.it/marzano/ieee-grs/index.html)

Italy Section of the Computer Society, Italy
(https://site.ieee.org/italy-cs/)

University of Cagliari, Italy
(https://unica.it/)

University of Perugia, Italy
(https://www.unipg.it)

University of Basilicata, Italy
(http://www.unibas.it)

Monash University, Australia
(https://www.monash.edu/)

Kyushu Sangyo University, Japan
(https://www.kyusan-u.ac.jp/)

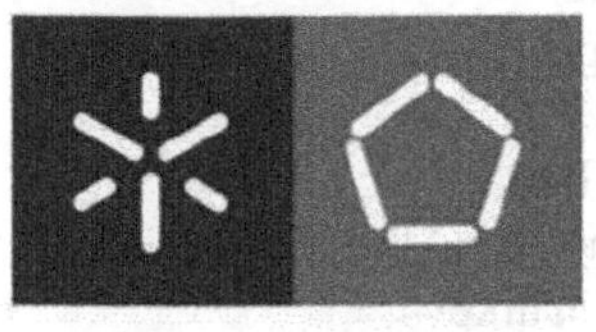

University of Minho, Portugal
(https://www.uminho.pt/)

Scientific Association Transport Infrastructures, Italy
(https://www.stradeeautostrade.it/associazioni-e-organizzazioni/asit-associazione-scientifica-infrastrutture-trasporto/)

Regione Sardegna, Italy
(https://regione.sardegna.it/)

Comune di Cagliari, Italy
(https://www.comune.cagliari.it/)

Referees

A. P. Andrade Marina	ISCTE, Instituto Universitário de Lisboa, Portugal
Addesso Paolo	University of Salerno, Italy
Adewumi Adewole	Algonquin College, Canada
Afolabi Adedeji	Covenant University, Nigeria
Afreixo Vera	University of Aveiro, Portugal
Agrawal Smirti	Freelancer, USA
Agrawal Akshat	Amity University Haryana, India
Ahmad Waseem	Federal University of Technology Minna, Nigeria
Akgun Nurten	Bursa Technical University, Turkey
Alam Tauhidul	Louisiana State University Shreveport, USA
Aleixo Sandra M.	CEAUL, Portugal
Alfa Abraham	Federal University of Technology Minna, Nigeria
Alvelos Filipe	University of Minho, Portugal
Alves Alexandra	University of Minho, Portugal
Amato Federico	University of Lausanne, Switzerland
Andrade Marina Alexandra Pedro	ISCTE-IUL, Portugal
Andrianov Sergey	Saint Petersburg State University, Russia
Anelli Angelo	CNR-IGAG, Italy
Anelli Debora	University of Rome, Italy
Annunziata Alfonso	University of Cagliari, Italy
Antognelli Sara	Agricolus, Italy
Aoyama Tatsumi	High Energy Accelerator Research Organization, Japan
Apduhan Bernady	Kyushu Sangyo University, Japan
Ascenzi Daniela	University of Trento, Italy
Asche Harmut	Hasso-Plattner-Institut für Digital Engineering GmbH, Germany
Aslan Burak Galip	Izmir Insitute of Technology, Turkey
Assumma Vanessa	Polytechnic University of Torino, Italy
Astoga Gino	UV, Chile
Atman Uslu Nilüfer	Manisa Celal Bayar University, Turkey
Behera Ranjan Kumar	National Institute of Technology, Rourkela, India
Badsha Shahriar	University of Nevada, USA
Bai Peng	University of Cagliari, Italy
Baia Alina-Elena	University of Perugia, Italy
Balacco Gabriella	Polytechnic University of Bari, Italy
Balci Birim	Celal Bayar University, Turkey
Balena Pasquale	Polytechnic University of Bari, Italy
Balletto Ginevra	University of Cagliari, Italy
Balucani Nadia	University of Perugia, Italy
Bansal Megha	Delhi University, India
Barazzetti Luigi	Polytechnic University of Milan, Italy
Barreto Jeniffer	Istituto Superior Técnico, Portugal
Basbas Socrates	Aristotle University of Thessaloniki, Greece

Berger Katja	Ludwig-Maximilians-Universität München, Germany
Beyene Asrat Mulatu	Addis Ababa Science and Technology University, Ethiopia
Bilancia Massimo	University of Bari Aldo Moro, Italy
Biondi Giulio	University of Firenze, Italy
Blanquer Ignacio	Universitat Politècnica de València, Spain
Bleil de Souza Clarice	Cardiff University, UK
Blečíć Ivan	University of Cagliari, Italy
Bogdanov Alexander	Saint Petersburg State University, Russia
Bonifazi Alessandro	Polytechnic University of Bari, Italy
Bontchev Boyan	Sofia University, Bulgaria
Borgogno Mondino Enrico	University of Torino, Italy
Borruso Giuseppe	University of Trieste, Italy
Bouaziz Rahma	Taibah University, Saudi Arabia
Bowles Juliana	University of Saint Andrews, UK
Braga Ana Cristina	University of Minho, Portugal
Brambilla Andrea	Polytechnic University of Milan, Italy
Brito Francisco	University of Minho, Portugal
Buele Jorge	Universidad Tecnológica Indoamérica, Ecuador
Buffoni Andrea	TAGES sc, Italy
Cabana David	International Marine Centre, Italy
Calazan Rogerio	IEAPM, Brazil
Calcina Sergio Vincenzo	University of Cagliari, Italy
Camalan Seda	Atilim University, Turkey
Camarero Alberto	Universidad Politécnica de Madrid, Spain
Campisi Tiziana	University of Enna KORE, Italy
Cannatella Daniele	Delft University of Technology, The Netherlands
Capolupo Alessandra	Polytechnic University of Bari, Italy
Cappucci Sergio	ENEA, Italy
Caprioli Caterina	Polytechnic University of Torino, Italy
Carapau Fermando	Universidade de Evora, Portugal
Carcangiu Sara	University of Cagliari, Italy
Carrasqueira Pedro	INESC Coimbra, Portugal
Caselli Nicolás	PUCV Chile, Chile
Castro de Macedo Jose Nuno	Universidade do Minho, Portugal
Cavallo Carla	University of Naples, Italy
Cerminara Iole	University of Basilicata, Italy
Cerreta Maria	University of Naples, Italy
Cesini Daniele	INFN-CNAF, Italy
Chang Shi-Kuo	University of Pittsburgh, USA
Chetty Girija	University of Canberra, Australia
Chiky Raja	ISEP, France
Chowdhury Dhiman	University of South Carolina, USA
Ciloglugil Birol	Ege University, Turkey
Coletti Cecilia	Università di Chieti-Pescara, Italy

Coni Mauro	University of Cagliari, Italy
Corcoran Padraig	Cardiff University, UK
Cornelio Antonella	Università degli Studi di Brescia, Italy
Correia Aldina	ESTG-PPorto, Portugal
Correia Elisete	University of Trás-os-Montes and Alto Douro, Portugal
Correia Florbela	Polytechnic Institute of Viana do Castelo, Portugal
Costa Lino	Universidade do Minho, Portugal
Costa e Silva Eliana	ESTG-P Porto, Portugal
Costantini Alessandro	INFN, Italy
Crespi Mattia	University of Roma, Italy
Cuca Branka	Polytechnic University of Milano, Italy
De Doncker Elise	Western Michigan University, USA
De Macedo Mourelle Luiza	State University of Rio de Janeiro, Brazil
Daisaka Hiroshi	Hitotsubashi University, Japan
Daldanise Gaia	CNR, Italy
Danese Maria	CNR-ISPC, Italy
Daniele Bartoli	University of Perugia, Italy
Datola Giulia	Polytechnic University of Torino, Italy
De Luca Giandomenico	University of Reggio Calabria, Italy
De Lucia Caterina	University of Foggia, Italy
De Morais Barroca Filho Itamir	Federal University of Rio Grande do Norte, Brazil
De Petris Samuele	University of Torino, Italy
De Sá Alan	Marinha do Brasil, Brazil
De Souto Marcilio	LIFO, University of Orléans, France
De Vito Saverio	ENEA, Italy
De Wilde Pieter	University of Plymouth, UK
Degtyarev Alexander	Saint Petersburg State University, Russia
Dell'Anna Federico	Polytechnic University of Torino, Italy
Dell'Ovo Marta	Polytechnic University of Milano, Italy
Della Mura Fernanda	University of Naples, Italy
Deluka T. Aleksandra	University of Rijeka, Croatia
Demartino Cristoforo	Zhejiang University, China
Dereli Dursun Ahu	Istanbul Commerce University, Turkey
Desogus Giulia	University of Cagliari, Italy
Dettori Marco	University of Sassari, Italy
Devai Frank	London South Bank University, UK
Di Francesco Massimo	University of Cagliari, Italy
Di Liddo Felicia	Polytechnic University of Bari, Italy
Di Paola Gianluigi	University of Molise, Italy
Di Pietro Antonio	ENEA, Italy
Di Pinto Valerio	University of Naples, Italy
Dias Joana	University of Coimbra, Portugal
Dimas Isabel	University of Coimbra, Portugal
Dirvanauskas Darius	Kaunas University of Technology, Lithuania
Djordjevic Aleksandra	University of Belgrade, Serbia

Duma Doina Cristina	INFN-CNAF, Italy
Dumlu Demircioğlu Emine	Yıldız Technical University, Turkey
Dursun Aziz	Virginia Tech University, USA
Dvarioniene Jolanta	Kaunas University of Technology, Lithuania
Errico Maurizio Francesco	University of Enna KORE, Italy
Ezugwu Absalom	University of KwaZulu-Natal, South Africa
Fattoruso Grazia	ENEA, Italy
Faginas-Lago Noelia	University of Perugia, Italy
Falanga Bolognesi Salvatore	ARIESPACE, Italy
Falcinelli Stefano	University of Perugia, Italy
Farias Marcos	National Nuclear Energy Commission, Brazil
Farina Alessandro	University of Pisa, Italy
Feltynowski Marcin	Lodz University of Technology, Poland
Fernandes Florbela	Instituto Politecnico de Bragança, Portugal
Fernandes Paula Odete	Instituto Politécnico de Bragança, Portugal
Fernandez-Sanz Luis	University of Alcala, Spain
Ferreira Ana Cristina	University of Minho, Portugal
Ferreira Fernanda	Porto, Portugal
Fiorini Lorena	University of L'Aquila, Italy
Flora Amedeo	University of Basilicata, Italy
Florez Hector	Universidad Distrital Francisco Jose de Caldas, Colombia
Foddis Maria Laura	University of Cagliari, Italy
Fogli Daniela	University of Brescia, Italy
Fortunelli Martina	Pragma Engineering, Italy
Fragiacomo Massimo	University of L'Aquila, Italy
Franzoni Valentina	Perugia University, Italy
Fusco Giovanni	University of Cote d'Azur, France
Fyrogenis Ioannis	Aristotle University of Thessaloniki, Greece
Gorbachev Yuriy	Coddan Technologies LLC, Russia
Gabrielli Laura	Università Iuav di Venezia, Italy
Gallanos Theodore	Austrian Institute of Technology, Austria
Gamallo Belmonte Pablo	Universitat de Barcelona, Spain
Gankevich Ivan	Saint Petersburg State University, Russia
Garau Chiara	University of Cagliari, Italy
Garcia Para Ernesto	Universidad del Pais Vasco, EHU, Spain
Gargano Riccardo	Universidade de Brasilia, Brazil
Gavrilova Marina	University of Calgary, Canada
Georgiadis Georgios	Aristotle University of Thessaloniki, Greece
Gervasi Osvaldo	University of Perugia, Italy
Giano Salvatore Ivo	University of Basilicata, Italy
Gil Jorge	Chalmers University, Sweden
Gioia Andrea	Polytechnic University of Bari, Italy
Gioia Dario	ISPC-CNT, Italy

Giordano Ludovica	ENEA, Italy
Giorgi Giacomo	University of Perugia, Italy
Giovene di Girasole Eleonora	CNR-IRISS, Italy
Giovinazzi Sonia	ENEA, Italy
Giresini Linda	University of Pisa, Italy
Giuffrida Salvatore	University of Catania, Italy
Golubchikov Oleg	Cardiff University, UK
Gonçalves A. Manuela	University of Minho, Portugal
Gorgoglione Angela	Universidad de la República, Uruguay
Goyal Rinkaj	IPU, Delhi, India
Grishkin Valery	Saint Petersburg State University, Russia
Guerra Eduardo	Free University of Bozen-Bolzano, Italy
Guerrero Abel	University of Guanajuato, Mexico
Gulseven Osman	American University of The Middle East, Kuwait
Gupta Brij	National Institute of Technology, Kurukshetra, India
Guveyi Elcin	Yildiz Teknik University, Turkey
Gülen Kemal Güven	Namk Kemal University, Turkey
Haddad Sandra	Arab Academy for Science, Technology and Maritime Transport, Egypt
Hanzl Malgorzata	Lodz University of Technology, Poland
Hegedus Peter	University of Szeged, Hungary
Hendrix Eligius M. T.	Universidad de Málaga, Spain
Higaki Hiroaki	Tokyo Denki University, Japan
Hossain Syeda Sumbul	Daffodil International University, Bangladesh
Iacovino Chiara	University of Basilicata, Italy
Iakushkin Oleg	Saint Petersburg State University, Russia
Iannuzzo Antonino	ETH Zurich, Switzerland
Idri Ali	University Mohammed V, Morocco
Ignaccolo Matteo	University of Catania, Italy
Ilovan Oana-Ramona	Babes-Bolyai University, Romania
Isola Federica	University of Cagliari, Italy
Jankovic Marija	CERTH, Greece
Jorge Ana Maria	Instituto Politécnico de Lisboa, Portugal
Kanamori Issaku	RIKEN Center for Computational Science, Japan
Kapenga John	Western Michigan University, USA
Karabulut Korhan	Yasar University, Turkey
Karaca Yeliz	University of Massachusetts Medical School, USA
Karami Ali	University of Guilan, Iran
Kienhofer Frank	WITS, South Africa
Kim Tai-hoon	Beijing Jiaotong University, China
Kimura Shuhei	Tottori University, Japan
Kirillov Denis	Saint Petersburg State University, Russia
Korkhov Vladimir	Saint Petersburg University, Russia
Koszewski Krzysztof	Warsaw University of Technology, Poland
Krzysztofik Sylwia	Lodz University of Technology, Poland

Kulabukhova Nataliia	Saint Petersburg State University, Russia
Kulkarni Shrinivas B.	SDM College of Engineering and Technology, Dharwad, India
Kwiecinski Krystian	Warsaw University of Technology, Poland
Kyvelou Stella	Panteion University of Social and Political Sciences, Greece
Körting Thales	INPE, Brazil
Lal Niranjan	Mody University of Science and Technology, India
Lazzari Maurizio	CNR-ISPC, Italy
Leon Marcelo	Asociacion de Becarios del Ecuador, Ecuador
La Rocca Ludovica	University of Naples, Italy
La Rosa Daniele	University of Catania, Italy
Lai Sabrina	University of Cagliari, Italy
Lalenis Konstantinos	University of Thessaly, Greece
Lannon Simon	Cardiff University, UK
Lasaponara Rosa	CNR, Italy
Lee Chien-Sing	Sunway University, Malaysia
Lemus-Romani José	Pontificia Universidad Católica de Valparaiso, Chile
Leone Federica	University of Cagliari, Italy
Li Yuanxi	Hong Kong Baptist University, China
Locurcio Marco	Polytechnic University of Bari, Italy
Lombardi Andrea	University of Perugia, Italy
Lopez Gayarre Fernando	University of Oviedo, Spain
Lops Pasquale	University of Bari, Italy
Lourenço Vanda	Universidade Nova de Lisboa, Portugal
Luviano José Luís	University of Guanajuato, Mexico
Maltese Antonino	University of Palermo, Italy
Magni Riccardo	Pragma Engineering, Italy
Maheshwari Anil	Carleton University, Canada
Maja Roberto	Polytechnic University of Milano, Italy
Malik Shaveta	Terna Engineering College, India
Maltinti Francesca	University of Cagliari, Italy
Mandado Marcos	University of Vigo, Spain
Manganelli Benedetto	University of Basilicata, Italy
Mangiameli Michele	University of Catania, Italy
Maraschin Clarice	Universidade Federal do Rio Grande do Sul, Brazil
Marigorta Ana Maria	Universidad de Las Palmas de Gran Canaria, Spain
Markov Krassimir	Institute of Electrical Engineering and Informatics, Bulgaria
Martellozzo Federico	University of Firenze, Italy
Marucci Alessandro	University of L'Aquila, Italy
Masini Nicola	IBAM-CNR, Italy
Matsufuru Hideo	High Energy Accelerator Research Organization (KEK), Japan
Matteucci Ilaria	CNR, Italy
Mauro D'Apuzzo	University of Cassino and Southern Lazio, Italy

Mazzarella Chiara	University of Naples, Italy
Mazzarino Marco	University of Venice, Italy
Mazzoni Augusto	University of Roma, Italy
Mele Roberta	University of Naples, Italy
Menezes Raquel	University of Minho, Portugal
Menghini Antonio	Aarhus Geofisica, Italy
Mengoni Paolo	University of Florence, Italy
Merlino Angelo	Università degli Studi Mediterranea, Italy
Milani Alfredo	University of Perugia, Italy
Milic Vladimir	University of Zagreb, Croatia
Millham Richard	Durban University of Technology, South Africa
Mishra B.	University of Szeged, Hungary
Misra Sanjay	Covenant University, Nigeria
Modica Giuseppe	University of Reggio Calabria, Italy
Mohagheghi Mohammadsadegh	Vali-e-Asr University of Rafsanjan, Iran
Molaei Qelichi Mohamad	University of Tehran, Iran
Molinara Mario	University of Cassino and Southern Lazio, Italy
Momo Evelyn Joan	University of Torino, Italy
Monteiro Vitor	University of Minho, Portugal
Montisci Augusto	University of Cagliari, Italy
Morano Pierluigi	Polytechnic University of Bari, Italy
Morganti Alessandro	Polytechnic University of Milano, Italy
Mosca Erica Isa	Polytechnic University of Milan, Italy
Moura Ricardo	CMA-FCT, New University of Lisbon, Portugal
Mourao Maria	Polytechnic Institute of Viana do Castelo, Portugal
Mourão Moura Ana Clara	Federal University of Minas Gerais, Brazil
Mrak Iva	University of Rijeka, Croatia
Murgante Beniamino	University of Basilicata, Italy
Muñoz Mirna	Centro de Investigacion en Matematicas, Mexico
Nedjah Nadia	State University of Rio de Janeiro, Brazil
Nakasato Naohito	University of Aizu, Japan
Natário Isabel Cristina	Universidade Nova de Lisboa, Portugal
Nesticò Antonio	Università degli Studi di Salerno, Italy
Neto Ana Maria	Universidade Federal do ABC, Brazil
Nicolosi Vittorio	University of Rome, Italy
Nikiforiadis Andreas	Aristotle University of Thessaloniki, Greece
Nocera Fabrizio	University of Illinois at Urbana-Champaign, USA
Nocera Silvio	IUAV, Italy
Nogueira Marcelo	Paulista University, Brazil
Nolè Gabriele	CNR, Italy
Nuno Beirao Jose	University of Lisbon, Portugal
Okewu Emma	University of Alcala, Spain
Oluwasefunmi Arogundade	Academy of Mathematics and System Science, China
Oppio Alessandra	Polytechnic University of Milan, Italy
P. Costa M. Fernanda	University of Minho, Portugal

Parisot Olivier	Luxembourg Institute of Science and Technology, Luxembourg
Paddeu Daniela	UWE, UK
Paio Alexandra	ISCTE-Instituto Universitário de Lisboa, Portugal
Palme Massimo	Catholic University of the North, Chile
Panaro Simona	University of Portsmouth, UK
Pancham Jay	Durban University of Technology, South Africa
Pantazis Dimos	University of West Attica, Greece
Papa Enrica	University of Westminster, UK
Pardede Eric	La Trobe University, Australia
Perchinunno Paola	Uniersity of Cagliari, Italy
Perdicoulis Teresa	UTAD, Portugal
Pereira Ana	Polytechnic Institute of Bragança, Portugal
Perri Damiano	University of Perugia, Italy
Petrelli Marco	University of Rome, Italy
Pierri Francesca	University of Perugia, Italy
Piersanti Antonio	ENEA, Italy
Pilogallo Angela	University of Basilicata, Italy
Pinna Francesco	University of Cagliari, Italy
Pinto Telmo	University of Coimbra, Portugal
Piroddi Luca	University of Cagliari, Italy
Poli Giuliano	University of Naples, Italy
Polidoro Maria João	Polytecnic Institute of Porto, Portugal
Polignano Marco	University of Bari, Italy
Politis Ioannis	Aristotle University of Thessaloniki, Greece
Pollino Maurizio	ENEA, Italy
Popoola Segun	Covenant University, Nigeria
Pratelli Antonio	University of Pisa, Italy
Praticò Salvatore	University of Reggio Calabria, Italy
Previtali Mattia	Polytechnic University of Milan, Italy
Puppio Mario Lucio	University of Pisa, Italy
Puttini Ricardo	Universidade de Brasilia, Brazil
Que Zeli	Nanjing Forestry University, China
Queiroz Gilberto	INPE, Brazil
Regalbuto Stefania	University of Naples, Italy
Ravanelli Roberta	University of Roma, Italy
Recanatesi Fabio	University of Tuscia, Italy
Reis Ferreira Gomes Karine	INPE, Brazil
Reis Marco	University of Coimbra, Portugal
Reitano Maria	University of Naples, Italy
Rencelj Marko	University of Maribor, Slovenia
Respondek Jerzy	Silesian University of Technology, Poland
Rimola Albert	Universitat Autònoma de Barcelona, Spain
Rocha Ana	University of Minho, Portugal
Rocha Humberto	University of Coimbra, Portugal
Rocha Maria Celia	UFBA Bahia, Brazil

Rocha Maria Clara	ESTES Coimbra, Portugal
Rocha Miguel	University of Minho, Portugal
Rodriguez Guillermo	UNICEN, Argentina
Rodríguez González Alejandro	Universidad Carlos III de Madrid, Spain
Ronchieri Elisabetta	INFN, Italy
Rosi Marzio	University of Perugia, Italy
Rotondo Francesco	Università Politecnica delle Marche, Italy
Rusci Simone	University of Pisa, Italy
Saganeiti Lucia	University of Basilicata, Italy
Saiu Valeria	University of Cagliari, Italy
Salas Agustin	UPCV, Chile
Salvo Giuseppe	University of Palermo, Italy
Sarvia Filippo	University of Torino, Italy
Santaga Francesco	University of Perugia, Italy
Santangelo Michele	CNR-IRPI, Italy
Santini Francesco	University of Perugia, Italy
Santos Rafael	INPE, Brazil
Santucci Valentino	Università per Stranieri di Perugia, Italy
Saponaro Mirko	Polytechnic University of Bari, Italy
Sarker Iqbal	CUET, Bangladesh
Scaioni Marco	Politecnico Milano, Italy
Scorza Francesco	University of Basilicata, Italy
Scotto di Perta Ester	University of Naples, Italy
Sebillo Monica	University of Salerno, Italy
Sharma Meera	Swami Shraddhanand College, India
Shen Jie	University of Michigan, USA
Shou Huahao	Zhejiang University of Technology, China
Siavvas Miltiadis	Centre of Research and Technology Hellas (CERTH), Greece
Silva Carina	ESTeSL-IPL, Portugal
Silva Joao Carlos	Polytechnic Institute of Cavado and Ave, Portugal
Silva Junior Luneque	Universidade Federal do ABC, Brazil
Silva Ângela	Instituto Politécnico de Viana do Castelo, Portugal
Simonetti Marco	University of Florence, Italy
Situm Zeljko	University of Zagreb, Croatia
Skouteris Dimitrios	Master-Up, Italy
Solano Francesco	Università degli Studi della Tuscia, Italy
Somma Maria	University of Naples, Italy
Sonnessa Alberico	Polytechnic University of Bari, Italy
Sousa Lisete	University of Lisbon, Portugal
Sousa Nelson	University of Algarve, Portugal
Spaeth Benjamin	Cardiff University, UK
Srinivsan M.	Navodaya Institute of Technology, India
Stankova Elena	Saint Petersburg State University, Russia
Stratigea Anastasia	National Technical University of Athens, Greece

Šurdonja Sanja	University of Rijeka, Croatia
Sviatov Kirill	Ulyanovsk State Technical University, Russia
Sánchez de Merás Alfredo	Universitat de Valencia, Spain
Takahashi Daisuke	University of Tsukuba, Japan
Tanaka Kazuaki	Kyushu Institute of Technology, Japan
Taniar David	Monash University, Australia
Tapia McClung Rodrigo	Centro de Investigación en Ciencias de Información Geoespacial, Mexico
Tarantino Eufemia	Polytechnic University of Bari, Italy
Tasso Sergio	University of Perugia, Italy
Teixeira Ana Paula	University of Trás-os-Montes and Alto Douro, Portugal
Teixeira Senhorinha	University of Minho, Portugal
Tengku Izhar Tengku Adil	Universiti Teknologi MARA, Malaysia
Teodoro Maria Filomena	University of Lisbon, Portuguese Naval Academy, Portugal
Tesoriere Giovanni	University of Enna KORE, Italy
Thangeda Amarendar Rao	Botho University, Botswana
Tonbul Gokchan	Atilim University, Turkey
Toraldo Emanuele	Polytechnic University of Milan, Italy
Torre Carmelo Maria	Polytechnic University of Bari, Italy
Torrieri Francesca	University of Naples, Italy
Torrisi Vincenza	University of Catania, Italy
Toscano Domenico	University of Naples, Italy
Totaro Vincenzo	Polytechnic University of Bari, Italy
Trigo Antonio	Instituto Politécnico de Coimbra, Portugal
Trunfio Giuseppe A.	University of Sassari, Italy
Trung Pham	HCMUT, Vietnam
Tsoukalas Dimitrios	Centre of Research and Technology Hellas (CERTH), Greece
Tucci Biagio	CNR, Italy
Tucker Simon	Liverpool John Moores University, UK
Tuñon Iñaki	Universidad de Valencia, Spain
Tyagi Amit Kumar	Vellore Institute of Technology, India
Uchibayashi Toshihiro	Kyushu University, Japan
Ueda Takahiro	Seikei University, Japan
Ugliengo Piero	University of Torino, Italy
Valente Ettore	University of Naples, Italy
Vallverdu Jordi	University Autonoma Barcelona, Spain
Vanelslander Thierry	University of Antwerp, Belgium
Vasyunin Dmitry	T-Systems RUS, Russia
Vazart Fanny	University of Grenoble Alpes, France
Vecchiocattivi Franco	University of Perugia, Italy
Vekeman Jelle	Vrije Universiteit Brussel (VUB), Belgium
Verde Rosanna	Università degli Studi della Campania, Italy
Vermaseren Jos	Nikhef, The Netherlands

Vignoli Giulio	University of Cagliari, Italy
Vizzari Marco	University of Perugia, Italy
Vodyaho Alexander	Saint Petersburg State Electrotechnical University, Russia
Vona Marco	University of Basilicata, Italy
Waluyo Agustinus Borgy	Monash University, Australia
Wen Min	Xi'an Jiaotong-Liverpool University, China
Westad Frank	Norwegian University of Science and Technology, Norway
Yuasa Fukuko	KEK, Japan
Yadav Rekha	KL University, India
Yamu Claudia	University of Groningen, The Netherlands
Yao Fenghui	Tennessee State University, USA
Yañez Manuel	Universidad Autónoma de Madrid, Spain
Yoki Karl	Daegu Catholic University, South Korea
Zamperlin Paola	University of Pisa, Italy
Zekeng Ndadji Milliam Maxime	University of Dschang, Cameroon
Žemlička Michal	Charles University, Czech Republic
Zita Sampaio Alcinia	Technical University of Lisbon, Portugal
Živković Ljiljana	Ministry of Construction, Transport and Infrastructure and Institute of Architecture and Urban & Spatial Planning of Serbia, Serbia
Zoppi Corrado	University of Cagliari, Italy
Zucca Marco	Polytechnic University of Milan, Italy
Zullo Francesco	University of L'Aquila, Italy

Contents – Part V

International Workshop on Ecosystem Services: Nature's Contribution to People in Practice. Assessment Frameworks, Models, Mapping, and Implications (NC2P 2020)

International Workshop on Open Knowledge for Socio-economic Development (OKSED 2020)

Short Papers

International Workshop on Geomatics in Forestry and Agriculture: New Advances and Perspectives (GeoForAgr 2020)

Evaluation of Meteorological Data-Based Models for Potential and Actual Evapotranspiration Losses Using Flux Measurements

Mirka Mobilia(✉) and Antonia Longobardi

University of Salerno, Via Giovanni Paolo II 132, 84084 Fisciano, Italy
lncs@springer.com

Abstract. Evapotranspiration is a key process within the hydrological cycle, so it requires an accurate assessment. This work aims at assessing monthly scale performances of six meteorological data-based methods to predict evapotranspiration by comparing model estimates with observations from six flux tower sites differing for land cover and climate. Three of the proposed methodologies use a potential evapotranspiration approach (Penman, Priestley-Taylor and Blaney-Criddle models) while the additional three an actual evapotranspiration approach (the Advection-Aridity, the Granger and Gray and the Antecedent Precipation Index method). The results show that models efficiency varies from site to site, even though land cover and climate features appear to have some influence. It is difficult to comment on a general accuracy, but an overall moderate better performance of the Advection-Aridity model can be reported within a context where model calibration is not accounted for. If model calibration is further taken into consideration, the Granger and Gray model appears the best performing method but, at the same time, it is also the approach which is mostly affected by the calibration process, and therefore less suited to evapotranspiration prediction tools dealing with a data scarcity context.

Keywords: Actual evapotranspiration · Potential evapotranspiration · Ameriflux · Fluxnet · Tereno earth observation

1 Introduction

Evapotranspiration (ET) is a key process within the hydrological cycle [1, 2]. It represents a critical parameter in many different applied hydrology studies [3] and uncertainties in its assessment propagate through the hydrological soil-water balance. For this reason, a correct assessment of ET is essential. Eddy covariance (EC) towers represent the best available techniques for determining the ET fluxes but they are expensive to establish and maintain. For these reasons, in the past, many authors have introduced various data-based approaches for actual (AET) and potential (PET) ET modeling [4–6]. Meteorological data-based models for potential evapotranspiration estimation include radiation-based and temperature-based approaches. Among the first type of approaches, the Priestley

O. Gervasi et al. (Eds.): ICCSA 2020, LNCS 12253, pp. 3–18, 2020.
https://doi.org/10.1007/978-3-030-58814-4_1

and Taylor (PT) [7], Turc (TRC) [8], and Abtew (AB) [9] methods are the most common. Among the temperature-based methods, Hargreaves (H) [10], Thornthwaite (TW) [11], Blaney- Criddle (BC) [12] and Linacre (LN) [13] formulations can be listed. The first category requires the solar radiation as the main meteorological variable for the simulation while the second class uses the temperature. A third category is represented by the combination of the previous methods, which couples energetic components, such as net radiation and air temperature, with atmospheric drivers, including air humidity and wind speed. Among these, the Penman (P) model [14, 15] is a universally accepted approach to evaluate potential ET. Concerning actual evapotranspiration, one of the best-known approaches within the class of meteorological data-based methods is the Antecedent Precipitation Index (API) model [16]. Actual evapotranspiration data driven models also include complementary models among which the Advection-Aridity (AA) model [17], the Granger and Gray (GG) model [18], the Complementary Relationship Areal Evaporation (CRAE) model [19], and the modified Advection-Aridity (MAA) model [20]. Considering the large number of proposed approaches, the choice of the most appropriate method for simulating evapotranspiration fluxes is an important issue to be addressed so, in time, many researchers have performed detailed comparative studies [21]. The overall results of the comparative studies suggested that there is not a single approach able to outperform other modeling methods for a particular biome. Given these premises, practical and scientific interest and continuation in this direction appear then encouraged. Within this framework, the current paper presents a comparative analysis where six models and six experimental sites have been taken into consideration. PT, P and BC formulations have been considered for the assessment of potential evapotranspiration, while the AA model, the GG approach and the API model have been considered among actual evapotranspiration empirical relationships. Six experimental sites, belonging to the AMERIFLUX, FLUXNET, and TERENO platforms, have been selected as case studies. They differ in terms of climate type, specifically temperate Oceanic and Mediterranean, and in terms of land covers, specifically forests (FOR), grasslands (GRA) and croplands (CRO). Testing and comparing the performance of the six models for the six experimental sites, it was possible to provide recommendations about the most suited method to be applied in the case of a calibrated and non-calibrated approach and furthermore it was possible to identify, for each model, which is the importance and impact generated by the calibration itself.

2 Materials and Methods

2.1 The Case Studies

Experimental data have been used to compare the relative performance of the selected approaches for evapotranspiration assessment. Six EC towers have been selected for this purpose, belonging to the TERENO (http://teodoor.icg.kfa-juelich.de/overview-en), FLUXNET (http://fluxnet.fluxdata.org/), and AMERIFLUX global networks (http://ameriflux.lbl.gov/). They are representative of specific biomes as they focus on the combination of three different land covers which are grassland, cropland and forests and two climatic regions namely the Mediterranean and the Oceanic climate. According to the Koppen classification [22], the Mediterranean climate (Cs) is characterized by hot, dry summers and cool, wet winters with the highest percentage of rain in the year. The Mediterranean climate includes the subtypes "Csa" and "Csb" where the letter "a" represents an average temperature in the warmest month above 22 C, while "b" indicates the average temperature in the warmest month below 22 C. The oceanic climate (Cf) has cool but not cold winters and warm summers, precipitation is evenly distributed throughout the year. Cf splits in "Cfa" and "Cfb" too. Six sites with the selected biomes have been analyzed in the present research including "us-twt" in California, "us-arm" in Oklahoma, "us-fwf" located in Arizona, "de-rur" and "de-hai" in Germany, "us-me3" in Oregon. Figure 1 shows the location of the stations, the identification number (ID) and the corresponding platforms.

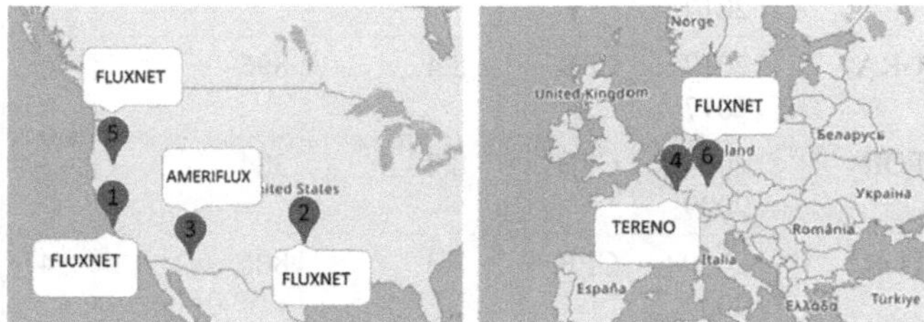

Fig. 1. Location of the investigated flux towers in U.S.A. and Europe.

As an additional climate characterization, which will help the discussion of the results, the moisture index (IM) has been estimated. The moisture index [11], previously calculated for the six sites, allows to classify the climate conditions of various geographical areas. Table 1 represents climate types together with the range of their IM values:

Table 1. Thornthwaite's climate types according to moisture index I_M.

Climatic Type	I_M
Per Humid	>100
B4) Humid (Strongly)	from 81 to 100
B3) Humid	from 61 to 80
B2) Humid (Moderate)	from 41 to 60
B1) Humid (Mild)	from 21 to 40
C2) Moist Sub-humid	from 0 to 20
C1) Dry Sub-humid	from −20 to 0
D) Semi-arid	from −40 to −21
E) Arid	from −60 to −41

Additional details for each site are listed in Table 2, including relevant references and Thornthwaite moisture index (IM).

Table 2. Experimental sites and their main characteristics

ID	Name	Vegetation type	Record period	Climate	Mean annual temperature (°C)	Mean annual Precipitation (mm)	IM (–)	References
1	us-twt	CRO	2009 to 2014	CSA	14.6	344	−65	[23]
2	us-arm	CRO	2003 to 2012	CFA	15.3	646	−40	[24]
3	us-fwf	GRA	2006 to 2012	CSB	8.4	539	−7	[25]
4	de-rur	GRA	2012 to 2017	CFB	8.4	895	68	[26]
5	us-me3	FOR	2004 to 2009	CSB	8.2	384	−30	[27]
6	de-hai	FOR	2000 to 2007	CFB	8.3	806	47	[28]

2.2 Model Description and Evaluation

Estimates from six models have been compared with observational data. Three potential evapotranspiration models and three actual evapotranspiration models have been selected. They are briefly described in the following.

Potential Evapotranspiration Approaches. In order to model baseline PET, Penman (P) equation known as a combination-type technique, Priestley–Taylor (PT) method among the radiation-based models and Blaney–Criddle (BC) equation belonging to the class of temperature-based approaches, have been proposed. Penman (P) formulation can be written as:

$$PET_P = \frac{1}{\lambda}\left[\frac{\Delta}{\Delta+\gamma}(R_n - G_{soil})\right] + \left[\frac{\gamma}{\gamma+\Delta}E_A\right] \tag{1}$$

where Δ is the slope of the saturation vapor pressure–temperature curve (kPa °C^{-1}), γ represents the psychrometric constant (kPa °C^{-1}), λ represents the latent heat of vaporization (MJ kg^{-1}), and E_A represents the drying power of the air, which is expressed as:

$$E_A = 2.6(1 + 0.54u)(e_s - e_a) \tag{2}$$

where u represents the wind speed (ms^{-1}), 2.6(1 + 0.54·u) is the wind function f(u), e_s represents the saturation vapor pressure (kPa), e_a represents the vapor pressure (kPa), Rn represents the net radiation (MJ m^{-2} d^{-1}) and G_{soil} represents the soil heat-flux density at the soil surface (MJ m^{-2} d^{-1}).

Priestley–Taylor formulation is given as:

$$PET_{PT} = \frac{1}{\lambda} \cdot \alpha \left[\frac{\Delta}{\Delta + \gamma} (R_n - G_{soil}) \right] \quad (3)$$

where α represents the advection correction coefficient, with a value of 1.26.

The usual form of the Blaney-Criddle equation is:

$$PET_{BC} = \mathrm{k}p(0.46 \cdot T_{mean} + 8) \quad (4)$$

where p is the percentage of total daytime hours for the considered period (daily or monthly) out of total daytime hours of the year, k is the monthly consumptive use coefficient.

Actual Evapotranspiration Approaches. Three meteorological data-based models have been used to quantify actual evapotranspiration losses: the AA-model, the GG model and the API model. The Advection-Aridity model, the Granger and Gray model are two of the most broadly used approaches among the class of complementary relationship (CR). Actual evapotranspiration derived by the AA method results from Eq. (5):

$$AET_{AA} = (2\alpha - 1)\frac{1}{\lambda}\left[\frac{\Delta}{\Delta + \gamma} (R_n - G_{soil}) \right] - \left[\frac{\gamma}{\gamma + \Delta} E_A \right] \quad (5)$$

According to the GG model, actual evapotranspiration can be estimated instead as follows:

$$AET_{GG} = \left[\frac{\Delta \cdot G}{\Delta + \gamma} \left(\frac{R_n - G_{soil}}{\lambda} \right) \right] + \left[\frac{\gamma \cdot G}{\gamma + \Delta \cdot G} E_A \right] \quad (6)$$

where G is the relative evaporation parameter expressed as:

$$G = \frac{1}{0.793 + 0.20e^{4.902D}} + 0.006D \quad (7)$$

In the previous equation, D is the relative drying power:

$$D = \frac{E_A}{E_A + R_n} \quad (8)$$

The third model selected in the present analysis for estimating actual evapotranspiration is the API model. According to this model, the actual evapotranspiration rates are expressed as:

$$AET_{API} = \frac{1}{\lambda} \cdot \alpha_{API} \left[\frac{\Delta}{\Delta + \gamma} (R_n - G_{soil}) \right] \quad (9)$$

The dimensionless coefficient, α_{API}, is expressed as a threshold function of the Antecedent precipitation index (API). Given a threshold value of the API equal to 20 mm, if the current API value is lower than or equal to the threshold API, then:

$$\alpha_{API} = 0.123(API) - 0.0029(API)^2 - 0.0000056(API)^3 \quad (10)$$

If the current API value is larger than the threshold API, then:

$$\alpha_{API} = 1.26 \tag{11}$$

API is given by the following formula:

$$API = \sum_{t=-1}^{-i} P_t k^{-t} \tag{12}$$

where i represents the considered number of antecedent days, k represents the decay constant, and P_t represents rainfall during day t.

Models Evaluation. Monthly scale ET losses modeled using the above described meteorological data-based approaches are in the following compared to the observed ET fluxes from the EC measurements, for purpose of model evaluation. The comparison will help to test the ability of the models to predict actual evapotranspiration fluxes but, even more importantly, it helps to detect the limitations of each approach. For an overall model evaluation, three goodness-of-fit statistics have been accounted for. These are the normalized root mean square error (RMSEd) as a measure of error intensity, the index of agreement (d) as a measure of patterns agreement, the correlation coefficient (r) as a measure of correlation between observed and modelled variables. They are estimated as follows:

$$RMSE(mm) = \left[\frac{1}{n}\sum_{i=1}^{n}\left(ET_{mod,i} - ET_{EC,i}\right)^2\right]^{\frac{1}{2}} \tag{13}$$

$$RMSEd(-) = \frac{RMSE(mm)}{\overline{ET}_{EC}} \tag{14}$$

$$d(-) = 1 - \frac{\sum_{i=1}^{n}\left|ET_{mod,i} - ET_{EC,i}\right|}{\sum_{i=1}^{n}\left(\left|ET_{mod,i} - \overline{ET}_{EC,i}\right| + \left|ET_{obs,i} - \overline{ET}_{EC,i}\right|\right)} \tag{15}$$

$$r(-) = \frac{Cov(ET_{mod}, ET_{EC})}{\sigma(ET_{mod})\sigma(ET_{EC})} \tag{16}$$

where n represents the length of the monthly sample, $ET_{mod,i}$ and $ET_{EC,i}$ respectively represent the monthly values of the modeled and the observed (i.e., derived from EC fluxes) evapotranspiration fluxes, and σ is the ET standard deviation.

3 Results

3.1 Monthly AET Prediction Models Results

Although all the six models present similar temporal ET patterns, substantial differences in the magnitude of evapotranspiration water losses exist among them, with an exception for one site (de-rur ID4). At a first visual inspection (Fig. 2), all methods appear to overestimate the ET_{EC} measurements but for a quantitative assessment of models' performances in predicting monthly scale ET losses, the goodness-of-fit indices evaluation is reported in Table 3. Furthermore, Fig. 3 illustrates the goodness-of-fit indices for the best performing method for each experimental site.

Table 3. Goodness of fit indices for the different models and experimental sites. In bold the best-performing methods for each site.

Site	Models	RMSEd(−)	d(−)	r(−)	Site	Models	RMSEd(−)	d(−)	r(−)
us-twt (CRO- Csa) ID1	API	0.42	0.73	0.83	de-rur (GRA-Cfb) ID4	API	0.18	0.89	0.99
	AA	0.43	0.69	0.80		AA	0.29	0.80	0.97
	GG	0.29	0.81	0.91		GG	0.21	0.87	0.99
	P	0.67	0.63	0.87		P	0.41	0.74	0.99
	PT	0.26	0.82	0.93		PT	0.20	0.88	0.99
	Blaney-Criddle	0.54	0.57	0.91		Blaney-Criddle	1.23	0.33	0.98
us-arm (CRO- Cfa) ID2	API	1.24	0.47	0.69	us-me3 (FOR- Csb) ID5	API	1.94	0.37	0.75
	AA	0.67	0.57	0.70		AA	1.28	0.49	0.79
	GG	1.12	0.49	0.71		GG	1.97	0.35	0.72
	P	2.54	0.18	0.58		P	2.78	0.24	0.66
	PT	1.24	0.47	0.69		PT	1.99	0.36	0.72
	Blaney-Criddle	2.21	0.19	0.61		Blaney-Criddle	2.67	0.19	0.73
us-fwf (GRA- Csb) ID3	API	0.95	0.55	0.82	de-hai (FOR- Cfb) ID6	API	1.34	0.59	0.96
	AA	0.63	0.54	0.85		AA	0.81	0.75	0.94
	GG	1.21	0.48	0.77		GG	1.41	0.56	0.95
	P	2.68	0.19	0.70		P	2.05	0.38	0.95
	PT	0.97	0.53	0.81		PT	1.34	0.59	0.96
	Blaney-Criddle	2.05	0.22	0.83		Blaney-Criddle	3.43	0.20	0.96

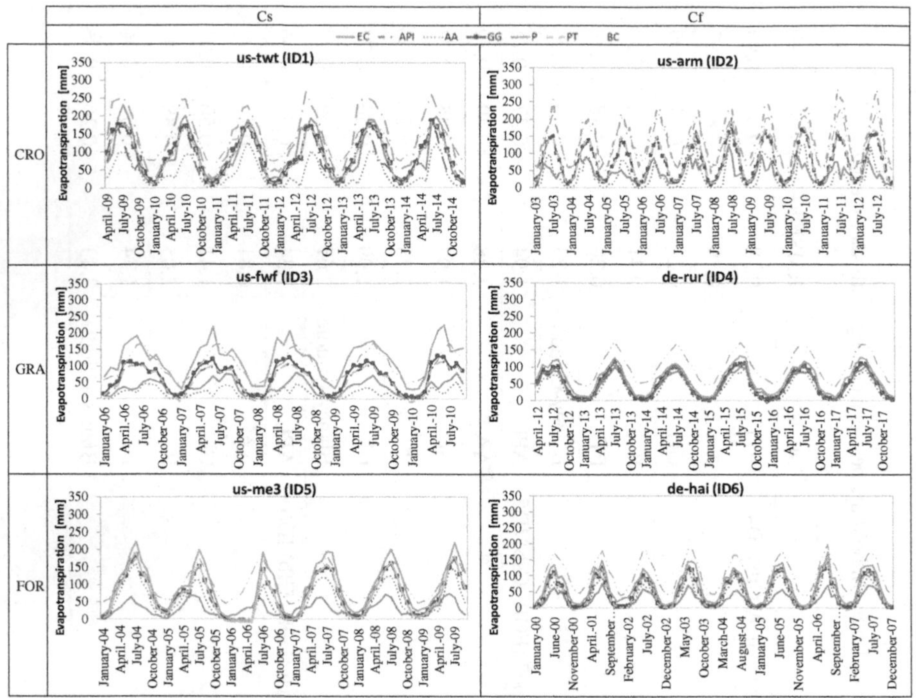

Fig. 2. Monthly patterns of observed and modelled evapotranspiration by using API, AA, GG, PM, PT, BC methods

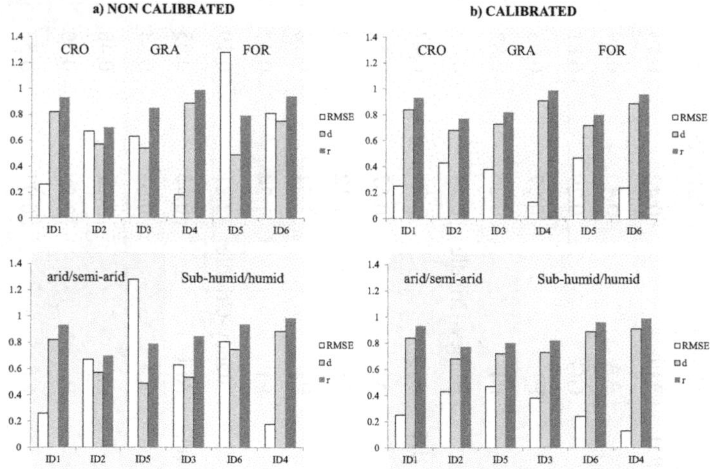

Fig. 3. GOF statistics for the best performing method for each site in the case of a) non calibrated approach and b) calibrated approach with reference to land cover and moisture index IM

The results underline the following key issues:

1. Overall and evidently the PET models result the worst-performing since they return the largest ET overestimation.
2. Among PET approaches, PT-model represents an exception to the rule as it is not only the best performing among PET models but also presents a fitting comparable to AET prediction methods (in particular to the API method). In addition, for the site us-twt (ID1), the Priestley-Taylor approach has been found to be the best performing method;
3. AET models are better able to predict ET rather than the PET ones. Among these, AA approach appears to be characterized by the lowest errors in most of the investigated cases (ID 2, 6, 3, 5) and comparable in the remaining (ID 1, 4).
4. The use of Antecedent Precipitation Index approach better describes the monthly scale evapotranspiration demands in only one case (ID4). Anyway, it should be considered that, for this particular site, the errors associated to all AET methods are comparable with each other.
5. Forest cover type systems (ID5 and ID6) seem associated to the largest prediction errors (larger RMSE and lower r and d) over the studied sites (Fig. 3 upper right panel);
6. Regardless for the land cover type, systems ID3, ID4 and ID6 featured by humid and sub-humid climate conditions seem associated to the lowest prediction errors (lowest RMSE and largest r and d) as illustrated in Fig. 3 lower right panel;
7. Finally, ET values result generally overestimated by all the models with significant percentages error (on average RMSE = 64%). This evidence points to the need to use a calibration procedure to improve meteorological data-based modeling of ET processes as described in the following paragraph.

3.2 AET Models Calibration

The previous analysis has shown large model uncertainties in ET assessment. Possible explanation for the significant errors can be found in the lack of a site-specific calibration of the model parameters so, in order to optimize the evapotranspiration estimates, the calibration of such parameters has been further introduced. As a confirmation of this, many authors in the past have argued about the need for the calibration of the model parameters in order to improve ET prediction [29]. In this study, the calibration process has concerned only the AET models since they have been proven to better perform than the PET ones. The parameters subject to the calibration are the wind function f(u) (for the AA method), the relative evaporation parameter G (for the GG method) and the α-coefficient (for both the API and the AA methods). A moderate range of variability has been reported for such parameters in the relevant literature. Concerning the PT proportionality constant, the proposed values range between 1.05 and 2.20 [30, 31]. As regard to the wind function, there have been many studies dealing with this issue that suggested $a_w = 0.37$ and $b_w = 0.22$ [32], or $a_w = 1.313$ and $b_w = 1.381$ [33] or $a_w = 0.1954$ and $b_w = 0.4703$ [34]. With reference to G, this parameter was empirically derived from several authors [35]. In the current study, the API and the GG approaches have been calibrated in a one-step approach (compared to the AA as later described) where, at the monthly scale, the best match between the eddy covariance ET (ET_{EC}) and the observed data has been achieved minimizing model errors. The calibrated formulations of the relative evaporation, G_{CAL}, and the calibrated Priestley-Taylor coefficient α_{CAL} resulting from this calibration process, has been shown in Table 4. The calibration of AA model consists of two phases [36] since it presents a two-terms structure. For the calibration of the term linked to the drying power of advected air, only the data from the moist days have been used. Moist days have been identified on the base of soil water content higher than a threshold value of 20% [37]. The wind function has been iteratively calibrated until the measured and modelled values of ET during the well-watered days reach the largest match. In the second step, the calibration of α has been performed for the whole period of observation regardless of dry and wet days. In Table 4, the calibrated wind function and Priestley-Taylor coefficient have been shown for each site. As evident in Table 4, α_{CAL}, for the calibrated API model, is similar to 1.26 in the cases of ID1 and ID4, whereas significantly deviates from it for the remaining cases. In the case of the AA model, α_{CAL} is more likely similar to the 1.26 standard coefficient. The calibrated parameter G, assumes for ID4 and ID6 a formulation similar to the one originally used in GG model, in the other cases, the constants remarkably differ from their non-calibrated values. In the end, as regard to the wind function, the calibration process returns for each site a value of b_w about ten times lower than 0.54 which is the non-calibrated parameter.

Table 4. Goodness of fit indices for the different experimental sites. Comparison is made between calibrated models and the non-calibrated best performing models (Table 3).

Site	Models	RMSEd(−)	d(−)	r(−)	Calibrated parameters
us-twt (CRO-Csa) ID1	API_{cal}	0.25	0.84	0.93	$\alpha_{cal} = 1.33$
	AA_{cal}	0.32	0.81	0.92	$\alpha_{cal} = 1.46$; $f(u)_{cal} = 3.2(1 + 0.029u)$
	GG_{cal}	0.27	0.84	0.92	$G_{cal} = 1/(1.5 + 3 \cdot 10^{(-6)} e^{27.3D}) + 0.044 \cdot D$
	PT	0.26	0.82	0.93	–
us-arm (CRO-Cfa) ID2	API_{cal}	0.48	0.61	0.69	$\alpha_{cal} = 0.57$
	AA_{cal}	0.64	0.50	0.73	$\alpha_{cal} = 1.22$; $f(u)_{cal} = 4.3(1 + 0.02u)$
	GG_{cal}	0.43	0.68	0.77	$G_{cal} = 1/(0.55 + 0.035 e^{13.02D}) + 0.061 \cdot D$
	AA	0.67	0.57	0.70	–
us-fwf (GRA-Csb) ID3	API_{cal}	0.38	0.73	0.82	$\alpha_{cal} = 0.77$
	AA_{cal}	0.47	0.71	0.80	$\alpha_{cal} = 1.30$; $f(u)_{cal} = 4.2(1 + 0.012u)$
	GG_{cal}	0.39	0.72	0.80	$G_{cal} = 1/(0.77 + 1.68 e^{3.15D}) + (0.0881 \cdot D)$
	AA	0.63	0.54	0.85	–

(continued)

Table 4. (*continued*)

Site	Models	RMSEd(−)	d(−)	r(−)	Calibrated parameters
de-rur (GRA-Cfb) ID4	API_{cal}	0.15	0.90	0.99	$\alpha_{cal} = 1.22$
	AA_{cal}	0.21	0.87	0.98	$\alpha_{cal} = 1.25$; $f(u)_{cal} = 2.53(1 + 0.054u)$
	GG_{cal}	0.13	0.91	0.99	$G_{cal} = 1/(1.2 + 0.2e^{4.3D}) + 0.012 \cdot D$
	API	0.18	0.89	0.99	–
us-me3 (FOR-Csb) ID5	API_{cal}	0.59	0.65	0.73	$\alpha_{cal} = 0.57$
	AA_{cal}	0.65	0.64	0.78	$\alpha_{cal} = 0.92$; $f(u)_{cal} = 1.88(1 + 0.0035u)$
	GG_{cal}	0.47	0.72	0.80	$G_{cal} = 1/(3.63 + 0.005e^{22.62D}) + 0.07 \cdot D$
	AA	1.28	0.49	0.79	–
de-hai (FOR-Cfb) ID6	API_{cal}	0.30	0.87	0.96	$\alpha_{cal} = 0.56$
	AA_{cal}	0.42	0.84	0.95	$\alpha_{cal} = 1.03$; $f(u)_{cal} = 3.10(1 + 0.0005u)$
	GG_{cal}	0.24	0.89	0.96	$G_{cal} = 1/(3.93 + 0.395e^{4.09D}) + 0.0069 \cdot D$
	AA	0.81	0.75	0.94	–

The accuracy of the AET values provided by the calibrated models (API_{CAL}, AA_{CAL}, GG_{CAL}), has been tested and compared to that resulting from the best performing model (before calibration process) by using the goodness of fit indices suggested in the paragraph 2.2. Results are illustrated in Table 4. In addition, for comparative purpose, the monthly patterns of modelled evapotranspiration resulting from the same models reported in Table 4, have been shown in Fig. 4. From the monthly patterns illustrated in Fig. 4, as expected, it can be seen that monthly evapotranspiration losses provided by the calibrated approaches appear to be more consistent with the EC measurements, also compared to the best-performing method prior to calibration. This circumstance is also supported by the goodness-of-fit assessment (Table 4) which allows to quantitatively assess whether the local calibration improves the confidence in ET estimates derived from the API, AA and GG models. Similarly, to the case of non-calibrated approaches, systems featured by sub-humid/humid climate conditions (Cfb) seem associated to the lowest prediction errors (Fig. 3 lower right panel) as well as forest cover type seems associated to the largest errors (Fig. 3 upper right panel). Overall, the GG_{cal} model appears the best performing calibrated model, while AA_{cal} is the least accurate model probably because of the complex calibration procedure.

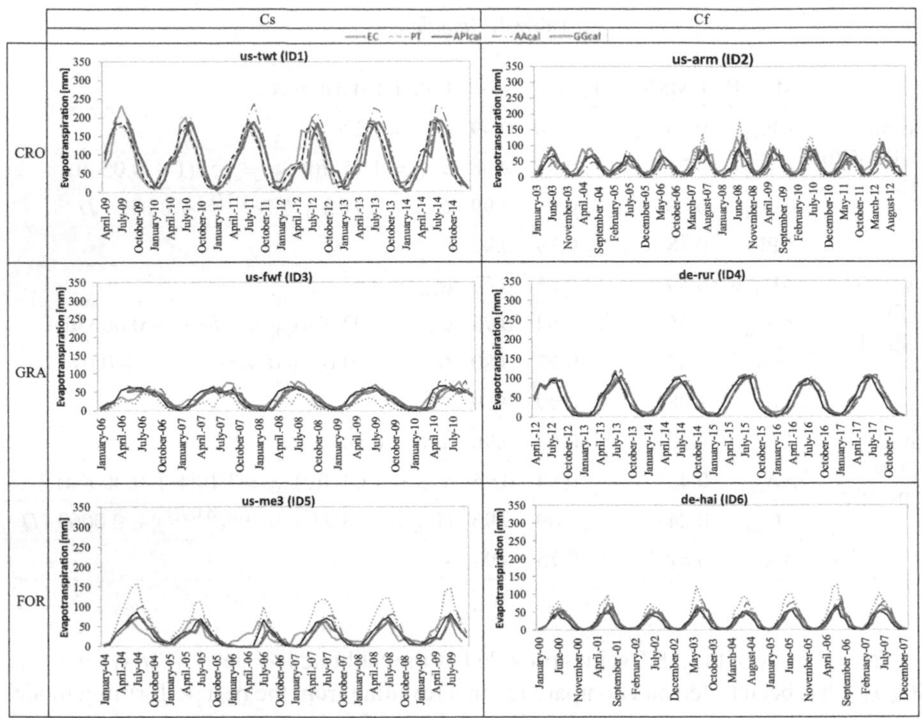

Fig. 4. Monthly patterns of modelled and observed evapotranspiration by using API_{CAL} method compared to the best performing model before calibration process.

The improvement determined by the model parameters calibrated can be better detected with reference to Fig. 5. RMSE, d and r variations are computed as the relative differences between the non-calibrated and the calibrated approaches.

RMSE variations are overall positive, entailing a reduction of RMSE after the calibration for each method and for each site, thus an improvement in model performance. Similarly, d and r variations are overall negative, entailing an increase in d and r after the calibration for each method and for each site, thus an improvement in model performance. Variations in RMSE and d are considerably larger than variations in r, and they are particularly large in the case of the FOR land cover. Among the applied models, the GG which appeared the best performing calibrated model, is the approach most affected by the calibration, with RMSE variation up to 83% and d reduction up to 106%.

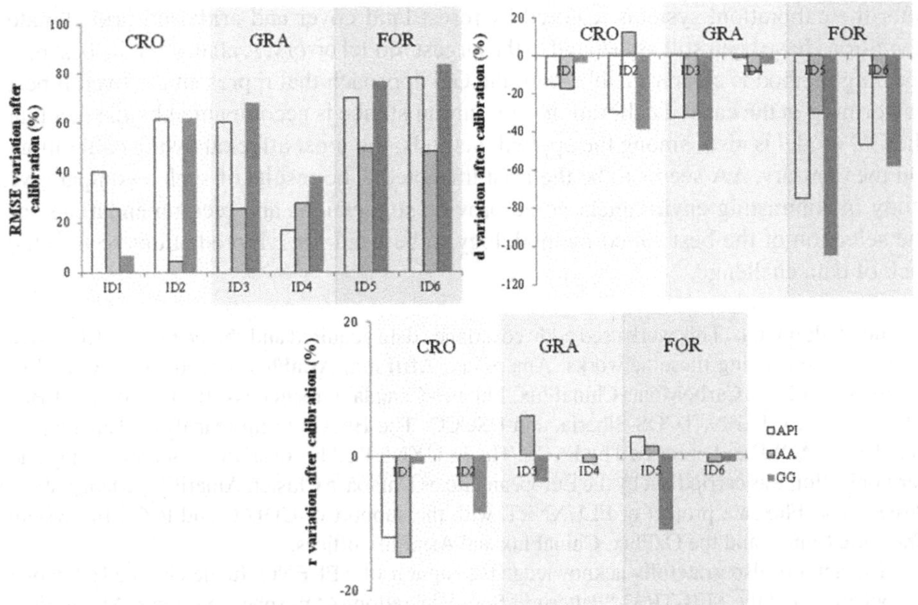

Fig. 5. RMSE, d and r variation caused by model parameters calibration.

4 Conclusion

The performance of six meteorological data-based evapotranspiration models has been evaluated using high-quality dataset of selected eddy covariance towers from FLUXNET, AMERIFLUX and TERENO platforms, characterized by different land covers and climate conditions. AET fluxes have been computed using three models: the GG, the AA and the API models. With regard to the PET approaches, a temperature-based method (i.e. Blaney–Criddle equation), a radiation-based model (Priestley–Taylor methodology) and a combination-type technique (Penman equation) have been tested. Even though it appeared difficult to comment on a general accuracy of the models, varying from site to site, and in finding a single modelling scheme which would be more appropriate for a specific combination of climate and vegetation type, some general tendencies have been detected. AET models have been obviously found to be better in modelling the eddy covariance ET estimates. In a non-calibrated approach, the AA model appeared the best performing method in almost all investigated cases. Systems featured by forest land cover and arid/semi-arid climate conditions have been associated to the largest model errors. Average RMSE, d and r amount to about 64%, 68% and 87%, highlighting the need for a calibration in order to improve model efficiency. Model parameters calibration involved the wind function f(u) for the AA method, the relative evaporation parameter G for the GG method, and the α-coefficient for both the API and the AA methods. Particularly for what concerned the AA method, the calibration process was particularly complex, and all the calibrated parameters significantly deviate from standard coefficients definition. The results of the calibration were obviously an increase in models' efficiency, with average RMSE, d and r that amount to about 32%, 80% and 88% after calibration. Nevertheless, after the calibration, systems featured by forest land cover and arid/semi-arid climate conditions have been still associated to the largest model errors. A change in the best performing method is clearly visible, with the GG approach that represent the overall best performing in the case of calibration. This circumstance is accompanied by the fact that the GG model is also, among the applied methods, the most affected by the calibration. On the contrary, AA seems to be the least impacted. The results of such a comparative study in contrasting environment could provide suggestions and recommendations for the selection of the best suited methodology to be used for ET predictions to face the lack of data challenge.

Acknowledgments. This work used eddy covariance data acquired and shared by the FLUXNET community, including these networks: AmeriFlux, AfriFlux, AsiaFlux, CarboAfrica, CarboEuropeIP, CarboItaly, CarboMont, ChinaFlux, Fluxnet-Canada, GreenGrass, ICOS, KoFlux, LBA, NECC, OzFlux-TERN, TCOS-Siberia, and USCCC. The ERA-Interim reanalysis data are provided by ECMWF and processed by LSCE. The FLUXNET eddy covariance data processing and harmonization was carried out by the European Fluxes Database Cluster, AmeriFlux Management Project, and Fluxdata project of FLUXNET, with the support of CDIAC and ICOS Ecosystem Thematic Center, and the OzFlux, ChinaFlux and AsiaFlux offices.

The authors also gratefully acknowledge the support of TERENO, funded by the Helmholtz Association, and the SFB-TR32 "Pattern in Soil–Vegetation–Atmosphere Systems: Monitoring, Modeling and Data Assimilation", funded by the Deutsche Forschungsgemeinschaft (DFG).

This research has been supported by the U.S. Department of Energy's Office of Science (Grant No. DE-FG02-06ER64318 and DE-AC02-05CH11231 for the AmeriFlux core site) and the US Department of Energy (Grant DE-SC0012194) and Agriculture and Food Research Initiative of the US Department of Agriculture National Institute of Food and Agriculture (Grants 2013-67003-20652, 2014-67003-22065, and 2014-35100-22066) for our North American Carbon Program studies, "Carbon cycle dynamics within Oregon's urban-suburban-forested-agricultural landscapes".

We would like to thank you for providing data, the Office of Biological and Environmental Research of the US Department of Energy under contract No. DE-AC02-05CH11231 as part of the Atmospheric Radiation Measurement Program (ARM) and California Department of Water Resources; USDA/AFRI Funding for AmeriFlux data resources was provided by the U.S. Department of Energy's Office of Science.

References

1. Longobardi, A., Khaertdinova, E.: Relating soil moisture and air temperature to evapotranspiration fluxes during inter-storm periods at a mediterranean experimental site. J. Arid Land **7**(1), 27–36 (2015)
2. Mobilia, M., Longobardi, A.: Model details, parametrization, and accuracy in daily scale green roof hydrological conceptual simulation. Atmos. **11**(6), 575 (2020)
3. Sartor, J., Mobilia, M., Longobardi, A.: Results and findings from 15 years of sustainable urban storm water management. Int. J. Saf. Sec. En. **8**(4), 505–514 (2018)
4. Makkink, G.F., Van Heemst, H.D.J.: The actual evapotranspiration as a function of the potential evapotranspiration and the soil moisture tension. Njas-wagen J. Life sc. **4**(1), 67–72 (1956)
5. Caprio, J.M.: The solar thermal unit concept in problems related to plant development and potential evapotranspiration. Phenol. Season. Mod. **8**, 353–364 (1974)

6. Bair, W., Robertson, G.W.: A new versatile soil moisture budget. Can. J. Plant Sci. **46**(3), 299–315 (1996)
7. Priestley, C.H.B., Taylor, R.J.: On the assessment of surface heat flux and evaporation using large-scale parameters. Mon. Weather Rev. **100**(2), 81–92 (1972)
8. Turc, L.: Estimation of irrigation water requirements, potential evapotranspiration: a simple climatic formula evolved up to date. Ann. Agron. **12**(1), 13–49 (1961)
9. Abtew, W.: Evapotranspiration measurements and modeling for three wetland systems in south Florida. J. Am. Water Resour. As. **32**(3), 465–473 (1996)
10. Hargreaves, G.: Preciseness of estimated reference crop evapotranspiration. J. Irrig. Drain. Eng. **115**(6), 1000–1007 (1989)
11. Thornthwaite, C.W.: An approach toward a rational classification of climate. Geogr. Rev. **38**, 55–94 (1948)
12. Blaney, H.F., Criddle, W.D.: Determining water requirements in irrigated areas from climatological and irrigation data. Soil Conserv. Serv. **96**, 48 (1950)
13. Linacre, E.T.: A simple formula for estimating evaporation rates in various climates, using temperature data alone. Agric. Meteorol. **18**(6), 409–424 (1977)
14. Penman, H.L.: Natural evaporation from open water, bare soil and grass. Proc. R. Soc. Lond. Series Math. Phys. Sci. **193**(1032), 120–145 (1948)
15. Penman, H.L.: Vegetation and hydrology. Soil Sci. **96**(5), 357 (1963)
16. Marasco, D.E., Culligan, P.J., McGillis, W.R.: Evaluation of common evapotranspiration models based on measurements from two extensive green roofs in New York city. Ecol. Eng. **84**, 451–462 (2015)
17. Mobilia, M., Longobardi, A., Sartor, J.F.: Including a-priori assessment of actual evapotranspiration for green roof daily scale hydrological modelling. Water **9**(2), 72 (2017)
18. Granger, R.J., Gray, D.M.: Evaporation from natural nonsaturated surfaces. J. Hydrol. **111**(1–4), 21–29 (1989)
19. Xu, Z.X., Li, J.Y.: Estimating basin evapotranspiration using distributed hydrologic model. J. Hydrol. Eng. **8**(2), 74–80 (2003)
20. Szilagyi, J., Hobbins, M.T., Jozsa, J.: Modified advection-aridity model of evapotranspiration. J. Hydrol. Eng. **14**(6), 569–574 (2009)
21. Fisher, J.B., Tu, K.P., Baldocchi, D.D.: Global estimates of the land–atmosphere waterflux based on monthly AVHRR and ISLSCP-II data, validated at 16 FLUXNET sites. Remote Sens. Environ. **112**, 901–919 (2008)
22. Köppen, W.: Das geographische System der Klimate. Handbuch der Klimatologie, Borntraeger (1936)
23. Knox, S.H., Matthes, J.H., Sturtevant, C., Oikawa, P.Y., Verfaillie, J., Baldocchi, D.: Biophysical controls on interannual variability in ecosystem-scale CO2 and CH4 exchange in a California rice paddy. J. Geophys. Res. Biogeosci. **121**(3), 978–1001 (2016)
24. Lokupitiya, E., et al.: Incorporation of crop phenology in simple biosphere model (SiBcrop) to improve land-atmosphere carbon exchanges from croplands. Biogeosci. **6**(6), 969–986 (2009)
25. Dore, S., et al.: Recovery of ponderosa pine ecosystem carbon and water fluxes from thinning and stand-replacing fire. Global Change Biol. **18**(10), 3171–3185 (2012)
26. Borchard, N., et al.: Spatio-temporal drivers of soil and ecosystem carbon fluxes at field scale in an upland grassland in Germany. Agric. Ecosyst. Environ. **211**, 84–93 (2015)
27. Kwon, H., Law, B.E., Thomas, C.K., Johnson, B.G.: The influence of hydrological variability on inherent water use efficiency in forests of contrasting composition, age, and precipitation regimes in the Pacific Northwest. Agric. Meteorol. **249**, 488–500 (2018)
28. Rebmann, C., et al.: Quality analysis applied on eddy covariance measurements at complex forest sites using footprint modelling. Theo. Appl. Climatol. **80**(2–4), 121–141 (2005)

29. Tabari, H., Grismer, M.E., Trajkovic, S.: Comparative analysis of 31 reference evapotranspiration methods under humid conditions. Irrig. Sci. **31**(2), 107–117 (2013)
30. McNaughton, K.G., Black, T.A.: A study of evapotranspiration from a Douglas fir forest using the energy balance approach. Water Resour. Res. **9**(6), 1579–1590 (1973)
31. Cristea, N.C., Kampf, S.K., Burges, S.J.: Revised coefficients for priestley-taylor and makkink-hansen equations for estimating daily reference evapotranspiration. J. Hydrol. Eng. **18**(10), 1289–1300 (2013)
32. Kohler, M.A., Nordenson, T.J., Fox, W.E.: Evaporation from Pans and Lakes. US Government Printing Office, United States (1955)
33. McMahon, T.A., Peel, M.C., Lowe, L., Srikanthan, R., McVicar, T.R.: Estimating actual, potential, reference crop and pan evaporation using standard meteorological data: a pragmatic synthesis. Hydrol. Earth Syst. Sci. **17**(4), 1331–1363 (2013)
34. Hobbins, M.T., Ramirez, J.A., Brown, T.C.: The complementary relationship in estimation of regional evapotranspiration: an enhanced advection-aridity model. Water Resour. Res. **37**(5), 1389–1403 (2001)
35. Kim, H., Kaluarachchi, J.J.: Estimating evapotranspiration using the complementary relationship and the Budyko framework. J. Water Clim. Change **8**(4), 771–790 (2017)
36. Crago, R.D., Qualls, R.J., Feller, M.: A calibrated advection-aridity evaporation model requiring no humidity data. Water Resour. Res. **46**(9), 1–8 (2010)
37. Crago, R., Brutsaert, W.: A comparison of several evaporation equations. Water Resour. Res. **28**(3), 951–954 (1992)

GNSS Network RTK for Automatic Guidance in Agriculture: Testing and Performance Evaluation

Fabio Radicioni[1(✉)], Aurelio Stoppini[1], Raffaella Brigante[2], Andrea Brozzi[3], and Grazia Tosi[1]

[1] Department of Engineering, Perugia University, 06125 Perugia, Italy
{fabio.radicioni,aurelio.stoppini,grazia.tosi}@unipg.it
[2] Civil Engineer, 06125 Perugia, Italy
[3] Environmental Engineer, 06125 Perugia, Italy

Abstract. The paper reports the results of a research on validation and optimization of automatic and semi-automatic guidance systems for agricultural machinery based on Real-Time positioning services provided by GNSS Networks (NRTK). The research is based on experimental campaigns performed on test areas, located in Umbria (central Italy) on the land of six farming companies.

The tests have interested many processes of the agricultural work carried out in different seasons and environmental conditions, by means of agricultural machinery of various size, power and characteristics. For the performance evaluation of different guidance systems and positioning methods, reference solutions obtained in post-processing with geodetic GNSS receivers have been utilized.

To reach generalized conclusions, appropriate parameters have been defined and evaluated in order to compare the quality of the results of tests performed with different equipment and conditions, and to quantify the economic benefits achieved through the GNSS guidance systems. Further tests have been performed to evaluate the ability of machine control systems to acquire a series of useful agronomic and geometric data during the work to be included in a farm-level GIS, including the three-dimensional geometry of the crops, the creation of reports about processes and treatments and the optimization of the machine paths and related agricultural activities.

Keywords: Precision agriculture · Machine control · Automatic guidance · GNSS real time positioning · Network RTK

1 Introduction

The control and guidance systems for agricultural machinery based on Real-Time GNSS positioning have emerged in the latest years as a significant cost reduction and increased productivity factor [1, 2].

The few-meters positioning accuracy supplied by a single GNSS receiver in standalone mode is not sufficient for precise agriculture, where it is necessary to achieve a

O. Gervasi et al. (Eds.): ICCSA 2020, LNCS 12253, pp. 19–35, 2020.
https://doi.org/10.1007/978-3-030-58814-4_2

decimeter or, for some applications, sub-decimeter accuracy [3, 4]. This is possible if the receiver placed on the equipment is able to acquire a code (DGNSS, accuracy < 1 m) or code/phase (RTK or NRTK, accuracy < 5 cm) RTCM correction stream via Ntrip protocol.

Most of the RTCM-based systems used in agriculture need a GNSS base station (located in a point with known coordinates) that sends RTCM corrections to the on-board receiver through a radio modem (base/rover RTK). In Italy and other European countries, the transmission power of a private radio signal is limited by law to a maximum of 0.5 Watts, which strongly limits the covered area and makes it necessary to locate the base in the proximity of the rover.

In the present research RTCM correction was not sent by a base station, but by means of the Control Center of the regional GNSS permanent network (GPSUMBRIA) [5]. This approach (Network RTK or NRTK) has the considerable advantage of covering very large areas without the need (and the cost) of a base station [6].

One of the purposes of this research was to test the applicability, the coverage and the reliability of NRTK approach on agricultural applications. The position obtained in real time from GNSS systems is used for driving the agricultural machines during the fieldwork. The GNSS guidance can be "assisted" (semi-automatic) or fully automatic, even if the driver is always on board for security reasons.

The experiments have compared three guidance modes: manual, assisted and automatic [7, 8]. The tests have been performed during different agricultural processes and the results have been compared for evaluating the geometric accuracy and the operator stress. The research has been carried out in the frame of a Rural Development Plan (PSR) promoted by the Umbria Regional Council and financed by UE, and has developed into a series of successive steps. The first step has been the individuation of test areas for each company of the project, then digital maps have been acquired and implemented on a GIS (software platform Topcon SGIS) integrating them with other metadata information (cultivation sheets with environmental and agronomic parameters). Preliminary inspections have been carried out in the test areas to check the coverage by the Network RTK positioning services and testing protocols have been developed. The relevant amount of experimental data collected has made possible to develop a deep and wide analysis, the results of which are described in this paper.

2 GNSS Infrastructures and NRTK Positioning Services

The NRTK technique is based on the existence of an infrastructure (Network of GNSS permanent stations) offering positioning services by sending RTCM correction messages. Each user sends to the network Control Center a service access request including his approximate position in NMEA format. The Control Center sends a custom RTCM correction stream based on the user location. One of the most common correction type is VRS, creating a "Virtual Reference Station" in the proximity of the user [9]. There are alternative approaches (MAC, FKP,...) but the results are similar (a real-time 3D positioning with accuracy < 5 cm) with comparable efficiency [10].

The experimentation described in the present paper has been supported by the GNSS network GPSUMBRIA realized since 2004 by the University of Perugia and the Regional

Administration of Umbria including 13 GNSS permanent stations (Fig. 1), with a short average spacing (about 40 km) giving the network a redundancy which permits to overcome malfunctions of some stations [5, 11]. All stations are equipped with geodetic multicostellation/multisignal receivers with choke-ring antennas.

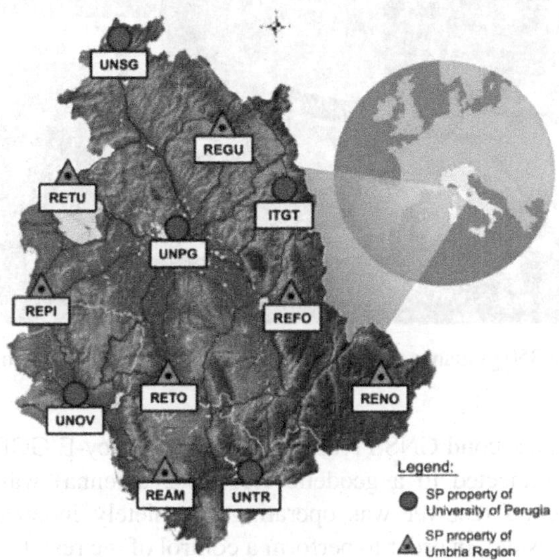

Fig. 1. The GNSS network GPSUMBRIA

The GPSUMBRIA network has the primary function of maintaining a stable reference frame for the whole region, consistent with the official datum ETRF2000. It also provides public and private users a wide range of positioning services in post-processing and real-time, distributed free of charge to promote the use of this infrastructure supporting technological innovation in various fields of work. For further information, please refer to [5] and [11].

3 Instruments and Machines Used in the Tests

For the experimental campaign tractors of different characteristics were used, all equipped with the GNSS guidance system Topcon System 350, including an AGI-4 receiver and a X30 console (Fig. 2). Some tractors were equipped with a Topcon AES-25 electric steering wheel, other machines used the included servo-assisted steering wheel, appropriately interfaced with the guidance system. An estimated cost for the complete system is of about 20000 €; if the tractor is already equipped with the electric steering wheel the cost is considerably reduced.

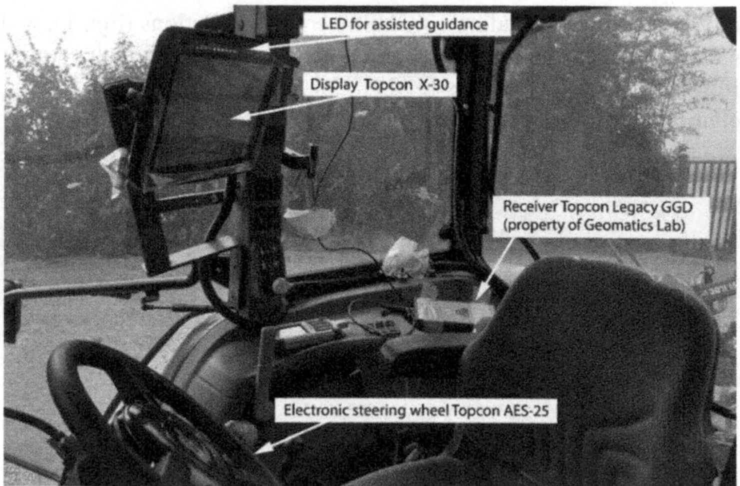

Fig. 2. Topcon 350 guidance system mounted on a tractor participating to the tests

During the tests a second GNSS receiver (Topcon Legacy-E GGD, dual-frequency GPS/GLONASS, connected to a geodetic LegAnt-2 antenna) was installed in the machines. This second receiver was operating completely independently from the machine guidance system, in order to perform a control of the results without any interference (Fig. 3). The planimetric and height offsets between the two different antennas were appropriately measured and taken into account.

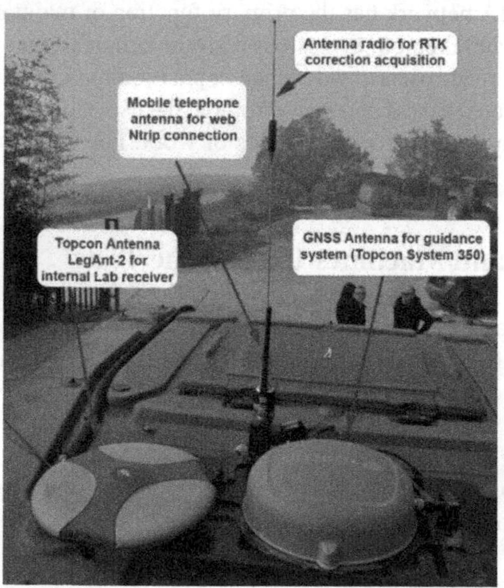

Fig. 3. GNSS receivers and antennas mounted on the top of a tractor cabin

The tests have been performed using tractors of various sizes and types, wheeled and tracked, for different agricultural processes. The control receiver (Topcon Legacy) has been used as rover for kinematic post-processing, acquiring GNSS raw data during the test sessions. In the proximity of each test area a second Topcon Legacy receiver has been installed, as base station for the determination of the rover trajectories (Fig. 4). For both receivers the sampling frequency was set to 1 Hz (1 measure or "epoch" per second). The base stations coordinates have been calculated from post-processed static GNSS solutions with connection to GPSUMBRIA network.

Fig. 4. Base-Rover post-processing for control purposes

4 Execution of the Tests

The tests here presented have been carried out in two different locations. The first test area (Fig. 5), located near Spina (Perugia) and characterized by a slope of about 9,5% with East exposure, has interested sowing, fertilizing and harrowing operations. The second site is a flat ground near Tavernelle (Perugia) which was interested only by harrowing process (Fig. 6).

Fig. 5. Sowing in manual mode (left) and automatic mode (right)

Fig. 6. Harrowing in manual mode (left) and automatic mode (right)

The agricultural processes were performed in three driving modes (e.g. Figs. 5, 6):

- manual;
- assisted;
- automatic.

In manual mode the operator has a complete control of the vehicle and proceeds with the usual methods based on alignment by sight. In assisted mode a row of LEDs shows the deviation from the ideal line and the correction is performed manually by the operator according to the LED indication. In automatic mode, the trajectory correction is automatically performed by the electric steering wheel and the operator only has to control the vehicle speed.

The trajectories followed by the machines were computed in two different ways:

- recording by the machine guidance system the positions calculated in real time;
- post-processing kinematic solutions obtained from the data gathered by the control GNSS receivers (Fig. 4).

A psychologist observed the reactions of the tractor drivers during part of the tests to evaluate the state of psycho-physical stress.

5 Data Processing

The post-processing of the GNSS data for control purposes was performed with the Topcon Tools 8.2.3 software (Fig. 7). The steps of the calculation were the following:

- computation of the 3D coordinates of the base stations by static GNSS connection with two permanent stations of the GPSUMBRIA network;
- assuming as fixed the coordinates of the base stations, GNSS kinematic computation of the trajectories of the tractors (3D position each second).

The processing was performed in the datum ETRF2000, the same of the positions obtained in real time by the on board GNSS guidance system.

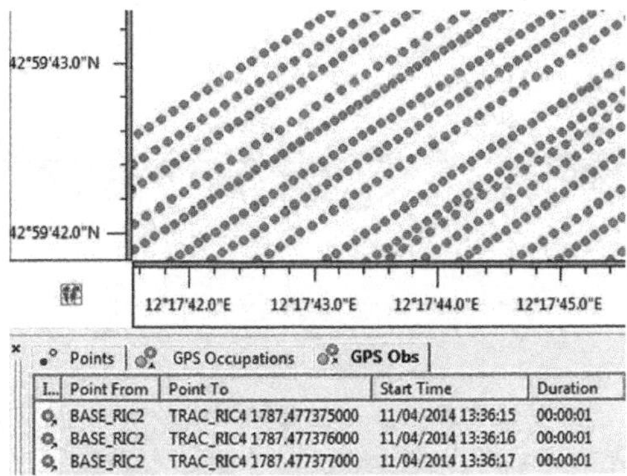

Fig. 7. Topcon tools post-processing solution of a tractor trajectory (example)

The post-processing trajectories were superimposed on the test areas ortophotos in GIS for a rapid check. Then, a comparison with the trajectories recorded by the guidance system was carried out.

The post-processing coordinates are referred to the antenna phase center. To compare them with the positions calculated in real time by the guidance system, the horizontal and vertical offsets were considered. The comparison also required an alignment of epochs, formats and units. A very good agreement was found between post-processing and real time solutions, at a few centimeters level.

5.1 Evaluation of the Efficiency of the Guidance System

In order to evaluate the efficiency of GNSS-supported guidance systems with respect to the manual guide, the following analysis was carried out:

- the trajectories were divided into individual rectilinear strips, excluding the initial and the final parts, affected by the U-turns of the tractor;
- for each strip the transverse displacements of each position with respect to a straight line indicating the hypothetical ideal path were evaluated;
- a statistical analysis was performed on the transverse displacements;
- a comparison between the results of the three different driving systems (manual, assisted and automatic) was finally performed.

In Fig. 8 are shown, as example, some graphs comparing the transverse deviations from the average straight line. The results have been grouped for tests performed under the same experimental conditions (test area, tractor, accessories, type of agricultural process, soil conditions) with the three different guidance systems.

The statistical parameters referring to Fig. 8 are summarized in Table 1. The mean value of the transverse deviation is always zero because the values are computed with respect to the average straight line, assumed as the ideal path.

The graphs A, B and C refers to test series effected with narrow wheels tractors on a variable slope terrain. The tests of the group A were carried out on dry terrain, while for

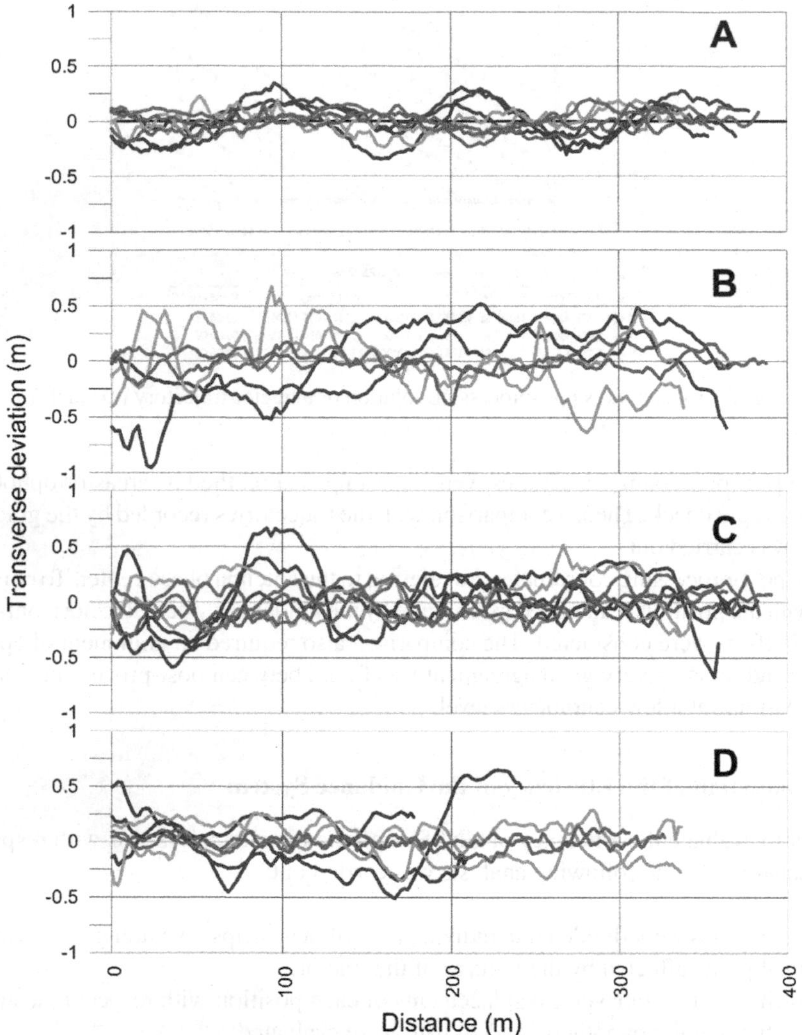

Fig. 8. Transverse deviations from an average rectilinear path vs. distance for different processes and machines: A) Sowing, wheeled tractor; B) Fertilization, wheeled tractor; C) Harrowing, wheeled tractor; D) Harrowing, rubber tracked tractor. Colour legend: blue = manual drive, green = assisted drive, red = automatic drive. (Color figure online)

the graphs B and C the driving conditions were quite difficult due to the moistened and muddy soil. The graph D refers to a test group performed with a rubber tracked tractor on a flat and dry ground (Fig. 6).

It can be seen that with the manual system there are relevant transverse displacements from the average ideal path, up to some decimetres for a trajectory of some hundreds of meters. An exception is the sowing process (graph A) where the traditional alignment aid (Fig. 5, left) helps to obtain a good accuracy even in manual mode.

Table 1. Statistical parameters of the experimental transverse deviations for different guidance systems on various test groups (referring to Fig. 8 graphs)

A - Sowing, wheeled tractor			
Parameter	Manual	Assisted	Automatic
Mean (m)	0,00	0,00	0,00
RMS (m)	0,16	0,09	0,08
RMS %	100	58	53
Max (m)	0,35	0,23	0,20
Min (m)	−0,35	−0,24	−0,23
V_{med} (m/s)	2,32	2,09	2,33
B - Fertilizing, wheeled tractor			
Parameter	Manual	Assisted	Automatic
Mean (m)	0,00	0,00	0,00
RMS (m)	0,31	0,24	0,10
RMS %	100	76	31
Max (m)	0,52	0,67	0,23
Min (m)	−0,95	−0,63	−0,38
V_{med} (m/s)	2,66	2,87	2,30
C - Harrowing, wheeled tractor			
Parameter	Manual	Assisted	Automatic
Mean (m)	0,00	0,00	0,00
RMS (m)	0,25	0,18	0,12
RMS %	100	73	48
Max (m)	0,67	0,51	0,24
Min (m)	−0,67	−0,30	−0,31
V_{med} (m/s)	2,66	2,98	2,72
D – Harrowing, rubber tracked tractor			
Parameter	Manual	Assisted	Automatic
Mean (m)	0,00	0,00	0,00
RMS (m)	0,26	0,16	0,06
RMS %	100	61	22
Max (m)	0,65	0,29	0,14
Min (m)	−0,51	−0,40	−0,18
V_{med} (m/s)	1,97	1,62	1,40

The deviations are reduced with the assisted driving system. With respect to manual driving, with the assisted guidance the RMS value reduces in the range of 58% to 76%.

In other situations (e.g. graph B) the driver seems to have difficulties to follow the system indications.

The automatic system always provided the most accurate results, with the smallest transverse deviations: RMS value of 6 cm in the most favourable case (graph D) and 12 cm in the worst one (graph C). With respect to manual drive, with the automatic guidance the RMS value reduces consistently (22% to 53%).

The deviations obtained in automatic mode are in good agreement with the accuracy level of a NRTK positioning (a few centimetres). However, in some cases the graphs show higher deviations. This is due to the fact that the graphs show the actual, raw results of tests carried out in the field. As already mentioned, in the B and C tests the tractor had narrow tyres and the ground was muddy and sloping. In such condition lateral displacements up to 20-25 cm are likely, because the steering, the mechanics and the inertia of the tractor make impossible to prevent the wheels from slipping down into the side grooves.

5.2 Evaluation of the Benefit of the Guidance System in Terms of Areas

In order to carry out an economic assessment of the actual benefit obtained by a precision guidance system, the main parameter to evaluate is the gaps and/or overlaps area between adjacent processed "strips", and its percentage on the total area worked. This concept is graphically expressed in Fig. 9. The costs are in fact generally proportional to the areas actually worked. Therefore, the processing extra costs are proportional to the overlaps and the losses due to lack of process are proportional to the gaps.

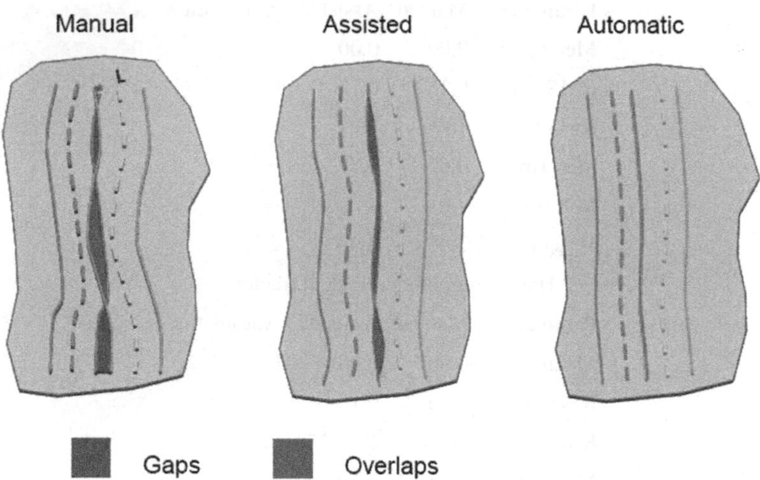

Fig. 9. Gaps and overlaps between contiguous processed strips

In this study, we started from an *a posteriori* evaluation and subsequently tried to define parameters and indexes for an *a priori* estimate of the benefits.

For the *a posteriori* evaluation we proceeded as follows. Starting from the trajectory axes and considering the width of the processed strip (different according to the type of equipment towed by the tractor), the footprints on the ground of the processed areas have been traced in a graphical environment (CAD and/or GIS). From the footprints, the actual areas of overlaps and gaps has been determined. Overlaps are defined as intersections between contiguous strips areas. Gaps are defined as difference between supposed total area and actually processed total area for each pair of contiguous strips.

The areas of overlaps and gaps were compared with the total area, in order to evaluate the actual benefits or losses related to different guidance systems.

Table 2 and Fig. 10 summarise the results for the same tests of Table 1 and Fig. 8.

Table 2. Evaluation of gaps and overlaps between contiguous processed strips for different guidance systems on various test groups (referring to the graphs of Fig. 10)

Tractor	Process	Guidance	Area (m^2)	Gaps (m^2)	Overlaps (m^2)	Gaps %	Overlaps %
wheeled	sowing	manual	11566	516	60	4,5	0,5
wheeled	sowing	assisted	8644	342	83	4,0	1,0
wheeled	sowing	automatic	9553	143	107	1,5	1,1
wheeled	fertilizing	manual	10468	0	973	0,0	9,3
wheeled	fertilizing	assisted	10672	17	43	0,2	0,4
wheeled	fertilizing	automatic	12474	63	0	0,5	0,0
wheeled	harrowing	manual	12448	0	2032	0,0	16,3
wheeled	harrowing	assisted	10595	166	181	1,6	1,7
wheeled	harrowing	automatic	8689	120	107	1,4	1,2
tracked	harrowing	manual	9873	2	1043	0,0	10,6
tracked	harrowing	assisted	7960	50	343	0,6	4,3
tracked	harrowing	automatic	7038	49	68	0,7	1,0

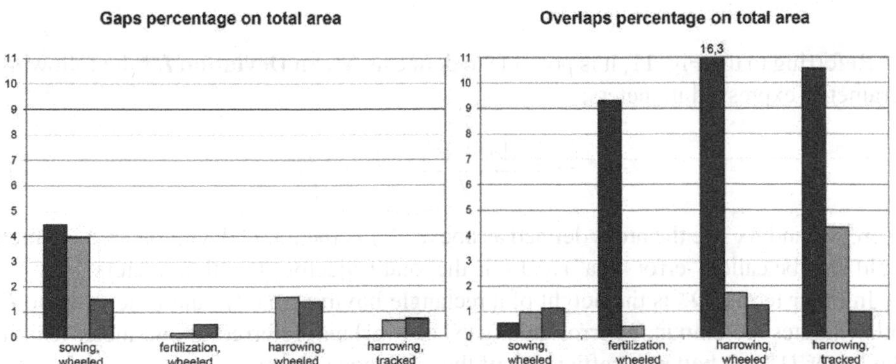

Fig. 10. Gaps and Overlaps percentage on total processed area for different guidance systems on various test groups (referring to Table 2). Legend: blue = manual drive, green = assisted drive, red = automatic drive. (Color figure online)

It can be noticed that with manual guidance, to avoid gaps strong overlaps often occurred (10% and more of the processed area), with a consequent relevant increase of the costs for processing and consumption of seeds and fertilizer. With the GNSS-guided systems, the overlaps are greatly decreased. However, in few cases gaps occur more than with manual drive but with a small percentage, around 1% or less.

6 Analysis and Parameterization of the Results

It can be useful to define some parameters that synthetically express the efficiency of a guidance system for agriculture and evaluate *a priori* the savings achievable by adopting a high accuracy GNSS guidance system.

Overlaps and gaps are caused by transversal deviations of the tractor from the ideal trajectory.

To assess their entity, the graphs have been analysed in terms of areas between the actual trajectory and the ideal one for all the guidance systems.

Figure 11 shows an example graph of the transversal deviations in which the positive error areas (A_P) and the negative ones (A_N) of the ideal trajectory have been highlighted.

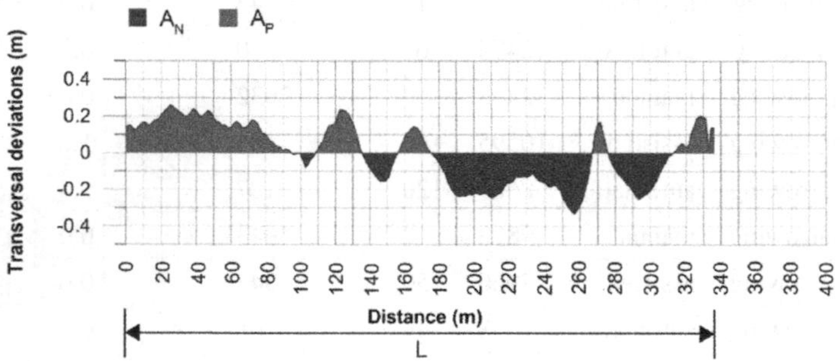

Fig. 11. Areas between the actual trajectory and a straight ideal line

Referring to the Fig. 11, it is possible to define as **Mean Deviation *D**** the following parameter, expressed in meters:

$$D^* = \frac{\sum(|A_P| + |A_N|)}{L} = \frac{A_D}{L} \tag{1}$$

where A_P and A_N are the areas defined as above, A_D is the total "deviation area" (which could also be called "error area") and L is the total trajectory length in meters.

In other terms, D^* is the height of a rectangle having area A_D and base equal to L, and evaluates the amount of error area (gaps or overlaps) referred to one-meter length. The lower D^*, the better the efficiency of the guidance system.

The Mean Deviation D^* can be expressed as a percentage $D^*\%$, representing the percentage of the deviation area for a unit width strip (1 m):

$$D^*\% = D^* \cdot 100 \tag{2}$$

The results obtained with different driving systems in the tests previously described have been analysed in terms of the parameters defined above. The mean values of the D*% parameter for the analysed strips is shown in the following graph.

The parameterization in terms of Mean Deviation (Fig. 12) helps to obtain a good summary of the results of the research.

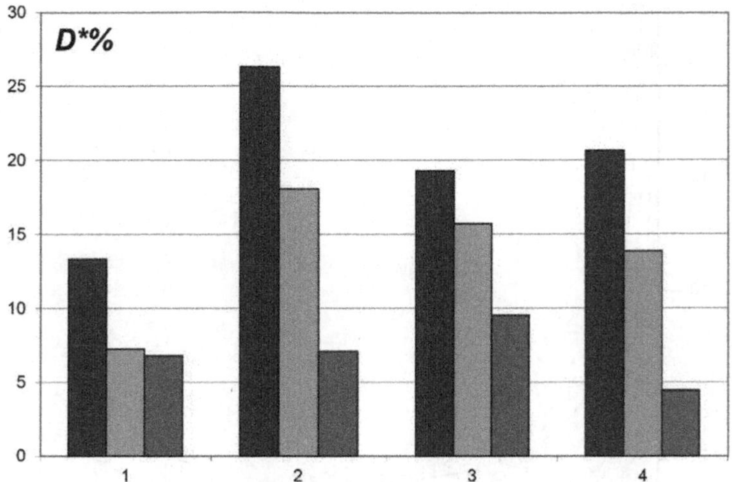

Fig. 12. Mean values of Mean Deviation *D*%* trend for different guidance systems on various test groups: 1 sowing, 2 fertilizing, 3 harrowing (wheeled tractor), 4 harrowing (tracked tractor). Legend: blue = manual drive, green = assisted drive, red = automatic drive. (Color figure online)

It is clear as the automatic guidance is the most advantageous one, leading to obtain *D*%* values on the 5-10% order, whilst for manual guidance *D*%* is in the 15-25% range. The reduction of the error areas in automatic mode compared to manual driving varies from ½ to ¼ factor.

The assisted guidance has shown results between manual and automatic driving, showing some difficulties to calibrate the system and highly driver-depending.

The evaluations carried out by psychologists indirectly confirm these results, advising a higher stress for the driver in assisted guide compared to the manual one.

The *D** parameter allow to evaluate the savings achievable with the installation of a GNSS automatic guidance system.

As define, D*% is referred to a unit width strip (S = 1 m) but actually the width of the field strip processed is different depending on the accessory towed by the tractor.

For a generic width S and length L strip, it is possible to define a **Deviation Index *ID*** as the percentage of the error area on the total area processed (A_T):

$$ID = \frac{A_D}{A_T} \cdot 100 = \frac{D^* \cdot L}{S \cdot L} \cdot 100 = \frac{D^*\%}{S} \tag{3}$$

where A_T, the total field area processed for one strip, is:

$$A_T = S \cdot L \tag{4}$$

The graph on Fig. 13 refers to the expression (3) and represents the trend of the percentage of the error area as a function of the width of the processed strip and of the *D*%* value and was drawn using an interpolation function.

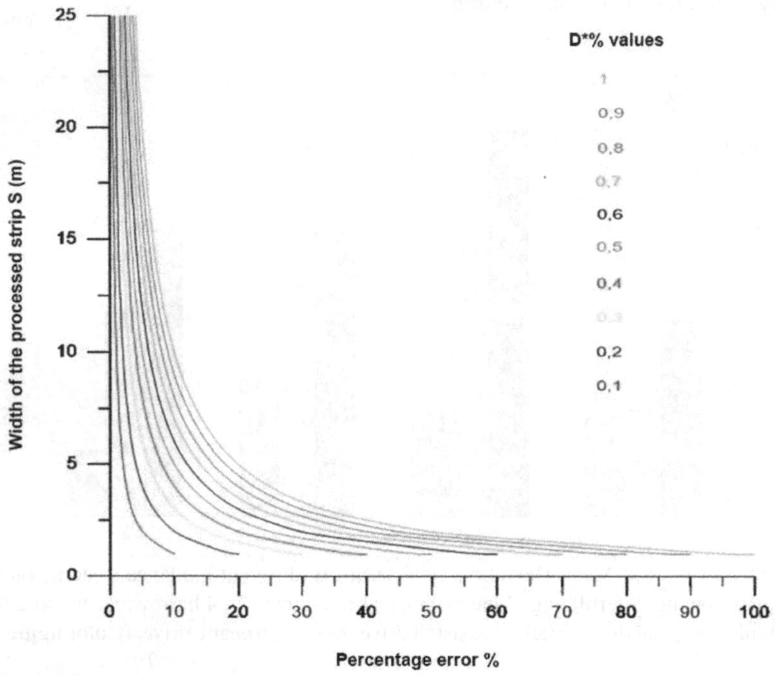

Fig. 13. Graph for the ID evaluation

The ID percentage value can be estimated according to the width *S* of the processed strip and the *D*%* value that can be assumed in relation to the guidance system adopted.

This graph shows how much the width of the field strip varying the D*% parameter can influence the process efficiency in terms of error percentage, so as to be able to determine the increase or the reduction of costs and times for the process.

To use this graph and define the cost reduction, by switching from one driving mode to another one, it is first necessary to estimate D*% value in manual and automatic guidance for a certain process and the strip width S. Entering the graph with S and D*%, the error area percentage is determined.

Two examples of the use of the graph in Fig. 13 follow. For a width of S = 5 m:

- in manual guidance (D* = 0.2), area percentage error 4% (m)
- in automatic guidance (D* = 0.1), area percentage error 2% (m)

For a width of S = 20 m:

- in manual guidance (D* = 0.2), area percentage error 1% (m)
- in automatic guidance (D* = 0.1), area percentage error 0.5% (m)

From the cost of the product supplied (fertilizer, treatment, ...) per unit area, it is possible to evaluate the savings due to automatic guidance. For a width of 5 m and a parcel of 100 ha, considering a hypothetical product cost of 400 €/ha, in manual guidance the extra costs are equal to 16 €/ha for a total of 1,600 €; with automatic guidance these values are halved, so there would be a saving of 800 € for this single process.

6.1 Code Correction (DGNSS) and EGNOS

In order to evaluate the efficiency of the guidance systems, the code correction modes (DGNSS - EGNOS) were also tested. The results are summarized in Fig. 14, expressed in terms of D*% parameter as defined in the previous chapter. It can be noticed that with assisted guidance, the code correction from GPSUMBRIA network (DGPS) provided a mean deviation parameter of about 0.50; with the same guidance mode, the code correction from the EGNOS [12] gave a slightly better result, with an average D*% of about 0.35. As expected, phase corrections produce better results than code ones, and confirm as the most suitable approach for obtaining good results, especially with automatic guidance system.

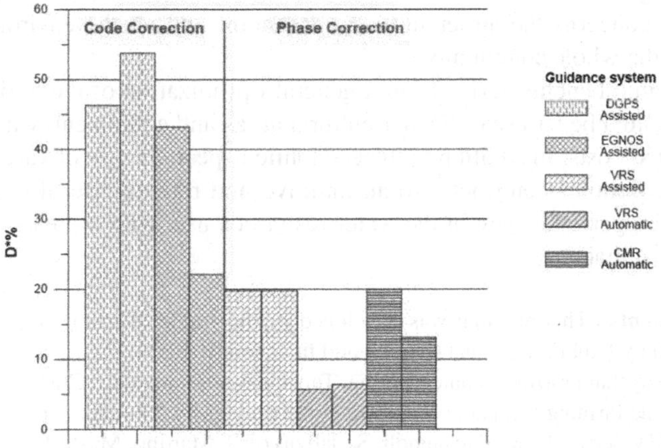

Fig. 14. Graph of mean deviation D*% for different correction mode

7 Final Remarks

The results obtained from this research have highlighted many aspects of the GNSS techniques application in precision agriculture and are encouraging: the advantages of the adoption of these techniques appeared clearly. GNSS NRTK technology based on real-time corrections and applied to agricultural equipment brings significant benefits under several points of view.

The use of network corrections compared to the base/rover ones shows remarkable advantages in terms of accuracy, greater reliability and stability as well as the possibility of covering a large territory operating in a global reference system. The analyses carried out on different driving modes show how the automatic mode reduces the D *% parameter of about 50% with respect to manual guidance; automatic guide is more precise and it is preferred by the operators, since less stressful.

A study was later carried out to evaluate the theoretical error area percentage based on S and D *% parameter in order to provide a tool to early analyse how much one driving mode is more efficient than another one. The tables and graphs developed show that as the width of the processed strip increases, there is an asymptotic reduction in the theoretical errors area percentage. On the contrary for reduced processed strip widths, the difference between the percentage error area of a manual guidance and the automatic one is much greater. The error area percentage therefore decreases as the width of the processed strip increases, reaching error percentage values between the various driving modes that are always less wide.

The accuracies achievable in assisted and automatic driving modes were assessed through the application of different types of real-time signal correction. Tests on code correction (DGPS, EGNOS) show a lower accuracy compared to the one achievable with phase correction. The VRS real-time correction gave the best accuracy results with both the assisted and automatic guidance.

Precision agriculture has a dual positive impact: on the economic-managerial front, which mostly concerns the agricultural entrepreneur, and on the environmental one, which affects the whole community.

The economic benefits derive from a general optimization of the agricultural procedures and from a better use of the agricultural areas and equipment, with a reduction of the associated costs. In addition to the economic aspect, the use of variable intensity agricultural procedures contributes to an intuitive and rational use of chemical products and to a bigger efficiency in the water resources use, with a greater reduction in environmental impacts.

Acknowledgements. This research was developed in the frame of Rural Development Plans (PSR) promoted by Umbria Regional Council and financed by EU.

We want to say thanks to the technical partner Topcon Positioning Italy, Cratia-Confagricoltura Umbria and all the farming companies involved in the project: FIA Foundation in Perugia, Blasi, Arnaldo Caprai Winery, Alviero Giovagnoli, Sodalizio of S. Martino, Mastri Birrai Umbri.

References

1. Bauer, W.D., Schefcik, M.: Using differential GPS to improve crop yields. GPS World **5**(2), 38–41 (1994)
2. Blackmore, S.B., Stout, B., Wang, M., Runov, B.: Robotic agriculture – the future of agricultural mechanisation? In: J. Stafford, V. (ed) 5th European Conference on Precision Agriculture, Uppsala, Sweden, pp. 621–628. Wageningen Academic Publisher, The Netherlands (2005)
3. Dijksterhuis, H.L., Van Willigenburg, L.G., Van Zuydam, R.P.: Centimetre-precision guidance of moving implements in the open field: a simulation based on GPS measurements. Comput. Electron. Agric. **20**(3), 185–197 (1998). https://doi.org/10.1016/S0168-1699(98)00016-7

4. Pérez-Ruiz, M., Upadhyaya, S.K.: GNSS in precision agricultural operation. In: Boukour Elbahhar, F., Rivenq, A. (eds.) New Approach of Indoor and Outdoor Localization Systems, CH-1, pp. 3–26. InTech, Rijeka, Croatia (2012). https://doi.org/10.5772/50448
5. Radicioni, F., Stoppini, A.: Umbria's new multi-constellation GNSS network. GeoMedia **23**(4), 6–11 (2019). ISSN:1128-8132
6. Fastellini, G., Radicioni, F., Stoppini, A.: Network Corrections for Machine Control. GPS World, pp. 32–40 (2009). ISSN:1048-5104
7. Bell, T.: Automatic tractor guidance using carrier-phase differential GPS. Comput. Electron. Agric. **25**(1–2), 53–66 (2000). https://doi.org/10.1016/S0168-1699(99)00055-1
8. Perez-Ruiz, M., Carballido, J., Agüera, J., Gil, J.A.: Assessing GNSS correction signals for assisted guidance system in agricultural vehicles. Precis. Agric. **12**(5), 639–652 (2011). https://doi.org/10.1007/s11119-010-9211-4
9. Wubbena, G., Bagge, A., Schmitz, M.: RTK Networks based on Geo ++ ® GNSMART - concepts, implementation, results. In: Proceedings of the 14th International Technical Meeting of the Satellite Division of The Institute of Navigation (ION GPS 2001), Salt Lake City, Utah, pp. 368–378 (2001)
10. Takac, F., Zelzer, O.: The Relationship Between Network RTK Solutions MAC, VRS, PRS, FKP and i-MAX. Proc. of the 21st International Technical Meeting of the Satellite Division of The Institute of Navigation (ION GNSS 2008), Savannah, Georgia, pp. 348–355 (2008)
11. Ciarapica, A., Radicioni, F., Stoppini, A.: Implementazione delle nuove costellazioni e segnali nella rete GPSUMBRIA. Atti Conferenza ASITA 2019, pp. 247–254 (2019) – ISBN:978-88-941232-5-8
12. EGNOS and Galileo for agriculture. EGNOS documentation. https://egnos-user-support.essp-sas.eu/new_egnos_ops/sites/default/files/documents/EGNOS_GALILEO_Agriculture.pdf

The Contribution of Remote Sensing and Silvicultural Treatments to the Assessment of Decline in an Oak Deciduous Forest: The Study Case of a Protected Area in Mediterranean Environment

Fabio Recanatesi[1](✉), Matteo Piccinno[2], Benedetta Cucca[1], Carlo Maria Rossi[1], and Maria Nicolina Ripa[1]

[1] Department of Agricultural and Forestry Sciences (D.A.F.N.E.), Tuscia University, Viterbo, Italy
{fabio.rec,benedetta.cucca,nripa}@unitus.it, carlomariarossivt@gmail.com

[2] Department of Landscape Planning, University of "La Sapienza" (D.I.A.P.), Rome, Italy
matteo.piccinno@uniroma1.it

Abstract. Thanks to their ability to produce ecosystem services, forest ecosystems have a significant social, economic and environmental impact on the development of many regions in the world, especially when located in urban and peri-urban areas.

Today, increased forest vulnerability is being reflected in a larger number of severe decline episodes associated mainly with drought. In this context, the Mediterranean area shows high forest vulnerability and a subsequent decline in its natural renewal rate.

In this scenario, the aim of the present research is to assess sustainability of a protected pristine deciduous oak forest near Rome, developing a forest health condition monitoring tool based on the application of multispectral satellite data, and through the identification of silvicultural models appropriate for promoting natural forest renewal.

The preliminary results of this research indicate how the exclusion of wildlife through fenced areas significantly favors the natural renewal of the forest, especially when silvicultural actions such as thinning are carried out. It has also been ascertained through the use of multispectral satellite data that there is a widespread decline in the health vegetative state of the deciduous oak surfaces, due to a widespread senescence of the forest. In the addressed study area, the Natural State Reserve of Castelporziano (Rome), data and results from this research can work as an important decision tool for sustainable forest management.

Keywords: Protected area · Risk assessment · Oak decline · Remote sensing · NDVI · GIS · Sentinel-2 · Landsat 5

O. Gervasi et al. (Eds.): ICCSA 2020, LNCS 12253, pp. 36–49, 2020.
https://doi.org/10.1007/978-3-030-58814-4_3

1 Introduction

The Mediterranean forest area is one of the world's biodiversity hotspots. In the last centuries, mainly due to human activities, approximately 70% of the original Mediterranean forests and shrub-lands were destroyed and, since 1990, the remaining cover has been listed in critical or endangered conditions [1, 2]. For these reasons, the Mediterranean basin has been identified as a key area for its high vulnerability as an area especially vulnerable to these predicted changes, with greater increases in temperature and aridity due to its geographical position between the arid subtropical climates of North Africa and the climates of Central Europe [3–6].

In this scenario, deciduous oak forest is one of the most vulnerable Mediterranean landscape, especially along the coastal area. Deciduous oak decline is defined as a condition characterized by episodes of premature, progressive loss of tree or stand vigor without obvious evidence of physical injury or attack by a primary disease or pest and in which several damaging agents interact and bring about a serious decline in tree health conditions [7–10]. In this context, driving factors of tree decline are numerous, including abiotic, biotic and anthropogenic ones. Climatic anomalies, namely increasing temperatures, repeated and prolonged periods of drought, as well as recurring wildfires are among the most important factors involved in this phenomenon. With regards to drought-induced oak dieback, two non-mutually exclusive mechanisms are involved: (i) hydraulic failure due to a drastic loss of xylem conductivity and (ii) carbon starvation when carbon demands are not met [11, 12]. As with other Mediterranean forests, oak deciduous forest growth was favored by precipitation from autumn of the year prior to ring formation to spring of the year of ring formation, whereas high temperatures during spring limited growth [13].

In Italy, isolated oak decline cases have been observed since the end of the last century. First identified in northeastern Italian forests, where Quercus robur L. was the most affected species, such decline spread thereafter in central and southern Italy, mainly on Quercus cerris L., Quercus frainetto Ten. and Quercus pubescens Willd., in both pure and mixed forests. The phenomenon affected most coastal Mediterranean ecosystems, for which summer water availability is usually the major limiting factor [14].

Today, common survey tools used in the field of Geographic Information Systems (GIS) show limitations for detecting the different phases of tree decline. Oak mortality and severe decline can be easily observed through the visual interpretation of aerial photos. Nonetheless, it is difficult to identify trees that are in early stage of decline, i.e. the trees that are still green but are beginning to defoliate [15]. These trees may die back in the next few years or become more vulnerable when next stress occurs and, for this reason, the affected areas need to be detected and treated to prevent huge ecological and economical losses.

Therefore, an efficient monitoring tool for environmental risk assessment is needed for planning effective strategies to support sustainable forest management, especially in protected areas.

With this aim, in the present research, an innovative tool for environmental risk management was developed to identify the most suitable silvicultural treatments for clearing the way to natural renewal processes of the forest. Moreover, to promote a sustainable preservation of these natural environments in the future, from 2015 a high frequency remote sensing monitoring system was arranged based on Sentinel-2 and Landsat-5 multispectral images and NDVI index [16–18].

At this purpose, satellite imagery provides an efficient means to retrieve information on the status and extent of forest resources and changes thereof. The large area coverage and high spatial resolution of newly launched optical and radar satellite systems offer new opportunities to remotely estimate and access land cover information on a wall-to-wall basis. At the same time, the high temporal resolution and capacity to acquire data on a weekly basis improves the capability to detect most recent land cover changes such as health status. The utilization of dense time series of multi-temporal and multi sensorial satellite imagery, which the European Space Agency (ESA) Sentinel-2 missions data is well suited for, can address challenges caused by phenological changes of forest canopies between the seasons and data availability restrictions due to clouds [19].

2 Materials and Methods

2.1 Study Area

The study area of Castelporziano (E 41°440 40.4000; N 12°230 59.4900, datum WGS84) is characterized by an incredibly rich natural environment and the presence of several cultural heritages. From the fifth century onwards, it was under the control of the Vatican State, until the nineteenth century, when it became a hunting estate of the Italian Royal family. Finally, at the end of World War II, Castelporziano was chosen as the presidential estate of the Italian Republic, thanks to its notable environmental and cultural value.

The presidential estate of Castelporziano obtained the status of Nature State Reserve in 1999. It covers over 6,000 ha, extending south–southwest of Rome towards the Tyrrhenian Sea (Fig. 1). There are two sites of community importance (SCIs) within the nature reserve: the coastal area (IT6030027) and the lowland oak woodland (IT6030028). This area, including the neighboring territory of Castelfusano, represents what remains of the forest system which once characterized the delta of the River Tiber and its neighboring zones. The area is mostly flat, except for some smooth slopes toward North which rise to a height of no more than 80 m a.s.l.. The coastline is characterized by a dune system, comprising ancient red sands and more recent grey sands. Within the dune system, several temporary water bodies are present, due to seasonal rain and the subsequent rising of the aquifer. Thanks to the presence of typical hydrosoils, this physical conformation has an important ecological role. Its vegetation type was once very common, but has now almost disappeared not only in the territory of Rome, but also along many Tyrrhenian coastal areas.

The territory has remained substantially unchanged over the last few centuries, allowing an undisturbed growth of the vegetation, which was able to develop and mature considerably. For these reasons, but also due to its concentration of very ancient plants (e.g., Quercus cerris L., Quercus pubescens Willd., Quercus robur L.) classified as "monumental trees" [20, 21] according to age and size criteria (many of them are more than 400 years old), Castelporziano stand out in the Mediterranean area for its unique environment.

From a climatic point of view, the site is classified as Mediterranean, referring to the climatic data of Rome—Collegio Romano (N 41°53'55" – E 12°28'50"), with a hot and

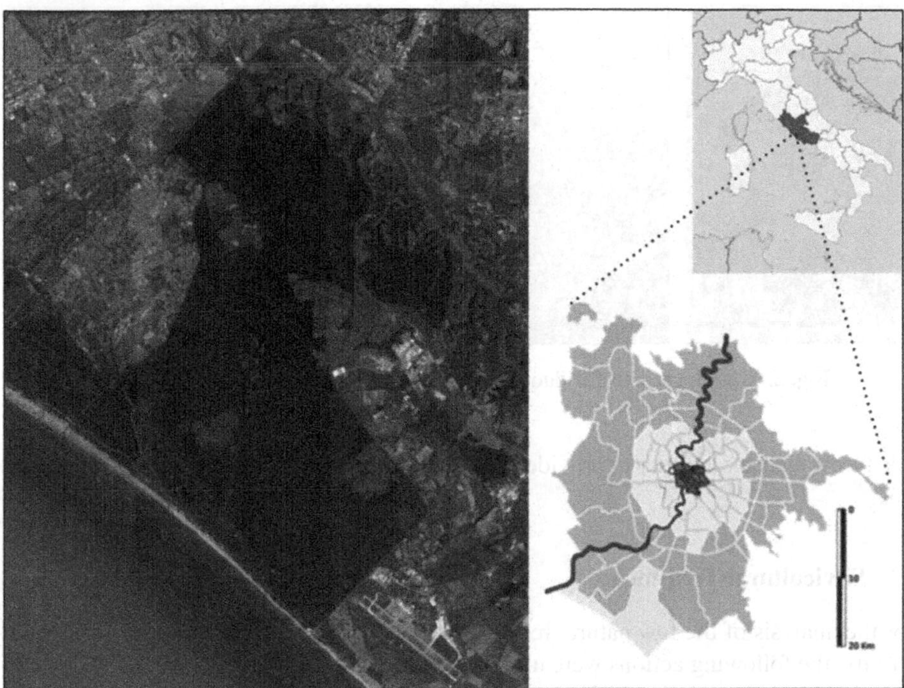

Fig. 1. Study area of castelporziano (E 41°440 40.4000; N 12°230 59.4900, datum WGS84): On the left, aerial photo and borders (red line); on the right, a territorial description of the study area (yellow), tiber river (blue), municipality of rome (dark gray), and city of rome (light gray and black). (Colour figure online)

dry period between May and September. The mean annual total precipitation in Rome (1862–2013) is 711 mm, while the mean annual temperature is 16.1 °C [22].

Throughout the last three decades, this unique environment showed a significant diffuse decline in forest health conditions and in its natural renewal capacity, Fig. 2 shows several examples of the dieback detected in Castelporziano. In this regard, the current Forest Plan Management – (FPM) [23, 24] has identified the following limiting factors to the sustainability and growth of deciduous oak woods: (i) senescence of the forest; (ii) high pressure of wildlife; (iii) lack of forest natural renewal.

Themes (ii) and (iii) are closely related, in fact, the protected area of Castelporziano is strongly affected by wild mammals impact [25]. Mainly the boars (Sus scrofa majori) caused the lacking of plant species recruitment in the deciduous oak forests [26] and a change in the structure of the humus systems. The populations of the ungulates have in general high density and are regulated by density-independent (oak seed productivity) and density-dependent factors. Their increase in the last times are due to lacking of predators, both man and animals.

To deal with these limiting factors, several actions were conducted for the acquisition of field data and remote sensing. This allowed to better understand the ongoing process of

Fig. 2. Castelporziano deciduous oak forest: different rates of health decline.

oak-forest dieback in order to provide useful advice in the management of the protected area.

2.2 Silvicultural Treatments

For the analysis of the low natural renewal rate of deciduous oak forest due to wildlife activity, the following actions were undertaken: (i) in 2012, a forest parcel (FP) located inside the study area, named "Campo di Rota" (12 ha surface), was fenced to exclude it from wildlife pressure; (ii) in 2013 this FP was divided in three test parcels (TP) named: A, B and C, two of them (TP-A and TP-B) were subjected to different rate of silvicultural thinning to promote the natural renewal of the forest and one of them (TP-C) treated as witness area; (iii) from 2013 to 2018, three square sample areas (SA), each one with a surface of 25 m2 and located under a mature oak canopy, have been monitored to quantify the natural renewal degree by annual seedlings counting.

2.3 Field Data

The effects on natural renewable capability derived by the different silvicultural models applied in the fenced area in 2013 differ according to their harvested intensity. In TP-A (6 ha), TP-B (4 ha) and TP-C (2 ha), a 70%, 90% and 0% (witness area) thinning of the dominated layer of the forest mainly characterized by Mediterranean scrub and with an average volume of 350 m3 ha-1 [24] was performed respectively. To quantify the effects of different silvicultural treatments on the natural renewal of the deciduous oak forest, three SAs have been positioned in each TP. Starting from 2013, the naturally regenerated oak seedlings were counted every year in August.

The census of natural renewal was carried out by analyzing the variation in the number of plants year by year throughout the observation period. To achieve this goal, tags were placed to distinguish the plants according to their year of birth.

In Fig. 3 the fenced area of Campo di Rota is show with the three TP (A, B and C) and their relative SAs (1, 2 and 3).

Fig. 3. On left, Campo di Rota experimental fenced forest parcel (FP) (red dotted line) with the three test parcels (TP): A, B and C and the sample areas (SAs) (not in scale) for the census of the natural renewal of the oak forest: SA-1, SA-2 and SA-3. The blue dots indicate the presence of oak's canopy at Sentinel-2 grid scale. On the right, examples of oak natural renewal referred to 2013 detected in: SA-1 and SA-2. (Colour figure online)

2.4 Satellite Data

Starting by 2015, a remote sensing-assisted risk rating tool was adopted to assess the health status of the deciduous oak's canopy for the whole study area (about 4.000 ha).

Specifically, to better understand the ongoing crown dieback, a georeferenced database for the deciduous oak forest was developed at Sentinel-2 grid scale (100 m2) using the GIS software program Qgis2.4.0 Chugiak, with the goal of detecting presence or absence of deciduous oak crown [27].

In fact, due to the high heterogeneity in terms of spatial distribution and silvicultural structures in Castelporziano oak forest, a preliminary analysis was carried out on the forest canopy cover, on a grid scale (100 m2), to specifically identify the cover of the deciduous oak canopy.

To achieve this, we used a Sentinel-2 derived grid with a spatial resolution of 100 m2. This allowed us to apply the NDVI specifically to detect the health condition of only the deciduous oak canopy.

To reach this goal, a georeferenced database was set up using: (i) information provided by the Castelporziano forest management plan (FMP) concerning the different heights referred to the dominant and dominated layers of the forest; (ii) CHM LiDAR data to separate dominant and dominated stand forest; and (iii) a diachronic set of multispectral Sentinel-2 and Landsat-5 images.

The analysis of the dominant and dominated layers of the forest was carried out by consulting the FMP of Castelporziano at the FP scale, in terms of height referred to dominant forest (oak) and dominated forest layers (Mediterranean scrub and/or bare soil).

Table 1. Main silvicultural characteristics of the FPs analyzed

Castelporziano deciduous oak forest structures	ID code	Surface (ha)	Mean Oak canopy cover (%)	Average height (m)		Forest canopy composition	
				Dominant layer of the forest	Dominated layer of the forest	Deciduous Oaks	Non-Deciduous Oaks
Transitional forests of deciduous oaks and Ostrya carpinifolia	21	156	73	9	7, 5	Qc; Qc; Qr; Qp	Pl; Qi; Ac; Fo; Cr; Pp
Transitional forests of deciduous oaks and Mediterranea scrub	22	181	62	8, 5	6, 5	Qc; Qf; Qr; Qp	E; Pl; Cr; Co
Transitional forests with prevalence of deciduous and mixed oaks	24	294	69	8, 5	7	Qr; Qf; Qc; Qp	Pp; Pl; Co; Qs; Qi; Qpt; Um
Coppice of deciduous oaks with Ostrya carpinifolia	31	53	77	9, 5	6, 5	Qf; Qr; Qc	Ca; Um; Cb; Co
Coppice of deciduous oaks with Mediterranean scrub	32	288	81	7, 5	6	Qf; Qc ; Qr	Pp; Qs; Qcr; Qi; Pl; E; Ct; E; Cr; Mc
Forest of deciduous oaks	41	21	8	11	7, 5	Qc; Qr;	Um; Co; Fo; Pl
Forest of deciduous oaks and Ostrya carpinifolia	42	512	37	9, 5	6	Qf; Qr; Qc	Qi; Co; Qs; Qcr; Pp; Cb; Um; Fo; Pl
Forest of deciduous oaks and Mediterranean scrub	43	664	18	11, 5	4, 5	Qf; Qc; Qpt; Qp	P; Pl; Qs; Co; Qcr; Qi; Ln; Ac

Legend: Qp Quercus pubescens; Qf Quercus frainetto; Qr Quercus robur; Qc Quercus cerris; Qi Quercus ilex; Qcr Quercus crenata; Qs Qurcus suber; Co Carpinus orientalis; Pp Pinus pinea; Cb Carpinus betulus; Um Ulmus minor; Fo Fraxinus oxycarpa; Pl Phillyrea latifolia; Qpt Qurercus petraea; Ln Laurus nobilis; Ac Acer campestre; E Erica spp.; Cr Crataegus spp.; Mc Myrtus communis

Using this information, we have separated the dominant layer from the dominated forest layer, reclassifying the CHM LiDAR data for each FP, Table 1 shows the main forest structures of the analyzed FPs.

In this way, we obtained a binary layer that represents the dominant position of the forest characterized by evergreen and deciduous oaks. In Table 1 the main silvicultural parameters are shown for the eight forest structures analyzed [28].

Finally, to remove evergreen canopy trees from our analysis, represented by evergreen oaks and stone pine, we compared the NDVI value detected for the winter and summer season using the 8 and 4 bands provided by Sentinel-2 data. The result of this methodology allowed us to obtain a grid mask relative to the canopy of the deciduous oak forest of Castelporziano.

The achievement of this georeferenced database was necessary considering the high spatial heterogeneity in terms of density of deciduous oaks at the FP scale as shown in Fig. 4.

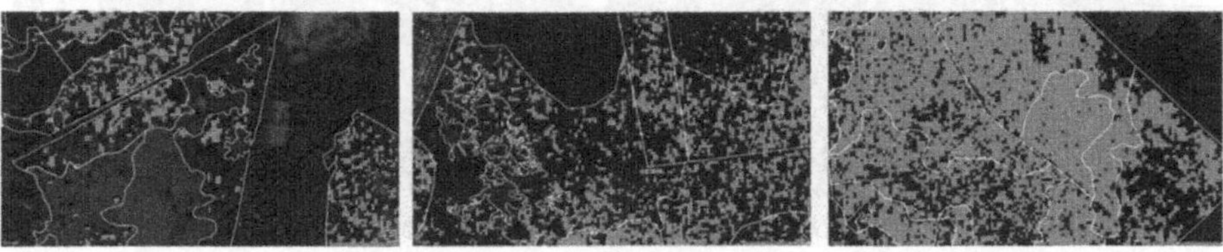

Fig. 4. Castelporziano deciduous oak forest: examples of heterogeneous distribution of oak canopy cover detected at the forest parcel (FP) scale (white line). The green dots represent cells of the Sentinel-2 grid with presence of deciduous oak's canopy. (Colour figure online)

To arrange a monitoring program for assessing the risk related to the ongoing crown decline in Castelporziano, the forest health status has been investigated applying NDVI index in diachronic way from 2015 to present [29]. For this purpose, a georeferenced dataset of multispectral images referred to the month of July, has been acquired by Sentinel-2 from 2015 to present and, to investigate the historical trend concerning the NDVI index, a series of Landsat-5 historical data was used for the years 1989, 2000 and 2009 [30]. All the multispectral data, Sentinel-2 and Landsat-5, provided by Copernicus Open Access Hub (https://www.copernicus.eu/en), were analyzed only to the grid cells in which the presence of oak canopy had been previously detected. Figure 5 shows an example concerning the method used to determine the vegetative health condition of the deciduous oak forest using NDVI index with Sentinel-2 images. Obviously, by using the "mask" of the deciduous oak canopy, at the scale of the grid Sentinel (100 m2), the surface investigated with the Landsat data (resolution of 900 m2) is lower.

3 Results and Discussion

The preliminary results regarding the effect of fenced areas on natural renewal capability have showed a positive effect on natural renewal of deciduous oak forest. In SA-1 and SA-2, in fact, a substantial high number of acorns have sprouted while, in the same

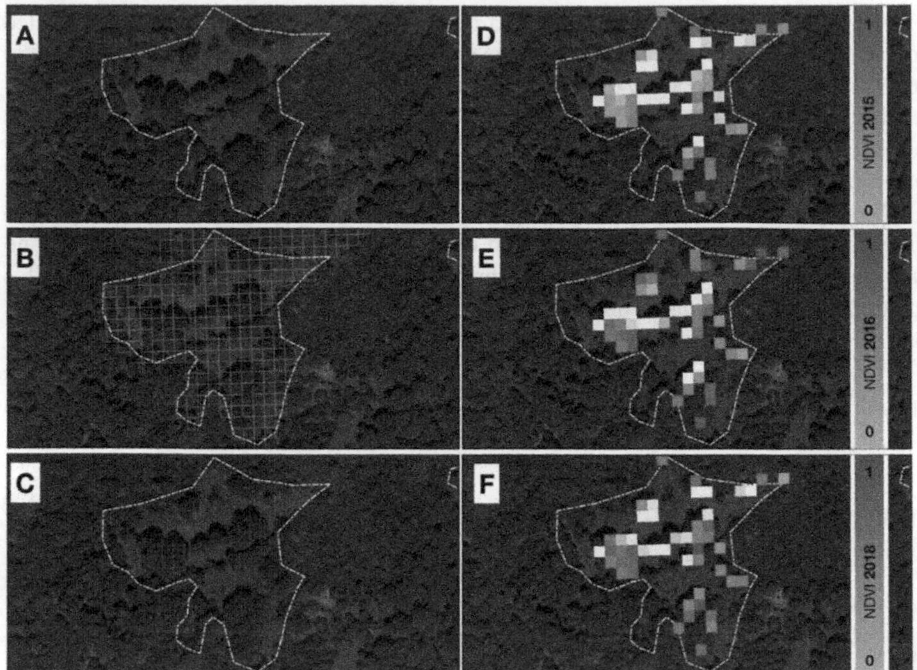

Fig. 5. (A) Forest Parcel (FP) (white line); (B) Sentinel-2 grid "mask"; (C) presence of oak deciduous canopy (red squares); (D, E and F) NDVI values detected for deciduous oak canopy for years: 2015, 2016 and 2017. (Colour figure online)

period, in the SA-3, not subject to forestry thinning, the effect of high density of the trees, the lack of light at the ground level and the competition for water availability due to the presence of high density of Mediterranean scrub, have played as limiting factor in natural renewing of the deciduous oak forest. Moreover, for the non-treated SA the seedlings of each year have presented a vegetative vigor not longer than three years that demonstrates how the high density of dominated layer of the forest does not allows a natural renewal of deciduous oak.

Concerning the effect of the different silvicoltural treatments carried out, comparing the two sample areas, it is clear that in SA-1 the response of natural renewal, in terms of oak seeds sprouting, is better than in SA-2 one as shown in Fig. 6. In fact, the number of annual seedlings, counted year by year, have showed a different mortality rate in the observed period. The SA-1, reduced by the 70% of its volume in 2013, presents a better micro climatic condition in terms of light and soil moisture available for the natural renewal and, for the same reason, the trees density rate produces a limiting factor in the introduction of other species such as those referred to the Mediterranean scrub.

Regarding the monitoring system carried out with Sentinel-2 images and based on the specifically application of the NDVI index on deciduous oak canopy, a diffuse decline was detected from 2015 to 2018, as Fig. 7 shows. For these time series data, in fact, the

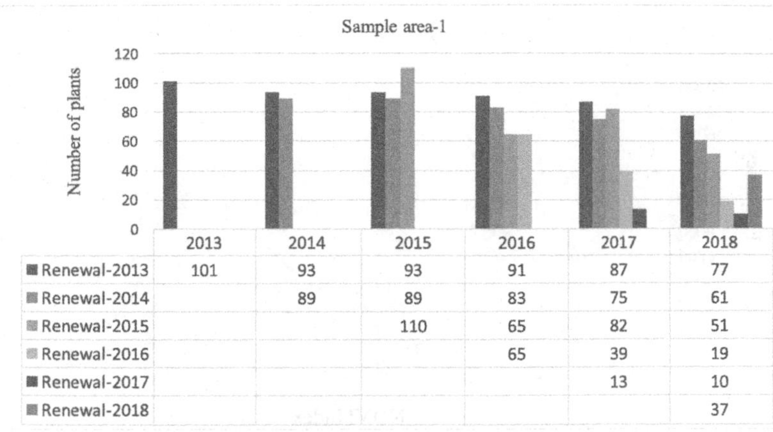

Sample area-1
Number of plants
120
100
80
60
40
20
0
2013 2014 2015 2016 2017 2018
Renewal-2013 101 93 93 91 87 77
Renewal-2014 89 89 83 75 61
Renewal-2015 110 65 82 51
Renewal-2016 65 39 19
Renewal-2017 13 10
Renewal-2018 37

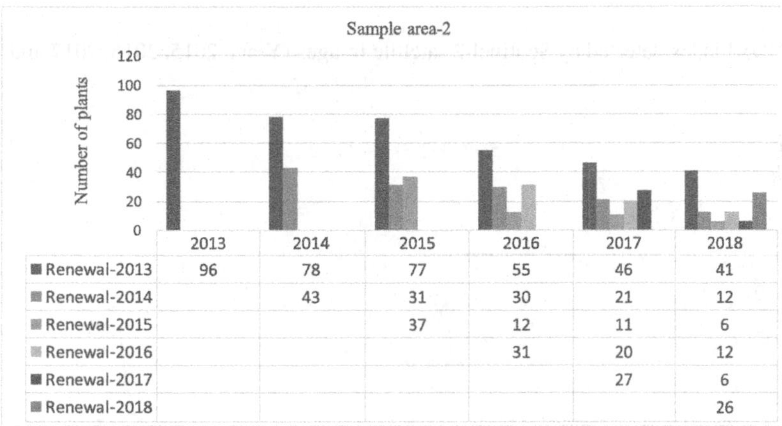

Sample area-2
Number of plants
120
100
80
60
40
20
0
2013 2014 2015 2016 2017 2018
Renewal-2013 96 78 77 55 46 41
Renewal-2014 43 31 30 21 12
Renewal-2015 37 12 11 6
Renewal-2016 31 20 12
Renewal-2017 27 6
Renewal-2018 26

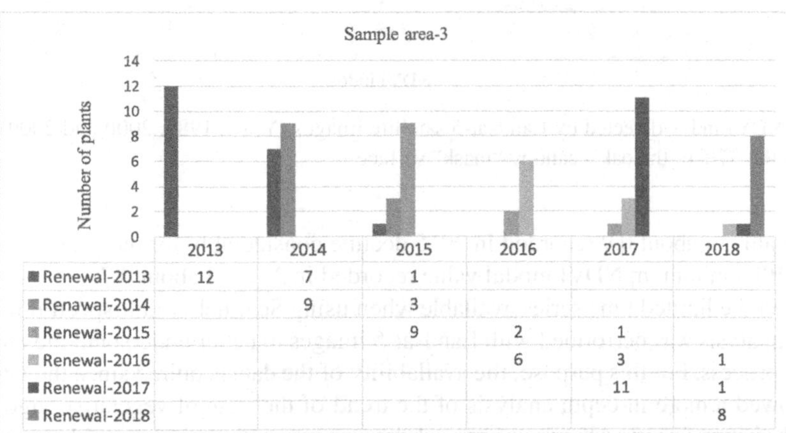

Fig. 6. Number of seedlings and mortality rate in the sample area (SA): 1, 2 and 3 for the period 2013-2018.

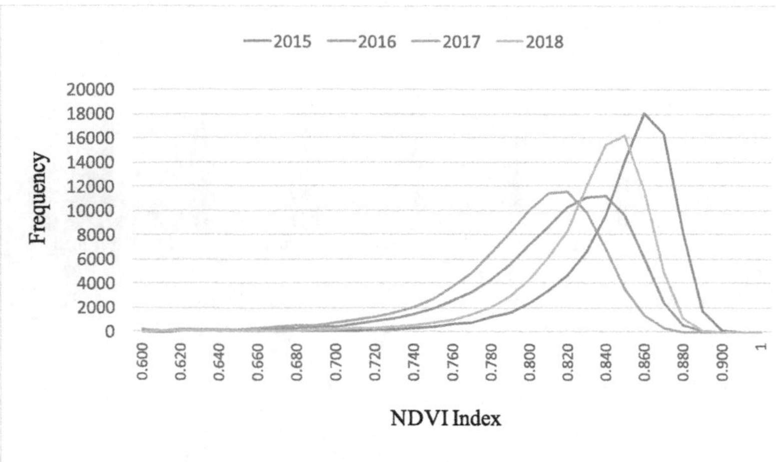

Fig. 7. NDVI index detected by Sentinel-2 satellite images (Years: 2015, 2016, 2017 and 2018).

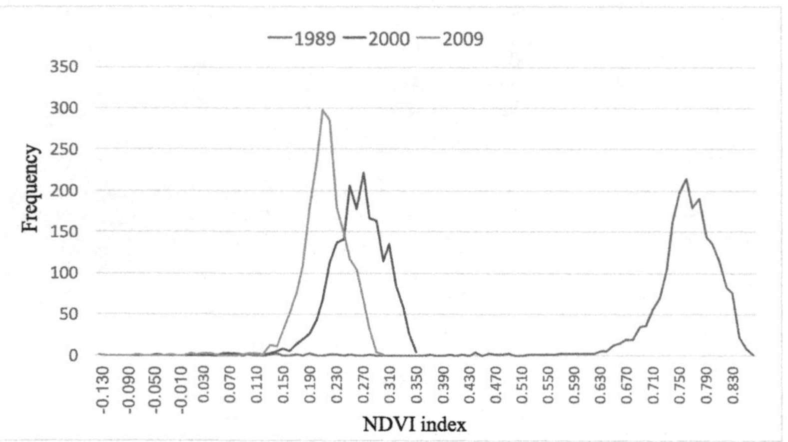

Fig. 8. NDVI index detected by Landsat-5 satellite images (Years: 1989, 2000 and 2009). Data refers to the 37% of the oak's canopy "mask" surface.

modal value of about 0.9 recorded in 2015 decline considerably for the years 2016 and 2018 with a minimum NDVI modal value recorded in 2017 of about 0.7.

Given the limited time series available when using Sentinel-2 multispectral images, further analysis was performed with Landsat-5 images to better understand the ongoing decline process. For this purpose, the availability of the data acquired since the late 80 s has allowed a more in-depth analysis of the trend of the state of vegetative vigor over time, shown in Fig. 8. Also for historical data on vegetative vigor, a widespread and progressive decline in the conditions of deciduous oak forests is confirmed. Referring to the modal values, it appears clear that from the end of the 80 s to 2009 there was a significantly reduction in NDVI modal values that from 0.77 in 1989 decreased until 0.21

in 2009. Although is not possible to directly compare the NDVI index values analyzed by Landsat-5 and Sentinel-2 data, because of their difference in the width of the spectral bands, results show that in the last thirty years the trend in vegetative health conditions of the studied area getting worse significantly.

4 Conclusion

The dieback of oak forest stands in the Mediterranean environment is today a very important topic within the scientific community. Especially for protected areas located in urban and peri-urban areas, these environments must be preserved with versatile and efficient analysis tools for the implementation of forest management operations.

In this research, we report the preliminary results from the application of different silvicultural treatments to facilitate the natural renewal of a protected forest. To monitor vegetation decline, a multispectral images dataset was created using Sentinel-2 and Landsat-5 satellites.

Census of seedlings carried out in the three sample areas showed that the competition for the light and soil moisture represent a limiting factor to natural renewal. Where the thinning (SA-3) of the forest has not been performed, the species of the dominated forest stand do not allow light to reach the ground, thus preventing seedlings from surviving.

In contrast, in the areas subjected to silvicultural treatment through the thinning of the dominated plan of the forest, the natural production of seedlings has been favored. In particular, the SA-1 was found to be the most efficient and this probably depends on a better density of plants compared to SA-2 where, the removal of 90% of the dominated layer, has favored the spread of the Mediterranean scrub limiting the development of oak seedlings over time.

Undoubtedly, the acquired data must be implemented over time to shed light on the ongoing process. Overall, the data acquired are intended to provide helpful specific indications for forest planning strategies of the protected area.

The monitoring of ongoing health decline based on remote sensing of multispectral images according to NDVI index is an effective tool that, thanks to the high frequency of acquisition offered by Sentinel-2, allows a monitoring concerning vegetative conditions, In addition, the arrangement of a grid layer "mask", relative to the presence/absence of oak canopy enables accurate analysis that, given the spatial heterogeneity of the plants in the Mediterranean environment, becomes an unavoidable operation to build up accurate and effective information at the scale of the forest particle.

Acknowledgments. The authors thank the General Secretariat of the Presidency of the Republic, the management of the Estate of Castelporziano, the Scientific-Technical Commission of Castelporziano that enabled these studies and the publication of the data.

Conflicts of Interest. The authors declare no conflict of interest.

Funding. This research was funded by the National Academy of Sciences (Rome), within the monitoring program of the presidential Estate of Castelporziano.

References

1. Millennium Ecosystem Assessment. Ecosystems and human well-being: Synthesis. Island Press, Washington, DC (2005) (ISBN 1–59726-040-1)
2. FAO and Plan Bleu. State of Mediterranean Forests 2018. Food and Agriculture Organization of the United Nations, Rome and Plan Bleu, Marseille (2018) ISBN FAO: 978-92-5-131047-2
3. Acacio, V., Holmgren, M., Rego, F., Moreira, F., Nohren, G.: Are drought and wildfires turning Mediterranean cork oak forest into persistent shrublands? Agroforestry Syst. **76**, 389–400 (2009)
4. Di Filippo, A., et al.: Climate change and oak growth decline: Dendroecology and stand productivity of a Turkey oak (Quercus cerris L.) old stored coppice in Central Italy. Ann. For. Sci. **67**, 706–710 (2010). https://doi.org/10.1051/forest/2010031
5. Gentilesca, T., et al.: Drought-induced oak decline in the western Mediterranean region: An overview on current evidences, mechanisms and management options to improve forest resilience. iForest Biogeosci. For. **10**, 796–806 (2014)
6. Colangelo, M., et al.: A multy proxy assessment of dieback causes in a Mediterranean oak species. Tree Physiol. **37**, 617–631 (2017)
7. Food and Agriculture Organization of the United Nations (FAO). Decline and Dieback of Trees and Forest; FAO Forestry Paper; FAO: Rome, Italy 1994
8. Natalini, F., Alejano, R., Vázquez-Piqué, J., Canellas, I., Gea-Izquierdo, G.: The role of climate change in the widespread mortality of holm oak in open woodlands of Southwestern Spain. Dendrochronologia **38**, 51–60 (2016)
9. Conte, A.L., et al.: Oak decline in the mediterranean basin: a study case from the southern apennines (Italy). Plant Sociol. **56**, 69–80 (2019). https://doi.org/10.7338/pls2019562/05
10. Di Filippo, A.: Climate change and oak growth decline: dendroecology and stand productivity of a turkey oak (Quercus cerris L.) old stored coppice in central italy. Ann. For. Sci. **67**, 1–14 (2010)
11. Costa, A., Pereira, H., Madeira, M.: Analysis of spatial pattern of oak decline in cork oak woodland in Mediterranean conditions. Ann. For. Sci. **204**, 16–26 (2010)
12. Manes, F., Seufert, G., Vitale, M.: Ecophysiological studies of Mediterranean plant species at the Castelporziano Estate. Atmos. Environ. **13**, 51–60 (2010)
13. Romagnoli, M., et al.: Climate factors and oak decline based on tree-ring analysis. a case study of peri-urban forest in the Mediterranean area. Urban For. Urban Gree. **34**, 17–28 (2018)
14. Maselli, F.: Monitoring forest conditions in a protected Mediterranean coastal area by the analysis of multiyear NDVI data. Remote Sens. Environ. **89**, 423–433 (2004)
15. Modica, G., et al.: Using landsat 8 imagery in detecting cork oak (Quercus suber L.) woodlands: a case study in Calabria (Italy). J. Agric. Eng. **47**, 205–215 (2016)
16. Bannari, A., Morin, D., Bonn, F.: A review of vegetation indices. Remote Sens. Rev. **13**, 95–120 (1995)
17. Ogaya, R., Barbeta, A., Başnou, C., Peñuelas, J.: Satellite data as indicators of tree biomass growth and forest dieback in a Mediterranean holm oak forest. Ann. For. Sci. **72**(1), 135–144 (2014). https://doi.org/10.1007/s13595-014-0408-y
18. Korhonen, L., Petteri, P.K., Rautiainen, M.: Comparison of Sentinel-2 and Landsat 8 in the estimation of boreal forest canopy cover and leaf area index. Remote Sens. Env. **195**, 259–274 (2017)
19. Haeusler, T., Enble, F., Gomez, S.: Satellite based monitoring of forest resources compliant with red + and zero deforestation. Responsible land governance: Towards an evidence based approach. Annual World Bank Conference and Poverty. Washington DC, March 20–24 (2017)
20. Recanatesi, F., Tolli, M., Ripa, M.N., Pelorosso, R., Gobattoni, F., Leone, A.: Detection of landscape patterns in airborne LIDAR data in the nature reserve of Castelporziano (Rome). J. Agric. Eng. **44**, 472–477 (2013)

21. Recanatesi, F.: Variation in land use/ land cover changes (LULCCs) in a peri-urban Mediterranean nature reserve: the estate of Castelporziano (Rome). Rendiconti Lincei **26**, 517–526 (2015)
22. Bianco, P.M., Martelli, F., Pignatti, S.: Clima. In: La Vegetazione Della Tenuta Presidenziale Di Castelporziano. Accademia Nazionale delle Scienze, pp. 453–455 (2001)
23. Giordano, E., Capitoni, B., Eberle, A., Maffei, L., Musicanti, A., Recanatesi, F., Torri, V.: Piano di gestione forestale della tenuta presidenziale di castelporziano [forest management plan of the presidential estate of castelporziano]. Segretariato Generale della Presidenza della Repubblica-Commissione Tecnico-Scientifica della Tenuta Presidenziale di Castelporziano **3**, 131–398 (2006)
24. Scrinzi, G., Presutti Saba, E., Colle, G.: Accademia Nazionale delle Scienze. Indirizzi Gestionali E Obiettivi D'intervento Per Le Classi Colturali Della Foresta Della Tenuta Presidenziale Di Castelporziano. Roma, Italy (2016)
25. Focardi, S., et al.: Monitoring populations of a guild of ungulates: implications for the conservation of a relict Mediterranean forest. Rendiconti Lincei **26**(3), 535–544 (2015). https://doi.org/10.1007/s12210-015-0439-9
26. Fanelli, G., Tescarollo, P.: The reneval of deciduous arboreous species in Castelporziano. Ricerche sulla complessità di un ecosistema forestale costiero mediterraneo. Scritti e documenti XXXVII, Seconda Serie Vol. II. Accademia Nazionale delle Scienze, pp. 607–622 (2006)
27. Recanatesi, F., Giuliani, C., Rossi, C.M., Ripa, M.N.: A remote sensing-assisted risk rating study to monitor pinewood forest decline: the study case of the Castelporziano state nature reserve (Rome). Smart Innov. Syst. Technol. **100**, 68–75 (2018)
28. Recanatesi, F., Giuliani, C., Ripa, M.N.: Monitoring mediterranean oak decline in a peri-urban protected area using ndvi and sentinel-2 images: the case study of Castelporziano state natural reserve. Sustainability **10**, 1–10 (2018)
29. Chiesi, M., et al.: Integration of ground and satellite data to model Mediterranean forest processes. Int. J. Appl. Earth obs. Geoinf. **13**, 504–515 (2011)
30. Deshayes, M., et al.: The contribution of remote sensing to the assessment of drought effects in forest ecosystems. Ann. For. Sci. **63**, 579–595 (2006). https://doi.org/10.1051/forest:2006045

Evaluating the Potential of Vegetation Indices in Detecting Drought Impact Using Remote Sensing Data in a Mediterranean Pinewood

Benedetta Cucca(✉), Fabio Recanatesi, and Maria Nicolina Ripa

Department of Agricultural and Forest Sciences (DAFNE), University of Tuscia, Viterbo, Italy
benedetta.cucca@unitus.it

Abstract. The Mediterranean ecosystem represents an important natural resource, being able to produce ecosystem services, has both economic and social repercussions, especially if located in urban and peri-urban areas.

In the last decades, increased forest vulnerability is being reflected in a larger number of severe decline episodes associated mainly with drought conditions. In this context, the Mediterranean area shows high forest vulnerability and a subsequent decline in its natural renewal rate.

In this context, the objective of this research is to evaluate the different vegetation indices to monitor the effect of drought on the health of the Castelporziano pine wood. For this purpose, we used the NDVI, NDII and NMDI, provided by ESA Sentinel-2 images and field observations, to monitor the health status of a historic pinewood that has recently been affected by a rapid spread of parasites (*Tomicus destruens Woll.*).

The application of these indices, on the scale of the entire pinewood, showed that the NDVI and NDII indices differentiate better the changes in vegetative health status for the observed period than the NMDI.

Moreover, NDVI and NDII were applied, based on the classifications made, to volume and age classes. Ultimately, these preliminary results require further studies to better understand the potential and limiting factors of the indices used in monitoring pinewoods under stress due to aridity.

Keywords: Vegetation index · Remote sensing · Sentinel-2 · Mediterranean forest · Castelporziano nature state reserve

1 Introduction

The Mediterranean region is rich in species and the bio geographical origin is the result of a combination of climate, soil and anthropic use of the landscape through the centuries, moreover it represents an attraction for tourism [1].

It is characterized by landscape fragmentation that causes an increase in environmental vulnerability, due to large increases in population, rising living standards, the development of irrigated agriculture and new activities (particularly tourism related)

O. Gervasi et al. (Eds.): ICCSA 2020, LNCS 12253, pp. 50–62, 2020.
https://doi.org/10.1007/978-3-030-58814-4_4

which have led to an improve of anthropogenic pressure on the Mediterranean environment [2, 3]. Moreover, the Mediterranean basin is considered to be one of the most endangered environments due to climate change, which has exacerbated these pressures in a negative way, as the current rate of climate change is much faster than in the past and involves a higher risk of extreme weather events, such as prolonged periods of drought, frequent and severe storms and rising temperatures [4, 5]. The combination of the effects of climate change, anthropogenic pressures (such as overexploitation of forest resources, human-induced fire and deforestation) and other aspects, such as land use and pollution, will have an effect on Mediterrean Forest vegetation, and the impacts are expected to affect the structure and operation of forest ecosystem, as well as ecosystems services (ES) they currently provide [6, 7].

The serious negative consequences of prolonged heat waves and dry spell include forest dieback, which can be caused by starvation of carbohydrate reserves or hydraulic failure as well as result in an increased risk of pest/pathogen attacks, which might contribute to reduced productivity and increased forest mortality [8].

Drought is a complex phenomenon that cannot be traced back to a single definition, in fact there are several according to the discipline that studies it. From the literature it is possible to deduce that there are 3 main physical ways to define drought: (i) meteorological, (ii) agricultural, and (iii) hydrological [10–13]. In general, these different definitions of droughts are linked in this way: low rainfall and the consequent increase in temperature (meteorological drought), which results in a deficit of water content in the soil and stream flow, (hydrological drought) and finally affects the water content of plants, (agricultural drought), [14, 15].

In this context it is widely acknowledged that the pinewood-decline is a phenomenon that is taking place in the Mediterranean basin [8, 9]. Indeed, the increased vulnerability of forests to high temperatures combined with drought condition is a phenomenon that is well studied and coincides with the mortality of species, and this phenomenon also contributes to the expansion of other adverse phenomena, such as pathogen pest, and other disturbing events [11].

At this regard, the arrangement of replicable methodologies for the monitoring of the health conditions of forest ecosystems, especially in the Mediterranean area, is increasingly becoming an effective tool to support management decisions.

Among the different methods of monitoring forest ecosystems, remote sensing is certainly the most widely used thanks to the ability of providing synoptic information for very large areas and with frequent acquisition [9–16].

Remote sensing is a non-invasive and non-destructive tool that allows repeated survey sessions without any damage to the objects studied. It is also used in forestry for the mapping of forest areas subject to deterioration, or for the evaluation of damage caused by pathogens. Traditionally, for the study of the physiological conditions of vegetation, spectral indices from remote-sensing data are widely used to evaluate the structure and functioning of terrestrial ecosystems [17].

In the field of remote sensing applications, scientists have developed vegetation indices for qualitatively and quantitatively evaluating vegetative covers using multispectral measurements. The multispectral response of vegetated areas presents a complex moisture of vegetation, soil brightness, environmental effects, shadow, soil color and moisture [18–20].

Several Vegetation Indices have been developed during recent decades, [18] and the most widely used in monitoring general health conditions of forestry surface is the normalized difference vegetation index (NDVI). In practice, NDVI is indicative of plant photosynthetic activity and has been found to be highly related to green leaf area index (LAI), thanks those properties NDVI can be used as an indicator of possible vegetation stress, due to water storage, indeed water availability is the main limiting factor for vegetation processes and therefore controls leaf pigment content and integrity [9].

Some specific indices have been used to detect the effects of drought, such, for instance, NDII [21] and NMDI [22].

The aim of this research is to evaluate the effectiveness of the main vegetation indices proposed in the literature, in order to monitor the effects of drought in a Mediterranean pinewood located in a peri-urban protected area in the Metropolitan area of Rome, the Nature State Reserve of Castelporziano.

2 Material and Method

2.1 Study Area

The study area is represented by the pinewood of Castelporziano (41°42’50”N - 12°24’03”E), a State Nature Reserve located in a peri-urban area of the municipality of Rome, (Fig. 1). Castelporziano presents a total surface area of 6.000 ha and its land use is characterized mainly by forest and to a lesser extent by agricultural activities.

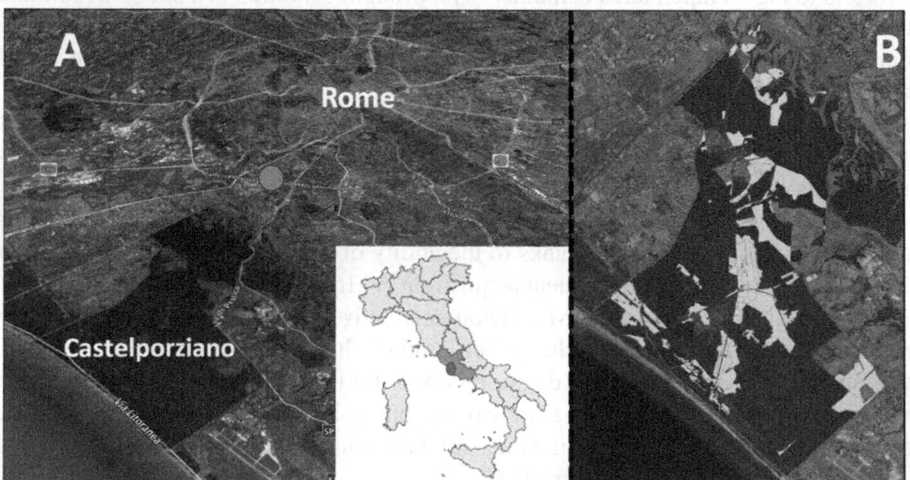

Fig. 1. Study area. [A]: The Nature State Reserve of Castelporziano and the metropolitan area of Roma. [B]: Pinewood (green) of Castelporziano. The blue dot indicate the rain gauge of EUR meteorological station. (Color figure online)

This territory is the last remnant of the ancient Mediterranean coastal forest, in which the predominant species are broadleaf oaks (4.000 ha) and Pinewood (900 ha) mainly characterized by *Pinus pinea* L. In particular, the pinewood of Castelporziano, with numerous trees aged over one hundred years or more, is the last remaining example today of mature pinewood along the Tyrrhenian coast [2, 3]. Furthermore, it is listed in the Habitat Directive with two Sites of Community Importance (SCI) and the whole territory is classified as a Special Protection Area (SPA). In October 2016, the ongoing environmental monitoring program in the Castelporziano Pinewood, carried out by remote sensing of multispectral Sentinel-2 images, allowed the detection of a diffuse dieback in several areas. This phenomenon, very probably, was caused by arid conditions that favored a sudden infestation of *Tomicus destruens* Woll, resulting, in several areas, in a severe and rapid decline of the forest.

2.2 Meteorological Data

Meteorological data were acquired from a meteorological station of the Italian National Hydrological Service located in Rome, exactly in the EUR district, 6 km far from the Estate of Castelporziano. The meteorological data set consisted of series of daily temperatures, (maximum and minimum), and precipitation from 1980 to 2018.

The Bagnouls Gaussen's diagram, (Fig. 2) shows the monthly average of temperatures and precipitation and the area between the two curves indicates the length and drought period. As can be seen from the graph, this period falls in the summer months, which makes the climate typically Mediterranean [23].

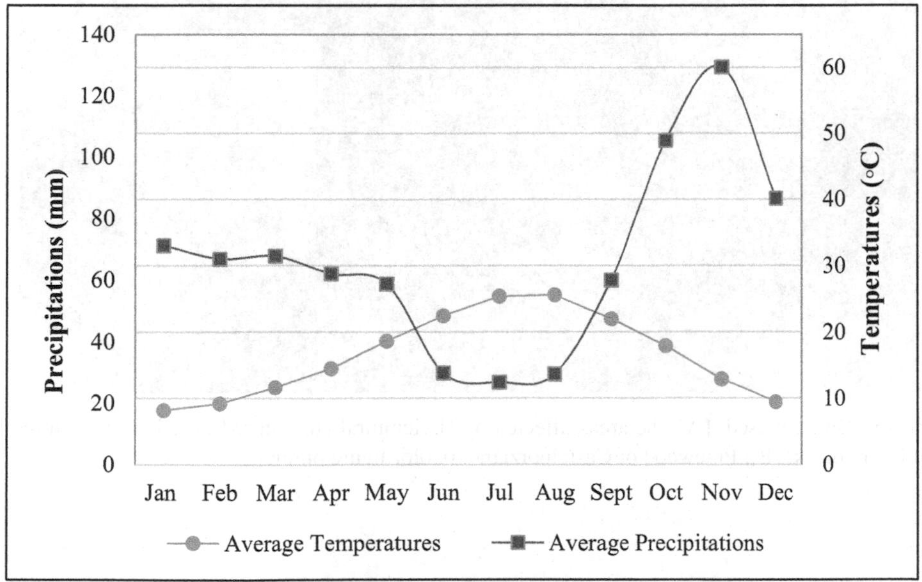

Fig. 2. Bagnouls Gaussen diagram for the years 1980–2019.

2.3 Data Set Used

We used a set of Level 1C Sentinel-2 satellite images, with top of atmosphere reflectance, (band 4, band 8, band 8a, band 11 and band 12) referring to the period: 30 August 2015, 24 August 2016, 24 August 2017, 19 August 2018 and 19 August 2019. These images are provided by Copernicus open access Hub of the European Space Agency (ESA). The Sentinel-2 images spatial resolution is 10, 20 or 60 m depending on the bands.

The acquired images were processed to level 2A Bottom of Atmosphere (BOA) using ESA Snap Sentinel-2 Toolbox with additional Sen2Cor, plug-in for atmospheric and topographic correction. Geometric distortion of the analyzed images was corrected with the rectified 10 m Digital Model Terrain (DTM) provided by the Italian Ministry of Environment.

The data concerning the forest inventory were acquired by the Observatory Laboratory of the Mediterranean ecosystem of Castelporziano [24]. It contains data related to the dendrometric characteristics of the pinewood, such as volume, age, etc.…

For this analysis, the health conditions of the pinewood were considered good in 2015 so this will be used as a reference scenario. In addition, areas inside the Pinewood were eliminated from the analysis as they were affected by silvicultural cuts (Fig. 3) carried out in 2017.

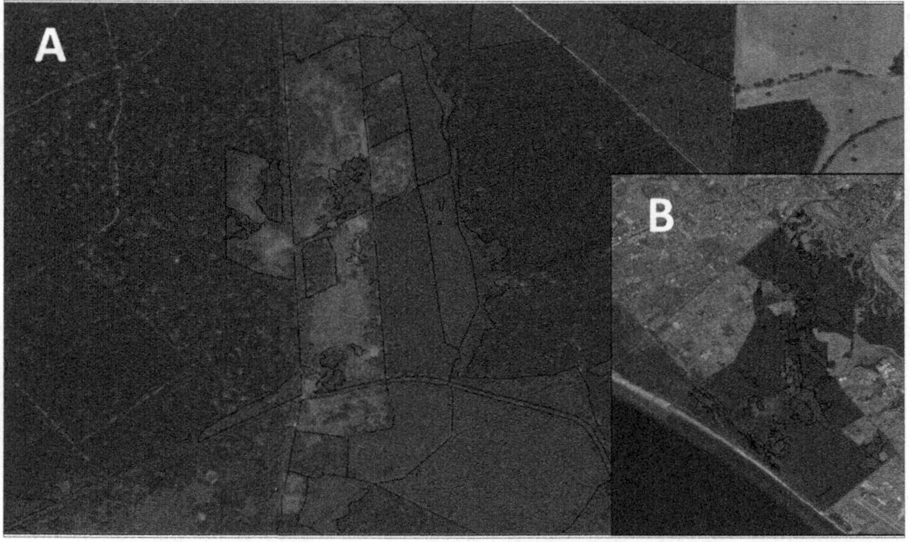

Fig. 3. Data set used. [A]: the areas affected by silvicultural cuts (in red), the border of forest units (in black) [B]: Pinewood of Castelporziano. (Color figure online)

To better understand the potential of the indices used in monitoring pinewood health conditions, we reclassified the surface according to their volume and age [24]. At this aim, the pinewood was classified according to dendrometric criteria, into 3 volume classes and 3 age classes (Fig. 4) at Forest Unit Parcel (FUP) scale.

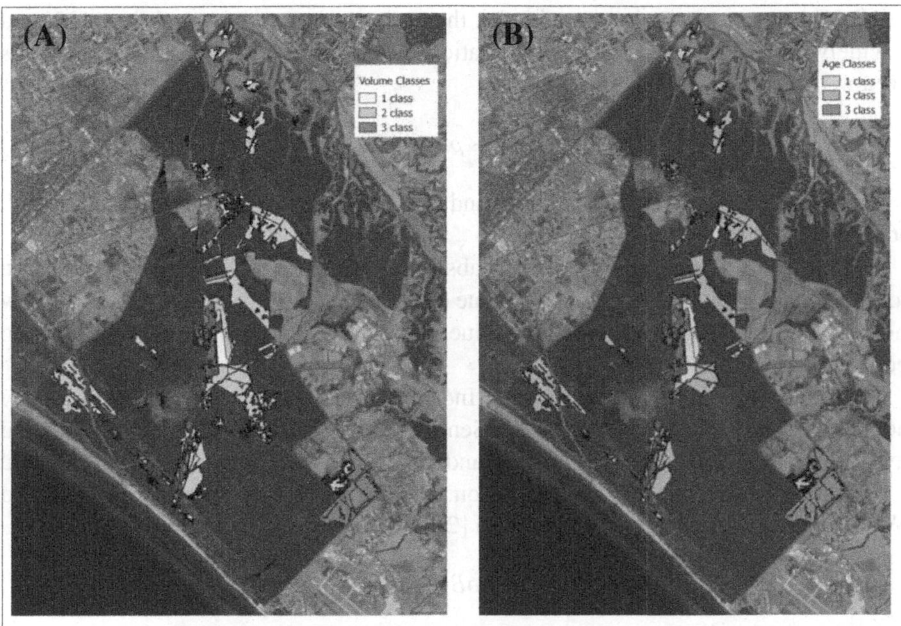

Fig. 4. Classification of Pinewood, [A]: Volume classes; [B]: Age classes

This classification is shown in Table 1.

Table 1. Classification of the pine forest according to its volume and age.

	Volume	Age
1 class	0–200 m^3 ha^{-1}	0–40 years
2 class	201–400 m^3 ha^{-1}	41–80 years
3 class	400–625 m^3 ha^{-1}	>80 years

2.4 Index Used

To assess the potential of mapping drought using Sentinel-2 data, three spectral indices were chosen to calculate: NDVI, (Normalized Difference Vegetation Index), NDII (Normalized Difference Infrared Index) and NMDI (Normalized Multi-band Drought Index).

NDVI is a remote sensing-based index that measure vegetation conditions [25] and its widely used to monitoring health vegetation condition [26]. The formula of NDVI is given in (Eq. 1):

$$NDVI = \rho B8 - \rho B4 / \rho B8 + \rho B4 \tag{1}$$

We used Sentinel 2 data, so the NIR band is ρ B8, (842 nm), and RED band is ρ B4, (665 nm).

Under healthy conditions, the light is absorbed by chlorophyll so the reflectance in the Red band decreases, increasing the value of the ratio. On the contrary, in case of low photosynthetic activity, the absorbance value in the red is higher and therefore the ratio decreases [17].

NDII, Normalized Difference Infrared Index [21], it's highly correlated with canopy and leaf water content [15]. In the case of Sentinel-2 data, the NIR band and SWIR band have different spatial resolutions, as 10 m and 20 m, so the SWIR bands were resampled to 10 m, before carrying out the calculation. NDII is defined as Eq. 2, using NIR and SWIR reflectance as 850 nm and 1610 nm [27]:

$$NDII = \rho B8a - \rho B11 / \rho B8a + \rho B11 \tag{2}$$

Finally, in this research, we used the Normalized Multi-band Drought Index, NMDI. This index was proposed for monitoring soil and vegetation moisture from space [22].

NMDI uses 860 nm channel as the reference, and to detect the absorbance of water it uses the difference between two SWIR channel, centered at 1640 nm and 2130 nm. NMDI formula is given (Eq. 3):

$$NMDI = \rho B8 - (\rho B11 - \rho B12) / \rho B8 + (\rho B11 - \rho B12) \tag{3}$$

3 Results

In the observed period, 2015–2019, the vegetation indices NDVI, NDII and NMDI were applied to the entire pinewood area and their temporal trend is shown in the following figures (Figs. 5, 6, and 7). To emphasize better the results, 2015 was taken as a reference of the health status of the pinewood as it did not show episodes of deterioration, and subsequent observations were stretched and compared to 2015.

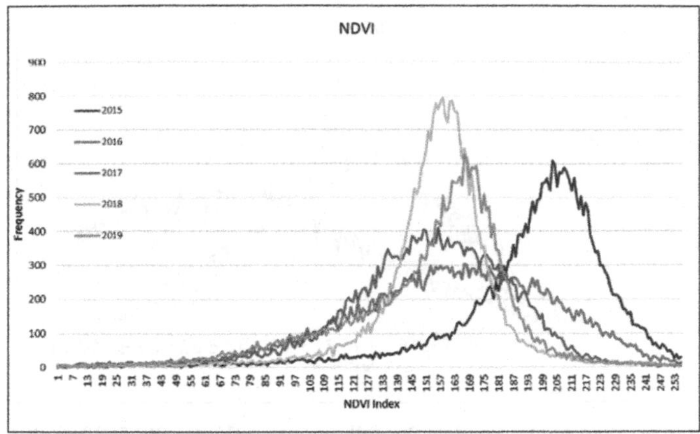

Fig. 5. NDVI index detected by Sentinel-2 satellite images (Years: 2015, 2016, 2017, 2018 and 2019).

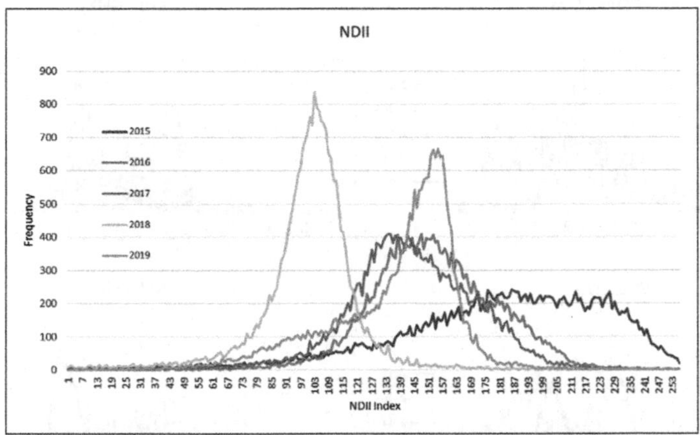

Fig. 6. NDII index detected by Sentinel-2 satellite images (Years: 2015, 2016, 2017, 2018 and 2019)

Observing preliminary results, the indices that showed the best effectiveness in terms of detecting the diachronic health conditions are the NDVI and the NDII indices. Considering that, these two indices were subsequently applied according to the classification made previously referred to volume and age classes of the pinewood, this to better investigate their capability in detecting health conditions in several forest structures phases. In Fig. 8 the results obtained are shown according to the volume classes and in Fig. 9 according to the age classes.

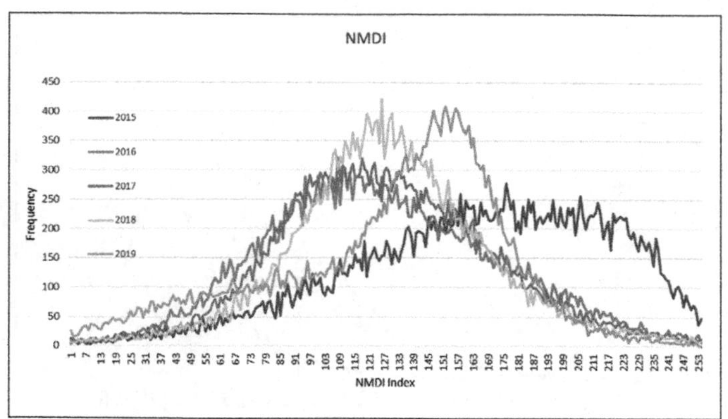

Fig. 7. NMDI index detected by Sentinel-2 satellite images (Years: 2015, 2016, 2017, 2018 and 2019)

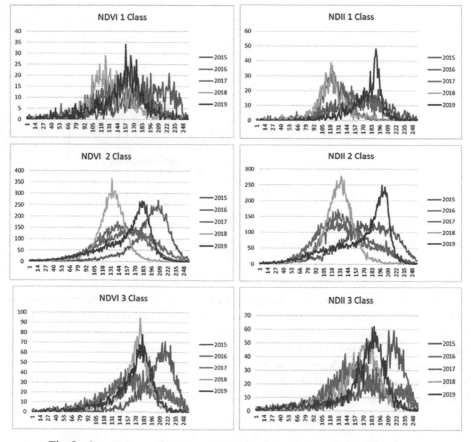

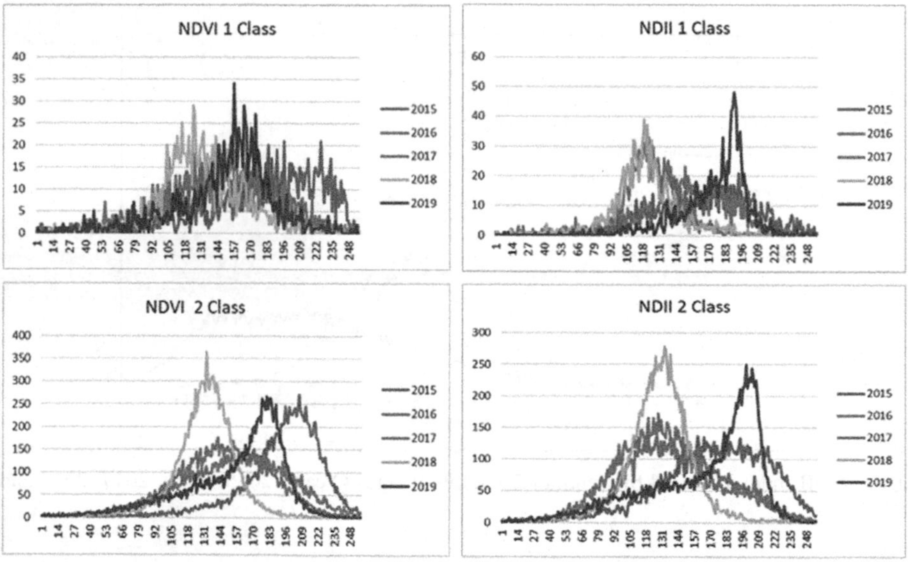

Fig. 8. Comparison of NDVI and NDII vegetation indices by volume classes.

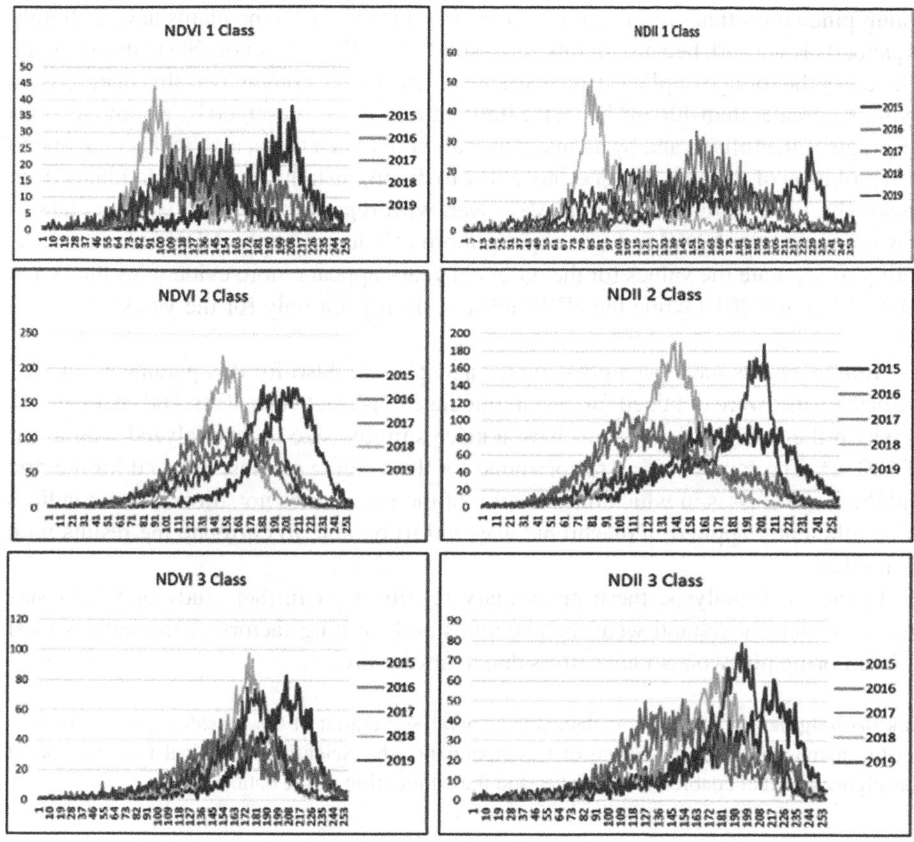

Fig. 9. Comparison of NDVI and NDII vegetation indices by age classes.

4 Discussion and Conclusion

The preliminary results obtained in this research show how the three applied vegetation indices present a different efficiency in detecting the health conditions of the studied pinewood in climatic drought conditions. At the scale of the whole pinewood it is evident that the NDVI and NDII index better differentiate the changes in vegetative health status for the observed period, this aspect emerges from the analysis of the modal values referred to the distribution of the cells frequencies based on their values. At this regard, the NDVI and NDII index, except for the years 2016 and 2017, significantly differentiate the variation in overall vegetative conditions. On the contrary, the NMDI index shows a lower variability of the data for all the years observed. This aspect clearly emerges from the over-lapping of the frequency curves in which, especially for the years: 2016, 2017, 2018 and 2019, the area of the curves presents a high overlap.

Instead, as regards the results obtained by the NDVI and NDII index applied to the different volume and age classes, it was found that: in the case of the volume classes, a better differentiation of the data is obtained for the intermediate volume class, i.e. the one included between 200 and 400 m^3 ha^{-1}. This mainly depends on two factors: (i) in young pinewoods that present a low volume (0–200 m^3 ha^{-1}) the plants have a slightly expanded crown and, because of this, the resolution of the cell is not able to discriminate efficiently the foliage of plants from the soil surface. (ii) For pinewoods that instead have a volume greater than 400 m^3 ha^{-1}, the limiting factor is represented by a homogeneous coverage of the foliage and by an interpenetration between them, also in this case due to the resolution of the cell, that does not allow to distinguish the healthy individuals from those who have suffered a decline. Moreover, with regard to the third volume class, it was noted that the NDVI index is slightly more efficient than the NDII index since its ability to separate the values for the observed years appears more evident for the years: 2015, 2018 and 2019 while the NDII index is significant only for the years: 2018 and 2019.

Similar results have been obtained for age groups. Also for this parameter, in fact, the best results were obtained for the intermediate class, between 40 and 80 years of age, in which the foliage of the plants have a more suitable size to be analyzed with a cell of 100 m^2. The same limiting factor, found for the volume classes, is found for the first and third age classes in which the structure of the forest does not allow the two indices to be efficiently applied in diachronic way and to be able to correlate the results with each other.

In the final analysis, these preliminary results need further study and field surveys to better understand what the potentials and limiting factors of the indices used in monitoring pinewoods under stress due to aridity are.

Acknowledgments. The authors thank the General Secretariat of the Presidency of the Republic, the management of the Estate of Castelporziano, the Scientific-Technical Commission of Castelporziano that enabled these studies and the publication of the data.

Funding. This research was funded by the National Academy of Sciences (Rome), within the monitoring program of the presidential Estate of Castelporziano.

Conflicts of Interest. The authors declare no conflict of interest.

References

1. Sluiter, R., de Jong, S.M.: Spatial patterns of Mediterranean land abandonment and related land cover transitions. Landscape Ecol. **22**, 559–576 (2007). https://doi.org/10.1007/s10980-006-9049-3
2. Recanatesi, F., Tolli, M., Ripa, M.N., Pelorosso, R., Gobattoni, F., Leone, A.: Detection of landscape patterns in airborne LIDAR data in the nature reserve of Castelporziano (Rome). J. Agricultural Eng. **XLIV**, 472–477 (2013). https://doi.org/10.4081/jae.2013.(s1):e94
3. Recanatesi, F.: Variations in land-use/land-cover changes (LULCCs) in a peri-urban Mediterranean nature reserve: the estate of Castelporziano (Central Italy). Rendiconti Lincei **26**(3), 517–526 (2014). https://doi.org/10.1007/s12210-014-0358-1
4. Grenon, M., Batisse, M.: Futures for the Mediterranean basin: the Blue Plan (1989)
5. IPCC. Climate Change 2014: Impacts, Adaptation, and Vulnerability. Part A: Global and Sectoral Aspects. Contribution of Working Group II to the Fifth Assessment Report of the Intergovernmental Panel on Climate Change, p. 1435. Cambridge University Press, Cambridge UK (2014)

6. Recanatesi, F., Giuliani, C., Ripa, M.: Monitoring Mediterranean Oak decline in a peri-urban protected area using the NDVI and Sentinel-2 images: the case study of Castelporziano State Natural Reserve. Sustainability **10**(9), 3308 (2018). https://doi.org/10.3390/su10093308
7. Bleu, P.: State of Mediterranean forests 2018. Food & Agriculture Org (2019)
8. Rita, A., et al.: The impact of drought spells on forests depends on site conditions: the case of 2017 summer heat wave in southern Europe. Glob. Change Biol. **26**(2), 851–863 (2020)
9. Maselli, F.: Monitoring forest conditions in a protected Mediterranean coastal area by the analysis of multiyear NDVI data. Remote Sens. Environ. **89**(4), 423–433 (2004). https://doi.org/10.1016/j.rse.2003.10.020
10. Prieto-Recio, C., Martin-Garcia, J., Bravo, F., Deizo, J.J.: Unravelling the associations between climate, soil properties and forest management in *Pinus Pinaster* decline in the Iberia Peninsula. Forest Ecol. Manag. **356**, 74–83 (2015). https://doi.org/10.1016/j.foreco.2015.07.033
11. Rodriguez-Vallejo, C., Navarro-Cerrillo, R.M.: Contrasting response to drought and climate of planted and natural pinus pinaster aiton forests in Southern Spain. Forests **10**(7), 603 (2019). https://doi.org/10.3390/f10070603
12. Wilhite, D.A., Glantz, M.H.: Understanding the drought phenomenon: the role of definitions. Water Int. **10**(3), 111–120 (1985)
13. Mishra, A.K., Singh, V.P.: A review of drought concept. J. Hydrol. **391**, 202–216 (2010). https://doi.org/10.1016/j.jhydrol.2010.07.012
14. Zhang, Y., et al.: Monitoring and estimating drought-induced impacts on forest structure, growth, function, and ecosystem services using remote-sensing data: recent progress and future challenges. Environ. Rev. **21**(2), 103–115 (2013). https://doi.org/10.1139/er-2013-0006
15. Zargar, A., Sadiq, R., Naser, B.: A review of drought indices. Environ. Rev. **19**, 333–349 (2011). https://doi.org/10.1139/a11-013
16. Modica, G., Pollino, M., Solano, F.: Sentinel-2 imagery for mapping cork oak (*Quercus suber* L.) distribution in Calabria (Italy): capabilities and quantitative estimation. In: Calabrò, F., Della Spina, L., Bevilacqua, C. (eds.) ISHT 2018. SIST, vol. 100, pp. 60–67. Springer, Cham (2019). https://doi.org/10.1007/978-3-319-92099-3_8
17. Ogaya, R., Barbeta, A., Başnou, C., Peñuelas, J.: Satellite data as indicators of tree biomass growth and forest dieback in a Mediterranean holm oak forest. Ann. Forest Sci. **72**(1), 135–144 (2014). https://doi.org/10.1007/s13595-014-0408-y
18. Bannari, A., Morin, D., Bonn, F.: A review of vegetation indices. Remote Sens. Rev. **13**, 95–120 (1995). https://doi.org/10.1080/02757259509532298
19. Kogan, F.N.: Application of vegetation index and brightness temperature for drought detection. Adv. Space Res. **15**(11), 91–100 (1995). https://doi.org/10.1016/0273-1177(95)00079-t
20. Deshayes, M., Guyon, D., Jeanjean, H., Stach, N., Jolly, A., Hagolle, O.: The contribution of remote sensing to the assessment of drought effects in forest ecosystems. Ann. Forest Sci. **63**(6), 579–595 (2006)
21. Hardisky, M., Klemas, V., Smart, R.: The influences of soil salinity, growth form, and leaf moisture on the spectral reflectance of spartina alterniflora canopies. Photogram. Eng. Remote Sens. **49**, 77–83 (1983)
22. Wang, L., Qu, J.J.: NMDI: a normalized multi-band drought index for monitoring soil and vegetation moisture with satellite remote sensing. Geophys. Res. Lett. **34**(20) (2007). https://doi.org/10.1029/2007gl031021
23. Blasi, C.: Fitoclimatologia del lazio. Fitosociologia **27**, 151–175 (1994)
24. Scrinzi, G., Presutti Saba, E., Colle, G.: Indirizzi Gestionali e Obiettivi d'Intervento per le classi colturali della faoresta della tenuta presidenziale di Castel Porziano. Accademia Nazioanle delle Scienze, Roma, Italy (2016)

25. Rouse, J.W., Haas, R.H., Deering, D.W., Sehell, J.A.: Monitoring the vernal advancement and retrogradation (Greenwave effect) of natural vegetation. Final Rep. RSC 1978-4, Remote Sensing Center, Texas A&M Univ., College Station (1974)
26. Gilabert, M.A., González-Piqueras, J., Martínez, B., Maselli, F., Menenti, M., Brivio, P.A.: Theory and applications of vegetation indices. Remote sensing optical observations of vegetation properties. Research Signpost, Scarborough, Toronto, Canada, pp. 1–43 (2010)
27. Zhang, C., et al.: Retrieving leaf and canopy water content of winter wheat using vegetation water indices. IEEE J. Sel. Top. Appl. Earth Observations Remote Sens. **11**(1), 112–126 (2018). https://doi.org/10.1109/jstars.2017.2773625

Unsupervised Burned Area Mapping in a Protected Natural Site. An Approach Using SAR Sentinel-1 Data and K-mean Algorithm

Giandomenico De Luca[1], Giuseppe Modica[1(✉)], Carmen Fattore[2], and Rosa Lasaponara[3]

[1] Dipartimento di Agraria, Università degli Studi Mediterranea di Reggio Calabria, Località Feo di Vito, 89122 Reggio Calabria, Italy
{giandomenico.deluca,giuseppe.modica}@unirc.it

[2] DiCEM, Università degli Studi della Basilicata, Via Lanera 20, 75100 Matera, Italy
carmen.fattore@imaa.cnr.it

[3] Istituto di Metodologie per l'Analisi Ambientale, Consiglio Nazionale delle Ricerche, C.da S. Loja, 85050 Tito Scalo, Italy
rosa.lasaponara@imaa.cnr.it

Abstract. This paper is focused on investigating the capabilities of SAR S-1 sensors for burned area mapping. To this aim, we analyzed S-1 data focusing on a fire that occurred on August 10th, 2017, in a protected natural site. An unsupervised classification, using a k-mean machine learning algorithm, was carried out, and the choice of an adequate number of clusters was guided by the calculation of the silhouette score. The ΔNBR index calculated from optical S-2 based images was used to evaluate the burned area delimitation accuracy. The fire covered around 38.51 km^2 and also affected areas outside the boundaries of the reserve. S-1 based outputs successfully matched the S-2 burnt mapping.

Keywords: Burned area detection · Sentinel-1 · SAR · Machine learning · K-mean clustering · Silhouette score · PCA · Radar burn difference (RBD) · Radar burn ratio (RBR) · Normalized burn ratio (NBR) · Protected natural site · Forest fire

1 Introduction

In the Mediterranean Basin, wildfires represent one of the primary disturbances, which causes economic damages and significant changes in landscapes, forests, and environmental ecosystems [1]. In the south of Italy, the 2017 fire-season has been one of the worse of the last decades because of the large number of burned woodlands and their extent [2, 3], also favored by the drought climatic trend of that year. Protected natural sites are environments characterized by higher ecological value and biodiversity and are among the most vulnerable contexts. For this reason, the aspect concerning post-fire management is one of the most critical issues for the safeguarding of flora and fauna. Timely and accurate detection and quantification of burned areas are the first operational

O. Gervasi et al. (Eds.): ICCSA 2020, LNCS 12253, pp. 63–77, 2020.
https://doi.org/10.1007/978-3-030-58814-4_5

step after the fire occurrence for assessing the damage and addressing the post-event management [3–6]. Moreover, this step is fundamental also for the subsequent implementing medium and long-term territorial planning strategies, in order to predict and manage irreversible forest and landscape degradation processes, and land cover changing [7–12]. In this context, remote sensing (RS) techniques provide reliable tools and techniques for monitoring and quantifying the location and the impact of burned areas with particular reference to satellite platforms [4]. The majority of studies on the detection of burned areas has been based on multi-spectral (MS) (i.e., optical) satellite data [4]. However, these platforms are sensitive to some environmental conditions, such as sunlight and cloud cover, representing a limitation, especially for areas frequently affected by the presence of clouds [3, 13]. Therefore, methods based on data acquired by cloud-independent sensors at high spatial and temporal resolutions are needed. Among them, Synthetic Aperture Radar (SAR) sensors provide an efficient system for discriminating events that cause changes in objects on the Earth's surface [4, 14–18]. To detect burned areas, radar technology exploits the variations in microwaves backscatter caused by the modification of the structure and moisture content of the vegetation cover and soil [6, 15, 19–21]. However, due to its intrinsic characteristics and the high sensitivity of the radar signal to surface conditions, it can be altered and rich in so-called "noises" [19, 22]. Referring to the SAR data, a significant parameter characterizing them is the used polarization [20]. Its complexity of processing causes that this sensor is not widely used compared to optical ones [23]. There are several space missions that provide satellite constellations operating SAR imaging useful for Earth's environmental and fire monitoring purposes [4].

Copernicus missions by European Space Agency (ESA) provides free high spatial and temporal resolution data both from SAR sensors (Sentinel-1, S-1) and from MS optical sensors (Sentinel-2, S-2) (https://sentinel.esa.int/web/sentinel/home). The S-1 constellation comprises two polar-orbiting satellites (S-1A and S-1B) performing C-band radar imaging. The aim of this work is to investigate the capabilities of SAR S-1 sensors for mapping a burned forest area, performing an unsupervised image classification approach using the k-mean machine-learning algorithm. This phase was anticipated by a series of pre-processing steps aimed to 1) reducing the noise of the radar images by calculating the backscatter time average of pre and post-fire datasets; 2) calculation of radar burn difference (RBD) and radar burn ratio (RBR) indices; 3) texture feature extraction; 4) data reduction by means of principal components analysis (PCA) transformation; 5) calculation of the silhouette score to define the number of clusters. Validation of mapping was carried out using the delta normalized burn ratio (ΔNBR) difference index, carried out using S-2 data as a reference map. A post-processing improvement was necessary to reduce commission errors, filtering smaller clusters and ruling out from errors other small fires occurred all over the scene. The fast-and-easy k-mean algorithm produced a correct overlap of the burned area equal to 82.18%; however, several small commission errors throughout the rest of the scene persisted.

2 Study Area and Dataset

The proposed methodology was tested in a study area located in the central area of Sicily (South of Italy, 37° 43'N; 14° 39'9E), the "Rossomanno-Grottascura-Bellia" regional nature reserve (Fig. 1). The large part of the woodland was covered by broadleaves (genus *Eucalyptus*) and coniferous (mainly *Pinus pinea* L. and *Pinus halepensis*, Mill) essences. The event occurred on august 10th 2017, and covered 38.51 km^2, also affecting neighboring and similar forest areas outside the boundaries of the reserve.

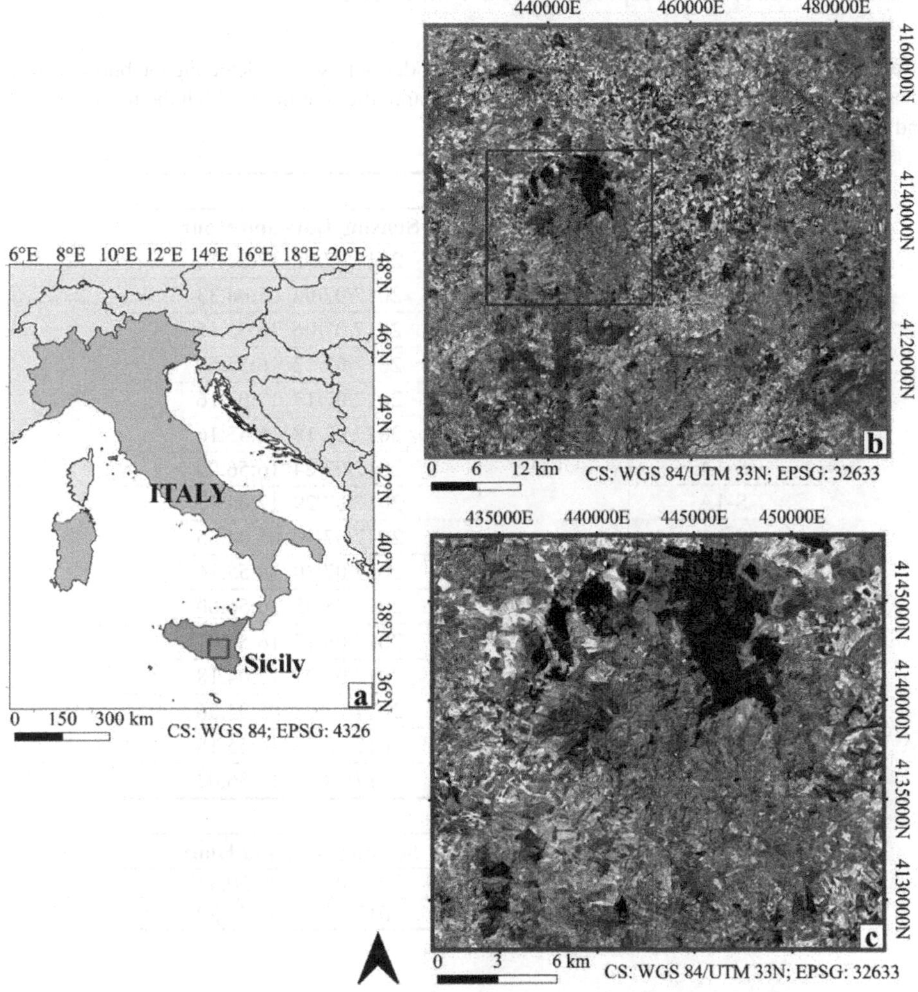

Fig. 1. Location of the study area in Italy (a). Map b is an overview of the study area of and its size is equal to the area of the clipped subset of Sentinel-1 data used in the subsequent processing. The darker area, indicated with a blue box in b and showed in detail in c (Sentinel-2 image on August 16th, 2017 false-color composite), represents the study burned area.

For the purpose of our study, Sentinel-1A/B ground range detected (GRD) dual-polarized (vertical-vertical VV, and vertical-horizontal VH polarizations) temporal series, acquired in interferometric wide (IW) mode, were downloaded through the Copernicus Open Access Hub (https://scihub.copernicus.eu/). In total, we acquired two S-1 image-datasets formed by eleven images for the pre-fire period (around for one month before) and five images for the post-fire period (around for one month after) (Table 1). Besides, we downloaded two Sentinel-2A Level-1C images acquired before and after the fire, respectively, in order to obtain the reference map based on the optical vegetation index. The acquisition dates of the two optical images correspond to the first (pre-fire) and last (post-fire) dates, respectively, of S-1 time-series.

Table 1. Characteristics of Sentinel-1 and Sentinel-2 dataset used for detecting the burned study area. The red lines separate the data acquired before and after the fire for both the missions (S-1 and S-2), respectively.

Sentinel-1 SAR		
Mission-Orbit	**Product**	**Sensing Date and Hour**
S-1A	IW Level-1 GRD	2017/07/05 17:04:16
S-1A		2017/07/06 05:04:33
S-1B		2017/07/06 16:55:15
S-1A		2017/07/12 16:55:59
S-1A		2017/07/17 17:04:16
S-1B		2017/07/18 16:55:16
S-1A		2017/07/24 16:56:00
S-1A		2017/07/29 17:04:17
S-1A		2017/07/30 05:04:35
S-1B		2017/07/30 16:55:16
S-1A		2017/08/05 16:56:00
S-1A	IW Level-1 GRD	2017/08/17 16:56:01
S-1A		2017/08/22 17:04:18
S-1A		2017/08/23 05:04:36
S-1B		2017/08/23 16:55:18
S-1A		2017/08/29 16:56:02
Sentinel-2 MS		
Mission-Orbit	**Product**	**Sensing Date and Hour**
S-2A	Level-1C	2017/07/07 09:50:31
S-2B	Level-1C	2017/08/31 09:50:29

3 Methods

3.1 Data Pre-processing

Sentinel-1. The S-1 data pre-processing was performed (separately for the pre and post-event datasets) and using the Sentinel-1 Toolbox implemented in the ESA- SNAP v.7.0 software (http://step.esa.int/main/toolboxes/snap/). The pre-processing started whit the application of the orbit (file automatic downloaded by SNAP), and then the thermal noise was removed.

Images were radiometric calibrated and converted to gamma (γ_0) and sigma (σ_0) noughts backscatter standard conventions. Terrain correction was carried out by an auto-downloaded digital elevation model (DEM) obtained from the shuttle radar topography mission (SRTM). In this step, a pixel resampling of 10 m $\times$ 10 m and a map projection to WGS84/UTM zone 33 N were performed. All images were clipped in a subset area of 3667 km^2 (Fig. 1-b).

The same pre-processing procedures were separating applied to each time-series dataset, pre- and post-fire, respectively. Each of the two derived temporal datasets was subject to two separately layer stacking.

Due to the speckle noise, using single backscattering images may not provide clear discrimination of the burned area, whereas the use of standard speckle reduction filters may instead reduce useful information [24–26]. For this reason, in order to reduce speckle noise effects, the backscatter time average was calculated separately for the two-time data series (before and after the fire), for each calibration nought (γ_0 and σ_0) and each polarization (VH and VV) [3].

Thus, at the end of this first pre-processing step, we had the following eight layers of data output:

- Post- and pre-fire average-γ_0-VH
- Post- and pre-fire average-γ_0-VV
- Post- and pre-fire average-σ_0-VH
- Post- and pre-fire average-σ_0-VV

A second layer stack was performed in order to put all these layer-bands into a unique stack. These individual layers were used to compute the RBD (Eq. 1) (the difference between pre and post-fire backscattered time average for each polarization) and the RBR (Eq. 2) (ratio of the backscattering coefficients between pre to post-fire for each polarization) [3, 27]:

$$\mathrm{RBD}_{\mathrm{xyn}} = \text{Post-fire average}_{\mathrm{xyn}} - \text{Pre-fire average}_{\mathrm{xyn}} \tag{1}$$

$$\mathrm{RBR}_{\mathrm{xyn}} = \text{Post-fire average}_{\mathrm{xyn}} / \text{Pre-fire average}_{\mathrm{xyn}} \tag{2}$$

Where xy represents a specific polarization (VV or VH) and n a specific calibration nought type (γ_0 or σ_0). RBD and RBR were computed for each VV and VH polarization and for each γ_0 and σ_0 nought, thus forming the first eight raster index layers (Table 2).

For each of these index layers, the GLCM (Grey Level Co-occurrence Matrix) mean and the variance texture features were computed and appended as new informative layers, thus generating a final dataset consisting of 24 images (Table 2).

Sentinel-2. The S-2 MS data were also processed in ESA-SNAP Sentinel-2 Toolbox. The Level-2A products (Bottom-of-Atmosphere) were generated from Level-1C using Sen2Cor SNAP plugin. Then, resampling to 10 m $\times$ 10 m pixel size, map projection, and clipping on the same area of S-1 data were carried out. The classic normalized burn ratio (NBR), based on the two burn sensitive bands (near-infrared NIR and short-infrared

Table 2. The twenty-four Sentinel-1 layers obtained after the pre-processing steps. The first eight are the index layers, based on the RBD and RBR indices, and computed between pre- and post-fire backscatter time average, for each calibration nought and each polarization. Layers from 9th to 24th represent the GLCM texture features (Mean and Variance) computed for each S-1 index layer.

Index Layers				
	Index	**Calibration nought**	**Polarization**	**n**
	RBD	γ_0	VH	1
			VV	2
		σ_0	VH	3
			VV	4
	RBR	γ_0	VH	5
			VV	6
		σ_0	VH	7
			VV	8
Texture Features Layers				
GLCM	**Index**	**Calibration nought**	**Polarization**	**n**
Mean	RBD	γ_0	VH	9
			VV	10
		σ_0	VH	11
			VV	12
	RBR	γ_0	VH	13
			VV	14
		σ_0	VH	15
			VV	16
Variance	RBD	γ_0	VH	17
			VV	18
		σ_0	VH	19
			VV	20
	RBR	γ_0	VH	21
			VV	22
		σ_0	VH	23
			VV	24

SWIR) [28], was computed for pre- and post-fire datasets, in order to obtain the temporal difference index (ΔNBR, Eq. 3):

$$\Delta NBR = \text{Pre-fire NBR} - \text{Post-fire NBR} \tag{3}$$

This index was used as a reference layer since it allows us to identify better the burned areas perimeter than other methods [28].

3.2 Data Preparation and Image Classification

Considering of the high number of input data layers, a principal component analysis (PCA) was performed to reduce the dimension of the dataset without losing the original information [29].

An unsupervised classification of all scene, using the k-mean algorithm, was carried out on the first transformed PCA outputs that reached a high enough cumulative variance (greater than or equal to 99.95%). One of the main issues, when a clustering algorithm is going to be performed, is the setting of the number of clusters. To deal with this, the silhouette score [30], implemented in scikit-learn library (https://scikit-learn.org) [31], was performed (Eq. 4). It is based on the separation distance between clusters, measured by:

$$\text{Silhouette Score} = (\mathrm{b_i}-\mathrm{a_i})/\max(\mathrm{a_i},\mathrm{b_i}) = [-1,\ 1] \quad (4)$$

Where i is the value of a single-pixel contained in a cluster, a is the average dissimilarity (mean distance) of i to all other objects of the same cluster, and b is the average dissimilarity to the nearest cluster that i is not a part of [30]. This coefficient measure how close each point in a cluster is to the points in neighboring clusters, for a given number of clusters, and the computation of its average results a simple method to address the choice of k-value (number of clusters) [30]. Its value can be in a range from 1 (maximum separation, best k-value) to −1 (minimum separation, worst k-value). We calculated the mean of the silhouette score for different k-values (range from 2 to 20).

3.3 Post-processing Enhancement and Clustering Accuracy

The errors of the burned area mapped using S-1 layers were detected, taking as reference the ΔNBR calculated using optical data. Since a time-average was used, several small fire-events or surface-changes that occurred during that time-frame could lead to an erroneous assessment of commission errors. To reduce this issue, a post-processing improvement was carried out, applying a semi-automatic filter in order to eliminate clusters that had an area less than 0.1 km^2. The resulting clusters were analyzed, matching them with the reference ΔNBR map, in order to interpret the errors and justify some of them, excluding from errors clusters that contained a mean value of the ΔNBR pixels average greater than or equal to 0.1 (conventional burned/not-burned threshold [32]).

The classification of commission errors was performed and distinguished on two levels:

1. The commission errors relating to the entire scene, represented by all the clusters outside the burned study area boundary, which were incorrectly labeled with the burned area class.
2. The commission errors relating to the study area, represented by the overestimated pixels incorrectly classified as burned.

4 Results and Discussions

4.1 Data Implementation and Clustering

Figure 2 shows the result layers, only for the gamma (γ_0) backscatter convention, of the S-1 images pre-processing in both polarizations (VV and VH). Added to the result layers in sigma (σ_0), the resulted 24 images were reduced using a PCA transformation.

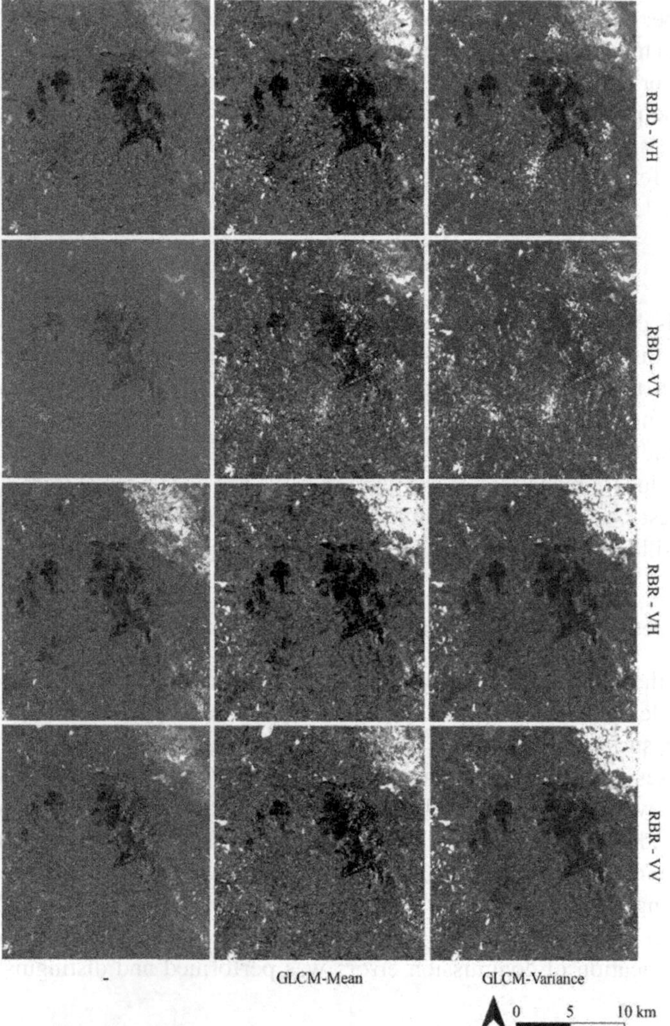

Fig. 2. Details of resulting S-1 based layers after pre-processing steps (for gamma γ_0 backscatter nought). The first column shows the index layers (RBD and RBR), computed between pre- and post-fire backscatter time average, for each polarization (VH and VV). The second and third columns represent the GLCM texture features (Mean and Variance, respectively) computed for each previous S-1 index layer. The rows denote the combination index-polarization.

It is noticeable how some images present a more well-defined area of low backscatter (black area), presumably indicative of the burned area, compared to the others. A clear difference is observed using different polarizations, with cross-polarization (VH) images presenting a sharper and more differentiated scene. The best scenes seemed to be the two VH polarized indexes (RBD and RBR), where the GLCM mean texture was extracted.

This confirms the relevance of these texture features as additional useful information layers for classification.

In Table 3, several statistics parameters of the first five PCs are reported. The first five principal components (PCs) that reached a cumulative variance of 99.98% were chosen as the input layer in the classification process (Fig. 1). Over this value, as shown in Fig. 3, the PCs lose the importance of their information useful for the discrimination of objects on the scene. This allowed to drastically reduce the number of layers, without losing useful information and thus speeding up the computational process [29].

Table 3. Statistics of the first five principal components (PCs)

PC	Min	Max	Mean	St dev	Variance [%]	Cumulative variance [%]
PC 1	0.37	7938.00	901.73	664.31	78.28	78.28
PC 2	0.25	126.00	37.35	11.37	17.80	96.08
PC 3	0.00	7938.00	958.86	894.79	3.14	99.22
PC 4	0.00	126.00	36.72	14.86	0.62	99.84
PC 5	0.37	7938.00	885.64	671.40	0.14	99.98

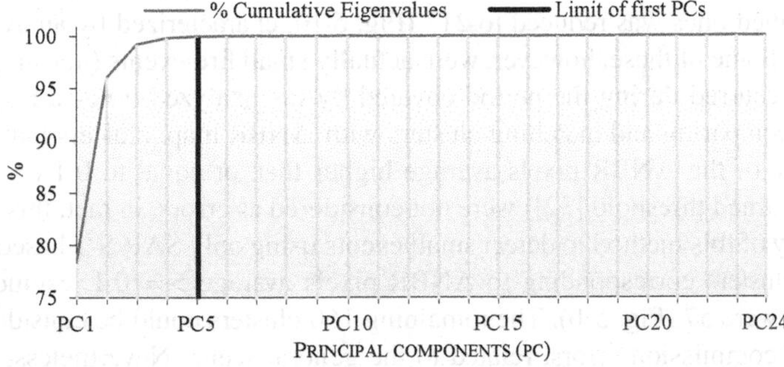

Fig. 3. Cumulative variance [%] of eigenvalues for the analyzed twenty-four principal components (PCs).

Figure 4 shows the trend of the averaged silhouette score calculated for different k-values (ranging from 2 to 20).

It is evident that for lower values of k the silhouette score, therefore the separation of the clusters, is higher. Silhouette analysis was be used in the preliminary choice of the most suitable number of clusters. A k-value of 3 was finally chosen, given that we only needed the "burned" land-use class. The rest of the scene fell into "non-burned" class.

4.2 Clustering Accuracy

The clustering process using k-mean was very fast, with a computation time of a few minutes. The clusters resulting from the entire scene are shown in Fig. 5-a. From a

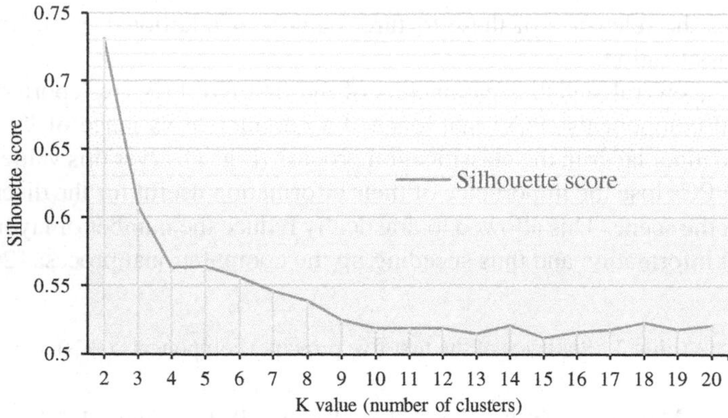

Fig. 4. Silhouette score for a range of k-value (number of clusters) between 2 and 20

visual assessment of the first result, it was evident that the burned area was clearly outlined. However, commission errors occurred, represented by small clusters across the entire scene (Fig. 5-a). These were composed of 46,708 clusters belonging to the class related to the study area (burned class), whit a maximum dimension range from 100 m^2 to 0.95 km^2, and only three others exceeding 1 km^2 (max 2.12 km^2). Applying the semi-automatic filter, small clusters were deleted, and the number of remaining wrong-classified ones was reduced to 217 (Fig. 5-b), characterized by an average area of 0.26 km^2. Some of these, however, were actually small fire-events (not subject of this study) that occurred during the period covered by the analyzed time-series. This was ascertained comparing and matching clusters with ΔNBR map: clusters that contained a mean value of the ΔNBR pixels average higher than or equal to 0.1 (conventional burned/not-burned threshold [32]) were not considered as errors, in fact, this confirmed the capability of this method to detect small events using only SAR S-1 based data. The number of clusters corresponding to ΔNBR pixels average >= 0.1, excluding study burned area, were 57 (Fig. 5-b). The remaining 160 clusters could be considered as the first level of commission errors, related to the general scene. Nevertheless, with their mean area of 0.24 km^2, they represented minimal areas if compared whit study burned area (Fig. 5-b). However, most of these clusters (85%) maintain ΔNBR pixels average values greater than 0. In fact, the NBR time-difference, as already mentioned, is the classic used to classify fire severity [28, 32]. However, this index exploits the SWIR reflectance increase also caused by the lower moisture content of the detected surface and higher exposure of the soil [15]. This means that, since the SAR sensor is sensitive to changes in humidity and surface roughness [21, 33], it is possible that it detected soil tillage, irrigated fields, etc., widespread in an area with a strong agricultural vocation.

In Fig. 5-c the vectorized study burnt area delimited by the proposed approach is presented, superimposed, and compared with the reference burned area derived by ΔNBR. The map in Fig. 5-d shows the areas relating to the correct overlap between the detected burned area with SAR and the reference area, the omission error, and the commission (relating only to the study area) error. The total area detected was of 38.87 km^2, of which, the 82.18% was the correct overlap, the remaining 17.82%

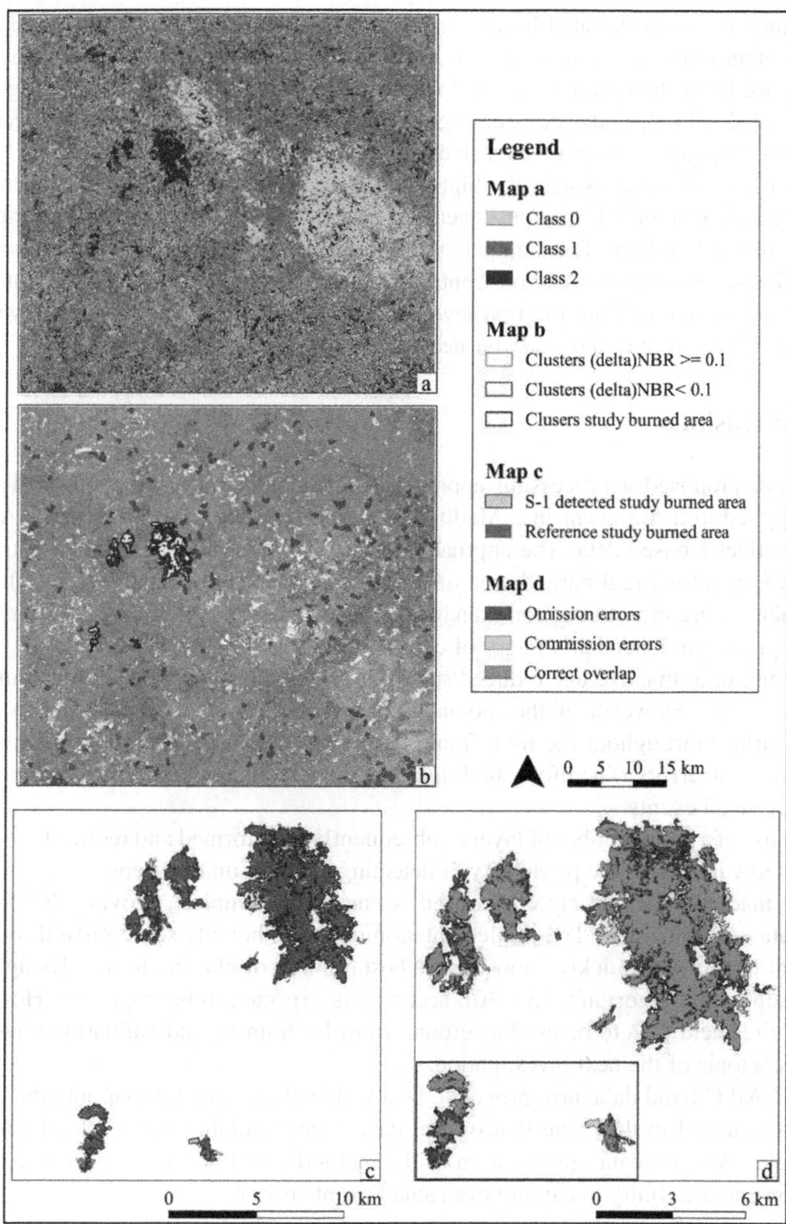

Fig. 5. a) Clustering result of the entire scene, showing the three classes set by choice of the k parameter value ($k = 3$). b) The remaining class-2 clusters after eliminating the smaller ones (<0.1 km). In blue the boundary of the burned area detected; in orange, the clusters representing small fires occurred during the time-frame (corresponding to ΔNBR >= 0.1) (not considered errors); red clusters wrongly classified (first level of commission errors). c) Comparison between study burned area detected by SAR and the reference one ΔNBR derived. d) Area correctly detected (green); areas omitted (red); overestimated areas (yellow). (Color figure online)

represented the overestimated burned area (commission). A surface corresponding to 17.09% of the reference burned area was not be detected (omission). The level of overlap is high (82.18%). It represents a good result if compared to other works using SAR data [3, 17, 22, 34, 35], also considering the use of a straightforward machine learning algorithm [36] applied over an extensive area.

The use of PCs that explain the higher variance, resulting from the transformation of a large number of information layers, has probably contributed to achieving this good result. Only relative few small areas appear to be under omission and commission errors. These lasts represent errors centralized only on the study burned area and are considered separately from the first level of commission errors related to the wrong-classified clusters out of the study burned area.

5 Conclusions

This work proposed a processing approach for the rapid mapping of burned wild-areas applied to a fire event in a Mediterranean protected natural site using SAR C-band Sentinel-1 based data. The approach detected most of the burned area boundary (82.18%), on a total real burned area of 38.51 km^2. This is important for an effective and enhanced fire monitoring and management in vulnerable environments since these sensors provide independent images of cloud cover.

The use of a time average reduced speckle noise without losing useful information from the images. However, all the anomalies detectable by the SAR sensor and occurred on the surface throughout the time-frame have been detected, increasing the number of commission errors. Therefore, highlighting the potential of this sensor in detecting relatively small events.

The use of a large number of layers, subsequently transformed and reduced via PCA, undoubtedly increased the possibility of detecting changes on the scene.

The machine learning algorithm used is one of the simplest, proving that S-1 C-band data can be trusted. The implementation of the Silhouette score proved to be an excellent method for quickly choosing the best number of clusters to use. Using more robust supervised algorithms [37–40], accuracy is expected to be improved. However, this requires field data to be used as ground-truth for training and validation phases. It could be a topic of the next investigation.

S-1 SAR C-band data have proven to be a viable alternative for mapping the extent of the fire, useful in the event that optical data is not available due to cloud cover or fire smoke. A significant optimization of the method could provide for an increase in precision and the ability to capture even small events better.

Acknowledgments. Giandomenico De Luca was supported by the European Commission through the European Social Fund (ESF) and the Regione Calabria.

References

1. Chuvieco, E.: Earth Observation of Wildland Fires in Mediterranean Ecosystems. Springer, Heidelberg (2009). https://doi.org/10.1007/978-3-642-01754-4

2. San-Miguel-Ayanza, J., et al.: Forest Fires in Europe, Middle East and North Africa 2017. Publications Office of the European Union (2018)
3. Lasaponara, R., Tucci, B.: Identification of burned areas and severity. IEEE Geosci. Remote Sens. Lett. **16**, 917–921 (2019). https://doi.org/10.1109/LGRS.2018.2888641
4. Chuvieco, E., et al.: Historical background and current developments for mapping burned area from satellite earth observation. Remote Sens. Environ. **225**, 45–64 (2019). https://doi.org/10.1016/j.rse.2019.02.013
5. Lizundia-Loiola, J., Otón, G., Ramo, R., Chuvieco, E.: A spatio-temporal active-fire clustering approach for global burned area mapping at 250 m from MODIS data. Remote Sens. Environ. **236**, 111493 (2020). https://doi.org/10.1016/j.rse.2019.111493
6. Pepe, A., et al.: Exploitation of copernicus sentinels data for sensing fire-disturbed vegetated areas. In: IGARSS 2018 - 2018 IEEE International Geoscience and Remote Sensing Symposium, Valencia, pp. 7589–7592 (2018). https://doi.org/10.1109/IGARSS.2018.8518272
7. Modica, G., et al.: Using Landsat 8 imagery in detecting cork oak (Quercus suber L.) woodlands: a case study in Calabria (Italy). J. Agric. Eng. **47**, 205–215 (2016). https://doi.org/10.4081/jae.2016.571
8. Fichera, C.R., Laudari, L., Modica, G.: Application, validation and comparison in different geographical contexts of an integrated model for the design of ecological networks. J. Agric. Eng. **46**, 52–61 (2015). https://doi.org/10.4081/jae.2015.459
9. Di Fazio, S., Modica, G., Zoccali, P.: Evolution trends of land use/land cover in a mediterranean forest landscape in Italy. In: Murgante, B., Gervasi, O., Iglesias, A., Taniar, D., Apduhan, B.O. (eds.) ICCSA 2011. LNCS, vol. 6782, pp. 284–299. Springer, Heidelberg (2011). https://doi.org/10.1007/978-3-642-21928-3_20
10. Modica, G., Merlino, A., Solano, F., Mercurio, R.: An index for the assessment of degraded mediterranean forest ecosystems. Forest Syst. (2015). https://doi.org/10.5424/fs/2015243-07855
11. Gulinck, H., et al.: The fourth regime of open space. Sustainability **10**, 1–15 (2018). https://doi.org/10.3390/su10072143
12. Choudhury, A.M., et al.: Photogrammetry and remote sensing for the identification and characterization of trees in urban areas (2019). https://doi.org/10.1088/1742-6596/1249/1/012008
13. Ruiz-Ramos, J., Marino, A., Boardman, C.P.: Using sentinel 1-SAR for monitoring long term variation in burnt forest areas. In: International Geoscience and Remote Sensing Symposium, pp. 4901–4904 (2018). https://doi.org/10.1109/IGARSS.2018.8518960
14. Belenguer-Plomer, M.A., Tanase, M.A., Fernandez-Carrillo, A., Chuvieco, E.: Burned area detection and mapping using Sentinel-1 backscatter coefficient and thermal anomalies. Remote Sens. Environ. **233**, 111345 (2019). https://doi.org/10.1016/j.rse.2019.111345
15. Tanase, M.A., Santoro, M., De La Riva, J., Pérez-Cabello, F., Le Toan, T.: Sensitivity of X-, C-, and L-band SAR backscatter to burn severity in Mediterranean pine forests. IEEE Trans. Geosci. Remote Sens. **48**, 3663–3675 (2010). https://doi.org/10.1109/TGRS.2010.2049653
16. Tanase, M.A., et al.: Burned area detection and mapping: intercomparison of sentinel-1 and sentinel-2 based algorithms over tropical Africa. Remote Sens. **12**, 334 (2020). https://doi.org/10.3390/rs12020334
17. Donezar, U., et al.: Applicability of the multitemporal coherence approach to sentinel-1 for the detection and delineation of burnt areas in the context of the copernicus emergency management service. Remote Sens. **11** (2019). https://doi.org/10.3390/rs11222607
18. Santi, E., et al.: The potential of multifrequency SAR images for estimating forest biomass in mediterranean areas. Remote Sens. Environ. **200**, 63–73 (2017). https://doi.org/10.1016/j.rse.2017.07.038

19. Lillesand, T., Kiefer, R., Chipman, J.: Remote Sensing and Image Interpretation, 7th edn. Wiley, New York (2015)
20. Imperatore, P., et al.: Effect of the vegetation fire on backscattering: an investigation based on sentinel-1 observations. IEEE J. Sel. Top. Appl. Earth Obs. Remote Sens. **10**, 4478–4492 (2017). https://doi.org/10.1109/JSTARS.2017.2717039
21. Stroppiana, D., et al.: Integration of optical and SAR data for burned area mapping in mediterranean regions. Remote Sens. **7**, 1320–1345 (2015). https://doi.org/10.3390/rs70201320
22. Belenguer-Plomer, M.A., Chuvieco, E., Tanase, M.A.: Sentinel-1 based algorithm to detect burned areas. In: Conference 11th EARSeL Forest Fires SIG, Chania, Greece (2017)
23. Baghdadi, N., Zribi, M.: Land Surface Remote Sensing in Agriculture and Forest (2016)
24. Richards, J.A.: Remote Sensing with Imaging Radar. SCT. Springer, Heidelberg (2009). https://doi.org/10.1007/978-3-642-02020-9
25. Mansourpour, M., Rajabi, M.A., Blais, J.A.R.: Effects and performance of Speckle noise reduction filters on active Radar and SAR images. ISPRS Int. J. Geo-Inf. **XXXVI-1/W41**, 1–6 (2006)
26. Santoso, A.W., Pebrianti, D., Bayuaji, L., Zain, J.M.: Performance of various speckle reduction filters on synthetic aperture radar image. In: 2015 4th International Conference on Software Engineering and Computer Systems, ICSECS 2015, Virtuous Softw Solut Big Data, pp. 11–14 (2015). https://doi.org/10.1109/ICSECS.2015.7333103
27. Tanase, M.A., Kennedy, R., Aponte, C.: Radar burn ratio for fire severity estimation at canopy level: an example for temperate forests. Remote Sens. Environ. **170**, 14–31 (2015). https://doi.org/10.1016/j.rse.2015.08.025
28. Lanorte, A., Danese, M., Lasaponara, R., Murgante, B.: Multiscale mapping of burn area and severity using multisensor satellite data and spatial autocorrelation analysis. Int. J. Appl. Earth Obs. Geoinf. **20**, 42–51 (2012). https://doi.org/10.1016/j.jag.2011.09.005
29. Richards, J.A.: Remote Sensing Digital Image Analysis, 5th edn. Springer, Heidelberg (2013). https://doi.org/10.1007/978-3-642-30062-2
30. Rousseeuw, P.J.: Silhouettes: a graphical aid to the interpretation and validation of cluster analysis. J. Comput. Appl. Math. **20**, 53–65 (1987). https://doi.org/10.1016/0377-0427(87)90125-7
31. Pedregosa, F., et al.: Scikit-learn: machine learning in python. J. Mach. Learn. Res. **12**, 2825–2830 (2011)
32. Keeley, J.E.: Fire intensity, fire severity and burn severity: a brief review and suggested usage. Int. J. Wildl. Fire **18**, 116–126 (2009). https://doi.org/10.1071/WF07049
33. Santi, E., Dabboor, M., Pettinato, S., Paloscia, S.: Combining machine learning and compact polarimetry for estimating soil moisture from C-band SAR data. Remote Sens. **11** (2019). https://doi.org/10.3390/rs11202451
34. Gimeno, M., San-Miguel-Ayanz, J., Schmuck, G.: Identification of burnt areas in mediterranean forest environments from ERS-2 SAR time series. Int. J. Remote Sens. **25**, 4873–4888 (2004). https://doi.org/10.1080/01431160412331269715
35. Martinis, S., Caspara, M., Plank, S., Clandillon, S., Haouet, S.: Mapping burn scars, fire severity and soil erosion susceptibility in southern France using multisensoral satellite data, pp. 1099–1102 (2017)
36. Ismail, M.H.: Evaluating supervised and unsupervised techniques for land cover mapping using remote sensing data. Geogr. Malaysian J. Soc. Space **5**, 1–10 (2009)
37. Lapini, A., Pettinato, S., Santi, E., Paloscia, S., Fontanelli, G., Garzelli, A.: Comparison of machine learning methods applied to SAR images for forest classification in mediterranean areas. Remote Sens. **12**(3), 369 (2020). https://doi.org/10.3390/rs12030369
38. Phiri, D., Morgenroth, J.: Developments in landsat land cover classification methods: a review. Remote Sens. **9**, 967 (2017). https://doi.org/10.3390/rs9090967

39. Ma, L., et al.: A review of supervised object-based land-cover image classification. ISPRS J. Photogramm. Remote Sens. **130**, 277–293 (2017). https://doi.org/10.1016/j.isprsjprs.2017.06.001
40. Santi, E., et al.: Machine-learning applications for the retrieval of forest biomass from airborne P-Band SAR data. Remote Sens. **12**(5), 804 (2020). https://doi.org/10.3390/rs12050804

Websites

41. ESA Sentinel Homepage. https://sentinel.esa.int/web/sentinel/home. Accessed 19 Mar 2020
42. Copernicus Sci Hub Homepage. https://scihub.copernicus.eu/. Accessed 22 Jan 2020
43. ESA SNAP Homepage. http://step.esa.int/main/toolboxes/snap/. Accessed 19 Mar 2020
44. Scikit-learn Homepage. https://scikit-learn.org. Accessed 20 Mar 2020

Using Sentinel 2 Data to Guide Nitrogen Fertilization in Central Italy: Comparison Between Flat, Low VRT and High VRT Rates Application in Wheat

Francesco Santaga, Paolo Benincasa, and Marco Vizzari(✉)

Department of Agricultural, Food, and Environmental Sciences, University of Perugia, 06121 Perugia, Italy
{francescosaverio.santaga,marco.vizzari,paolo.benincasa}@unipg.it

Abstract. The goal of this research was to compare traditional and variable rate technology (VRT) nitrogen (N) fertilization in winter wheat (*Triticum aestivum L.*). The study was developed over two years in two different fields (one field per year). Three different N fertilization approaches applied to the second fertilization were compared by integrating NDVI (Normalized Difference Vegetation Index) data from Sentinel 2 satellites (S2), grain yield, and protein content. In both fields used for the experimentation, the three treatments were defined as follows: 1) a standard rate (Flat-N) derived by an N balance approach; 2) a variable rate based on S2 NDVI, where the maximum rate was equal to the standard rate (Var-N-low); 3) a variable rate based on S2 NDVI, where the average rate was equal to the standard rate (Var-N-high). An inverse linear relationship between NDVI and N-rates was applied to calculate VRT doses on the assumption that NDVI and other correlated VIs, before the second N fertilization, are directly related to crop N nutritional status. Results show that differences between treatments in terms of NDVI, grain yield, and protein content were very low and generally not significant, suggesting that a low-N management approach, even using simple linear models based on NDVI and VRT, may considerably improve the economic and environmental sustainability of N fertilization in winter wheat. Further experiments are necessary to better explore the proposed approaches and compare them, by example, with the NDVI proportional methods that could be more suitable when the crop growth is mainly influenced by limiting factors other than N nutrition status.

Keywords: NDVI · Remote sensing · GIS · Precision farming · Variable rate technology · Yield mapping · Protein content

1 Introduction

Precision agriculture (PA) is mainly aimed at improving economic and environmental sustainability of cropping systems by reducing inputs and increasing temporal and spatial use efficiencies of the main cultivation operation like tillage, irrigation, fertilizers, pesticides and herbicides (see e.g. references [1–3]).

O. Gervasi et al. (Eds.): ICCSA 2020, LNCS 12253, pp. 78–89, 2020.
https://doi.org/10.1007/978-3-030-58814-4_6

PA integrates various modern and advanced technologies to achieve a well-timed in-season and between-seasons crop management [4]. These technologies include Geographic Information System (GIS), Global Navigation Satellite System (GNSS), agronomic modeling, variable rate technology (VRT), yield mapping and Remote Sensing (RS) from various platform such us UAVs (Unmanned Air Vehicles), airborne variable rate technology (VRT), yield mapping and advanced data processing.

Remote sensing of vegetation mainly relies on the detection on the green (495–570 nm) and red (620–750 nm) portions of the visible spectrum, the red-edge (680–730 nm), near and mid-infrared bands (850–1700 nm) [5, 6]. A plethora of algebraic formulas are available to combine these bands and calculate several Vegetation Indices (VIs) for investigating vegetation status and define coherent crop management according to more or less advanced approaches (see e.g. references [7–9]). In this context, the most used index, because of its ease of calculation and interpretation, is still the NDVI (Normalized Difference Vegetation Index), a normalized difference between reflectance of Red and Near-Infrared (NIR) spectral bands [10]. It varies between 0 and 1 in vegetated areas, increasing with LAI (Leaf Area Index), chlorophyll content, and plant N-nutritional status (see e.g. references [11–14]). The NDVI has been widely applied to assess wheat N-nutritional status and yield, with encouraging results [15–17].

The Sentinel-2 satellites (S2) are equipped with a multispectral sensor (MSI) including 13 spectral bands, with a spatial resolution ranging from 10 m to 60 m, an average temporal resolution of 5 days, and a radiometric resolution of 12 bit enabling the image to be acquired over a range of 0 to 4095 potential light intensity values with an accuracy error less than 5%. Visible and NIR bands have a spatial resolution of 10 m. Such features make the S2 a very relevant source of Spatio-temporal information for supporting precision agriculture [18].

N is the main nutrient of the vast majority of crops, including wheat. Increasing the N rate generally increases crop yield since it increases the grain number and size [1]. However, increasing the N rates reduces the N uptake efficiency (NUE) and increases the amount of residual N in the soil which is exposed to leaching risks [11, 19] and may cause severe environmental impacts on near-surface and deep aquifers [20]. In this regard, while traditional flat-rate approaches typically tend to over- or under-apply fertilizers, with map-based VRT precision fertilization it is possible to modify and optimize the distribution and improve the economic and environmental sustainability of the crops. A wide number of researches deals with wheat N nutrition and precision N fertilization, but most of them propose quite complex models that result not easily adoptable by PA non-specialists.

In PA, grain yield mapping is possible thanks to combines equipped with GNSS and yield tracking systems [21]. To produce yield maps, the harvested quantities are georeferenced and linked with the corresponding reference area on the ground calculated by multiplying the working width by the area length (working speed * time interval). Yield mapping accuracy is very variable and is mainly influenced by flow sensor calibration, combined speed changes, grain flow variations, and grain moisture. Despite many limitations and possible spatial and quantitative inaccuracies [22], this technology provides interesting information about the spatial heterogeneity of yields.

Grain protein development is physically based on the deposition of plant N and its translocation to grain during the filling process and the N content at the anthesis stage was found to be indicative for the final grain protein content [23]. Consequently, optimal N-fertilization management results very important for both quantitative and qualitative properties of yield.

While many studies have combined VIs (derived from various remote or proximal sensors) and VRT crop fertilization, only a small quantity of research integrates yield mapping sensors, and, to our knowledge, probably very few studies have combined VIs, VRT fertilization, and yield mapping in a PA case study and, in particular, to assess the effects of different variable N-rate treatments on winter wheat.

In this framework, this study carried out over two years and in two different experimental fields, was aimed at comparing two different VRT N fertilization treatments (based on Sentinel 2 and easily-applicable approaches) versus a traditional standard flat N rate in terms of crop NDVI trend, grain yield, and protein content. The research also investigates the possible relationships existing between quantitative and qualitative features of yield and the NDVI to assess its forecasting potential.

2 Materials and Methods

2.1 Study Areas

The experiments were carried out over two consecutive cropping seasons, in two different fields owned by two farms: in 2017–2018 on a 14 ha plain field in Tiber valley, near Deruta, Umbria, Italy (170 m a.s.l., 42°95'07" N, 12°38'18" E) owned by the FIA – "Fondazione per l'Istruzione Agraria" farm (Fig. 1, Field 1) and in 2018-2019 on a 10 ha plain field in Mugnano, Umbria, Italy (227 m a.s.l., 43°04'57" N, 12°21'74" E) (Fig. 1, Field 2) owned by the "Sodalizio di San Martino" farm. Both fields are characterized by a soil gradient related to proximity to a stream (located at the east of the Field 1 and at the west of Field 2).

The climate is the Mediterranean, characterized by a dry season between May and September and a cold and rainy season from October-November to March-April. The cropping season 2017–2018 was unusually rainy in December and March, while temperatures were generally higher than the poly-annual trend except for a very cold end of February (Fig. 2a). The cropping season 2018–2019 was particularly favorable for crops, with winter rainfall in the seasonal average and temperatures above the average (Fig. 2b).

The experimental crop was rainfed winter wheat (*Triticum aestivum L.)* sown in the first half of November. The previous crop had been pea (*Pisum sativum Asch et Gr*) in Field 1 and sunflower (*Helianthus annuus L.*) in Field 2. The crop was managed according to ordinary practices, while weeds and diseases were controlled chemically.

2.2 Experimental Design

The experiments were based on the comparison in terms of NDVI trend, yield, and protein content, of three different N fertilization, approaches applied to the second fertilization in wheat. In both fields used for the experimentation, the three treatments

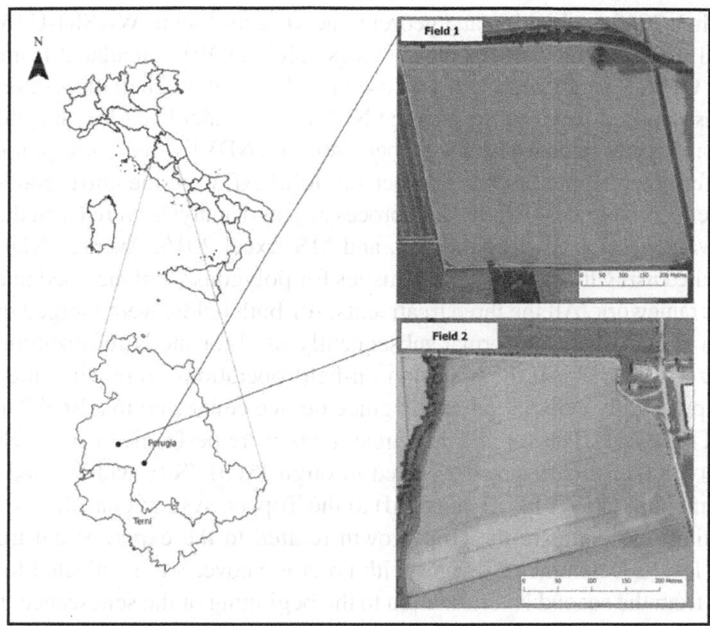

Fig. 1. The geographical location of the study areas.

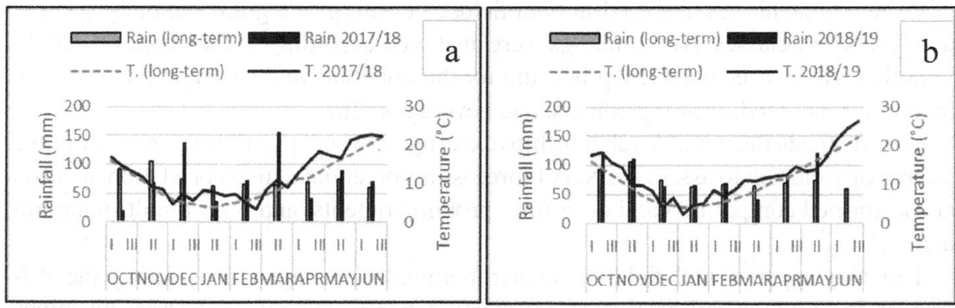

Fig. 2. Monthly cumulated rainfall and average temperatures per decade during the wheat growing season 2017–2018 (a) and 2018–2019 (b), and in the long term (temperature 1951–2018, rainfall 1921–2018).

under investigation were defined as follows: 1) a standard rate (Flat-N) derived by an N balance approach; 2) a variable rate based on S2 NDVI, where the maximum rate was equal to the standard rate (Var-N-low); 3) a variable rate based on S2 NDVI, where the average rate was equal to the standard rate (Var-N-high). An inverse linear relationship between NDVI and VRT N-rates was adopted both in Var-N-low and Var-N-high on the assumption that NDVI and other correlated VIs (e.g. NIR/Red simple ratio), before the second N fertilization (7–8 Feekes' stage), are directly related to crop N nutritional status [12, 16, 24]. For both fields, to calculate the VRT rates, a Level 2A Sentinel-2 image, collected before the second fertilization (respectively March 22nd, 2018 for Field

1 and March 3, 2019 for Field 2) and georeferenced according to WGS84-UTM32, was downloaded from The Copernicus Open Access Hub. NDVI, calculated from bands 4 and 8 using QGIS Raster Calculator, was used for the N rates calculation. A linear relationship was imposed between the average NDVI value calculated for all experimental units and fertilizer-N rates where the 5° percentile of NDVI value corresponded to the maximum fertilizer-N rate and the 95° percentile of NDVI value corresponded to the minimum fertilizer-N rates. All the data processing and analysis were carried out using QGIS software, version 3.10 64 bit [25], and MS Excel 2016. Average NDVI values were calculated using the SAGA "grid statistics for polygons" tool included in the QGIS processing framework. All the three treatments, for both fields, were merged in a single prescription map in shapefile format subsequently used for the N fertilization with the VRT fertilizer spreader. All the precision on-field operations were performed using a tractor equipped with a GNSS automatic guide device connected to a Real-Time Kinematic (RTK) network. The variable rate treatments were performed using a Sulky 40+ (ECONOV) VRT fertilizer spreader linked through ISOBUS (a widely used software protocol compliant to ISO 11783 standard) to the Topcon system console.

To monitor and compare the crop growth related to the experimental treatments, all relevant level 2A Sentinel-2 images with no cloud cover were collected for the two study areas from the second N fertilization to the beginning of the senescence. In total, 7 images were collected for Field 1 and 10 images for Field 2. Average NDVI values and standard deviations were then calculated for each plot using the SAGA "grid statistics for polygons" tool included in the QGIS processing framework.

Protein content was analyzed in both fields according to a grain sampling scheme based on NDVI classes. All samplings were analyzed according to the official Kjeldahl method, a widely used chemical procedure for the quantitative determination of protein content in food, feed, feed ingredients, and beverages [26].

To investigate the possible relationships existing between quantitative and qualitative features of yield and to assess the NDVI forecasting potential a final correlation analysis was performed comparing yield quantities, protein contents, and NDVI multi-temporal data.

The two experimental fields were agronomically managed considering the differences in terms of soil properties, fertilization practices, and the harvest machines available in the two farms.

2.2.1 Field 1

To account for the possible unknown spatial actors, the 14 ha experimental area of the field was divided into 168 plots of about 700 square meters each (35 m long, 21 m wide) grouped in 28 zones. Thus, the three treatments were laid down according to a randomized design with 2 replicates per treatment in each zone for a total of 56 replicates per treatment in the whole study area (Fig. 3).

N fertilization (as urea) was split into two applications. The first application occurred on 18 January 2018 with 30 kg N ha^{-1}, while the second one, occurred on 26 March 2018 and, according to the general methodology, was managed according to the three experimental theses: 1) a standard rate of 120 kg N ha^{-1} (Flat-N) derived by an N balance (the relatively high rate is justified by the very rainy winter); 2) a variable rate of 60 to

120 kg N ha^{-1}, calculated using the linear model applied to S2 NDVI of 22 March 2018 (i.e., four days before the second fertilization), where the maximum rate was equal to the standard rate (Var-N-low); 3) a variable rate of 90 to 150 kg N ha^{-1}, based on S2 NDVI, where the medium rate was equal to the standard rate (Var-N-high).

Harvest was carried out on 26 June 2018 for the Field 1 using a combined harvester Claas Lexion 630 equipped with a Topcon YieldTrakk system (processing data from the optical sensor measuring grain mass flow and moisture sensors), which produced a georeferenced yield map as an ESRI polygon shapefile. The combine harvester had a cutting width of 7.50 m and was equipped with a tilt sensor to correct the effect of slope on the sensor readings. Initial on-field calibration was performed on the combine to adjust for the actual working width and measure the unit weight of grain, which was used by the system to convert the measured mass flow (l/s) to Mg. The shapefile generated by the yield tack system was overlapped in QGIS on the experimental units to calculate the average yield values. This averaging procedure and the subsequent averaging to calculate a mean yield value for each treatment type, attenuated the possible inaccuracies generated by the yield track system.

Protein content was measured on 20 June 2018 (i.e., six days before the final harvest). To reduce the number of samples, the sampling scheme was defined according to three classes of NDVI for a total of 36 field samples, then merged two by two to obtain 18 lab samples.

2.2.2 Field 2

In this field, due to the lack of a harvester equipped with a yield track system, larger experimental units were defined. To account for the possible, not measured spatial factors, the three treatments were laid down in 14 experimental units according to a randomized design with 4 replicates per treatment (Fig. 3). N fertilization (as urea) was split into three applications. The first application occurred on 16 January 2019 with 40 kg N ha^{-1}, while the second N fertilization, occurred on 18 March 2019 and, according to the general methodology, was managed according to the three experimental treatments: 1) a standard rate of 100 kg N ha^{-1} (Flat-N) derived by an N balance; 2) a variable rate of 50 to 100 kg N ha^{-1}, calculated using the linear model applied to S2 NDVI of 2 March 2019 (i.e., three days before the second fertilization), where the maximum rate was equal to the standard rate (Var-N-low); 3) a variable rate of 85 to 115 kg N ha^{-1}, based on S2 NDVI and calculated using the AGROSAT model, where the medium rate was equal to the standard rate (Var-N-high). The VRT N rates were calculated on a sub-scheme basis including 120 plots of about 460 square meters each (22 m long, 21 m wide) within the 14 experimental units. The last N application was made on 6 May 2019 with 30 kg N ha^{-1}.

To measure yield, harvest, carried out on 8 July 2019, was performed separately collecting and weighing the yield by each experimental unit. This procedure, even though very time-consuming, allowed us to obtain very accurate yield data for each experimental unit and treatment.

To measure protein content, 28 samplings (each consisting of 4 sub-samples), two for each experimental unit, were collected on 26 June 2019 (i.e., twelve days before final harvest).

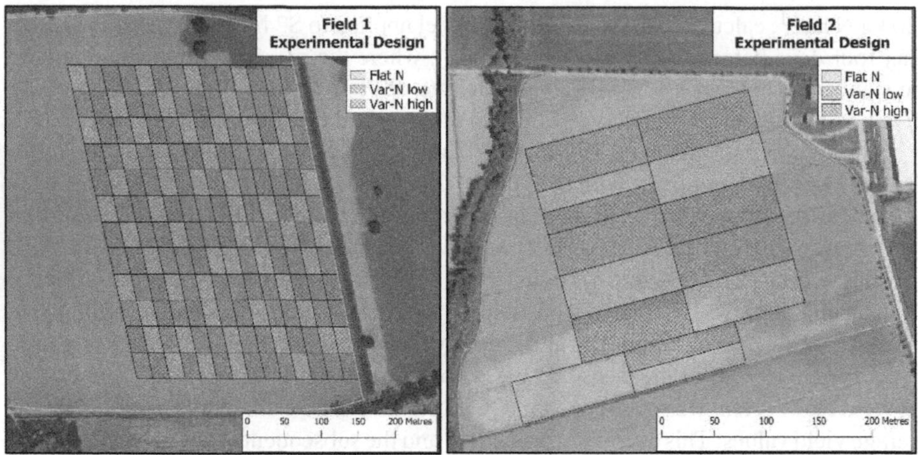

Fig. 3. Experimental layout. Flat-N (derived by an N balance), Var-N-low (variable-rate with the maximum rate equal to the standard rate), Var-N-high (variable-rate with the medium rate equal to the standard rate)

3 Results and Discussion

3.1 VRT Treatments and NDVI Trends

The NDVI and the prescription maps used for the VRT treatments of the second N fertilization in the two fields are shown in Fig. 4. In both cases can be observed an NDVI spatial trend (with a more relevant range in the Field 1) apparently related to the textural gradients of the two fields (Fig. 5). In all the field portions, both where the NDVI was high before N fertilization and where it was low, the index showed a further moderate increase up to nearly or over 0.9, highlighting a very good crop vigor. After the second fertilization, the trend of NDVI was slightly affected by fertilization treatments only in the second field while no differences can be observed in Field 1. This could indicate that the nitrogen rate was probably above the crop requirements in all the treatments, highlighting a potential N excess in the higher dosage theses, and probably that the field heterogeneity was not due to a real nitrogen nutritional deficiency but to intrinsic factors of the fields. This could explain the same NDVI trend of the three treatments in both fields, apart from slight differences which decrease with the crop growth in the Field 2).

3.2 Grain Yield and Quality

The yield map for Field 1, exported from the yield-track system, and the yield map for Field 2, showing the yield quantities measured in each experimental unit, are reported in Fig. 6. The relevant yield difference between the two fields can be related, besides the different soil features, to the meteorological trend of the two years (Table 1). This was characterized, in the first year, by intense rainy events during March (which generated considerable stress during the most important crop growth stage) and, in the second year, by very favorable and mild temperatures together with a good quantity and well-distributed rains which determined a very high yield in all over Central Italy. Concerning

Fig. 4. NDVIs calculated from Level 2A Sentinel-2 image and N prescription maps developed by integrating the three different experimental treatments.

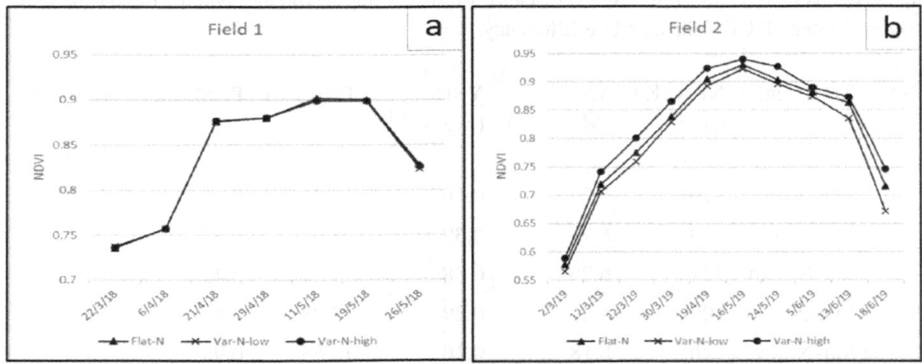

Fig. 5. NDVI time series analysis for the three N fertilization treatments in the two experimental fields

the three treatments under investigation, In Field 1, they did not differ significantly for total yield (Table 1), and no relationship was found between the N rate and yield ($R^2 = 0.087$). Similarly, no correlation was found between N treatments and protein content ($R^2 = 0.001$). Even though the slight difference in protein content of Flat-N and Var-N-low treatments was statistically significant ($p = 0.02$), it did not appear relevant from the agronomic viewpoint. Similarly, in Field 2, no evident relationship was found between the N rate and yield ($R^2 = 0.174$), and no correlation was found between N treatments and protein content ($R^2 = 0.150$). Finally, in both fields, grain yield was very weakly correlated to NDVI only in Field 1 at any time of NDVI measurements (Table 2).

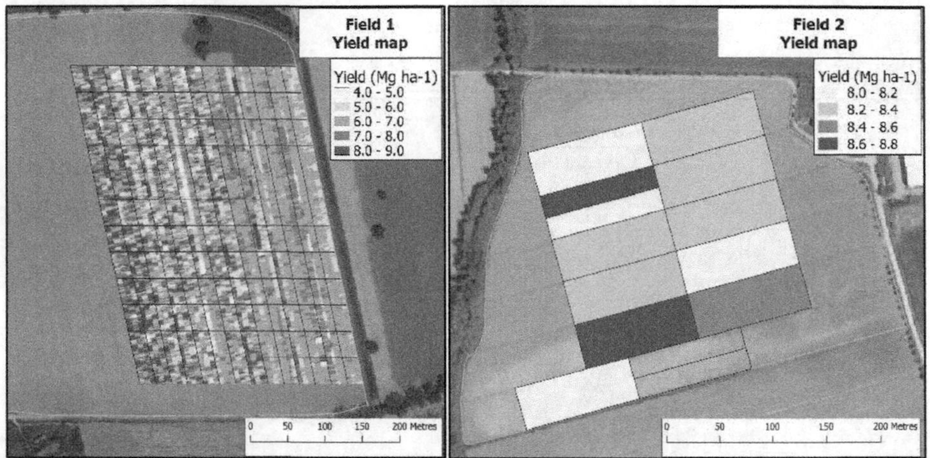

Fig. 6. Yield maps of the two experimental fields.

Table 1. Grain yield, protein content, and Nitrogen Use Efficiency (yield) for the three N fertilization treatments in the two fields: Flat-N, Var-N-low, and Var-N-high. NRA: Average N rate, YA: Average Yield, YSD: St. Dev. Yield, PCA: Average Protein Content; PCSD St. Dev. Protein Content, NUE: Nitrogen Use Efficiency.

Field	Treatment	NRA (Kg ha^{-1})	YA (Mg ha^{-1})	YSD (Mg ha^{-1})	PCA (%)	PCSD (%)	NUE (Kg Yield/Kg N rate)
1	Flat-N	120	6.74	0.36	9.4	0.31	56.2
	Var-N-low	90	6.73	0.39	8.9	0.37	74.8
	Var-N-high	121	6.76	0.38	9.2	0.48	55.9
2	Flat-N	100	8.41	0.29	13.88	0.50	84.1
	Var-N-low	76	8.18	0.16	13.53	0.98	107.6
	Var-N-high	101	8.33	0.21	14.18	0.43	82.5

Table 2. Correlation between yield and NDVI (at any time of measurement) plotted over all the 168 plots of Field 1 and over all the 12 plots of Field 2.

Field 1		Field 2	
Date	R^2	Date	R^2
22 Mar	0.29	05 Mar	0.12
6 Apr	0.26	22 Mar	0.04
21 Apr	0.24	19 Apr	0.05
29 Apr	0.19	16 May	0.10
11 May	0.19	05 Jun	0.00
26 May	0.27	13 Jun	0.06
31 May	0.26	18 Jun	0.02

In the two case studies, the N rate increase did not translate in an NUE (Nitrogen Use Efficiency) increase as this was probably limited by the other factors. This would indicate that, in some cases, the N rate could be conveniently and more efficiently directly related to the NDVI [27], on the assumption that lower NDVI values could indicate that other soil features, besides N availability, are limiting factors for obtaining higher yields. The similar NDVI trend observed in all the three treatments and in both fields (Fig. 4), could also support this evidence, or at least, indicate that the 20 kg N ha^{-1} of difference among treatments was not significant for NDVI analysis. In this view, VRT nitrogen fertilization can only partially mitigate the heterogeneity of production determined by environmental factors such as soil nitrogen and water availability. Thus, the alternative approach of providing a nitrogen supply proportional to the crop NDVI deserves to be considered when factors other than N nutrition status, as it is with sandy soils where NDVI and yield may be limited by low N availability and water retention [28].

4 Conclusions

Our study compared two VRT N fertilization treatments (based on Sentinel 2 NDVI) with a standard flat N rate in terms of crop NDVI trend, grain yield, and protein content. Results suggest that a VRT approach with a lower overall N rate may be more efficient, producing the same grain yield and comparable protein content with a lower N input. Var-N-low treatment in some cases could determine a lower protein grain content. In this regard, the economic trade-off between lower N fertilization costs and decreased yield value due to lower grain protein content should be determined by the farmers. This evidence is consistent with the result of Raun et al. [29] which reports that the VRT technique improves the NUE by 15% in average compared to the standard flat rates. In specific contexts, the N-rate reduction results environmentally and economically very relevant since it could reduce water pollution (still a critical issue in Umbria and all over the world). However, further experiments are necessary to further explore the proposed approaches and compare them, by example, with the NDVI proportional methods that may result more suitable when the crop growth is mainly influenced by other limiting factors different than N nutrition status.

Acknowledgements. This research was developed within the project "*RTK 2.0 - Prototipizzazione di una rete RTK e di applicazioni tecnologiche innovative per l'automazione dei processi colturali e la gestione delle informazioni per l'agricoltura di precisione*" – RDP 2014–2020 Umbria – Meas. 16.1. The authors wish to thank the farms "Fondazione per l'Istruzione Agraria" (Casalina di Deruta, province of Perugia, Italy) and "Sodalizio San Martino" (Mugnano, Province of Perugia, Italy) for their valuable support during all the experimental stages.

References

1. Benincasa, P., et al.: Reliability of NDVI derived by high resolution satellite and UAV compared to in-field methods for the evaluation of early crop N status and grain yield in wheat. Exp. Agric. 1–19 (2017). https://doi.org/10.1017/s0014479717000278
2. Bongiovanni, R., Lowenberg-Deboer, J.: Precision agriculture and sustainability. Precis. Agric. **5**, 359–387 (2004). https://doi.org/10.1023/B:PRAG.0000040806.39604.aa
3. Bora, G.C., Nowatzki, J.F., Roberts, D.C.: Energy savings by adopting precision agriculture in rural USA. Energy Sustain. Soc. **2**, 1–5 (2012). https://doi.org/10.1186/2192-0567-2-22
4. Liaghat, S., Balasundram, S.K.: A review: the role of remote sensing in precision agriculture. Am. J. Agric. Biol. Sci. **5**, 50–55 (2010). https://doi.org/10.3844/ajabssp.2010.50.55
5. Im, J., Jensen, J.R.: Hyperspectral remote sensing of vegetation. Geogr. Compass **2**, 1943–1961 (2008). https://doi.org/10.1111/j.1749-8198.2008.00182.x
6. Modica, G., et al.: Using landsat 8 imagery in detecting cork oak (Quercus suber L.) woodlands: a case study in Calabria (Italy). J. Agric. Eng. **47**, 205–215 (2016). https://doi.org/10.4081/jae.2016.571
7. Silleos, N.G., Alexandridis, T.K., Gitas, I.Z., Perakis, K.: Vegetation indices: advances made in biomass estimation and vegetation monitoring in the last 30 years. Geocarto Int. **21**, 21–28 (2006)
8. Xue, J., Su, B.: Significant remote sensing vegetation indices: a review of developments and applications. J. Sens. **2017** (2017). https://doi.org/10.1155/2017/1353691
9. Mulla, D.J.: Twenty five years of remote sensing in precision agriculture: key advances and remaining knowledge gaps. Biosyst. Eng. **114**, 358–371 (2013). https://doi.org/10.1016/j.biosystemseng.2012.08.009
10. Rouse, J.W., Hass, R.H., Schell, J.A., Deering, D.W.: Monitoring vegetation systems in the great plains with ERTS. In: Third ERTS Symposium. NASA, vol. 1, pp. 309–317 (1973). citeulike-article-id:12009708
11. Muñoz-Huerta, R.F., et al.: A review of methods for sensing the nitrogen status in plants: advantages, disadvantages and recent advances. Sensors **13**, 10823–10843 (2013). https://doi.org/10.3390/s130810823
12. Cabrera-Bosquet, L., Molero, G., Stellacci, A., Bort, J., Nogués, S., Araus, J.: NDVI as a potential tool for predicting biomass, plant nitrogen content and growth in wheat genotypes subjected to different water and nitrogen conditions. Cereal Res. Commun. **39**, 147–159 (2011). https://doi.org/10.1556/crc.39.2011.1.15
13. Carlson, T.N., Ripley, D.A.: On the relation between NDVI, fractional vegetation cover, and leaf area index. Remote Sens. Environ. (1997). https://doi.org/10.1016/S0034-4257(97)00104-1

14. Solano, F., Di Fazio, S., Modica, G.: A methodology based on GEOBIA and WorldView-3 imagery to derive vegetation indices at tree crown detail in olive orchards. Int. J. Appl. Earth Obs. Geoinf. **83**, 101912 (2019). https://doi.org/10.1016/j.jag.2019.101912
15. Sultana, S.R., et al.: Normalized difference vegetation index as a tool for wheat yield estimation: a case study from Faisalabad, Pakistan. Sci. World J. **2014**, 1–8 (2014). https://doi.org/10.1155/2014/725326
16. Zhu, Y., Yao, X., Tian, Y.C., Liu, X.J., Cao, W.X.: Analysis of common canopy vegetation indices for indicating leaf nitrogen accumulations in wheat and rice. Int. J. Appl. Earth Obs. Geoinf. **10**, 1–10 (2008). https://doi.org/10.1016/j.jag.2007.02.006
17. Cao, Q., et al.: Active canopy sensing of winter wheat nitrogen status: an evaluation of two sensor systems. Comput. Electron. Agric. (2015). https://doi.org/10.1016/j.compag.2014.08.012
18. Zheng, Q., Huang, W., Cui, X., Shi, Y., Liu, L.: New spectral index for detecting wheat yellow rust using sentinel-2 multispectral imagery. Sensors **18**, 868 (2018). https://doi.org/10.3390/s18030868
19. Spiertz, J.H.J., Nitrogen, J.H.J.S., Agronomy, A.: Nitrogen, sustainable agriculture and food security. A review. To cite this version: HAL Id: hal-00886486 (2010)
20. Vizzari, M., Modica, G.: Environmental effectiveness of swine sewage management: a multicriteria AHP-based model for a reliable quick assessment. Environ. Manag. **52**(4), 1023–1039 (2013). https://doi.org/10.1007/s00267-013-0149-y
21. Ross, K.W., Morris, D.K., Johannsen, C.J.: A review of intra-field yield estimation from yield monitor data. Appl. Eng. Agric. **24**, 309–317 (2008)
22. Arslan, S., Colvin, T.S.: Grain yield mapping: yield sensing, yield reconstruction, and errors. Precis. Agric. **3**, 135–154 (2002). https://doi.org/10.1023/A:1013819502827
23. Zhao, C., Liu, L., Wang, J., Huang, W., Song, X., Li, C.: Predicting grain protein content of winter wheat using remote sensing data based on nitrogen status and water stress. Int. J. Appl. Earth Obs. Geoinf. **7**, 1–9 (2005). https://doi.org/10.1016/j.jag.2004.10.002
24. Vian, A.L., et al.: Nitrogen management in wheat based on the normalized difference vegetation index (NDVI). Ciência Rural **48**, 1–9 (2018). https://doi.org/10.1590/0103-8478cr20170743
25. Quantum GIS Development Team Quantum GIS Geographic Information System (2017)
26. Labconco, C.: A Guide to Kjeldahl Nitrogen Determination Methods and Apparatus. Labconco Corporation (1998)
27. Raun, W.R., et al.: Optical sensor-based algorithm for crop nitrogen fertilization. Commun. Soil Sci. Plant Anal. **36**, 2759–2781 (2005). https://doi.org/10.1080/00103620500303988
28. Vizzari, M., Santaga, F., Benincasa, P.: Sentinel 2-based nitrogen VRT fertilization in wheat: comparison between traditional and simple precision practices. Agronomy **9**, 278 (2019). https://doi.org/10.3390/agronomy9060278
29. Raun, W.R., et al.: Improving nitrogen use efficiency in cereal grain production with optical sensing and variable rate application contribution from the Oklahoma agric. Exp. Stn. Agron. J. **94**, 815–820 (2002). https://doi.org/10.2134/agronj2002.8150

International Workshop on Collective, Massive and Evolutionary Systems (IWCES 2020)

A Learning Based Approach for Planning with Safe Actions

Rajdeep Niyogi[1(✉)], Saurabh Sharma[1], Michal Vavrecka[2], and Alfredo Milani[3]

[1] Indian Institute of Technology Roorkee, Roorkee 247667, India
rajdpfec@iitr.ac.in, saurabhsharma090394@gmail.com

[2] Czech Technical University, 166 36 Prague 6, Czechia
vavrecka@fel.cvut.cz

[3] University of Perugia, 06123 Perugia, Italy
milani@unipg.it

Abstract. Given a configuration involving some objects in an environment, the planning problem, considered in this paper, is to find a plan that rearranges these objects so as to place a new object. The challenging aspect here involves deciding when an object can be placed on top of another object. Here only defining standard planning operators would not suffice. For instance, using these operators we can come up with actions that may be performed at a state but it should not be performed. So we introduce the notion of *safe actions* whose outcomes are consistent with the laws of physics, commonsense, and common practice. A safe action can be performed if a robot performing the action knows the knowledge of the situation. We developed a knowledge engine using a supervised learning technique. However, unlike the common task of learning functions, our approach is to *learn predicates*–that evaluate to binary values. By learning such a predicate a robot would be able to decide whether or not an object A can be placed on top of another object B. We give a method to handle new objects for which the predicates have not been learned. We suggest a nondeterministic planning algorithm to synthesize plans that contain only safe actions. Experimental results show the efficacy of our approach.

Keywords: Planning · Learning · Predicate · Safe actions

1 Introduction and Motivation

Service robots are used to manipulate objects to achieve goal directed activities in automated/smart environments (e.g., home, cafeteria, office) [1–4]. In order to accomplish goals, a robot should possess the following skills: (i) perceptual skills which refer to the ability to acquire information from the environment, (ii) motor skills which refer to the ability to actuate in the environment, and (iii) cognitive skills which refer to the ability to synthesize plans to achieve a goal [5]. Planning is the reasoning side of acting [6]. In order to perform a simple action like pick-and-place, a robot should apply commonsense, physics knowledge, and

O. Gervasi et al. (Eds.): ICCSA 2020, LNCS 12253, pp. 93–105, 2020.
https://doi.org/10.1007/978-3-030-58814-4_7

take into account the current situation or context [7]. For certain tasks, in order for planning to be successful, the agent should learn some relationships of the objects.

Consider a table, in a kitchen, that is divided into four locations where each location is occupied with a plate; assume for simplicity that all the plates are identical and only one object can occupy each location. There is no other free space available. If a human is asked to place a cup on the table, she would possibly do any one of the following: (i) place the cup on any plate, (ii) pick any plate and place it on top of an adjacent plate, or make a tower of all the plates and then place the cup in a vacant location. There are different perspectives for looking at this task. These are, for instance, grasping which is concerned with how to hold the cup (by the handle of the cup or by one side); placing which refers to how the hand should move between the objects to place the cup, and if both the cup and plate are made of glass then care should be taken to place the cup softly on the plate; and capability of picking the cup (a weak hand may not be able to pick the cup properly). In this paper we take a different perspective which is not about these physical abilities required for placing an object; rather it is about reasoning when an object can be placed on top of another object. Humans have acquired this cognitive skill from their experience with handling objects of different types, observation, and/or learning from situations.

When a human asks the home robot to place the cup on the table, she expects the robot not just to place it somewhere on the table, but to first tidy up the table and then keep the cup. The goal states would be to place the cup on top of either plate A, plate B, plate C, or plate D. Such goal states correspond to the above mentioned point (i). Let us reconsider the kitchen situation described above but now all the locations are occupied by a cup and the task is to place another cup on the table. In this case none of the goal states (place the cup on top of either cup A, cup B, cup C, or cup D) is feasible since it is not a common practice of keeping a cup on top of another cup.

If a robot can place a cup on a plate, it can as well place a cup on another cup; nothing precludes this from happening. A robot is expected to perform safe actions. Informally, a safe action does not violate the laws of physics, commonsense, or common practice. For instance, the action of placing a cup on top of another cup is not a safe action, whereas placing a cup on a plate is a safe action. Thus if we wish to make the robots act like humans, it becomes imperative that they are embedded with adequate knowledge base that enables them to act autonomously and not just merely perform actions. This requires the robot to know (by learning) the commonsense knowledge of the situation (e.g., Do not put a cup on a cup or Clean the table before placing cups) and also physical knowledge (e.g., If you place a laptop on a cup then it will fall). Anyone who is used to a kitchen environment would first tidy up the table and then place the cup. This is the intent of the request and this corresponds to the goal state discussed above for point (ii). Here again if we replace the plates with cups, since a cup is normally not placed on top of another cup, a vacant location cannot be created and thus the request cannot be fulfilled.

For the planning scenarios described above, a precondition may hold, but an action should not be performed. We emphasize here that it is not the case that an action cannot be performed; rather it is the case where an action should not be performed. Here, only an operator definition will not suffice. So we introduce the notion of safe actions whose outcomes are consistent with physics, commonsense, and common practice. A safe action can be performed if a robot performing the action knows the knowledge of the situation. We developed a knowledge engine using a supervised learning technique. However, unlike the common task of learning functions, our approach is to learn predicates–that evaluate to binary values. By learning such a predicate a robot would be able to decide whether or not an object A can be placed on top of another object B. Once the robot learns the predicate, planning can be carried out and the plans contain only safe actions.

The remaining part of the paper is organized as follows. The preliminaries are given in Sect. 2. Predicate learning is given in Sect. 3. The proposed planning algorithm is given in Sect. 4 and the experimental results are given in Sect. 5. Related work is given in Sect. 6. The conclusions are given in Sect. 7.

2 Preliminaries

Definition 1 *(Planning domain). A planning domain can be formally defined as* $D = \langle S, A, s_0, \delta, F \rangle$ *where* S *is a nonempty finite set of states* $S \subseteq 2^{AP}$ *where* AP *is a nonempty finite set of atomic propositions or ground predicates for a domain,* A *is a nonempty finite set of executable actions,* s_0 *is the initial state,* δ *is a transition function* $\delta : S \times A \to S$, F *is a set of final states* $F \subseteq S$.

Definition 2 *(Planning problem). Given a planning domain D, a planning problem is to find a plan (a sequence of actions) which when executed at an initial state would lead to a final state.*

2.1 Planning Operator

A planning operator O is defined using preconditions $pre(O)$ and postconditions $post(O)$. The semantics of a planning operator O is given as follows: O is applicable at a state s if $pre(O)$ holds at s, and $post(O)$ holds in the resulting state s'. Thus a planning operator transforms one state to another. An action is a ground instance of an operator.

In the standard Blocks-world domain, the blocks are assumed to be identical in shape and size. An operator to put an object x on top of another object y (say, by a robot hand) can be defined as follows where $clear(y)$ means that nothing is on top of y and $handempty$ means that the robot is not holding any object.

put-on-top(x, y)
$precondition : holding(x) \wedge clear(y) \wedge x \neq y$
$postcondition : on(x, y) \wedge handempty \wedge not(clear(y))$

Consider a simple situation in this domain where the blocks B are C are placed on a table, and a robot is holding block A. By performing put-on-top(A,B), A is placed on top of B; similarly by performing put-on-top(A,C), A is placed on top of C. In this domain there is no additional constraint for placing one block on top of another block, and so any block can be placed on top of another subject to satisfying the preconditions. Let us consider an instance of the operator say put-on-top($laptop, cup$). If the precondition holds in a state, this action can be performed at the state and in the resulting state the *laptop* would be on top of the *cup*. Although an action can be performed at a state if the preconditions hold in the state, it should not be performed at the state in this case; the resulting configuration is unstable and the *laptop* may fall. Thus when arbitrary objects are considered, the above operator definition will not be suitable since an agent performing the action should know or decide whether it would be appropriate to place one object on top of another. In the following we suggest variants of the put-on-top operator to see if such reasoning can be captured at the syntactic level.

2.2 Limitations of Planning Operators

Situation I: An operator that would allow placing an object on top of another object when both the objects are of the same type.

put-on-top-same-type(x, y)
$precondition : (type(x) = type(y)) \wedge holding(x) \wedge clear(y) \wedge x \neq y$
$postcondition : on(x, y) \wedge handempty \wedge not(clear(y))$

For example, when both the objects are, say, plate or book, the operator would be applicable at a state where the precondition holds. However, when both the objects are cup then this operator should not be performed.

Situation II: An operator that would allow placing an object on top of another object when both the objects are of different type.

put-on-top-diff-type(x, y)
$precondition : (type(x) \neq type(y)) \wedge holding(x) \wedge clear(y) \wedge x \neq y$
$postcondition : on(x, y) \wedge handempty \wedge not(clear(y))$

This operator should not be performed when $x = laptop$ and $y = cup$.

Thus, operator definition alone is not sufficient for the problem under consideration.

Safe Action: An action a, applicable at state s ($pre(a)$ holds at s), is considered safe if $post(a)$ is consistent with physics, commonsense, and common practice.

Safe Plan: A safe plan is a plan that consists of only safe actions.

The problems with the operators defined in Situations I and II are that they are not safe. Thus in order to define an operator for placing one object on top of another object we first define a predicate $CAN\_PLACE(A, B)$ which is true if A can be placed on B, false otherwise.

put-on-top-safe(x, y)

$precondition : CAN\_PLACE(x, y) \wedge holding(x) \wedge clear(y) \wedge x \neq y$
$postcondition : on(x, y) \wedge handempty \wedge not(clear(y))$

Thus in order for a robot to perform safe actions, it should know or learn the truth/falsity of the CAN_PLACE predicate. We suggest an approach for learning this predicate in the next section.

3 Predicate Learning

The predicate $CAN\_PLACE(A, B)$ is true if A can be placed on B, false otherwise. An important property of the predicate is that it is not symmetric in general, $CAN\_PLACE(A, B)$ does not imply $CAN\_PLACE(A, B)$. From the truth/falsity of the $CAN\_PLACE(A, B)$ predicate, no conclusion be made about the predicate $CAN\_PLACE(A, B)$ since these two predicates are not logically connected at all, in general.

The CAN_PLACE predicate instances are to be learned for all the pairs of objects. For instance, $CAN\_PLACE(cup, cup)$, $CAN\_PLACE(cup, plate)$, $CAN\_PLACE(cup, stapler)$, etc. Thus, if there are n objects, the total number of instances of the predicate would be n^2 and this many predicates should be learned.

The robot has to decided if an object A can be placed on top of another object B based solely on 2D images of the objects. An image in RGB format is first converted to gray scale. This is done since two images of an object with different colors would be classified into its unique category (denoted by an integer identifier ID). An existing object recognition techniques is used for the purpose. We have taken 10 categories of objects and for each category around 60 images are taken from Caltech vision, Bing image search, and Google image search.

A neural network (NN) is used for learning the predicate. The network structure will consist of an initial layer of size 2 (corresponding to a pair of objects), followed by a variable number of hidden layers, and a final output layer of size 1. The training of the NN is done by taking input pairs (e.g., ID_A, ID_B) and providing the output which is the associated truth value of the predicate instance $CAN\_PLACE(A, B)$. The predicates learned for a set of objects are shown in the Table 1, where A is an object from a column, B is an object from a row in $CAN\_PLACE(A, B)$. Any object in the set can be placed on a 'book'. A 'cup' can also be placed on a 'plate', so the cell CAN_PLACE(cup,plate) is 1.

3.1 Handling a New Object

Once a robot has learned the CAN_PLACE predicate it can decide if an object A can be placed on another object B. If a robot is faced with new object(s) for which the predicates have not been learned, the robot would get stuck and the goals cannot be accomplished. At some point of time a robot would always encounter a new object. So it is not possible to anticipate all such objects in advance and learn the corresponding predicates. Thus we suggest a method for mapping a new object to some known object (for which a predicate has already

Table 1. Learned predicate instances.

$CAN\_PLACE(A, B)$	Cup	Plate	Stapler	Laptop	Book
Cup	0	0	0	0	0
Plate	1	1	0	0	0
Stapler	0	0	0	0	0
Laptop	0	0	1	0	1
Book	1	1	1	1	1

been learned) based on some physical properties (Table 2) of the object which are easily observable. These properties are:

1. Overall shape: The overall shape of an object can be either simple or complex. Examples of objects with simple shapes are book, plate. Examples of objects with complex shapes are stapler, cup. There are some objects (e.g., laptop) that can be both simple and complex depending on its state. The numbers 1, 2 are used to represent complex shape and simple shape respectively.
2. Base shape: It can be either simple or complex. Simple shapes are circle (characterized by the top view of a cup), rectangle (characterized by book, laptop). Stapler is an example of a complex shape. The numbers 1, 2, 3 are used to represent circle, rectangle, and complex shape respectively.
3. Base area: It is calculated in sq. cm.

Table 2. Sample data set of objects of different category.

Overall shape	Base shape	Base area	Category
2	2	153	Book
1	2	600	Laptop
1	3	500	Stapler

Whenever a robot picks an object, it can easily identify these properties of the object. Supervised learning (SVM) is used to learn these properties corresponding to given categories. The testing data set consists of 20 vectors for each category. The results of learning the properties corresponding to each category are shown in Table 3. For example, out of the 20 vectors for 'laptop', 15 are correctly classified as 'laptop' and 5 are incorrectly classified as 'book'.

When a new object (other than these five categories) is encountered, these three properties of the object are identified. Based on these properties, the new object is mapped to an object in the closest category for which the predicate is known, i.e., book, laptop, cup, plate, and stapler. Now the new object is treated as the object in the category. If the new object is a "newspaper" the properties are identified as:

Table 3. Learning the physical properties of each category.

True class\predicted class	Cup	Plate	Stapler	Laptop	Book
Cup	20	0	0	0	0
Plate	0	19	1	0	0
Stapler	0	1	19	0	0
Laptop	0	0	0	15	5
Book	0	0	0	5	15

1. Overall Shape is simple, so the value is 2.
2. Base Shape is rectangle, so the value is 2.
3. Base area of a newspaper can be calculated by measuring its length and width. For a normal newspaper which is half folded, its length is 42 cm and width is 33 cm. So the area is 42 × 33 i.e., 1386 sq.cm.

The newspaper with properties represented as a vector [2, 2, 1386] is mapped to a laptop. So for deciding if a newspaper can be placed on a cup reduces to deciding if a laptop can be placed on top of a cup for which the predicate $CAN\_PLACE(laptop, cup)$ is already known.

4 Proposed Planning Approach

Definition 3 *(Planning problem with safe actions). Given a planning domain D, a configuration involving some objects in an environment, the planning problem is to find a safe plan that rearranges these objects so as to place a new object.*

We assume that all objects can be placed on the table: $\forall x. CAN\_PLACE(x, table)$ holds. Let $TOWER_y$ denote a tower of objects with y at the bottom of the tower, and putdown($TOWER_y$) be an action that removes all the objects on top of y including y.

Planning algorithm:
Plan-to-place-object
Input: an object x to be placed in an Environment E
Output: $PLAN$-that consists of safe actions or failure
begin
while there exists an object x to be placed in E **do**
$PLAN := \emptyset$
  Case 1: Place x in E without rearrangement.
  if there exists an object y in E such that
    $(CAN\_PLACE(x, y) \wedge clear(y))$ hold
    then report success with $PLAN$:= put-on-top-safe(x, y)
  else report failure
  Case 2: Place x in E by rearranging only top objects.

if there exists objects y', y, z in E such that
$(CAN\_PLACE(y,z) \wedge clear(z) \wedge on(y,y') \wedge CAN\_PLACE(x,y'))$ hold
then report success with
$PLAN$:= put-on-top-safe(y, z);put-on-top-safe(x, y')
else report failure
Case 3: Place x within a tower of objects in E.
if there exists objects y, y' in the tower such that
$(on(y,y') \wedge CAN\_PLACE(x,y') \wedge CAN\_PLACE(y,x))$ hold
then report success with
$PLAN$:= putdown($TOWER_y$);put-on-top-safe(x, y');
put-on-top-safe($TOWER_y, x$)
else report failure
od
end

Features of the Algorithm: The algorithm is nondeterministic since for a given initial configuration different plans are possible for placing a particular object. For instance, if every region has only one plate and the goal is to place a cup, then both Case 1 and Case 2 holds. In this scenario any one of the cases would be considered nondeterministically and the corresponding plan would be returned. Similarly, if every region has a tower of $k > 1$ plates, and the goal is to place another plate, then all the three cases hold. Thus for the design of the algorithm, the nondeterminism is necessary (and not based on choice) since we only want to achieve the goal and moreover no goal configuration is given as input. This aspect differentiates the planning problem considered in this paper with conventional planning problems where an initial and goal configuration is given as input. Finally, the order of execution of the Cases is irrelevant.

4.1 Illustration of the Algorithm

We illustrate the working of the algorithm by taking different situations. The environment E consists of n-regions. In the following examples there are 4 regions that are named R1 (top left), R2 (top right), R3 (bottom right), R4 (bottom left).

1. Goal: place a stapler. There is no space available in any region and the stapler cannot be placed on top of any object. This is an instance of Case 2. So the steps involved are: first, remove the plate from R1 and place it on top of the plate in R2; now place the stapler in R1 (Fig. 1).
2. Goal: place a plate. There is no space available in any region and the stapler cannot be placed on top of any object. This is an instance of Case 3. So the steps involved are: first, remove the cup from R4; then place the plate on top of the book in R4; now place the cup on top of plate in R4 (Fig. 2).
3. Goal: place a cup. There is no space available in any region and a cup cannot be placed on top of a cup. Neither Case 2 nor Case 3 is applicable. So the object cannot be placed in any region (Fig. 3).

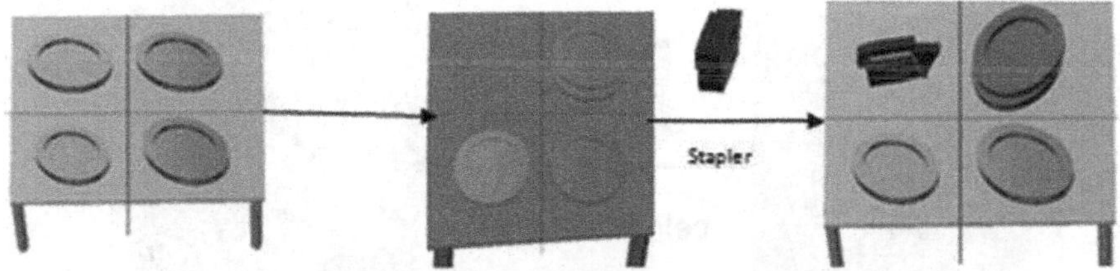

Fig. 1. Planning using Case 2.

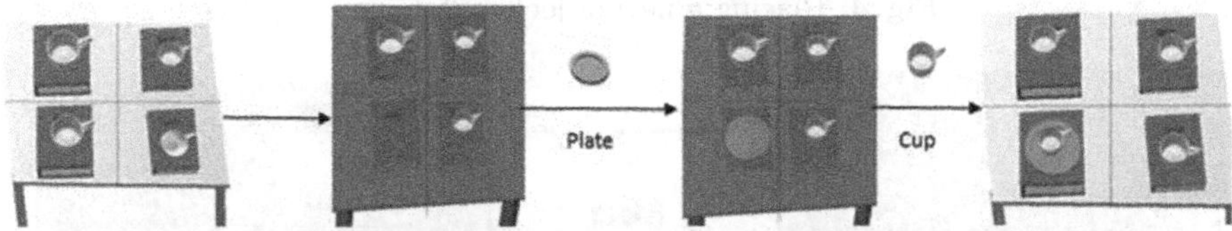

Fig. 2. Planning using Case 3.

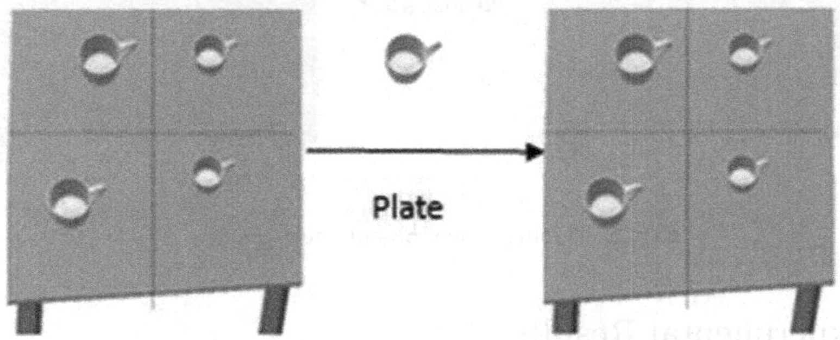

Fig. 3. No rearrangement is possible.

4.2 Placing a New Object for Which the Predicate has Not Been Learned

1. Goal: place a cellphone. Since no predicate is learned for cellphone, so overall shape, base shape, and base area are identified for cellphone and the final vector is [2, 2, 150] which is closest to a book. Thus the problem reduces to placing a book. This is an instance of Case 2. The steps involved are: first, remove plate on top of R1; then place it on top of plate in R4; now cellphone is placed in R1 (Fig. 4).
2. Goal: place a newspaper. Since no predicate is learned for newspaper, so, overall shape, base shape, base area are identified for newspaper and the final vector is [2, 2, 550], which is closest to a book. Thus the problem reduces to placing a book. This is an instance of Case 3. The steps involved are: first, remove cup from R1; then place newspaper on top of book already present in R1; now place cup on top of R1 (Fig. 5).

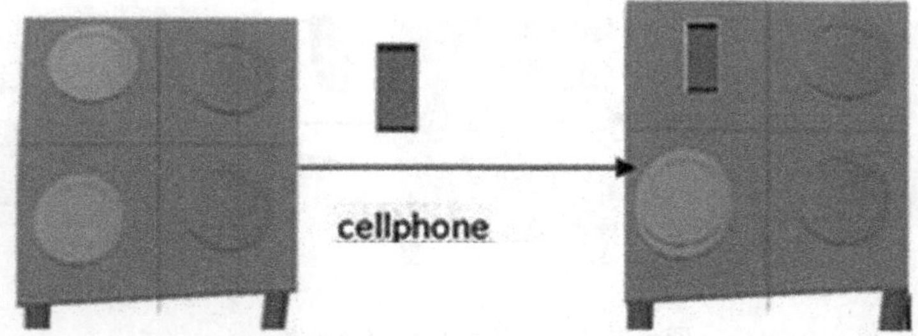

Fig. 4. Placing a new object: cellphone.

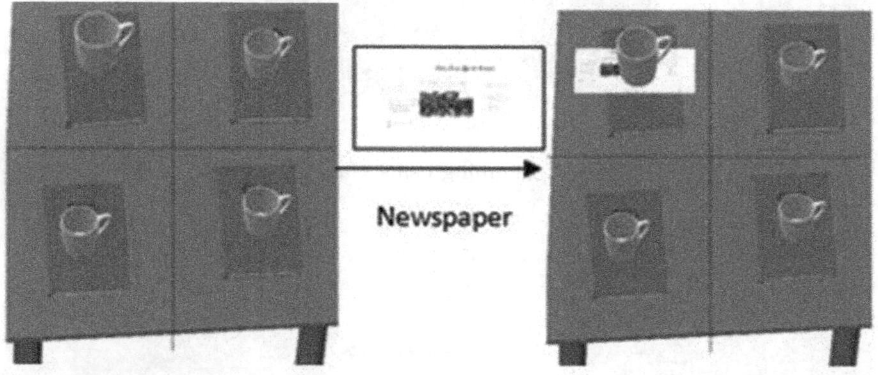

Fig. 5. Placing a new object: newspaper.

5 Experimental Results

All the experiments are performed using MATLAB on a personal computer having the configuration–Intel core i5 @ 2.5 GHz with 4 GB RAM.

I) We considered different initial configurations and for each configuration, different objects were selected for placing by fixing the number of regions. The average planning time taken for different instances is shown in Fig. 6. The time taken increases almost linearly with the number of objects.

II) We took different initial configurations and for each configuration, the number of regions was varied for a fixed number of objects to be placed in the configuration. The average planning time taken for different instances is shown in Fig. 7a and 7b. The time taken decreases almost logarithmically with the number of regions.

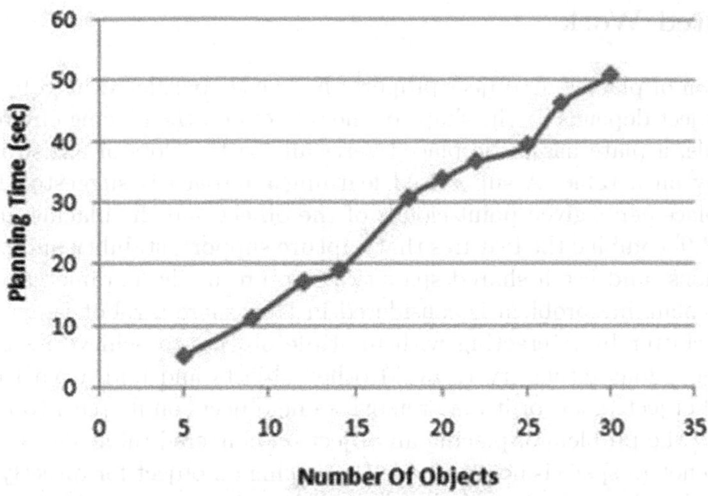

Fig. 6. Planning time versus number of objects.

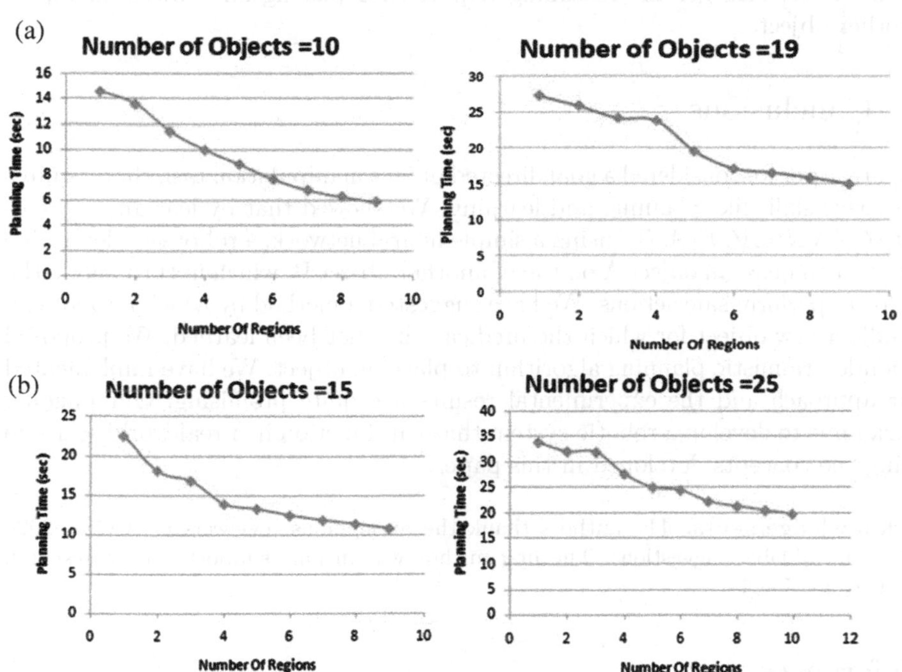

Fig. 7. (a) Planning time versus number of regions for #objects 10, 19. (b) Planning time versus number of regions for #objects 15, 25.

6 Related Work

The problem of placing an object properly has been considered in [8,9]. How to place an object depends on the shape of the object and the placing environment. For example, a plate has to be placed vertically in the slots of a dish rack but horizontally on a table. A supervised learning approach is suggested for finding good placements given point-clouds of the object and the placing area. The methods [8,9] combine the features that capture support, stability and preferred configurations, and use a shared sparsity structure in the parameters. A rearrangement planning problem is considered in [10] where a robot is expected to work in a clutter by interacting with multiple objects to achieve its goal. For this the robot may either try to avoid other objects and find a path to reach the desired object (goal) or it may remove some objects on its path to reach the goal. In [11] the problem of placing an object on cluttered table surfaces is considered. If enough space is not available for placing an object for directly placing an object, the planning algorithm suggested in [11] tries to find a sequence of linear push actions so as to obtain the necessary space. However, none of these works [8–11] consider the reasoning required for placing one object on top of another object.

7 Conclusions

In this paper we considered a goal directed object manipulation task that requires cognitive skills like planning and learning. We showed that by learning a predicate $CAN\_PLACE(A, B)$, using a simple neural network, a robot can determine whether to place an object A on top of another object B, which in turn allows the robot to perform safe actions. We have suggested a method by which a robot can handle a new object for which the predicate has not been learned. We proposed a nondeterministic planning algorithm to place an object. We have implemented our approach and the experimental results are quite promising. Our ongoing work aims to develop a robotic system that can function in a real world scenario using the concepts developed in this paper.

Acknowledgements. The authors thank the anonymous reviewers of ICCSA 2020 for their valuable suggestions. The first author was in part supported by a research grant from Google.

References

1. Wilson, G., et al.: Robot-enabled support of daily activities in smart home environments. Cogn. Syst. Res. **54**, 258–272 (2019)
2. Abdulkareem, A., Ogunlesi, V., Afolalu, S.A., Onyeakagbu, A.: Development of a smart autonomous mobile robot for a cafeteria management. Int. J. Mech. Eng. Technol. **10**(1), 1672–1685 (2019)

3. Ersen, M., Oztop, E., Sariel, S.: Cognition-enabled robot manipulation in human environments: requirements, recent work, and open problems. IEEE Robot. Autom. Mag. **24**(3), 108–122 (2017)
4. Kemp, C.C., Edsinger, A., Torres-Jara, E.: Challenges for robot manipulation in human environments [grand challenges of robotics]. IEEE Robot. Autom. Mag. **14**(1), 20–29 (2007)
5. Huamán Quispe, A., Ben Amor, H., Christensen, H.I.: A taxonomy of benchmark tasks for robot manipulation. In: Bicchi, A., Burgard, W. (eds.) Robotics Research. SPAR, vol. 2, pp. 405–421. Springer, Cham (2018). https://doi.org/10.1007/978-3-319-51532-8_25
6. Ghallab, M., Nau, D., Traverso, P.: Automated Planning: Theory and Practice. Elsevier, Amsterdam (2004)
7. Beetz, M., Besler, D., Haidu, A., Pomarlan, M., Bozcouglu, K.A., Bartels, G.: KnowRob 2.0: a 2nd generation knowledge processing framework for cognition-enabled robotic agents. In: ICRA, pp. 512–519 (2018)
8. Jiang, Y., Zheng, C., Lim, M., Saxena, A.: Learning to place new objects. In: ICRA, pp. 3088–3095 (2012)
9. Jiang, Y., Lim, M., Zheng, C., Saxena, A.: Learning to place new objects in a scene. Int. J. Robot. Res. **31**(9), 1021–1043 (2012)
10. King, J.E., Cognetti, M., Srinivasa, S.S.: Rearrangement planning using object-centric and robot-centric action spaces. In: ICRA, pp. 3940–3947 (2016)
11. Cosgun, A., Hermans, T., Emeli, V., Stilman, M.: Push planning for object placement on cluttered table surfaces. In: IROS, pp. 4627–4632 (2011)

Service Composition in a Context-Aware Setting with Functionally Equivalent Services

Sujata Swain and Rajdeep Niyogi(✉)

Indian Institute of Technology Roorkee, Roorkee 247667, India
sujataswain019@gmail.com, rajdpfec@iitr.ac.in

Abstract. Context-aware systems play a vital role in facilitating our daily life activities. The development of context-aware systems is an inherently complex task. These systems adapt to context change and provide a composed service to satisfy user requests. This paper aims to provide a complete sketch of a context-aware system. To illustrate the working of the proposed system, we consider a context-aware e-learning application that provides different types of study material according to the context. When context changes, a new plan is obtained to satisfy the user request. We implement and evaluate the context-aware e-learning system with the different phases of the proposed system. The experimental results show the efficacy of the approach.

Keywords: Context change · Classical planning · Functionally equivalent · QoS-aware

1 Introduction

Nowadays the pervasive computing is a promising approach for facilitating the daily life activities/tasks. The users may have various smart devices in their vicinity. Therefore, the ubiquity of smart devices helps to satisfy the daily life activities, by modeling the resources as services and by integrating the services in their vicinity. However, the interaction and management of all various devices and services is considered as a challenging task. The context-aware system is an emerging solution to alleviate such challenges. The main goal of context-aware systems is to acquire the context information, to utilize that information and provide the appropriate services to the current context. It will supervise the user's interaction with the ubiquitous environment for automating users' repetitive actions [1]. A context-aware application aims to satisfy the user request/goal G anywhere and anytime, even if a context changes, i.e., for all possible contexts $c = \{c_1, c_2, \ldots, c_k\}$ in a given domain, find a plan π such that plan $\pi \models_c G$. This is shown in Fig. 1. For example, a context-aware system can detect that a user never read a message while driving, and thus a text to voice translation service read the message header through a voice box in the car whenever he/she is driving.

O. Gervasi et al. (Eds.): ICCSA 2020, LNCS 12253, pp. 106–119, 2020.
https://doi.org/10.1007/978-3-030-58814-4_8

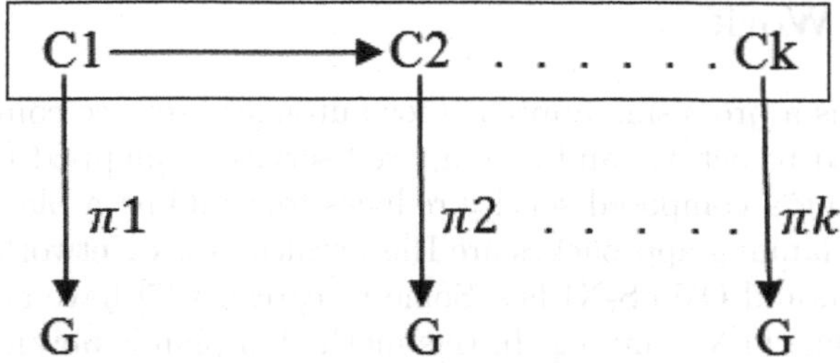

Fig. 1. Goal maintenance with context change

With the proliferation of services suitable automatic service composition algorithms are required to not only synthesize correct plans from thousands of services but also satisfy the quality requirements of the users. The user request can be associated with some end-to-end QoS requirements like maximum price the user can spend, minimum reliability needed for the composition. Therefore, a QoS-aware service composition approach should select services to build an optimal composed service that meets the end-to-end QoS constraints [2]. Meta-heuristic approaches [3] have proved to be one of the most promising techniques for QoS-aware service composition [4]. There exists some automated planning based approaches to address the problem of QoS-aware service composition [5]. However these approaches have the following drawbacks: they cannot deal with more than one QoS parameter and they are not designed to handle context changes. In this paper, we propose a complete architecture of the context-aware system.

The main contributions of this work are as follows:

- OWL-S description abstract service is transformed into planning domain. User request, context, and inputs are also transformed into the planning problem. The produced domain and problem are described using well-established standards, such as PDDL.
- A flexible planner can be employed which has the functionality to get a plan, such as Blackbox planner. A plan contains a set of actions which are the abstract services description.
- The user's context may change during execution time. A replanning component is considered to obtain a new plan according to a new context.
- The functionally equivalent services are modeled using a meta-reasoner tree, which may greatly impact on the unavailability of abstract service.
- The above mentioned approaches would be shown with the help of a context-aware e-learning application. In this case study, we also see how a composed service changes when the context changes.

The rest of this paper is organized as follows. Related work is discussed in Sect. 2. The proposed approach is given in Sect. 3. A case study is given in Sect. 4. The implementation and experimental results are given in Sect. 5. We conclude the paper in Sect. 6.

2 Related Work

AI planning [6] is a promising approach for automatic service composition. Services are mapped to actions and a composed service is mapped to a plan. The problem of finding a composed service reduces to a finding a plan. Some of the well-known AI planning approaches are Hierarchical Task Network (HTN) planning, Graphplan, and OWLS-XPlan. Some researchers [7] have adopted service composition using HTN planning. In this method, a plan is obtained by decomposing a complex task into simple sub-tasks. HTN planners (SHOP and SHOP2) are used to obtain a plan. In [7], a context-aware service composition framework based on planning is suggested. The approach uses HTN planning to obtain a plan and the composed service is based on user request, service context, and user context. User context information includes user location. Service context information includes response time, availability, and throughput. Some researchers have adopted service composition using OWLS-Xplan [8]. An OWL-S service composition planner, called OWLS-Xplan is proposed for service composition [8]. Xplan, a hybrid planner, is a combination of Fast Forward (FF) planning and Hierarchical Task Networking (HTN) planning methods.

Different service providers provide services with the same functionality to solve a simple task but offering different QoS parameters, such as price, time, reliability, and availability, etc. QoS-aware service composition approaches provide an optimal composite service to satisfy a user request [9]. These approaches consider a set of predefined simple tasks and a set of candidate services corresponding to a simple task. The QoS-aware service composition approaches select a service from the set of candidate services corresponding to a simple task. Several researchers proposed service composition using genetic algorithm methods [10]. Many researchers adopted particle swarm optimization algorithms for QoS-aware service composition [11]. Some researchers adopted fruitfly optimization algorithm (FOA) for service composition [4]. In [12], a hybrid genetic algorithm (HGA) which combines the genetic algorithm and fruitfly optimization algorithm is proposed and applied to select services. This method has good feasibility, optimality and low execution time.

3 An Adaptive Context-Aware Service Composition Approach

In this section, we present our proposed system that aimed at enabling context-aware service composition application. This is achieved by generating an abstract composed service, selecting an optimal concrete composed service, and adapting to the context changes in the environment. The proposed context-aware service composition system is shown in Fig. 2. The components of the proposed system are discussed below.

Translation Phase: This phase prepares all the required inputs for the upcoming phases. This phase contains two modules: domain translation and problem translation. Input to domain translation module is OWL-S description of

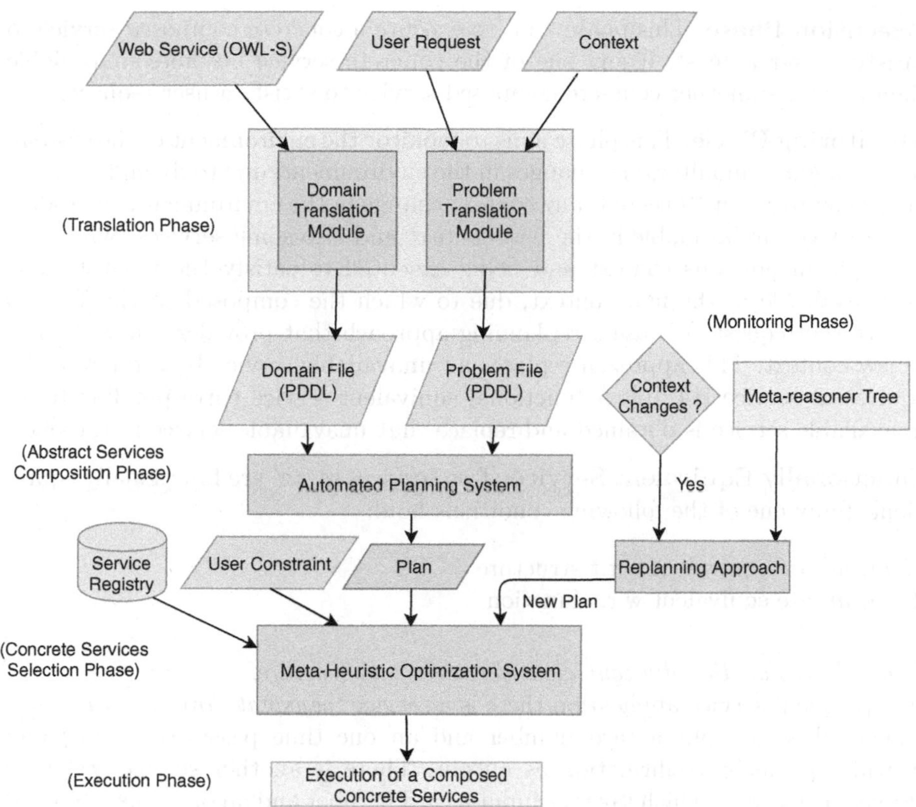

Fig. 2. Architecture of the proposed QoS-based context-aware system

abstract services that are located in the service repository. It translates the OWL-S description of an abstract service into an action of Domain PDDL. The translation phase collects user's request, user's inputs and also collects context of the environment through sensors. The problem translation module constructs an initial state from the user's inputs and context, whereas, from the user's request, it constructs a goal state. The combination of initial state and goal state is Problem PDDL.

Abstract Services Composition Phase: This phase aims to get an abstract composed service (plan) from Domain PDDL and Problem PDDL. Blackbox planner [18] is used to obtain a plan. A plan is a sequence of actions (services).

Concrete Services Selection Phase: This phase aims to get an optimal concrete composed service corresponding to an abstract composed service (plan). It retrieves the sets of concrete services (CS) corresponding to the abstract services from the service repository. It gets the global constraints ($GCst$) and user's preference (w) on QoS attribute which are provided by a user. It uses a meta-heuristic approach to obtain an optimal concrete composed service.

Execution Phase: This phase aims to execute a concrete composed service to satisfy a user request. If any one of the concrete service becomes unavailable then it selects another concrete composed service to satisfy a user request.

Monitoring Phase: This phase aims to monitor the environment of the system. It continuously monitors the changes in the environment, due to dynamic nature of the environment. If there is any context change in the environment, then some new services are available in the new context and also some services (which are available in previous context and being executed to satisfy the request) may be unavailable in the new context, due to which the composed service fails to satisfy the request. We use a replanning approach that provides a new plan in a new context. This approach replaces an unavailable service by a functionally equivalent service [14–16]. A functional equivalent service corresponding to an unavailable service is obtained and replace that unavailable service in the plan.

Functionally Equivalent Service: Two services m, m' are functionally equivalent if any one of the following conditions hold:

1. m, m' are equivalent w.r.t structure
2. m, m' are equivalent w.r.t function

Example-1: Functionally equivalent service w.r.t structure.
In a payment service application there is a service '*payment through credit card*' which takes as input a card number and an one time password (OTP) and provides payment confirmation as output. There is another service '*payment through debit card*' which takes as input a card number and an one time password (OTP) and provides payment confirmation as output. These two services are functionally equivalent w.r.t structure as it takes same inputs and provides same outputs. In Fig. 3, Service A and Service B are functionally equivalent w.r.t structure, if $I_1 = I_3$ and $I_2 = I_4$ and $O_1 = O_2$.

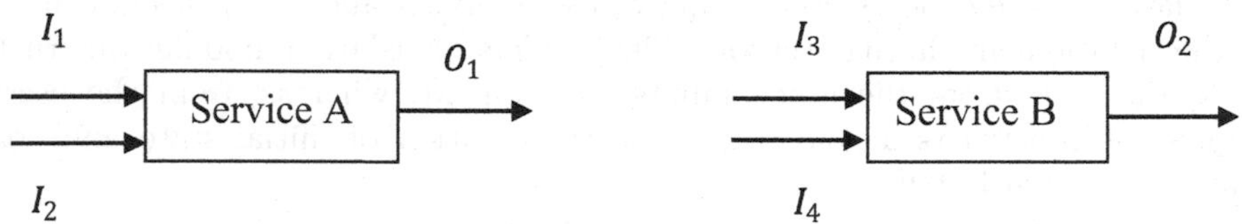

Fig. 3. Representation of services based on input and output

Example-2: Functionally equivalent service w.r.t function.
According to [13], a service can be anything e.g., hardware devices, network resources, a piece of computation, and even a human being. A medicine domain is presented in [14], where medicine is considered as a service. 'Lupiclor' is a

medicine used for hypertension. There is another medicine 'Lorvas' which is also used for hypertension disease. Doctor is an expert in the medicine domain and he/she can decide whether two medicines are equivalent or not. Doctor may recommend the use of 'Lorvas' medicine in place of 'Lupiclor' medicine. If Lorvas can be used in place of Lupiclor, then these two medicines are functionally equivalent w.r.t function as they are used for hypertension disease.

4 Case Study

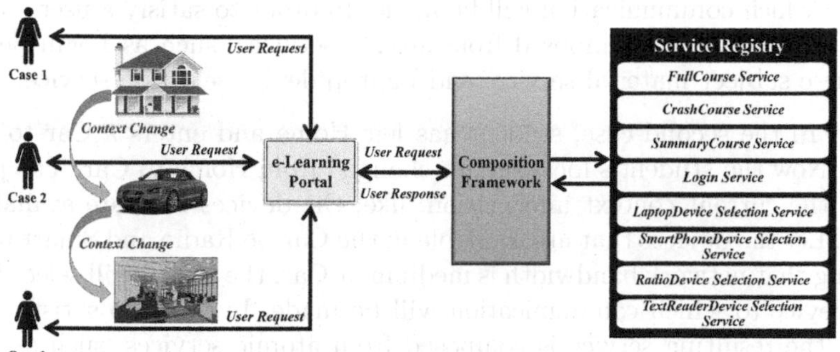

Fig. 4. Context-aware e-Learning application (CEA)

An e-learning domain as a context-aware application, named as Context-aware e-Learning Application (CEA) is considered. This application helps in the learning process of a student and saves time and effort for preparing notes. When a user makes a request regarding a subject she wants to study, the portal uses a composition framework to combine different atomic services. There are different atomic services in this system: login service, subject material service, and device selection service. Each of them accepts certain inputs and produces certain outputs.

User requests are enriched with context information. For example, the portal takes into account the following context types: student's location, number of days remaining for the examination and the computing device in use. These contexts can be sensed by a module in the application. The CEA delivers lectures based on the number of days remaining for the examination and the best device available at the student's location. Let X be the number of days remaining before the first examination and course duration be 5 months (150 days approximately). Let the CEA provide a course material α where

$$\alpha = \begin{cases} Fullcoursematerial & if\ 30 \leq X < 150 \\ Crashcoursematerial & if\ \ 2 \leq X < 30 \\ Summarycoursematerial & if\ \ 0 \leq X < 2 \end{cases}$$

Figure 4 describes the following three cases.

Case 1. In the first case, student is at Home. Student has the subscription to the e-Learning portal. The portal provides the login service which allows it acquires the information about some information the subscribed user. The portal provides student's requested subject material through the best device available at Home. The portal receives the context information like, student's location, number of days remaining before the examination, and devices available at that location. Let the number of days remaining before the examination be 45; the full course subject material service will be selected by the portal. Let the devices that are available at home be the Laptop and Smartphone. The devices are ranked according to screen size, memory, and network bandwidth. Assuming that network bandwidth is high at Home, the portal will select Laptop as the device to which communication will be made. In order to satisfy a user request, the resulting service is composed from atomic services, such as Login Service, Full course subject material service, and Laptop device selection service.

Case 2. In the second case, student has left Home and enters a Car to go to College. Now the student's location has changed from Home to Car. The portal receives the current context information, like, the devices that are available in the Car. Let the devices that are available in the Car be Radio and Smart phone. Assuming that network bandwidth is medium at Car, the portal will select Radio as the device to which communication will be made. In order to satisfy a user request, the resulting service is composed from atomic services, such as Login Service, Full course subject material service, and Radio device selection service.

Case 3. In the third case, student has left Car and enters into the Classroom. Now student's location has changed from Car to Classroom. The portal receives the current context information, like, the devices that are available in the Classroom. Let the devices that are available with the student be Text reader and Smart phone. Assuming that network bandwidth is low at Classroom, the portal will select Text reader as the device to which communication will be made. In order to satisfy a user request, the resulting service is composed from atomic services, such as Login Service, Full course subject material service, Text reader device selection service.

5 Experimental Results

We implement the proposed system in a context-aware e-learning application (CEA). The system is developed with the help of different tools. These are protege, automated planner, MATLAB, and Eclipse IDE (a Java-based platform). Protege is an ontology editor, which contains OWLS-editor, SPARQL query language, semantic web rule language (SWRL) and pellet reasoner as inference engine. Experiments are run on the Intel Core i5 2.53 GHz machine with 4 GB of RAM.

Table 1 shows the various devices that are registered to be used at specific location. For example, devices 'SonyLaptop' and 'SamsungSmartPhone' are registered at location 'Home', devices 'StereoRadio' and 'SamsungSmartPhone' are registered at location 'Car', devices 'Kindle' and 'SamsungSmartPhone' are registered at location 'Classroom'. When the location does not match any one of Home/Car/Classroom, then 'SamsungSmartPhone' is selected.

Table 1. Device registry corresponding to the location.

Location	Device
Home	Laptop, SmartPhone
Car	SmartPhone, Radio
Classroom	Textreader, SmartPhone
Any other location	SmartPhone

The various services are available in registry, as shown in Fig. 5.

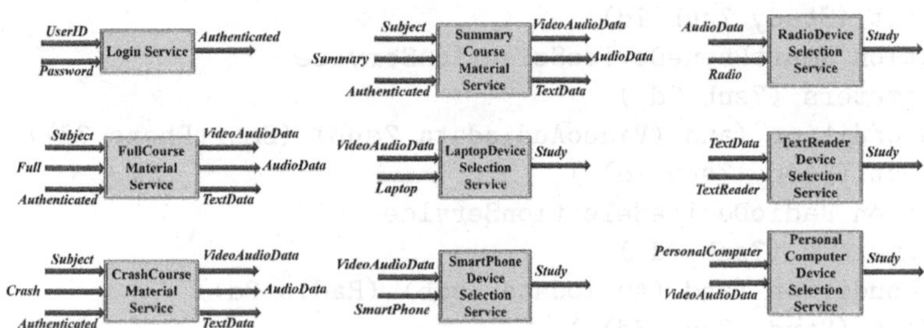

Fig. 5. Services in registry

The user request is *to study Computer Network.*

5.1 Translation Phase

Service descriptions are translated to Domain PDDL. A service is translated into an action in Domain PDDL. Inputs and outputs of a service are translated into the preconditions and effects of an action respectively. The Domain PDDL is shown below.

```
( define (domain EducationSystem_Domain)
(:types location device service subject - object user - agent)
(predicates: (UserId ?u)(Password ?p)
(Authenticated ?u)(Subject ?sub)
(Full ?f) (Crash ?c) (Summary ?s)
(VideoAudiodata ?sub) (Audiodata ?sub) (Textdata ?sub)
(Laptop ?d)(SmartPhone ?d) (Radio ?d))
(Study ?sub ?d))
```

```
(:action LoginService
:parameters (?u - UserId ?p - Password )
:precondition (and (UserId ?u)(Password ?p))
:effect (Authenticated ?u))
(:action FullCourseMaterialService
:parameters (?u - Authenticated ?sub - Subject ?f - Full )
:precondition (and (Authenticated ?u)(Subject ?sub)(Full ?f))
:effect (and (VideoAudiodata ?sub) (Audiodata ?sub) (Textdata
?sub) ))
(:action CrashCourseMaterialService
:parameters (?u - Authenticated ?sub - Subject ?c - Crash )
:precondition (and (Authenticated ?u)(Subject ?sub)(Crash ?c))
:effect (and (VideoAudiodata ?sub) (Audiodata ?sub) (Textdata
?sub) ) )
(:action LaptopDeviceSelectionService
:parameters (?sub ?d )
:precondition (and (VideoAudiodata ?sub) (Laptop ?d))
:effect (Study ?sub ?d))
(:action SmartPhoneDeviceSelectionService
:parameters (?sub ?d )
:precondition (and (VideoAudiodata ?sub) (SmartPhone ?d))
:effect (Study ?sub ?d) )
(:action RadioDeviceSelectionService
:parameters (?sub ?d )
:precondition (and (Audiodata ?sub) (Radio ?d))
:effect (Study ?sub ?d) )
 ... )
```

A user request, input, and context are translated into Problem PDDL. User provides his user id ('sujata'), password ('swain') and submits his request ('to study CN'). The application obtains the location information ('Home') and number of remaining days to the examination ('Full'). From the device registry, the application selects a device available at that location ('SonyLaptop'). The Problem PDDL is shown below.

```
(:init
(UserId sujata)
(Password swain)
(Subject CN)
(Full CN-full)
(Laptop SonyLaptop) )
(:goal (Study CN SonyLaptop) )
```

5.2 Planning Phase

In this phase, a Blackbox planner is used to obtain a plan. Blackbox planner takes Domain and Problem PDDL as input. Blackbox planner obtains a plan, which contains a sequence of actions. Actions are same as services. The Blackbox plan is shown below. It contains Login service, Full course material service, Laptop device selection service. These services are composed to satisfy a user request.

```
Begin plan
1 (loginservice sujata swain)
2 (fullcoursematerialservice sujata cn cn-full)
3 (laptopdeviceselectionservice cn sonylaptop)
End plan
```

The composed service structure of the plan is shown in Fig. 6.

Fig. 6. A composed service for a user request in CEA when user's location is Home

Fig. 7. A composed service for a user request in CEA when user's location is car and SmartPhone is selected

5.3 Selection Phase

In this phase, the concrete services are selected corresponding to the abstract services. We use a meta-heuristic selection algorithm called hybrid genetic algorithm (HGA) [12], to obtain a list of composed concrete service ($CCSs$). We have used QWS dataset [17] of real web services. The dataset contains 2507 rows and 9 columns. A row represents a concrete web service, and a column represents a QoS attribute. The QoS attributes are response time, availability, and throughput, the likelihood of success, reliability, compliance, best practices, latency, and documentation. In our experiments, we consider 2500 rows (2500 concrete web services) and 4 columns (4 attributes). We consider four QoS attributes: response time, latency, availability and reliability. We consider that each QoS attribute is given equal preference. The stopping criterion for HGA algorithm is maxItr = 300.

In CEA application, a plan contains three number of abstract services. These are login service, full course material service, and laptop device selection service. Therefore, the chromosome size is 3. The population size is the number of concrete services corresponding to an abstract service. The population size should be less than or equal to 2500/chromosome size. We have considered population size is 350 ($\leq$2500/3). These services contain 350 concrete services in each. After applying HGA algorithm, the five best composed concrete services are given in Table 2. The first row can be interpreted as: 151 denotes 151st concrete service of the login service, 182 denotes 182nd concrete service of the full course material service, 311 denotes 311st concrete service of the laptop device selection service, and the value of objective function is 2.4224.

Table 2. Concrete services selection in CEA application.

Login service (AS1)	Full course material service(AS2)	Laptop device selection service (AS3)	Value of objective function
151	182	311	2.4224
338	182	311	2.4235
106	182	311	2.4339
79	182	311	2.4461
79	149	311	2.4472

5.4 Monitoring Phase

When a context changes, some concrete services may become unavailable. Due to which, some selected abstract services may not have any concrete services. Let AS_i be an abstract service that is unavailable due to context change. To handle such situation, a replanning strategy is suggested. We describe the replanning strategy through two cases.

Case-1: User's context (location) changes from Home to Car and available network bandwidth is high.

When the user's context changes, there may be a change in the set of available services and resources. In CEA application, we take user's location as context. When the location changes from Home (c) to a Car (c'), a set of available devices also changes, due to which the request cannot be satisfied. In CEA application, the user submits her request for the full course material of a subject. At that time user's location is at 'Home'. The proposed system provides the full course material through 'Laptop'. While providing the material, user's location changes from 'Home' to 'Car'. Let 'Laptop' be not available at the 'Car'. Due to which, Laptop device selection service becomes unavailable. Available devices at Car: SamsungMobile (SmartPhone), StereoRadio (Radio). Due to high network bandwidth available, SamsungMobile is selected to display the output. The application obtains a new plan for the unavailable service. The application generates a new problem PDDL for an unavailable service at the new context. The new Problem PDDL is generated as shown below.

```
(:init
(UserId sujata)
(Password swain)
(Subject CN)
(Full CN-full)
(SmartPhone SamsungMobile) )
(:goal (Study CN SamsungMobile) )
```

A new plan is obtained for the unavailable service using Blackbox planner. The obtained new plan is shown below.

```
Begin plan
1 (loginservice sujata swain)
2 (fullcoursematerialservice sujata cn cn-full)
3 (smartphonedeviceselectionservice cn samsungmobile)
End plan
```

The composed service structure of the plan is shown in Fig. 7.

Case 2: Full course service becomes unavailable.
Sometime only context information cannot help to obtain a new plan for the unavailable service. Therefore, a meta-reasoner is required to obtain the functionally equivalent services to an unavailable service. In CEA application, a meta-reasoner tree is implemented by ontology in protege tool. The functionally equivalent services are becomes siblings in the meta-reasoner tree.

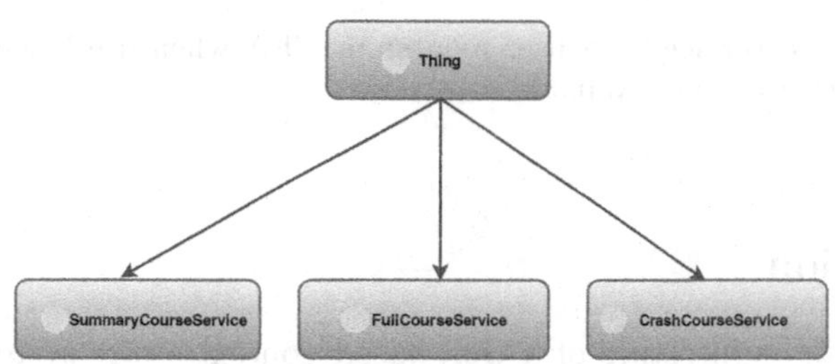

Fig. 8. Meta-reasoner tree of CEA application

In the CEA application, FullCourseService, CrashCourseService, and SummaryCourseService are providing lecture materials of a subject. As, we know these are providing a full description, a brief description, and a summary description respectively. Therefore these services are becoming the siblings in the meta-reasoner tree, as shown in Fig. 8.

A user has requested for FullCourseService of a subject CN, let's say S. However, there is no concrete service available to satisfy S. The existing system fails under this circumstance. The application gets the siblings of S, i.e., CrashCourseService (let's say, S_1) and SummaryCourseService (let's say, S_2). The service S_1 or S_2 are FE services of a service S. Therefore, CrashCourseService (S_1) or SummaryCourseService(S_2) can be substituted in the place of FullCourseService

(S) in the plan. The meta-reasoner provides the type 'Crash' which is functionally equivalent with the type 'Full'. The application generates a new Problem PDDL as shown below.

```
(:init
(UserId sujata)
(Password swain)
(Subject CN)
(Crash CN-Crash)
(Laptop SonyLaptop) )
(:goal (Study CN SonyLaptop) )
```

A new plan is obtained for the unavailable service using Blackbox planner. The obtained new plan is shown below.

```
Begin plan
1 (loginservice sujata swain)
2(crashcoursematerialservice sujata cn cn-crash)
3 (laptopdeviceselectionservice cn sonylaptop)
End plan
```

The composed service structure of the plan is shown in Fig. 9.

Fig. 9. A composed service for a user request in CEA when user's location is home and full course service is not available

6 Conclusion

We developed an architecture of a QoS based context-aware system. As a case study we considered a context-aware e-learning application that provides different types of study material according to the context. When context changes, a functionally equivalent service is replaced in place of an unavailable service using automated planning. The experimental results show the efficacy of the approach.

Acknowledgements. The authors thank the anonymous reviewers of ICCSA 2020 for their valuable suggestions. The second author was in part supported by a research grant from Google.

References

1. Chihani, B., Bertin, E., Jeanne, F., Crespi, N.: Context-aware systems: a case study. In: Cherifi, H., Zain, J.M., El-Qawasmeh, E. (eds.) DICTAP 2011. CCIS, vol. 167, pp. 718–732. Springer, Heidelberg (2011). https://doi.org/10.1007/978-3-642-22027-2_60

2. Alrifai, M., Risse, T., Nejdl, W.: A hybrid approach for efficient Web service composition with end-to-end QoS constraints. ACM Trans. Web (TWEB) **6**(2), 1–31 (2012)
3. Osman, I.H., Kelly, J.P.: Meta-heuristics theory and applications. J. Oper. Res. Soc. **48**(6), 657–657 (1997)
4. Zhang, Y., Cui, G., Wang, Y., Guo, X., Zhao, S.: An optimization algorithm for service composition based on an improved FOA. Tsinghua Sci. Technol. **20**(1), 90–99 (2015)
5. Peer, J.: A PDDL based tool for automatic web service composition. In: Ohlbach, H.J., Schaffert, S. (eds.) PPSWR 2004. LNCS, vol. 3208, pp. 149–163. Springer, Heidelberg (2004). https://doi.org/10.1007/978-3-540-30122-6_11
6. Ghallab, M., Nau, D., Traverso, P.: Automated Planning: Theory and Practice. Elsevier, Amsterdam (2004)
7. Omid, M.: Context-aware web service composition based on AI planning. Appl. Artif. Intell. **31**(1), 23–43 (2017)
8. Klusch, M., Gerber, A., Schmidt, M.: Semantic web service composition planning with OWLS-Xplan. In: Proceedings of the 1st International AAAI Fall Symposium on Agents and the Semantic Web, pp. 55–62 (2005)
9. Singh, R.P., Pattanaik, K.: An approach to composite QoS parameter based web service selection. Procedia Comput. Sci. **19**, 470–477 (2013)
10. Amiri, M.A., Serajzadeh, H.: QoS aware web service composition based on genetic algorithm. In: IEEE Fifth International Symposium on Telecommunications, pp. 502–507 (2010)
11. Ludwig, S.A.: Applying particle swarm optimization to quality-of-service-driven web service composition. In: IEEE 26th International Conference on Advanced Information Networking and Applications, pp. 613–620 (2012)
12. Seghir, F., Khababa, A.: A hybrid approach using genetic and fruit fly optimization algorithms for QoS-aware cloud service composition. J. Intell. Manuf. **29**, 1–20 (2016)
13. Lee, C., Ko, S., Lee, S., Lee, W., Helal, S.: Context-aware service composition for mobile network environments. In: Indulska, J., Ma, J., Yang, L.T., Ungerer, T., Cao, J. (eds.) UIC 2007. LNCS, vol. 4611, pp. 941–952. Springer, Heidelberg (2007). https://doi.org/10.1007/978-3-540-73549-6_92
14. Swain, S., Niyogi, R.: Smartmedicist: a context-aware system for recommending an alternative medicine. Int. J. Pervasive Comput. Commun. **14**(2), 147–164 (2018)
15. Swain, S., Niyogi, R.: Context-aware service composition with functionally equivalent services for complex user requests. In: Barolli, L., Amato, F., Moscato, F., Enokido, T., Takizawa, M. (eds.) AINA 2020. AISC, vol. 1151, pp. 1089–1100. Springer, Cham (2020). https://doi.org/10.1007/978-3-030-44041-1_94
16. Swain, S., Niyogi, R.: An ontology based approach for satisfying user requests in context aware settings. In: IEEE 30th International Conference on Advanced Information Networking and Applications, pp. 1130–1137 (2016)
17. Al-Masri, E., Mahmoud, Q.H.: QoS-based discovery and ranking of web services. In: IEEE Proceedings of 16th International Conference on Computer Communications and Networks, pp. 529–534 (2007)
18. Kautz, H., Selman, B.: BLACKBOX: a new approach to the application of theorem proving to problem solving. In: Workshop on Planning as Combinatorial Search (AIPS 1998), vol. 58260, pp. 58–60 (1998)

Formal Verification of a Distributed Algorithm for Task Execution

Amar Nath and Rajdeep Niyogi(✉)

Indian Institute of Technology Roorkee, Roorkee 247667, India
anath@cs.iitr.ac.in, rajdpfec@iitr.ac.in

Abstract. In a dynamic environment, the accomplishment of a mission composed of multi-robot tasks is quite a challenging problem. To execute collaborative tasks successfully, robots may need to be present at the location of the task. However, the required robots may not be present at the location of the task. A distributed algorithm has been proposed recently for such task execution. A model checker can analyze the behavior of the algorithm. In this paper, we formally model the algorithm using the PRISM model checker. We identify some interesting safety and liveness properties of the algorithm and perform extensive simulations of the algorithm. The results validate that the behavior of the algorithm is as expected.

Keywords: Task execution · Distributed algorithm · Formal verification · PRISM model checker

1 Introduction

A growing trend in the robotics community is to use a group of robots working in collaboration with each other (called multi-robot system (MRS) [1]) to accomplish tasks instead of using a single robot. The use of MRS provides better scalability, reliability, flexibility, and helps perform the tasks faster and in a cheaper way than single robot systems. MRS can be beneficial in search and surveillance applications, especially in areas that are difficult or impossible for humans to access. Another benefit of MRS is that they have better spatial distribution.

Execution of certain tasks (e.g., moving a heavy object) requires several robots' collective effort since no individual robot possesses all the skills required to achieve the task. Such tasks are to be executed in a dynamic environment, where the location and state of the robots change with time, the robots may enter and exit the environment, the location of static objects change with time as well, and no robot has global knowledge. When a task has to be executed in such an environment, the robots required to perform the task may not be available at the location of the task. So the robots should communicate and coordinate with each other in order to gather the required number of robots

O. Gervasi et al. (Eds.): ICCSA 2020, LNCS 12253, pp. 120–131, 2020.
https://doi.org/10.1007/978-3-030-58814-4_9

at the location of the task. For this, a distributed algorithm has recently been suggested in [2], and it has been implemented on a multi-robot simulator [14].

The algorithm suggested in [2] forms a coalition on task detection. The process of coalition formation starts on task detection (at runtime), but coalition cannot be formed in every run of the algorithm. The state and location of the robots play an important role in a coalition formation. A multi-robot system deployed in a real-world scenario should behave as expected. Incorrect behavior of the MRS would harm safety aspects and might also cause economic losses. For an MRS supposed to operate in a dynamic environment, it becomes imperative that any probable incorrect behavior is detected before the system is deployed on a real robotics system. Formal verification [3] is a process of checking whether a design satisfies the requirements.

Model-checking is a popular formal verification technique for automatically verifying the correctness properties of finite-state systems. Formal verification technology has been mostly successful and widely used in industry and space applications. Quantitative verification [4,5], allows reasoning in terms of quantitative properties, for instance, can a robot reach the desired location within, say, ten units of time, or what is the probability that a coalition would be formed. PRobabilistIc Symbolic Model checker (PRISM) [4,5], a probabilistic model checker, is a tool for formal modeling and analysis of systems that exhibit random or probabilistic behavior. It is used to analyze systems from many different application domains like communication, randomized distributed algorithms, and many others [4,5].

The rest of the paper is structured as follows. The related work is given in Sect. 2. The distributed algorithm [2] is described in Sect. 3. The formal modeling and verification of the algorithm are given in Sect. 4. The verification results are given in Sect. 5. Conclusions are made in Sect. 6.

2 Related Work

There are many model checking tools (e.g., SPIN [6], UPPAAL [7], MCMAS [8], and PRISM [4]) to formally verify different properties of a system. The work [9] considers the application of formal verification for checking whether the robotic application tasks are schedulable with respect to given hardware. The work [10] describes tools that automatically convert autonomy software into formal models that are then verified using model checking. This approach has been applied for task description language for mobile robotic systems. The work [11] considers some languages suitable for the specification and analysis of MRS. A comparison of these languages is made with respect to their ability to express some features of MRS like foraging and flocking.

PRISM based model checking has been done in [12] for verifying a team formation protocol [13] involving a network of interconnected agents with certain resources. We are not aware of any works that use the PRISM model checker for verifying the distributed algorithm for task execution in a multi-robot setting proposed in [2].

3 A Distributed Algorithm for Task Execution in a Dynamic Environment [2]

We consider the formal verification of an existing distributed algorithm for task execution in a dynamic environment [2]. A brief description of the algorithm [2] is given below.

In a dynamic environment $\mathcal{E}$, let a robot i detects a task $\tau = \langle \nu, l, t, k, \Psi \rangle$ at location l, and the robot i has sub-set of skills, required to execute the task, i.e., $\psi_i \supseteq \tau.\Psi$. The skills set for robots and tasks are represented as ψ and Ψ respectively. The elements of the task τ, i.e., ν, l, t, k, Ψ are defined as; ν is the name of a task (e.g., move (carry) box B to location l', lift desk D), $l \in L$ is the location where the task is arrived/detected, t is the time at which the task arrived, k is the number of robots required to execute the task, and Ψ is the skill/capability vector required to execute the task.

The task τ may not be executed by a robot i, and hence a team of robots needs to be formed before starting the execution of a task. However, all the robots may not be present at that location. No robot knows the states, locations, and skills of other robots (i.e., the absence of global knowledge). Thus, the robots should communicate among themselves in order to acquire relevant information for task execution without the intervention of any central authority. This necessitates the design of a distributed approach for task execution in such dynamic environments. In order to form a team for the execution of task τ, the robot i that is called an initiator, start the coalition/team formation process—the rest of the robots besides initiators called non-initiator.

An initiator i broadcasts a Request message and waits for some time, say Δ. It is assumed that a broadcast message would be delivered only to the robots present in the environment at that time. A non-initiator j, who has the necessary skills, will send either a Willing message or an Engaged message if its state is Idle or Promise respectively. Otherwise, it will ignore the Request message. The initiator increases its counter c when it receives a Willing message. After Δ time has elapsed, i checks if there are enough robots available to form a team ($c \geq k-1$). If yes, i select the members for the team and sends *Confirm* messages to them, *Not-Required* message to $(c-(k-1))$ non-initiators, if any. If no, i sends a *Not-Required* message to all c non-initiators who expressed their willingness to help. Depending on its queue status, i will change its state from Ready to Idle or Promise. The selected non-initiators gather at the task location and start the execution of a task. When robots change their state to Busy from either Ready or Promise, it is assumed that robots jointly start the execution of the task.

A non-initiator robot works as follows. The computations are done based on the current state that may be Idle, Promise, Busy, and Ready. Within a state, the type of message is checked, and appropriate actions are taken. For example, when state is Idle, if a Request message is received, it becomes Promise, the identifier of the sender is enqueued, and $flag$ is set to true; all these actions are done atomically (denoted by $\langle \ldots \rangle$). Now, the robot sends a Willing message to the sender (initiator), and $flag$ is set to false. A robot j maintains a local queue Q, which keeps the senders' identifiers based on the incoming Request messages.

Q is used to avoid starvation since more than one initiator may send Request messages at the same instant of time. The boolean variables $flag$ and $flag'$ are used to control the sending of Willing and Engaged messages respectively.

In order to ensure that the algorithm [2] satisfies some properties, formal verification is required. In this paper, the formal verification of the algorithm is done using PRISM.

4 Formal Verification of the Algorithm [2] with PRISM Model Checker

Model-checking is a formal, automatic technique to verify whether or not system design models satisfy given requirements [3]. In other words, it is a problem of establishing whether or not a given formula ϕ is true in a given model $\mathcal{M}$. Model-checking involves three phases:

- Modeling: to convert a design into a formalism so that mathematical computation and logical deduction can be performed.
- Specification: to specify the properties that the model should satisfy.
- Verification: to verify whether the model satisfies the specification [15].

A qualitative model checker gives "yes" or "no" as output. A quantitative (or probabilistic) model checker, on the other hand, gives the result "yes" or "no," or some probability as an output. In probabilistic model checking, the models encode the probability of making a transition between states instead of simply the existence of such a transition.

4.1 Modeling of the Distributed Algorithm in PRISM

The most important activity of the distributed algorithm for task execution in a dynamic environment is coalition formation. In coalition formation, a robot starts the coalition on task detection, if it can not execute the task alone. The task cannot be executed until coalition formation. We need to ascertain whether the algorithm described in Sect. 3 satisfies some properties.

4.2 PRISM Model

We model the distributed algorithm [2] using PRISM model checker [4]. In order to demonstrate the procedure clearly, we assume that at some point in time t, 5 robots ($\text{Robot}_1 \ldots \text{Robot}_5$) are present in the environment. In the environment several tasks ($\tau_1 \ldots \tau_m$) may arrive, and the task may be detected by any robot. The modeling captures the scenarios (given in Fig. 1), where a task τ can be detected by some robot. The model takes care of possibilities of task detection by different robots at different time. In Fig. 1-a, Robot_1 is the initiator robot and it forms the coalition with Robot_2 and Robot_3. Similarly, in Figs. 1-b, 1-c, 1-d and 1-e, Robot_2, Robot_3, Robot_4 and Robot_5 are acting as initiators respectively.

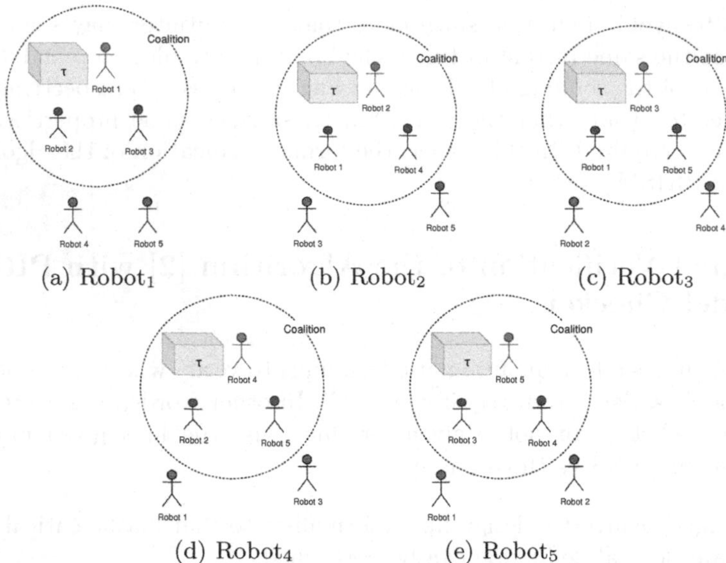

(a) Robot_1 (b) Robot_2 (c) Robot_3

(d) Robot_4 (e) Robot_5

Fig. 1. Different scenarios of robots detecting tasks and forming their corresponding coalitions

Data Structure: The data structure in the model consists of global variables and local variables. pInt is a global variable to denote the probability with which a robot detects a task. The global variable pOt denotes the probability with which an initiator stops its coalition formation process because it does not receive a sufficient number of willing messages within a predefined period. The representation in PRISM is given below.

```
mdp
const double pInt = .2; // probabaility; a robot detects a task
const double pOt = .1; //probabaility of timeout without team formation
const N = 5; //Total no of robots =5
```

The local variables of each robot are used to control the local aspects of the robots. The variable "state" is an integer which is used to capture the states of a robot during the task execution; 0,1,2,3 denotes Idle, Ready, Promise, and Busy respectively. The variable q1 is for placing the request received by a robot. The value of variable k, represents the total number of robots required for task execution. The variable c is used a count the number of Willing messages received by an initiator.

```
//Robot1 states, i.e., {0=Idle, 1=Ready, 2=Promise, 3=Busy}
state1:[0..3]; //queue
q1:[0..5];//queue
c1:[0..4] init 0; //Variable to records the no. of willing messages
k1:[0..3] init 3;//The required no. of robots required to execute a task
```

The sending of the messages is controlled by Boolean variables as discussed below. All the Boolean variables are initialized to false. The Boolean variable Send_request_12 denotes that it is a Request message which is sent from $Robot_1$ to $Robot_2$. Similarly, the other variables are constructed. The variable Send_confirm_12 is used to control the sending of Confirm message, from $Robot_1$ to $Robot_2$. Similarly, other message variables are used for sending different messages, i.e., Willing, Not-required and Engaged. The variables wr21, wr31, wr41, and wr51 are used to keep track of robots, who has sent the Willing to the $Robot_1$.

```
//The messages
Send_request_12 : bool init false; Send_confirm_12 : bool init false;
Send_request_13 : bool init false; Send_confirm_13 : bool init false;
Send_request_14 : bool init false; Send_confirm_14 : bool init false;
Send_request_15 : bool init false; Send_confirm_15 : bool init false;

Send_willing_12 : bool init false; Send_eng_12 : bool init false;
Send_willing_13 : bool init false; Send_eng_13 : bool init false;
Send_willing_14 : bool init false; Send_eng_14 : bool init false;
Send_willing_15 : bool init false; Send_eng_15 : bool init false;

Send_notreq_12 : bool init false; wr21 : bool init false;
Send_notreq_13 : bool init false; wr31 : bool init false;
Send_notreq_14 : bool init false; wr41 : bool init false;
Send_notreq_15 : bool init false; wr51 : bool init false;
```

Key Procedure: We constructed PRISM modules for every robot, present in the environment, and behaving according to the algorithm described in Sect. 3. A PRISM model for task detection by a $Robot_1$ is given below. The $Robot_1$ detects a task with probability with, say, 0.2 (pInt). As soon as it detects a task, it changes its state from Idle to Ready and acts as an initiator. In Ready state, the initiator, start the coalition formation process by broadcasting the Request messages to all other robots.

```
//task detection
[](state1 = 0)&(task1_detected = true) -> pInt:(state1' = 1) &
    (Initiator1'=true)+ (1-pInt):(state1' = 0);
//broadcasting the request
[](state1 = 1) & (Initiator1=true) -> (state1' = 1)
    &(Send_request_12'=true) & (Send_request_13'=true) &
    (Send_request_14' =true) & (Send_request_15' =true);
```

After sending the request to all other robots, the initiator receives either Willing or Engaged messages. When an initiator receives the Willing message from a non-initiator, it increments its counter c. If the sufficient number of

Willing messages are received within a specific period of time, then a coalition is formed successfully, as shown below.

```
//recept of willing message, but condition is not satisfied
[](state1= 1)&(Initiator1=true)& (Send_willing_21=true)& (c1 < k1-1)
    &(wr21=false) -> (state1' = 1)&(c1' = c1 +1)&(wr21'=true);
[](state1= 1)&(Initiator1=true)& (Send_willing_31=true)& (c1 < k1-1)
    &(wr31=false) -> (state1' = 1)&(c1' = c1 +1)&(wr31'=true);
[](state1= 1)&(Initiator1=true)& (Send_willing_41=true)& (c1 < k1-1)
    &(wr41=false) -> (state1' = 1)&(c1' = c1 +1)&(wr41'=true);
[](state1= 1)&(Initiator1=true)& (Send_willing_51=true)& (c1 < k1-1)
    &(wr51=false) -> (state1' = 1)&(c1' = c1 +1)&(wr51'=true);

//receipt of engaged message in any condition, it is just ignored
[](state1 = 1)&(Initiator1=true) & (Send_eng_21=true) -> (state1' = 1);
[](state1 = 1)&(Initiator1=true) & (Send_eng_31=true) -> (state1' = 1);
[](state1 = 1)&(Initiator1=true) & (Send_eng_41=true) -> (state1' = 1);
[](state1 = 1)&(Initiator1=true) & (Send_eng_51=true) -> (state1' = 1);
```

If a sufficient number of willing messages are received, the initiator sends Confirm or Not-required messages depending on the current situation. The selection of the desired robot for a coalition formation is formed at run time. The PRISM code for coalition formation is given below. The sending of either Confirm or Not-required message is also decided at runtime. Similarly, PRISM code for other robots has been constructed.

5 Verification Results

The efficiency of the distributed algorithm designed for task execution in a dynamic environment (given in Sect. 3) depends on the successful coalition formation process. The coalition formation is done via asynchronous message passing. The efficient coordination via communication is the key to success for the algorithm. In a dynamic environment, if coalitions for tasks are formed quickly, tasks may be executed successfully.

The initial conditions produced by the PRISM model checker is shown in Fig. 2. The initial PRISM snapshot illustrates all the labels present in the model. In addition, the built-in labels "init" and "deadlock" are also included. Selecting a label from the list highlights all states in the current path which satisfy it. It clear from Fig. 2, that the model is properly initialized, and no deadlock is present in the model at this moment in time (Fig. 3). The model is ready for verification.

5.1 Modeling Using PRISM

In order to analyze a PRISM model, it is necessary to specify one or more properties. PRISM's property specification is based on Computational Tree Logic (CTL) [3].

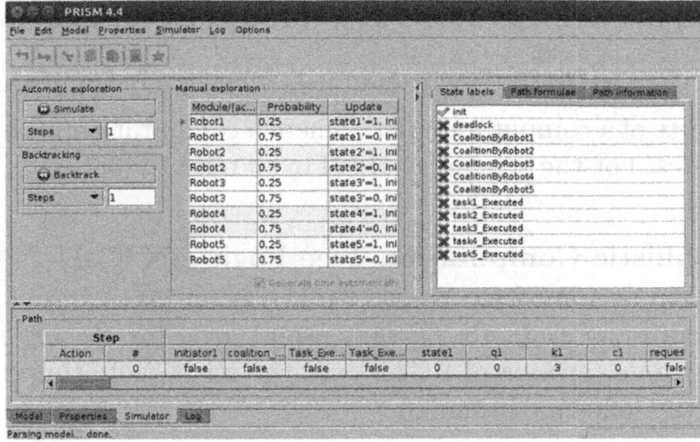

Fig. 2. Initial conditions of the model in PRISM model checker

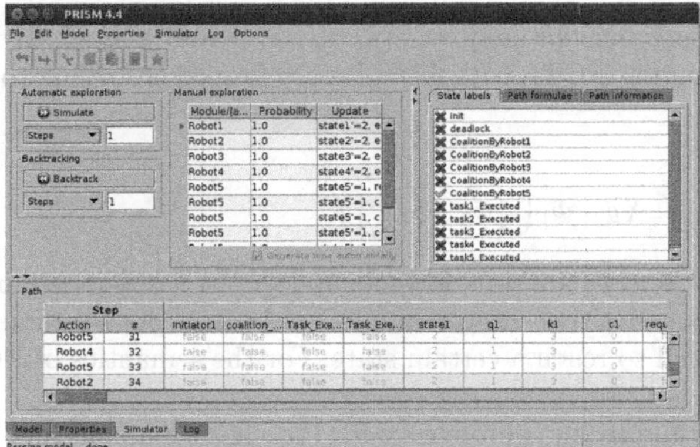

Fig. 3. A coalition is formed by Robot_5

5.1.1 Computation Tree Logic (CTL)

CTL has a two-stage syntax where formula in CTL are classified into *state* and *path* formulas. CTL *state formula* over the set *AP* of an atomic proposition are formed according to the following grammar [3].

$$\Phi ::= true \mid p \in AP \mid \Phi_1 \wedge \Phi_2 \mid \neg\Phi \mid E\varphi \mid A\varphi$$

where, *AP* is the set of atomic propositions, *E* and *A* are the path quantifiers– "for some path" and "for all path" respectively and φ is a *path formula.* CTL *path formula* are formed according to the following grammar:

$$\varphi ::= X\Phi \mid F\Phi_1 \mid G\Phi_1 \mid \Phi_1 \bigcup \Phi_2;$$

where Φ, Φ_1 and Φ_2 are the state formula and X, F, G, U are the temporal operators to denote "next", "some time in the future", "always in the future", and "until" operator respectively. $F\Phi$ and $G\Phi$ are dual operators where, $F\Phi = true \text{ U } \Phi$ and $G\Phi = \neg F \neg \Phi$.

Intuitively, *state formula* express a property of a state, while a *path formula* express a property of a computation path where a computation path is an infinite sequence of states. For the semantics of CTL we refer to [3].

5.1.2 Probabilistic Computation Tree Logic (PCTL)

Probabilistic Computation Tree Logic (PCTL) is an extension of CTL with a probability operator *(P)* [3]. PCTL is a useful logic for stating soft deadline properties. The *state formula* of PCTL over the set AP of atomic propositions are defined by the following grammar.

$$\Phi ::= true \mid p \in AP \mid \Phi_1 \wedge \Phi_2 \mid \neg\Phi \mid P_{\bowtie k}\ (\varphi)$$

where, φ is a *path formula* and $\bowtie \in \{<, \leq, >, \geq\}$ and $k \subseteq [0,\ 1]$ is an interval with rational bounds. PCTL *path formulae* are formed according to the following grammar:

$$\varphi ::= X\Phi \mid \Phi_1 \bigcup \Phi_2 \mid \Phi_1 \overset{\leq n}{\bigcup} \Phi_2$$

Where Φ, Φ_1, and Φ_2 are state formula and $\bigcup^{\leq n}$ is a "bounded until" operator where $n \in \mathbb{N}$ is a positive integer number reflecting the maximum number of transitions needed to reach a certain state. For the semantics of PCTL we refer to [3].

Some safety and liveness properties for the algorithm, specified in PCTL are given below.

- **Safety property:** Safety property has the form:
  $\mathrm{P}_{\bowtie k}$ G $(\Phi_1 \rightarrow \Phi_2)$ which is equivalent to $\mathrm{P}_{\bowtie k}$ G $((\neg\Phi_1) \vee \Phi_2)$
  We identified the following safety property for the distributed algorithm designed for task execution in a dynamic environment.
  1. Robot_1 sends Confirm messages in Ready state, after receiving sufficient number of Willing messages. This property can be expressed in PCTL as:
     S_1 : $P_{>0}$`G (!((state1=1)&((Send_confirm_12=true)|(Send_confirm_13=true)`
     `|(Send_confirm_14=true)|(Send_confirm_15=true)))|(c1>=(k1-1)))`
  2. If Robot_1 is in Promise state, and it receives a Confirm message, then its next state will be Busy.
     S_2 : $P_{>0}$ `G (!((state1 = 2)&((Send_confirm_21=true)|(Send_confirm_31=true)`
     `|(Send_confirm_41=true)|(Send_confirm_51=true)))|` ($P_{>0}$ `X(state1=3)))`
- **Liveness property:**
  Liveness property has the form:
  $\mathrm{P}_{\bowtie k}$ G $((\Phi_1 \rightarrow P_{\bowtie k} F\Phi_2)$ which is equivalent to $\mathrm{P}_{\bowtie k}$ G $((\neg\Phi_1) \vee P_{\bowtie k} F\Phi_2))$

1. If Robot_1 broadcasts a request message then eventually it must receive either Willing or Engaged messages.

   L1 : $P_{>0}$ G (!((Send_request_12=true)|(Send_request_13=true)|(Send_request_14=true) |(Send_request_15=true))|$P_{>0}$ F(((Send_willing_21=true)|(Send_willing_31=true) |(Send_willing_41=true)|(Send_willing_51=true))|((Send_eng_21=true)| (Send_eng_31=true)|(Send_eng_41=true)|(Send_eng_51=true))))
2. If Robot_1 detects a task, eventually it forms the coalition successfully with probability greater than zero. The coalition may not form every time as at some time, other robots might be busy doing other activities, and hence, condition $(c \geq (k-1))$ might not be satisfied.

   L2 : $P_{>0}$[true U (coalition_Formation1 = true)]
3. Every task in the environment is detected by a robot and eventually it is executed by a team of robots with some probability greater than 0. The task τ_1 is detected by Robot_1 and eventually Robot_1 goes to Busy state to execute the task. After finishing the task, the label "Task_ExecutionFinish1=true" becomes true.

   $P_{>0}$[true U "task1_Executed"] can be rewritten as:

   L3 : $P_{>0}$[true U ((Initiator1=true)& (Task_ExecutionFinish1=true))]

The verification of a system that is complex and has a large number of variables is quite challenging. Due to the large state space exploration, the PRISM model checker demands a huge amount of memory to store the explored states. In the case of low memory, the discrete-event simulator built into PRISM can be used to generate approximate results for PRISM properties, a technique called statistical model checking. To verify some of the identified properties (e.g., S_1, L_1 and L_2), we have used this technique for verification. Essentially, statistical model checking is achieved by sampling: generating a large number of random paths through the model, evaluating the result of the given properties on each run, and using this information to generate an approximately correct result. This approach is particularly useful on very large models when normal model checking is infeasible. This is because the discrete-event simulation is performed using the PRISM language model description, without explicitly constructing the corresponding probabilistic model.

PRISM supports four different methods for performing statistical model checking: CI (Confidence Interval), ACI (Asymptotic Confidence Interval)-for large sample size, APMC (Approximate Probabilistic Model Checking), SPRT (Sequential Probability Ratio Test).

We use ACI sampling methodology for verification; the ACI method uses the Normal distribution. This method is appropriate when the number of samples is significant (because we can get a reliable estimation of the variance from the samples) but maybe less accurate for small samples (Figs. 4 and 5).

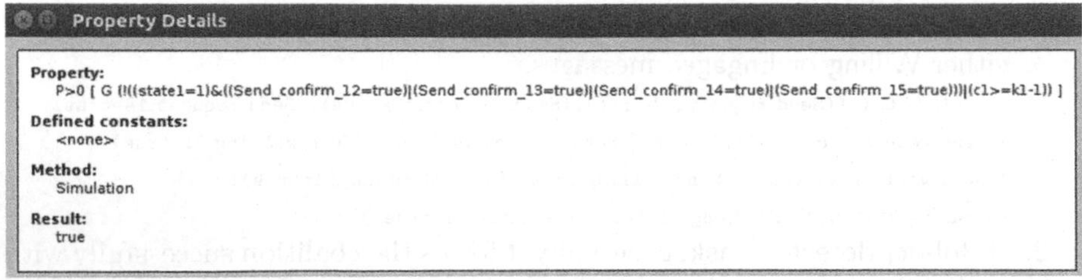

Fig. 4. Result for the safety property S_1

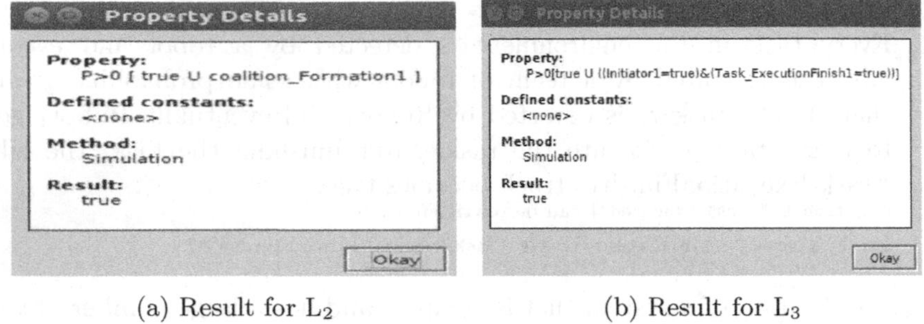

(a) Result for L_2 (b) Result for L_3

Fig. 5. Results for the liveness properties

6 Conclusion

In this paper, we considered the problem of verifying a distributed algorithm designed for task execution in a dynamic environment. The correctness of the algorithm is guaranteed by formally verifying the algorithm with probabilistic model checking. We identified some important safety and liveness properties of the algorithm. We constructed the algorithm's model in the PRISM model checker and verified the algorithm's properties. Extensive experiments were performed with a varying number of agents. The results are quite encouraging, and it confirms the expected execution of the algorithm.

Acknowledgements. The authors thank the anonymous reviewers of ICCSA 2020 for their valuable suggestions. The second author was in part supported by a research grant from Google.

References

1. Yan, Z., Jouandeau, N., Cherif, A.A.: A survey and analysis of multi-robot coordination. Int. J. Adv. Rob. Syst. **10**(12), 399 (2013)
2. Nath, A., Arun, A.R., Niyogi, R.: An approach for task execution in dynamic multirobot environment. In: Mitrovic, T., Xue, B., Li, X. (eds.) AI 2018. LNCS (LNAI), vol. 11320, pp. 71–76. Springer, Cham (2018). https://doi.org/10.1007/978-3-030-03991-2_7

3. Baier, C., Katoen, J.-P.: Principles of Model Checking. MIT Press, Cambridge (2008)
4. Kwiatkowska, M., Norman, G., Parker, D.: PRISM: probabilistic symbolic model checker. In: Field, T., Harrison, P.G., Bradley, J., Harder, U. (eds.) TOOLS 2002. LNCS, vol. 2324, pp. 200–204. Springer, Heidelberg (2002). https://doi.org/10.1007/3-540-46029-2_13
5. Kwiatkowska, M., Norman, G., Parker, D.: PRISM 4.0: verification of probabilistic real-time systems. In: Gopalakrishnan, G., Qadeer, S. (eds.) CAV 2011. LNCS, vol. 6806, pp. 585–591. Springer, Heidelberg (2011). https://doi.org/10.1007/978-3-642-22110-1_47
6. Holzmann, G.: Spin Model Checker, the: Primer and Reference Manual. Addison-Wesley Professional, Boston (2003)
7. Larsen, K.G., Pettersson, P., Yi, W.: Uppaal in a nutshell. Int. J. Softw. Tools Technol. Transf. **1**(1–2), 134–152 (1997)
8. Lomuscio, A., Qu, H., Raimondi, F.: MCMAS: a model checker for the verification of multi-agent systems. In: Bouajjani, A., Maler, O. (eds.) CAV 2009. LNCS, vol. 5643, pp. 682–688. Springer, Heidelberg (2009). https://doi.org/10.1007/978-3-642-02658-4_55
9. Foughali, M., Berthomieu, B., Dal Zilio, S., Hladik, P.-E., Ingrand, F., Mallet, A.: Formal verification of complex robotic systems on resource-constrained platforms. In: 2018 IEEE/ACM 6th International FME Workshop on Formal Methods in Software Engineering (FormaliSE), pp. 2–9. IEEE (2018)
10. Simmons, R., Pecheur, C., Srinivasan, G.: Towards automatic verification of autonomous systems. In: Proceedings 2000 IEEE/RSJ International Conference on Intelligent Robots and Systems (IROS 2000) (Cat. No. 00CH37113), vol. 2, pp. 1410–1415. IEEE (2000)
11. De Nicola, R., Di Stefano, L., Inverso, O.: Towards formal models and languages for verifiable multi-robot systems, arXiv preprint arXiv:1804.08091 (2018)
12. Chen, T., Kwiatkowska, M., Parker, D., Simaitis, A.: Verifying team formation protocols with probabilistic model checking. In: Leite, J., Torroni, P., Ågotnes, T., Boella, G., van der Torre, L. (eds.) CLIMA 2011. LNCS (LNAI), vol. 6814, pp. 190–207. Springer, Heidelberg (2011). https://doi.org/10.1007/978-3-642-22359-4_14
13. Gaston, M.E., desJardins, M.: Agent-organized networks for dynamic team formation. In: Proceedings of the Fourth International Joint Conference on Autonomous Agents and Multiagent Systems, pp. 230–237. ACM (2005)
14. Pinciroli, C., et al.: Argos: a modular, multi-engine simulator for heterogeneous swarm robotics. In: 2011 IEEE/RSJ International Conference on Intelligent Robots and Systems, pp. 5027–5034. IEEE (2011)
15. Sultan, K.I.: Modeling and verifying probabilistic social commitments in multi-agent systems. Ph.D. thesis, Concordia University (2015)

Semantic Similarity Measures for Topological Link Prediction

Giulio Biondi[1] and Valentina Franzoni[2](✉)

[1] Department of Mathematics of Computer Science, University of Florence, 50134 Florence, Italy
giulio.biondi@unifi.it

[2] Department of Mathematics of Computer Science, University of Perugia, 06123 Perugia, Italy
valentina.franzoni@dmi.unipg.it

Abstract. The semantic approach to data linked in social networks uses information extracted from node attributes to quantify the similarity between nodes. In contrast, the topological approach exploits the structural information of the network, e.g., nodes degree, paths, neighbourhood breadth. For a long time, such approaches have been considered substantially separated. In recent years, following the widespread of social media, an increasing focus has been dedicated to understanding how complex networks develop, following the human phenomena they represent, considering both the meaning of the node and the links structure and distribution. The link prediction problem, aiming at predicting how networks evolve in terms of connections between entities, is suitable to apply semantic similarity measures to a topological domain. In this paper, we introduce a novel topological formulation of semantic measures, e.g., NGD, PMI, Confidence, in a unifying framework for link prediction in social graphs, providing results of systematic experiments. We validate the approach discussing the prediction capability on widely accepted data sets, comparing the performance of the topological formulation of semantic measures to the conventional metrics generally used in literature.

Keywords: Unified view · Complex networks · Graph-based link prediction · Structural link prediction · Ranking-based approach

1 Introduction

For a long time, the semantic and topological approaches to the similarity in complex networks have been considered substantially separated. The semantic approach uses information extracted from node attributes to quantify the similarity between nodes, while the topological approach exploits the structural information of the network, e.g., nodes degree, paths, neighbourhood [4,7]. A set of techniques have been proposed in the literature for the link prediction, based on topological or semantic similarity. The idea behind both approaches is

O. Gervasi et al. (Eds.): ICCSA 2020, LNCS 12253, pp. 132–142, 2020.
https://doi.org/10.1007/978-3-030-58814-4_10

that similar nodes will develop a link in the future. Such similarity is structural in the topological approach, feature-based in the semantic approach, but can be applied to the same data. The link prediction problem, aiming at predicting how networks evolve in terms of connections between entities, is usually addressed with a topological approach. Still, we consider also suitable to apply the semantic approach to a topological domain. Formally, the link prediction problem consists in predicting the evolution of a given network at time t in terms of new links that will appear in the network in a future time t'. Forecasting a new link can be valuable for recommending, advertising or generating support, e.g., analysing social networks. E.g., in co-authorship networks, nodes represent authors, links represent co-authorship and prediction forecasts collaborations. Although the two approaches have been integrated into hybrid similarity frameworks, a dichotomy still exists, and the most significant interest in link prediction literature has been devoted to the topological approach, easier to exploit, and domain-independent. The key idea is that the web-based similarity measures use statistics from a search engine which can be interpreted in terms of the structure of the Web (i.e., of the indexing network of search engines). Therefore, such measures indirectly embed a measure of documents' neighbourhood topology. This work shows how semantic similarity measures (i.e., average confidence, PMI, NGD, X-squared) can be reformulated in a topological view and used in an associated graph for link prediction, starting from the concept that a substantial equivalence exists between the two approaches to the Link Prediction problem [9,12]. The advantages of modelling both classes of similarities in a single comprehensive model are apparent: a unified model provides the opportunity to use semantic measures in a topological framework and vice versa. In the first section, we introduce the link prediction problem in our unified framework. In the second section, we present a mapping of the semantic measures to the topological domain. In the third and fourth sections, we experimentally validate the proposed approach, discussing the prediction capability on widely accepted data sets, comparing the performance of the topological formulation of semantic measures to the conventional metrics generally used in literature. In the fifth section, conclusions are drawn.

2 Mapping Semantic Measures in a Topological Domain

2.1 Previous Research

In previous works [9,12] we studied the feasibility of a bidirectional mapping from topological measures to semantic formulations and vice versa and demonstrated the correctness of the unified approach. The comparison has been conducted on web-based semantic proximity measures, emphasizing their ability to express topological concepts by exploiting the capabilities of search engines. In a preliminary phase we performed an in-depth analysis of such measures. We extended the comparison to other proximity measures that can be applied to a web-based domain even if they are not created for that context, obtaining promising results on Pointwise mutual information (PMI) [26]; Normalized Google Distance (NGD) [6]; PMING distance [8], which is a combination of the previous sensibly improving measuring performances in clustering; Confidence; Average Confidence, seen as a combination of directional Confidence either way; Chi-square. Such measures have been tested on image classification, using image metadata and captions, and on text-based emotion recognition. A proximity model for randomized Heuristic Semantic Search (HSW) [14] has been experimented in several variations to guide the navigation through network links, where semantic measures can be used as heuristics to choose the step-by-step path instead of a random or a rule-based selection from candidate nodes, ranked using an aggregation function on the results of several random tournaments. Previous contributions also include the extension of the context-based Image Semantic Similarity [10] to a new class of set similarity measure to be used on social communities, using different combination schemes. The study of distances based on random walks, which are robust and computationally efficient for context extraction in large unknown graphs, lead to exciting results in terms of topological goals, e.g., convergence, path length, and minimal solution. Such models and techniques have been systematically tested on benchmark data sets, e.g., social networks, bibliographic repositories, recommender systems, and semantic associations between terms and emotional tags. The previous work laid the foundation for investigating algorithms for ranking graph nodes for many applications, including link prediction and reconstruction.

2.2 Topological Formulation of Semantic Similarity

We start considering as information source a search engine S, providing statistics about the occurrence, co-occurrence and probability of terms in a context [13], i.e. the frequency of single terms and terms pairs, used in web-based semantic proximity measures. Consider the terms-to-documents graph $G_S = (V, E)$ indexed by the search engine. Typify G_S as a bipartite graph where the set $V = T \cup D$ can be partitioned in two subsets. Vertices in T represent indexed terms, vertices in D represent the indexed documents. The edges $(u, v) \in E$ are the occurrences of terms in documents, i.e. (u, v) is the relation "u occurring in document v". For each edge in G_S, the property $\forall (u, v) \in E, u \in T \wedge v \in D$ is hold, i.e. G_S is bipartite.

If we consider the sample graph G_S shown in Fig. 1, it is apparent that all the information required by the semantic similarity measures can be defined in terms of neighbourhood and graph parameters of G_S, with the constraint of knowing the considered entities, i.e., the *frequency/occurrence* of a term u, the *co-occurrence* of u and v, and the corresponding *probabilities*

$$f(u) = |\Gamma(u)| \tag{1}$$

and

$$f(u, v) = |\Gamma(u) \cap \Gamma(v)|. \tag{2}$$

In such formulation $\Gamma(u)$ is the set of documents that contain a term u, and a document d is a common neighbour of the terms u and v, $d \in \Gamma(u) \cap \Gamma(v)$, if d contains both terms. Conversely, $\Gamma(d)$ is the set of terms contained in a given document d and $t \in \Gamma(d_1) \cap \Gamma(d_2)$, if t occurs in both d_1 and d_2.

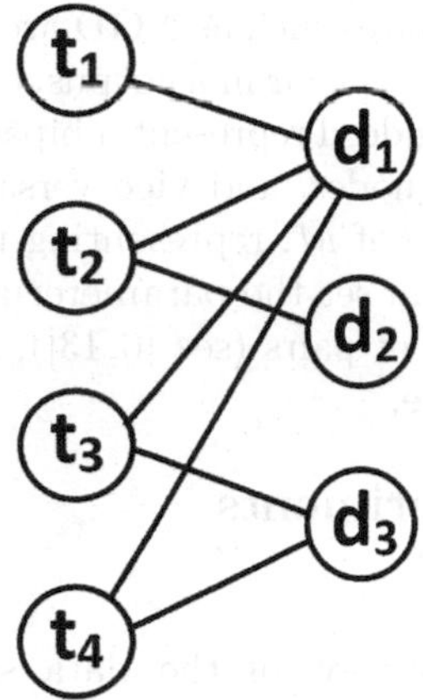

Fig. 1. An example of terms-to-documents graph

Topological Confidence. The *Confidence index (CF)* [2] formulation is straightforward in terms of topology:

$$similarity(u,v)_{TConf} = \frac{|\Gamma(u) \cap \Gamma(v)|}{|\Gamma(u)|} \tag{3}$$

The original Confidence index *TConf* is not symmetric; thus, we define the Average Topological Confidence [13]:

$$similarity(u,v)_{AvgTConf} = \frac{1}{2}\left(\frac{|\Gamma(u) \cap \Gamma(v)|}{|\Gamma(u)|} + \frac{|\Gamma(u) \cap \Gamma(v)|}{|\Gamma(v)|}\right) \tag{4}$$

Topological Pointwise Mutual Index. The Pointwise Mutual Index (PMI) [5] can be expressed topologically as:

$$similarity(u,v)_{TPMI} = \log_2\left(|V| \cdot \frac{|\Gamma(u) \cap \Gamma(v)|}{|\Gamma(u)| \cdot |\Gamma(w)|}\right) \tag{5}$$

Topological Normalized Google Distance. The Normalized Google Distance topological formulation results in [6]:

$$similarity(u,v)_{TNGD} = \frac{\max(\log|\Gamma(x)|, \log|\Gamma(y)|) - \log(|\Gamma(x) \cap \Gamma(y)|)}{\log M - \min(\log|\Gamma(x)|, \log|\Gamma(y)|)} \tag{6}$$

Chi-squared Coefficient χ^2. The Chi-squared Coefficient χ^2 [20] can be adapted as follows:

$$similarity(u,v)_{T\chi^2} = \frac{|\Gamma(u) \cap \Gamma(v)| * (|V| - |\Gamma(u) \cup \Gamma(v)|) - |\Gamma(u) * \Gamma(v)|}{(|\Gamma(u) \cap \Gamma(v)| + |\Gamma(u)|)(|\Gamma(u) \cap \Gamma(v)| + |\Gamma(v)|)} * \frac{|V|}{(|\Gamma(u)| + |V| - |\Gamma(u) \cup \Gamma(v)|)(|\Gamma(v)| + |V| - |\Gamma(u) \cup \Gamma(v)|)} \tag{7}$$

Web-based similarity measures such as NGD are explicitly designed to count the frequencies with which terms occur in a corpus, e.g. the documents indexed in a search engine; such corpora indeed represent a bipartite graph, where document nodes are connected to word nodes, and vice versa. In some cases we will not be able to know the real value of M, representing the total number of indexed documents. In this case, we can set the parameter as a random number greater than any occurrence of terms or pairs (see [6,13]), $M > |V|$, because it simply serves as a normalisation value.

3 Design of the Experiments

3.1 Data Sets

This section contains an overview of the data sets, which represent social networks, in particular email correspondence and co-authorship. For each of them, the size after preprocessing, in terms of nodes and edges, is shown in Table 1. The size of the data sets analyzed varies from a few hundreds of nodes (*radoslaw-email, email-EU-core*) to thousands (netscience, ego-Facebook, ca-GrQc, feather-lastfm-social) up to tens of thousands (*CA-HepPh, CA-HepTh, CA-AstroPh*); all of them can be considered sparse with respect to the number of edges. The data sets come from three widely accepted sources, i.e. *Stanford Large Network Dataset Collection* [18], *The Koblenz Network Collection* [16] and *The Network Repository* [24].

Table 1. Data sets statistics

Data set	$\|V\|$	$\|E\|$	Reference
Netscience	1461	2742	[23]
CA-GrQc	5241	14484	[17]
CA-HepPh	12006	118489	[17]
CA-HepTh	9875	25973	[17]
CA-AstroPh	18771	198050	[17]
ia-radoslaw-email	167	3250	[22]
ego-facebook	4039	88234	[21]
email-eu-core	986	16864	[17,28]
feather-lastfm-social	7624	27806	[25]

3.2 Preprocessing

Before the evaluation process, data sets are cleaned and randomised; the following elements are removed since they are not exploited in our approach:

- multiple edges between the same pair of nodes;
- self-loops;
- additional information associated with edges, e.g. text attributes.

3.3 *k*-fold Validation and the 0-Tail Issue

A k-fold validation is performed on each data set, choosing $k = 10$. This setup implies examining particular cases that might appear. The most relevant issue to consider is that entities can appear as 0-degree nodes because all the incident edges have been moved in $E_{TE}(k)$. Therefore, the calculated value for pairs including such nodes may be incorrect for some measures, while others are not affected. In particular:

- In Average Confidence, the degrees of nodes appear as denominators in a fraction; thus, if at least one of them is zero, the case in which the predicted value is infinite is replaced with 0.
- In Jaccard, if both nodes have degree 0, the predicted value is $\frac{0}{0}$, which evaluates to NaN and is replaced with 0.
- In PMI, it is enough to have a 0-degree node to get a $\frac{0}{0}$ value, again NaN, replaced with $-\infty$.
- In NGD, in case of division by zero, the value is replaced with $+\infty$.
- In χ^2, NaN values are replaced with 0.

This solution is correct from the logical point of view, because calculating neighbourhood-based similarity measures between two nodes u and v when one, or even both of them, have degree 0, i.e. have no neighbourhood, leads to a 0-tail [3]. The table containing the prediction values is sorted to produce the ranking induced by similarity measures; in case of distance measures, e.g. NGD, it is sufficient to reverse the rank order prior to the evaluation.

3.4 Evaluation Metrics and Approach-Dependent Considerations

In our approach, Link Prediction can be seen as a Binary Classification (BC) problem because each edge in the E_{POT} set either belongs or not to E_{TE}, used to test the prediction. The following quantities are defined to evaluate the performances of our classification model in the BC view:

- $TP(TN)$: number of positive (negative) instances correctly classified
- $FP(FN)$: number of misclassified negative (positive) instances
- $P_{real} = TP + FN$: number of positive instances
- $N_{real} = TN + FP$: number of negative instances
- $P_{alg} = TP + FP$: number of instances classified as positive
- $N_{alg} = TN + FN$: number of instances classified as negative

The length of P_{alg} and N_{alg} depends on a threshold $\tau = |E_{TE}|$ [19]. Links appearing in the top $|E_{TE}|$ positions in the rank are thus classified as positive, i.e. likely to appear at time $t + 1$. The fraction of links also appearing in $|E_{TE}|$ constitutes the TP set, while the remaining links correspond to the FP set. On the other hand, edges ranked lower than $|E_{TE}|$ are classified as negative, and part of them will not be included in the $|E_{TE}|$, forming the TN set. The remainder composes the FN set. The traditional evaluation metrics for classification are *Accuracy*, *Precision*, *Recall* and *F1*. It is worth noticing that the choice of our threshold $\tau = |E_{TE}|$ induces additional constraints. In particular, the number of FP instances is equal to FN; therefore, in our approach to the link prediction problem, Precision, Recall and F1 all assume the same values and can be considered equal.

Further considerations are required regarding Accuracy. Our algorithm evaluates the similarity measures for each edge in the set $E_{POT} = E_{FULL} \setminus E_{TR}$, which cardinality is $|E_{POT}| = |E_{FULL}| - |E_{TR}| = |V| \cdot (|V| - 1)) - |E_{TR}|$. The cardinality of the set E_{TE} is an upper bound for the TP, FP and FN, usually small if compared to $|E_{POT}|$. Since $|E_{POT}| = TP + TN + FP + FN$, it follows that $TN \gg TP + FP + FN$. Recalling that accuracy is defined as $ACC = \frac{TP+TN}{TP+FP+TN+FN}$, and given that TN represents the highest quota of the total edges, its value will always be ≈ 1, thus losing its significance. Since Precision considers the top $|E_{TE}|$ edges in the rank induced by similarity measures and counts the positive hits to evaluate performances, in some cases it could produce excessively low scores, not reflecting the real performance of the ranking as a whole. Due to our constraints and considerations, we decided to focus on an additional evaluation metric. Considering the position of the FN values in the rank, to detect whether most of them lay close to the τ ranking position (i.e., the frontier) or, instead, towards the bottom, it is useful to plot the Receiver Operating Characteristic (ROC) curve and calculate the Area Under the Curve (AUC) [27] value. A random predictor with uniform distribution returns AUC values close to 0.5; a higher value denotes a ranking where the positive edges are generally located in the upper section, and 1 indicates perfect rank. Since the accuracy is not significant in our case, we focus on precision and AUC in order to have more general, inter-dataset, key performance indicators.

4 Experimental Results

In the experiments, the mapped measures have been compared to conventional, widely used topological measures for Link Prediction, i.e. Common Neighbours [19], Jaccard [15], Adamic Adar [1] and Resource Allocation [29]. In Tables 2 and 3 the results are averaged on 10 folds; in bold, the best mapped semantic measure for each data set.

Results show that the performance of the mapped semantic measures is generally comparable to topological measures. The χ^2 index delivers highest Precision among the mapped measures in five out of nine experiments, with the remainder equally divided between Average Confidence and NGD. The reason for the higher Precision of AA and RA lies in the information about the neighbourhood up to a distance of 2 links traversal. CN and Jaccard, as well as our mapped measures, exploit only the direct neighbourhood of nodes, and their performance can be therefore compared. The exception is PMI [11], which is not a suitable correlation metric when only a few observations are provided. It is not surprising that the worst performances of semantic-derived measures are obtained with the smallest data sets, where node degree is in the order of few tens or hundreds.

Table 2. Average precision over 10 fold

	CN	Jaccard	AA	RA	Random	AvgConf	NGD	PMI	X2
netscience	0.4478	0.4967	0.6634	0.6823	0.0000	0.4847	**0.4967**	0.1948	0.4916
CA-GrQc	0.3594	0.3521	0.4873	0.5472	0.0001	0.3234	0.3170	0.0554	**0.3368**
CA-HepPh	0.5084	0.5654	0.5894	0.7790	0.0002	0.5410	0.4594	0.0359	**0.5744**
CA-HepTh	0.2179	0.1333	0.3399	0.3361	0.0000	**0.1274**	0.1262	0.0461	0.1231
CA-AstroPh	0.3813	0.3389	0.4490	0.6309	0.0001	0.3213	0.2637	0.0433	**0.3465**
ia-radoslaw	0.4058	0.2634	0.4138	0.4237	0.0320	**0.2748**	0.0308	0.0003	0.0889
Ego-facebook	0.3121	0.3238	0.3273	0.4457	0.0010	0.2767	0.2342	0.0038	**0.3203**
Email-eu-core	0.1995	0.2001	0.2230	0.2654	0.0032	0.0656	0.0938	0.0020	**0.1656**
feather-lastfm	0.1380	0.0074	0.1646	0.1595	0.0001	0.0050	**0.0083**	0.0009	0.0061

Table 3. Average AUC over 10 fold

	CN	Jaccard	AA	RA	Random	AvgConf	NGD	PMI	X2
netscience	0.9335	0.9336	0.9338	0.9338	0.4960	**0.9337**	0.9335	0.9332	0.8819
CA-GrQc	0.9218	0.9218	0.9221	0.9221	0.5019	**0.9219**	0.9218	0.9213	0.8942
CA-HepPh	0.9806	0.9816	0.9815	0.9821	0.5011	**0.9815**	**0.9815**	0.9794	0.9773
CA-HepTh	0.9019	0.9019	0.9022	0.9022	0.4998	**0.9019**	**0.9019**	0.9017	0.8856
CA-AstroPh	0.9885	0.9888	0.9892	0.9895	0.4993	**0.9887**	0.9883	0.9868	0.9861
ia-radoslaw	0.9146	0.8619	0.9167	0.9205	0.5002	**0.8457**	0.6606	0.4620	0.7631
Ego-facebook	0.9925	0.9907	0.9936	0.9949	0.4985	**0.9910**	0.9866	0.9588	0.9905
Email-eu-core	0.9390	0.9298	0.9440	0.9489	0.5002	**0.9203**	0.8918	0.8498	0.9126
feather-lastfm	0.8474	0.8465	0.8478	0.8478	0.4953	0.8463	0.8460	0.8450	**0.8586**

Table 4. 10-fold precision, Netscience data set

Fold	CN	Jaccard	AA	RA	Random	AvgConf	NGD	PMI	X2
0	0.4255	0.5018	0.6545	0.68	0	0.4945	0.5055	0.2109	0.5055
1	0.4836	0.4873	0.6509	0.6836	0	0.4655	0.4873	0.1673	0.48
2	0.4891	0.5547	0.7117	0.7372	0	0.5438	0.5657	0.1825	0.5438
3	0.4197	0.4416	0.6241	0.6606	0	0.4343	0.4453	0.1934	0.438
4	0.4161	0.5219	0.6569	0.6788	0	0.5109	0.5109	0.2226	0.5073
5	0.4489	0.4599	0.6606	0.6715	0	0.4635	0.4489	0.1861	0.4526
6	0.4562	0.4927	0.6679	0.6715	0	0.4891	0.4964	0.208	0.4964
7	0.4453	0.4964	0.6642	0.6752	0	0.4781	0.5	0.1825	0.4964
8	0.4526	0.5037	0.6715	0.6788	0	0.4818	0.5037	0.2007	0.4927
9	0.4416	0.5073	0.6715	0.6861	0	0.4854	0.5037	0.1934	0.5037

Regarding the AUC, the best performances are obtained with Average Confidence, which is also comparable to topological alternatives. In all but few cases, the mapped measures achieve consistent results on all the data sets.

In Table 4, the results of the 10-fold validation process are provided for the Netscience data set. It is apparent that all the measures show a coherent behaviour across all the folds, with only a few exceptions; such behaviour is shared across all the experiments.

5 Conclusion

In this paper, we introduce a new framework for the Link Prediction problem, aiming at giving a unified view of the two currently investigated approaches, topological and semantic. Our framework allows the use of semantic proximity measures to perform Link Prediction in a topological domain by remapping them according to a formal rule. Experiments have been held on data sets of different sizes, spanning from hundreds to tens of thousands of nodes. Different types of networks are represented, e.g., collaboration and e-mail, to evaluate the performance of semantic measures, i.e. Average Confidence, PMI, NGD, and X2, in a topological context. As a general conclusion, our experimental evidence shows that Average Confidence is comparable to classical topological ranking measures in terms of AUC; while χ^2 returns better Precision. We also observed that, in agreement with the literature, the applicability of measures derived from web-based semantics improves as the size of the network increases.

References

1. Adamic, L.A., Adar, E.: Friends and neighbors on the web. Soc. Netw. **25**(3), 211–230 (2003). https://doi.org/10.1016/S0378-8733(03)00009-1
2. Agrawal, R., Imieliundefinedski, T., Swami, A.: Mining association rules between sets of items in large databases. In: Proceedings of the 1993 ACM SIGMOD International Conference on Management of Data, SIGMOD 1993, pp. 207–216. Association for Computing Machinery, New York (1993). https://doi.org/10.1145/170035.170072
3. Chiancone, A., Franzoni, V., Li, Y., Markov, K., Milani, A.: Leveraging zero tail in neighbourhood for link prediction, pp. 135–139 (2016). https://doi.org/10.1109/WI-IAT.2015.129
4. Chiancone, A., Franzoni, V., Niyogi, R., Milani, A.: Improving link ranking quality by quasi-common neighbourhood, pp. 21–26 (2015). https://doi.org/10.1109/ICCSA.2015.19
5. Church, K.W., Hanks, P.: Word association noms, mutual information, and lexicography. In: Proceedings of the 27th Annual Conference of the Association for Computational Linguistics, vol. 16, no. 1, pp. 22–29 (1989). https://doi.org/10.3115/981623.981633
6. Cilibrasi, R., Vitanyi, P.: The google similarity distance, arxiv.org or clustering by compression. IEEE J. Trans. Inf. Theory **51**(4), 1523–1545 (2004)

7. Franzoni, V., Chiancone, A., Milani, A.: A multistrain bacterial diffusion model for link prediction. Int. J. Pattern Recogn. Artif. Intell. **31**(11) (2017). https://doi.org/10.1142/S0218001417590248
8. Franzoni, V., Milani, A.: PMING distance: a collaborative semantic proximity measure, vol. 2, pp. 442–449 (2012). https://doi.org/10.1109/WI-IAT.2012.226
9. Franzoni, V., Milani, A.: Structural and semantic proximity in information networks. In: Gervasi, O., et al. (eds.) ICCSA 2017. LNCS, vol. 10404, pp. 651–666. Springer, Cham (2017). https://doi.org/10.1007/978-3-319-62392-4_47
10. Franzoni, V., Milani, A., Pallottelli, S., Leung, C., Li, Y.: Context-based image semantic similarity, pp. 1280–1284 (2016). https://doi.org/10.1109/FSKD.2015.7382127
11. Franzoni, V.: Misure di prossimità semantica per il Web. Master's thesis (2012)
12. Franzoni, V.: A unifiying approach to semantic and topological similarity in information networks. Ph.D. thesis (2017)
13. Franzoni, V., Milani, A.: PMING distance: a collaborative semantic proximity measure. In: Proceedings - 2012 IEEE/WIC/ACM International Conference on Intelligent Agent Technology, IAT 2012, vol. 2, pp. 442–449 (2012). https://doi.org/10.1109/WI-IAT.2012.226
14. Franzoni, V., Milani, A.: Heuristic semantic walk. In: Murgante, B., et al. (eds.) ICCSA 2013. LNCS, vol. 7974, pp. 643–656. Springer, Heidelberg (2013). https://doi.org/10.1007/978-3-642-39649-6_46
15. Jaccard, P.: Étude comparative de la distribution florale dans une portion des Alpes et des Jura. Bulletin del la Société Vaudoise des Sciences Naturelles **37**(JANUARY 1901), 547–579 (1901). https://doi.org/10.5169/seals-266450
16. Kunegis, J.: Konect: the koblenz network collection. In: Proceedings of the 22nd International Conference on World Wide Web, WWW 2013, Companion, pp. 1343–1350. Association for Computing Machinery, New York (2013). https://doi.org/10.1145/2487788.2488173
17. Leskovec, J., Kleinberg, J., Faloutsos, C.: Graph evolution: densification and shrinking diameters. ACM Trans. Knowl. Discov. Data **1**(1), 2-es (2007). https://doi.org/10.1145/1217299.1217301
18. Leskovec, J., Krevl, A.: SNAP Datasets: Stanford large network dataset collection, June 2014. http://snap.stanford.edu/data
19. Liben-Nowell, D., Kleinberg, J.: The link-prediction problem for social networks. J. Am. Soc. Inform. Sci. Technol. **58**(7), 1019–1031 (2007). https://doi.org/10.1002/asi.20591
20. Manning, C.D., Schütze, H., Weikurn, G.: Foundations of statistical natural language processing. SIGMOD Rec. (2002). https://doi.org/10.1145/601858.601867
21. McAuley, J., Leskovec, J.: Learning to discover social circles in ego networks. In: Proceedings of the 25th International Conference on Neural Information Processing Systems, NIPS 2012, vol. 1, pp. 539–547. Curran Associates Inc., Red Hook (2012)
22. Michalski, R., Palus, S., Kazienko, P.: Matching organizational structure and social network extracted from email communication. In: Abramowicz, W. (ed.) BIS 2011. LNBIP, vol. 87, pp. 197–206. Springer, Heidelberg (2011). https://doi.org/10.1007/978-3-642-21863-7_17
23. Newman, M.E.J.: Finding community structure in networks using the eigenvectors of matrices, May 2006. https://doi.org/10.1103/PhysRevE.74.036104
24. Rossi, R.A., Ahmed, N.K.: The network data repository with interactive graph analytics and visualization. In: AAAI (2015). http://networkrepository.com
25. Rozemberczki, B., Sarkar, R.: Characteristic functions on graphs: birds of a feather, from statistical descriptors to parametric models (2020)

26. Turney, P.D.: Mining the web for synonyms: PMI-IR versus LSA on TOEFL. In: De Raedt, L., Flach, P. (eds.) ECML 2001. LNCS (LNAI), vol. 2167, pp. 491–502. Springer, Heidelberg (2001). https://doi.org/10.1007/3-540-44795-4_42
27. Yang, Y., Lichtenwalter, R.N., Chawla, N.V.: Evaluating link prediction methods. Knowl. Inf. Syst. **45**(3), 751–782 (2014). https://doi.org/10.1007/s10115-014-0789-0
28. Yin, H., Benson, A.R., Leskovec, J., Gleich, D.F.: Local higher-order graph clustering. In: Proceedings of the 23rd ACM SIGKDD International Conference on Knowledge Discovery and Data Mining, KDD 2017, pp. 555–564. Association for Computing Machinery, New York (2017). https://doi.org/10.1145/3097983.3098069
29. Zhou, T., Lu, L., Zhang, Y.C.: Predicting missing links via local information. Eur. Phys. J. B **71**(4), 623–630 (2009). https://doi.org/10.1140/epjb/e2009-00335-8

International Workshop on Large Scale Computational Science (LSCS 2020)

Large Scale Automatic Computations for Feynman Diagrams with up to Five Loops

E. de Doncker[1(✉)], F. Yuasa[2], O. Olagbemi[1], and T. Ishikawa[2]

[1] Western Michigan University, Kalamazoo, MI 49008, USA
{elise.dedoncker,omofolakunmiel.olagbemi}@wmich.edu
[2] High Energy Accelerator Research Organization (KEK), 1-1 OHO, Tsukuba, Ibaraki 305-0801, Japan
{fukuko.yuasa,tadashi.ishikawa}@kek.jp
http://www.cs.wmich.edu/elise

Abstract. We give results by automatic integration methods for finite and UV-divergent 4-loop diagrams and a finite 5-loop case with massless internal lines. Non-adaptive methods include DE (Double Exponential), and Quasi-Monte Carlo (QMC) techniques. The latter are based on optimal lattice rules, implemented in Cuda-C for GPUs; or, for execution on PEZY/ Exascaler, the host program is written in C++ and the kernel is generated using the Goose compiler interface. DE is executed on similar hardware as QMC, with or without parallel libraries for MPI. Transformations are incorporated to alleviate or smoothen singularities on the boundaries of the domain. For adaptive integration we use the ParInt package layered over MPI on a cluster, as well as a new adaptive scheme that performs GPU evaluations of the cubature rules. For the UV-divergent diagram we apply a nonlinear extrapolation on a sequence of integral approximations generated for dimensional regularization. Some results are verified using computationally intensive symbolic/numerical evaluations with pySecDec.

Keywords: Feynman loop diagrams · Adaptive/non-adaptive integration · High performance computing · Dimensional regularization

1 Introduction

1.1 Feynman Loop Integrals

After the discovery of the Higgs particle in the Large Hadron Collider (LHC) experiment at CERN, the Standard Model of particle physics has been investigated precisely to find a tiny deviation of the experimental observations from theoretical predictions.

With marked improvements in the technology of high energy physics experiments, accurate theoretical predictions are required more than ever, with an increased importance of higher order corrections in the perturbation method.

O. Gervasi et al. (Eds.): ICCSA 2020, LNCS 12253, pp. 145–162, 2020.
https://doi.org/10.1007/978-3-030-58814-4_11

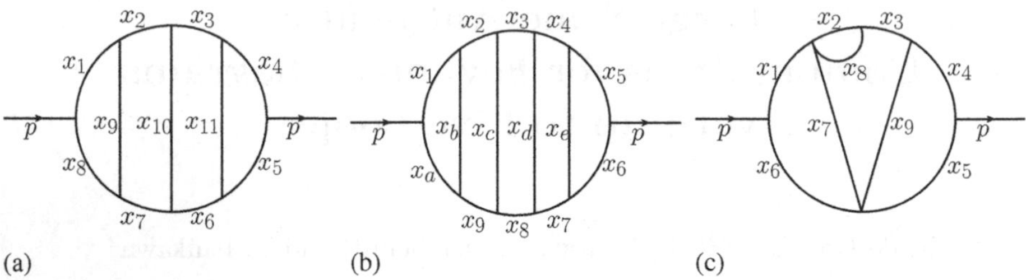

Fig. 1. (a) 4-loop $N = 11$ [4], (b) 5-loop $N = 14$ [4], (c) 4-loop $N = 9$ [4]

In particular, these will play a crucial role in the precise investigation of the Higgs sectors and electroweak interactions in both upcoming HL-LHC (High-Luminosity LHC) and future Linear Collider experiments.

In calculating higher order corrections to observables, the Feynman diagrammatic approach is commonly used today since a prescription for the approach has been well established. Feynman loop integrals emerge in the course of the calculations. The one-loop level has been studied completely in an analytic manner by 't Hooft and Veltman [18] and there are already several computer programs to evaluate one-loop integrals (such as LoopTools [17]). For corrections including multi-loop integrals with various mass and momentum values, a general and analytic treatment is not possible so that a numerical approach is mandatory. Various approaches have been proposed and their implementations have been published, for example, pySecDec [5] utilizes symbolic/algebraic manipulations and numeric calculations. It is further reported that Forcer [34], a FORM program, has been used for the computation of challenging loop problems such as the five-loop beta function for Yang-Mills theory with fermions [32,33].

As the number of loops increases, the number of dimensions of integration increases in general as well as the degree of difficulty. Thus numerical multi-dimensional integration is one of the key ingredients in the computation of higher order corrections. An excellent example of the successful application of large-scale numerical methods is the computation of the full two-loop electroweak corrections to the muon anomalous magnetic moment [19]. The methods presented in this paper are fully numerical and based on adaptive or non-adaptive multi-dimensional integration techniques, with the goal of enabling an accurate high-performance evaluation of Feynman Integrals at the multi-loop level with any masses and momenta.

A scalar Feynman integral in Feynman parameter (Euclidean) space can be represented by $\mathcal{F} = (4\pi)^{-\nu L/2}\mathcal{I}$ where

$$\mathcal{I} = \Gamma(N - \frac{\nu L}{2})\,(-1)^N \int_{\mathcal{C}_N} \prod_{r=1}^{N} dx_r\, \delta(1 - \sum x_r) \frac{C^{N-\nu(L+1)/2}}{(D - i\varrho C)^{N-\nu L/2}} \tag{1}$$

$$= \Gamma(N - \frac{\nu L}{2})\,(-1)^N \int_{\mathcal{S}_{N-1}} \prod_{r=1}^{N-1} dx_r\, \frac{C^{N-\nu(L+1)/2}}{(D - i\varrho C)^{N-\nu L/2}} \tag{2}$$

where L and N denote the number of loops and internal lines, respectively; C and D are polynomials determined by the topology of the corresponding diagram and physical parameters, and we let $\varrho = 0$ as D does not vanish in the interior of the domain for the current application. The space-time dimension is $\nu = 4 - 2\varepsilon$ where ε is a parameter that tends to zero for regularization. Whereas the integral representation (1) extends over the N-dimensional unit cube $\mathcal{C}_N$, the integral (2) over the $d = (N-1)$-dimensional unit simplex $\mathcal{S}_d = \{\mathbf{x} \in \mathcal{C}_d \mid \sum_{j=1}^{d} x_j \leq 1\}$ is obtained by eliminating the δ-function.

We will treat the diagrams of Fig. 1, including: (a) a finite 4-loop diagram ($N = 11$), (b) a finite 5-loop diagram ($N = 14$), and (c) a UV-divergent 4-loop diagram ($N = 9$).

1.2 UV Singularities

The polynomial C in the denominator may vanish at the boundaries of the domain, giving rise to an ultra-violet (UV) singularity in case the exponent $N - \nu(L+1)/2 = N - (2-\varepsilon)(L+1)$ is negative. We incur this situation for the diagram of Fig. 1(c) with $N = 9$ massless internal lines and $L = 4$ loops, where the integral satisfies an expansion of the form

$$\mathcal{I} = \mathcal{I}(\varepsilon) = \gamma(\varepsilon) \sum_{k \geq \kappa} C_k \varepsilon^k \tag{3}$$

with $\kappa = -1$ as given by [4]. For regularization we will generate an approximate sequence to $\{\varepsilon_\ell \mathcal{I}(\varepsilon_\ell)\}$ as $\varepsilon_\ell \to 0$ (i.e., space-time dimension $\nu \to 4$).

With the goal of obtaining the limit numerically, we use the ϵ-algorithm [41] for a nonlinear extrapolation, and an implementation based on the code of *qext()* from the QuadPack package [30]. The computation produces a triangular table, with a sequence based on integral approximations as the entry sequence in the first column. The *qext()* procedure computes a new lower diagonal when a new entry is available, together with a measure of the distance of each element from preceding neighboring elements. Then *qext()* returns the new lower diagonal element with the smallest value of the distance estimate as the extrapolation result.

1.3 Automatic Integration

Classic automatic integration software includes HALF [7], QuadPack [30], Adapt [14], Dcuhre [3] and Cuba [16]. An automatic integration method is supplied with a specification of the integral including the dimension, domain and integrand function, as well as an error tolerance and a bound on the allowed amount of work, such as the maximum number of integrand evaluations to be performed in the course of the integration. While the procedure acts as a black-box, the computation aims to deliver an approximation to the integral and an error estimate.

Defining the integrand on the domain $\mathcal{D}$ as a vector function with s components, $f : \mathcal{D} \subset \mathbb{R}^d \to \mathbb{R}^s$, the integral can be represented by $\mathcal{I} = \mathcal{I}f =$

$\int_{\mathcal{D}} f(\mathbf{x})\, d\mathbf{x}$. Using $\mathcal{Q}$ and E_a for the final integral approximation and absolute error estimate, respectively, a possible target accuracy requirement is

$$||\mathcal{Q} - \mathcal{I}|| \le E_a \le t = \max\{t_a, t_r||\mathcal{I}||\} \tag{4}$$

(in infinity norm), where t_a and t_r are the user-specified absolute and relative error tolerances. Unless otherwise noted it is assumed that $s = 1$.

1.4 Transformations

Since we rely on the loop integral representation (2) over a simplex domain, a transformation is needed from the simplex to the unit cube. Unless otherwise stated we transform the integral over $\mathcal{S}_d$ of (2) to $\mathcal{C}_d$ by the coordinate transformation

$$x_j = (1 - \sum_{k=1}^{j-1} x_k)\, y_j, \quad 1 \le j \le d \tag{5}$$

so that $\mathbf{y} \in \mathcal{C}_d$ and the Jacobian is $\prod_{j=1}^{d-1}(1 - \sum_{k=1}^{j-1} x_k)$.

For Fig. 1(c) we use the following simplex-to-cube transformation that also aims to reduce singular behavior on the boundaries,

$$\begin{aligned}
x_1 &= y_1\, y_2\, y_5\, y_6 & x_6 &= y_1\, y_2\, y_5\, y_{6m} \\
x_2 &= y_{1m}\, y_3\, y_4 & x_7 &= y_1\, y_2\, y_{5m} \\
x_3 &= y_{1m} y_{3m} & x_8 &= y_{1m}\, y_3\, y_{4m} \\
x_4 &= y_1 y_{2m} y_7 y_8 & x_9 &= y_1\, y_{2m}\, y_{7m} \\
x_5 &= y_1 y_{2m} y_7 y_{8m} & &
\end{aligned} \tag{6}$$

with $y_{jm} = 1 - y_j$, $\sum_{k=1}^{d+1} x_k = 1$ and Jacobian $y_1^5\, y_{1m}^2\, y_2^2\, y_{2m}^2\, y_3\, y_5\, y_7$.

Furthermore, while lattice rules are applied with a periodizing transformation of the integrand, we select a transformation that also suppresses singularities on the boundaries of the domain. In some cases these transformations also improve the performance of adaptive methods for dealing with boundary singularities. We make use of Sidi's $\sin^{\mathrm{m}}$-transformations [36] for $m = 4$ and 6,

$$\Psi_4(t) = t + (-8\sin(2\pi t) + \sin(4\pi t))/(12\pi), \quad \Psi_4'(t) = \frac{8}{3}\sin^4(\pi t) \tag{7}$$

$$\Psi_6(t) = t - (45\sin(2\pi t) - 9\sin(4\pi t) + \sin(6\pi t))/(60\pi), \quad \Psi_6'(t) = \frac{16}{5}\sin^6(\pi t) \tag{8}$$

Subsequently in this paper, the adaptive methods ParInt and ParAdapt will be discussed in Sects. 2 and 3, respectively. A double exponential (DE) transformation is used in a non-adaptive technique as described in Sect. 4.1. Quasi-Monte Carlo (QMC) approaches based on lattice rules are covered briefly in Sect. 4.2, also including embedded lattice rules and stochastic families of rules. Finally, results for the diagrams of Fig. 1 are given in Sect. 5.

2 Adaptive Multivariate Integration – ParInt

The ParInt package provides a parallel automatic integration method implemented in C and layered over MPI (Message Passing Interface [23]). ParInt allows for integration over hyper-rectangular and simplex regions. The adaptive strategy continually refines the integration domain by region subdivisions in a distributed task partitioning algorithm, cf. [10,13]. In view of the global termination criterion (4), the strategy adheres to a class of the meta-algorithm termed global adaptive [31]. With the notations of Sect. 1.3, the accuracy requirement to be attained for the integral $\mathcal{I}$ is given by (4), and the termination criterion tested in the course of the computations is of the form $E_a \leq t = \max\{t_a, t_r||\mathcal{Q}||\}$, where $\mathcal{Q}$ is the current overall integral approximation.

For estimating the integral and error over each subregion, the integration rules are linear combinations of function values, $\sum_{j=1}^{n} w_j f(\mathbf{x}_j)$. An integration rule is of polynomial degree of accuracy k if it integrates all polynomials of degrees through k exactly and does not integrate all polynomials of degree $k+1$ exactly. For hyper-rectangular regions, ParInt provides basic rules of polynomial degrees 7 and 9 [2,14].

The given domain is initially distributed over a number of processes (workers), each of which successively selects its largest error subregion, subdivides (bisects it) and integrates over the parts. The selected region is thereby deleted from the worker's local heap, and the children regions are inserted. The contributions of the selected region to the integral and to the error estimate are replaced by those of the children regions. The resulting differences are accumulated into updates for the overall integral and error estimate, and eventually sent to the controller process. Executed on a separate process, the controller may also perform as a worker.

The update messages from the workers further contain information on their busy or idle status, which is used to initiate load balancing, where work is sent from busy to idle or near-idle workers. As an additional feature, specifying a maximum heap size leads to maintaining a double-ended heap (deap) data structure where low-priority elements are deleted when adding regions, in order to maintain constant size once the maximum heap size is reached.

3 ParAdapt

ParAdapt, based on Adapt [14], targets global adaptive integration over hyper-rectangu- lar regions in moderate dimensions, say $d \geq 10$, by performing its (degree 7) rule evaluations on GPU [27,28]. The number of function evaluations per region, $2^d + 2d(d+2) + 1$, ranges between 1,265 and 33,279 for dimensions $d = 10$ to 15. Apart from the integration rule, fourth divided differences are computed through the region center in each coordinate direction, in order to gauge in which directions the integrand varies most. In ParAdapt the selected region can be subdivided into 2, 4 or 8 subregions of equal volume by halving the sides corresponding to the coordinate directions of the largest, second-largest and third-largest divided difference. Subdivision into 16 is done by subdividing into 8 as above and choosing one of the remaining directions in a round-robin manner.

The rule evaluations over the children regions are performed on the GPU simultaneously. The rule points for the unit d-cube as the standard region are stored on the GPU and properly scaled for each subregion, i.e., the point $\tilde{\mathbf{p}}$ in $\mathcal{C}_d$ is mapped to the hyper-rectangle with edges from a_j to b_j in the jth coordinate direction as $p_j = a_j + (b_j - a_j)\tilde{p}_j$. Thus each rule point $\tilde{\mathbf{p}}$ has an image $\mathbf{p}$ in each of the children regions.

As outlined for CUDA programming in [35], the threads are laid out over a rectangular array where each row represents a block, and the width of a block corresponds to the number of threads per block. Figure 2 depicts a one-dimensional (x) grid, where we denote the number of blocks (array height) $g = gridDim.x$, and the number of threads per block (array width) $b = blockDim.x$. The blocks are indexed by $blockIdx.x = 0, 1, \ldots, g-1$ (row numbers). The thread ID within a block is $threadIdx.x$ (column number). Globally the threads are numbered consecutively in a row-major fashion as indicated by the *tids* (global thread IDs) listed in the grid cells.

blockIdx.x	*tids*			
0	0	1	...	$b-1$
1	b	$b+1$	...	$2b-1$
2			...	
.				
.				
.				
$g-2$	$(g-2)b$	$(g-2)b+1$	...	$(g-1)b-1$
$g-1$	$(g-1)b$	$(g-1)b+1$	...	$gb-1$

Fig. 2. Threads layout in blocks; block IDs and global thread IDs (*tid*) are shown.

Then grid cell (i, j) corresponds to $tid = ib + j$ (i.e., grid cell $(blockIdx.x, threadIdx.x)$ corresponds to $tid = blockIdx.x * blockDim.x + threadIdx.x$). Following $tid = gb - 1$ the *tids* wrap around, so that grid cell $(0, 0)$ corresponds to $tid = 0, bg, 2bg, \ldots$, and grid cell (i, j) to $tid = ib + j, ib + j + bg, ib + j + 2bg, \ldots$

We assign the function evaluations for a point $\mathbf{p}$ in successive subregions to successive *tids*. Figure 3 shows two blocks, (*0* and *1*), with the global *tids*, and *ptIndex* and *rgnIndex* assigned to each *tid*, for $r = numRgns$ regions ($0 \le rgnIndex < r$) and assuming that r divides the number of threads per block b (this can be adjusted in case r does not divide b). The global *tids* indexing the block elements are written in italics outside the blocks, as well as the block numbers. An example for $r = 4$ regions and $b = 256$ is also given. In this case, two blocks handle 128 points of the integration rule applied in four regions.

	0	*1*	⋯	*r−1*	*r*	*r+1*	⋯	*2r−1*	⋯			⋯	*b−1*	*tid*
0	0	1	⋯	$r-1$	0	1	⋯	$r-1$	⋯	0	1	⋯	$r-1$	*rgnIndex*
	0	0	⋯	0	1	1	⋯	1	⋯	$\frac{b}{r}-1$	$\frac{b}{r}-1$	⋯	$\frac{b}{r}-1$	*ptIndex*
1	0	1	⋯	$r-1$	0	1	⋯	$r-1$	⋯	0	1	⋯	$r-1$	*rgnIndex*
	$\frac{b}{r}$	$\frac{b}{r}$	⋯	$\frac{b}{r}$			⋯		⋯	$\frac{2b}{r}-1$	$\frac{2b}{r}-1$	⋯	$\frac{2b}{r}-1$	*ptIndex*
	b	*b+1*	⋯				⋯		⋯			⋯	*2b−1*	*tid*

	0	*1*	*2*	*3*	*4*	*5*	*6*	*7*	⋯	*252*	*253*	*254*	*255*	*tid*
block 0	0	1	2	3	0	1	2	3	⋯	0	1	2	3	*rgnIndex*
	0	0	0	0	1	1	1	1	⋯	63	63	63	63	*ptIndex*
block 1	0	1	2	3	0	1	2	3	⋯	0	1	2	3	*rgnIndex*
	64	64	64	64	65	65	65	65	⋯	127	127	127	127	*ptIndex*
	256	*257*	*258*	*259*	*260*	*261*	*262*	*263*	⋯	*508*	*509*	*510*	*511*	*tid*

Fig. 3. Relationship between *tid*, *rgnIndex* and *ptIndex* for $r = numRgns$ regions. It is assumed that r divides the number of threads per block b. The second array shows an example for $r = 4$ regions and $b = 256$.

```
while(tid < N) {
    ptIndex = tid/numRgns;
    rgnIndex = tid − ptIndex ∗ numRgns;
    // get original point p̃ from point list at ptIndex
    // and region information at rgnIndex
    for (j = 0; j < d; j++)  p[j] = a[j] + ( b[j] − a[j] ) ∗ p̃[j];  // scaling
    funvls = f(p); // evaluate function
    sumWeightsFunvls += weights[ptIndex] ∗ funvls;  // rule sum accumulation
        . . .  // accumulation for error estimate
    tid += blockDim.x ∗ gridDim.x;
}
```

Fig. 4. Kernel with function evaluation and accumulation of partial rule sum

For a given *tid* the algorithm can thus determine *ptIndex* to reference the integration points and weights, and *rgnIndex* for properly scaling the point and applying its contribution to the weighted sum of function values for the required region. Denoting the total number of points over the r regions resulting from a subdivision by $N = rn$, where n is the number of points in the rule sum, the rule evaluation loop of the CUDA kernel roughly conforms to the description of Fig. 4. Only the accumulation of the partial rule sum pertaining to the integral approximation (into *temp_sumWeightsFunvls*[*ptIndex*]) is shown. Further accumulations are needed for the error estimate.

The *sumWeightsFunvls* values across a block are stored in a cache array that is shared by all threads in the block. A regular reduction operation as outlined in [35] then leaves the results for the r regions in the first r threads in the block. The $(gridDim.x) \times r$ values over all blocks are returned from the kernel, and summed further into the r region results.

4 Non-adaptive Integration

4.1 Double-Exponential Method

The double-exponential method (DE) [38,39] transforms the one-dimensional integral

$$\int_0^1 f(x)\,dx = \int_{-\infty}^{\infty} f\left(\phi(t)\right)\phi'(t)\,dt, \qquad \text{using}$$
$$x = \phi(t) = \frac{1}{2}(\tanh(\frac{\pi}{2}\sinh(t)) + 1), \qquad \phi'(t) = \frac{\pi\cosh(t)}{4\cosh^2(\frac{\pi}{2}\sinh(t))} \tag{9}$$

in order to obtain a very rapid decrease of the Jacobian in the transformed integrand as $|t|$ increases. This renders the integral suitable for a trapezoidal rule approximation, leading to the integral approximation

$$I_h^{N_{eval}} = \sum_{k=-N_-}^{k=N_+} f(\phi(kh))\,\phi'(kh) \tag{10}$$

with mesh size h. The number of function evaluations is $N_{eval} = N_- + N_+ + 1$. The formula (9) is used in a product manner for multivariate integration.

4.2 Lattice Rules

Rank-1 lattice rules provide an integral approximation over the unit cube of the form

$$\mathcal{Q}f = \mathcal{Q}(\mathbf{z}, n)f = \frac{1}{n}\sum_{j=0}^{n-1} f(\{\frac{j}{n}\mathbf{z}\}) \tag{11}$$

where $\mathbf{z}$ is a generator vector with components $z \in \mathcal{Z}_n = \{1 \le z < n \mid gcd(z,n) = 1\}$, and $\{\mathbf{x}\}$ denotes a vector obtained by taking the fractional part of each component of $\mathbf{x}$ (see [37]). Classically n was taken prime [20,21] (so that $\mathcal{Z}_n = \{1, 2, \ldots, n-1\}$); extensions to non-prime n are given in [24,26]. We precomputed the generators $\mathbf{z}$ for various n in [8,9,11,12], using the component by component (CBC) algorithm [25,26] either directly or via Lattice Builder [22].

We further use a sequence embedding of lattice rules defined in [37], based on a rank-1 rule Q_0 and where each rule of the sequence applies a scaled copy of Q_0 to the subregions obtained by subdividing $\mathcal{C}_d$ into m equal parts in each of r coordinate directions. Denoting

$$\mathcal{Q}_r f = \mathcal{Q}_r^{(m)}(\mathbf{z}, n)f = \frac{1}{m^r n}\sum_{k_r=0}^{m-1} \cdots \sum_{k_1=0}^{m-1}\sum_{j=0}^{n-1} f(\{\frac{j}{n}\mathbf{z} + \frac{1}{m}(k_1, \ldots, k_r, 0, \ldots, 0)\}) \tag{12}$$

for n and m relatively prime, the points of Q_r are embedded in Q_{r+1} for $0 \le r < d$. Q_r has $m^r n$ points and is of rank r for $1 \le r \le d$, and Q_d is composed of m^d scaled copies of Q_0. An error estimate for Q_d is calculated using a sequence of rules $Q^{(i)}$, $1 \le i \le d$, of order $m^{d-1}n$ and embedded in Q_d [37].

A stochastic family of rules can be considered as proposed by Cranley and Patterson [6], by adding a random vector $\mathbf{\Delta}$ to the integration points,

$$\mathcal{Q}(\mathbf{z}, n, \mathbf{\Delta})f = \frac{1}{n}\sum_{j=0}^{n-1} f(\{\frac{j}{n}\mathbf{z} + \mathbf{\Delta}\}) \tag{13}$$

Averaging over a number of randomized (shifted) rule sums of the form (13) where $\mathbf{\Delta}$ has a multivariate uniform random distribution on $\mathcal{C}_d$ yields an integral approximation that has the integral $\mathcal{I}f$ as its expected value [37]. An error estimate is given in terms of the standard deviation.

5 Numerical Results

5.1 4-Loop Finite Diagram

The 4-loop diagram $G[4b]$ from [4] shown in Fig. 1(a), with $N = 11$ massless internal lines and integrand $C^{1+5\varepsilon}/D^{3+4\varepsilon}$ in (2), corresponds to an expansion

$$\mathcal{I}(\varepsilon) = G[4b] \sim -(-s)^{-3-4\varepsilon}\Gamma(3+4\varepsilon)\,(C_0 + C_1\varepsilon + \ldots) \tag{14}$$

For the finite diagram, the constant C_0 in (14) can be computed by setting $\varepsilon = 0$. The analytic value is $C_0 = 35\,\zeta(7) \approx 35.2922$. The value given for C_0 in [4] is 35.10. In [11] we reported 35.16 computed by a lattice rule with about 400M (million) points after a Sidi Ψ_6 transformation. Table 1 gives results by various lattice rules and embedded lattice rules (for $m = 1$ or 2 in (12)) on GPU and PEZY accelerators.

The GPU program is implemented in CUDA C and executed on the *thor* cluster at WMU, where the host process runs on a node with Intel Xeon E5-2670, 2.6 GHz dual CPU, and the lattice rule is evaluated on a Kepler-20m GPU, using 64 blocks and 512 or 1024 threads per block. The K20m has 2496 CUDA cores and 4800 MBytes of global memory. The lattice generator vector $\mathbf{z}$ is precomputed and communicated as a one-dimensional array of length d from the main program to the CUDA kernel. GPU results for lattice rules ($m = 1$) are given for n = 400M and 5^{13} points, and embedded versions with $m = 2$ for n = 10M and 100M. Note that the multiple M represents the next higher prime rounded down to the indicated multiple of a million function evaluations. Apart from the integral approximation, an absolute error estimate is also listed for $m = 2$. Furthermore, the implementation of the singular integrand C/D^3 requires testing that the denominator does not vanish before performing the division. We test $|D|^3 > Thr$, where (threshold) Thr is given in Table 1. A small positive value needs to be assigned particularly for $m > 1$, in view of the proximity of rule points to the boundaries of the domain.

Further results in Table 1 are obtained on the Suiren2 system of the High Energy Accelerator Research Organization (KEK) in Tsukuba, Japan, which is based on the PEZY-SC2 accelerator [29,40] and uses direct liquid immersion cooling. The configuration has 48 Xeon D-16C 1.3 GHz nodes and 8 PEZY-SC2

Table 1. Results of lattice and embedded lattice rules for $G[4b]$

n	m	*Result*	*Time[s]*	*Accel.*	*Thr*
400M	1	35.162005	1.83	K20m	0
5^{13}	1	35.163998	5.56	K20m	0
10M	2	35.265933	86.85	K20m	1.0 e-48
100M	2	35.279573	558.75	K20m	1.0 e-48
100M	2	35.279573	8.85	SC2	1.0 e-48
400M	2	35.289696	28.77	SC2	1.0 e-60
5^{13}	2	35.272921	83.82	SC2	1.0 e-48

boards per node. The node interconnect is Infiniband EDR. Each PEZY-SC2 board has 64 GB of memory, and the total amount of memory is 26,880 GB. The PEZY-SC2 programming model utilizes a kernel in an OpenCL-like language (PZCL) and a host program in C++. However, we generated the kernels via the Goose compiler interface [15], which takes a program instrumented with Goose compiler directives to parallelize the code. The SC2 results in Table 1 are obtained using 8 nodes and 8 tasks/node.

Table 2 provides results from ParAdapt on K20m GPU for $r = 4$, 8 and 16 regions per subdivision ($\#R = r$), various total numbers of integrand evaluations ($\#Ev$ in $B =$ billion), numbers of blocks ($\#Bks = g$) and threads per block ($\#TpB = b$) (where the notations r, g and b were introduced in Sect. 3). Entries with multiple values of $\#Bks$ and $\#TpB$ (separated by commas) are included with execution times (separated by '/') or a range of times.

All Table 2 runs are for threshold $Thr = 0$. Results for ParAdapt with up to 10B evaluations and $Thr = 1.0$ e-48 were included in [27]. This typically yields slightly lower integral approximations than $Thr = 0$, e.g., with 10B evaluations and $Thr = 1.0$ e-48 the result is 35.278714, and with $Thr = 1.0$ e-60 the result is 35.298195. Integral approximations for high numbers of evaluations are reported for comparison and do not change significantly, but the error estimate (bound) decreases. Some ParInt (long double) results obtained on the *thor* cluster with 64 processes on 4 nodes are also given.

For confirmation we further ran pySecDec 1.4.3 [5], which gave: 35.2379 ± 0.0175 using Vegas, and 35.2906 ± 0.0013 with QMC Korobov rank-3. With pySecDec 1.4.1 we previously calculated 35.2417 ± 0.0176 with Vegas. The number of sectors generated was 1968.

5.2 5-Loop Finite Diagram

The integrand for the 5-loop diagram $G[5]$ of Fig. 1(b) with $N = 14$ massless internal lines is $C^{2+6\varepsilon}/D^{4+5\varepsilon}$ in (2), and the expansion given in [4] is

$$\mathcal{I}(\varepsilon) = G[5] \sim (-s)^{-4-5\varepsilon}\Gamma(4+5\varepsilon)\,(C_0 + \ldots) \tag{15}$$

Table 2. Results of adaptive methods for $G[4b]$

ParAdapt						
#R	#Ev[B]	Result	E_a	Time[s]	#Bks	#TpB
4	15	35.329827	1.430 e-01	598–784	10,20,32,64	128,256,512
4	100	35.302547	4.828 e-02	8795	10	512
4	500	35.294968	1.931 e-02	32950	10	512
8	1	35.152057	9.861 e-01	28.0/27.1	64/20	128/512
8	10	35.307276	2.416 e-01	267.8/257.3	64/20	128/512
8	100	35.300016	5.906 e-01	2618/2517	64/20	128/512
8	500	35.294643	2.270 e-02	12897/20148	64/20	128/512
8	800	35.293851	1.722 e-02	20944	64	128
16	10	35.303108	3.956 e-01	166–193	64,40	128,512,256
16	100	35.303019	1.015 e-01	1695	64	256
16	200	35.299403	6.732 e-02	3263	64	256
16	500	35.296194	3.916 e-02	8481	64	256
16	800	35.294992	2.966 e-02	13656	64	256
ParInt						
	100	35.326279	1.50 e-01	3913		
	500	35.301808	5.98 e-02	19585		
	1000	35.297771	3.97 e-02	39195		
	2000	35.295374	2.61 e-02	78354		

with $C_0 = 40.53$. For the finite diagram we let $\varepsilon = 0$. Our computational experiments indicate a somewhat higher answer than 40.53, i.e., ≈ 42 rounded.[1] The analytic value is $42\,\zeta(9) \approx 42.0844$.

Table 3 displays results of large ParAdapt runs on Intel Xeon E5-2670, 2.6 GHz dual CPU with K20m (on *thor*), for 4 or 8 regions evaluated simultaneously on the GPU. The integral approximations, estimated absolute and relative errors, and times in seconds are shown. Sidi's Ψ_4 transformation was used. Some long double ParInt runs on 4 nodes/64 processes of the *thor* cluster are also listed.

With pySecDec 1.4.1 [5] we calculated an integral value of 41.9105 ± 0.0460 using Vegas; 27320 sectors were produced. The elapsed times were roughly around 40 h to generate the sectors, 40 h to compile, and 20.5 h for the integration. Using QMC Korobov rank-3 delivered the following results:

(i) 42.0941 ± 0.0221 obtained with pySecDec as an average over 32 randomized shifts of the form (13) in the range of 41.7559 to 42.3096, on AMD EPYC 7501 using 128 threads, in a computation time of about 14 days;

[1] For those interested in English literature, "42" is the answer to the Ultimate Question of Life, the Universe and Everything, cf., Douglas Adams, "The Hitchhiker's Guide to the Galaxy" [1].

Table 3. Results of adaptive methods for $G[5]$

ParAdapt					
r	*#Ev[B]*	*Result*	E_a	E_r	*Time[s]*
4	400	42.585786	1.183 e+00	2.778 e-02	5858
4	800	42.441678	8.972 e-01	2.114 e-02	10643
4	2000	42.323422	6.061 e-01	1.432 e-02	41105
4	4000	42.257989	4.401 e-01	1.041 e-02	67445
8	800	42.451987	9.765 e-01	2.300 e-02	11728
8	1200	42.387342	8.246 e-01	1.945 e-02	19593
8	2000	42.324564	6.621 e-01	1.564 e-02	19593
8	2500	42.300792	5.999 e-01	1.418 e-02	24671
8	3000	42.283284	5.527 e-01	1.307 e-02	29956
8	4000	42.257705	4.843 e-01	1.146 e-02	53734
ParInt					
	200	43.318466	1.59 e+00	3.670 e-02	8060
	1000	42.606834	8.97 e-01	2.105 e-02	40574
	2000	42.438615	7.06 e-01	1.666 e-02	81612

(ii) 42.1227 ± 0.0215, averaged over 32 shifts ranging from 41.891 to 42.3492, and run on Intel(R) Xeon(R) CPU E5-2687W v4 @ 3.00 GHz using 48 threads. The outputs for both (i) and (ii) include intermediate status reports; (ii) has one "status = exceeded max number of iterations" while (i) has six.

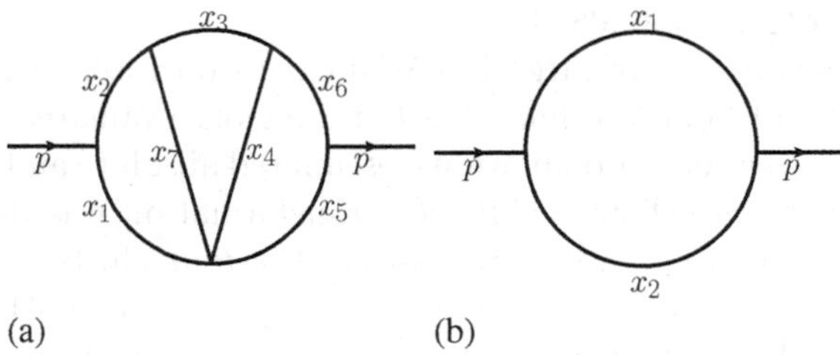

Fig. 5. Diagrams constituting Fig. 1(c)

5.3 4-Loop UV-Divergent Diagram

The diagram corresponding to $G[4a]$ in [4] and shown in Fig. 1(c) has $N = 9$ massless internal lines, leading to the integrand $C^{-1+5\varepsilon}/D^{1+4\varepsilon}$ in (2) and the expansion

$$\mathcal{I}(\varepsilon) = G[4a] \sim -\frac{1}{\varepsilon}(-s)^{-1-4\varepsilon}\Gamma(1+4\varepsilon)\,B(1-\varepsilon,1-\varepsilon)(C_{-1}+C_0\varepsilon+C_1\varepsilon^2+\ldots) \tag{16}$$

where $C_{-1} = 20\,\zeta(5) \approx 20.73855510$ and $C_0 = 50\,\zeta(6) - 80\,\zeta(5) - 4\,\zeta(3)^2 \approx -37.86683051$. With reference to Fig. 1(c), the diagram can be considered as consisting of two parts, given by Fig. 5(a) and (b). Figure 5(a) corresponds to the diagram 6(a) in [13] and gives rise to $C_{-1}+\ldots$, while the second part corresponds to $\frac{1}{\varepsilon}B(1-\varepsilon,1-\varepsilon)$ in Eq. (16). In [13] we were able to compute the integral for diagram Fig. 5(a) as 20.73855508 ≈ 20.73855510 with $E_a = 9\times10^{-8}$ by ParInt using 50B evaluations in 90 s (double) and 181 s (long double precision).

Our goal is to approximate the factor C_{-1} of $1/\varepsilon$ for the combined diagram of Fig. 1(c) directly. For an examination of the integrand, the polynomials C an D in the Feynman integral representation (2) are given by

$$\begin{aligned} C &= x_{28}x_{459}(x_{16}x_{37}+x_3x_7)+x_{167}(x_2x_{459}x_8+x_{28}x_{45}x_9)\\ D &= x_2x_8(x_{45}x_6x_7+x_4x_5x_{167}+x_{16}x_5x_9+x_{56}x_7x_9+x_1x_6x_{459})\\ &\quad + x_{28}((x_1x_5+x_4x_6)x_7x_9+x_3(x_{16}x_4x_5+x_1x_{45}x_6+(x_4x_5+x_{45}x_6)x_7\\ &\quad + (x_{16}x_5+x_1x_6)x_9+x_{56}x_7x_9)+x_4x_5(x_7x_9+x_{16}x_{79})+x_1x_6(x_7x_9+x_{45}x_{79})) \end{aligned} \tag{17}$$

with $x_9 = 1-\sum_{k=1}^{8} x_k$ and $x_{i_1\ldots i_j} = \sum_{k=i_1}^{i_j} x_k$ (where the indices i_1 to i_j are in increasing order). It can be seen that C and D vanish at boundaries of the 8-dimensional unit simplex, including: $C = D = 0$ if $x_2 = 0$ and $x_8 = 0$, or if $x_1 = 0$, $x_6 = 0$ and $x_7 = 0$, or if $x_4 = 0$, $x_5 = 0$ and $x_9 = 0$. Upon further inspection, the transformation (6) has a smoothening effect. After substitution, the C and D polynomials are factored as

$$\begin{aligned} C &= y_1^2\, y_{1m}\, y_2\, y_{2m}\, y_3\, A_1\\ D &= y_1^3\, y_{1m}\, y_2\, y_{2m}\, y_3\, A_2 \end{aligned} \tag{18}$$

where A_1 and A_2 are polynomials of the y_i variables. This produces a factor

$$\tilde{f} = \frac{(y_1^2\, y_{1m}\, y_2\, y_{2m}\, y_3)^{-1+5\varepsilon}}{(y_1^3\, y_{1m}\, y_2\, y_{2m}\, y_3)^{1+4\varepsilon}} = y_1^{-5-2\varepsilon}(y_{1m}\, y_2\, y_{2m}\, y_3)^{-2+\varepsilon} \tag{19}$$

that is partially cancelled out by the Jacobian $J = y_1^5\, y_{1m}^2\, y_2^2\, y_{2m}^2\, y_3\, y_5\, y_7$ in the transformed integrand, since

$$\tilde{f}J = y_1^{-2\varepsilon}(y_{1m}\, y_2\, y_{2m})^{\varepsilon}\, y_3^{-1+\varepsilon}\, y_5\, y_7. \tag{20}$$

As $\varepsilon \to 0$, the factor $y_3^{-1+\varepsilon}$ is especially problematic, and it determines the integrand behavior near $y_3 = 0$. This can be addressed by a simple transformation of the form

$$x = \varphi(t) = t^{\frac{1}{\varepsilon}} \tag{21}$$

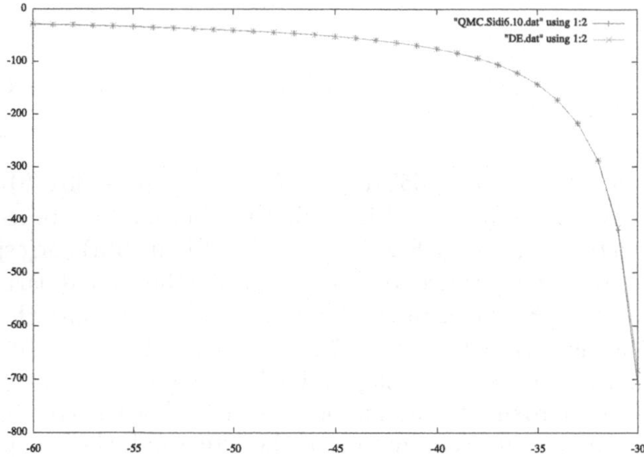

Fig. 6. Integration results $\varepsilon\mathcal{Q}(\varepsilon)$ as a function of $-\ell$ for $\varepsilon = 1.05^{-\ell}$

which alleviates the singularity (assuming g is smooth) in the integral

$$\begin{aligned}\int_0^1 x^{-1+\varepsilon} g(x)\,dx &= \int_0^1 t^{\frac{-1+\varepsilon}{\varepsilon}} \varphi'(t)\,g(\varphi(t))\,dt \\ &= \frac{1}{\varepsilon}\int_0^1 t^{-\frac{1}{\varepsilon}+1}\,t^{\frac{1}{\varepsilon}-1} g(\varphi(t))\,dt = \frac{1}{\varepsilon}\int_0^1 g(\varphi(t))\,dt \end{aligned} \tag{22}$$

For example, the transformation $x = t^2$ eliminates the singularity in $\int_0^1 1/\sqrt{x}\,dx$.

One numerical approach for regularization replaces ε by a small value; Fig. 6 displays integration values $\varepsilon\mathcal{Q}(\varepsilon)$ as ε decreases (from right to left). The horizontal axis is labeled with the exponents $(-\ell)$ of $\varepsilon = 1.05^{-\ell}$ and the vertical axis shows the approximations converging to $-C_{-1}$. Data plotted as '+' are obtained with QMC for the original integrand with C and D given by (17), and a lattice rule with 5^{13} points [12] after a Ψ_6 transformation. The '$\times$' values are computed with DE, cf. (10) with an even number of evaluations $N_{evals} = 128$, mesh size $h = 0.052565$ for the third dimension, and $N_{evals} = 32$, mesh size $4h$ for the other dimensions, and the integrand is coded using transformation (6) (without (21)). Figure 6 shows good agreement of the two methods for the range of $\varepsilon = 1.05^{-30} \approx 0.231378$ to $1.05^{-60} \approx 0.0535357$.

Table 4 gives a nonlinear extrapolation by the ϵ-algorithm [41] to $\varepsilon\mathcal{I}(\varepsilon)$ as $\varepsilon \to 0$ for the $G[4a]$ expansion (16). The entry sequence $\varepsilon_\ell\mathcal{Q}(\varepsilon_\ell)$ is computed with ParInt in long double precision, for the geometric sequence of $\varepsilon_\ell = 1.2^{-\ell}, \ell = 12, 13, \ldots$. ParInt is executed using 64 processes on 4 cluster nodes over MPI with 16 procs/node, and the maximum number of integrand evaluations set at 100B. The cube-to-simplex transformation (6) is applied, together with the substitution (21) in the y_3-direction for improving the accuracy. In Table 4, the entry sequence is given in the first column, followed by the corresponding absolute and relative error estimates in columns 2 and 3, respectively, the extrapolation results in columns 4–5, and the time in seconds in column 6.

Table 4. Extrapolation to $\varepsilon\mathcal{I}(\varepsilon)$ as $\varepsilon \to 0$ for $G[4a]$ diagram

$-\ell$	$R_\ell = -\varepsilon_\ell \mathcal{Q}(\varepsilon_\ell)$	E_a	E_r	*Extr. #*	*Extrapol. result*	*Time (s)*
−12	53.45672718118757	0.0461	0.000862			1004.5
−13	43.22634363076326	0.0120	0.000278			1013.6
−14	38.32164736111470	0.0153	0.000400	1	33.804663	998.2
−15	33.26266821115664	0.00917	0.000276	2	199.14802	1000.7
−16	30.41639542582190	0.00631	0.000207	3	26.755147	999.5
−17	28.33223869037645	0.00632	0.000223	4	22.632701	1001.0
−18	26.76557914867488	0.00555	0.000208	5	21.977077	1000.3
−19	25.56825964014690	0.00610	0.000238	6	21.354362	997.8
−20	24.63846007737136	0.00556	0.000226	7	20.423179	995.1
−21	23.90564850811475	0.00492	0.000206	8	20.470130	994.2
−22	23.32114992156617	0.00356	0.000153	9	20.145763	1001.1
−23	22.85256745147067	0.00304	0.000133	10	20.232313	1018.1
−24	22.47414242303327	0.00267	0.000119	11	20.149453	1025.0
−25	22.16670775499503	0.00228	0.000103	12	20.733395	1023.4
−26	21.91616295171026	0.00182	8.29 e-05	13	20.751014	1025.0

Note that the extrapolated results are selected from the extrapolation table by the ϵ-algorithm procedure. Furthermore, the differences between consecutive entry elements R_ℓ increase at the $4th$ entry element ($R_4 - R_3 \approx 5.06$) and decrease from there on, contributing to the spurious behavior at the $2nd$ extrapolation. However, the ϵ-algorithm achieves the extrapolation to $\varepsilon\mathcal{I}(\varepsilon)$, notwithstanding the steep behavior of the integrand over the small range of ε.

On a programming note, obtaining results for this type of integration problem with vanishing denominators requires that checks are implemented to protect against arithmetic exceptions in the function subprogram (such as division by 0). The integrand is set to zero in the vicinity of the singularity. However, the computation is sensitive to the value of the threshold as the function is evaluated for values of the denominator closer to zero, so that tests are needed that take the machine constants into account, such as the underflow and overflow numbers and machine precision.

6 Conclusions

We improved on numerical results in the literature for the loop integrals corresponding to two finite diagrams, 4-loop with $N = 11$ and 5-loop with $N = 14$, and obtained results for a 4-loop UV-divergent diagram with $N = 9$ internal lines. We found good agreement between different tools, using adaptive (ParInt and ParAdapt) and non-adaptive (DE and QMC) integration. ParAdapt, which performs its rule evaluations on GPU, appears to be a viable tool for dimensions

≥ 10. For lower dimensions, the number of points in the degree 7 rules is fairly low to justify the execution on GPU, although in future versions this may be addressed, e.g., by new adaptive schemes that enable generating multiple regions more effectively for the GPU application. Good agreement was also found with recent runs of the symbolic/numeric pySecDec system [5], which took multiple days with MC, or two weeks with QMC for the 5-loop diagram.

Acknowledgments. We acknowledge the support from the National Science Foundation under Award Number 1126438 that funded the cluster used for the computations with ParInt and ParAdapt in this paper. Furthermore we rely on the Grant-in-Aid for Scientific Research (17K05428) of JSPS, and on partial support by the Large Scale Computational Sciences with Heterogeneous Many-Core Computers, Grant-in-Aid for High Performance Computing with General Purpose Computers from MEXT (Ministry of Education, Culture, Sports, Science and Technology-Japan). We also sincerely thank the reviewers of this paper for their valuable comments.

References

1. Adams, D.: The Hitchhiker's Guide to the Galaxy. Pocket Books, Simon & Shuster, Inc. (1981). ISBN 0-671-52721-5
2. Berntsen, J., Espelid, T.O., Genz, A.: An adaptive algorithm for the approximate calculation of multiple integrals. ACM Trans. Math. Softw. **17**, 437–451 (1991)
3. Berntsen, J., Espelid, T.O., Genz, A.: Algorithm 698: DCUHRE-an adaptive multi-dimensional integration routine for a vector of integrals. ACM Trans. Math. Softw. **17**, 452–456 (1991)
4. Binoth, T., Heinrich, G.: Numerical evaluation of multi-loop integrals by sector decomposition. Nucl. Phys. B **680**, 375 (2004). hep-ph/0305234v1
5. Borowka, S., Heinrich, G., Jahn, S., Jones, S.P., Kerner, M., Schlenk, J.: A GPU compatible quasi-Monte Carlo integrator interfaced to pySecDec. Comput. Phys. Commun. **240**, 120–137 (2019). Preprint: arXiv:1811.11720v1 [hep-ph]. https://arxiv.org/abs/1811.11720. https://doi.org/10.1016/j.cpc.2019.02.015
6. Cranley, R., Patterson, T.N.L.: Randomization of number theoretic methods for multiple integration. SIAM J. Numer. Anal. **13**, 904–914 (1976)
7. De Ridder, L., Van Dooren, P.: An adaptive algorithm for numerical integration over an n-dimensional cube. J. Comput. Appl. Math. **2**(3), 207–210 (1976)
8. de Doncker, E., Almulihi, A., Yuasa, F.: High speed evaluation of loop integrals using lattice rules. J. Phys.: Conf. Series (JPCS) IOP Series **1085**, 052005 (2018). http://iopscience.iop.org/article/10.1088/1742-6596/1085/5/052005
9. de Doncker, E., Almulihi, A., Yuasa, F.: Transformed lattice rules for Feynman loop integrals. J. Phys.: Conf. Series (JPCS) IOP Series **1136**, 012002 (2018). https://doi.org/10.1088/1742-6596/1136/1/012002
10. de Doncker, E., Genz, A., Gupta, A., Zanny, R.: Tools for distributed adaptive multivariate integration on NOW's: PARINT1.0 release. In: Supercomputing 1998 (1998)
11. de Doncker, E., Yuasa, F., Almulihi, A.: Efficient GPU integration for multi-loop Feynman diagrams with massless internal lines. In: Okada, H., Atluri, S.N. (eds.) ICCES 2019. MMS, vol. 75, pp. 737–747. Springer, Cham (2020). https://doi.org/10.1007/978-3-030-27053-7_62

12. de Doncker, E., Yuasa, F., Almulihi, A., Nakasato, N., Daisaka, H., Ishikawa, T.: Numerical multi-loop integration on heterogeneous many-core processors. In: The Journal of Physics: Conference Series (JPCS), IOP Series (ACAT 2019) (2019, to appear)
13. de Doncker, E., Yuasa, F., Kato, K., Ishikawa, T., Kapenga, J., Olagbemi, O.: Regularization with numerical extrapolation for finite and UV-divergent multi-loop integrals. Comput. Phys. Commun. **224**, 164–185 (2018). https://doi.org/10.1016/j.cpc.2017.11.001
14. Genz, A., Malik, A.: An adaptive algorithm for numerical integration over an n-dimensional rectangular region. J. Comput. Appl. Math. **6**, 295–302 (1980)
15. Goose - GRAPE9-MPx - for goose version 1.5.0: K & F Computing Research Co. (2014). (in Japanese)
16. Hahn, T.: Cuba - a library for multidimensional numerical integration. Comput. Phys. Commun. **176**, 712–713 (2007). https://doi.org/10.1016/j.cpc.2007.03.006
17. Hahn, T., Pérez-Victoria, M.: Automated one-loop calculations in four and D dimensions. Comput. Phys. Commun. **118**(2–3), 153–165 (1999). hep-ph/9807565
18. 't Hooft, G., Veltman, M.: Scalar one-loop integrals. Nucl. Phys. B **153**, 365–401 (1979)
19. Ishikawa, T., Nakazawa, N., Yasui, Y.: Numerical calculation of the full two-loop electroweak corrections to muon (g-2). Phys. Rev. D **99**, 073004 (2019)
20. Korobov, N.M.: The approximate computation of multiple integrals. Dokl. Akad. Nauk SSSR **124**, 1207–1210 (1959). (Russian)
21. Korobov, N.M.: Properties and calculation of optimal coefficients. Doklady Akademii Nauk SSSR **132**, 1009–1012 (1960). Russ. Eng. trans. Soviet Math. Doklady **1**, 696–700
22. L'Equyer, P., Munger, D.: Algorithm 958: lattice builder: a general software tool for constructing rank-1 lattice rules. ACM Trans. Math. Softw. **42**(2), 15:1–15:30 (2016)
23. MPI. http://www-unix.mcs.anl.gov/mpi/index.html
24. Niederreiter, H.: Existence of good lattice points in the sense of hlawka. Monatshefte für Mathematik **86**, 203–219 (1978)
25. Nuyens, D., Cools, R.: Fast algorithms for component-by-component construction of rank-1 lattice rules in shift-invariant reproducing kernel Hilbert spaces. Math. Comput. **75**, 903–920 (2006)
26. Nuyens, D., Cools, R.: Fast component-by-component construction of rank-1 lattice rules with a non-prime number of points. J. Complex. **22**, 4–28 (2006)
27. Olagbemi, O.E.: Scalable algorithms and hybrid parallelization strategies for multivariate integration with ParAdapt and CUDA. Ph.D. thesis, Western Michigan University (2019)
28. Olagbemi, O.E., de Doncker, E.: Scalable algorithms for multivariate integration with ParAdapt and CUDA. In: Proceedings of 2019 International Conference on Computational Science and Computational Intelligence. IEEE Computer Society (2019). https://american-cse.org/csci2019/pdfs/CSCI2019-14dQVW1stBtXVEInMQPd3t/558400a481/558400a481.pdf
29. PEZY Computing/Exascaler Inc. http://www.exascaler.co.jp/
30. Piessens, R., de Doncker, E., Überhuber, C.W., Kahaner, D.K.: QUADPACK. A Subroutine Package for Automatic Integration. Springer Series in Computational Mathematics, vol. 1. Springer, Heidelberg (1983). https://doi.org/10.1007/978-3-642-61786-7
31. Rice, J.R.: A metalgorithm for adaptive quadrature. J. Assoc. Comput. Mach. **22**, 61–82 (1975)

32. Ruijl, B., Herzog, F., Ueda, T., Vermaseren, J.A.M., Vogt, A.: The R^*-operation and five loops calculations. In: 13th International Symposium on Radiative Corrections (2017)
33. Ruijl, B., Herzog, F., Ueda, T., Vermaseren, J.A.M., Vogt, A.: The R^*-operation and combinatorial challenges at five loops. J. Phys.: Conf. Series (JPCS) IOP Series **1085**, 052006 (2018). https://doi.org/10.1088/1742-6596/1085/5/052006
34. Ruijl, B., Ueda, T., Vermaseren, J.A.M.: Forcer, a FORM program for the parametric reduction of four-loop massless propagator diagrams. Technical report, 2017-019, Nikhef (2017). arXiv:1704.06650 [hep-ph]
35. Sanders, J., Kandrot, E.: CUDA by Example: An Introduction to General-Purpose GPU Programming. Pearson, London (2010)
36. Sidi, A.: A new variable transformation for numerical integration. Int. Ser. Numer. Math. **112**, 359–373 (1993)
37. Sloan, I., Joe, S.: Lattice Methods for Multiple Integration. Oxford University Press, Oxford (1994)
38. Sugihara, M.: Optimality of the double exponential formula - functional analysis approach. Numer. Math. **75**(3), 379–395 (1997)
39. Takahasi, H., Mori, M.: Double exponential formulas for numerical integration. Publ. Res. Inst. Math. Sci. **9**(3), 721–741 (1974)
40. Torii, S., Ishikawa, H.: ZettaScaler: liquid immersion cooling manycore based supercomputer. Technical report, ExaScaler Inc., PEZY Computing K. K. (2017)
41. Wynn, P.: On a device for computing the $e_m(s_n)$ transformation. Math. Tables Aids Comput. **10**, 91–96 (1956)

Performance Evaluation of Strassen Matrix Multiplication Supporting Triple-Double Precision Floating-Point Arithmetic

Tomonori Kouya(✉)

Shizuoka Institute of Science and Technology,
2200-2 Toyosawa, Fukuroi 437-8555, Japan
kouya.tomonori@sist.ac.jp

Abstract. The Strassen matrix multiplication can be categorized into divide-and-conquer algorithms, and they are known as the most efficient algorithms. We previously implemented them supporting multiple precision floating-point arithmetic using MPFR and Bailey's QD libraries and have shown their effectiveness in our papers and open-source codes. In preparation for a future release, we have introduced an optimized triple-word floating-point arithmetic proposed by Fabiano et al., and we found its utility in our implementation of multiple precision matrix multiplication. In this paper, we demonstrate the effectiveness of the Strassen triple-double precision matrix multiplication through performance evaluation compared to those based on QD and MPFR libraries.

Keywords: Triple-word precision arithmetic · Matrix multiplication · Strassen algorithm

1 Introduction

All types of scientific computations require precise numerical results that satisfy users owing to their performance levels. If the targeting problems are ill-conditioned and cannot be solved with the standard IEEE 754 double precision floating-point arithmetic (binary64), then multiple precision floating-point arithmetic with a longer mantissa than binary64 must be used for their precise solutions. In this case, a reliable and stable multiple precision library, such as QD [3] by Bailey et al. or MPFR [4], should be chosen to solve the problems on the current computational environment. The QD library, which is one of the multi-component models of multiple precision floating-point arithmetic, supports only two types of floating-point arithmetic: double-double (DD, 106 bits of mantissa) and quad-double (QD, 212 bits). The QD library performs better for the same mantissa lengths than the MPFR, which supports any length of mantissa, based on the optimized natural number kernels of GNU MP (GMP) [5].

Triple-double (TD, 159 bits = 53 bits×3), which is based on triple-word arithmetic proposed by Flippo et al., is a type of multi-component model including

O. Gervasi et al. (Eds.): ICCSA 2020, LNCS 12253, pp. 163–176, 2020.
https://doi.org/10.1007/978-3-030-58814-4_12

QD. They are expected to be faster than MPFR for the same length of mantissa and also offer a mid-level performance and accuracy when compared to DD and QD. Numerical experiments have shown a good performance TD computation compared with CAMPARY [2], which supports any length of mantissa based on binary32 and binary64.

We have already released multiple precision matrix multiplication library, BNCmatmul [10] using divide-and-conquer algorithms, including Strassen, and parallelized various precision matrix multiplication based on DD, QD, and MPFR libraries with OpenMP [7,8]. In comparison with Rgemm in MPLAPACK (MBLAS) [6], it produces better performance for large-sized matrices. We introduced TD arithmetic to BNCmatmul and then confirmed that TD matrix multiplication requires approximately five times larger computational time than DD and about half the computational time of QD.

In this paper, we describe the software layers of BNCmatmul and MBLAS, analyze how to parallelize the Strassen algorithm, compare the performance of BNCmatmul with Rgemm of MBLAS, and implement TD arithmetic based on triple-word arithmetic. Then, we carry out numerical experiments of TD Strassen matrix multiplication and compare their performance and accuracy with DD and QD on both Ryzen and Corei7 computational environments. Finally, we conclude our tasks and present our future works.

2 Structure of BNCmatmul and Its Performance

We have already released BNCmatmul, which features parallelized Strassen and Winograd multiple precision matrix multiplication based on OpenMP, QD-based C inline functions and MPFR. By utilizing the divide-and-conquer algorithms to reduce the number of arithmetic algorithms, high efficiency for large size matrix multiplications has been achieved over Rgemm in MBLAS and MPLAPACK.

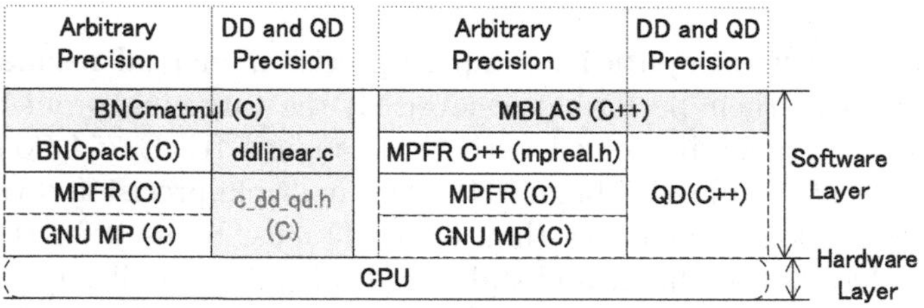

Fig. 1. Software layers of BNCmatmul and MPLAPACK(MBLAS)

In Fig. 1, we illustrate the differences and similarities of the software structure between BNCmatmul and MPLAPACK. Both these libraries are based on QD or QD-based C inline functions for DD and QD accuracy and MPFR for arbitrary accuracy. MPLAPACK is completely written in C++ and its classes (QD and MPFR C++). In contrast, BNCmatmul is written in C-language, QD-based inline C functions (c_dd_qd.h), and original MPFR functions. Our implementation of the TD arithmetic is appended to c_dd_qd.h, reusing the same error-free transformation as incline C functions for the DD and QD arithmetic.

In the remaining section, the parallelized Strassen algorithms are explained and the performance of matrix multiplication provided by BNCmatmul is compared with Rgemm of MBLAS.

3 Parallelized Strassen and Winograd Algorithms

For given matrices A and B, the Strassen and Winograd algorithms for matrix multiplication $C := AB$, being categorized in the divide-and-conquer algorithms, can reduce the number of additions and multiplications compared to the normal matrix multiplication, particularly for large-sized matrices. Thus, these algorithms provide better performance when used together with large multiple precision floating-point arithmetic. We confirmed their efficiency through benchmark tests and applications of LU decomposition [7,8].

The algorithms we implemented in BNCmatmul and those in parallelization are illustrated in Fig. 2 and Fig. 3, where A, B and C are divided as

$$A := \begin{bmatrix} A_{11} & A_{12} \\ A_{21} & A_{22} \end{bmatrix}, \; B := \begin{bmatrix} B_{11} & B_{12} \\ B_{21} & B_{22} \end{bmatrix}$$
$$\Longrightarrow C := AB = \begin{bmatrix} C_{11} & C_{12} \\ C_{21} & C_{22} \end{bmatrix}.$$

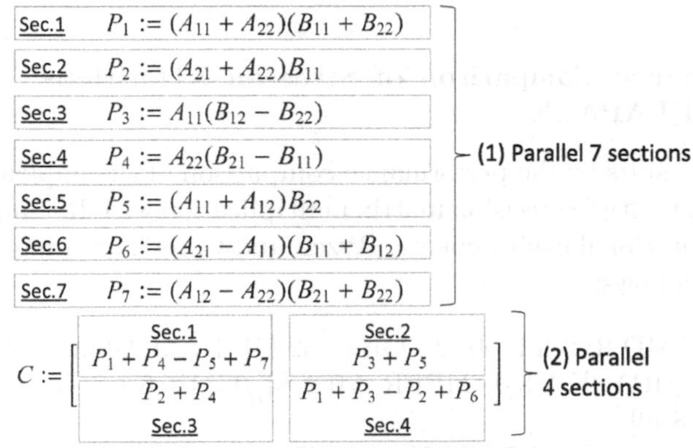

Fig. 2. Parallelized Strassen algorithm

The Strassen and Winograd matrix multiplications we implemented were parallelized in each parallelizable part of those constructed with groups of `omp section`. Although the Winograd matrix multiplication is less complex than the Strassen matrix multiplication, the part of recursive self-calls of both algorithms

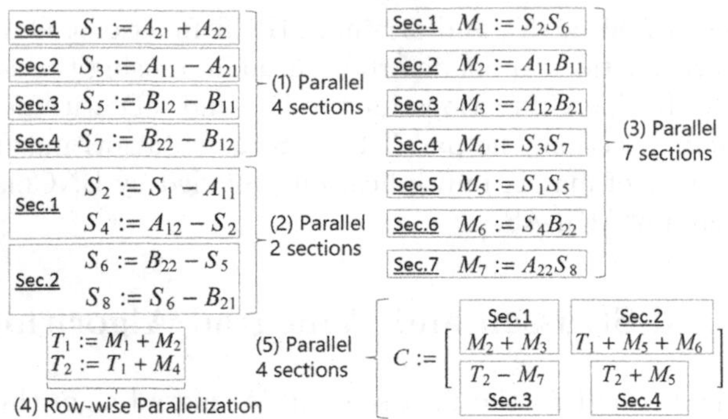

Fig. 3. Parallelized Winograd algorithms

can be divided and executed on seven threads. When the size of the matrices does not fit the Strassen and Winograd algorithms, our implementation requires parallelized dynamic padding and peeling to produce user-defined size of matrix products. Although it is well known that the number of computations of the Winograd algorithm is lesser than that of Strassen, no significant difference in computational time or effectiveness of parallelization was observed among these algorithms in DD, QD, and MPFR arbitrary precision arithmetic. Therefore, we focus on the Strassen algorithm in the rest of this paper.

Parallelization of the Strassen and Winograd matrix multiplication mentioned above can present effectiveness in DD and QD precision arithmetic, except in the case of MPFR, where our implementation produced lower performance than Rgemm.

3.1 Performance Comparison of Strassen Algorithms with MPLAPACK

We depict our results by the performance comparison of the implemented parallelized Strassen multiple precision matrix multiplication with Rgemm of MBLAS. The two computational environments, Ryzen and Corei7, are prepared for those evaluations as follows:

Ryzen AMD Ryzen 1700 (2.7 GHz), 32 GB RAM, Ubuntu 16.04.5 x86_64, GCC 5.4.0, MPACK 0.8.0, MPFR 4.0.2 [4]/GMP 6.1.2 [5], QD 2.3.22 [3], BNCpack 0.8 [9]

Corei7 Intel Core i7-9700K (3.6GHz), 16 GB RAM, Ubuntu 18.04.2 x86_64, GCC 7.3.0, MPACK 0.8.0, MPFR 4.0.2 [4]/GMP 6.1.2 [5], QD 2.3.22 [3], BNCpack 0.8 [9]

C++ options `g++ -O3 -std=c++11 -fopenmp`

MPLAPACK, which was downloaded from GitHub on December 2019, was installed with QD and MPFR/GMP libraries included in it. BNCmatmul is also commonly utilized with these libraries. Strassen algorithms are recursively called until the number of rows or columns of divided matrices is less than or equal to 32.

MBLAS of MPLAPACK provides the same type of functions and order of arguments as the original reference BLAS. The elements of matrix are supposed to be stored as column-major order. The Rgemm used in comparison, is one of the functions in MBLAS to calculate $C := \alpha AB + \beta C$, so we set $\alpha = 1$ and $\beta = 0$ to obtain the result of a simple matrix multiplication of $C := AB$. All the elements of the matrices are stored along with in column-major layout for the benefit of Rgemm.

Aside from that, our implemented matrix multiplication functions are supposed to utilize matrices along with row-major layout and written in C-language, but we used common benchmark programs written in C++ to compare them with Rgemm.

The square matrices A and B, used in our benchmark tests, are as follows:

$$A = \left[\sqrt{5}\,(i+j-1)\right]_{i,j=1}^{n},\quad B = \left[\sqrt{3}\,(n-i)\right]_{i,j=1}^{n}.$$

Due to all the positive real elements of A and B, precise elements of C can be derived through our benchmark tests of $C := AB$, and the lack of one or two significant decimal digits were found in all sizes and precision arithmetic.

QD-Based Matrix Multiplication. Figure 4, illustrates the performance comparison of serial Strassen, DD and QD matrix multiplication with Rgemm. These graphs depict plots of the ratio of computational time with those of Rgemm/Strassen. Thus, the plotted number over 1 means that our Strassen matrix multiplication is faster than Rgemm. In these figures, we show the thresholds of dimension and ratio (≥ 1) such as $767, 1.04$ in DD matrix multiplication on Ryzen7, over which our Strassen matrix multiplication is faster than Rgemm. Currently, there is no existence of parallelized Rgemm with the QD library, and those figures illustrate the results of serial matrix multiplication. As per the graphs, we can understand that our Strassen matrix multiplication is faster for large-sized matrices in any cases of DD or QD.

In Fig. 5, we illustrate the efficiency of our parallelized Strassen matrix multiplication. These figures plot the performance improvement ratio of computational time with 2, 4, and 8 threads against serial computational time. According to these figures, our parallelized Strassen matrix multiplication can achieve expected efficiency for both DD and QD arithmetic.

Due to these results for both DD and QD computations, TD Strassen matrix multiplication can be expected to show similar efficiency and performance improvement.

MPFR-Based Matrix Multiplication. For comparison with MPFR-based matrix multiplication, we illustrate our MPFR-based Strassen matrix multiplication against Rgemm in Fig. 6. MPFR Rgemm is parallelized with OpenMP and provides expected improvement. The Strassen implementation and Rgemm ratio

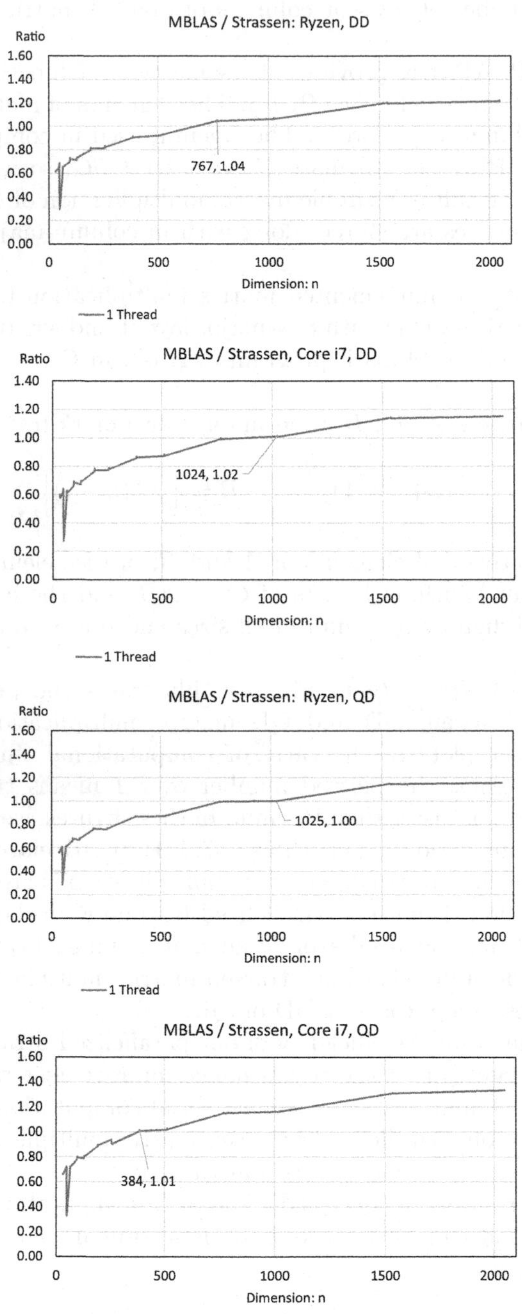

Fig. 4. Comparison of DD and QD matrix multiplication: BNCmatmul/Rgemm vs. Dimension of square matrices

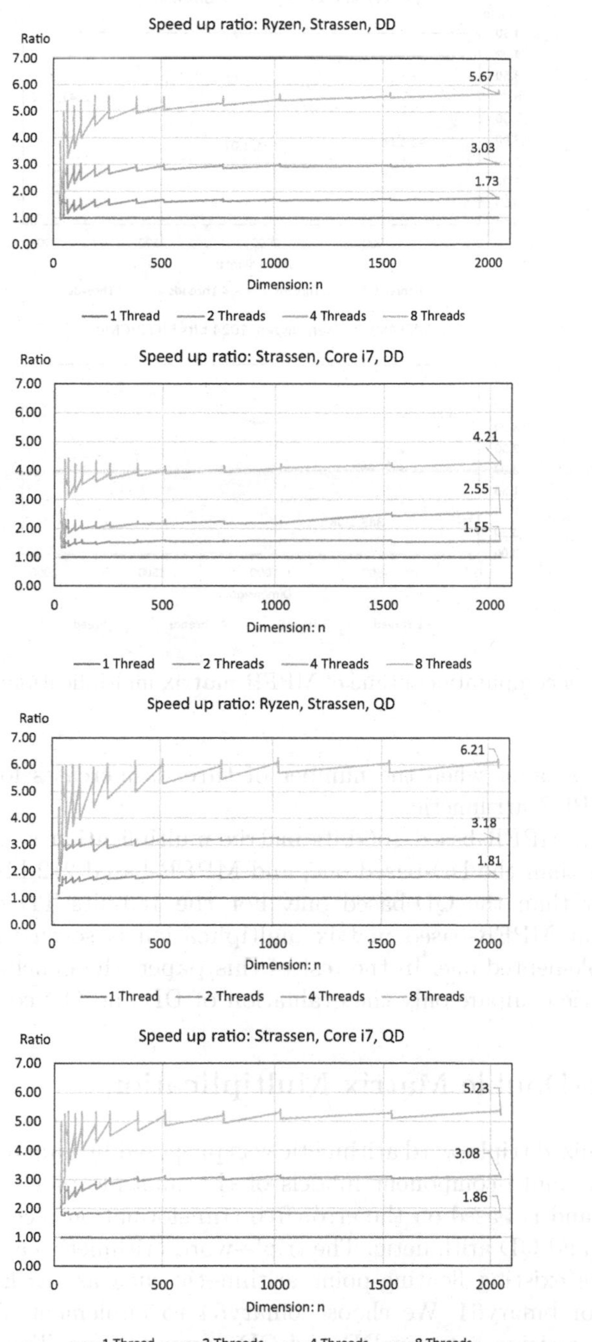

Fig. 5. Performance improvement ratio of parallelized DD an QD Strassen matrix multiplication

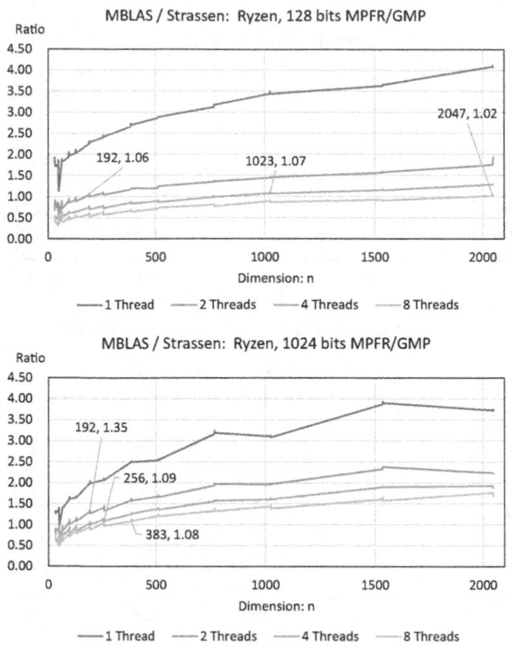

Fig. 6. Ratio of computational time of MPFR matrix multiplication: Rgemm/Strassen

will become smaller when the number of threads increases for both 128- and 1024-bits MPFR arithmetic.

Primarily, MPFR-based 106-bits matrix multiplication is approximately 18 times slower than the DD-based one, and MPFR-based 212-bits one about two times slower than the QD-based one. For the 159-bits TD computation, we observed that MPFR-based matrix multiplication is seven times slower than our TD-implemented one. In the rest of this paper, the benchmark tests of the TD arithmetic compare only the evaluation of DD and QD computations.

4 Triple-Double Matrix Multiplication

A well-optimized triple-word arithmetic was proposed by Fabiano et al. [1], which is one of the multi-component models of the multiple precision floating-point arithmetic, and is based on the error-free transformation techniques commonly used in DD and QD arithmetic. The triple-word arithmetic can be implemented by using the existing floating-point arithmetic such as IEEE single precision (binary32) or binary64. We choose binary64 to implement TD arithmetic as the middle precision between DD and QD computations. The TD matrix multiplication we implemented utilizes TD addition (TDadd) and TD multiplication (TDmul) in which they proposed a set of TD arithmetic. In the remaining section, we describe the algorithms for TD and its related arithmetic.

Error-free transformation algorithms: QuickTwoSum, TwoSum and TwoProd-FMA (Algorithm 1–3) are used as pieces to construct the TD arithmetic. In this paper, the entire floating-point variables are binary64, and $\oplus$, $\ominus$, $\otimes$ and FMA mean standard binary64 arithmetic.

Algorithm 1 (s, e) := QuickTwoSum(a, b)

$s := a \oplus b$
$e := b \ominus (s \ominus a)$
return (s, e)

Algorithm 2 (s, e) := TwoSum(a, b)

$s := a \oplus b$
$v := s \ominus a$
$e := (a \ominus (s \ominus v)) \oplus (b \ominus v)$
return (s, e)

TwoProd functions are implemented in two ways: one with utilizing Split function of binary64 value and another with utilizing fused multiply-add (FMA) arithmetic. In our implementation of TD arithmetic, we choose TwoProd-FMA because it is the simplest and native FMA arithmetic that is available on both Ryzen and Core i7 computational environments.

Algorithm 3 (p, e) := TwoProd(a, b)

$p := a \otimes b$
$e :=$ FMA$(a, b, -p)$ $(= a \times b - p)$
return (p, e)

4.1 Algorithms of TD Arithmetic

Triple-word precision floating-point numbers are constructed by three pieces of existing floating-point numbers. We express each element of triple-word floating-point number as $x := (x_0, x_1, x_2)$, in which all the pieces x_i $(i = 0, 1, 2)$ are expressed with binary64.

Renormalization: VecSum and VSEB(k). All types of triple-word arithmetic require renormalization just before returning the results as correct triple-word floating-point number. For this process, Fabiano et al. proposed the combination of VecSum (Algorithm 4) and VSEB(k) (VecSumErrBlanch, Algorithm 5).

Algorithm 4 $(e_0, ..., e_{n-1}) := \text{VecSum}(x_0, ..., x_{n-1})$

$s_{n-1} := x_{n-1}$
for $i = n - 2$ to 0 **do**
  $(s_i, e_{i+1}) := \text{TwoSum}(x_i, s_{i+1})$
end for
$e_0 := s_0$
return $(e_0, ..., e_{n-1})$

Algorithm 5 $(y_0, ..., y_{k-1}) := \text{VSEB}(k)(e_0, ..., e_{n-1})$

$j := 0$
$\epsilon_0 := e_0$
for $i = 0$ to $k - 3$ **do**
  $(r_i, \epsilon_{i+1}^t) := \text{TwoSum}(\epsilon_i, e_{i+1})$
  if $\epsilon_{i+1}^t \neq 0$ **then**
    $y_j := r_i$
    $\epsilon_{i+1} := \epsilon_{i+1}^t$
    $j := j + 1$
  else
    $\epsilon_{i+1} := r_i$
  end if
end for
$(y_j, y_{j+1}) := \text{TwoSum}(\epsilon_{k-2}, e_{k-1})$
$y_{j+2} := 0, ..., y_{k-1} := 0$
return $(y_0, ..., y_{k-1})$

TDadd and TDmul. TDadd (Algorithm 6), addition of two triple-word numbers, add $x := (x_0, x_1, x_2)$ and $y := (y_0, y_1, y_2)$, and then produce the sum $r = (r_0, r_1, r_2) := x + y$. At first, it merges x and y and then executes VecSum and VSEB(3) to renormalize and return r.

Algorithm 6 $r := \text{TDadd}(x, y)$

$(z_0, ..., z_5) := \text{Merge}(x_0, x_1, x_2, y_0, y_1, y_2)$
$(e_0, ..., e_5) := \text{VecSum}(z_0, ..., z_5)$
$(r_0, r_1, r_2) := \text{VSEB}(3)(e_0, ..., e_5)$
return (r_0, r_1, r_2)

Fabiano et al. proposed two types of triple-word multiplications, one is more accurate and the other one is faster. We choose the faster version of multiplication (Algorithm 7) due to the lesser number of computations.

TDadd and TDmul are only required for matrix multiplication. For this, we implement the arithmetic with error-free transformation functions, which have been prepared in `c_dd_qd.h`. Therefore, we can compare the performance and accuracy of DD, QD, and TD matrix multiplications with common the single inline C library.

Algorithm 7 $r := \text{TDmul}(x, y)$

$(z_{00}^{\text{up}}, z_{00}^{\text{lo}}) := \text{TwoProd}(x_0, y_0)$
$(z_{01}^{\text{up}}, z_{01}^{\text{lo}}) := \text{TwoProd}(x_0, y_1)$
$(z_{10}^{\text{up}}, z_{10}^{\text{lo}}) := \text{TwoProd}(x_1, y_0)$
$(b_0, b_1, b_2) := \text{VecSum}(z_{00}^{\text{lo}}, z_{01}^{\text{up}}, z_{10}^{\text{up}})$
$c := \text{FMA}(x_1, y_1, b_2)$
$z_{31} := \text{FMA}(x_0, y_2, z_{10}^{\text{lo}})$
$z_{32} := \text{FMA}(x_2, y_0, z_{01}^{\text{lo}})$
$z_3 := z_{31} \oplus z_{32}$
$s_3 := c \oplus z_3$
$(e_0, e_1, e_2, e_3) := \text{VecSum}(z_{00}^{\text{up}}, b_0, b_1, s_3)$
$r_0 := e_0$
$(r_1, r_2) := \text{VSEB}(2)(e_1, e_2, e_3)$
return (r_0, r_1, r_2)

The complexity of DD, TD, and QD arithmetic are shown in Table 1. The addition and multiplication of DD and QD arithmetic are fast (sloppy) versions in the QD library.

Table 1. Number of elementary arithmetic

	$\oplus$, $\ominus$	$\otimes$	FMA	if	Machine epsilon
DDadd and DDmul	21	3	1	0	1.2e–32
TDadd and TDmul	80	3	5	8	1.4e–48
QDadd and QDmul	294	13	10	10	1.5e–64

The total amount of computations shows that TDadd and TDmul require about 3.8 times more complexity compared to that of DDadd and DDmul, and they require about 0.3 times compared with QDadd and QDmul. We can expect a mid-level performance and accuracy between DD and QD arithmetic.

4.2 Benchmark Tests for TD-Based Matrix Multiplication

The computational time (unit: second) obtained through our benchmark tests with 1023–1025 and 2047–2049 dimensional square matrix multiplications are shown in Fig. 7. In these figures, we can see each seconds of DD, TD, and QD Strassen matrix multiplication. The Ryzen and Corei7 processors have 8 cores, and, thus, we depict serial and parallelized computational time with OpenMP with 8 threads. Table 2 shows maximum relative errors in all elements of C generated from computations of Fig. 7, so we can confirm that our matrix multiplications obtained expected accuracy with DD, TD and QD arithmetic.

According to these figures, any dimensional TD matrix multiplication requires about five times of DD and approximately half of QD for serial and

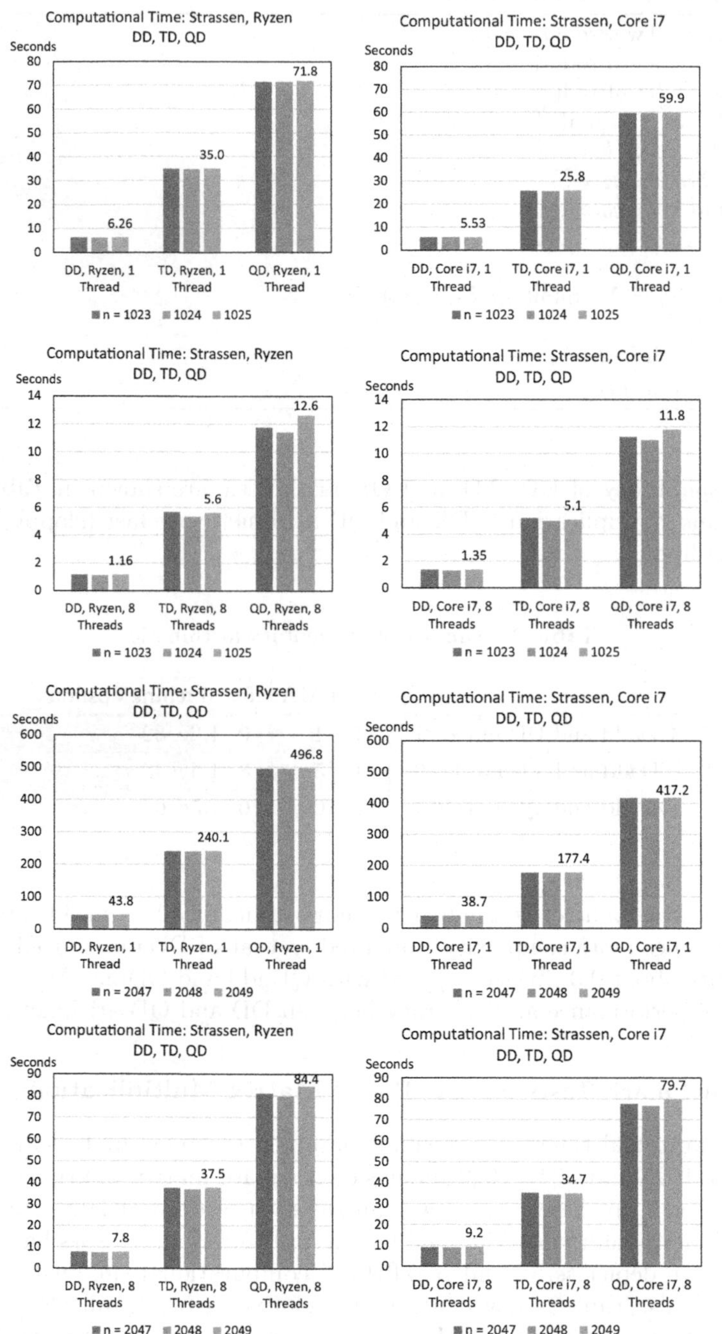

Fig. 7. Computational time (unit: second) of TD Strassen matrix multiplication

Table 2. Maximum relative error of elements of C arisen by Strassen algorithm

Dimension	1023	1024	1025
DD	4.8e–30	4.3e–30	3.4e–30
TD	1.3e–46	1.3e–46	1.4e–46
QD	4.3e–63	4.7e–63	5.0e–63
Dimension	2047	2048	2049
DD	9.3e–30	9.9e–30	1.1e–29
TD	3.2e–46	4.0e–46	3.4e–46
QD	1.2e–62	1.1e–62	9.8e–63

parallel cases. These ratios against DD and QD matrix multiplications are reasonable, as shown in Table 1.

The performance improvement ratio of TD Strassen matrix multiplication is illustrated in Fig. 8.

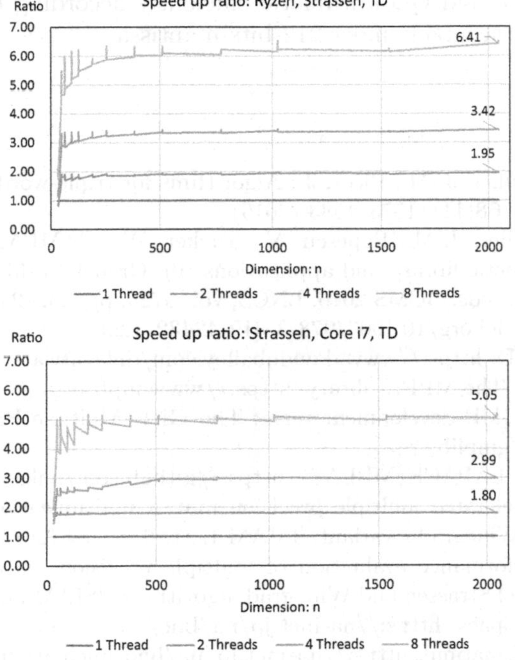

Fig. 8. Performance improvement ration of parallelized TD Strassen matrix multiplication

For any dimensional square matrices, parallelized TD Strassen shows similar level of speedup ratio against the number of OpenMP threads compared with Fig. 5.

5 Conclusion and Future Works

We implemented TD arithmetic based on Fabiano et al.'s proposed triple-word floating-point arithmetic and demonstrated that we can obtain the expected performance and accuracy for TD Strassen matrix multiplication. They require approximately five times more computational time compared to DD matrix multiplication and about half computational time against QD. The parallelization improvement ratio with OpenMP can be achieved at the expected levels as compared with DD and QD computations. Currently, the QD library does not contain a TD class; thus, we cannot compare our TD matrix multiplication with MPLAPACK, but our TD matrix multiplication would be faster than Rgemm of MPLAPACK for larger sizes of matrices if TD class existed.

For future works, we will release a new BNCmatmul, including TD implementation, and verify the efficiency for TD of LU decomposition. We can also customize DD, TD, and QD arithmetic efficiently according to users' requirements and achieve accuracy under 212-bits mantissa.

References

1. Fabiano, N., Muller, J.-M., Picot, J.: Algorithms for triple-word arithmetic. IEEE Trans. Comput. **68**(11), 1573–1583 (2019)
2. Joldes, M., Muller, J.-M., Popescu, V., Tucker, W.: CAMPARY: cuda multiple precision arithmetic library and applications. In: Greuel, G.-M., Koch, T., Paule, P., Sommese, A. (eds.) ICMS 2016. LNCS, vol. 9725, pp. 232–240. Springer, Cham (2016). https://doi.org/10.1007/978-3-319-42432-3_29
3. Bailey, D.H.: QD. https://www.davidhbailey.com/dhbsoftware/
4. MPFR Project, The MPFR library. https://www.mpfr.org/
5. Granlaud, T.: GMP development team: The GNU Multiple Precision arithmetic library. https://gmplib.org/
6. Nakata, M.: MPLAPACK(MBLAS). https://github.com/nakatamaho/mplapack
7. Kouya, T.: Accelerated multiple precision matrix multiplication using Strassen's algorithm and Winograd's variant. JSIAM Lett. **6**, 81–84 (2014)
8. Kouya, T.: Performance evaluation of multiple precision matrix multiplications using parallelized Strassen and Winograd algorithms. JSIAM Lett. **8**, 21–24 (2016)
9. Kouya, T.: BNCpack. https://na-inet.jp/na/bnc/
10. Kouya, T.: BNCmatmul. https://na-inet.jp/na/bnc/bncmatmul-0.2.tar.bz2

Acceleration of Boltzmann Equation for Core-Collapse Supernova Simulations on PEZY-SC Processors

Hideo Matsufuru[1(✉)] and Kohsuke Sumiyoshi[2]

[1] High Energy Accelerator Research Organization (KEK), 1-1 Oho, Tsukuba, Ibaraki 305-0801, Japan
hideo.matsufuru@kek.jp

[2] National Institute of Technology, Numazu College, 3600 Ooka, Numazu, Shizuoka 410-8501, Japan
sumi@numazu-ct.ac.jp

Abstract. Performing large scale numerical simulations is essential to understand the explosion mechanism of core-collapse supernovae. It is mandatory to solve a multi-physics system described by coupled equations of hydrodynamics and neutrino-radiation transfer in multi-dimensions. Since the neutrino transfer is in principle governed by the Boltzmann equation in six-dimensional coordinates, numerical simulations require large computational resources. In this work, we focus on the acceleration of the Boltzmann equation by exploiting the PEZY-SC processors. The PEZY-SC processor possesses many-core MIMD cores on each chip, and works as an accelerator device similarly to GPUs. We examine two simulation codes for the neutrino transport in the supernova simulations. One is a radiation-hydrodynamics code under the spherical symmetry. The second is a 6D Boltzmann equation solver applied to two-dimensional space. We examine the bottlenecks of these codes and offload them to the PEZY-SC devices. The performance is measured on the Suiren Blue and Suiren2 systems at KEK.

Keywords: Many-core accelerator · PEZY-SC · Boltzmann equation · Supernova explosion · Radiation-hydrodynamics

1 Introduction

Core-collapse supernova explosions are phenomena that occurs at the end of stellar life whose mass is larger than 10 times the solar mass. The gravitational compression of Fe core and the subsequent core bounce launches the shock wave that leads to the explosion. Despite the long history of investigations based on this general idea, the detailed mechanism of the core-collapse supernova explosion is still elusive, because only prohibitively large-scale numerical simulations can explore the multi-dimensional mechanism with multi-physics in multi-scale [1,2]. Precise understanding of the supernova explosion is one of the essential

O. Gervasi et al. (Eds.): ICCSA 2020, LNCS 12253, pp. 177–192, 2020.
https://doi.org/10.1007/978-3-030-58814-4_13

issues in astrophysics in order to reveal the origin of heavy elements, the formation of compact objects (neutron stars or black holes), and observation of neutrino bursts and gravitational waves.

Among the ingredients of this multi-physics system, the Boltzmann equation for the neutrino radiation regulates the scale of numerical simulations, since its time evolution is described by a six-dimensional (space and neutrino momentum) distribution function. Increasing the resolution of space and neutrino momentum, the numerical cost rapidly increases. Fully six-dimensional computation of the Boltzmann equation has become feasible only recently. To provide quantitative theoretical prediction at the level demanded for comparison with observational data, however, it is essential to systematically study variety of massive stars and the effect of many components of microphysics, such as the equation of state for the dense matter and the neutrino reaction processes.

Recent supercomputers are categorized into two types. One is massively parallel clusters whose nodes are composed of multi-cores and shared memory, such as the K-computer and the forthcoming Fugaku supercomputer in Japan. The other type makes use of the arithmetic accelerators, such as GPUs, and are becoming popular for its high cost performance. Most of supernova simulations have been performed on the former, presumably because the latter requires involved implementation of code to offload the tasks to the accelerator devices. In our previous work, we offloaded the bottlenecks of the Boltzmann equation in supernova simulations to GPUs and achieved substantial acceleration [3,4].

In this work we investigate another accelerator architecture, the PEZY-SC processors. The PEZY-SC processors are novel many-core architecture that share several advantages with GPUs while also have distinct features, such as the threads working as MIMD processing elements. To exploit their potentially high arithmetic performance, understanding of their characteristic structure is important. It is worth establishing the knowledge; which kinds of applications are suitable to this architecture and how to optimize the codes.

We examine two types of the Boltzmann equation solvers. One is the radiation-hydrodynamics code under the spherically symmetry, *i.e.*, on one-dimensional spatial coordinate [5,6]. This code was also used in our previous studies on GPUs [3,4]. The second code is a multi-dimensional Boltzmann equation solver [7], which is a basis of recent large-scale simulations.

From a numerical point of view, three types of problems are examined: (1) A linear equation solver for a block tridiagonal matrix whose block matrices are dense, (2) Determination of the inverse of dense block matrices, and (3) Computation of neutrino reaction processes which are represented as integration of reaction rates over the energy and angles of neutrinos. We examine whether these bottlenecks can be accelerated by offloading to the PEZY-SC processors. As shown below, although effect of offloading is restricted by the bandwidth of device memory, one needs to employ optimization techniques to properly exploit the potential performance of hardware under this limitation. Establishing such recipes is also useful to prepare for future architecture including the next generation of the PEZY-SC processor.

This paper is organized as follows. Next section summarizes the formulation to investigate the supernova explosion focusing on the structure as computational problems. In Sect. 3 we summarize the features of PEZY-SC processors and the programming environment. The implementation of codes and the results of performance measurement are described in Sects. 4 and 5 for one- and two-dimensional simulations, respectively. Section 6 is devoted to our conclusion.

2 Formulation

2.1 Boltzmann Equation

For numerical simulations of supernovae, one needs to solve the evolution of the stellar matter at high temperature and density and the radiation transfer of neutrinos generated by the weak interaction simultaneously. The former is described by hydrodynamics under the gravitational effect governed by the general relativity. The latter is described by the Boltzmann equation, since the neutrinos are not always in statistical equilibrium and thus their distribution is not always isotropic and equilibrium values, therefore, a function of spatial coordinates and their momentum. Leaving the details of these formulation to literature [5–8], here we briefly summarize the costly parts in numerical simulations.

The general relativistic Boltzmann equation for the neutrino distribution function is written as

$$\frac{dx^\mu}{d\tau}\frac{\partial f_\nu}{\partial x^\mu} + \frac{dp^i}{d\tau}\frac{\partial f_\nu}{dp^i} = \left(\frac{\delta f_\nu}{\delta \tau}\right)_{\text{coll}} \tag{1}$$

where x^μ are the space-time coordinates and p^i the momentum coordinates, τ the affine parameter (specific time). This equation describes the conservation of the neutrino distribution function, and thus rewritten as an evolution equation. The left hand side describes the time derivative of f_ν and advection terms. The collision term, the right hand side, represents the change of the neutrino number caused by the weak interaction with matter. This term is composed of several reaction processes [9], and computationally demanding.

To solve the Boltzmann equation, the discrete ordinate (S_N) method is adopted through finite differencing the spatial and momentum coordinates. We adopt a fully implicit differencing for time advance since the equation is stiff with largely different time scales due to energy dependence of the interaction. In contrast to the explicit scheme where the time step is constrained by the Courant number, it is advantageous to increase the step size to follow the time evolution in a long time scale. However, it is numerically expensive to solve a linear equation with a large sparse matrix at each time step for time advancing. This linear equation solver tends to be the primary bottleneck of our simulations.

2.2 Spherically Symmetric (1D) Simulation

For one-dimensional simulation, *i.e.* under the spherical symmetry, coupled equations of hydrodynamics and neutrino transfer under general relativistic geometry can be solved [5,6]. In this case the evolution equation contains both the degrees of freedom of the neutrino radiation and hydrodynamics. Under the spherical symmetry, the neutrino distribution function is a function of the radial coordinate r, the neutrino energy E_ν, and the angle of neutrino momentum against the radial direction θ_ν. Four neutrino species are treated ($N_\nu = 4$): electron neutrino ν_e and μ-neutrino ν_μ, and their anti-neutrinos $\bar{\nu}_e$ and $\bar{\nu}_\mu$. In addition to the distribution function $f_\nu(r, E_\nu, \theta_\nu)$ for each neutrino species, eleven hydrodynamical variables, such as the temperature and entropy, are evolved simultaneously in the time evolution equation. We discretize radial coordinate, neutrino angle, and energy to N_r, $N_{\rm ang}$, and N_{E_ν} grids, respectively. Thus at each radial point there are $N_{E_\nu} \cdot N_{\rm ang} \cdot N_\nu$ neutrino degrees of freedom and $N_{\rm hyd} = 11$ hydrodynamical variables. Typically $N_r = O(100)$, $N_{\rm ang} = O(10)$, $N_{E_\nu} = O(10)$ are adopted currently, while ten times higher resolutions are demanded for more quantitative investigation.

In the implicit scheme, the most costly part of numerical simulation is a linear equation solver for the coefficient matrix of the time evolution equation. From the above equation, the coefficient matrix results in a tri-diagonal form,

$$M = \begin{pmatrix} B_1 & C_1 & 0 & & \cdots & \\ A_2 & B_2 & C_2 & 0 & & \\ 0 & A_3 & B_3 & C_3 & & \\ \vdots & & \ddots & \ddots & \ddots & 0 \\ & & 0 & A_{n-1} & B_{n-1} & C_{n-1} \\ 0 & \cdots & & 0 & A_n & B_n \end{pmatrix}, \tag{2}$$

where $n = N_r$ is the number of radial grids. At each radial point, i, the block matrices A_i, B_i, C_i are dense matrices of rank $N_{\rm max} = N_{E_\nu} N_{\rm ang} N_\nu + N_{\rm hyd}$.

In the case of one-dimensional simulations, direct methods for the linear equation are also applicable [10]. We instead adopt an iterative solver algorithm based on the Krylov subspace method as a preparation to the multi-dimensional simulations. We employ the BiCGStab algorithm with the weighted Jacobi-type preconditioner [11]. The preconditioning is represented as

$$x_{k+1} = \omega[-M_D^{-1}(M - M_D)x_k + M_D^{-1}b] + (1-\omega)x_k \tag{3}$$

where ω is the weight parameter, M_D the block-diagonal part of M in Eq. (2). Since M_D^{-1} is also in a block diagonal form, it can be determined preceding to the solver algorithm. The procedure to determine the weight parameter ω is described in Ref. [11]. Here we just note that it suffices to determine several small eigenvalues approximately by applying the Arnoldi algorithms to a Krylov subspace of degree around 20. The preconditioning is performed by repeatedly applying the operation (3), $N_{\rm Jacobi}$ times, which is practically determined. $N_{\rm Jacobi} = 25$ sufficiently works in the present case.

2.3 Multi-dimensional Simulation

In our multidimensional simulations, the hydrodynamics of stellar matter and the Boltzmann equation of neutrinos are solved not in parallel but sequentially at each substep of the time evolution. Thus we focus on the Boltzmann equation for the neutrino radiation transfer [7], as a benchmark code of the coupled system with the hydrodynamics under the gravity [12]. The neutrino distribution is a function of spatial coordinate $x = (r, \theta, \phi)$ and neutrino energy and two angles, $(E_\nu,\ \theta_\nu,\ \phi_\nu)$. Applying the discrete ordinate method and employ the implicit differencing scheme for the time advancing, the structure of numerical problem is similar to that of the spherically symmetric case. The coefficient matrix of the time evolution equation takes a similar form to Eq. (2), while the subdiagonal blocks exist in not only r-direction but also θ- and ϕ-directions. These subdiagonal block matrices, $A_x^{(r)}$, $A_x^{(\theta)}$, $A_x^{(\phi)}$ and $C_x^{(r)}$, $C_x^{(\theta)}$, $C_x^{(\phi)}$ represent the advection of neutrinos. Contrary to the 1D case, these subdiagonal block matrices are not dense but just diagonal in the neutrino energy and angles. As a linear equation solver for this coefficient matrix, we currently adopt an iterative algorithm without preconditioning, while its application is straightforward.

2.4 Related Works

Use of GPUs in the simulations of core-collapse supernovae has been progressed mainly for application to the hydrodynamics. As for the simulation code including the neutrino transport, the VERTEX code was ported to GPUs by employing CUDA of NVIDIA [13]. Its most time consuming part was one reaction term in the collision term of the Boltzmann equation and offloaded to GPUs. On the Kepler architecture, the target kernel was accelerated by factor of 54 which resulted in 1.8 times acceleration of the whole simulation time compared to the execution on the host processors.

In our previous work [3,4], we offloaded the bottlenecks of the supernova simulations under the spherical symmetry to GPUs and demonstrated their efficiency. In Ref. [3] the iterative linear equation solver was offloaded by implementing with OpenACC and exploiting cuBLAS library provided by NVIDIA. In successive work [4] the other time consuming parts, the computation of the collision term and the inversion of the block matrices, were also offloaded by using CUDA framework. The present work is based on these results.

3 Pezy-SC Processor

3.1 Architecture

The PEZY-SC processors are novel many-core architecture provided by Pezy Computing K.K. The processor is hierarchically composed of PEs (Processing Elements) each launches eight MIMD threads. Being equipped in a liquid immersion cooling system "ZettaScaler" provided by ExaScaler Inc., it achieves high power efficiency as awarded in the Green500 list several times [14]. Currently two generations of the PEZY-SC processors are available: PEZY-SC and PEZY-SC2. Hereafter we call the former as PEZY-SC1 for distinction. We develop our simulation codes for PEZY-SCs on the Suiren Blue and Suiren2 systems at KEK whose features are summarized in Table 1.

Table 1. Specification of the Suiren Blue and Suiren2 systems at KEK.

System	Suiren Blue (64 nodes)	Suiren2 (48 nodes)
Accelerator	PEZY-SC1	PEZY-SC2 (700 MHz)
Peak DP performance/device	1.5 TFlops	2.8 TFlops
Number of PE/device	1024	1984
Number of threads per PE	8	8
Number of PE per City	16	16
Size of local memory/PE	16 KB	20 KB
L1 cache	2 KB/2PE	2 KB/PE
L2 cache	64 KB/City	64 KB/City
L3/Last Level cache	2 MB/Prefecture	40 MB/device
Device memory size	16 GB	64 GB
Device memory bandwidth	102 GB/s	76.8 GB/s
Host-device network/device	PCIe Gen3 ×8	PCIe Gen3 ×8

Each node of the Suiren Blue system is composed of an Intel Xeon E5-2618Lv3 host processor and four PEZY-SC1 processors connected by the PCIe Gen3 with 8 lanes. The PEZY-SC1 device possesses 1024 PEs that are hierarchically installed in units of Village (four PEs), City (four Villages), Prefecture (16 Cities) so that four Prefectures compose one device. Each PE launches 8 threads that share the local memory of PE. The peak performance of one PEZY-SC processor is 1.5 and 3 TFlops for double and single precision arithmetics, respectively. The device memory bandwidth is 102 GB/s. The L1 cache is shared by 2PEs, L2 by 16 PEs in a City, and L3 by 16 Cities in a Prefecture.

Each node of the Suiren2 system is composed of an Intel Xeon D1571 host processor and eight PEZY-SC2 processors connected by the PCIe Gen3 with 8 lanes. While the number of cores is 2048 in the architecture design, current products disable 64 PEs to increase the yield of the processor chip. Furthermore the clock cycle is reduced from 1 GHz in the design to 700 MHz for stable operation. The structure of PEZY-SC2 device is similar to that of PEZY-SC. The last level cache assigns 32 MB for access from PEs and 8 MB for PCIe.

Although the arithmetic performance of the PEZY-SC2 processor is higher than that of PEZY-SC1, the latter has better memory bandwidth. The primary bottleneck of our application is regulated by the device memory bandwidth. Thus we mainly use the PEZY-SC1 processor for developing the code, and at the last stage measure the performance on the PEZY-SC2 processors for comparison.

3.2 Programming Environment

As the programming environment, Pezy Computing provides PZCL SDK which is a subset of the OpenCL framework while includes extensions to exploit the PEZY-SC architecture. We use the PZCL SDK 4.1 on Suiren Blue and 5.0 on Suiren2. For PEZY-SC1 there are two addressing modes in PZCL, 32-bit and 64-bit. In this work we use the latter considering our target size of simulations.

There are several functions added to the OpenCL standard to make use of the hierarchical structure of the PEZY-SC architecture. It is essential to understand such structure and corresponding functions to achieve desired performance. Here we summarize the several such features and techniques.

Hierarchical Synchronization. PZCL provides functions to synchronize the threads at several levels. Synchronization of threads in the Village, City, and the whole device are performed by calling built-in functions. Synchronization at other levels, such as in PE or Prefecture, is provided as assembly commands. Since the threads of PEZY-SC work as MIMD processes, memory access timing may differ thread by thread. Explicit synchronization of threads before memory access may increase the memory access performance by inducing coalesced access.

Hierarchical Cache. In the PEZY-SC architecture, the cache coherence is assured on user's responsibility. Thus flushing the cached data must explicitly be done by function calls. Similarly to the synchronization, there is a built-in function to flush the data at each level of the cache.

Changing Threads. Eight threads within PE execute the commands in turn in two bunches each containing four threads. These execution bunches are explicitly exchanged by a built-in function of PZCL, `chgthread()`. Putting this function after the device memory access may partially hide the memory access latency.

Local Memory. Each PE has a local memory shared by the threads in that PE. Usually this local memory is used as stack areas of the threads. It is possible to use this memory area as a shared memory of the threads by changing the size of stack area before launching the kernel using an API function in PZCL. The freed memory area can be accessed by directly referring the memory address.

3.3 Related Works

There have been several published works on utilizing the PEZY-SC processors including the porting and performance evaluation of libraries and simulation codes [15–18] as well as application to scientific studies [19,20]. Among these works, the problem of lattice QCD simulations [15] has similarity to this work and gives insights on the optimization of our code. In a viewpoint of efficiency in porting a codes to new architecture, Ref. [21] designs the OpenACC on PEZY-SC as an alternative programming framework to the currently available PZCL/OpenCL. In addition to these works, several projects to make use of the PEZY-SC processors are in progress.

4 Results of 1D Simulation

4.1 Implementation and Numerical Setup

Our base code is described in Fortran and parallelized with MPI. In our previous works on GPUs [3,4], we employed OpenACC or CUDA after porting the bottleneck parts into the C language. For PEZY-SC processors we can make use of these C codes as the starting point to develop the code in PZCL. Since there is almost direct correspondence between the CUDA and PZCL kernels, the first step of porting to the latter is rather straightforward, while thereafter optimization specific to the PEZY-SC architecture is required.

The scale of 1D simulation is determined by the parameters N_r, N_{E_ν}, and $N_{\rm ang}$. While currently typical values of these parameters are (N_r, N_{E_ν}, $N_{\rm ang}$) = (256, 14, 6), we aim at increasing them up to (1024, 16, 8) or (1024, 24, 12) within acceptable cost. In Table 2, we summarize the elapsed time budget for ingredients of one Newton-Raphson iteration, that is repeated a few times within each time step, executed at $N_r = 256$ and with four MPI processes. The first part of Table 2 shows the result of execution on the host processor of Suiren Blue. As already mentioned in Sect. 1, there are three bottlenecks in our numerical simulation: (1) Iterative linear equation solver for the coefficient matrix of the time evolution equation, (2) Inversion of the block dense matrices of the coefficient matrix used in the weighted Jacobi-type preconditioning for the iterative solver, and (3) Calculation of the collision term of the Boltzmann equation. In the same way as the GPU case [3,4], we offload these parts to the Pezy-SC processors and optimize the corresponding kernel codes. Result for the PEZY-SC processor is also summarized in Table 2. In the following subsections, we explain the details of implementation and discuss these results.

Table 2. Time budget of one Newton-Raphson iteration on Suiren Blue system with four MPI processes.

(N_{E_ν}, $N_{\rm ang}$)	Elapsed time [sec]			
	(14, 6)	(16, 8)	(24, 12)	(32, 16)
Host (Suiren Blue)				
Hydrodynamics	0.0024	0.0037	0.0086	0.013
Advection term	0.022	0.029	0.069	0.12
Collision term	1.93	4.32	27.0	104
Matrix setup (inverse)	5.63	19.3	219	1217
Matrix setup (Arnoldi)	0.51	0.93	4.59	15.6
Iterative solver	9.37	14.9	71.9	213
PEZY-SC (Suiren Blue)				
Collision term	2.49	7.00	36.28	148
Matrix setup (inverse)	0.28	0.89	8.87	47.3
Matrix setup (Arnoldi)	0.16	0.24	0.89	2.57
Iterative solver	2.00	2.57	11.52	32.5
Matrix data conversion	0.44	0.95	6.72	21.2

4.2 Linear Equation Solver

Matrix-vector multiplication. The primary bottleneck of our numerical simulation is the linear equation solver for the coefficient matrix of the evolution equation. As noted in Subsect. 2.2, M in Eq. (2), $M - M_D$, and M_D^{-1} are the matrices in the preconditioned iterative solver. Since the determination of M_D^{-1} is the subject of Subsect. 4.3, here we regard M_D^{-1} as already determined explicitly. In the following we summarize the implementation of the matrix-vector multiplication, $y = Mx$, and optimization techniques applied.

Task Assignment. Since the MPI parallelization is done in the radial coordinate, each device processes them in units of the block in Eq. (2). We assign one block (one values of r) of vector y to one City, *i.e.* the 16 PEs sharing the L2 cache. For our present setup, $N_r = 256$ and four MPI processes, this is a practical choice, since each device processes the number of vector blocks equal to the number of Cities in the case of PEZY-SC1.

Boundary Communication. The boundary data of the vector x must be exchanged before the matrix is multiplied. Although this communication can be overlapped with the bulk part of the matrix-vector operation, we currently adopt the blocking communication since this overhead is relatively small as comparing the performance of M_D^{-1} and $M - M_D$.

Padding. The rank of the block matrices is $N_{\rm max} = N_{\rm ang} N_{E_\nu} N_\nu + N_{\rm hyd}$, and $N_{\rm hyd} = 11$ is always fractional with respect to the number of threads. Such an alignment may affect the memory access performance. We thus extend the arrays to $\tilde{N}_{\rm hyd} = 16$ by padding the matrices with unity and the vectors with zero.

Coalesced Access. The layout of the components of the block matrices is important for memory access performance. Representing the index of matrix component A_{ij} as an inline function `index(i,j)`, `index=i+Nmax*j` is a standard layout. Assigning computation of the component y_i to each thread, this layout corresponds to the coalesced access. However, this implies the access in `j`-loop is not continuous. Better performance is achieved with modified indexing, expressing in the C language,

$$\texttt{index} = (\texttt{i\%nth}) + \texttt{nth} * (\texttt{j} + \texttt{Nmax} * (\texttt{i/nth})), \tag{4}$$

where $\texttt{nth} = 8$ is the number of threads in PE.

Unrolling. The loaded value of x_j is reused by unrolling the `i`-loop. Considering the size of $N_{\rm max}$, $N_{\rm unroll} = 3$, 5, and 10 seem appropriate for $(N_{E_\nu}, N_{\rm ang}) = (14, 6)$, (16, 8), and (24, 12), respectively. We implemented the code with these three values of $N_{\rm unroll}$, and found that $N_{\rm unroll} = 3$ always shows the best performance. Since the number of rows processed in each thread may be different, the MIMD feature of the PEZY-SC thread is efficient in this implementation.

The performance of the matrix-vector multiplication for these matrices is displayed in Fig. 1. As already noted, no sizable effect of communication is observed

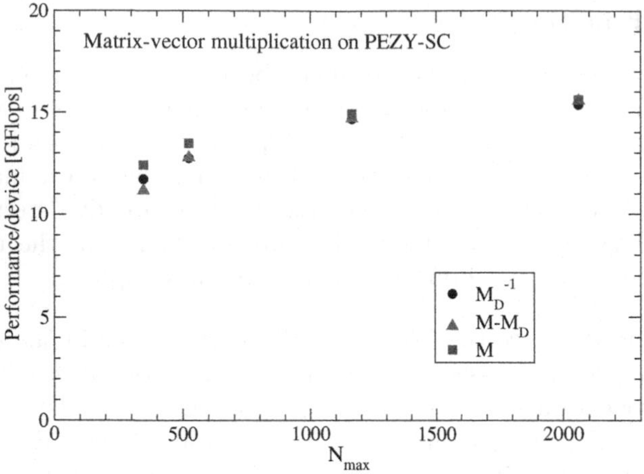

Fig. 1. The performance of the matrix-vector multiplication on PEZY-SC processor.

in the performance of M_D^{-1} and other two matrices. There is a tendency that M acquires better performance than M_D^{-1} in spite of the communication overhead. This can be explained as the effect of cached data of the right hand side vector x. Assuming complete reuse of cached data, the byte-per-flop of the bulk part of these matrices is about 4. Considering the device memory bandwidth, about 25 GFlops is the performance limit of the matrix multiplication. Ref. [15] estimated the sustained bandwidth of the device memory for the 'axpy' operation (`y = a*x+y`) which results in about 50 GB/s, half the peak bandwidth. We therefore realize that our code is sufficiently optimized. Compared to the result for NVIDIA Tesla P100 GPU (4.7 TFlops FP64 peak performance and 720 GB/s device memory B/W) in our previous work [3], the performance of the matrix-vector multiplication on PEZY-SC is about 10% of that on P100. This is explained by the less memory bandwidth of PEZY-SC than the latter.

The elapsed time of the whole iterative solver is shown in Table 2. For two small matrix sizes, acceleration is substantial even considering the overhead of matrix data conversion that includes the change of matrix layout and data transfer from the host to device. The latter is performed once before the iterative solver and takes 10% of the quoted time. This is reasonable considering about 8 GB/s of PCIe bandwidth. For larger sizes, this overhead becomes sizable, even considering that number of iteration until the convergence strongly depends on the parameters and the stage of time evolution. One needs to appropriately choose the number of MPI processes and devices so that this overhead becomes negligibly small compared to the iteration time.

Arnoldi Method. As a by-product of acceleration of matrix-vector multiplication, the Arnoldi method used to determine the weight parameter ω in Eq. (3) is also accelerated, since the consumed time is dominated by construction of the Krylov subspace rather than the Arnoldi algorithm itself. The former part is offloaded to the accelerator devices and the resultant Hessenberg matrix is transferred to the host processor. The Arnoldi algorithms is performed at the host by calling the DGEEV routine of the LAPACK library with negligible numerical cost. The time budget of this part is denoted as 'matrix setup (Arnoldi)' in Table 2. Comparing to the results on the host processor, sufficient acceleration is achieved.

Result for PEZY-SC2 Processor. Finally we briefly summarize the performance result on the Suiren2 system. We do not quote the measured values of performance explicitly, since our code is not optimized for the PEZY-SC2 processor. We rather observe the qualitative difference of the performance on these two generations without changing the code. Among the parameter sets in Table 2, the largest size does not run presumably due to the required memory size exceeding that of the system. For the matrix-vector multiplication, we assigned one block on each r to one City. With this setup and present parameter values, not all the PEs of PEZY-SC2 are used. The performance of the matrix-vector multiplication on PEZY-SC2 becomes about 60% of those on PEZY-SC1. This is explained with the difference of the device memory bandwidth displayed in Table 1 and that the PEs are not saturated by the launched threads. Accordingly the values of elapsed time for the linear solver, the Arnoldi method, and the matrix data conversion increase several tens of percent from those on PEZY-SC1.

4.3 Inversion of Dense Block Matrices

The block diagonal matrix M_D^{-1} is repeatedly applied in the preconditioning and thus it needs to be efficient to determine preceding to the iterative solver. To determine $M_D^{-1} = \{B_i^{-1} | i = 1, \ldots, n\}$ from $M_D = \{B_i | i = 1, \ldots, n\}$, the original code adopts the LU decomposition by calling the DGETRF and DGETRS routines in the LAPACK library. As shown in Table 2, this computation rapidly becomes costly as the matrix size increases, and thus worth to offload. It is however nontrivial to parallelize the LU decomposition efficiently on many-core processors. We instead employ an alternative algorithm, the blocked Gauss-Jordan elimination method [22]. The algorithm is represented as follows.

$$(B||A) = \left(\begin{array}{c||c|c} B_{00} & A_{01} & A_{02} \\ \hline B_{10} & A_{11} & A_{12} \\ \hline B_{20} & A_{21} & A_{22} \end{array}\right) \rightarrow \left(\begin{array}{c|c||c} B_{00} & 0 & A_{02} \\ \hline 0 & 0 & 0 \\ \hline B_{20} & 0 & A_{22} \end{array}\right) + \left(\begin{array}{c} -A_{01}A_{11}^{-1} \\ \hline A_{11}^{-1} \\ \hline -A_{21}A_{11}^{-1} \end{array}\right) (B_{10}|I||A_{12}), \quad (5)$$

where B_{ij} and A_{ij} are block matrices. Setting the size of A_{11} to be $b \times b$, each application of Eq. (5) extends the size of B part by b columns and rows. Starting from the original matrix A, *i.e.* $B = 0$, repeated application of Eq. (5) finally arrives at $B = A^{-1}$. A_{11}^{-1} can be determined by unblocked Gauss-Jordan method.

While the Gauss-Jordan elimination is nothing but a rearrangement of the LU decomposition, its blocked form can be parallelized to threads in units of the block size b. Only A_{11}^{-1} must be solved on a single thread. Thus the value of b is a tunable parameter. In this work, we set $b = 8$ considering the number of threads per PE. On each PE, A_{11} is loaded from the device memory to the local memory, and one thread solve A_{11}^{-1} with the unblocked Gauss-Jordan algorithm. After obtaining A_{11}^{-1}, remaining computation in each step of Eq. (5) can be performed in parallel. We assign them so that each City (16 PEs) inverts one block matrix B_i. As shown in Table 2, adopting the Gauss-Jordan algorithm and offloading to the PEZY-SC processor achieve sufficient acceleration of computational time. However, as the matrix size increases, elapsed time of this process rapidly increases. For (N_{E_ν}, $N_{\rm ang}$) larger than (24, 12), rearrangement of the number of devices and the number of PEs to solve each block matrix is desirable. Comparing these results to those for NVIDIA Tesla P100 GPU [4], the elapsed time of the matrix inversion is just about 40% larger than the latter. This implies the optimization on PEZY-SC works better than on P100, and is worth to feed back to the latter.

Result for PEZY-SC2 Processor. In the same way as for the matrix-vector multiplication, in our setup the launched threads do not saturate all the PEs of PEZY-SC2. Presumably this explains that the measured values of elapsed time for the blocked Gauss-Jordan algorithm on PEZY-SC2 are almost the same as those on PEZY-SC1.

4.4 Collision Term

Calculation of the collision term of the Boltzmann equation (1) is composed of several physical processes [9]. Table 3 summarizes the neutrino reaction processes included in this work. The first column is abbreviation of the physical process described in the second column. The third column shows the elapsed time measured on the host processors of Suiren Blue with four MPI processes. The last four processes, *esc*, *pap*, *plp*, *nbr*, are dominant, and thus the target of offloading. Indeed on GPUs sufficient acceleration has been achieved [4].

At the radial point r, the reaction rate of neutrino species ν is represented as $R^\nu_{\rm int}(E'_\nu, \theta'_\nu, E_\nu, \theta_\nu, r)$, where ($\theta_\nu$, E_ν) and (θ'_ν, E'_ν) are neutrino momentum angle and energy before and after the interaction, respectively. The contributions to the coefficient matrix and the source vector of the linear equation are obtained by multiplying $R_{\rm int}$ with the kinematic factors, neutrino distribution function under the matter environment, and integrating it over θ'_ν and E'_ν. Thus the calculation is performed in two steps: (a) Determination of the reaction rate $R^\nu_{\rm int}$, and (b) Calculation of the contribution to the collision term. In each step, each thread undertakes a contribution to each (r, E_ν, θ_ν) point of $R^\nu_{\rm int}$ or the collision term. These tasks are flatly assigned to the threads of device using all the resources, in contrary to the matrix-vector operations. This is mainly for simplicity of porting, since the calculation of the reaction rate is much more involved than the latter.

Table 3 shows the elapsed time on PEZY-SC1 and PEZY-SC2 for the parameter set (N_r, N_{E_ν}, $N_{\rm ang}$) $= (256, 14, 6)$. The data calculated on the devices are transferred to the host and changed to the data layout on the host, at the cost of the time quoted as 'data conversion' in Table 3. The result of Table 3 indicates that in spite of substantial acceleration in the *esc* process, there is almost no advantage in total by offloading these processes to PEZY-SC1. This is the case also for the larger matrix sizes as listed in Table 2.

Table 3. Elapsed time budget in the calculation of collision term at $(N_r, N_{E_\nu}, N_{\rm ang}) = (256, 14, 6)$, with four MPI processes on the host processor of Suiren Blue, PEZY-SC1, and PEZY-SC2.

Abbrev.	Physics process	Elapsed time [sec]		
		Host	PEZY-SC1	PEZY-SC2
ecp	Absorption/emission of ν_e on nucleons	0.06		
aecp	Absorption/emission of $\bar{\nu}_e$ on nucleons	0.06		
nsc	Neutrino scattering on nucleons	0.10		
csc	Coherent scattering of neutrino on nuclei	0.02		
ecpa	Absorption/emission of ν_e on nuclei	0.06		
esc	Scattering with electrons	0.94	0.37	0.04
pap	Neutrino pair creation/annihilation	0.25	0.42	0.04
plp	Plasmon process	0.28	0.42	0.04
nbr	Bremsstrahrung	0.22	0.42	0.04
	Data conversion	–	0.21	0.25

On the other hand, for the PEZY-SC2 processors, computation is much more accelerated than PEZY-SC1. On PEZY-SC2, the memory access performance is improved for non-coalesced access compared to PEZY-SC1. This explains the results displayed in Table 3 and implies the potential improvement on PEZY-SC1 by rearranging the data layout and task assignment. Thus considering the data conversion overhead, there is a substantial gain in offloading to the PEZY-SC2 processors. For larger two sizes, we observe the acceleration slightly less than a factor of two.

5 Results of 2D Simulation

5.1 Implementation and Numerical Setup

Our base code of the multi-dimensional Boltzmann solver is described in Fortran and parallelized with MPI. Applying the same strategy as the 1D code, we first convert the bottleneck parts of the code into the C language and then modify them to the kernels working on the PEZY-SC processors. The codes to setup the device environment, transfer the data, and launch the kernels in the 1D simulation are almost directly reused. Although the code is applicable to all the one, two, and three dimensional spaces, here we examine the performance of the code in two-dimensional space as a prototype of practical application.

As a benchmark setup, we adopt the numbers of grids in spatial coordinates, $N_r = 256$ and $N_\theta = 128$ (and $N_\phi = 1$). For the numbers of neutrino's momentum grids, (N_{θ_ν}, N_{ϕ_ν}, N_{E_ν}), we consider two sets (6, 12, 14) and (8, 16, 16) as values practically feasible. We measure the performance of the code with four MPI processes each handles one PEZY-SC device. As noted in Subsect. 2.3, we employ an iterative solver without preconditioning. Thus the inversion of the dense block matrices is not the subject of present consideration. For the collision term, we offloaded the processes *ecp*, *nsc*, *csc*, *ecpa*, and *pap* in Table 3. However, the observed elapsed time for these processes on the Suiren Blue system exhibits no advantage of offloading. The situation is similar to the 1D case, and we do not discuss further the offloading of the collision term in multi-dimensional code, considering the effort of implementation not deserving the gain. Thus we focus on the matrix-vector multiplication in the iterative linear equation solver.

5.2 Matrix-Vector Multiplication

The structure of the matrix M of the form Eq. (2) implies that the multiplication of block diagonal part, $M_D = \{B_i | i = 1, \ldots, n\}$ where $n = N_r \times N_\theta \times N_\phi$, to a vector is the dominant arithmetic operations, since B_i are dense matrices while the block matrices A_i and C_i are diagonal in the present case. Thus the byte-per-flop of $y_i = B_i x_i$, about 4 for the double precision arithmetics, is the representative of the matrix M multiplied to a vector x. Considering the device memory bandwidth of the PEZY-SC processor, about 25 GFlops is a guideline of the performance limit.

We apply the same prescription described in Subsect. 4.2 except for padding. $N_{\rm unroll} = 8$ provides the best performance for the present case. The sustained performance of the matrix-vector multiplication on the PEZY-SC1 processors is 14.2 GFlops and 13.4 GFlops for $(N_{\theta_\nu}, N_{\phi_\nu}, N_{E_\nu}) = (6, 12, 14)$ and (8, 16, 16), respectively. These values of performance are slightly less than the corresponding results of one-dimensional setup displayed in Fig. 1, presumably due to the structure of present matrix. The offloading substantially improve the elapsed time of the linear equation solver. For example, for $(N_{\theta_\nu}, N_{\phi_\nu}, N_{E_\nu}) = (6, 12, 14)$, the time for 22 BiCGStab iterations is improved from 25.2 s to 7.0 s (iteration) + 1.5 s (data conversion). The more the number of iteration is required, the more acceleration is acquired.

For the PEZY-SC2 processors, we execute the same code as on the PEZY-SC1 changing only the total number of PEs from 1024 to 1984, since the number of spatial grids is enough larger than the number of Cities. We obtain the sustained performance 14.4 and 15.4 GFlops for $(N_{\theta_\nu}, N_{\phi_\nu}, N_{E_\nu}) = (6, 12, 14)$ and (8, 16, 16), respectively. The better values of performance than those on PEZY-SC1 may imply that the memory access pattern of the present matrix is more suitable to the PEZY-SC2 architecture. We realize that our optimization prescriptions effectively apply also to the linear equation solver in the multi-dimensional Boltzmann equation code.

6 Conclusion

In this work, we examined viability of the PEZY-SC processors applied to the Boltzmann equation solver in the core-collapse supernova simulations. For one-dimensional code, we offloaded three bottlenecks to the PEZY-SC devices. For the iterative linear equation solver and inversion of dense block matrices, we achieved sufficient acceleration by offloading, while for the former the sustained performance is restricted by the device memory bandwidth. For the computation of the collision term, however, we judged it is not practical to extend application because the achieved acceleration seems not to deserve large effort of porting and optimizing the code of this part. The good performance exhibited by the PEZY-SC2 processor seems to indicate the architecture is developing in promising direction. For the multi-dimensional Boltzmann equation solver, we demonstrated that the linear equation solver is offloaded efficiently by applying the prescriptions learnt in developing the one-dimensional code.

In conclusion, the PEZY-SC processors are attractive many-core architecture which potentially accelerates some kinds of applications. There are commonly applicable prescriptions to improve the performance, as examined in Sect. 4. For extensive application, however, two issues are to be settled. One is the device memory bandwidth worse than recent GPUs. This would be much improved in the next generation of the PEZY-SC processor. The other is the porting efficiency, which is crucial for application to wide area of researches. Efficient libraries and frameworks such as the OpenACC [21] are strongly desired.

Acknowledgment. The authors are grateful to A. Imakura, H. Okawa, T. Takiwaki and S. Yamada for HPC researches on core-collapse supernovae, to T. Aoyama, K-I. Ishikawa, T. Ishikawa, N. Kurosawa, R. Sakamoto, Y. Yamaura for development of code on PEZY-SC processors and for maintaining the Suiren Blue and Suiren2 systems. This work was supported by the Large Scale Computational Sciences with Heterogeneous Many-Core Computers in grant-in-aid for High Performance Computing with General Purpose Computers in MEXT, Grant-in-Aid for the Scientific Research from the Ministry of Education, Culture, Sports, Science and Technology (MEXT), Japan (15K05093, 17H06357, 17H06365, 19K03837, 20H01905), HPCI Strategic Program of Japanese MEXT, research programs at K-computer of the RIKEN AICS and Post-K project (Project ID: hp180111, hp180179, hp180239, hp190100, hp190160, hp200102, hp200124), the Particle, Nuclear and Astro Physics Simulation Program (Nos. 2019-002, 2020-004) of Institute of Particle and Nuclear Studies, KEK.

References

1. Kotake, K., et al.: Core-collapse supernovae as supercomputing science: a status report toward 6D simulations with exact Boltzmann neutrino transport in full general relativity. Prog. Theor. Exp. Phys. **2012**, 01A301 (2012). https://doi.org/10.1093/ptep/pts009
2. Janka, H.-T., Melson, T., Summa, A.: Physics of core-collapse supernovae in three dimensions: a sneak preview. Ann. Rev. Nucl. Part. Sci. **66**, 341–375 (2016). https://doi.org/10.1146/annurev-nucl-102115-044747
3. Matsufuru, H., Sumiyoshi, K.: Simulation of supernova explosion accelerated on GPU: spherically symmetric neutrino-radiation hydrodynamics. In: Gervasi, O., et al. (eds.) ICCSA 2018. LNCS, vol. 10962, pp. 440–455. Springer, Cham (2018). https://doi.org/10.1007/978-3-319-95168-3_30
4. Matsufuru, H., Sumiyoshi, K.: Accelerating numerical simulations of supernovae with GPUs. In: 2018 Sixth International Symposium on Computing and Networking Workshops (CANDARW) (2018). https://doi.org/10.1109/CANDARW.2018.00056
5. Yamada, S.: An Implicit Lagrangian code for spherically symmetric general relativistic hydrodynamics with an approximate Riemann solver. Astrophys. J. **475**, 720–739 (1997). https://doi.org/10.1086/303548

6. Yamada, S., Janka, H.-T., Suzuki, H.: Neutrino transport in type II supernovae: Boltzmann solver vs. Monte Carlo method. Astron. Astrophys. **344**, 1468–1470 (1999). arXiv:astro-ph/9809009
7. Sumiyoshi, K., Yamada, S.: Neutrino transfer in three dimensions for core-collapse supernovae I. static configurations. Astrophys. J. Suppl. **199**, 17 (2012). https://doi.org/10.1088/0067-0049/199/1/17
8. Shibata, M., Nagakura, H., Sekiguchi, Y., Yamada, S.: Conservative form of Boltzmann's equation in general relativity. Phys. Rev. D **89**, 084073 (2014). https://doi.org/10.1103/PhysRevD.89.084073
9. Bruenn, S.W.: Stellar core collapse: numerical model and infall epoch. Astrophys. J. Suppl. **58**, 771–841 (1985). https://doi.org/10.1086/191056
10. Sumiyoshi, K., Ebisuzaki, T.: Performance of parallel solution of a block-tridiagonal linear system on Fujitsu VPP500. Parallel Comput. **24**, 287–304 (1998). https://doi.org/10.1016/S0167-8191(98)00007-6
11. Imakura, A., Sakurai, T., Sumiyoshi, K., Matsufuru, H.: A parameter optimization technique for a weighted Jacobi-type preconditioner. JSIAM Lett. **4**, 41–44 (2012). https://doi.org/10.14495/jsiaml.4.41
12. Nagakura, H., et al.: Simulations of core-collapse supernovae in spatial axisymmetry with full Boltzmann neutrino transport. Astrophys. J. **854**, 136 (2018). https://doi.org/10.3847/1538-4357/aaac29
13. Dannert, T., Marek, A., Rampp, M.: Porting large HPC applications to GPU clusters: the codes GENE and VERTEX. Adv. Parallel Comput. **25**, 305–314 (2014). https://doi.org/10.3233/978-1-61499-381-0-305
14. The Green500 site. https://www.top500.org/green500/
15. Aoyama, T., et al.: First application of lattice QCD to pezy-SC processor. Procedia Comput. Sci. **80**, 1418–1427 (2016). https://doi.org/10.1016/j.procs.2016.05.457
16. Yoshifuji, N., Sakamoto, R., Nitadori, K., Makino, J.: Implementation and evaluation of data-compression algorithms for irregular-grid iterative methods on the PEZY-SC processor. In: 2016 6th Workshop on Irregular Applications: Architecture and Algorithms (IA3), pp. 58–61 (2016)
17. Haribara, Y., Ishikawa, H., Utsunomiya, S., Aihara, K., Yamamoto, Y.: Performance evaluation of coherent Ising machines against classical neural networks. Quantum Sci. Technol. **2**, 044002 (2017). https://doi.org/10.1088/2058-9565/aa8190
18. Hishinuma, T., Nakata, M.: pzqd: PEZY-SC2 acceleration of double-double precision arithmetic library for high-precision BLAS. In: Okada, H., Atluri, S.N. (eds.) ICCES 2019. MMS, vol. 75, pp. 717–736. Springer, Cham (2020). https://doi.org/10.1007/978-3-030-27053-7_61
19. Yamazaki, T., Igarashi, J., Makino, J., Ebisuzaki, T.: Real-time simulation of a cat-scale artificial cerebellum on PEZY-SC processors. Int. J. High Perform. Comput. Appl. **33**, 155–168 (2017). https://doi.org/10.1177/1094342017710705
20. Sasaki, T., Hosono, N.: Particle number dependence of the n-body simulations of moon formation. Astrophys. J. **856**, 175(14pp) (2018). https://doi.org/10.3847/1538-4357/aab369
21. Tabuchi, A., et al.: Design and preliminary evaluation of omni OpenACC compiler for massive MIMD processor PEZY-SC. In: Maruyama, N., de Supinski, B.R., Wahib, M. (eds.) IWOMP 2016. LNCS, vol. 9903, pp. 293–305. Springer, Cham (2016). https://doi.org/10.1007/978-3-319-45550-1_21
22. Quintana, E.S., Quintana, G., Sun, X., van de Geijn, R.: A note on parallel matrix inversion. SIAM J. Sci. Comput. **22**, 1762–1771 (2001). https://doi.org/10.1137/S1064827598345679

International Workshop on Land Use Monitoring for Sustanability (LUMS 2020)

Shrinking Phenomena in Italian Inner Mountainous Areas. Resilience Strategies

Francesco Rotondo[1(✉)], Giovanni Marinelli[2], and Luca Domenella[2]

[1] DICEA, Politechnic University of Marche, Via Brecce Bianche 12, 60131 Ancona, Italy
f.rotondo@univpm.it

[2] SIMAU, Polytechnic University of Marche, Via Brecce Bianche 12, 60131 Ancona, Italy
{g.marinelli,domenella}@univpm.it

Abstract. Several factors have been identified by literature as the cause of shrinkage. These factors are often closely linked to spatial features. There are some contexts in which various causes overlap and amplify as in the case of the mountain or foothill areas of Central Italy, which is the case study of this work. The areas of the Marche region in Central Italy, affected by the severe earthquake of 2016, actually feature multiple shrinking causes. In this region, small and medium-sized towns play a determinant role in structuring urban systems with their influence over local communities and organizations.

This research work intends to describe the main characteristics of the territory under study, as well as the shrinking causes detected by the analyses. It then tries to identify the strategies in place and to compare them with those already covered by literature, assessing both weaknesses and strengths.

Keywords: Small and medium-sized towns · Urban strategies · Shrinking cities

1 Shrinking Phenomena in Mountain and Foothill Areas: First Elements of Analysis

Growth and degrowth cycles have characterized all cities throughout history. Even the cities that industrial civilization has accustomed us to think characterized by ever-growing demographic trends such as the capitals of the western states have experienced moments of decline throughout their long history, as the case of Rome teaches.

Similarly there are cities, which due to calamitous events or significant economic changes, have been abandoned (this is the case, in Italy, of some municipalities in the inner areas of the Southern Apennines such as Craco or the Central Apennines, such as for example, Santo Stefano di Sessanio) and today they present themselves as real ghost towns.

In contemporary cities, many have investigated the possible causes [1, 2], which in a nutshell can be summarized in four main ones:

The work is an integrated fruit of authors collaboration, also if the paragraph 1 have to attributed to Francesco Rotondo, the paragraph 2 to Luca Domenella, the paragraph paragraph 3 to Giovanni Marinelli.

O. Gervasi et al. (Eds.): ICCSA 2020, LNCS 12253, pp. 195–206, 2020.
https://doi.org/10.1007/978-3-030-58814-4_14

- economic decline, loss of employment, de-industrialization;
- suburbanization and changes in the settlement system;
- aging and decline of the natural balance;
- pollution, and particularly unfavorable environmental context.

To these main causes, we can add natural disasters that suddenly determine the impossibility of living in the affected places and, finally, as in the case of small and medium-sized municipalities in the inner areas, the distance from services and places of significant economic production, which they cause isolation and abandonment. Often these causes occur concurrently, in some cases one of them becomes prevalent.

This work deals with medium and small cities in demographic decline in the inner areas of the central Apennines of the Marche Region, which, already characterized by abandonment phenomena, were hit in 2016 by a severe earthquake that accelerated and aggravated the phenomena already in place.

Therefore, after a brief illustration of how the inner areas have been defined in the related strategy developed by the Italian state and the relationships between the problems of the inner areas and the more general ones of the shrinking cities, the case study of the central Italian areas, affected by the 2016 earthquake, will be illustrated, drawing possible general indications on the investigated phenomena.

In line with the place based approach proposed by Fabrizio Barca (Statistician and economist, as President of the OECD Committee for territorial policies and advisor of the European Commission, he coordinated public administrators and scholars in the design of a new method of intervention for territories that are lagging behind: the "place-based approach") to the European Commission [3, 4] Italy has developed a National Strategy for the Inner Areas which in most cases consist of small and medium municipalities of the Apennines from North to South Italy.

The "National Strategy for Inner Areas" interprets the territory of the Italian inner areas as a set of project areas, treated as local inter-municipal systems each with its own territorial identity defined by social, economic, geographical, demographic and environmental characters. Each project area, selected through an open preliminary investigation between the Region and the State, is asked to develop a Project area development strategy or "Area strategy" Fig. (2).

The selection process of the inner areas - which affect more than 60% of the national territory and 23% of the Italian population - took place through a public investigation procedure, carried out by all the central Administrations collected in the National Inner Areas Committee and by the Region (or autonomous province) concerned.

In order to define the concept of inner areas, the national territory was divided at municipal level not according to a minimum population criterion, nor according to altimetric parameters, but according to a criterion of capacity to offer some essential ser- vices, which have been identified in the presence in the territory of an institution of upper secondary school, a first level hospital structure and a railway station classified not less than the "Silver" category. Based on the coexistence of these three requirements, the "urban poles" and the "inter-municipal poles" have been identified, made up of those neighboring municipalities in which the three essential services were "jointly" present Fig. 1.

Fig. 1. Entrance to the abandoned city of Craco in the Basilicata region in the southern Apennines (photo by the author).

Consequently, the municipalities not included in the poles have been classified according to an "accessibility" indicator, calculated in terms of minutes of travel to reach the nearest pole: the limits have been set in less than 20 min (peri-urban areas or belt), between 20 and 40 min (intermediate areas), between 40 and 75 min (peripheral areas) and over 75 min (outermost areas).

Municipalities with access times over 20 min from the nearest pole have been classified as "inner areas".

The strategy aims to create new income possibilities and to ensure the inhabitants greater accessibility to essential services, as well as to improve the maintenance of the territory itself. It is aimed at financing "pilot interventions" for the rebalancing of the offer of basic services in the inner areas of the country, with priority reference to local public transport, education and socio-health services.

The identification of the inner areas of the country starts from a polycentric reading of the Italian territory, that is, a territory characterized by a network of municipalities or aggregations of municipalities (service offer centers) around which gravitate areas characterized by different levels of spatial periphery. Inner areas are defined as those that are significantly distant from the centers offering essential services (education, health and mobility), rich in important environmental and cultural resources and highly diversified by nature and following secular anthropization processes.

In the case of the Marche region, the inner areas on the border with the Umbria and Lazio regions were affected in 2016 by a strong earthquake that destroyed many homes and public buildings, which will be discussed below, which aggravated and accelerated the shrinkage phenomena already in place. A few years after the earthquake, the Municipalities are still facing the transition from the emergency phase, characterized by a mainly sectoral-operational approach, linked to the temporary nature of solutions,

Fig. 2. The inner areas in Italy. UVAL-UVER processing of data from the ministry of health, ministry of education and FS. The blue area indicates the study area of this work: the inner areas of the Marche region affected by the 2016 earthquake.

to the phase in which implementation urban planning schemes are developed[1]. These plans may envisage public and private building refurbishment interventions, related to

---

[1] Reference regulatory framework: Special Commissioner's Order no. 25: Criteria for the delimitation of urban centers and special interest centers that were most severely affected by the earthquake that occurred on August 24, 2016; Special Commissioner's Order no. 39: implementation planning guidelines related to reconstruction of historic town centers and urban centers that were most severely affected by the earthquake that occurred on August 24, 2016.

building aggregates or individual structural units[2]. This choice was motivated by the desire to avoid losing the local community, in most contexts mainly made up of over 65 elderly people [12], and to fight against depopulation.

2 2016 Earthquake, Urban and Territorial Crisis, Policy and Governance

A severe earthquake struck Central Italy in 2016, affecting four regions, 10 provinces and 139[3] Municipalities, up to a total of approximately 8,000 km2, reaching 6.5 Mw magnitude with the shock recorded on October 30th, which caused the destruction of highly valuable historic centers. The earthquake of 2016 reached a far greater intensity than the previous earthquake that occurred in L'Aquila in 2009, which was regarded as the "fifth most severe disaster in the modern history of Italy", not in terms of the number of victims, but because of the intensity of the earthquake (with the highest peak reaching a 6.3 Mw magnitude) in the affected area.

The Marche Region was the most severely affected region out of the four regions within the area struck by the earthquake, with extensive damage in 86 out of a total of 139 municipalities (3,978 km2 of affected regional surface). The toll was very high: with more than 104,000 damaged buildings, 54,000 evacuated buildings and 32,000 displaced people, of whom 28,500 benefited from Autonomous Accommodation contributions (CAS) since the very beginning and about 3,400 people hosted in accommodation facilities along the Adriatic coast[4].

To avoid the depopulation of the areas affected by the earthquake, and to reconnect people to their places of origin, so- called Emergency Housing Facilities (SAE) have progressively been built since August 2017 (in 28 municipalities located within the area struck by the earthquake), temporarily accommodating over 4,400 people Fig. (3).

The earthquake impact analysis on the housing system (source: Marche Region, June 2018) shows that among the 86 municipalities within the Marche seismic area, 16 municipalities feature more than 30% of the population accommodated in temporary housing solutions (CAS, accommodation facilities and SAE), including 9 municipalities with more than 50% of displaced people due to the earthquake.

The town of Camerino is among the most heavily damaged municipalities, with over 3,500 displaced inhabitants out of a resident population of about 6,850 inhabitants (census dated July 31, 2016), in addition to the non-permanently resident university population Table 1.

[2] Reference regulatory framework: Special Commissioner's Order no. 19: Measures designed to restore and rebuild buildings severely damaged or destroyed by the earthquake that occurred on August 24, 2016, for residential use, according to anti-seismic rules.

[3] On January 1st, 2017 the Municipality of Valfornace was established from the merger of the municipalities of Fiordimonte and Pievebovigliana. The number of municipalities located within the seismic area fell to 139, compared to 140 municipalities set out by decrees Dl 186/2016 and 8/2017.

[4] Variable data surveyed on a monthly basis, source: Osservatorio Sisma (Earthquake Observatory), Marche Region. https://sisma2016.gov.it/.

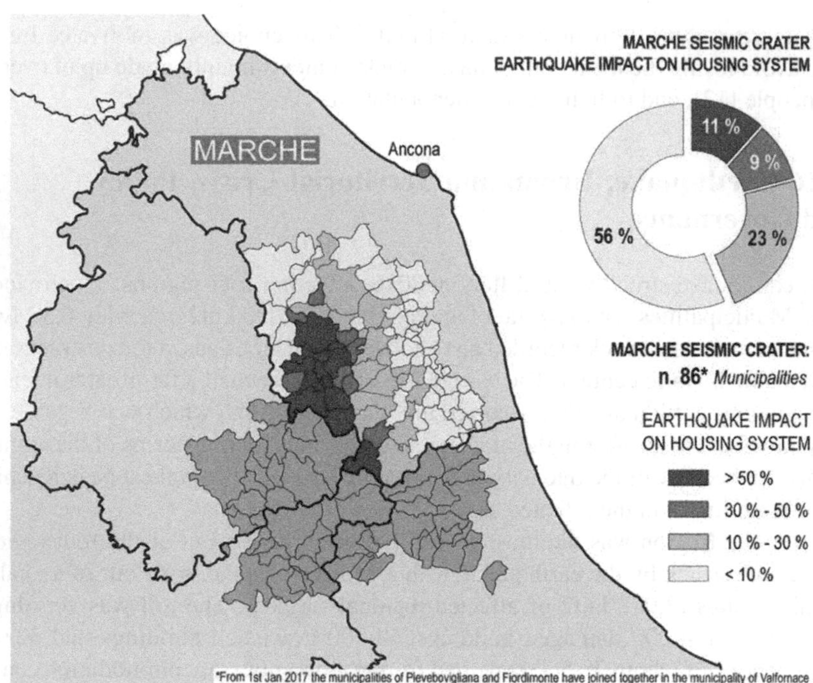

Fig. 3. Marche Region, impact of the earthquake on the housing system; data source: statistics office - Marche Region, http://statistica.regione.marche.it/

Table 1. Table captions should be placed above the tables. data source: statistics office - Marche Region, http://statistica.regione.marche.it/

EARTHQUAKE IMPACT ON HOUSING SYSTEM: Municipalities with population in emergency housing solutions	N. Municipalities	Territorial surface (km^2)	Resident population (on 31/07/2016)	POPULATION IN EMERGENCY HOUSING SOLUTIONS (June 2018)						POPULATION IN EMERGENCY HOUSING SOLUTIONS
				People with contribution for renting accommodation (CAS)		N. people in hotel	N. people in other accommodation facilities	N. people in emergency housing (SAE)	TOTAL population	
				N people	N. households					
MORE THAN 50 % of the population	9	655,5	13.965	5.445	3.005	482	341	2.331	8.599	27,79%
BETWEEN 30% e 50% of the population	7	213,1	4.874	1.380	642	78	7	428	1.893	6,12%
BETWEEN 10% e 30% of the population	21	1.114,9	62.881	10.689	4.706	247	22	458	11.416	36,89%
LESS THAN 10% of the population	49	1.994,7	266.753	8.983	3.843	20	15	20	9.038	29,21%
TOTAL MARCHE SEISMIC CRATER	86	3.978,3	348.473	26.497	12.196	827	385	3.237	30.946	100,00%

Finally, 7 municipalities were heavily affected with more than one third of uninhabitable buildings, including the Town of Caldarola with 749 inhabitants out of 1,806 residents (census dated July 31, 2016), while 21 municipalities feature a total loss of housing functionality of city centers higher than 10%, with 11,416 inhabitants being provided with emergency housing solutions out of 62,881 residents in the area at the time of the earthquake.

A significant earthquake impact, in terms of distribution, has been recorded in the remaining 49 municipalities located in the area affected by the earthquake in the Marche region (about 50% of the territory within the area struck by the earthquake in the Marche region), with an overall incidence of displaced people below 10% of the resident population, and with more than 9,000 people accommodated in temporary emergency solutions Table 2.

Table 2. Marche Region, the earthquake impact on the housing system. Details of the most severely affected municipalities. data source: statistics office - Marche Region, http://statistica.regione.marche.it/

MUNICIPALITY	Territorial surface (km²)	Resident population (on 31/07/2016)	POPULATION IN EMERGENCY HOUSING SOLUTIONS (June 2018)						POPULATION IN EMERGENCY HOUSING SOLUTIONS	EARTHQUAKE IMPACT ON HOUSING SYSTEM: Municipalities with population in emergency housing solutions
			People with contribution for renting accommodation (CAS)		N. people in hotel	N. people in other accommodation facilities	N. people in emergency housing (SAE)	TOTAL population		
			N people	N households						
Arquata del Tronto (AP)	92,2	1.160	468	245	41		418	927	79,91%	
Camerino (MC)	129,9	7.008	2.965	1.791	239	305	18	3.527	50,33%	
Castelsantangelo sul Nera (MC)	70,7	274	69	42	11		108	188	68,61%	
Fiastra (MC)	57,7	552	208	94	7		130	345	62,50%	
Muccia (MC)	25,9	915	331	155	16	10	396	753	82,30%	MORE THAN 50 % of the population
Pieve Torina (MC)	74,8	1445	578	274	37	3	516	1134	78,48%	
Ussita (MC)	55,3	447	101	51	11		177	289	64,65%	
Valfornace (MC)	48,6	1058	375	182	46		225	646	61,06%	
Visso (MC)	100,4	1106	350	171	74	23	343	790	71,43%	
total	655,5	13965	5445	3005	482	341	2331	8599		
Bolognola (MC)	25,9	138	49	23	5		12	66	47,83%	
Caldarola (MC)	29,2	1806	464	214	32		253	749	41,47%	
Cessapalombo (MC)	27,6	508	163	80	11	7	20	201	39,57%	
Gagliole (MC)	24,1	632	215	88	3		4	222	35,13%	BETWEEN 30% e 50% of the population
Monte Cavallo (MC)	38,5	132	21	9			20	41	31,06%	
Montegallo (AP)	48,5	529	198	101	3		44	245	46,31%	
Pioraco (MC)	19,5	1129	270	127	24		75	369	32,68%	
total	213,1	4874	1380	642	78	7	428	1893		
Acquacanina (MC)	26,8	122	37	23				37	30,33%	
Acquasanta Terme (AP)	138,4	2885	753	356	19		6	778	26,97%	
Amandola (FM)	69,5	3623	487	225	3	13	2	505	13,94%	
Camporotondo di Fiastrone (MC)	8,8	557	122	43	2		17	141	25,31%	
Castelraimondo (MC)	44,8	4578	638	280	18		25	681	14,88%	
Colmurano (MC)	11,2	1260	181	78				181	14,37%	
Cossignano (AP)	15,0	976	94	41				94	9,63%	
Force (AP)	34,3	1321	203	83			14	217	16,43%	
Gualdo (MC)	22,2	812	189	76	1		20	210	25,86%	
Monte San Martino (MC)	18,5	757	91	33				91	12,02%	
Montefortino (FM)	78,6	1162	294	123				294	25,30%	BETWEEN 10% e 30% of the population
Montemonaco (AP)	67,8	586	145	72				145	24,74%	
Palmiano (AP)	12,7	189	22	12				22	11,64%	
Roccafluvione (AP)	60,6	1994	231	111				231	11,58%	
San Ginesio (MC)	78,0	3479	810	371	33	9	92	944	27,13%	
San Severino Marche (MC)	194,3	12716	2053	897	108		214	2375	18,68%	
Santa Vittoria in Matenano (FM)	26,2	1325	231	94				231	17,43%	
Sarnano (MC)	63,2	3280	576	245	52		43	671	20,46%	
Serrapetrona (MC)	37,6	954	168	70	11		25	204	21,38%	
Smerillo (FM)	11,3	366	60	24				60	16,39%	
Tolentino (MC)	95,1	19939	3304	1449				3304	16,57%	
total	1.114,9	62881	10689	4706	247	22	458	11416		

The vast majority of the population residing in areas affected by the earthquake in 2016, despite the serious inconvenience experienced so far, decided not to leave their respective towns, although a gradual demographic decline and depopulation process had al- ready been in place even before the earthquake.

The earthquake has further aggravated and accelerated the depopulation process taking place in these areas, reducing even further the minimum habitability standards, in terms of accessibility and provision of basic services, as already broadly pointed out by the National Strategy for Inner Areas [5].

While the decision to provide temporary settlements (Emergency Housing Solutions) to the people affected by the earthquake proved to be, on the one hand, a complex and potentially uneconomic operation especially in these foothill and mountain areas, on the other hand it was motivated by the will not to weaken the local community, predominantly consisting of elderly people aged over 65 [6] and to try to prevent the affected areas from becoming more and more desolate.

The goal would instead be to set up temporary housing areas according to new criteria and guidelines leading to a greater integration with the community and with the landscape. In the event of the occurrence of a future earthquake, it would therefore be necessary to assess in advance the identification and setting up of emergency preparedness areas (waiting, sheltering-admission, gathering), in addition to those guidelines already envisaged by the Civil Protection provisions set out by CLE (Limit Emergency Condition: accessibility and access to the areas, number of aggregate objects interfering with the area in question, first aid facilities, formal and dimensional information, accessibility, service infrastructure, morphology and location of the area, type of soil, type of instability, possible landslides, groundwater, surface water, hazards and danger of flood areas. It is therefore necessary to design a stable prevention and early warning system throughout the territory and to identify equipped areas that may play a dual role: both during the ordinary daily-phase and in the emergency phase during a seismic crisis. Ultimately, the new criteria should be able to ensure integration with the context and the landscape, in order to ensure a better level of connectivity with the existing environment, protect and enhance natural and historical heritage and check the compatibility between temporary functions and pre-earthquake daily functions Fig. (4) and Fig. (5)

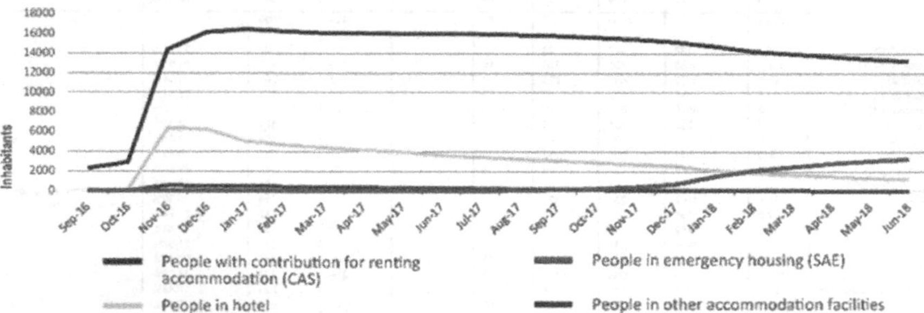

Fig. 4. Region Marche, emergency stage: dynamic housing response. data source: statistics office - Marche Region, http://statistica.regione.marche.it/

3 Resilience Strategies: Programs for Building Back Better, Safety and Disaster Preparedness

The increasing awareness of the high vulnerability of Italian urban systems is triggering off a growing demand for safety, bringing environmental risk prevention and managemen tissues in the public spotlight.

The weakly effective predominantly building-centered approach on safety is highlighting the inherent limitations of a sectoral approach, which neglects the relationships between settlement contexts and urban functional systems.

Fig. 5. Marche Region, temporary housing solutions, examples of settlements

The building risk mitigation interventions (not always consciously) involve an urban impact and for this reason they should be evaluated and readjusted taking into account the spatial, hierarchical and functional organization of the urban context in which they are implemented.

Ensuring the effectiveness and efficiency of risk mitigation actions undoubtedly is the key objective in terms of safety. Therefore it becomes necessary to identify suitable methodologies to relate the urban environment not only to environmental aspects, but also to cultural and economic issues, engaging local communities and individual citizens in the decision-making process, since the promotion of safety to face natural hazards means not just preventing or limiting the damage caused by natural disasters, but also investing on competitiveness and quality of life in our country [7]. Ultimately, the post-earthquake phase should lead to a paradigm shift in the lifestyle of this wide territory based on: a permanent protection of the urban-territorial risk; a networked technological service system providing better services to the local community and businesses; a new functional relationship system between small towns in areas affected by the earthquake and urban centers outside of the earthquake-stricken areas (through transport incentives, cooperative firms, itinerant services for manufacturing activities, etc.) strengthening of cooperation relations and economic and social exchange between communities living in the mountain, hillside and coastal areas.

In conclusion, marginal territorial systems that are not easily accessible, such as inland areas, regional and urban planning should focus on mitigation of risks, seismic vulnerability and the consequent need for changing lifestyles. Therefore, the new strategic land use objectives should include future visions shared by many small towns, circular economic processes associated with new forms of governance based on advanced technological networks providing regional and supra-regional remote protection and assistance.

Despite a few legislative innovations developed within regional contexts (Umbria Regional Law no. 11/05, Marche Regional Law no. 61/08, Emilia-Romagna Regional Law no. 20/2000 and no. 6/2009, Calabria Regional Law no. 19/2002), a clear-cut separation between urban planning and risk planning still remains in Italy [7].

The current legislation envisages only partially the need for prevention within ordinary spatial governance planning, except for the Umbria Regional planning law, which has introduced the so-called Minimum Urban Structure to serve as an essential tool to reduce seismic vulnerability at an urban scale, through goals and actions to be implemented by means of the General Master Plans.

According to the Sendai Framework for Disaster Risk Reduction (2015–30) [12], an interdisciplinary and holistic approach for an appropriate disaster risk management is necessary, based on the awareness that the severity of a natural disaster is closely related to the choices that are made and that concern specific questions pertaining to each individual or having a relevant wide spatial scope, such as life lifestyles; the approach underlying the preservation and enhancement of natural and cultural resources; agroforestry and pastoral activities management; handicraft and industrial manufacturing systems; urban and infrastructural growth planning and design [8].

It is therefore necessary that the Disaster Risk Reduction approach becomes an integral part of the regulations that are immediately enforceable by the Regions and municipalities located within the area affected by the earthquake, to manage and monitor all the lengthy reconstruction process stages, being the only regulatory tool available to supplement the risk "component" in the urban and regional planning project.

This awareness is increasing more integrated in European territorial governance policies. Hence, urban planning cannot relinquish its responsibility in giving its contribution in achieving the above mentioned objectives.

The United Nations Office for Disaster Risk Reduction [12] underlines the following key factors to focus on:

1. Ensure the preparedness of individuals, communities and economic and social organizations to deal with and cope up with natural disasters and related risks by means of appropriate measures to increase the response capacity, and therefore the resilience of local communities;
2. Post-disaster interventions meant to build better, conceiving reconstruction as an opportunity to be seized to mitigate the impact of future disasters. All this is summed up in the slogan Building Back Better [9], i.e. a principle that applies not only to buildings or physical infrastructure but to a much broader attitude.

In this context, the "action plan" launched by the Italian Government, which was established under the coordination of the Extraordinary Emergency Commissioners and centered on Commissioners' Ordinances, was fully implemented only with reference to temporary intervention objectives intended to cope up with the emergency situation; more specifically in accordance with the Law 229/2016 (Civil Protection Law) and the various ordinances, it was designed to meet emergency housing needs, to be swiftly implemented through "unitary and homogeneous" procedural models throughout the area affected by the earthquake, regardless of the varied settlement articulation and different (historical, cultural and natural) landscape features that characterize the Central Apennines spatial contexts [10] Fig. (6).

Even before the 2016 earthquake, the Italian State had paid a special attention to the Apennine area, i.e. a large portion of the national territory, which although rich in environmental resources and landscapes, as well as cultural and local know-how, has undergone a marginalization process that has resulted into a decline in population and employment, along with an inadequate land use and protection.

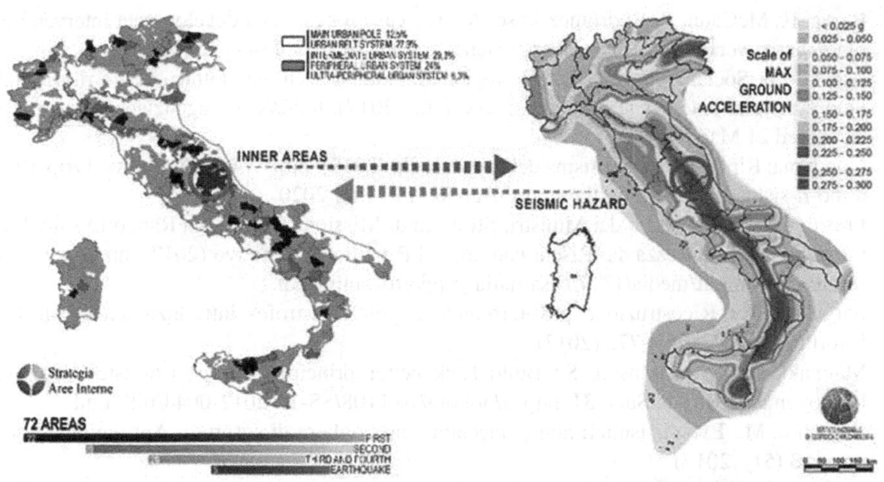

Fig. 6. Case study localization in inner areas and in seismic hazard Italian map

Based on the National Strategy for Inner Areas classification already discussed (see paragraph 1), it has been assessed that Italian inner areas account for 52% of municipalities, 23% of the population and about 60% of the Country's entire territory [11].

At the end of the evaluation process, 72 areas were initially selected, characterized by particularly low-density population levels (2001–2011 census period), and by a 4.4% population decrease compared to an average 4.3% population increase in Italy. The depopulation trend was confirmed in the 2011–2017 period, with a further loss of residents by 3.2% in only six years (as against an average Italian population growth by 1.9%). This trend makes it even more urgent to strengthen the commitment and actions to ensure a prompt implementation and enforcement of planned actions within the area-wide strategies.

In outlining this geographical mapping, National Authorities have carried out a major spatial consultation operation and building of a new multi-level governance system, in which Regional and Provincial Authorities have demonstrated their ability to listen to the local communities' needs and to choose socio-economic policy priorities in agreement with the Central Government.

References

1. Haase, A., Bernt, M., Großmann, K., Mykhnenko, V., Rink, D.: Varieties of shrinkage in European cities. Euro. Urban Reg. Stud. **23**(1), 86–102 (2016)
2. Wolff, M., Wiechmann, T.: Urban growth and decline: europe's shrinking cities in a comparative perspective, 1990–2010. Euro. Urban Reg. Stud. **25**(2), 122–139 (2017)
3. Barca, F.: An agenda for a reformed cohesion policy. A place-based approach to meeting European Union challenges and expectations. Independent Report, prepared at the request of Danuta Hübner, Commissioner for Regional Policy. http://www.europarl.eu-ropa.eu/meetdocs/2009_2014/documents/regi/dv/barca_report_/barca_report_en.pdf. Accessed 20 Feb 2020

4. Barca, F., McCann, P., Rodríguez-Pose, A.: The case for regional development intervention: place-based versus place-neutral approaches. J. Reg. Sci. **52**, 134–152 (2012)
5. Agency for Social Cohesion, Schede regionali, Analisi socio-economica del territorio italiano e delle risorse per le politiche di coesione (2017). http://www.agenziacoesione.gov.it. Accessed 21 Mar.2020
6. Nomisma: Ripartire dopo il sisma del centro Italia (2019). https://www.nomisma.it/ripartire-dopo-il-sisma-del-centro-italia-report. Accessed 21 Mar 2020
7. Presidenza del Consiglio dei Ministri: Struttura di Missione Casa Italia Rapporto sulla Promozione della sicurezza dai Rischi naturali del Patrimonio abitativo (2017). http://www.casaitalia.governo.it/media/1317/casa-italia_rapporto-online.pdf
8. Sargolini, M.: Ricostruzione post-terremoto e post-catastrofe- introduzione. Urbanistica Informazioni **272**, 769–772 (2017)
9. Mannakkara, S., Wilkinson, S.: Build back better principles for post-disaster structural improvements. Struct. Surv. **31**. https://doi.org/10.1108/SS-12-2012-0044/full/html
10. Sargolini, M.: Eventi sismici: non ci facciamo più cogliere di sorpresa. Agriregionieuropa, anno **13** (51) (2017)
11. Labonia, D., Costantini, S: la strategia nazionale per le aree interne: una strategia integrata e multilivello. In: Formez PA (ed.) L'associazionismo intercomunale nelle aree interne, (2019). http://focus.formez.it/sites/all/files/formez_azioni_40.pdf
12. United Nations, Third UN World Conference on Disaster Risk Reduction in Sendai, Japan, (2015). https://www.undrr.org/publication/sendai-framework-disaster-risk-reduction-2015–2030

Evaluating Socio-spatial Exclusion: Local Spatial Indices of Segregation and Isolation in Naples (Italy)

Maria Cerreta[(✉)], Giuliano Poli, and Maria Reitano

Department of Architecture, University of Naples Federico II, via Toledo 402, 80134 Naples, Italy
{maria.cerreta,giuliano.poli}@unina.it, maria.reitano@virgilio.it

Abstract. This research aims at evaluating socio-spatial exclusion, through selected spatial indices of isolation and segregation, within the Municipality of Naples (Italy), where entire communities, living in social housing districts, face critical conditions of social isolation and exclusion from the processes of urban development. The methodological approach investigates the scientific landscape in the fields of policy evaluation, policy analysis and planning, detecting the accepted standards for measuring urban segregation, as well as spatial multi-dimensional indicators and indices, able to tackle complex urban issues, related to social isolation processes, within the urban system. The selection of the global spatial indices of Dissimilarity, Isolation and Exposure, and their application at the local level are tested, using mesh blocks as minimum spatial units. The results identify different clusters within the selected urban territory, expression of the various critical conditions and effect of the many housing policies, during the second half of the last century, that highlight how some policy decision has reinforced segregation dynamics. The research is developed within the framework of the European project HERA Joint Research Programme "Public Spaces: Culture and Integration in Europe", "PuSH: Public Space in European Social Housing".

Keywords: Socio-spatial segregation · Spatial indices · GIS-based evaluation method · Spatial analysis

1 Introduction

Segregation in contemporary cities is to be considered as a global phenomenon of socio-spatial exclusion and isolation among social groups [1], depending, in many cases, on urbanisation processes, that cause increasingly inequalities between wealthy and deprived urban districts [2]. Residential segregation is understood through the combination of income inequality, internal or international migration flows [3, 4], welfare regimes and social housing policy [5], and urban sprawl [6]. Urban expansion processes are often related to phenomena of social segregation and dispersion, deriving from government's inability to establish affordable housing and transport prices, for each population group,

O. Gervasi et al. (Eds.): ICCSA 2020, LNCS 12253, pp. 207–220, 2020.
https://doi.org/10.1007/978-3-030-58814-4_15

according to their income level [7]. Discriminatory processes in social housing policy systems have defined different housing pathways for different social groups, including issues like ownership and housing conditions [8].

The progressive developments of IT have been leading to the whole implementation of spatially explicit data at the global level, directing research towards a multi-dimensional vision of urban phenomena. This vision entailed a redefinition of investigation techniques and tools, which have been implemented by the Organisation for Economic Co-operation and Development (OECD) through the design of guidelines for the integration of multi-dimensionality and complexity of the environmental, political and social issue in practices [9]. The last proposed model concerns the composite indicators [10, 11], as single parameters combined into a synthetic index and determined by the selection of key criteria for understanding the issues analysed.

Composite indicators are, therefore, used to ideally measure those multi-functional concepts that in a complex context cannot be made explicit through simple data and indicators without a significant loss of information. These approaches emphasise the choice of prescription models in terms of mathematical or statistical aggregation procedures, and entail potentials and critical aspects which are inherent substantially to: (i) the definition of shared criteria and objectives at the basis of the information selection process, (ii) the use of a methodology of transparent aggregation, (iii) the explicit explanation and sharing within the context of investigation or political fields, and, finally, (iv) the quality of the available data [9].

During the last ten years, indicators and targets for social inclusion and cohesion have been defined at European and national levels [12, 13]. Indices of Deprivation have been elaborated [14–18] to assess social deprivation and exclusion, according to access to social benefits and services, health care services provisioning, income distribution and housing ownership, level of unemployment, perceived quality of life. All these indicators and indices underline the multi-dimensional aspect of social exclusion analysis [19–21].

Another significant issue is related to the concept of segregation and, in particular, the spatial segregation. A first attempt to define a multi-dimensional measure refers to exposure [22] and dissimilarity indices [23], evaluating residential segregation of different social groups: the first one refers to the potential contact among different social groups; the second one is a measure of evenness among different social groups. These definitions have been further developed, according to the integration of social and spatial dimensions [24].

This paper proposes a preliminary application of the local spatial indices of dissimilarity and exposure, processing statistical data about unequal income distribution on Census tracts, considering the district of Ponticelli, on the outskirts of Naples, Italy.

The following main questions drive the research:

1. How do spatial data, indicators and indices aid to understanding segregation as a complex phenomenon within decision-making processes oriented to new local policies and plans?
2. How to assess socio-spatial segregation within the city?
3. How do urban social housing plans relate to this phenomenon?

The goal is to study the best-fit approach, within the scientific literature, to represent urban segregation and, thus, evaluate the effects of policy and planning processes on the hotspots. The preliminary outcome allows us to test the methodology at different geographical scales.

The first part of the paper (Sect. 2) shows a literature review through the scientific landscape method. The second part (Sect. 3) defines the methodological approach for studying and assessing the urban segregation; the third (Sect. 4) introduces the case study; the fourth (Sect. 5) analyses the preliminary outcome of the research, while the last (Sect. 6) highlights pros and cons of the applied methodology.

1.1 Literature Survey: A Scientific Landscape Map

A literature survey has been implemented and visualised through the bibliometric approach of the scientific landscapes provided by van Eck and Waltman [25] (Fig. 1).

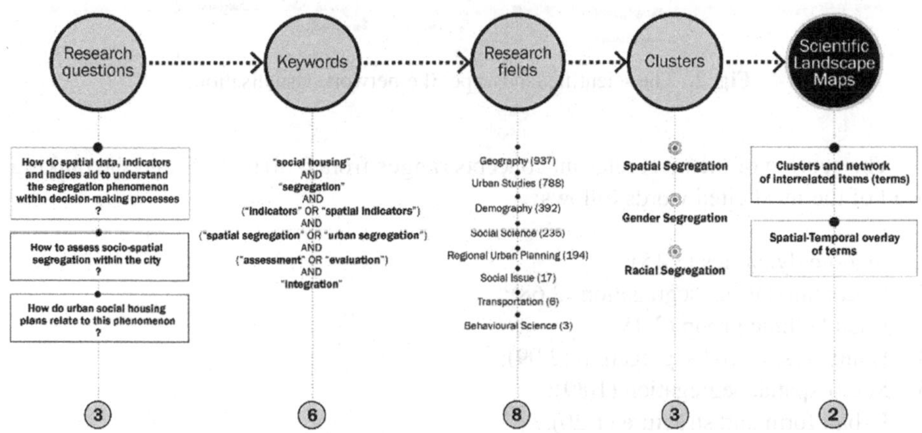

Fig. 1. The methodological steps for the scientific landscape maps.

The search has been led on WOS and SCOPUS database, selecting open access articles in the last three decades. The considered keywords and related logical operators are: "social housing" AND "segregation" AND ("indicators" OR "spatial indicators") AND ("urban segregation" OR "spatial segregation") AND ("assessment" OR "evaluation") AND "integration".

The most consistent fields with the research issues have been selected within WOS categories related to Urban Studies, Regional Urban Planning, Geography and Demography. The overall number of articles is 2.949, of which 796 open access publishing.

Through the network visualisation of the scientific landscape, three clusters of segregation topics have been detected and referred to as: "spatial segregation", "gender segregation" and "racial segregation" core-themes. The distance between two items (words) in the visualisation approximately indicates the relatedness of the items in terms of co-citation links. The weight of clusters indicates the number of term occurrences in the scientific literature (Fig. 2).

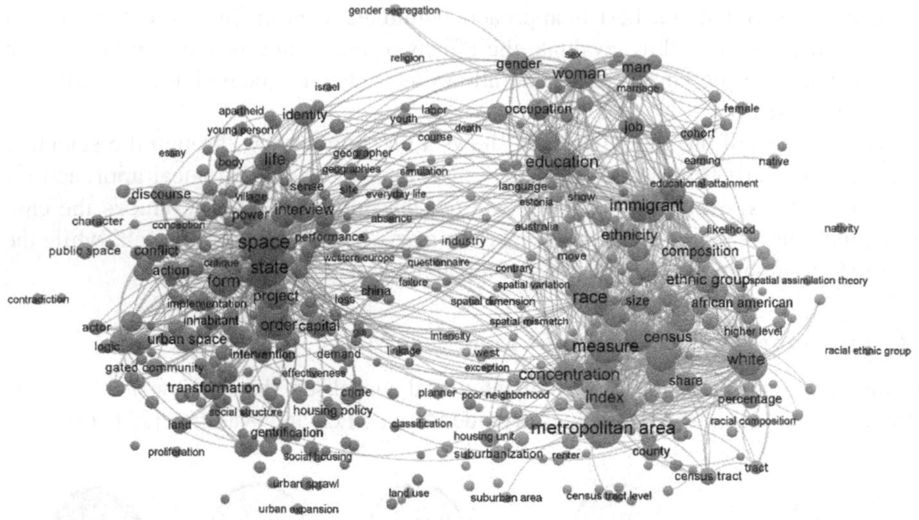

Fig. 2. The scientific landscape: the network visualisation.

The scoring of the most relevant concepts ranges from 0.30 to 3.15, and the ranking head of the most cited words follows:

1. Income dynamics (3.15);
2. Occupational sex segregation (2.68);
3. Racial ethnic group (2.45);
4. Ethnic residential segregation (2.09);
5. Socio-spatial segregation (1.89);
6. Urban form and structure (1.20).

Figure 3 displays a migration of scientific interest in the segregation phenomena from racial and gender issues to a spatial one. Weight and colour of clusters indicate the average number of publication per year that contains the terms mentioned above.

Through the selection of most-cited keywords and concepts, it has been possible to gather and analyse the goal-focused literature in recent years.

The literature study focus is shifting from urban areas and sectors - spatial dimension - where social groups are concentrated - social dimension - to segregation patterns of population clusters - socio-spatial dimension - within the city [26].

The score of 1.89 referring to “Socio-spatial segregation”, along with its temporal dynamics (Fig. 3), highlights a new research trend combining social and spatial segregation where: social segregation includes racial, gender, religious, ethnic, class and income disparities, occurring within the urban space; spatial segregation refers to the residential separation of different social groups [27]; the dependences between the two concepts regard their dialectic relation and a multi-dimensional urban issue [28].

The criteria for evaluation of segregation dynamics by Duncan & Duncan 1955 and Bell 1954 are further developed through four spatial criteria of evenness, clustering,

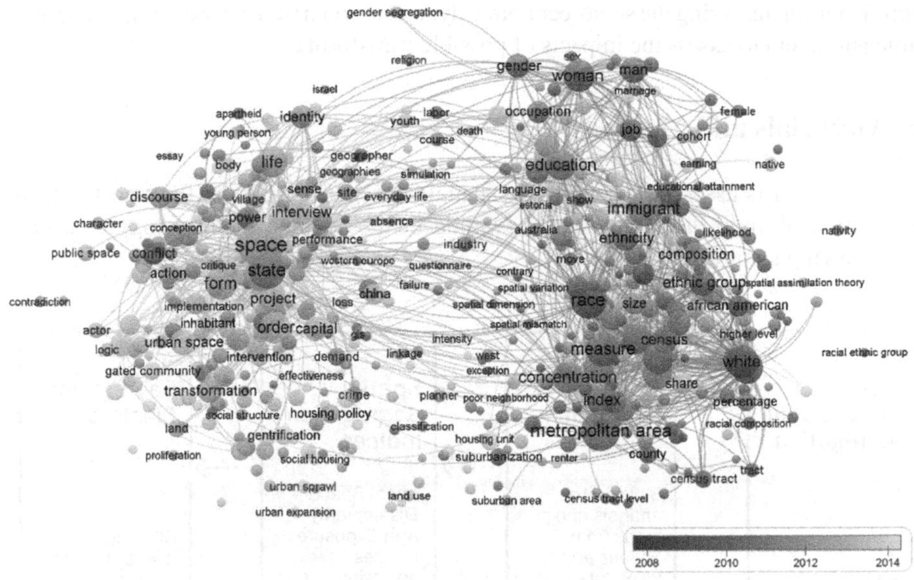

Fig. 3. The average number of publication per year.

exposure and isolation [29], and through complex measures, focusing on the integration of spatial and social dimensions [30–32], and the possibility to spatialise values at different geographic scales: global indices are developed, expressing a measure of segregation for the entire city [33]; local indices derive from the latter, as measures of segregation in different areas, implying the possibility to map segregation patterns within the urban territory [34–36]. Reardon and O'Sullivan [32] propose two spatial segregation measures: one associates the concepts of spatial evenness and clustering, referring to the distribution of different population groups; the other one combines exposure and isolation, underlining the possible contact among different population groups.

According to these measures, Feitosa et al. [24] develop four global or generalised indices of urban segregation and verify their application at the local level:

- Spatial Dissimilarity index, D(m) refers to the comparison of a social group with the entire urban population;
- Spatial Exposure index, P(m,n) indicates the potential contact between two population groups;
- Spatial Isolation index, Q(m) indicates the potential contact among people belonging to the same population group;
- Spatial Neighbourhood Sorting index, NSI refers to population disparities among different study areas.

Local indices allow to detect and map different degrees of segregation, that the global ones are not able to capture, calculating local population intensity, through a kernel function [24, 37]. The classification and evaluation of the above indices are particularly significant for analysing the socio-economic dynamics of territory concerning the spatial dimension, and to assess the impacts of possible transformations.

2 Materials and Methods

The main aim is assessing urban socio-spatial segregation pattern, through the local application of multi-dimensional indices. Indeed, the adopted methodology considers the following steps (Fig. 4):

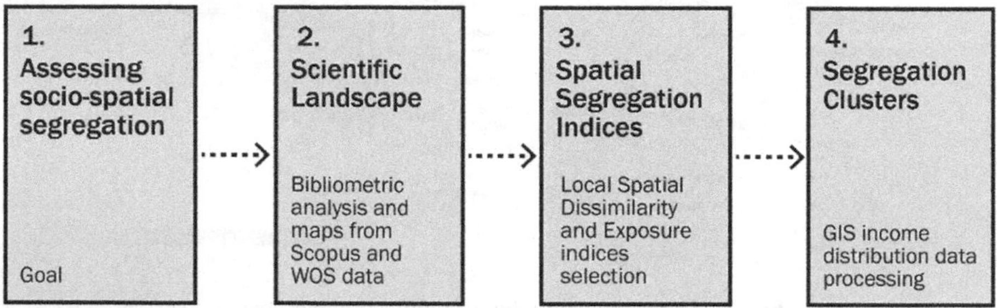

Fig. 4. The methodological steps to assess the urban socio-spatial segregation

1. Methodological goal definition;
2. Scientific landscape analysis;
3. Spatial segregation indices selection;
4. Segregation clusters identification.

The first step identifies the research goal and drives the methodological process towards the interpretation of urban segregation as a multi-dimensional issue, to be understood through social and spatial aspects.

The second step analyses and describes the scientific landscape, and allows, through the bibliometric analysis, to investigate the main issues, to select indicators and indices of segregation and to support the decision-making processes, focusing on the impacts that urban planning policies can have on socio-spatial exclusion.

According to the literature survey, in the third methodological step, two spatial segregation indices have been selected and provided at different scales in a GIS environment: Local Spatial Dissimilarity index *d(m)*; Local Spatial Exposure index *p(m)* [24]. They are processed using unequal income distribution data, and their application is tested at the local level, according to their scientific definition, through the computation of a kernel function.

Indeed, a locality is an aerial unit, that can be represented through its centroid, and kernel density is a geostatistical analysis tool, estimating the intensity of a phenomenon on a surface from punctual events [38]. Using a kernel estimator implicates the setting of a bandwidth of the analysed phenomenon: this allows to explore different scales of segregation analysis and to define to what territorial scale intra-urban segregation patterns emerge [39].

Local Spatial Dissimilarity index *d(m)* is a measure of how the population of each locality differs, on average, from the population composition as a whole. It varies from 0 to 1, where 0 stands for the minimum degree of evenness and 1 for the maximum degree, that is how much clustered a social group is within the urban territory.

$$d(m) = \sum m \frac{N_j}{2NI} \left| t_{jm} - t_m \right| \quad (1)$$

Where:

- *m* is the population group;
- *N* is the total population of the city;
- *Nj* is the total population in areal unit j;
- *I* = $\sum$*m (tm)(1 – tm)*;
- *tm* is the proportion of group m in locality j;
- *tjm = Ljm/Lj*;
- *Ljm* is the total population intensity of group m in locality j;
- *Lj* = $\sum$*j k(Nj)* is the local population intensity in locality j;
- *k* is the kernel estimator which estimates the influence of each areal unit on the locality j.

Local Spatial Exposure index *p(m)* of group *m* to group *n* measures the average proportion of group *n* in the localities of each member of group *m.* It expresses the potential contact between the two population groups (m,n) and ranges from 0 (minimum exposure or isolation) to 1 (maximum exposure).

$$p(m, n) = \sum j \frac{N_{jm}}{N_m} \left(\frac{L_{jn}}{L_J} \right) \quad (2)$$

Where:

- *m* is a population group;
- *n* is a population group;
- *Njm* is the population of group m in areal unit j;
- *Nm* is the population of group m in the study region;
- *Ljn* is the local population intensity of group n in locality j;
- *Lj* = $\sum$*j k(Nj)* is the local population intensity in locality j;
- *k* is the kernel estimator which estimates the influence of each areal unit on the locality j;
- *Nj* is the total population in areal unit j.

The fourth step of the methodological process is related to segregation clusters identification, detecting segregation patterns of population clusters within the urban territory, and addresses the further development of the research toward the assessment of urban segregation dynamics.

3 Case Study

The detection of segregation patterns related to the marginality of social housing districts in Naples (Italy) has been explored applying the local indices of segregation to the case study, through a cross-scale approach, taking into account the municipality, district and housing settlement levels (Fig. 5). The case study of "Lotto O", in the neighbourhood of Ponticelli, in the periphery of Naples, allows investigating on social deprivation of people living in housing districts, which resulted from the national resettlement policies, established after a disastrous earthquake had occurred in 1980.

Fig. 5. The geographical scale of "Lotto O" in Ponticelli, Naples (Italy).

After the rebuilding phase, the housing policy did not enable a resettlement process, supporting people's recovery and social integration. The results are unlivable housing conditions, informal building settlements, social isolation and exclusion from the processes of urban development.

At the municipality level, the comparison with other peripheral districts of Naples, subjected to social housing plans, during the second half of the last century, as well, supports the territorial analysis towards the interpretation of the urban segregation dynamics, which resulted in the socio-spatial exclusion of the most vulnerable population, living in social housing settlements.

4 Results

The two selected indices process data about no income population that derive from the population census, provided by the Italian Statistics National Institute [40] at the mesh block level. Rather than just spatialise population data, the selected spatial indices take into account both the social and the spatial dimensions, constituting, indeed, composite indicators, capable of elaborating together different measures. This operation allows to map multi-dimensional indices, referring to the socio-spatial dimensions of clustering and isolation, and to detect urban processes of gentrification and social exclusion, which often shape the city space through gated-communities and enclosed housing settlements. Furthermore, the local indices application provides insights on urban segregation patterns, allowing to identify differences at a very fine scale of analysis. To grasp local specificities within the urban territory, the research sets up a cross-scale territorial analysis, aiming at comparing the data, according to three different scales, the municipality, district and housing settlement levels. In this paper, the results deriving from the first level of territorial analysis, the municipal one, are presented. The indices are computed, setting a bandwidth of 0.9 within a distance of 1000 sqm, as mean distance among the centroids of Naples Census tracts, as it is shown in Fig. 6, where the adopted kernel density function is mapped. As a consequence, the first spatial level to which the urban segregation pattern results evident and is to be analysed is defined.

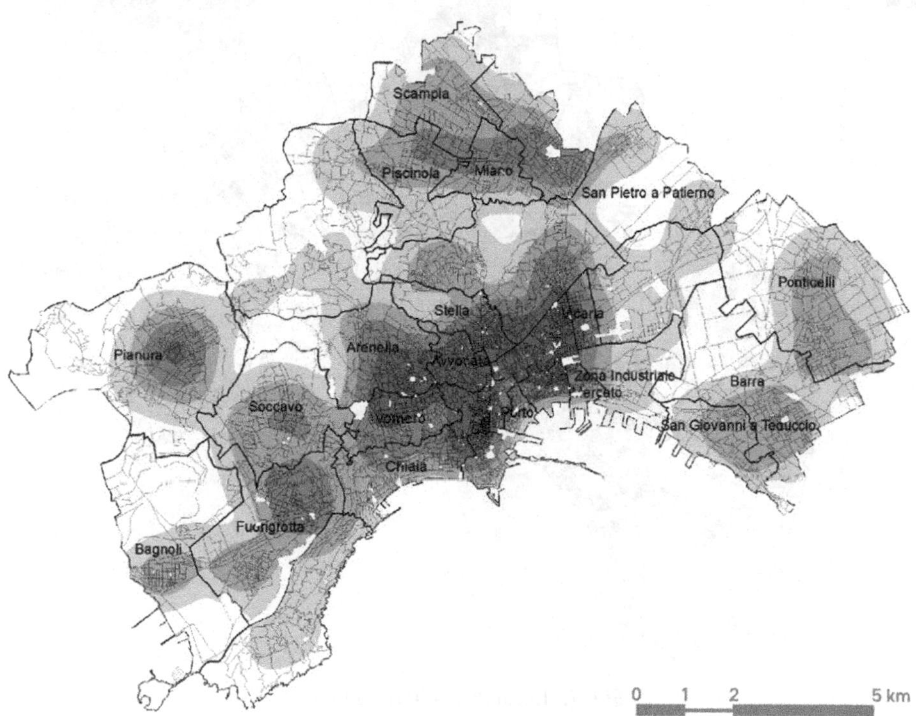

Fig. 6. Kernel density estimation

The local dissimilarity index (Fig. 7) measures how much clustered the group of population with no income is, compared to Naples population as a whole. Clusters emerge in different urban areas: within Scampia district - northern area - that was very much affected by housing policies, between the 60s and 70s, and where many social issues related to deprivation and unlivable housing conditions have arisen, during the last years;

within Pianura district - western peripheral area - which, constituting an autonomous municipality until the 20s, was subjected to urbanisation processes after a community of local workers has settled, defining it as a workers' district; within Ponticelli district - eastern peripheral area - that has a very hybrid fabric, combining industrial and rural areas with different housing settlements, built during the 50s–80s. In "Lotto O", constituting one of these settlements in Ponticelli, dissimilarity values express a medium-high level of no income population segregation. Other smaller clusters are detected within central residential areas and the south-eastern harbour area.

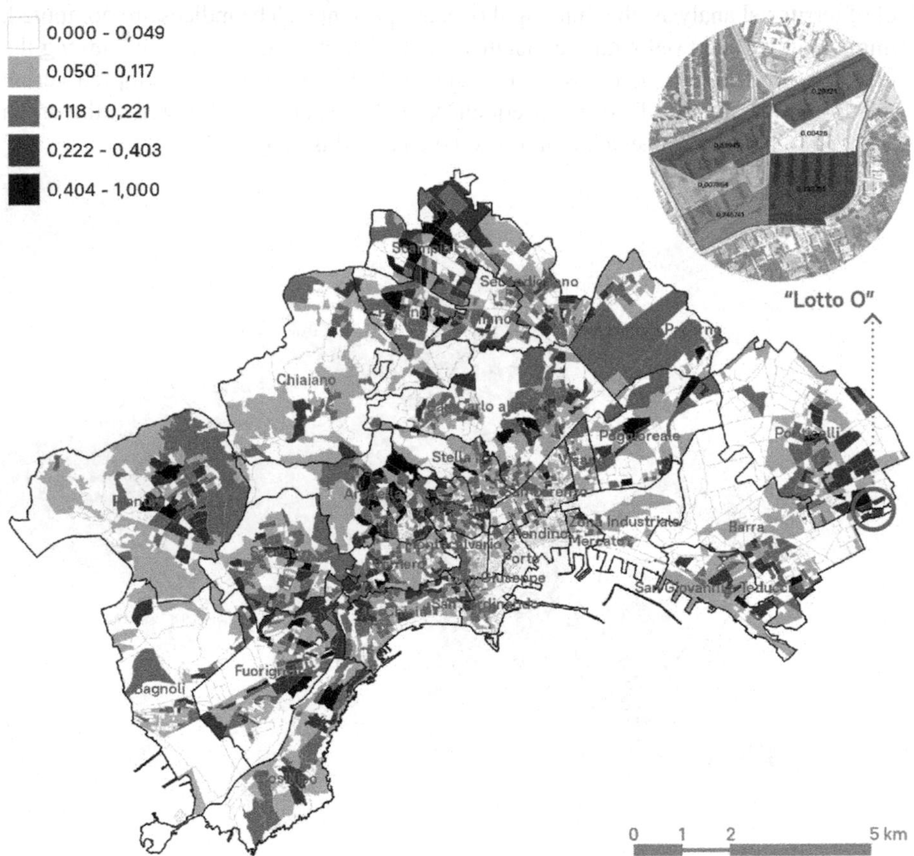

Fig. 7. Local dissimilarity index

The local exposure index (Fig. 8) measures the potential contact between the group of population with no income and the one with an income, that is to say, how much isolated the second group is from the first one. Indeed, two vast urban areas result to be the most enclosed ones: the city central area, comprehending Vomero, Arenella, Colli Aminei and San Carlo all'Arena districts, where exposure values are the lowest ones within the urban territory; the south-western area, including Posillipo and Chiaia districts. These areas represent residential districts, differently subjected to middle-class gentrification processes.

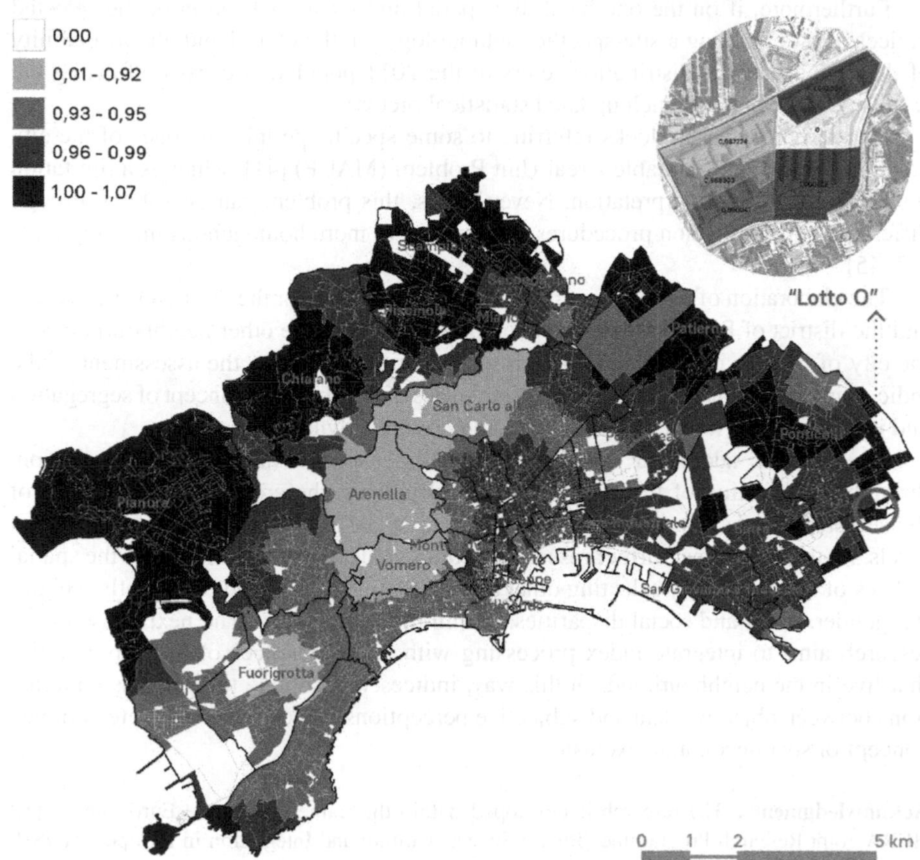

Fig. 8. Local exposure index

Fuorigrotta and Soccavo residential districts result to be very isolated, as well. Middle exposure values are to be found within Naples historic downtown and the south-eastern neighbourhoods, underlining the presence in these areas of a very mixed population. High exposure values feature all the inner peripheral districts, including Ponticelli and "Lotto O" settlement, reflecting a higher density of no income population at the neighbour level. In this perspective, this index can be understood as a measure of no income people vulnerability.

5 Conclusions

The research, focusing on the spatial and local application of segregation indices, underlines the multi-dimensionality and complexity of the phenomenon and the need to evaluate it, through appropriate measures, to address decision-making processes better. Indeed, the results show how urban segregation dynamic is, in many cases, to be related to the negative impacts of social housing and planning policies.

Furthermore, if on the one hand, the spatial and local application of the selected indices allows building a site-specific methodology, on the other hand, the availability of data about income distribution refers to the 2011 population census, affecting the results, with a not very much updated statistical picture.

Moreover, the mesh blocks referring to some specific peripheral zones of the city are affected by the Modifiable Areal Unit Problem (MAUP) [41], which is a limitation for the correct data interpretation. Nevertheless, this problem can be solved through different data aggregation procedures or resorting to more homogenous mapping units [42–45].

The elaboration of the segregation and isolation indices for the "Lotto O" settlement and the district of Ponticelli, allow to compare them with the other neighbourhoods of the city of Naples, understanding the different aspects. Besides, the assessment of the indices underlines the peculiarities of the area, describing how the concept of segregation and isolation are strictly connected to socio-economic dynamics.

The study is addressed towards a multi-dimensional evaluation of segregation, through the selection of further indicators and indices; the cross-scale application of the selected indices, aiming at computing them at the district and housing settlement levels. At the same time, further researches could go deep in the definition of the spatial indices of segregation by selecting other indicators to be processed, differently weighting gender, racial and social disparities, within the urban space. The next phase of the research aims to integrate index processing with the preferences of the communities that live in the neighbourhood. In this way, indices will be able to synthesise interactions between objective data and subjective perceptions that can return a more complex concept of socio-economic exclusion.

Acknowledgments. The research is developed within the framework of the European project HERA Joint Research Programme "Public Spaces: Culture and Integration in Europe", "PuSH: Public Space in European Social Housing", that involves the University of Copenhagen, Denmark (project leader prof. E. Braae), the Norwegian University of Life Sciences, Norway, (research unit coordinator prof. Inger-Lise Saglie), the ETH Zürich, Switzerland (research unit coordinator prof. Marie Antoinette Glaser), and the University of Naples Federico II (research unit coordinator prof. Laura Lieto).

References

1. Peach, C.: Does Britain have ghettos? Trans. Inst. Br. Geograph. **21**(1), 216–235 (1996)
2. Safier, M.: Managing division. City **2**(8), 188–190 (1997)
3. Malmberg, B., Andersson, E., Östh, J.: How does segregation vary between different urban areas? Using a k-nearest neighbor approach to segregation measurement. In: 23rd ENHR Conference, pp. 5–8. University of Toulouse, France (2011)
4. Sleutjes, B., De Valk, H.: Residential segregation patterns of migrant groups in Dutch cities: the role of scale. NIDI Working Paper (2015)

5. Kadi, J., Ronald, R.: Market-based housing reforms and the 'right to the city': the variegated experiences of New York, Amsterdam and Tokyo. Int. J. Hous. Pol. **14**(3), 268–292 (2014)
6. Ramos, F.R., Biderman, C.: Urban sprawl and spatial segregation in Sao Paulo Metropolitan Region. In: Anais do XLI Encontro Nacional de Economia [Proceedings of the 41st Brazilian Economics Meeting]. ANPEC, Brazil (2014)
7. Muth, R.F.: Numerical solution of urban residential land-use models. J. Urban Econ. **2**(4), 307–332 (1975)
8. Robinson, D., Pearce, S.: Housing market renewal and community cohesion. Queen's Printer and Controller of Her Majesty's Stationery Office, UK (2009)
9. OECD: Handbook on Constructing Composite Indicators. Methodology and user guide (2008). www.oecd.org/publishing/corrigenda
10. Cerreta, M., Poli, G.: Landscape services assessment: a hybrid multi-criteria spatial decision support system (MC-SDSS). Sustainability **9**(8), 1311 (2017)
11. Poli, G.: A hybrid evaluation framework for multi-functional landscapes. Theoretical approaches and operative tools for sustainability. Ph.D Thesis, University of Naples Federico II (2018). http://www.fedoa.unina.it/12154/
12. Atkinson, A.B., Marlier, E., Nolan, B.: Indicators and targets for social inclusion in the European Union. JCMS J. Common Market Stud. **42**(1), 47–75 (2004)
13. Schmeets, H., Coumans, M.: The assessment of social cohesion and social exclusion in the Netherlands. In: UNESCO Workshop on Measuring and Assessing Inclusive Social Policies (2013)
14. Salmond, C., Crampton, P., Sutton, F.: NZDep91: a New Zealand index of deprivation. Aust. N. Z. J. Public Health **22**(7), 835–837 (1998)
15. Carr-Hill, R., Chalmers-Dixon, P.: A Review of Methods for Monitoring and Measuring Social Inequality, Deprivation and Health Inequality. University of York, UK (2002)
16. Salmond, C., Crampton, P., Atkinson, J.: NZDep 2006 index of deprivation (Dept of Public Health, trans.). University of Otago, Wellington (2007)
17. Neri, A.R.: The importance of indices of multiple deprivation for spatial planning and community regeneration. The example of the welsh index of multiple deprivation and the related communities first programme for the Italian system. Ital. J. Plann. Pract. **2**(2), 34–65 (2014)
18. Atkinson, J., Salmond, C., Crampton, P.: NZDep2013 Index of Deprivation. Department of Public Health, University of Otago, Wellington, NZ (2014)
19. Levitas, R., Pantazis, C., Fahmy, E., Gordon, D., Lloyd, E., Patsios, D.: The Multi-Dimensional Analysis of Social Exclusion: A Research Report for the social Exclusion Task Force. University of Bristol, Bristol (2007)
20. Perchinunno, P., Rotondo, F., Torre, C.M.: A multivariate fuzzy analysis for the regeneration of urban poverty areas. In: Gervasi, O., Murgante, B., Laganà, A., Taniar, D., Mun, Y., Gavrilova, Marina L. (eds.) ICCSA 2008. LNCS, vol. 5072, pp. 137–152. Springer, Heidelberg (2008). https://doi.org/10.1007/978-3-540-69839-5_11
21. Balena, P., Sannicandro, V., Torre, C.M.: Spatial multicrierial evaluation of soil consumption as a tool for SEA. In: Murgante, B., et al. (eds.) ICCSA 2014. LNCS, vol. 8581, pp. 446–458. Springer, Cham (2014). https://doi.org/10.1007/978-3-319-09150-1_32
22. Bell, W.: A probability model for the measurement of ecological segregation. Soc. Forces **32**(4), 357–364 (1954)
23. Duncan, O.D., Duncan, B.: A methodological analysis of segregation indexes. Am. Sociol. Rev. **20**(2), 210–217 (1955)
24. Feitosa, F.F., Camara, G., Monteiro, A.M.V., Koschitzki, T., Silva, M.P.: Global and local spatial indices of urban segregation. Int. J. Geogr. Inf. Sci. **21**(3), 299–323 (2007)
25. van Eck, N.J., Waltman, L.: Accuracy of citation data in Web of Science and Scopus. arXiv preprint arXiv:1906.07011 (2019)

26. Driedger, L.: Changing boundaries: sorting space, class, ethnicity and race in Ontario. Can. Rev. Sociol. Revue canadienne de sociologie **40**(5), 593–621 (2003)
27. Van Kempen, R., Şule Özüekren, A.: Ethnic segregation in cities: new forms and explanations in a dynamic world. Urban Stud. **35**(10), 1631–1656 (1998)
28. Soja, E.W.: The socio-spatial dialectic. Ann. Assoc. Am. Geogr. **70**(2), 207–225 (1980)
29. Massey, D.S., Denton, N.A.: The dimensions of residential segregation. Soc. Forces **67**(2), 281–315 (1988)
30. Morrill, R.L.: On the measure of spatial segregation. In: Geography Research Forum, pp. 25–36 (1991)
31. Wong, D.W.: Formulating a general spatial segregation measure. Profess. Geogr. **57**, 285–294 (2005)
32. Reardon, S.F., O'Sullivan, D.: Measures of spatial segregation. Sociol. Methodol. **34**(1), 121–162 (2004)
33. Wong, D.W.: Measuring multiethnic spatial segregation. Urban Geogr. **19**(1), 77–87 (1998)
34. Wong, D.: Enhancing segregation studies using GIS. Comput. Environ. Urban Syst. **20**(2), 99–109 (1996)
35. Wong, D.W.: Modeling local segregation: a spatial interaction approach. Geogr. Environ. Model. **6**(1), 81–97 (2002)
36. Wong, D.W.: Spatial decomposition of segregation indices: a framework toward measuring segregation at multiple levels. Geogr. Anal. **35**(11), 179–194 (2003)
37. Reardon, S.F., et al.: The geographic scale of metropolitan racial segregation. Demography **45**(3), 489–514 (2008)
38. Danese, M., Lazzari, M., Murgante, B.: Kernel density estimation methods for a geostatistical approach in seismic risk analysis: the case study of Potenza hilltop town (Southern Italy). In: Gervasi, O., Murgante, B., Laganà, A., Taniar, D., Mun, Y., Gavrilova, M.L. (eds.) ICCSA 2008. LNCS, vol. 5072, pp. 415–429. Springer, Heidelberg (2008). https://doi.org/10.1007/978-3-540-69839-5_31
39. Monkkonen, P., Zhang, X.: Innovative measurement of spatial segregation: comparative evidence from Hong Kong and San Francisco. Reg. Sci. Urban Econ. **47**(07), 99–111 (2014)
40. ISTAT (Italian National Institute for Statistics). Censimento della popolazione e delle abitazioni (2011). https://www.istat.it/it/archivio/104317
41. Openshaw, S.: The modifiable areal unit problem. In: Concepts and Techniques in Modern Geography, vol. 38. GeoBooks, Norwick (1984)
42. Cerreta, M., Inglese, P., Malangone, V., Panaro, S.: Complex values-based approach for multidimensional evaluation of landscape. In: Murgante, B., et al. (eds.) ICCSA 2014. LNCS, vol. 8581, pp. 382–397. Springer, Cham (2014). https://doi.org/10.1007/978-3-319-09150-1_28
43. Cerreta, M., Panaro, S., Poli, G.: A knowledge-based approach for the implementation of a SDSS in the Partenio Regional Park (Italy). In: Gervasi, O., et al. (eds.) ICCSA 2016. LNCS, vol. 9789, pp. 111–124. Springer, Cham (2016). https://doi.org/10.1007/978-3-319-42089-9_8
44. Mele, R.; Poli, G.: The effectiveness of geographical data in multi-criteria evaluation of landscape services. Data **2**(9), 1–11 (2017). https://doi.org/10.3390/data2010009
45. Cerreta, M., Mele, R., Poli, G.: Urban vulnerability assessment: towards a cross-scale spatial multi-criteria approach. In: Gervasi, O., et al. (eds.) ICCSA 2018. LNCS, vol. 10962, pp. 502–517. Springer, Cham (2018). https://doi.org/10.1007/978-3-319-95168-3_34

Sustainable Local Development and Smart Specialisation Strategies: Recent Developments in Agri-food Research and Innovation Partnerships in Puglia, Italy

Manuela Persia, Pasquale Balena, Alessandro Bonifazi(✉), Maria Immacolata Marzulli, Antonio Orlando, and Carmelo M. Torre

Polytechnic University of Bari, 70126 Bari, Italy
m.persia86@gmail.com, {pasquale.balena,alessandro.bonifazi, carmelomaria.torre}@poliba.it, mi.marzulli@gmail.com, a.orlando.it@gmail.com

Abstract. This paper investigates how agri-food research and innovation (R&I) activity may interact with sustainable local development processes. The focus is on smart specialisation strategies and partnerships between agri-food business and research organisations, established under the open innovation paradigm. An exploratory study is carried out on recent (2010–19) agri-food R&I activity in Puglia (Italy), covering both projects and patents carried out by 47 research centres (affiliated to any of 11 research institutions) and 40 agri-food enterprises. Beside project data analysis based on categorisation, the methodology applied social network analysis to partnerships. Findings point to Sustainable Manufacturing and Human and Environmental Health being the prevalent target areas of innovation activity, thus resulting in some form of sustainable agricultural intensification, with a bias towards Industrial Biotechnology, Advanced Materials and Nanotechnology. Open innovation approaches seem to be still phasing in, and the innovation potential of agri-food enterprises appears to be largely untapped. Future research may address the friction between industry-driven smart specialisation strategies and place-based innovation patterns that harness the intangible potential of social and relational capital.

Keywords: Agri-food sector · Open innovation · Smart specialisation · Food Systems · European innovation partnerships

1 Introduction

Researchers and innovators have been confronted with many challenges and wicked problems while aiming to support food and nutrition security for all [25, 30].

Sustainable development-oriented policy making has increasingly payed attention to food security and nutrition – as framed by Agenda 2030's Goal 2 "End hunger, achieve food security and improved nutrition and promote sustainable agriculture" and other mutually reinforcing goals [19, 28].

O. Gervasi et al. (Eds.): ICCSA 2020, LNCS 12253, pp. 221–236, 2020.
https://doi.org/10.1007/978-3-030-58814-4_16

Against the background of these ambitious goals set by the global community, major challenges still need to be tackled, which include [11, 24]:

- pressure of a growing world population (expected to be about 9 billion by 2050 with 70% of the population in urban areas);
- climate change and other global environmental changes;
- economic inequalities and political instability;
- food safety issues and adverse nutrition behaviours and lifestyles, resulting in an increase in the rate of non-communicable, diet-related diseases (including coronary heart disease, stroke, and diabetes).

On top of delivering on unprecedented output targets, food systems are therefore expected to become fully nutrition-sensitive and planetary-boundaries compatible.

To that end, the "knowledge transfer" paradigm has inexorably shown its limitations, giving way to alternative approaches to knowledge exchange, learning and innovation.

Under the European Innovation Partnership "Agricultural Productivity and Sustainability" (EIP-AGRI), funded by the European Commission (EC)[1], an "interactive innovation model" became popularised: in its most advanced terms, knowledge is co-created by farmers, scientists, advisers, enterprises, NGOs and other stakeholders.

On the operational level, Agricultural Knowledge and Innovation Systems (AKIS) are understood as means to analyse and manage how farming practices, business models, regulations and funding programmes, expertise and research outputs interact within a country or a region [20]. It is apparent from the outcomes of an EU-funded research project [21] that the overall strength and the degree of integration of AKIS vary significantly across Europe (Fig. 1).

Fig. 1. An overview of the state of Agricultural Knowledge and Innovation Systems (as of 2014) in Europe. Source: EIP-AGRI [16], adapted after Knierim and Prager [21].

Within the rapidly evolving field of research and innovation studies, the Open Innovation (OI) concept has been recently gaining momentum, and it may be defined as "*a*

[1] https://ec.europa.eu/eip/agriculture/en.

distributed innovation process based on purposively managed knowledge flows across organizational boundaries, using pecuniary and nonpecuniary mechanisms in line with the organization's business model" [6]. OI also considers the central role that users play in both value creation and as the beneficiaries of innovative products and services, thus including a well-functioning ecosystem that allows co-creation, whose members interact "*along and across industry and sector-specific value chains to co-create solutions to socio-economic and business challenges*" [12, 13: 13].

The links between the OI approach and the agri-food sector have been broadly explored in recent years. Under the auspices of a recent call for solutions promoted by a non-profit organisation[2], these links have been conceptualised as to include:

- shared value across food networks
- Internet of Things as a solution for precision agriculture
- tracing and tracking using blockchain
- climate change and variability adaptation strategies
- circular economy applied to agriculture.

On the whole, OI in the agri-food sector entails concerted efforts to: a) shift attention from the conceptual and operational framing of "knowledge transfer" to triggering "open innovation processes"; b) highlight any specificity of the agri-food sector with respect to OI approaches and; c) investigate synergies and frictions between agriculture/ rural development policy and regional innovation strategies.

As for the second and third issues, the lines of research carried out at the European Commission-Joint Research Centre's Institute for Prospective Technological Studies may help develop a comprehensive framework focusing on knowledge sharing: by 2016, a total of 85 EU regions had selected over 270 agri-food-related smart specialisation priorities – the most frequently identified being novel agri-food technologies, agri-food and tourism, and food with higher added value [5, 7].

Both European Innovation Partnerships and Smart Specialisation Strategies were launched by the EU in an attempt to place following research questions innovation at the heart of its integrated strategy for smart, sustainable and inclusive growth [14] – and framed in the Europe 2020 Flagship Initiative "Innovation Union" [15].

Hence, by prioritising agri-food innovations for strategic investments, some regions signalled the importance of the agri-food sector for their sustainable local development trajectories, within a broader trend towards harnessing the European Regional Development Fund to develop research and innovation capacity across Europe.

Based on activities carried out in the framework of the Interreg V-A Greece-Italy "Innovative Networks for the Agrifood Sector" project (Innonets), this paper aims at presenting some preliminary analyses concerning recent (2010–2019) research&innovation (R&I) activities (covering both projects and patents) in the agri-food sector in the Puglia region (Italy). Moving from a survey of research organisations and programmes, the work addresses the following research questions:

[2] Fondazione Giacomo Brodolini, Social Roots programme: www.socialroots.eu.

1. what is the focus of R&I activity in the agri-food sector in the target area?
2. is R&I activity evolving towards open innovation approaches?
3. is the regional smart specialisation strategy playing a role in linking R&I activity to sustainable local development?

To that purpose, the following Section introduces the context for R&I activity in the study area, while Sect. 3 illustrates the methodology adopted by the research team. After reporting on the preliminary results in Sect. 4, the paper closes with a brief discussion and some concluding remarks.

2 The Context of Research and Innovation Activity in Puglia, Italy

Puglia lies in South-eastern Italy; it stretches over almost 20.000 km^2 and hosts around 4 million inhabitants. It is mostly flat, except for the Monti Dauni range and the Gargano headland, which face each other across the main plain in the North (Tavoliere). Once dominated by extensive agriculture and few prominent trading centres, Puglia evolved into a mixed economy with a growing service sector and few industrial poles. There are 257 municipalities, mainly medium to small towns, grouped into a Metropolitan city (Bari) and five provinces.

According to the regional Smart Specialisation Strategy[3], the most promising agri-food research areas in Puglia concern traceability, quality and safety, biotechnologies, advanced sensor and microsystem technologies for precision farming, as well as a diversified array of technologies and methods for food preservation and processing. Among the many research initiatives that have been surveyed, production-driven R&I activities seem to prevail over processing- and marketing-oriented ones.

A preliminary investigation of innovation clusters in the agri-food sector identified 4 policy-driven clusters – one with a regional remit (the Agri-food Regional Cluster-D.A.RE.) and three local clusters, each covering the territory of 1 to 3 provinces and reflecting the local specialisation patterns:

- Jonico Salentino Agri-food cluster;
- Terre Federiciane Agri-food cluster;
- Plant nursery and Flower growing Cluster.

Moreover, the links between R&I supply and demand may be described following the outcomes of a recent study on innovation needs in the agri-food sector in Puglia[4] [26], and therefore investigated along 7 focus areas covering, among others, both traditional supply chains (such as the wine and oil's) and more innovative topics – having a bearing on food safety and sustainable agriculture.

[3] Adopted on 1 August 2014 by means of Resolution n. 1732 of the Regional Council of Puglia, concerning *"Strategia regionale per la Specializzazione intelligente - approvazione dei documenti strategici 'SmartPuglia 2020' e 'Agenda Digitale Puglia2020.'"*

[4] Commissioned by the regional government and carried out by the then National Institute for Agricultural Economics (INEA), now merged into the CREA-Council for research in agriculture and the analysis of agrarian economics.

The three main categories that may help trace either thematic or territorial links that hinge on R&I activities in Puglia are shown in Fig. 2, along with a few examples drawn from the abovementioned sources.

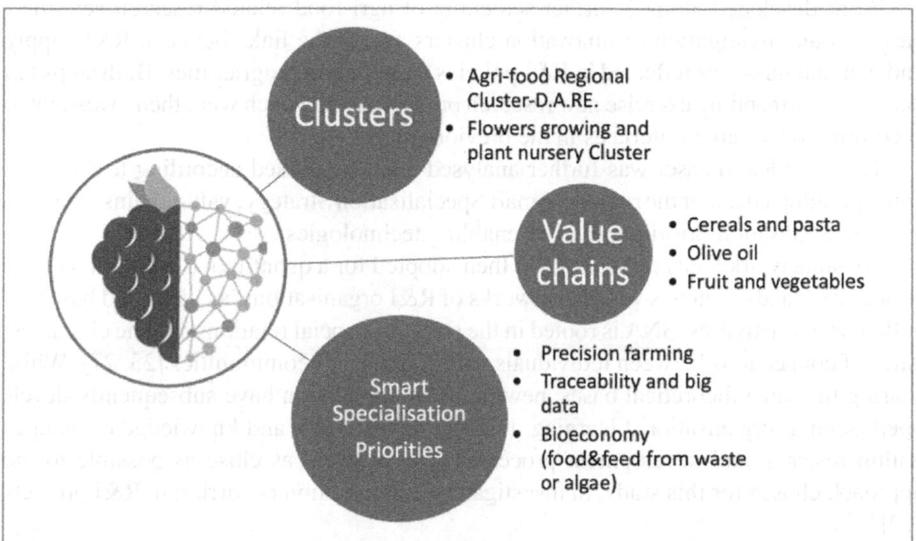

Fig. 2. A schematic conceptualisation of the main thematic or territorial links emerging from the R&I activity in the agri-food sector.

With a view to investigating the links between R&I activity in the agri-food sector and sustainable local development, it might be useful to sketch the spatial distribution of cultivated areas, by identifying the main crops and some specialisations that appear to be remarkable in terms of either local prevalence or market concentration at national level. By way of an example, within the framework of a prominent prevalence of a few cultivations at the regional level (with arable land accounting for almost 50% of the total utilised agricultural land, olive groves for about 33%, and vineyards for somewhat less than 10%), these are unevenly distributed across the provincial territories. Moreover, some specialisations on individual agri-food products – which would not stand out in regional statistical accounts of crop categories – are worth an in-depth analysis to screen for innovation potentials, given their remarkable share even at national level (it is the case of, among others, cherries, tomatoes and artichokes, which accounted, respectively, for 35%, 35% and 31% of the overall national production in 2012).

3 Methodology

The research design moved from a mapping exercise of all R&I centres and institutions with an active interest in the agri-food sector, located in the Puglia region. These were investigated and illustrated by focusing on both their organisation and outputs, according to a simplified framework, covering:

- a list of recently funded projects;
- awarded patents;
- active laboratory and spin-offs.

Work developed along a further screening of agri-food related research activities, based on an investigation of innovation clusters and of the links between R&I supply and demand links – as reflected in R&I policies and funding programmes. Both steps fed back into the mapping exercise new research organisations, which were then investigated according to the same criteria as in the previous step.

The complete dataset was further analysed and categorised according to the main concepts adopted under the regional Smart Specialisation Strategy: value chains, clusters, smart specialisation priorities and key enabling technologies.

Social network analysis (SNA) was then adopted for a quantitative evaluation of the structure of, and dynamics within, networks of R&I organisations, as identified based on collaborative activities. SNA is rooted in the studies of social relations and the characteristics of connections between individuals within groups or communities [23, 27]. While sharing the same theoretical bases, new fields of application have subsequently developed, such as organisational learning, management studies, and knowledge exchanges within research and development processes [29] or even, as close as possible to the approach chosen for this study, in investigating collaboration occurring in R&I projects [10].

SNA supported the ex-post analysis of the network of relationships between R&I partners, aiming to identify collaborative social phenomena which may have emerged, consciously or unconsciously, and to discuss their dynamics.

The *degree centrality* and the *betweenness centrality* indicators were applied to Nodes (R&I organisations, including both research centres and agri-food firms) and Edges were weighed according to the number of projects each couple of organisations collaborated on. Moreover, macro-descriptors of the like of the *average path length*, the *clustering coefficient* and the *degree distribution* were chosen to analyse the whole network. The Gephi Tools open source software package was used both to measure the indicators and to draw the network diagrams, based on Fruchterman-Reingold layout algorithms [1].

Geospatial data analysis was performed with Kepler.gl, a high-performance web-based application for visual exploration of large-scale geolocation data sets [2, 31]. In Fig. 3 we provide a step-by-step visual representation of the research process.

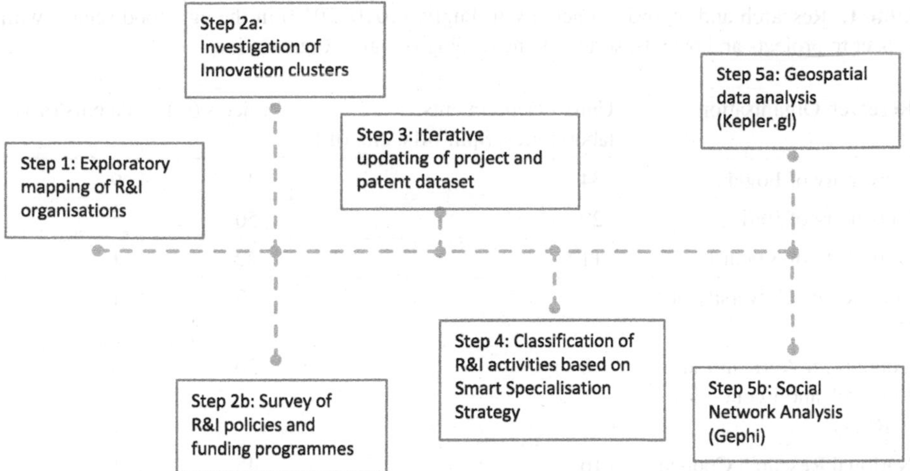

Fig. 3. The main steps in the research workflow.

4 Results

Following a survey of R&I activity, 145 projects (including permanent research facilities that focus on the agri-food sector) and 17 patents were identified. These are listed in Table 1, as sorted according to the main research organisation (out of the total 11) that was involved in the activity.

The full dataset allows a breakdown of the R&I activity carried out at each organisation into their internal departments and centres. Most R&I organisations are public bodies, state-controlled or publicly funded hybrid organisations, with a few exceptions. Within larger organisations, it is interesting to note that agri-food related R&I activity sometimes involves units that focus on different areas, such as information technology and health, thus signalling an interdisciplinary approach.

Among the Spin-offs that carry out applied research in the agri-food sector, Sinagri (University of Bari) and Innovative Solution (Polytechnic University of Bari) are those that are currently active in the largest number of projects. The latter also developed a relevant patent.

R&I outputs were subsequently sorted according to the main categories of thematic links, to track trends and specialisation patterns. With respect to value chains, Fig. 4 concerns both projects and patents: beside the main value chains of interest in the region, Labelling and Logistics have been singled out from other cross-cutting topics (which still account for 35% of the total activity), because of their relevance to territorial cooperation and market internationalisation.

Fruit and vegetables (15%), olive oil (13%) and wine (11%) are the most represented value chains, with most activities dealing with productivity enhancement or quality control. Most of the 17 patents concern the processing of cereals and flours to produce low-gluten pasta (23%), the development of a novel biodegradable-food-packaging material (18%), and innovative methods to produce canned fruit (18%).

Table 1. Research and innovation activity in Puglia (2010–2019) in the agri-food sector, with respect to projects and patents, sorted by the leading research organisation.

Research Organisation	Units - Departments, laboratories, Spin-offs, *etc.* (n.)	Projects (n.)	Patents (n.)
University of Foggia	34	44	9
University of Bari	20	50	5
University of Salento	11	22	1
Polytechnic University of Bari	4	13	1
Council for Agricultural Research and Economics (CREA)	8	30	0
National Research Council (CNR)	16	45	1
Animal Health Research Institute of Puglia and Basilicata (IZSPB)	4	11	0
CIHEAM/IAMB - Mediterranean Agronomic Institute of Bari	1	19	0
CMCC Foundation - Euro-Mediterranean Research Centre on Climate Change	1	1	0
"Giovanni Basile Caramia" Centre for research, development and training in agriculture	1	8	0
Bonassisa Lab	1	3	0
Total	101	246*	17

*This count is redundant, when compared to the previously mentioned figure of 145 projects, because some projects were carried out by two or more partners.

As for the priorities identified by the Region's Smart Specialisation Strategy – adopted in the wake of the EU 2020 smart, sustainable and inclusive agenda – only *Sustainable Manufacturing* and *Human and Environmental Health* were significantly represented in both projects (around 40% each) and patents (around 50% each), while *Digital, creative and inclusive communities* were only relevant to 17% of projects.

The concentration of patents in a few areas is also observed when Key Enabling Technologies are adopted as categorisation principles (Fig. 5), although in this case only one category is prevalent in both projects and patents (*Industrial Biotechnology*),

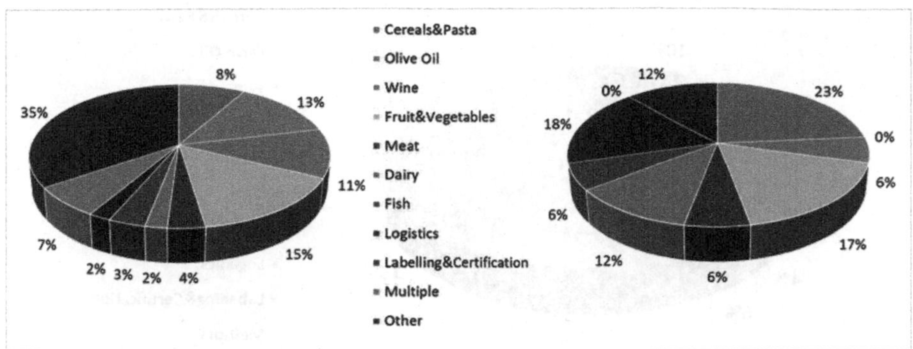

Fig. 4. R&I activity in the agri-food sector in Puglia (2010–19), sorted according to value chains. Projects on the left, Patents on the right.

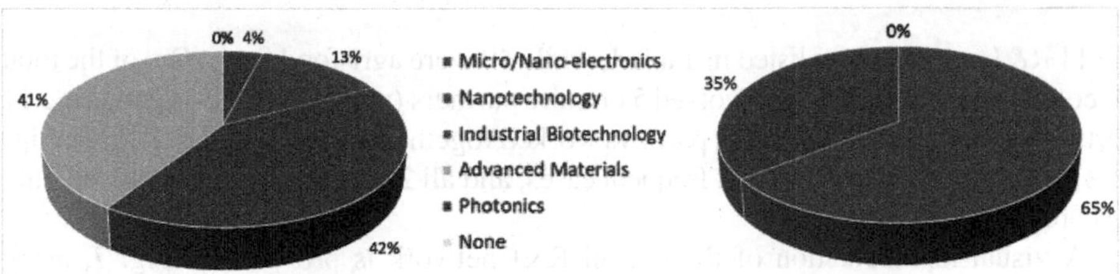

Fig. 5. R&I activity in the agri-food sector in Puglia (2010–19), sorted according to Key Enabling Technologies. Projects on the left, Patents on the right.

whereas *Advanced Materials* (for projects) and *Nanotechnology* (for patents) proved to be the dominant categories accounting, respectively, for 41% and 65% of the activities.

4.1 The Shaping of Research and Innovation Networks

Partnerships are key to R&I activity, although only one third of the surveyed projects involved two or more partners. Based on this subset, a major difference may be appreciated, that is, the share of projects focusing on no particular value chain is significantly lesser, whereas the breakdown among the other items is similar in proportion (Fig. 6).

The most remarkable difference in the distribution of collaborative projects over smart specialisation priorities, when compared to the whole sample, concerns a significant increase in the share of *Sustainable Manufacturing* (more than 30%) to the detriment of *Human and Environmental Health.* Similar trends, yet of a lesser magnitude, may be observed for Key Enabling Technologies – with *Micro/Nano-electronics* and *Advanced Materials* increasing, while *Nanotechnology* and *Industrial Biotechnology* are less represented in collaborative projects. Most of the partnerships sought to develop innovative technologies and materials aimed at boosting either resource-efficiency, or the recycle and reuse of waste and by-products.

Turning to SNA for a quantitative analysis, an overall network of 87 partners was detected – 47 of which were departments, laboratories or Spin-offs affiliated to any of

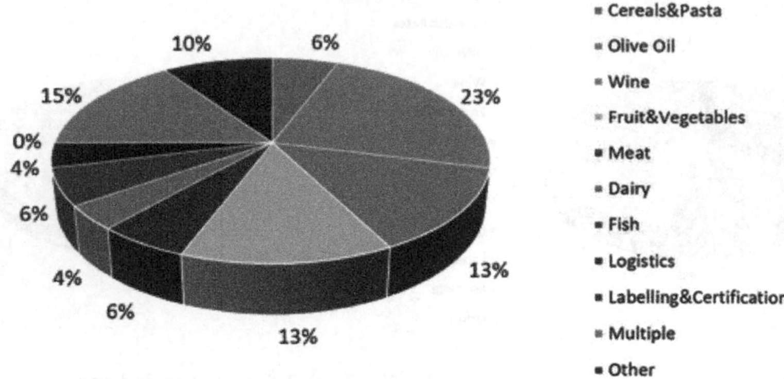

Fig. 6. R&I projects in the agri-food sector in Puglia (2010–19), carried out by partnerships of two or more organisations, and sorted according to value chains. *Cfr*. Fig. 4.

the 11 R&I organisations listed in Table 1, while 40 were agri-food firms. Out of the total 52 collaborative projects, 23 involved 5 or more partners (with two projects gathering 11 partners each), while four or less partners worked together in 29 initiatives. Partnerships of 2 or 3 members were the most frequent cases, and all 2-partner projects involved only research organisations.

A visual representation of the overall R&I network is provided in Fig. 7, using the *degree centrality indicator* and showing weighted edges, based on the Fruchterman-Reingold Layout algorithms. Beside the apparent centrality of about 10 highly connected organisations – in equal share, research centres (among which, four are hyper-connected to each other) and agri-food firms – there appear to be two relatively homogenous network components with gradually decreasing interconnectedness. A negligible number of nodes, mostly research centres, are peripheral or relatively isolated, since the edges of lower-degree nodes tend to spread over large areas of the network.

The centrality of the core component is reinforced by the observation that the involved nodes (all representing research organisations) have the highest values for both degree and node strength (since edges are weighted according to the number of projects each couple of organisations is collaborating on), and also relatively high values of *betweenness centrality*.

4.2 The Spatial Dimension of Innovation Networks

The contribution of R&I to territorialisation processes was first investigated by searching for the role of agri-food clusters, established under a regional law: 16 projects fall within the Regional Agri-food Cluster-D.A.RE., which therefore appears to play a key role in fostering R&I in its target thematic area, while only one project involves the Plant nursery and Flower growing Cluster and none concerns the other two clusters ("Jonico Salentino" and "Terre Federiciane" Agri-food clusters), despite the affiliation of both agri-food business and research organisations.

A further attempt to unravel the spatial links of agri-food R&I activity across the Puglia region moved from mapping projects and patents onto the location of the

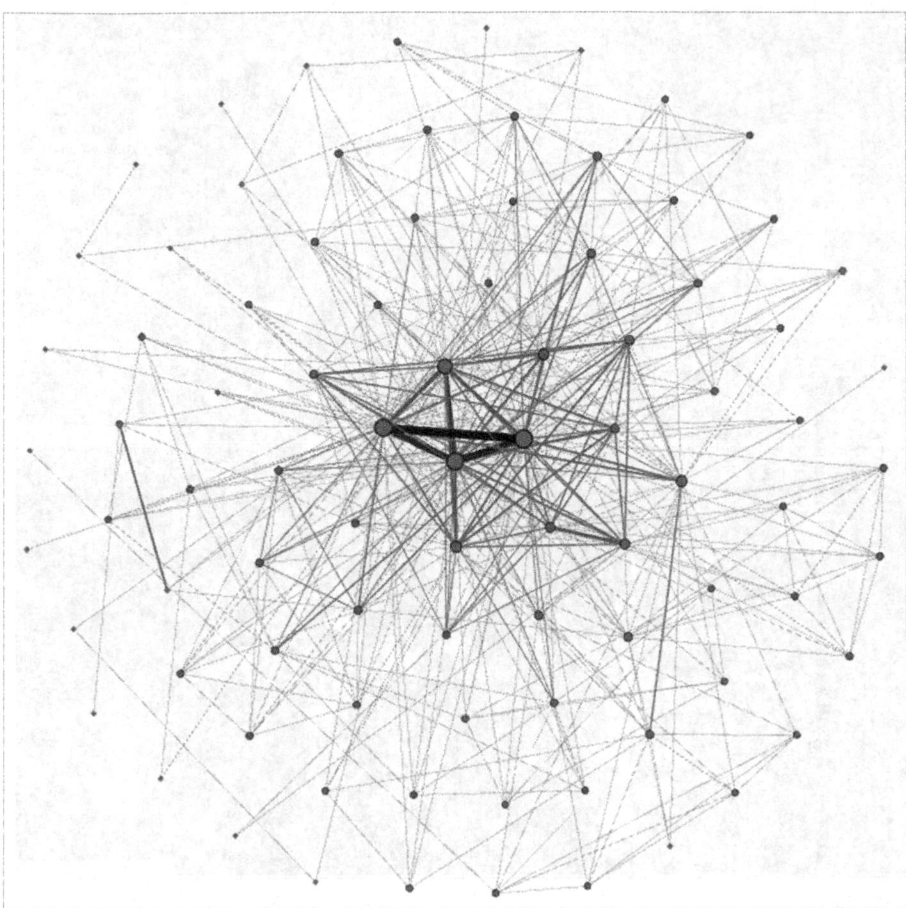

Fig. 7. The network of collaborative R&I projects diagram, based on the *degree centrality* indicator, weighted edges and Fruchter-man-Reingold Layout algorithms. Nodes representing research centres are red, agri-food business green. (Color figure online)

intermediate-level unit within the relevant organisations and drawing a corresponding topographic network accordingly. A very preliminary outcome of such efforts, supported by the Kepler.gl web application, is included in Fig. 8.

4.3 The Role of Agri-Food Business in R&I Networking

A focus on the involvement of agri-food firms in R&I activity revealed contrasting trends. On the one hand, there are very few firms engaging in R&I activity (40 out of a total 80,000+ in the region), and yet most of them participated in at least five projects, thus suggesting that they have been building up innovation capacity over time. Moreover, although their average *betweenness centrality* is lower, they don't show the polarisation that may be observed for research organisations, whose average values are driven by a few very high values. When the analysis is limited to the sub-network based on those

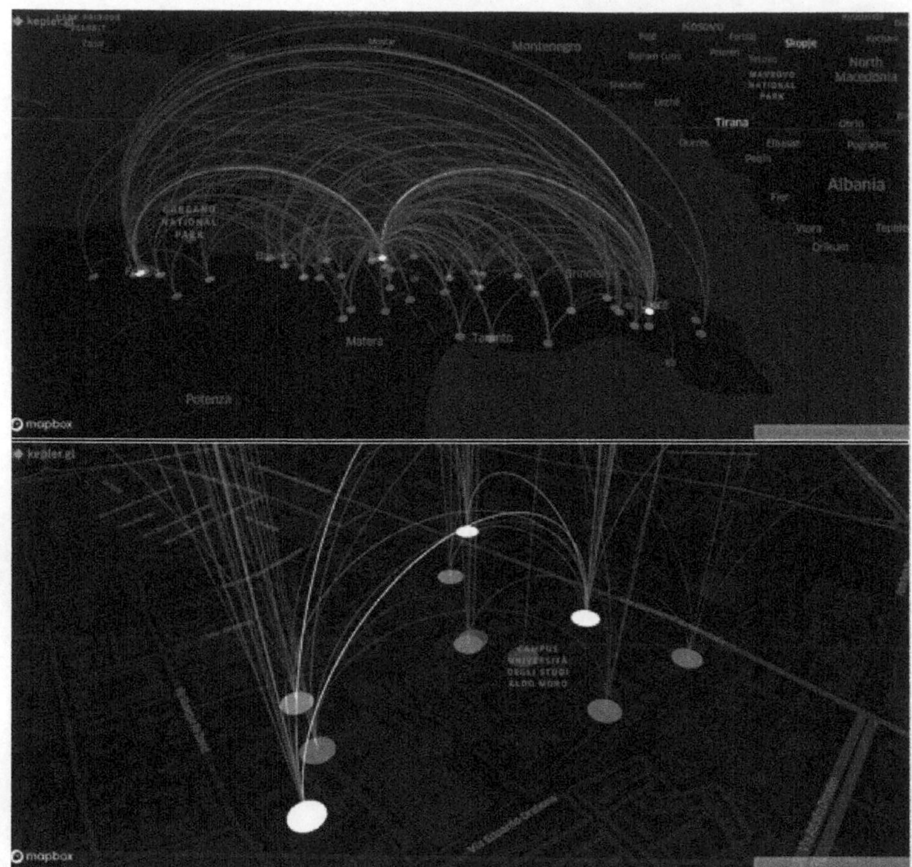

Fig. 8. A spatial visualisation of the R&I network in Puglia, built with Kepler.gl: in the top panel, the whole network; in the bottom panel, a dense cluster of research centres (in Bari).

R&I projects that involve at least one firm, the number of active research organisations drops from 47 to 25 (since 22 research centres only collaborate with other research organisations) and a relatively more fragmented network structure emerges (Fig. 9), as corroborated by the moderately higher value of *average path length* (2.47 vs 2.17) and the considerably lower value for the *clustering coefficient* (0.48 vs 0.83).

A core component is still manifest, although it now appears to include both research centres and agri-food firms, in almost equal share. Two smaller components are visible on the right side, loosely connected to the core, and only connected to each other through the intermediation of two research centres, which therefore have a relatively high betweenness centrality. It is also worth pointing to an organisation that has been grouped under the agri-food firms though in fact being a consultancy (Agriplan): it shows as high degree and centrality values as those of the core research centres.

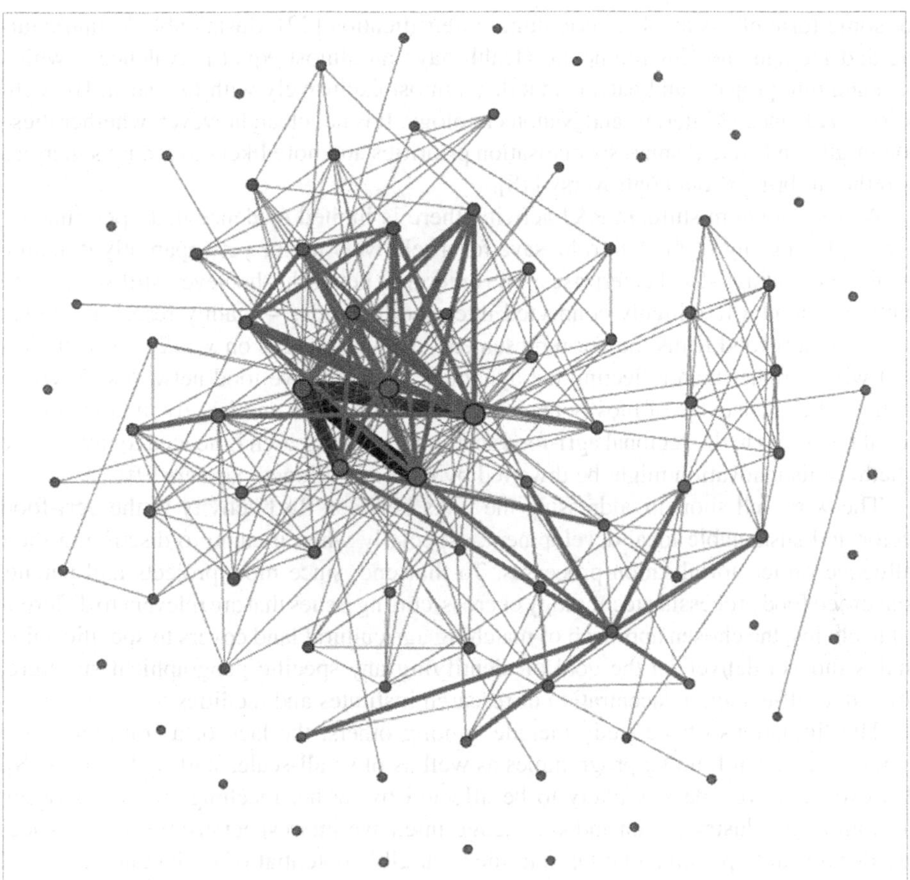

Fig. 9. The R&I sub-network of collaborative projects in Puglia that involve at least one agri-food business. The same methodological remarks as in Fig. 7 apply. Nodes representing research centres are red, agri-food business green. (Color figure online)

5 Discussion and Conclusions

This paper discusses the potential role of agri-food R&I activity in contributing to sustainable local development, by bridging smart specialisation strategies and agriculture and rural development policy. A focus on open innovation, understood as the co-creation of knowledge and innovative products, services or policies within flexible networks of research institutes, agri-food firms, civil society organisations and public-sector bodies [5, 6].

An exploratory study was carried out concerning recent (2010–19) agri-food R&I activity in Puglia (Italy), yielding a dataset that comprise 145 projects and 17 patents – developed by 47 research centres (affiliated to any of 11 research institutions) and 40 agri-food enterprises.

The preliminary results show that R&I activity in the agri-food sector in Puglia tend to focus on the main value chains (Fruit and vegetables, olive oil and wine), by aiming for some form of sustainable agricultural intensification [22]. Sustainable Manufacturing and Human and Environmental Health have an almost equal prevalence – which translate into projects and patents that deal almost exclusively with Industrial Biotechnology, Advanced Materials and Nanotechnology. It is not clear, however, whether these potentially ambivalent smart specialisation priorities are more likely to secure synergies or rather to bring about controversy [18].

As for paradigm shifts in R&I activity, there is limited evidence that open innovation is playing any significant role, save for a relatively minor yet apparently dynamic involvement of agri-food enterprises. The emerging networks, however, still seem to be centred around a few highly connected intermediate nodes – mainly research centres but some agri-food firms too are represented – in what verges on *small-world* models [17] which, rather than reflecting the dynamics of alternative food networks [3] could point to the persistence of mostly uncharted R&I directions and largely untapped relational resources in the regional agri-food sector. Further research is needed to investigate whether this innovation might be thwarted by better positioned partners [9].

The work fell short in addressing the links between R&I activity in the agri-food sector and sustainable local development, especially when it came to discussing their influence on territorialisation processes. To that end, since most projects and patents concerned food processing technology or cross-cutting issues that are relevant to different value chains, the chosen approach of matching agricultural land covers to specific value chains did not deliver on the goal of identifying any specific geographical structure, beyond a self-evident concentration of research institutes and facilities.

The limitations of the study include, among others, the lack of a comprehensive review of national funding programmes as well as of small-scale, start-up business [8]. However, this weakness is likely to be affected by farther-reaching friction between the dominant industry-driven and knowledge-intensive smart specialisations, and place-based innovation patterns that tap into the intangible potential of social and relational capital [4].

Further developments of this research may, therefore, aim at tracing innovation practice-in-action in the agri-food sector in a transboundary context, within the territorial cooperation networks whose innovation capacity the Innonets project is expected to enhance.

Acknowledgements. The authors declare that the contents of the paper are based on data and information collected within the "Innovative Networks for the Agrifood Sector-Innonets" Project (http://interreginnonets.eu), co-funded by European Union, European Regional Development Funds (E.R.D.F.) and by National Funds of Greece and Italy, in the framework of the Interreg V-A Greece –Italy Programme.

References

1. Bastian, M., Heymann, S., Jacomy M.: Gephi: an open source software for exploring and manipulating networks. In: Third International AAAI Conference on Weblogs and Social Media (2009). https://www.aaai.org/ocs/index.php/ICWSM/09/paper/view/154. Accessed 22 June 2020

2. Borruso, G., Bertazzon, S., Favretto, A., Murgante, B., Torre, C.M. (eds.): Geographic Information Analysis for Sustainable Development and Economic Planning: New Technologies. IGI Global, Hershey (2013). http://doi.org/10.4018/978-1-4666-1924-1
3. Brinkley, C.: The small world of the alternative food network. Sustainability **10**, 2921 (2018)
4. Capello, R., Kroll, H.: From theory to practice in smart specialization strategy: emerging limits and possible future trajectories. Eur. Plann. Stud. **24**, 1393–1406 (2016)
5. Cavicchi, A., Ciampi Stancova, K.: Food and Gastronomy as Elements of Regional Innovation Strategies. European Commission, Joint Research Centre, Institute for Prospective Technological Studies, Spain. EUR 27757 EN (2016). https://doi.org/10.2791/284013
6. Chesbrough, H., Bogers, M.: Explicating open innovation: clarifying an emerging paradigm for understanding innovation. In: Chesbrough, H., Vanhaverbeke, W., West, J. (eds.) New Frontiers in Open Innovation, pp. 3–28. Oxford University Press, Oxford (2014)
7. Ciampi Stancova, K., Cavicchi, A.: Dynamics of Smart Specialisation Agrifood Transregional Cooperation, JRC Technical reports, JRC107257 (2017). https://doi.org/10.2760/020864
8. Cillo, V., Rialti, R., Bertoldi, B., Ciampi, F.: Knowledge management and open innovation in agri-food crowdfunding. Br. Food J. **121**, 242–258 (2019)
9. Colurcio, M., Wolf, P., Kocher, P., Russo Spena, T.: Asymmetric relationships in networked food innovation processes. Br. Food J. **114**(5), 702–727 (2012). https://doi.org/10.1108/00070701211229981
10. Enger, S.G., Gulbrandsen, M.: Orchestrating collaborative projects: inside ICT networks in horizon 2020. In: Science and Public Policy, pp. 1–14 (2020). https://doi.org/10.1093/scipol/scaa021
11. European Academy Science Advisory Council (EASAC): Policy Report 34, December 2017, Opportunities and challenges for research on food and nutrition security and agriculture in Europe (2017). ISBN: 978-3-8047-3811-9
12. European Commission: Europe's future: Open Innovation, Open Science, Open to the World-Reflection of the RISE Group. Publications Office of the European Union, Luxembourg (2017)
13. European Commission: Europe's future: Open Innovation, Open Science, Open to the World-a vision for Europe. Publications Office of the European Union, Luxembourg (2016)
14. European Commission: Europe 2020, A strategy for smart, sustainable and inclusive growth - Brussels, 03/03/2010, COM (2010) 2020 (2010)
15. European Commission: Europe 2020 Flagship Initiative Innovation Union - Brussels, 06/10/2010, COM (2010) 546 final (2010)
16. European Innovation Partnership Agriculture (EIP-Agri): Agricultural knowledge and innovation systems-stimulating creativity and learning. EIP-Agri Service point publication (2018). www.eip-agri.eu. 22 June 2020
17. Ferligoj, A., Doreian, P., Batagelj, V.: Positions and roles. In: The SAGE Handbook of Social Network Analysis, pp. 434–446. SAGE, London (2011)
18. Garnett, T., Godfray, C.: Sustainable intensification in agriculture. Navigating a course through competing food system priorities. In: Food Climate Research Network and the Oxford Martin Programme on the Future of Food. University of Oxford, UK (2012)
19. Garrett, J.L., Ruel, M.T.: Nutrition and SDG 11: Healthy diets, nutrition and urban settlements. In: The Alliance of Bioversity International and the International Center for Tropical Agriculture (CIAT), Rome, Italy (2020). https://hdl.handle.net/10568/107124
20. Knierim, A., et al.: The AKIS Concept and its Relevance in Selected EU Member States. Outlook Agric. **44**, 29–36 (2015)

21. Knierim, A., Prager, K.: Agricultural Knowledge and Information Systems in Europe: Weak or Strong, Fragmented or Integrated? (2015). A report submitted in the framework of the PRO-AKIS Project and available at https://430a.uni-hohenheim.de/en/pro-akis. Accessed 12 May 2020
22. Lee, D.R., Barrett, C.B., McPeak, J.G.: Policy, technology, and management strategies for achieving sustainable agricultural intensification. Agric. Econ. **34**, 123–127 (2006)
23. Moreno, J.L.: Who Shall Survive? Foundations of Sociometry, GroupPsychotherapy, and Sociodrama. Nervous and Mental Disease Publishing Co., Washington, D.C. (1934)
24. Pretty, J., et al.: The top 100 questions of importance to the future of global agriculture. Int. J. Agric. Sustain. **8**, 219–236 (2010)
25. Rittel, H.W.J., Webber, M.M.: Dilemmas in a general theory of planning. Pol. Sci. **4**, 155–169 (1973)
26. Schiralli, M., et al.: I fabbisogni di innovazione dell'agricoltura pugliese: Risultati e proposte dei Tavoli di approfondimento tecnico-scientifico - Linee Guida per la ricerca e sperimentazione in agricoltura 2009–2011. Regione Puglia e INEA, Bari-Roma (2012). ISBN 9788881452972
27. Scott, J.: Social Network Analysis. Sage, London (2012)
28. Torre, C.M., Morano, P., Tajani, F.: Saving soil for sustainable land use. Sustainability **9**, 350 (2017). https://doi.org/10.3390/su9030350
29. Tortoriello, M., Reagans, R., McEvily, B.: Bridging the knowledge gap: the influence of strong ties, network cohesion, and network range on the transfer of knowledge between organizational units. Org. Sci. **23**(4), 1024–1039 (2012)
30. Van Latesteijn, H.C., Rabbinge, R.: Wicked problems in sustainable agriculture and food security, the TransForum experience. Int. Food Agribus. Manage. Rev. **15**, 89–94 (2012)
31. Yoshida, T., et al.: Chapter 7 - Spatial modeling and design of smart communities. In: Yamagata, Y., Yang, P.P.J. (eds.) Urban Systems Design-Creating Sustainable Smart Cities in the Internet of Things Era, pp. 199–255. Elsevier, Amsterdam (2020). https://doi.org/10.1016/B978-0-12-816055-8.00007-5

International Workshop on Machine Learning for Space and Earth Observation Data (MALSEOD 2020)

An Approach to Classify Burned Areas Using Few Previously Validated Samples

Olga O. Bittencourt, Fabiano Morelli, Cícero A. S. Júnior, and Rafael Santos(✉)

INPE – National Institute for Space Research, Av. dos Astronautas, 1758, São José dos Campos, SP 12227-010, Brazil
{olga.bittencourt,fabiano.morelli,cicero.junior,rafael.santos}@inpe.br
http://www.inpe.br

Abstract. Monitoring the large number of active fires and their consequences in such an extensive area such as the Brazilian territory is an important task. Machine Learning techniques are a promising approach to contribute to this area, but the challenge is the building of rich example datasets, whose previous examples are unavailable in many areas. Our aim in this article is to move towards the development of an approach to detect burned areas in regions for which there is no previously validated samples. We deal with that by presenting some experiments to classify burned areas through Machine Learning techniques that combine remote sensing data from nearby areas and it can distinguish between burned and non burned polygons with good results.

Keywords: Remote sensing · Burned forest classification keyword · Forest fire survey and monitoring

1 Introduction

Brazil recorded more than 197,000 active fires within its 851 million hectares of are between January and December of 2019 [6]. This represents an increase of around 48% compared to the number of active fires recorded throughout 2018. Among the six biomes in the country, the Cerrado (savannas and scrub forests), a biodiversity-rich region that occupies around 204 million hectares, was the most affected biome – it recorded more than 63,000 active fires in this period. It is estimated that it lost almost half of its original vegetation cover.

Monitoring this large number of active fires and their consequences in such an extensive area such as the Brazilian territory is an important task, and requires the involvement of policy makers, environmentalists and the scientific community. Several studies cover the fire-related aspects and their economic, social, and environmental impacts [3,9,12,18]. They agree with the need for reliable information about the extent and location (both in space and time) of the areas affected by the fire.

O. Gervasi et al. (Eds.): ICCSA 2020, LNCS 12253, pp. 239–254, 2020.
https://doi.org/10.1007/978-3-030-58814-4_17

The National Institute for Spatial Research (INPE), part of the Brazilian Ministry of Science, Technology, Innovation and Communications, is the official institute responsible for monitoring forest fires and reporting information in Brazil. INPE's monitoring is done by remote sensing and it is developed in two independent ways, using different satellite images' resolutions. Low-resolution images (with pixels larger than 300 m) are used to generate daily data products. The active fire monitoring, for example, is done this way for the whole country. Medium-resolution images (with pixel' sizes around 30 m) are used for less frequent but more accurate studies. The burned areas' estimation is done this way, but only for the Cerrado biome. With these distinct views, it is possible to offer products such as estimation of burned area and the prediction of the risk of fire on vegetation. These products can be used to prevent, monitor, combat and create actions to analyze the impacts of burning, to estimate the emission of pollutants and to reduce the damage caused by fire. However, other biomes that also had a high number of active fires, do not have this more accurate monitoring of burned areas.

The general approach used by INPE's estimation of burned area with medium-resolution images is to compare consecutive images of the same regions. Figure 1 illustrates fragments of three consecutive remote sensing images. They are in a band combination applied to Landsat 8, displayed as a red, green, blue (RGB). Areas change over time and some are highlighted on the right side of the figure. The objective is to detect spectral changes and to determine the changes caused by fires. As part of the official data, it is necessary to present the quality of indication at least 95% of success. And, to ensure this quality, nowadays, it is necessary for manually verify the data before the publication.

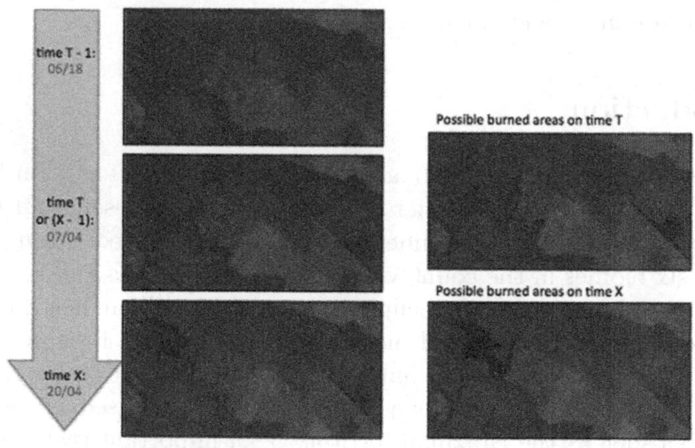

Fig. 1. Fragments of three consecutive Landsat images.

Recent studies [2,5,12] present challenges and new advances in fire monitoring. However, there is no generic automatic model for the problem of classifying burned data in continuous monitoring on a global scale, as the Brazilian whole territory. A consensus is that to develop and evaluate more automatic approaches, it is important to have a rich knowledge database about previous occurrences of burned areas. Unfortunately, many Brazilian regions, and even biomes, have few validated burned area studies and datasets, such as Amazon and Caatinga (a dry shrub-land biome). The major challenge of this approach is the need for previously validated data from the same area – validated data is data that was evaluated by a specialist, which is very time consuming. Thus, to expand the analysis to the whole country, a new approach is essential.

Our aim in this article is to move towards the development of an approach to detect burned areas in biomes or regions for which there is no previously validated data. We deal with that by presenting some experiments to classify burned areas through Machine Learning techniques that combine remote sensing data from nearby areas and it can distinguish between burned and non burned polygons in areas without samples or with few previously validated remote sensing data. Figure 2 details some examples of polygons of the fragments highlighted in Fig. 1. The red polygons are burned examples and the blue polygons, caused by crops, are non burned areas.

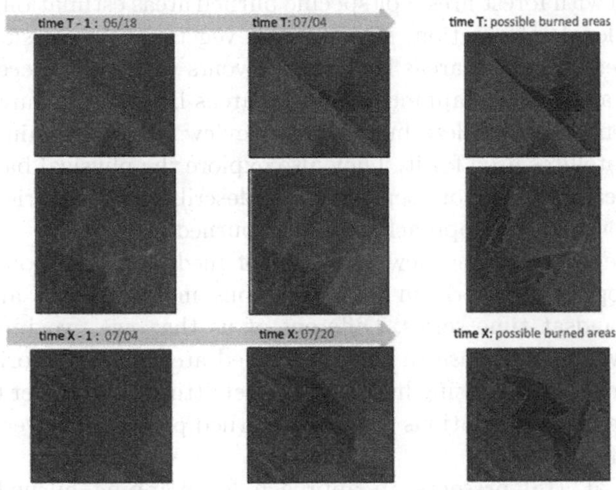

Fig. 2. Detailed examples of burned and non burned polygons. (Color figure online)

The proposed approach is validated over a large study area in the Brazilian Cerrado and Caatinga against reference data derived from classifications done by experts by INPE. The good results of the experiments contribute to propose using the approach to adapt data from nearby areas.

This paper is organized in the following sections: Section 2 shows related work and how remote sensing is used to monitor burned areas. Section 3 presents the proposed approach and explains the dataset. Section 4 presents the experiments for some classification models and discuss the results. Section 5 presents the conclusions and future work.

2 Burned Areas Mapping by Remote Sensing Monitoring

The use of remote sensing images collected in different wavelengths is the most efficient way to monitor fires in places with great territorial extension or areas of difficult access. The spectral data present different information for each type of target and for the different regions of the electromagnetic spectrum that are changed after vegetation burning. Furthermore, remote sensing images frequently provides recent information. In Brazil, for example, it is the most efficient fire monitoring means, with the lowest cost. In recent years, new generations of satellites (e.g. Landsat 8, Sentinel-2 and CBERS-4 – the China-Brazil Earth Resources Satellite) were developed to provide better resolution images and more precise georeferencing. Features and advances made possible by these new satellites generation, and some strategies to combine them to improve cloud-free observations may be found in [11].

There are some projects that monitor fire events and related information in many places around the world. The SERV-FORFIRE (Integrated Services And Approaches For Assessing Effects Of Climate Change) [8] project is one of them that presents collaborative efforts of the international community of remote sensing to deal with forest fires. For specific burned areas estimation, they employ and combine local information, such as soil, vegetation and risk management database to detect burned areas in extreme events with high success.

Inside the automatic mapping of burned areas literature, Chuvieco et al. [5] present a recent and complete burned area review with the main wavelengths, sensors, and satellites used for it. They also explore the physical basis for detecting burned areas from remote sensing data, describes the historical trends and summarizes some recent approaches to map burned areas.

Studies are applying the new advances of medium resolution data. Liu et al. [12] developed an algorithm for continuous monitoring of annual burned areas using Landsat time series. Different of us that use two images comparison and knowledge database to classify burned areas, their algorithm is based on burned pixel detection using harmonic model fitting with longer time series. It allows breakpoint identifications to detach burned pixels with overall accuracies at around 80%.

Pereira et al. [18] presents an approach for mapping burned areas using automated sample selection based on active fires and One-Class Support Vector Machine (SVM) supervised learning model. They present the advances of using automatic detection with good overall accuracies and some limitations such as the dependence of the images' contrast. This study shows the feasibility of using machine learning techniques for the burned areas mapping problem.

Andrade et al. [1] proposed a semiautomatic approach to classify burned areas through the use of neural networks. Previous results decreased the number of polygons wrongly classified and showed the viability of using Neural Networks in the classification process. Mithal et al. [16] employ machine learning approaches in the problem of burned areas mapping. They present a three-step approach to map burned areas in tropical areas which compares data from two low resolution (500 m) successive images from Moderate Resolution Imaging Spectroradiometer

(MODIS), feeds it into a proprietary algorithm to classify these data and perform a final processing step for detection of burned areas. According to the authors, although it has many errors in indicating correct burned areas, it is a promising global approach that brings a more comprehensive assessment of tropical fires.

Bittencourt et al. [2] proposed a strategy to classify burned areas by using a Machine Learning approach. They used a one-year knowledge dataset to classify unknown data in the same region. Extending their work, we employ an approach through the use of Machine Learning (ML) classification models to classify which areas have changed in a comparison of two different acquisition moments. The main difference is that our work is focused on providing to extend strategies to INPE's machine learning classification process to classify areas with few historic datasets. Previous results show the difficulty of choosing one specific model to answer our burn classification problem. To contribute to the understanding of this problem, our work is related to the effort to develop automated approaches to classify burned areas with few previously validated data.

3 Proposed Approach

We hypothesize that knowledge databases with lots of previously validated data can characterize and classify regions in nearby areas. Our aim in this article is to contribute to the development of an approach to detect burned areas with no previously validated data. We treat this problem by proposing a strategy that employs machine learning techniques based on a knowledge database from classified regions to classify near regions. We defined the process to determine relevant features and experimented with the approach on an applicable dataset.

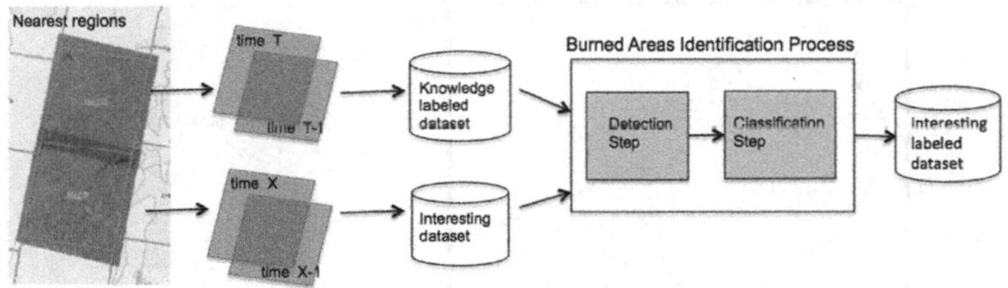

Fig. 3. General view of burned areas identification process.

The general idea of the whole burned areas identification process, illustrated in Fig. 3, is based on remote sensing data evaluation and classification, and it is composed by two steps: the first is to detect spectral changes in two consecutive images of the same region in a limited period. This first step has high reliability and it was developed and is being used at INPE.

The resulting database is composed of polygons extracted by the burned areas mapping algorithm [15]. This process detects candidate burned polygons every two weeks with high reliability for medium resolution images (30 m). It compare images from the same region to different dates, with the standard temporal difference being a 16-day. The ones that present interference like noise or many clouds are discarded and an image before this one is used, with 32, 48 or at most 64 days difference. At intervals greater than this, the vegetation starts the recovering process and it is not possible to detect relevant changes.

However, some of these changed regions are deforestations, crops, and clouds, and, to be officially considered as burned areas and reported, it needs to be labeled in order to ensure the quality of at least 95% of success in the indication of burned areas. This is done in a second step that defines if the detected change is due to fire, based on a knowledge database of previously detected changes of the same region.

The most recent INPE's published official result of burned areas estimation in the Cerrado employed a further evaluation process to separate the confirmed burned areas dataset. The result of this process is a huge validated knowledge database from the Cerrado biome that is composed of a set of changed areas that can be caused by many factors, with some of them being burn occurrences. The results are good and reliable but the manual evaluation is expensive and time-consuming. Other strategies to create an automatic evaluation must ensure the quality of results.

3.1 Data

The dataset used in this paper's experiment was acquired through INPE's Fire Monitoring Program [7] that uses images from Landsat satellites. The data cover part of the Cerrado biome, as shown in Fig. 4.

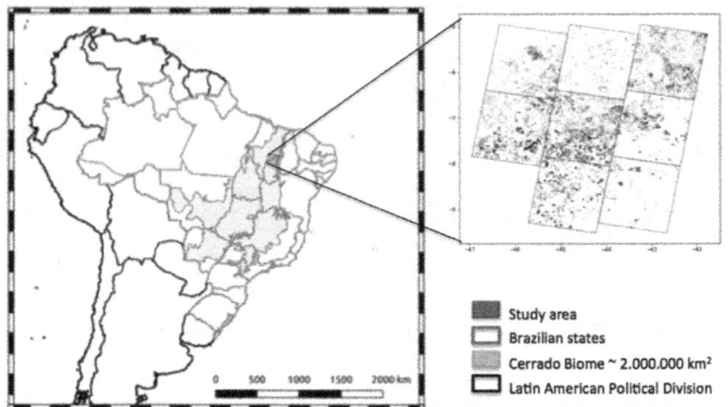

Fig. 4. Fragment of Brazilian territory covering the Cerrado biome and highlighting eight Landsat path/rows. (Color figure online)

The Landsat Program [22] stands out among Earth observation satellites that provide medium-resolution orbital images of the same area every 16 days since the 1980s. It provides environmental data with all corrections processed, such as spectral band values and spectral vegetation indices.

Landsat imagery is separated by paths and rows. The red parallelogram in Fig. 4, the study area of this work, illustrates a fragment of an image position with a set of eight path/rows illustrated in Fig. 4. Light gray highlights indicate the Cerrado delimitation and dark gray indicates protected areas. Every single pixel in the image corresponds to a square cell of 30 m × 30 m on the terrain and each complete image represents a coverage area of 18,500 × 18,500 ha. As each original Landsat image contains the reflectance spectra for each pixel in a digital image, the polygons are composed of a set of pixels.

The parallelograms in Fig. 4 illustrates the eight path/rows and the polygons detected as change between two consecutive images. The central parallelogram corresponds to path 220 and row 065, named by 220/065 path/row, part of the Cerrado biome in the states of Maranhão and Piauí, in Brazilian territory. The complete dataset is composed of positive and negative examples of burned areas occurrences, in a total of 118881 polygons. Confirmed burned areas (positive examples) are represented in red and non burned areas (negative examples) are represented in blue. These latter are polygons detected by the reference algorithm and that were discarded by experts because they were not caused by fires, such as clouds, crops, and deforestations.

The polygons' set was developed by the evaluation of a set of 80 images of the 2018 year. The data ranging is from April to October. Other months correspond to the rainiest period in that region. This makes it difficult to compare consecutive images without a huge portion of clouds and because that period is less prone to the existence of active fires. There are 10 images of each path/row on the following sets: 219/064, 219/065, 219/066, 220/064, 220/065, 220/066, 221/065 and 219/066. In this work, the area division is indicated by path/rows because it is simple to simulate a real process and to facilitate data visualization process.

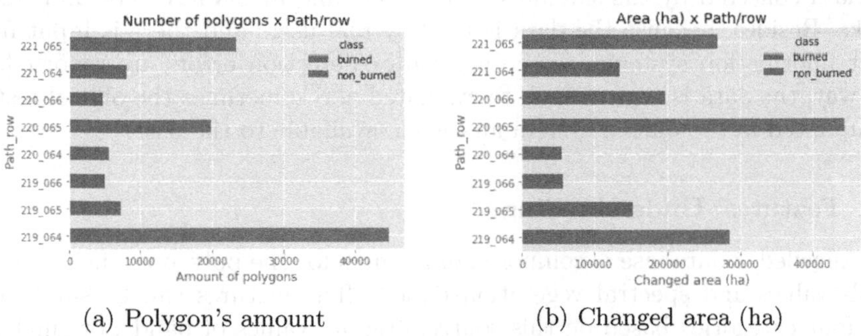

(a) Polygon's amount (b) Changed area (ha)

Fig. 5. Polygon's amount and changed area by path/row

The study area contains 118881 polygons that cover around 1594211 ha (around 14761155 soccer fields). From those, 75060 correspond to confirmed burned polygons totaling 1133059 ha and 43821 are areas changed due to other factors, which we call non burned polygons, and which total area is 461151 ha. Figure 5 illustrates the total number of polygons and the area occupied by changed areas by month in each year.

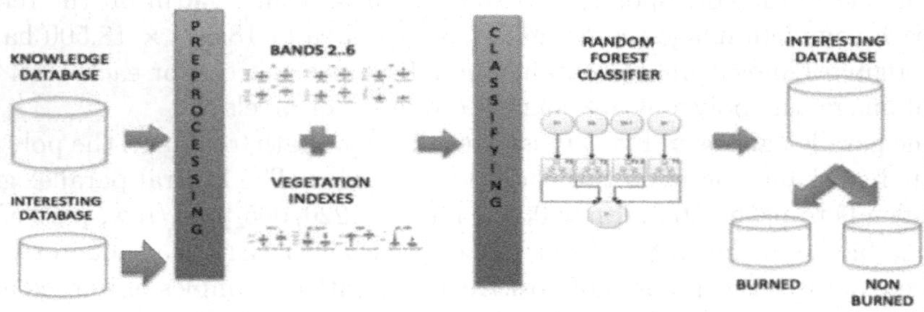

Fig. 6. General view of classification step.

Figure 6 illustrates the general Burned Classification Process. It starts with the comparison of an image I on a time T with an image J on a previous time (T-1). Adjacent pixels on the image I detected as change are grouped in a polygon. For each polygon on the image I, it is computed the medians of each spectral band. After that, it is computed the medians of each spectral band on the same polygon's area on the image J and the differences between values on time T related to time T-1 are estimated.

We obtained the dataset available in early December to build our knowledge base and run experiments from that release. However, as work is in operation and with continuous development, as advances are made within the INPE's research, some advances are introduced into the system, for example, improvements in the data collected by the satellites and also enhancements in clouds and smoke masks. Besides, because the data is used by real users and there is input from other information systems, some omission or detection errors are reported. In this way, the data is reprocessed, re-evaluated and sometimes the official results are updated in the official system and made available to the user.

3.2 Features' Understanding

The knowledge database is composed of features for the polygons, their spectral bands values and spectral vegetation indices. The features can be subdivided into four categories based on this source: original values of bands, original values of spectral indices, values computed of bands' values differences and values computed from spectral indices differences. In this study, b4 denotes data from Landsat band 4, b5 corresponds to data from Landsat band 5 and so on. There are two direct sets of features based on the value of bands. The first set is composed of the median values of each pixel that make up the polygon. The features indicated without suffixes correspond to the median value observed on the day of the satellite's passage.

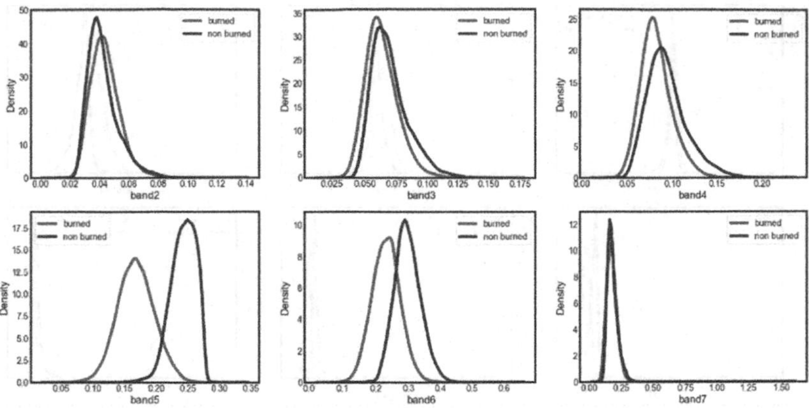

Fig. 7. Histogram of spectral bands b2, b3, b4, b5, b6 and b7 original values, for polygons labeled as burned and non burned.

Figure 7 shows the frequency distributions of original values of spectral bands data from b2 to b7 for all 118881 evaluated polygons. The distributions, except for b5 and b6, are unimodal and similar for burned and non burned polygons. The variability of data is within known specifications limits on the literature [5] for each band. We highlight bands b5 and b6 to differentiate between burned and non burned data because the curves and the mean of burns and non-burns are different.

The differences that appear in the bands, in general, are small with the highest concentrations around 0. The plots show some outliers that focused on the positive part of most of the sets. They are common to the data and that will be kept on to avoid tendency results. Except for the plots of bands 5 and 6, the shape of the burning curve is similar to the format of the non burning graph. This indicates the difficulty of performing linear separation of these sets using these data.

Features indicated with the suffix "_dif" correspond to differences between the median value of the pixels on each polygon in the passage and the medium value of pixels of the region bounded by that polygon in the previous date used in the comparison. Figure 8 shows an overview of the different values of spectral bands data from b2 to b7.

All of these histograms are unimodal and, except for data from bands 2 and 3, the curves are asymmetric. The curves on burned and non burned sets are more similar than original features and outliers are presented in bands b5, b6, and b7. The mean values are concentrated around 0, which demonstrates small differences between data on the previous date.

Another set of attributes of each polygon is composed of eight spectral vegetation indices already used in burned literature. They are: Burn Area Index (BAI) [4], Char Soil Index (CSI) [13], Global Environment Monitoring Index (GEMI) [19], Mid-Infrared Burn Index (MIRBI) [21], Normalized Burn Ratio

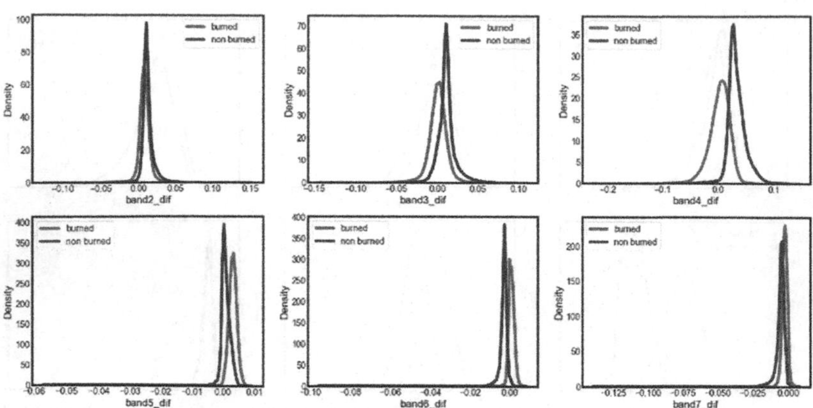

Fig. 8. Histogram of difference between spectral bands b2, b3, b4, b5, b6 and b7 original values and spectral bands previous values, for polygons labeled as burned and non burned.

(NBR) [10], Normalized Difference Vegetation Index (NDVI) [20], and Normalized Difference Water Index (NDWI) [14].

A summary of the vegetation indices applied in this approach is described above.

$$
\begin{aligned}
NDVI &= \frac{b5 - b4}{b5 + b4},\\
NBR &= \frac{b5 - b7}{b5 + b7},\\
MIRBI &= 10 * b7 - 9.8 * b6 + 2,\\
NDWI &= \frac{b3 - b6}{b3 + b6},\\
BAI &= \frac{1}{(0.1 - b4)^2 + (0.06 - b5)^2},\\
CSI &= \frac{b2}{b6},\\
GEMI &= \frac{n * (1 - 0.25 * n) * (b5 - 0.125)}{1 - b5}\\
&\quad with\, n = \frac{2 * b7^2 - b5^2 + 1.5 * b7 + 0.5 * b5}{b7 + b5 + 0.5},\\
GEMIL &= \frac{n * (1 - 0.25 * n) * (b5 - 0.125)}{1 - b5},\\
&\quad with\, n = \frac{2 * b6^2 - b5^2 + 1.5 * b6 + 0.5 * b5}{b6 + b5 + 0.5}
\end{aligned}
$$

They present good results in preliminary experiments, which are not presented in this article.

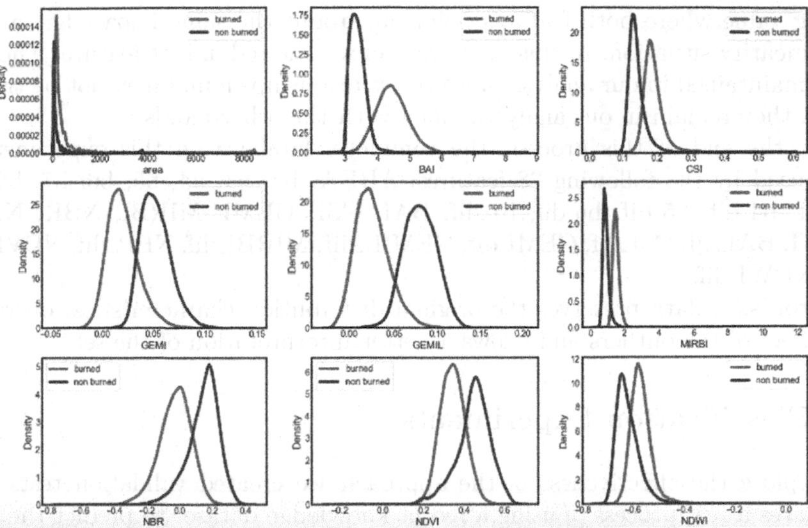

Fig. 9. Histogram of area (ha) and spectral indices original values, for polygons labeled as burned and non burned.

Figure 9 presents the histograms of the spectral vegetation indices and the area of each polygon. Some features present outliers and attributes, GEMIL, NBR and NDVI present differentiation between burned and non burned set but it is still not simple to do a linear cut between the sets. These curves present larger ranges between data. Features AREA and BAI present larger ranges. Curves on these histograms present mean values with more distinction between burn and non burned sets. No feature is alone sufficient to characterize the burn set but it can contribute to correctly distinguish the two sets.

The last set of features is based on the difference between the current indices and the values of indices on the previous images. After this set we have the following set of 29 features: AREA, b2, b3, b4, b5, b6, b7, b2_dif, b3_dif, b4_dif, b5_dif, b6_dif, b7_dif, BAI, CSI, GEMI, GEMIL, MIRBI, NBR, NDVI, NDWI, BAI_dif, CSI_dif, GEMI_dif, GEMIL_dif, MIRBI_dif, NBR_dif, NDVI_dif, and NDWI_dif.

3.3 Data Processing

The strategy in the data processing is to have a smaller set of relevant attributes to reduce the volume of analyzed data and the processing time while maintaining a low error rate improving the prediction performance of the classifiers.

The first step is the normalization of the set of features to have different features on the same scale. That will accelerate the learning process.

After that, the second step is the evaluation of the correlation between each pair of features. We consider correlations are greater than 97,5% represents a strong value where both features point out about the same knowledge, a multicollinearity situation. In this case, we remove the redundant feature. The rest were maintained in our analysis since the relationships found may not be trivial. Thus, they remain in our analysis, along with the other bands.

At the end of this process, the complete database on this experiment is composed by the following 28 features: AREA, b2, b3, b4, b5, b6, b7, b2_dif, b3_dif, b4_dif, b5_dif, b6_dif, b7_dif, BAI, CSI, GEMI, MIRBI, NBR, NDVI, NDWI, BAI_dif, CSI_dif, GEMI_dif, GEMIL_dif, MIRBI_dif, NBR_dif, NDVI_dif, and NDWI_dif.

Processed data preserves the original distribution characteristics, decreases the effect of the outliers and allows a better interpretation of the set.

4 Classification Experiments

To explore the effectiveness of the approach we created validation tests that simulates a real process of using a recent knowledge dataset to predict the classification to a nearest regions dataset. Our approach is a classification problem solved through a supervised learning class of problems, where a model is trained with a labeled dataset. We explored our approach in five experiments that alternate training and testing datasets. The features of the training dataset are used to create a model. In the testing set, the features excluding the labeled class, are used to predict the class based on the created model. We employed all polygons from some path/rows to test all polygons from other path/rows. No data is repeated in the training and the testing dataset.

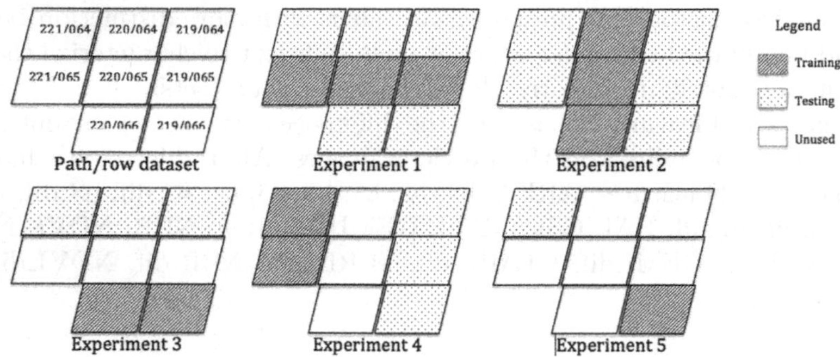

Fig. 10. Complete path/rows positions and each experiment training and testing sets

Figure 10 illustrates the complete path/rows positions and detaches the training and testing sets in each experiment. Experiments 1 and 2 show a global view of the set and they are done with all adjacent path/rows. In experiments 3 and 4, the idea is to test if more distant data than adjacent path/rows would affect the results. Experiment 5 simulates the more distant path/rows available in this dataset.

- Experiment 1: Three central path/rows on the same row compose the training set. Other rows compose the testing set.
  - Training: 219/065, 220/065, 221/065.
  - Testing: 219/064, 219/066, 220/064, 220/066, 221/064.
- Experiment 2: Three central path/rows on the same path compose the training set. Other paths compose the testing set.
  - Training: 220/064, 220/065, 220/066.
  - Testing: 219/064, 219/065, 219/066, 221/064, 221/065.
- Experiment 3: The 066 row is the training and the 064 row is the testing.
  - Training: 219/066, 220/066.
  - Testing: 219/064, 220/064, 221/064.
- Experiment 4: The 221 path is the training and the 219 path is the testing.
  - Training: 221/064, 221/065.
  - Testing: 219/064, 219/065, 219/066.
- Experiment 5: The 219/066 path/row is the training data and the 221/064 path/row is the testing set.
  - Training: 219/066.
  - Testing: 221/064.

Table 1. Number of polygons in each experiment divided by training and testing sets.

Experiment	Training			Testing		
	Burned	Non Burned	Total	Burned	Non Burned	Total
1	21327	8870	30197	22494	66190	88684
2	24473	24079	48452	17348	50981	68329
3	13342	45144	58486	4006	5837	9843
4	12021	45114	57135	10473	21076	31549
5	1566	3501	5067	5409	2690	8099

Table 1 illustrates the number of polygons in each experiment. All of them have distinct amounts of data and some of them are more balanced than others. However, it is possible to see on previous histograms the different sets, on the majority of plots, do not present large variations within the same class.

4.1 Random Forest Model Classifier

This model consists of an ensemble of simple tree decision classifiers used to determine the outcome. Each simple tree employs a set of decision rules to separate the classes and, the ensemble votes for the most popular class. Random Forest is a robust algorithm that minimizes the errors in specific trees.

We chose this classifier because it showed good results in previous works and it has simple interpretability. We performed experiments using the Scikit-learn environment [17]. The main parameters used on the model are a set of 64 trees in the forest, 5 as the minimum number of instances in leaves and the indication to the classifier to balance the number of examples in each class.

To evaluate the performance of the classifier in the problem of predicting unlabeled data, we analyze the following metrics: the accuracy (the proportion of true results among the total number of cases examined), the precision (the proportion of predicted positives related to real positive), the recall (the proportion of actual positives correctly classified) and the F1 score (the harmonic mean between precision and recall).

Table 2. General overview of each experimental result

Experiment	Accuracy	Precision	Recall	F1 score
1	98	99	94	97
2	98	99	94	97
3	97	93	99	96
4	99	97	98	98
5	97	96	98	97

Table 2 shows a general overview of the results. All analyzed metrics' values are higher than 93%. This indicates that it is possible to predict the class of the polygon with high accuracy, near to reaching our initial aim of 95% of success in each metric.

The training dataset has a different distribution than the test/validation dataset and population. As a real problem, we consider wide margins between training and test, but the results outperform previous experiments. In addition to this challenge, our database is not error-free. Some areas are ambiguous and even experts have doubts in certain places. In such cases, if the experts have not sure in certain areas, they are classified as non burned, further increasing the variability within the class.

These results indicate that for these sets, the approach was able to recover most of the burned areas and to indicate that areas identified as burned had few false positives. It is possible to note that, in these experiments, adjacent path/rows show results close to the results of the most distant orbits. New experiments with more orbits and more distant sets will be necessary to better analyze this result.

5 Conclusions and Results

This work aims to show directions and to add value for the construction of an automated high-performance environment to be able of dealing with the extensive Brazilian territory and the complexity of generating data to build knowledge bases for the classification of fire data and non burned.

We know it is a challenging task to perform this kind of test for large scale areas. Besides, there is the complexity, and, in some cases, the impossibility to generate train datasets. Then, we must advance in creating a fast and accurate automated classifier with little manual interference that can detect fires by combining data from more than one biome. It may treat and classify areas with sparse data. And with each new set of data generated by a satellite image can be autofitted to classify new data from nearby path/rows with the same accuracy.

In this article, we presented the approach, applied it in nearby regions and obtained accuracy close to 95%. Our results show that it is feasible to use the strategy of the near set to help characterize the sets in places with poor data or missing data. We believe that this can be improved with more tests in different areas to propose the minimum values of path/rows and polygons that validate the approach.

To the next steps, it is important to continue investigating whether data closer has a better answer and how far it is possible to apply the strategy with high accuracy. So, to this approach to be incorporated into the standard procedure to test new areas is needed.

We know that different types of vegetation, soil, seasonal effects, and other local characteristics may enrich the evaluation. For future work, we suggest incorporating other data products related to the fire risk, soil models and vegetation to generate a more precise characterization of fires. However, we show that the available data on LandSat is able of taking a step towards evaluating data in regions with little validated data using readily available data. Work continues to be improved. We are testing the most appropriate strategy to treat doubtful cases and working on the model's adaptability to all other Brazilian biomes.

Acknowledgements. This study was supported by National Council for Scientific and Technological Development (CNPq)/Coordination of Associated Laboratories (COCTE/INPE) (no. 300587/2017-1).

References

1. de Andrade, R.N., Bittencourt, O., Morelli, F., Santos, R.: Classificação semi-automática de áreas queimadas com o uso de redes neurais. In: XVIII Brazilian Symposium on Geoinformatics - GeoInfo 2017, pp. 92–97 (2017)
2. Bittencourt, O.O., Morelli, F., dos Santos Júnior, C.A., Santos, R.: Evaluating classification models in a burned areas' detection approach. In: Misra, S., et al. (eds.) ICCSA 2019. LNCS, vol. 11622, pp. 577–591. Springer, Cham (2019). https://doi.org/10.1007/978-3-030-24305-0_43
3. Bowman, D., et al.: Fire in the earth system. Science **324**, 481–484 (2009)
4. Chuvieco, E., Martín, M.: Cartografí de grandes incendios forestales en la península ibérica a partir de imágenes noaa-avhrr. Serie Geográfica **7**, 109–128 (1998)
5. Chuvieco, E., et al.: Historical background and current developments for mapping burned area from satellite earth observation. In: Remote Sensing of Environment (2019)
6. Instituto Nacional de Pesquisas Espaciais (INPE): Programa de monitoramento de queimadas. http://www.inpe.br/queimadas/portal. Accessed 28 Jan 2018

7. Instituto Nacional de Pesquisas Espaciais (INPE): Programa de monitoramento de queimadas, área queimada, resolu cão 30m. https://prodwww-queimadas.dgi.inpe.br/aq30m/. Accessed 28 Jan 2018
8. JPI Climate and European Union: Serv-for fire integrated services and approaches for assessing effects of climate change and extreme events for fire and post fire risk prevention. https://servforfire-era4cs.eu/
9. Katagis, T., Gitas, I., Toukiloglou, P., Veraverbeke, S., Goossens, R.: Trend analysis of medium- and coarse-resolution time series image data for burned area mapping in a Mediterranean ecosystem. Int. J. Wildland Fire **23**, 668–677 (2014)
10. Key, C., Benson, N.: Landscape assessment: Ground measure of severity, the composite burn index; and remote sensing of severity, the normalized burn ratio. In: FIREMON: Fire Effects Monitoring and Inventory System, pp. 1–51 (2006)
11. Li, J., Roy, D.: A global analysis of sentinel-2a, sentinel-2b and Landsat-8 data revisit intervals and implications for terrestrial monitoring. Remote Sens. **9**, 902 (2017)
12. Liu, J., Heiskanen, J., Maeda, E.E., Pellikka, P.K.: Burned area detection based on Landsat time series in savannas of southern Burkina Faso. Int. J. Appl. Earth Obser. Geoinf. **64**, 210–220 (2018)
13. Smith, A.M.S., Drake, N.A., Wooster, M.J., Hudak, A.T., Holden, Z.A., Gibbons, C.J.: Production of Landsat ETM+ reference imagery of burned areas within Southern African savannahs: comparison of methods and application to MODIS. Int. J. Remote Sens. **28**, 2753–2775 (2007)
14. McFeeters, S.: The use of normalized difference water index (NDWI) in the delineation of open water features. Int. J. Remote Sens. **17**, 1425–1432 (1996)
15. Melchiori, E., Setzer, A.W., Morelli, F., Libonati, R., Cândido, P.d.A., Jesús, S.C.d.: A Landsat-TM/OLI Algorithm for Burned Areas in the Brazilian Cerrado: Preliminary Results, pp. 1302–1311. Imprensa da Universidade de Coimbra (2014)
16. Mithal, V., Nayak, G., Khandelwal, A., Kumar, V., Nemani, R., Oza, N.C.: Mapping burned areas in tropical forests using a novel machine learning framework. Remote Sens. **10**, 69 (2018)
17. Pedregosa, F., et al.: Scikit-learn: machine learning in Python. J. Mach. Learn. Res. **12**, 2825–2830 (2011)
18. Pereira, A.A., et al.: Burned area mapping in the Brazilian savanna using a one-class support vector machine trained by active fires. Remote Sens. **9**(11), 1161 (2017)
19. Pinty, B., Verstraete, M.: GEMI: a non-linear index to monitor global vegetation from satellites. Vegetation **101**, 15–20 (1992). https://doi.org/10.1007/BF00031911
20. Rouse Jr., J.W., Haas, R.H., Schell, J.A., Deering, D.W.: Monitoring Vegetation Systems in the Great Plains with ERTS. NASA Special Publication, vol. 351, p. 309 (1974)
21. Trigg, S., Flasse, S.: An evaluation of different bi-spectral spaces for discriminating burned shrub-savannah. Int. J. Remote Sens. **22**, 2641–2647 (2001)
22. United States Geological Survey (USGS): Science Data Lifecycle. https://earthexplorer.usgs.gov. Accessed 18 Oct 2018

Total Solar Irradiance Forecasting with Keras Recurrent Neural Networks

Amita Muralikrishna[1,2](✉), Luis E. A. Vieira[1], Rafael D. C. dos Santos[1], and Adriano P. Almeida[1]

[1] National Institute of Space Research, Av. dos Astronautas, 1758, São José dos Campos, Brazil
{luis.vieira,rafael.santos,adriano.almeida}@inpe.br

[2] Federal Institute of Education, Science and Technology of São Paulo, Route Presidente Dutra km 145, São José dos Campos, Brazil
amita@ifsp.edu.br

https://www.inpe.br, https://sjc.ifsp.edu.br

Abstract. The prediction of solar irradiance at the top of the atmosphere is useful for research that analyzes the behavior and response of the different layers of the Earth's atmosphere to variations in solar activity. It would also be useful for the reconstruction of the measurement history (time series) of different instruments that suffered from time failures and discrepancies in scales due to the calibration of equipment. In this work we compare three Keras recurrent neural network architectures to perform forecast of the total solar irradiance. The experiments are part of a larger proposal for modularization of the prediction workflow, which uses digital images of the Sun as input, and aims to make the process modular, accessible and reproducible.

Keywords: Recurrent neural network · Total solar irradiance · Keras

1 Introduction

The energy the Earth receives from the Sun is what drives life and many of the processes on the planet. Many of the studies of this relationship and its consequences requires constant monitoring of the Sun, in order to investigate its activity and to try to predict certain types of events on Earth. The main way to study this energetic influence is through the radiation received by the Sun in the form of temperature and irradiation over time.

Recurrent neural networks (RNNs) have shown to be a powerful tool for dealing with time series or data of a sequential nature. New architectures have emerged to further improve the prediction capabilities of the network. This work proposes to perform the prediction of one of the measures of data from the Sun, the total solar irradiance (TSI), using as the input for the network 40 parameters extracted from areas that measure sunspots and active regions. Two types of images of the Sun are used for that.

O. Gervasi et al. (Eds.): ICCSA 2020, LNCS 12253, pp. 255–269, 2020.
https://doi.org/10.1007/978-3-030-58814-4_18

A workflow describes the whole procedure, based on [21], organizing the steps in modules. The purpose is to make it available for the validation of the results, the execution of more experiments with the same data, or even a new one, and the modification of modules by other researchers with different techniques for tasks like identification, classification and the prediction itself. The intention is, therefore, to make the workflow modular, accessible and reproducible.

As options for experiments with RNNs, the simplest architecture - SimpleRNN (Simple Recurrent Neural Network) - is used, as well as those created to solve the problem of vanishing gradient, LSTM (Long Short Term Memory) and GRU (Gated Recurrent Unit). This work presents their performance for different net configurations.

2 Sun Activity, Sunspots and Active Regions

The Sun owes much of its activity to its rotation and consequent complexity generated in its magnetic field. The events resulting from this activity can be observed under different types of records, in different layers of the star. The presence and the evolution of active regions and sunspots are two important indicators of disturbances in the solar magnetic field. And when studying the effects of this disturbances from the Earth, the TSI is also an important indicator [11].

The sunspots appear visually distinct on the surface of the Sun because they are darker and colder regions, emitting less energy than the rest of the surface [14]. They are formed by two regions: the umbra, a central and darker region, and the penumbra, which thrives around the umbra in only half of the spots, and has a lighter, gray coloration [5]. And the active regions are directly related to the presence of sunspots and can be observed in moments of time that precede and accompany the birth of the spots and can still be visible after their disappearance.

Figure 1 shows a morning record from 2011 November 9th of the SDO (Solar Dynamics Observatory) HMI (Helioseismic and Magnetic Imager) instrument[1] through two types of images, collected in different wavelengths. Active regions are visible in the image on the left, where the opposite colored pixels represent opposite polarities of the solar magnetic field lines, and with more extensive areas than those of the corresponding sunspots, present in the image on the right, at the same instant of time. The presence of sunspots occurs in areas where the magnetic field is most concentrated and intense, but the active regions extend over the entire area where the field disturbance is visible.

Data extracted from both types of images in Fig. 1 will be combined and used at the beginning of the procedure developed to forecast solar irradiance in this work.

[1] SDO webpage: https://sdo.gsfc.nasa.gov/mission/.

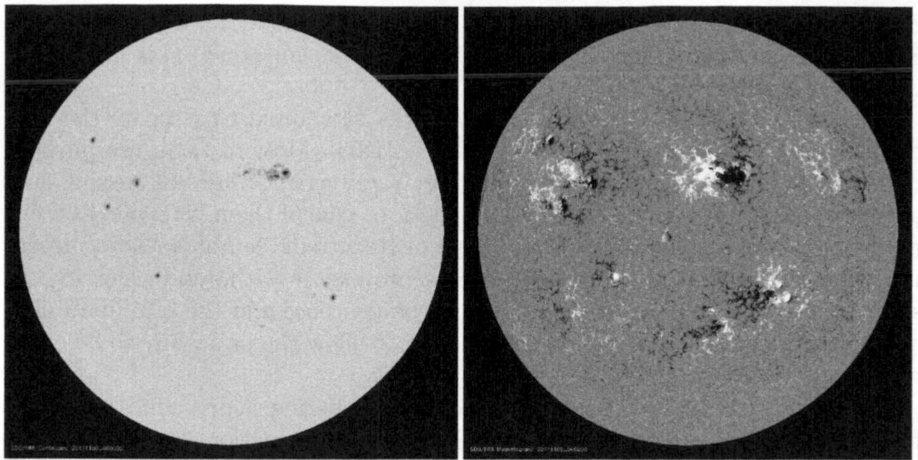

Fig. 1. On the left, an image with sunspots, and on the right, another image with active regions, both registered in the same time on 2011, November 9th.

3 TSI Forecasting

The solar irradiance can be defined as a certain amount of solar radiation per unit area.

When measured on the ground, the solar irradiance is different from when measured at the top (outside) of the Earth atmosphere, since its emission at different wavelengths varies according to the physical and chemical properties of the Earth's atmosphere layers [24].

The solar irradiance measured at the top of the Earth's atmosphere is considered an influential parameter in studies of the atmosphere layers properties' and the consequences of the disturbances they suffer from the influence of solar activity [3]. Other relevant studies about weather and climate on Earth recognized the great influence of solar irradiation for the creation of climate models, as, for example, [4,6,22].

For the second form of irradiance there are two measures: the spectral solar irradiance (SSI), defined by a range of wavelengths covered by solar radiation and received by Earth at a distance of 1 AU[2]; and the TSI: radiation emitted by Sun in all spectral regions, equivalent to the integral of all SSI spectral bands centered per second in 1 m^2 at 1 AU.

The TSI, focus of this work, has a history of measurements performed by instruments on board of different satellites. However, this collection of measurements has gaps in the time series discrepancies (Fig. 2), due to problems such as calibration and degradation of the equipment, which prevents studies that require a long and continuous period of data. Since 2003, TSI measures have

[2] 1 AU (Astronomical Unit) is the average distance between Sun and Earth, outside the Earth's atmosphere.

been collected by the instrument TIM (Total Irradiance Monitor) on board the SORCE (Solar Radiation and Climate Experiment) mission[3]. This data set is used in this work.

In order to solve this problem, many works attempted to estimate the irradiance curve with different methods [2,8,17,21,23]. Most of them use physical models that allow the reconstruction of time fractions of TSI or SSI missing data and not specifically the task of series prediction. One of them [21], whereas, can predict continuous TSI values using a type of Recurrent Neural Network present in a proprietary software. Although it presents results with good accuracy, the software restrictions such as the need for a paid license and the incompatibility of toolboxes between different versions does not allow the procedure to be easily distributed and reproduced.

The aim of this work is in the direction of offering a procedure that performs the TSI estimation, which can allow its reconstruction, but also predict its future variation six hours in advance, using neural networks implemented in free programming languages and libraries.

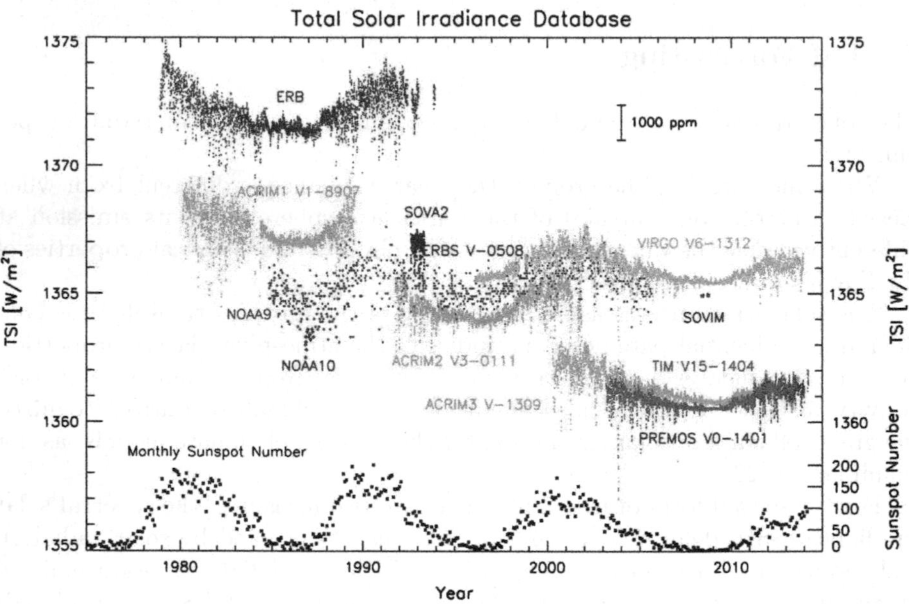

Fig. 2. History of TSI measurements by different instruments on board satellites, as their calibration discrepancies and faults. Measurements performed by TIM were initiated in 2003. The monthly averages of the number of sunspots are also displayed and confirms the influence of the solar activity on the TSI variation [16].

[3] SORCE webpage: http://lasp.colorado.edu/home/sorce/.

3.1 Forecasting Workflow

The complete workflow for solar irradiance prediction (in this work, specifically TSI) begins with the processing of two types of solar images (as shown in Fig. 1, collected by NASA's SDO mission), both of which are records of the solar photosphere (essentially the solar "surface"):

- The continuum images: corresponding to those visible to the human eye, which record the sunspots;
- The magnetograms: which allows the visualization of the active regions, through the polarity of the solar magnetic field.

A set of both images are downloaded considering the desired time period, and then a merged procedure of identification, classification and calculation of the disturbed areas over both is performed. In the sequence, a data matrix is prepared with the calculated and classified areas which are used as input to the neural network that will perform a supervised training, presenting as desired output the TSI values observed for an instant of 6 h ahead. The workflow tasks, separated into modules, where each black outlined block represents a module, can be seen in Fig. 3. This figure also suggests, through the dash outlined boxes, replacement options for some of the tasks.

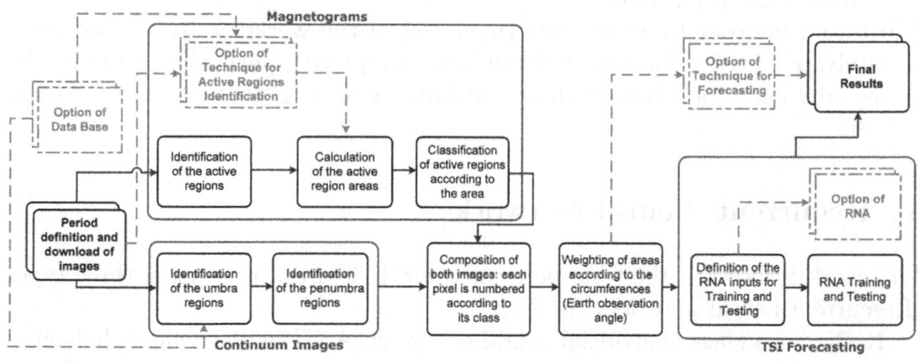

Fig. 3. Complete workflow for processing the solar images and predicting TSI.

Parallel to the specific objective of comparing the performances of different Recurrent Neural Networks architectures in TSI forecasting, this work is part of a larger proposal that aims to share the complete procedure, with the partial and final results, in a modular way, in order to allow modifications on steps of the procedure and extensions that includes other preprocessing and classification approaches.

3.2 Modularity and Reproducibility

Research in areas such as Space Geophysics uses computational tools and techniques to process and analyze data, focused on generating quality final results. However, the detailed record of the entire analytical workflow that was adopted to arrive at such results, and its availability for reuse, is also a valuable tool, and could bring a series of benefits for the researchers.

This concept is already used in other scientific areas. Bioinformatics researchers, for example, can share robust and reliable workflows in the cloud, joined by a large volume of data, that can be reused by a research community who need the same data and processing [7,18,19].

This work is the beginning of a proposal for the modularization of the solar images analysis process, with the final objective of making available a solar irradiance prediction workflow that is, mainly:

Accessible: available on a free platform, language and libraries in the cloud, so that it can be used by an interested researcher, offering with it all the necessary processing devices like operating system, software and libraries, with the originally used versions;

Reproducible: with notebook commented codes that can be: re-executed to validate the developed procedures and the partial and final results obtained; or edited to, for example, allow the reuse of the workflow to process and analyze other input data;

Modular: in order to allow parts (modules) of the workflow to be used separately, or edited to have part of the process replaced, purposing, for example, the creation of new tests with new techniques or tools that perform the same task.

4 Recurrent Neural Networks

This work focuses on the tests performed for TSI forecasting using three types of recurrent neural networks (RNNs).

RNNs are a class of artificial neural networks (ANN) with dynamic behavior, which consider the existing dependency between the instances of entry. This is what differentiates them from the traditional Feed Forward Networks, which treat the inputs as independent from each other.

In order to generate internal memory devices, RNNs also have connections between neurons of the same layer, different from the traditional Feed Forward, in which the connections exist only between the different layers. What happens basically in this new architecture is that the output of a neuron can be fed back into the neuron itself [9].

This flexibility of RNNs allows them to be used in language processing problems such as speech recognition, language modeling, machine translation [10], price monitoring [20] and time series in general, cases in which considering the historical context of the inputs can be an essential differential in the forecast quality.

Essentially, the RNNs follow the basic functioning of other ANNs, regarding the internal processing of neurons, which results in the weighted sum of the input over which an activation function is applied. However, besides the traditional matrix of weights, the simple types of RNNs have another matrix of weights that is used exclusively in the processing of the feedback coming from the previous processing moments.

In Fig. 4, it is possible to visualize the basic process which occurs in a recurrent neuron to calculate its state h in the time instant t, given the input at the same time ($x^{(t)}$) and its previous state ($h^{(t-1)}$), generating its output ($o^{(t)}$). On the left of the picture a briefer representation is made and on the right the unfolding of the process considering instants of time from $t-1$ to $t+1$. In addition to this information, the figure also distinguishes the three weight matrices, with U the input layer weight matrix, V the output layer weight matrix and W the weight matrix applied to the feedback signals [9].

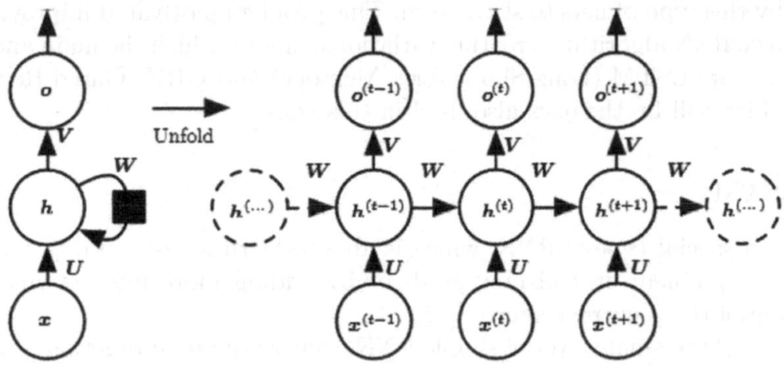

Fig. 4. Basic working of a simple class of RNNs neuron [9].

Equations 1a–1c formalize the operations indicated in Fig. 4, where we observe that the cell in the state $h^{(t-1)}$ that receives and processes the input $x^{(t-1)}$, in addition to transmitting the result as output ($o^{(t-1)}$) to the next layer, also uses it as input to update its own state to $h^{(t)}$. Therefore, when that same cell receives the next entry $x^{(t)}$, it has the memory of the previous entry $x^{(t-1)}$. And so the process continues, successively, until it processes all the input instances.

The activation function commonly used in recurrent layers is the hyperbolic tangent ($tanh$), to deal with nonlinearity of data. Equations 1b and 1c show, respectively, the weighted sum on which the activation function $tanh$ with the respective weight matrices is applied, and then the calculation of the output of each recurring neuron.

$$h^{(t)} = f\left(h^{(t-1)}, x^{(t)}\right) \tag{1a}$$

$$h^{(t)} = tanh\left(Wh^{(t-1)} + Ux^{(t)}\right) \tag{1b}$$

$$o^{(t)} = Vh^{(t)} \tag{1c}$$

The training algorithm normally used in RNNs is Backpropagation Through Time, adapted from the traditional backpropagation used in multilayer perceptrons, but, in this case, using the time instants as the basis for the backpropagation. It makes the calculations of the chain rule more complex, since the backpropagation of the error must reach not only the neurons of the previous layer in question, but all those who influenced them with the feedback through time. Thus, the large number of steps through which the error is retropropagated generates a drastic reduction in the value of the gradient, approaching zero, resulting in the so-called vanishing gradient problem, in which the weights begin not to suffer significant updates, not contributing then to the learning process [13].

The operation of the simple recurrent nets architectures, like Keras SimpleRNN, tested in this work, is based on the previously described functioning and does not deal with the vanishing gradient problem, which limits the memory offered by this type of nets to short term. This problem motivated improvements in the basic RNN algorithm, creating variations, among which the main and most used today are LSTM (Long Short-Term Memory) and GRU (Gated Recurrent Unit), which will be the ones also used in this work.

4.1 LSTM

LSTM is a special type of RNN, which is able to learn long-term dependencies, solving the problem of vanishing gradient by adding more interactions in the processing of the recurrent neuron [12].

Instead of the single layer of simple RNNs, where the *tanh* function is applied on the weighted sum between the input and the previous state, LSTMs have more layers interacting in a very specific way, each one with its own matrix of weights [10]:

Forget Gate f: Defines how much of the previous state $h^{(t-1)}$ should be allowed to pass on. Activates the signal with sigmoid function (Eq. 2).

$$f = \sigma\left(W^{(f)}h^{(t-1)} + U^{(f)}x^{(t)}\right) \tag{2}$$

Input Gate i: Defines how much of the newly computed state with the x^t entry will be kept for the next instants of time. Activates the signal with sigmoid function (Eq. 3).

$$i = \sigma\left(W^{(i)}h^{(t-1)} + U^{(i)}x^{(t)}\right) \tag{3}$$

Output Gate o: Defines how much of the internal state $h^{(t-1)}$ is desired to be exposed for the next layer. Activates the signal with sigmoid function (Eq. 4).

$$o = \sigma\left(W^{o}h^{(t-1)} + U^{o}x^{(t)}\right) \tag{4}$$

Internal Hidden State g: It is computed based on the current entry $x^{(t)}$ and the previous state $h^{(t-1)}$ of the neuron, similar to what happened in the elements of Simple RNNs, using the function *tanh* (Eq. 5).

$$g = tanh\left(W^{(g)}h^{(t-1)} + U^{(g)}x^{(t)}\right) \tag{5}$$

After obtaining the results of *f*, *i*, *o* and *g*, the so-called Cell-State is calculated ($c^{(t)}$), given by Eq. 6, in which a combination is made between the long-term memories and the most recent ones, through the Forgot gate and the Input gate. This way, their values are weighted in order to ignore the desired memories (with value 0) or making them relevant (with value 1).

$$c^{(t)} = \left(c^{(t-1)} \otimes f\right) \oplus (g \otimes i) \tag{6}$$

The output h of the neuron is finally calculated as a function of the Cell-State value, after applying the *tanh* function to it, and then determining, through the value of the output gate, how much this output is relevant to this instant of time (Eq. 7).

$$h^{(t)} = tanh\left(c^{(t-1)} \otimes o\right) \tag{7}$$

4.2 GRU

It can be considered that the GRU is a variation of LSTM and very similar to it, with the advantage of having a considerably simpler gates structure than LSTM. GRUs are composed of only two gates: **Update** and **Reset**, which are able to be trained, respectively, to define how much of the older information should be kept, and to merge the new information entries with the previous memories. Equations 8a–8d summarize the computations that take place in GRU cells [10].

$$z = \sigma\left(W^{(z)}h^{(t-1)} + U^{(z)}x^{(t)}\right) \tag{8a}$$

$$r = \sigma\left(W^{(r)}h^{(t-1)} + U^{(r)}x^{(t)}\right) \tag{8b}$$

$$c = tanh\left(W^{(c)}\left(h^{(t-1)} \otimes r\right) + U^{(c)}x^{(t)}\right) \tag{8c}$$

$$h^{(t)} = (z \otimes c) \oplus \left((1-z) \otimes h^{(t-1)}\right) \tag{8d}$$

According to some works, LSTM and GRU are networks that have shown themselves to be very similar in terms of performance [15]. In this work, both of the architectures, as well as the Simple RNN, will be tested to see which will bring better results for the TSI forecast.

5 Results

Experiments were performed with Keras library for Python RNN architectures layers: SimpleRNN, LSTM and GRU.

As training and validation data set, it was used the period from 2011 November 05 to 2012 March 30, which presented records of quiet and disturbed sun activity. They had 6-h temporal resolution, making a total of 588 time instants, from which 80% were used as training set and 20% as validation set.

The networks fixed configuration involved: 40 input parameters, a recurrent layer and a linear output layer (Keras Dense layer) with a neuron, to predict a single TSI value. The nets parameters that were varied in the experiments were: number of recurrent hidden neurons, batch size, time steps, the use of Dropout (an algorithm to prevent the over-fitting problem in neural networks training process [1].) and the net architecture.

5.1 Varying Hidden Units

For all the architectures, experiments were made varying the recurrent layer hidden numbers, considering two experiment groups:

Few units without a dropout layer: For the first batch of experiments, few units were used, from 1 to 8, taking as basis [21]. For each different number of hidden units, five complete training processes were done, being adopted as fixed parameters: batch size of 5 and 1 time step. The Fig. 5 shows the least Validation Root Mean Square Error (RMSE) variation obtained in five training processes for each hidden unit number.

Many units with a dropout layer: For the second batch of hidden units experiments, 10 to 80 units were used, with 5 full training processes for each configuration. This time, a Dropout layer was added to the net, trying to prevent over-fitting, that was observed on the first group of hidden units tests. An initial dropout rate of 0.2 was assumed. The Fig. 5 shows the results for this experiment.

The first class of tests showed that low quantities of hidden units, specifically one unit, brought better accuracy results. However, the experiment with more units and the use of Dropout layer brought even better accuracy, besides of faster convergence with 20% of the epochs that were needed in the first group of tests.

The second group also presents less variability in RMSE for the same batch of tests.

In most of cases, in both groups of tests, specially in the second one, the GRU and LSTM nets performance looked very similar, bringing minor error than the SimpleRNN.

5.2 Varying Batch Number and Dropout Rates

For droptout rates varying tests, rates from 0% to 50% were used, considering that 50% is the higher recommended rate in Keras documents. The results with

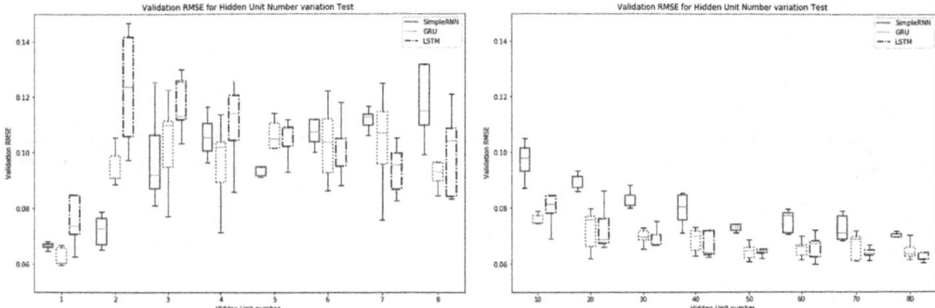

Fig. 5. Validation RMSE for hidden units number experiment. On the left, units from 1 to 8, and on the right, units from 10 to 80.

GRU and LSTM, the architectures which presented minor RMSE, did not show a considerable variance for the different dropout rates, but the higher rate showed a significantly less RMSE. Therefore, once a big number of hidden units was used, a rate of 50% was chosen for the subsequent experiments.

The batch number variation was defined calculating different percentages of the training data length. It started on 0.5% and was increased until 50%.

Tests were made for few as for many hidden units and both showed not a considerable difference in performance throughout, but a little worst performance over the batch size increasing in both test groups. Therefore, even though bigger size batches result in faster training processes, smaller batches were opted for the subsequent tests.

5.3 Varying Time Step

This set of tests was made varying the number of time steps in the input data composition. All previous tests used only one time step, what means that only the input at time t was being used for predicting the output at time $t+1$ (6 h ahead).

When using more time steps, more previous time instants are used. For example, when using 3 time steps, for predicting the output at time $t+1$, the input at times t, $t-1$ and $t-2$ are used.

Figure 6 shows the results obtained for the three net architectures (on the left) when varying the time step from 1 to 5. The same figure (right side) shows the performance comparison between the two architectures that showed best performance.

The tests for 2 and 3 time steps gave a minor value for RMSE, maybe suggesting time dependence between the Sun activity and TSI. More experiments should be done to confirm that relationship.

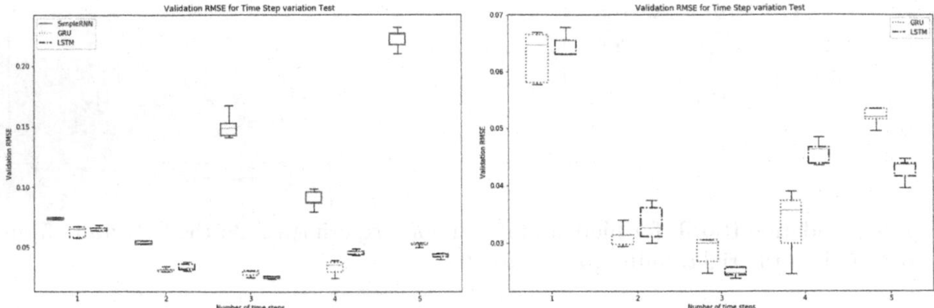

Fig. 6. Validation RMSE for time step varying experiment. On the left, the comparison between the three different architectures, and on the right, the comparison between only the GRU and LSTM.

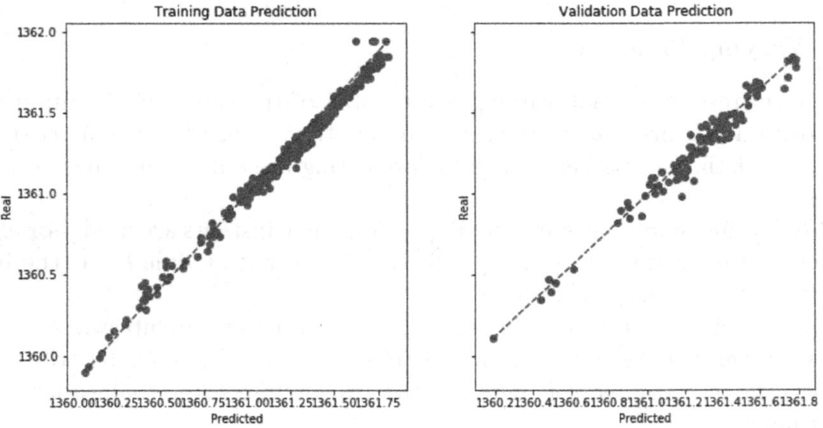

Fig. 7. TSI Training and Validation data prediction comparing the desired data to the obtained from GRU net.

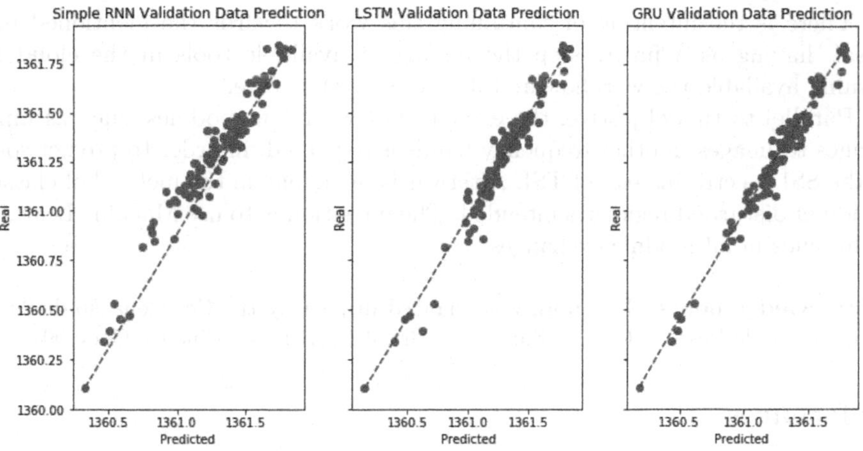

Fig. 8. TSI Validation data prediction comparing the performances between LSTM, GRU and SimpleRNN.

5.4 Forecast Accuracy

In an attempt to combine the best results obtained in the experiments described above, the last training steps were conducted using the considered best parameters.

Figure 7 shows, for one of these trainings, the relationship between the desired and obtained TSI values for the training and the validation data. Figure 8 shows the validation performance for each architecture for the same training parameters.

6 Conclusions and Future Works

In some experiments, the GRU net showed a slightly better performance, but in the most of them LSTM and GRU showed almost the same performance.

The SimpleRNN, for the first experiments, showed good results too, but in subsequent tests, it presented considerably worse performance than the two other architectures.

The time steps varying results suggest a better investigation over the time dependency period between the sun activity and its consequences at the top of the Earth's atmosphere.

Further tests are considered necessary to arrive at a final configuration for the TSI forecast. For that, it is intended to train a larger set of data after finding a satisfactory way of linking long periods of data, considering the existing gaps between them. The use of new practices to better analyze the network performance for different configurations is considered too for the continuity of this work.

There is the intention of continuing this work towards the mentioned proposal, having as a future step the testing of available tools in the cloud for turning available the workflow and its modular structure.

Parallel to this objective, the exchange of workflow modules, such as input images to images in other frequency bands is expected, in order to predict some of the SSI spectra instead of TSI. Afterwards, a change in the method of classification of disturbed regions is intended. The intention is to use Machine Learning techniques in all module exchanges.

Acknowledgements. This work was financed in part by the Coordenação de Aperfeiçoamento de Pessoal de Nível Superior - Brasil (CAPES) - Finance Code 001.

References

1. Baldi, P., Sadowski, P.J.: Understanding dropout. In: Advances in Neural Information Processing Systems, pp. 2814–2822 (2013)
2. Ball, W.T., Krivova, N.A., Unruh, Y.C., Haigh, J.D., Solanki, S.K.: A new SATIRE-S spectral solar irradiance reconstruction for solar cycles 21–23 and its implications for stratospheric ozone. J. Atmos. Sci. **71**(11), 4086–4101 (2014)
3. Burrell, A.G., Yeoman, T.K., Stephen, M., Lester, M.: Influence of solar irradiance on polar ionospheric convection. In: AGU Fall Meeting Abstracts (2016)
4. Coddington, O., Lean, J.L., Pilewskie, P., Snow, M., Lindholm, D.: A solar irradiance climate data record. Bull. Am. Meteorol. Soc. **97**(7), 1265–1282 (2016)
5. Echer, E., Rigozo, N.R., Nordemann, D.J.R., Vieira, L.E.A., Prestes, A., de Faria, H.H.: O Numero de Manchas Solares, Índice da Atividade do Sol. Rev. Bras. Ensino Física **24**(2), 157–163 (2003)
6. Ermolli, I., et al.: Recent variability of the solar spectral irradiance and its impact on climate modelling. arXiv preprint arXiv:1303.5577 (2013)
7. Fjukstad, B., Bongo, L.A.: A review of scalable bioinformatics pipelines. Data Sci. Eng. **2**(3), 245–251 (2017)
8. Gómez, J.R., Vieira, L.A., Dal Lago, A., Palacios, J., Balmaceda, L.A., Stekel, T.: Modelling short-term Solar Spectral Irradiance (SSI) using coronal electron density and temperature profiles based on solar magnetic field observations. Proc. Int. Astron. Union **12**(S327), 82–85 (2016)
9. Goodfellow, I., Bengio, Y., Courville, A.: Deep Learning. MIT Press, Cambridge (2016). http://www.deeplearningbook.org
10. Gulli, A., Pal, S.: Deep Learning with Keras. Packt Publishing Ltd., Birmingham (2017)
11. Hathaway, D.H.: The solar cycle. Living Rev. Solar Phys. **7** (2010). https://doi.org/10.12942/lrsp-2010-1
12. Hochreiter, S., Schmidhuber, J.: LSTM can solve hard long time lag problems. In: Advances in neural information processing systems, pp. 473–479 (1997)
13. Hochreiter, S.: Recurrent neural net learning and vanishing gradient. Fuzziness Knowl.-Based Syst. Int. J. Uncert. **6**(2), 107–116 (1998)
14. Hoyt, D.V., Schatten, K.: The Role of the Sun in Climate Change. Oxford University Press, Oxford (1997)
15. Jozefowicz, R., Zaremba, W., Sutskever, I.: An empirical exploration of recurrent network architectures. In: International Conference on Machine Learning, pp. 2342–2350 (2015)

16. Kopp, G.: An assessment of the solar irradiance record for climate studies. J. Space Weather Space Clim. **4**, A14 (2014)
17. Krivova, N.A., Vieira, L.E.A., Solanki, S.K.: Reconstruction of solar spectral irradiance since the Maunder minimum. J. Geophys. Res.: Space Phys. **115**(A12), 1–11 (2010)
18. Leipzig, J.: A review of bioinformatic pipeline frameworks. Brief. Bioinf. **18**(3), 530–536 (2017)
19. O'Connor, B.D., et al.: The Dockstore: enabling modular, community-focused sharing of Docker-based genomics tools and workflows. F1000Research **6**, 52 (2017). https://doi.org/10.12688/f1000research.10137.1
20. Pinheiro, C.A.O., Senna, V.D.: Multivariate analysis and neural networks application to price forecasting in the Brazilian agricultural market. Ciência Rural **47**(1), 1–7 (2017)
21. Vieira, L.E.A., de Wit, T.D., Kretzschmar, M.: Short-term forecast of the total and spectral solar irradiance. arXiv preprint arXiv:1111.5308 (2011)
22. Williamson, C.E., et al.: Solar ultraviolet radiation in a changing climate. Nat. Clim. Change **4**(6), 434–441 (2014)
23. Yeo, K.L., Ball, W.T., Krivova, N.A., Solanki, S.K., Unruh, Y.C., Morrill, J.: UV solar irradiance in observations and the NRLSSI and SATIRE-S models. J. Geophys. Res. Space Phys. **120**(8), 6055–6070 (2015)
24. Yiğit, E., Knížová, P.K., Georgieva, K., Ward, W.: A review of vertical coupling in the atmosphere-ionosphere system: effects of waves, sudden stratospheric warmings, space weather, and of solar activity. J. Atmos. Solar-Terrestrial Phys. **141**, 1–12 (2016)

Assessing Satellite Image Time Series Clustering Using Growing SOM

Rodrigo de Sales da Silva Adeu(✉), Karine Reis Ferreira, Pedro R. Andrade, and Lorena Santos

National Institute for Space Research (INPE), Astronautas Avenue 1758, São José dos Campos 12227-010, São Paulo, Brazil
{rodrigo.adeu,karine.ferreira,pedro.andrade,lorena.santos}@inpe.br,
http://www.inpe.br/

Abstract. Mapping Earth land use and cover changes is crucial to understand agricultural dynamics. Recently, analysis of time series extracted from Earth observation satellite images has been widely used to produce land use and cover information. In time series analysis, clustering is a common technique performed to discover patterns on data sets. In this work, we evaluate the Growing Self-Organizing Maps algorithm for clustering satellite image time series and compare it with Self-Organizing Maps algorithm. This paper presents a case study using satellite image time series associated to samples of land use and cover classes, highlighting the advantage of providing a neutral factor (called spread factor) as a parameter for GSOM, instead of the SOM grid size.

Keywords: Growing Self-Organized Map · Land use and cover · Machine learning

1 Introduction

Technologies and methods of remote sensing and digital image processing play a crucial role in the identification, mapping, assessment and monitoring of land use and cover changes. In the last years, the use of remote sensing image time series analysis to produce land use and cover information has increased greatly [6]. Bi-temporal or traditional change detection approaches are commonly used to detect complex underlying processes, but time series derived from Earth observation satellite images has been used as an alternative to facilitate this task [10].

In order to classify Earth observation image time series to produce land use and cover change maps, machine learning methods such as Support Vector Machine (SVM) and Random Forest (RF) have been used [11]. Most of these methods are based on supervised learning algorithms, requiring a training step that uses labeled land use and cover samples. A crucial challenge on this task is the selection of representative samples to obtain a good classification accuracy.

To better select land use and cover samples from satellite image time series, Santos et al. [13] propose a method based on Self-Organizing Maps (SOM) neural network [8] for time series clustering. Such method estimates the land use

O. Gervasi et al. (Eds.): ICCSA 2020, LNCS 12253, pp. 270–282, 2020.
https://doi.org/10.1007/978-3-030-58814-4_19

and cover samples quality from the satellite image time series clusters created by SOM.

Despite its advantages, SOM has a characteristic that limits its potential. It uses a predefined and fixed network architecture in terms of number and arrangement of neural processing elements. Simulations have to be run several times on different network sizes to find an appropriate network structure [5]. This work aims to contribute to land use and cover research area by validating an approach that avoids this additional parameter. Growing SOM (GSOM) was originally proposed to address the SOM characteristic of predetermining the map size [1]. This paper evaluates GSOM as an alternative to traditional SOM for satellite image time series clustering.

2 Self-Organizing Map (SOM)

A Self-Organizing Map (SOM) is an unsupervised neural network. SOM maps a high dimensional space onto a low-dimensional space preserving its neighbourhood topology. SOM is composed by input and output layers, with the latter generally being a two-dimensional grid.

Each element of a grid is called neuron. An important property of SOM is that the neurons are organized in a way that they maintain a similar neighbourhood, that is, neurons that have similar characteristics are close in the output layer. Figure 1 shows the structure of SOM.

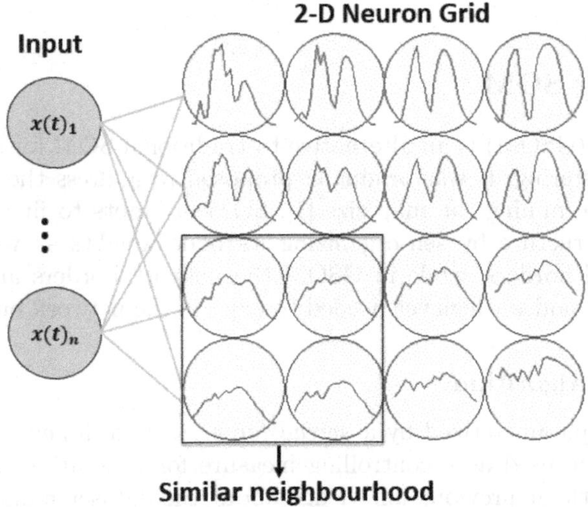

Fig. 1. SOM structure

Each neuron j has a n-dimensional weight vector $w_j = [w_1, \ldots, w_n]$ associated to it. An input $x(t) = [x(t)_1, \ldots, x(t)_n]$ is associated to most similar neuron to it through distance metrics, as Euclidean distance. The distance D_j is computed between a input vector and each neuron j for all the neurons in the output layer (Eq. 1).

$$D_j = \sum_{i=1}^{N} \sqrt{(x(t)_i - w_j)^2}. \tag{1}$$

Once we have with all distances between a input and all neurons, the minimum distance is determined the Best-Matching-Unit (BMU), i.e. the neuron d_b with weight vector closer to $x(t)$ (Eq. 2):

$$d_b = min\{D_1, \ldots, D_j\}. \tag{2}$$

The BMU and its neighbours within a radius r must be updated. The weights are adjusted to increase the similarity with the input vector, the update is given by:

$$w_j(t) = w_j(t) + \alpha(t) \times h_{b,j}(t)[x(t)_i - w_j(t)], \tag{3}$$

In Eq. 3, $\alpha(t)$ is the learning rate, set as $0 < \alpha(t) < 1$ and $h_{b,j}$ is a neighbourhood function. The SOM mapping ends when all input vectors are presented to output layer. During each time, the $\alpha(t)$ must be reduced and the neighbourhood function reduce the radius of the neighborhood. There are several ways to reduce the value of $\alpha(t)$ and the radius of the neighbours. They can be found in [9].

3 Growing SOM

Growing SOM (GSOM) is an alternative to traditional SOM for satellite image time series clustering. It was originally proposed to address the SOM requirement of predetermining the map size [1]. SOM attempts to fit a data set into a predefined structure by self-organizing its node weights as well as possible within its fixed borders, while in GSOM the network borders are expandable, generating new nodes whenever needed to expand the network outwards.

3.1 GSOM Algorithm

The GSOM is parameterized by a *spread factor*, a data dimensionality neutral factor. It can be used as a controlling measure for generating maps with different sizes, without previous knowledge about the dataset number of samples or attributes. The GSOM learning algorithm has three phases:

Initial phase: At the initialization phase, GSOM network starts with four neurons with randomly assigned weight vectors. All the initial neurons are boundary nodes and have opportunity to grow. In Fig. 2, the four initial neurons are connected with lines and the available positions are shown via dashed circles.

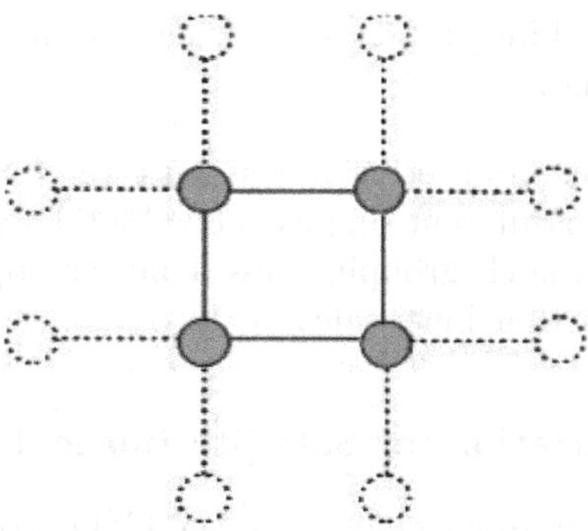

Fig. 2. Initial GSOM with four neurons. Source: [14]

Growing phase: At this phase, the time series data are presented to the network. The weight vector that is closest to the input vector mapped (the winner neuron), is selected based on a distance function. The winner neuron accumulative error is calculated according to a distance function between the input vector and the winner neuron weight vector. This error indicates the distance between the input vector and the weight vector of neurons. When the accumulative error of a neuron exceeds a *growing threshold* (calculated based on the spread factor), and the candidate neuron is on the grid boundary, new neurons are added in the available free positions around the candidate neuron in the grid, as showed on Fig. 3. If the winning neuron is not on the grid boundary, the accumulated error of the neighbors are updated according to the winner distance, giving the non-boundary nodes some ability in initiating node growth.

Smoothing phase: In order to fine-tune the weight vectors and to improve the map smoothness, a smoothing phase is applied after growing [14]. No new nodes are added during this phase. The intent is to smooth out any existing quantization error, mainly in the nodes grown at the growing phase latter

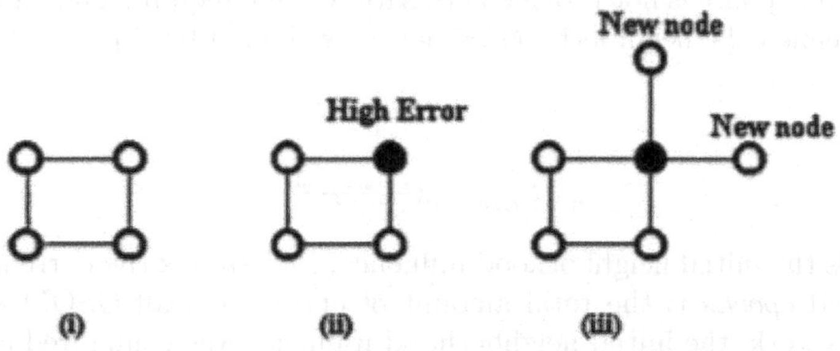

Fig. 3. New node generation from the network boundary. Source: [1]

stages [1]. The smoothing phase stops when the nodes error values in the map become very small.

Depending on the clusters present in the data, the GSOM map generated by this process develops into different shapes. The GSOM shape represents the data grouping, and therefore, such grouping has a better opportunity of attracting the user attention for further investigation [1].

3.2 GSOM Customization for Satellite Image Time Series

In this paper, we propose minor changes in the GSOM described by Alahakoon et al. [1]. These changes aim to fit the algorithm to work with satellite image time series.

During the network weights adaptation, the described learning rate states that it needs to be a function that gradually takes higher values as the map grows and the number of nodes becomes larger [1]. The suggested function is described by Eq. (1) with $R = 3.8$, and $n(t)$ is the number of neurons on a given iteration t.

$$(\frac{1-R}{n(t)}) \tag{4}$$

The use of this learning rate function resulted on a classification accuracy decrease. In order to improve the accuracy, this function was replaced by the function described by Eq. 2, that gradually takes minor values as the number of iterations increase:

$$e^{(\frac{-iteration}{epochs})}, \tag{5}$$

with *iteration* representing the current iteration number and *epochs* representing the total amount of epochs.

Alahakoon et al. [1] states that the GSOM starting neighborhood selected for weight adaptation is smaller compared to the SOM, and weight adaptation is carried out with reducing neighborhood until neighborhood is unity. But a function for initializing and reducing the neighborhood influence during the growing and smoothing phase is not provided. To satisfy these requirements, after several tests, we defined the neighborhood influence as showed by Eq. (3):

$$e^{(\frac{-d}{2\times\sigma^2})}, \tag{6}$$

$$\sigma = ini \times e^{(\frac{-iteration}{epochs})}, \tag{7}$$

where *ini* is the initial neighborhood influence, *iteration* is the current iteration number, and *epochs* is the total amount of epochs. On all GSOM executions used in this work, the initial neighborhood influence was configured as 0.6.

4 Case Study: SOM X GSOM Comparative

In order to check the accuracy of GSOM for satellite image time series clustering and to compare it with SOM, we implemented both SOM and GSOM in Python [12], with the changes proposed in this paper. We then executed a case study using the same time series data set described in Santos et al. [13]. In this case study, we applied both Python algorithms to this data set and compare the results.

4.1 Data Set

The satellite image time series data set used in our case study is shown in Fig. 4. This data set is composed by 2215 ground samples of land use and cover classes, including natural vegetation and agricultural, for the Mato Grosso state in Brazil. These samples refer to nine distinct land use and cover classes: (1) Cerrado, (2) Pasture, (3) Forest, (4) Soy-Corn, (5) Soy-Cotton, (6) Soy-Fallow, (7) Soy-Millet, (8) Fallow-Cotton and (9) Soy-Sunflower.

Each sample has a spatial location (latitude and longitude), start and end date that corresponds to agricultural year (from August to September) and the corresponding sample class label. For each sample spatial location, we got the time series associated to that location or pixel from a satellite image collection ordered in time, as shown in Fig. 4. In this work, we used satellite images of the MODIS (Moderate-Resolution Imaging Spectroradiometer) sensor of the NASA satellite Terra, including its product MOD13Q1. Each time series has multiple attributes that was generated by EVI, NDVI, NIR and MIR attribute concatenation. These ground samples were collected by [11].

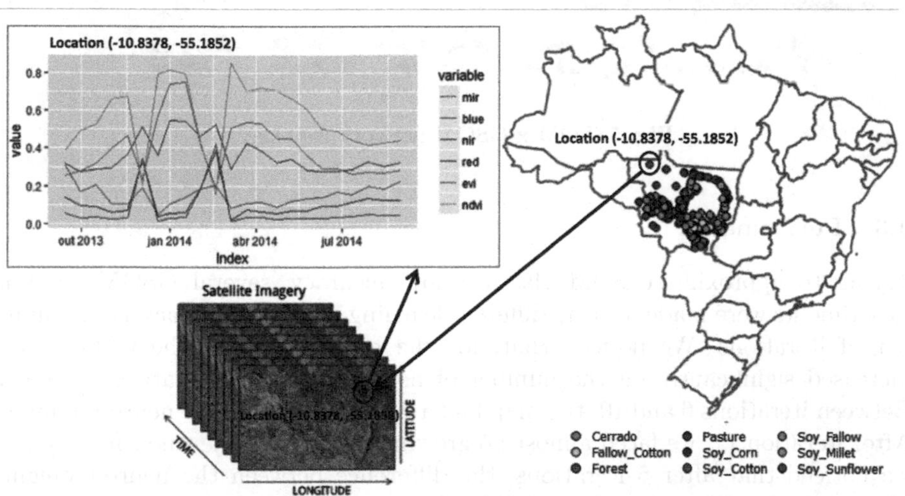

Fig. 4. Satellite image time series data set associated with land use and cover samples. Source: [4]

4.2 Network Topology

SOM uses a fixed network architecture in terms of number and arrangement of neural processing elements which have to be predefined. To better estimate the SOM network size, a preliminary study about the number of attributes, classes separability and number of data samples needs to be done. On the other hand, GSOM requires only a spread factor as an input parameter. The spread factor is a neutral number between 0 and 1 that defines how much the network needs to grow.

Figure 5 shows the networks create by SOM (using a fixed 25×25 grid) and GSOM (using a spread factor 1 and number of iteration 15; 10 iterations for growing and 5 iterations for smoothing). Both algorithms achieved similar classification accuracy, but with different network topologies. In the SOM case, as the grid size is always prefixed, the cluster distribution can differ, but the grid will always have the same size. On the other hand, in the GSOM case, we can observe the grid growing to fit the data.

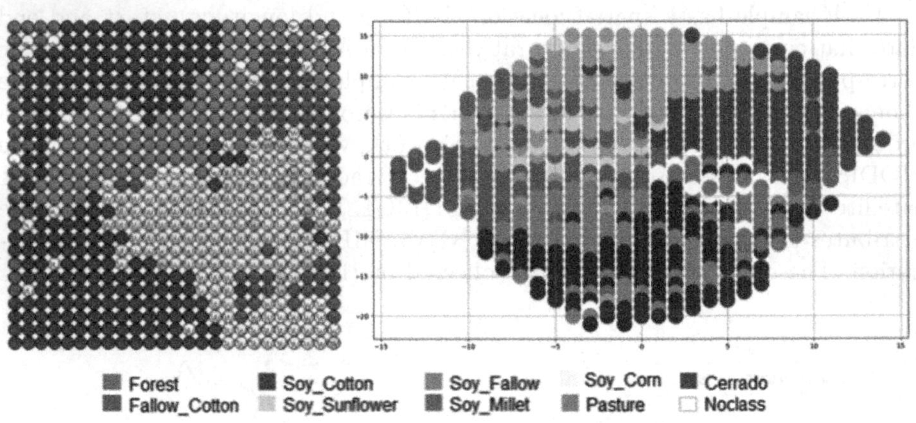

Fig. 5. SOM x GSOM network topology.

4.3 Performance

Trying to approximate SOM classification accuracy, several GSOM running experiments were made, testing different learning rates, spread factors and number of iterations. We noticed that, for the given data set, the GSOM map increased significantly on the number of neurons between iterations 1 and 5. Between iterations 6 and 10, the map had a small growing of the neuron number. After iteration 11, we faced almost no growing. Analyzing the smoothing phase, we noticed that after 5 iterations, the difference between the neuron weights after each iteration were above 0.001. This facts lead us to fix the number of iterations on growing phase in 10, and the number of iterations on smoothing phase in 5.

As the SOM algorithm has a fixed grid, each iteration takes approximately the same time to run. On the GSOM growing phase, the increasing number of neurons implies on variable time spent on each iteration. Figure 6 illustrates the time spend by SOM (with 25×25 fixed grid) and GSOM parametrized with 10 Growing iterations and 5 Smoothing iterations. Both algorithms were executed 10 times, using the same learning rate and the same neighborhood update functions.

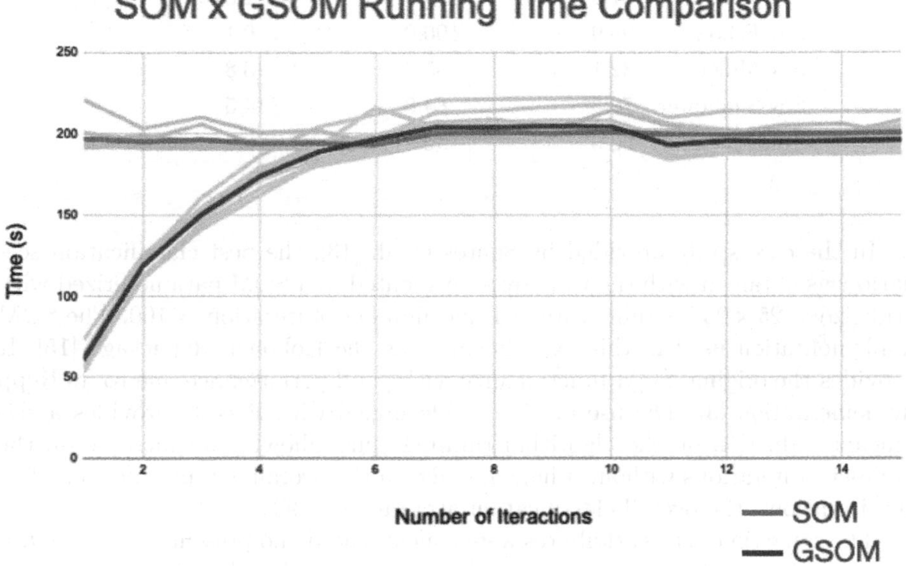

Fig. 6. SOM x GSOM performance comparison.

4.4 Cluster Accuracy

After the unsupervised clustering provided by SOM, each neuron is analyzed, and the samples associated to this neuron are counted. All neurons used by SOM are labeled, using the label of the majority samples associated to it. After that, we are now able to check the accuracy of each neuron, and consequently, the whole map accuracy.

In order to compare the cluster accuracy, the same implementation of SOM and GSOM algorithms were executed 10 times, using the same learning rate and the same neighborhood update functions. As the Python implementation slows down the overall solution performance, only 15 iterations of each algorithms were ran. Before that, several GSOM executions were ran in order to generate a grid map with almost the same neurons quantity of a 25×25 SOM. The results are showed on Table 1. We noticed that, besides a small classification increment, GSOM presents significant results of +11.7% and +14.5% on Fallow-Cotton and Soy-Sunflower clustering respectively.

Table 1. 15 SOM iterations x 15 GSOM iterations - Accuracy for each cluster.

Cluster	SOM accuracy	GSOM accuracy	GSOM – SOM
Cerrado	96.4	97.6	1.2
Fallow-Cotton	84.1	95.8	11.7
Forest	98.4	98.4	0.0
Pasture	88.9	93.8	4.9
Soy-Corn	86.1	87.2	1.1
Soy-Cotton	91.1	93.9	2.8
Soy-Fallow	99.9	100.0	0.1
Soy-Millet	82.1	85.9	3.8
Soy-Sunflower	70.3	84.8	14.5
Total accuracy	90.0	92.8	2.8

In the case study provided by Santos et al. [13], the best classification scenario was obtained with the time series presented to a SOM parameterized with grid size $= 25 \times 25$, learning rate $= 1$ and number of iteration $= 100$. The SOM implementation used in this experiments was the Kohonen R package [15]. It provides the original SOM functionality with good performance due to its Rcpp implementation [3]. The use of C++ code mixed with R code provides a significant reduction on the algorithm running time, allowing an increase on the number of iterations without a huge impact on the overall execution time. After 100 iterations, the overall classification accuracy was 93%.

The same time series attributes were concatenated and presented to a GSOM, parameterized with spread factor $= 1$, learning rate $= 1$ and number of iteration $= 15$ (10 iteration for growing and 5 iteration for smoothing). The overall cluster accuracy of GSOM was 93%. The cluster accuracy for each cluster is presented in Table 2. We can notice that, despite of a small classification decrease on Fallow-Cotton and Pasture clusters, GSOM presents a significant increment of the Soy-Sunflower clustering accuracy of +11.7%. Also, the overall sample cluster was pretty similar and stated as 93.0% for both algorithms.

5 GSOM Neighborhood Analysis

A relevant SOM property that needs to be validated during the GSOM tests is the neighborhood topography maintenance. On a regular SOM, similar satellite image time series are grouped into nearness neighborhoods, even if these time series are labeled as different classes. The distribution on the SOM grid over the iterations tends to cluster satellite image time series of a specific sample on the same closer neighborhood. On the specific case of satellite image time series associated to land use and cover ground samples, the neighborhood maintenance in the clustering process is useful to identify sampling outliers.

Table 2. 100 SOM iterations x 15 GSOM iterations - Accuracy for Each Cluster.

Cluster	SOM accuracy	GSOM Accuracy	GSOM – SOM
Cerrado	97.3	98.2	0.9
Fallow-Cotton	85.7	82.3	−3.4
Forest	99.3	98.5	−0.8
Pasture	97.3	94.5	−2.8
Soy-Corn	84.0	84.4	0.4
Soy-Cotton	95.5	95.2	−0.3
Soy-Fallow	100.0	100.0	0.0
Soy-Millet	90.3	88.9	−1.4
Soy-Sunflower	76.9	88.6	11.7
Total accuracy	93.0	93.0	0.0

In this case study, we can conclude that GSOM also keeps this property, as shown in Fig. 7. The map highlights the nearest neighbors of Neuron 1 (N1). We also point out some random distant neighbors in blue (N593, N607, N610, and N615). Analyzing the distance between the weight vectors of Neuron 1 and the weight vectors of the nearest and some distant random neighbors, we can notice that the distance between the neuron weights grows as we move away from the comparing source. We can visually inspect the time series generated by each of this neurons weights, to check the distance between the nearest neighbors and the distant ones, as shown in Fig. 8.

The sum of the difference between Neuron 1 weights of its nearest neighbors is 26.94. As we move away from Neuron 1, this distance grows. As an example, the distance between the selected distant random neurons weights and Neuron 1 weights is 57.15. These distances are summarized on Table 3. This property was analysed for other neurons in the map and similar results were found.

Table 3. Distance between Neuron 1 weights and its nearest/farther neighbors.

N1 - Nearest	Distance	N1 - Farther	Distance
N1 - N0	7.27	N1 - N593	14.80
N1 - N3	5.67	N1 - N607	16.43
N1 - N5	6.28	N1 - N615	13.95
N1 - N4	7.72	N1 - N610	11.97
Neighborhood distance	26.94	Neighborhood distance	57.15

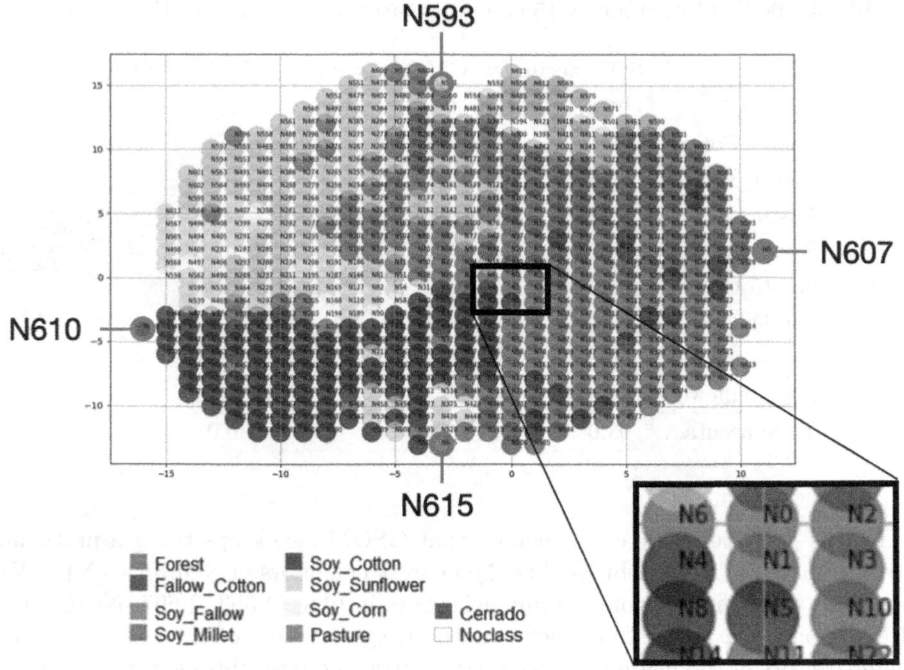

Fig. 7. GSOM grid sample extract - neighborhood analysis.

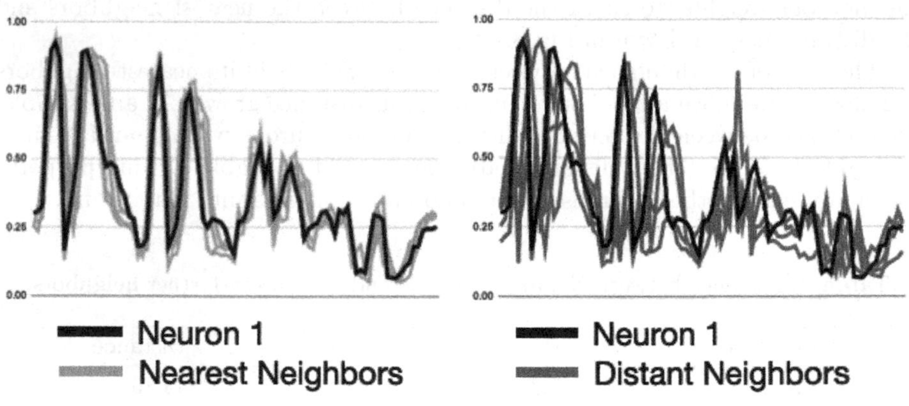

Fig. 8. Neighborhood Analysis - Nearest x Random Distant Neighbors.

6 Final Remarks

For the given satellite image time series clustering problem, on the given data set (Mato Grosso State, Brazil vegetation ground samples), GSOM seems to be a suitable alternative to SOM. After small customization and adaptation, the GSOM generated map grew as expected, reaching the same amount of neurons of the equivalent SOM, but with a different network topology. GSOM also keeps an important characteristic of SOM, the neurons neighborhood influence.

The cluster accuracy reached by GSOM was similar to the equivalent SOM. It also had a small advantage on the overall clustering time, thanks to its growing phase, when the neuron number is smaller than SOM. We were also able to test the main GSOM characteristic that initiates this work, which was the capability of clustering the dataset without specifying the grid size. The Spread Factor usage was a simple and effective task, allowing users without previous algorithm knowledge to cluster the data.

The source code used in this work and the dataset files are available on GitHub [7]. The current implementation is a prototype, that will be evolved in order to become a consolidated product in the future. Future works also include applying the GSOM algorithm to other land use and cover time series datasets, in order to confirm the benefits showed on the experiment presented in this work.

References

1. Alahakoon, D., Halgamuge, S.K., Srinivasan, B.: Dynamic self-organizing maps with controlled growth for knowledge discovery. IEEE Trans. Neural Netw. **11**, 601–614 (2000)
2. Bagan, H., Wang, Q., Watanabe, M., Yang, Y., Ma, J.: Land cover classification From Modis EVI time-series data using SOM neural network. Int. J. Remote Sens. **2**, 4999–5012 (2005)
3. Eddelbuettel, D., François, R.: Rcpp: seamless R and C++ integration. J. Stat. Softw. **40**, 1–18 (2011)
4. Ferreira, K.R., Santos, L., Picoli, M.C.A.: Evaluating distance measures for image time series clustering in land use and cover monitoring. In: Machine Learning for Earth Observation Workshop (2019)
5. Flexer, A.: On the use of self-organizing maps for clustering and visualization. J. Intell. Data Anal. **5**, 373–384 (2001)
6. Gomez, C., White, J.C., Wulder, M.A.: Optical remotely sensed time series data for land cover classification: a review. ISPRS J. Photogramm. Remote Sens. **116**, 55–72 (2016)
7. GSOM Python Implementation Repository. https://github.com/rodrigosales/GSOM. Accessed 3 May 2020
8. Kohonen, T., Schroeder, M.R., Huang, T.S.: Self-Organizing Maps, 3rd edn. Springer, Heidelberg (2001). https://doi.org/10.1007/978-3-642-56927-2
9. Natita, W., Wiboonsak, W., Dusadee, S.: Appropriate learning rate and neighborhood function of self-organizing map (SOM) for specific humidity pattern classification over Southern Thailand. Int. J. Model. Optim. **6**, 61 (2016)
10. Pasquarella, V.J., Holden, C.E., Kaufman, L., Woodcock, C.E.: From imagery to ecology: leveraging time series of all available Landsat observations to map and monitor ecosystem state and dynamics. Remote Sens. Ecol. Conserv. **2**, 152–170 (2016)
11. Picoli, M., et al.: Big earth observation time series analysis for monitoring Brazilian agriculture. ISPRS J. Photogramm. Remote Sens. **145**, 328–339 (2018)
12. Python Software Foundation. Python Language Reference, version 3.7.2. http://www.python.org

13. Santos, L., Ferreira, K.R., Picoli, M., Camara, G.: Self-organizing maps in earth observation data cubes analysis. In: Vellido, A., Gibert, K., Angulo, C., Martín Guerrero, J.D. (eds.) WSOM 2019. AISC, vol. 976, pp. 70–79. Springer, Cham (2020). https://doi.org/10.1007/978-3-030-19642-4_7
14. Vasighi, M., Abbasi, S.: Multiple growing self-organizing map for data classification. In: International Symposium on Artificial Intelligence and Signal Processing (2017)
15. Wehrens, R., Buydens, L.: Self and Super-Organizing Maps in R: the Kohonen Package. J. Stat. Softw. **21**, 1–19 (2007)

International Workshop on Building Multi-dimensional Models for Assessing Complex Environmental Systems (MES 2020)

The Estimation of the Optimal Level of Productivity for Sponsors in the Recovery and Enhancement of the Historical-Architectural Heritage

Luigi Dolores[1(✉)], Maria Macchiaroli[1], Gianluigi De Mare[1], Antonio Nesticò[1], Gabriella Maselli[1], and Elena Merino Gómez[2]

[1] University of Salerno, Via Giovanni Paolo II, 132, Fisciano, SA, Italy
{ldolores,mmacchiaroli,gdemare,anestico,gmaselli}@unisa.it
[2] Nebrija University, Calle Pirineos, 55, 28040 Madrid, Spain
emerino@nebrija.es

Abstract. The paper explores the theme of sponsorship aimed at enhancing the historical-architectural heritage, analyzing the point of view of companies. Specifically, a static analysis model proposed in a previous paper, whose objective is to establish the optimal amount to invest in sponsorship to maximize business profit, is integrated with an innovative model that allows the company to assess the degree of financial efficiency of the investment, i.e. its productivity Υ. The latter depends on a series of variables that characterize both the monument to be enhanced, the location in which it is located, and the sponsorship strategy adopted by the company. However, in the case of sponsorship of recovery/restoration work, the critical variable that most affects the efficiency of the investment is the number of visitors to the location where the monument is located (direct audience). This is because as the number of visitors increases, the level of exposure to the sponsorship message increases. Therefore, we assume two functional relationships, one linear and the other logarithmic, which correlate financial efficiency to the average number of visitors. In this way, the advantage of the company is twofold. On the one hand, it has the opportunity to maximize profits by investing the optimal amount of sponsorship. On the other hand, it can choose the level of productivity of the investment by deciding to finance the monument of a specific location according to its degree of exposure.

Keywords: Sponsorship · Historical-architectural heritage · Sponsorship productivity · Sponsorship financial effectiveness · Direct audience · Profit maximization

---

L. Dolores, M. Macchiaroli, G. De Mare, A. Nesticò, G. Maselli and E. M. Gómez—The six authors contributed equally to this work.

O. Gervasi et al. (Eds.): ICCSA 2020, LNCS 12253, pp. 285–299, 2020.
https://doi.org/10.1007/978-3-030-58814-4_20

1 Introduction

In the last decade in Italy, public administrations have established multiple sponsorship relationships with private entities to carry out different types of public action interventions. The main sector in which there is a high use of sponsorship is certainly that of cultural heritage [1–4]. In this sector, the public intervention has proved insufficient due to the recent economic crisis and the consequent cuts in public spending [5–7]. The sponsorship contract establishes a collaborative relationship between public and private actors, generating clear advantages for both parties. In particular, the public body acquires the necessary resources to protect and enhance the cultural heritage, while the private entrepreneur obtains a considerable return on advertising as well as incentives of various kinds and tax relief. The recent spread of the instrument among private companies is mainly due to its strong social impact in terms of advertising. Sponsorship contributes to the diffusion of the company name and its products, often being more effective than other promotional strategies of the marketing mix [8].

The main form of sponsorship in the cultural sphere consists essentially in the donation of money, the supply of goods or the provision of services necessary for the implementation of interventions to upgrade the historical-architectural heritage. According to Nelli and Bensi [9], this type of sponsorship is the most suitable to give prestige to the company and improve its image as it allows the sponsor to create consensus in the local community. However, it has some limitations, such as the reduced visibility offered to the sponsor (it is not always appropriate to place a company brand next to monuments or buildings of artistic and cultural value), the not always optimal relationship with the mass media (often these initiatives can obtain a limited media resonance because part of the public does not accept the commercial exploitation of the image of monuments), the difficult integration of sponsorship with other forms of communication. According to Peluso [10], these limitations are due to the difficult adaptation of the contractual model of sponsorship to the cultural sphere. It is a contract of an essentially mercantile nature initially used only in the sports and broadcasting sectors. For that reason, the commercial activity of the sponsor is badly suited to the cultural and historical asset being upgraded. The historical-architectural heritage belongs to the community, which is itself represented by it. For this reason, the territorial communities do not always recognize themselves in the goods or services that the sponsor intends to advertise. However, if social responsibility objectives prevail over purely commercial ones [11], there is generally positive perception of the initiative promoted and therefore successful sponsorship. There must be an affinity of values and complementarity of objectives between the company's communication strategy and the cultural project for sponsorship to be effective. The sponsoring company can thus obtain a series of benefits: ensure greater visibility, strengthen its image and reputation, improve internal relations, strengthen relations with stakeholders, consolidate its impact on the territory [12]. These benefits coincide with the company's corporate communication objectives. No less important are the marketing objectives, measurable in terms of financial performance, that the company intends to achieve through sponsorship. Improving the company's visibility, image and reputation often lead to an increase in demand for the goods or services it offers. When a company intends to pursue a specific marketing objective, the message of sponsorship is mainly addressed to the final consumer. In this case, the aim is to achieve an increase in turnover and, therefore, in profits [13–15].

The objective of this work is to analyze the financial aspects of sponsorship, contextualizing the tool only in the marketing field. Specifically, a static analysis model proposed in a previous work, whose objective is to estimate the optimal amount to invest in sponsorship to maximize business profit [16], is integrated with a new model that allows the company to choose the level of financial efficiency of the investment. Not only is it, therefore, possible to determine the optimal sponsorship budget that allows the company to obtain the highest possible profit, but the amount needed is also commensurate with the degree of productivity of the investment, a parameter that depends not only on the organizational and management skills of the company but also on the characteristics of the sponsorship activity and the sponsored object.

The elaboration of the model for the estimation of the optimal level of productivity for companies sponsoring interventions for the redevelopment of the historical-architectural heritage can be summarized in three phases. In the first phase, the critical variables that influence the financial efficiency of the sponsorship are identified. In the second phase, two different functional relationships (linear and logarithmic) are hypothesized that correlate each critical variable to a parameter Υ representative of the rate of variation of the marginal productivity of the sponsorship. For the sake of simplicity, the only variable direct audience (number of visitors in the location of interest) is considered, since the latter in the case of sponsorship of recovery/restoration work is the one that has the greatest impact on the efficiency of the investment. And in fact, visitors to the location where the building is located are the main recipients of the sponsorship message, by viewing the billboards posted on the scaffolding of the building site. Consequently, there is a high probability that some of the new consumers of the products offered by the sponsoring company will coincide with some of the visitors to the location of interest. The latter, understanding the social usefulness of the sponsored initiative, may decide to purchase the goods offered by the sponsoring company instead of those offered by competing companies. In the third and final phase, the parameter Υ is introduced in the static analysis model to estimate the optimal budget that the company should invest in sponsorship. In this case, the productivity of the sponsorship is no longer linked solely to the company's historical data, i.e. only to the management strategies adopted in the past but can be defined by the company according to the desired level of direct public exposure to the sponsorship message. The static model has therefore been refined through an innovative procedure that allows estimating the productivity parameter Υ of sponsorship.

The ex-ante model proposed aims to show companies the right methods to follow during the sponsorship planning phase about the choice of the monument (and therefore the location) to match their image. In this way, it is possible to encourage the use of the tool for efficient enhancement of the historical-architectural heritage.

The model will be validated in a next work applying it to a company already active in the field of cultural sponsorship. For this company, the financial efficiency of the sponsorship will be estimated for several levels of direct audience.

2 State of Art

The main question underlying the construction of the model concerns the definition of the critical variables that influence the financial efficiency of the investment. It is therefore fundamental to identify those characteristics on which the success of the sponsoring activity depends, and which produce an increase in demand for the goods/services offered by the sponsoring company. To this end, a survey of the reference literature has been carried out to determine those parameters which, according to the most authoritative scholars of sponsorship, can contribute positively to the growth of sales volume.

Most of the studies conducted so far in the international arena have given little space to cultural sponsorship, framing the instrument from a general point of view or only in the sports and broadcasting fields. Most of these studies identify the set of criteria that influence the effectiveness of sponsorship communication objectives. However, it has rarely been examined how these parameters could affect the financial efficiency of the investment [17]. Over the years, several classifications of effectiveness criteria have been proposed, with greater emphasis on those most used by companies in the process of selecting sponsorship opportunities [9]. Although they condition the overall effectiveness of the investment, it is reasonable to think that many of these criteria may also affect the financial efficiency of the sponsorship. This is because the communication objectives of sponsorship may influence the marketing objectives. For example, an increase in brand awareness could generate an increase in sales volumes. Therefore, certain effectiveness criteria can also be used in assessing the monetary feasibility of the investment [3, 18].

Meenaghan [19] has identified the main criteria of effectiveness by systematizing them into the following classes: the ability to achieve objectives, the ability to convey the desired image, media coverage potential, the funding required, target audience coverage, hospitality opportunities, executive preferences, required geographic coverage, internal staff knowledge of the chosen sponsorship, type of sponsorship, exclusivity, the potential for bad publicity, organization of the sponsored activity, other criteria. These classes of criteria refer to sponsorship in general and not specifically to the cultural sphere. The same can be said for the criteria most used by the companies identified by Duncan [20], which are the following: target audience, brand image strengthening, extendibility, brand involvement, cost-effectiveness, presence of other sponsors. The study shows that companies pay little attention to economic criteria as they are more difficult to evaluate, preferring those that express the communicational character of sponsorship. Nelli and Bensi [9] identify four classes of criteria based on their relevance to companies. The classes proposed are the following: fairly important criteria (amount of costs, geographical coverage, level of coverage of the target group, the exclusivity of sponsorship, TV and press coverage), less important criteria (duration of the sponsorship, secondary media coverage, cost per contact, the link between sponsor and sponsee), irrelevant criteria (fiscal benefits of sponsorship).

Table 1 shows the classifications of the sponsorship criteria of Meeneghan [19], Duncan [20] and Nelli and Bensi [9].

Once the main criteria proposed in the literature have been identified, it remains to be established which of them have the greatest influence on the financial performance of sponsorship. Empirical studies conducted by Meenaghan [21] show that consumers who actively participate in a sponsored event are more likely to buy the products offered

Table 1. Three different classifications of sponsorship criteria

Meeneghan's criteria (1983)	
1. The ability to fulfil objectives	a) Broad corporate objectives b) Product related objectives c) Sales objectives
2. The potential to project the desired image	
3. Sponsorship choice and company/product compatibility	a) Product linked b) Product image linked c) Corporate image linked d) Non-linked
4. Media coverage potential	a) Television b) Other
5. The founding requirement	
6. Target audience coverage	
7. The opportunity for guest hospitality	
8. Executive preference	
9. Geographical coverage required	a) Local/regional b) National c) International
10. Staff knowledge of chosen sponsorship	
11. Sponsorship type	a) New/Established b) Once-off/Longer term
12. Solus position	
13. The potential of adverse publicity	
14. The organization of the sponsored activity	
15. Other criteria	
Duncan's criteria (2002)	
1. Target audience	
2. Brand image reinforcement	
3. Extendability	
4. Brand involvement	
5. Cost-effectiveness	
6. Other sponsors	
Nelli and Bensi's criteria (2005)	
1. Fairly important criteria	a) Amount of costs b) Geographical coverage c) Coverage of the target group d) Exclusivity of sponsorship e) Tv and press coverage
2. Less important criteria	a) Duration of the sponsorship b) Secondary media coverage c) Cost per contact d) sponsor/sponsee connection
3. Irrelevant criteria	e) Fiscal benefits of sponsorship

by the sponsor than those who do not attend the initiative. Similarly, those who are involved in an activity financed or organized by a sponsor are twice as likely to change their preferences as those who are not. This behavior has been recorded especially for those brands that offer "low involvement" products on the market. Gwinner [22] states that when the sponsoring company offers this type of goods the image of the sponsored event/activity positively influences the attitude towards the brand. In the case of "high involvement" products, the attitude towards the sponsor remains unclear according to studies conducted so far.

We can, therefore, say that those who are personally involved in a sponsored activity can more easily grasp its image values and associate them with the sponsor. So, sponsorship produces better effects for those who actively participate in the initiative promoted. Differently, in the case of the uninvolved public, the effects of sponsorship are generally rather limited. This trend is supported by empirical studies by Grohs et al. [23] which show that the degree of brand awareness of the sponsor by public increases with increasing exposure and level of involvement in the sponsored initiative.

In the case of sponsorships aimed at the restoration/recovery of the historical-architectural heritage, the exposure takes place mainly by the direct vision of the advertising posters posted on the scaffolding of the construction sites or through the mass media that publicize the promoted initiative. However, although it is difficult to measure, it can be assumed that the level of public involvement is higher if the sponsorship message is received directly on-site and not through the mass media. Moreover, the media contribution is generally rather small when the object of the recovery/restoration work is a so-called "minor monument" or a building of historical-architectural value little known to the community. In fact, in the context of Italian cities, recently there has been an increase in the number of cases of sponsorships aimed at the enhancement of monuments and historical buildings of lesser renown than those that were subsidized until some time ago (for instance, the Colosseum). In these cases, the critical variable that most affects the financial results of the sponsorship is the direct audience, i.e. the number of visitors to the location where the building is located. For this reason, in the study phase of the productivity parameter of the sponsorship, the critical variable direct audience was considered above all. However, the proposed functional relationships, which relate the sponsorship productivity with the number of visitors of a certain location, can also be used to explain how other critical variables (for instance, media coverage) can influence the financial performance of the company.

3 Method

Having established that the number of visitors to the location of interest is the main critical variable, we can refine the static model by introducing the estimation of the productivity parameter Υ. By this, the study can ideally be divided into two phases: the static analysis phase of the sponsorship investment and the phase of choosing the level of productivity desired by the company.

3.1 Static Analysis Phase

The static analysis phase of the sponsorship investment consists of the refinement of a model proposed by Bucci, Castellani and Figini [24] through the modalities explained in a previous publication [25]. The objective of this phase is to estimate the optimal sponsorship budget that allows the company to maximize profits. Specifically, it is assumed that the company's production is represented by the Cobb-Douglas function below [26]:

$$R = TK^{\alpha}L^{\beta}S^{\Upsilon}. \tag{1}$$

Where R is used to indicate the company's revenues, K, L and S represent the production factors labour, capital and sponsorship respectively, and the coefficients $0 < \alpha < 1$, $0 < \beta < 1$ and $0 < \Upsilon < 1$ measure the production elasticity and the diminishing returns of the individual factors of production. T, on the other hand, is the firm's technical progress constant. For simplicity the price of the good offered by the enterprise is normalized to 1.

The coefficients T, α, β and Υ, which represent the rate of change in marginal productivity of capital, labour and sponsoring, can be estimated using the log-linearity condition of the Cobb-Douglas function. And, in fact, known the historical series of K, L and S, the multiple linear regression applied to the linearized production function, reported below, returns the value of the four unknown variables:

$$LN\,R = LN\,T + \alpha LN\,K + \beta LN\,L + \Upsilon LN\,S. \tag{2}$$

The coefficients T, α, β and Υ estimated through the regression are the trend coefficients, i.e. those which would occur if the company did not decide to change either the productivity levels of the three inputs or the technology adopted.

The total profit of the company is represented by the following equation:

$$\pi = TK^{\alpha}L^{\beta}S^{\Upsilon} - rK - wL - sS, \tag{3}$$

where rK, wL and sS represent capital cost, labour cost and sponsorship cost respectively, while r, w and s are their respective unit costs [27, 28]. From the condition of the first order, obtained by placing zero the derivative concerning S of the profit function, we can solve the optimization problem:

$$S^{*} = \left(s/\left(\Upsilon T\,K^{\alpha}L^{\beta}\right)\right)^{(1/(\Upsilon-1))}. \tag{4}$$

Equation (4) allows estimating S^*, i.e. the optimal number of sponsored restorations capable of maximizing company profits. Multiplying S^* by the unit cost of sponsorship s (cost of a single restoration) results in the optimal investment in sponsorship (sS^*), which can also be expressed as a percentage of turnover. Finally, by replacing S^* with S in Eq. (3) it is possible to estimate the maximum profit achievable for the company.

The optimization problem is thus solved, and therefore the static analysis phase is finished. Figure 1 shows the logic of the static analysis phase.

In the next subsection, the innovative phase is introduced that allows the company to choose the productivity level of the sponsorship.

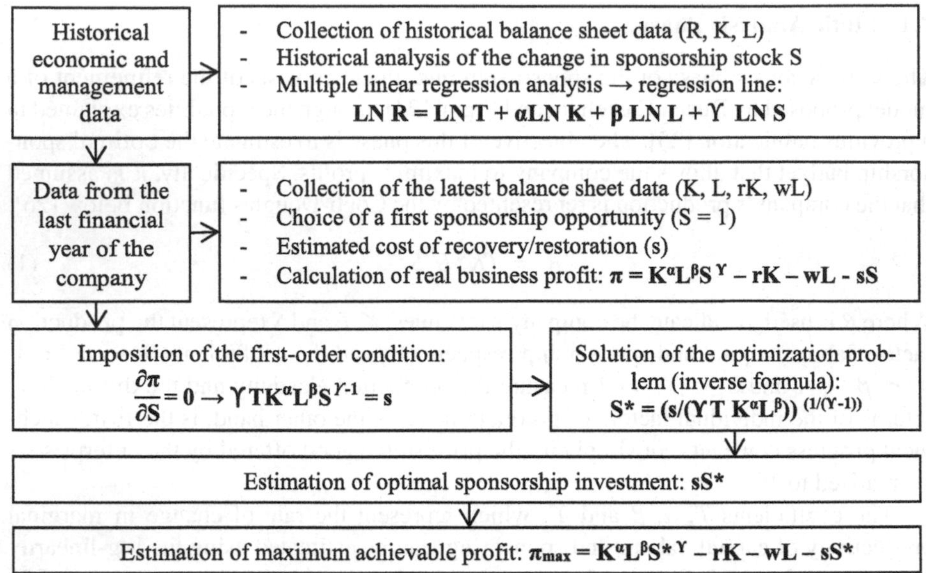

Fig. 1. Flow chart of the logical steps of the static analysis phase (own processing)

3.2 Productivity Level Choice Phase

At this point, the second phase takes over, i.e. one that allows the company to choose the level of productivity it considers most appropriate. As mentioned above, the parameter Υ represents the rate of variation of the marginal productivity of the sponsorship, i.e. the variation of the production output obtained following a unitary variation of the sponsorship stock *S*. In the applications proposed so far, Υ used in the static analysis is the trend estimated through the multiple linear regression. However, if sponsorship were to become more efficient it would increase its marginal productivity, i.e. the parameter Υ. As a result, the maximum achievable profit would become higher. The sponsoring company to increase the Υ of the sponsorship must, therefore, act on the critical variables that influence the financial efficiency of the investment. In the specific case of sponsorship aimed at enhancing the historical-architectural heritage, the main critical variables that can influence consumer choices (and therefore the productivity rate of the investment) have been identified, classifying them in the following categories:

- **Location features:** number of visitors to the location of interest (direct audience) *n*; location relevance to the community *rl*; target audience coverage *ta*.
- **Monument features:** popularity of the architect/designer *ap*; architectural quality *qa*; local relevance of the monument *rc*; national and international relevance of the monument *rni.*
- **Sponsorship features:** billboard size *dc*; media coverage *cm;* sponsor's organizational capacity *co;* congruence between the brand image and the monument image *ci;* ability to convey the desired image *id*; funding required *fr*.

The classes of critical variables considered are summarized in Table 2.

Table 2. Classes of critical variables of the historical-architectural heritage sponsorship

Location features	
Number of visitors to the location (direct audience)	n
Location relevance to the community	rl
Target audience coverage	ta
Monument features	
Popularity of the architect/designer	ap
Architectural quality	qa
Local relevance of the monument	rc
National and international relevance of the monument	rni
Sponsorship features	
Billboard size	dc
Media coverage	cm
Sponsor's organizational capacity	co
Brand image/monument image congruence	ci
Ability to convey the desired image	id
Funding required	fr

Therefore, the Υ parameter, representing the degree of efficiency of sponsorship, is a function of the variables introduced above:

$$\Upsilon = f(n,\ rl,\ ta,\ ap,\ qa,\ rc,\ rni,\ dc,\ cm,\ co,\ ci,\ fr). \tag{5}$$

For the so-called "minor monuments" located in small towns, the characteristics of the monument to be restored become negligible, as well as most of the characteristics of the sponsorship (such as, for example, media coverage). In the limit condition, the financial efficiency of the sponsorship will depend solely on the parameter n representative of the number of visitors to the location of interest. The essential requirement to obtain a return on the sponsorship investment is the public exposure of the initiative. We consider, therefore, that the contribution of the other critical variables is negligible. The Υ function, therefore, becomes the following:

$$\Upsilon = f(n). \tag{6}$$

We will, therefore, have different values of Υ as the location hosting the monument changes as the average monthly number of visitors changes. In particular, we hypothesize two different types of functions that correlate Υ with n. The first function proposed is the following linear type:

$$\Upsilon = an + b. \tag{7}$$

In the absence of visitors, the sponsorship would be ineffective, so when $n = 0$ we have $\Upsilon = 0$. This means it must necessarily be $b = 0$. The line identified, therefore, passes through the origin of the axes. Moreover, known n for the location of interest, it can be assumed that its corresponding Υ is the trend estimated with the regression. Once this correspondence is established, it is possible, once measured n for other locations, to estimate with linear proportion the parameter Υ representative of the financial effectiveness of other sponsorship opportunities. Considering then two different locations and known for the first location the effectiveness of sponsorship Υ_A (mail equal to Υ estimated with the regression) and the average number of monthly visitors n_A and for the second location the average number of monthly visitors n_B, it is possible to estimate Υ_B in the following way:

$$\Upsilon_B = \Upsilon_A n_B / n_A. \tag{8}$$

The second function proposed is logarithmic:

$$\Upsilon = aLN(n + b) \tag{9}$$

In the case of the logarithmic function, it is assumed that the growth of Υ as n increases is less than proportional. That is, as the number of visitors increases, consumers' purchasing intention increases, but marginal purchases decrease. Again, the observation that when $n = 0$ we have $\Upsilon = 0$ applies. This means that it must necessarily be $b = 1$. The logarithmic function will then pass through the origin of the Cartesian axes. Considering then two different locations and known for the first location the effectiveness of the sponsorship Υ_A (mail equal to Υ estimated with the regression) and the average number of monthly visitors n_A and for the second location the average number of monthly visitors n_B, you can estimate Υ_B in the following way:

$$\Upsilon_B = (LNn_B / LNn_A) / \Upsilon_A \tag{10}$$

The static model is now applicable for both locations, and therefore for the two different levels of direct audience. For each level of exposure, it is, therefore, possible to estimate the optimal sponsorship budget that maximizes the company's profit.

Figure 2 shows the logic of the sponsorship productivity level selection phase.

Similarly, linear or logarithmic relationships can also be assumed for other critical variables that influence the efficiency of the investment [29–33].

The logarithmic function, given the less than proportional growth, is more conservative than the linear one. As the degree of exposure of the message to the public increases, the level of efficiency of sponsorship grows more and more slowly until it stabilizes.

It can also be assumed that, should the company decide to use the mass media to increase the exposure of the sponsorship, both curves, linear and logarithmic, would shift to the right, no longer starting from zero but the number of contacts reached through radio, TV, web, newspapers, etc.

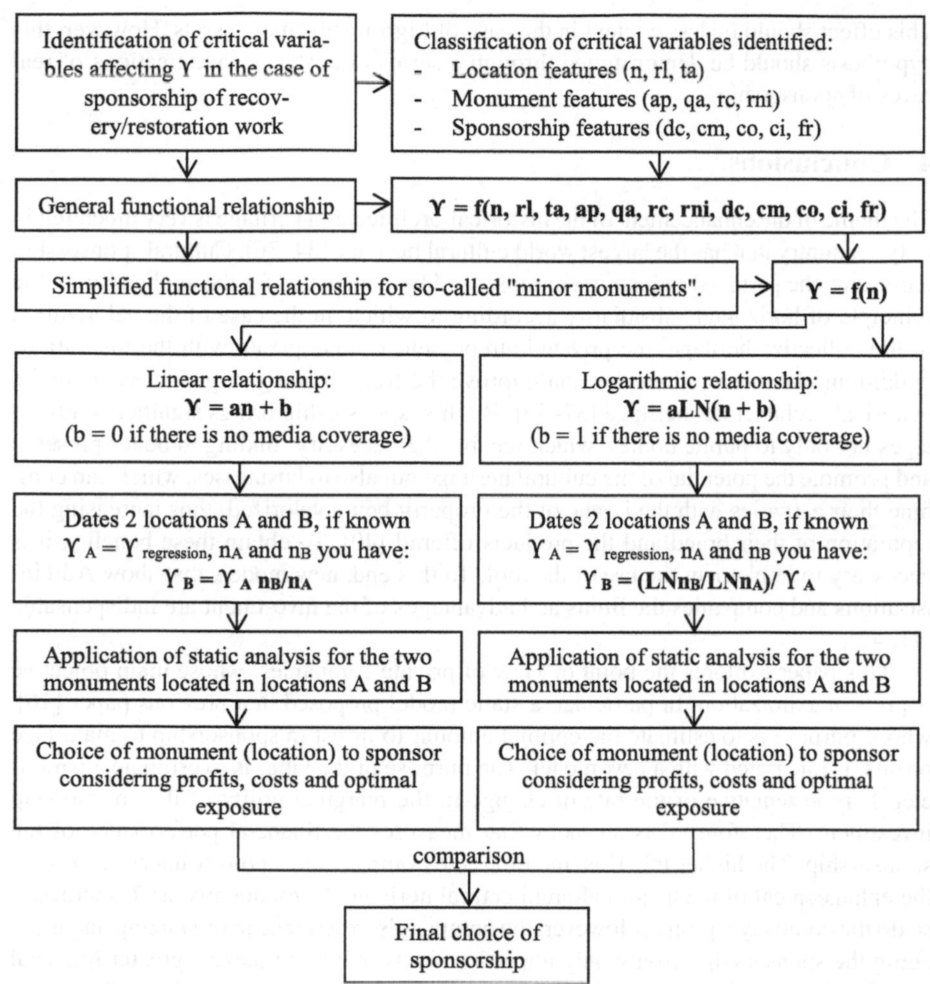

Fig. 2. Flow chart of the logical steps of the sponsorship productivity level selection phase (own processing)

The overall model, which includes both phases, allows the company to choose both the desired level of sponsorship productivity Υ and the right sS^* amount to invest to achieve the highest possible profit.

At this point, it would remain to be defined which of the two functional relationships, linear or logarithmic, is more representative of reality. Considering what Gwinner stated [22], one could think of applying the linear model, in which the effects of direct audience strongly affect the efficiency of sponsorship, to those companies that offer goods with low involvement, and the logarithmic model, in which the degree of productivity grows more slowly as exposure increases, to those companies that offer goods with high involvement. In fact, in the case of low-involvement goods, the image of the sponsored event, which depends on the level of exposure, positively influences the attitude towards the brand.

This effect should be less evident in the case of high-involvement assets. However, this hypothesis should be demonstrated through a series of posterior investigations of real cases of sponsorship.

4 Conclusions

The theme of the enhancement of the historical-architectural heritage is very much felt in Italy, a country that has the largest world cultural heritage [34–36]. Cultural sponsorship represents the partnership instrument most used by companies for the application of the principle of horizontal subsidiarity according to which, in the case of the valorization of the collective heritage, the private entrepreneur can cooperate with the institutions in defining the interventions that can improve the fruition and give greater value to the historical-architectural heritage [37–39]. By this, sponsorship brings significant advantages not only to public bodies, which receive the necessary funding to better preserve and promote the potential of the cultural heritage but also to businesses, which can combine their activities with the image of the property being valorized, thus increasing the reputation of their brand and the products offered [40]. To obtain these benefits, it is necessary to implement the use of the tool. To this end, new models that show Administrations and companies the limits and advantages of the investment are indispensable [41, 42].

This paper explores the point of view of private companies, whose main objective is profit maximization. In particular, a static model proposed in a previous paper [16], whose purpose is to estimate the optimal amount to invest in sponsorship to maximize profits, is integrated with a new model. The purpose of the latter is to estimate a parameter Υ representative of the rate of change in the marginal utility of the sponsorship investment. Therefore, Υ is an index that measures the financial performance of the sponsorship. The higher the Υ is, the more the company can sponsor interventions for the enhancement of the historical-architectural heritage. Consequently, as Υ increases, so do the company's profits. However, the company's experience in organizing and managing the sponsorship activity only improves if it is willing to make a greater financial sacrifice. In short, the company has to invest a higher amount to enhance its performance. The higher cost of the investment is necessary if you want to improve the brand's ability to increase its reputation and image by changing the critical variables that affect the productivity of sponsorship. These variables, in the case of sponsorship aimed at enhancing the historical-architectural heritage, have been systematized into three classes: location features, monument features, sponsorship features. It is assumed that in the case of sponsorship of monuments or buildings with historical-cultural value, the critical variable that most affects the efficiency of the sponsorship is the number of visitors n of the location of interest. Therefore, two functions have been proposed, one linear and the other logarithmic, which correlate the parameter of productivity Υ to the number of visitors n. In both cases, as n increases, Υ also increases. In the case of a linear function, the n parameter has a greater weight on the productivity of the sponsorship. Differently, the logarithmic function is more restrictive than the linear function since the growth of Υ is less than proportional.

The model supports companies that want to evaluate the convenience of sponsorship investment. However, it may also be useful to public administrations. In fact, the public authorities can match the advertising fee (i.e. the surcharge of the restoration cost) of each location to its attractiveness expressed in terms of exposure to the sponsorship message [43].

With this work, some of the theoretical limits of the previous version of the static model have been overcome. However, there are still some critical issues that depend on the basic assumptions adopted. In the future, not only will an attempt be made to overcome these critical points, but more weight will also be given to the other variables that may influence the financial performance of the sponsorship investment starting from an empirical observation on real cases. Moreover, the model, here formulated only on a theoretical basis, will be validated through its application to a company active in the field of sponsorship for the valorization of historical-architectural heritage.

References

1. Piperata, G.: Sponsorizzazione ed interventi di restauro sui beni culturali. Aedon – Riviste di arti e diritto online 1 (2005). https://doi.org/10.7390/20060
2. Fiore P., Nesticò A., Macchiaroli M.: The energy improvement of monumental buildings. An investigation protocol and case studies. Valori e Valutazioni **16**, 45–55 (2016). ISSN 2036-2404
3. Nesticò, A., Macchiaroli, M., Pipolo, O.: Historic buildings and energetic requalification a model for the selection of technologically advanced interventions. In: Gervasi, O., et al. (eds.) ICCSA 2015. LNCS, vol. 9157, pp. 61–76. Springer, Cham (2015). https://doi.org/10.1007/978-3-319-21470-2_5
4. Cassalia, G., Tramontana, C., Calabrò, F.: Evaluation approach to the integrated valorization of territorial resources: the case study of the Tyrrhenian area of the Metropolitan City of Reggio Calabria. In: Calabrò, F., Della Spina, L., Bevilacqua, C. (eds.) ISHT 2018. SIST, vol. 101, pp. 3–12. Springer, Cham (2019). https://doi.org/10.1007/978-3-319-92102-0_1
5. Tramontana, C., Calabrò, F., Cassalia, G., Rizzuto, M.C.: Economic sustainability in the management of archaeological sites: the case of Bova Marina (Reggio Calabria, Italy). In: Calabrò, F., Della Spina, L., Bevilacqua, C. (eds.) ISHT 2018. SIST, vol. 101, pp. 288–297. Springer, Cham (2019). https://doi.org/10.1007/978-3-319-92102-0_31
6. Della Spina, L.: Historical cultural heritage: decision making process and reuse scenarios for the enhancement of historic buildings. In: Calabrò, F., Della Spina, L., Bevilacqua, C. (eds.) ISHT 2018. SIST, vol. 101, pp. 442–453. Springer, Cham (2019). https://doi.org/10.1007/978-3-319-92102-0_47
7. Della Spina, Lucia: Scenarios for a sustainable valorisation of cultural landscape as driver of local development. In: Calabrò, Francesco, Della Spina, Lucia, Bevilacqua, Carmelina (eds.) ISHT 2018. SIST, vol. 100, pp. 113–122. Springer, Cham (2019). https://doi.org/10.1007/978-3-319-92099-3_14
8. Cavaliere, S.: Le sponsorizzazioni e la tutela del patrimonio culturale. Amministrazione in cammino – Rivista elettronica di diritto pubblico, di diritto dell'economia e di scienza dell'amministrazione a cura del Centro di ricerca sulle amministrazioni pubbliche "Vittorio Bachelet" (2012)
9. Nelli, R.P., Bensi, P.: La sponsorizzazione e la sua pianificazione strategica – Modelli di funzionamento e processi di selezione, 1st edn. Vita e Pensiero, Milano (2005). ISBN 9788834312353
10. Peluso, S.: La sponsorizzazione dei beni culturali: opportunità e crescita dello strumento alla luce del caso Colosseo. Gazzetta dell'Ambiente **5**(19), 117–142 (2013)

11. Deigh, L., Farquhar, J., Palazzo, M., Siano, A.: Corporate social responsibility: engaging the community. Qual. Mark. Res. **19**(2), 225–240 (2016). https://doi.org/10.1108/QMR-02-2016-0010
12. Moneta, F., Romenti, S.: Nuovi strumenti per un rapporto strategico tra cultura e impresa: un modello di valutazione delle sponsorizzazioni e partnership culturali. 14° Rapporto Annuale Federculture 2018. Gangemi Editore, Rome (2018). ISBN 978-88-492-3660-6
13. Severino, F.: Il fundresing per la cultura: cosa offrire alle imprese. Aedon, Rivista di arti e diritto on line 1 (2007). https://doi.org/10.1446/24413
14. Giua, M.: L'apporto delle imprese alla cultura fra sponsorizzazione e mecenatismo. Aedon, Rivista di arti e diritto on line 3 (2000). https://doi.org/10.1446/12733
15. Fantin, A.: La sponsorizzazione dei beni culturali: nuovi orizzonti del partenariato pubblico privato. Il capitale culturale: Stud. Value Cult. Herit. **2**, 115–131 (2011). http://dx.doi.org/10.13138/2039-2362/110
16. Dolores, L., Macchiaroli, M., De Mare, G.: Sponsorship for the sustainability of historical-architectural heritage: application of a model's original test finalized to maximize the profitability of private investors. Sustainability **9**(10), 1750 (2017). https://doi.org/10.3390/su9101750
17. Eventi Aziendali Homepage. http://www.eventiaziendali.it/approfondimenti/view/la-sponsorizzazione-culturale-elementi-per-il-calcolo-dellefficacia/68. Accessed 08 Mar 2020
18. De Mare, G., Granata, M.F., Nesticò, A.: Weak and strong compensation for the prioritization of public investments: multidimensional analysis for pools. Sustainability **7**(12), 16022–16038 (2015). https://doi.org/10.3390/su71215798
19. Meenaghan, T.: Commercial sponsorship. Eur. J. Mark. **17**(7), 5–73 (1983). https://doi.org/10.1108/EUM0000000004825
20. Duncan, T.: IMC: Using Advertising & Promotion to Build Brands. McGraw-Hill Education, Boston (2002). ISBN 0071123318 (pbk.) - 025621476X (alk. paper)
21. Meenaghan, T.: Understanding Sponsorship Effects. Psychol. Mark. **18**(2), 95–122 (2001). https://doi.org/10.1002/1520-6793(200102)18:2%3c95:AID-MAR1001%3e3.0.CO;2-H
22. Gwinner, K.: A model of image creation and image transfer in event sponsorship. Int. Mark. Rev. **14**, 145–158 (1997). https://doi.org/10.1108/02651339710170221
23. Grohs, R., Wagner, U., Vsetecka, S.: Assessing the effectiveness of sport sponsorships — an empirical examination. Schmalenbach Bus. Rev. **5**(2), 119–138 (2004). https://doi.org/10.1007/BF03396689
24. Bucci, A., Castellani, M., Figini, P.: L'investimento in Sponsorizzazione delle Imprese: Un'analisi Economica in Termini Statici e Dinamici. Rivista di Politica Economica **93**, 183–224 (2003)
25. Dolores, L., Macchiaroli, M., De Mare, G.: A dynamic model for the financial sustainability of the restoration sponsorship. Sustainability **12**(4), 1694 (2020). https://doi.org/10.3390/su12041694
26. Cobb, C.W., Douglas, P.H.: A theory of production. Am. Econ. Rev. **18**, 139–165 (1928). https://www.jstor.org/stable/1811556
27. Nesticò, A., Maselli, G.: A protocol for the estimate of the social rate of time preference: the case studies of Italy and the USA. J. Econ. Stud. **47**(3), 527–545 (2020). https://doi.org/10.1108/JES-02-2019-0081
28. Nesticò, A., Maselli, G.: Declining discount rate estimate in the long-term economic evaluation of environmental projects. J. Environ. Account. Manag. **8**(1), 93–110 (2020). https://doi.org/10.5890/JEAM.2020.03.007
29. Nesticò, A., He, S., De Mare, G., Benintendi, R., Maselli, G.: The ALARP principle in the cost-benefit analysis for the acceptability of investment risk. Sustainability **10**(12), 1–22 (2018). https://doi.org/10.3390/su10124668

30. De Mare, G., Nesticò, A., Macchiaroli, M.: Significant appraisal issues in value estimate of quarries for the public expropriation. Valori e Valutazioni **18**, 17–23 (2017). ISSN 20362404
31. Nesticò, A., De Mare, G., Fiore, P., Pipolo, O.: A model for the economic evaluation of energetic requalification projects in buildings. a real case application. In: Murgante, B., Misra, S., Rocha, A.M.A.C., Torre, C., Rocha, J.G., Falcão, M.I., Taniar, D., Apduhan, B.O., Gervasi, O. (eds.) ICCSA 2014. LNCS, vol. 8580, pp. 563–578. Springer, Cham (2014). https://doi.org/10.1007/978-3-319-09129-7_41
32. Manganelli, B., De Mare, G., Nesticò, A.: Using genetic algorithms in the housing market analysis. In: Gervasi, O., et al. (eds.) ICCSA 2015. LNCS, vol. 9157, pp. 36–45. Springer, Cham (2015). https://doi.org/10.1007/978-3-319-21470-2_3
33. Macchiaroli, M., Pellecchia, V., D'Alpaos, C.: Urban water management in Italy: an innovative model for the selection of water service infrastructures. WSEAS Trans. Environ. Dev. **15**, 463–477 (2019). ISSN: 1790-5079. E-ISSN: 2224-3496
34. Forte, F.: Historic, artistic and cultural patrimony for a "habitable city": incentives for care. In: Mondini, G., Fattinnanzi, E., Oppio, A., Bottero, M., Stanghellini, S. (eds.) SIEV 2016. GET, pp. 233–243. Springer, Cham (2018). https://doi.org/10.1007/978-3-319-78271-3_19
35. Fidone, G.: Il ruolo dei privati nella valorizzazione dei beni culturali: Dalle sponsorizzazioni alle forme di gestione. Aedon, Rivista di arti e diritto on line 1–2 (2012). https://doi.org/10.7390/37869
36. Antoniucci, V., Marella, G.: The influence of building typology on the economic feasibility of urban developments. Int. J. Appl. Eng. Res. **12**(15), 4946–4954 (2017)
37. Principio di sussidiarietà. In Wikipedia Homepage. https://it.wikipedia.org/wiki/Principio_di_sussidiariet%C3%A0. Accessed 11 Mar 2020
38. Forte, F.: The role of private in preserving cultural heritage: sponsorship. In: Gambardella, C., Listokin, D. (eds.) Development and Preservation in large cities: an international perspective. La scuola di Pitagora, Naples (2014). ISBN 978-88-6542-389-9
39. Canesi, R., Marella, G.: Residential construction costs: an Italian case study. Int. J. Appl. Eng. Res. **12**(10), 2623–2634 (2017)
40. Forte, F.: From bata to prada: appraisal approach in new retail design. IOP Conf. Ser. Mater. Sci. Eng. **603**(3), 032018 (2019). https://doi.org/10.1088/1757-899X/603/3/032018
41. Nesticò, A., De Mare, G., Frusciante, B., Dolores, L.: Construction costs estimate for civil works. a model for the analysis during the preliminary stage of the project. In: Gervasi, O., et al. (eds.) ICCSA 2017. LNCS, vol. 10408, pp. 89–105. Springer, Cham (2017). https://doi.org/10.1007/978-3-319-62404-4_7
42. De Mare, G., Nesticò, A., Macchiaroli, M., Dolores, L.: Market prices and institutional values. In: Gervasi, O., Murgante, B., Misra, S., Borruso, G., Torre, C.M., Rocha, A.M.A.C., Taniar, D., Apduhan, B.O., Stankova, E., Cuzzocrea, A. (eds.) ICCSA 2017. LNCS, vol. 10409, pp. 430–440. Springer, Cham (2017). https://doi.org/10.1007/978-3-319-62407-5_30
43. Dolores, L., Macchiaroli, M., De Mare, G.: A model for defining sponsorship fees in public-private bargaining for the rehabilitation of historical-architectural heritage. In: Calabrò, F., Della Spina, L., Bevilacqua, C. (eds.) ISHT 2018. SIST, vol. 101, pp. 484–492. Springer, Cham (2019). https://doi.org/10.1007/978-3-319-92102-0_51

Evaluating the Urban Quality Through a Hybrid Approach: Application in the Milan (Italy) City Area

Alessandra Oppio[1(✉)], Marta Bottero[2], Federico Dell'Anna[2], Marta Dell'Ovo[3], and Laura Gabrielli[4]

[1] Department of Architecture and Urban Studies, Politecnico Di Milano, Via Bonardi 3, 20133 Milan, Italy
alessandra.oppio@polimi.it

[2] Department of Regional and Urban Studies and Planning, Politecnico di Torino, Corso Mattioli 39, 10125 Turin, Italy

[3] Department of Architecture, Built Environment and Construction Engineering, Politecnico di Milano, via Bonardi 9, 20133 Milan, Italy

[4] Department of Architecture and Arts, IUAV University of Venice, Dorsoduro 2206, 30123 Venice, Italy

Abstract. Urban planning can support the optimal exploitation of the resources available in an urban system with specific reference to the accessibility of goods and services by an increase of the quality of the public space. In this perspective, knowing the economic effects generated by urban planning choices can be fundamental to guide decision-making processes. For this purpose, a research work which proposes a method for defining a synthetic index through the Multi-Attribute Value Theory to describe urban quality is presented. The synthetic index proposed in this study reflects the public open spaces, accessibility and provision of services qualities of the urban context. Besides, this study estimates these advantages through the hedonic prices method, analyzing the residential market. The combined methodology has been applied in detail to three districts located in the Municipality of Milan (Italy). The simultaneous reading of the indices used to spatialise the urban quality levels allows identifying the extrinsic characteristics of the three neighbourhoods analyzed. Considering the changes induced on house prices, the results of the hedonic models show that the economic impacts generated by low levels of urban quality are significant. Accordingly, the policies that aim to transform the existing urban fabric become fundamental for the creation of economic and social value.

Keywords: Multi-criteria decision analysis · Hedonic prices method · Urban policy

The original version of this chapter was revised: the presentation of the authors' names corrected. The correction to this chapter is available at https://doi.org/10.1007/978-3-030-58814-4_66

O. Gervasi et al. (Eds.): ICCSA 2020, LNCS 12253, pp. 300–315, 2020.
https://doi.org/10.1007/978-3-030-58814-4_21

1 Introduction

The 17 Sustainable Development Goals (SDGs) adopted in 2015 by all United Nations Member States highlighted how cities today represent the most challenging context for quality of life, environmental sustainability, health and social inclusion. Their strategic role in ensuring the quality of life in our society and the wellbeing of the population is moreover described by the Lancet 2019 Report - an annual update about five fields of research (climate change impacts, exposures and vulnerability; adaptation, planning and resilience for health; mitigation actions and health co-benefits; economics and finance; public and political engagement). Today, 55% of the population lives in an urban area, and the percentage is expected to increase to 68% by 2050 [1]. In this context, sustainable urbanization is the key to sustain and manage the negative consequences related to this trend and, in fact, the 11th SDG is focused on promoting more inclusive, resilient and sustainable cities in order to improve their overall quality. Moreover, the effects of urban quality involves different dimensions – social, environmental, economic – as well as multiple scales – regional, metropolitan, sub-metropolitan, neighbourhood [2].

The current contribution aims at assessing the value of the urban quality by considering both multi-dimensional aspects and the marginal price, in order to explore its connection with home prices.

Many studies have been carried on to prove the correlation between property prices and extrinsic (location, neighbourhood's quality, etc.) as well as intrinsic (structural features, systems, etc.) characteristics [3–5]. D'Acci [4, 6] provided an in-depth literature review aimed at showing how the quality of the location influences the property prices such as the proximity to green spaces, a pleasant view, the quality of the open spaces, the presence of traffic, noise, pollution, the accessibility, the proximity to services etc. The concept of urban quality considered within this research is the one connected with the concept of urban design in order to better focus on how cities can be planned and answer to contemporary demands. In detail, by analyzing the definition of urban quality provided by urban design studies presented by Oppio et al. [7, 8], the paper will focus on the contribution of public open spaces, accessibility and provision of services to the urban quality of three different neighbourhoods located in the city of Milan (Italy) to understand how it finally influences the house market price. The study proposes a multi-methodological evaluation framework based on the integration of a Multi-Attribute Value Theory (MAVT) model [9] with the hedonic prices (HP) method [10].

The paper is divided into six sections. After an introduction where the research question has been elicited, the second section will present the integrated evaluation framework composed by the spatial analysis and HP method; the third one will introduce the case study while the fourth one the application of the two methodologies. Section five and six are devoted to the discussion of the results and the conclusions.

2 The Integrated Evaluation Framework

Figure 1 presents the integrated evaluation framework developed in order to answer the research question previously elicited. The flowchart is divided into two main parts. Since the quality of open spaces deals with several spatial elements, a Spatial Multiple Criteria Decision Analysis (MCDA) has been firstly defined in order to combine spatial data provided through Geographical Information Systems (GIS) and decision maker's preferences into value maps, whereas in the second phase, the econometric model has been developed to estimate the marginal price of urban quality.

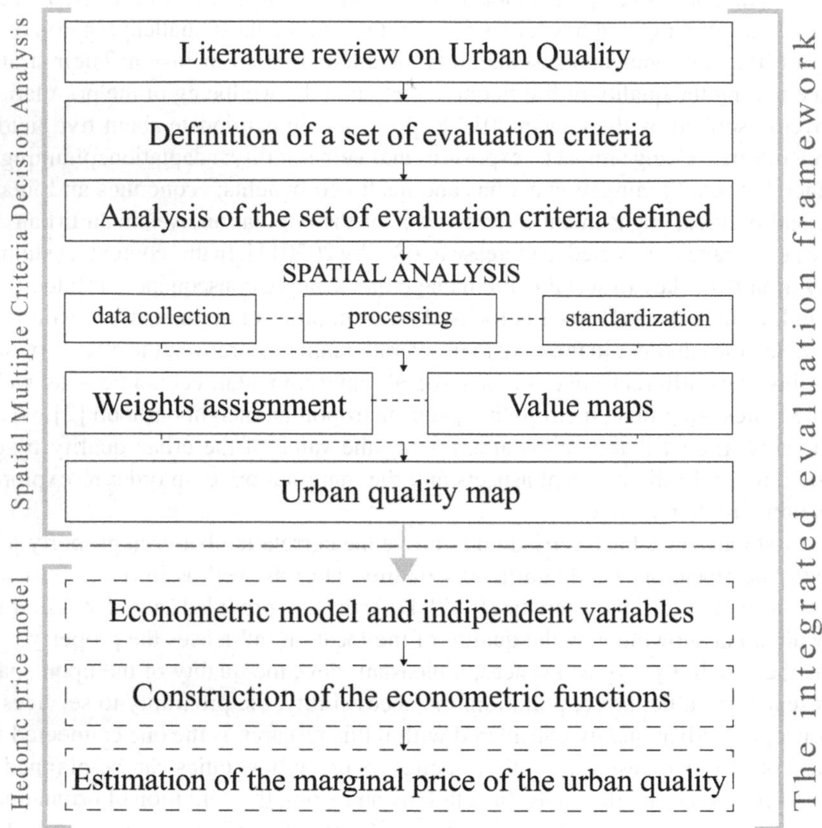

Fig. 1. The integrated evaluation framework

2.1 Spatial MCDA

The first phase of research has been carried on by focusing on the definition of urban quality through an in-depth literature review. As previously mentioned, it has been decided to conceive the urban quality by considering the definition given by the urban design approach meant as the study about the physical settings of the built environment, the morphological layout, consideration of intangible and visual values, the social context, etc. [11–14]. Once the urban quality has been defined, it has been possible to investigate its drivers in order to frame a set of criteria with the objective to measure the propensity of a place to generate urban quality. In this sense, given the hierarchical multi-attribute concept characterizing the urban quality, several attributes of a different nature have been considered. The literature review provided by Oppio et al. [7, 8] allowed to define a complete framework composed by three criteria, namely Accessibility, Supply of services and Public open spaces, divided into sub-criteria as presented in Fig. 2. For what concerns the five sub-criteria analyzed within the public open space dimensions, a total of twenty-six indicators have been further identified in order to better specify and measure their complexity.

Fig. 2. Set of criteria.

Considering the spatial nature of the criteria involved in the decision problem [15] and the results obtained by recent applications of MCDA method for the evaluation of urban quality [7, 8, 16–18] the use of Multi-Attribute Value Theory (MAVT) in the Geographic Information Systems (GIS) domain is proposed.

A compensative and additive model has been selected since a trade-off has to be defined among the dimensions and it is not possible to maximize all the aspects involved [19]. To this purpose, the MAVT has been adopted since it addresses problems with a finite set of alternative options evaluated with respect to conflicting objectives [20]. By combining the MAVT with the GIS domain, it is possible to clearly visualize the spatial relationships among strengths and weaknesses of the area under investigation [15], to organize and store a huge quantity of geographical data and to conduct operations directly useful for the decision process, inside a georeferenced environment [21]. Assumed the potentials previously pointed out, given the spatial nature of the problem and the multifaceted aspects to consider, a spatial MCDA model is proposed and divided into the traditional phases of a decision making process [22]:

1. Intelligence: it identifies the problem to be solved in order to frame a consistent set of criteria that allows understanding which kind of data has to be collected and which geo-operation has to be processed;
2. Design: it involves the standardization procedure and the weights' assignment;
3. Choice: it consists of data overlay, visualization of partial value maps and the overall urban quality map.

2.2 Hedonic Prices Method

To give an economic value to the urban quality indexes measured in the first phase of the analysis, we used the hedonic prices (HP) method based on Rosen's theory [10]. The HP method is based on the estimate of a multiple regression model in which the observed price of an asset is explained by the set of characteristics that describe it. In real estate, the price of buildings depends on intrinsic and structural features of the asset and extrinsic features related to the neighbourhood where it is located. In particular, the estimated coefficients explain the contribution, positive or negative, of each of the characteristics to the formation of the asset's market price. To obtain the hedonic price of each characteristic, it is necessary to identify a hedonic price function f which establishes a relationship between the price P of the good and all the characteristics that influence this value. This relationship can be schematized according to the Eq. (1), as follows:

$$y = f(x_1, x_2, \ldots, x_n) + e \tag{1}$$

where y is the dependent variable that represents the property price, x_i is the i-th independent variable that contributes to the formation of the value of the asset, e is the error term.

The HP method has been widely used to investigate the effects of urban quality on real estate prices. Glumac et al. [23], starting from a dataset of Luxembourg real estate transactions, investigated the relationship between quality improvements influence and the price of land. Boscacci et al. [24] valued the positive effects generated by the redevelopment of the Navigli area in Milan by a hedonic model. D'Acci [4] estimated the qualitative benefits perceived from the site's characteristics in Turin (Italy), focusing on the proximity to the centre and the increase in site quality. Rosato et al. [25] proposed a hybrid model based on HP method and Multi-Attribute Analysis to test the effects of the MOSE project (Electromechanical Experimental Module) for the protection of Venice (Italy) on real estate prices. Dell'Anna et al. [26] compared the effect of accessibility features on Turin and Barcelona property prices.

3 Case Study

The study area selected to apply the integrated evaluation framework previously defined is the city of Milan (Italy) and in detail three neighbourhoods located on the north-eastern side of the Municipality, from the centre to the administrative border (Fig. 3). The choice to measure the urban quality of neighbourhoods located on this diagonal axis is relevant since it allows to understand whether it differs from central to suburban areas. More, in detail:

- Brera is located in the city centre and is one of the most significant touristic spots in Milan. The area is mainly traffic-free and is easily accessible by public transports.
- Loreto is located at the border of the old city and is characterized by a high urban density. It is one of the most multi-ethnic districts of Milan, and in the last period, it has been populated with artists and young people.

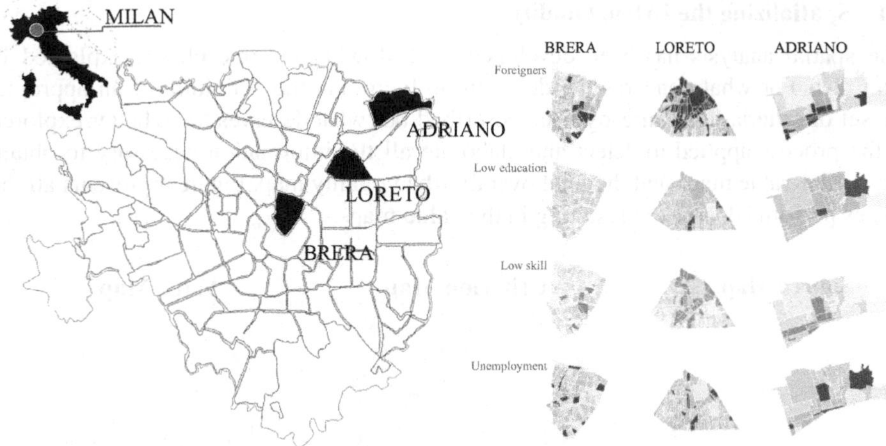

Fig. 3. Case study analyzed and social characteristics

- Adriano is located in the outskirt of the Municipality and is characterized by a not uniform urban shape. Nowadays it is at the centre of policies for its urban regeneration given its original character as a mainly residential district.

The diagonal axis here described well represents three dissimilar neighbourhoods with different location features. Both Loreto and Adriano are undergoing significant changes for what concerns the population and urban fabrics.

The limit of each district has been identified according to the administrative division into Nuclei di Identità Locale (NIL, Centres of Local Identity) as the Municipality of Milan has defined them.

4 Application

Given the objective of the contribution to evaluate urban quality considering three main aspects, namely, the public open spaces quality, the accessibility and provision of services, multidimensional indicators have been defined either in the form of objective or subjective indicators.

Objective indicators are based on the attainment of various basic objectives of the product/service. In contrast, subjective indicators are employed more at the individual level and measure the individual's level of satisfaction with the product/service, that is, they represent a subjective perspective that lays on an introspective and personal experience-based concept.

The general objective of this study is related to the conceptualization of urban quality and to the investigation of an evaluation process able to standardize the evaluation of urban quality levels. This would ensure the replicability of the model, thus contributing to the optimization of the city performance.

4.1 Spatializing the Urban Quality

The spatial analysis has been developed by following the tree phases explained in Sect. 2.1. For what concerns the decision problem and the definition of an appropriate set of criteria it has already been described but what deserves to be better explored is the process applied to detect and elaborate all the information necessary to obtain the partial value maps and the final overall urban quality map. Figure 4 presents all the stages performed aimed at resulting in the value maps.

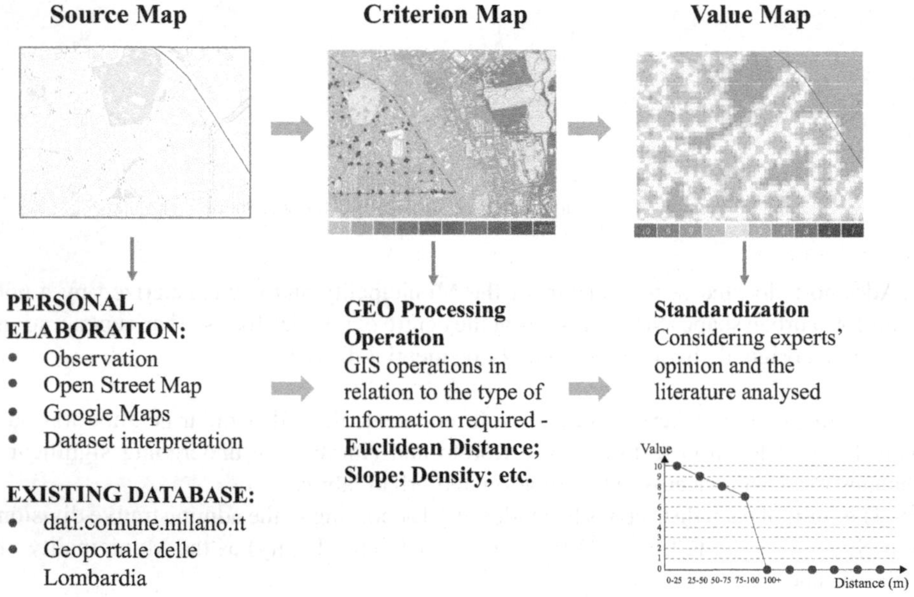

Fig. 4. Process to elaborate value maps

As already mentioned, the sub-criteria have been further measured by indicators, each requiring specific data that have been collected, mainly by the use of GIS maps developed by the Municipality of Milan and by other sources such as direct observation, Open Street Map and Google Maps (Source map). The work has been carried out with the support of the software ArcGIS and with the Spatial Analyst tool that allows performing the Spatial MCDA. The Geoprocessing operations have been carefully selected considering the information required and mainly two processes have been applied: the Euclidean Distance and the Density. The Criterion maps obtained and the information have been subsequently standardized by the support of experts and by analysing researches developed previously. The standardization procedure allowed to transform the unit of measurement of the selected sub-criteria in comparable units. According to the software used and to the geo-operation applied to the original data it is possible to assign a dimensionless score, from 0 to 10 (where 0 is the worst and 10 is the best score), to different performances considering how much they satisfy the specific requirement. The results of this phase are the Value maps where it is already possible to visualize the most suitable area in relation to the criterion or indicator investigated.

To aggregate the partial Value maps and result in the overall Urban quality map, the criteria weight elicitation has been performed. A focus group has been organized with 13 experts of different fields, asking to weight criteria considered and using the point allocation method. They decided to assign a different weight to the sub-criteria within the Public open space criterion (Physical setting 33%, Connectivity 25%, Vitality 23%, Meaning 13%, Protection 16%), The same weight has been attributed to the sub-criteria belonging to Accessibility and Supply of Services. To visualize a neutral scenario, the three criteria have been considered with the same importance.

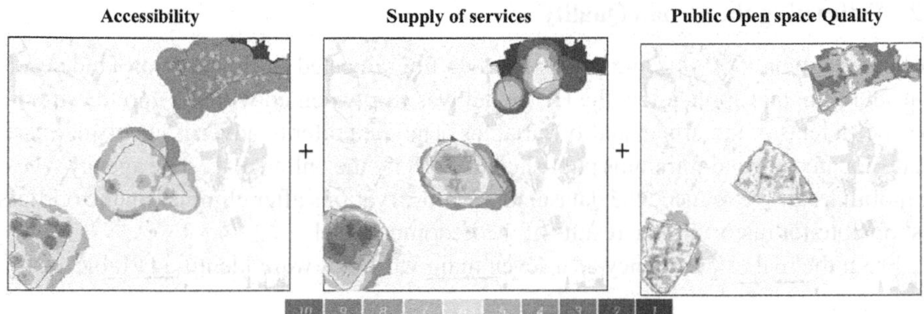

Fig. 5. Partial Value maps

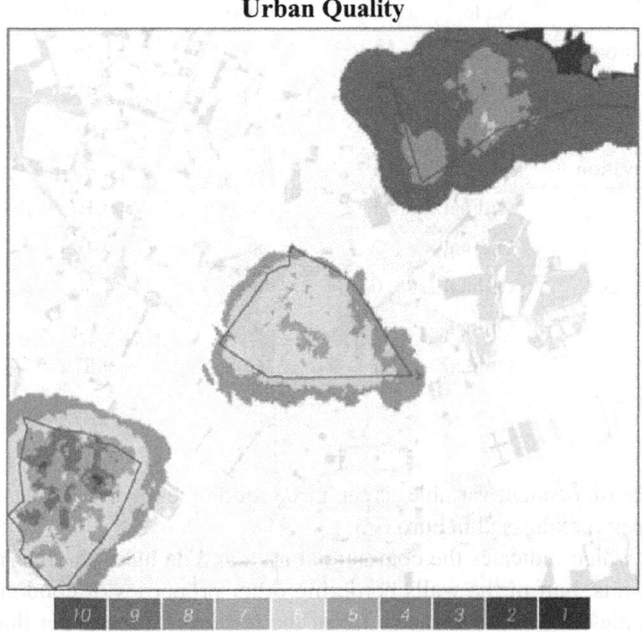

Fig. 6. Overall Urban quality map

Once the weights' assignment has been performed, it is possible to proceed with the aggregation of the sub-criteria, to visualize the partial value maps of the criteria involved (Fig. 5) and finally by aggregating them to visualize the overall Urban quality map (Fig. 6). The aggregation has been carried on considering the MAVT explained previously.

From both the partial maps and the overall, it is evident the predominance of cells with high value in the city core while moving toward the suburb, the value tends to decrease.

4.2 Estimating the Urban Quality

Collected around 350 offering prices for dwellings located in the three urban districts considered in this application, the HP model was implemented with the aim to estimate the coefficients of the urban quality variables. The data refer to advertisements of apartments located in condominiums published in 2018 by the online real estate agency www.immobiliare.it. We reduced the dataset to 338 observations after eliminating the outliers responsible for distorting the results of the hedonic model.

From the real estate agency ads, seven main variables were identified (Table 1):

Table 1. Descriptive statistics of variables (338 observations)

Variables	Measure	Min	Max	Mean	SD
Asking price (€)	Scale	59,000	2,800,000	505,201	500,261
Floor area (m^2)	Scale	25	300	96.95	49.56
Number of bathrooms	Scale	1	3	1.45	0.62
Dwelling's level	Scale	0	11	2.48	2.08
Energy class	Scale	1	5	1.61	1.043
State of conservation	Ordinal	1	4	2.63	0.77
Year range	Ordinal	1	8	4.10	2.149
Accessibility	Ordinal	2	8	4.49	1.88
Supply of services	Ordinal	0	8	4.56	2.07
Open spaces	Ordinal	1	4	2.63	0.59
Urban quality	Ordinal	1	6	3.57	1.434

- Asking price (dependent variable) is the price recommended by the real estate agent for the property, expressed in euro (€).
- Floor area, which indicates the commercial area and includes the internal walls, the perimeter walls, half of the walls bordering other properties or condominiums, half of the balconies, 1/3 of the terraces, 1/5 of the terraces on the upper floor, expressed in m^2.
- Number of bathrooms counts the bathrooms in the apartment.

- Dwelling's level indicates the level of the floor where the property is located in the condo, where the ground floor and mezzanine floor is equal to 0, the first floor is worth 1, and so on.
- Energy class indicates the energy performance of the property, and it is based on the Energy Performance Certificate (EPC) promoted in 2010 by the European Directive EPBD 2010/31/EU. According to EPC, 1 indicates a property in class G, 2 in class F, and so on [27].
- State of conservation specifies the maintenance status of the dwelling (1 = Poor/To be restored; 2 = Good; 3 = Restored; 4 = New/Under construction) [28].
- Year range variable clusters the properties according to the age class of construction of the buildings where they are located (before 1900 = 1, 1901–1920 = 2, 1921–1945 = 3, 1946–1960 = 4, 1961–1975 = 5, 1976–1990 = 6, 1991–2005 = 7, after 2005 = 8) [29].

We implemented the offer price dataset with the disaggregated urban quality (Accessibility, Supply of services, Public Open space Quality) variables, and their aggregated value (Urban Quality), according to properties' location, in order to measure the spillover effect of housing prices.

Before carrying out hedonic regressions, a correlation test of the dataset variables was carried out (Table 2). If a multivariate linear regression function specifies the hedonic price function, the explanatory variables should be hypothetically independent of each other. Otherwise, multicollinearity between independent variables is present. The validity of the regression model cannot be separated from the choice of explanatory variables to be included in the calculation, which must influence the formulation of the price. In detail, Pearson's test showed that a strong correlation exists between the floor area and the number of bathrooms, as expected. The calculation of the correlation index highlighted the presence of collinearity between urban quality variables.

Furthermore, the State of conservation is correlated both with the Energy class and the year of construction, as foreseeable. Besides, the urban quality variables are strongly correlated with the Year range and Energy class variables. Starting from the hypothesis that real estate developments have followed the urban dynamics of the city of Milan, these last characteristics are uniformly distributed in the neighbourhoods. Given the results of the collinearity test, some variables have not been included in the model. In the presence of this phenomenon, the equation used may not be significant and produce distorting effects in the results of the estimate. Consequently, it was decided to comprise the aggregated Urban Quality (UQ) variable and to discard the Year range and Energy class as predictors.

5 Discussion of the Results

The HP theory does not indicate the perfect function type to adopt in the regression model. Rosen claimed that the function is rarely linear. This situation occurs only when the property is a perfectly divisible asset. The most frequently used regression functions are the semi-logarithmic and logarithmic forms. In the case of the semi-logarithmic form, the coefficient can be interpreted as the percentage variation of the property's

Table 2. Correlation analysis

		Floor area	Number of bathrooms	Dwelling's level	Energy class	State of conservation	Year range	Accessibility	Supply of services	Open spaces	Urban quality
Floor area	Pearson corr.	1	.743**	.114*	.026	-.057	-.039	.325**	.227**	.198**	.298**
	Sign.		.000	.037	.638	.294	.471	.000	.000	.000	.000
Number of bathrooms	Pearson corr.	.743**	1	.105	.214**	.084	.063	.258**	.188**	.189**	.260**
	Sign.	.000		.054	.000	.124	.245	.000	.001	.000	.000
Dwelling's level	Pearson corr.	.114*	.105	1	.156**	.024	.129*	.014	-.072	-.037	-.040
	Sign.	.037	.054		.004	.665	.018	.792	.188	.503	.465
Energy class	Pearson corr.	.026	.214**	.156**	1	.430**	.472**	-.151**	-.202**	-.028	-.172**
	Sign.	.638	.000	.004		.000	.000	.005	.000	.611	.001
State of conservation	Pearson corr.	-.057	.084	.024	.430**	1	.300**	.028	-.057	-.076	-.022
	Sign.	.294	.124	.665	.000		.000	.611	.299	.163	.693
Year range	Pearson corr.	-.039	.063	.129*	.472**	.300**	1	-.401**	-.425**	-.299**	-.435**
	Sign.	.471	.245	.018	.000	.000		.000	.000	.000	.000
Accessibiliy	Pearson corr.	.325**	.258**	.014	-.151**	.028	-.401**	1	.736**	.550**	.900**
	Sign.	.000	.000	.792	.005	.611	.000		.000	.000	.000
Supply of services	Pearson corr.	.227**	.188**	-.072	-.202**	-.057	-.425**	.736**	1	.659**	.917**
	Sign.	.000	.001	.188	.000	.299	.000	.000		.000	.000
Open spaces	Pearson corr.	.198**	.189**	-.037	-.028	-.076	-.299**	.550**	.659**	1	.719**
	Sign.	.000	.000	.503	.611	.163	.000	.000	.000		.000
Urban quality	Pearson corr.	.298**	.260**	-.040	-.172**	-.022	-.435**	.900**	.917**	.719**	1
	Sign.	.000	.000	.465	.001	.693	.000	.000	.000	.000	

** = significant at 0.01
* = significant at 0.05

price following an extra-unit of the independent characteristic. Two different regression models based on Ordinary Least Square (OLS) have been applied considering "Offering price" as the dependent variable in logarithmic scale (LN Price).

Table 3 shows the results of the semi-log model computed via OLS estimator, introducing as an independent variable the UQ in the ordinal scale, from the worst level (UQ 1) to the best (UQ 6). In the first model, the coefficients of the variables have obtained the expected sign. The four explanatory variables identified above are statistically significant and show adequate amounts and signs. From these results, it is possible to deduce the marginal percentage value of the predictors. The size of the apartment (Floor area variable) positively affects the price of the properties (β = 0.01). Referring to the Dwelling's level variable, it is possible to deduce that living on a high floor is seen as an advantage, influencing the property price by 4.6% for each additional floor. The state of conservation strongly affects the price (β = 0.151). The UQ seems to be the characteristic that most influences the price of the properties, with a percentage of 27.6%. It is not surprising that this variable significantly affects the market price, as it represents the extrinsic characteristics relating to the urban belt, the neighbourhood, the accessibility of the area where a property is located, and the services available. This result agrees with the literature, which emphasizes that these positional characteristics can influence the price of properties from 15% to 35% [30].

Table 3. Regression model results – Nonlinear model (OLS)

	Non-standardized coefficients		t	Sign.
	β	SE		
Constant	10.310	0.100	102.601	0.000
Floor area	0.010	0.000	21.787	0.000
Dwelling's level	0.046	0.010	4.481	0.000
State of conservation	0.151	0.028	5.472	0.000
Urban quality	0.276	0.016	17.744	0.000
LN Price (mean)	R^2	Adjusted R^2	SE of estimate	
12.764	0.781	0.778	0.39	

The second regression model wants to check if UQ levels can affect real estate asset differently. For this reason, the UQ variable has been discretized in dichotomous variables, one for each level. UQ level 6 has been excluded from the hedonic model in order to verify the potential benefits generated by the minimum requirements of UQ in terms of population appreciation. In fact, from a political point of view, urban quality is undoubtedly one of the decisive elements in improving the perception of safety and wellbeing among the inhabitants [31]. If then the interventions in the booming part of the city of Milan have a strong significance linked to tourism promotion, the actions of public policies in the most degraded areas assume fundamental importance in improving the quality of life. With this in mind, ensuring interventions to improve urban quality is one of the fundamental tasks of the Public Administration. Table 4 shows the results of the second hedonic model. By comparing the performance parameters of the two models, it is possible to confirm that the second model explains more significant deviance between observed and fitted values (Adjusted $R^2 = 0.806$). The explanatory variables assume statistical significance and congruous signs. By focusing on the variables of the UQ levels, it is possible to confirm that an appreciation exists with respect to the UQ levels 1, 2, 3 and 4. Compared to the UQ level 5, the consumer is no longer willing to pay for higher UQ levels. According to the decreasing marginal utility theory, once the maximum utility level represented by the UQ level 5 is reached, any other increases will probably bring disutility, decreasing the level of individual satisfaction. These results confirm that an appreciation for the characteristics considered in the UQ index exists and it is reflected in the real estate market of the city of Milan. From the results, a real estate unit can double its market price if it is located in an area characterized by a high level of urban quality (beta coefficient of UQ level 1 = 1.00).

Table 4. Regression model results – Nonlinear model (OLS)

	Non-standardized coefficients		t	Sign.
	β	SE		
Constant	11.803	0.120	98.174	0.000
Floor area	0.010	0.000	23.473	0.000
Dwelling's level	0.041	0.010	4.101	0.000
State of conservation	0.132	0.026	5.025	0.000
Urban quality level 1	−1.000	0.101	−9.928	0.000
Urban quality level 2	−0.910	0.086	−10.598	0.000
Urban quality level 3	−0.744	0.083	−8.934	0.000
Urban quality level 4	−0.413	0.081	−5.105	0.000
Urban quality level 5	0.156	0.081	1.918	0.056
LN Price (mean)	R^2	Adjusted R^2	SE of estimate	
12.764	0.810	0.806	0.364	

6 Conclusions

The methodology proposed within this contribution and applied to three different neighbourhoods in the Municipality of Milan aimed at assessing the value of the urban quality, both considering monetary and non-monetary methodologies.

One of the strengths of the methodological approach adopted can be detected, in fact, in the combination of qualitative and quantitative methodologies which allows on one side to catch the drivers of urban quality and on the other to assess them accurately. One of the possible outcomes of the study could be supporting policies concerning urban regeneration and planning. By making the monetary value of urban quality explicit, Public Administration, investors, developers and urban designers can easily consider the economic impact of their choices when designing cities and neighbourhoods. For example, the results obtained lead to reflect on the economic effects generated by urban transformations, in particular of areas with low quality of public and private services. In the case study, the main problems have been detected in the Adriano district, which is attributable to that part of the city which grew up around the 90s without a global vision but somewhat disconnected and unfinished. In this kind of areas, the neighbourhood scale approach is almost impossible and insufficient. For this reason, supported by the analysis provided and the value maps, it is clear how punctual interventions are not enough and should be accompanied in some way by different actions based on a strategy that operates through the urban context.

Another outcome of the research is the definition of a synthetic index able to represent features about extrinsic characteristics of the neighbourhood and as a result, to improve information into the real estate market. This notion can become strategic in decision-making processes regarding urban development where the private sector is involved and moreover in public-private negotiations to understand the benefits produced by a higher level of urban quality.

At the same time, some limits are present, and other aspects should be deepened.

The datasets of observation should be expanded in order to validate better the results obtained and provide more robust conclusions. A higher number of observations could allow to describe better the incidence of the three variables (Accessibility, Supply of Services and Public Open Space Quality) in achieving the urban quality and evaluate their marginal price.

Finally, future studies could be related to the development of a Choice-Experiment to calculate consumers' willingness to pay for the different characteristics of the urban quality and to compare the results with those obtained by performing the HP model. In fact, according to Louviere et al. [32], an approach that integrates Revealed Preferences (RPs) and Stated Preferences (SPs) approaches can limit the errors of the unobserved variables that characterize RPs.

References

1. United Nations Department of Economic and Social Affairs: 68% of the world population projected to live in urban areas by 2050, says UN. https://www.pc.gov.au/research/supporting/non-market-valuation

2. Weziak-Białowolska, D.: Quality of life in cities - empirical evidence in comparative European perspective. Cities **58**, 87–96 (2016). https://doi.org/10.1016/j.cities.2016.05.016
3. Carmona, M.: Place value: place quality and its impact on health, social, economic and environmental outcomes. J. Urban Des. **24**, 1–48 (2019). https://doi.org/10.1080/13574809.2018.1472523
4. D'Acci, L.: Quality of urban area, distance from city centre, and housing value. Case study on real estate values in Turin. Cities **91**, 71–92 (2019). https://doi.org/10.1016/j.cities.2018.11.008
5. Simonotti, M.: La stima immobiliare. UTET, Turin (1997)
6. D'Acci, L.: Monetary, subjective and quantitative approaches to assess urban quality of life and pleasantness in cities (hedonic price, willingness-to-pay, positional value, life satisfaction, isobenefit lines). Soc. Indic. Res. **115**(2), 531–559 (2013). https://doi.org/10.1007/s11205-012-0221-7
7. Oppio, A., Bottero, M., Arcidiacono, A.: Assessing urban quality: a proposal for a MCDA evaluation framework. Annal. Oper. Res. 1–18 (2018). https://doi.org/10.1007/s10479-017-2738-2
8. Oppio, A., Bottero, M., Giordano, G., Arcidiacono, A.: A multi-methodological evaluation approach for assessing the impact of neighbourhood quality on public health. Epidemiologia e Prevenzione **40**, 249–256 (2016). https://doi.org/10.19191/EP16.3-4.P249.092
9. Montibeller, G., Franco, A.: Decision and risk analysis for the evaluation of strategic options. In: O'Brien, F.A., Dyson, R.G. (eds.) Supporting Strategy: Frameworks, Methods and Models, pp. 251–284. Wiley, West Sussex (2007)
10. Rosen, S.: Hedonic prices and implicit markets: product differentiation in pure competition. J. Polit. Econ. **82**, 34–55 (1974). https://doi.org/10.1086/260169
11. Punter, J.: Developing urban design as public policy: best practice principles for design review and development management. J. Urban Des. **12**, 167–202 (2007). https://doi.org/10.1080/13574800701306195
12. Carmona, M., Heath, T., Tiesdell, S., Oc, T.: Urban design today. In: Public Places Urban Spaces, pp. 3–19 (2010)
13. Dias, N., Curwell, S., Bichard, E.: The current approach of urban design, its implications for sustainable urban development. Procedia Econ. Financ. **18**, 497–504 (2014). https://doi.org/10.1016/s2212-5671(14)00968-x
14. Urban Design Group: What is Urban Design? http://www.udg.org.uk/about/what-is-urban-design
15. Dell'Ovo, M., Capolongo, S., Oppio, A.: Combining spatial analysis with MCDA for the siting of healthcare facilities. Land Use Policy **76**, 634–644 (2018). https://doi.org/10.1016/j.landusepol.2018.02.044
16. Munda, G.: Measuring sustainability: a multi-criterion framework. Environ. Dev. Sustain. **7**, 117–134 (2005). https://doi.org/10.1007/s10668-003-4713-0
17. Blečić, I., Cecchini, A., Congiu, T., Fancello, G., Trunfio, G.A.: Evaluating walkability: a capability-wise planning and design support system. Int. J. Geogr. Inf. Sci. **29**, 1350–1374 (2015). https://doi.org/10.1080/13658816.2015.1026824
18. Nijkamp, P., Teresa, M., Ciuffo, B., Torrieri, F.: Sustainable urban land use and transportation planning: a cognitive decision support system for the Naples metropolitan area. Int. J. Sustain. Transp. **1**, 91–114 (2007). https://doi.org/10.1080/15568310601091981
19. Dell'Ovo, M., Oppio, A.: Bringing the value-focused thinking approach to urban development and design processes: the case of foz do tua area in Portugal. Valori e Valutazioni **23**, 91–106 (2019)
20. Keeney, R.L., Raiffa, H.: Decision Making with Multiple Objectives Preferences and Value Tradeoffs, New York (1976)

21. Malczewski, J.: GIS-based multicriteria decision analysis: a survey of the literature. Int. J. Geogr. Inf. Sci. **20**, 703–726 (2006). https://doi.org/10.1080/13658810600661508
22. Simon, H.A.: Theories of bounded rationality. In: McGuire, C.B., Radner, R. (eds.) Decision and Organization. North-Holland Pub. Co., Amsterdam (1972)
23. Glumac, B., Herrera-Gomez, M., Licheron, J.: A hedonic urban land price index. Land Use Policy **81**, 802–812 (2019). https://doi.org/10.1016/j.landusepol.2018.11.032
24. Boscacci, F., Camagni, R., Caragliu, A., Maltese, I., Mariotti, I.: Collective benefits of an urban transformation: Restoring the Navigli in Milan. Cities **71**, 11–18 (2017). https://doi.org/10.1016/j.cities.2017.06.018
25. Rosato, P., Breil, M., Giupponi, C., Berto, R.: Assessing the impact of urban improvement on housing values: a hedonic pricing and multi-attribute analysis model for the historic centre of Venice. Buildings **7**, 112 (2017). https://doi.org/10.3390/buildings7040112
26. Dell'Anna, F., Bravi, M., Marmolejo-Duarte, C., Bottero, M.C., Chen, A.: EPC green premium in two different European climate zones: a comparative study between Barcelona and Turin. Sustain. (Switzerland) **11**, 5605 (2019). https://doi.org/10.3390/su11205605
27. European Commission: Directive 2010/31/UE, Energy Performance of Building Directive Recast (EPBD recast). https://eur-lex.europa.eu/legal-content/EN/TXT/HTML/?uri=CELEX:32010L0031&from=it
28. Bottero, M., Bravi, M., Dell'Anna, F., Mondini, G.: Valuing building energy efficiency through Hedonic Prices Method: are spatial effects relevant? Valori e Valutazioni **21**, 27–40 (2018)
29. Ballarini, I., Corgnati, S.P., Corrado, V.: Use of reference buildings to assess the energy saving potentials of the residential building stock: the experience of TABULA project. Energy Policy **68**, 273–284 (2014). https://doi.org/10.1016/j.enpol.2014.01.027
30. Forte, C., De' Rossi, B.: Principi di economia ed estimo. Etas libri (1979)
31. Gabrielli, L., Giuffrida, S., Trovato, M.R.: From surface to core: a multi-layer approach for the real estate market analysis of a central area in Catania. In: Gervasi, O., Murgante, B., Misra, S., Gavrilova, M.L., Rocha, A.M.A.C., Torre, C., Taniar, D., Apduhan, B.O. (eds.) ICCSA 2015. LNCS, vol. 9157, pp. 284–300. Springer, Cham (2015). https://doi.org/10.1007/978-3-319-21470-2_20
32. Louviere, J.J., Hensher, D.A., Swait, J.D.: Combining sources of preference data. In: Stated Choice Methods. pp. 227–251. Cambridge University Press (2000)

Universal Design-Based Framework to Assess Usability and Inclusion of Buildings

Erica Isa Mosca(✉) and Stefano Capolongo

Politecnico di Milano, Ponzio Street 31, 20133 Milan, Italy
ericaisa.mosca@polimi.it

Abstract. Universal Design (UD) offers different sets of principles that can be used as reference in design practice to meet the needs of the vast majority of a population. However, there is a lack of an accountable approach to measure and analyze the built environment through UD performance.

This study aims to develop an evaluation framework to assess UD in public buildings to determine, in addition to accessibility requirements, the usability and inclusion of projects for different users.

Multicriteria Decision Analysis (MCDA) was adopted as research methodology to systematically and scientifically develop the framework, which was structured based on knowledge derived from: an in-depth literature review on UD evaluation and workshops with stakeholders and experts. The selection and comparison of a pool of criteria is described including the cognitive mapping technique for translating information gathered by workshops.

A hierarchical framework was created, consisting of three main categories of UD (i.e. physical-spatial quality, sensorial-cognitive quality, and social quality), eight criteria (i.e. usability, functionality, safety/security, wayfinding, understanding, environmental factors, well-being, and social inclusion), and 21 indicators. The proposed framework can be considered as an innovative approach in the field of accessible design evaluation since it explores the relation among a multiplicity of aspects, including human performance and social factors, to evaluate the quality of UD buildings.

Keywords: Design for All · Inclusive design · MCDA · Universal design · Workshop · Cognitive mapping technique

1 Introduction

Universal Design (UD) strategy aims to meet the needs of the greatest number of people, regardless of age, gender, physical and cultural features, abilities or disabilities. Architect R. Mace introduced UD in 1985 [1] as a strategy that encourages designing environments or products that are usable by the vast majority of a population, without adaptation or stigma. It refers to a universal human experience since all individuals can be impaired by "temporary impairments" (e.g. age, broken limb, pregnancy) or "situational impairments" generated by the built environment (e.g. inaccessible transportation or public buildings, negative attitudes, and limited social support) [2].

O. Gervasi et al. (Eds.): ICCSA 2020, LNCS 12253, pp. 316–331, 2020.
https://doi.org/10.1007/978-3-030-58814-4_22

In architecture, UD overcomes architectural barriers where accessibility is the minimum design requirement [3]. Accordingly, UD offers people with different needs the possibility to use and enjoy a space in a dignified way, providing all users the same experience despite different design solutions.

In this study, UD and Design for All (DfA), which is design that aims for diversity, social inclusion, and equality [4], are considered equal since both are driven by the same objectives even though they come from the American and European contexts, respectively [5]. These design strategies aim to promote diversity and develop projects that overcome all kinds of impairments: physical (e.g. dexterity, movement, static and dynamic stamina), sensorial (e.g. sight, hearing, touch), cognitive (e.g. memory, understanding), and social (e.g. social participation, culture, religion, etc.) [6, 7].

1.1 Problem Definition

Although physical, cognitive, or social inclusion can affect users' well-being, architectural environments are still not often designed to consider users' needs and experiences within space [8]. Ways to link UD knowledge and practice are also still inadequate [9, 10]. In many cases, the lack of consideration for users' needs can negatively influence users and compromise the performance of the entire service [11]. The inclusion of social aspects only at the end of the design process has tangible effects on individuals' well-being, furthermore this can generate extra cost and time for adjustments to disable situations [12]. For these reasons, it is fundamental to evaluate the usability and inclusion of projects before and after construction. There is an urgent need to study and develop specific evaluation tools based on performance, which allow designers to assess and compare project features in terms of usability and inclusion [13].

In this context, UD evaluation explores how well a building works for a wide range of users [14]. It overcomes the focus on architectural barriers and specific categories of users concerned with accessibility and underlines UD variables that positively influence people's well-being. As such, clear criteria and indicators are needed to better understand the impacts of the environment on users' behavior and well-being [15]. As Preiser states, "a rigorous and accountable approach must be taken in measuring and analyzing" based on UD performance [16], clear features are therefore needed to assess the usability and inclusion of built environment.

1.2 Objective of the Study

The evaluation systems currently used for the assessment of building performance, such as Leadership in Energy and Environmental Design (LEED) [17] and the Building Research Establishment's Environmental Assessment Method (BREEAM) [18], check the presence of certain technical, design, and system aspects through a series of indicators and a specific scoring method. These tools provide a reliable evaluation of overall aspects of a building (e.g. indoor air quality, thermal comfort). This approach has been followed aiming at developing a framework to measure how universally designed buildings are in terms of usability and social inclusion. The purpose is to fix the basis for an evaluation method that can be applied to new buildings and renovations (i.e. project audit) or in Post-Occupancy Evaluation (POE) [14] to objectively define the priority of interventions in existing buildings. Accordingly, the study addresses the following research questions:

i) What are the most prevalent criteria used to measure UD building performance?
ii) How can these aspects be adopted to generate an evaluation framework for UD?

Section 2, in particular, describes the general methodology on which the framework is built (i.e. Multicriteria Decision Analysis (MCDA)) and the specific methods used for its development (i.e. literature review and workshops with users and experts). Section 3 explores the results generated from each of the methods that enable the development of the framework. Section 4 presents the final discussion, while Sect. 5 contains the conclusion with future perspectives.

2 Methodology

2.1 Multicriteria Decision Analysis Approach

As previously stated, the main objective of this study is to provide a UD evaluation of building design based on outcomes that can improve the well-being of as many users as possible, instead of merely focusing on specific categories of users. The application of this concept to the evaluation of public buildings involves a plurality of users with various physiological, sensorial, cognitive, and emotional needs and circumstances [19], which in turn adds complexity to the evaluation process. This process must thus consider several quantitative and qualitative aspects related to social factors and human performance.

For this reason, the study focuses on multicriteria methodologies since they can be used to structure and solve complex decision and planning problems involving multiple qualitative and quantitative criteria and the analysis and comparison of the full range of aspects related to a project [20]. The MCDA approach [21] delivers specific models that can solve issues of real situations through eight main steps [20]. This study adopted the second step "identifying objectives and criteria" to systematically develop the framework. After establishing a decision context (i.e. first step) [20], which in this case is UD evaluation with related stakeholders, the second step involved breaking down the issue into different objectives or criteria to define the structure of an evaluation framework [20]. The described criteria are parameters for evaluating a system through quantitative, qualitative, or descriptive measures that represent its main features. After selection, criteria were organized in a hierarchical framework (i.e. decision tree), which consisted of criteria and indicators clustered in high-level and lower-level objectives. This evaluation is therefore characterized by a performance-based approach, such as UD, that focuses on the achievement of objectives rather than on the prescription of rules [22].

The research is developed through different phases, shown in Fig. 1, that allow to elaborate the contents of the framework (i.e. categories, criteria, indicators) through knowledge assembled from two methods: a literature review and a workshop with stakeholders.

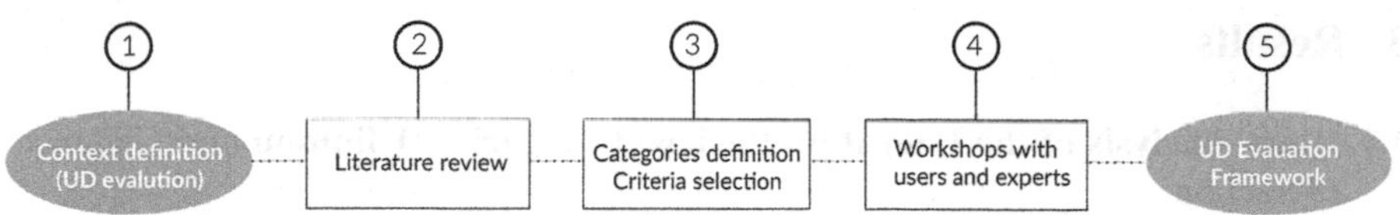

Fig. 1. Methodology flow chart

2.2 Literature Review

A literature review was conducted to investigate current and existing studies on UD and DfA evaluation methods and tools. This analysis aims to explore existing knowledge on UD and DfA assessments and collect data to systematically and scientifically select items for the development of a decisional and assessment UD framework.

The Scopus database was used to search for articles, using a specific three-level set of keywords: *Universal Design* OR *Design for All* OR *Inclusive Design* OR *Accessibility* AND *Evaluation* OR *Assessment* OR *Performance* AND *Architecture* OR *Built environment.* Eligibility criteria were used to select and include or exclude them from the analysis. Articles were excluded if they related to case studies because they contain results that are too specific or pertain to an "education" issue, especially because there are fields under UD and DfA related more to education and learning than design.

Twenty-three articles were included in the final analysis, subdivided into four main categories: evaluation theories, criteria, methods, and tools. The analysis revealed that there are different sets of criteria to assess UD and DfA adopted by different evaluation methods found in the literature. The specific methodology and results of the literature study have been described in a previous work [22]. This study compares criteria to identify the most prevalent topics.

2.3 Workshops: Stakeholders' Analysis and Cognitive Mapping Approaches

When defining criteria in MCDA, the involvement of different perspectives is a typical approach suggested for the development of assessment frameworks [21]. Since UD is a discipline based on users' needs, it is fundamental to include a plurality of viewpoints in the framework definition as such accommodates different possible approaches to a problem. In this study, stakeholders (i.e. users and experts) were involved through workshops that aim to determine if some of the main objectives were excluded or if they overlap with the criteria in the literature review. In particular, the paper proposed the stakeholder analysis [23] to identify which actors should be involved in the workshop and the cognitive mapping technique [24] to organize content. Recent studies have combined these methods to ensure a more inclusive approach in the identification of relevant objectives and criteria [25]. Stakeholders represent actors interested in the decision-making process as they either directly affect or are affected by its resolution. Meanwhile, the cognitive mapping method is well suited for complex problems; it provides a well-arranged systematization of available concepts for the structuring of decision trees [26].

3 Results

3.1 Data Analysis of the Literature Review: Categories Definition and Criteria Selection

Many evaluation tools for accessibility and usability highlight the spectrum of disabling situations for users in any given building setting [28]. This approach can work in private space evaluation, such as a home [3]. Conversely, public buildings bring extensive complexity to the evaluation because of the plurality of space settings and users involved [22]. For this reason, the criteria analysis in this study did not focus on users' disabilities, but rather worked with performance criteria that represent the main objectives to develop environments universally usable and enjoyable for a wider number of users.

Different evaluation tools for UD building features are often based on the *Seven Principles of Universal Design* [29]. These principles refer to human performances, particularly usability issues and aspects related to people's perception of the space (e.g. sensory and cognitive issues) [28]. However, the in-depth literature review provided an overview of different criteria sets in UD (see Table 1) and highlighted social issues over human factors as important aspects that differentiate UD from other user-centered approaches. Social factors ensure evaluation or design for people's needs, thus contributing to their overall well-being and overcoming basic accessibility.

These aspects were introduced in Preiser's *Habitability Framework* [16], specifically in the third order of needs related to social and experiential factors, and in Lawton's *Need Satisfaction Behavior Framework* [30]. Moreover, Sanford proposed adding two principles to the original ones: social and contextual integration [31]. Similarly, Froyen's *Aspects of Universal Design Patterns* [3] extended the *Seven UD Principles* with elements of comfort quality (e.g. light, acoustic properties, and thermal comfort) and features related to wellness (e.g. privacy and esthetic appeal). More recently, the new definition of UD proposed by Steinfeld and Maisel clearly introduced social and health factors, defining it as "a process that enables and empowers a diverse population by improving human performance, health and wellness, and social participation" [7]. Accordingly, the *Eight Universal Design Goals* [7] have been formulated to update the UD principles and identify measurable outcomes where "health" and "wellness" represent the intersection of human performance and social factors. Finally, the *Accessibility Goals* available in the ISO GUIDE 71:2014 [32] were included in this analysis since they aim to provide an approach for the identification and development of standards for project design and evaluation.

Categories Definition

The previous analysis based on the literature review described how UD projects strive to design for diversity and consider all kinds of impairments (e.g. physical, sensorial, cognitive, and social). This is reflected in the analysis of the evaluation criteria sets in the literature, which concerns three main categories (see Fig. 2): two related to human performances (i.e. physical aspects and sensorial-cognitive aspects) and one focused on social aspects. Accordingly, it is possible to define three UD categories in relation to the theories and criteria sets previously analyzed:

Table 1. Criteria sets resulted from the literature review analysis

Universal design principles [29]	Habitability framework [16]		Need satisfaction behaviour [30]	Universal d esign patterns – aspects [30]	Universal design goals [7]		Accessibility goals [32]
Equitable use	Regulations	Health	Security/Safety	Security measure	Human performance	Body fit	Suitability for the widest range of users
Flexibility in use		Safety	Function	Ergonomic measure		Comfort	Conformity with user expectations
Simple and intuitive use		Security	Cognition	Size and Space for approach and use		Awareness	Support for individualization
Perceptible information	Technological knowledge	Functional	Comfort	Light		Understanding	Approachability
Tolerance for error			Order	Acoustic properties			Perceivability Understandability
Low physical effort		Efficiency	Autonomy	Thermal comfort		Wellness	Controllability
Size and Space for approach and use		Workflow	Privacy	Perceptible Information			Usability
			Stimulation	Visual Information	Social participation		Error tolerance
	Social factors	Psychological/Social	Affiliation	Wayfinding		Social integration	Equitable use
		Cultural	Individuality	Identification		Personalization	Compatibility with other systems
		Aesthetic	Spirituality	Privacy		Cultural appropriateness	

- Physical-Spatial Quality: the capability of the environment to foster easy, comfortable, functional, and safe use of space and objects. This means being able to physically interact with a system;
- Sensory-Cognitive Quality: the capability of the environment to foster orientation, comprehension of the service, and comfort of users. This refers to the features that impact peoples' senses and cognition;
- Social Quality: the ability of the environment to enhance well-being and inclusion. It considers emotional stimuli and social integration among users.

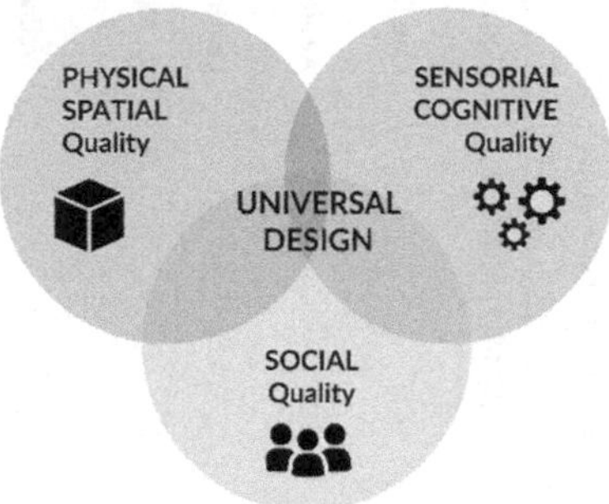

Fig. 2. Framework's categories: physical-spatial quality, sensorial-cognitive quality, social quality.

Criteria Selection

MCDA suggests grouping criteria into a series of sets to separate distinguishable components of the overall objective for the decision [20]. This procedure is helpful when there is a large number of criteria to compare to the current study; it enables shifting from a list of criteria to a hierarchical framework through a comparison aimed at understanding the redundancy of criteria.

Figure 3 shows the complete list of analyzed criteria clustered according to the three categories, as well as their frequency, to develop a preliminary selection and comparison. The different criteria had an average presence of 50%. This value was defined as the exclusion thresh-old value. Nine of the 20 criteria had a frequency lower that the limit value. The criteria selected, considering only their frequency are safety and security, size and space for approach and use, usability, functionality/flexibility, understanding, perceptible information, comfort (environmental factors), health/wellness, and social integration.

	CRITERIA	UD Principles [31]	Habitability Framework[19]	Need Satisfation Behaviour [32]	Universal Design Patterns [34]	Universal Design Goals [10]	Accessibility Goals [35]	N°	%
PHYSICAL/SPATIAL QUALITY	Safety and Security	Error Tollerance	x	x	x		Error Tollerance	5	83%
	Equitable Use	x					x	2	33%
	Size and Space for Approach and Use	x			x	Body fit	Approachability	4	67%
	Usability	Low physical effort	x				x	3	50%
	Ergonomics				x			1	17%
	Functionality/Flexibility	x	x	x			Support for individualization	4	67%
	Autonomy		Efficiency	x				2	33%
	Personalization					x		1	17%
SENSORY/COGNITIVE QUALITY	Workflow		x	Order				2	33%
	Understanding	Simple and intuitive in use		Understanding /Awareness	Identification	x	x	5	83%
	Perceptible Information	x			Perceptible and Visual Information/ Wayfinding		Perceivability	3	50%
	Comfort (Environmental Factors)			x	Light/Acoustic/ Thermal comfort	x		3	50%
	Stimulation			x				1	17%
SOCIAL QUALITY	Health/Wellness		x	Spirituality		x		3	50%
	Aesthetic		x			x		2	33%
	Cultural Appropriateness		x			x		2	33%
	Social Integration		Psycological Social factors	Affiliation		x	Suitability for the widest range of use	4	67%
	Privacy			x	x			2	33%
	Individuality			x				1	17%
	Controllability						x	1	17%

Fig. 3. Criteria selection and comparison

3.2 Data Analysis from Workshops with Stakeholders: Cognitive Mapping

This section shows how stakeholder analysis and cognitive mapping were used for the definition of objectives that characterize the multicriteria model. Workshops were conducted to understand stakeholders' needs, objectives, and expectations [23] regarding the UD project and compare these with criteria found in the literature review.

The study involved experts, such as designers whose work relates to disability, accessibility, and UD, since they have more technical knowledge about accessible design and can provide specific data about UD building features that impact people's well-being. Moreover, users with impairments (e.g. motor, sight, hearing, and mental) were involved to identify needs that designers often ignore and utilize user experiences to improve the environment for all. For instance, people with sensory problems can provide interesting feedback regarding sensorial quality, such as "wayfinding" criteria. Considering the scope of the research, which is improving the environment performance under three different UD categories found in the literature (i.e. physical-spatial, sensorial-cognitive, and social quality), the stakeholders were divided according to the area they belong to, as shown in Fig. 4.

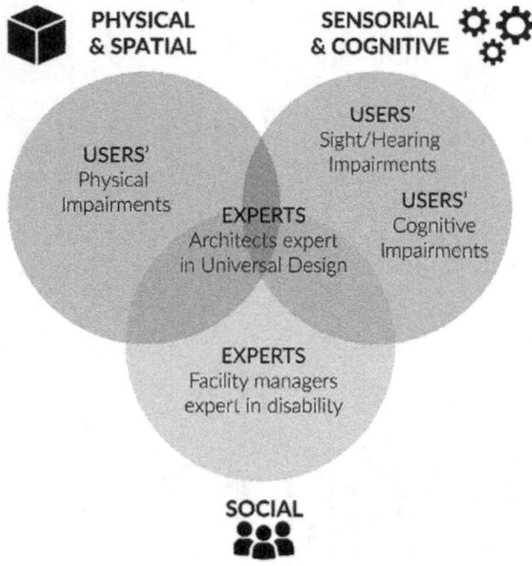

Fig. 4. Stakeholders' analysis in relation to categories.

With the aim of fostering creativity, the workshop's interactive setting (i.e. five participants at most) was used to build the cognitive map. Five workshops were conducted, one with experts (i.e. architects and designers specialized on accessibility and UD) and four with users with motor, sight, hearing, or cognitive impairments. The workshops lasted approximately two hours and consisted of the following phases:

- Introduction: The research topic was described to the participants.
- Feedback: The participants were asked the question, "What are the most important aspects that should be present in a Universal Design space?"
- Post-it session: A common discussion was conducted so that participants can share ideas about major needs and expectations. Meanwhile, post-it are hang on a panel by the facilitator of the workshop to fix the main concepts (e.g. problems, goals, etc.)
- Analysis: The main concepts discussed were reviewed together to find relations and define criteria and indicators.

The cognitive mapping technique was used to compare the results of the workshops. In this study, the final maps summarized the outputs of the post-it phase (i.e. repetitive concepts were eliminated, and similar concepts were merged). Figure 5 presents an example of a cognitive map of the results of the workshop with people with physical impairments. In Fig. 5, the gray boxes represent the main objectives (i.e. criteria) mentioned in the workshop, while the white boxes refer to characteristics that enable the achievement of the main objectives (i.e. indicators).

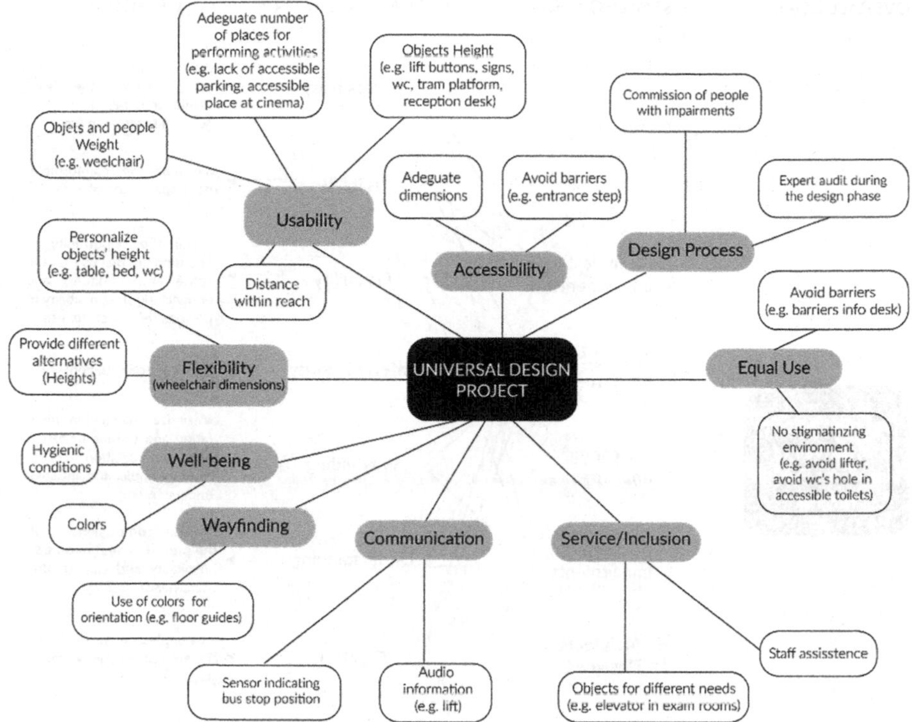

Fig. 5. Cognitive map of the workshop with people with physical impairments.

3.3 Universal Design Objectives in Relation to the Needs of Different Users

The five workshops supported the identification of users' and experts' objectives regarding a UD environment. Figure 6 clearly highlights that the objectives of people with visual impairments referred mostly to aspects related to sight, such as orientation, communication and light. Meanwhile, the objectives of people with motor impairments were more related to the use of the space and furniture.

The cognitive maps derived from information gathered during the workshops were converted into a unique hierarchical structure to identify information that overlap or differ from any group. The decision tree generated (see Fig. 6) shows the overall goal, the stakeholders involved, the set of criteria obtained from the literature and the stakeholder's objectives identified in the workshops. Moreover, this analysis reveals that 'usability' is related to the use of both space and object and it includes the criteria 'size and space for approach and use'.

3.4 Universal Design Assessment Framework: Categories, Criteria and Indicators

The previous analysis enabled the development of a hierarchical model of criteria that represents a preliminary attempt to define a framework, also called decision tree, of UD measurable objectives.

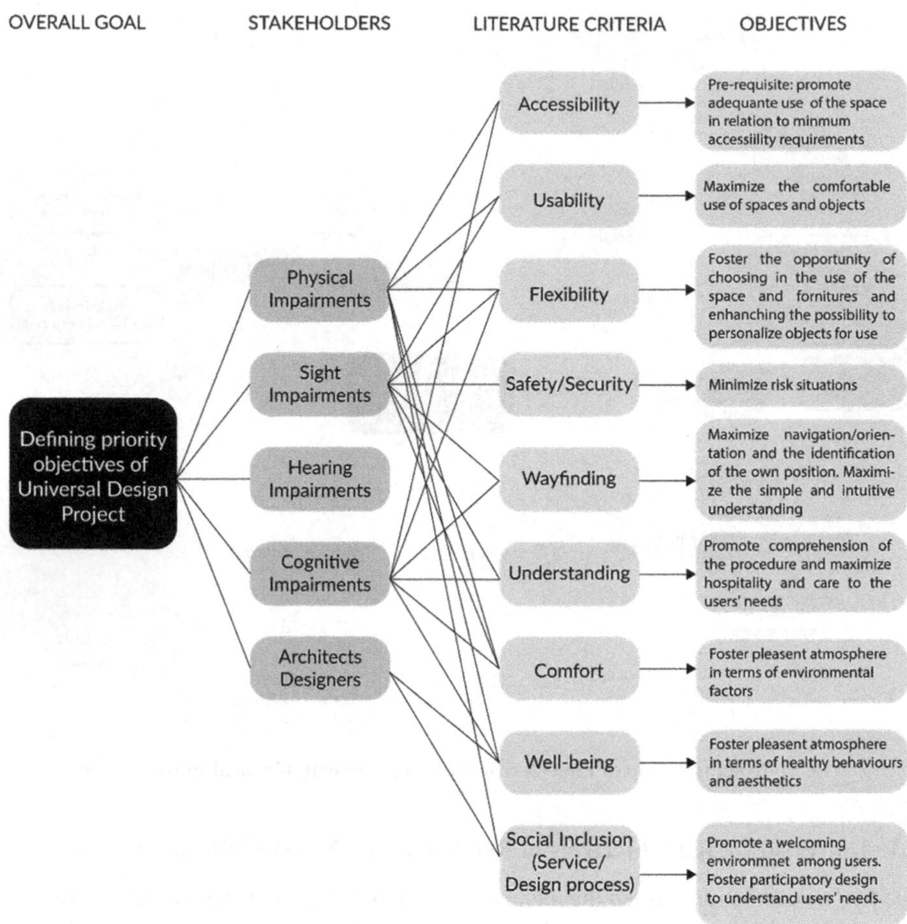

Fig. 6. Hierarchical structure of the objectives expressed by the stakeholders resulted by the comparison of the cognitive maps.

Table 2 shows the proposed framework developed from the previous analysis. The framework is composed of three main categories, a set of eight criteria, and 21 indicators. The *physical-spatial quality* category refers to the way people interact with the space in a physical way. The *sensorial-cognitive quality* category focuses on activities that involve the senses and the intellect as orientation in a space. The *social quality* category concerns attention given to meeting users' needs and wishes in diverse contexts and tending to individuals' health (i.e. wellness) and behavior (i.e. social inclusion). The eight criteria can be described as follows based on information gathered from the studies analyzed in the literature review and the workshops:

- Usability: to use environments, facilities, and objects to ensure the comfort of different users (e.g. distance, dimension, weight, number of people, etc.). Usability includes accessibility, which is considered a pre-requisite;

Table 2. Proposed evaluation framework of Universal Design buildings' performance

Categories	Criteria	Indicators
1. Physical-spatial quality	1.2 Usability	Equal use of the environment
		Equal use of furniture
	1.3 Functionality	Flexibility/Personalization
		Low physical effort
		Flows/Distribution
	1.4 Safety/Security	Minimize risk situations
		Maximize security perception
2. Sensorial-cognitive quality	2.1 Wayfinding	Visual information (signs, colors, map, landmark)
		Perceptible information (tactile, sound)
	2.2 Understanding	Information easy to understand (symbols, language, color contrast)
		Communication (awareness, ICT)
	2.3 Environmental factors	Illumination (natural/artificial)
		Acoustics
		Thermal comfort
		Indoor air quality
3. Social quality	3.1 Well-being	Health promotion and Physical activity
		Hygienic conditions
		Aesthetic quality (colors, materials)
	3.2 Social Inclusion	Cultural appropriateness
		Social relation (integration and privacy)
		Inclusive design process

- Functionality: to satisfy the preferences of different users through flexibility and adaptation of space and furniture in terms of use and time (i.e. maintainability);
- Safety/Security: to guarantee safety and security of different users in both emergency and common situations, by minimizing risks without stigmatized solutions;
- Wayfinding: to orientate users with visual, tactile, and verbal information to help them determine their own position in a space;
- Understanding: to communicate information in an effective and simple way through different methods, regardless of the environmental conditions or the cognitive and sensory abilities of users;

- Environmental Factors: to evaluate the indoor comfort conditions of a building's environment by analyzing air quality, thermal comfort, acoustics, and lighting;
- Well-being: to transfer positive emotions to different users through healthy behaviours, physical activity and the design of the environment and its soft qualities, pleasantness, and esthetics;
- Social Inclusion: to foster active participation of different users during the design process, guarantee the same experience for all users, reinforce the cultural values of any design project, and treat all groups with dignity and respect.

Finally, the indicators of Table 2 come from both the analysis of the literature and the information gathered with the different cognitive maps of the workshops. Each indicator is evaluated by the presence or absence of specific requirements, as a checklist, by means of a binary scale. In this way, a score is assigned to each indicator in relation to the characteristics' presence.

4 Discussions

The present work proposes a UD performance-based evaluation framework aimed at assessing the quality of the built environment to improve its usability and social inclusion for a wider number of users. According to the MCDA, the framework is composed of 21 indicators and eight main criteria (i.e. usability, functionality, safety/security, wayfinding, understanding, comfort, well-being, social inclusion) divided into three categories: physical-spatial quality, sensory-cognitive quality, and social quality.

The study represents a first attempt to investigates the actual meaning of UD criteria that, as showed by the analysis, still overlap or lack of clear features needed to assess the built environment in terms of usability and inclusion. In this sense, the literature review explored existing studies and provided the basic UD criteria, while the workshops with the cognitive mapping technique enabled the gathering of evidence regarding stakeholders' objectives through a participative approach.

The proposed framework can be considered an innovative approach in the field of accessible design, since it takes into account social factors, in addition to physical, sensorial and cognitive aspects, which are basically considered in different evaluation tools of accessible design. The framework can be used in practice as a decision support system (DSS) at the beginning of the design process. For example, the framework can be adopted for focus group discussions with different stakeholders as a reference to determine if the proposed design solution takes into account the different objectives of a UD project in relation to physical, sensory/cognitive, and social quality.

Nevertheless, this research has limitations. For instance, the workshop used to identify objectives and enhance knowledge from the literature review are limited in number. The validation of the framework can be an opportunity to expand the discussion by engaging more experts or conducting a focus group with different stakeholders in one meeting.

Furthermore, the analysis was conducted at criteria level, considering the environment as a whole, but deeper considerations can emerge when examining specific buildings spaces. One possibility is to experiment the framework proposed focusing on the different building's areas considered in the evaluation (e.g. entrance, horizontal circulation, rooms, etc.). As such, a possible research line is the adoption of the evaluation framework to gather more information about each criterion by focusing on different space settings that characterize a typology of public building (e.g. schools, hospitals, workplaces, etc.).

5 Conclusions

The present study describes the development of a design evaluation framework, which can be considered a starting point when measuring UD building performance using a rating system. The system can help inform choices amid different alternatives and suggest interventions to increase buildings' usability and inclusion. Accordingly, a performance-based approach can prevent subjective evaluation and overcome prescriptive regulations, allowing the comparison of different building solutions.

In this regard, two main research lines can be followed: (1) developing a DSS to be used during the design process involving stakeholders to improve the usability and inclusion of new buildings and renovations and (2) developing a tool for POE to objectively define the priority of interventions in existing buildings. In both cases, the tool can produce new evidence-based design knowledge to suggest guidelines used from the beginning of the design process to support designers and avoiding extra time, extra costs, and disabling situations.

Acknowledgements. The authors of this paper want to show their great gratitude to all the participants to the workshops and people who supported the organization. In particular, the associations that made it possible to conduct this study are: Lega per i Diritti delle Persone con Disabilità (LEDHA) Milano, Unione Italiana Lotta alla Distrofia Muscolare (UILDM) Milano, Associazione Nazionale Subvedenti (ANS) Milano, Solidarietà in Rete (SIR), Associazione Italiana Sclerosi Multipla (AISM) Milano and Design for All Italia. The study is part of the doctoral research of E.M. at the Department of Architecture, Built environment and Construction engineering of Politecnico di Milano.

References

1. Mace, R.: Universal Design. Barrier-Free Environments for Everyone. Designers West, Los Angeles (1985)
2. Goldsmith, S.: Designing for the Disabled: The New Paradigm. Architectural Press, Oxford (1997)
3. Froyen, H., Verdonck, E., De Meester, D., Heylighen, A.: Mapping and documenting conflicts between Users and Built Environments. In: Proceedings of Include, Include 2009. Helen Hamlyn Centre, London (2009)
4. European Institute for Design and Disability (EIDD): Stockholm Declaration (2004). http://dfaeurope.eu/what-is-dfa/dfa-documents/the-eidd-stockholm-declaration-2004/
5. Watchorn, V., et al.: An integrated literature review of the current discourse around universal design in the built environment – is occupation the missing link? Disabil. Rehabili. **17**, 1–12 (2019)

6. Buti, L.B.: Ask the Right Question. A Rational Approach to Design for All in Italy. Springer, Cham (2019). https://doi.org/10.1007/978-3-319-96346-4
7. Steinfeld, E., Maisel, J.L.: Universal Design: Creating Inclusive Environments. Wiley, Hoboken (2012)
8. Capolongo, S.: Social aspects and well-being for improving healing processes' effectiveness. Ann Ist Super Sanità **52**(1), 11–14 (2016)
9. Ielegems, E., Herssens, J., Vanrie, J.: A V-model for more. An inclusive design model supporting interaction between designer and user. In: Proceedings of the 20th International Conference on Engineering Design, ICED, vol. 9 (DS 80-09), pp. 259–268 (2015)
10. Mosca, E.I., Herssens, J., Rebecchi, A., Capolongo, S.: Inspiring architects in the application of design for all: knowledge transfer methods and tools. J. Access. Des. All **9**(1), 1–24 (2019)
11. Buffoli, M., Bellini, E., Bellagarda, A., Di Noia, M., Nickolova, M., Capolongo, S.: Listening to people to cure people: the LpCp – tool, an instrument to evaluate hospital humanization. Ann Ig. **26**(5), 447–455 (2014). https://doi.org/10.7416/ai.2014.2004
12. Afacan, Y., Erbug, C.: An interdisciplinary heuristic evaluation method for universal building design. Appl. Ergon. **40**, 731–744 (2009)
13. Bottero, M.C., et al.: A multidisciplinary sustainability evaluation system for operative and in-design hospitals. In: Capolongo, S., Bottero, M.C., Buffoli, M., Lettieri, E. (eds.) Improving Sustainability During Hospital Design and Operation: A Multidisciplinary Evaluation Tool. GET, pp. 31–114. Springer, Cham (2015). https://doi.org/10.1007/978-3-319-14036-0_4
14. Preiser, W.F.E.: The evolution of post-occupancy evaluation: toward building performance and universal design evaluation. In: Preiser, W.F.E., Ostroff, E. (eds.) Learning from Our Buildings: A State-of-the-Practice Summary of Post-Occupancy Evaluation. The National Academies Press, Washington, DC (2001)
15. Brambilla, A., Rebecchi, A., Capolongo, S.: Evidence based hospital design. A literature review of the recent publications about the EBD impact of built environment on hospital occupants' and organizational outcomes. Ann. Ig **31**, 165–180 (2019)
16. Preiser, W.F.E.: Toward universal design performance assessments. In: Preiser, W.F.E. (ed.) Universal Design Handbook. Mcgraw-Hill, New York (2010)
17. USGBC (2009) LEED for new construction and major renovations. USGBC, Washington. https://www.usgbc.org/drupal/legacy/usgbc/docs/Archive/General/Docs1095.pdf
18. BRE Global Ltd. (2018) Breeam UK New Construction. Non-domestic Buildings (United Kingdom), BRE, Watford (2018). https://tools.breeam.com/filelibrary/Consultations/SD5078_DRAFTUK_nondom_NC_2018-manual.pdf
19. Mosca, E.I., Herssens, J., Rebecchi, A., Strickfaden, M., Capolongo, S.: Evaluating a proposed Design for All (DfA) manual for architecture. Adv. Intell. Syst. Comput. **776**, 54–64 (2019)
20. Department for Communities and Local Government (DCLG): Multicriteria Analysis: a manual London (2009). http://eprints.lse.ac.uk/12761/1/Multi-criteria_Analysis.pdf
21. Roy, B.: Multicriteria Methodology for Decision Aiding, vol. 12. Springer, Cham (2013)
22. Mosca, E.I., Capolongo, S.: Towards a universal design evaluation for assessing the performance of the built environment. In: Transforming our World Through Design, Diversity and Education, vol. 256, pp. 771–779 (2019)
23. Dente, B.: Understanding Policy Decisions. SAST, pp. 1–27. Springer, Cham (2014). https://doi.org/10.1007/978-3-319-02520-9_1
24. Eden, C.: Analyzing cognitive maps to help structure issues or problems. Eur. J. Oper. Res. **159**(3), 673–686 (2004)
25. Ferretti, V.: From stakeholders analysis to cognitive mapping and Multi Attribute Value Theory: an integrated approach for policy support. Eur. J. Oper. Res. **253**, 524–541 (2016)
26. Mendoza, G.A., Prabhu, R.: Evaluating multi-stakeholder perceptions of project impacts: a participatory value-based multi-criteria approach. Int. J. Sustain. Dev. World Ecol. **16**(3), 177–190 (2009)

27. Iwarsson, S.: The Housing Enabler: an objective tool for assessing accessibility. Br. J. Occup. Ther. **62**(11), 491–497 (1999)
28. Sanford, J.A.: Assessing universal design in physical environment. In: Mpofu, E.T.O. (ed.) Rehabilitation and Health Assessment: Applying ICF Guidelines. Springer, New York (2009)
29. Connell, B.R., et al.: The Principles of Universal Design, CUD. NC State University, Raleigh (1997)
30. Lawton, M.P.: Designing by degree: assessing and incorporating individual accessibility needs. In: Preiser, W.F.E., Ostroff, E. (eds.) Universal Design Handbook. McGraw-Hill, New York (2001)
31. Sanford, J.A.: Universal Design as a Rehabilitation Strategy: Design for the Age. Springer, Cham (2012)
32. ISO/ICE: GUIDE 71:14(E) Guide for addressing accessibility in standards (2014). https://www.iec.ch/webstore/freepubs/isoiecguide71%7Bed2.0%7Den.pdf

Urban Ecosystem Services: A Review of Definitions and Classifications for the Identification of Future Research Perspectives

Caterina Caprioli(✉), Marta Bottero, and Giulio Mondini

Interuniversity Department of Regional and Urban Stu
dies and Planning (DIST), Politecnico di Torino, Castello del Valentino: Viale Pier Andrea Mattioli, 39, 10125 Turin, TO, Italy

{caterina.caprioli,marta.bottero,giulio.mondini}@polito.it

Abstract. Thanks to many initiatives, such as the Millennium Ecosystem Assessment (MEA), The Economics of Ecosystems and Biodiversity (TEEB) and EU target for 2020 on Biodiversity, the topic of ecosystem services has received even more attention both in the academic and political debate. On the contrary, the research on urban ecosystems and urban ecosystem services has yet been relatively modest compared to other ecosystems, like wetlands or forests. However, the relevance of topic requires more efforts in this field also because, in most cases, urban ecosystem services have been studied individually, without considering their role in governance and planning processes. In this context, the present paper has the aim at giving a perspective of the state of the art of the research on urban ecosystem services with a focus on the different definitions and classifications emerging from the literature, as well as of examples of indicators for their valuation. The work highlights the gaps in the research to support the definition of future research perspectives and analysis, in particular for the adoption of valuation approaches able to guide the decision-making process in urban areas and for ensuring the consideration of urban ecosystem services in spatial planning policies and actions.

Keywords: Ecosystem services · Land-use planning · Decision-making · Evaluation methods · Resilient city

1 Introduction

Why should we talk about ecosystem services and urban ecosystem services in cities?

As it is well known, cities worldwide are responsible for more than 70% of energy-related emissions and United Nations predict that by 2050 over 70% of the world population will live in urban areas [1]. In particular, in the EU, almost three out of four citizens still live in cities and the number will further grow [2].

O. Gervasi et al. (Eds.): ICCSA 2020, LNCS 12253, pp. 332–344, 2020.
https://doi.org/10.1007/978-3-030-58814-4_23

All these people need an inclusive, healthy, resilient, safe and sustainable living environment [3–5]. As a consequence, demands on natural capital and ecosystems services is going to increase steadily in our urbanized planet [6–8].

However, the way of how to achieve these challenges is not completely clear. As pointed by Gómez-Baggethun and Burton [9], the research on urban ecosystem services still represents an open frontier in the wider context of ecosystem services researches, even if many studies have been conducted over the years on their role and importance. Just think that very recent researches have been funded by the EU – i.e. the Mapping and Assessment of Ecosystems and their Services (MAES) [3] and the EnRoute project [10] – which are pilot project mainly focused on the role of urban ecosystems and urban ecosystem services. These two contributions are closely related and in line with the EU target for 2020 on Biodiversity [11], which requires the restoration and maintenance of ecosystems and related services through an increase in knowledge of ecosystems, promoting the use of green infrastructure and reducing the loss of biodiversity and services.

As Gómez-Baggethun and Burton [9] pointed, cities, as any other social-ecological system, depend on ecosystems and their components to sustain long-term conditions for life [12], health [13, 14], security [15], good social relations [16] and other important aspects of human well-being [9, 17]. Cities depend on ecosystems beyond the limits of the city itself, but also benefit from urban ecosystems within the city [18].

In this context, the paper aims at developing a perspective of the state of the art of the research in the context of urban ecosystem services with a focus on the different definitions and classifications emerging from the literature. In this way, it is possible to start from the very baseline context in order to support the definition of future research perspectives and analysis, in particular for the adoption of valuation approaches able to guide the decision-making process in urban areas for ensuring the consideration of urban ecosystem services in spatial planning policies and actions.

2 Literature Review and First Insights

The approach used in this research was based on a review of main scientific publications on the topic of urban ecosystem services, including quantitative and qualitative content analyses. The review considers only scientific articles published in English from the Scopus database with the aim at highlighting the main trends of the research in this context, but in particular to give a more comprehensive view on the definitions of urban ecosystem services in literature for guiding future challenges of the research in this field. The analysis and collection of papers were performed between October 2019 and February 2020. The result is a number equal to 2,747 documents by limiting the search to title, abstract and keywords, using the string search (TITLE-ABS-KEY ("ecosystem services" AND (cities OR city OR "urban areas" OR "urban area")) AND (LIMIT-TO (LANGUAGE, "English"))). The string considers both the term urban areas and cities, even if the two have a different meaning, in particular in the context of ES valuation, as we discussed in detail in the next section. This is a precautionary choice to avoid losing documents related to the valuation of ecosystem services at the city scale which represent the point of view of this research more than at the territorial one.

As it is possible to see in Fig. 1, the research on urban ecosystem services started around 1995, but the first main relevant publication on this topic is in 1999 the work by Bolund and Hunhammar [18]. Then, we have to wait until 2005 for a number of publications per year greater than 10, and 2011 for an increase in the number of documents that overcomes a hundred. These two moments of breakthroughs in the literature production are not incidental, because they exactly correspond to the two major initiatives in the field of ecosystem services, which are the Millennium Ecosystem Assessment (MEA) [19] and The Economics of Ecosystems and Biodiversity (TEEB) [17]. These studies, within the research project URBES (Urban Biodiversity and Ecosystem Services) [20] developed from 2012 to 2015 and the CICES (Common International Classification of Ecosystem Services) [21] proposed in 2009, have led to an increasing interest in the academic and ever more attention in the political debate on ecosystem services, as shown by the Management Plan - Environment DG of 2012 [22].

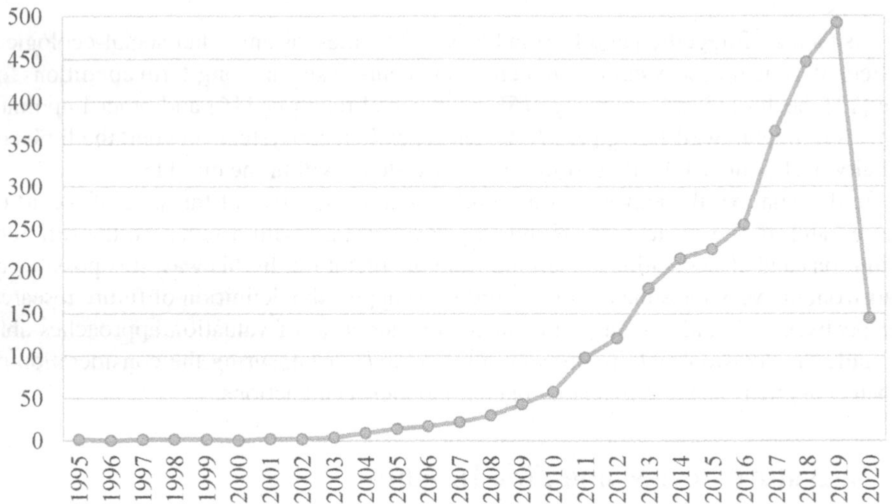

Fig. 1. Urban ecosystem services publications over the years (Scopus database)

From the literature review, it is possible to underline that the attention on ecosystem services in urban contexts is lower than the one at territorial scale, as also testified by the work of Assennato et al. [23]. Urban soils are very often perceived as a resource that can be freely managed to meet citizens' needs [24]. Moreover, compared to other ecosystems, like wetlands or forests, the focus on urban ecosystems has yet been relatively modest [9] and, in most cases, they have been studied individually. The same result is also evidence from the Luederitz et al. [25] peer-review, that shows how intensive is the literature on forests and wetlands (but also rivers and lakes) compared to street greenery, parks or green-roofs (see in particular [25] p. 105). The analysis of single ecosystem services is also demonstrated by the recent reviews on ecosystem services in urban areas, such as the work of Lundy and Wade [26] on water, the research of Wang et al. [27] on the indoor environment, the review of Salmond et al. [28] on ecosystems services and disservices provided by street trees or the research of Perrotti and Stremke [29] on the benefits provided by green infrastructure, in particular for a more energy-efficient and less carbon-intensive urban metabolism.

The analysis of single ecosystem services is combined, in the majority of cases, with the consideration only of the economic value dimension. Monetary values have been extensively examined in the literature, while the description or measurement of symbolic, cultural, identity and other non-economic values remains largely unexplored [9, 30–32].

An exception in this context is the extensive literature review developed by Luederitz et al. [25] which tries to bridge the gap analyzing the different perspectives to be considered in urban ecosystem services research. Due to the inherently complex and interdisciplinary nature of ecosystem services analysis [33], it is necessary to cover the wide range of perspectives from which such research can be conceptualized and undertaken. The challenges concern the achievement not only of ecological modelling and economic assessment but also issues such as governance, planning and stakeholder involvement [25].

A change of course is, therefore, necessary for this field. If the ecological studies have covered most of the attention in the literature, the governance aspects represent the less considered, as it emerges from Luederitz review [25]. This is tremendously problematic since without proper institutional and organizational structures or policy instruments is quite difficult to achieve the performances required, to control decision-making process in planning and to manage the course of actions of transformations in urban contexts.

3 Classifications and Definitions Emerging from the Literature

Starting from the wider considerations emerging from the previous analysis of the literature, this section has the aim to highlight the different classifications and definitions on the topic of urban ecosystem services. The literature review shows two main different classifications provided by Bolund and Hunhammar in 1999 [18] and Baggethun et al. [9], instead an in-depth analysis on research groups and European projects on urban ecosystem services adds to the previous classifications, other two interesting ones (SUITMAs group and, MAES and EnRoute projects). These four are presented and extensively analyzed in this paper.

However, to better clarify what we mean when talking about urban ecosystem services, it is necessary to take a step back illustrating the single meanings of "urban" "ecosystem" and "ecosystem services". Starting from "ecosystem", it can be defined as "a set of interacting species and their local, non-biological environment functioning together to sustain life" [34]. For the "urban" environment, it is possible to define the city as a single ecosystem or a set of different individual ecosystems which compose it, such as green areas or rivers [18, 35]. "Ecosystem services" are, then, defined by De Groot et al. [36] and the Millennium Ecosystem Assessment (MEA) [19] as benefits that humans obtain from ecosystem functions, whereas Costanza [37] and The Economics of Ecosystems and Biodiversity (TEEB) [17] as direct and indirect contributions from ecosystems to human well-being. Or even, following Daily et al. [33] "ecosystem services" are the conditions and processes through which the natural ecosystems - and the species that compose such systems - support and satisfy human life allowing the conceptualization and management of the relationship and interactions between men and environment in the wider context of sustainability. All these definitions highlight the relevant degree of interdependence between humans and the rest of nature [38].

The meaning of "urban ecosystem services" is strongly based on the previous definitions by simply restricting the area of interest. In fact, if ecosystems - both inside and outside urban areas - are often modified to provide specific ecosystem services to inhabitants [39], "urban ecosystem services" are those services that are directly produced by ecological structures within urban areas or peri-urban regions.

If there is essentially a shared vision on the definitions of all these terms and concepts, the analysis of the literature shows a less clear perspective in term of classifications of urban ecosystem services. This could be explained for different reasons. Firstly, the researches have started, of course, from different moments of history in the analysis of ecosystem services. As an example, the first paper of Bolund and Huhammar [18] is strongly based on the work of Costanza [37], instead, the work of Gómez-Baggethun and Burton [9] was based on the classifications emerging from MEA [19] and TEEB [17] (and the work of Dobbs et al. [40]). Secondly, and probably more important, it is the fact that the limit between urban and non-urban, and so, between ecosystem services and urban ecosystem services, is often blurred and not easily delineated. As a consequence, it is not that surprising that different perspectives exist and the two definitions (ecosystem services and urban ecosystem services) increasingly tend to converge.

Figure 2 illustrates schematically the literature considered in this paper for understanding the different classifications of urban ecosystem services, with also the connection with the previous works from which they are derived. The authors themselves specify in their contributions the previous references used for conducting their research on urban ecosystem services.

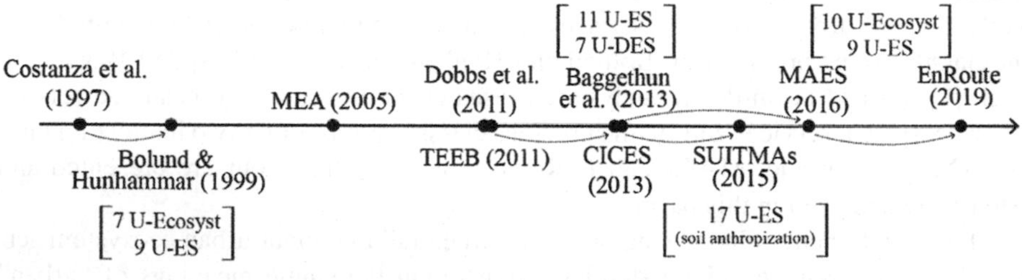

Fig. 2. Timeline framework of urban ecosystem services classification

First Classification. The first classification on urban ecosystem services was performed by Bolund and Hunhammar in 1999 [18]. As mentioned before, this paper represents one of the first attempts and without no doubt the first most relevant contribution on this topic. For the identification of the ecosystem services related to the urban context, the authors started from the 17 ecosystem services defined by Costanza et al. [37]. In particular, Bolund and Hunhammar [18] identified 7 urban ecosystems (trees, lawns/parks, urban forests, cultivated land, wetlands, lakes/sea, and streams) and 9 related urban ecosystem services (air filtering, micro-climate regulation, noise reduction, rainwater drainage, sewage treatment, recreational and cultural values, food production and erosion control).

Second Classification. Gómez-Baggethun and Barton [9] proposed an alternative classification. Starting from the previous categorizations of ecosystem services [19, 33, 36] and in particular from the 22 ecosystem services defined by TEEB (2010) [17], the authors used the same four categories (provisioning, regulating, habitat, and cultural and amenity services), identifying 11 ecosystem services and 7 examples of disservices for the urban context. In particular, these services are especially important in the urban context, as they provide a direct impact on health and security. The services considered are:

- for provisioning: food supply
- for regulating: water flow regulation and runoff mitigation, urban temperature regulation, noise reduction, air purification, moderation of environmental extremes, waste treatment, climate regulation, pollination and seed dispersal
- for cultural: recreation and cognitive development
- for supporting: animal sighting (habitat for biodiversity).

Instead, the examples of disservices reported are air quality problems, view blockage, allergies, accidents, fear and stress, damages on infrastructure, habitat competition with humans.

Apart from the different number of urban ecosystem services considered, the two works differ in the final objective of the research. The first classification comes from a more site-specific analysis, where Stockholm is taken as an exemplary case study for analyzing this topic. In fact, Bolund and Hunhammar [18] clearly underline how some services (in particular food production and erosion control) should not be considered for the specific area under analysis. This local perspective could have, in some way, limited the selection of different services. On the contrary, the second work has the aim to provide a more global perspective on this theme, considering both European and non-European case studies and literature references for identifying a list as comprehensive as possible.

Third Classification. More in line with the second classification, it is the work of SUITMAs (Soil of urban, industrial, traffic, mining and military areas), a research group founded in 1998 to promote soil science in heavily populated areas [24]. In this case, the focus is more on the assessment of the ecosystem services in urban contexts than on the identification of a list of services. However, it is interesting to notice that compared to the previous classification, this one considers a greater number of services, 16 against 11 of Bolund & Hunhammar [18], following the CICES classification [21]:

- for provisioning: food production, non-food biomass, reservoir of minerals, freshwater supply;
- for regulating: water storage, runoff and flood control, pollution attenuation, global climate, local climate, biodiversity, invasive species, air purification, noise control;
- for cultural: recreation/tourism, archives of human history, landscape, education.

The relevant aspect of this classification, however, is related to how the urban ecosystem services are evaluated. The evaluation is based on the level of the anthropization of the soils. More details on this aspect are given in the next chapter of the paper.

Fourth Classification. The last (and more recent) classification considered in this paper is the one from the EU project MAES (Mapping and Assessment of Ecosystems and their Services Urban ecosystems) [3] and EnRoute project (Enhancing Resilience of Urban Ecosystems through Green Infrastructure) [10]. The first one is mainly focused on the identification of the list of urban ecosystem services, through different methodological steps:

1. a preliminary list of ecosystem services emerging from the analysis of the literature and an online questionnaire with different stakeholders on the measurement and policies related to urban ecosystem services;
2. an additional contribution of researchers and stakeholders on real examples mapping and assessment of ecosystem services based on some European cities;
3. interactive discussions on the content of step 1 and 2;
4. synthesis and reporting phase.

The final result of these steps is a set of indicators for measuring the following urban ecosystem services:

- for provisioning: food supply, water production
- for regulating: air purification, climate change regulation (reduction of CO2), temperature regulation, noise mitigation, water flow regulation and runoff mitigation, insect pollination
- for cultural: recreation, education

The second project, the EnRoute project [10], started from the work of MAES [3], intending to test the applicability of the framework of indicators identified in the previous research. In particular, the work consisted in testing, in different EU cities, the role of six policies for spreading and maintaining urban ecosystem services, with a particular focus on mapping and evaluating urban green infrastructures and related actions.

It is important to notice that interesting reflections have been emerged from the EnRoute project [10], in particular for what concerns the definition of a proper scale for studying urban ecosystem services. In fact, as mentioned before, one of the main criticalities and difficulties when referring to urban ecosystem services is setting the boundaries for evaluating the benefits and impacts of such services, as well as also the boundaries of what is urban and what is not. The project underlined for each indicator the proper scale of measurement, distinguishing between core city and functional urban area. This second scale is specifically defined during the EnRoute project [10], as a specific operational spatial extension able to takes into account the city and its surroundings, in a view of the interdependence of cities and external landscape, constituting an urban ecosystem in itself.

4 Discussion

The previous paragraph has shown the different classifications emerging from the analysis of the literature. This section, instead, has the aim of providing a guide for the evaluation of the different urban ecosystem services resulting from the previous investigations. Moreover, starting from this list, it is possible to give some suggestions for future perspectives and key challenges for the research.

Table 1 reports the list of urban ecosystem services provided by the authors of the paper considered. For each class, it is reported the main reference from which these services derived, and the indication of the urban ecosystem considered in the classification of each author. This table gives a preliminary framework for valuating in a comprehensive way urban ecosystem services also by connecting them to the more general ecosystem services framework at the territorial scale provided over the time by Costanza et al. 1997, TEEB [17] and CICES [21].

The analysis of the literature shows a quite homogeneous way to evaluate such urban ecosystem services, strongly focused on the measurement of ecological and biophysical values of those services. A different approach is found in the third classification where the quantification of the urban ecosystem services is based on the potential of each soil category, which can be arranged according to a gradient of anthropization and the capability to support vegetation [24]. The categorization is based on 4 different groups ranging from soils with little changes compared to the corresponding natural soils - i.e., the pseudo-natural SUITMAs, often covered by urban forest or urban and suburban agriculture, to extremely modified soils usually not considered as soils by many scientists - i.e. sealed soils by SUITMAs - [24]. Intermediate categorizations are dumping site SUITMAs - sporadically re-vegetated - and engineered SUITMAs - deliberately vegetated - [24]. However, also in this case, the ecological and biophysical perspective is dominant.

Another difference emerging from this research comparison, it is the attempt of the EnRoute project in implementing and testing different actions and policies in specific cities in order to verify their effect and suitability. Even if such measures are limited to the enhancement of green infrastructure, it is a step forward for increasing the awareness of the importance of this topic in the governance of cities.

In fact, the connections between ecosystem processes and functions and human well-being are complex and the valuation of benefits and impacts of ecosystem services require to adopt a pluralistic approach [38]. Different values of ecosystem services may be captured and measured to inform urban and transformation planning [9]: ecological and biophysical elements, economic and insurance values, social and cultural aspects [17, 41]. However, if biophysical and economic values are widely experimented and studied in the literature (as also showed in Table 1), more efforts are needed for measuring socio-cultural values. This happens because emotional and symbolic values are cannot be adequately captured by common metaphors or monetary metrics [42, 43], making the assessment more complicated. It is for that reason, as underlined by Saarikoski et al. [44], that recent trends of the literature highlight the necessity to adopt alternative approaches for evaluating ecosystem services, such as multicriteria analysis (MCDA). MCDA, in general, perform better than monetary valuation in many aspects, such as the consideration of multiple dimensions – spanning from ecological to economic values from cultural

Table 1. Comparative table of the urban ecosystem services taxonomy considered in the literature

I		II		III		IV
Ecosystem Services	**Urban Ecosystem Services**	**Ecosystem Services**	**Urban Ecosystem Services**	**Ecosystem Services**	**Urban Ecosystem Services**	**Urban Ecosystem Services**
Costanza et al. 1997	**Bolund & Hunhammar 1999**	**TEEB (2011)**	**Gómez - Baggethun & Barton 2013**	**CICES (2013)**	**SUITMAs (2015)**	**MAES (2016), EnRoute (2019)**
Food production	x	Food	x	Biomass: - Nutrition - Materials from plants, algae, animals for agriculture	x	x
Raw materials		Raw materials		Biomass (fibres and other materials for direct use and processing)	x	
Water regulation	x	Water	x	Water: Materials (non-drinking)	x	x
Water supply				Water - nutrition (drinking)	x	x
-		Medical resources		Biomass (fibres and other materials for direct use and processing)		
-				Biomass (genetic materials from all biota)		
-				Biomass: - fibres and other materials from for direct use and processing - energy sources Mechanical energy (animal based)		
Climate regulation	x	Local climate and air quality	x x	Atmospheric composition and climate regulation	x x	x
Gas regulation	x	Carbon sequestration and storage	x	Mediation of gaseous/air flows	x x	x x
-	x		x	-	x	x
Disturbance regulation		Moderation of extreme events	x	-		
Waste treatment	x	Waste-water treatment	x	Mediation: - waste, toxics and other nuisances by biota - waste, toxics and other nuisances by ecosystems		
Nutrient cycling						
Erosion control & sediment retention	x	Erosion prevention and maintenance of soil fertility		Mediation of mass flows	x	x
Soil formation				Soil formation and composition		
Pollination		Pollination	x	Lifecycle maintenance, habitat and gene pool protection		x
Biological control		Biological control		Pest and disease control	x	
Refugia		Habitat for species	x			
Genetic resources		Maintenance of genetic diversity		Lifecycle maintenance, habitat and gene pool protection	x	
Recreation	x	Recreation and mental and physical health	x	Physical and experiential interactions	x	x
-		Tourism			x	
Cultural	x	Aesthetic appreciation and inspiration for culture, art & design		- Intellectual and representational interactions - Other cultural outputs (existence, bequest)	x	x
-		Spiritual experience and sense of place		Spiritual and/or emblematic	x	

Disservices
- air quality problems
- view blockage
- allergies
- accidents
- fear and stress
- damages on infrastructure
- habitat competition with humans

to moral aspects of a policy or management problem, and the creation of an open and transparent public debate on the pros and cons of alternative courses of action, including the distribution of gains and losses across beneficiaries of ecosystem services [44].

The importance of integrating multiple perspectives in research on urban ecosystem services is fundamental in order to improve decisions on the protection and enhancement of the environment, to monitor the impacts of interventions on human well-being, to support urban planning and design, and the determination of policies [44]. Moreover, the consideration of multiple values into decision-making processes still represent an underexplored field of research and, therefore, a very challenging perspective for assessing more comprehensively the analysis of urban ecosystem services [45].

5 Conclusion

Urban ecosystems and urban ecosystem services are becoming a fundamental topic of research, since the demand of natural capital is going to increase steadily in our urbanized planet. People who live in urban areas need an even more health, sustainable and environmental recreative living space. Moreover, ecosystem services could be used as a tool and opportunity that cities have to bringing positive changes, such as saving municipal costs, strengthening local (green) economies, improving the quality of life and ensuring livelihoods [17].

The present analysis has shown some common aspects and limits of the current literature on urban ecosystem services. As a consequence, we want to highlight the following recommendations for further research on this topic:

1. It is necessary a unique and shared classification of the ecosystem services provided by urban areas. Probably, the attempt to reduce the list of ecosystem services to be as general as possible is not the right way, but a more comprehensive lists of services and disservices could be used by cities as a checklist for describing their specific characteristics. In this way, both smaller and bigger cities can refer to the same framework, but they can tailor it to their specificities. Moreover, it is necessary to pay more attention on the scale of the intervention and the scale of the effects when urban ecosystem services are valuating.
2. A more holistic view of the research on urban ecosystem services is required, in order to consider all the interrelations between ecosystems in urban areas. This perspective can support public administrations and decision-makers in the definition of shared and complete actions in achieving higher level of ecosystem services performance.
3. A multi-aspects consideration of benefits and impacts of (urban) ecosystem services should be implemented in the research. The analysis of only biophysical and ecological aspects or the translation of benefits in monetary values is limited. There is a need to integrate in the valuation also socio-cultural aspects, through the adoption of non-monetary approaches and the co-participation of different stakeholders in the measurement of benefits of these services.
4. Public bodies and local administrators should identify a plan of actions for increasing the level of (urban) ecosystem services providing and avoiding the loss of these services through compensation measure to be implemented inside or outside the

area under transformation. This is possible only through the adoption of multi-methodological evaluation approaches able to give a rigorous description of the state-of-art and of the future implementations.

Overall, the key challenges of the future research on ecosystem services concern the interdisciplinarity, multi-dimensionality, multi-spatiality and temporality of the problem and the role that these services have and will have in the future of our cities [45]. In this context, only through the adoption of different evaluation tools and methodologies, in particular in their combination, can give the necessary 'value pluralism' perspective [9] in the study of (urban) ecosystem services, thus supporting the decision-making process in the definition of urban and territorial transformations. More insights on this theme are given in Caprioli et al. [45] and future perspectives of this research will explore the combination of ecological and economic measurement with cultural and moral aspects of a policy or management problem using the urban ecosystem services taxonomy proposed in this paper. If the consideration of ecological and economic aspects is widely explored in last years, more efforts are needed in the valuation of social and cultural aspects of (urban) ecosystem services. Multicriteria Analysis (MCDA) can represent an interesting approach for analyzing more intangible components of (urban) ecosystem service valuation, as also testified by the recent trends of the literature [44].

References

1. United Nations: World Urbanization Prospects: The 2018 Revision (2019). https://doi.org/10.18356/b9e995fe-en
2. EuroStat: Urban Europe. Statistics on Cities, Towns and Suburbs. Stat. books Eur. Union (2016). https://doi.org/10.2785/91120
3. European Union: Mapping Ecosystem Services. Publications Office of the European Union, Luxembourg (2016)
4. Assumma, V., Bottero, M., Monaco, R.: Landscape economic attractiveness: an integrated methodology for exploring the rural landscapes in piedmont (Italy). Land **8**(7), 105 (2019). https://doi.org/10.3390/land8070105
5. Bottero, M., Datola, G., De Angelis, E.: A system dynamics model and analytic network process: an integrated approach to investigate urban resilience. Land **98**, 242 (2020). https://doi.org/10.3390/land9080242
6. Ayres, R.U., van den Bergh, J.C.J.M.: A theory of economic growth with material/energy resources and dematerialization: Interaction of three growth mechanisms. Ecol. Econ. **55**(1), 96–118 (2005). https://doi.org/10.1016/j.ecolecon.2004.07.023
7. Guo, Z., Zhang, L., Li, Y.: Increased dependence of humans on ecosystem services and biodiversity. PLoS One **5**, e13113 (2010). https://doi.org/10.1371/journal.pone.0013113
8. Krausmann, F., Gingrich, S., Eisenmenger, N., Erb, K.-H., Haberl, H., Fischer-Kowalski, M.: Growth in global materials use, GDP and population during the 20th century. Ecol. Econ. **68**(10), 2696–2705 (2009). https://doi.org/10.1016/j.ecolecon.2009.05.007
9. Gómez-Baggethun, E., Barton, D.N.: Classifying and valuing ecosystem services for urban planning. Ecol. Econ. **86**, 235–245 (2013). https://doi.org/10.1016/j.ecolecon.2012.08.019
10. Maes, J., Zulian, G., Günther, S., Thijssen, M., Raynal, J.: Enhancing Resilience Of Urban Ecosystems through Green Infrastructure. Final Report, Luxembourg (2019). https://doi.org/10.2760/602928

11. Biodiversity Strategy. https://ec.europa.eu/environment/nature/biodiversity/strategy/index_en.htm. Accessed 18 Jan 2020
12. Odum, E.P.: Fundamentos de Ecologia (2007)
13. Maas, J.: Green space, urbanity, and health: how strong is the relation? J. Epidemiol. Commun. Health **60**(7), 587–592 (2006). https://doi.org/10.1136/jech.2005.043125
14. Tzoulas, K., et al.: Promoting ecosystem and human health in urban areas using Green Infrastructure: a literature review. Landsc. Urban Plan. **81**(3), 167–178 (2007). https://doi.org/10.1016/j.landurbplan.2007.02.001
15. Costanza, R., Mitsch, W.J., Day, J.W.: A new vision for New Orleans and the Mississippi delta: applying ecological economics and ecological engineering. Front. Ecol. Environ. **4**(9), 465–472 (2006). https://doi.org/10.1890/1540-9295(2006)4[465:ANVFNO]2.0.CO;2
16. European Environment Agency: Green infrastructure and territorial cohesion (2011). https://doi.org/10.2800/88266
17. TEEB (The Economics of Ecosystems & Biodiversity): Mainstreaming the economics of nature?: A synsthesis of the approach, conclusions and recommendations of TEEB (2010)
18. Bolund, P., Hunhammar, S.: Ecosystem services in urban areas. Ecol. Econ. **29**(2), 293–301 (1999). https://doi.org/10.1016/S0921-8009(99)00013-0
19. Millennium Ecosystem Assessment: Living Beyond Our Means: Natural Assets and Human Well-being Statement from the Board (2005). https://doi.org/10.2111/RANGELANDS-D-13-00013.1
20. Elmqvist, T.: The URBES Project. Factsheet 1 (2015)
21. Haines-Young, R., Potschin, M.: Common International Classification of Ecosystem Services (CICES): Consultation on Version 4, August-December 2012 (2013)
22. European Commission: Management Plan - Environment DG (2012)
23. Assennato, F., et al.: Azione B1 - I servizi ecosistemici del suolo - Review (2015)
24. Morel, J.L., Chenu, C., Lorenz, K.: Ecosystem services provided by soils of urban, industrial, traffic, mining, and military areas (SUITMAs). J. Soils Sediments **15**(8), 1659–1666 (2015). https://doi.org/10.1007/s11368-014-0926-0
25. Luederitz, C., et al.: A review of urban ecosystem services: six key challenges for future research. Ecosyst. Serv. **14**, 98–112 (2015). https://doi.org/10.1016/j.ecoser.2015.05.001
26. Lundy, L., Wade, R.: Integrating sciences to sustain urban ecosystem services. Prog. Phys. Geogr. Earth Environ. **35**(5), 653–669 (2011). https://doi.org/10.1177/0309133311422464
27. Wang, Y., Bakker, F., de Groot, R., Wörtche, H.: Effect of ecosystem services provided by urban green infrastructure on indoor environment: a literature review. Build. Environ. **77**, 88–100 (2014). https://doi.org/10.1016/j.buildenv.2014.03.021
28. Salmond, J.A., et al.: Health and climate related ecosystem services provided by street trees in the urban environment. Environ. Health **15**(S1), S36 (2016). https://doi.org/10.1186/s12940-016-0103-6
29. Perrotti, D., Stremke, S.: Can urban metabolism models advance green infrastructure planning? Insights from ecosystem services research. Environ. Plan. B Urban Anal. City Sci. **47**(4), 678–694 (2020). https://doi.org/10.1177/2399808318797131
30. Chan, K.M.A., et al.: Where are cultural and social in ecosystem services? A framework for constructive engagement. BioScience **62**(8), 744–756 (2012). https://doi.org/10.1525/bio.2012.62.8.7
31. Lautenbach, S., Kugel, C., Lausch, A., Seppelt, R.: Analysis of historic changes in regional ecosystem service provisioning using land use data. Ecol. Indic. **11**(2), 676–687 (2011). https://doi.org/10.1016/j.ecolind.2010.09.007
32. Larondelle, N., Haase, D.: Urban ecosystem services assessment along a rural-urban gradient: a cross-analysis of European cities. Ecol. Indic. **29**, 179–190 (2013). https://doi.org/10.1016/j.ecolind.2012.12.022

33. Daily, G.C., et al.: Ecosystem services in decision making: time to deliver. Front. Ecol. Environ. **7**(1), 21–28 (2009). https://doi.org/10.1890/080025
34. Moll, G., Petit, J.: The urban ecosystem: putting nature back in the picture. Urban For. **14**, 8–15 (1994)
35. Rebele, F.: Urban ecology and special features of urban ecosystems. Glob. Ecol. Biogeogr. Lett. **4**(6), 173–187 (1994). https://doi.org/10.2307/2997649
36. De Groot, R.S., Wilson, M.A., Boumans, R.M.J.: A typology for the classification, description and valuation of ecosystem functions, goods and services. Ecol. Econ. **41**(3), 393–408 (2002). https://doi.org/10.1016/S0921-8009(02)00089-7
37. Costanza, R., et al.: The value of the world's ecosystem services and natural capital. Nature. **387**(6630), 253–260 (1997)
38. Costanza, R., et al.: Twenty years of ecosystem services: how far have we come and how far do we still need to go? Ecosyst. Serv. **28**, 1–16 (2017). https://doi.org/10.1016/j.ecoser.2017.09.008
39. Gutman, P.: Ecosystem services: foundations for a new rural-urban compact. Ecol. Econ. **62**(3–4), 383–387 (2007). https://doi.org/10.1016/j.ecolecon.2007.02.027
40. Dobbs, C., Escobedo, F.J., Zipperer, W.C.: A framework for developing urban forest ecosystem services and goods indicators. Landsc. Urban Plan. **99**(3–4), 196–206 (2011). https://doi.org/10.1016/j.landurbplan.2010.11.004
41. Bottero, M., Dell'Anna, F., Nappo, M.: Evaluating tangible and intangible aspects of cultural heritage: an application of the PROMETHEE method for the reuse project of the Ceva–Ormea Railway. In: Mondini, G., Fattinnanzi, E., Oppio, A., Bottero, M., Stanghellini, S. (eds.) SIEV 2016. Green Energy and Technology. GET, pp. 285–295. Springer, Cham (2018). https://doi.org/10.1007/978-3-319-78271-3_23
42. Martinez-Alier, J., Munda, G., O'Neill, J.: Weak comparability of values as a foundation for ecological economics. Ecol. Econ. **26**(3), 277–286 (1998). https://doi.org/10.1016/S0921-8009(97)00120-1
43. Norton, B.G., Hannon, B.: Environmental values. Environ. Ethics **19**(3), 227–245 (1997). https://doi.org/10.5840/enviroethics199719313
44. Saarikoski, H., et al.: Multi-criteria decision analysis and cost-benefit analysis: comparing alternative frameworks for integrated valuation of ecosystem services. Ecosyst. Serv. **22**, 238–249 (2016). https://doi.org/10.1016/j.ecoser.2016.10.014
45. Caprioli, C., Bottero, M., Zanetta, E., Mondini, G.: Ecosystem services in land-use planning: an application for assessing transformation scenarios at the local scale. In: Bevilacqua, C., Calabrò, F., Della Spina, L. (eds.) New Metropolitan Perspectives. NMP 2020. Smart Innovation, Systems and Technologies, vol. 178, pp. 1332–1341. Springer, Cham (2021). https://doi.org/10.1007/978-3-030-48279-4_124

Complex Projects Assessment. The Impact of Built Environment on Healthcare Staff Wellbeing

Andrea Brambilla[1], Alessandro Morganti[1(✉)], Göran Lindahl[2], Andrea Riva[3], and Stefano Capolongo[1]

[1] Department ABC Architecture Built Environment Construction Engineering, Design & Health Lab, Politecnico di Milano, via Ponzio 31, 20133 Milan, Italy
alessandro.morganti@polimi.it

[2] Department of Architecture and Civil Engineering, Centre for Healthcare Architecture, Chalmers University of Technology, Göteborg, Sweden

[3] School of Architecture Urban Planning Construction Engineering, Politecnico di Milano, Milan, Italy

Abstract. Projects, plans and programmes for complex environments such as healthcare facilities need to be designed with specific consideration of the multitude of users, technologies and policies in order to address a sustainable and resilient development. Several Evidence Based Design (EBD) studies highlight the deep interrelation between built and natural systems with human or organizations-related outcomes, but the effect on healthcare staff such as Medical Doctors (MD) is still underexplored. The paper investigates the assessment of self-reported satisfaction and wellbeing of MDs in healthcare facilities. A multidimensional assessment model composed of 53 Likert scale questions has been developed from literature review and existing tools, and submitted to a statistically significant sample of workers in 2 different office settings of an Italian hospital. Since MDs spend a considerable amount of their working time in offices, the qualities of such space are very important. The study highlights and confirms that localization, indoor environment, natural and artificial light are relevant drivers for staff satisfaction and wellbeing. Further investigations on a wider and diverse sample are encouraged.

Keywords: Evaluation survey · Hospital staff · User satisfaction

1 Background

1.1 Complex Environments and Unexplored Areas of Research

Projects, plans, and programs for complex environments such as healthcare facilities need to be designed with specific consideration of the multitude of users, technologies and policies in order to address sustainable and resilient development. In complex building types, such as hospitals, there is the demand for overall quality and several

O. Gervasi et al. (Eds.): ICCSA 2020, LNCS 12253, pp. 345–354, 2020.
https://doi.org/10.1007/978-3-030-58814-4_24

theories, tools and methodologies have been developed to assess the qualities of the physical environment [1–4]. Since 1980 s scholars and researchers conducted multiple studies in order to demonstrate how the built environment has a significant effect on the final users, including and with a specific focus on patients and their families, clinicians, nurses and the entire medical staff. Environmental psychology theories and Evidence Based Design (EBD) have focused on explaining the influence of natural and built environment on human health [5, 6]. Recent literature in the field from environmental psychology, architecture and public health, highlights that environmental conditions i.e. acoustics, temperature, safety and security and layout issues are never neutral, yet they have an either positive or negative impact on occupant's outcome and performances [6–9]. This relationship is considered as fundamental for the concept of "usability", that consider buildings as support medium of their occupant activities [10]. Literature reviews show adequately which are the gaps and open points that should be investigated to evaluate in a more accurate way healthcare qualities, highlighting the deep interrelation between built and natural systems with human and organizational outcomes [11]. To the best of our knowledge the effect of the built environment on healthcare staff such as Medical Doctors (MD) is still an underexplored field of study, since many researches just focus on patients [12]. Nevertheless, in the medical field, several researches highlight how clinical work is actually very stressful for the medical staff, and how this can lead to bad health conditions. There is also evidence that clinicians who suffer from work-related stress are more prone to relational problems, anxiety, burnout, substance abuse, to develop depression syndrome and assume antidepressant drugs, or even get to suicide [13]. In literature it is also showed how burnout and depressive syndrome have an indirect bad influence on healthcare systems and on patient's care [14, 15]. All these effects can have consequences on patients, such as higher wrong diagnosis rates, wrong drug prescriptions and many other medical errors, that can then pass on the satisfaction and the wellbeing both of patients, about their care path, both of clinicians about the overall clinical results they obtained. MDs are indeed considered as a fundamental part of the hospital workforce and therefore their workplace should be adequately designed in order to improve satisfaction, productivity and so a consequent benefit for patients. Two principal typologies of support spaces are identified for the MD such as the examination room, where the medical doctor evaluates the patients, and the medical office, meant as the administrative work station, on which this study is focused [16]. The activities carried out in the medical office can concern the clinical report update, the setting of the therapeutic plan or the radiology exams request for the patient, and where clinicians usually meet patients and their parents to discuss the therapeutic plan. It is reasonable to conclude that these offices can be considered the physician workplace [17]. Nevertheless, when focusing on MD workplaces in healthcare facilities and the impact on their wellbeing and health outcomes, emerges an uncovered research area [12]. As different studies, reviews and workplace regulations show, the use of a comfortable and customizable work environment can contribute to maximize productivity, reduce fatigue and discomfort, limiting the risk of occupational illnesses. In healthcare settings this means an increased security level of services provided to the patient, directly and indirectly influencing the healthcare system's performances. At the same time, the workplace physical environment can provide many stressing factors, such as annoying lighting, undue noises, inappropriate equipment location or space overcrowding. The scientific literature on workplaces largely shows the benefits that specific layouts and physical features have on workers' wellbeing [18, 19], laying the foundations of systematic evaluation tools adopted by quality certifications for these specific spaces. This knowledge is rarely transferred to healthcare workplaces, despite the deep impact it could have on both medical staff and patients. Starting from these bases, the gap is calling for qualitative and quantitative studies that investigate the impact of the hospital environment as enhancer or reducer of MDs performances and wellbeing, and this research proposes a comprehensive methodology to tackle it.

1.2 Aim of the Study

The aim of this study is to assess and compare two different medical office settings from the same hospital, evaluate the perceived wellbeing and relate impacts that these environments have on MDs that regularly use them. This study identifies specific features to care about when designing, refurbishing or operating medical office spaces within the overall hospital facility management. These selected features could be also proposed as criteria for a systematic evaluation of healthcare workplaces, that is now lacking.

2 Methodology

The research methodology has been structured into three phases: survey development, empirical phase and data analysis as shown in Fig. 1.

2.1 Survey Development

Starting from some existing and validated assessment tools, commonly used in organizational and architectural fields, and the available literature on the topic, an assessment survey has been developed. Six evaluation tools from excellence certifications that are considered the gold standards for qualitative analysis have been selected: three from the environmental field (Leed, Breeam, Casbee) and three from the managerial field (JCI, CQC, ACSQHC). In parallel, it has been conducted a literature review about the quality evaluation of hospital spaces, sorting all the publications in the macro-areas described by Ulrich et al. in 2008. Among these few articles, only the ones that focus on medical offices were selected and analyzed. From the critical integration between elements considered in the literature and the ones considered in the tools analyzed, this research proposes an assessment model for the evaluation of medical staff support areas in hospitals. The tool is structured as a questionnaire and is described in the following paragraphs.

Assessment Model Structure

A specific survey has been elaborated in order to evaluate the qualities of medical offices. The anonymous survey has been submitted to the selected sample, both as paper and as digital version. The questionnaire is composed by 53 items: 45 items are issued as multiple-choice questions, 8 items are issued as open-ended questions. The questions are structured in order to explore the impact of eight built environment variables on four psychological and physical wellbeing outcomes domains (Table 1).

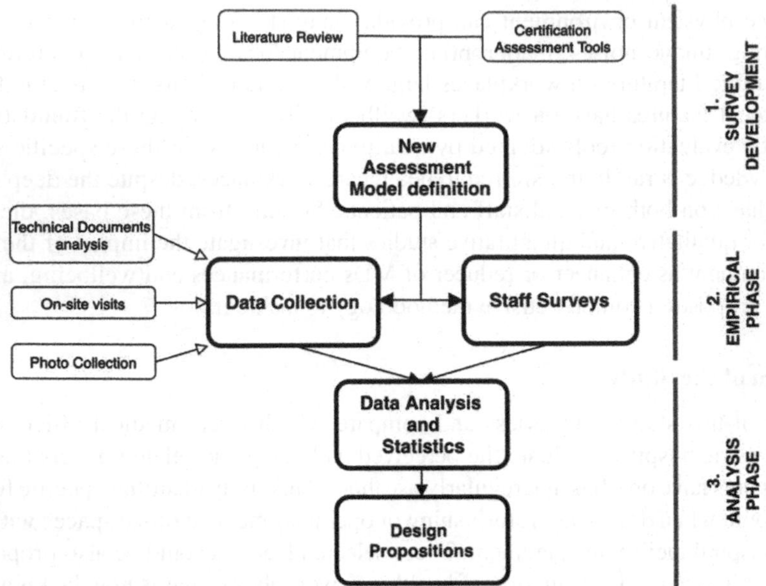

Fig. 1. Flow chart of the methodological process followed

Table 1. Assessment framework of environmental features and MD wellbeing domains

Environmental features	Wellbeing domains
1. Localization	a. Overall satisfaction
2. Indoor environment	b. Work performances
3. Natural light	c. Daily fatigue
4. Artificial light	d. Stress
5. Temperature	
6. Humidity	
7. Acoustics	
8. Ventilation	

The questions are structured as a Likert scale model: each item is a question to whom the user can answer stating their agreement/disagreement degree. The interviewer can choose a value from 1 to 5, declaring how much he/she agrees that the built environment feature has an impact on his/her wellbeing domain. Value 1 stands for "I completely disagree" and value 5 stands for "I completely agree" [20].

2.2 Empirical Phase

The empirical phase has been developed into two sub-phases: an observational phase and an experimental phase. During the observational phase the support areas selected were analyzed, considering the daily activities that are carried out in those spaces. The experimental phase was applied to two main typologies of medical offices. The data collection was carried on through the analysis of technical documents, on-site visits and photo collection. The on-site visits were conducted in weekly working-days during the daily activities. During the experimental phase the assessment model was proposed to medical staff through a questionnaire, in order to collect feedback from users about the quality of the medical offices considered.

Site and Settings
The tool was applied in selected hospital wards from a medium-large size University Hospital in Lombardy Region, Italy. The choice of the structure was motivated by the presence of two different typologies of medical offices, that differ in terms of localization, spatial layout and indoor settings. The structure derives from the union of a monobloc building (divided into three principal sectors A, B and C) and some foreparts located behind it, named "the diamonds" because of their shape. In this study the medical offices located in sectors A and C have been included. The choice of these two sectors was due to the different characteristics they have in terms of layout distribution and physical elements we can find in medical offices. Offices in sector A are hereafter called Type-A offices, and offices in sector C are hereafter called Type-C offices. A detailed description of the two settings is provided in Table 2.

2.3 Analysis Phase

Data collected during on-site visits and through the questionnaire have been analyzed, extracting descriptive statistics that led to qualitative considerations.

Data collection and sample size
The sample has been calculated with the Creative Research Systems online tool "Sample Size Calculator" (https://www.surveysystem.com/sscalc.htm) promoted by the Italian Public Health and Epidemiology portal. Considering the total staff population in the hospital counting 670 individuals (2017 data), 149 Medical Doctors have been included in the survey, since 75 of them were allocated in sector A, and 74 in sector C. Data have been collected between 18 and 28 February 2019 through direct interviews to the staff and online forms.

Data Analysis
Data gathered through the questionnaire have been analyzed with the software IBM SPSS Statistics v.25. Firstly the data collected have been submitted to descriptive analysis through frequencies observation, to detect the number of occurrences of each answer chosen by the respondents calculated as average, median and standard deviation. Secondly, the T-Student statistical test was applied, which allowed to compare the obtained average values from each item for type-A and type-C medical offices, and to highlight only the results where a significant difference between the two setting was present. This approach allowed to focus the analysis only on the parameters that had a significant difference in values between the two groups, looking at the averages obtained. Therefore, just the results related to Localization; Indoor environment; Natural light; Artificial light will

Table 2. Characteristics of the two office typologies included in the study

Type-A OFFICES	Type-C OFFICES
• Located in the foreparts, filtered from patients corridor; • Single and multiple workstations (3-4 MDs); • Absence of art or natural elements; • North or West orientation; • Neon lights from ceiling; • Limited control of the temperature by the users • Standard acoustic insulation	• Located inside the wards, within the patients' corridor; • Multiple workstations (3-4 MDs); • Absence of art or natural elements; • South orientation; • Neon lights from the ceiling; • Limited control of the temperature by the users • Standard acoustic insulation
Type-A OFFICES	**Type-C OFFICES**

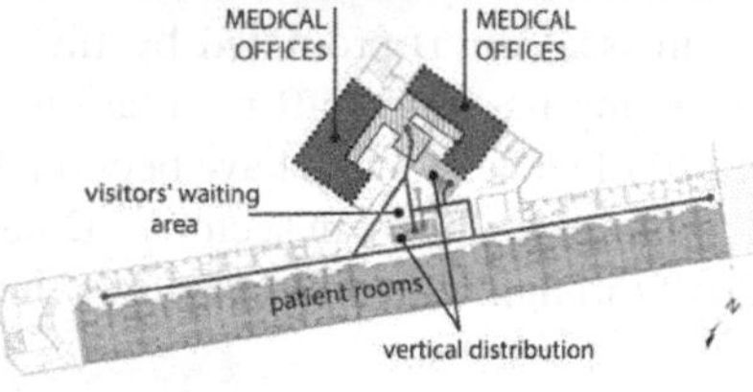

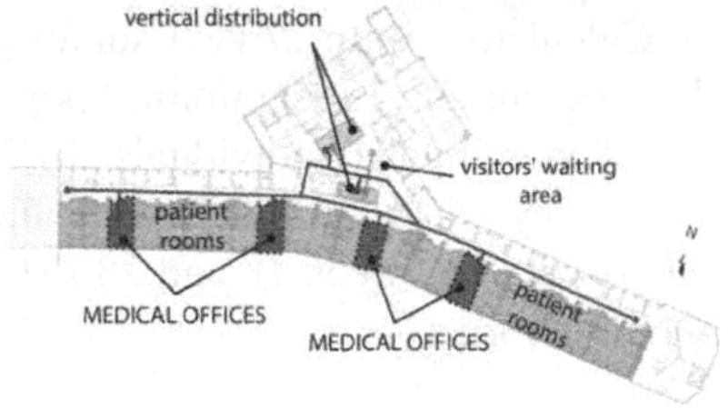

be discussed. The remaining four built environment parameters (Temperature; Humidity; Acoustics; Ventilation) have not been considered, because no significant differences between the two office settings emerged.

3 Results and Discussion

3.1 Demographic and Job-Related Data

58,1% of the sample is represented by female MD while 41,9% is male. In terms of age, the population is homogeneously distributed with a minority of over 50 (20,9%) while under 30 (most likely resident doctors) and 31–50 years old practitioners are respectively 39,2% and 39,9%. More than half of the sample (53,4%) stated that in average he/she spend more than 30 h per week inside the medical offices, 31,1% spend between 11 and 29 h and only 15,5% spend 10 h or less. Most of MDs spend up to 75% of their working-week time in offices, therefore the quality of built environment where they stay should be seriously taken into account.

3.2 Indoor Environment

Several data suggest a great impact of indoor built environment on MD's wellbeing. Indeed, from the data collected, only 12% of the respondents from type-A medical offices are satisfied with the current indoor quality characteristics of the workspaces; equally, in type-C medical offices only 19% are satisfied with the spaces they use every day. The current characteristics of both medical offices A and C do not contribute to improving work performance, according to 89.3% of the respondents from type-A medical offices and 87.8% from type-C medical offices, respectively. The same environments seem to have a bad influence on daily fatigue in 60% of the interviews for A-offices and in 55.4% for C-offices. 66 out of 75 physicians say that the indoor environment of type-A workplaces does not help in reducing stress levels, and 68 physicians affirm the same for type-C workplaces. The low overall satisfaction in both offices about the indoor environment and his influences on work activities could be related to office settings. Both type-A and type-C offices have a net surface between 14 and 18 m^2, and are organized to host between 2 and 3 doctors, and in some cases an examination bed. These office dimensions could be inadequate and undersized for hosting both medical consultations and workstations for more than one doctor. This study confirms that the current characteristics of the workspace and the type of furniture in both medical offices do not help, or even worsen overall work quality and the wellbeing of doctors that have been interviewed. Size, furniture, colors, the possibility of customize the space are all characteristics to be taken into account in such healthcare workplaces.

3.3 Localization

More than half of the physicians interviewed (65.3%) believe that the location of type-A medical offices ensures adequate visual privacy, while the situation is opposite for type-C medical offices, where 60.8% of physicians point it as a missing quality. Similarly, the localization of type-A studies helps improving work performance in 41.4% of cases and reducing stress levels in 34.6%, while the localization of type-C offices does not improve work performance in 77% of cases and does not reduce work stress in 83.7% physicians' opinion. The analysis shows that the specific localization of workspaces has a negative impact on privacy levels, work performance, daily fatigue, stress and personal satisfaction in Type-C settings which are located inside the ward, in opposition to Type-A settings which, although very close to the ward are more protected. These results underline that an effective study of layouts, with a correct functional distribution of public spaces and healthcare flows, can significantly influence the working wellbeing of medical staff, improving their efficiency and decreasing negative consequences related to the daily workload. These design choices are fundamental to ensure adequate visual privacy for conversations between medical staff and patients or their family members. An adequate location of medical offices ensures a greater level of visual privacy for healthcare professionals, that can perform certain activities without being interrupted, thus improving work performances.

3.4 Natural Lighting

Only 17.3% of physicians are satisfied with natural lighting provided in Type-A offices, while almost half (47.3%) of them are satisfied with natural lighting in Type C offices. This seems to have a negative impact on daily fatigue (60%) and stress (65.3%) in Type A studies, while a degree of indifference on effects of natural light in Type-C offices prevails. The analysis strongly shows a very low satisfaction about natural lighting in type-A medical offices, in opposition to a good satisfaction in type-C offices. In addition to a different facade orientation (north and west for the Type-A and south for the Type C), the results for natural light satisfaction are also due to the design of the windows. Indeed, the presence of ribbon-like windows in type-A offices does not allow an outward vision or direct enlightenment of workstations, unlike the vertical ones that are present in type-C offices. The lack of adequate natural lighting has a negative impact on visual comfort and wellbeing of medical staff and their activities [21]. As can be seen from the data analysis, window type and door frames with vertical development are therefore preferable to horizontal ones (ribbon). The indoor natural lighting conditions are influenced not only by the orientation of the façade but also by the window size as well as by other parameters such as the relationship between the window and the floor surface, the furniture position, the colors, etc.

3.5 Artificial Lighting

Artificial lighting in type-A offices is considered qualitatively and quantitatively unsatisfactory by 41.4% of physicians, while it is the opposite for type-C offices where satisfaction for artificial lighting is found in 39.2% of respondents. For both type A and type C workplaces, in most cases artificial lighting seems to have no impact on daily fatigue (48% for type A and 45.9% for type C) or on work performance (48% type A and 52.7% type C). On the contrary, it has a negative impact on stress in both type A (53.4%) and type C (46%) settings. Under the same conditions of artificial lighting, the level of satisfaction is opposite for the two medical offices, in favor of type-C ones: this is probably linked to the fact that the presence of a greater source of natural light contributes to medical staff satisfaction.

4 Conclusions and Further Development

The study highlights and confirms that built environment characteristics are very important for MDs satisfaction, productivity and wellbeing. In particular localization, natural and artificial light and the indoor environment emerged as driving factors able to positively or negatively influence indoor wellbeing. The research could lead to some design propositions able to support designers or hospital technical managers in the project phase, refurbishing or renovating MD workspaces prioritizing the most influent parameters, in order to improve overall satisfaction and performance. Further investigations are encouraged on a wider sample of healthcare professionals, including nurses and socio-sanitary workers, analyzing other typologies of workspaces that support different healthcare daily activities.

Acknowledgments. We acknowledge the Medical Direction in the figure of Dr. N.O. and Dr. L. R. for supporting the research, sharing the questionnaire with the medical staff of the hospital and providing technical information.

References

1. Faroldi, E., Fabi, V., Vettori, M.P., Gola, M., Brambilla, A., Capolongo, S.: Health tourism and thermal heritage: assessing Italian spas with innovative multidisciplinary tools. Tourism Anal. **24**, 405–419 (2019). https://doi.org/10.3727/108354219X15511865533121
2. Elf, M., Nordin, S., Wijk, H., Mckee, K.J.: A systematic review of the psychometric properties of instruments for assessing the quality of the physical environment in healthcare. J. Adv. Nurs. **73**, 2796–2816 (2017)
3. de Castro, M.F., Mateus, R., Bragança, L.: Healthcare building sustainability assessment tool - sustainable effective design criteria in the portuguese context. Environ. Impact Assess. Rev. **67**, 49–60 (2017)
4. Brambilla, A., Buffoli, M., Capolongo, S.: Measuring hospital qualities. a preliminary investigation on health impact assessment possibilities for evaluating complex buildings. Acta Bio Medica Atenei Parmensis **90**, 54–63 (2019). https://doi.org/10.23750/abm.v90i9-S.8713
5. Shannon, M.M, Nordin, S., Bernhardt, J., Elf, M.: Application of theory in studies of healthcare built environment research. HERD. 193758671990110 (2020)
6. Ulrich, R.S., Berry, L.L., Quan, X., Parish, J.T.: A conceptual framework for the domain of evidence-based design. HERD **4**, 95–114 (2010)
7. Fontaine, D.K., Briggs, L.P., Pope-Smith, B.: Designing humanistic critical care environments. Crit. Care Nurs. Q. **24**, 21–34 (2001)
8. Uhlig, P.N., Brown, J., Nason, A.K., Camelio, A., Kendall, E.: System innovation: concord hospital. Jt Comm. J. Qual. Improv. **28**, 666–672 (2002)
9. Casalino, L.P., Crosson, F.J.: Physician satisfaction and physician well-being: should anyone care? Prof. Professionalism **5** (2015)
10. Lindahl, G., Blakstad, S.H., Hansen, G., Nenonen, S.: USEframe – a framework to understand and map usability research. In: Proceedings of the Nordic Facilities Management Conference, 22–23 August 2011. CFM/DTU (2011)
11. Elf, M., Anåker, A., Marcheschi, E., Sigurjónsson, Á., Ulrich, R.S.: The built environment and its impact on health outcomes and experiences of patients, significant others and staff—a protocol for a systematic review. Nurs. Open **7**(3), 895–899 (2020)
12. Bluyssen, P.M.: Towards an integrated analysis of the indoor environmental factors and its effects on occupants. Intell. Build. Int. 1–9 (2019)
13. Wallace, J.E., Lemaire, J.B., Ghali, W.A.: Physician wellness: a missing quality indicator. Lancet **374**, 1714–1721 (2009)
14. Firth-Cozens, J., Greenhalgh, J.: Doctors' perceptions of the links between stress and lowered clinical care. Soc. Sci. Med. **44**, 1017–1022 (1997)
15. Williams, E.S., Skinner, A.C.: Outcomes of physician job satisfaction: a narrative review, implications, and directions for future research. Health Care Manage. Rev. **28**, 119–139 (2003)

16. Ulrich, R.S., et al.: A review of the research literature on evidence-based healthcare design. HERD **1**, 61–125 (2008)
17. Tucker, A.L., Spear, S.J.: Operational failures and interruptions in hospital nursing. Health Serv. Res. **41**, 643–662 (2006)
18. Candido, C., Kim, J., de Dear, R., Thomas, L.: BOSSA: a multidimensional post-occupancy evaluation tool. Build. Res. Inf. **44**, 214–228 (2016)
19. Forooraghi, M., Miedema, E., Ryd, N., Wallbaum, H.: Scoping review of health in office design approaches. JCRE. ahead-of-print (2020)
20. Likert, R.: A technique for the measurement of attitudes. Arch. Psychol. **22**(140), 55 (1932)
21. Origgi, L., Buffoli, M., Capolongo, S., Signorelli, C.: Light wellbeing in hospital: research, development and indications. Ann. Ig. **23**, 55–62 (2011)

An Analytic Network Process (ANP)-Based Approach for Investigating Alternative Planning Scenarios of Mining Activities in Piedmont Region

Vanessa Assumma(✉), Marta Bottero, Giulio Mondini, and Elisa Zanetta

Interuniversity Department of Regional and Urban Studies and Planning, Politecnico di Torino, 10125 Turin, Italy
{vanessa.assumma,marta.bottero,giulio.mondini}@polito.it, elisa.zanetta@gmail.com

Abstract. The paper aims to explore a set of future scenarios in the context of the Strategic Environmental Assessment (SEA) for the adoption of the Regional Plan for Mining Activities in Piedmont region (Italy). The study investigates the use of a Multicriteria Decision Analysis technique (MCDA), namely the Analytic Network Process (ANP), with the aim to support the definition of the best sustainable scenario. The ANP model evaluates a protocol of objectives and strategies in order to explore their complex relations and to guide the evaluation of alternative planning scenarios. The paper shows how the ANP model may be considered a suitable support to aid the decision-making process in better understanding the full range of impacts generated by mining activities on the territory, thus supporting the creation of integrated and sustainable planning policies at regional scale.

Keywords: ANP · Regional planning · Decision-making process

1 Introduction

Anthropogenic activities represent the main driving forces that generates pressures on the environment, that is ever more fragile and sensitive to changes. The pressures determine impacts on both abiotic and biotic components, and their intensity solicits the environment to respond, transform and adapt itself [1].

Despite mining activities represent an important pillar for the economic development and competitiveness of a region, these are considered as very impacting on the environment during their life cycle and after their closure: soil erosion, water pollution, noise and vibrations, acid drainage [2], loss of soil ecosystem services are some significant effects of the shrinking of scarce resources [3, 4]. Despite the crisis that affected mining industry in recent years, that caused the closure of several quarries [5], this still play a very important role into the national and regional economy.

The latest report by SNPA [6] has given an overview of the current trends and possible future scenarios for limiting the impacts on the environment, according to the

O. Gervasi et al. (Eds.): ICCSA 2020, LNCS 12253, pp. 355–365, 2020.
https://doi.org/10.1007/978-3-030-58814-4_25

SD Goals targets [7]. The progressive transition toward a model of Circular Economy (CE) with the European Circular Economy package [8] is transforming the relations between economy and environment [9] with positive signals also in the mining industry. Grande and colleagues [10] have introduced the term of "Circular Mining" as adaptation of the circular economy paradigm to the mining industry, with the aim at promoting a novel concept of mining industry "technical feasible, economically profitable and environmentally sustainable".

Over the last years, a domain to regulate the planning of mining industry in a more efficacy and transparent way is emerged, in terms of release of mining grants, reopening of quarries, environmental recovery, relation with landscape, protected areas and so on. In Italy, the power on mining activities has been transferred to the regions through the D.P.R. no. 616/1977, D.lgs. no. 112/1998 and D.lgs no. 83/2012 [11–13], even if most of the regions have not yet provided a regional plan in the field. There are some regions that have adopted a regional plan of new generation in subject and/or that are moving for it. Piedmont Region has recently adopted the Regional Law no. 23/2016, that introduces the Regional Plan of Mining Activities (Piano Regionale delle Attività Estrattive - PRAE) to regulate the planning and management of the existing mining activities and the potential open of new sites and extensions, according to the sustainability and circular economy principles [14].

The adoption of a regional plan requires the procedure of Strategic Evaluation Assessment (SEA), for evaluating the possible impacts generated by the regional plan on environment and its components [15, 16]. The SEA procedure must favor a wide participation of actors and stakeholders, with different visions and expertises, and in this sense the use of decision aiding tools may help them to envision future scenarios for the activation of regional policies and actions [17, 18].

In this sense, the Multicriteria Decision Analysis (MCDA) has been retained a reliable supporting tool to be considered within the SEA procedure of the regional plan. Among the different MCDA methods, the present study proposes a methodological contribution based on the adoption of the Analytic Network Process (ANP) to investigate the relations between the objectives and strategies of the Regional Plan of Mining Activities, thus guiding the definition of the best sustainable scenario. In this way, the actors and stakeholders may easily identify the priorities to be traduced in actions that will be activated in the most sustainable scenario.

2 Methodology

As already said, MCDA has been widely recognized as a useful approach for supporting decision problems in various and different fields, e.g. environmental assessments, urban and territorial planning, being able to guide the decision-making process for achieving common planning goals, by considering multidimensional aspects and different points of view. The MCDA counts many applications that carried promising outcomes for environmental and social challenges [19, 20] regeneration of downgraded industrial areas [21] strategies for net-zero energy districts [22] landscape ecology and economics [23] urban resilience [24], urban development and design processes [25].

In the present research, the Analytic Network Process (ANP) has been proposed [26] because reveals particularly suitable for this type of decision problem. More in details, the ANP model is considered an evolution of the simpler Analytic Hierarchy Process (AHP) because represents the decision problem as a network in which the elements of the problem are linked through interdependency relationships and at different levels [27]. In this research work, the network allows the exploration of the relations between strategies belonging to different objectives, thus aiding the evaluator to identify the direct and/or indirect effect determined by a strategy and the potential synergies with the connected ones for reaching shared regional goals. For these reasons, this application may carry an added value on the current knowledge and practice.

From the methodological point of view, the ANP requires a network structure to represent the problem, as well as pairwise comparisons to establish the relationships within the structure. To develop an ANP model, it is necessary to carry out five fundamental steps that can be described as follows:

1) Structuring of the decision-making process. This step involves defining the main objective of the evaluation and identifying groups or "clusters" constituted by various elements (i.e. nodes) that influence the decision, and alternatives or options from which to choose. The network model has been then structured through the software Superdecisions (http://www.superdecisions.com/);
2) Pairwise comparisons. In this phase pairwise comparisons are developed in order to establish the relative importance of the different elements, with respect to a certain component of the network. The comparisons are based on the use of a 1–9 points scale where the value 1 indicates equal importance between two elements, whereas the value 9 indicates that one element is extremely more important than the other;
3) Supermatrices formation. The third step consists of the progressive formation of three supermatrices: the initial or unweighted supermatrix, the weighted supermatrix and, finally, the limit supermatrix. The unweighted supermatrix contains all the eigenvectors that are derived from the pairwise comparison matrixes of the model. The eigenvector obtained from the cluster level comparison, with respect to the control criterion, is applied to the initial supermatrix as a cluster weight and the result is the weighted supermatrix. The supermatrix elements allow a resolution to be made concerning of the interdependencies that exist between the elements of the network;
4) Final priorities. In this step the weighted supermatrix is raised to a limiting power to converge and to obtain a long-term stable set of weights that represents the final priority vector;
5) Sensitivity analysis. The last step consists in carrying out the sensitivity analysis on the outcome of the model in order to test its robustness and to verify the stability of the results.

The 5 steps of the method will be detailed in the next section with reference to the application on the considered case study.

3 Application

The paper illustrates an ongoing study considering the application of a ANP model for the evaluation of the Regional Plan of Mining Activities of Piedmont Region. The present application is based on a simulation of the real decision-making process in which an experts' panel for the evaluation of the network's elements in order to explore the suitability of the ANP approach, to support the definition of intervention priorities and the assessment of alternative planning scenarios. Following the methodology, the first step of the method is finalized to structure the decision problem and it is represented by the elements described below.

- Clusters: they represent the objectives introduced by the Regional Law of Piedmont no. 23/2016 (Table 1);
- Nodes: they represent the strategies considered by each objective. Given the high number of nodes, it has been retained useful in some clusters to merge those strategies considered as redundant. In Table 1, the symbol * means that the strategies belonging to the i-th objective have been merged for facilitating the experts in the comparisons. In fact, it is reasonable to evaluate at least 2 and maximum 8 strategies, for each objective, to prevent incoherent comparisons;
- Alternatives: they represent planning scenarios that must be evaluated at level of clusters and nodes. According to the literature in the context of scenario planning, experts normally use a recognizable set of scenarios, i.e. inertial, tendential and strategic scenarios that should consider the desiderata of actors and stakeholders involved into the process [28, 29]. In our case, we adapted the scenarios that have been identified by actors and stakeholders during the SEA scoping phase (see Table 2).

Figure 1 illustrates the structuring of the ANP model elaborated through the software Superdecisions.

Once having defined the elements of the network, it is possible to identify the relationships. These can be "external" when these occur between two or more elements of the network, and "internal" (i.e. loop), when relationships exist between nodes belonging to the same cluster.

Table 1. Objectives and strategies as cluster and nodes of the ANP model. (Elaboration from Regional Law Piedmont no. 23/2016).

Clusters (i.e. Objectives)	Nodes (i.e. Strategies)
a) Definition of guidelines for a correct balance between environmental values, such as territory, environment landscape, and the mining activity and the reference market.	8*
b) Protection and safeguard of the fields under cultivation, those recognized and the relative resources, considering mineral deposits and mining as primary resources for the socio-economic development of the territory.	6*
c) Valorization of cultivated materials through their integral use and adequate to their specific features.	6*

(*continued*)

Table 1. *(continued)*

Clusters (i.e. Objectives)		Nodes (i.e. Strategies)
d) Unification of the mining activities on the entire territory of the region.		4
e) Orientation of mining activities towards a better balance between industrial production and optimization of interventions for the purpose of recovering and valorizing deteriorated and disused sites.		8*
f) Promotion, protection and qualification of the work and business.		4
g) Facilitation of the recovery of inert aggregates coming from construction and demolition, as well as the use of inert recycling materials.		5
h) Insurance of monitoring mining activities.		3
i) Facilitation of environmental and economic synergies arising from interventions by arrangement and maintenance of river auctions and hydroelectric basins.		8
j) Indications for the supply of the materials required for the realization of public works.		7
Total	10	59

Table 2. Set of alternative scenarios considered in the ANP model.

Alternative scenarios	Description
1) Inertial scenario	It envisages the maintenance of the planning in force, applying the new provisions deriving from current regulations. No Regional Plan on mining activities is provided.
2) Limiting scenario	It is very preserving versus the environment and landscape and it limits the release of new authorizations, that could determine the closure of the existing mining activities.
3) Trend scenario	It envisages all the objectives of the Regional Law, balancing the needs between territorial values, mining activities and the reference market with the promotion, protection and qualification of work and businesses.

Subsequently, the pairwise comparison method is used to investigate the importance of the various network elements. In the present simulation, a questionnaire was proposed to a panel of experts with expertise on regional and urban planning and management of mining activities, asking them to evaluate pairwise the network elements at the clusters level and then at the nodes level. Moreover, the software allowed to the experts to evaluate coherently the network elements, thanks to the Consistency Ratio index (CR)

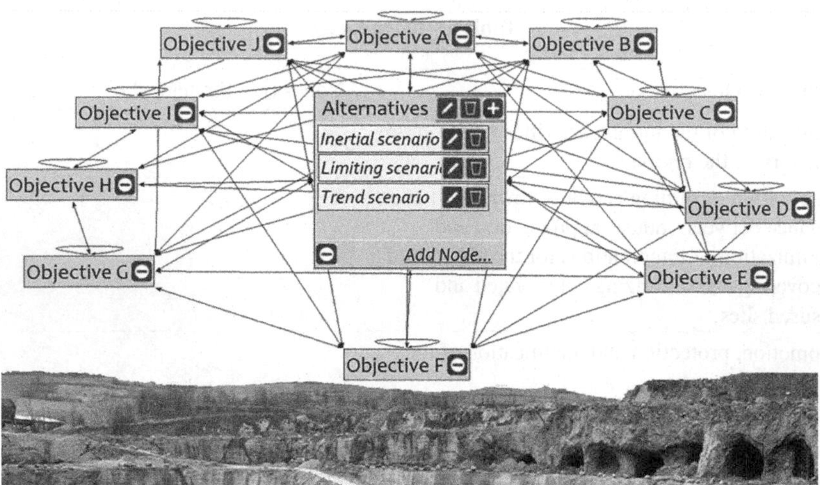

Fig. 1. Structuring of the objectives of the Regional Law 23/2016 according to the ANP model (Elaboration through Superdecisions software)

that ensures the comparisons be coherent and not contradictory. In fact, the comparisons are coherent when CR index is less or equal to 10%. As an example, Table 3 reports the comparison matrix derived from the comparisons of the strategies belonging to the objective D "Unification of mining activities on the entire territory of the region" with reference to the Trend scenario.

Table 3. Comparisons between the nodes in objective D with reference to trend scenario.

Nodes	d.1	d.2	d.3	d.4	Priorities
d.1 Give guidelines on the main opportunities for increasing the technology of the abatement techniques that may be used in the various types of mining activities in the region	1	4	1/5	1/3	0.13833
d.2 Give guidelines for the definition of actions related to the problems of stability of the excavation fronts, with reference to their conformation, in the meanwhile and at the end of the cultivation process	1/4	1	1/5	1/5	0.06075
d.3 Define the regional distribution of the mining activities of the three sectors, and in particular of the first one, whose activities are more diffused and less constrained for the mining distribution	5	5	1	2	0.49891
d.4 Verify the location of mining activities with respect to landscape components, cities and their development, natural protected areas and infrastructure systems	3	5	1/2	1	0.30201
	CR ratio:				0.07710

The experts comparisons were converted by Superdecisions as vectors and then it was possible to elaborate three supermatrices: 1) the initial supermatrix collects the vectors at node and cluster levels; 2) the weighted supermatrix aggregates both vectors of nodes and clusters; 3) the limit supermatrix multiplies these vectors for themselves until when the vectors became stable (see Fig. 2). In this way, it was possible to obtain the ranking of final priorities of the objectives and strategies considered in the planning process. Lastly, a sensitivity analysis on the ANP model was performed to test its reliability through the software function "ANP Sensitivity" on some strategies that revealed crucial for the present application [26].

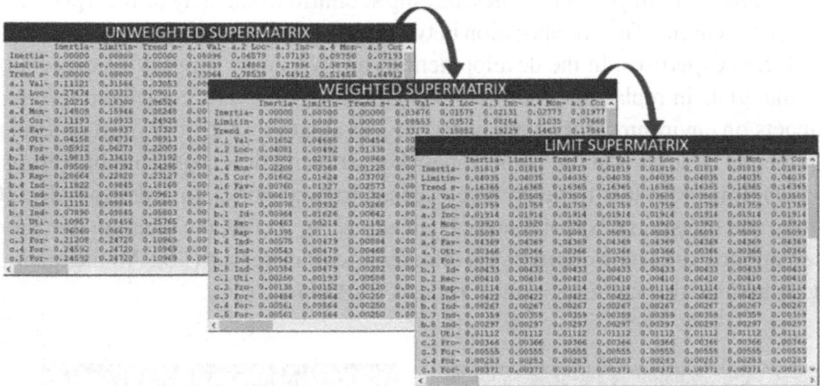

Fig. 2. Elaboration of the supermatrices to calculate the final priorities.

4 Discussion of Results

As shown in Fig. 3a, from the elaboration of the preliminary results coming for the methodological exploration, the ANP application is useful to identify some strategies emerged as relevant for the future policies of the region on mining activities. According to the obtained results, the valorization and safeguard of natural resources, such as the water bodies and ecosystems, play a transversal importance that must be considered by policy decisions (a.1); this may be achieved through a major sensitivity to the localization of new mining activities with respect to the environmental components (a.4.) and a more balanced regional planning between mining activities and other sectoral plans (e.g. Landscape Regional Plan or Waste Management Regional Plan) (a.5). Furthermore, it is important for mining activities to achieve the circular economy purposes (a.6.). These strategies reveal crucial in all considered scenarios. A suitable representation of those areas in that are located mining activities and the potential extension areas is the fundamental basis on which to base the cognitive analyzes of the regional territory (b.3) and it is closely related to the building of a regional infrastructure system that integrates various data sources (h.1.). The formulation of guidelines to favor an integral use of the resource in all phases of the extracting process (c.3), and to valorise and mantain the sawing sludge (c.4) may aid on one hand on the maximization of the performance of the resource and on the other hand the reduction of processing costs. It is important to distribute mining sites at regional level and according to the three sectors (i.e. aggregates, industrial materials, ornamental stones) (d.3.), in coherence with the landscape components, cities, protected areas and infrastructures (d.4.). The creation of alternative solutions to new wells (e.3) and the progressive ecological recovery of brownfields habitats (e.4, i.4) look toward the zeroing of the land take in Piedmont region. A protocol of environmental sustainability for mining activities (f.1.) and the promotion of local materials may aid the competitiveness of the region (f.3.). The diffusion of alternative materials (g.1) and the progressive integration of certified recycled materials in the market (j.1.) may facilitate the recovery of aggregates deriving from demolitions and recycling processes; these strategies reveal very important for the Limiting scenario which may be incorporated also in the Trend scenario. The collaboration between the Departments of Regione Piemonte, with different expertises, in the development of analysis may support the estimation of treated materials in replacement of quarry materials (g.4.), thus contributing to reduce the impacts on environmental components. The evaluation of a work must consider the environmental benefits and the balance between construction costs and marketing revenues (i.7). It is important to favor the closeness to new works, in order to reduce CO_2 emissions and transport costs of materials on site (j.5); finally, the creation of synergies between public works may optimize the interchange of materials (j.6). All the mentioned strategies assume relevant importance as basis for the new plan.

Strategies	Normalized by Cluster	Limiting
a.1	0,142	0,035
a.4	0,159	0,039
a.5	0,206	0,051
a.6	0,177	0,044
a.8	0,153	0,038
b.3	0,337	0,011
c.1	0,371	0,011
c.3	0,185	0,006
d.3	0,373	0,020
d.4	0,423	0,023
e.3	0,185	0,011
e.6	0,141	0,008
f.1	0,334	0,015
f.3	0,281	0,013
g.1	0,256	0,024
g.4	0,266	0,025
h.1	0,526	0,059
i.4	0,163	0,006
i.7	0,211	0,007
j.1	0,283	0,020
j.5	0,184	0,013
j.6	0,212	0,015

a

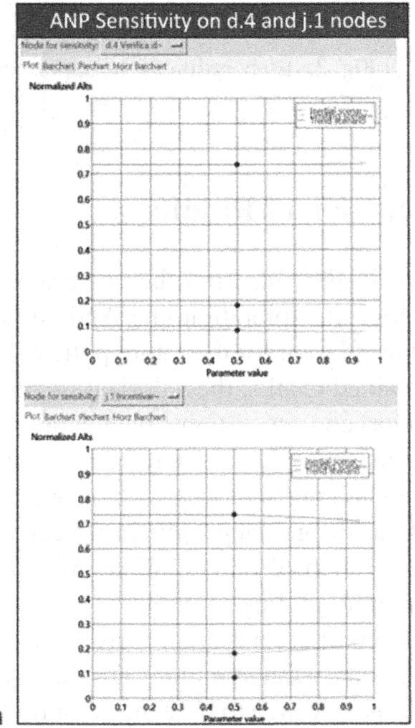

b

Fig. 3. Relevant priorities derived from the limit supermatrix (a) and sensitivity analysis on some significative nodes (b).

Figure 3a reports the priorities of all strategies as resulting from the preliminary investigation illustrated in the present paper. The synthesis of the final priorities, will be performed in the real evaluation process. We give in Fig. 3c some plots of the sensitivity analysis that testify the stability of the results of the model.

5 Conclusions

The paper has illustrated the methodological application of the ANP model within the SEA procedure for the design of the regional plan on mining activities in Piedmont Region.

From the presented study, the ANP model has appeared as particularly effective to support the decision-making process in the assessment of future scenarios of plans and programs, thanks to its dynamic approach to define the various relations between objectives and strategies.

From a methodological point of view, the many comparisons, due also to the transversal relations of strategies, have implied an effort of the experts in this evaluation. In this sense, for the real application it could be useful to reduce further the number of strategies before the building of the ANP model, such as through a Multivariate Redundancy Analysis (MRA) [30].

The next step of this research work will be the involvement of real actors and stakeholders to validate the results obtained through the survey. Subsequently, a focus group will be organized for aiding the real actors and stakeholders to share the role and the importance of the objectives and strategies to orient the regional planning on mining activities toward the best sustainable scenario, thus enforcing the performance of the future plan.

The authors will implement the ANP model with GIS methods [31] to aid both actors and stakeholders to better visualize the final model's outputs. This integration could aid the decision makers for example to identify the suitable areas for the localization of new quarry activities as well as for the recovery of inactive mines; in this sense, the authors consider the role of geodatabases crucial as an opportunity to take this promising research path [18]. In addition, the authors will consider the Geo-Design methods [32] to facilitate actors and stakeholder to visualize the priority strategies in the region, thus envisioning shared scenarios to support the regional planning.

Acknowledgements. This work has been developed within the research project related to the Strategic Environmental Assessment of the Regional Plan for mining activities of Piedmont Region (Scientific Coordinator: Prof. Giulio Mondini, Interuniversity Department of Urban and Regional Studies and Planning, Politecnico di Torino).

References

1. Cutter, S.L.: Resilience to what? Resilience for whom? Geogr. J. **182**(2), 110–113 (2016)
2. Onwe, R., Abraham, E.: Environmental problems of surface and underground mining: a review. Int. J. Eng. Sci. (IJES) **4**(12), 12–20 (2015). ISSN 2319 – 1813
3. Millennium Ecosystem Assessment (MEA): Millennium ecosystem assessment ecosystems and human well-being: current state and trends assessment. Island Press, Washington

4. Baveye, P.C., Baveye, J., Gowdy, J.: Soil "ecosystem" services and natural capital: critical appraisal of research on uncertain ground. Front. Environ. Sci. **4**, 1–41 (2016). https://doi.org/10.3389/fenvs.2016.00041
5. Zanchini, E., Nanni, G. (eds.): Legambiente: Rapporto Cave. I numeri e gli impatti economici e ambientali delle attività estrattive nel territorio italiano. Le opportunità e le sfide nella direzione dell'economia circolare (2017) https://www.legambiente.it/sites/default/files/docs/rapporto_cave_2017.pdf. Accessed 01 Mar 20
6. Sistema Nazionale per la Protezione dell'Ambiente (SNPA). Rapporto Consumo di suolo, dinamiche territoriali e servizi ecosistemici (Report on Land take, territorial dynamics and ecosystem services) (2019). https://www.snpambiente.it/2019/09/17/consumo-di-suolo-dinamiche-territoriali-e-servizi-ecosistemici-edizione-2019/. Accessed 01 Mar 20
7. United Nations: Transforming Our World: the 2030 Agenda for the Sustainable Development (2015). https://www.unric.org/it/images/Agenda_2030_ITA.pdf. Accessed 01 Mar 20
8. European Commission: Closing the loop - An EU action plan for the Circular Economy, Com (2015) 614 communication from the commission to the European Parliament, the Council, the European Economic and Social Committee and the Committee of the Regions. European Commission, Brussels (2015). https://eur-lex.europa.eu/legal-content/EN/TXT/?uri=CELEX:52015DC0614. Accessed 01 Mar 20
9. Pearce, D.W., Turner, R.K.: Economics of Natural Resources and the Environment. Johns Hopkins Press, Baltimore (1990)
10. Grande, J.A., et al.: The paradigm of circular mining in the world: the Iberian Pyrite belt as a potential scenario of interaction. Environ. Earth Sci. **77**(10), 1–6 (2018). https://doi.org/10.1007/s12665-018-7577-1
11. D.P.R. no. 616/1977. Attuazione della delega di cui all'articolo 1 della legge 22 luglio 1975, n. 382. http://legislature.camera.it/_bicamerali/questreg/norme/dpr616.htm. Accessed 01 Mar 20
12. Parlamento Italiano: D.lgs. no. 112/1998, Conferimento di funzioni e compiti amministrativi dello Stato alle regioni ed agli enti locali, in attuazione del capo I della legge 15 marzo 1997, n. 59. Gazzetta Ufficiale n. 92 del 21 aprile 1998 - Supplemento Ordinario n. 77. http://www.parlamento.it/parlam/leggi/deleghe/98112dl.htm. Accessed 01 Mar 20
13. Parlamento Italiano: D.lgs 83/2012, Misure urgenti per la crescita del Paese
14. Regione Piemonte: Legge regionale n. 23 17 novembre 2016, Disciplina delle attività estrattive: disposizioni in materia di cave (2016). http://arianna.consiglioregionale.piemonte.it/. Accessed 01 Mar 20
15. European Commission: Directive 2001/42/EC of the European Parliament and of the Council on the Assessment of the Effects of Certain Plans and Programmes on the Environment, Brussels (2001)
16. Dlgs 152/2006 – Testo Unico Ambiente http://www.isprambiente.gov.it/it/garante_aia_ilva/normativa/normativa-ambientale/Dlgs_152_06_TestoUnicoAmbientale.pdf. Access 01 Mar 20
17. Bottero, M., Mondini, G. (eds.): Valutazione e sostenibilità. Piani, programmi, progetti, Celid, Torino (2009)
18. Bottero, M.C., Polo Pérez, I., Taddia, G., Lo Russo, S.: A geodatabase for supporting planning and management of mining activities: the case of Piedmont Region. Environ. Earth Sci. **79**(4), 1–12 (2020). https://doi.org/10.1007/s12665-020-8815-x
19. Bottero, M., Ferretti, V., Pomarico, S.: Assessing different possibilities for the reuse of an open-pit quarry using the Choquet integral. J. Decis. Anal. **21**(1–2), 25–41 (2014)
20. Mondini, G.: Integrated assessment for the management of new social challenges. Valori Valutazioni **17**, 15–17 (2016)

21. Becchio, C., Bottero, M., Corgnati, S.P., Dell'Anna, F.: A MCDA-based approach for evaluating alternative requalification strategies for a net-zero energy district (NZED). In: Zopounidis, C., Doumpos, M. (eds.) Multiple Criteria Decision Making. MCDM, pp. 189–211. Springer, Cham (2017). https://doi.org/10.1007/978-3-319-39292-9_10
22. Bottero, M., Caprioli, C., Berta, M.: Urban problems and patterns of change: the analysis of a downgraded industrial area in Turin. In: Mondini, G., Oppio, A., Stanghellini, S., Bottero, M., Abastante, F. (eds.) Values and Functions for Future Cities. GET, pp. 385–401. Springer, Cham (2020). https://doi.org/10.1007/978-3-030-23786-8_22
23. Assumma, V., Bottero, M., Monaco, R., Soares, A.J.: An integrated evaluation methodology to measure ecological and economic landscape states for territorial transformation scenarios: an application in Piedmont (Italy). Ecol. Indicat. **105**, 156–165 (2019). https://doi.org/10.1016/j.ecolind.2019.04.071
24. Bottero, M., Datola, G., Monaco, R.: Exploring the resilience of urban systems using fuzzy cognitive maps. In: Gervasi, O., et al. (eds.) ICCSA 2017. LNCS, vol. 10406, pp. 338–353. Springer, Cham (2017). https://doi.org/10.1007/978-3-319-62398-6_24
25. Dell'Ovo, M., Oppio, A.: Bringing the value-focused thinking approach to urban development and design processes: the case of Foz do Tua area in Portugal. Valori Valutazioni **23**, 91–106 (2019). ISSN 20362404
26. Saaty, T.L.: Decision making—the analytic hierarchy and network processes (AHP/ANP). J. Syst. Sci. Syst. Eng. **13**, 1–35 (2004). https://doi.org/10.1007/s11518-006-0151-5
27. Bottero, M., Lami, I., Lombardi, P.: Analytic Network Process. La valutazione di scenari di trasformazione urbana e territoriale. Alinea Editrice, Firenze (2008)
28. Godet, M.: The art of scenarios and strategic planning: tools and pitfalls. Technol. Forecast. Soc. Change **65**, 3–22 (2000)
29. Amer, M., Daim, T.U., Jetter, A.: A review of scenario planning. Futures **46**, 23–40 (2013). https://doi.org/10.1016/j.futures.2012.10.003
30. Whitley, B.E., Kite, M.E. (eds.): Principles of Research in Behavioral Science. Routledge, New York (2013). ISBN 978-0-203-08521-9
31. Malczewski, J., Rinner, C. (eds.): Multicriteria Decision Analysis in Geographic Information Science. Advances in Geographic Information Science. Springer, Heidelberg (2015). https://doi.org/10.1007/978-3-540-74757-4
32. Steinitz, C.: A Framework for Geodesign: Changing Geography by Design. ESRI Press (2012)

Exploring the Redundancy Capacity Through a System Dynamics Approach

Marta Bottero, Giulia Datola(✉), and Elena De Angelis

Interuniversity Department of Regional and Urban Studies and Planning, Politecnico di Torino, Turin, Italy

{marta.bottero,giulia.datola,elena.deangelis}@polito.it

Abstract. Current urban agenda is interested in developing urban strategies to enhance urban resilience for cities. This paper examines the concept of urban resilience applied in the context of urban planning with specific attention to which are the capacities that make urban systems resilient. The knowledge and the understanding of these capacities are fundamental to set up suitable strategies. However, only few frameworks consider urban resilience and its capacity within the complexity of urban system. Through an in-depth literature review, this paper aims at providing a methodological framework both to recognize these capacities and analyze which are the main factors that mainly contribute to the achievement of these ability. The paper illustrates the first step of the application of a System Dynamics approach to analyze the redundancy capacity in order to define which are the key variables to enhance this capacity and also to determine which can be the impacts on the urban systems as a whole of the redundancy.

Keywords: Urban resilience · Resilience capacities · System Dynamics Model · Causal loop · Decision-making

1 Introduction

The concept of urban resilience is actually a fundamental objective of the new urban agenda [1–6]. Urban resilience concept is defined as the capacity of the city to adapt, change and absorb in face to a disturbance, within all its dimensions [7]. Global community is interested in enhancing urban resilience for cities, to make them able to face with both natural and man-made hazards [8]. An increasing attention in applying resilience in urban planning is demonstrated by both the growing number of different campaigns [1–3] and by the development of new evaluation frameworks to measure urban resilience [9–16].

Different resilience approaches [17–20] (e.g. engineering, ecological, economical) describe the characteristics, that a system should have to be resilient [21, 22]. These characteristics (i.e. capacities) are namely robustness, stability, flexibility, resourcefulness, coordination capacity, redundancy, diversity, foresight capacity, independence, connectivity and interdependence, collaboration capacity, agility, adaptability, self-organization, creativity and innovation, efficiency, and equity [22, 23]. However, only

O. Gervasi et al. (Eds.): ICCSA 2020, LNCS 12253, pp. 366–378, 2020.
https://doi.org/10.1007/978-3-030-58814-4_26

few frameworks include these capacities in the evaluation. As an example, the "resilience matrix" proposed by Fox-Lent [24] and subsequently implemented by Sharifi [25]. The purpose is constructing a matrix in which urban resilience indicators are putted in relation with the resilience capacities, to aware planners and decision makers of the importance of each ability and characteristic [22, 26–28].

This paper analyses and recognizes the set of the characteristics that can influence urban resilience enhancement (Sect. 2). Based on the existing evaluation methods [11, 26, 29–31], it also proposes a general framework to collect urban resilience indicators within urban resilience capacities. In detail, this paper applies this framework to recognize those urban resilience indicators related to the redundancy. Moreover, the application of System Dynamics approach [32–35] has been proposed to analyze the mutual influences between redundancy and its referred criteria, to analyze this capacity within the complexity of urban systems [32]. The results is a causal loop in which mutual influences have been identified, underling also which can be the effects of the redundancy capacity on the city as a system [35].

2 Urban Resilience Qualities

As above mentioned, the main characteristics that make a city resilient have to be determined to properly define and evaluate strategies to enhance urban resilience. This section illustrates and describes those capacities that urban systems should have to maintain or enhance their resilience. This list is the result of a literature review about resilience characteristics, described both in different resilience approaches [22, 36] and in several urban resilience campaigns [13].

Figure 1 illustrates the capacities of resilient systems, recognised in different approaches, such as ecology, sustainability and climate change [22].

In details, this dissertation is focused on those capacities referred to urban resilience, which can be summarised as follow:

- Reflexive. Reflective systems accept changings in continuous. To being reflexive, systems need mechanisms able to evolve continuously. The objective is be able to modify standards or norms in according to emerging evidences. As a result, people and institutions analyze and systematically learn from their past experiences, to base future decision-making [13];
- Robust. Robust systems include well-conceived, constructed and managed physical assets. The target is being able to withstand the impacts of hazard events without significant damages. In details, robust design foresees potential failures in systems [13];
- Redundant. Redundancy includes also diversity, or rather the presence of different ways to achieve needs. Redundancy can be explained with the repetition of the same elements, in order to guarantee the functionality of the systems in case of emergency events [13];
- Flexible. Flexibility is the capacity to react to unexpected events [37]. The lack of flexibility characterizes often the disaster management systems. In fact, flexibility implies the ability of the systems to change, evolve and adapt in response to evolving

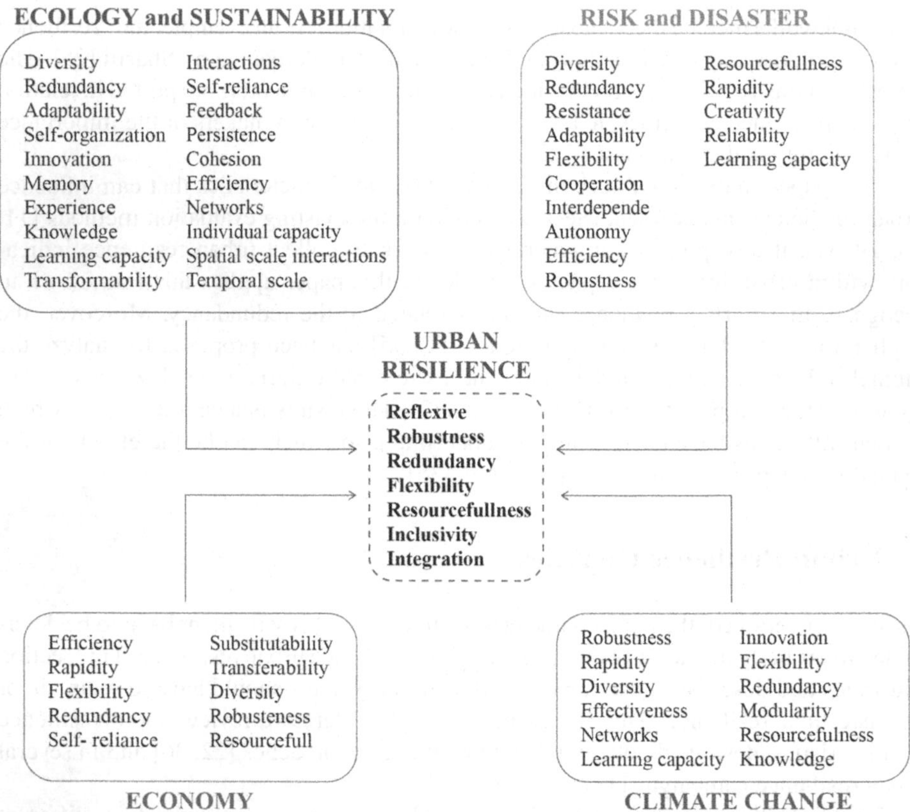

Fig. 1. Approach to collect urban resilience capacities (elaboration from Galderisi 2010)

situations [38]. Furthermore, it may favor decentralization and modular approaches for the management of infrastructure and ecosystem management [13];

- Resourceful. This capacity includes the ability of the system to anticipate future conditions and in setting priorities. It also implicates that both citizens and institution should be able to achieve their goals or meet their needs during a shock or when under stress [13];
- Inclusive. It is referred to the consultation and the engagement of communities, in order to reduce also the social vulnerability [13];
- Integrated. Integration and alignment between city systems promote consistency in decision-making and ensure that all investments are mutually supportive to a common outcome. Integration is evident within and between resilient systems, and across different scales of their operation. Exchange of information between systems enables them to function collectively and respond rapidly through shorter feedback loops through the city [13].

3 Redundancy Indicators

As mentioned in the first section, this paper analyses the capacity of redundancy. This capacity is related to the ability of the urban system to keep a satisfactory level of performance following an unexpected event. It is related to the presence of different elements with the same function, ensuring the continuity in case some elements fails [39, 40] and it is fundamental to ensure the continuity of urban performances. Table 1 lists a multi-dimensional set of urban resilience indicators, which are referred to redundancy. They are the result of an in-depth literature review about urban resilience indicators [16, 25, 29–31]. In detail, the literature review has been carried out through the support of the Scopus platform, using the keywords "urban resilience indicators", "resilience capacities" and "redundancy capacity". Moreover, different resilience assessment approaches [13, 41, 42] and several case studies have been analyzed [43, 44], to better understand how these indicators can be applied in the evaluation.

Table 1. Urban resilience indicators referred to redundancy capacity

Dimension	Criteria	Description	Unit	Capacity	Impact	Source
Social	Access to internet services	Percentage or number of household with access to broadband internet services	[num./%]	Robust, Redundant, Inclusive	+	Cutter et al. 2014
	Accessibility to public transport	Number of public transportation stop/1000 inhabitants.	[num.]	Inclusive, Redundant	+	Cutter et al. 2014
	Quantity of service facility	Number of service facility in the municipality	[num.]	Inclusive, redundant	+	Adapted from Cutter et al. 2014
	Number of hospital	Number of hospital per 10.000 person	[num.]	Inclusive, redundant	+	Cutter et al. 2014
	Public space	Surface of public space, open for public use	[hectares/m^2]	Redundant		Adapted from UNISDR 2015
	Accessibility to food distribution	Percentage of population which can access to food serves	[%]	Inclusive, Redundant	+	Adapted from Mercycrop 2016

(*continued*)

Table 1. *(continued)*

Dimension	Criteria	Description	Unit	Capacity	Impact	Source
Environment	Water supply	Number of different supply sources providing at least 5% of water supply capacity	[num.]	Redundant, Flexible	+	OECD, 2018; Cutter et al. 2014
	Diversity renewable energy	Number of different source of renewable energy	[num.]	Redundant, Flexible	+	Feldmeyer, 2019; Eurostat 2017
Economic	Diversification of economic business	Number of people or percentage of population not employed in the first economic sector	[num./%]	Redundant, Resourceful	+	Adapted from Cutter et al. 2010
Infrastructure	Emergency points/recovery points	Number of emergency point located in the municipal territory per 10.000 population	[num.]	Redundant	+	Feldemeyer 2019
	Arterial roads	Kilometres of main streets	[km linear]	Redundant	+	Cutter et al. 2014
	Multifunctional spaces	Surface or number of space with multifunctional characteristics that can be adapted	[hectares/m^2]	Redundant	+	Cutter et al. 2014
Governance	Risk assessment report	Presence or not of risk assessment report in urban development policy	[0–1]	Redundant	+	Arup 2015
	Climate action plan	Presence or not of climate action plan in urban development policy	[0–1]	Redundant	+	Cutter et al. 2014

For this reason, this paper provides a method to collect and describe these criteria considering: (1) dimension, (2) description, (3) unit, (4) capacity, (5) impact (Positive "+" or negative "−"), and (6) source, in order to combine and integrate the different information provided in literature [13, 16, 25, 29–31, 41]. The objective is underling the capacities to which they are referred to, putting in evidence which can be their possible influence.

4 System Dynamics Approach

System Dynamics Model are both computer-aided and theoretical approach applied to analyze dynamic and complex systems by the identification of the mutual interdependences between variables [46]. SDMs are based on the System Dynamics approach. The methodology of the System Dynamics (SD) has been introduced by Forrester at the end of '50s to analyze and improve the understanding of complex systems [33–35]. SD is based on feedback concepts to handle non-linearity and multi-loop that characterize complex systems. In fact, it is considered as a suitable tool to examine and illustrate the functioning of complex systems through the identification of the interdependent relationships between their variables [47]. Furthermore, it can be applied to model and simulate the behavior of complex dynamic systems to understand and analyze their dynamics and design development policies [35, 44–46]. System dynamics is a tool for understanding the change of a dynamic system over time. This approach can help in understanding the impacts of various factors on defined objectives in a system and provide useful information for decision makers [29, 35, 46, 48–52].

In details, there are six steps through analyze and describe complex systems through the SD approach [35, 43]. These phases are:

1. Identify the problem;
2. Develop a dynamics hypothesis, explaining the cause of the problem;
3. Create a basic structure of a causal graph;
4. Argument the causal graph with more information;
5. Convert the augmented causal graph into a system dynamics flow graph;
6. Translate a system dynamics flow into SD models

4.1 Causal Loop

Defined the variables of the system, the following step is developing the causal loop diagram, identifying the relationships and feedback loops between variables [42, 43]. The causal loop diagram illustrates the feedback structure of the system. It represents the reference mode that causes the dynamic behavior of the system [34]. It is also a tool to represent the relationships between variables. In detail, the relationships between variables can be either positive or negative. A positive relationship means that the variables will change in accordance to each other. Instead, the negative relationship implicates that the variables will change in opposite way.

The process to structure the causal loop diagram can be described within these phases:

- Define the problem and the objective;

- Identify the most important elements of the systems;
- Identify the secondary important elements of the systems;
- Identify the tertiary important elements of the systems;
- Define the cause-effect relationships.

As an example, Fig. 2 illustrates the causal loop referred to the population. Two different loops are identified, loop "R+" and "B−". Loop "R+" is a positive loop. It means that the population will grow with births, and the number of birth will increase with the population augment. It is a reinforcing loop, or rather the variable will change in the same direction over time [34]. Loop "B−" means that the number of deaths will grow with the population and the population will decrease as the death increasing.

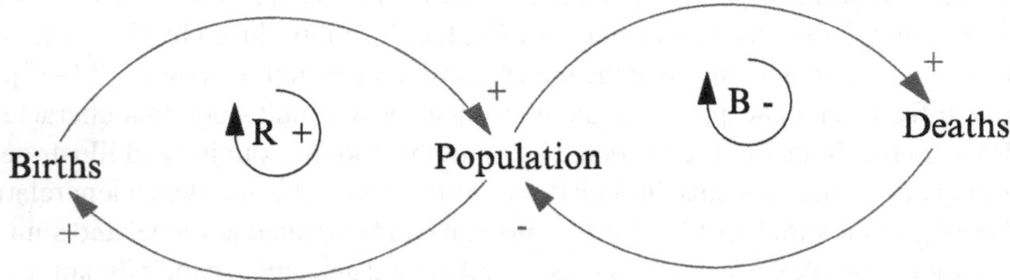

Fig. 2. Causal loop diagram of population (Bala et al. 2017)

5 Analyzing Redundancy Through System Dynamics Approach

As mentioned in the first section, cities are complex, adaptive and dynamic systems [35]. It implies that their multi-dimensional components are influencing each other, determining the evolution of cities over time [47, 48]. It is fundamental to provide a tool able to consider how different elements can influence each other and how factors can impact on a defined objective, in accordance to urban resilience enhancement [10]. This paper proposes the employment of the causal loop diagram to determine both how urban resilience indicators can influence the redundancy, and how redundancy should affect these variables. This choice has been also made in accordance to the fact that resilience can be interpreted as the result of different capacities that are mutually interrelated [53].

The challenge is providing a framework able to manage this complexity, to support decision makers in the identification of the key variables and their possible impacts on the city as whole, within urban resilience enhancement. Figure 3 illustrates the causal loop developed to analyze the redundancy. This causal loop has been developed following the phases mentioned in the previous section (Sect. 4.1). Firstly, the objective has been clarified, or rather "analyze how the variables can influence the redundancy and how the employment of the redundancy concept in urban development strategy could affect city as a whole". Secondly, the most important elements of the examined issue have been determined (Table 1). For this phase, all indicators listed in Table 1 have been identified as the most important elements of the system. Thirdly, the causal loop between the most important variables have been designed. The mainly loops identified among redundancy and variables are: (1) Infrastructure for internet service "A"; (2) Arterial roads "B"; Emergency points "C", Number of hospital "D". Secondly, also some loops between variables themselves have been recognized: loop "E" among "infrastructure for internet services" and "quantity of services"; "F" among "renewable energy" and "diversity in renewable energy" and "G" between "diversification of economic business" and "economic development". Furthermore, through this causal loop diagram, also some secondary variables of the city have been identified, namely: (1) vulnerable people, (2) road demand, (3) road improvement rate, (4) urban area, (5) soil consumption, (6) renewable energy, (7) offer of public transport. These variables are not listed in Table 1, because they do not influence redundancy in directly way. However, they are connected to the primary variable (Table 1) and they can influence the redundancy through both a reinforcing loop or by a negative influence.

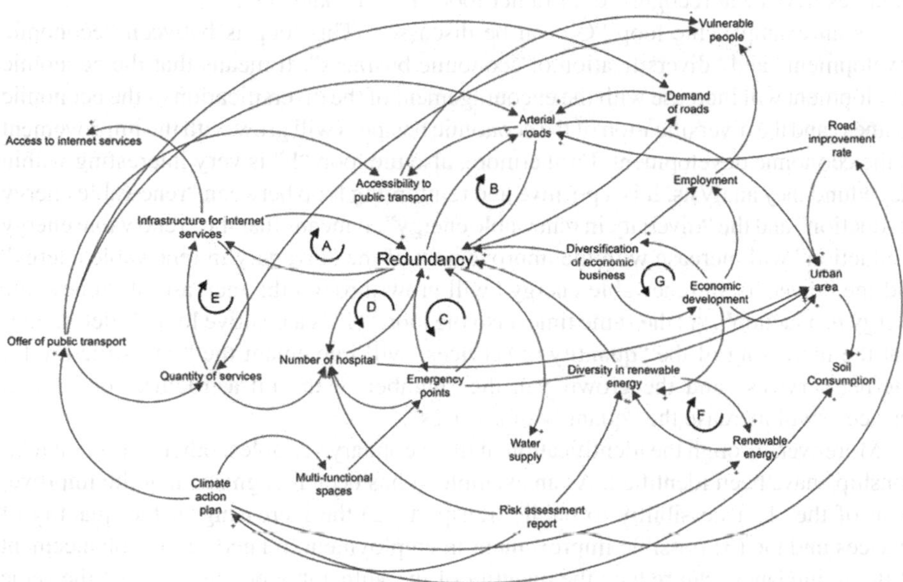

Fig. 3. Causal loop of redundancy

6 Discussion

The causal loop processing (Fig. 3) has been useful to determine:

- The loops between redundancy and indicators;
- The mutual relationships and loops among the considered indicators

Through the development of the causal loop, it was possible to reason about how the considered indicators (Table 1) can influence redundancy and how redundancy can influence these variables, within the objective of enhancing urban resilience. As illustrated in Fig. 3, different loops have been identified. Positive loops, namely "A", "B", "C" and "D" have been identified among redundancy and four indicators, or rather (1) infrastructure for internet services, (2) arterial roads, (3) emergency points and (4) number of hospitals. As an example, loop "A" means that the implementation of the redundancy in urban development strategy will increase the number of the infrastructure for internet services and the growing in the infrastructure for internet services will improve the redundancy capacity. Equally, for loop "B", "C" and "D", the redundancy implementation will increase the number of hospitals, number of arterial roads, and the number of emergency points and the growing of these elements will improve the redundancy capacity. Thus, these causal loops are reinforcing loops [34], that means that the variables will change in the same direction over time.

As above mentioned, also the secondary variables have been identified during the causal loop drawing. Consequently, three loops among the primary and secondary variables have been recognized, or rather loop "E", "F" and "G".

As an example, the loop "G" can be discussed. This loop is between "economic development" and "diversification of economic business". It means that the economic development will increase with the encouragement of the diversification of the economic business and the diversification of the economic business will grow with the improvement of the economic development. Furthermore, also the loop "F" is very interesting within the redundancy analysis. It is a positive and reinforcing loop between "renewable energy production" and the "diversity in renewable energy". It means that the "renewable energy production" will increase with the improvement of the "diversity in renewable energy" and the "diversity in renewable energy" will grow through the increase of "renewable energy production". As the same time, also the loop "G" is a positive loop. It determines that the increasing of the "quantity of services" will implement the "infrastructure for internet services" and the growing in the "number of the infrastructure for internet services" will increase the "quantity of services".

Moreover, through the identification of the secondary variables, other important relationships have been identified. As an example, it has been recognised that the improvement of the (1) accessibility to public transport, (2) the increasing of the quantity of services and the (3) possible improvement in employment, related to the enhancement of the redundancy, can reduce the quantity of the vulnerable people [54]. At the same time, it is also possible to underline that the redundancy enhancement should have negative impacts on the environmental dimension. In fact, the growing of (1) main roads, (2) number of hospitals and (3) emergency points could increase the surface of the urban area and consequently the soil consumption rate. These consequences are also in accordance to the issues underlined by Walker related to the conflicts between resilience and sustainability [55]. In this sense, the causal loop diagram (Fig. 3) has been fundamental to underline how the capacity of the redundancy can have both positive and negative impacts on the urban system, as a whole.

7 Conclusions and Future Developments

The paper recognizes the capacities that make a city resilient (Sect. 2) [23] and provides a multi-dimensional set of urban resilience indicators referred to the redundancy capacity

(Table 1). Moreover, it illustrates a preliminary application of SD approach to analyze the relationships between the redundancy and its variables, through the development of the causal loop diagram (Fig. 3). The illustrated application can be considered as preliminary step in the SD employment to analyze urban resilience within its capacities. It has been useful to underline its suitability in managing complexity and in identifying the probable impacts of different factors on the same objective [34]. Considering the recognized potentialities, the future development of this research should be organized with a sequential organization. Firstly, the causal loop (Fig. 3) has to be translated into the stock and flow diagram. It is necessary to evaluate the consistency of the redundancy impacts on the urban system over time [56]. Secondly, a System Dynamics Model that embrace all urban resilience capacities with their indicators will be processed. The challenge is providing a general evaluation framework, that is able to analyze urban resilience within its capacities [57], managing cities as complex and adaptive systems [35]. The final objective is proposing an evaluation tool to assess urban development strategies [46, 54, 55], considering their probable impacts on urban system over time. Thus, this research can support the definition of actions and policies for urban resilience enhancement, predicting their probable effects [62]. Furthermore, this general framework should be integrated with the multi-criteria analysis [58, 60, 61], to consider the specific characteristic of context both in the evaluation and in setting developing strategies [57–59].

References

1. Mart, C., et al.: A Midterm Monitoring and Evaluation Report of 100 Resilient Cities and the participation of (2018)
2. Event, N.: Making Cities Resilient 2030 Introduction & Background. 2030, 1–19
3. Helena, M.V., Dilanthi, A., Richard, H.: Making Cities Resilient: from awareness to implementation. Int. J. Disaster Resil. Built Environ. **4**, 5–8 (2013). https://doi.org/10.1108/17595901311299035
4. UNISDR (United Nations Office for Disaster Risk Reduction): Sendai Framework Data Readiness Review 2017, Disaster-related Data for Sustainable Development (2017)
5. UNISDR: Hyogo Framework for Action 2005–2015. In: United Nations International Strategy for Disaster Reduc (2005). https://doi.org/10.1017/CBO9781107415324.004
6. Masnavi, M.R., Gharai, F., Hajibandeh, M.: Exploring urban resilience thinking for its application in urban planning: a review of literature. Int. J. Environ. Sci. Technol. **16**(1), 567–582 (2018). https://doi.org/10.1007/s13762-018-1860-2
7. Meerow, S., Newell, J.P., Stults, M.: Defining urban resilience: a review (2016). https://doi.org/10.1016/j.landurbplan.2015.11.011
8. World Economic Forum: The Global Risks Report 2018 13th Edition (2013). ISBN 978-1-944835-15-6
9. Tremml-Werner, B.: The Comparative Framework. Spain, China and Japan in Manila, 1571-1644, 43–90 (2018). https://doi.org/10.1515/9789048526819-003
10. Ilmola, L.: Approaches to measurement of urban resilience. In: Yamagata, Y., Maruyama, H. (eds.) Urban Resilience. ASTSA, pp. 207–237. Springer, Cham (2016). https://doi.org/10.1007/978-3-319-39812-9_11
11. Moghadas, M., Asadzadeh, A., Vafeidis, A., Fekete, A., Kötter, T.: A multi-criteria approach for assessing urban flood resilience in Tehran. Iran. Int. J. Disaster Risk Reduct. **35**, 101069 (2019). https://doi.org/10.1016/j.ijdrr.2019.101069

12. Quinlan, A.E., Berbés-Blázquez, M., Haider, L.J., Peterson, G.D.: Measuring and assessing resilience: broadening understanding through multiple disciplinary perspectives. J. Appl. Ecol. **53**, 677–687 (2016). https://doi.org/10.1111/1365-2664.12550
13. Da Silva, J., Moench, M.: City Resilience Framework. Arup (2014). http://www.seachangecop.org/files/documents/URF_Bo
14. Resilience, C.: City Resilience Index
15. Sellberg, M.M., Wilkinson, C., Peterson, G.D.: Resilience assessment: a useful approach to navigate urban sustainability. Ecol. Soc. **20**, 43 (2015)
16. Sharifi, A.: A critical review of selected tools for assessing community resilience. Ecol. Indic. (2016). https://doi.org/10.1016/j.ecolind.2016.05.023
17. Meerow, S., Newell, J.: Resilience and complexity: a bibliometric review and prospects for industrial ecology. J. Ind. Ecol. **19** (2015). https://doi.org/10.1111/jiec.12252
18. Adger, W.: Social and ecological resilience: are they related? Prog. Hum. Geogr. **24**, 347–364 (2000). https://doi.org/10.1191/030913200701540465
19. Kantsler, V., Steinberg, V.: Orientation and dynamics of a vesicle in tank-treading motion in shear flow. Phys. Rev. Lett. **95** (2005). https://doi.org/10.1103/PhysRevLett.95.258101
20. Rose, A.: Economic resilience to natural and man-made disasters: multidisciplinary origins and contextual dimensions. Environ. Hazards **7**, 383–398 (2007). https://doi.org/10.1016/j.envhaz.2007.10.001
21. Lazarević, E.V., Kekovi, Z., Antoni, B.: Insearch of the principles of resilient urban design: implementability of the principles in the case of the cities in Serbia. Enery Build. **158**, 1130–1138 (2018). https://doi.org/10.1016/j.enbuild.2017.11.005
22. Galderisi, A.: Urban resilience: a framework for empowering cities in face of heterogeneous risk factors. A|Z ITU J. Faculty Architect. **11**, 36–58 (2014)
23. Cutter, S.L.: The landscape of disaster resilience indicators in the USA. Nat. Hazards **80**(2), 741–758 (2015). https://doi.org/10.1007/s11069-015-1993-2
24. Fox-Lent, C., Bates, M.E., Linkov, I.: A matrix approach to community resilience assessment: an illustrative case at Rockaway Peninsula. Environ. Syst. Decis. **35**(2), 209–218 (2015). https://doi.org/10.1007/s10669-015-9555-4
25. Sharifi, A., Yamagata, Y.: Urban resilience assessment: multiple dimensions, criteria, and indicators. In: Yamagata, Y., Maruyama, H. (eds.) Urban Resilience. ASTSA, pp. 259–276. Springer, Cham (2016). https://doi.org/10.1007/978-3-319-39812-9_13
26. Sharifi, A., Yamagata, Y.: Principles and criteria for assessing urban energy resilience: a literature review (2016). https://doi.org/10.1016/j.rser.2016.03.028
27. Sharifi, A., Yamagata, Y.: Resilient urban planning: major principles and criteria. Energy Procedia (2014). https://doi.org/10.1016/j.egypro.2014.12.154
28. Cutter, S.L., et al.: A place-based model for understanding community resilience to natural disasters. Glob. Environ. Chang. (2008). https://doi.org/10.1016/j.gloenvcha.2008.07.013
29. Figueiredo, L., Honiden, T., Schumann, A.: OECD Regional Development Working Papers 2018/02 Indicators for Resilient Cities (2018)
30. Cutter, S.L., Burton, C.G., Emrich, C.T.: Disaster resilience indicators for benchmarking baseline conditions. J. Homel. Secur. Emerg. Manag. (2010). https://doi.org/10.2202/1547-7355.1732
31. Feldmeyer, D., et al.: Indicators for monitoring urban climate change resilience and adaptation. Sustainability **11**(10), 2931 (2019)
32. Forrester, J.W.: Principles of Systems. Productivity Press, Portland (1990)
33. Forrester, J.W.: Industrial Dynamics. MIT Press, Cambridge (1961)
34. Bala, B.K., Arshad, F.M., Noh, K.M.: Systems thinking: system dynamics. In: System Dynamics: Modelling and Simulation. pp. 15–35. Springer, Singapore (2017). https://doi.org/10.1007/978-981-10-2045-2_2

35. Batty, M.: Cities as Complex Systems: Scaling, Interaction, Networks, Dynamics and Urban Morphologies. Work. Pap. CASA Work. Pap. (131). Cent. Adv. Spat. Anal. (UCL), London (2012). https://doi.org/10.1007/978-0-387-30440-3_69
36. Leichenko, R.: Climate change and urban resilience, 164–168 (2011). https://doi.org/10.1016/j.cosust.2010.12.014
37. Godschalk, D.: Urban Hazard Mitigation: Creating Resilient Cities. Nat. Hazards Rev. **4** (2003). https://doi.org/10.1061/(ASCE)1527-6988(2003)4:3(136)
38. Gibson, C.A., Tarrant, M.: A "conceptual models" approach to organisational resilience: gibson and tarrant discuss the range of inter-dependant factors needed to manage organisational resilience. Aust. J. Emerg. Manag. **25**, 6–12 (2010)
39. Chuvarayan, A., Martel, I., Peterson, C.: A Strategic Approach for Sustainability and Resilience Planning within Municipalities (2006)
40. Bruneau, M., et al.: A framework to quantitatively assess and enhance the seismic resilience of communities. Earthq. Spectra **19** (2003). https://doi.org/10.1193/1.1623497
41. Fu, X., Wang, X.: Developing an integrative urban resilience capacity index for plan making. Environ. Syst. Decis. **38**(3), 367–378 (2018). https://doi.org/10.1007/s10669-018-9693-6
42. O'Connell, D., Walker, B., Abel, N., Grigg, N.: The Resilience, Adaptation and Transformation Assessment Framework: From Theory to Application (2015). https://doi.org/10.13140/RG.2.1.4301.4564
43. Suárez, M., Gómez-Baggethun, E., Benayas, J., Tilbury, D.: Towards an urban resilience index: a case study in 50 Spanish cities. Sustain. (2016). https://doi.org/10.3390/su8080774
44. Tabibian, M., Rezapour, M.: Assessment of urban resilience; a case study of Region 8 of Tehran city, Iran. Sci. Iran. **23**, 1699–1707 (2016). https://doi.org/10.24200/sci.2016.2240
45. UNISDR: Making Cities Resilient Report 2012 (2012). https://doi.org/10.1177/0956247814522154
46. Rouwette, E., Vennix, J.: System dynamics and organizational interventions. Syst. Res. Behav. Sci. **23**, 451–466 (2006). https://doi.org/10.1002/sres.772
47. Sterman, J.: Business Dynamics, System Thinking and Modeling for a Complex World 19 (2000). http://lst-iiep.iiep-unesco.org/cgi-bin/wwwi32.exe/[in=epidoc1.in]/?t2000=013598/(100)
48. Park, M., Kim, Y., Lee, H., Han, S., Hwang, S., Choi, M.: Modeling the dynamics of urban development project: focusing on self-sufficient city development. Math. Comput. Model. **57**, 2082–2093 (2013). https://doi.org/10.1016/j.mcm.2011.05.058
49. Wu, D., Ning, S.: Dynamic assessment of urban economy-environment-energy system using system dynamics model: a case study in Beijing. Environ. Res. **164**, 70–84 (2018). https://doi.org/10.1016/j.envres.2018.01.029
50. Tan, Y., Jiao, L., Shuai, C., Shen, L.: A system dynamics model for simulating urban sustainability performance: a China case study. J. Clean. Prod. **199**, 1107–1115 (2018). https://doi.org/10.1016/j.jclepro.2018.07.154
51. Forrester, J.W.: Urban Dynamics. MIT Press, Cambridge (1979)
52. Alfeld, L.E., Graham, A.K.: Introduction to Urban Dynamics. Wright-Allen Press, Cambridge (1976)
53. Norris, F.H., Stevens, S.P., Pfefferbaum, B., Wyche, K.F., Pfefferbaum, R.L.: Community resilience as a metaphor, theory, set of capacities, and strategy for disaster readiness. Am. J. Commun. Psychol. **41**, 127–150 (2008). https://doi.org/10.1007/s10464-007-9156-6
54. Joakim, E., et al.: Using system dynamics to model social vulnerability and resilience to coastal hazards. Int. J. Emerg. Manag. **12**, 366 (2016). https://doi.org/10.1504/IJEM.2016.079846
55. Walker, B., Salt, D., Reid, W.: Resilience Thinking: Sustaining Ecosystems and People in A Changing World. Bibliovault OAI Repos. Univ. Chicago Press (2006)

56. Datola, G., Bottero, M., De Angelis, E.: How urban resilience can change cities: a system dynamics model approach. In: Misra, S., et al. (eds.) ICCSA 2019. LNCS, vol. 11622, pp. 108–122. Springer, Cham (2019). https://doi.org/10.1007/978-3-030-24305-0_9
57. Kuznecova, T., Romagnoli, F.: System Dynamics approach within the context of city resilience and urban metabolism (2014). https://doi.org/10.3846/enviro.2014.125
58. Bottero, M., Comino, E., Dell'Anna, F., Dominici, L., Rosso, M.: Strategic assessment and economic evaluation: the case study of Yanzhou Island (China). Sustainability (2019). https://doi.org/10.3390/su11041076
59. Assumma, V., Bottero, M., Datola, G., De Angelis, E., Monaco, R.: Dynamic models for exploring the resilience in territorial scenarios. Sustainabilty (2020). https://doi.org/10.3390/su12010003
60. Roy, B., Vincke, P.: Multicriteria analysis: survey and new directions. Eur. J. Oper. Res. **8**, 207–218 (1981)
61. Figueira, J., Greco, S., Ehrgott, M.: Multiple criteria decision analysis, state of the art surveys. Mult. Criteria Decis. Anal. State Art Surv. **78** (2005). https://doi.org/10.1007/b100605
62. Bottero, M., Caprioli, C., Cotella, G., Santangelo, M.: Sustainable cities: A reflection on potentialities and limits based on existing eco-districts in Europe. Sustainability (2019). https://doi.org/10.3390/su11205794

International Workshop on Ecosystem Services: Nature's Contribution to People in Practice. Assessment Frameworks, Models, Mapping, and Implications (NC2P 2020)

Use of Landscape Metrics and Multi-criteria Analysis to Identify Landscape Units Concerning of Vegetation of Quadrilátero Ferrífero - MG

Lourdes Manresa Camargos(✉), Nicole Andrade da Rocha(✉), and Ana Clara Mourão Moura(✉)

Universidade Federal de Minas Gerais (UFMG), Av. Antônio Carlos, 6.627, Belo Horizonte, Brazil

loumcamargos@hotmail.com, nicarocha.jf@gmail.com, anaclara@ufmg.br

Abstract. This article had the main objective to identify Landscape Unities corresponding to the vegetation in the Quadrilátero Ferrífero area, in Minas Gerais. The study looks to contribute with the identification of homogeneous areas in the shape of territorial unities, for the composition of methods about the territorial strategic planning. For this, nuclear area landscape metrics were used, shape index and fractal connectivity, identified as the main metrics which depict quality and vegetation fractal embrittlement condition. Afterward, a Multicriterial Analysis by Evidence Weight according to the priority level for each metric, for integration of the analysis and identification of the greater values fractal bearing in mind the three aspects. As a result, two main unities were obtained: notable vegetation landscape; and vegetation with a higher vulnerability to transformation. Was observed a concentration of notable landscapes of vegetation on the central and southeast Quadrilatero's areas, mainly at the Serra do Gandarela, Serra da Moeda and Serra do Caraça. In counterpart, the areas corresponding to the south and north of the Quadrilatero, besides being closer to the urban centers, has shown to be more likely to be transformed due to the isolation of the fragments. Stem from this analysis, the importance of the Conservation Units maintenance is bolstered, which are fundamental to the natural resource's protection. The landscape metrics is rated as an important tool of landscape analysis through pattern identification and the understanding of the dynamics of a geographic region. At last, the multicriteria analysis is understood as an important tool for supporting the decision making, being able to evaluate different variables to obtain interest rankings, in agreement with the demanded objectives.

Keywords: Landscape metrics · Multicriteria analysis · Strategic planning

1 Introduction

Studies on landscape and territory must understand the relationships of the environment and its dynamics, about the potentialities and vulnerabilities related to anthropic action,

O. Gervasi et al. (Eds.): ICCSA 2020, LNCS 12253, pp. 381–393, 2020.
https://doi.org/10.1007/978-3-030-58814-4_27

as well as about the cultural values that elect notable values. For this, is necessary to have an integrated view of the physical and biological factors of natural systems and their interactions with socioeconomic and political factors [1].

The study of landscape ecology is a way of identifying existing changes and conditions of the landscape, through the identification and characterization of fragments in the territory, analyzing the spatial distribution and the forms they present.

It is an area of knowledge that proposes the study of the structure, function and change of these heterogeneous regions, seeking to identify patterns of changes and study the dynamics of a geographical region through metrics of the landscape [2].

In addition, Landscape Ecology aims to characterize the most suitable fragments for environmental conservation and compose the spatial arrangements necessary to achieve biodiversity, species balance and the gene flow that constitutes the landscape mosaic, in order to allow a balance between green areas and human occupation [3, 4].

The quantitative data of the landscape structure are termed as indexes or metrics of Landscape Ecology. When quantifying the composition and configuration of the landscape, these data allow the comparison between landscapes or between the same landscape at different times, allowing the identification of the functional processes and ecological patterns of the landscapes, allowing to measure the spatial distribution of the patches, evaluating both the fragment individually, such as the general structure of the area and the role of each fragment in the set, with regard to size, density, isolation, distance, connectivity and complexity of the shape [5, 6].

In this sense, this article seeks to combine landscape metrics and multicriteria analysis in order to understand the landscape configuration, identifying vulnerabilities and potentialities.

Multicriteria analysis is a method of spatial analysis that is based on the integration of data according to the objectives of analysis, taking into account multiple criteria, making a simplification of the spatial complexity involved through layers of information of the main variables that characterize the phenomenon [7, 8].

Thus, through the recognition of landscape patterns, the article presents a reproducible script to identify Landscape Units of the Quadrilátero Ferrífero referring to the areas with remarkable landscape and areas that have greater vulnerability of transformation.

The choice for the landscape of the Quadrilátero Ferrífero as an object of analysis is justified due to its landscape complexity and its richness in natural resources, mainly its water resources. The area is the birthplace and cradle of important water resources, of mountains that are a reference for the landscape of Minas Gerais and of transition between the Atlantic Forest and the Cerrado, with emphasis on the rupestrian field vegetation that is located together with the crests of the saws.

The Quadrilátero Ferrífero (Fig. 1) is in the center-southeast portion of Minas Gerais and occupies an area of about 18,000 km^2. The area is home to 52 municipalities, including the capital, Belo Horizonte.

The region has great environmental, mineral and geological importance in the state, having as its landscape reference the Serra do Gandarela, Serra da Piedade, Serra do Curral, Serra Rola Moça, Serra da Moeda, Serra do Ouro Branco and Serra do Caraça.

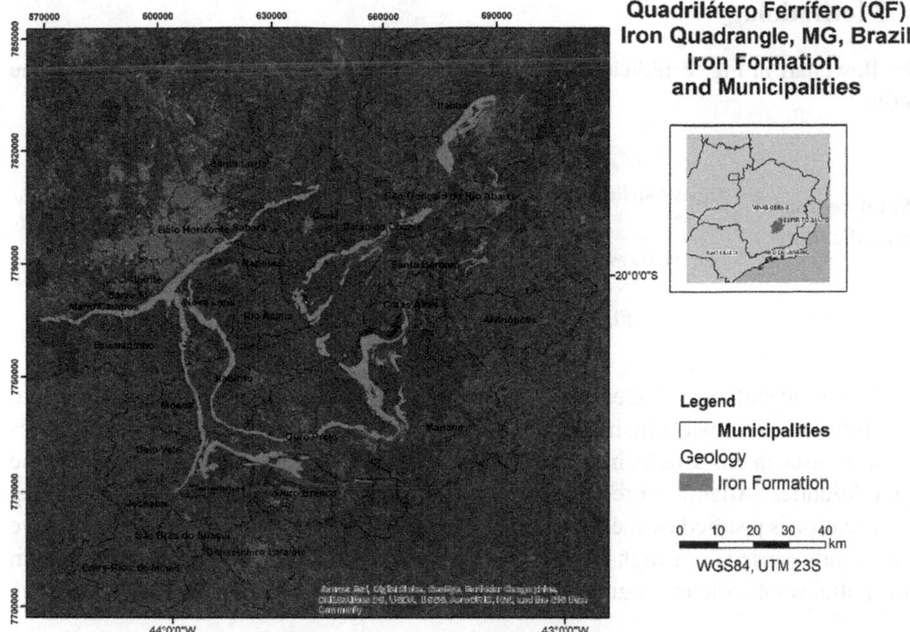

Fig. 1. Location of Quadrilátero Ferrífero

The limit of the Quadrilátero Ferrífero used in the present work corresponds to the boundaries of the municipalities where iron was found and was defined during studies by the Geoprocessing Laboratory of the School of Architecture at UFMG. This delimitation was made because the Quadrilátero Ferrífero itself is only the delimitation of the ferriferous area, but for territorial planning purposes it was decided to carry out the cut including the municipalities.

The Quadrilátero Ferrífero is a priority area for biodiversity conservation in Minas Gerais, being classified as an "Area of Special Biological Importance" [9]. The region's vegetation is composed of the transition between the Cerrado and Atlantic Forest biomes, with emphasis on the vegetation of Campos Rupestres. For this reason, the forests and fields of that region are extremely important for the maintenance of wild flora and fauna, especially of endemic, rare and endangered species.

Currently, Serra do Gandarela is one of the last physical and natural remnants in good condition present in the Quadrilátero Ferrífero. The region is of great importance due to the existence of aquifer recharge fields, its heterogeneous morphology, flora with species of Campos, Cerrado and Atlantic Forest, remnants of primary forests, in addition to the existence of geological heritage [10].

As it is a region of conflicts of interest, this work seeks to identify the Landscape Units of vegetation in the Quadrilátero Ferrífero, as a contribution to studies of strategic planning proposition, aiming at the protection or requalification of fragments. In this article, the metrics of the landscape calculated from the land cover data for the Campos and Atlantic Forest will be considered, as they are the main components of the local vegetation.

2 Methodology

The flowchart in Fig. 2 indicates the methodological steps in the development of the study.

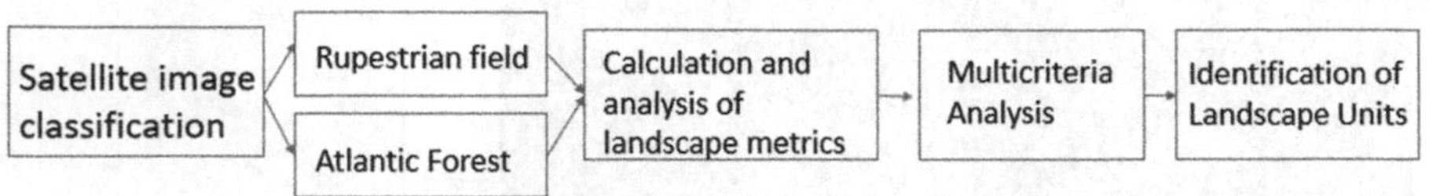

Fig. 2. Methodological flowchart

First, to identify the classes used, the soil cover map of IDE SISEMA (state Spatial Data Infrastructure) was obtained and a reclassification was made to obtain the classes that were used in this article, namely the Campos Rupestres (Rupestrian Fields) and the Mata Atlântica (Atlantic Forest), as shown in Fig. 3. The option to adopt an existing classification is justified by the intention of working with official data, although we have also already carried out a high-quality classification with the use of RapidEye images in 5 m spatial resolution and digital processing.

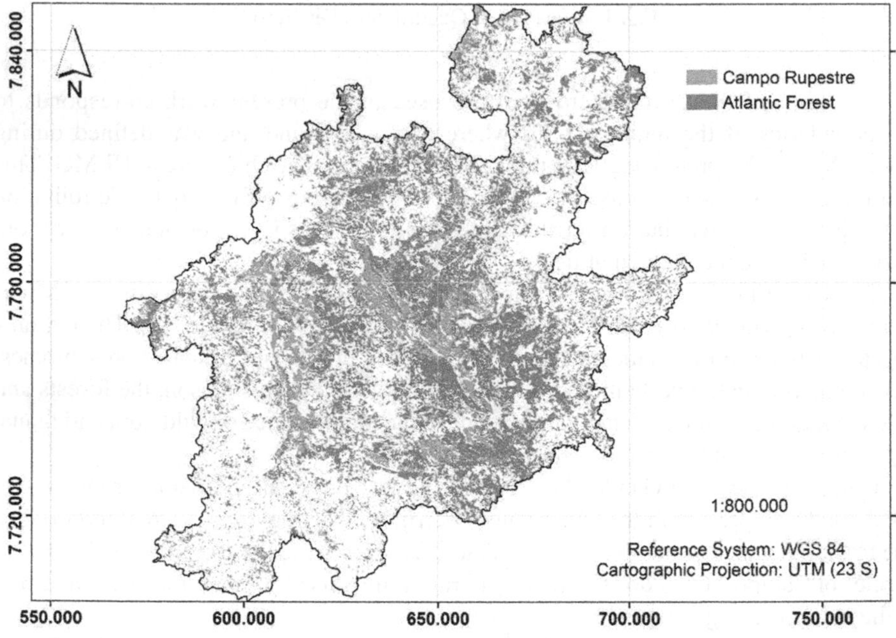

Fig. 3. Land cover classes

We chose to analyze the Campos Rupestres and Mata Atlântica class separately, as it is understood that each ecosystem represents a different importance, having different characteristics of fauna and flora.

Among the set of metrics indicated by the studies of Landscape Ecology, three were chosen, due to previous studies that indicated them as "drivers" variables, main indicators of the conditions of the fragments [11, 12].

The main landscape metrics used were extracted from the categories of area, shape and connectivity, using the metrics described in Fig. 4. This step was performed in the ArcGIS 10.7 software, with the Patch and V-Late Beta 2.0 extensions.

Fig. 4. Landscape metrics - (a) - core area: the fragment on the left has a less robust core than the one on the right due to the elongation of the shape and proximity of the internal area to the edges; (b) - shape index: perimeter/area ratio that makes the fragment on the right more exposed to transformations, (c) - connectivity: favoring stepping-stones. Source: MOURA, 2010 [13].

Finally, the Multicriteria Analysis step was performed using the Evidence Weights method, generating a classificatory index to identify landscape units according to the degree of importance of vegetation preservation in the Quadrilátero Ferrífero. The study is also applicable to the choice of areas for requalification since it indicates a hierarchy between the most qualified and protected fragments versus the most fragile and at risk of transformation.

3 Partial Results and Discussion

The results and discussions are related to the products of the methodological steps, which are, respectively: calculation and analysis of landscape metrics and multicriteria analysis to identify landscape units.

3.1 Analysis of Landscape Metrics

Core Area: The core area metric allowed us to calculate which fragments have an internal protected area greater than 500 m, signaled by the red color in Fig. 5. In this sense, these fragments are of great relevance, as they are more protected from the external actions of the edge effect, which are changes in the structure, composition or abundance of a fragment in its border or edge.

Therefore, they are fragments that must be prioritized in the definition of the most notable vegetation landscapes of the Quadrilátero Ferrífero from the data of the core area, the regions with lesser or greater presence of protected internal areas of the forest and rupestrian fields are identified, as shown in Fig. 5.

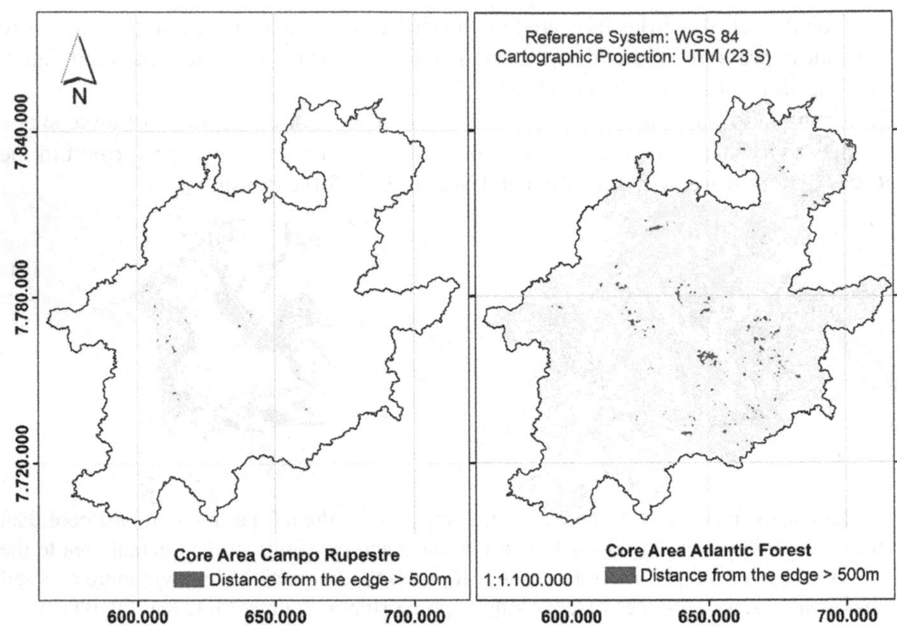

Fig. 5. Core area metric (Color figure online)

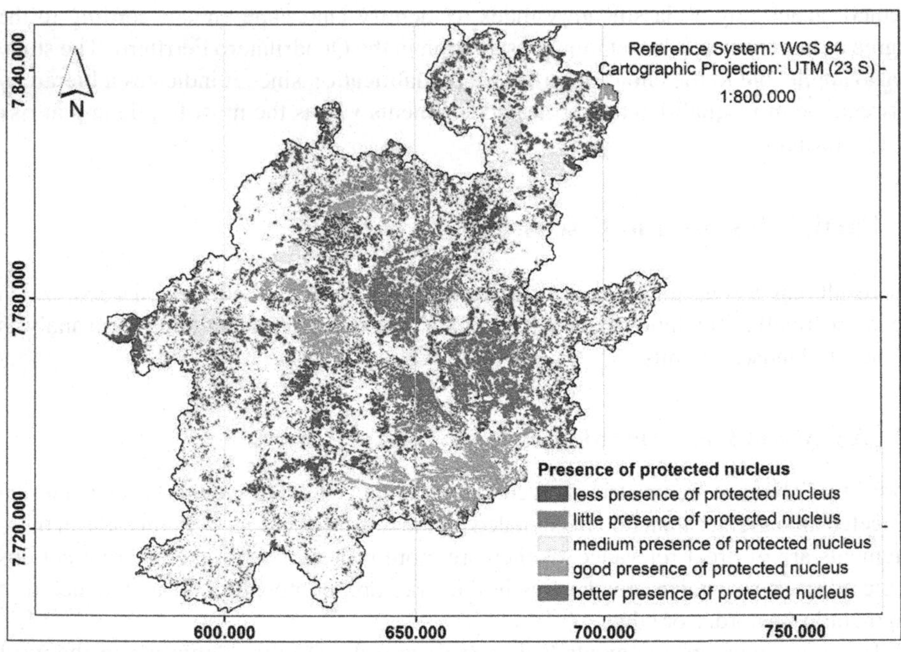

Fig. 6. Presence of protected nucleus

Thus, the regions that have a nuclear area with a distance from the edge greater than 500 m, are those that have a more protected core. Once the nuclei were located, fragments that have these conditions were selected, ranked according to the number of nucleus areas contained in them (Fig. 6).

Shape - Shape Index: The purpose of analyzing the shape index is to check if the fragments have problems caused by the edge effect. The closer to 1, the more regular or more circular the fragments are [14] and the more distant from 1, the more irregular and more propitious to the edge effect.

The shape index is calculated to represent the perimeter/area ratio of the fragments. In this sense, the more regular the shape, the larger the internal area of the fragment and the smaller the interaction with the surrounding matrix. Therefore, it will also be less prone to the edge effect.

Therefore, it is understood that the closer to 1 the shape index, the more regular and protected the fragments are (Fig. 7). To a degree of importance, fragments with a shape index close to 1 (dark green) are more notable than very irregular fragments (light green), which are possibly already subject to the external actions of the edge effect.

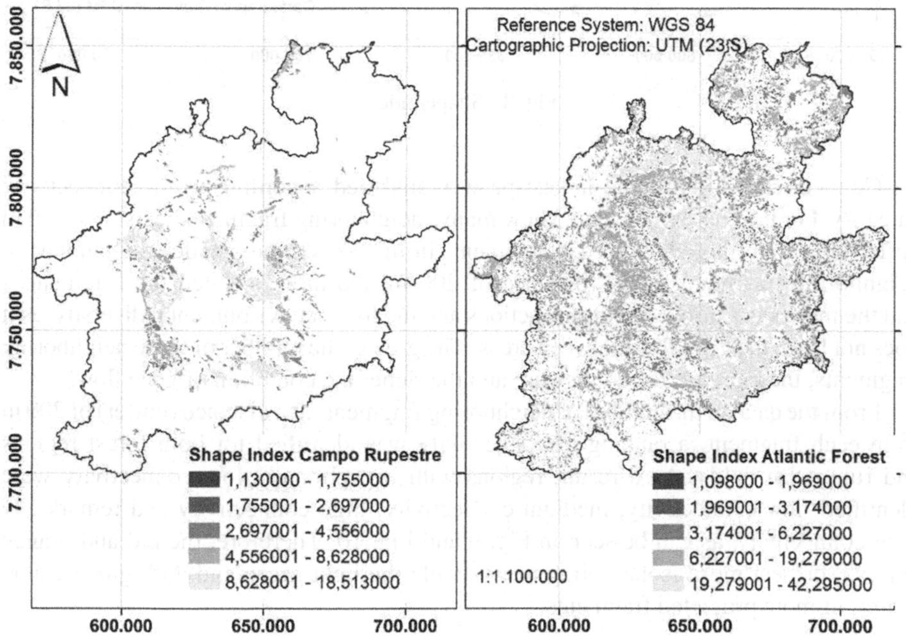

Fig. 7. Shape Index Metric (Color figure online)

From the data of the shape index metric, fragments with irregular, irregular and regular shapes from the regions of the Atlantic Forest and rupestrian fields were identified (Fig. 8). In this sense, the more regular the fragment, the more protected the border effect will be.

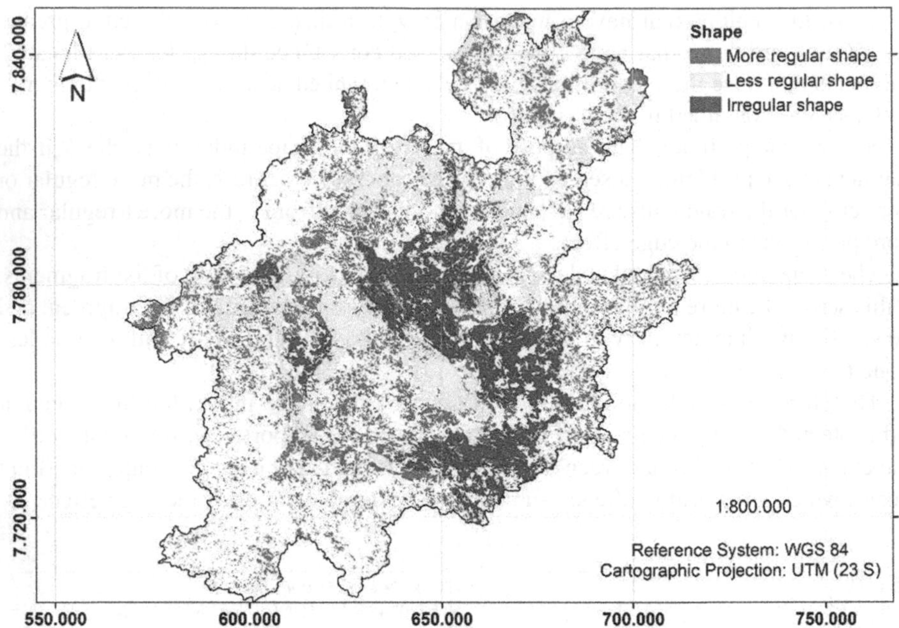

Fig. 8. Shape index

Connectivity: Finally, the landscape was analyzed according to the connectivity category. For this, it was calculated how many 'neighboring fragments' exist in a 200 m buffer area from the edge of each fragment. In this sense, the smaller the number of neighboring fragments at this distance of 200 m, the more isolated the fragment is and the more susceptible to external actions and the loss of environmental diversity, as it does not favor the gene flow between areas. The greater the number of these neighboring fragments, the more protected they are and the richer the condition of gene flow.

From the data on the number of neighboring fragments at a distance (buffer) of 200 m from each fragment, a ranking of connectivity was identified for both forest regions and rupestrian fields. As a result, regions with exceptionally low connectivity were identified; low connectivity; medium connectivity; high connectivity and remarkably high connectivity, as can be seen in Fig. 9 and Fig. 10. Therefore, the red and orange colors represent more isolated fragments, while the light green and dark green colors represent more protected fragments.

3.2 Multicriteria Analysis

Multicriteria Analysis is a method of spatial analysis that has been widely used mainly in the last twenty years in a digital way (although it was already used in an analog way in the 1960s by McHarg, 1969). It is based on the systemic approach and is based on data integration according to the objectives of analysis, considering multiple criteria [7].

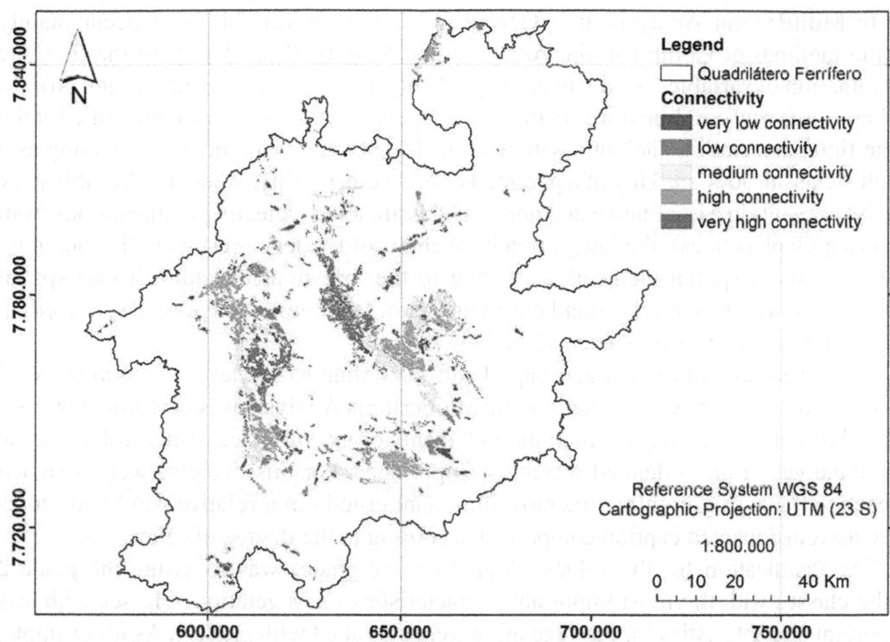

Fig. 9. Campo rupestre connectivity.

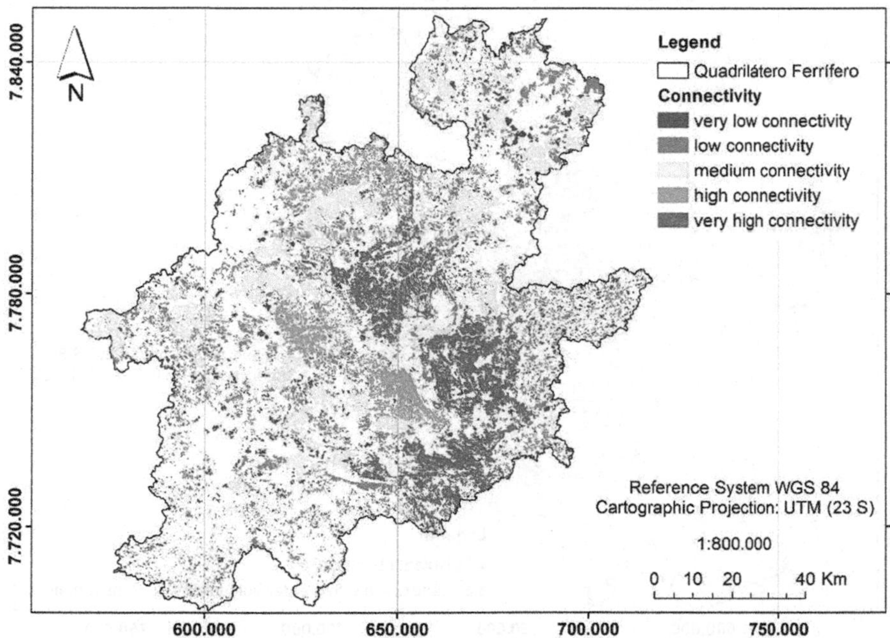

Fig. 10. Atlantic forest connectivity

In Multicriteria Analysis, the stage of integration of variables can occur mainly by the methods of Combinatorial Analysis and Weights of Evidence. In the first, the combination of variables occurs in pairs, gradually, as the researcher judges the process and proposes new combinations. In the second method, all variables are integrated at the same time, associating each one with a defined importance weight, and obtaining as a result a classification ranking of a potential or of a vulnerability. While the Combinatory Analysis results in a qualitative and nominal classification (selecting compositions from the research objectives), the integration by Weights of Evidence results in the hierarchy of the analyzed spatial elements according to the investigated values. Those spatial elements of higher hierarchy stand out in the set of variables studied, placed according to the relative importance of each variable in the set.

For the identification of Landscape Units according to the level of importance of the Quadrilátero Ferrífero vegetation, the Multicriteria Analysis was performed by Evidence Weights, a method in which the judgments of the variables of interest are made simultaneously from a defined weight of importance. For this, weights were assigned to each variable (highlighting the most important criteria in a relative way) and scores were assigned to each caption component according to the degree of relevance.

The justification for the values adopted for the grades was to assign the grade 2 to the classes with the most important characteristics for vegetation. Classes with less important characteristics for the vegetation were classified with grade 1. As for example, for classes with index values of a form closer to 1 (more regular and protected forms)

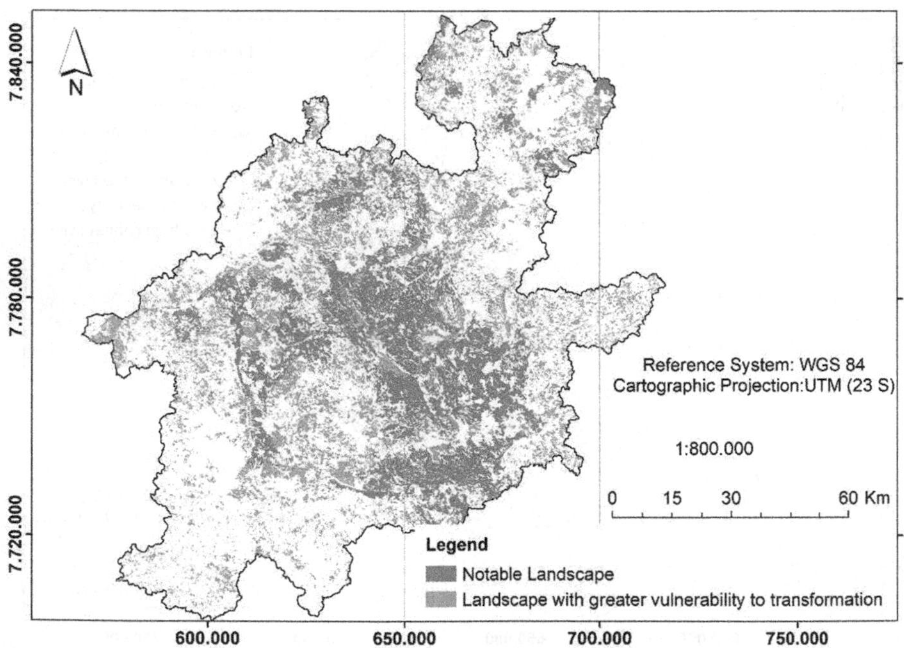

Fig. 11. Map of landscape units

was given a score of 2, while for index values of more distant forms of 1 (a more irregular and unprotected form) a score of 1 was given.

Once the marks were assigned to the legend components, it was necessary to define the weights for each variable, so that map algebra could be performed. The team decided that the variables would have different importance, depending on the specialist knowledge about the area. The assignment of weights can be done by data-driven or knowledge-driven, in processes of listening or taking opinions [15]. For this work, the team judged the connectivity metric as the most important, weighing 50%. The metric of form was considered with a weight of 20% and the metric of nuclear area, with a weight of 30%.

Thus, combining the variables generated by the calculation of landscape metrics, according to their degree of importance, it was possible to obtain the following Landscape Units in the Quadrilátero Ferrífero represented in Fig. 11.

4 Conclusions

The studies of the vegetation cover through the network of its fragments are particularly important to know the characteristics of a landscape, through the identification of patterns and the dynamics of a geographic region. With that, it is also possible to understand how society deals with environmental preservation and conservation issues. The characterizations of the existing conditions are the basis for the construction of opinions and decision making.

This article stands out by combining studies of landscape metrics with multicriteria analysis, presenting the potential of combining these methodologies in the identification of landscape units, assisting researchers and managers in the identification of areas that require greater attention and that need policies and preservation projects.

With the combination of the two methodologies it was possible to identify two main units in the Quadrilátero Ferrífero: remarkable landscapes of vegetation; and vegetation with greater vulnerability to transformation and that need attention regarding the loss of green areas.

In the development of the study of landscape metrics, it was identified which fragments have protected cores and which have unprotected cores; fragments with a more regular shape and fragments that have a more irregular shape and are more susceptible to the edge effect; and, finally, which fragments are most connected to each other and which are most disconnected.

It was observed that fragments with greater connectivity coincide with fragments with a more protected core, both present in central spots of the Quadrilateral. However, the most regular fragments are also the most isolated fragments (less connectivity) and have a poorly protected core. It is also noticed that these last more isolated fragments, are more spread along the Quadrilátero Ferrífero and are smaller in area, when compared with the large central green patches.

Finally, to identify the two landscape units in the studies of green areas in the region, the Multicriteria Analysis method was used to arbitrate weights of importance for each metric or variable in the systemic approach of integrating values. The connectivity metric was judged to be the most important, with a weight equal to 50%, the form metric was considered to have a weight of 20% and the core area metric to a weight of 30%.

As a result, there was a concentration of remarkable landscapes of vegetation in the central and southeastern area of the Quadrilátero corresponding, for the most part, to the Serras do Gandarela, Serra da Moeda and Serra do Caraça. On the other hand, the areas to the south and north of the Quadrilátero, in addition to those close to urban centers, were more susceptible to transformation. Based on this analysis, the importance of maintaining the Conservation Units is reinforced, which are fundamental for the protection of natural resources.

It should be noted that the process presented here is defensible and reproducible. Defensible because it applies a clear model for choosing variables in the form of metrics, defining notes in the form of classifying the legend components and deciding on the relative weights of the variables involved. These are decisions that can be revised at any time in stages of calibration vis-a-vis with each reality and with the research objectives. For this same reason, they are reproducible processes, since a user can easily obtain satellite images and perform their classifications, if there is no classification of available ground cover for their territory, followed by the application of integration metrics and algebras. In the case study in question, ArcGIS software was used, but the processes could also be executed with free applications, such as QGis and Fragstats.

The partial and final results obtained are integrated with other studies of landscape analysis, being a first step for the characterization of the physical and anthropic conditions of the environmental landscape.

Acknowledgments. The authors would like to thank the CNPq support through the project "Geodesign and Parametric Modeling of Territorial Occupation: Geoprocessing for the proposal of a Master Plan for the Landscape for the Quadrilátero Ferrífero-MG", Process 401066/2016-9, Edital Universal 01/2016 and FAPEMIG PPM-00368-18.

References

1. Filho, B.S.S.: Análise de Paisagem: Fragmentação e Mudanças. Departamento de Cartografia, Centro de Sensoriamento Remoto – Instituto de Geociências – UFMG, Belo Horizonte (1998)
2. Martins, É.S., et al.: Ecologia da Paisagem: Conceitos e Aplicações Potenciais no Brasil. Documentos, vol. 121, pp. 1–35, Platina, DF (2004)
3. Forman, R.T.T., Godron, M.: Landscape Ecology. Wiley, New York (1986)
4. Metzger, J.P.: O que é Ecologia de Paisagens? Biota Neotrópica, vol. 1, pp. 1–9 (2001)
5. Lucas, D.F.: Análise Espacial das Fragmentos Florestais no Município de São Gonçalo do Rio Abaixo/MG. Curso de Especialização em Geoprocessamento, Instituto de Geociências, Universidade Federal de Minas Gerais, Belo Horizonte (2011)
6. Rocha, N.A.: Geoprocessamento na parametrização de áreas verdes urbanas: Contribuições ao Plano de Cobertura Vegetal e Arborização Urbana. Tese doutorado, Escola de Arquitetura, Universidade Federal de Minas Gerais, Belo Horizonte (2019)
7. Moura, A.C.M.: Jankowski, P.: Contribuições aos estudos de análise de incertezas como complementação às análises multicritérios - "Sensitivity analysis to suitability evaluation". Revista Brasileira de Cartografia (2016), vol. 68/4, Edição Especial Geoinformação e Análise Espacial, pp. 665–684. Sociedade Brasileira de Cartografia, Geodésia Fotogrametria e Sensoriamento Remoto (2015)

8. Rocha, N.A., Casagrande, P., Moura, A.C.M.: Análise Combinatória e Pesos de Evidência na produção de Análise de Multicritérios em modelos de avaliação. Geografía y Sistemas de Información Geográfica, Argentina (2018)
9. Fundação Biodiversitas: Biodiversidade em Minas Gerais. Belo Horizonte (2005). http://www.biodiversitas.org.br/atlas/. Accessed 17 Aug 2019. McHarg, I.: Design with Nature, p. 208. Wiley, New York (1969)
10. Fonseca, C.O.: A dinâmica espacial da Serra do Gandarela e entorno a partir da formação de territórios: análise e representações coremáticas. Dissertação (Mestrado em Geografia). Universidade Federal de Minas Gerais, Belo Horizonte (2014). http://www.bibliotecadigital.ufmg.br/dspace/bitstream/handle/1843/IGCC-9SYMQ8/disserta__o_charles_de_oliveira_fonseca.pdf?sequence=1. Accessed 20 Nov 2017
11. Fonseca, B.M., Ribas, R.P., Moura, A.C.M.: Aplicação dos conceitos e métricas de ecologia da paisagem na gestão da paisagem urbana. Paisagem e Ambiente, vol. 38, pp. 71–85. São Paulo (2016)
12. Rocha, N.A.; Borges, J.L.C.; Moura, A.C.M.: Conflitos das dinâmicas de transformação urbana e ambiental à luz da ecologia da paisagem. PARC: Pesquisa em Arquitetura e Construção, vol. 7, pp. 23–34, São Paulo (2016)
13. Moura, A.C.M.: Estudo exploratório de aplicação de métricas de paisagem na caracterização da dinâmica de transformação regional – potenciais de transformação das manchas urbanas. In: VIII Encontro Nacional da Associação Brasileira de Estudos Regionais e Urbanos - ENABER, 2010, Juiz de Fora - MG. Anais do VIII Encontro Nacional da Associação Brasileira de Estudos Regionais e Urbanos - ENABER. São Paulo (USP), Associação Brasileira de Estudos Regionais e Urbanos (ABER), pp. 1–22 (2010)
14. Forman, R.T.T.: Land mosaics: The Ecology of Landscapes and Region, 632 p. Cambridge Press, New York (1995)
15. Moura, A.C.M.: Reflexões metodológicas como subsídio para estudos ambientais baseados em Análise de Multicritérios. In: XIII Simpósio Brasileiro de Sensoriamento Remoto, 2007, Florianópolis. Anais do XIII Simpósio Brasileiro de Sensoriamento Remoto. São José dos Campos: Instituto Nacional de Pesquisas Espaciais, vol. 1, pp. 2899–2906 (2007)

Locally-Provided and Globally-Relevant Ecosystem Services: A Needed Distinction for Quantification

Dani Broitman(✉)

Technion - Israel Institute of Technology, 3200003 Haifa, Israel
danib@technion.ac.il

Abstract. Ecosystem services are defined as benefits obtained by humans from ecosystem functions and processes. Although the different types of ecosystem services are well defined, their measurement and quantification has remained controversial despite long last research efforts. A particularly elusive and often neglected aspect of ecosystem services quantification has been a proper identification of the beneficiaries. We argue that a clear-cut distinction between locally-provided and globally-relevant ecosystem services are necessary in order to manage a meaningful debate about ecosystem services quantification. Using a detailed spatial analysis of land-use change and residential location in The Netherlands over almost two decades, we operationalize the distinction between two types of services provided by "green" land uses (protected natural areas, agricultural areas and parks). Recreational services available to nearby dwellers are used as an example of locally-provided ecosystem services, while carbon sequestration exemplifies the globally-relevant category. The conclusion is that while monetary value can be justified as a proxy measure of globally-relevant ecosystem services, non-monetary approaches are appropriate for locally-provided ecosystem services. The distinction between both types of ecosystem services is useful also for policy-making purposes: Quantification of locally-provided services is well suited for spatial planning in general and urban planning in particular, but globally-relevant services assessment (specially its monetary approach) is more informative at national and supranational levels.

Keywords: Ecosystem services · Locally-provided · Globally-relevant · Quantification

1 Introduction

Since the concept of ecosystem services has been coined, the quest for an adequate method for their assessment, measurement and valuation is a central research goal in the area [17–19]. After more than two decades of intensive research efforts, the definition and categorizations of the different types of ecosystem services are well defined and widely agreed [38, 47]. The quantification and valuation efforts, in comparison, are either questioned in principle [37, 46], or are actively being discussed without an apparent

O. Gervasi et al. (Eds.): ICCSA 2020, LNCS 12253, pp. 394–404, 2020.
https://doi.org/10.1007/978-3-030-58814-4_28

convergence towards an agreed ground [16, 50]. It is not surprising thus, that a recent review of about a decade of scientific literature about the valuation of ecosystem services in urban areas [5] found that most of the studies are based on diverse types of non-monetary valuations.

One of the basic problems behind the quantification of ecosystem services is that not always is clear to whom are they provided [44]. Indeed, a particularly elusive and often neglected aspect of ecosystem services quantification has been a proper identification of the beneficiaries (for example, [20, 21]). In a world where more than half of the world population live in urban areas, cities are the places where people obtain most of the benefits from ecosystems [36], and therefore make sense to focus on them. On one hand, cities consume ecosystem services provided by areas located both nearby and far away, sometimes exerting a large influence remotely [41]. But natural and semi-natural areas also abound within and around urban boundaries, and therefore cities also consume ecosystem services produced locally [7]. This dual nature of ecosystem services through the prism of whom is able to use them lie in the suggested clear-cut distinction between locally-provided and globally-relevant ecosystem services. Carbon sequestration by a plot of forest, for example, provides few services for the people living in the area, since the same service can be provided by other, nearby and similar plots. But the accumulation of these localized services affects ultimately every human being on the planet through the atmospheric carbon balance. The decreased water storage capacity of a parcel under development is not an issue from the owner's viewpoint, but the accumulation of developed land is significant for all the inhabitants of the watershed. These are examples of globally-relevant ecosystem services. Locally-provided ecosystem services are the opposite: These affect exclusively people located in a narrow area of influence and are completely irrelevant for outsiders. Services relevant at short distances (as aesthetic landscapes, recreational opportunities in natural areas nearby or noise reduction by tree canopies) are examples of locally-provided services. In the same manner that a single place can be the source of several ecosystem services (provisioning, regulating, etc.) it can offer globally-relevant and locally-provided services simultaneously. The difference between them is conceptual and affects the way in which they can be accounted. We claim than in order to manage a meaningful debate about ecosystem services quantification (and even monetization of part of them) a clear-cut distinction between locally-provided and globally-relevant ecosystem services is necessary. The operationalization of the suggested framework is performed using a detailed spatial analysis of land-use change and residential location in The Netherlands over almost two decades, quantizing services provided by "green" land uses (protected natural areas, agricultural areas and parks). Recreational services available to nearby dwellers are used as an example of locally-provided ecosystem services, while carbon sequestration exemplifies the globally-relevant category.

This paper is structured as follows: Sect. 2 presents a short review of the literature on urban green areas and their associated ecosystem services. Section 3 describes the study area, data and methods used in the research, which results are presented in Sect. 4. Section 5 summarizes discussing the significance of the results and concludes with respect to the research questions.

2 Ecosystem Services of Green Infrastructures in Urban Areas

The term urban green infrastructure designs the network of interconnected natural, semi-natural and artificial green areas within and around cities, emphasizing quality, quantity and multifunctional roles [48]. As such, urban green infrastructures provide a wide range of ecosystem services [29] ranging from wellbeing, positive physical and mental health effects [27], urban biodiversity conservation [34] and micro-climatic regulation [14]. Additional services provided by green infrastructures are runoff reduction [26] and local pollution abatement [39]. These services seem to be highly valuable since city dwellers are willing to pay high prices to live near green infrastructures [4, 15, 25]. However, not all the ecosystem services provided by urban green infrastructures are relevant for a dedicated quantification in the relatively constrained spatial context of urban and peri-urban areas [10].

In this research, we focus on the quantification of two different services provided by urban green infrastructures. The locally-provided ecosystem service is the provision of cultural services in the broadest sense: Non-material benefits obtained by people when they are in contact with natural, semi-natural or open areas. These services include mental and physical health, as mentioned previously, but also recreational opportunities [3, 32]. The globally-relevant service provided by urban green infrastructures that will be quantified by this research is carbon sequestration, that belongs to the regulating services category.

People in general, and urban dwellers in particular, appreciate the locally-provided services offered by urban green infrastructure [45]. In order to evaluate the relative preferences of people for the different types of green infrastructures discussed in this research, we rely on the literature about recreational and landscape value perception. Parks with moderately dense vegetation located in urban areas are appreciated by urbanites [6], while those perceived as natural are more valuated [40]. Landscapes of mixed rural-natural areas are more valuable than large scale agriculture landscapes [24], while natural landscapes are generally more appreciated than farm environments [33, 49].

Urban green infrastructure contributes to the balance of greenhouse gases, a globally-relevant ecosystem service, via carbon sequestration [29]. However, at a local level, the carbon balance itself and the amount of carbon eventually sequestered depend greatly on the type of green area, the specific land use and the land management [35]. For example, carbon sequestration by agricultural soils is greatly influenced by local climate, the crop type and the agricultural practices [23]. A large part of the available assessment of carbon sequestration by soils provides global figures [23] and focus more on stocks of carbon rather than on sequestration flows [30], measures that are not appropriated for our approach. Although the literature on carbon storage flows by urban green infrastructure is scarce, there are economic and quantitative assessments related to urban parks [1, 28].

3 Methods

3.1 Study Area

This research focuses on selected ecosystem services provided by different land uses in The Netherlands at the national level, during the period 2000–2017. In that period,

The Netherlands experienced processes of population growth and residential development. Part of the new residential stock was developed converting previous non-urban land uses into residential land, but an additional large share was built within existing urban areas, increasing the residential density [8, 9]. This dual type of residential development reflects partially the influence of the long last Dutch planning tradition that aims simultaneously to provide enough land for residential development while protecting existing open spaces in general [2, 22]. In addition, European nature conservation initiatives as Natura 2000, to whom The Netherland is committed, and local initiatives as the National Ecological Network, aim to maintain a cohesive network of natural areas and corridors between them [31]. These spatial policies contribute with a modest expansion of natural areas and further constrain residential extensions.

3.2 Data

The Dutch Central Bureau of Statistics (CBS) maintains a comprehensive set of spatial data sources, covering the entire national territory using square cells of 100 ms. These spatial data sets are consistent along time and are available for several years, in particular for the study period, in 2000 and 2017. The first dataset contains the number of housing units and the number of inhabitants in each cell during both years [13]. In the context of this research, we are interested in the number of inhabitants residing in a certain cell, regardless the type of dwelling (detached houses, apartments, etc.). The number of individual inhabitants is rounded to the nearest multiple of five, and cells with less than five inhabitants are rounded to zero, in order to maintain anonymity in scarcely populated areas. For these reasons, there is a certain mismatch between the total national population and the aggregate population of the spatial data set. The second dataset contains highly detailed vector data describing land uses observed in both years [11, 12].

3.3 Ecosystem Services Quantification

In the first step we define the predominant land use in each cell, based on the spatially explicit land use datasets. The original vector data are converted into a 25 square meter raster dataset, and then aggregated into the predominant land uses at a resolution of 100 square meters, using 38 land use types. For the purpose of this research, three land use types are considered part of the green infrastructure: Land used for nature conservation, agricultural land and parks. These land use types were retrieved directly from the predominant land use dataset. The fourth relevant land use is residential land, that is defined as each cell populated by 5 or more inhabitants according to the residential and the dwelling dataset from the CBS. In case of mismatch between both datasets (i.e., cells with more than 5 inhabitants in which the predominant land use is natural, agricultural or parks) the cell is defined as residential, overriding the processed land-use data by the original CBS data about population and dwellings.

At this point the spatial data required for the quantification of the globally-relevant ecosystem services is available: The green infrastructure at the national level, both within residential areas and outside them, is well defined as either natural, agricultural or park areas. For the quantification of the locally-provided ecosystem services, additional steps are required. A range of 500-meter distance from the place of residence to the nearest green area is a widely accepted metric for green area's accessibility [42, 43, 51]. Therefore, the residential cells located within a buffer of 500 meters from natural, agricultural or park areas were identified, and the inhabitants living there are considered beneficiaries of the cultural ecosystem services provided by the green infrastructures. Inhabitants, thus, can be classified in eight mutually exclusive categories: (a) People receiving services exclusively by one green land use (natural or agricultural or park areas). (b) People receiving services simultaneously by two green land uses (natural and agriculture, for example, or other bilateral combinations). (c) People receiving services by all three green land uses (living in places located near natural, agricultural and park areas). (d) Inhabitants deprived of any ecosystem service provided by the green infrastructure, i.e. living far from all the three green land uses.

The quantification of the globally-relevant service (carbon sequestration) is performed using the scarce data available in the literature [1, 28], assigning monetary values to the carbon sequestration capacity of each green land use. The quantification of the locally-provided services (cultural services and particularly recreation) is performed assigning to each inhabitant a different value according to its location regarding the green infrastructure. As the literature about landscape preferences suggests, it seems that the most valuable areas are natural, followed by parks and finally by agricultural landscapes. The respective values were defined following this ordinal principle. We assume also that the services received from different types of green areas are additive. However, it is important to stress that all the assigned values used for specific cell by cell valuation, are, by definition, not accurate. These values (defined in Table 1) are used only to illustrate the suggested quantification method.

4 Results

During the period 2000–2017, the Dutch residential population[1] grew by about 4.5%. The land devoted to residences, parks and nature conservation expanded by 5.5%, 2.5% and 18.4% respectively. The agricultural land, which is by far the largest land-use considered in this research, shrank by 3.1%. Figure 1 shows the main land uses focused on a small region. In addition, it illustrates how the locations near green infrastructures are defined: Cells within the residential areas that are located at a distance shorter than 500 meters from natural, agricultural or park areas are considered as places accessible to the urban green infrastructure.

Once the relevant areas are identified, it is possible to summarize them. For the globally-relevant ecosystem service (carbon sequestration) the total extension of the natural, agricultural and park areas, whether near residential areas or not, is the main variable. In comparison, for the locally-provided ecosystem service (cultural services), it is necessary to calculate how many persons enjoy accessibility to green infrastructures. The most important figures for the quantification of the analyzed ecosystem services are summarized in Table 2.

[1] By residential population we denominate the population included in the CBS dataset [13]. Due to the round off to the nearest multiple of 5 and the removal of cells in which less than 5 persons live, there are differences between the official Dutch population figures and the aggregated figures presented here.

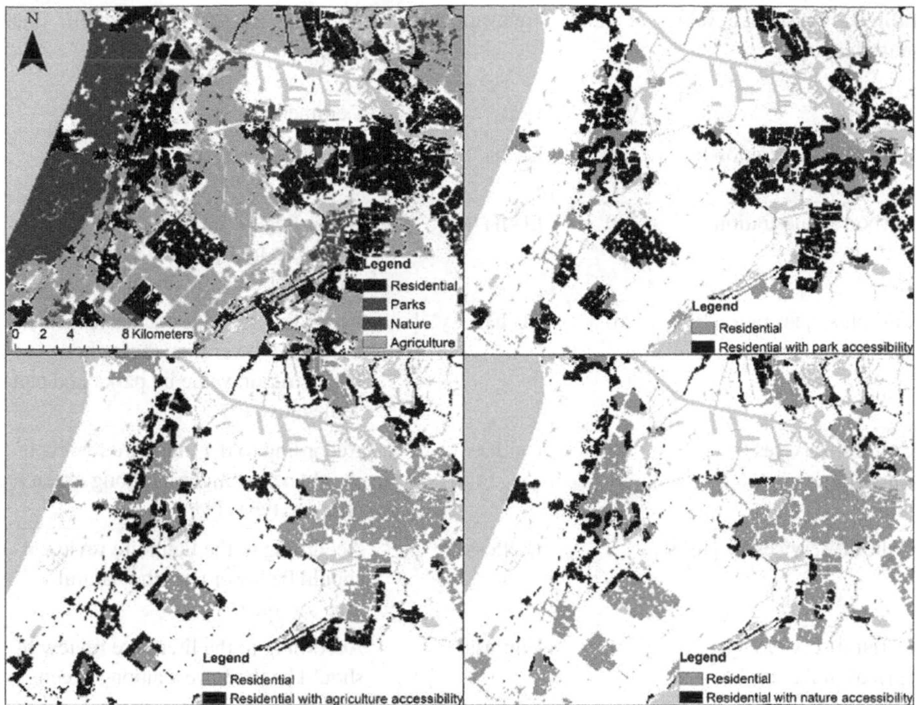

Fig. 1. Land uses in the urban area of Amsterdam and Haarlem (upper-left). Within the residential areas, there are places located near parks (upper-right), near agricultural areas (lower-left) and near nature conservation areas (lower-right). "Near" means located at less than 500 m from one of these green infrastructures.

The last step of the calculation involves the values defined in Table 1. Assuming that agreed values for each type of ecosystem service are available, the carbon sequestration contribution of a certain land type that is the area multiplied by the carbon capacity per hectare. Regarding cultural and recreational services from green structure, the accessibility measure is calculated for each inhabitant. For example, if it is far away from all types of green areas its index is 0, if its location is near a park only, its index is 2. Table 3 summarizes the changes observed in the provisioning of both ecosystem services according to the values defined in Table 1.

The absolute values of the calculated ecosystem services are not reported since the figures in which they are based (Table 1) are illustrative and, therefore, are inaccurate by definition and used only as a reference. The added value of the suggested clear-cut distinction between locally-provided and globally-relevant ecosystem services is the conceptual framework in which reliable and accepted figures of services (defined in units per hectare) can be simply plugged in a table in order to obtain a multi-dimensional valuation of ecosystem services. In this case study, we analysed only two services provided by the same land-uses, showing their temporal valuation during a period of time. Doing so, we obtain sensible results circumventing the problem of the lack of reliable services valuation per hectare. The extension of the framework to the quantification of additional locally-provided and globally-relevant ecosystem services is straightforward.

Table 1. Illustrative values of globally-relevant and locally-provided services used for their quantification.

Service	Value	Unit	Comment
Carbon sequestration by parks	126	EU ha^{-1} y^{-1}	Calculated from [1]
Carbon sequestration by natural areas	200	EU ha^{-1} y^{-1}	According to the literature review it should be higher than the carbon sequestration value by parks (*)
Carbon sequestration by agricultural areas	50	EU ha^{-1} y^{-1}	According to the literature review it should be lower than the carbon sequestration value by parks and can be negative (*)
Cultural services by natural areas	3	Unitless	According to the literature review it should be the highest among green land use types (**)
Cultural services by parks	2	Unitless	According to the literature review it should be lower than the natural area's value (**)
Cultural services by agricultural areas	1	Unitless	According to the literature review it should be the lowest among green land use types (**)

(*) Accurate values are not available. The chosen value is used only for reference.
(**) Recreational and landscape value perception. The chosen value is used only for reference.

5 Discussion

The analysis, mapping and quantification of ecosystem services in urban areas has attracted considerable research interest in the last years producing very detailed and comprehensive studies [20, 21]. However, two aspects related to ecosystem services in urban areas remain elusive: The first is that the beneficiaries of the produced ecosystem services are not clearly identified. The second aspect, closely related to the first, is that the meaning of "urban ecosystem services" (compared to simply "ecosystem services" without additional superlatives) is unclear. The underlying and implicit definition of the existing research is that any ecosystem service produced in urban areas is "urban". But this raises the question of the urban area's boundary definition: Different boundaries necessarily will result in different assessments. Moreover, there is no reason to assume that a patch of vacant land located within an administratively defined urban area should provide different services than an identical patch located further away, outside the urban area. The water storage capacity of both patches is relevant at the regional level regarding flood prevention and at the aquifer level regarding recharging. If the patch happens to be included in an urban area or not is irrelevant. On the other hand, there are services that are inherently local. A winter puddle visited by the neighbors does not offer the same cultural, educational and recreational ecological services than a similar but inaccessible one. In order to manage a meaningful discussion about ecosystem services (in

Table 2. Land uses providing globally-relevant services and number of people receiving locally-provided services.

	2000	2017
Nature conservation area (square kilometers)	2,935	3,097
Parks (square kilometers)	193	229
Agricultural land (square kilometers)	23,436	22,714
People living in residential areas accessible to natural areas only	224,160	239,345
People living in residential areas accessible to parks only	3,413,625	4,158,015
People living in residential areas accessible to agricultural areas only	2,657,965	2,327,520
People living in residential areas accessible both to natural and agricultural (but not to parks)	1,620,310	1,483,225
People living in residential areas accessible both to natural areas and parks (but not to agriculture)	441,840	583,065
People living in residential areas accessible both to agricultural areas and parks (but not to nature)	3,562,975	3,542,760
People living in residential areas accessible to all types of green areas (nature, agriculture and parks)	1,593,980	1,693,385
People living in residential areas inaccessible to any type of green areas (i.e., farther than 500 meters from nature and agriculture and parks)	1,253,010	1,414,720

Table 3. Change of globally-relevant and locally-provided services during the period 2000–2017 according to the illustrative values in Table 1.

Change during the period 2000–2017	By whom	Value
Provision of carbon sequestration	Natural areas	2.5%
	Park areas	18.4%
	Agricultural areas	−3%
	Total green areas	−0.4%
Provision of cultural and recreational services	Natural areas	3%
	Park areas	10.7%
	Agricultural areas	−4.5%
	Total green areas	4.8%

general, and urban, in particular) quantification, we argue that a clear-cut distinction is required. On one hand, locally-provided ecosystem services, focused on the people that usufruct them (or are able to use them) and depend on the accessibility of the source of the service to the beneficiaries. On the other hand, globally-relevant ecosystem services may affect people in the source's vicinity, but are relevant at larger scales (regional and even global). Globally-relevant services are provided regardless of the willingness of the potential beneficiaries to use them. Some locally-provided services are optional (as recreational services) while others are compulsive (as noise reduction or local air purification). Globally-relevant services may be quantified in geophysical terms (carbon sequestration, water storage, cooling capacity, etc.) or in monetary terms if there are markets for them (as in the case of carbon trade). Locally-provided services quantification depends on the beneficiaries and their location, and can be expressed in abstract ordinal scales (assigning larger values to more attractive supply). Monetary approaches are less appropriate for locally-provided ecosystem services [10].

From a policy-making perspective, the quantification of locally-provided services is well suited for spatial planning in general and urban planning in particular. The increase observed in the provision of cultural and recreational services by urban green infrastructure in the Netherlands is an evidence of a well-managed aspect of urban planning. Temporal comparisons of the same type, but at different administrative levels (provinces, municipalities, etc.) may shed light on the performance of the local government regarding the provision of locally-provided ecosystem services. The behavior of globally-relevant services as carbon sequestration over time is more relevant at the national level, in particular if an established market exists for the service and the country should be committed to achieve well-defined goals in the international arena, as is the case with carbon trade agreements.

The methodology developed in this research is fully portable, in the sense that it can be applied to any urban or metropolitan context, subjected to the availability of the required data. The test case described in this research was based on comprehensive and detailed spatial data, but the methods can be easily adapted to more coarse spatial data and to specific metropolitan areas. As such, the suggested methodology has a potential contribution for the research of urban ecosystem services.

This research demonstrates the usefulness of the suggested framework using a test case of the variation of two ecosystem services (one locally-provided and the other globally-relevant) during a period of time. We believe that the suggested clear-cut differentiation will contribute to defining clearer grounds to the ecosystem services quantification discussion. Since several services of both types can be provided by the same area, such differentiation allows for a refined monitoring of the implications of ongoing or planned land use changes. In addition, it allows for the use of multi-objective optimization techniques for the enhancement of ecosystem service provision.

References

1. Aevermann, T., Schmude, J.: Quantification and monetary valuation of urban ecosystem services in Munich. Germany. Zeitschrift für Wirtschaftsgeographie **59**(3), 188–200 (2015)
2. Alterman, R.: The challenge of farmland preservation: lessons from a six-nation comparison. J. Am. Plann. Assoc. **63**(2), 220–243 (1997)
3. Andersson, E., Tengö, M., McPhearson, T., Kremer, P.: Cultural ecosystem services as a gateway for improving urban sustainability. Ecosyst. Serv. **12**, 165–168 (2015)
4. Asabere, P.K., Huffman, F.E.: The relative impacts of trails and greenbelts on home price. J. Real Estate Financ. Econ. **38**(4), 408–419 (2009). https://doi.org/10.1007/s11146-007-9089-8
5. Atif, S.B., et al.: Identification of key-trends and evaluation of contemporary research regarding urban ecosystem services: a path towards socio-ecological sustainability of urban areas. Appl. Ecol. Environ. Res. **16**(3), 3545–3581 (2018)

6. Bjerke, T., Østdahl, T., Thrane, C., Strumse, E.: Vegetation density of urban parks and perceived appropriateness for recreation. Urban Forest. Urban Greening **5**(1), 35–44 (2006)
7. Bolund, P., Hunhammar, S.: Ecosystem services in urban areas. Ecol. Econ. **29**(2), 293–301 (1999)
8. Broitman, D., Koomen, E.: Residential density change: densification and urban expansion. Comput. Environ. Urban Syst. **54**, 32–46 (2015)
9. Broitman, D., Koomen, E.: The attraction of urban cores: densification in Dutch city centres. Urban Stud. 57, 1920–1939 (2019). 0042098019864019
10. Broitman, D., Czamanski, D., Malkinson, D.: Cities and nature. Int. Rev. Environ. Resour. Econ. **12**(1), 47–83 (2018)
11. CBS: Bestand bodemgebruik productbeschrijving. Centraal Bureau voor de Statistiek, Voorburg/Heerlen (2008)
12. CBS (2015). https://data.overheid.nl/dataset/58880-bestand-bodemgebruik-2015
13. CBS: Kaart van 100 meter bij 100 meter met statistieken (2017). https://www.cbs.nl/nl-nl/dossier/nederland-regionaal/geografische-data/kaart-van-100-meter-bij-100-meter-met-statistieken. Accessed 27 Nov 2019
14. Chang, C.R., Li, M.H., Chang, S.D.: A preliminary study on the local cool-island intensity of Taipei city parks. Landscape Urban Plann. **80**(4), 386–395 (2007)
15. Conway, D., Li, C.Q., Wolch, J., Kahle, C., Jerrett, M.: A spatial autocorrelation approach for examining the effects of urban greenspace on residential property values. J. Real Estate Financ. Econ. **41**(2), 150–169 (2010). https://doi.org/10.1007/s11146-008-9159-6
16. Cordier, M., Agúndez, J.A.P., Hecq, W., Hamaide, B.: A guiding framework for ecosystem services monetization in ecological–economic modeling. Ecosyst. Serv. **8**, 86–96 (2014)
17. Costanza, R., Folke, C.: Valuing ecosystem services with efficiency, fairness and sustainability as goals. In: Postel, S. et al. (eds.) Nature's Services: Societal Dependence on Natural Ecosystems, pp. 49–70. Island Press, Washington, D.C. (1997)
18. Costanza, R., et al.: The value of the world's ecosystem services and natural capital. Nature 387(6630), 253–260 (1997)
19. De Groot, R.S., Wilson, M.A., Boumans, R.M.: A typology for the classification, description and valuation of ecosystem functions, goods and services. Ecol. Econ. **41**(3), 393–408 (2002)
20. Derkzen, M.L., van Teeffelen, A.J., Verburg, P.H.: Quantifying urban ecosystem services based on high-resolution data of urban green space: an assessment for Rotterdam, the Netherlands. J. Appl. Ecol. **52**(4), 1020–1032 (2015)
21. Elmqvist, T., et al.: Benefits of restoring ecosystem services in urban areas. Current Opinion Environ. Sustain. **14**, 101–108 (2015)
22. Faludi, A., van der Valk, A.J.: Rule and Order Dutch Planning Doctrine in the Twentieth Century, vol. 28. Springer, Dordrecht (2013). https://doi.org/10.1007/978-94-017-2927-7
23. Freibauer, A., Rounsevell, M.D., Smith, P., Verhagen, J.: Carbon sequestration in the agricultural soils of Europe. Geoderma **122**(1), 1–23 (2004)
24. García-Llorente, M., Martín-López, B., Iniesta-Arandia, I., López-Santiago, C.A., Aguilera, P.A., Montes, C.: The role of multi-functionality in social preferences toward semi-arid rural landscapes: an ecosystem service approach. Environ. Sci. Policy **19**, 136–146 (2012)
25. Gibbons, S., Mourato, S., Resende, G.M.: The amenity value of English nature: a hedonic price approach. Environ. Resour. Econ. **57**(2), 175–196 (2014). https://doi.org/10.1007/s10640-013-9664-9
26. Gómez-Baggethun E., et al.: Urban ecosystem services. In: Elmqvist, T., et al. (ed.) Urbanization, Biodiversity and Ecosystem Services: Challenges and Opportunities, pp. 175–251. Springer, Dordrecht (2013). https://doi.org/10.1007/978-94-007-7088-1_11
27. Grahn, P., Stigsdotter, U.A.: Landscape planning and stress. Urban Forest. Urban Greening **2**(1), 1–18 (2003)

28. Gratani, L., Varone, L., Bonito, A.: Carbon sequestration of four urban parks in Rome. Urban Forest. Urban Greening **19**, 184–193 (2016)
29. Grunewald, K., Xie, G., Wüstemann, H.: The multiple benefits of urban green—ecosystem services assessment. In: Grunewald, K., Li, J., Xie, G., Kümper-Schlake, L. (eds.) Towards Green Cities. CN, pp. 43–104. Springer, Cham (2018). https://doi.org/10.1007/978-3-319-58223-8_3
30. Harper, R.J., Tibbett, M.: The hidden organic carbon in deep mineral soils. Plant Soil **368**(1–2), 641–648 (2013). https://doi.org/10.1007/s11104-013-1600-9
31. Jongman, R.H.: Nature conservation planning in Europe: developing ecological networks. Landscape Urban Plann. **32**(3), 169–183 (1995)
32. Kabisch, N., Haase, D.: Green justice or just green? Provision of urban green spaces in Berlin, Germany. Landscape Urban Plann. **122**, 129–139 (2014)
33. Kaltenborn, B.P., Bjerke, T.: Associations between environmental value orientations and landscape preferences. Landscape Urban Plann. **59**(1), 1–11 (2002)
34. Kattwinkel, M., Biedermann, R., Kleyer, M.: Temporary conservation for urban biodiversity. Biol. Cons. **144**(9), 2335–2343 (2011)
35. Lal, R.: Soil carbon sequestration to mitigate climate change. Geoderma **123**(1–2), 1–22 (2004)
36. Marcotullio, P., Piracha, A., King, C. Urban ecosystems and the Millennium Ecosystem Assessment: Towards an Inclusive Framework: UNU (No. 105). IAS working paper (2003)
37. Masood, E., Garwin, L.: Audacious bid to value the planet whips up a storm. Nature **395**, 430 (1998)
38. Millennium Ecosystem Assessment - MEA: Ecosystems and Human Well-being: Synthesis. Island Press, Washington, DC (2005)
39. Nowak, D.J., Crane, D.E., Stevens, J.C.: Air pollution removal by urban trees and shrubs in the United States. Urban Forest. Urban Greening **4**(3–4), 115–123 (2006)
40. Ode, Å., Fry, G., Tveit, M.S., Messager, P., Miller, D.: Indicators of perceived naturalness as drivers of landscape preference. J. Environ. Manage. **90**(1), 375–383 (2009)
41. Rees, W.E.: Ecological footprints and appropriated carrying capacity: what urban economics leaves out. Environ. Urbanization **4**(2), 121–130 (1992)
42. Sarkar, C.: Residential greenness and adiposity: findings from the UK Biobank. Environ. Int. **106**, 1–10 (2017)
43. Sarkar, C., et al.: Exploring associations between urban green, street design and walking: results from the Greater London boroughs. Landscape Urban Plann. **143**, 112–125 (2015)
44. Satz, D., et al.: The challenges of incorporating cultural ecosystem services into environmental assessment. Ambio **42**(6), 675–684 (2013). https://doi.org/10.1007/s13280-013-0386-6
45. Shwartz, A., Turbé, A., Simon, L., Julliard, R.: Enhancing urban biodiversity and its influence on city-dwellers: an experiment. Biol. Cons. **171**, 82–90 (2014)
46. Silvertown, J.: Have ecosystem services been oversold? Trends Ecol. Evol. **30**(11), 641–648 (2015)
47. TEEB – The Economics of Ecosystems and Biodiversity (2011). TEEB Manual for Cities: Ecosystem Services in Urban Management. www.teebweb.org
48. Tzoulas, K., et al.: Promoting ecosystem and human health in urban areas using Green Infrastructure: a literature review. Landscape Urban Plann. **81**(3), 167–178 (2007)
49. Van den Berg, A.E., Koole, S.L.: New wilderness in the Netherlands: an investigation of visual preferences for nature development landscapes. Landscape Urban Plann. **78**(4), 362–372 (2006)
50. Venkatachalam, L.: Environmental economics and ecological economics: where they can converge? Ecol. Econ. **61**(2–3), 550–558 (2007)
51. Villeneuve, P.J., et al.: A cohort study relating urban green space with mortality in Ontario, Canada. Environ. Res. **115**, 51–58 (2012)

Spatial Distribution of Surface Temperature and Land Cover: A Study Concerning Sardinia, Italy

Sabrina Lai, Federica Leone(✉), and Corrado Zoppi

Dipartimento di Ingegneria Civile, Ambientale e Architettura (DICAAR), University of Cagliari, Cagliari, Italy
{sabrinalai,federicaleone,zoppi}@unica.it

Abstract. Land surface temperature (LST) is a key climate variable that has been studied mainly at the urban scale and in the context of urban heat islands. By analyzing the connection between LST and land cover, this study shows the potential of LST to analyze the relation between urbanization and heating phenomena at the regional level. Land cover data, drawn from Copernicus, and LST, retrieved from Landsat 8 satellite images, are analyzed through a methodology that couples GIS and regression analysis. By looking at the Italian island of Sardinia as a case study, this research shows that urbanization and the spatial dynamics of heating phenomena are closely connected, and that intensively farmed areas behave quite similarly to urban areas, whereas forests are the most effective land covers in mitigating LST, followed by areas covered with Mediterranean shrubs. This leads to key policy recommendations that decision-makers could implement to mitigate LST at the regional scale and that can, in principle, be exported to regions with similar climate and land covers. The significance of this study can be summed up in its novel approach to analyzing the relationship between LST and land covers that uses freely available spatial data and, therefore, can easily be replicated in other regional contexts to derive appropriate policy recommendations.

Keywords: Land Surface Temperature (LST) · Land cover · Afforestation · Green urban grids · Regression models

1 Introduction

Fast changes aimed at promoting social and economic development have characterized international land cover dynamics in the last few decades [1]. Land cover features are related not only to rapid urbanization, but also to processes of higher anthropization, such as the transformation of forests into agricultural areas or transitions from woodlands and shrubs to new predominantly homogeneous agrarian land [2]. According to the National

This article is extracted from: Lai, S., Leone, F, Zoppi, C.: Spatial distribution of surface temperature and land cover: A study concerning Sardinia, Italy. Sustainability 12(8), 3186, 20 pp. (2020). https://doi.org/10.3390/su12083186.

O. Gervasi et al. (Eds.): ICCSA 2020, LNCS 12253, pp. 405–420, 2020.
https://doi.org/10.1007/978-3-030-58814-4_29

Institute for Environmental Protection [3], artificial land cover in Italy increased by 0.21% in 2018, that is by 23,033 km^2.

Land cover changes, and especially transitions from natural and semi-natural areas to artificial land covers, affect regional and local temperatures [4]. In fact, although urban areas and their surroundings receive the same amount of solar radiation, the local temperatures differ because different surface materials have different heat capacity [5]. From this perspective, land surface temperature (LST) is a significant parameter for investigating the effects of land covers on local temperatures.

Hofierka et al. [6] define LST as "the radiative skin temperature of the ground", affected by solar reflectance, thermal emissivity, and heat capacity. In other words, LST combines interactions between land surface and atmosphere with ground–atmosphere energy fluxes. Therefore, understanding how land cover changes affect climate represents a key element in international debates [7] that highlight that land cover can significantly affect quality of life, that is human health and safety, through its influence on LST [8]. The impacts on climate conditions generated by land-cover change processes can be effectively analyzed by assessing the relations between the spatial distribution of LST and that of land covers. The influence of land use/land cover changes on LST variation has been studied by various authors [4, 9–12]. Feizizadeh et al. [4] analyze the relations between LST and land use/land cover in Maraqeh County (Iran), using a method based on the application of the Surface Energy Balance Algorithm for Land (SEBAL) to Landsat Enhanced Thematic Mapper (ETM+) imagery. Chaudhuri and Mishra [9] compare land use/land cover and LST differences between India and Bangladesh by analyzing satellite images corresponding to different time periods and by using intensity analysis. Zullo et al. [10] study the relationship between LST variations and the increase in urbanized areas from 2001 to 2011 in the Po Valley. Guha et al. [11] investigate the relationship between LST and two indexes, that is the normalized difference vegetation index (NDVI) and the normalized difference built-up index (NDBI) in Florence and Naples by using Landsat 8 data. Stroppiana et al. [12] focus on the relationship between spatio-temporal LST variation and land cover, topography, and potential solar radiation in four southern Italian regions.

Although various authors have studied the relations between land use/land cover and LST, further analysis may provide more accurate parameters in order to understand this complex relationship [13] at a wider scale. Moreover, a mere understanding of this relation is not sufficient to deal with climate change, while new policies and strategies should be included within spatial planning at the regional and local levels.

In this study, the connections between anthropization and natural conditions and the spatial taxonomy of LST are analyzed in order to assess whether, and to what extent, land covers and their transitions affect the spatial layout of heating phenomena at the regional level, in the case study of Sardinia, Italy. The methodological approach applied in this study, which is based on a cross-sectional spatial inferential analysis, provides results that can be used in two ways. On the one hand, the differential impacts of different land cover types on LST are characterized with reference to the LEAC classification, and the most critical land covers related to heating phenomena are identified. On the other hand, a number of planning policies concerning land cover changes are defined, with the ultimate aim of decreasing LST.

The study is structured into five sections. The first section identifies the wider context and the debates to which the study is contributing. The second section describes the study area, data, and methodology used in this study. The third section presents the results that are discussed in the fourth section, where the main findings are interpreted and compared with findings from similar studies. The fifth section provides recommendations in terms of strategies and policies, and proposes concluding remarks and future directions of the research.

2 Materials and Methods

2.1 Study Area

With a size of 24,000 km^2 and approximately a 1,850-km long coastline, Sardinia is one of the major Mediterranean islands. The island, which from an administrative point of view is an Italian autonomous region populated by around 1.6 million inhabitants, is taken as the spatial context for this study because its climate homogeneity and self-containment allow for a pretty straightforward identification of the regional boundaries.

2.2 Data

Landsat 8 OLI (Operational Land Imager) and TIRS (Thermal Infrared Sensor) images are freely available from the US Geological Survey website [14]. For spatial criteria, a bounding box having minimum latitude 38.8, maximum latitude 41.4, minimum longitude 8, maximum longitude 10 was selected; for temporal criteria, the spring interval spanning from 15 April 2019 to 31 May 2019 was chosen. The five selected multi-band images are listed in Table 1. The cell size of the thermal bands (10 and 11), for each image, was 30 meters.

Table 1. Landsat 8 Operational Land Imager-Thermal Infrared Sensor (OLI-TIRS) images selected for this study.

Image code	Date	Scene
LC08_L1TP_193031_20190523_20190604_01_T2	May 23, 2019	193
LC08_L1TP_193032_20190523_20190604_01_T1	May 23, 2019	193
LC08_L1TP_193033_20190523_20190604_01_T1	May 23, 2019	193
LC08_L1TP_192032_20190516_20190521_01_T2	May 16, 2019	192
LC08_L1TP_192033_20190516_20190521_01_T1	May 16, 2019	192

2018 land cover data, provided in both raster and vector formats with a minimum mapping unit (MMU) of 25 hectares, classed following the CORINE third-level nomenclature [15], were retrieved from the Land Monitoring Service [16] of the European Union's Copernicus Earth Observation Program.

Finally, a Digital Terrain Model (DTM) is available for Sardinia from the regional geoportal [17] and its cell size equals 10 meters.

2.3 Methodology

The methodological approach of this study develops as follows. First, LST was extracted and mapped. Secondly, land covers and elevation data were processed so as to build a spatial dataset comprising the three layers; such dataset was next used to feed a multiple regression analysis to estimate the relationships between different land covers and LST. A graphical summary of the methodology adopted in this study is provided in Fig. 1.

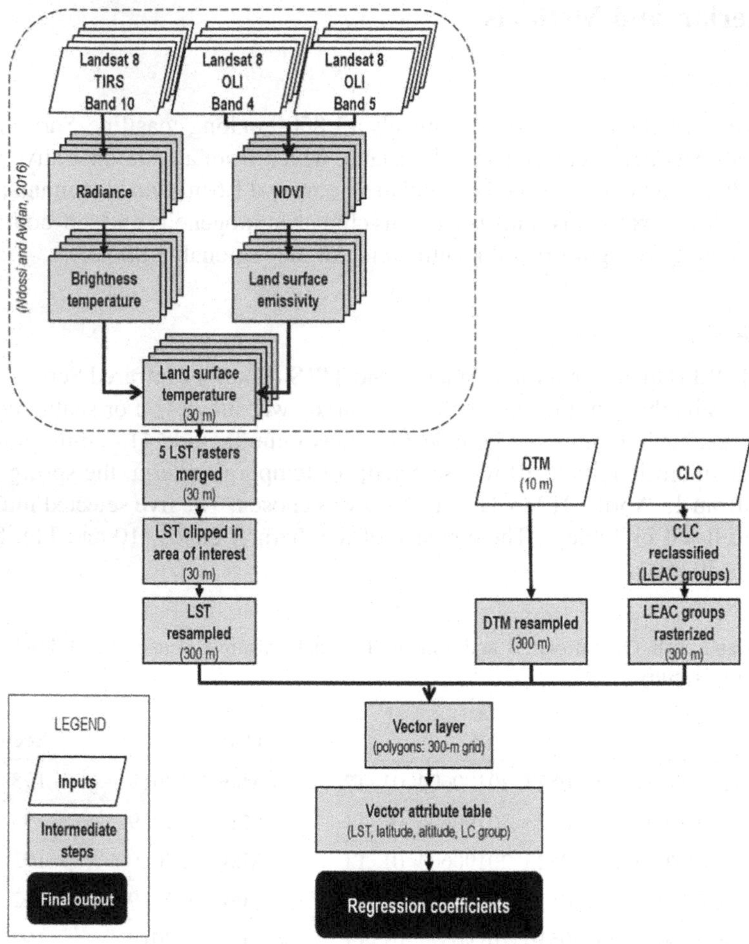

Fig. 1. Graphical summary of the methodology.

LST Extraction and Mapping at the Regional Scale

A QGIS plugin implemented by Ndossi and Avdan [18] was used in this study. For each image listed in Table 1, a five-step process was therefore performed through the plugin. In the first step, the top-of-atmosphere spectral radiance was calculated for each pixel [19]; subsequently, the top-of-atmosphere spectral radiance was converted into the top-of-atmosphere brightness temperature [19]. Next, the NDVI was calculated using Landsat 8's bands 4 and 5 images as inputs [20]; NDVI makes it possible to calculate, in the fourth step, Land Surface Emissivity (LSE) through various algorithms. Among those implemented in the plugin, Zhang, Wang, and Li's algorithm [21], which builds upon van de Griend and Owe's findings concerning the correlation between LSE and NDVI [22], was chosen here because it was reported to yield the best results [18] for LST retrieval. Finally, in the fifth step, LST was calculated using the so-called "Planck function" [23], which has been reported to be "easier to use in comparison to the other algorithms as it does not require atmospheric variables" [18] (p. 28). Through these steps, five LST raster maps (one for each Landsat image listed in Table 1 and each having resolution 30 meters) were obtained. The five LST images were then merged, so as to obtain a single LST image for the whole region (in the case of overlapping pixels, the maximum LST value, consistently corresponding to pixels belonging to scene 193 produced on May 23 was retained), which was next resampled to a 300-m cell size so as to lower the resolution, hence reducing computational efforts in the subsequent steps.

Land Covers and Elevation

From the European 2018 CLC vector dataset, polygons concerning Sardinia were first extracted and next reclassified based on the LEAC classification defined by the EEA [24] (p. 98) and used for land cover accounts. Table 2 shows the LEAC-related macroclasses as groups of the 44 third-level classes of the CLC dataset.

Table 2. CORINE land cover classes and groups.

	LEAC groups	CORINE Land Cover Classes			
URB	Artificial (urbanized) areas	1.*			
APC	Arable and permanent crops	2.1.*	2.2.*	2.4.1	
MCP	Mosaic crops and pastures	2.3.*	2.4.2	2.4.3	2.4.4
FSW	Forests, shrubs, and woodlands	3.1.*	3.2.4		
HNGS	Heathland, natural grasslands, and sclerophyllous vegetation	3.2.1	3.2.2	3.2.3	
OPSP	Open spaces with sparse or absent vegetation	3.3.*			
WAT	Water bodies and wetlands	4.*	5.* (except 523-sea)		

The asterisk (*) marks any sub-classes of a given class, or any sub-sub-classes of a given sub-class.

Next, the resulting layer was converted into a raster map with a cell size of 300 meters (where the grid was the same as that of the resampled LST). Each cell was assigned a value corresponding to the prevailing land cover group.

As for elevation, the regional DTM was resampled so as to obtain a new raster file with the same cell size and grid as the LST and land cover group raster images. As for the resampling technique, linear interpolation, appropriate for continuous data [25] as elevation, was used to derive the cell's altitude.

Input Table for the Regression

A vector layer (shapefile) was created. Polygons in this shapefile spatially coincide with pixels belonging to the three raster maps derived as per the previous subsubsections; hence, every polygon is a 300 m by 300 m square in the projected reference system EPSG 32632 [26]. Each polygon was then assigned the following attributes: the LST value of the corresponding cell, its prevailing land cover group, and its altitude. Furthermore, the latitude of the polygon's centroid (in the reference system EPSG 32632) was added, since the temperature is expected to be dependent on the latitude. Finally, a field taking the value 1 (pixels pertaining to scene 193) or 0 (pixels only pertaining to scene 192) was added. The pixels featuring in both scenes were regarded as belonging to scene 193.

Land Covers and LST

The polygons described in the previous subsubsection were identified as the spatial units for estimating a multiple linear regression which takes the following form:

$$LST = \beta_0 + \beta_1 URB + \beta_2 APC + \beta_3 MCP + \beta_4 FSW + \beta_5 HNGS + \beta_6 OPSP + \beta_7 ALTIT + \beta_8 LATD + \beta_9 W \quad (1)$$

where:

- explanatory variables from URB through to OPSP, which represent the LEAC groups, are dichotomous variables; each variable can take either of the two values, 1 or 0, according to whether the area size of a LEAC group in a cell takes the largest value with respect to the area sizes of the other groups; therefore, if in a cell the URB group shows the largest area size, the variable URB equals 1, otherwise it equals 0, and so on; each coefficient estimated by regression (1), β_i, i = 1, …, 6, identifies the change in LST related to a cell in case it shows the largest area size identified by the variable associated to the coefficient β_i (i.e., URB, APC, etc.) with respect to the basic condition that the largest area size of the cell is identified by the variable WAT (Wetlands and water bodies); the coefficients estimated by regression (1), β_i, i = 1, …, 6, define a taxonomy of the zone types based on the quantitative contribution to LST expressed by the values of β_i, i = 1, …, 6;
- ALTIT is the altitude in meters related to the polygon;
- LATD is the latitude in meters of the polygon's centroid;
- W (standing for "West") is a dichotomous variable which can take either of the two values, 1 or 0.

The results from the multiple linear regression were used to identify the quantitative effects of different land covers on LST and their ordinal ranking; for each LEAC group, the rank depended on the value of the coefficients βi, i = 1, …, 6, of regression (1).

That being so, the surface, whose equation was unknown, representing an n-dimensional phenomenon, e.g., a spatial phenomenon, as a functional relation between n variables, was approximated, point by point, by the point neighborhood identified by the tangential hyperplane. The neighborhood shared by the surface, whose equation was unknown, and by the tangential hyperplane, whose equation was known, was identified by the linear relation between the covariates, as a locally identified approximation of the unknown general relation between the factors. A multiple linear regression such as (1) provided the estimates of the coefficients of the linear equation, which demonstrated the trace of a tangential hyperplane over a nine-dimensional unknown surface which represented the functional relation between LST and its covariates [27].

The variables ALTIT and LATD were used to control the impacts of the altitude and latitude of a cell on the LST; as a consequence, if the estimates of the coefficient β_7 and β_8 were significant with reference to their *p*-values, this would entail that the altitude and latitude generate effects on the LST, whose expected signs are negative, since it is expected that the higher the altitude, or the greater the latitude, the lower the LST, everything else being equal. Finally, the variable W was used to control the impact of the date of the satellite images, which should show a systematic difference between May 23, 2019 and May 16, 2019, since May 23 was a clear sunny day whereas May 16 was partly cloudy. That being so, the cells whose LSTs were extracted on May 23, belonging to scene 193 and hence located on the western side of the island, should show higher LSTs than the others, everything being equal, and the expected sign of W should be positive.

A standard significance test based on p-values was implemented as regards the coefficients of the regressions, to detect whether they are significantly different from zero. If p-values were lower than 5%, then the explanatory variables' effects on LST could confidently be considered important.

3 Results

The outcomes of the methodological approach discussed in the second section are presented as follows. In the first subsection, the spatial layout of the LST taxonomy is described; in the next subsection, the estimates of regression model (1) are reported and the effects of different LEAC macroclasses on LST are presented, which define an ordered scale whose lowest level is represented by water bodies and wetlands and upper level by urbanized land.

3.1 LST Spatial Taxonomy Results

Some outputs of the LST extraction process are shown in Fig. 2, which clearly shows that some parts of the island were covered by clouds when the Landsat images where produced—this locally affected both NDVI and LST values. Hence, such pixels (25,099 out of 266,818) were subsequently removed; Fig. 3 shows the spatial distribution of LST minus the cloudy cells, of LEAC groups, and of elevation that were used to develop the matrix that fed the regression.

3.2 Regression Results

The estimates of the regression identify the impacts of the land cover macroclasses of the LEAC on the LST. The estimates of the coefficients of the Boolean covariates define

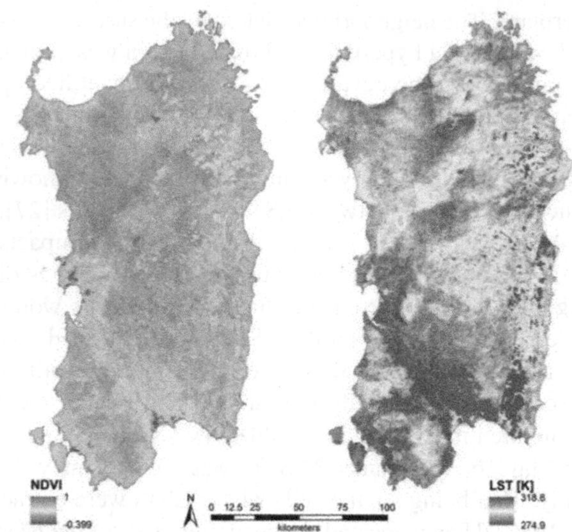

Fig. 2. Spatial layout of NDVI and LST in Sardinia, May 2019.

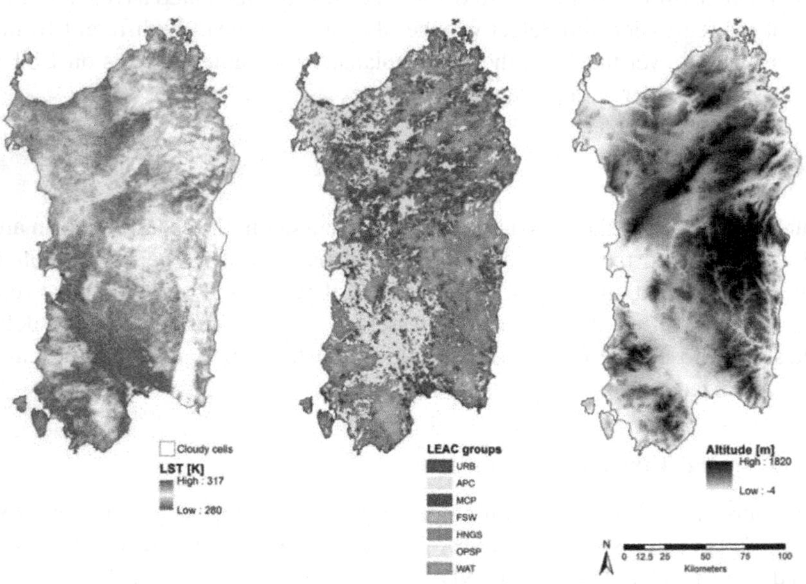

Fig. 3. Spatial layout of LST with cloudy cells removed, of LEAC groups, and of elevation.

the differential effects of each variable on LST change with respect to "Water bodies and wetlands", whose effect on LST is the lowest among the LEAC macroclasses. Table 3 shows the results of the regression model.

The estimates of the coefficients of the altitude and latitude variables are significant in terms of p-value hypothesis testing, and they show the expected sign. As a consequence,

Table 3. Regression results.

Explanatory variable	Coefficient	Standard deviation	t-statistic	*p*-value	Mean of the explanatory variable
URB	8.918	0.0531	167.991	0.000	0.032
APC	8.515	0.0460	185.274	0.000	0.269
MCP	7.413	0.0465	159.529	0.000	0.228
FSW	4.786	0.0476	100.556	0.000	0.150
HNGS	6.272	0.0463	135.428	0.000	0.293
OPSP	7.349	0.0602	122.113	0.000	0.017
ALTIT	−0.00638	−0.0000218	−292.404	0.000	317.248
LATD	−0.0000157	−0.0000000781	−200.735	0.000	4,438,355.893
W	4.311	0.0242	178.260	0.000	0.951

Dependent variable: LST: Mean: 302.230 K; Standard deviation: 3.801; Adjusted R-squared: 0.571.

it can be stated that the higher the altitude, or the larger the latitude, the lower the LST. On average, an increase of 100 m in altitude will imply a decrease of 0.64 K in temperature, whereas an increase of 10 km in latitude will entail a decrease of 0.16 K in temperature. Moreover, the coefficient of the dichotomous variable W is significant and it shows the expected sign as well, which implies that, on average, a cell whose LST was related to the satellite images taken on May 23 is 4.3 K higher than the LST of a cell whose LST was related to the satellite images taken on May 16.

Therefore, the estimates of the three control variables' coefficients are significant and show the expected sign, and, that being so, it is pretty straightforward to identify the implications concerning the differential effects on LST derived from the six LEAC macroclasses on the basis of the estimated coefficients of the six dichotomous variables from URB through OPSP.

The estimated coefficients of the six dichotomous variables are significant with respect to the standard test based on p-values described at the end of Sect. 2. The estimates of the coefficients entail the following implications, which all assume the condition "everything else being equal". First, the highest effect on LST is shown by URB. The estimated coefficient implies that, on average, urbanized (artificialized) cells present an LST higher by: 8.9 K than WAT cells (water bodies and wetlands); 0.4 K than APC cells (arable and permanent crops); 1.5 K than MCP cells (mosaic crops and pastures) and OPSP (open spaces with sparse or absent vegetation); 2.6 K than HNGS cells (heathland, natural grasslands, and sclerophyllous vegetation); 4.1 K than FSW (forests, shrubs, and woodlands). Secondly, intensive farming (APC) generates impacts on LST similar to urbanization, even though it is not characterized by the soil-sealing phenomenon. Thirdly, extensive farming and pastures (MCP), and bare land or poorly vegetated soils (OPSP) are correlated to lower LST, and their impacts on LST are similar to each other. Fourthly, the two LEAC non-agricultural vegetated macroclasses are the most effective as regards mitigation of the land surface heating phenomenon. Forests, shrubs, and woodlands (FSW) show the largest positive impact on LST mitigation.

4 Discussion

The ordered scale of the effects of the LEAC macroclasses on LST derived from the estimates of the regression model shows a number of aspects consistent with the findings reported in the current literature. The most relevant impact on increases in LST is represented by urbanized land, whose differential effect on LST with respect to water bodies and wetlands is about 9 K. Several reasons can explain this outcome. Sealed soils either limit or prevent air circulation and the impact of downwind cooling [28]. In heavily urbanized areas, the thermal comfort of vegetated areas is almost completely missing [29]. Artificial surfaces make evapotranspiration almost impossible, and, as a result, LST and air temperature are comparatively higher than in non-artificial surfaces [30]. In addition, the surface materials used in urban areas have higher radiant temperatures [13]. The increasingly frequent heat-wave and heat-island phenomena would be mitigated by the canopies of woodland trees and shrubs, which are rare or absent in urbanized areas [31].

In relation to intensive farming, the outcomes of the regression model show that the impact on LST increase generated by intensive farming areas is only slightly lower than that of urbanized land, that is, about 8.5 K higher than that of the water bodies and wetlands LEAC macroclass. Indeed, the areas belonging to the APC macroclass reveal conditions that are very similar to those of the URB macroclass. Even though the soil is not sealed, arable land and permanent crops generate negative effects on downwind cooling and air circulation which make LST comparatively higher than those of the other LEAC macroclasses except artificial land. Even the thermal comfort and evapotranspiration provided by areas characterized by intensive agriculture are very low with respect to that of the other LEAC macroclasses, with the exception of the URB macroclass, since in artificial areas trees are almost totally absent and soils are generally covered by dense low-growing vegetation [32].

HNGS shows lower LST compared to other macroclasses due to the presence of vegetation that reduces the amount of stored heat in the soil through transpiration [33]. In fact, vegetation affects the microclimate through shading that prevents incoming solar radiation reaching the land surface through evapotranspiration and by affecting air movement and heat exchange [29].

The results of this study reveal that forests, shrubs, and woodlands show the larger positive impact on LST mitigation. According to a study carried out by Walawender et al. [34] in relation to Krakow, forests and waters show low values of LST. However, their behavior changes during the year. In March, before the period of growth between germination and flowering, waters show considerably lower values of LST compared to forests. In May, when the vegetative period is just beginning in Poland, the LST values of forests are slightly lower than the values of waters. In June and August, at the end of the vegetative period, forests and waters take the same values. This different behavior is caused by evapotranspiration that is superior at the peak of the vegetative period when air temperature goes up. The same study shows that the LST of arable land, pastures, and permanent crops is affected by seasons. At the beginning of the vegetative period, the LST of arable land is slightly higher than the mean values. Before the vegetative period, the LST values of permanent crops and grassland are higher than the mean values. This temperature variation can be explained through the state in which arable land is kept after the planting period, that is not covered by any vegetation. In April–May, during the early vegetative season, arable land shows the same thermal properties as bare soil, and its LST values are higher than areas covered with vegetation.

On the other hand, pastures are perennial; therefore, the early vegetative period is characterized by a closed canopy different from the bare soil that characterizes arable land in the same vegetative period. Moreover, the capacity of regenerating living biomass is strongly connected with precipitations that limit a constant forage production during the vegetation period [35].

It must be noted that lowering LST in rural areas has relevant implications in terms of mitigation of water shortages and of the entailed negative economic impacts and social problems [36]. As per Sruthi and Aslam [37], LST and NDVI are strictly negatively correlated in agricultural areas, which implies that the higher the LST, the lower the vegetation density. This outcome is particularly important with regards to periods of drought, characterized by productivity decline determined by poor rains and soil humidity [37]. In turn, the decline in productivity can possibly generate significant consequences in terms of economic and social unrest [38]. This is an outstanding issue with reference to Sardinia, where agricultural area comprises about one half of the regional land (11,500 km^2) and employment in agriculture is about 7.5% of total employment (41,000 people) [39].

5 Conclusions

A number of policy recommendations are implied by the outcomes of this study.

First, high LSTs in the consolidated fabric of cities, towns, and small villages, which may possibly develop into heat islands and waves, can be mitigated through the implementation of widespread urban microscale operations, such as the planting of trees, the increase in the endowment of urban green zones through the plantation of new areas and/or the enlargement of existing ones [29]. Other microscale measures consist of the realization of green facades and walls, and green and blue urban grids. There are several examples of these planning policies implemented in different urban contexts. A pioneer and outstanding primer is the London Green Grid [40].

The microscale planning measures aimed at decreasing LST in urbanized contexts are based on the provision of ecosystem services regulating LST. The implementation of these measures implies the integration of different kinds of planning policies, in order to induce virtuous behaviors on behalf of the local communities, organized groups of residents, building enterprises, and public administrations. A central issue is that the value of urban land is strictly related to its permitted building volume, whether it is residential or devoted to services or infrastructure. That being so, the plantation of new green areas and/or the enlargement of existing ones, which imply that these areas would decrease their value substantially by losing their building potential, should be implemented through the integration of appropriate planning measures. On the one hand, it is necessary to enact a regulatory system whose rules should state that new settlements, and, perhaps, existing ones, have to be endowed with a certain amount of vegetated areas, either by devoting part of the facades and roofs to greenery, or by binding more-or-less large areas to be part of blue or green grids, such as in the case of East London [41]. On the other hand, a system of financial incentives should be put in place so as to make buildings endowed with green facades and roofs, as well as the realization of green and blue grids in the existing urban neighborhoods and in the new developments, attractive in terms of private investment [42]. Finally, public commitment to the increase in the urban endowment of blue and green grids and infrastructure should be identified clearly through the implementation of public planning policies, for example through compulsory purchase orders concerning municipal areas where urban greening plans, such as the East London Green Grid, are to be implemented [43].

Secondly, as regards non-artificial land, the most effective LEAC macroclasses in lowering LST are forests, shrubs, and woodlands (FSW) and heathland, grasslands, and sclerophyllous vegetation (HNGS),whereas the impacts of intensive and extensive agriculture-related land covers (APC and MCP), and of open spaces (OPSP) are very close to the negative impact of urbanized land. A pretty straightforward implication is that the LEAC macroclasses characterized by the lowest degree of anthropization, such as FSW and HNGS, should be targeted by public policies in order to implement the mitigation of the land surface heating phenomenon. Policy measures should aim at supporting stepwise transitions from APC, MCP, and OPSP to HNGS and FSW.

Afforestation is the main road to identify the implications of the regression model results as regards lowering LST in rural areas [44]. Moreover, for afforestation, a distinction should be made between high-rent intensive arable land (ARA) and low-rent mosaic farmland and pastures (MCP) [45]. Transitions from agriculture to forests are not likely to take place in cases of ARA, whereas they are more likely in cases of MCP, since the comparatively high rents of forest farming are a relevant incentive towards land cover change [45]. Policy measures aiming at implementing a decrease in LST should be based on targeting both ARA and MCP, as follows. A system of afforestation incentives should be implemented, targeting rural areas on the basis of agricultural rent, with the aim of encouraging low-rent farmers to turn into forest farmers. It is highly likely that these incentives are effective in cases of rural areas classified as either MCP or OPSP, whereas high-rent farming, which mainly takes place in ARA, should be less interested in implementing land cover changes [46]. From this perspective, a fundamental role has to be played by national, regional, and local administrations in order to identify the optimal size of afforestation-related land cover transitions and of public investment in terms of financial feasibility [47]. Public commitment to decrease LST in rural areas is very important as regards the effectiveness of planning policies, and it should be visible to the local communities through, for instance, the direct purchase of private rural land, such as low-rent croplands or abandoned, poorly vegetated open spaces, in order to develop afforestation processes [48].

The methodological approach defined and implemented in this study as regards the Sardinian region provides estimates of the quantitative size of the impact of public policies concerning urban and rural contexts. Moreover, the methodology defined and implemented in this study can be easily exported to other national and European regional contexts, since worldwide and free satellite images the enable the identification of the spatial distribution of LST are available, and the CORINE land-cover-based LEAC taxonomy is available for all European countries.

As regards the outcomes of this study, there are two main directions for future research in the field of spatial planning policies to decrease LST and mitigate the connected problems, which consist of heat waves and heat islands, and quality of life in rural and urban areas. On the one hand, a network of direct, on-site observations would be of fundamental importance as regards the validation of the spatial layout of LST, which would make feasible the experimental implementation of planning policies aimed at generating impacts on LST. No planning experiment could be developed in the absence of a validated baseline dataset related to LST. On the other hand, tests and pilot projects involving municipal administrations would be very useful to test the effectiveness of policies such as the afforestation or urban blue and green grids. Researchers in the field of sustainability-oriented planning and local public administrations should therefore lobby local, national, and international funding agencies so as to secure enough funds to implement experimental programs concerning decreasing LST, including pilot actions and local tests.

Acknowledgments. The study was implemented within the Research Program "Paesaggi rurali della Sardegna: pianificazione di infrastrutture verdi e blu e di reti territoriali complesse" [Rural landscapes of Sardinia: Planning policies for green and blue infrastructure and spatial complex networks], funded by the Autonomous Region of Sardinia for the period 2019–2021, under the provisions of the call for the presentation of "Projects related to fundamental or basic research" of the year 2017, implemented at the Department of Civil and Environmental Engineering and Architecture (DICAAR) of the University of Cagliari, Italy.

Sabrina Lai, Federica Leone, and Corrado Zoppi collaboratively designed this study. Individual contributions are as follows: Federica Leone wrote Sections "Introduction" and "Discussion"; Sabrina Lai wrote Sections "Study area", "Data", "LST Extraction and Mapping at the Regional Scale", "Land Covers and Elevation" "Input Table for the Regression" and "LST Spatial Taxonomy Results"; Corrado Zoppi wrote Sections "Land Covers and LST", "Regression Results", and "Conclusions".

References

1. Nguyen, T.M., Lin, T.-H., Chan, H.-P.: The environmental effects of urban development in Hanoi, Vietnam from satellite and meteorological observations from 1999–2016. Sustainability **11**, 1768 (2019). https://doi.org/10.3390/su11061768
2. Kim, Y.-H., Baik, J.-J.: Spatial and temporal structure of the urban heat island in Seoul. J. Appl. Meteorol. **44**, 591–605 (2005). https://doi.org/10.1175/JAM2226.1
3. Munafò, M. (ed.): Consumo di suolo, dinamiche territoriali e servizi ecosistemici. Edizione 2019; Report SNPA 08/19 [Land Take, Territorial Dynamics and Ecosystem Services. 2019 Edition. SNPA Report SNPA 08/19, 2019]. SNPA: Atlanta, GA, USA (2019). ISBN 978-88-448-0964-5
4. Feizizadeh, B., Blaschke, T., Nazmfar, H., Akbari, E., Kohbanani, H.R.: Monitoring land surface temperature relationship to land use/land cover from satellite imagery in Maraqeh County Iran. J. Environ. Plann. Manage. **56**, 1290–1315 (2013). https://doi.org/10.1080/09640568.2012.717888

5. Fonseka, H.P.U., Zhang, H., Sun, Y., Su, H., Lin, H., Lin, Y.: Urbanization and its impacts on land surface temperature in Colombo metropolitan area, Sri Lanka, from 1988 to 2016. Remote Sens. **11**, 957 (2019). https://doi.org/10.3390/rs11080957
6. Hofierka, J., Gallay, M., Onačillová, K., Hofierka Jr., J.: Physically-based land surface temperature modeling in urban areas using a 3-D city model and multispectral satellite data. Urban Clim. **31**, 100566 (2020). https://doi.org/10.1016/j.uclim.2019.100566
7. Wang, C., Li, Y., Myint, S.W., Zhao, Q., Wentz, E.A.: Impacts of spatial clustering of urban land cover on land surface temperature across Köppen climate zones in the contiguous United States. Landscape Urban Plann. **92**, 103668 (2019). https://doi.org/10.1016/j.landurbplan.2019.103668
8. Alfraihat, R., Mulugeta, G., Gala, T.: Ecological evaluation of urban heat island in Chicago City, USA. J. Atmos. Pollut. **4**, 23–29 (2016). https://doi.org/10.12691/jap-4-1-3
9. Chaudhuri, G., Mishra, N.B.: Spatio-temporal dynamics of land cover and land surface temperature in Ganges-Brahmaputra delta: a comparative analysis between India and Bangladesh. Appl. Geogr. **68**, 68–83 (2016). https://doi.org/10.1016/j.apgeog.2016.01.002
10. Zullo, F., Fazio, G., Romano, B., Marucci, A., Fiorini, L.: Effects of urban growth spatial pattern (UGSP) on the land surface temperature (LST): a study in the Po Valley (Italy). Sci. Total Environ. **650**, 1740–1751 (2019). https://doi.org/10.1016/j.scitotenv.2018.09.331
11. Guha, S., Govil, H., Dey, A., Gill, N.: Analytical study of land surface temperature with NDVI and NDBI using Landsat 8 OLI and TIRS data in Florence and Naples city Italy. Eur. J. Remote Sens. **51**, 667–678 (2018). https://doi.org/10.1080/22797254.2018.1474494
12. Stroppiana, D., Antoninetti, M., Brivio, P.A.: Seasonality of MODIS LST over Southern Italy and correlation with land cover, topography and solar radiation. Eur. J. Remote Sens. **47**, 133–152 (2014). https://doi.org/10.5721/EuJRS20144709
13. Ding, H., Shi, W.: Land-use/land-cover change and its influence on surface temperature: a case study in Beijing City. Int. J. Remote Sens. **34**, 5503–5517 (2013). https://doi.org/10.1080/01431161.2013.792966
14. USGS: Science for a Changing World—EarthExplorer. https://earthexplorer.usgs.gov/. Accessed 11 Apr 2020
15. Kosztra, B., Büttner, G., Hazeu, G., Arnold, S.: Updated CLC Illustrated Nomenclature Guidelines. Environment Agency Austria, Vienna (2019)
16. CLC 2018. https://land.copernicus.eu/pan-european/corine-land-cover/clc2018. Accessed 11 Apr 2020
17. DTM Passo 10 Metri [DTM Sampling Rate 10]. http://webgis2.regione.sardegna.it/catalogodati/card.jsp?uuid=R_SARDEG:JDCBN. Accessed 11 Apr 2020
18. Ndossi, M.I., Avdan, U.: Application of open source coding technologies in the production of land surface temperature (LST) maps from landsat: a PyQGIS plugin. Remote Sens. **8**, 413 (2016). https://doi.org/10.3390/rs8050413
19. USGS. Using the USGS Landsat Level-1 Data Product. https://www.usgs.gov/land-resources/nli/landsat/using-usgs-landsat-level-1-data-product. Accessed 11 Apr 2020
20. Townshend, J.R.G., Goff, T.E., Tucker, C.J.: Multitemporal dimensionality of images of normalized difference vegetation index at continental scales. IEEE Trans. Geosci. Remote Sens. **GE-23**, 888–895 (1985). https://doi.org/10.1109/tgrs.1985.289474
21. Zhang, J., Wang, Y., Li, Y.: A C++ Program for retrieving land surface temperature from the data of Landsat TM/ETM + band6. Comput. Geosci. **32**, 1796–1805 (2006). https://doi.org/10.1016/j.cageo.2006.05.001
22. van de Griend, A.A., Owe, M.: On the relationship between thermal emissivity and the normalized different vegetation index for natural surfaces. Int. J. Remote Sens. **14**, 1119–1131 (1993). https://doi.org/10.1080/01431169308904400
23. Artis, D.A., Carnahan, W.H.: Survey of emissivity variability in thermography of urban areas. Remote Sens. Environ. **12**, 313–329 (1982). https://doi.org/10.1016/0034-4257(82)90043-8

24. EEA. land accounts for Europe 1990–2000: towards integrated land and ecosystem accounting; European environment agency Report no. 11. Office for Official Publications of the European Communities, Luxembourg (2006). ISBN 92-9167-888-0
25. ArcGis Help. Resample. https://pro.arcgis.com/en/pro-app/tool-reference/data-management/resample.htm. Accessed 11 Apr 2020
26. EPSG 32632. https://epsg.io/32632. Accessed 11 Apr 2020
27. Wolman, A.L., Couper, E.: Potential consequences of linear approximation in economics. Fed. Reserve Bank Richmond Econ. Q. **89**, 51–68 (2003)
28. Oke, T.R.: The urban energy balance. Prog. Phys. Geogr. **12**, 471–508 (1988). https://doi.org/10.1177/030913338801200401
29. Geneletti, D., Cortinovis, C., Zardo, L., Blam Adel, E.: Planning for Ecosystem Services in Cities. Springer, Dordrecht (2019). https://doi.org/10.1007/978-3-030-20024-4
30. Demuzere, M., et al.: Mitigating and adapting to climate change: Multi-functional and multi-scale assessment of green urban infrastructure. J. Environ. Manage. **146**, 107–115 (2014). https://doi.org/10.1016/j.jenvman.2014.07.025
31. Fischer, E.M., Schär, C.: Consistent geographical patterns of changes in high-impact European heatwaves. Nat. Geosci. **3**, 398–403 (2010). https://doi.org/10.1038/ngeo866
32. Irmak, A. (ed.): Evapotranspiration. Remote Sensing and Modeling. IntechOpen, London, UK (2012). https://doi.org/10.5772/725
33. Youneszadeh, S., Amiri, N., Pilesjo, P.: The effect of land use change on land surface temperature in the Netherlands. In: Proceedings of the International Conference on Sensors & Models in Remote Sensing & Photogrammetry, Kish Island, Iran, 23–25 November 2015, vol. 41, pp. 745–748 (2015)
34. Walawender, J.P., Szymanowski, M., Hajto, M.J., Bokwa, A.: Land surface temperature patterns in the urban agglomeration of Krakow (Poland) derived from landsat-7/ETM + data. Pure. appl. Geophys. **171**(6), 913–940 (2013). https://doi.org/10.1007/s00024-013-0685-7
35. Feldhake, C.M., Glenn, D.M., Peterson, D.L.: Pasture soil surface temperature response to drought. Agron. J. **88**, 652–656 (1996). https://doi.org/10.2134/agronj1996.00021962008800040025x
36. Mokhtari, A., Mansor, S.B., Mahmud, A.R., Helmi, Z.M.: Monitoring the impacts of drought on land use/cover: a developed object-based algorithm for NOAA AVHRR time series data. J. Appl. Sci. **11**, 3089–3103 (2011). https://doi.org/10.3923/jas.2011.3089.3103
37. Sruthi, S., Aslam, M.A.M.: Agricultural drought analysis using the NDVI and land surface temperature data: A case study of Raichur District. Aquatic Proc. **4**, 1258–1264 (2015). https://doi.org/10.1016/j.aqpro.2015.02.164
38. Dodo, M.K.: Examining the potential impacts of climate change on international security: EU-Africa partnership on climate change. SpringerPlus **3**(1), 1–18 (2014). https://doi.org/10.1186/2193-1801-3-194
39. Centro Studi di Confagricoltura [Study Center of the Italian Confederation of Agriculture]. L'agricoltura Nelle Regioni d'Italia—2015—Sardegna [The Agriculture in the Italian Regions—2015—Sardinia]. http://www.confagricoltura.it/DownLoadFileUrl.php/url=backend@@comunicazioni@@file_upload@@allegato@@1701171100150_20_sardegna.pdf/nomefile=20_sardegna.pdf. Accessed 11 Apr 2020
40. Mayor of London: London's Urban Heat Island: A Summary for Decision Makers. Greater London Authority, City Hall (2006)
41. Jenning, V., Larson, L., Yun, J.: Advancing sustainability through urban green space: cultural ecosystem services, equity, and social determinants of health. Int. J. Environ. Res. Public Health **13**, 196 (2016). https://doi.org/10.3390/ijerph13020196
42. Webster, C.: The new institutional economics and the evolution of modern urban planning: Insights, issues and lessons. Town Plann. Rev. **76**, 455–502 (2005). https://doi.org/10.3828/tpr.76.4.5

43. Fors, H., Frøik Molin, J., Murphy, M.A., Konijnendijk van den Boschab, C.: User participation in urban green spaces—For the people or the parks? Urban Forest. Urban Greening **14**, 722–734 (2015). https://doi.org/10.1016/j.ufug.2015.05.007
44. Wall, S.: Small-scale forestry and rural development: the intersection of ecosystems, economics and society. In: Proceedings of IUFRO 3.08 Conference Hosted by Galway-Mayo Institute of Technology, Galway, Ireland, 3–6 July 2006. COFORD, Dublin, Irish (2006)
45. Kumm, K.I., Hessle, A.: Economic comparison between pasture-based beef production and afforestation of abandoned land in Swedish forest districts. Land **9**, 42 (2020). https://doi.org/10.3390/land9020042
46. Hyytiainen, K., Leppanen, J., Pahkasalo, T.: Economic analysis of field afforestation and forest clearance for cultivation in Finland. In: Proceedings of the International Congress of European Association of Agricultural Economists, Ghent, Belgium, 26–29 August 2008
47. Zavalloni, M., D'Alberto, R., Raggi, M., Viaggi, D.: Farmland abandonment, public goods and the CAP in a marginal area of Italy. Land Use Policy press (2019). https://doi.org/10.1016/j.landusepol.2019.104365
48. Brouwer, R., Lienhoop, N., Oosterhuis, F.: Incentivizing afforestation agreements: institutional-economic conditions and motivational drivers. J. Forest Econ. **21**, 205–222 (2015). https://doi.org/10.1016/j.jfe.2015.09.003

Soil Ecosystem Services and Sediment Production: The Basilicata Region Case Study

Angela Pilogallo(✉), Lucia Saganeiti, Francesco Scorza, and Beniamino Murgante

University of Basilicata, Viale dell'Ateneo Lucano 10, 85100 Potenza, Italy
angela.pilogallo@unibas.it

Abstract. The conservation of soil and multiple ecosystem services it provides, is crucial for human well-being, for pursuing many of the Sustainable Development Goals and for addressing some of the most important challenges of our society. However several factors contribute to soil degradation, including climatic characteristics, lithological and morphological features and transformation processes. Only the last ones can be governed and that is the reason why spatial planning needs tools and analyses to interpret the role of land use changes in complex dynamics such as the erosive phenomena. This work presents the results obtained from the implementation of the InVEST SDR module on the territory of Basilicata Region and considering the evolution occurred between 1990 and 2018. Our outcomes show an intensification of erosion phenomena mainly along the Apennine chain and the coastal area of the Tyrrhenian Sea. Although this area corresponds to the higher average rainfall erosivity over the entire period, the most significant soil loss occurs in correspondence with unfavorable land use changes. The negative connotation typically associated with deforestation, conversion of agricultural soils to arable lands and thinning or total loss of vegetation becomes a measurable quantity, at least from one of several points of view.

Keywords: Soil ecosystem services · Land degradation · Soil conservation · InVEST SDR module

1 Introduction

Soil is the core of terrestrial ecosystems and the provider of most of ecosystem services (ES) [1]. Even if the type, the intensity and the quality of these ES depends on the specific environmental characteristics [2, 3], soil is essential for agricultural production and plays a key role in regulating carbon cycle [4] and in preserving biodiversity [5, 6].

Contributing in the removal of significant topsoil and, consequently, in the loss of nutrients and carbon stock and in porosity variations, erosion is actually recognized as one of the most critical threat to soil properties and functions [7]. Unfortunately a detrimental mix of morphological, climatic and soil characteristics [8], makes the Mediterranean basin particularly exposed to erosive phenomena [9]. Furthermore, because of increasing anthropic pressures, land use changes and climate conditions under actual global changes, the Mediterranean basin is expected to be a critical desertification hotspot [10].

O. Gervasi et al. (Eds.): ICCSA 2020, LNCS 12253, pp. 421–435, 2020.
https://doi.org/10.1007/978-3-030-58814-4_30

Although it is recognized that soil functions must necessarily be preserved in order to pursue sustainable development [11] and despite soil scientists have highlighted for decades the need to overcome the piecemeal legislative approach [4], nowadays a fully integration of soil ES into decision-making processes at different levels of governance regarding land use and management [12] is still missing.

The purpose of this work is to evaluate the differences in terms of sediment generation occurred in the Basilicata region between 1990 and 2018 considering both land use and climatic changes. According to the European Soil Bureau [13] the study area, whose territory is characterized by a predominantly mountainous morphology and the widespread presence of clayey hills, includes many catchments that fall within the highest erosion risk classes. Some areas of the region, where erosion phenomena are so evident that they represent a threat to settlements and infrastructure, have been the focus of a number of studies aimed at investigating the role of agricultural policies [14, 15], the increase in the frequency of heavy rainfall events [16] or in inter-annual precipitations variability [17].

The Region's attitude to land degradation [18], the expected climate changes and ongoing land-use modification trends require a regional study to be carried out in order to define a basis for monitoring future erosion trends and design policies aimed at preserving soil ES provision.

We used Sediment Delivery Ratio (SDR) InVEST module [19], a spatially-explicit tool able to model soil erosion and sediment transport and deposition phenomena. The results of the elaboration are precisely related to changes in land use, in order to highlight the domains in which spatial planning can act on the regional scale.

2 Materials and Methods

Erosion is a natural phenomenon to which a number of factors contribute: morphological and soil characteristics, climate, vegetation cover, fire occurrence, land management and cultural practices, land use changes. As the topic is considered of relevant importance in order to support the most basic ES for the survival of humankind [20], it is important to carry out assessments at the regional scale.

The difficulty in finding detailed and spatialized data related to each of the above mentioned quantities, has led to the increasing usage of models that are both simple and scientifically credible such as the SDR InVEST module, useful to represent the spatial variability in sediment retention service also considering non-linear responses to land use changes [21].

The study area, the model on which the tool is based and the phases of data collection and processing of the layers needed for the model running, are described below.

2.1 Study Area

The soils of Southern Italy, as well as most of the Mediterranean lands [9], are prone to erosive phenomena so that Rendell, 1986 [22] defined them as *the inevitable results of a combination of high relative relief, erodible soils and climate.*

The Basilicata Region (Fig. 1), which covers a total area of about 10,000 km^2, is more than 46% mountainous and just over 45% hilly, while only 8% is characterized by a flat morphology.

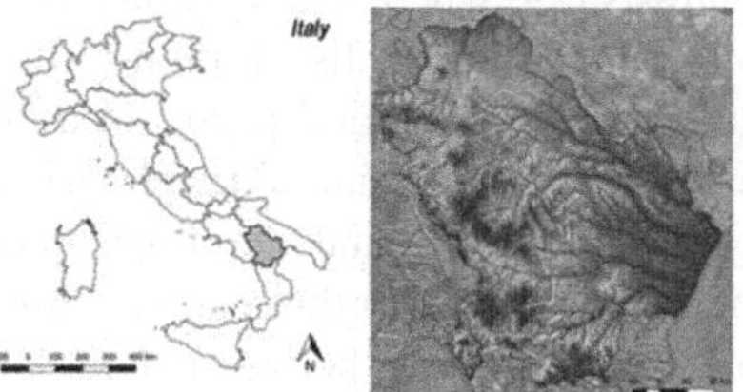

Fig. 1. Basilicata region's physical map

Analyzing the changes in land use in the Basilicata region from 1990 to 2018 (Fig. 2), it emerges that the most significant losses occurred in woodlands (−12,500 ha), agricultural mosaic (−27,500 ha) and meadows (−5,500 ha). On the other hand, an increase has been recorded in the classes related to bare lands (+13,600 ha) and shrublands (+7,000 ha) but, above all, from arable lands (−21,400 ha). Less significant on the regional scale were the transitions towards residential and industrial land uses which, however, due to their dynamic characteristics have been studied by the authors in several works [23–25].

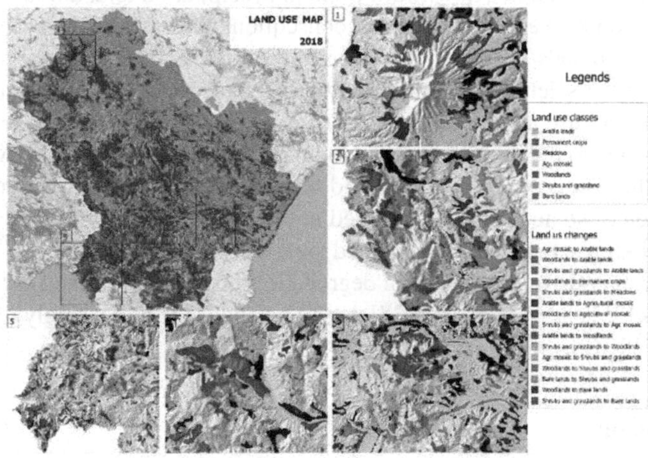

Fig. 2. Land use map at 2018 for the Basilicata region. The detail boxes represent the main land use changes in some areas of the regional territory

Altogether the territory, which from both the geological and structural points of view represents one of the most complex and varied among the Apennine regions [26], is composed of a western sector, on average more elevated due to the presence of the Apennine Chain and an eastern area, mainly characterized by the hilly morphology and often subject to erosive phenomena which, in some territorial areas, have given rise to badlands [27]. The flat areas can be identified mainly along the Ionian coast, originating from the continuous build-up of eroded material carried downstream by the branched and dense hydrographic network [28].

The topographic complexity of the study area inevitably influences its climatic features, characterized by contrasts [29] where the Apennine reliefs intercepts the Atlantic perturbations and affects the precipitation distribution [30]. In fact, the territory falls partly in the temperate and cold climate, and partly in the Mediterranean, linked to two distinct pluviometric regimes: the Ionian side, characterized by perturbed fronts less frequent and with a lower intensity; and the Tyrrhenian side exposed instead to perturbations, coming from the west and north-west, and affected by greater rainfall.

The average annual precipitation varies between about 500 mm and over 2000 mm and has a typically Mediterranean seasonal distribution: generally about 35% of rainfall is concentrated in winter, 30% in autumn, 23% in spring and only 12% in summer. The trend of rainfall during the year is subject to strong variations with a considerable part of the precipitations concentrated in a few days and characterized by very high intensity.

The temperature trend is also characterized by strong excursions with very hot summers and cold winters. The average of the minimum temperatures varies between about −10 and −2 °C while the average of the maximum temperatures is between 31 and about 39 °C. A recent study [29] revealed an increase in both minimum and maximum temperatures during the 1951–2010 period, leading to an average growth in minimum temperature of approximately 1.1 °C and a raise in the number of very warm days per year that became markedly stronger since 1971. It is worth considering that this increase in temperatures correspond to a downward trend in precipitation total amount [30], implying conditions conducive to aridity and all consequent processes such as landslides [31], gully [32] and badlands [33] erosion. Some of these areas have been the subject of in-depth study by the scientific community, which has extensively documented the role of changes in land use and management. In some cases this growth in territorial vulnerability was due to the introduction of Common Agricultural Policy (CAP) measures that favored the recovery of shrubland and badlands for wheat cultivation [34] or the implementation of some measures included in the Reg. CE 2078/92 that which implies a 20-year period of set-aside for remodeled areas [35].

To further man-driven pressures in degradation prone areas, linked for examples to deforestations [36] and overgrazing [37], has to be added the increasingly relevant threat of wild fires [38–40].

2.2 Methodology

Although the scientific bibliography is rich in relationships and models for the evaluation of soil loss [41, 42], an increasing attention [43, 44] is paid to tools and models capable to assess not only on-site effects but even off-site impacts [45], strengthening a more systemic approach to territorial governance [46]. The understanding of these dynamics constitutes the necessary basis for the design of policies and strategies aimed at ensuring the delivery of the above mentioned ES by the landscape.

The tool used in this work, the InVEST Sediment Delivery Ratio (SDR) module, allows the spatially-explicit representation of the annual average soil loss and then to compute the sediment delivery ratio which is the part of the soil loss that actually reaches the hydrographic network.

For each of the *i*-pixels, the annual total amount of soil loss - expressed in $tons \cdot ha^{-1} \cdot yr^{-1}$ - is assessed using the Revised Universal Soil Loss Equation (RUSLE) [47]:

$$usle_i = R_i \cdot K_i \cdot LS_i \cdot C_i \cdot P_i$$

where R_i is the rainfall erosivity ($MJ \cdot mm(ha \cdot hr)^{-1}$), K_i is the soil erodibility ($ton{\cdot}ha \cdot hr\ (MJ{\cdot}ha{\cdot}mm) - 1$), LS_i is the slope length gradient factor, C_i is the crop management parameter and P_i is a factor depending on support practices.

The SDR ratio is then calculated following the following expression [46]:

$$SDR_i = \frac{SDR_{max}}{1 + exp\left(\frac{IC_0 - IC_i}{k}\right)}$$

where SDR_{max} represents the maximum theoretical SDR set by default equal to 0.8 and IC_0 and k are calibration factors set by default equal to 0.5 and 2, respectively. IC_i, according to Borselli et al. [48], constitutes a measure of the connectivity assessment based on landscape's information and it's useful to describe the hydrological linkage between sediments' sources and destinations, among which hydrographic network's components.

Although SDR module is scientifically based on the theory of hydrological connectivity [49], it requires a small number of input layers and provides ease of implementation for this reason proving to be useful in predicting the impacts related to land use changes [50]. Data needs for running SDR model are indeed a Land Use/Land Cover (LULC) map, the Digital Elevation Model (DEM) of the study area, two raster dataset with the rainfall erosivity (R) and the soil erodibility (K) indexes for each pixel and a biophysical table summarizing the values of the *C* and *P* parameters assigned to each land use class.

The detailed building of the dataset is described below.

Rainfall Erosivity (*R*)

R factor is a parameter significant of the rainfall energy as an erosive agent [51] and it represents the rain potential ability to cause soil loss [52]. As stated by Diodato, 2004 [53], its assessment is tedious and time-consuming because it accounts for the product of the total kinetic energy of a rainfall multiplied by its maximum intensity of 30 min of rain [54].

However, since the purpose of this work is to define the changes that occurred in the period 1990–2018 and the necessary data are not all available for this time series, an experimental relationship [55] was used:

$$R = 0.0483P^{1.61}$$

where *P* is the average annual precipitation in mm.

These datasets were made available by the Basilicata Civil Protection Functional Center in relation to the pluviometric stations located within the regional territory and

Fig. 3. Rainfall erosivity maps related to 1990 and 2018

those ones located in Calabria, Campania and Apulia Regions closer to the regional borders. Results can be seen in Fig. 3. *Rainfall erosivity maps related to 1990 and 2018*

Soil Erodibility Factor (K)
The K factor is significant of the soil erodibility (Mg·h·MJ − 1·mm − 1), that is a measure of the susceptibility of soil particles to detach from the ground and be transported by rainfall and runoff [54]. Being representative of the susceptibility to soil erosion, the K-factor is a complex synthesis of a combination of phenomena such as the splash during rainfall and intensive events, runoff along the upper soil layer - including transportability of sediments - and seepage into the soil [56]. For these reason, *K* factor is a function of the soil structure [57], the permeability [58], the total amount of organic matter [59], the granulometry [60], the water contents in topsoil [61], and a number of quantities that vary over time even in response to major upheavals such as fires [62–64]. An accurate estimation thus requires intensive and time-consuming field measurements [65] that have resulted in a continuous investigation and testing of experimental methods and estimation procedures based on a limited number of soil features [66].

In this work, the raster dataset of K-factor was provided by the JRC's European Soil Data Centre (ESDAC) [67] as a result of a study aimed at generate a harmonized high-resolution soil erodibility map for EU-25 member States.

Biophysical Table: The Crop Management (C) and the Support Practice (P) Factors
As already mentioned in the methodology, one of the inputs required by the model is a table specifying the *C* and *P* parameters' values for each land use class.

C-factor represents a ratio between soil loss from a certain LULC class and the fallow condition [68] and it's useful to consider differences in infiltration capacities between vegetated and tilled bare fallow areas. Limiting the rainfall impact on soil surface, vegetation cover and an appropriate crop management thus influence runoff and soil erosion [69]. RUSLE original model [56] consider *C*-factor as a product of following variables: land use, soil moisture, canopy cover, surface's cover and roughness. Its value ranges from 0, corresponding to non-erodible surface, and 1, that represent bare land with no vegetation. In the present work, given the regional working scale and the lack of detailed data related to the type of management of agricultural practices (e.g.

conservation/ridge tillage, no till practices), it was decided to adopt the values proposed by Panagos et al., 2015 [70], which are variable according to LULC.

P-factor is significant of the adoption of supporting agricultural management practices, such as fields contouring, terracing and strip cropping, that contribute in reducing the runoff and, consequently, limit the soil erosion [71, 72]. Since the model requires only one value for each land use class and not a spatially distributed value layer, it was decided to use the values calculated for Italy, and equal to 0.9519, as part of work carried out on the European scale [73].

3 Results and Discussion

The first result obtained from the implementation of the SDR module is a map of the spatial distribution within the regional territory of the annual soil loss gradient (t/ha).

Figure 4 shows through a color gradient representing the intensity of erosive phenomena, the comparison between the outcomes obtained in 1990 and 2018. Uncolored portions of land correspond to land use classes that do not contribute to sediment production (watercourses and bodies of water, artificial surfaces) [74, 75]. Both maps highlight the areas that show a greater attitude to give rise to erosive phenomena: the northern part of the regional territory, the south-western part overlooking the Tyrrhenian coast and the slopes located along the eastern part of the Apennine chain, corresponding to the middle valleys of the main rivers of the Basilicata region. Our outcomes, furthermore, confirm what assessed by European Soil Bureau [13] that declared an average annual soil loss ranging from 5 and 10 t/ha in the province of Potenza and ranging from 3 and 5 t/ha in the province of Matera. Although the analysis carried out at the regional scale necessarily uses less detailed dataset than the studies at the basin scale, the maximum value obtained, equal to 282 t/ha/yr, is comparable to what found in the Candelaro basin (Apulia Region) in which a maximum equal to 210 t/ha/yr was assessed [76]. In fact, it should be noted that the western part of the regional territory falls entirely within the first province and that, as can also be seen from our results, the area along the Ionian coast contributes very little to erosion phenomena, also thanks to the very low slopes that compensate for the negative role of intensive agriculture.

An useful comparison can be made with outcomes derived from Morgan, 1992 [77] which assessed average loss in an individual rainstorm, throughout the European territory, ranging from 20 to 40 t/ha with a frequency of once every two or three years and in more than 100 t/ha during extreme events. However, the comparison suggests an intensification of the intensity of erosion processes above all along the Apennine chain.

Based on the analysis of the values measured by primary catchment area (Table 1), it can be seen that the maximum value of annual soil loss has increased in all basins falling in the Basilicata region, excluding the Cavone catchment. However, these increases do not always correspond to a growth in the average value: this is the case for the Bradano, and Basento basins. On the other hand, erosive phenomena seem to be attenuating in the Cavone basin, which is the only one to record a decrease both in the average and in the maximum value.

In order to understand the changes that have occurred in terms of the intensity of erosion phenomena, a map has been produced representing the difference between

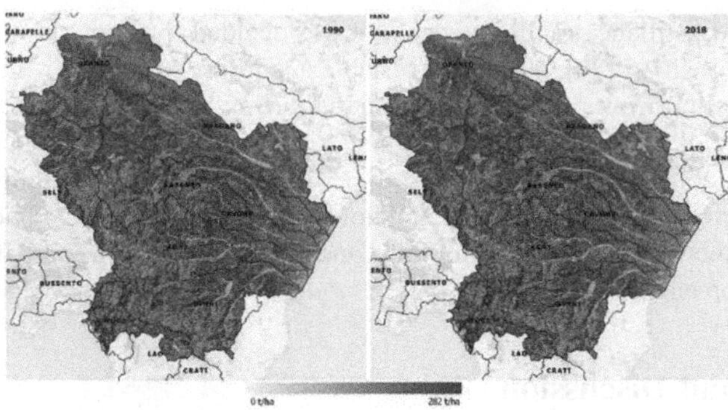

Fig. 4. Comparison between the distribution of annual soil loss (t/ha) in 1990 e 2018, respectively

Table 1. Soil loss values (t/ha/yr^{-1}) for 1990 and 2018 resulting for each of the river basins of the Basilicata region

Catchment	Maximum value		Mean value		Standard Deviation		Variance		Median value	
	1990	2018	1990	2018	1990	2018	1990	2018	1990	2018
Ofanto	215.3	240.6	2.2	2.4	4.4	4.6	19.6	21.6	0.7	0.8
Bradano	231.4	241.3	2.3	2.1	4.4	4.0	19.0	16.2	0.8	0.7
Lato	7.0	7.7	0.3	0.3	0.5	0.5	0.3	0.2	0.1	0.1
Sele	336.9	512.1	3.1	3.6	6.6	7.6	43.7	57.1	0.5	0.8
Basento	332.6	400.3	2.6	2.5	5.5	5.2	30.0	27.4	0.5	0.6
Cavone	307.4	286.0	3.0	2.7	6.1	5.5	36.7	30.7	0.8	0.7
Agri	378.2	744.2	2.7	3.0	6.4	8.7	41.1	76.1	0.3	0.3
Sinni	640.9	955.9	3.3	3.5	8.1	10.2	64.9	103.9	0.3	0.3
Bussento	58.1	80.5	1.3	1.8	6.3	8.8	40.2	77.2	0.0	0.0
Noce	990.7	1377.9	5.3	11.0	13.0	32.6	169.2	1059.7	0.5	0.6
Lao	537.0	1305.7	5.3	7.1	13.8	20.6	190.9	424.9	0.4	0.4

2018 and 1990 soil loss (Fig. 5). A positive difference corresponds to a worsening of the conditions predisposing to erosion (red gradients), while a negative difference is significant by a decrease in soil loss (green gradients). For the areas where this difference is most evident, more detailed boxes have also been set up. The first detail window (Fig. 5 - box 1) frames the area of the Vulture Mount where the increase in soil loss mainly concerns the sectorial side of the Mount. To this worsening in terms of soil conservation, the deforestation of large areas changed into permanent crops, arable lands, shrubs and grasslands has been determinant. More heterogeneous is the change in the most western part of the region (Fig. 5 - box 2) where three types of changes have contributed most to the increase in soil loss: from shrubs to bare lands, from woodlands to agricultural mosaic and from this last class to arable lands. A substantial improvement in soil stability conditions is shown by detail window 3 (Fig. 5 - box 3), which frames a portion of territory between the Sinni and Agri river basins. In the more northern part of the box, the decrease in soil loss is related to a change from arable lands to woodlands while in Southern part, it is more linked to a transformation from agricultural mosaic to shrubs and grasslands.

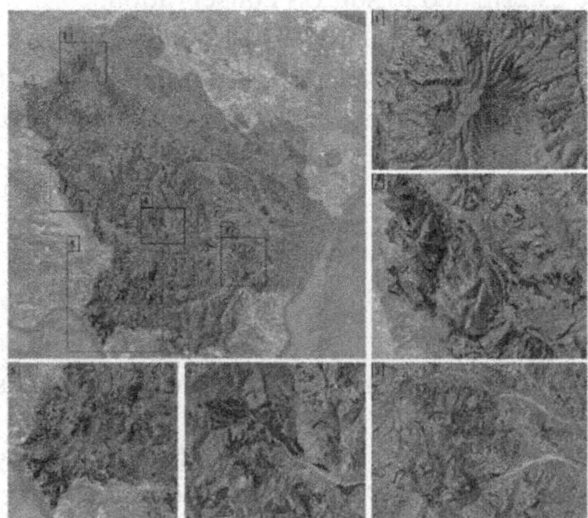

Fig. 5. Differences in annual soil loss occurred between 2018 and 1990. Green graduation represents an improvement (i.e. a decrease in erosion intensity), red graduation represents an increase in erosive phenomena. (Color figure online)

Figure 5 - Box 4, shows an area belonging to a mountainous catchment area where changes in land use have brought about changes in erosion phenomena that vary according to altitude. Along the slopes, in fact, the changes have led to the reduction of shrubs and stable grassland in favor of agricultural classes of land use (arable lands, meadows and agricultural mosaic). This has led to an increase in soil loss. In the riparian lands, closer to the watercourses, the establishment of agricultural mosaic and the evolution of bushes in the woods has led to a stabilization of the slopes with consequent improvement of erosion phenomena. The area overlooking the Tyrrhenian coast (Fig. 5 - Box 5), finally, appears to be strongly affected by an increase in erosion phenomena and soil loss linked to the decrease of wooded land and vegetated areas (mainly shrubs and meadows) that covered the highest part of the reliefs characterized by relevant slopes.

4 Conclusions

The need to protect the soil and its functions is all the more evident as not only does the provision of many ES depend on them [78], but they are considered crucial for obtaining many of the UN 2030 Sustainable Development Goals [79] and relevant keys for the most important challenges for our society such as poverty alleviation, mitigation of regional disparities and climate change mitigation [2, 80]. The importance of the issue of soil protection and limiting land degradation is particularly crucial for spatial planning, as it is in charge of the governance of land use change. The results obtained for the Basilicata Region indeed confirm that, despite the intensity of erosion phenomena are significantly influenced by the characteristics linked to the pluviometric regime and the rainfall erosivity, the soil use and coverage play an important role.

As highlighted by Mallinis et al. [81], mapping the spatial distribution of erosive processes and the consequent assessment of the soil loss in relation to different time extents, constitute the starting point for the implementation of erosion control measures and the design of policies oriented to soil ES conservation.

In this regard, since the issue of land degradation is complex and transversal with respect to different sectors, it is considered particularly useful to deepen it through the ES approach [82–86], capable of supporting a comprehensive, dynamic and scalable assessment framework to support and to make more operational the Sustainable Planning [87–91].

References

1. Kibblewhite, M.G., Ritz, K., Swift, M.J.: Soil health in agricultural systems (2008). https://doi.org/10.1098/rstb.2007.2178
2. Pereira, P., Bogunovic, I., Muñoz-Rojas, M., Brevik, E.C.: Soil ecosystem services, sustainability, valuation and management (2018). https://doi.org/10.1016/j.coesh.2017.12.003
3. Dominati, E., Patterson, M., Mackay, A.: A framework for classifying and quantifying the natural capital and ecosystem services of soils. Ecol. Econ. **69**, 1858–1868 (2010). https://doi.org/10.1016/j.ecolecon.2010.05.002
4. Stringer, L.: Can the UN Convention to combat desertification guide sustainable use of the world's soils? Front. Ecol. Environ. **6**, 138–144 (2008). https://doi.org/10.1890/070060
5. Udawatta, R.P., Gantzer, C.J., Jose, S.: Agroforestry practices and soil ecosystem services. In: Soil Health and Intensification of Agroecosystems, pp. 305–333. Elsevier Inc. (2017). https://doi.org/10.1016/B978-0-12-805317-1.00014-2
6. Pascual, U., et al.: On the value of soil biodiversity and ecosystem services. Ecosyst. Serv. **15**, 11–18 (2015). https://doi.org/10.1016/j.ecoser.2015.06.002
7. Gregory, A.S., et al.: A review of the impacts of degradation threats on soil properties in the UK. Soil Use Manag. **31**, 1–15 (2015). https://doi.org/10.1111/sum.12212
8. Raclot, D., Bissonnais, Y.L., Annabi, M., Sabir, M.: Sub-chapter 2.3.3. Challenges for mitigating mediterranean soil erosion under global change. In: The Mediterranean region under climate change, pp. 311–318. IRD Éditions (2018). https://doi.org/10.4000/books.irdeditions.23538
9. García-Ruiz, J.M., Nadal-Romero, E., Lana-Renault, N., Beguería, S.: Erosion in Mediterranean landscapes: changes and future challenges. Geomorphology **198**, 20–36 (2013). https://doi.org/10.1016/j.geomorph.2013.05.023
10. Salvati, L., Zitti, M., Perini, L.: Fifty years on: long-term patterns of land sensitivity to desertification in Italy. L. Degrad. Dev. **27**, 97–107 (2016). https://doi.org/10.1002/ldr.2226
11. Keesstra, S.D., et al.: The significance of soils and soil science towards realization of the united nations sustainable development goals. Soil **2**, 111–128 (2016). https://doi.org/10.5194/soil-2-111-2016
12. Jónsson, J.Ö.G., Davídsdóttir, B.: Classification and valuation of soil ecosystem services (2016). https://doi.org/10.1016/j.agsy.2016.02.010
13. Van der Knijff, J.M., Jones, R.J.A., Montanarella, L.: European soil bureau soil erosion risk assessment in Italy (2000)

14. Clarke, M.L., Rendell, H.M.: The impact of the farming practice of remodelling hillslope topography on badland morphology and soil erosion processes. Catena **40**, 229–250 (2000). https://doi.org/10.1016/S0341-8162(99)00047-8
15. Capolongo, D., Mannaerts, C.M.: Analyzing temporal changes in climate erosivity using a simplified rainfall erosivity model in Basilicata (Southern Italy) hydroclimate reconstrucion in the last centuries view project. Artic. J. Hydrol. (2008). https://doi.org/10.1016/j.jhydrol.2008.04.002
16. Bentivenga, M., Piccarreta, M.: Geomorphology of Pisticci area (Basilicata, Southern Italy). J. Maps. **12**, 220–226 (2016). https://doi.org/10.1080/17445647.2016.1193776
17. Piccarreta, M., Capolongo, D., Boenzi, F., Bentivenga, M.: Implications of decadal changes in precipitation and land use policy to soil erosion in Basilicata, Italy. Catena. 138–151 (2006). https://doi.org/10.1016/j.catena.2005.11.005
18. Pascale, S., et al.: Landslide susceptibility mapping using artificial neural network in the urban area of senise and san costantino albanese (Basilicata, Southern Italy). In: Murgante, B., et al. (eds.) ICCSA 2013. LNCS, vol. 7974, pp. 473–488. Springer, Heidelberg (2013). https://doi.org/10.1007/978-3-642-39649-6_34
19. Sediment Delivery Ratio—InVEST 3.6.0 documentation. http://data.naturalcapitalproject.org/nightly-build/invest-users-guide/html/sdr.html#quantitative-valuation. Accessed 27 Mar 2020
20. Borrelli, P., et al.: An assessment of the global impact of 21st century land use change on soil erosion. Nat. Commun. **8**, 1–13 (2017). https://doi.org/10.1038/s41467-017-02142-7
21. Hamel, P., Chaplin-Kramer, R., Sim, S., Mueller, C.: A new approach to modeling the sediment retention service (InVEST 3.0): case study of the Cape Fear catchment, North Carolina, USA. Sci. Total Environ. **524–525**, 166–177 (2015). https://doi.org/10.1016/j.scitotenv.2015.04.027
22. Rendell, H.M.: Soil erosion and land degradation in southern Italy. In: Fantechi, R., Margaris, N.S. (eds.) Desertification in Europe, pp. 184–193. Springer, Netherlands (1986). https://doi.org/10.1007/978-94-009-4648-4_19
23. Saganeiti, L., Pilogallo, A., Scorza, F., Mussuto, G., Murgante, B.: Spatial indicators to evaluate urban fragmentation in basilicata region. In: Gervasi, O., et al. (eds.) ICCSA 2018. LNCS, vol. 10964, pp. 100–112. Springer, Cham (2018). https://doi.org/10.1007/978-3-319-95174-4_8
24. Saganeiti, L., Pilogallo, A., Faruolo, G., Scorza, F., Murgante, B.: Territorial fragmentation and renewable energy source plants: which relationship? Sustain. **12**, 1828 (2020). https://doi.org/10.3390/SU12051828
25. Scorza, F., Saganeiti, L., Pilogallo, A., Murgante, B.: Ghost Planning: the inefficiency of energy sector policies in a low population density region. Arch. DI Stud. URBANI E Reg. In press (2020)
26. Cotecchia, V., Del Prete, M.: Essai de zonage géotechnique d'une région de structure complexe dans le sud des Apennins (Basilicate) avec particuliere référence a la stabilité des pentes. Bull. Int. Assoc. Eng. Geol.- Bull. l'Assoc. Int. Géol. l'Ingénieur **15**(1), 51–58 (1977). https://doi.org/10.1007/BF02592647
27. Liberti, M., Simoniello, T., Carone, M.T., Coppola, R., D'Emilio, M., Macchiato, M.: Mapping badland areas using LANDSAT TM/ETM satellite imagery and morphological data. Geomorphology **106**, 333–343 (2009). https://doi.org/10.1016/j.geomorph.2008.11.012
28. Grippa, A., et al.: Use of the HVSR method to detect buried paleomorphologies (filled incised-valleys) below a coastal plain: the case of the Metaponto plain (Basilicata, southern Italy) (2011). https://doi.org/10.4430/bgta0011
29. Piccarreta, M., Lazzari, M., Pasini, A.: Trends in daily temperature extremes over the Basilicata region (southern Italy) from 1951 to 2010 in a Mediterranean climatic context. Int. J. Climatol. **35**, 1964–1975 (2015). https://doi.org/10.1002/joc.4101

30. Piccarreta, M., Pasini, A., Capolongo, D., Lazzari, M.: Changes in daily precipitation extremes in the Mediterranean from 1951 to 2010: the Basilicata region, southern Italy. Int. J. Climatol. **33**, 3229–3248 (2013). https://doi.org/10.1002/joc.3670
31. Lazzari, M., Piccarreta, M.: Landslide disasters triggered by extreme rainfall events: the case of montescaglioso (Basilicata, Southern Italy). Geosciences **8**, 377 (2018). https://doi.org/10.3390/geosciences8100377
32. Lazzari, M., Geraldi, E., Lapenna, V., Loperte, A.: Natural hazards vs human impact: an integrated methodological approach in geomorphological risk assessment on the Tursi historical site, Southern Italy. Landslides **3**, 275–287 (2006). https://doi.org/10.1007/s10346-006-0055-y
33. Piccarreta, M., Capolongo, D., Miccoli, M.N., Bentivenga, M.: Global change and long-term gully sediment production dynamics in Basilicata, southern Italy. Environ. Earth Sci. **67**, 1619–1630 (2012). https://doi.org/10.1007/s12665-012-1603-5
34. Capolongo, D., Pennetta, L., Piccarreta, M., Fallacara, G., Boenzi, F.: Spatial and temporal variations in soil erosion and deposition due to land-levelling in a semi-arid area of Basilicata (Southern Italy). Earth Surf. Process. Landform. **33**, 364–379 (2008). https://doi.org/10.1002/esp.1560
35. Costantini, E.A.C., Lorenzetti, R.: Soil degradation processes in the Italian agricultural and forest ecosystems (2013). https://doi.org/10.4081/ija.2013.e28
36. Oliver, S.: The causes of erosive land degradation in the Basilicata Region of Italy (1999). https://www.jstor.org/stable/40573338. https://doi.org/10.2307/40573338
37. Kelly, C., et al.: Community resilience and land degradation in forest and shrubland socio-ecological systems: evidence from Gorgoglione, Basilicata, Italy. Land use policy. **46**, 11–20 (2015). https://doi.org/10.1016/J.LANDUSEPOL.2015.01.026
38. Lanorte, A., Belviso, C., Lasaponara, R., Cavalcante, F., De Santis, F., Aromando, A.: Satellite time series and in situ data analysis for assessing landslide susceptibility after forest fire: preliminary results focusing the case study of pisticci (Matera, Italy). In: Murgante, B., et al. (eds.) ICCSA 2013. LNCS, vol. 7972, pp. 652–662. Springer, Heidelberg (2013). https://doi.org/10.1007/978-3-642-39643-4_47
39. Lasaponara, R., et al.: Spatial open data for monitoring risks and preserving archaeological areas and landscape: case studies at Kom el Shoqafa, Egypt and Shush, Iran. Sustainability **9**, 572 (2017). https://doi.org/10.3390/su9040572
40. Lasaponara, R., Tucci, B., Ghermandi, L.: On the use of satellite sentinel 2 data for automatic mapping of burnt areas and burn severity. Sustainability **10**, 3889 (2018). https://doi.org/10.3390/su10113889
41. Nearing, M.A., Lane, L.J., Lopes, V.L.: Modeling Soil Erosion. Routledge (2018). https://doi.org/10.1201/9780203739358-6
42. Pandey, A., Himanshu, S.K., Mishra, S.K., Singh, V.P.: Physically based soil erosion and sediment yield models revisited (2016). https://doi.org/10.1016/j.catena.2016.08.002
43. Ali, K.F., De Boer, D.H.: Spatially distributed erosion and sediment yield modeling in the upper Indus River basin. Water Resour. Res. **46** (2010). https://doi.org/10.1029/2009WR008762
44. Diodato, N., Grauso, S.: An improved correlation model for sediment delivery ratio assessment. Environ. Earth Sci. **59**, 223–231 (2009). https://doi.org/10.1007/s12665-009-0020-x
45. de Vente, J., et al.: Predicting soil erosion and sediment yield at regional scales: where do we stand? (2013). https://doi.org/10.1016/j.earscirev.2013.08.014
46. Vigiak, O., Borselli, L., Newham, L.T.H., McInnes, J., Roberts, A.M.: Comparison of conceptual landscape metrics to define hillslope-scale sediment delivery ratio. Geomorphology **138**, 74–88 (2012). https://doi.org/10.1016/j.geomorph.2011.08.026

47. Renard, K.G., Foster, G.R., Weesies, G.A., Porter, J.P.: RUSLE: revised universal soil loss equation. J. Soil Water Conserv. **46**, 30–33 (1991)
48. Borselli, L., Cassi, P., Torri, D.: Prolegomena to sediment and flow connectivity in the landscape: a GIS and field numerical assessment. Catena **75**, 268–277 (2008). https://doi.org/10.1016/j.catena.2008.07.006
49. Borselli, L., Torri, D., Poesen, J., Iaquinta, P.: A robust algorithm for estimating soil erodibility in different climates. Catena **97**, 85–94 (2012). https://doi.org/10.1016/j.catena.2012.05.012
50. Jamshidi, R., Dragovich, D., Webb, A.A.: Estimating catchment-scale annual soil loss in managed native eucalypt forests, Australia. For. Ecol. Manage. **304**, 20–32 (2013). https://doi.org/10.1016/j.foreco.2013.04.032
51. Panagos, P., et al.: Rainfall erosivity in Europe. Sci. Total Environ. **511**, 801–814 (2015). https://doi.org/10.1016/j.scitotenv.2015.01.008
52. Ekern, P.C.: Rainfall intensity as a measure of storm erosivity. Soil Sci. Soc. Am. J. **18**, 212–216 (1954). https://doi.org/10.2136/sssaj1954.03615995001800020025x
53. Diodato, N.: Estimating RUSLE's rainfall factor in the part of Italy with a Mediterranean rainfall regime. Eur. Geosci. Union. **8**, 103–107 (2004)
54. Wischmeier, W.H., Smith, D.D.: Predicting rainfall erosion losses - a guide to conservation planning (1978)
55. Renard, K.G., Freimund, J.R.: Using monthly precipitation data to estimate the R-factor in the revised USLE. J. Hydrol. **157**, 287–306 (1994). https://doi.org/10.1016/0022-1694(94)90110-4
56. Renard, K.G., Foster, G.R., Weesies, G.A., Mccool, D.K., Yoder, D.C.: Predicting soil erosion by water: a guide to conservation planning with the revised universal soil loss equation (Rusle) (1997)
57. Pintaldi, E., D'Amico, M.E., Stanchi, S., Catoni, M., Freppaz, M., Bonifacio, E.: Humus forms affect soil susceptibility to water erosion in the Western Italian Alps. Appl. Soil. Ecol. **123**, 478–483 (2018). https://doi.org/10.1016/j.apsoil.2017.04.007
58. Saganeiti, L., Pilogallo, A., Faruolo, G., Scorza, F., Murgante, B.: Energy landscape fragmentation: Basilicata Region (Italy) study case. In: Misra, S., et al. (eds.) ICCSA 2019. LNCS, vol. 11621, pp. 692–700. Springer, Cham (2019). https://doi.org/10.1007/978-3-030-24302-9_50
59. Six, J., Elliott, E.T., Paustian, K.: Soil structure and soil organic matter II. A normalized stability index and the effect of mineralogy. Soil Sci. Soc. Am. J. **64**, 1042–1049 (2000). https://doi.org/10.2136/sssaj2000.6431042x
60. Loch, R.J., Rosewell, C.J.: Laboratory methods for measurement of soil erodibilities (K factors) for the universal soil loss equation. Aust. J. Soil Res. **30**, 233–248 (1992). https://doi.org/10.1071/SR9920233
61. Wall, G.J., Dickinson, W.T., Rudra, R.P., Coote, D.R.: Seasonal soil erodibility variation in southwestern Ontario. Can. J. Soil Sci. **68**, 417–424 (1988). https://doi.org/10.4141/cjss88-038
62. Giovannini, G., Vallejo, R., Lucchesi, S., Bautista, S., Ciompi, S., Llovet, J.: Effects of land use and eventual fire on soil erodibility in dry Mediterranean conditions. For. Ecol. Manage. **147**, 15–23 (2001). https://doi.org/10.1016/S0378-1127(00)00437-0
63. Moody, J.A., Martin, D.A.: Post-fire, rainfall intensity-peak discharge relations for three mountainous watersheds in the western USA. Hydrol. Process. **15**, 2981–2993 (2001). https://doi.org/10.1002/hyp.386
64. Lanorte, A., et al.: Integrated approach of RUSLE, GIS and ESA Sentinel-2 satellite data for post-fire soil erosion assessment in Basilicata region (Southern Italy). Geomat. Nat. Hazards Risk. **10**, 1563–1595 (2019). https://doi.org/10.1080/19475705.2019.1578271

65. Myronidis, D.I., Emmanouloudis, D.A., Mitsopoulos, I.A., Riggos, E.E.: Soil erosion potential after fire and rehabilitation treatments in Greece. Environ. Model. Assess. **15**, 239–250 (2010). https://doi.org/10.1007/s10666-009-9199-1
66. Bagarello, V., di Stefano, C., Ferro, V., Giordano, G., Iovino, M., Pampalone, V.: Estimating the USLE soil erodibility factor in sicily South Italy. Appl. Eng. Agric. **28**, 199–206 (2012). https://doi.org/10.13031/2013.41347
67. Panagos, P., Meusburger, K., Ballabio, C., Borrelli, P., Alewell, C.: Soil erodibility in Europe: a high-resolution dataset based on LUCAS. Sci. Total Environ. **479–480**, 189–200 (2014). https://doi.org/10.1016/j.scitotenv.2014.02.010
68. Kinnell, P.I.A.: Event soil loss, runoff and the universal soil loss equation family of models: a review (2010). https://doi.org/10.1016/j.jhydrol.2010.01.024
69. Lee, S.: Soil erosion assessment and its verification using the universal soil loss equation and geographic information system: a case study at Boun, Korea. Environ. Geol. **45**, 457–465 (2004). https://doi.org/10.1007/s00254-003-0897-8
70. Panagos, P., Borrelli, P., Meusburger, K., Alewell, C., Lugato, E., Montanarella, L.: Estimating the soil erosion cover-management factor at the European scale. Land Use Policy **48**, 38–50 (2015). https://doi.org/10.1016/j.landusepol.2015.05.021
71. Foster, G.R., Highfill, R.E.: Effect of terraces on soil loss: USLE P factor values for terraces. J. Soil Water Conserv. **38**, 48–51 (1983)
72. Karydas, C.G., Sekuloska, T., Silleos, G.N.: Quantification and site-specification of the support practice factor when mapping soil erosion risk associated with olive plantations in the Mediterranean island of Crete. Environ. Monit. Assess. **149**, 19–28 (2009). https://doi.org/10.1007/s10661-008-0179-8
73. Panagos, P., Borrelli, P., Meusburger, K., van der Zanden, E.H., Poesen, J., Alewell, C.: Modelling the effect of support practices (P-factor) on the reduction of soil erosion by water at European scale. Environ. Sci. Policy **51**, 23–34 (2015). https://doi.org/10.1016/j.envsci.2015.03.012
74. Nolè, G., Lasaponara, R., Lanorte, A., Murgante, B.: Quantifying urban sprawl with spatial autocorrelation techniques using multi-temporal satellite data. Int. J. Agric. Environ. Inf. Syst. **5**, 20–38 (2014). https://doi.org/10.4018/IJAEIS.2014040102
75. Elfadaly, A., Attia, W., Qelichi, M.M., Murgante, B., Lasaponara, R.: Management of cultural heritage sites using remote sensing indices and spatial analysis techniques (2018). https://doi.org/10.1007/s10712-018-9489-8
76. Karydas, C., Bouarour, O., Zdruli, P.: Mapping spatio-temporal soil erosion patterns in the Candelaro River Basin, Italy, using the G2 model with Sentinel2 imagery. Geosciences **10**, 89 (2020). https://doi.org/10.3390/geosciences10030089
77. Morgan, R.P.C.: Soil conservation options in the UK. Soil Use Manag. **8**, 176–180 (1992). https://doi.org/10.1111/j.1475-2743.1992.tb00917.x
78. Greiner, L., Keller, A., Grêt-Regamey, A., Papritz, A.: Soil function assessment: review of methods for quantifying the contributions of soils to ecosystem services. Land use policy **69**, 224–237 (2017). https://doi.org/10.1016/j.landusepol.2017.06.025
79. Jónsson, J.Ö.G.: Soil: ecosystem services, economic analysis and sustainability indicators (2019)
80. Salvati, L., Mancini, A., Bajocco, S., Gemmiti, R., Carlucci, M.: Socioeconomic development and vulnerability to land degradation in Italy. Reg. Environ. Chang. **11**, 767–777 (2011). https://doi.org/10.1007/s10113-011-0209-x
81. Mallinis, G., Gitas, I.Z., Tasionas, G., Maris, F.: Multitemporal monitoring of land degradation risk due to soil loss in a fire-prone mediterranean landscape using multi-decadal landsat imagery. Water Resour. Manag. **30**(3), 1255–1269 (2016). https://doi.org/10.1007/s11269-016-1224-y

82. Scorza, F., Pilogallo, A., Saganeiti, L., Murgante, B., Pontrandolfi, P.: Comparing the territorial performances of renewable energy sources' plants with an integrated ecosystem services loss assessment: a case study from the Basilicata region (Italy). Sustain. Cities Soc. **56**, 102082 (2020)
83. Attolico, A., Smaldone, R., Scorza, F., De Marco, E., Pilogallo, A.: Investigating good practices for low carbon development perspectives in basilicata. In: Gervasi, O., et al. (eds.) ICCSA 2018. LNCS, vol. 10964, pp. 763–775. Springer, Cham (2018). https://doi.org/10.1007/978-3-319-95174-4_58
84. Mazzariello, A., Pilogallo, A., Scorza, F., Murgante, B., Las Casas, G.: Carbon stock as an indicator for the estimation of anthropic pressure on territorial components. In: Gervasi, O., et al. (eds.) ICCSA 2018. LNCS, vol. 10964, pp. 697–711. Springer, Cham (2018). https://doi.org/10.1007/978-3-319-95174-4_53
85. Pilogallo, A., Saganeiti, L., Scorza, F., Las Casas, G.: Tourism attractiveness: main components for a spacial appraisal of major destinations according with ecosystem services approach. In: Gervasi, O., et al. (eds.) ICCSA 2018. LNCS, vol. 10964, pp. 712–724. Springer, Cham (2018). https://doi.org/10.1007/978-3-319-95174-4_54
86. Saganeiti, L., Favale, A., Pilogallo, A., Scorza, F., Murgante, B.: Assessing urban fragmentation at regional scale using sprinkling indexes. Sustain. **10** (2018). https://doi.org/10.3390/su10093274
87. Casas, G.L., Scorza, F.: Sustainable planning: a methodological toolkit. In: Gervasi, O., et al. (eds.) ICCSA 2016. LNCS, vol. 9786, pp. 627–635. Springer, Cham (2016). https://doi.org/10.1007/978-3-319-42085-1_53
88. Scorza, F., Grecu, V.: Assessing sustainability: research directions and relevant issues. In: Gervasi, O., et al. (eds.) ICCSA 2016. LNCS, vol. 9786, pp. 642–647. Springer, Cham (2016). https://doi.org/10.1007/978-3-319-42085-1_55
89. Dvarioniene, J., Grecu, V., Lai, S., Scorza, F.: Four perspectives of applied sustainability: research implications and possible integrations. In: Gervasi, O., et al. (eds.) ICCSA 2017. LNCS, vol. 10409, pp. 554–563. Springer, Cham (2017). https://doi.org/10.1007/978-3-319-62407-5_39
90. Murgante, B., Borruso, G., Lapucci, A.: Sustainable development: concepts and methods for its application in urban and environmental planning. Stud. Comput. Intell. **348**, 1–15 (2011). https://doi.org/10.1007/978-3-642-19733-8_1
91. Las Casas, G., Murgante, B., Scorza, F.: Regional local development strategies benefiting from open data and open tools and an outlook on the renewable energy sources contribution. In: Papa, R., Fistola, R. (eds.) Smart Energy in the Smart City. GET, pp. 275–290. Springer, Cham (2016). https://doi.org/10.1007/978-3-319-31157-9_14

International Workshop on Open Knowledge for Socio-economic Development (OKSED 2020)

Smart Communities and Knowledge Sharing as Main Tools to Achieve Common Purposes

Luigi Mundula[1(✉)] and Flavia Marzano[2]

[1] DICAAR – Department of Civil and Environmental Engineering and Architecture, University of Cagliari, Via Marengo 2, Cagliari, Italy
luigimundula@unica.it

[2] Link Campus University, Via del Casale di S. Pio V, 44, Rome, Italy
flavia.marzano@gmail.com

Abstract. As reaction to globalization and the loosing of landmark caused by the huge data and information availability in the "net" and by the mass media proliferation, the research of an identity and the need of a feeling of belonging is stronger and stronger in today society. The information and communication technologies (ICT's) - which initially helped to erase socio-territorial boundaries and to strengthen a feeling of belonging to a single community in which we are all interlinked and interdependent – have now become the main tools for building local, and smart, communities. These, in addition to being places of confrontation, are also and above all places for sharing subjective and objective knowledge (and therefore for continuous learning). There are several experiences going towards this direction (i.e. creating shared spaces built around shared values that emerge to deal with problems felt as "public") ranging from analytical, investigative, critical and vindictive dimensions to proposals, monitoring, evaluation, deliberation, on the most varied topics: from the abandonment of public buildings (such as confiscated property), to security and the protection of territories. These are thus defined spaces in which, through self-organization and civic hacking dynamics, problems that are perceived as public are discussed and public goods are co-produced. These last are intended not as goods produced or owned by a public administration, but as the result of a process of social interaction. Digital technologies in this contest are tools by which social practices of re-appropriation and collective redefinition of public goods are nourished.

Keywords: Social interactions · Digital technologies · Smart communities

This paper is the result of the joint work of the authors. For Italian evaluation purposes Luigi Mundula takes responsibility for Sects. 2 and 4, and Flavia Marzano for Sects. 1 and 3.

O. Gervasi et al. (Eds.): ICCSA 2020, LNCS 12253, pp. 439–452, 2020.
https://doi.org/10.1007/978-3-030-58814-4_31

1 Introduction

"The best ideas are common property" (Seneca)

In the presidency conclusions of the Lisbon European Council (March 2000) [16], the first sentence in the chapter "Preparing the transition to a competitive, dynamic and knowledge-based economy" was "*an information society for all*".

The Lisbon Council issues were defined in 1999 in a document which motivates the need for *e*Europe as follows [6]:

Why *e*Europe now? *e*Europe [9] is a political initiative to ensure the European Union fully benefits for generations to come from the changes the Information Society is bringing. These changes, the most significant since the Industrial Revolution, are far-reaching and global. They are not just about technology. They will affect everyone, everywhere.

Bringing communities, both rural and urban, closer together, creating wealth, sharing knowledge [1, 14, 26], they have huge potential to enrich everyone's lives.

And the same document defines key objectives of *e*Europe:

- Bringing every citizen, home and school, every business and administration, into the digital age and online.
- Creating a digitally literate Europe, supported by and entrepreneurial culture ready to finance and develop new ideas.
- Ensuring the whole process is socially inclusive, builds consumer trust and strengthens social cohesion.

Starting from these statements, we may understand how innovation and technologies can (and must) support sharing of knowledge and inclusion.

2 Innovation and Knowledge Diffusion

Knowledge sharing is closely linked to innovation and in particular to its dynamics, namely the processes that lead to its diffusion. This theme has been and still is at the center of the theoretical debate. An invention, that is, the purely creative act, which does not turn into an (product, process, organization) innovation does not have economic value and therefore does not produce effects on the socio-economic system. An innovation that is adopted by a few other players produces limited effects. The more widespread an innovation is, the more effects it produces. The theoretical models and approaches differ according to whether they identify linear processes and sequences over time (the phases follow one another in sequential order) or non-linear (interactive models with feedback from one phase to another).

Nonlinear models, developed starting from systemic theory [15, 22, 34] emphasize the interactions between actors, competences, knowledge and information flows that distinguish the different phases of the innovative process. In these models the central role is played by knowledge, skills (especially tacit) and learning processes that arise from the contact of people and the knowledge and skills incorporated in them.

In traditional theoretical models of the innovation economy, the representation of the innovation diffusion is an S-shaped curve. This representation is inspired by the theory of the product life cycle, characterized by an introduction phase, a development phase, a maturation phase and a decline phase. Likewise, an innovation or a new technology would know an introduction phase, a slow growth phase, a rapid growth phase and a maturity phase (which can also lead to a decline of innovation unless subsequent improvements). If the first phase can be characterized by radical innovations, the subsequent ones are mostly characterized by incremental and adaptive innovations.

The S-shape and above all the times of the different phases and the slopes of the different arches are influenced by various factors. The times of introduction (of adoption of a new product or of a new production technology) vary from innovation to innovation and from technology to technology, from enterprise to enterprise from society (of individuals) to society (of individuals). The same is true for large-scale deployment times. The S-curve could therefore take very different forms. Among the models that have attempted to explain the mechanisms for spreading innovation we find the one centered on the idea of imitation. This model transfers the epidemiological model of propagation developed in the medical sciences to the social sciences. The diffusion would take place by contagion (given by physical proximity and contacts between people) according to a speed of diffusion that varies according to the technology, the sector and the market.

Still on the topic of dynamics, a particularly important problem is that of technology transfer (particular method of spreading innovation and knowledge).

Technology transfer is the result of a set of operations that lead a company to "move" the point of application of a technology to a) another company (also a branch); b) to another country through the sale of its know-how and technical assistance. Technology transfer can be differentiated into:

- transfer of technical elements (machines, infrastructures, …)
- transfer of techniques in the strict sense (machines, production processes, with related user manuals, …)
- transfer of techniques in a broad sense (transmission of know-how and training)
- "global" technology transfer (the three previous components jointly)

The complex nature of technology undoubtedly explains one of the greatest difficulties of technology transfer, to the extent that this transfer does not imply, in the majority of cases, the modification or delocalization of the whole of the technological structure, but only of some of its elements. The success of the technology transfers, on the other hand, would require a shift of all the components of the technology (material, informative and organizational elements).

Since this rarely happens (in particular specific knowledge and know-how are difficult to transfer), those who "receive" technology are always in a position of dependence.

The transfer of knowledge opens a controversial chapter, that of protecting the rights of those who produce it: intellectual property rights (IPRs). Nowadays, the wealth of nations no longer resides in the earth and gold, but in knowledge. The ownership of factories, mineral reserves, properties and gold is quickly replaced by the ownership of intellectual products or "intellectual property".

Studies on the effects of IPRs on economic development assume knowledge as a non-competing asset. Consequently, the production of knowledge is associated with a higher rate of social return than the private one, thus determining a systematic under investment in knowledge. The political choice to solve the problem was to grant the "knowledge producer" the possibility of selling his innovation temporarily exclusively (e.g. patents, trademarks, copyrights). The idea behind this protection would stimulate innovation by guaranteeing a short-term monopoly associated with an improvement in long-term social well-being. The trade-off between the short and long term allows to derive the optimal length of the IPRs [7]. The IPRs system varies significantly from country to country. The level of protection of IPRs in a given country can be explained by associating it with its level of economic development and its historical and cultural path [30].

Least developed countries offer the lowest standards of protection for their lesser capacity to create innovation and have therefore traditionally preferred a rapid dissemination of knowledge at the expense of protecting IPRs. As countries rise on the scale of development, they adopt higher standards of protection both because they have more resources dedicated to the creation of innovation and because they represent more attractive markets for the more advanced countries and therefore face increasing pressures for protection from the outside. IPRs are therefore now part of the institutional infrastructure of developed countries as they aim to encourage private investment in research and development (R&D) and in other inventive or creative activities.

Many of the developed countries have pushed towards greater protection of intellectual property rights (Intellectual Property Rights - IPRs) through bilateral, regional and multilateral actions. In this context, the Agreement on Trade Related Aspects of Intellectual Property Rights, including Trade in Counterfeit Goods (the TRIPS Agreement), negotiated during the Uruguay Round (1986–94) of the trade negotiations, emerged as one of the three multilateral agreements (together with GATT and GATS) which outlined the fundamental structure according to which the World Trade Organization (WTO) operates. The TRIPS Agreement is based on pre-existing international conventions but in addition establishes minimum protection standards for all forms of IPRs and establishes procedures in the event of disputes, also providing for multilateral sanctions in cases of non-compliance with the rules laid down in the agreement.

The argument that is often proposed in support of this globally uniform regulation of intellectual property law is that such a system of rules would favor investment, research and technology transfer in developing countries.

However, some authors [5, 8, 24] believe that with the TRIPs Agreement the international monopoly of "knowledge producers" has been increased to the detriment of consumers, generating a distribution conflict between the North (innovator and knowledge producer) and the South (consumer of knowledge and technology). According to this approach, in terms of distribution of social well-being [29] the North, by increasing its level of monopoly, determines a very serious imbalance by extracting a part of the surplus of the South.

Based on these considerations, the South will tend to adopt a less restrictive IPRs policy than that of the North, indirectly supporting imitation and playing a global free-rider role rather than supporting a IPRs policy harmonization program.

Starting from even more radical positions, Vandana Shiva [31] argues that the birth of intellectual property rights is linked to the attempt by more developed nations to use them as the main tool of their own economic growth and for the control of world trade and markets International.

In this scenario, the digital revolution has led to the appearance of a new protagonist: the Creative Commons licenses.

Creative Commons are an important cultural and legal phenomenon, thanks to which the principles of copyleft born in the IT field (Free and Open Source Software) have expanded to creative works in general (open content). Creative Commons is a project born in the USA which belongs to a non-profit association (based in San Francisco) and which is structured in a series of decentralized communities scattered around the world.

Creative Commons (CC) licenses are based on copyright and apply to any work protected by it. The fundamental prerequisite for being able to grant a work under a Creative Commons license is to be the owner of all the rights granted with the license or to have an explicit authorization/request from the owner of the rights (for example the publisher).

Creative Commons licenses allow the author to define the rights that the author reserves towards the users of the document, according to the "some rights reserved" model.

Creative Commons licenses are ideally structured in two parts: the first part indicates the freedoms granted by the author for his own work; the second, however, exposes the conditions of use of the work itself.

The two freedoms are:

Share → Freedom to copy, distribute or transmit the work
Reworking → Freedom to readjust the work

The conditions of use of the work, which the user of the work must undergo in order to be able to use it freely, are four (Attribution; ShareAlike; Derivatives; Non-Commercial) and each is associated with a graphic symbol in order to make it easier to recognize. The combination of these four clauses gives rise to the Creative Commons licenses in use (Table 1). Once applied, the Creative Commons license is irrevocable.

3 Open Source, Open Data, Communities and Influencers

When speaking of "knowledge sharing" in the world of digital technologies, one might certainly start from the great experiences of the free software and open source communities or, for simplicity, FOSS (Free and Open Source Software) to avoid the error, unfortunately still common, of understanding "free software" as costless software while the word free in this context derives from freedom, and above all freedom to share [20].

Table 1. Creative Commons License

Sigla	Descrizione
CC BY	It allows you to distribute, modify, create works derived from the original, even for commercial purposes, provided that the authorship of the work is recognized to the author
CC BY-SA	It allows you to distribute, modify, create works derived from the original, even for commercial purposes, provided that the authorship of the work is recognized to the author and that the new work is given the same licenses as the original (therefore each derivative will be commercial use allowed) This license, in some ways, can be traced back to the copyleft licenses of free and open source software
CC BY-ND	It allows you to distribute the original work without any modification, even for commercial purposes, provided that the authorship of the work is recognized to the author
CC BY-NC	It allows you to distribute, modify, create works derived from the original, on condition that the authorship of the work is recognized to the author, but not for commercial purposes. Anyone who modifies the original work is not required to use the same licenses for derivative works
CC BY-NC-SA	It allows you to distribute, modify, create works derived from the original, but not for commercial purposes, provided that the authorship of the work is recognized to the author and that the new work is attributed the same licenses as the original (therefore to each derivative commercial use will not be allowed)
CC BY-NC-ND	This license is the most restrictive: it only allows you to download and share the original works on condition that they are not modified or used for commercial purposes, always attributing the authorship of the work to the author
CC Zero (CC0)	With a CC0 license, the author knowingly renounces all rights to his work. The functioning and effectiveness of this type of license depends on the type of work and the relative current regulations, but in general it acts as an unconditional waiver of one's rights to his work, which automatically becomes public domain

But let's see the definition given by the Free Software Foundation [10]:

"Free software" means software that respects users' freedom. Roughly, it means that the users have the freedom to run, copy, distribute, study, change and improve the software. Thus, "free software" is a matter of liberty, not of price. To understand the concept, you should think of "free" as in "free speech," not as in "free beer".

We sometimes call it "libre software," borrowing the French or Spanish word for "free" as in freedom, to show we do not mean the software is costless.

Below is the definition of free software freedoms (https://www.gnu.org/philosophy/free-sw.html.en#f1):

A program can be defined as "free software" if the program's users have the following four essential freedoms:

- The freedom to run the program as you wish, for any purpose.
- The freedom to study how the program works, and change it so that it does your computing as you wish. Access to the source code is a precondition for this.
- The freedom to redistribute copies so that you can help others.
- The freedom to distribute copies of your modified versions to others. By doing this you can give the whole community a chance to benefit from your changes. Access to the source code is a precondition for this.

It is therefore evident that the sharing of knowledge is the basis of free software and the communities that were born around these principles are communities that share, often as volunteers, time and skills.

Thanks to the type of licenses with which it is released and the collaborative methods with which it is developed, open source software becomes an innovation enabler contributing to the technological independence of Europe and the development of European companies. It is no coincidence that the European Parliament already on 29 October 2015 issued a resolution that "calls for the systematic replacement of proprietary software by auditable and verifiable open-source software in all the EU institutions".

Many European countries then followed up on this resolution with national regulations.

Public Administrations (PAs) buying software have to ensure the respect of many different constraints at least from the legal, technical and economical points of view.

Nevertheless PAs cannot forget that they are spending public money for the public interest, so they also have to ensure the respect of some "common" rules.

The development of technologies can be seen at least from three different points of view:

- technical: computer technologies (hardware and software) are more and more evolved and responding to customer requirements and needs
- easiness of use: evolution of technologies has brought simplification of interfaces and of man machine interaction tools
- economical: strong enhancement of the price/performance ratio

Technologies are evolving very fast and not always democratically; the risk is that too few suppliers control the market making technologies an instrument of power rather than a tool for progress.

Many population groups are weaker for social, physical, age, gender, income or culture reasons. For these groups access to technologies is not insured simply by technical evolution.

The role and the vision of politicians and an appropriate choice of policies are essential to lower the digital divide and to fill the gap between technologies and citizens giving people the full capacity to control and use new tools and avoiding the risk of new monopolies.

PAs can turn risks into opportunities, granting to citizens and enterprises the reduction of discriminating conditions and making them participate to economical, technological and social evolution processes.

In this phase PAs and in particular the local PAs have big duties and big opportunities to act in the direction of bridging the digital divide [19]!

PAs in buying software must assure:

- Pluralism, competition and security
- Integration with the software already in use
- "Continuity" of data (possibility of reading data also in the future)
- Interoperability and cooperation
- Availability of source code at least for inspection and traceability (even in case of proprietary code)

PAs in buying software must:

- Be proprietary of the "structure of data"
- Get better price/performance solutions
- Get a good price/performance maintenance
- Verify the TCO (Total Cost of Ownership and possibly the Social TCO)
- Buy software based on Open Standards
- Be sure to be able to change software supplier (paying attention to avoid lock-in)
- Be sure that the software acquired will not have any "backdoors"

In giving information, PAs must grant to citizens

- Transparency
- Privacy (GDPR)
- Accessibility (both in the sense of availability of documents and in the sense of accessibility for people with disabilities)
- Possibility to read public documents without having to buy any software (or license)
- Possibility to export data and documents in open formats
- Open Government Data

How can this be done[18]?
Most of the previous requirements can be easily obtained by adopting:

- Open Standards (OS)
- Open Source Software (OSS) solutions, but, in some case, it is essential that adoption of OS and OSS solutions be made compulsory by law in order to grant that the following requirements be totally satisfied:
  - Efficient and easy interoperability
  - Extended reusability of software and solutions [23]
  - Permanent access to data and information (Open Government Data)
  - Independence from suppliers
  - Verifiability of content and procedures

And what is the advantage for citizens?
Acquisition of FOSS by PAs may help in:

- reducing the digital divide
- increasing internal ICT competences and forming communities among PAs
- favouring sustainable economic and social development of the territory

Beyond this minimal and common level of requirements, each Administration will be able to adopt its own policies adding more compulsory rules like, for instance, the following:

- PAs when buying software developed on their own specifications have to acquire the source code and be proprietary of it;
- PAs owning software developed on their own specifications, have to give it for free with the source code and documentation to any other PA that can adapt it to its own needs.

3.1 Open by Default!

Speaking about openness, it is clear that Open Data [2] is also the basis for knowledge sharing: "Open data is data that can be freely used, shared and built-on by anyone, anywhere, for any purpose." (Open Knowledge Foundation)

The key features of openness defined by the Open Knowledge Foundation are:

- *Availability and access*: the data must be available as a whole and at no more than a reasonable reproduction cost, preferably by downloading over the internet. The data must also be available in a convenient and modifiable form.
- *Reuse and redistribution*: the data must be provided under terms that permit reuse and redistribution including the intermixing with other datasets. The data must be machine-readable.
- *Universal participation*: everyone must be able to use, reuse and redistribute — there should be no discrimination against fields of endeavour or against persons or groups. For example, 'non-commercial' restrictions that would prevent 'commercial' use, or restrictions of use for certain purposes (e.g. only in education), are not allowed.

In 2009 President Obama in a Memorandum declared:

"My Administration is committed to creating an unprecedented level of openness in Government. We will work together to ensure the public trust and establish a system of transparency, public participation, and collaboration. Openness will strengthen our democracy and promote efficiency and effectiveness in Government."

Open Government, Open Data, Open Access, Open Source, Open Standard, Open Innovation (H. Chesbrough) and any other way of sharing and collaborating without the "owner attitude" are the only way to ensure sustainability replacing the pernicious Not Invented Here syndrome (NIH) with Proudly Found Elsewhere [6]!

There are many examples of collaboration [21] in these areas and perhaps the best known worldwide is Wikipedia [35].

"Wikipedia is a multilingual online encyclopaedia created and maintained as an open collaboration project by a community of volunteers using a wiki-based editing system … Initially an English-language encyclopaedia, versions of Wikipedia in other languages were quickly developed. With 6.1 million articles, the English Wikipedia is the largest among the more than 300 Wikipedia encyclopedias. Overall, Wikipedia comprises more than 53 million articles attracting 1.5 billion unique visitors per month."

In some ways even social networks can be used as tools for the immediate sharing of knowledge even if this obviously implies less scientific rigor of information.

Finally, bloggers and influencers are another important vehicle of communication and knowledge sharing but, of course, they are going to tell us what they want to show us from their own point of view.

In summary, technologies are a great tool for sharing knowledge, and visions and policies can and must be a tool to encourage it.

4 Digital Sharing for the Territorial Fruition

Communities can take advantage of the forms of sharing made possible by new technologies to strengthen their resilient response to the shocks and stresses to which they are subjected: together with the traditional environmental, social and economic dimensions of sustainability, the literature also recognizes the important role played, in particular, by GIS tools [4], and especially by web mapping solutions.

Although traditional (paper) maps are still a vital source of information for the use of the territory, the context of GeoWeb 2.0 [17, 36] has opened up new perspectives that were largely unexplored until a few years ago. Technological advances such as the introduction of AJAX [11], the massive use of GPS and the spread of OGC standards for the interoperability of web mapping [25] have ushered in the era of neogeography [34], in which users become producers (and no longer pure consumers) of geospatial data. In this phase, defined by Plewe [28] as the third generation of web mapping, applications have become interactive and usable as their desktop counterparts[1].

The fourth generation of web mapping has focused on three-dimensional virtualization of the Earth's globe such as Nasa World Wind, Google Earth and Microsoft Bing, offering users a more realistic and engaging experience. The advent of these public web services with global coverage of digital images has opened up the world of geospatial mapping via the Internet to the world community. The ability to generate maps has extended far beyond the small group of web developers and mapping experts [27].

[1] Examples of such applications related to Italian slow tourism include: slow itineraries in Italian parks (http://www.parks.it/itinerari/Eindex.php); GiroParchi, which shows nature trails through the Gran Paradiso National Park and the Mont Avic Natural Park in Val d'Aosta, Italy (http://www.giroparchi.it/it/map/wrap); the Web viewer Contrat de Rivière Haute-Sûre, (http://www.crhs-sig.eu/mapserver_crhs/index.php?lang=en); Via Alpina, centered on a series of slow tourist routes along the Alps (http://www.via-alpina.org); the Swiss national portal for slow tourism (http://map.wanderland.ch/?lang=en); one web viewer on the most interesting slow tourism routes in Europe (http://maps.peterrobins.co.uk/routes.html) and another on the Via Francigena (http://www.viefrancigene.org/en/map).

Following the idea of Plewe's four generations of web mapping, Tsou [32] described a fifth generation based on cloud computing, advanced Internet applications (Rich Internet Applications - RIA)[2] and crowdsourcing. Instead of striving for ever more powerful hardware and increasingly sophisticated software, users can access cloud computing and cloud storage resources and services. Web mapping solutions, which integrate crowdsourcing data from users, allow users to be much more involved in the applications themselves. It is therefore evident that the center of the development of web mapping goes beyond information and data and substantially concerns the interactions of people on a global level.

User participation has also been the enabling factor for neogeography and is traditionally associated with the definition of Volunteered Geographic Information or VGI [12].

Consistent with this perspective, according to [13], the network initially appeared as the network of documents, was then transformed into a network of people and is now developed as a data network and social networks, through which they create real smart communities: in other words, communities are enriched by the contribution of users thanks to the support of new technologies and the network. The latter web transition focuses on a stronger connection involving people and data, i.e. interpersonal interactions around information and knowledge, which includes community mapping processes, location-based activities, dynamic processes and interactions, etc., in a geographical context[3].

The traces left by smart communities are not only physical traces on the territory, but also useful information for knowing the state of the places. This aspect is of particular relevance precisely in those contexts characterized by a certain degree of danger or which have been affected by catastrophic events, in that it transforms smart communities into resilient communities, that is, in places where infrastructure, architecture and services are developed to respond to everyone's needs, especially the most vulnerable groups, and where the opportunities are equally distributed in an environmentally friendly way. In this perspective, the main elements at stake are: systems and social agents. The systems include: the natural environment, physical infrastructure, social institutions and knowledge of places. The agents are, however, the actors who shape the systems: individuals, families, private companies and civil society organizations. Hence, a complete resilience strategy is one that adopts a collaborative approach, suitable for guiding and supporting the forces of the system and social agents. And here workspaces open on the second and third elements of resilient systems: ability to self-organize and ability to learn and adapt.

---

[2] RIA refers to a web programming environment that provides an intuitive user interface and access to powerful widgets and tools (e.g. Google Web Toolkit and Adobe FLEX).

[3] Examples of this type in the field of slow tourism are MapMyHike (http://www.mapmyhike.com), a crowdsourcing platform that collects hiking routes from people (also loaded via a mobile app); PisteCiclabili, where users can upload traces of Italian cycle paths (http://www.piste-ciclabili.com); GPSaCavallo, focused on horse trails (http://www.gpsacavallo.com); Wikiloc, which offers free GPS routes and waypoints that members can upload and share and which is integrated with Google Maps and Google Earth (https://it.wikiloc.com).

In addition to being places of confrontation, smart communities are also and above all places for sharing subjective and objective knowledge (and therefore continuous learning) and become particularly important in contexts that are vulnerable or characterized by a certain degree of risk. Collaborative mapping experiences are now different in this direction in order to create shared spaces built around shared values that emerge to face problems felt as "public". They are experiments that take on different dimensions and different themes from time to time. They range from analytical, investigative, critical and claiming dimensions to propositional, monitoring, evaluative, deliberative, on the most varied themes: from the abandonment of public buildings (such as confiscated assets), to the security and safeguard of the territories.

This is how spaces are articulated in which, through dynamics of self-organization and civic hacking, issues felt as public are discussed and public goods are co-produced. The latter understood not as goods produced or owned by a public administration, but as the result of a process of social interaction. Digital technologies become tools through which social practices of collective re-appropriation and redefinition of public goods are nourished.

From this point of view there is a connection with the civic sense that mobilizes people around public problems and the practices that these mobilizations determine. People who commit themselves to the co-production of possible solutions and, often, to the implementation of the operational tools through which to define or produce them.

In this sense, the forms of slow tourism associated with forms of digital sharing, in particular those of track route sharing [3], represent the possibility of triggering a process of territorial resilience which must be the local response in the name of transformation and change in the way to approach the territories. However, this potential does not lie only in acquiring an independent recognition and identity thanks to the increase in the tracks loaded or by the followers, but rather in being able to take root in the territory, intersecting with the already existing slow paths (both trekking and biking) present in these platforms, building a capillary and dynamic network of crossing the territory capable of innervating it and developing new connections and, therefore, a new perspective of socio-economic development.

The real big challenge is represented by continuous learning that can only come from the integration between a top-down functionalist vision with a bottom-up vision, based on design processes that start from the person and the reference context (person centered in place design). It is therefore a question of enabling a strong combination of formal and informal learning. Data, information and perceptions can only be shared and can only be considered a common good.

Only once the productive fabric has been reconstituted and has corresponded to a process of territorial integration can it be said that this "formula" will have borne fruit, stimulating the economic development of the territories and the reconstitution of the social fabric. This "formula" can therefore be the way to trigger an economic development of the territory and, in turn, to encourage the reconstitution of the social fabric, as well as the rediscovery and enhancement of local resources.

References

1. Ahmed, Y.A., Ahmad, M.N., Ahmada, N., Zakariaa, N.H.: Social media for knowledge-sharing: a systematic literature review. Telematics Inform. **37**, 72–112 (2018)
2. Aliprandi, S.: Il fenomeno open data, Indicazioni e norme per un mondo di dati aperti, Ledizioni (2014)
3. Balletto, G., Milesi, A., Ladu, M., Borruso, G.: Dashboard for supporting slow tourism in green infrastructures. A methodological proposal in Sardinia. Sustainability **12**, 3579 (2020)
4. Baud, R.: The concept of sustainable development: aspects and their consequences from a socio-philosophical perspective. YES (Youth Encounter on Sustainability) Summer Course Material, ACTIS, ETH Zürich (2008)
5. Chin, J., Grossman, G.M.: Intellectual property rights and north-south trade. In: Jones, R.W., Kreuger, A.O. (eds.) The Political Economy of International Trade. Basil Blackwell, Cambridge (1990)
6. Concas, G., De Petra, G., Gallus, G.B., Ginesu, G., Marchesi, M., Marzano, F.: Contenuti aperti, beni comuni. McGraw Hill, Milano (2009)
7. de Benedictis, L.: Trips, trattative commerciali, teoria economica ed evidenza empirica. In: Guerrieri, P. (ed.) Libero scambio e regole multilaterali. Il Mulino, Bologna (2003)
8. Deardorff, A.V.: Welfare effects of global patent protection. Economica **59**, 35–51 (1992)
9. eEurope: an information society for all (2005). https://eur-lex.europa.eu/LexUriServ/LexUriServ.do?uri=COM:2002:0263:FIN:EN:PDF
10. Free Software Foundation. https://www.fsf.org/. Accessed 02 June 2020
11. Garrett, J.J.: Ajax. A New Approach to Web Applications (2005). http://www.adaptivepath.com/ideas/ajax-new-approach-web-applications. Accessed 29 Nov 2019
12. Goodchild, M.F.: Citizens as sensors: the world of volunteered geography. GeoJournal **69**(4), 211–221 (2007). https://doi.org/10.1007/s10708-007-9111-y
13. Hall, W., Tiropanis, T.: Web evolution and Web science. Comput. Netw. **56**, 3859–3865 (2012)
14. Kaur, S., Misra, S.C.: Social Networking and Knowledge Sharing in Organizations. In: Encyclopedia of Information Science and Technology, Fourth edn (2018)
15. Le Moigne, L.: Progettazione della complessità e complessità della progettazione. In: Bocchi G., Ceruti M. (a cura di), La sfida della complessità, Feltrinelli, Milano, pp. 97–99 (1985)
16. Lisbon European Council. https://www.europarl.europa.eu/summits/lis1_en.htm
17. Maguire, D.J.: GeoWeb 2.0 and volunteered GIS. In: Workshop on Volunteered Geographic Information, Santa Barbara (CA), pp. 104–106 (2007)
18. Marzano, F.: Dieci anni di Open Source nella Pubblica Amministrazione Italiana: finalmente ci siamo! In: Le soluzioni Open Source per la Pubblica Amministrazione. Le esperienze nella regione Umbria, pp. 13–16, Franco Angeli, Milano (2013)
19. Marzano, F.: FLOSS e Pubblica Amministrazione. In: Finalmente Libero. Software libero e standard aperti per le pubbliche amministrazioni, pp. 1–32. McGraw Hill, Milano (2008)
20. Marzano, F.: Il FLOSS nella pubblica amministrazione. In: Il software libero in Italia, pp. 82–99. ShaKe edizioni (2009)
21. Marzano, F.: Why we is better than me. In: "Yes WE STEM" (eBook 2016)
22. Maturana, H.R., Varela, F.J.: Autopoiesi e cognizione. La realizzazione del vivente. Marsilio, Bologna (2001)
23. Official website of the European Union: share and reuse Interoperability solutions for public administrations, business and citizens https://joinup.ec.europa.eu/
24. Panagariya, A.: TRIPs and the WTO: an uneasy marriage. In: Paper Presented at a Seminar at the World Trade Organization, Geneva, 20 July (1999)
25. Peng, Z.R., Tsou, M.H.: Internet GIS. Wiley, Hoboken (2003)

26. Petrucco, C.: Partecipazione e condivisione di conoscenza negli apprendimenti on-line - Participation and knowledge sharing in online learning, JO - FORMAZIONE & INSEGNAMENTO. Rivista internazionale di Scienze dell'educazione e della formazione (2015)
27. Piana, C.: Open source, software libero e altre libertà. Un'introduzione alle libertà digitali, Ledizioni (2018)
28. Plewe, B.: Web cartography in the United States. Cartogr. Geogr. Inf. Sci. **34**(2), 133–136 (2007)
29. Primo Braga, C.A., Fink, C., Sepulveda, C.P.: Intellectual Property rights and economic development. Discussion Paper 402, World Bank, Washington D.C. (1999)
30. Primo Braga, C.A., Fink, C.: How stronger protection of intellectual property rights affects international trade flows (1999). https://elibrary.worldbank.org/doi/pdf/10.1596/1813-9450-2051
31. Shiva V: Protect Or Plunder? Understanding Intellectual Property Rights. Global issues (2001)
32. Tsou, M.T.: Revisiting web cartography in the United States: the rise of user-centered design. Cartogr. Geogr. Inf. Sci. **38**, 250–257 (2013)
33. Turner, A.J.: Introduction to Neogeography. O' Reilly Media, Sebastopol, USA (2006)
34. von Bertanlaffy, L.: Teoria generale dei sistemi. Fondamenti, sviluppi, applicazioni, ILI (1968)
35. Wikimedia https://www.wikimedia.org/
36. Yadav, P., Deshpande, S., Sengupta, R.: Animating maps: visual analytics meets GeoWeb 2.0. In: Griffith, Daniel A., Chun, Y., Dean, Denis J. (eds.) Advances in Geocomputation. AGIS, pp. 75–84. Springer, Cham (2017). https://doi.org/10.1007/978-3-319-22786-3_8

The Impact of the COVID-19 Outbreak on the Socio-Economic Issues of the Black Sea Region Countries

George Abuselidze[1(✉)] and Lela Mamaladze[2]

[1] Batumi Shota Rustaveli State University, Ninoshvili, 35, 6010 Batumi, Georgia
george.abuselidze@bsu.edu.ge

[2] Iv. Javakhishvili Tbilisi State University, University, 2, 0186 Tbilisi, Georgia

Abstract. The COVID-19 appeared in Hubei Province (China) at the end of 2019 and it was assessed as a global pandemic in March 2020. Because of pandemic radically transformed the existing reality and created a completely new Pandeconomic (economic, social and political) challenges to the world. There were restricted international air, land and sea traffic, as well as domestic traffic, cultural and sports events, social events and economic activities as part of the activities taken by the states against the spread of the virus.

The aim of the research is to study the impact of the current pandemic situation on the socio-economic issues of the Black Sea Region countries. The paper systematically analyzes economic processes of the Black Sea Region countries in the domestic and international context. In addition, the analysis of the planned anti-crisis activities outlines future prospects and develops recommendations. It is likely that the crisis caused by the pandemic will last longer than COVID-19 itself. Consequently, the results presented in the study and the recommendations developed based on the research have a practical purpose in eliminating the Pandeconomic crisis.

Keywords: COVID-19 Outbreak · Crisis · Socio-economic issues · Pandeconomy · Black Sea Region

1 Introduction

The research concludes the analysis of 1940–2004 cases show that given the current social, economic, or ecological conditions under globalization, there is a much greater risk that the disease will acquire the potential for a pandemic at the present time[1]. For example, the increase in population density [1] and the increased contacts between humans and animals [2] the frequency of international flights and interstate traffic – are the small list of factors that increase the likelihood of transmitting the infection.

[1] According to the World Health Organization, a pandemic means a situation where the spread of the disease extends beyond a state and becomes international, involving the world, and infecting large numbers of people [48].

O. Gervasi et al. (Eds.): ICCSA 2020, LNCS 12253, pp. 453–467, 2020.
https://doi.org/10.1007/978-3-030-58814-4_32

Consequently, measures and restrictions taken by government to prevent pandemic call into question international or local economic relations, business entities and labor issues face many challenges.

Under the conditions of globalization, the world is evolving rapidly and the social, economic or political environment is undergoing constant transformation. Consequently, the discussion of historical experience highlights the difference factors of the economic impact compared to the modern world and it allows us to develop recommendations that are as close as possible to reality.

2 Research Methods

2.1 Analysis of Recent Research

The paper is based on both quantitative and qualitative methods of research. To answer the research question the study includes to analyze the scientific publications on the relevant topic. In particular, the global financial and economic crises and their impact on the socio-economic situation of individual countries [3–9], economic recessions caused by a pandemic [10–17], financial-economic policy (activities) against crisis and fragmentary approaches among them [18–26]. The results of the surveys conducted by the leading research organization, economic models and statistical data [27–49].

2.2 Research Methodology

The research methodology is based on the 2006 model developed by the Center for Applied Macroeconomic Analysis, Global Macroeconomic Consequences of pandemic influenza (2006), which describes how the epidemic is causing the global economic crisis and declining GDP [50]. The study also used a model presented by economists from the National Bureau of Economic Research in 2016. The calculation of the results is based on the analysis of all cases of epidemics from the 18th century to the present. The model is related to the scale of epidemic and the decline in income. It is noteworthy that this model also takes into account the specific factors due to which events in developing and developed countries face to different scenarios [51]. In conclusion, some practical recommendations have been developed on the theoretical and methodological research of the issue. Short and long-term recommendations based on the scientific analysis of the problem are important because it helps the states maintain stability during the economic crisis.

3 The Impact of Pandemics on the Economy – A Historical Review

From a historical perspective, once in every 10 years, the world economy is going through a certain process of renewal. Existing trends have led to intensive development of processes, such as market adjustment and more balanced economy and markets. It is noteworthy that throughout history, the population has been constantly struggling with global economic recessions or pandemics at different times of century (see Fig. 1).

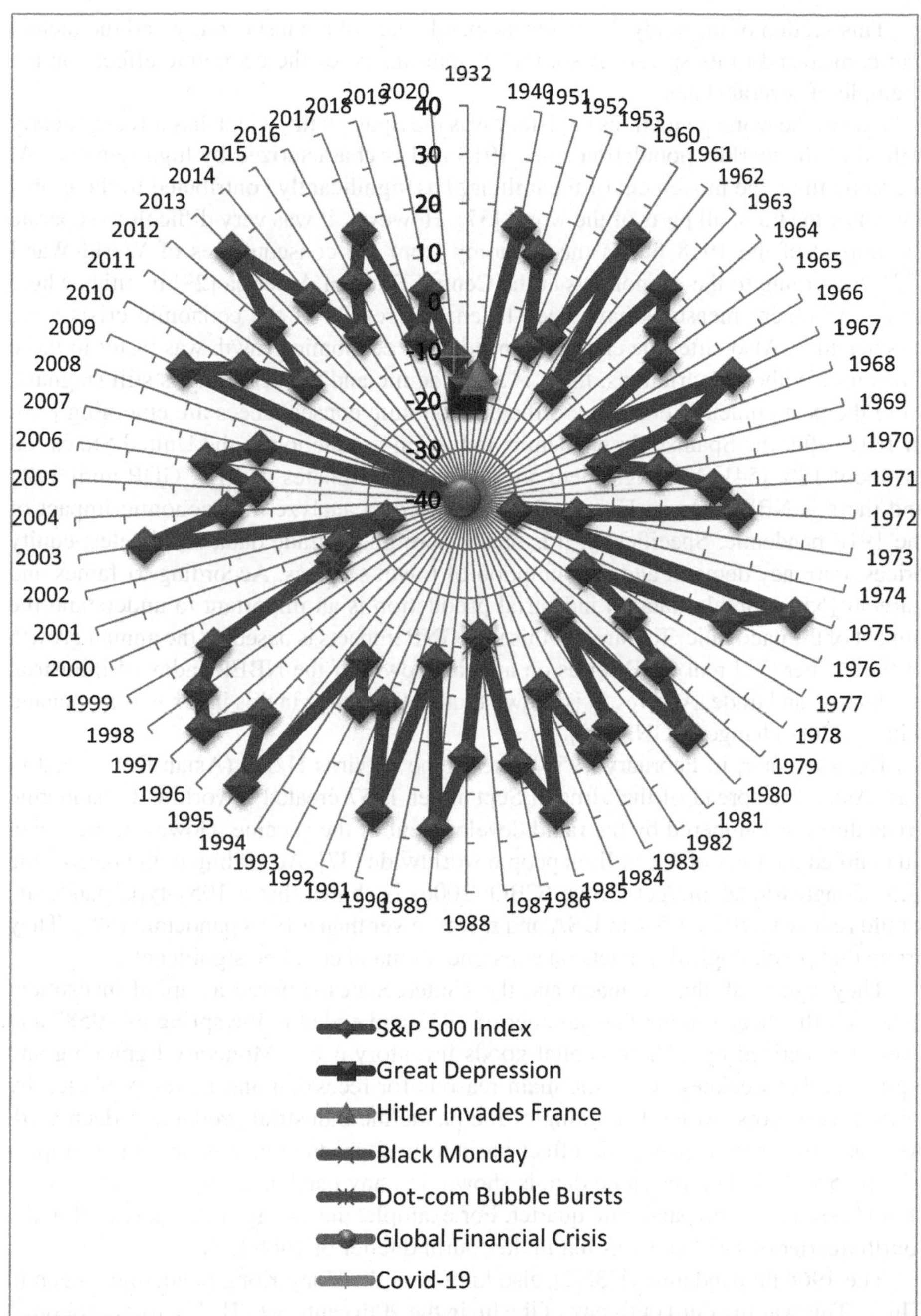

Fig. 1. How the covid-19 crash compares to historic market falls. Source: Created by the authors based on IMF World Economic Outlook data, Financial Times and papers [3, 10]

This section of the study discusses the pandemics of the last century and the factors that contributed to its spread. Also, this chapter analyzes the economic effects on the example of several states.

One of the worst pandemics in history was the Spanish flu, which has affected nearly a third of the world's population since 1918 and is characterized by high lethality. At the same time, the movement of the military has significantly contributed to the global spread of the flu in all parts of the world [37]. However, it was very difficult to separate the impact of the 1918 flu on the economy from the consequences of World War I [52]. According to the economists at the Central Bank of America [29] in cities where strict and urgent measures have been taken; the results of the economic crisis were less negative. Also, after the end of the pandemic, economic growth was faster in these cities too. Without restrictions, there is an epidemic and the economy is still stagnant, so in the post-epidemic era, more difficult economic consequences are emerging [53]. In 1918, after the Spanish flu pandemic, industrial production in the United States fell by about 18% [54]. Although there are no official estimates of BEA GDP until 1929 and there is NBER Macro History Database used to analyze the economic impact of the 1918 pandemic. Specifically, it is meant here goods trade data, retail sales, equity prices, currency demand and consumption of travel services. According to James and Sargent [55], monthly data on industrial production is an important to understand the impact of the pandemic. To translate this into GNP impacts is based on the annual growth of the Romer [72] real GNP series on annual growth of the NBER index of industrial production and trade. As a result is shown that a 1% change in this index was associated with a 0.26% change in GNP [55].

Decades later, in February 1957, a new type of virus H2N2 (Asian flu) spread in East Asia. The spread of the virus in September 1957 created a worldwide pandemic crisis that was hampered by the rapid development of the vaccine. However, the Asian flu claimed the lives of 1.1 million people worldwide [37]. According to the data of the U.S. Congressional Budget Office (CBO: 2006) is shown that a 1957-type pandemic would reduce GDP by 1.5% in USA and it was lower than a 1918 pandemic (5%). They argue that psychological impacts on consumer demand could be significant.

They also think that "Canada and the United States suffered a capital investment recession that began in the late summer of 1957 and ended in the spring of 1958" and was characterized by a sharp capital goods inventory cycle. Monetary tightening and equity market weakness were the main reasons for recession and it was predicted by leading indicators. At the beginning of the pandemic industrial production decreased. And as a final result, pandemic effect on industrial production was an annual impact of −0.15%. Based on the same data is shown that any pandemic impacts on economy should be clear in the pandemic quarter. For example, the savings rate decreased in the fourth quarter of 1957 and was flat in the fourth quarter of 1968 [55].

The 1968 flu pandemic (H3N2), also known as the Hong Kong pandemic, began in China. This was the third outbreak of the flu in the 20th century [37]. The total economic cost was estimated at $4.6 billion in 1968 or $34 billion today in USA. Because of the U.S. spent $225 million on Medicare (1968 dollars, $1.7 billion in 2020). The second wave of the pandemic in the U.S. considered a mild recession with GDP decreasing by only 0.6% and unemployment peaked right after the recovery began at 6.1% [56].

It should be noted that this period in the United States coincided with political tensions and public protests. In addition, the U.S. was involved in one of the largest-scale military confrontations - the Vietnam War. Given these factors, the period of recovery of the damage caused by the pandemic and the stabilization of the situation took much longer [57].

In April 2009, the H1N1 virus appeared in Europe. The case of "swine flu" has spread to almost all Western countries. In June 2009, members of the World Health Organization declared a new flu pandemic for the first time in 41 years [37]. From an economic perspective, based on research of The Economist, losses range from 0.5% to 1.5% of GDP in affected countries [41]. According to the same data, it took less than six months to spread the 2009 pandemic, while in 1918, 1957 and 1968 it took much more than six months, which was facilitated by the factors discussed above. During the 20th Century almost every countries experienced on the one hand a big wave of GDP per capita growth and on the other hand a huge decline in GDP per capita growth. It considers only a particular economic development measure [58]. Most papers analyze the impact of various factors on GDP. However, almost nothing is said about the impact of the global pandemic on the GDP. In summary, economic losses (reduced demand, delayed production, reduced supply, and unemployment) are caused by measures to prevent the spread of the virus. The threat was posed by the modern world in 2020, when the World Health Organization declared March 11 a new coronavirus infection pandemic.

4 Pandemic and its Impact on the Black Sea Region

Given the scale of the pandemic, leading international organizations have conducted studies that predict the negative impact of Covid-19 on economic activity. In particular,

- According to the International Labor Organization (ILO), unemployment in the world will increase significantly as a result of the virus. Compared to 2019, when the number of unemployed was 188 million, it will increase by 5.3 million in the small range of the spread of a virus; Unemployment will rise by 13 million in the medium range of the virus and by 24.7 million in the high range of the virus [57].
- According to the study by the Organization for Economic Co-operation and Development (OECD), the following scenarios are presented: a) Economic growth in 2020 will be reduced by 0.5% to 2.4% if the economic effects of the virus peak in the first quarter. b) In another case, global economic growth in 2020 (2.9% according to the old forecast) could be reduced by half, or 1.5%. According to the report, China's economic growth will slow to 4.9%, the Eurozone's 0.8% and the US's 1.9% due to the spread of the coronavirus [59].
- According to Bloomberg, global economic growth slowed by 1.2% in the first quarter of 2020. According to the same study, the economic result could include recessions in the United States, the Eurozone, Japan, and China, totaling $ 2.7 trillion in losses [15].
- According to the latest analysis proposed by the UN, the growth of the global economy after COVID-19 will be reduced by at least 2.5% and the damage will reach about a trillion dollars. In the worst case, this number could be double. The biggest damage will be to oil and other exporting countries. At least a 1% reduction in the economic growth rate of such countries is expected [44].

- According to the OSCE report, due to the decrease in world trade, the growth of the world economy will be reduced to 2.4% from the previous forecast of 2.9% [59].

Statista.com publishes the sectors of the economy that have suffered the most from the pandemic. There are: 1) manufacturing, 2) travel and transportation 3) retail, 4) energy and resources, 5) high tech and telecommunications, 6) healthcare and life sciences, 7) non-profits, 8) media and entertainments, 9) universities and colleges, 10) banking, financial sectors and insurances and 11) public sector [60].

According to the study by small open economies [10], the economic downturn is expected to be as high as –5%. As for the countries of the Black Sea Region, according to the publication of George Wisan (Coordinator of the Black Sea Security Program of the Romanian Energy Center), "The region's resilience will be tested in a way it hasn't before and the political and economic impact will likely be felt long after the pandemic is over" [45] and in the present study, the case of each state in the Black Sea Region is discussed.

4.1 Georgia

In the case of Georgia, a large part of GDP is occupied by the tourism industry, which is also characterized by a high rate of employment and plays an important role in reducing the trade balance. Georgia ranks among the world's leading countries in the share of the tourism sector in GDP (approximately 11%). Therefore, it plays an important role in terms of foreign exchange inflows to Georgia [61] and, consequently, the stability of the GEL exchange rate. Revenue from tourism in January 2020 was 17% higher than the previous year. So, the negative impact of the pandemic was evident in the following month, and became more apparent in the following period [40].

According to 2019 data, in the most important 15 investors are the United States, China and Japan. The economic impact of the viral outbreak in existing countries can directly affect Georgia. In particular, there is a danger of a significant reduction in foreign direct investment [30].

The case of Georgia, as a developing country, international money transfers play an important role in terms of the significant share of GDP, as well as the inflow of foreign currency and the impact of the national currency on the exchange rate. The share of money transfers in Georgia's GDP is 13.5% (2019 Preliminary, Geostatic). In March 2020, the money transferred to Georgia decreased by 9% to $ 125.9 million. One of the factors contributing to the decline is the economic shock caused by COVID-19. The amount of remittances decreased from the countries where the pandemic was widespread - Russia (28.32%), Italy (8.66%), Greece (1.81%) and Spain (18.56%). Instead, in March 2020, $ 20.4 million (62.1 million GEL) was sent abroad from Georgia, which is 10.1% more than in March 2019 ($ 18.5 million). All this once again confirms the theoretical provisions of the direction of capital movement during crises. In addition, a significant portion of the population is self-employed. Also, employed in the sector of the economy whose activities have been restricted due to the threat of the spread of the pandemic (e.g., restaurants, aesthetic centers, non-food stores). Business entities left without income could not take responsibility for providing their employees with wages in a pandemic.

Consequently, being left without paying a large amount of the citizens further exacerbates the difficult economic background.

4.2 Russia

Russia is one of the world's leading producers of crude oil and natural gas. In 2019, 29.6% of Russia's total exports were crude oil, 18.3% was recycled oil, and 4.3% was natural gas. In total, the share of these three products exceeds 50% of total exports [62]. In the OSCE report on March, the growth rate of the Russian economy was revised and reduced. If the expected economic growth at the beginning of the year was 1.6%, which was reduced by four tenths [59]. The Russian economy is significantly affected by falling oil prices due to reduced demand and declining exports.

It should be noted that the issue of depreciation of the Russian ruble. If at the beginning of the year $ 1 was the equivalent of 66 Russian rubles, in March this figure was replaced by 80.9 Russian rubles [63].

According to the data from Russia's Center for Macroeconomic Analysis and Short-term Forecasting indicate negative 20% of GDP for Q1 2020 and up to 15 million unemployed. Consulting Company Finexpertiza's report estimates, that a full month of closures and self-isolation will cost private sector businesses Rs. 530 billion rubles. Business losses in terms of unrealized income are estimated at Rs. 917 billion a week and Rs. 5.5 trillion a month, which is 5% of GDP [38].

Millions of Russians are at risk of losing their jobs. Official unemployment rate could hit 15% by the end of the year, up from its current level of 4.6%. According to various estimates, between three and five million jobs across the country were at risk and on the other hand, unemployment rate of between 10 and 15% was possible—equivalent to 7–10 million out of work.

Economists of The Moscow Times note that the economic crisis could be worse than any Russia has experienced since Putin came to power 20 years ago [42].

4.3 Turkey

In the opinion of some experts (Erdemir, A., Lechner, J. A.) Ankara's finances were weak before the pandemic. In addition, combination of external debt and a public health crisis could spell disaster [64]. It should be noted that economic growth in Turkey last year was only 0.9%. Unemployment is high and inflation is low, also, foreign exchange reserves and foreign direct investment are declining. In addition, Turkey is involved in the hostilities in Syria and Libya [65].

The suspension of certain sectors of the economy due to the pandemic has affected Turkey in the following areas:

- Unemployment has risen as a result of the suspension of certain sectors of the economy. Turkey's unemployment rate was 13.7% in 2019, a 2.7% rise compared to the previous year [66]. In 2020 it increased to 13.8% in January compared to 13.7% again [67].
- Turkey's tourism industry has been growing at an unprecedented speed for the last three years [43]. Due to the suspension of international traffic, the tourism industry also faced problems, with revenues accounting for 12% of the Turkish economy and

employing more than a million people [65]. Turkey's income from tourism is expected to decline this year by 10–20 billion dollars [34].
- Turkey depended for its imports on East Asia, which accounted for 23% of total imports in 2019. Most of those imports were factory goods used by Turkey [34].

The country's foreign trade volume grew 3.6% year-on-year to $98.4 billion in the first quarter of 2020. The export was choked January–March after seeing a 4% rise in the first two months [28]. As a result of declining exports, production also declined.

According to the World Bank, 1) Turkey's economy will grow by 0.5% this year and it will be 3% points lower than planned. 2) Growth will pick up steam in 2021–22 to hit 4%. 3) 11% inflation is expected in 2020, caused by declining energy prices, exchange rate pressures and monetary easing. As for the longer-term forecast, 9% is expected in 2021 and 8.5% in 2022. 4) Fiscal deficit is estimated to expand to 4.5% of GDP in 2020 to 2.9% of GDP by 2022 [68].

4.4 Ukraine

The COVID-19 epidemic reached Ukraine when the country has a poor national economic landscape. The slowed or stopped production and a decline in trade caused by pandemic can only worsen the situation. Ukraine's economy had started slowing down at the end of 2019. The effects of the pandemic on the economy will also be influenced by oil prices on and the ensuing panic affecting the financial indexes, which pushed devaluation of the national currency [47].

Ukraine is also an exporter of primary commodities (for example, metals) and the price for them is going to fall significantly due to falling demand in world markets [46]. The reasons were a global drop in prices of and demand for iron ore and steel, which are important parts of Ukraine's GDP. At the beginning of 2020 industrial production fell 5.1% [47].

According to the gravitational model of international trade developed by the Foreign Trade Analytical Center Trade, there is expected a 15–25% drop in exports and imports, which means a decrease in exports by $ 7.5–12.5 billion and imports by $ 9–15 billion in 2020 [46].

4.5 Bulgaria

According to the World Bank (2009) industry accounts for 23.8% of the GDP, and 30% of the workforce is employed in the industrial sector. The agricultural sector represents 3.6% of GDP and employs 7% of the workforce. Also, tourism sector accounting for 11.7% of GDP and 11% of total employment [69]. Measures against the spread of the pandemic in Bulgaria, as well as in other states, include partial or complete cessation of the above sectors, which has a negative impact on the overall economic picture.

According to the IMF, unemployment rate was estimated at 4.2% in 2019, down from 5.2% the previous year. IMF experts note that the rate being currently estimated to increase to 8% in 2020 and decrease to 4.5% in 2021 [69]. Bulgaria's real GDP growth could reach 5% next year. According to the financial group KBC's optimistic scenario, Bulgaria's economy could shrink by 4% this year, while the pessimistic scenario forecasts a 12% decline [39]. Raiffeisen Bank International's economic experts forecast a 3.9% economic downturn in Bulgaria in 2020 [33]. IMF report (April, 2020) estimates due to the outbreak of the pandemic, GDP growth is expected to fall to –4% in 2020 and pick up to 6% in 2021 [69].

Finance Minister Vladislav Goranov said a press conference was held in March 2020 that "If the period of isolation continues for three months in total, our economy will recover by the end of 2021" [70].

4.6 Romania

Romania had starts 2020 in bad economic conditions, namely, huge twin deficits, high financing needs, crippled infrastructure, a workforce crisis, and political turmoil [71]. The beginning of the pandemic in China played an important role to effect of the textile industry in Romania. Because of China was the main supplier for material. After that when Italy was affected, Romanian factories that have business relations with Italy were highly affected [35].

In early March, more than a million people lost their jobs in Romania. To this were added hundreds of thousands of Romanians who returned to Romania after losing their jobs in Italy, Spain, and the United Kingdom [31]. The Romanian economy is expected to unemployment narrow 10.1% in 2020. According to the data from IMF, growth should rebound to 3.9% in 2021 [32].

5 Overall Findings and Recommendations

The overall conclusion of this study showed that coronavirus has a negative impact on almost every sector of the economy. However, following the example of the Black Sea Region countries will be particularly affected: tourism, manufacturing, finance, retail, entertainment, leisure and the oil industry too in the case of Russia (see Fig. 2).

It should be noted that the prevalence rate and increased probability of the spread of the pandemic from the last century to the present day is confirmed by studies supported by practical examples [49]. Therefore, it is necessary to develop recommendations on the one hand, to minimize the economic damage caused by the pandemic and, on the other hand, to restore the economy.

In many developed countries, there is a strategy that describes the rules of behavior during a large-scale epidemic. (For example, Pandemic Influenza Plan developed by U.S. Department of Health and Human Service). The strategy should include:

- Developing the factors influencing the country's economic sectors;
- Establish practical methods of solving the problem based on scientific research;
- Determine real activities by the government to avoid potential threats to the crisis;
- The use of additional political and economic instruments to solve current crisis caused by pandemic.

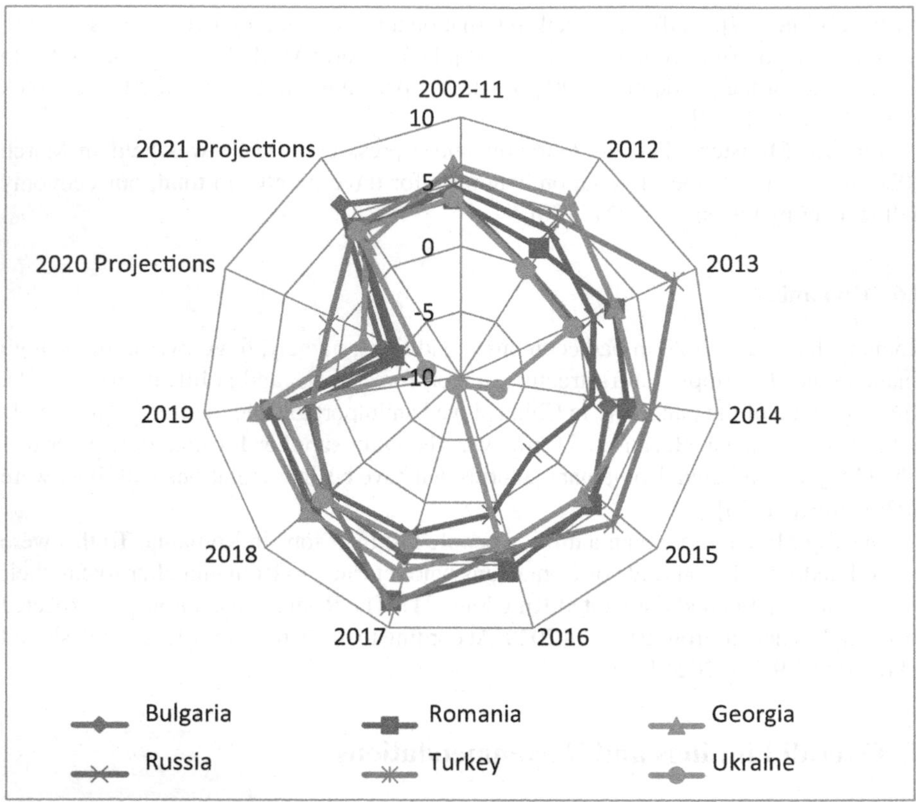

Fig. 2. Emerging market and developing economies: real GDP. Source: Created by the authors based on IMF World Economic Outlook data and papers [3, 10]

6 Conclusions

The paper discusses the changing reality caused by the global pandemic in the economic, political and social spheres. Restrictions on economic activity as a result of the coronavirus spread have posed new challenges to countries around the world, including the Black Sea Region. The aim of the research was to analyze the impact of the COVID-19 Outbreak on the Black Sea Region countries' socio-economic conditions. To better understand the situation, we discussed the pandemics that have taken place over the last hundred years and their economic effects on several states. Accordingly, the study was based on an analysis of domestic and international economic processes in each state described above.

In this research is used a model in which growth of GDP is the dependent variable. So, this study analyzed GDP changes on the example of each state in the Black Sea Region. Accordingly, the study compared data on the impact of the current pandemic on the socio-economic situation in the Black Sea Region - before and during the pandemic. Also, the leading industry in GDP by share was analyzed. Conclusions developed in this paper will also play a major role in post-pandemic and future pandemics.

The current situation can be called a Pandeconomic [10]. Because in the future, scientists will further expand the scope of recommendations to avoid and/or alleviate crises caused by global pandemics. Therefore, the results presented in the study and the recommendations developed based on it have both theoretical and practical purposes in order to alleviate the economic crises arising from the global pandemic in the future.

References

1. Jones, K.E., et al.: Global trends in emerging infectious diseases. Nature **451**(7181), 990–993 (2008). https://doi.org/10.1038/nature06536
2. Morse, S.S., et al.: Prediction and prevention of the next pandemic zoonosis. The Lancet **380**(9857), 1956–1965 (2012). https://doi.org/10.1016/s0140-6736(12)61684-5
3. Abuselidze, G., Mamaladze, L.: U.S-Turkey crisis and its impact on the economy of the black sea region. In: E3S Web of Conferences, vol. 135, p. 03077 (2019). https://doi.org/10.1051/e3sconf/201913503077
4. Arnold, P.J.: Global financial crisis: the challenge to accounting research. Account. Organ. Soc. **34**(6–7), 803–809 (2009). https://doi.org/10.1016/j.aos.2009.04.004
5. Benatar, S.R., Gill, S., Bakker, I.: Global health and the global economic crisis. Am. J. Public Health **101**(4), 646–653 (2011). https://doi.org/10.2105/AJPH.2009.188458
6. Bilorus, O.: World structural crisis and transformations of the global financial system. Econ. Ann.-XXI **07–08**(1), 4–7 (2014)
7. Ciro, T.: The Global Financial Crisis: Triggers, Responses and Aftermath, pp. 1–266. Routledge (2016)
8. Kattel, R.: Financial and economic crisis in Eastern Europe. J. Post Keynes. Econ. **33**(1), 41–60 (2010). https://doi.org/10.2753/PKE0160-3477330103
9. Kotz, D.M.: The financial and economic crisis of 2008: a systemic crisis of neoliberal capitalism. Rev. Radical Polit. Econ. **41**(3), 305–317 (2009). https://doi.org/10.1177/0486613409335093
10. Abuselidze, G., Slobodianyk, A.: Pandeconomic crisis and its impact on small open economies: a case study of COVID-19. In: Murgul, V., Pukhkal, V. (eds.) EMMFT 2019. AISC, vol. 1258, pp. 718–728. Springer, Cham (2021). https://doi.org/10.1007/978-3-030-57450-5_61
11. Baker, B.K.: The impact of the International Monetary Fund's macroeconomic policies on the AIDS pandemic. Int. J. Health Serv. **40**(2), 347–363 (2010). https://doi.org/10.2190/HS.40.2.p
12. Calomiris, C.W.: The Great Depression and other "contagious" events. In: The Oxford Handbook of Banking, 1st edn. (2012). https://doi.org/10.1093/oxfordhb/9780199640935.013.0027
13. Claessens, S., Forbes, K.: International financial contagion: an overview of the issues and the book. In: Claessens, S., Forbes, K.J. (eds.) International Financial Contagion. Springer, Boston (2001). https://doi.org/10.1007/978-1-4757-3314-3_1
14. Madhav, N., Oppenheim, B., Gallivan, M., Mulembakani, P., Rubin, E., Wolfe, N.: Pandemics: Risks, Impacts, and Mitigation. Disease Control Priorities, 3rd edn., vol. 9. Improving Health and Reducing Poverty Published (2017). https://doi.org/10.1596/978-1-4648-0527-1
15. Orlik, T., Rush, J., Cousin, M., Hong, J.: Coronavirus Could Cost the Global Economy $2.7 Trillion (2020). https://www.bloomberg.com/graphics/2020-coronavirus-pandemic-global-economic-risk/. Accessed 17 Mar 2020

16. Peckham, R.: Economies of contagion: financial crisis and pandemic. Econ. Soc. **42**(2), 226–248 (2013). https://doi.org/10.1080/03085147.2012.718626
17. Sułkowski, Ł.: Covid-19 pandemic; recession, virtual revolution leading to de-globalization? J. Intercult. Manag. **12**(1) (2020). https://doi.org/10.2478/joim-2020-0029
18. Abuselidze, G.: Modern challenges of monetary policy strategies: inflation and devaluation influence on economic development of the country. Acad. Strat. Manag. J. **18**(4), 1–10 (2019)
19. Abuselidze, G., Kizinidze, M.: Influence of central bank regulations on interbank competition in association with EU. In: E3S Web of Conferences, vol. 135, p. 04037 (2019). https://doi.org/10.1051/e3sconf/201913504037
20. Abuselidze, G., Mamuladze, L.: The peculiarities of the budgetary policy of Georgia and the directions of improvement in association with EU. In: SHS Web of Conferences, vol. 73, p. 01001 (2020). http://doi.org/10.1051/shsconf/20207301001
21. Abuselidze, G.: Optimality of tax policy on the basis of comparative analysis of income taxation. Eur. J. Sustain. Dev. **9**(1), 272–293 (2020). https://doi.org/10.14207/ejsd.2020.v9n1p272
22. Abuselidze, G., Gogitidze, I.: Tax policy for business entities under the conditions of association with the European Union: features and optimization directions. In: E3S Web of Conferences, vol. 166, p. 13013 (2020). https://doi.org/10.1051/e3sconf/202016613013
23. Favero, C.A., Giavazzi, F.: Is the international propagation of financial shocks non-linear?: evidence from the ERM. J. Int. Econ. **57**(1), 231–246 (2002). https://doi.org/10.1016/S0022-1996(01)00139-8
24. Goldin, I., Vogel, T.: Global governance and systemic risk in the 21st century: lessons from the financial crisis. Glob. Policy **1**(1), 4–15 (2010). https://doi.org/10.1111/j.1758-5899.2009.00011.x
25. Prokhorova, V., Protsenko, V., Abuselidze, G., Mushnykova, S., Us, Y.: Safety of industrial enterprises development: evaluation of innovative and investment component. Sci. Bull. Nat. Min. Univ. **5**, 155–161 (2019). https://doi.org/10.29202/nvngu/20195/24
26. Slobodianyk, A., Abuselidze, G.: Prospective of provision of dairy products for the population of Ukraine. In: E3S Web of Conferences, vol. 135, p. 01019 (2019). https://doi.org/10.1051/e3sconf/201913501019
27. Abuselidze, G., Slobodianyk, A.: Analysis and control of bankruptcy and reorganization processes: case studies using accounting data. In: E3S Web of Conferences, vol. 164, p. 09036 (2020). https://doi.org/10.1051/e3sconf/202016409036
28. Daily Sabah: Turkey's foreign sales choked by pandemic as exports drop nearly 18% in March (2020). https://www.dailysabah.com/business/economy/turkeys-foreign-sales-choked-by-pandemic-as-exports-drop-nearly-18-in-march. Accessed 15 Apr 2020
29. Dizikes, P.: The data speak: stronger pandemic response yields better economic recovery. MIT News Office (2020). http://news.mit.edu/2020/pandemic-health-response-economic-recovery-0401. Accessed 08 Apr 2020
30. Economic Policy Research Center: COVID-19: Economic Consequences of the World and for Georgia (2020). http://eprc.ge/uploads/brosh/COVID__fin-geo.pdf. Accessed 28 Apr 2020
31. Emerging Europe: Postcard from Romania: the most gentle of lockdowns, and Easter, make me anxious (2020). https://emerging-europe.com/from-the-editor/postcard-from-romania-the-most-gentle-of-lockdowns-and-easter-make-me-anxious/. Accessed 15 Apr 2020
32. Euractiv: Romania still establishing how best to lift lock-down measures (2020). https://www.euractiv.com/section/coronavirus/short_news/romania-update-covid-19/. Accessed 07 May 2020
33. Euronews: Covid-19: what are the consequences for small and medium enterprises across Europe? (2020). https://www.euronews.com/2020/04/03/covid-19-what-are-the-consequences-for-small-and-medium-enterprises-across-europe. Accessed 09 Apr 2020

34. EPC: Consequences of Coronavirus Pandemic on Turkish Economy (2020). https://epc.ae/topic/consequences-of-coronavirus-pandemic-on-turkish-economy. Accessed 16 Apr 2020
35. Fair Wear: Covid-19 impact and responses: Romania (2020). https://www.fairwear.org/covid-19-dossier/covid-19-guidance-for-production-countries/covid-19-impact-and-responses-romania/. Accessed 16 Apr 2020
36. Intelinews: Turkey's one-year foreign debt repayment obligations down 3% m/m to $175bn at end-Aug (2018). https://www.intellinews.com/turkey-s-one-year-foreign-debt-repayment-obligations-down-3-m-m-to-175bn-at-end-aug-150380/. Accessed 29 Mar 2020
37. Publika: The most famous pandemics in the last 100 years (2020). https://publika.ge/article/bolo-100-wlis-yvelaze-cnobili-pandemiebi/. Accessed 05 Apr 2020
38. Russia Briefing: The Social & Economic Impact of Covid-19 on Russia and Recovery Potential (2020). https://www.russia-briefing.com/news/social-economic-impact-covid-19-russia-recovery-potential.html/. Accessed 25 Apr 2020
39. SeeNews: Bulgaria's economy could shrink 10% in 2020 due to COVID-19 – KBC (2020). https://seenews.com/news/bulgarias-economy-could-shrink-10-in-2020-due-to-covid-19-kbc-693410. Accessed 15 Apr 2020
40. Tabula: What awaits the economy during the Coronavirus crisis and what the government plans to do (2020). http://www.tabula.ge/ge/story/166721-ra-elis-ekonomikas-koronavirusis-krizisis-pirobebshi-da-ras-gegmavs-mtavroba. Accessed 24 Mar 2020
41. The Economist: The cost of swine flu (2009). https://www.economist.com/news/2009/07/27/the-cost-of-swine-flu. Accessed 27 Mar 2020
42. The Moscow Times: Analysts Fear the Economic Impact of Russia's April Coronavirus Shutdown Will Be Catastrophic (2020). https://www.themoscowtimes.com/2020/04/02/russia-economy-coronavirus-analysts-fear-economic-impact-russias-april-coronavirus-shutdown-catastrophic-a69851. Accessed 14 Apr 2020
43. TRT World: In pictures: Turkey's booming tourism sector takes a hit from coronavirus (2020). https://www.trtworld.com/turkey/in-pictures-turkey-s-booming-tourism-sector-takes-a-hit-from-coronavirus-34845. Accessed 05 Apr 2020
44. UNCTAD: The Coronavirus Shock: A Story of Another Global Crisis Foretold and What Policymakers Should Be Doing About It (2020). https://bit.ly/2WwcW5O. Accessed 15 Apr 2020
45. Visan, G.: The Black Sea and COVID-19. Middle East Institute (2020). https://www.mei.edu/publications/black-sea-and-covid-19. Accessed 15 Apr 2020
46. VOX Ukraine: Impact of COVID-19 on Global Economy and Ukraine's Foreign Trade (2020). https://voxukraine.org/en/impact-of-covid-19-on-global-economy-and-ukraine-s-foreign-trade/. Accessed 15 Apr 2020
47. Willson Center: Projected Impact of COVID-19 on Ukraine's Economy (2020). https://www.wilsoncenter.org/blog-post/projected-impact-covid-19-ukraines-economy. Accessed 15 Apr 2020
48. World Health Organization: What is a pandemic? (2010). https://www.who.int/csr/disease/swineflu/frequently_asked_questions/pandemic/en/. Accessed 15 Mar 2020
49. World Health Organization: Ten threats to global health in 2019 (2019). https://www.who.int/news-room/feature-stories/ten-threats-to-global-health-in-2019. Accessed 15 Mar 2020
50. McKibbin, W.J., Sidorenko, A.A.: Global macroeconomic consequences of pandemic influenza. Centre for Applied Macroeconomic Analysis (CAMA), Crawford School of Public Policy, Australian, National University (2006)
51. Fan, V.Y., Jamison, D.T., Summers, L.H.: The inclusive cost of pandemic influenza risk. NBER Working Papers, National Bureau of Economic Research Recession, Cambridge (2016). https://doi.org/10.3386/w22137

52. First Channel: The new coronavirus is very different from the 1918 Spanish flu - how and why? (2020). https://1tv.ge/news/akhali-koronavirusi-dzalian-ganskhvavdeba-1918-wlis-espanuri-gripisgan-rogor-da-ratom/. Accessed 28 Mar 2020
53. BPN: The economic impact of the "Spanish flu" on the world 100 years ago - what countries should consider (2020). https://www.bpn.ge/article/67646-espanuri-gripis-ekonomikuri-epekti-100-clis-cinandel-msoplioze-ra-unda-gaitvaliscinon-kveqnebma/. Accessed 10 Apr 2020
54. Kalmikov, A.: Quarantine will kill business and the economy: is that so? The answer has been known for 100 years, since the time of the "Spanish". BBC News (2020). https://www.bbc.com/russian/features-52126987. Accessed 05 Apr 2020
55. James, S., Sargent, T.: The economic impact of an influenza pandemic. Finance Canada, Working paper 2007-04 (2006)
56. Krier, B.: Recent pandemics and historic precedents for COVID-19. Ben Franklin Technology Partners of Central & Northern Pennsylvania (2020). https://cnp.benfranklin.org/most-older-americans-might-not-realize-they-have-already-lived-through-several-pandemics/. Accessed 17 Apr 2020
57. International Labor Organization: How will COVID-19 affect the world of work? (2020). https://www.ilo.org/global/topics/coronavirus/impacts-and-responses/WCMS_739047/lang--en/index.htm. Accessed 07 May 2020
58. Bergeaud, A., Cette, G., Lecat, R.: GDP per capita in advanced countries over the 20th century. Banque de France Working Paper No. 549 (2015). https://doi.org/10.2139/ssrn.2602267
59. Boone, L.: Coronavirus: the world economy at risk. OECD Economic Outlook (2020). https://doi.org/10.1787/7969896b-en. https://www.oecd.org/economic-outlook/. Accessed 25 Apr 2020
60. Statista: Projected coronavirus (COVID-19) impact index by industry and dimension - minor (1) to severe (5) in 2020 (2020). https://www.statista.com/statistics/1106302/coronavirus-impact-index-by-industry-2020/. Accessed 25 Apr 2020
61. Abuselidze, G.: European integration of Georgia and financial-economic condition: achievements and challenges. Eur. J. Sustain. Dev. **8**(1), 53–69 (2019). https://doi.org/10.14207/ejsd.2019.v8n1p53
62. Brodzicki, T.: Resource curse and the potential impact of COVID-19: the case of Russia (2020). https://bit.ly/2Wuwk31. Accessed 06 Apr 2020
63. Bloomberg (2020). https://bloom.bg/2IZkrdv. Citied in: Economic Policy Research Center (2020). COVID-19: Economic Consequences of the World and for Georgia. http://eprc.ge/uploads/brosh/COVID__fin-geo.pdf. Accessed 28 Apr 2020
64. Foreign Policy: The Coronavirus Will Destroy Turkey's Economy (2020). https://foreignpolicy.com/2020/04/08/the-coronavirus-will-destroy-turkeys-economy/. Accessed 15 apr 2020
65. Batiashvili, Z.: Complications Caused by the Coronavirus in Turkey and Their Influence on Georgia. GFSIS (2020). https://www.gfsis.org/ge/blog/view/1065. Accessed 20 Apr 2020
66. Ahval. Unemployment in Turkey rose by almost 1 million in 2019 – TurkStat (2020). https://ahvalnews.com/turkish-unemployment/unemployment-turkey-rose-almost-1-million-2019-turkstat. Accessed 26 Mar 2020
67. Asharq Al-Awsat Newspaper: Turkey Unemployment Concerns Rise over Coronavirus (2020). https://aawsat.com/english/home/article/2228206/turkey-unemployment-concerns-rise-over-coronavirus. Accessed 15 Apr 2020
68. Anadolu Agency: World Bank: Turkish economy to grow 0.5% in 2020 (2020). https://www.aa.com.tr/en/economy/world-bank-turkish-economy-to-grow-05-in-2020/1798602. Accessed 12 Apr 2020

69. Bulgaria: Economic and Political Overview (2020). https://www.nordeatrade.com/no/explore-new-market/bulgaria/economical-context. Accessed 06 May 2020
70. BalkanInsight: Bulgaria Prepares for Worst-Case Economic Scenario (2020). https://balkaninsight.com/2020/03/31/bulgaria-prepares-for-worst-case-economic-scenario/. Accessed 09 Apr 2020
71. Business Review: Coronavirus to take high toll on Romanian economy (2020). https://business-review.eu/money/finance/br-analysis-coronavirus-to-take-high-toll-on-romanian-economy-209743. Accessed 22 Apr 2020
72. Romer, C.D.: World War I and the postwar depression: a reinterpretation based on alternative estimates of GNP. J. Monetary Econ. **22**(1), 91–115 (1988). https://doi.org/10.1016/0304-3932(88)90171-7

Integrated Data and Service Platforms for Smart Energy Networks as a Key Component for Smart Cities

Jan-Philipp Exner[1(✉)], Michelle Krämer[1], Dirk Werth[1], Andreas Eitel[2], Jochen Britz[3], and Boris Brandherm[3]

[1] August-Wilhelm-Scheer Institut für digitale Produkte und Prozesse, Saarbrücken, Germany
Jan-Philipp.Exner@aws-institut.de

[2] Fraunhofer Institute for Experimental Software Engineering IESE, Kaiserslautern, Germany
Andreas.Eitel@iese.fraunhofer.de

[3] German Research Center for Artificial Intelligence, Saarbrücken, Germany
Boris.Brandherm@dfki.de

Abstract. In the light of the German national energy system transformation, the so-called "Energiewende", the requirements for a sustainable energy supply based on renewables are very complex. To address this topic, the project Designetz develops approaches to test how decentralized renewable energy sources and the need for electrical energy can affect the respective network infrastructure levels and how an intelligent information communication technology (ICT) infrastructure can look like, to meet the demands of the energy network of the future, also in the context of smart cities. First results indicate that a transformation towards an increasingly decentralized energy supply is necessary and, particularly in view of the volatility, demands corresponding requirements of the ICT infrastructure. It will be shown how the classic producer-consumer constellation is changed and a multitude of prosumers, i.e. actors, who are both producers and consumers of electricity, arise, and how they can be integrated into the grid structure. Core functionalities will be demonstrated with an integrated data and service platform which also allows the possible integration of supplementary services. In addition, the potential interdependencies from a more decentralized energy network towards regional and urban planning patterns will be assessed.

Keywords: Renewable energies · Smart grid · Smart cities · Data and service platform

1 Introduction

The share of renewable energies in Germany was growing permanently in the last decades due to technological developments, but the national "Energiewende" (energy system transformation) [12] defined a new relevance of this topic.

O. Gervasi et al. (Eds.): ICCSA 2020, LNCS 12253, pp. 468–483, 2020.
https://doi.org/10.1007/978-3-030-58814-4_33

On June 6, 2011, the German Federal Government decided to shut down eight nuclear power plants immediately and to phase out nuclear energy gradually until 2022 due to a change in perception of Nuclear energy. In General, the political goal is to move away from nuclear energy and fossil fuels towards renewables-in the next decades.

The transformation from central to decentralized energy supply in the course of decarbonizing energy production and the phase-out of nuclear energy, imposes major challenges for the energy supply in Germany. These challenges can't only be overcome by installing hardware. According to the Federal Ministry of Economics and Energy, who started the SINTEG (National Smart Energy Showcases) projects in 2016, digitization approaches are seen as necessary development, to utilize efficiency potential and to develop a blueprint for a functioning, safe and efficient energy system of the future. One of the five SINTEG projects is Designetz. This focuses on an energy system transformation kit that contributes to the efficient system of the future with individual solutions [9]. The broad consideration of these topics also reflects the complex interactions towards other sectors such as mobility and urban planning. The greater the amount of energy fed to the grid from low-voltage levels by ordinary citizens, the more integrated concepts such as smart cities should be taken into account.

The paper is organized as follows: Sect. 2 presents the theoretical framework for a global decentralized energy system based on renewable energies. Section 3 exemplifies some of the Designetz approaches. Section 4 focusses on the interactions between the various scales of regional and urban planning and defines necessary points for further research by the integration into the real world. Finally, Sect. 5 concludes and provides some highlights.

2 Theoretical Framework

In order to achieve the primary goals of the national energy transformation, it is crucial to establish a subsidiarity of energy production and consumption, a flexible and adaptable infrastructure, as well as a secure and safe distribution. This embraces the conceptual goals of the project, the future composition of the energy network as well as the appearance of prosumers and the respective security issues. In previous decades, electrical energy in Germany was mainly generated by central power plants based on fossil fuels and has so far been primarily centralized by some large producers such as nuclear or coal-fired power plants. With the introduction of the German energy transition and the emergence of more renewable energies, electricity generation is becoming more heterogeneous, decentralized and dynamic [1,21]. Hence, the classic producer-consumer constellation changes towards a multitude of prosumers, i.e. actors who simultaneously are producers and consumers of electricity. The use of renewable energies also leads to strong weather-related fluctuations in electricity production [21]. This means that the impact on the energy network infrastructure is inevitable, and the fundamental question must be, how the networks can be kept stable in the event of dynamic feed-in. In addition to conventional energy network expansion, the focus is on IT-based management of the available flexibility in the energy system. The power feed-in of distributed renewables and the demand of electrical power increase on the distribution level confront low-voltage grids by challenges ranging from unmonitored overloads over violations of the voltage range to back-feeding of electrical energy. Additionally, the volatility of loads and renewable energies makes it difficult to predict future grid states, to plan preventive measures, and to apply them if needed. These factors have a particular impact on the energy network infrastructure and raising the question, how the networks could remain stable. In order to address these points, one can physically expand the electrical grid and storage infrastructure, the power grid or by the means of digitization, make the existing grid smarter and more efficient. This paper exemplifies how to design the ICT backbone for the German energy network in 2035 with IT-supported management of the available flexibilities in the energy system. The results were achieved in the project Designetz, which is funded by the Federal Ministry of Economics and Technology and is one of the largest German research projects on energy system transformation.

2.1 Conceptual Goal of Designetz

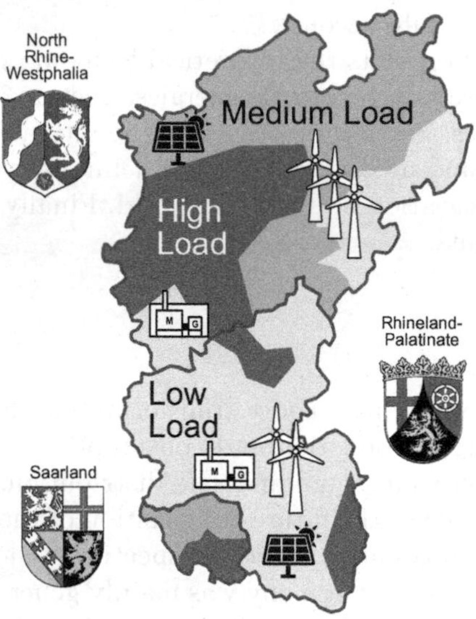

Fig. 1. Project area Designetz

The project area of Designetz embraces an exemplary mixed region with photovoltaic and wind facilities and areas, which have partly high renewable surpluses and nearby load centers (see Fig. 1). The project faces many individual solutions in twenty new demonstration projects as well as in eleven already existing projects, that are to be combined in a joint solution. Designetz develops technologies to balance the production and the usage of electricity between the regions by leveraging the flexibility of the aforementioned demonstration projects.

The project showcases the use of digital technologies to master the technical and economic challenges of the energy transition. It develops secure and efficient processes that are suitable for mass business and tests innovative technologies and market mechanisms for flexible and intelligent networks and markets. In order to successfully roll out the energy transition, there must be an interaction between the countries and technology-open standardized technological solutions in order to ensure penetration not only across Germany, but also at an international level. To develop these solutions, it makes sense to learn from pioneering regions that are already facing the challenges of integrating a high proportion of renewable energy. SINTEG promotes the learning process of complex interaction in so-called project showcases.

The goal of the SINTEG program is also to gain practical experience for the future development of the legal framework. For this purpose, the Federal Government has passed a regulation with "experiment options". The regulation gives the project showcases the opportunity to test new technologies, processes and business models without economic disadvantages, for example, the digitization and the coupling of electricity and heat. This enables innovations to get from the laboratory to the practical test and finally to the market more quickly. With SINTEG, a "real laboratory" is created for the intelligent energy supply of the future.

2.2 The Value of Flexibility in the Smart Grid

In a power grid, generation and consumption must be in balance. This also applies to a sustainable and decentralized grid and an appropriate ICT system for a sustainable grid must therefore have a local, decentralized optimization of flexibility to make this possible. The transforming energy system will lead to an increasing number of prosumers and more and more actors will show flexible generation and consumption behavior. Hence, the development of a flexibility management scheme is essential. In addition, it will be the task of network operators to assess the effects of generation and consumption behavior, to keep the network stable and, if necessary, to compensate for network bottlenecks. At the same time, market participants such as aggregators and traders must also be considered. An ICT system for energy flexibility management must therefore enable existing and potentially new stakeholders to be dynamically linked [7]. Flexibility in the energy market is defined as follows: It is the change of feed or withdrawal in response to an external signal (price signal or activation) with the aim of providing a service in the energy system [6].

As the share of renewable energies in electricity generation increases, the residual load approaches zero on many days, in many hours and then increases significantly within a short period of time. It is therefore necessary to make the participants in the system more flexible in order to be able to efficiently guarantee a reliable power supply. This is especially important in terms of the growing number of prosumers. A prosumer [10] can simultaneously draw electricity and, for example, also produce it via the solar system on the roof and feed it into the grid. Hence, the energy system transformation overcomes the old separation into producer and consumer of electricity or heat. They can increasingly help to keep the entire electricity system stable and thus contribute to a reliable power supply. This can also be lucrative for every participant, if utilities offer electricity prices that reflect the changed electricity supply.

3 Implementation in the Context of Designetz

Flexibility describes the relative potential that the consumption behavior of installation dynamics generates according to the requirements of the network or the market. Due to the dynamic development of the energy sector and the increasing influence of digitization, the effects on business models and the new players in this area are becoming visible. The requirements for corresponding ICT infrastructure are examined in the officially financed SINTEG project named Designetz and are used as a blueprint for Germany's energy network in 2035. In this project the IT system plays a central role in the realization of the backbone of a future energy system. Hence, this one must be flexible, adaptable and expandable, and be able to integrate previously unknown actors and services to be able to do that. One of the key elements in this way is the development of an integrated data and service platform.

3.1 Integrated Data and Service Platform

In Designetz, the requirements for the ICT infrastructure are realized in an exemplary manner. Several data nodes (servers) will be connected to each other from local to regional to supra-regional level in terms of communication technology, taking the necessary decentralization of the solution into account. On each of these data nodes, a data and service platform is implemented as a service-oriented architecture. The advantage of this architecture lies in the combination of its modularity in order to offer the possibility of a needs-based design, combined with services for the basic functions such as data management and simple additional options for the current and future added value of services and functions. In addition, dedicated security frameworks are used to monitor and control communication between data nodes and between individual services, thus ensuring secure data exchange at all levels.

We have data *about* the power grid (so-called master data, like network topology and electricity equipment) and *from* the power grid (measurement data with different granularity and coverage). Both master data and measurement data are processed, aggregated, stored in and, as necessary, distributed to other databases. Furthermore, processes were also digitized (e.g., for booking and requesting flexibility options). Based on these data and processes, different services were developed: (i) "models" and "simulations" as a service, (ii) AI-based prediction methods for generation from photovoltaics and wind, peak-maintaining load curve forecasts for private households and at the local network transformer level, (iii) analysis methods such as for anomaly detection or network analysis, (iv) a power system simulation service with which, among other things, the current network status or resource loads (as a virtual sensor for non-existent sensors) can be calculated, (v) the Flex-Management System for evaluation, reservation, retrieval and visualization of flexibility options.

For these services to work, a data and service platform is required that enables services to access data, to communicate with each other and for the transparent integration of new data sources.

To meet these requirements, an integrated data and service platform has been developed that follows Industrie 4.0 guidelines [15]. In other words, the data and service platform is divided into two platforms: the software-defined platform, through which data sources such as sensors, actuators and existing data nodes can be integrated, and the service-oriented platform based on this,

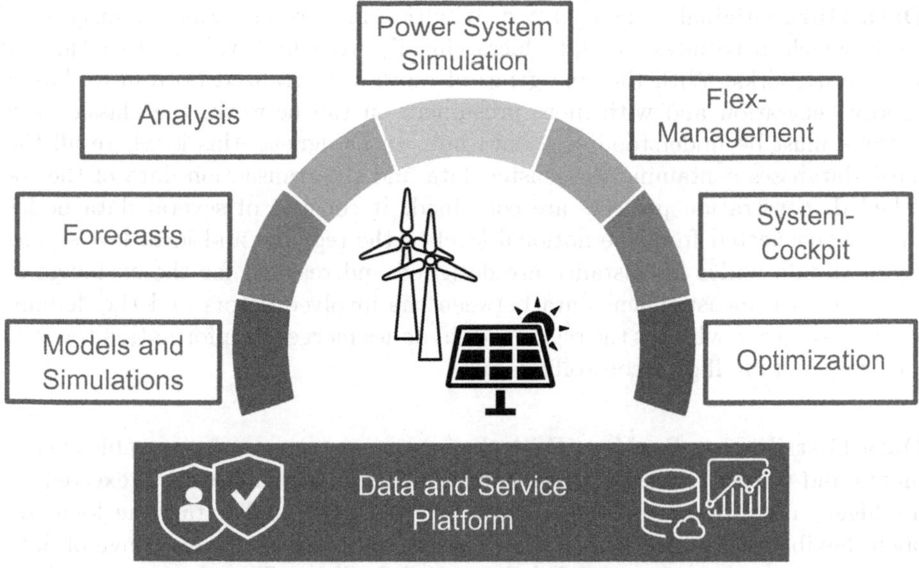

Fig. 2. Concept of the integrated data and service platform in the project

which provides the basis for the services mentioned before. Services must only be developed against this service-oriented platform (Fig. 2).

The service-oriented platform allows the flexible combination of services (service mashup) and thus an adaptation to different application scenarios in energy supply. This kind of data and service platform could also be a potential component of an urban platform for smart cities in the future. In addition to the privacy/data protection aspect, the possibilities of pseudonymization, anonymization and aggregation of data were investigated. The data and service platform transparently provides a security architecture and corresponding security mechanisms not only for itself but also for the data and services.

3.2 Data Infrastructure

The decentralized energy system of the future based on renewable energies and the increased use of flexibility leads to specific requirements. The involvement of numerous stakeholders with different interests and functions in such a system requires the definition of standardized processes and data formats. They will be based on clear and structured rules, which include specifications, how flexibility is offered, visualized and can be traded, i.e. in the context of the consideration, regarding for instance reservation or cancellation processes of flexibility products. These functions must be supported by an IT system that is scalable and implemented with uniform data technology.

Data Hub. Originally, the energy distribution in Germany was organized centrally which distributes the data hierarchically from high voltage to local low voltage networks. With the emergence of more decentralized bottom-up based energy generation and with more prosumers on the network, the classic data cascade must be understood as a data hub. In Designetz, this is where all the basic databases containing the master data and the transaction data of the so-called demonstration projects are combined. It consists of several data nodes that are connected from the national level to the regional and local levels. The regional data nodes for instance are designed and realized for the exchange of flexibility and measurement data between the involved actors and the demonstration projects, whereas the regional data nodes merge the information towards a central and intelligent controlling unit.

Data Distribution Service. With the increasing amount of renewable energy plants and to ensure the best use of flexibility, greater emphasis is exerted on intelligent networking and the exchange of energy-related data. The focus on open, flexible and secure IT infrastructure facilitates the easy exchange of data and the integration of new stakeholders and facilities. Therefore, the working group for Designetz implemented a uniform, open and secure integrated data and service platform. The platform fulfils the following three objectives: (1) an efficient, regulatory compliant data management, and (2) the cascading data hubs for flexibility options, network and meter data (the monitoring of the flexibility options is implemented prototypically within the framework of the Flex-Monitoring) and finally (3) a holistic security and data protection concept.

3.3 Services

In the following we want to present in more detail the services for monitoring and management of flexibility and various AI-based forecast services.

Monitoring and Management of Flexibilities. In Designetz, the demonstration projects are connected to the data nodes via appropriate interfaces. Relevant flexibility data can be exchanged using a uniform data model and structured processes that meet the requirements of all stakeholders. The necessary flexibility when expanding the data model can be ensured via document-oriented database structures. A central service in the Designetz-ICT system is a flexibility management component. This component coordinates the standard processes in the background, from the offer to the reservation to the call for flexibility. At the same time, the demonstration projects can use a monitoring function that provides a permanent overview of their own status as well as the overall system view and the retrieval of the processes involved. The flexibility management component also offers aggregation functions that support the creation of portfolios with various demonstration projects and enable their use as flexibility products in a future flexibility market. Initially, no such market is implemented in Designetz, but a network-related call for flexibility is realized through higher-level software.

Besides the passive monitoring, management of flexibilities offers further features. For instance, through an optimized combination of external procurement, generation, storage and consumption, it will be possible to generate business models for actors offering these necessary flexibilities as well as managers in terms of the net stability. By shifting loads or selling decentralized electricity flexibility, companies can react to the opportunities that arise on various energy markets. This means that operators trade their flexibility in line with the price signals on the energy trading markets.

Forecast. Various AI-based forecasting algorithms are available to predict the electrical behavior (power supply or consumption) of photovoltaic systems, and private households. 1) *Photovoltaic production*: Several methods for the prediction of the power output of photovoltaic systems are applied and combined in a meta-model for both day-ahead and intraday forecasts (see Fig. 3). A data set that consists of meteorological data (e.g., global radiation, temperature and humidity) and the measured power output of the photovoltaic systems over some years is used to create the models. The approaches considered include artificial neural networks, random forest, and case-based reasoning. 2) *Individual fine-grained load profiles of private households*: a peak-conserving forecast algorithm is available that tries to maintain peaks in order to achieve a forecast of a meaningful load profile. The forecast algorithm was initially developed and used in the project "Peer Energy Cloud" [7] for individual fine-grained load profiles of private households and was gradually improved in subsequent projects; it is resource-efficient in terms of data and computing requirements and thus suitable for embedded systems.

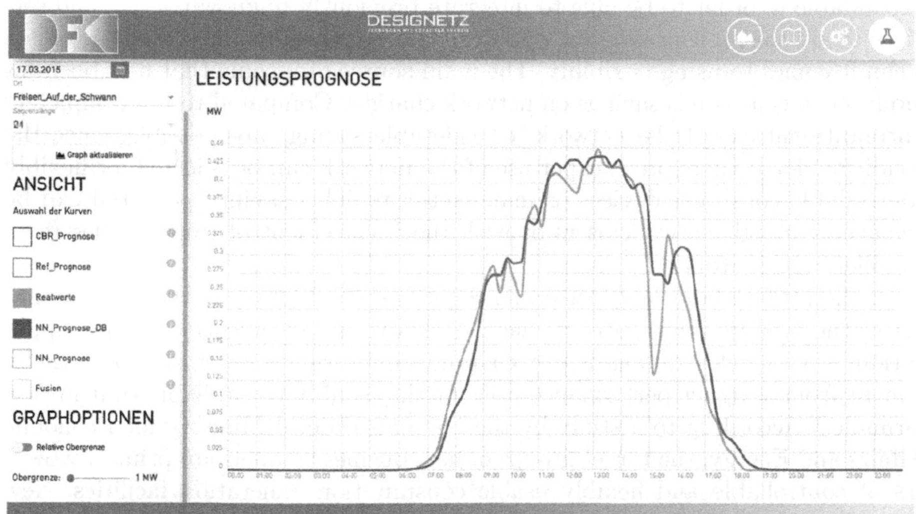

Fig. 3. Example of a forecast (in green) for the power generation of a photovoltaic system (day-ahead) and its subsequently measured values (in blue). On the left side of the dashboard other forecasts such as Case-based Reasoning and their combinations can be selected. (Color figure online)

3.4 Security and Privacy

The data and service platform itself was developed in a structured way according to Common Criteria (CC) – Evaluation Assurance Level (EAL) 4, taking into account BSI (German Federal Office for Information Security) conformity (security-by-design, privacy-by-design, resilience-by-design) [8]. The data and service platform is developed on the same evaluation assurance level as the smart meter in Germany. However, the smart meter is a monolithic system in contrast to the modular approach of the data and service platform. In addition to the privacy/data protection aspect, partners from Saarland University and CISPA (Helmholtz Center for Information Security) investigated the possibilities of pseudonymization, anonymization and aggregation of data. The data and service platform transparently implements a security architecture and corresponding security mechanisms not only for itself but also for the data and services. This includes, among other things, an innovative role and rights management as well as a comprehensive data usage control solution from Fraunhofer IESE for the (also downstream) usage control of data and services [14]. Due to the gateway character of the security components developed by the DFKI, a service no longer needs to implement corresponding security mechanisms itself.

3.5 Potential New Business Models

Due to the dynamic development of the energy sector and the increasing influence of digitization, there is already enormous growth in new players and business models. An IT system that plays a central role in realizing the backbone of a future energy system must therefore be able to be flexible, adaptable and expandable in order to be able to integrate previously unknown actors and services to do this. There are new opportunities for providers and end customers when it comes to using flexibility. The main source of income that new business models can generate is savings on network charges. Compared to the completely unconditional use of the network, considerable savings are possible, since the conditional and therefore cheaper use of the network can be selected for flexibly controllable consumer devices or manufacturers. This savings potential can be achieved through network users or with the involvement of third parties (e.g., supplier, aggregator).

If the ratio of labor and performance price shifts in favor of the performance price, there is another source of income. Above all, electricity-intensive applications such as electric heating or charging infrastructures for electric vehicles benefit from a higher performance price or the flexibly controllable shift in performance. According to a study by the German Federal Ministry for Economic Affairs and Energy, the target groups of new business models are primarily owners of controllable and flexibly usable consumption/generation facilities. New opportunities thus arise especially for, among other things, household customers who have controllable consumption, generation and/or storage facilities as prosumers, but also for mobility providers who can adapt the control of the unloading and loading of vehicles [21]. Smart meters are used to ensure the transparency of energy consumption and the timely monitoring of the utilization of the power grids [1]. This new field also gives rise to further new business models.

The companies provide CC certified services for the operation of smart meter gateways and not only in their entirety, but also some as "software as a service" or as a pure IT infrastructure. This range of offers enables the measuring point operators to buy the required services on the market. Overall, it can be said that lively competition and a wide range of services have arisen around the Smart Meter Gateway Administration. This enables flexible tariffs and complex delivery products (e.g., tenant electricity) as well as value-added services in the field of sub-metering (heat cost allocators, sensors, actuators). There are already a few offers for end consumers that combine a time-variable electricity tariff with the provision of an intelligent measuring system [11]. Cellular energy systems, so called Microgrids, are also seen as a promising future solution. Microgrids use all generation, consumption and flexibility capacities and only draw energy from the higher-level network at certain points [12]. Potential further thoughts are indicating connected marketplaces as well as different possibilities to monetize data from the service platforms. These aspects are especially important in the understanding of urban platforms also as service platforms. Shipworth for instance points out the potential peer-to-peer trading in accordance with blockchain and its disruptive nature [25]. In bringing these platforms and services together, the relevance of such connected urban platforms will grow significantly.

4 Further Implications on Energy Distribution and for Urban Planning

The upcoming section reflects the mentioned aspects in the light of regional and urban planning. With the use of a modular and integrated data and service platform, further development towards a more decentralized and bottom-up based energy network which offers the ability to attach services will be supported. The existing top-down oriented system will begin to disappear and the new situation will have flow-on effects to the way we plan our cites. In this way, the necessary interdisciplinary understanding of the issues will be more crucial in the future, especially at the local level, where district and housing energy grids are an essential part of every smart city concept.

4.1 Requirements for Creating a Smart, Effective and Resilient Grid

The previously mentioned aspects indicated that the classical distinction between producer and consumer will disappear and, in this way, every prosumer must be understood as an active part of the network. Whereas data and service platforms theoretically enable every household to act like a "little" powerplant within the network on a much smaller scale. The consequence is, that the complexity regarding the design of smart grids will also grow. Hence, in the light of the given requirements, there are some major challenges for realizing a smart energy grid for Germany in the future. First of all is the physical hardware site. Investments in the net infrastructure will be inevitable, because large, central fossil fuel power stations will be replaced increasingly with decentralized and unpredictable/volatile/uncertain/unreliable production. This raises questions regarding conventional storage capabilities as well as power-to-x approaches and innovative solutions (e.g., swarm batteries).

The second challenge concerns the distribution networks and their control infrastructure which will also face a serious transformation in terms of the need for digitization. The design of the infrastructure needs to fulfill reasonable control and adaptation functionalities and resist fluctuations at all levels as a resilient backbone on every level.

The last transformative challenge will be based on the fact that a digitized and decentralized electricity network with lots of prosumers will lead to the foundation of respective platforms and marketplaces [7]. The need to handle and manage flexibilities will be indispensable for the electricity grid to remain as stable and efficient as possible. The more effectively this smart optimization of the network works, the more cost savings regarding conventional structures can be achieved [2,13]. While the intelligence within the networks is at present not on the same quality level at all levels (for instance currently mainly on level of transmission grids and on the house level), this must be improved also for local grids.

In addition, ongoing trends such as the convergence with e-mobility will have an effect. The concept of smart cities for instance [4,19,22,24] differs by definition, but always, the convergence of all relevant urban sectors and the interdependencies to the power grid are crucial. Further, the market penetration of the transport sector with electric vehicles' both in individual, freight transport as well as public transport, requires a respective charging infrastructure that will affect the local grids. Besides the necessary investments in the local electricity distribution network, the traffic sector itself is very important. With a growing number of e-vehicles as part of the mobility system, their batteries could play their role as part of a decentralized storage unit for electricity in general and locally produced electricity based on renewable energies, especially for the charging supply network. In this light, the importance of flexibility, which allow dynamic pricing, is growing as well as their role as a crucial part of the energy network [23]. Though, the effects are not limited only on the individual transport, but also local public transport and the interdependencies between long-distance and freight transport will have to be taken into consideration. In addition, totally new approaches like mobile charging stations [26] could set the guidelines for highly complex requirements for urban infrastructure, in terms of modularity, granularity and flexibility. General questions will arise, such as the existing gas station network's suitability for large scale electric charging. The position of the charging stations and the associated parking facilities will also play a significant role in shaping the future street scene. In order to find suitable locations for local mobility points for car sharing, this is of great importance. More than that, the whole process of charging has to be scrutinized. In addition, further questions will emerge such as re-use of old petrol stations or the different space requirements for charging queues for traditional and e-vehicles. The batteries in e-vehicles could be used as decentralized storage, especially for locally generated electricity from renewables and thus play an important role in the charging grid on a local level in urban districts. The development of areas and districts requires a new, innovative, flexible and digitized energy supply, that can be implemented by integrating renewables, storage options and e-mobility equipment.

This raises the issue on how these approaches could be integrated organizationally. In the light of the development of integrated smart city solutions, cities face the challenge of the provision of urban data by city administrations and other members by respective portals (e.g., open data portals) [17]. For urban services and data, the question therefore arises how they can be efficiently provided, managed and controlled. This topic raised significant awareness in the last decade [16] focusing predominantly on aspects such as public services, governance [20] but not specifically in the light of energy purposes. In this way, these urban dashboards could evolve in the future from a passive component for just monitoring the urban environment towards an active component by integrating the functionalities of a data and service platform.

4.2 Influences on Various Regional and Urban Planning

Considered from a regional and urban planning perspective, the effects will also be significant. The relevant planning procedures were considered in the following section. One basic aspect is the uneven geographical distribution of areas which will produce renewable energies and those which will merely consume it. In Germany, the BauGB (Federal Building Code) sets the formal guidelines for type, degree of building, land use, and it further defines strategic goals for regional and urban planners. In this way, BauGB §1 paragraph 5 states, that urban planning should "contribute to ensuring a decent environment, [...] promote climate protection and adaptation, especially in urban development" [5]. Besides the standards from a formal point of view, the planning solutions comply with the requirements for the integration into the urban environment, especially in the light of design aesthetics.

In fact, the increased use of renewable energies will thus cause a demand for energy transport lines. If energy will be transported from regions with greater production capacity (e.g., offshore wind farms) towards regions with a locally high demand (e.g., industrial areas), the respective hard infrastructure must be installed. For instance, as shown by scientific debate wind energy has a tremendous potential – especially offshore farms [27] – for a fast and cost-efficient nationwide development of the electricity grid. Hence, the great wind potential is primarily found in mountainous and coastal areas, wind turbines are most profitable in these regions while being the most sparsely populated areas in Germany. Therefore, not only must the general question of the legitimacy of the construction be answered, but also the transport structures for energy have to be built. High voltage lines that have not yet been realized are still required, especially from industrialized north, such as Schleswig-Holstein, to the urban sprawl of consumers in the south, for example Bavaria or Baden-Württemberg. The formal obligations for the respective approval procedures and strategic development plans are inevitable and they will be a guideline for further plans on lower planning scales. The political debate in Germany showed [18] that determining the route for the new power lines in a consensus-oriented democratic system could be difficult. From a regional planning perspective, the focus on the provision of services is of public interest. However, this could include investments in the entire power grid, such as conventional grid extensions and the strategic planning of power plants. The resulting requirements will subsequently have an impact on the planning objects at local levels, e.g., traces or transformer substations, either for new locations or for retrofitting of existing ones.

Relevant aspects in this perspective are for instance the potential location finding process, the formal approval of combined heat and power plants and district-based energy storage on a more local level. This is particularly important since the focus on district-based considerations increases in many cities. This also includes the energy perspective, even towards concepts such as self-sufficiency. Other aspects must also be considered at the local level, which is mainly linked to the respective urban planning procedures and the building permit procedures at the district and housing levels. These are requirements for urban land use planning that will procure the installation of multimodal system stabilizers in urban areas, such as power-to-x systems for public utilities. This is of high relevance because the avoidance of emissions is now seen as an essential part of urban planning. In addition, the respective security issues and constraints, like the location in a district perspective for numerous power-to-x facilities or the effects of power chargers on local grid levels are still open questions. The effects in the local scale in terms of the building perspective will also be fundamental. In this perspective, the understanding of a smart city begins with the advent of smart and connected homes. Crucial parts in this perspective are the integration of battery storages in buildings or the respective voltage lines to charge e-mobility cars to fit the demands of in-house charging for e-vehicles [13]. Hence, a data and service platform based on flexibility as a key element for smart city or also smart home solutions. These should bring more adaptability for their users, and consequently, this does not only mean comfort in controlling the house but also to be an active part of the power grid network as a prosumer. This potential could be monetarized by emerging business models, focused also on prosumers.

5 Conclusion

The vision for a smart and secure energy grid of the future in Germany is decentralized, digitalized and decarbonized. In order to address these fields, the underlying architecture has to be adaptable, flexible and should use concepts such as data and services platforms as central components. Only with this focus, the digital net expansion will realize its potential. This is especially important in the light of the bigger share of renewable energies, because they will be unstable and the only way to handle this complexity comes along with the use of flexibilities, which need an almost totally digitized power grid network.

The vision in the project Designetz, which will achieve all of its results by 2021, is to take a look at the year 2035. It clarifies that, in addition to the pure IT-side and infrastructure consideration of requirements, that the business conditions will change for future networks. In the context of digitization, digitalization and digital transformation, this also means that the development of new business models based on new market mechanisms will emerge. The increasing number of actors and transactions, the resilience and high safety requirements for critical infrastructures, decentralized energy and IT infrastructures, as well as decentralized organization structures, such as contract processing, drastically increases the complexity of the energy network of the future. In the course of these complex requirements, blockchain-based solutions can also be a promising alternative through the use of smart contracts, especially in respective integration approaches in the urban platform.

In general, however, it should be noted that the network of the future needs to be as flexible as possible and must have a modular structure. The respective needs – considered in the light of an increasing share of renewable energies, will tend to increase in their complexity. There will always be a correlation between energy production and energy use, the more supply on local levels, the more complex the networks will be. The more tools such as data and service platforms will come to every household, the more it will be used and the more important it will be that these trends and developments has to be considered from planners from the energy side, as well as from urban planners or even architects. Consequently, new emerging trends, such as e-vehicles or new consumer-based business models in smart homes with smart meters will have to be part of every consideration and defining the necessity for integrated development concepts. Therefore, regional and urban planners must include energy issues in their decision making, and integrated master plans will contain energy plans as obvious as traffic plans on every scale. Especially the interaction with smart and electric mobility and their requirements [3]. In terms of a modular data and services platform, a first approach is exemplified in the context of Designetz and on the basis of the preliminary results, the authors of this study are confident they'll achieve a coherent concept for the blueprint of the energy network looking ahead to the year 2035.

Acknowledgement. This work was supported by the SINTEG-project Designetz funded by the German Federal Ministry of Economic Affairs and Energy (BMWi) under the grants 03SIN235, 03SIN231 and 03SIN222. The authors would like to kindly thank the project partners in Designetz, namely Hager Electro GmbH & Co KG, htw saar, innogy SE, IS Predict, Westnetz, and Saarland University for their valuable contributions.

References

1. Azad, S., et al.: Smart meter as a cornerstone for grid integration of renewable energies. In: 9th Solar & Storage Integration Workshop. Energynautics GmbH (2019)
2. Azad, S., et al.: Grid serving deployment of smart meter data in the context of distribution grid automation. In: 2019 IEEE PES Innovative Smart Grid Technologies Europe, pp. 1–6. IEEE (2019)
3. Azad, S., et al.: Increasing grid visibility on the basis of smart meters as a building block for grid integration of electromobility. In: 3rd E-Mobility Integration Symposium. Energynautics (2019)
4. Batty, M., et al.: Smart cities of the future. Eur. Phys. J. Spec. Top. **214**(1), 481–518 (2012). https://doi.org/10.1140/epjst/e2012-01703-3
5. Beck-Texte im dtv (ed.): Bundesbaugesetz: BauGB, 50 edn. Deutscher Taschenbuch Verlag, München (2018)
6. BNetzA: Flexibility in the electricity system. Bundesnetzagentur (2017)
7. Brandherm, B., Baus, J., Frey, J.: Peer Energy Cloud - Civil Marketplace for Trading Renewable Energies. In: Proceedings of the 2012 Eighth International Conference on Intelligent Environments (IE 2012). IEEE Computer Society (2012)
8. Britz, J., Alexandersson, J., Stephan, W.: UCH goes EAL4—the foundation of an eco system for ambient assisted living: ISO/IEC 15408 common criteria based implementation of the ISO/IEC 24752 universal control hub middleware. In: Wichert, R., Klausing, H. (eds.) Ambient Assisted Living. ATSC, pp. 83–96. Springer, Cham (2016). https://doi.org/10.1007/978-3-319-26345-8_8
9. Bundesministerium für Wirtschaft und Energie (BMWi): Förderprogramm SINTEG: "Schaufenster intelligente Energie - Digitale Agenda für die Energiewende". https://www.bmwi.de/Redaktion/DE/Artikel/Energie/sinteg.html
10. Bundesministerium für Wirtschaft und Energie (BMWi): Newsletter Energiewende - Was ist ein "Prosumer"?. https://www.bmwi-energiewende.de/EWD/Redaktion/Newsletter/2016/06/Meldung/direkt-erklaert.html
11. Bundesministerium für Wirtschaft und Energie (BMWi): Baustein für die Energiewende: 7 Eckpunkte für das "Verordnungspaket Intelligente Netze" (2014)
12. Bundesministerium für Wirtschaft und Energie (BMWi): Smart energy made in Germany. Federal Economics Ministry (2014)
13. Exner, J.P., Derouet, M., Linn, C., Werth, D.: Requirements for reliable and flexible smart grids as energy networks in smart cities. In: REAL CORP 2019 Proceedings, vol. 4, pp. 589–596. Karlsruhe (2019)
14. Feth, D., Jung, C.: 10 Jahre Forschung zu Datennutzungskontrolle am Fraunhofer IESE. Fraunhofer IESE (2019). https://blog.iese.fraunhofer.de/10-jahre-datennutzungskontrolle-am-fraunhofer-iese/
15. Kagermann, H., Riemensperger, F., Hoke, D., Schuh, G., Scheer, A.W.: Smart Service Welt: Recommendations for the Strategic Initiative Web-Based Services for Businesses. Acatech (2015)
16. Kitchin, R., Lauriault, T.P., McArdle, G.: Knowing and governing cities through urban indicators, city benchmarking and real-time dashboards. Reg. Stud. Reg. Sci. **2**(1), 6–28 (2015)
17. Kloeckl, K.: LIVE Singapore! Die Stadt als digitaler öffentlicher Raum. In: Die Stadt entschlüsseln: Wie Echtzeitdaten den Urbanismus verändern, pp. 86–100. Birkhäuser Verlag GmbH (2013)

18. Krack, J., Köppl, S., Samweber, F.: Die Akzeptanz des Netzausbaus in Deutschland. Energiewirtschaftliche Tagesfragen **1/2**, 101–107 (2017)
19. von Lojewski, H., Muniziger, T.: Smart cities und das Leitbild der europäischen Stadt. Städtetag aktuell, pp. 10–11 (2013)
20. Mannaro, K., Baralla, G., Garau, C.: A goal-oriented framework for analyzing and modeling city dashboards in smart cities. In: Bisello, A., Vettorato, D., Laconte, P., Costa, S. (eds.) SSPCR 2017. GET, pp. 179–195. Springer, Cham (2018). https://doi.org/10.1007/978-3-319-75774-2_13
21. Mika, B., Goudz, A.: Digitalisierung der Energiewende – Energiewende 2.0. Blockchain-Technologie in der Energiewirtschaft: Blockchain als Treiber der Energiewende, pp. 25–36. Springer, Heidelberg (2020). https://doi.org/10.1007/978-3-662-60568-4_4
22. Murgante, B., Borruso, G.: Smart city or smurfs city. In: Murgante, B., et al. (eds.) ICCSA 2014. LNCS, vol. 8580, pp. 738–749. Springer, Cham (2014). https://doi.org/10.1007/978-3-319-09129-7_53
23. Mwasilu, F., Justo, J.J., Kim, E.K., Do, T.D., Jung, J.W.: Electric vehicles and smart grid interaction: a review on vehicle to grid and renewable energy sources integration. Renew. Sustain. Energy Rev. **34**, 501–516 (2014)
24. Schweitzer, E., Schulze, R., Tünnemann, M.: Smart City Charta - Digitale Transformation in Kommunen nachhaltig gestalten. Bundesinstitut für Bau-, Stadt- und Raumforschung im Bundesamt für Bauwesen und Raumordnung, Bonn (2017)
25. Shipworth, D., Burger, C., Weinmann, J., Sioshansi, F.: Peer-to-peer trading and blockchains: enabling regional energy markets and platforms for energy transactions. In: Consumer, Prosumer, Prosumager, pp. 27–52. Elsevier (2019)
26. Volkswagen AG: Flexible Quick Charging Station (2020). https://www.volkswagenag.com/en/brands-and-models/group-components/flexible-charging-station.html
27. Weigt, H.: Germany's wind energy: the potential for fossil capacity replacement and cost saving. Appl. Energy **86**(10), 1857–1863 (2009)

Short Papers

Numerical Analysis of Single Jet Impinging a Flat and Non-flat Plate

Flávia V. Barbosa[1(✉)], Senhorinha F. C. F. Teixeira[2], and José C. F. Teixeira[1]

[1] MEtRICs I&D Centre, School of Engineering, University of Minho, Guimarães, Portugal
flaviab@dem.uminho.pt

[2] ALGORITMI I&D Centre, School of Engineering, University of Minho, Guimarães, Portugal

Abstract. The complexity of the flow field and heat transfer in jet impingement has led to several studies in order to increase the processes and products performance. Jet impingement is widely implemented, since it ensures high average heat transfer coefficients and the uniformity of the temperature over the target surface. However, the flow generated depends on several parameters related to the jet flow, such as jet velocity and temperature, and the target plate geometry. Complex impinging surfaces are identified in the majority of the applications, such as reflow soldering and cooling of turbines or solar systems. To increase the process efficiency, it is important to fully understand the interactions between the jet and the target surface. Considering the interest of this field, the present study is conducted to investigate the influence of the target surface on heat transfer in a single jet impingement process. To minimize the number of experiments, decreasing time and costs, the implementation of numerical tools is fundamental. In that sense, the impingement of the hot air jet over a flat and non-flat plate was predicted numerically using the ANSYS FLUENT software. The velocity and temperature profile were analyzed and the Nusselt number were compared for both cases. The results show the complexity of the flow generated in the vicinity of the step and the changes of the jet flow structure when it impinges a complex surface.

Keywords: Jet impingement · Heat transfer · Non-flat surface

1 Introduction

Jet impingement, a widely used technique in cooling and heating applications, is a complex heat transfer process that ensures high heat transfer rates over the target surface. However, one of the biggest issues of this forced convection process is the difficulty to obtain uniform temperatures over the impinging surface. If the complexity of the surface is increased, more hot/cold spots can appear, leading to product defects. In order to understand the influence of the target plate geometry on heat transfer performance, several studies have been conducted. Spring et al. [1] concluded that the use of large ribs mainly influence the interaction with crossflow to generate locally higher surface crossflow velocities and turbulence in the wake regions between ribs. In terms of ribs shape, Annerfeldt et al. [2] mentioned that triangle-shaped, wing-shaped, cylindrical and rectangular elements enhance the Nusselt number by a factor from 1 to 1.3 for cooling

O. Gervasi et al. (Eds.): ICCSA 2020, LNCS 12253, pp. 487–495, 2020.
https://doi.org/10.1007/978-3-030-58814-4_34

application. Brakmann et al. [3] analyzed the influence of micro cube shaped pins on the target surface and they found that pins increase the target area by 150% comparatively to a flat plate, resulting in an increase of the convective heat transfer between 135% and 142%. In terms of flow field, they observed that when the airflow passes through a pin, it will be separated inducing a vortex on the downstream side of the pin. This leads to a decrease of the heat transfer and to an increase of the pressure loss in this zone. Furthermore, Ligrani et al. [4] studied the influence of small-scale cylinders in the target plate, observing that the increase of the height of small cylinders leads to an increase of the local mixing, vorticity, turbulent thermal transport and thermal resistance, generating a substantial thermal insulation barrier. Buzzard et al. [5] proved that the average Nusselt number is increased by rectangular roughness of small height, since the increase of the height leads to an increase of the local vorticity and larger mixing. In addition, for laminar flows, plates with small roughness alone present higher Nusselt numbers than plates with a combination of small and large roughness. However, the reverse situation is observed when the flow is turbulent. According to Ren et al. [6], this is due to two reasons: first, in turbulent flows, the combination of large and small pins increases the mixing of the flow, increasing the convective heat transfer at the surface; second, in laminar flows, the extra material provided by large rectangles generates an insulating effect.

The numerical modelling of jet impingement has been implemented in several industrial sectors in order to minimize the number of experiments that force to stop entire production lines and involves huge costs and time waste. Several works have been conducted to select the numerical model which predicts with higher accuracy the jet impingement process. Hofman et al. [7] analyzed 13 turbulence models to determine which one predicts better the jet impingement process and they concluded that nearly all the models predict well the wall jet heat transfer, however almost all of them fail in predicting the local heat transfer near the stagnation region. The SST k-ω model with activated transitional flow option seems to be the model that presents the better predictions. Ortega-Casanova & Granados-Ortiz [8] also agreed that SST k-ω is more accurate in single jet impingement modelling, since it predicts the secondary maximum Nusselt number with accuracy. Ozmen & Ipek [9] demonstrated that Realizable k-ω turbulence model is capable to predict the flow and heat transfer characteristics with success in moderate values of nozzle-to-plate distances. Penumadu & Rao [10] revealed that the heat transfer characteristics are better predicted by SST k-ω model essentially due to its ability to accurately handle regions with high pressure gradients. According to these authors, the SST k-ω model was revealed both as accurate and computing time saving in engineering applications. These advantages make this model a good choice for the numerical modelling of jet impingement process.

In order to understand the influence of the target plate geometry on heat transfer performance, a numerical analysis using the Computational Fluid Dynamics software ANSYS FLUENT was performed. This study analyzes two different surfaces, a flat plate and a plate with a step using the SST k-ω turbulence model. Through these numerical simulations, velocity and temperature profiles over the surface are analyzed. The increased complexity of the flow profile due to the step surface is presented, showing the necessity to explore in detail the flow dynamics in the vicinity of non-flat surfaces. Through the numerical model presented in this work, optimization of the target surface and jet variables can be conducted in future works, in order to enhance the heat transfer over the impinging plate.

The numerical analysis of the jet flow structure, velocity and temperature is relevant for industrial applications that involve complex surfaces, providing a solution to minimize trial and error techniques still widely used in the industrial sector. Through the numerical model, the detailed study of the jet impingement process can be conducted prior manufacturing, and process optimization can be implemented in order to reduce nonuniform heat transfer over the target plate.

2 Numerical Modelling

2.1 Numerical Domain and Boundary Conditions

The computational domain, presented in Fig. 1, consists of a single jet impinging a flat and non-flat surface. The air flows through a circular nozzle, following a uniform velocity distribution, whose value depends on the Reynolds number required in the study, and at a constant temperature of about 120°C. Since the Mach number is below 0.3, the air jet flow is considered incompressible. After the impingement, the air flow escapes through the side walls. Considering this geometry and the flow parameters, the Reynolds number obtained in this study case is approximately 2,000. According to [11], this flow lies in the transition region. No-slip condition was implemented at both nozzle plate and target plate. A constant temperature of 25°C was specified to the target surface and insulated wall was defined at the nozzle plate. Pressure outlet boundary condition with zero initial gauge pressure was applied to the open sides of the domain.

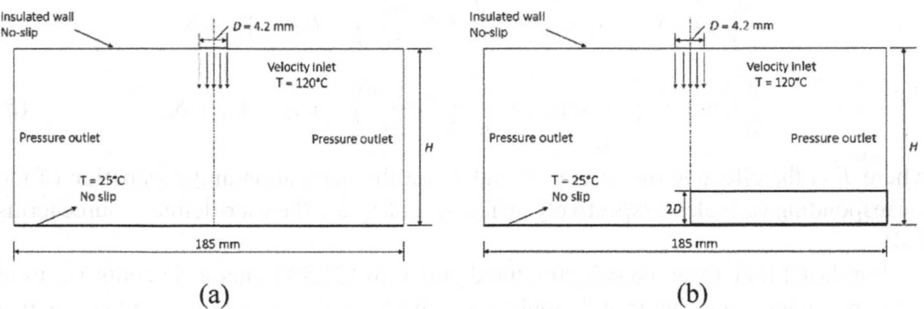

Fig. 1. Numerical domain (a) flat plate (b) step surface.

2.2 Mathematical Model

The governing equations solved by the CFD software FLUENT 19.1 are expressed by Eq. (1) to solve continuity equation, Eq. (2) and Eq. (3) to solve momentum and energy equations, respectively. Since the flow is incompressible, these equations can be written using vectors notation as follows:

$$\nabla \cdot u = 0 \tag{1}$$

$$\frac{\partial u}{\partial t} + u \cdot \nabla u = -\frac{1}{\rho}\nabla p + \mu \cdot \nabla^2 u \tag{2}$$

$$\frac{\partial T}{\partial t} + u \cdot \nabla T = \kappa \cdot \nabla^2 T \tag{3}$$

where u represents the velocity, p the fluid pressure field and T the temperature. The physical properties of the fluid are expressed by the constants ρ, μ and κ which represent the density, kinematic viscosity and diffusivity, respectively.

However, solving full Navier-Stokes equations is too much accurate and demands high computer resources. Since high level of accuracy are not required in this problem, averaged values seem to be enough. The method used to average Navier-Stokes equations is the Reynolds Averaged Navier Stokes (RANS). This method averages the continuity and momentum equations through the decomposition of the velocity by an average velocity $((\bar{u})$ and a fluctuating component $\left(u'\right)$. The unknown velocity fluctuation, u', induces a closure problem which must be solved by using a turbulence model. Considering the advantages pointed out in the previous section, the SST k-ω model was applied to numerically predict the behavior of a jet flow impinging on a flat and non-flat surface. This model, developed by Menter [12], applies the k-ω model in the near wall region and switches to the k-ε model in the far field, combining the advantages of both models. The combination of both SST and the k-ω turbulence models improves the near wall treatment since it gradually switches from a classical low-Reynolds formulation on fine meshes to a log-wall function formulation on coarser grids [13]. The turbulence kinetic energy, k, and the specific dissipation rate, ω, are expressed by Eq. (4) and (5) respectively:

$$\frac{\partial}{\partial t}(\rho k) + \frac{\partial}{\partial x_i}(\rho k u_i) = \frac{\partial}{\partial x_j}\left(\Gamma_k \frac{\partial k}{\partial x_j}\right) + G_k - Y_k + S_k \tag{4}$$

$$\frac{\partial}{\partial t}(\rho \omega) + \frac{\partial}{\partial x_i}(\rho \omega u_i) = \frac{\partial}{\partial x_j}\left(\Gamma_\omega \frac{\partial \omega}{\partial x_j}\right) + G_\omega - Y_\omega + S_\omega \tag{5}$$

where Γ is the effective diffusivity, G and Y are the generation and dissipation of the corresponding variables, respectively, while S_k and S_ω are the user-defined source terms [14].

For the CFD analysis a block-structured grid with 124,500 square elements was used combined with a bias factor of 8, applied near both the target and nozzle plates, which implies a greater refinement close to these walls. This mesh was selected since it ensures a mean wall y^+ value below 2, which according to [15], ensures the accuracy of the SST k-ω model.

The SIMPLE algorithm was used to solve the pressure-velocity coupling. This algorithm uses a relationship between velocity and pressure corrections to enforce mass conservation and to obtain the pressure field [16]. Regarding the spatial discretization of momentum, a second-order upwind was applied while for the dissipation rate and turbulent kinetic energy, a first order upwind was followed. The computational models were solved using a transient formulation based on a first-order implicit method and the convergence criterion of 1E-3 for continuity, momentum and turbulence equations and 1E-6 for energy equation.

3 Results and Discussion

3.1 Velocity Profile

Through the velocity profile, the three main regions identified by Martin [17] can be identified: the free jet region, the stagnation zone and the wall jet region. Between the free jet region and the stagnation zone, another zone can be stated, the decaying region. Viskanta [11] further subdivided this last region in two zones, the initial "developing zone" and the "fully developed zone". The free jet region, formed at the nozzle exit, is characterized by the interaction between the jet and the surrounding environment and presents the maximum velocity value, 12 m/s in this case. As the jet approaches the target plate, it loses axial velocity and turns. A stagnation region is induced, where the overall velocity is near zero [18]. The stagnation region is clearly identified in both flat and non-flat surface. However, as shown in Fig. 2 (b), the step induces a slight deviation of the flow, and an increased mixture between the jet flow and the surrounding air near the bottom of the step was identified. These results are in accordance with [19] and [20], who predicts the separation of the flow at the corner of the step followed by a reattachment downstream on the plate. This phenomenon induces a recirculation region which affects the wall heat transfer. Two stagnation points are identified in this case, located in the bottom and top of the step, while in the flat plate, Fig. 2 (a), this point occur at the jet axis.

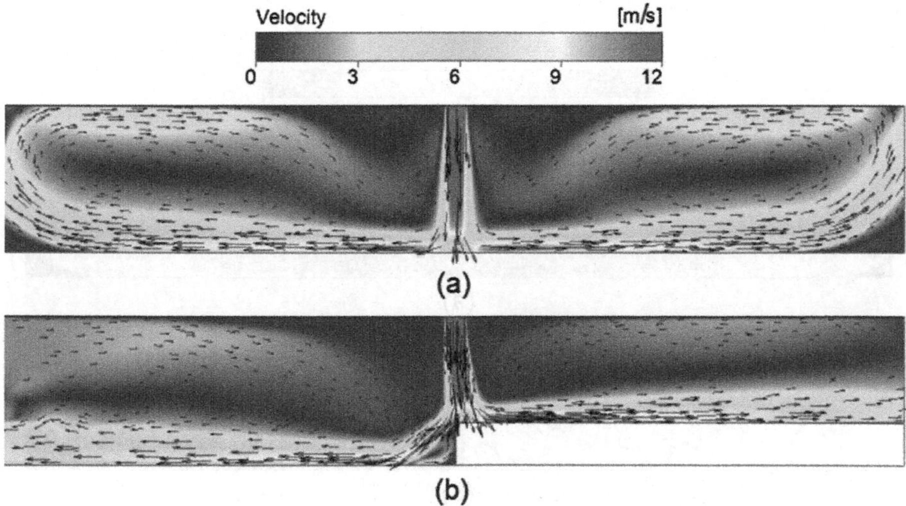

Fig. 2. Jet velocity profile (a) flat plate (b) step surface.

After the contact with the plate, the flow is divided into two streams moving in opposite radial directions along the surface. This wall jet region is characterized by a radial flow with a growing boundary layer [18], due essentially to the strong acceleration of the surrounding flow in the vicinity of the stagnation point. This phenomenon seems to be stronger over the step surface, leading to a flow acceleration and consequently to a reduction of the boundary layer thickness. Since this boundary layer has a decisive influence for the heat transfer coefficient [21], higher values are expected to be achieved in the non-flat plate case, near the step. The separation of the flow occurs when the boundary layer leaves the surface of the plate. Looking at Fig. 2, it seems that the separation point occurs first in the flat plate, showing that the turbulence generated by the step moves away this point from the centerline of the jet.

3.2 Temperature Profile

The temperature profile, presented in Fig. 3, demonstrated that the uniformization of the temperature field throughout the domain is achieved in the case of a flat plate. However, the step induces higher temperatures in the vicinity of the step, due to the development of a thinner boundary layer compared with the flat plate. In addition, the edge of the step interferes with the boundary layer development, a deceleration of the flow is observed, and consequently a decrease in temperature is identified in this region, which is not observed in the flat plate case. A cold point was also identified in the interface between the flat and step surface. This decrease on temperature can be minimized with a multiple jet impingement configuration. Figure 3 clearly show the shear layer detachment at the step corner, followed by the reattachment, as well as the recirculation vortex induced in the vicinity of the step. As mentioned by [22], this effect induce a decrease of the local heat transfer. These phenomena were also observed experimentally by [20] and [23], and numerically by [19].

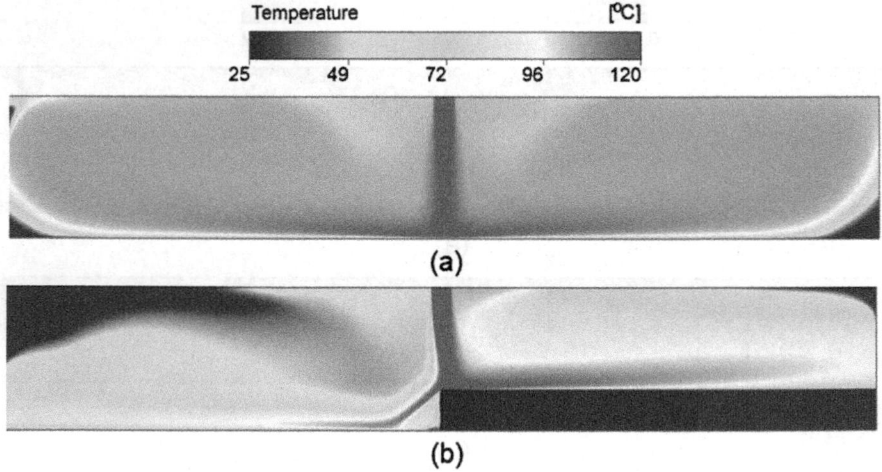

Fig. 3. Temperature profile (a) flat plate (b) step surface.

3.3 Nusselt Number

The Nusselt number variation over the target surface was analyzed and compared for both flat and non-flat plates. Since a larger Nusselt number represents a more effective convection [24], this property allows to analyze the heat transfer performance of the jet impingement. The Nusselt number, given by Eq. (6), represents the ratio between convection and conduction across a fluid.

$$\mathrm{Nu} = \frac{h \cdot D}{k_{air}} \tag{6}$$

where, D is the jet diameter, $k_{air,}$ the thermal conductivity of the air and h is the local convective heat transfer coefficient, obtained by the ratio between the heat flux by forced convection of the jet flow ($\dot{q}_j$) and the temperature difference between the target surface (T) and the jet at the inlet (T_j), as presented in Eq. (7):

$$h = \frac{\dot{q}_j}{\left(T - T_j\right)} \tag{7}$$

The results obtained numerically show the variation of the Nusselt number over the target plate at different jet axis distances. Figure 4 demonstrated that the peak value is reached at the stagnation point located at the jet axis. The step surface induces an increase of the local heat transfer value of approximately 50% compared with a non-flat plate. In terms of heat transfer average, an increase of 10% is observed at $0 < x/D < 2$. This increase due to non-flat surface was also identified in several studies [3, 5, 6, 8]. As mentioned by [23], this is increase is due to small recirculation zones present on the top of the step surface, as well as flow mixing resulting from the separation of flow streamlines near the edge of the upper surface on the step. However, due to the interference of the step edge, lower heat transfer values are recorded near the bottom of the step, essentially due to the recirculation zone. Increasing the distance from this region, the flow develops, and a secondary maximum is recorded at approximately $x/D = -3$. This secondary peak seems to occur due to the transition of the boundary layer from laminar to turbulent. The vortex generated near the bottom edge of the step interferes with the flow, moving away the secondary maximum from the jet axis. These results are in accordance with [20] and

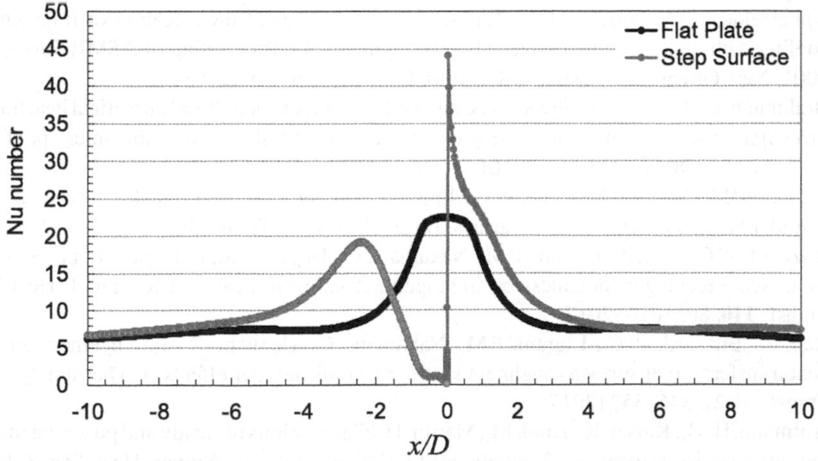

Fig. 4. Nusselt number variation over the target plate.

[23]. The transition region is followed by the wall jet region were a similar decrease of the Nusselt number is observed [25].

4 Conclusions

This work presents a numerical analysis of a single jet impinging a flat and non-flat surface. The results demonstrated the accuracy of the SST k-ω model, since the different regions of the jet were predicted with accuracy. The stagnation point, which is generally the most critical point to be numerically predicted, was clearly identified in both cases. The results show that the step surface generated an acceleration of the flow in the vicinity of the wall, leading to an increase of the heat transfer average of approximately 10% at a jet axis distance (*x/D*) between 0 and 2. The velocity and temperature profiles show that the step surface induce an acceleration of the flow in the vicinity of the step compared with the flat plate, leading to higher heat transfer values. However, in the left side of the step, a higher degradation of the heat transfer is observed compared with the flat plate. This effect can be minimized with a multiple jet configuration, showing that this process is more propitious to achieve uniform heat transfer profiles over the target surface, minimizing cold and hot spots.

Acknowledgments. The first author would like to express her gratitude for the support given by the Portuguese Foundation for Science and Technology (FCT) and the MIT Portugal Program. This work has been supported by FCT – Fundação para a Ciência e Tecnologia within the R&D Units Project Scope: UIDB/00319/2020 (ALGORITMI Center) and R&D Units Project Scope UIDP/04077/2020 (METRICS Center).

References

1. Spring, S., Xing, Y., Weigand, B.: An experimental and numerical study of heat transfer from arrays of impinging jets with surface ribs. J. Heat Transf. **134**(8), 082201 (2012)
2. Annerfeldt, M.O., Persson, J L., Torisson, T.: Experimental investigation of impingement cooling with tubulators or surface enlarging elements. In: Proceeding of ASME Turbo Expo 2001, New Orleans, Louisiana, USA, 2001-GT-0149, pp. 1–9 (2001)
3. Brakmann, R., Chen, L., Weigand, B., Crawford, M.: Experimental and numerical heat transfer investigation of an impinging jet array on a target plate roughened by cubic micro pin fins. J. Turbomach. **138**(11), 111010 (2016)
4. Ligrani, P.M., Ren, Z., Buzzard, W.C.: Impingement jet array heat transfer with small-scale cylinder target surface roughness arrays. Int. J. Heat Mass Transf. **107**, 895–905 (2017)
5. Buzzard, W.C., Ren, Z., Ligrani, P.M., Nakamata, C., Ueguchi, S.: Influences of target surface small-scale rectangle roughness on impingement jet array heat transfer. Int. J. Heat Mass Transf. **110**, 805–816 (2017)
6. Ren, Z., Buzzard, W.C., Ligrani, P.M., Nakamata, C., Ueguchi, S.: Impingement jet array heat transfer: target surface roughness shape, reynolds number effects. J. Thermophys. Heat Transf. **31**(2), 346–357 (2017)
7. Hofmann, H.M., Kaiser, R., Kind, M., Martin, H.: Calculations of steady and pulsating impinging jets - an assessment of 13 widely used turbulence models. Numer. Heat Transf. Part B Fundam. **51**(6), 565–583 (2007)

8. Ortega-Casanova, J., Granados-Ortiz, F.J.: Numerical simulation of the heat transfer from a heated plate with surface variations to an impinging jet. Int. J. Heat Mass Transf. **76**, 128–143 (2014)
9. Ozmen, Y., Ipek, G.: Investigation of flow structure and heat transfer characteristics in an array of impinging slot jets. Heat Mass Transf. **52**(4), 773–787 (2015). https://doi.org/10.1007/s00231-015-1598-z
10. Penumadu, P.S., Rao, A.G.: Numerical investigations of heat transfer and pressure drop characteristics in multiple jet impingement system. Appl. Therm. Eng. **110**, 1511–1524 (2017)
11. Viskanta, R.: Nusselt-reynolds prize paper - heat transfer to impinging isothermal gas and flame jets. Exp. Therm. Fluid Sci. **6**, 111–134 (1993)
12. Menter, F.R.: Two-equation eddy-viscosity turbulence models for engineering applications. AIAA J. **32**(8), 1598–1605 (1994)
13. Menter, F.R., Ferreira, J.C., Esch, T.: The SST turbulence model with improved wall treatment for heat transfer predictions in gas turbines. Int. Gas Turbine Congr. **2003**(1992), 1–7 (2003)
14. Wen, Z., He, Y., Cao, X., Yan, C.: Numerical study of impinging jets heat transfer with different nozzle geometries and arrangements for a ground fast cooling simulation device. Int. J. Heat Mass Transf. **95**, 321–335 (2016)
15. Xing, Y., Spring, S., Weigand, B.: Experimental and numerical investigation of heat transfer characteristics of inline and staggered arrays of impinging jets. J. Heat Transf. **132**(9), 092201 (2010)
16. Ferziger, J.H., Peric, M.: Computational Methods for Fluid Dynamics, 3rd edn. Springer, USA (1996). https://doi.org/10.1007/978-3-642-97651-3
17. Martin, H.: Heat and mass transfer between impinging gas jets and solid surfaces. Adv. Heat Transf. **13**, 1–60 (1977)
18. Ben Kalifa, R., Habli, S., Saïd, N.M., Bournot, H., Le Palec, G.: Parametric analysis of a round jet impingement on a heated plate. Int. J. Heat Fluid Flow **57**, 11–23 (2016)
19. Behnia, M., Ooi, A., Gregory, P.: Prediction of turbulent heat transfer in impinging jet geometries. Modell. Simul. Turbulent Heat Transf. **15**, 147–175 (2006)
20. Lee, D.H., Chung, Y.S., Ligrani, P.M.: Jet impingement cooling of chips equipped with multiple cylindrical pedestal fins. J. Electron. Packag. Trans. ASME **129**(3), 221–228 (2007)
21. Zuckerman, N., Lior, N.: Jet impingement heat transfer: physics, correlations, and numerical modeling. Adv. Heat Transf. **39**(06), 565–631 (2006)
22. Xu, P., Sasmito, A.P., Qiu, S., Mujumdar, A.S., Xu, L., Geng, L.: Heat transfer and entropy generation in air jet impingement on a model rough surface. Int. Commun. Heat Mass Transf. **72**, 48–56 (2016)
23. Chung, Y.S., Lee, D.H., Ligrani, P.M.: Jet impingement cooling of chips equipped with cylindrical pedestal profile fins. J. Electron. Packag. Trans. ASME **127**(2), 106–111 (2005)
24. Cengel, Y.A., Ghajar, A.J.: Heat and Mass Transfer: Fundamentals and Applications, Fifth Edit. McGraw-Hill Education, New York (2011)
25. Barbosa, F.V., Teixeira, S F C F., Teixeira J.C.F.: Influence of the nozzle-to-plate distance in a jet impinging a cold plate – a numerical approach. In.: Proceeding of ECOS 2019 - The 32nd International Conference on Efficiency, Cost, Optimization, Simulation and Environmental Impact of Energy Systems (2019)

Computational Models of Defect Clustering for Tethered Bilayer Membranes

Tomas Raila[1](✉), Marija Jankunec[2], Tadas Meškauskas[1], and Gintaras Valinčius[2]

[1] Institute of Computer Science, Vilnius University, Vilnius, Lithuania
tomas.raila@mif.vu.lt
[2] Life Sciences Center, Vilnius University, Vilnius, Lithuania

Abstract. This study deals with computational modeling of defect clustering effects observed in bilayer phospholipid membranes. Two defect clustering models (algorithms) are presented and compared with the random defect distribution approach. Specific defect distribution instances are evaluated using a simple methodology based on Voronoi diagrams and statistical properties of their sector areas. Computational experiments are performed by using the models to generate synthetic defect distributions with different parameter combinations. The proposed methodology is also validated against atomic force microscopy images of real membranes with defects.

Keywords: Voronoi diagrams · 2D point clustering · Computer simulation · Phospholipid membranes

1 Introduction

Tethered bilayer phospholipid membranes (tBLMs) are popular models of biological membranes and versatile biosensing platforms, enabling studies of protein-membrane and similar interactions in a controlled way. In ideal conditions, such bilayers attached to conductive surface should exhibit dielectric properties. However, this is not the case in real situations due to membrane defects appearing either naturally or being introduced by various pore-forming chemical compounds [1]. One of experimental techniques used to assess electrical properties of such defected membranes is electrochemical impedance spectroscopy (EIS) [9]. This approach has traditionally been used to probe basic macroscopic properties of bilayers, in contrast of microscopy techniques (such as atomic force microscopy - AFM), which can provide extensive visual and structural information. Some recent studies showed that by modeling EIS spectra analytically [8] or numerically [3], certain structural properties of membranes can also be estimated.

One particular study in this specific topic dealt with synthetic EIS spectra computed for 3D membrane models using finite-element analysis (FEA) [6,7].

O. Gervasi et al. (Eds.): ICCSA 2020, LNCS 12253, pp. 496–504, 2020.
https://doi.org/10.1007/978-3-030-58814-4_35

EIS spectral features were used to estimate basic properties of membrane defects, such as their size and density. Results indicated qualitative similarities of EIS response between regular and random defect distributions. Modeled EIS spectra and synthetic defect distributions were also compared to experimentally obtained AFM and EIS data, indicating a good fit in most situations. However, it was found that defect clusters cause inconsistencies between EIS spectra computed for synthetic and experimental defect distributions, preventing the proposed methodology from being applicable in such cases. This study goes further into the defect clustering phenomenon. We present two parameterized defect clustering models which are used to generate synthetic clustered defect distributions. They are numerically evaluated by applying a simple methodology based on Voronoi diagrams and their basic statistical properties. The main objective is to determine if the described models can be used to qualitatively differentiate clustered and random defect distributions. Another investigated question is whether the proposed methodology has the potential to be further developed to enable quantitative evaluation of defect clustering effects in tBLM membranes based on experimental AFM or EIS data. In addition to computational experiments carried out with synthetic data we also validate the methodology by using real defect distributions experimentally registered with AFM.

2 Defect Distribution Models

The basic defect distribution type, used in the current and previous [7] study is the random defect distribution (Fig. 1), in which defect center coordinates (X and Y) are sampled from uniform probability distribution, independently for each defect. Due to its simplicity, this model is used as the baseline against which two more complex defect clustering models are assessed. In order to numerically express the properties of any defect distribution case, we use Voronoi diagrams [5]. The statistical distributions of sector areas obtained from computing such diagrams are characterized in terms of four summary statistics: standard deviation (σ), skewness, kurtosis and median absolute deviation (MAD). All studied defect distributions are bounded by hexagonal shape of the modeling domain in the same way as the membrane models solved with FEA technique in earlier work [7].

2.1 Attraction Model

This method is based on the assumption that defects naturally attract each other and thus tend to cluster together. Such type of object interaction is fundamental and common in nature (i.e. gravitational and electromagnetic forces) and also applicable in biological membrane models [4]. In this model attraction takes effect if the distance between two defects is below the predefined threshold d_T, which can be expressed in one of two ways:

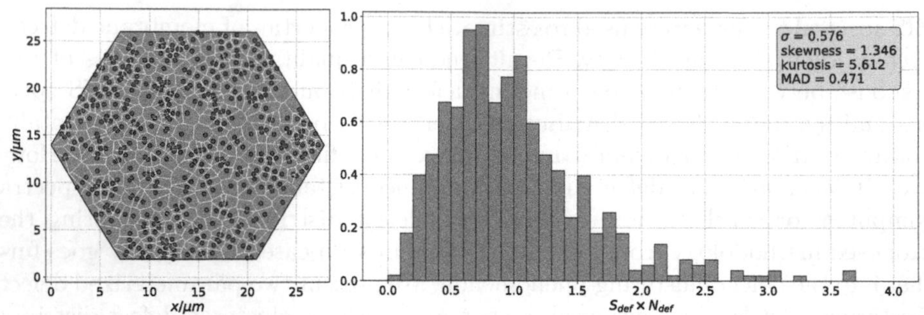

Fig. 1. Example of random defect distribution. Left: Voronoi diagram of defects in the modeling domain. Right: histogram of Voronoi sector areas (normalized with respect to defect density) and their statistics.

- Number of defect radiuses (of the attracting defect).
- Fixed distance in nanometers.

Generating a clustered defect distribution involves the following steps:

1. Coordinates of the first defect are picked randomly from uniform distribution.
2. For each of the subsequent defects:
   (a) Initial coordinates for the current defect with radius r_c are selected randomly from uniform distribution
   (b) Closest existing defect is selected and designated as the attractor with radius r_a.
   (c) Distance between the current and attractor defects is calculated.
   (d) If the distance is below the predefined threshold d_T and above the minimum distance $1.5 * (r_c + r_a)$, the current defect is shifted towards the attractor defect. Minimum distance is retained to avoid defect overlapping.
   (e) Otherwise, if the distance is below the minimum distance of $1.5*(r_c+r_a)$, the current defect is shifted away from the attractor defect until distance between their centers matches the minimum distance.
   (f) If the updated coordinates of the current defect fall outside the hexagon area, the defect is discarded.

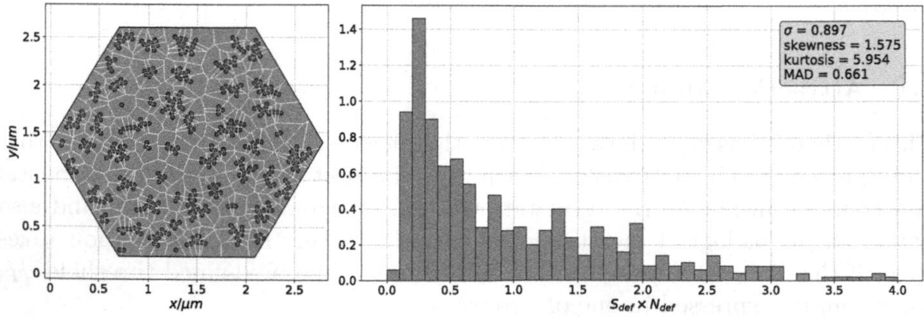

Fig. 2. Example of synthetic defect distribution generated using attraction model, where $d_T = 15$ (expressed in defect radiuses).

Figure 2 shows one example of synthetic clustered defect distribution, obtained by the described model. Distribution consists of 500 defects with equal radius (13 nm), dispersed with density of 100 defects per square micrometer. Such cases are characterized by tightly packed defect groups all containing a similar number of defects. This is reflected in the sector area histogram where the clustered defects represent a large number of small Voronoi sectors, in contrast with random distributions (Fig. 1).

2.2 LCN Model

This model is inspired by an idea that membrane defect clusters tend to form complex structures of varying size and shape, visually resembling clouds. This concept is relevant in computer graphics were various algorithms are used to procedurally generate cloud or smoke textures. For the implementation of this model we chose *lattice convolutional noise* (LCN) algorithm [2] and extended it by introducing two additional parameters by which the clustering effects are adjusted:

- Average relative cluster size: S
- Minimal probability of defect appearance: P

Parameter S is a positive real number which adjusts the scaling of LCN-generated initial image - smaller values correspond to a larger amount of small clusters. P is selected from $[0, 1]$ interval and represents the lower bound of probability field values. Defect distribution generation consists of the following steps:

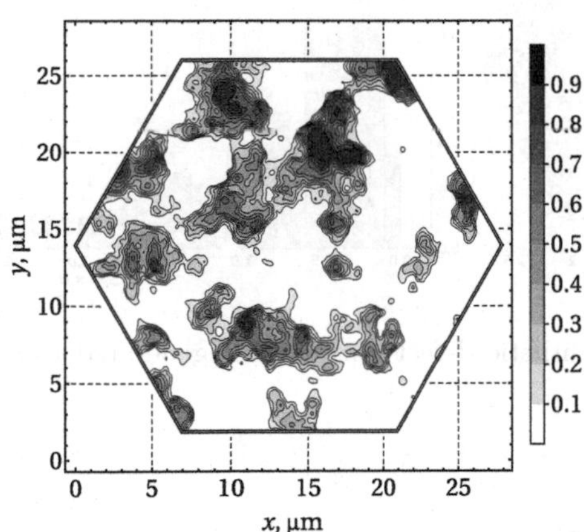

Fig. 3. Example of probability field generated with LCN algorithm.

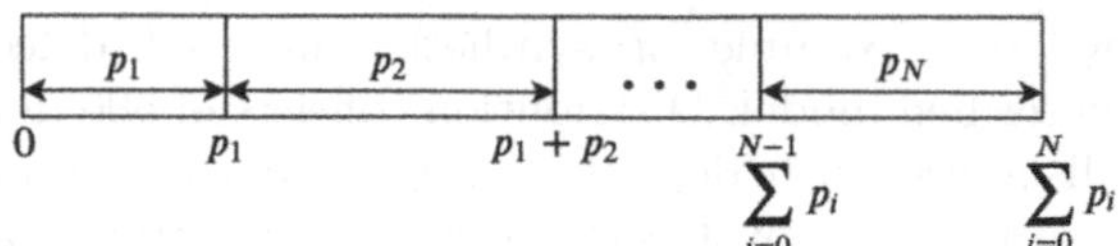

Fig. 4. Weighted roulette wheel selection of probability field pixels

1. By using the LCN algorithm a probability field of fixed resolution (i.e. 4096×4096) is generated and clipped by the hexagonal model domain shape (Fig. 3). Each pixel in the field corresponds to the probability p_i of defect appearing in that point.
2. Probability sum S_N is calculated for the field consisting of N points. Interval $[0; S_N]$ is divided into N subintervals, where each corresponds to probability p_i of respective pixel (Fig. 4).
3. For each defect a random number is uniformly sampled from interval $[0; S_N]$ and corresponding pixel of probability field is designated as the center of that defect.

This model produces clustered defect distributions (Fig. 5) which are visually distinct from the ones obtained by applying the attraction model (Fig. 2). Clusters exhibit different sizes and various irregularities which also reflected by statistical properties of Voronoi sector areas, where the majority of small sectors are offset by a number of very large ones.

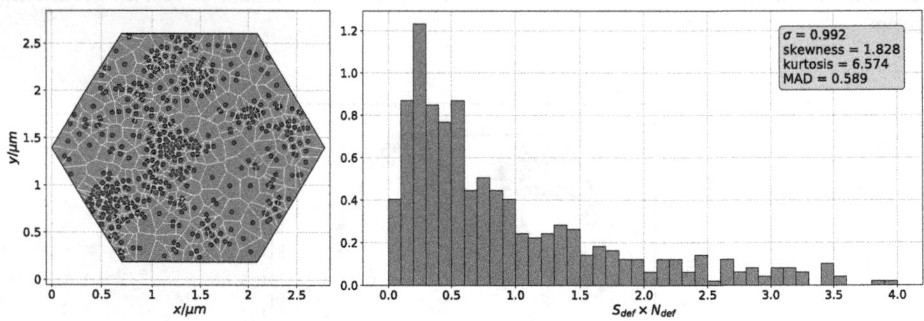

Fig. 5. Example of synthetic defect distribution generated using LCN model, where $S = 1$ and $P = 0.1$.

3 Experiments

3.1 Synthetic Data

In order to differentiate random and clustered defect distributions using a simple statistical approach, a number of synthetic defect distributions were generated by applying the proposed models with different parameter combinations

(Table 1). A total of 54 and 48 combinations for attraction and LCN models respectively were examined and summary statistics were computed for 100 independently generated cases for each option. In the same way, statistical properties of random defect distributions were determined from 100 independently generated cases. Each defect distribution consisted of 500 defects. Defect densities and sizes for attraction model were selected by likely scenarios examined in the earlier study [7]. Other values were chosen arbitrarily, to cover a wide range of visually different clustering cases. Sector areas in all cases were normalized with respect to defect density.

Table 1. Clustering model parameter values used in synthetic defect distribution generation.

Model type	Model parameter	Values
Attraction model	Defect density N_{def}	1; 10; 100
	Defect size R_{def} (nm)	0.5; 13; 25.5
	Attraction threshold[1] d_T	5; 10; 15; 20; 25; 30
LCN model	Min. probability P	0; 0.03; 0.06; 0.09; 0.12; 0.15
	Cluster size S	0.25; 0.5; 0.75; 1; 1.25; 1.5; 1.75; 2

[1] Expressed as the number of defect radiuses (R_{def}).

Standard deviation was chosen for the purpose of comparing clustered and random distributions. The baseline $\sigma = 0.54$ was found to be the average case for random defect distribution model, as determined from 100 independently generated instances. Attraction model results (Fig. 6) show very different σ trends for various defect size (R_{def}) and density (N_{def}) values. In case of small (0.5 nm) defects it is impossible to distinguish the clustered and random distributions. Similar issue applies for medium size (13 nm) defects with low density, although density increase introduces clear trend of σ growth depending on attraction threshold. Interesting effect of largest σ growth with medium defect density can be observed in largest (25 nm) defect case.

Figure 7 illustrates the dependency of standard deviation values by S and P parameters of LCN model. By decreasing the values of both parameters, standard deviation approaches the random distribution baseline, but does not cross that threshold. Although a clear increasing trend can be observed in all P cases, the specific clustering parameter values for a given clustered distribution cannot be unambiguously estimated just from the standard deviation of its Voronoi sector areas.

3.2 AFM Data

To validate the proposed methodology against real-world data, three AFM images of tBLMs affected with pore-forming toxin vaginolysin (VLY) were obtained. Each image covers membrane area of $6\,\mu\text{m} \times 6\,\mu\text{m}$, captured at

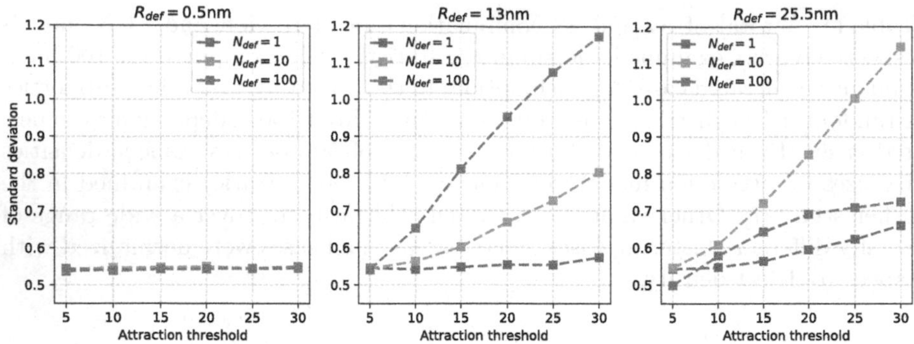

Fig. 6. Standard deviation values of Voronoi sector areas of generated synthetic defect distributions using attraction model.

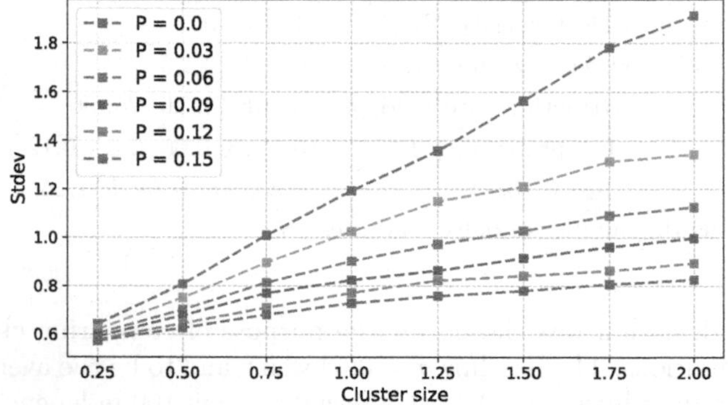

Fig. 7. Standard deviation values of Voronoi sector areas of generated synthetic defect distributions using LCN model with different parameter values.

1536 × 1536 resolution. Figure 8 illustrates one such example with Voronoi diagram overlaid on top of AFM image where several defect clusters, characterized by a large number of small sectors, can be observed. Coordinates of the defects present in each image were annotated manually by domain expert and Voronoi diagrams with corresponding statistical properties were computed for all cases (Table 2). Results show that experimentally registered defect distributions are significantly different from baseline random case in terms of standard deviation and MAD, although this does not apply for skewness and kurtosis.

Based on synthetic clustered distribution properties (Fig. 6 and 7) and baseline values of random distribution model, all three AFM-registered defect distributions can be classified as being clustered and distinct from random cases. However, unambiguously determining the more suitable clustering model and its parameters is not possible. Both attraction and LCN models can produce distributions with matching σ values, however, the attraction model depends more on the overall features of real defect distribution (defect size and density), which might be difficult to estimate or measure experimentally. As noted in earlier work [7], radiuses of membrane defects (introduced by VLY) usually fall in range from 13 nm to 25 nm. This fact might be useful in estimating attraction model parameters based on summary statistics (σ and others). On the other hand, the LCN algorithm does not depend on defect size and density parameters and can be considered as more versatile.

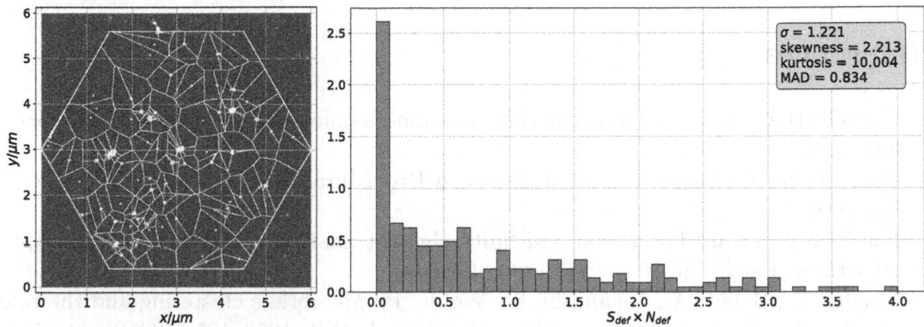

Fig. 8. Example of clustered defect distribution obtained from an AFM image of a real tBLM membrane sample.

Table 2. Statistical properties of Voronoi sector areas of experimentally registered defect distributions in comparison with random defect distribution properties.

Case ID	N	N_{def}	Stdev	Skewness	Kurtosis	MAD
AFM #1	234	10.01	1.22	2.21	10.00	0.83
AFM #2	148	6.33	1.12	1.80	6.52	0.70
AFM #3	235	10.05	0.88	1.21	4.25	0.79
Random	–	–	0.54	1.18	5.38	0.49

4 Results and Conclusions

In this work we presented two defect clustering algorithms and a simple methodology for evaluating clustering effects, based on Voronoi diagrams and statistical properties of their sector areas. Experiments with synthetic clustered defect distributions showed different σ and other property trends depending on model parameter combinations. LCN model was considered to be more versatile in differentiating the random and clustered defect distributions, although the results are only qualitative and the current approach is not yet applicable in deriving clustering parameters for a given specific defect distribution case. The usefulness of attraction model for this task also cannot be ruled out, although its applicability depends on defect size and density properties. Standard deviation of Voronoi sector areas proved to be useful in distinguishing between clustered and randomly-distributed defect cases. Although the small amount of available AFM data prevents the statistically-proven conclusions to be made, analysis tentatively proved the usefulness of the proposed methodology in evaluating the clustering effects in real tBLM membranes.

Next steps in this research direction would involve a more thorough statistical analysis with the larger amount of AFM data, further clustering model development and application of the methodology on experimental EIS data.

References

1. Cornell, B.A., et al.: A biosensor that uses ion-channel switches. Nature **387**, 580–583 (1997)
2. Ebert, D., et al.: Texturing and Modeling: A Procedural Approach, 3rd edn., December 2002
3. Kwak, K.J., et al.: Formation and finite element analysis of tethered bilayer lipid structures. Langmuir **26**, 18199–18208 (2010)
4. Mugler, A., Bailey, A., Takahashi, K., Wolde, P.: Membrane clustering and the role of rebinding in biochemical signaling. Biophys. J. **102**, 1069–1078 (2012). https://doi.org/10.1016/j.bpj.2012.02.005
5. Okabe, A., Boots, B., Sugihara, K., Chiu, S.: Spatial Tessellations: Concepts and Applications of Voronoi Diagrams, vol. 43, January 2000. https://doi.org/10.2307/2687299
6. Raila, T., Meškauskas, T., Valinčius, G., Jankunec, M., Penkauskas, T.: Computer modeling of electrochemical impedance spectra for defected phospholipid membranes: finite element analysis. In: Sergeyev, Y.D., Kvasov, D.E. (eds.) NUMTA 2019. LNCS, vol. 11974, pp. 462–469. Springer, Cham (2020). https://doi.org/10.1007/978-3-030-40616-5_44
7. Raila, T., Penkauskas, T., Jankunec, M., Dreižas, G., Meškauskas, T., Valinčius, G.: Electrochemical impedance of randomly distributed defects in tethered phospholipid bilayers: Finite element analysis. Electrochim. Acta **299**, 863–874 (2019)
8. Valinčius, G., Meškauskas, T., Ivanauskas, F.: Electrochemical impedance spectroscopy of tethered bilayer membranes. Langmuir **28**, 977–990 (2012)
9. Valinčius, G., Mickevičius, M.: Tethered phospholipid bilayer membranes: an interpretation of the electrochemical impedance response. In: Iglič, A., Kulkarni, C.V., Rappolt, M. (eds.) Advances in Planar Lipid Bilayers and Liposomes, vol. 21, pp. 27–61. Academic Press (2015). (Chap. 2)

Model of Post Fire Erosion Assessment Using RUSLE Method, GIS Tools and ESA Sentinel DATA

Gabriele Nolè[1(✉)], Valentina Santarsiero[1,3], Antonio Lanorte[1], Biagio Tucci[1], Vito Augusto Capurso[2], Francesco Vito Ronco[2], and Beniamino Murgante[3]

[1] IMAA-CNR, C. da Santa Loja, Zona Industriale, 85050 Tito Scalo, Potenza, Italy
{gabriele.nole,valentina.santarsiero,antonio.lanorte, biagio.tucci}@imaa.cnr.it

[2] Protezione Civile Puglia, via delle Magnolie, 14, 700026 Modugno, Bari, Italy
{v.capurso,f.ronco}@regione.puglia.it

[3] School of Engineering, University of Basilicata, Viale dell'Ateneo Lucano 10, 85100 Potenza, Italy
{valentina.santarsiero,beniamino.murgante}@unibas.it

Abstract. Soil erosion in fired areas is one of the main environmental problem involves degrading the quality of the soil and reducing the productivity of the affected lands. The aim of this work is to implement a procedure that analyzes the change detection of the potential soil eroded in a burned area, and discriminate the amount of potential soil loss. As part of the MESARIP project (in agreement with the Regional Civil Protection) in order to implement the analyses of soil erosion pre and post fire event, using Sentinel 2 data and with the RUSLE (Revised Universal Soil Loss Equation) method in a GIS open source environment, a graphical model has been developed. The application of the RUSLE requires a series of consequential spatial analysis elaborations and, according to this scheme, the model has been developed with the Graphical Modeler. QGIS contains in a single environment a multiplicity of tools and algorithms native to other open source GIS software, such as, for example, SAGA GIS and GRASS GIS. The user interface is very simple and requires basic and thematic input data such as DEM, MASK areas or vegetation indices etc. The advantages in the construction of the model can be identified in the standardization of map algebra operations and also in the speed of execution of the steps. Currently the model has been tested in some burned areas in 2019 located in the northern part of the Apulia Region and will be tested in operational mode during the 2020 summer season.

Keywords: Graphical modeler · RUSLE method · Soil erosion

1 Introduction

Soil erosion is a natural process which is responsible for landscape degradation. Forest vegetation generally is good for soil protection, however, human disturbances may

O. Gervasi et al. (Eds.): ICCSA 2020, LNCS 12253, pp. 505–516, 2020.
https://doi.org/10.1007/978-3-030-58814-4_36

accelerate erosion on territories with high relief energy. This processes represent one of the most serious environmental problem.

Climate change is also responsible for soil loss intensification. Several studies discuss how forestry activities [28] and land use change influence the sediment transport [2–4, 6, 8, 29, 31].

Soil erosion involves the detachment and transport of soil particles from the upper layers of the soil, degrading the quality of the soil and reducing the productivity of the affected lands. In fired areas this phenomenon is more evident as the effects of fire irreversibly degrade these soils.

Removing trees reduces evapotranspiration and rainfall interception leading to increased surface runoff. Furthermore without vegetation, soils become vulnerable to surface erosion. Most of the soil erosion study done by other researchers were based on the USLE/RUSLE [26, 27, 31] as a method to predict the soil loss, RUSLE takes into account several factors such as rainfall, soil erodibility, slope, land cover and erosion control practice for soil erosion prediction.

Remote sensing technologies can provide useful data for fire management, from risk estimation [5, 7, 13, 16, 22, 31], fire detection [18] to post fire monitoring [1, 14, 17] including burn area [4, 5, 27].

Puglia is, among the Italian regions, the least equipped with forests, despite this being among those most affected by incendiary phenomena. According to the estimates of the Regional Civil Protection, about 600 fires have been surrounded by forest police in 2019, of which 464 concern wooded areas.

The project "MESARIP satellite methodologies for the assessment of the risk of fires in the Puglia Region", in collaboration between the CNR IMAA and the Civil Protection Puglia, aims to provide tools and methodologies useful for the prevention, forecast and management of emergencies related to risk forest fires and interface also with the use of satellite technologies. The activities included in the project include that of estimating and studying fire severity and soil erosion in burnt areas.

The aim of this work is to implement a procedure that analyzes the change detection of the potential soil eroded in a burned area, and discriminate the amount of potential soil loss. In order to implement the analyses of soil erosion pre and post fire event, using ESA Sentinel 2 data and with the RUSLE (Revised Universal Soil Loss Equation) method in a GIS open source environment, a graphical model has been developed.

The graphical modeler has been developed using QGIS open source software and allows you to create complex models using a simple and easy-to-use interface.

QGIS contains in a single environment a multiplicity of tools and algorithms native to other open source GIS software, such as, for example, SAGA GIS and GRASS GIS. Thanks to this flexibility, the implemented model consists of elaborations that "point" to different software.

2 Material and Method

The study area covered by this work includes all the areas burned in 2019 in the Puglia region Apulia (see Fig. 1).

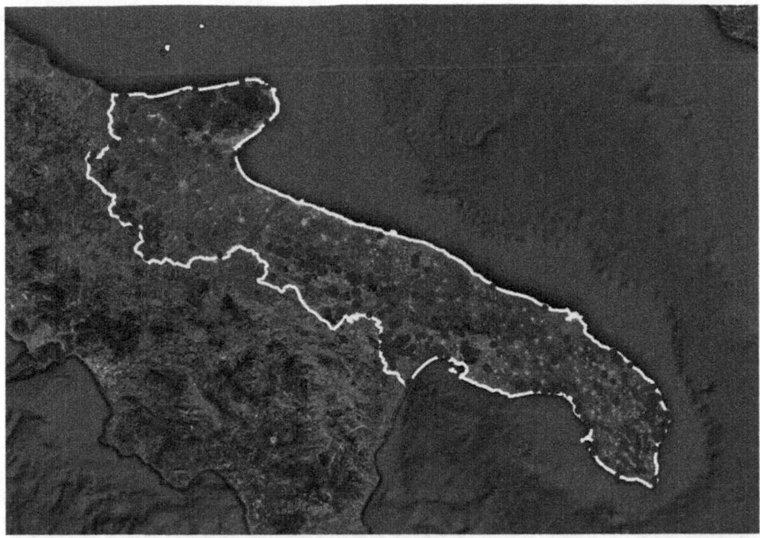

Fig. 1. Geographical localization of fire 2019 areas.

2.1 Fire Severity Assessment and RUSLE Methodology

After the fire, a series of spectrum changes takes place due to the fire consuming the vegetation, destroying the chlorophyll, leaving the soil bare, charring the roots and altering the soil's moisture. The reduction in chlorophyll results in an increase in the visible region of the electromagnetic spectrum and in a diminution in the near infrared region [12]. The NBR (Normalized Burn Ratio) combining information on the near infrared and the mid-infrared regions has been used in the discrimination of burned areas in the Mediterranean, using both a post-fire image and a bitemporal pre-/post-fire difference [12].

The severity of the fire was estimated using Sentinel 2 A and 2 B bands most sensitive to changes in the post-fire reflectance value (Band 8a and Band 12).

In order to assess fire severity degree, dNBR values was categorized. As it is known that dNBR ranges values are basically site-specific, fixed thresholds were not applied but [11] classification approach was adopted. These authors applied an unsupervised clustering algorithm [12] to objectively assign fire severity classes to dNBR on the base of data iterative partitioning [28]. This approach has benefits such as objectivity, possibility of use in case of unavailability of field data and minimizing the issues due outliers. In this study we selected six classes of dNBR: unburned; very low, low, moderate, high and very high. [14].

The dNBR index is used to produce the severity map of the fire on the ground. For each event analyzed, pre and post-fire images very close to the days of the event were used to capture the effects of first-rate fire on the ground. The dNBR index generated several spatial fire severity models related to different fire intensities for each study site. In Figs. 2 and 3, respectively, the images of the preview of the dNBR related to the webgis, the dNBR in grayscale contextualized to the study area, finally the dNBR with the symbology based on the values assumed by each pixel on a certain portion of the area.

Fig. 2. dNBR Lucera fire in grey scale.

Fig. 3. dNBR Lucera fire.

Many models have been developed in the past to predict areas that are susceptible to soil erosion, to predict soil loss, and to evaluate soil erosion-control practices and RUSLE is one of the most widely used soil erosion model worldwide. For this work RUSLE (Revised Universal Soil Loss Equation) has been applied, this is an empirical model, based on experimental data, which allows to stimulate the average rate of soil loss due to surface and channeled erosion (erosion of the rill).

The RUSLE [26–28] retains the same six factors of the USLE. The equation used for the calculation of both the USLE and the RUSLE is

$$A = R \times K \times LS \times C \times P \tag{1}$$

Where:
A = annual soil loss (Mg · ha −1 · year −1);
R = precipitation erosion factor (MJ · mm · ha −1 · h −1 · year −1);
K = soil erodibility factor (Mg · h · MJ −1 · mm −1);
LS = slope length factor and slope (dimensionless);
C = crop and cover management factor (dimensionless);
P = cultivation or anti-erosion (dimensionless) practice factor.

The erosion factor of the outflow of rainfall R (MJ · mm · ha − 1 · h − 1 · year-1), constitutes a measure of the rain energy considered as the main erosive agent [28–30]. It is calculated on the basis of the average monthly cumulated rainfall and was determined using the following formula [30]:

$$R = (1163,45 + 4,9 \times H - 35,2 \times NRE - 0.58 \times q) \tag{2}$$

where H (mm • y − 1) is the average value of the annual precipitation, q the altitude of the site (obtained from a DTM with 5 m resolution) and NRE the average annual value of the rainy events. The rainfall values come from the rainfall data of the Functional Center of the Puglia Region on which the average of the values over a few years was subsequently calculated, interpolated to have a value relating to the burnt areas.

K, or the soil erodibility factor (Mg • h • MJ − 1 • mm − 1), is significant of the susceptibility of soil particles to detachment and subsequent transport by rain and surface runoff. By changing the structure of the soil and its permeability, fire leads to a decrease in organic matter and therefore, ultimately, an increase in the K parameter [7]. In the present study, the reference value of the K factor is that obtained from the dataset contained in "Soil Erodibility in Europe High Resolution dataset" [30]. Larsen and MacDonald [17] point out, like other authors, that high severity fires increase the production and transport of sediments by several orders of magnitude. In this work the same criteria applied by [31] in Calabria have been used and therefore K has been multiplied by a factor between 1.6 (very low severity) and 2 (very high severity).

Factors L and S represent the effect of topography on soil erosion rate. The length of the slope (L) in RUSLE is defined as the distance between the point where the runoff begins and the point where sedimentation occurs or where the runoff water is channeled [29]. The increase in the value of eroded soil is proportional to the increase in the length of the slope. The slope steepness factor (S) also allows to consider the increase in erosive phenomena in relation to the angle of inclination of the slope. In fact, a greater slope corresponds to an increase in the flow velocity and, consequently, of the sediments produced and transported. The LS topographic factor was calculated with the support of the QGIS software starting from the DTM with a grid size of 5 m. For the calculation of the LS factor at a point r located along a hilly slope, the following equation was used [23]:

$$LS(r) = (\mu + 1)\,[a(r)/a0]\mu \times [sin\, b(r)/b0]^{n} \quad (3)$$

where a (r) [m2 · m − 1] is the area of the basin that contributes to the outflow in the section corresponding to point r per unit of width (specifically in the case studies we have calculated a (r) as a product of the QGIS functions "flow accumulation" and "pixel resolution"), b is the slope in radians, a0 = 22.1 m is the standard length USLE, b0 = 9% is the standard slope USLE while μ en are parameters that depend on the type of flow and the ground conditions. In this study n was assumed equal to 1.2 [14]. The parameter μ, indicative of the relationship between erosion within the grooves (rill) and that along the intermediate slopes (inter-rill), describes the erosive phenomenon which, while inside the impluvium depends on the surface runoff, along the intermediate and furrowed surfaces is a function of the energy with which rainfall impacts the soil. As part of this study, μ was calculated using the formula proposed by [22–24]:

$$\mu = \beta / (1 + \beta) \quad (4)$$

with a value of β varying between 0.5 (unburnt soil, pre-fire condition) and 1.0 (soil covered by fire with very high severity). A correct estimate of these parameters is important as the β value is quickly changed by the fire.

C factor reflects the effects of surface coverage and roofing management on soil erosion [31].

Plant cover and appropriate crop management reduce soil runoff and erosion [21] liby limiting the impact of rain on the soil surface. For non-erodible surface we assume C = 0, while the reference condition refers to bare soil (absence of vegetation) with a value of C = 1. For both the pre-fire and post-fire scenarios, the estimate of the factor C was carried out on the basis of the calculation of vegetation indices derived from satellite. In particular, the SAVI (Soil-Adjusted Vegetation Index) was used. Based on the statistical regression analysis performed by [12] the following equation is used:

$$C = -a \times SAVI + 1 \quad (5)$$

where C is the cover factor and a = 1.18

$$SAVI = [(NIR - RED) \times (1 + L)]/(NIR + RED + L) \quad (6)$$

where L is a correction factor and has been assumed equal to 0.5 while NIR and RED are the reflectance values in the near infrared and red bands. SAVI is calculated using the best Sentinel 2 images acquired pre and post-fire as close as possible, temporally, to the date of the fire. Following this procedure it is possible to expect an overestimation of the post-fire factor C, but considering the underlying operational purposes of this study, we consider this compromise acceptable.

The cultivation or anti-erosion practice factor (P) is an expression of the effects of agricultural management practices aimed at reducing water runoff and consequently soil loss. To determine the value of the P factor, the following equation is applied [3] exclusively to classes of agricultural vegetation (intensive and continuous arable crops, extensive crops and complex agricultural systems, olive groves, orchards, citrus groves, vineyards).

$$P = 0.2 + 0.03 \times S \tag{7}$$

where S is the slope (%) and the maximum value that P can reach is 1.0.

3 Result and Discussion

The application of the described methodology allowed to elaborate the fire severity maps of the study sites, which were subsequently used as input for the estimation of the parameters of the RUSLE model.

The study has been conducted using a modeling approach, already developed in the 70s–80s of last century (RUSLE model), implemented with digital techniques capable of managing and processing a large number of spatial data (GIS) [16, 17, 22, 24, 25], to obtain a cartographic elaborations as output.

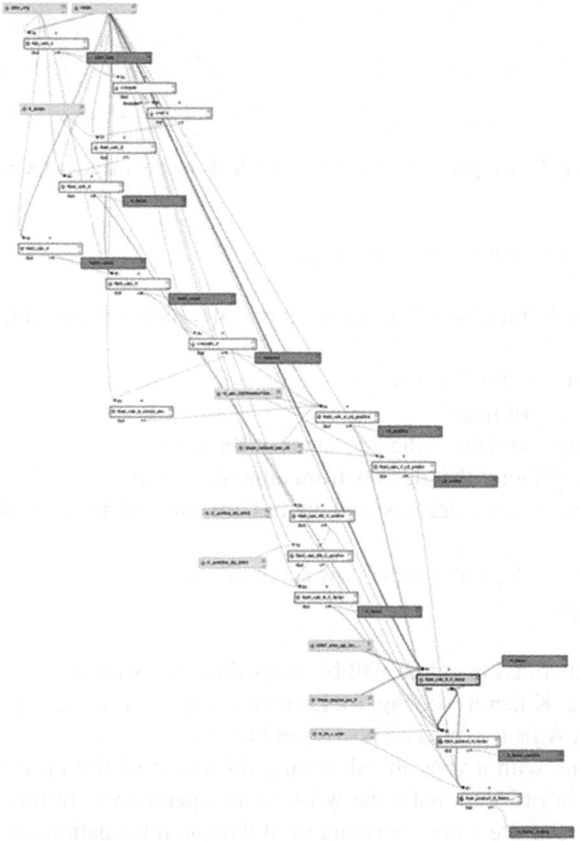

Fig. 4. A RUSLE model scheme made in QGIS.

The main part of the processes useful for obtaining the main maps of the RUSLE model was schematized by means of a spatial analysis workflow (See Fig. 4) in the graphic modeler of QGIS. This, in addition to allowing a clear definition of the sequence of the processes, avoids incurring changes in the fire-to-fire procedure.

Quantitative and semi-quantitative data in this paper has been collected from academic literature and websites. All data has been converted into raster at 10 m grid cell, so that spatial analysis can be done in the same cell size and map projection. In order to use it, it is necessary to create input maps that must be carefully analyzed (See Fig. 5).

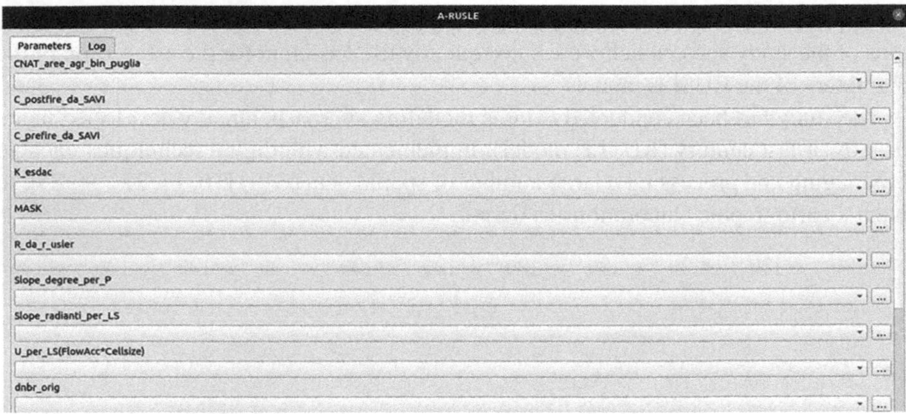

Fig. 5. Graphical interface for a RUSLE model made in QGIS.

Specifically, the required input maps are:

- the binary Agricultural Soil Map on the basis of which it is possible to calculate the P factor;
- pre and post fire Factor C maps;
- the original K-factor map;
- the MASK map that defines the perimeter of the fire;
- the map of the R factor that derives from annual rainfall;
- the slope expressed in degrees and in radians (useful for calculating P and LS respectively);
- the U map, which depends on the flow accumulation;
- the dNBR map.

The maps generated in output will be clipped on the perimeter of the fire, based on the mask, and are: K factor (see Fig. 6), LS (pre and post fire) (see Fig. 7), C factor (see Fig. 8), P Factor, A factor (pre and post) (see Fig. 9).

This was done with a view to calculating the effect of fire on erosion in the next summer season in order to make the work more operational. In this regard, in order to quickly locate the fire reports arriving in SOUP, an information entry and recording system has been implemented. The method could be to evaluate the fires that are reported

Fig. 6. K factor of Lucera Fire event of 06/07/2019.

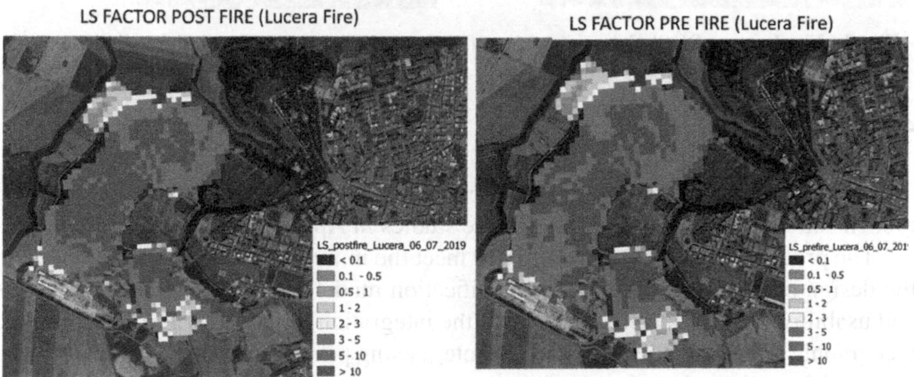

Fig. 7. LS factor PRE and POST of Lucera fire event of 06/07/08.

C FACTOR POST FIRE (Lucera Fire)

C_postfire_Lucera_06_07_2019

basso

alto

Fig. 8. C factor of Lucera fire event of 06/07/2019.

and recorded in SOUP through the formonline which are thus displayed directly on the webgis.

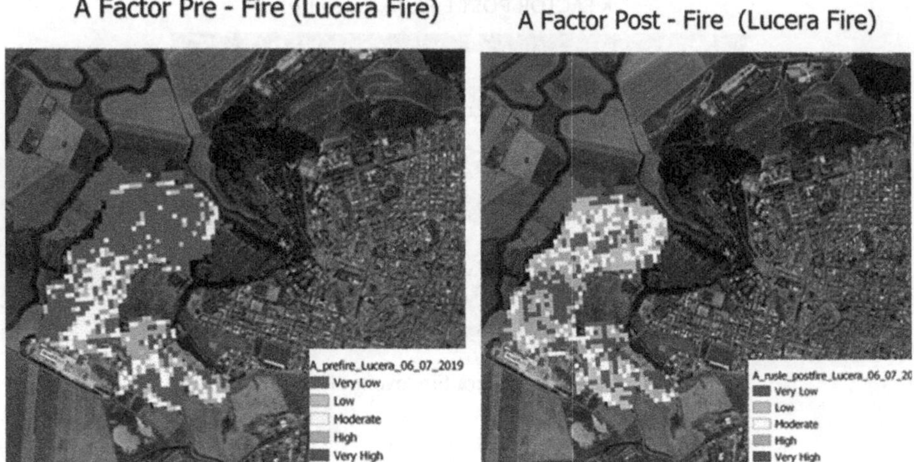

Fig. 9. Fire Lucera: RUSLE A pre and post fire factor. Annual post-fire soil erosion forecast.

4 Conclusions

This work in particular implements the use of the RUSLE model for predicting post-fire eroded soil in applications to different case studies in Apulia Region.

The products generated at the moment meet the minimum requirements assumed in the design phase: quality of the fire identification model, estimation of the parameters and usability of the product. In particular, the integration of the RUSLE model with the Geographic Information Systems and remote sensing provides a reliable estimate of the potential for soil erosion after the fire.

The integration of "classic" spatial data such as aerophotogrammetric data, raster and vector cartography, which have always been used by local authorities, today have a new life thanks to the integration with data collected in the field or acquired remotely (by drone or satellite).

This study point out, in fact, the interoperability of GIS software which allow you to manage data from different sources (satellite images, RUSLE data, cartographic data of the Puglia Region) in a single environment. Furthermore, the use of the model described in this paper presents innumerable advantages such as the speed in carrying out the study and estimation operations of the eroded soil by applying the RUSLE model, uniformity of spatial processes and processes and the standardization of these.

All the operations carried out are being evaluated between CNR researchers and experts from the Puglia Civil Protection to make the model itself easily applicable in near real time in the summer 2020.

The creation of data warehouses, such as the SIT PUGLIA of the Puglia Region (http://sit.puglia.it/portal/sit_portal) greatly enhance the sharing of geographic information and it is important to know them and use them to monitor and plan the actions to be put in place field on the territory.

References

1. Chuvieco, E., Martin, M.P., Palacios, A.: Assessment of different spectral indices in the red-near-infrared spectral domain for burned land discrimination. Int. J. Remote Sens. **23**(23), 5103–5110 (2002)
2. Fu, B.J., et al.: Assessment of soil erosion at large watershed scale using RUSLE and GIS: a case study in the Loess Plateau of China. Land Degrad. Dev. **16**(1), 73–85 (2005)
3. García-Ruiz, J.M., Nadal-Romero, E., Lana-Renault, N., Beguería, S.: Erosion in Mediterranean landscapes: changes and future challenges. Geomorphology **198**, 20–36 (2013)
4. García-Ruiz, J.M., et al.: Flood generation and sediment transport in experimental catchments affected by land use changes in the central Pyrenees. J. Hydrol. **356**(1–2), 245–260 (2008)
5. García, M.L., Caselles, V.: Mapping burns and natural reforestation using Thematic Mapper data. Geocarto Int. **6**(1), 31–37 (1991)
6. Giovannini, G., Vallejo, R., Lucchesi, S., Bautista, S., Ciompi, S., Llovet, J.: Effects of land use and eventual fire on soil erodibility in dry Mediterranean conditions. For. Ecol. Manage. **147**(1), 15–23 (2001)
7. Hall, R.J., Freeburn, J.T., De Groot, W.J., Pritchard, J.M., Lynham, T.J., Landry, R.: Remote sensing of burn severity: experience from western Canada boreal fires. Int. J. Wildland Fire **17**(4), 476–489 (2008)
8. Hartigan, J.A., Wong, M.A.: Algorithm AS 136: a k-means clustering algorithm. J. R. Stat. Soc. Ser. C (Appl. Stat.) **28**(1), 100–108 (1979)
9. Heredia, Á., Martínez, S., Quintero, E., Piñeros, W., Chuvieco, E.: Comparación de distintas técnicas de análisis digital para la cartografía de áreas quemadas con imágenes LANDSAT ETM+. GeoFocus. Revista Internacional de Ciencia y Tecnología de la Información Geográfica **3**, 216–234 (2003)
10. Holden, Z.A., Evans, J.S.: Using fuzzy C-means and local autocorrelation to cluster satellite-inferred burn severity classes. Int. J. Wildland Fire **19**(7), 853–860 (2010)
11. Kuo, K.T., Sekiyama, A., Mihara, M.: Determining C factor of universal soil loss equation (USLE) based on remote sensing. Int. J. Environ. Rural Dev. **7**(2), 154–161 (2016)
12. Lanorte, A., Danese, M., Lasaponara, R., Murgante, B.: Multiscale mapping of burn area and severity using multisensor satellite data and spatial autocorrelation analysis. Int. J. Appl. Earth Obs. Geoinf. **20**, 42–51 (2013)
13. Larsen, I.J., MacDonald, L.H.: Predicting postfire sediment yields at the hillslope scale: testing RUSLE and Disturbed WEPP. Water Resour. Res. **43**(11) (2007)
14. Lasaponara, R., Lanorte, A.: Multispectral fuel type characterization based on remote sensing data and Prometheus model. For. Ecol. Manage. **234**, S226 (2006)
15. Lee, S.: Soil erosion assessment and its verification using the universal soil loss equation and geographic information system: a case study at Boun Korea. Environ. Geol. **45**(4), 457–465 (2004)
16. Lisle, T.E., Napolitano, M.B.: Effects of recent logging on the main channel of North Fork Caspar Creek. In: Ziemer, R.R. [Tech. Coord.]. Proceedings of the conference on coastal watersheds: The Caspar Creek story. PSW-GTR-168. Pacific Southwest Research Station. USDA Forest Service, Albany, CA, pp. 81–85, May 1998
17. Miller, J.D., Nyhan, J.W., Yool, S.R.: Modeling potential erosion due to the Cerro Grande Fire with a GIS-based implementation of the Revised Universal Soil Loss Equation. Int. J. Wildland Fire **12**(1), 85–100 (2003)
18. Mitasova, H., Hofierka, J., Zlocha, M., Iverson, L.R.: Modelling topographic potential for erosion and deposition using GIS. Int. J. Geogr. Inf. Syst. **10**(5), 629–641 (1996)
19. Odeh, I.O.A., McBratney, A.B., Chittleborough, D.J.: Soil pattern recognition with fuzzy-c-means: application to classification and soil-landform interrelationships. Soil Sci. Soc. Am. J. **56**(2), 505–516 (1992)

20. Panagos, P., et al.: Rainfall erosivity in Europe. Sci. Total Environ. **511**, 801–814 (2015)
21. Panagos, P., Borrelli, P., Meusburger, K.: A new European slope length and steepness factor (LS-Factor) for modeling soil erosion by water. Geosciences **5**(2), 117–126 (2015)
22. Panagos, P., Meusburger, K., Ballabio, C., Borrelli, P., Alewell, C.: Soil erodibility in Europe: a high-resolution dataset based on LUCAS. Sci. Total Environ. **479**, 189–200 (2014)
23. Rauste, Y., Herland, E., Frelander, H., Soini, K., Kuoremaki, T., Ruokari, A.: Satellite-based forest fire detection for fire control in boreal forests. Int. J. Remote Sens. **18**(12), 2641–2656 (1997)
24. Renard, K.G.: Predicting soil erosion by water: a guide to conservation planning with the Revised Universal Soil Loss Equation (RUSLE). United States Government Printing (1997)
25. Renard, K.G., Foster, G.R., Weesies, G.A., Porter, J.P.: RUSLE: revised universal soil loss equation. J. Soil Water Conserv. **46**(1), 30–33 (1991)
26. Richards, G.D.: A general mathematical framework for modeling two-dimensional wildland fire spread. Int. J. Wildland Fire **5**(2), 63–72 (1995)
27. Shakesby, R.A.: Post-wildfire soil erosion in the Mediterranean: review and future research directions. Earth Sci. Rev. **105**(3–4), 71–100 (2011)
28. Sorriso-Valvo, M., Bryan, R.B., Yair, A., Iovino, F., Antronico, L.: Impact of afforestation on hydrological response and sediment production in a small Calabrian catchment. CATENA **25**(1–4), 89–104 (1995)
29. Surfleet, C.G., Ziemer, R.R.: Effects of forest harvesting on large organic debris in coastal streams. In: LeBlanc, J. (ed.) Conference on Coast Redwood Forest Ecology and Management, 18–20 June 1996, Arcata, California. Humboldt State University, pp. 134–136 (1996)
30. Terranova, O., Antronico, L., Coscarelli, R., Iaquinta, P.: Soil erosion risk scenarios in the Mediterranean environment using RUSLE and GIS: an application model for Calabria (southern Italy). Geomorphology **112**(3–4), 228–245 (2009)
31. Wischmeier, W.H., Smith, D.D.: Predicting rainfall erosion losses - a guide for conservation planning. U.S. Department of Agriculture, Agriculture Handbook No 537, p. 58, Hyattsville (MD) (1978)

A Mobile Small Sized Device for Air Pollutants Monitoring Connected to the Smart Road: Preliminary Results

Stefano Chiesa[1], Maurizio Pollino[2,3], and Sergio Taraglio[1](✉)

[1] Robotics Laboratory, ENEA, Rome, Italy
{stefano.chiesa,sergio.taraglio}@enea.it

[2] Analysis and Protection of Critical Infrastructures Laboratory, ENEA, Rome, Italy
maurizio.pollino@enea.it

[3] EISAC.it, Italian Node of the European Infrastructure Simulation and Analysis Centre, Rome, Italy

Abstract. The work in progress on a small sized air pollution monitoring system mountable on board urban vehicles is described. The system exchanges data exploiting a "Smart Road" infrastructure with a central computing facility, the Smart City Platform, a GIS-based Decision Support System designed to perform real time monitoring and interpolation of data with the aim of possibly issuing alarms with respect to different town areas. Early experimental data gathering in the Rome urban area and subsequent spline interpolation processing are presented. Thus, air pollutants distribution maps have been produced. Finally, protocols for data exchange have been designed. Work is in progress on algorithms for data fusion among different monitoring systems and interpolation of data for a geographically denser map.

Keywords: Air pollution · Smart Road · Monitoring · Mapping

1 Introduction

Human health is adversely affected by the exposure to air pollutants with chronic and long-term ailments ranging from upper respiratory irritation to deadly morbidity such as lung cancer or heart diseases [1]. The underlining cause is represented by the ever increasing energy consumption: most of it is still in the form of fossil fuels burning. This produces huge amounts of carbon dioxide (CO_2) contributing to the global warming of our planet, but, at the same time, it outputs a series of air pollutants of direct and harmful influence on human health: carbon monoxide (CO), sulphur dioxide (SO_2), nitrogen oxides (NO_x) and particulate matters of several sizes (PM_1, $PM_{2.5}$ and PM_{10}). In addition, long term exposure has been linked to premature mortality [2].

This problem has been tackled at a legislative level with the installation of monitoring systems in urban areas. Current systems are usually sparsely distributed in the urban area with a very low spatial resolution: in the area of Rome there are 13 monitoring stations,

O. Gervasi et al. (Eds.): ICCSA 2020, LNCS 12253, pp. 517–525, 2020.
https://doi.org/10.1007/978-3-030-58814-4_37

managed by ARPA Lazio environmental agency [3], of which 10 are inside the GRA ("Grande Raccordo Anulare", the beltway around the town). If an average radius of 9 km is considered for the GRA, it means that each station covers a surface of 25 km^2, if evenly distributed. If the whole surface of the municipality is considered (1,285 km^2), and all the available systems, this figure rises to 99 km^2. The situation is similar in most large towns around the world, e.g. in Beijing there are 22 stations each covering 113 km^2, in London 14 stations each covering 112 km^2 [4].

The sparseness of the data has had as a consequence the need for estimates of the pollutants in unmeasured areas using a variety of methods, e.g. spatial averaging, nearest neighbour, Inverse Distance Weighting (IDW), Spline interpolation, Kriging, Land-Use Regression (LUR) modelling, dispersion modelling, neural networks, etc. [4].

In recent years the availability of smaller pollution sensing devices and of the Global Navigation Satellite System (GNSS) has opened the way for small size mobile systems for the monitoring of air pollutants [5]. This increases the density of measurements, yet it does not solve the sparseness problem, since the mobile measurements are usually performed along the streets or in specific areas. In order to have a larger view, the same methods previously developed for interpolation of data of monitoring stations have been applied also in the case of mobile air pollution data [4].

The aim of this paper is to briefly describe the work in progress on an air pollutant monitoring system based on a mobile small sized device which can be carried by vehicles in the urban area: private cars, mass transport buses, service vehicles. The system is directly interfaced with an intelligent infrastructure, namely a "Smart Road", which relays the data to a central computing facility which can perform a real time monitoring and interpolation of data, possibly issuing alarms with respect to different areas of the town.

In Sect. 2 it is described the Smart Road infrastructure and its features and capabilities together with its use in the present scenario. In Sect. 3 the monitoring unit is described. In Sect. 4 some examples of data collection/exchange and interpolation processing are given together with a comparison with the actual data from the available fixed monitoring systems. In the last section the conclusions and comments are given with the direction towards which further work is foreseen.

2 The Smart Road

The Smart Road is a rather *fuzzy* concept which has gained the limelight in recent years together with its companions: Smart City, Smart District, Smart Building, Smart Home. They all describe the concept of pervasive computing: all the parts of the nowadays life can be made *smart* with the help of some processing power, communication and, above all, data. The trigger (and effect) of this smart wave is the so-called Internet of Things (IoT), i.e. the possibility to equip nearly every electronic device with communication and elaborative powers, together with an ever decreasing cost of computing power and storage memory. The Smart Road concept has been instantiated and implemented in different ways in different places, but it is intimately linked to the Intelligent Transportation System (ITS) framework [6]. The idea is that transport and mobility must be reconsidered as an integrated and above all dynamic system where control, information and management operate synergistically and synchronously [7].

For example, in Sweden the Smart Road is considered as an infrastructure able to recharge electric vehicles while they are moving in it [8, 9]. In Italy the main road administrator, ANAS (https://www.stradeanas.it/en), is currently making smart some sections of the Italian road network with an approach centred on the safety of the journey. They are equipping road-side street lights with sensors and with a wireless network to communicate with cars and passengers for traffic related warnings and to monitor road status [10].

ENEA is currently involved in a project to set up an experimental Smart Road in order to study applications and solutions for a better quality of life and energy saving. The basic architecture is shown in Fig. 1. Through the communication network of the roadside lamps, the electric/autonomous vehicle is able to dialog with the Smart City computing centre. In one direction the vehicle furnishes data gained with proprioceptive sensors (e.g. position, speed, battery charge, etc.) or exteroceptive ones (e.g. air temperature, pollution, road surface conditions, etc.) acting as a sort of mobile sensor device. In the other direction the vehicle may receive from the computing centre relevant information which it cannot directly and locally access: e.g. an alarm condition on the future path to be followed or a meteorological alert of any kind. In addition, the vehicle can receive instructions concerning its recharging, e.g. where and when, compatible with the overall status of the electrical grid and the wishes of the vehicle itself, such as being near to the trip destination.

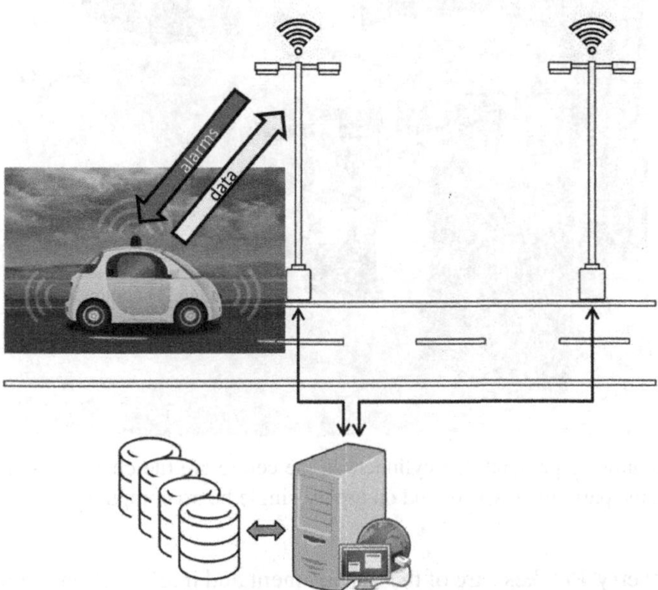

Fig. 1. The Smart Road architecture

The Smart Road aspect of interest in this work is that of air pollutants monitoring. The idea is that some vehicles in the town are equipped with a mobile air pollutant monitoring system. This system checks some chemicals with a given frequency and then transmits back the data to the central facility. The prototype system envisaged is small and light and can be conceivably mounted on almost any vehicle, however it may be mounted chiefly on mass transit buses or other service vehicles of the municipality. The central computing facility gathers data from the different mobile systems and interpolates data both spatially and temporally, greatly increasing the real time awareness of the pollution situation in the town.

3 The Monitoring System

The monitoring system is shown in Fig. 2. It is capable of detecting SO_2, CO, NO, NO_2, volatile organic compounds (VOC), O_3 and particulates in the three values of PM_1, $PM_{2.5}$ and PM_{10} and some atmospheric physical parameters such as temperature, humidity and pressure. At the same time, it is equipped with a GPS sensor, thus yielding georeferenced values. Table 1 lists the sensors on board the device.

In Fig. 2 it is possible to see the sensors sensitive to the individual chemical species (the cylinders in the centre of the image), the particulate sensor (the black box on the left) and above the chemical sensors the control and management electronic card based on the single-board computer Raspberry-Pi.

Fig. 2. Air monitoring payload: the cylinders in the centre are the chemical sensors, the black box on the left the particulate sensor and on top the single board computer

The Raspberry-Pi takes care of the management and interrogation of the sensors and provides the data to the Smart Road system via a WiFi internet connection, implementing a web service, which can be remotely accessed. The size of the device is about 10 × 17 × 9 cm, with a weight of around 500 g, it needs a power source in the range 7–36 V and a power of about 3 W.

The unit, mounted on the vehicle, will provide the intelligent infrastructure with georeferenced chemical and atmospheric concentration data with a given frequency,

Table 1. Air pollution sensors

Chemical	Model	Technology	Range
CO	DDScientific - GS+4CO	Electrochemical	0–2000 ppm
SO_2	SO2 4S CiTiceL	Electrochemical	0–20 ppm
VOC	Figaro TGS8100	Semiconductor	1–30 ppm (H2)
O_3	Alphasense OX-A431	Electrochemical	0–20 ppm
NO	DDScientific - GS+4NO	Electrochemical	0–250 ppm
NO_2	DDScientific - GS+4NO2	Electrochemical	0–30 ppm
Particulate	Alphasense OPC-N2	Optical	0.38÷17 μm

presently estimated in the order of once every few seconds in order not to saturate the available bandwidth.

4 Early Experimental Data Processing

4.1 Data Collection

Some experimental data collection has been performed mounting the system on the roof of a vehicle and driving it in the town of Rome. Two different modes of operation have been tested. In the first one (February 19, 2020, 11:00 AM) it has been followed a path in the neighbourhood of one of the fixed air pollution analyzers placed by the ARPA Lazio [11]. In the second (February 19, 2020, 11:25 AM) the route of a mass transport bus has been followed.

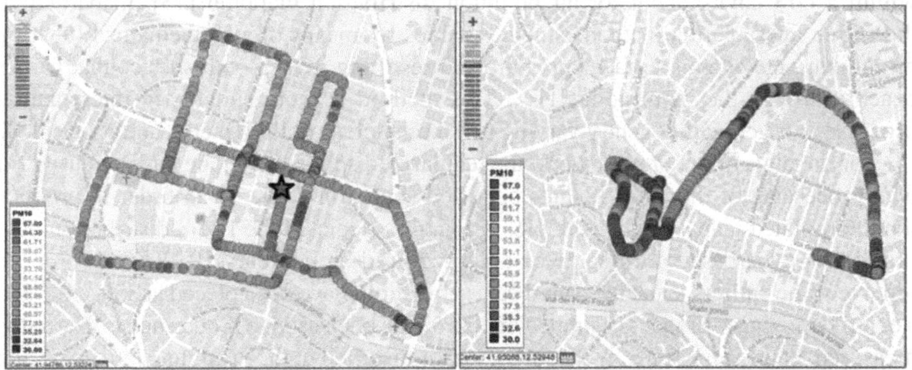

Fig. 3. Left: the collection of PM_{10} data in the neighbourhood of one of the fixed municipal monitoring systems (red star); right: the collection of PM_{10} following the route of bus n. 349

In the first mode the system has monitored a relatively small area with a relatively large number of samples. The idea was to simulate the contribution of many different air monitors installed on board several different cars. In addition, the location has been chosen such that there is a ground truth for the chemicals provided by the above-mentioned monitoring station ("Bufalotta" [11]). The second mode is intended to simulate the case in which the system equips a mass transit bus. In order to have a simulation very comparable to a real recording, the vehicle has followed a bus along its route, stopping behind it at every bus stop.

In Fig. 3 are shown the two examples of experimental data recording: on the left the collection of experimental data in the neighbourhood of the fixed municipal monitoring system, on the right a part of the route of a mass transit bus in the same neighbourhood. Both the displayed graphs are relative to the PM_{10} measurement in a northern semi peripheral part of Rome, as an example. The same type of graph can be provided for any of the on-board sensors.

4.2 Data Processing and Integration

The Smart Road conceived in the present work will allow the dialogue between a Smart City Platform (SCP, i.e. a suitable application to manage urban data, provide services and support local authorities) and the vehicles circulating in it. To this end, the system has been designed to send, in one direction, data collected from the vehicle to the SCP and, in the other, to provide alert messages or other information services. All these data can be managed in the SCP by means of a GIS-based Spatial Decision Support System (SDSS) [12]. Thus, the values recorded during the experimental activity have been processed in GIS environment with the aim of mapping the spatial distribution of air pollutants within the area of interest and sharing this information by means of the SCP.

All the data acquired by the vehicles are sent to the SDSS to be ingested and interpolated. Given the heterogeneity of the data, an exchange format based on JSON (JavaScript Object Notation) has been adopted.

Several techniques of spatial interpolation (IDW, spline, Kriging, etc.) can be used within a GIS environment for air pollution distribution mapping [13]. In particular, the spline interpolation method estimates values by means of a mathematical function minimizing the overall surface curvature and resulting in a smooth surface that passes exactly through the input points [14]. This method is more suitable in interpolation processes for generating gently varying surfaces such as pollution concentrations [15].

For the aims of the present work, the regularized spline technique has been used for data processing of the air pollutants collected (listed in Table 1), in order to produce the interpolated maps. As an example, in Fig. 4 is depicted the PM_{10} distribution map produced on the basis of the sample points acquired on February 19, 2020. In order to remove some outliers in the measured data a threshold have been placed at 80 $\mu g/m^3$ and a centred moving average, of sample window 5, has been used to reduce noise. The value measured, at the same time, by the PM_{10} sensor installed in the "Bufalotta" fixed station was 37 $\mu g/m^3$ (legal limit according to the Italian legislation: 40 $\mu g/m^3$). The official PM_{10} data from the fixed stations is posted just once a day as a daily average, thus the comparison is only indicative. According to the recent historical data [3], during the first six months of 2020 the PM_{10} exceeded 22 times the legal limit [16], notwithstanding the lockdown due to the Covid-19 emergency. For this reason, it is opportune to monitor it and analyse the relative trends and behaviour.

Fig. 4. PM_{10} distribution map: interpolation from data acquired (February 19, 2020) in the neighbourhood of a monitoring station ("Bufalotta") and following the route of bus n. 349

Finally, all the interpolated maps produced for the various pollutant values collected by the vehicles (in different times) can be integrated within the SDSS: here it is also possible to perform additional spatial analysis, by overlapping the pollutant distribution maps with other information layers about the urban area considered (e.g. meteo-climatic data, traffic conditions, etc.)

5 Discussion, Conclusions and Future Work

The central idea presented in this work concerns the availability of a much larger dataset than what presently available and in near real time, gathered with lightweight and small mobile monitoring systems. In many fields of application, the availability of a large quantity of data, even if of a lower quality, yields a non trivial contribution to the description of a state. The concept of data fusion in many different fields of application is an example of this approach: to estimate a measurement several different sensors of different characteristics and precisions can be exploited, all contributing in different degree to the final value [17].

Here a large number of experimental points sampled by several vehicles is a wealth not to be disregarded, even if the quality of the data is far from being optimal. The here employed low cost chemical sensors are usually affected by diverse sources of error [18]. Basically, they should be periodically calibrated. In the operative conditions envisaged, the monitoring system is placed on a bus or on a private car. Possibly, in the first case, a scheduled maintenance by the mass transit operator may be set up, but, in the second one, the calibration would be entrusted to the single citizen with a probably much worse result. A further problem is that of the measure itself on a vehicle, the reference data from static monitoring systems is not affected by any air flow, the data on a vehicle is clearly variable with the air flow due to the vehicle speed. This should be at least coarsely modelled in order to have better measurements.

Further work should be directed towards the integration and interpolation algorithms. On one side, a strategy to estimate the reliability of the data coming from the various mobile monitoring system should be set up on the basis of the characteristics of the single measuring system (e.g. time from last calibration, use, location, etc.). On the other, algorithms for data fusion are to be studied to fuse together data coming from different monitoring systems, static and mobile, and performing geographical interpolation, algorithm possibly based on Kalman filtering or neural networks, see e.g. [19, 20].

In this work the general setup of an air pollution monitoring system has been presented. The system is based on the use of light and small mobile monitoring devices able to yield in real time georeferenced pollution data through an intelligent infrastructure, the Smart Road. Some experimental tests to collect data in the town of Rome and some first experiments on data interpolation and exchange have been performed. Further work is in progress on the side of strategies and algorithms for the fusion of data coming from different monitoring systems and interpolation of data for a geographically denser map to be shared by means of the SDSS application.

Acknowledgements. This work has been partly carried out in the framework of the Triennial Plan 2019–2021 of the National Research on the Electrical System (*Piano Triennale 2019–2021 della Ricerca di sistema elettrico nazionale*), funded by the Italian Ministry of Economic Development.

References

1. Raaschou-Nielsen, O., et al.: Air pollution and lung cancer incidence in 17 European cohorts: prospective analyses from the European Study of Cohorts for Air Pollution Effects (ESCAPE). Lancet Oncol. **14**(9), 813–822 (2013)
2. European Commission: Material for Clean Air. European Commission, Brussels (2017)
3. ARPA Lazio (Agenzia Regionale per la Protezione Ambientale della Regione Lazio). http://www.arpalazio.gov.it/. Accessed 28 Feb 2020
4. Xie, X., et al.: A review of urban air pollution monitoring and exposure assessment methods. ISPRS Int. J. Geo-Inf. **6**(12), 389 (2017). https://doi.org/10.3390/ijgi6120389
5. Minet, L., Liu, R., Valois, M.-F., Xu, J., Weichenthal, S., Hatzopoulou, M.: Development and comparison of air pollution exposure surfaces derived from on-road mobile monitoring and short-term stationary sidewalk measurements. Environ. Sci. Technol. **52**(6), 3512–3519 (2018). https://doi.org/10.1021/acs.est.7b05059
6. Giannopoulos, G.A., Mitsakis, E., Salanova, J.M.: Overview of Intelligent Transport Systems (ITS) developments in and across transport modes. JRC Scientific and Policy Reports. Publications Office of the European Union, Luxembourg (2012). https://doi.org/10.2788/12881
7. Directive 2010/40/EU of the European Parliament and of the Council of 7 July 2010 (2010)
8. Smart Road "eRoadArlanda". https://eroadarlanda.se/. Accessed 24 Feb 2020
9. Smart Road "Gotland". https://www.smartroadgotland.com/. Accessed 24 Feb 2020

10. ANAS S.p.A.: Direzione Operation e Coordinamento Territoriale Infrastruttura Tecnologica e Impianti: SMART ROAD "La strada all'avanguardia che corre con il progresso". ANAS, Rome (2018). (in Italian)
11. ARPA Lazio: Bufalotta monitoring station. http://193.206.192.215/web/sh_cm.ricerca%3fp_staz%3d1205884 Accessed 28 Feb 2020
12. Taraglio, S., et al.: Decision Support System for smart urban management: resilience against natural phenomena and aerial environmental assessment. Int. J. Sustain. Energy Plan. Manag. **24**, 135–146 (2019). https://doi.org/10.5278/ijsepm.3338
13. Li, J., Heap, A.: A review of comparative studies of spatial interpolation methods in environmental sciences: performance and impact factors. Ecol. Inform. **6**, 228–241 (2011)
14. Greiner, H.: A survey on univariate data interpolation and approximation by splines of given shape. Math. Comput. Model. **15**(10), 97–108 (1991)
15. Kumar, A., Gupta, I., Brandt, J., Kumar, R., Dikshit, A.K., Patil, R.S.: Air quality mapping using GIS and economic evaluation of health impact for Mumbai City, India. J. Air Waste Manag. Assoc. **66**(5), 470–481 (2016)
16. ARPA Lazio (Agenzia Regionale per la Protezione Ambientale della Regione Lazio), PM_{10} measurements. http://www.arpalazio.net/main/aria/sci/qa/misure/PM10.php. Accessed 09 June 2020
17. Durrant-Whyte, H.: Multi sensor data fusion. Australian Centre for Field Robotics, The University of Sydney, NSW, Australia (2001)
18. Castell, N., et al.: Can commercial low-cost sensor platforms contribute to air quality monitoring and exposure estimates? Environ. Int. **99**, 293–302 (2017). https://doi.org/10.1016/j.envint.2016.12.007
19. Bertino, L., Evensen, G., Wackernagel, H.H.: Sequential data assimilation techniques in oceanography. Int. Stat. Rev. **71**(2), 223–241 (2003). https://doi.org/10.1111/j.1751-5823.2003.tb00194.x
20. Schneider, P., Castell, N., Vogt, M., Dauge, F.R., Lahoz, W.A., Bartonova, A.: Mapping urban air quality in near real-time using observations from low-cost sensors and model information. Environ. Int. **106**, 234–247 (2017). https://doi.org/10.1016/j.envint.2017.05.005

Using Google Trends, Gaussian Mixture Models and DBSCAN for the Estimation of Twitter User Home Location

Paola Zola[1(✉)], Paulo Cortez[2], and Maurizio Tesconi[1]

[1] Institute for Informatics and Telematics (IIT) of the National Research Council of Italy (CNR), Pisa, Italy
{paola.zola,maurizio.tesconi}@iit.cnr.it

[2] ALGORITMI Centre, Department of Information Systems, University of Minho, 4804-533 Guimarães, Portugal
pcortez@dsi.uminho.pt

Abstract. In this work we propose a novel approach to estimate the home location of Twitter users. Given a list of Twitter users, we extract their timelines (up to 3,200) using the Twitter Application Programming Interface (API) service. We use Google Trends to obtain a list of cities in which the nouns of a specific Twitter user are more popular. Then, based on word popularity, we sample the geographical coordinates (latitude, longitude) over all the world surface. Finally, the Gaussian Mixture Model and the DBSCAN clustering algorithms are implemented to estimate the users' geographic coordinates. The results are evaluated using the mean and median error computed on the Haversine distance. Competitive findings are achieved when compared with a baseline approach that estimated the users' location given the Google Trends city mode.

Keywords: Geostatistics · Gaussian Mixture Models · DBSCAN · Twitter · Google Trends

1 Introduction

Inferring Twitter users home location is a growing interest research topic given its importance for many real-world applications. For example, knowing the location of people is fundamental in event detection studies, recommendation systems, health care support systems, friendship network analysis and so on [3,4].

Assign a location to Twitter users based on their message contents is a non-trivial task. In fact, only a few percentage of tweet is geotagged [9] and users often do not add reliable information to their profile information. Research studies addressing the geolocation problem either apply unsupervised (i.e., based on text location dictionaries) or supervised approaches (i.e., models trained on a sample of geotagged tweets).

Differently, in this work, we propose a novel unsupervised learning tool aiming to infer Twitter users home location at coordinate-level that is based on Google

O. Gervasi et al. (Eds.): ICCSA 2020, LNCS 12253, pp. 526–534, 2020.
https://doi.org/10.1007/978-3-030-58814-4_38

Trends engine. The proposed approach exploits our previous work [11], where Google Trends (GT) was used to assign the home Country to Twitter accounts. The algorithm proposed in [11] firstly collected the users timelines to extract all nouns. The nouns collection, for each account, was then fetched to GT in order to determine the user's most probable country. In this paper we extend the GT applicability to a more fine grain location estimation level. In particular, we aim to assign to each Twitter account her home location in terms of geographic coordinates (latitude, longitude). The experiment are conducted on a dataset composed by 2,880 Twitter accounts with a verified location, and, for each user we consider all historical messages (up to 3,200 tweets). For each account, we extract the GT cities distribution passing, as keyword, the nouns (generic and proper) hold in the tweets collection. Having the cities distribution, we convert it on a synthetic world surface based on city polygon areas that respects the GT distribution. Then, the geographic sampled data points are used to fit two clustering algorithms: Gaussian Mixture Models (GMM) and the Density Based Spatial Clustering of Applications with Noise (DBSCAN).

The results are evaluated using mean and median absolute error computed on the Haversine distance from the ground truth users home location. The paper is organized as follows: Sect. 2 an overview of previous work about Twitter geolocation is proposed, then in Sect. 3 the proposed approach is explained and in Sect. 4 discusses the obtained results. Finally, Sect. 5 concludes the paper.

2 Overview on Twitter User Location Estimation

Approaches for social media users geolocation might be distinguish in two classes: word distribution (WD) and social network (SN) based. The first group (WD) analyzes the texts content identifying location indicative words (LIW) and/or using specific dictionaries for location entity recognition [8,9]. However, as argued in [8], focusing only on LIW and specific place mentions can discard important information linked to generic nouns. Users geolocation methods based on friendship social networks (SN) exploits users social interactions in order to infer the unknown location. A hybrid approach that merges WD and SN has been implemented in [2].

Focusing on WD approaches, which includes also our proposed method, initial studies mainly apply traditional natural language processing techniques [8], while recent researches adopt machine learning techniques [10]. Another feature to be considered is the location estimation granularity. In fact, previous works either focus on specific regions/countries [2,8] providing a street or coordinate level estimation or considered the entire world surface but predicting only the users' country [10,11]. Differently, in this work we apply clustering algorithms to assign to each user a probability distribution over the whole world map in order to estimate an unique point associated with the user home location.

3 Proposed Approach

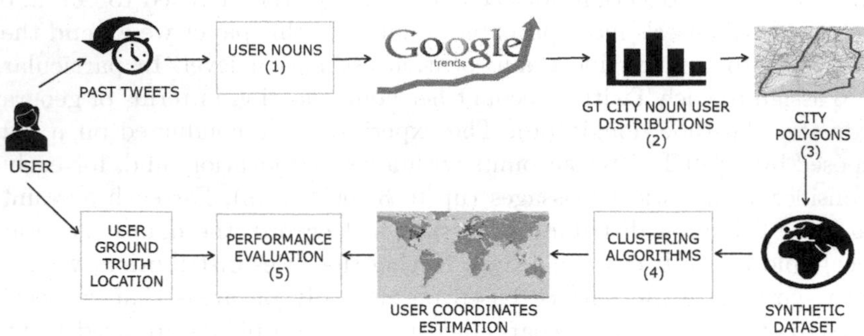

Fig. 1. Proposed approach

The proposed approach, which follows the one adopted in [11], is depicted in Fig. 1. The proposed algorithm is composed by five steps and it uses only tweet nouns assuming that they are the most representative part of speech able to identify different countries [8]. For user u, the proposed approach works by first identifying the sequence of all nouns $\mathbf{n}_u = \langle n_1, n_2, ..., n_{l_u} \rangle$ (phase (1) in Fig. 1). To obtain $\mathbf{n}_u$, the tweets are first preprocessed by transforming the text to lowercase and removing English stop words. For each noun $n_i \in \mathbf{n}_u$, a GT query is executed by using the `Pytrends` Python module. The GT query results for noun n_i is a sequence with integers confidence scores for the most frequent cities C that have typed the specific noun $n_i \in \mathbf{n}_u$ (phase (2) in Fig. 1).

Denoting C_u as the city distribution for a given user given all her nouns, we first locate these cities on the world surface, generating then samples of GT geographic data points that are used to fit a clustering model, with the final user location being estimated as the centroid of the largest cluster. To perform this operation, we computed the polygon areas $p(c)$ for all cities $c \in C$. The $p(c)$ is defined as a two-dimensional polygon where the edges correspond to the physical borders of the city c. The aim is to uniformly sample a certain number of two-dimensional points (latitude and longitude) in the city polygon representing the GT integer confidence scores generated for each city (phase (3) in Fig. 1). To obtain the cities polygons we downloaded the data from OpenStreetMap website[1]. If the specific $i-th$ city is not available on OpenStreetMap dataset we derived, as a proxy of the city polygon, the city surface built around the city centre coordinates. Given the coordinates of the $i-th$ city center, the circumference is computed considering a the radius equal to $r = \sqrt{\frac{A}{\pi}}$ where A correspond to the city area. The city centre coordinates (latitude and longitude)

[1] http://www.openstreetmap.org.

are derived from Wikidata[2]. The developed Python library for the city polygon definition is freely available on GitHub[3].

Once all city polygons are computed, we sample a finite number of points from each city polygons such that the GT data distribution is respected (e.g., there will be more points inside New York if the associated GT noun global scores are higher). The obtained GT noun city sampled geographic data points are then used to fit a clustering model (one for each user). Finally, the user location is estimated as the centroid of the largest cluster (phase (4) in Fig. 1).

In this paper we consider the GMM and the DBSCAN algorithms. The optimal number of clusters for the GMM is evaluated with the Bayesian Information Criteria (BIC). Moreover, we experimented different values associated with the maximum number of cluster in the model ranging in {5,10,20,30,50}, in order to evaluate how the algorithm performance changes given this parameter. For the DBSCAN algorithm we used the default parameters of `sklearn` Python module.

3.1 Clustering Algorithms

Gaussian Mixture Models (GMM) is a probabilistic model to represent the distribution of a population as a linear combination of Gaussian [1]. Usually, each Gaussian k in the GMM is called component. If each component in the mixture is interpreted as a cluster of the dataset then the GMM can be seen as a unsupervised learning algorithm for classification. Let's define K as the number of components in the GMM, α_k as the weight of the kth component, $\boldsymbol{\mu}_k$ and Σ_k the location and the scale parameter of the component k, then the GMM model for the random variable X has the following distribution:

$$p(X) = \sum_{k=1}^{K} \alpha_k \mathcal{N}(X|\boldsymbol{\mu}_k, \Sigma_k) \tag{1}$$

where $\sum_{k=1}^{K} \alpha_k = 1$.

The estimation is performed with the Expectation Maximization Algorithm (EM), an iterative procedure which alternates the computation of the expectation of the likelihood (E-step) with the maximization of the expectation of the likelihood (M-step) up to convergence. The only parameter that needs to be fixed in a GMM is the number of clusters K. In this work, we select the best K value according to the Bayesian Information Criterion (BIC) as performed in [2].

DBSCAN (Density Based Spatial Clustering of Applications with Noise) is a density based algorithm to cluster data in the presence of noise. It is particularly good in discovering clusters of arbitrary shape [6]. The intuition behind the DBSCAN is that relevant clusters should have a higher point density when compared with noise. Thus, isolated points are considered noise, while regions with

[2] https://www.wikidata.org/wiki/Wikidata:Main_Page.

[3] https://github.com/CostRagno/geopolygon.

an high density of points are considered clusters. Let's define $\boldsymbol{x}_i$, a threshold ϵ, D_i as the region of size ϵ centred in $\boldsymbol{x}_i$ and $dist(\boldsymbol{x}_i, \boldsymbol{x}_j)$ as a distance measure between two points. Then, the Eps-neighbourhood N_ϵ of $\boldsymbol{x}_i$ results:

$$N_\epsilon(\boldsymbol{x}_i) = \{\boldsymbol{x}_j \in D_i | dist(\boldsymbol{x}_i, \boldsymbol{x}_j) < \epsilon\}. \tag{2}$$

The DBSCAN algorithm is based on four main concepts:

- the point $\boldsymbol{x}_i$ is a core point if $\#N_\epsilon(\boldsymbol{x}_i) > N$, where N is the minimum number of points to consider a point as core point;
- the point $\boldsymbol{x}_j$ is directly density-reachable from $\boldsymbol{x}_i$ if point $\boldsymbol{x}_j \in N_\epsilon(\boldsymbol{x}_i)$ and $\#N_\epsilon(\boldsymbol{x}_i) > N$;
- the point $\boldsymbol{x}_j$ is density-reachable if there is a chain of points $\boldsymbol{x}_j, \boldsymbol{x}_{j+1} \ldots, \boldsymbol{x}_i$ such that $\boldsymbol{x}_{j+1}$ is directly-density reachable from $\boldsymbol{x}_j$;
- all points not reachable are considered noise.

Note that if the point $\boldsymbol{x}_i$ is reachable but $\#N_\epsilon(\boldsymbol{x}_i) < N$, then it is called a border point. The DBSCAN evaluates all the points in a dataset and it considers as part of a cluster all the reachable.

3.2 Evaluation

We assume a pure unsupervised learning approach, with no ground truth location data being used by the clustering methods during the estimation of the user location. Thus, the ground truth data is only used as an external attribute during the evaluation phase, for validation purposes, allowing to compute absolute error distances (phase (5) in Fig. 1). In particular, we adopt the Mean Absolute Error (MAE) and the Median Absolute Error (MdAE) on the Haversine distance measures expressed in Kilometres as proposed in [5]. The Haversine formula measures the great-circle distance between two points on a sphere given their longitudes and latitudes. The great-circle distance is the shortest distance between two points on the surface. Moreover, for comparison purposes, we computed as a baseline method the simple city mode for each user, given her GT cities distribution, extracting the city center coordinates.

4 Data and Results

4.1 Data

The dataset was collected between January and February 2018 and it is composed by 2,880 Twitter Users with a verified home location. The information regarding the ground truth country are based on a double check system that matched the metadata information (the address provided by the user in her Twitter account) and the analysis of location indicative words (LIW) given the historical tweets for each account [11]. The original dataset, freely available on GitHub[4], is composed by 3,298 accounts but, in this work, we keep only the

[4] https://github.com/paolazola/Twitter-country-geolocation.

accounts still available removing the suspended and deleted ones. For each Twitter user we then collected her timeline up to 3,200 according to the Twitter API restriction.

4.2 Experiment Results

We performed the GT query search for all 2,880 users according to the nouns extracted from their timelines. For each user, the performed queries resulted in a city distribution from which we sampled random data respecting the GT queries distribution. Then, the iterative procedure described in Sect. 3 is performed for GMM, with maximum number of clusters within the set {5,10,20,30,50}, and for the DBSCAN algorithm, until a unique location (pair of latitude and longitude) is extracted. Table 1 reports the MAE and MdAE values, expressed in kilometres (km), computed between the user home location estimated with different configurations of GMM and DBSCAN with respect to the ground truth. Moreover, Table 1 also shows the MAE and MdAE values obtained by the baseline method. From the results in Table 1 it is possible to notice two main aspects. The first one is that the best configuration of the GMM is the one with maximum number of cluster equal to 10. The second one is that if the MAE is considered, the GMM ($k = 10$) is the best model, while the best MdAE is achieved by DBSCAN. However, both models (GMM with $k = 10$ and DBSCAN) overperform the baseline for both MAE and MdAE distance measures. In particular, the MdAE of DBSCAN is $1,000$ km less than the MdAE of the baseline, denoting the competitive performance of the proposed approach. We also present an example of the user home location estimation for the GMM ($k = 10$) and the DBSCAN (Fig. 2). Figure 2 reports an example of corrected estimated user; the real user location is London and both GMM (k = 10) and DBSCAN derive the final estimation point with latitude $51.507, 51.500$ and longitude $-0.127, -0.144$ respectively for GMM (k = 10) and DBSCAN.

Table 1. Models results in terms of MAE and MdAE. The bold notation underlines the best models. The k in the GMM corresponds to the maximum number of clusters.

Model	MAE (km)	MdAE (km)
GMM (k = 5)	4582.34	2035.39
GMM (k = 10)	**4359.05**	1759.40
GMM (k = 20)	4796.14	2206.07
GMM (k = 30)	4806.32	2230.69
GMM (k = 50)	5143.23	3503.95
DBSCAN	4484.16	**1737.58**
Baseline	5326.58	2770.89

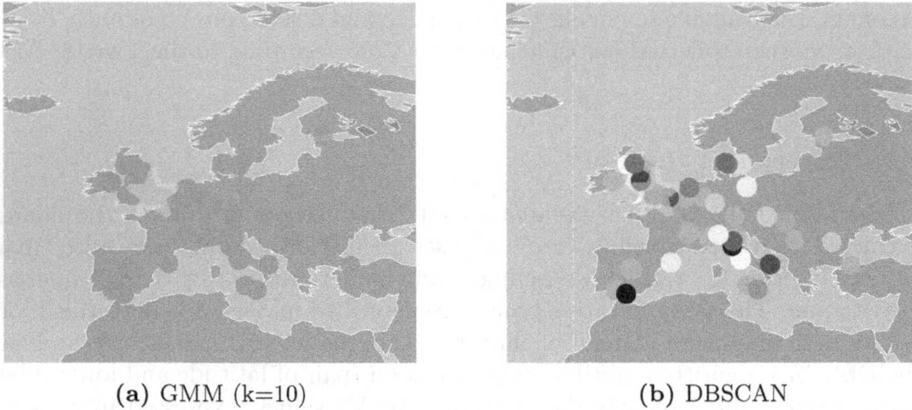

(a) GMM (k=10) (b) DBSCAN

Fig. 2. GMM (k = 10) and DBSCAN home location estimation for User#1. The different colours represent different clusters while the yellow star represents the true user location. In this case User#1 is from London and both DBSCAN and GMM (k = 10) predicted the correct location. (Color figure online)

Moreover, we have analyzed the distribution of the Haversine distance between the true location and the estimated points, revealing that some users are correctly located with an error of just few meters, while for others the estimation error is huge. In particular, we noticed that the largest location estimation errors are frequent among anglophone countries. In particular, Australian users are often estimated as if belonging to the United States. We highlight that this phenomenon, difficulty of anglophone country identification, is well known in the geolocation research field [7]. The estimation errors that involves Australia/New Zealand and United States might be related with the low population density in the Oceania continent, which results in a lower number of Australian cities from GT queries. Regarding this phenomenon, we noticed that DBSCAN performed better in clustering anglophone users. We report an example of this in Fig. 3, where the GMM ($k = 10$) predicted the user home location of User#2 in Chicago, United States while her home location is in Adelaide, Australia. For the same user, the DBSCAN model correctly predict the user home location in Adelaide, Australia. While interesting results were achieved for DBSCAN (in terms of MdAE values), we note that the algorithm was set with the default `sklearn` Python module parameters: ϵ equal to 0.5 and N equal to 5. Nevertheless, a deeper analysis of the DBSCAN hyperparameters will be analyzed in future works.

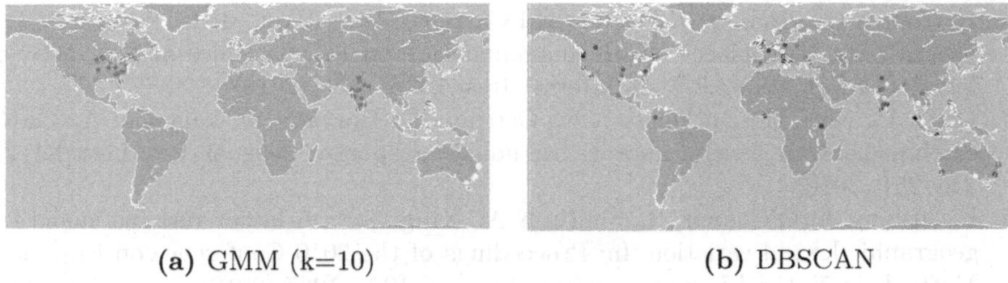

(a) GMM (k=10) (b) DBSCAN

Fig. 3. GMM ($k = 10$) and DBSCAN home location estimation for User#2. The different colours represent different clusters while the yellow star represents the true user location. In this case User#2 is from Adelaide. The GMM ($k = 10$) incorrectly predicted the user home location in United States while the DBSCAN predicted the correct location. (Color figure online)

5 Conclusions

Inferring Twitter user geolocation using only written texts is a challenging task that is fundamental for many social media analytics (e.g., event detection analysis, recommendation systems). Indeed, several works have addressed this task (e.g., [5]), but often these studies focus on a small world region, requiring geotagged labels to train supervised learning methods or rigid geographic dictionaries (LIW). In this work, we propose a novel method to infer Twitter users location considering the world surface using a pure textual based approach. The proposed approach is based on Google Trends (GT) city distributions associated with Twitter user nouns, which are used to fit clustering algorithms, namely GMM and DBSCAN. The aim of this work is to offer a valid and flexible method for users geolocation that can be applied to any language and do not rely on simple LIW. Competitive results were achieved by the clustering methods when compared with a baseline one (GT city mode) that lead the approach to be useful to determine users location for several applications such as marketing campaign and recommendation systems. Nevertheless, further research is needed in order to improve accuracy and reduce anglophone country mismatches (e.g., between Australia and United States of America). In future work, we intend to improve the quality of the proposed geolocation estimation methods by: studying the effect of the tuning of DBSCAN hyperparameters; considering other clustering algorithms (e.g., k-means); and weighting the GT noun city distribution data points with the city population density.

References

1. Banfield, J.D., Raftery, A.E.: Model-based Gaussian and non-Gaussian clustering. Biometrics **49**, 803–821 (1993)
2. Bakerman, J., Pazdernik, K., Wilson, A., Fairchild, G., Bahran, R.: Twitter geolocation: a hybrid approach. ACM Trans. Knowl. Discov. Data (TKDD) **12**(3), 34 (2018). https://doi.org/10.1145/3178112

3. Burton, S.H., Tanner, K.W., Giraud-Carrier, C.G., West, J.H., Barnes, M.D.: "Right time, right place" health communication on Twitter: value and accuracy of location information. J. Med. Internet Res. **14**(6), 156 (2012)
4. Earle, P., Guy, M., Buckmaster, R., Ostrum, C., Horvath, S., Vaughan, A.: OMG earthquake! Can Twitter improve earthquake response? Seismol. Res. Lett. **81**(2), 246–251 (2010)
5. Eisenstein, J., O'Connor, B., Smith, N.A., Xing, E.P.: A latent variable model for geographic lexical variation. In: Proceedings of the 2010 Conference on Empirical Methods in Natural Language Processing, pp. 1277–1287 (2010)
6. Ester, M., Kriegel, H.P., Sander, J., Xu, X., et al.: A density-based algorithm for discovering clusters in large spatial databases with noise. KDD **96**(34), 226–231 (1996)
7. Han, B., Cook, P., Baldwin, T.: Geolocation prediction in social media data by finding location indicative words. In: Proceedings of COLING 2012, pp. 1045–1062 (2012)
8. Middleton, S.E., Middleton, L., Modafferi, S.: Real-time crisis mapping of natural disasters using social media. IEEE Intell. Syst. **29**(2), 9–17 (2013). https://doi.org/10.1109/MIS.2013.126
9. Schulz, A., Hadjakos, A., Paulheim, H., Nachtwey, J., Möhlhäuser, M.: A multi-indicator approach for geolocalization of Tweets. In: Seventh International AAAI Conference on Weblogs and Social Media (2013)
10. Zubiaga, A., Voss, A., Procter, R., Liakata, M., Wang, B., Tsakalidis, A.: Towards real-time, country-level location classification of worldwide Tweets. IEEE Trans. Knowl. Data Eng. **29**(9), 2053–2066 (2017). https://doi.org/10.1109/TKDE.2017.2698463
11. Zola, P., Cortez, P., Carpita, M.: Twitter user geolocation using web country noun searches. Decis. Support Syst. **120**, 50–59 (2019). https://doi.org/10.1016/j.dss.2019.03.006

Lurking Reduction at School Through Virtual Communities of Practice: The Binario 9 ¾ Project

Fabio Sartori[1(✉)], Claudia Maga[1], Barbara Tosi[2], and Alessandro Varallo[2]

[1] DISCO, University of Milano-Bicocca, viale Sarca 336/14, 20126 Milan, Italy
fabio.sartori@unimib.it, c.maga@campus.unimib.it
[2] CSCI - Consorzio Scuola Comunità Impresa, via Ansaldi 4/a, 28100 Novara, NO, Italy
{tosi,varallo}@cscinovara.it

Abstract. The recent COVID-19 emergency has pointed out the importance of distance learning in modern Education. Indeed, although it cannot be considered a substitute of traditional didactic methodologies based on frontal lectures, it can be a valid integration, especially when addressed to those students characterized by learning disturbs and/or cultural barriers. In this paper we present a recent project, namely Binario 9 ¾, where distance learning has been implemented through virtual communities and storytelling adoption, to support impaired students of middle school to bridge the gap with others.

Keywords: Virtual communities of practice · Distance learning · Storytelling · Legitimate peripheral participation

1 Introduction

COVID-19 pandemic has caused the total closure of schools in about 192 world countries; it has been calculated the 91.4% of the total number of students in these countries stayed out of the school[1]. Consequently, distance learning has suddenly become the unique way for them to continue attendance of courses, despite problems in its implementation due to several reasons, from teachers' difficulties to revise their teaching styles to students' and their families' problems in acquiring necessary technological equipment. In Italy, the *educational emergency* originated from the pandemic has seen the arising of spontaneous *communities of practice*, composed of teachers, students and parents involved in the complex task of terminating the current school year.

Brown and Duguid (2001) defined *communities of practice* groups of people sharing knowledge and competencies about a given theme. This notion has been adopted to indicate the spontaneous arising of knowledge centers in organizations with respect to the classical business units clustering. According to Pan and Leidner (2003), CoPs facilitate the development of an environment characterized by *structured informality*. Finally,

[1] United Nations Education Scientific and Cultural Organization (2020). COVID-19 Educational Disruption and Response. Available at: https://en.unesco.org/covid19/educationresponse.

O. Gervasi et al. (Eds.): ICCSA 2020, LNCS 12253, pp. 535–543, 2020.
https://doi.org/10.1007/978-3-030-58814-4_39

the importance of CoP emerges from the fact that knowledge cannot be considered apart from the context where it develops. Every type of knowledge activity implies that *knowledge contributors* as well as *seekers* require a *community* to share general conversation, experimentation and experiences with other people carrying out the same kind of activities. Following these guidelines, two distinct roles emerge in the process of knowledge generation within CoPs: contributors and seekers. The former must be willing to part with their knowledge and share it via a *knowledge management system* (KMS); the latter typically log into the system, type keywords to search, retrieve and examine the results (Sutanto and Jiang 2013).

Indeed, knowledge contributors are *active* entities and knowledge seekers are *passive* entities in the KMS development: the way knowledge is modeled within the system is transparent to the knowledge seeker; he/she is not interested in its modification or maintenance. Indeed, this is a big limitation to the CoP potentialities in developing knowledge models, especially when the CoP is *virtual,* since the principle of *legitimate peripheral participation* (Lave and Wenger 2002) is not satisfied. Legitimate peripheral participation is the key aspect when developing technological solutions for CoPs promotion, aiming at transforming newcomers into contributors rather than passive *lurkers.* Yeow et al. (2006) highlight that lurkers are participants *who persistently refrain from engaging in the core activities that sustain a virtual community.* Arguably, as the perception of both periphery and participation are context-specific, the identification of a behavior as lurking is dependent upon technology constraints and group-specific norms.

In this paper we reflect about the relationship among the three entities above, i.e. knowledge contributors, knowledge seekers and lurkers, in the distance learning scenario. We'll present the methodological issues behind Binario 9 ¾, a project aiming at the support of middle school students characterized by difficulties in learning contents proposed by teachers, mainly due to poor level of inclusion into society. The intervention has allowed to develop a virtual community of practice, made of teachers, tutors and students, where the latter can exploit collections of exercises thought to enable them overcoming their difficulties in understanding concepts. Each lesson has been designed as a story, through which the student ideally moves from her/his initial lurking condition to the knowledge contributor one. The story contents have been validated by teachers involved in the community and, although their use with students has been postponed due to COVID-19 emergency, initial results are encouraging. The rest of the paper is organized as follows: Sect. 2 briefly reviews the literature about virtual communities of practice and storytelling, focusing on Education. Section 3 reflects about legitimate peripheral participation. Section 4 introduces our case study to show in practice how Binario 9 ¾ works. Finally, the paper concludes with some considerations about future works.

2 Motivation and Background

Virtual communities of practices can be meant as replacement of company web sites for information and commerce (Sutanto et al. 2011). Indeed, despite the existence of many tools for promoting such communities, how keeping the community alive is still an important research trend, form both the theoretical and practical points of view. Preece and Shneiderman (2009) highlighted that few of billions of people involved in on-line social activities take active part in generating contents, by writing reviews of products or services, uploading photos and/experiences of their travels, or expressing opinions about politics or social life.

The debate on how to improve the capability of participants to contribute is still important, although many results have been reached in the recent past, see e.g. (Ma and Agarwal 2007) and (Zhang and Zhang 2005). Blanchard and Markus (2004) introduced the term *Sense of Virtual Community* (SOVC) to measure the degree of involvement of people in a community. This means that the feeling of belonging to a community is not innate, but it must be developed within the community structure goals and rules. Indeed, technology plays a crucial role in improving SOVC. A person starting the collaboration within a community as a lurker could become a knowledge contributor in the future, if and only if he/she will be guided to understand the community structure, to share its goals, boundaries and rules. For instance, *rating-based ranking* positively affects knowledge seekers' attitude to extract and comment about the knowledge modeled in a KMS (Sutanto and Jiang 2013), as well as *algorithm-based approaches* to evaluate the quality of knowledge shared by contributors positively guide them to continue feeding the system.

Successful implementation of CoPs depend on three crucial factors, as proposed by Wang et al. (2008): *remove barriers* to participation of individuals; *support and enrich* the development of participants' uniqueness within the context of the community; *link that uniqueness* with the goal of the community. Moreover, technological supports for CoPs traditionally based on centralized architectures do not meet knowledge contributors' and seekers' behavior, although they facilitate easy control and management of knowledge. This aspect is highly relevant when we think on how cultivating virtual communities of practice for the Education domain: which features should be considered to develop *virtual community systems* (VCSs) suitable allowing the emerging of positive SOVC among participants?

Educational processes aim to the promotion integral health of persons; thus, it should be a right rather than a privilege during the whole life span development (Alberici 1998).

Contemporary socio-cultural context supports the idea of knowledge acquisition and management, not only as development of organizations, policies, methods of knowledge diffusion, but also as a community benefit. Starting from these considerations, we reflect about the concept of continuous learning within organizations and how to support it. In this methodological framework, we focus on *learning by doing paradigm* at school. Learning by doing methodology states that the learning process is the result of a continuous interaction between theory and practice, between experimental periods and theoretical elaboration moments. Learning by doing is articulated into four distinct steps (see Fig. 1), where practical phases, i.e. *concrete experience* and *experimentation*, are alternated with theoretical ones, i.e. *observation* and *reflection and creation* of abstract concepts: The result is a *lesson learned* that is applicable in the future. In our framework, a concrete experience can be represented by a *story*, which is a description of decision-making process about a problem to be solved. As reported in Denning (2006), *storytelling build trust, unlock passion, overcomes hierarchies due to its intrinsically collaborative nature and its capability to flatten the communication among people (or communities)*. A story is a narrative account of real or imagined event(s). Stories explain how things are, why they are, and the different roles and purposes involved. Stories are the building blocks of knowledge, the foundation of memory and learning. In the Knowledge Management literature (Bhardwaj and Monin 2006), stories are often considered as very profitable tools to make explicit tacit knowledge, with the possibility to exploit them in the process of generating collective creativity from individual creativity. Starting from these considerations, we have reflected on how promoting the creation of virtual communities capable to improve integration of students with special needs at school, focusing on those courses traditionally characterized by higher level of lurking conditions, like Math (Di Poccio 2018).

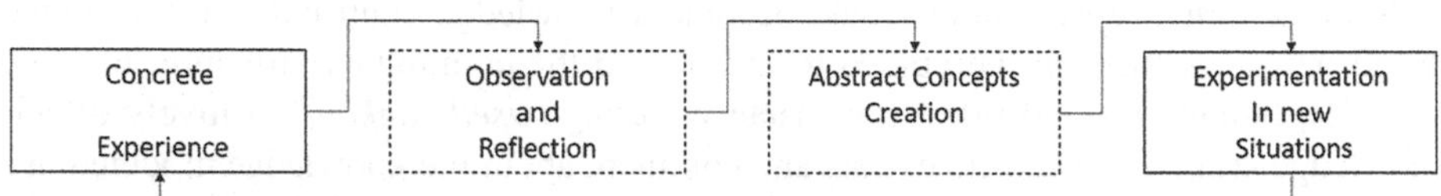

Fig. 1. The four steps of learning by doing

3 Legitimate Peripheral Participation

Legitimate Peripheral Participation (LPP) is the most crucial aspect of communities of practice: basically, it concerns the possibility for each member of the community to increase the global knowledge of it. Moving towards virtual communities this principle is hard to satisfy, being clear the distinction among, at least, three distinct roles, that are knowledge contributor, knowledge seeker and lurker. Indeed, the former has greater influence than the latter, being responsible for the maintenance of knowledge within the community. An interesting point is understanding how people can move from a role to another one: indeed, this possibility must be provided by the virtual community back-end, from both the organizational and technical points of view. Most of the times, a person can ac-quire credits based on his/her activity on the system (that is very often designed and implemented as a blog). This way, a user can enter the community at the lurker level improving it till the contributor one. Figure 2 shows a sketch of a virtual community from the LPP perspective: Knowledge contributors are fully integrated in the community; they participate to its definition and evolution. They can be the designer and/or developers of virtual community systems (VCS), that are the set of organizational and technical tools that enables people to interact with the community; knowledge seekers are partially integrated in the community, they can be defined borderline participants. They will occasionally act as contributors as well as lurkers, on the basis of topics discussed by the community; lurkers are outside the community, they will occasionally enter it to find solutions to their problems rather than to support it.

Virtual community systems are crucial to encourage the community growth: as highlighted by dashed lines in the figure, lurkers and knowledge seekers will be interested in the community activities if and only if the underlying tools will be able to capture them. Their nature and characteristics depend on the nature and characteristics of the

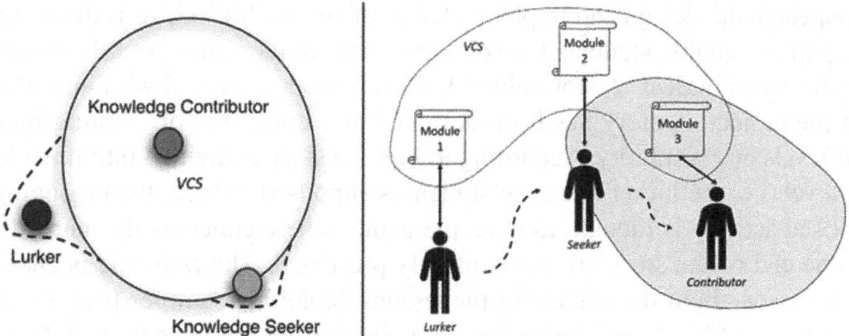

Fig. 2. On the left, Legitimate peripheral participation in Virtual Communities; on the right, the role of VCSs in the maintenance/growth of virtual communities.

community they serve and the problem to solve; anyway, their scope should be the maintenance and, possibly, growth of the virtual community by means of opportune modules dedicated to each role, as shown in right part of Fig. 2.

4 Case Study: The Binario 9 ¾ Project

Project Binario 9 ¾, funded in the frame of Italy-Switzerland V-A Interreg Programme 2014–2020, aims at promoting success at school and better learning opportunities for impaired students, focusing on immigrants. Indeed, there are still many differences between their conditions at school with respect to Italian or Swiss students: in Italy, the 2018 report[2] about "Invalsi test" results pointed out how foreign students obtain lower scores than Italian ones at the last year of middle school. Similar claim states for Swiss situation. The project has allowed to design and implement a comprehensive approach to reduce this impairment situation: in this paper we focus on the development of tools for reducing the gap between Italian students and their foreign colleagues in math, to improve the inclusion of the latter as well as their capability to access secondary schools programs.

As stated above, a virtual community of practice is characterized by three kinds of roles: knowledge contributors, knowledge seekers and lurkers. In the project, knowledge contributors are both domain experts and knowledge engineers: while domain experts provide the knowledge necessary to develop the virtual community system, knowledge engineers are responsible for modeling this knowledge into a suitable system. Domain experts are middle school teachers; they are responsible to indicate the topics the system should focus on; knowledge engineers are technicians. Knowledge seekers are tutors, i.e. people who have knowledge about the domain and how to use the developed VCS. Their task is supporting students with special learning needs in filling the gap with their peers. Students are lurkers in the project scenario; they are excluded from the community at the beginning, due to their difficulties in solving problems. We have based our choices on students with difficulties in understanding mathematics and Italian language. Thus, the

[2] See https://www.invalsi.it/invalsi/doc_evidenza/2018/Rapporto_prove_INVALSI_2018.pdf.

crucial aspect in the design and implementation of successful VCS was the definition of iterative paths to enable students to evolve from the initial status towards the others.

As introduced in Sect. 2, storytelling has been adopted to deal with virtual communities in the project. A story has been designed as a collection of learning modules at different levels of granularity. According to Fig. 2 a story is divided into three levels: at the first level (i.e. the lurker one), the student is supposed to be at the beginning. Here, the proposed activity is thought as a simple game, where concepts the students should learn at the end of the story are not explicitly presented. The rationale is enabling the student to reason about the content of the lessons exploiting samples from the concrete life. At the second level (i.e. the seeker one), the student who has passed the first step is invited to increase his/her level of competence about the lesson subject by means of a lecture, supported by a tutor. Here, he/she should be able to learn theoretical aspect of the concrete problem solved when staying at lurker level, by means of comparison between the usual training program at school and the reality. Tutor presence is crucial to this aim, to guide the student with special needs to develop the conceptual capability to build up virtuous connection between the two positions.

Last, but not least, the contributor level presents another game to the student, maybe the same as the first level one, but asking him/her to exploit theory to solve the problems. Doing so, the VCS tests the student about his/her capability to evolve from the initial condition, characterized by difficulties in understanding a problem due to the absence of necessary conceptual references, to the final one, where the student should be potentially able to design and implement similar stories for supporting his/her peers. Of course, a story could be partially followed according to the level of initial skills of the students, as well as the subject covered by it. Till now, fifteen stories have been completely developed, for a total of 45 learning modules on topics from arithmetic operations to solid geometry. All the stories are thought as chapters of a meta-story, that tells us about the summer holidays of a group of friends. In this way, we hope the students understand that Math is composed of different theoretical questions whose answers can generate new questions rather than isolated concepts. Such modules have been implemented into Scratch 3.0TM; this environment[3] has been chosen for two main reasons: the metaphor of program as a theatrical performance in terms of actors, scripts and stages is ideal for reproducing the narration of a story; most of students know Scratch since they studied basic notions at school, so we hope to promote the evolution towards the knowledge contributor role allowing them to explore how a story has been realized, in order to enable them to produce other stories on their own.

Figure 3 shows a sketch of a narration in the project: the sample concerns the surfaces area and perimeter topic. In Chapter 1, the story presents the friends at the end of holidays, asking the user to draw the most beautiful monument in the pictures. Monuments proposed have been chosen thanks to their aspect, characterized by the presence of figures studied at school, like triangles, rectangles, squares, and circles. Figures are drawn by the student exploiting a grid on the touchscreen and their areas and perimeters are calculated in terms of it too. Then, Chapter 2 proposes definitions, descriptions, and formulas of different kinds of figures, providing the tutor with guidelines to increase the under-standing of the topic by his/her student. Finally, Chapter 3 revises the sample

[3] https://scratch.mit.edu/discuss/topic/326861/.

of Chapter 1, asking the student to play tangram, recognize the figures composing the pictures and calculating the areas and perimeters of total surfaces by composition of single elements. Formulas learned following Chapter 2 must be applied and grid can be used to validate results.

Fig. 3. A story in the Binario 9 ¾ project

5 Conclusion and Future Works

In this paper we have introduced a conceptual and computational framework for the development of virtual communities in the Education domain. The Binario 9 ¾ project has been presented as a case study. The implementation phase of the project has finished on January 2020, as well as the definition of the Binario 9 ¾ virtual community members. Selected students are 30, only one of them is Italian. Eight students are at first grade, six at second grade and sixteen at third grade of middle school. Fourteen students are male, the rest are female. The community is completed by 13 tutors and two teachers; ten tutors are attending University, two the last two years at Secondary schools and one is working as teacher's aide. Teachers have developed a questionnaire to evaluate the initial level of students. Unfortunately, the COVID-19 emergency has stopped the project just at the beginning of the testing phase. Although the initial results are encouraging, an intense validation campaign will be implemented when restarting next September. This validation will be conducted from two perspectives at least: first, the effectiveness of the proposed VCS will be evaluated in terms of better understanding of topics by students. This step will be based on questionnaires prepared by virtual community teachers; second, the effectiveness of the proposed VCS in improving the maintenance and growth of the community will be measured too. This point will address our future research, being necessary to build up a bridge between the application of correct SOVC measures. Abfalter et al. (2012) proposed recently to adopt a revised version of SCI (Chavis et al. 1986), namely SCI^2 (Chavis et al. 2008): this index consists of 24 closed-ended items measured on Likert-like scale. The items are grouped into four dimensions: reinforcement of needs (RON), membership (MEM), influence (INF) and shared emotional connection (SEC). The total sense of community index ($TSOC^I$) is the summary of the Q_i, where Q_i is the value in the range [0…3] given by the user to the i-th question. In our study, we are interested in evaluating if virtual community systems can support communities of practice to evolve. To this aim, we will apply the notions of lurking, seeking, or contributing communities on the basis of their $TSOC^I$ value (Sartori et al. 2018).

Acknowledgements. Authors wish to thank the members of the Consortium for their support in the project: on the Italian side, *Fondazione Circolo dei lettori, Municipality of Novara, Consorzio Scuola Comunità Impresa* and *Associazione Next-Level*; on the Swiss side, *Alta Scuola Pedagogica dei Grigioni* and *Ufficio Orientamento professionale, negli studi e nella carriera Cantone Grigioni.*

References

Abfalter, D., Zaglia, M.E., Mueller, J.: Sense of virtual community: a follow up on its measurement. Comput. Hum. Behav. **28**(2), 400–404 (2012)

Alberici, A.: Towards the learning society: an italian perspective. In: International Perspectives on Lifelong Learning, pp. 236–244 (1998)

Bhardwaj, M., Monin, J.: Tacit to explicit: an interplay shaping organization knowledge. J. Knowl. Manage. **10**(3), 72–85 (2006)

Blanchard, A.L., Markus, M.L.: The experienced sense of a virtual community: characteristics and processes. ACM Sigmis Database **35**(1), 64–79 (2004)

Brown, J.S., Duguid, P.: Knowledge and organization: a social-practice perspective. Organ. Sci. **12**(2), 198–213 (2001)

Chavis, D., Lee, K., Acosta, J.: The sense of community (sci) revised: The reliability and validity of the sci-2. In: 2nd International Community Psychology Conference, Lisboa, Portugal (2008)

Chavis, D.M., Hogge, J.H., McMillan, D.W., Wandersman, A.: Sense of community through Brunswik's lens: a first look. J. Commun. Psychol. **14**(1), 24–40 (1986)

Denning, S.: Effective storytelling: strategic business narrative techniques. Strategy & Leadership (2006)

Di Poccio, A.M.: La narrazione digitale a supporto dellinsegnamento e del-lapprendimento. In Scuola Estiva di Formazione per i docenti del Primo Ciclo di Istruzione. Insegnare Matematica: didattica, inclusione e cooperazione, Quaderni nr. 3, pp.71–82. APAV (2018). ISBN 9788894350135

Lave, J., Wenger, E.: Legitimate peripheral participation in communities of practice. In: Supporting Lifelong Learning, vol. 1, pp. 111–126 (2002)

Ma, M., Agarwal, R.: Through a glass darkly: Information technology design, identity verification, and knowledge contribution in online communities. Inf. Syst. Res. **18**(1), 42–67 (2007)

Pan, S.L., Leidner, D.E.: Bridging communities of practice with information technology in pursuit of global knowledge sharing. J. Strateg. Inf. Syst. **12**(1), 71–88 (2003)

Preece, J., Shneiderman, B.: The reader-to-leader framework: Motivating technology-mediated social participation. AIS Trans. Hum. Comput. Interact. **1**(1), 13–32 (2009)

Sartori, F., Melen, R., Pinardi, S.: Cultivating virtual communities of practice in KAFKA. Data Technologies and Applications (2018)

Sutanto, J., Jiang, Q.: Knowledge seekers and contributors reactions to recommendation mechanisms in knowledge management systems. Inf. Manag. **50**(5), 258–263 (2013)

Sutanto, J., Kankanhalli, A., Tan, B.C.Y.: Eliciting a sense of virtual community among knowledge contributors. ACM Trans. Manage. Inf. Syst. (TMIS) **2**(3), 14 (2011)

Wang, C.-Y., Yang, H.-Y., Seng-cho, T.C.: Using peer-to-peer technology for knowledge sharing in communities of practices. Decis. Support Syst. **45**(3), 528–540 (2008)
Yeow, A., Johnson, S., Faraj, S.: Lurking: legitimate or illegitimate peripheral participation? ICIS 2006 Proceedings, p. 62 (2006)
Zhang, C., Zhang, C.: Discovering users' participant roles in virtual communities with the help of social interaction theories. In: PACIS 2005 Proceedings, p. 65 (2005)

The Navigation of Multi-itineraries for the Cultural Heritage Context

Yuri Palazzo(✉), Silvia Calegari, Paolo Avogadro, and Matteo Dominoni

University of Milano-Bicocca, DISCo,
Viale Sarca 336 Building 14, 20126 Milan, Italy
{silvia.calegari,paolo.avogadro,matteo.dominoni}@unimib.it,
y.palazzo@campus.unimib.it
http://www.idea.disco.unimib.it/, https://www.progettopollicina.eu/

Abstract. Itinerary planning is a challenging knowledge acquisition activity. An itinerary is an ordered list of points of interest (POIs) obtained after the analysis of several dimensions (e.g., current context, user preferences, etc.) that are jointly considered for a context-aware recommendation of customized paths. When the system returns many itineraries, it is difficult for a user to understand which of them is optimal. This is particularly true if they are returned by a single query, they present large overlaps, and the points of interest are new to the user.

This paper presents the *SearchPath* service which is a vertical application dedicated to the retrieval of indexed itineraries according to the geographic context and user's interests. The innovation underlying this service is the navigation of multi-itineraries where a path is considered according to several conceptual interconnected views. Moreover, a collection of cards for additional knowledge and multimedia information can be expanded for each of the POI. The *SearchPath* service has been integrated in the Pollicina project where cultural heritage itineraries have been defined by users during their learning activities.

Keywords: Cultural itineraries · Navigation maps · Metro map

1 Introduction

Nowadays the number of services dedicated to the promotion of tourism is growing. There is, in fact, an increasing demand for web-market applications which could help the users to plan their own personalized itineraries. The result of a query of one of these travel applications is often a collection of itineraries. Deciding which of them is more interesting is not a simple task, especially when the knowledge of the points of interest (POIs) is limited. Indeed, the definition of an itinerary should take into account several user preferences such as: available time, topics of interest, means of transport, etc.

An itinerary is in fact defined as a set of POIs linked with each other typically according to the geographical coordinates encoded as latitude/longitude

O. Gervasi et al. (Eds.): ICCSA 2020, LNCS 12253, pp. 544–552, 2020.
https://doi.org/10.1007/978-3-030-58814-4_40

pairs. In the literature, several works [1–3,6–10] address the task of identifying the optimal path from a pool of POIs, according to different features (the nearest POIs to the user, the means of transportation, the time available for the visit, etc.). In our case, the itineraries are built with a social suite called Educational Social Network (EduSN) defined in the Pollicina Project (POR FESR 2014–2020) [4,5]. The main goal of this project is to provide a collaborative tool which allows the students to create cultural paths connecting artworks belonging to different cultural institutions distributed in the territory following a theme provided by the teacher. This paper presents the *SearchPath* service, a vertical application dedicated to the retrieval of the relevant itineraries stored in the Pollicina's repository. A query defines the context which is used by the search engine to return the relevant itineraries by exploiting the BM25 similarity function. The result of a query is a set of cards of the itineraries with snippets including: title, a list of concepts, a list of cultural entities, etc. When a user selects a group of itineraries of interest from the results, it can be difficult to establish the relevant differences among the paths, especially in case when there are many overlapping POIs. The related problematic of the visualization of multi-itineraries is addressed with the help of different conceptual views in the form of metro maps. Each *view* captures a different knowledge aspect for the itinerary, according to a specific topic. Since the views are in the form of (partially) overlapping metro lines a user can immediately grasp the relevant conceptual differences among the itineraries. In this early phase of our work we focused on the user experience. At variance in respect to [7,9,10], the faceted search, the query results, and the itinerary preview are all shown in the same page, in order to facilitate query insertion and path selection. The *SearchPath* service is the only tourist application that supports a multi-path preview that enables the users to easily compare and select different paths. Other works present multi-path visualization services [1,2] but the paths cannot be selected incrementally by the user. The *SearchPath* service has also an educational aspect, since its collaborative topological view of the paths can be used to create conceptual maps showing links between topics. This helps to visually connect multiple information and topics. Such a tool is very useful within the flipped learning paradigm where the students collaborate for the construction of the itinerary among cultural objects by sharing ideas, material, and feedback under the supervision of a coach (the teacher). These itineraries are stored in the platform and they are available for all the scholastic institutions involved in the Pollicina project.

The *SearchPath* service is used by students and teachers to plan their cultural visits within Regione Lombardia (Italy) as the Pollicina project has been developed under the Regional Operational Program. The idea is to include cultural materials from the ICCD repository (http://www.iccd.beniculturali.it/) in order to define itineraries having POIs in the Italian territory, and later to externalize and personalize the use of the *SearchPath* service for tourism companies.

This paper is organized as follows. Section 2 presents the *SearchPath* service dedicated to the retrieval and navigation of multi-itineraries, Sect. 3 proposes a use case of the *SearchPath* service in the Pollicina project. Finally, in Sect. 4 the conclusions are stated.

2 The *SearchPath* Service

This section introduces the *SearchPath* service designed to support the users during their activity of searching cultural paths. As described in Sect. 1, it is possible to find in the literature several algorithms which establish optimal paths, according to multi-featured distances within a set of POIs. In our research instead, we focus on the management of sets of pre-made itineraries (see Sect. 3). The *SearchPath* service is a vertical application comprising offline and online phases. The offline phase is used for indexing the itineraries according to the standard approach presented in the information retrieval research context, whereas the online one is dedicated to the search, selection, and navigation of multi-itineraries. This means that, given a query, the vertical search engine is able to retrieve a set of relevant itineraries based on the BM25 similarity. The intuitive environment presented in this paper allows the users to access to several views of the selected itineraries by the adoption of an innovative mode of knowledge navigation. We present here an overview of the online phase:

Search: The user can express the information needs in a query facet form which contains three kinds of features that explicitly represent the request: (1) the identification of a specific POI (a user can directly write the name of the cultural institute of interest), (2) the address of interest, and (3) the concepts of interest. For sake of usability, the features (1) and (2) are collapsed in a unique field named *place* within the query facet form. If one inserts the name of the POI, this attribute is searched into its corresponding address via Google Places API. A user is supported during the insertion of the query with the adoption of a query suggestion methodology developed according to the vocabulary of the indexed itineraries. A query q is defined as $q := p \cup C$, where p is the *place* and $C = \{c_1, c_2, ..., c_n\}$ is the set containing all the concepts inserted by the user.

Selection: The result of the query is a ordered collection of itineraries, and the user can select one or more of them. Each itinerary is represented as a card with the following attributes: a title, a list of POIs with related preview images, and a list of concepts.

Navigation: there are two visualization modes for the selected itineraries:

1. *The Geographic Mode* is the default view of the service where the selected itineraries appear in the geographic map. Since a multi-itinerary selection is allowed, it is important to provide a clear visualization system in the map. For each itinerary, the service takes the latitude/longitude pairs of all POIs and sorts them at first by latitude and then by longitude. Finally, each pair of adjacent coordinates is connected by a unique edge. The color of each itinerary is generated with a pseudo-random procedure. A user can display the paths according to the selected means of transport: the order of the POIs

is fixed, but the trajectory between adjacent POIs can change according to the mean of transport (the default selection is "walking mode"). The user is geo-localized in order to facilitate the choice of the means of transport.

2. *The Topological Mode* returns a conceptual multi-view in the form of metro maps. A metro map is a form of visualization where collections of objects are arranged as lines where the order of the stops follows specific features of the objects. This visualization method is used to better understand information in many areas, including news, stories, research, legal cases and literature, because it summarizes different connections between the objects [11]. We implemented two possible topological itineraries, one based on the authors and the other on the cultural objects. The lines are identified with the same color used in the *Geographic Mode.* The stops (stations) are arranged in chronological order, following the birth date (for the author view) or the creation date (for the cultural object view). In addition, a list of cards is visualized when a user selects a stop. The cards correspond to all of the authors (or objects) of the itinerary associated with the specific station. The cards contain knowledge in the form of textual descriptions, multimedia content, technical information regarding the object, etc.

3 The Use Case: The Pollicina Project

Pollicina is a cultural navigator developed under the Regional Operational Program of the European Fund for Regional Development 2014–2020 (POR FESR 2014–2020) of the Regione Lombardia in Italy. The core idea of the project is to provide tools for creating customized cultural paths among different cultural institutions. Visits to cultural institutions are very popular, but they are usually confined within the institutions themselves, or their close surroundings. A person, however, might be interested in following specific ideas and interests which go beyond the collections of a single institution. Pollicina is an initial answer to these needs since it allows a user to browse through collections belonging to many sources and to produce trans-institutional cultural paths. Pollicina's most natural target includes scholastic institutions ranging from primary to high school. The classes are in fact one of the main sources of visitors for cultural institutions, and the problem of integrating specific study lines with the collections of the museums needed to be addressed. This project follows the Flipped Learning pedagogical approach. The idea is that a teacher should not impart information with a top-bottom approach, but rather provide the students with sufficient information and let them build collaboratively their own solutions. Within Pollicina, a coach (the teacher) defines a generic theme (for example, waterways in Lombardy) and associates more specific sub-themes for better filtering the research, providing a basic conceptual map. At the beginning the students enrich the conceptual map with their own ideas. Later, with the help of a search engine they are able to retrieve the cards related to the objects linked with the concepts. A user friendly interface allows them to drag and drop the cards on a table and complete the conceptual map. This phase is done collaboratively by the students, with an integrated peer-review process meant to define a minimum standard for the quality of the choices. A further collaborative step includes a pruning of the conceptual map, where the students decide the more relevant objects. At this point one can publish the cultural itinerary in order to use it as a guideline for a real visit of the objects, beyond the single institution. In large collaborative environments like schools it is possible to produce many cultural paths, even related to the same main theme. Once the repository starts to contain many of these paths, it becomes necessary to produce a navigator helping to understand the similarities and differences among them. In particular, such a system should provide quick and intuitive views of the structures of each path. This is at the basis of the present research where we introduce a service dedicated to the search, navigation and visualization for collections of paths.

3.1 The *SearchPath* Service for the Cultural Heritage Context

The *SearchPath* service has been developed according to the microservice architecture where the development of a single application is seen as a set of small services, each of which is run by its own process and it communicates via http API, allowing for a simple and agile integration with the Pollicina platform. The *SearchPath* user interface is a ReactJS hybrid app, that contains a navigation service based on the Google Maps APIs and a metro map interactive visualization developed with D3.js, a JavaScript library for producing dynamic, interactive data visualizations. The service works cross-browsers and cross-devices. In the following, we contextualize with an example the usage of the *SearchPath* service within the Pollicina project according to the steps described in Sect. 2.

Phase 1 - Search: John Doe, an architect, is visiting Milan for the first time, and he decides to have a walk in the city downtown. For this reason, he accesses the *SearchPath* service in order to visit some POIs near him. At start, a locator returns his position on the map. He inserts "Gallerie d'Italia" in the *place* field of the query, since the concierge of his hotel recommended it to him. He also inserts "architecture" as a topic of interest in the *concepts* input field. Since he enjoys urban sightseeing, he selects *walking* as a travel mode, and he starts the query by clicking the magnifying glass icon.

Phase 2 - Selection: As soon as the platform updates the screen, the locator for "Gallerie d'Italia" appears on the geographic map. At the same time the itineraries that match the criteria appear under the map as summary cards. Each summary card of an itinerary contains information such as title, associated concepts, associated POIs, etc. It also contains a *Show Itinerary* button. John clicks on the button of the itinerary entitled "Fashion Houses of Milan". As a result, a magenta border highlights the summary card. The sorted POIs of the itinerary are displayed on the map and they are connected with a magenta line. At this point, John clicks on another itinerary button. A green border appears around the card and a green path is added to the geographic map (see Fig. 1).

Phase 3 - Navigation: At the top right corner of the geographic map, there is a toggle button allowing to pass from the geographic to the metro map

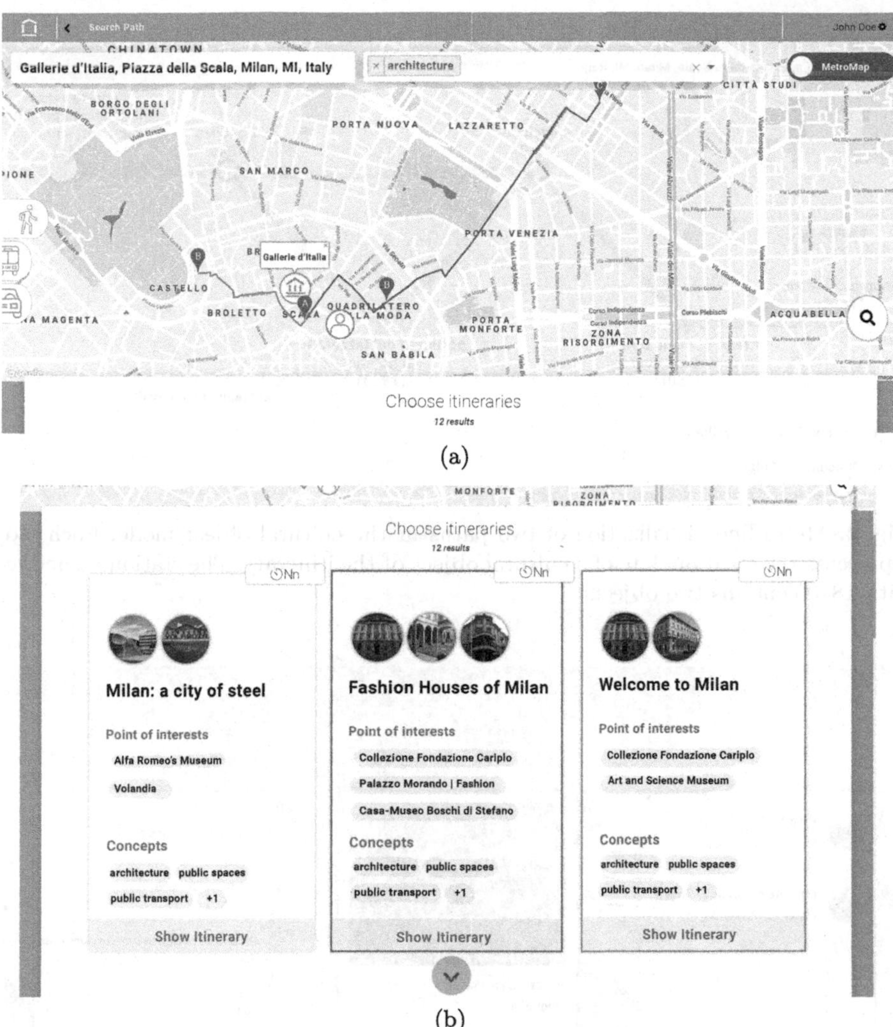

Fig. 1. (a) The query regarding "Gallerie d'Italia" (*place* field) and "architecture" (*concept* field). (b)Two of the returned itineraries have been selected and are shown on the *Geographic Mode.*

visualization. John clicks on it and the system shows the two selected itineraries as metro lines where the stations are the cultural objects sorted by the creation date. When a cultural object is present in two or more metro lines, that cultural object becomes an interchange station between the lines. The label of each station is composed by the title of the cultural object and the creation date year. If more cultural objects are associated with a single date, all of them are aggregated in a unique station/stop. In this case, the label indicates the number of objects (denoted with the term "badges"), and their creation date (Fig. 2).

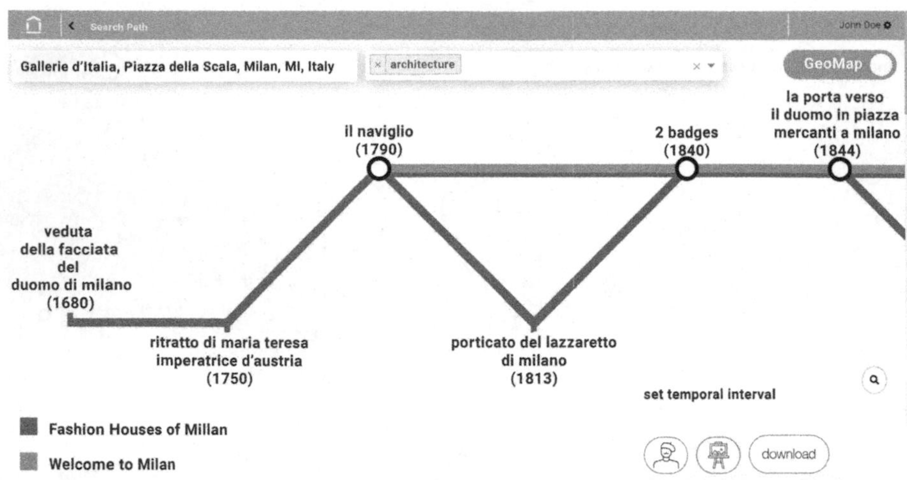

Fig. 2. Metro line visualization of two paths in the cultural object mode. Each stop represents the creation date of a cultural object of the itinerary. The station associated with 1840 contains two objects.

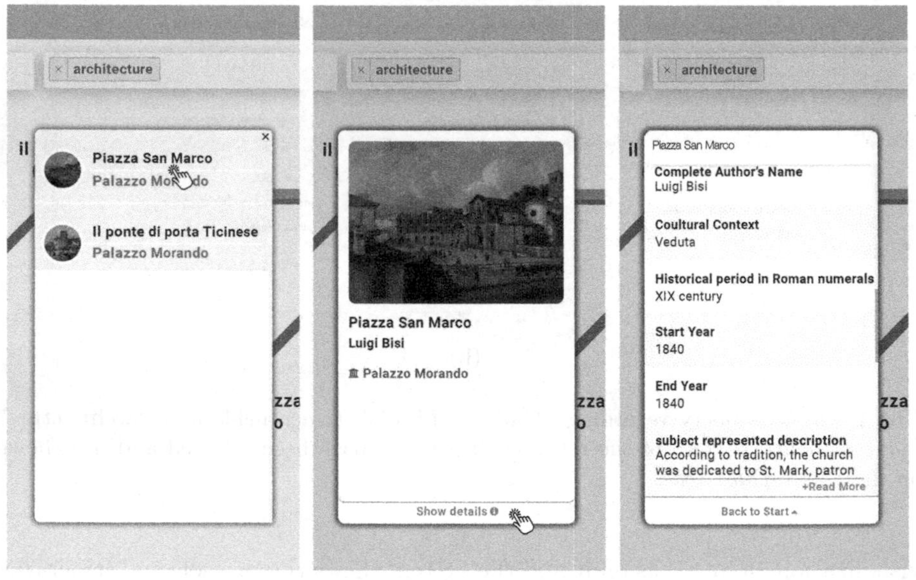

Fig. 3. (Left) The two possible badges related to the stop 1840 are shown in a modal. (Center) After clicking on "Piazza San Marco" one obtains a new modal with a summary of the card of the object. (Right) By expanding the card in the center, one can access to more detailed information regarding the selected badge.

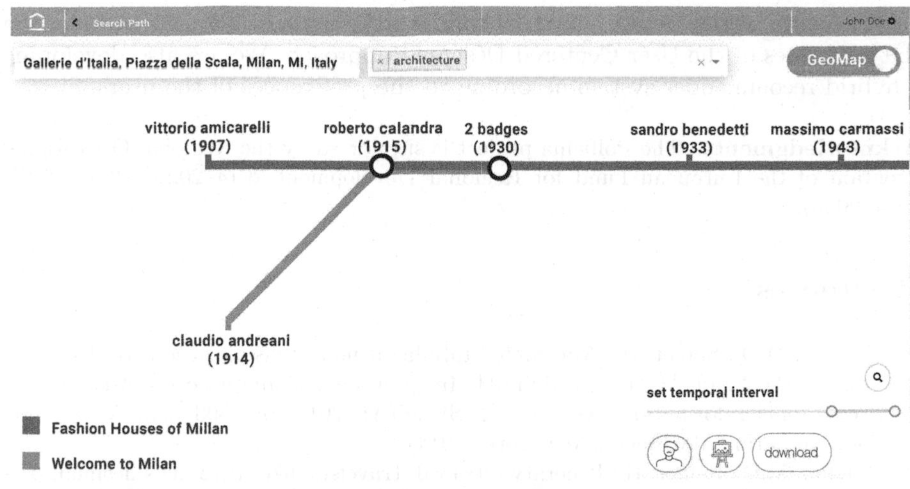

Fig. 4. The complementary metro map based on the author's birthdate.

John clicks on the interchange station among the lines corresponding to the year 1840. As a result, he obtains the two cultural badges of the stop. By clicking on one of them, John accesses to the knowledge of the cultural object: a painting named "Piazza San Marco" (Fig. 3). In addition, John has the possibility to switch to the metro visualization mode based on the authors or select an interval of time. With this second option, only those elements matching the time interval are used to form the metro map. He selects the author view and the time interval from 1900 to present since he is specialized on buildings of the 20th century. This new metro line mode (Fig. 4) shows that the itinerary "Fashion houses of Milan" is better suited to his interests.

4 Conclusions and Future Work

This paper presented the *SearchPath* service included in the Pollicina project. This service helps the users to navigate cultural heritage itineraries. At variance in respect with those articles devoted at finding an optimal path connecting POIs, we provide here a tool to search itineraries and to help the navigation when those itineraries are already existing. The problem at the time of choosing among multi-paths is exactly the fact that they share many features, and it is difficult for a user to understand which of them is more interesting. The *SearchPath* service provides two interacting systems for visualization: the *Geographic Mode*, and the *Topological Mode*. The *Geographic Mode* is the natural view showing the itineraries as routes among the POIs on the map; whereas the *Topological Mode* produces conceptual views in the form of metro maps, where the order of the POIs follows specific information. Having more views helps to disentangle the differences among the itineraries and supplements them with non trivial connections among POIs, like for example the periods of time.

As future works we are going to validate the *SearchPath* service following the guidelines of the User Centered Designed approach. We are also developing a hybrid recommender system according to the preferences of the users.

Acknowledgments. The Pollicina project is supported by the Regional Operational Program of the European Fund for Regional Development 2014–2020 (POR FESR 2014–2020).

References

1. Adelfio, M.D., Samet, H.: Automated tabular itinerary visualization. In: Proceedings of the 22nd ACM SIGSPATIAL International Conference on Advances in Geographic Information Systems, SIGSPATIAL 2014, pp. 593–596. Association for Computing Machinery, New York (2014)
2. Adelfio, M.D., Samet, H.: Itinerary retrieval: travelers, like traveling salesmen, prefer efficient routes. In: Proceedings of the 8th Workshop on Geographic Information Retrieval, GIR 2014. Association for Computing Machinery, New York (2014)
3. Bolzoni, P., Helmer, S., Wellenzohn, K., Gamper, J., Andritsos, P.: Efficient itinerary planning with category constraints. In: Proceedings of the 22nd ACM SIGSPATIAL International Conference on Advances in Geographic Information Systems, SIGSPATIAL 2014, pp. 203–212. Association for Computing Machinery, New York (2014)
4. Calegari, S., Avogadro, P., Meluso, F., Dominoni, M.: The pollicina project: a social learning management system to create personalized cultural itineraries. In: Misra, S., et al. (eds.) ICCSA 2019. LNCS, vol. 11619, pp. 489–503. Springer, Cham (2019). https://doi.org/10.1007/978-3-030-24289-3_36
5. Calegari, S., Dominoni, M.: The pollicina project: a collaborative and educational social suite to build cultural itineraries. In: Luigini, A. (ed.) EARTH 2018. AISC, vol. 919, pp. 225–234. Springer, Cham (2019). https://doi.org/10.1007/978-3-030-12240-9_24
6. Fogli, A., Sansonetti, G.: Exploiting semantics for context-aware itinerary recommendation. Pers. Ubiquitous Comput. **23**(2), 215–231 (2019). https://doi.org/10.1007/s00779-018-01189-7
7. Gavalas, D., Kasapakis, V., Konstantopoulos, C., Pantziou, G., Vathis, N.: Scenic route planning for tourists. Pers. Ubiquitous Comput. **21**(1), 137–155 (2016). https://doi.org/10.1007/s00779-016-0971-3
8. Jiaoman, D., Lei, L., Xiang, L.: Travel planning problem considering site selection and itinerary making. In: Proceedings of the 2018 Conference on Research in Adaptive and Convergent Systems, RACS 2018, pp. 29–36. Association for Computing Machinery, New York (2018)
9. Rajaonarivo, L., et al.: Recommendation of heterogeneous cultural heritage objects for the promotion of tourism. ISPRS Int. J. Geo-Inf. **8**(5), 230 (2019)
10. Schaller, R., Elsweiler, D.: Itinerary recommenders: How do users customize their routes and what can we learn from them? In: Proceedings of the 5th Information Interaction in Context Symposium, IIiX 2014, pp. 185–194. Association for Computing Machinery, New York (2014)
11. Shahaf, D., Guestrin, C., Horvitz, E., Leskovec, J.: Inf. Cartography. Commun. ACM **58**(11), 62–73 (2015)

Adsorption of Atoms on a Crystalline Ice Surface Model: Results from Periodic *ab Initio* Simulations

Stefano Ferrero[1(✉)], Berta Martínez-Bachs[1], Joan Enrique-Romero[1,2], and Albert Rimola[1]

[1] Departament de Química, Universitat Autònoma de Barcelona, Bellaterra, 08193 Barcelona, Catalonia, Spain
stefano.ferrero@uab.cat

[2] Université Grenoble-Alpes, CNRS, Institut de Planétologie et d'Astrophysique de Grenoble (IPAG), rue de la Piscine 414, 380008 Grenoble, France

Abstract. In cold and dense regions of the interstellar medium, such as molecular clouds, more than 200 gas-phase molecular species have been observed by means of infra-red and rotational spectroscopy techniques alongside solid sub-micrometer sized particles called dust grains. These grains are of uttermost importance because their surfaces serve as meeting points for chemical species that adsorb from the gas phase, diffuse and possibly react to form more complex molecules. These grains consist of a silicate or carbonaceous cores covered in layers of water dominated ices that contain other small volatile molecules such as CO, CO_2, NH_3, CH_3OH. Most of the ice components originate from the adsorption and reaction of bare atoms, e.g., H, C, N and O, on the grain surfaces. An important challenge in Astrochemistry is to characterize the thermodynamics and kinetics of the main reaction steps of the bare atoms forming the ice components on the grain surfaces. As a first step previous to the reaction of these atomic species, in this paper we present results based on quantum chemistry methods on the adsorption of atomic carbon, nitrogen and oxygen on a crystalline water ice surface model mimicking the icy grain surfaces.

1 Introduction

Surface chemistry plays a central role in Astrochemistry. Grain surface processes such as adsorption, diffusion and reactions are currently topics of great interest both for experimentalists and theoreticians of the field. Quantitative information such as binding energies (BE), diffusion energies and reaction rate constants are used as input data in astrochemical models that aim to reproduce the evolution of the chemical composition of the interstellar medium (ISM) [2]. However, the values implemented in these models are often roughly approximated, leading to

O. Gervasi et al. (Eds.): ICCSA 2020, LNCS 12253, pp. 553–560, 2020.
https://doi.org/10.1007/978-3-030-58814-4_41

incorrect predictions of the interstellar chemical evolution. Following the work of Shimonishi et al. [9] in which the adsorption of atomic C, N, O on different annealed 20-water molecule clusters was deeply investigated, here we explore the same adsorption processes on a periodic crystalline model for water ice. Our results are compared with those of Simonishi et al. as well as those from Wakelam et al. [13] in which BEs were calculated for a vast number of species (also for C, N and O) with a single water molecule. The aim of the work is to investigate the effect of the structural models used as water ice surfaces, including the size of the models, the structural state and the inclusion or not of periodicity, on the adsorption properties.

2 Computational Details

All the simulations were performed adopting the DFT formalism, using the CP2K software package [6]. Electronic structure calculations were carried out using the QUICKSTEP module, which employs the hybrid Gaussian and plane waves (GPW) approach (i.e., an hybrid scheme of Gaussian functions and plane waves as basis set) for the calculation of energies and forces [7,12]. In our DFT simulations we applied the norm-conserving GTH (Goedecker-Teter-Hutter) pseudopotentials, [3] replacing the core electrons and a triple-zeta valence basis set added with a single set of polarization Gaussian functions (TZVP) for valence electrons. The PBE DFT exchange-correlation functional in combination with the D3(BJ) Grimme's correction to account for dispersive forces (not taken into account in the pure PBE functional) was used [4,5,8].

Binding energies for the atomic species considered were calculated as:

$$-BE = \Delta E_{\text{int}} = E(SM) - E(S) - E(M) \tag{1}$$

in which the binding energy (BE) is the interaction energy (ΔE_{int}), with opposite sign, between the atom and the surface, $E(SM)$ is the energy of the optimized atom/slab adduct, $E(S)$ is the total energy of the optimized slab and $E(M)$ is the total energy of the atomic species. The BE values are not corrected for the basis set superposition error (BSSE).

3 Ice Surface Model

As a first step to simulate the atom adsorption processes on interstellar ice water, we adopted as ice model the P-ice system, a crystalline proton ordered water ice phase [1]. From its bulk structure, we cut a surface along the (010) plane. This surfaces slab model does not possess a net dipole moment along the z-axis, which ensures a electronic structure stability by increasing its thickness [11]. The PBE-D3(BJ)-optimized structure of the P-ice (101) surfaces (see Fig. 1) presents two main adsorption sites identified as dH (dangling hydrogen) and dO (dangling oxygen). We adopted a supercell model with unit cell parameters of $|\mathbf{a}| = 13.156$ Å and $|\mathbf{b}| = 14.162$ Å with the aim to simulate the adsorption of fully isolated atoms, i.e., without contributions from lateral interactions between replica images, this way mimicking the actual low gas densities of the ISM. The thickness of the slab model is 11 Å (corresponding to 3 water layers). To avoid fictitious interactions between slab replicas, the c parameter (represented by the non-periodic z direction) was set to 30.156 Å. During the optimizations, the cell parameters remained fixed. Integrals were evaluated only at the Γ point, namely, point $k = 0$ in the first Brillouin zone (so-called the central zone).

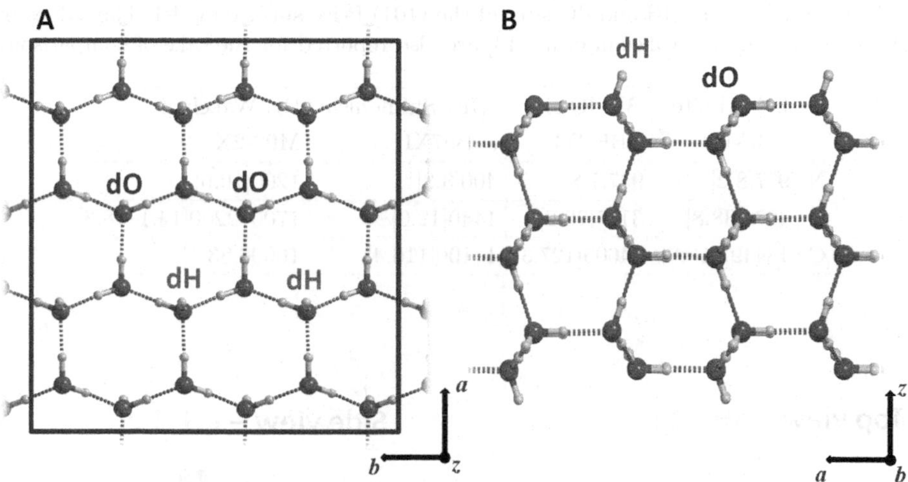

Fig. 1. Top view (A) of the first layer and side view (B) of the crystalline surface model, with dangling hydrogen (dH) and dangling oxygen (dO) sites highlighted in red and blue, respectively.

4 Adsorption of C, N and O

Several geometry optimizations were performed to simulate the atomic adsorptions on the crystalline water ice surface. For all cases, the initial guess structures consisted of the atoms placed over the centroid of the hexagon of the outermost water layer, rendering adsorption states either close to the dH or the dO sites. The adsorption of the atoms were simulated according to their electronic ground states, i.e., C(^3P), O(^3P) and N(^4S). In any case, adsorption does not lead to changes in the electronic states, that is, the first excited electronic states of the bare atoms (namely, singlet for C and O, and doublet for N) remain more unstable upon adsorption. These atoms do not possess any charge and electric dipole moment but can exhibit an electric quadrupole moment or higher moments since their electron density is not spherically symmetric around the nucleus. In our cases, C and O do possess a non-zero electric quadrupole moment whereas N has a null quadrupole moment but a non-zero octupole moment. Accordingly, the interactions between these atoms and the surface are expected to be weak through a physisorption mechanism. Figure 2, Fig. 3 and Fig. 4 show the PBE-D3(BJ)-optimized structures of the computed complexes for every atom on both dH and dO sites. Table 1 reports the calculated BE values for these atoms, the comparison of which with those of Simonishi et al. and Wakelam et al. is also reported.

Table 1. Calculated BE values, given in Kelvin and in kJ mol^{-1} (in square brackets) of N, O and C on the dH and dO sites of the (101) P-ice surface model. The values by Shimonishi et al. [9] Wakelam et al. [13] are also reported for the sake of comparison.

	BE dH site PBE-D3	BE dO site PBE-D3	⟨BE⟩ Shimonishi ω-B97XD	BE Wakelam M06-2X
N	977[8.2]	937[7.8]	400[3.3]	1200[10.0]
O	4673[38.8]	3177[20.2]	1440[12.0]	1700–2200[14.1–18.3]
C	18449[153.2]	14605[127.3]	14100[116.4]	10000[83.1]

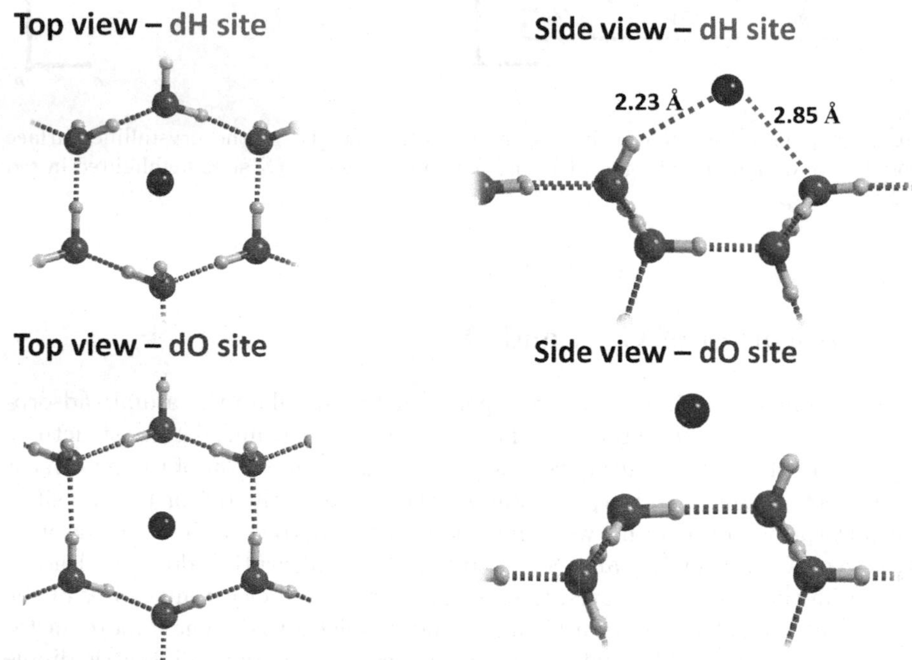

Fig. 2. Top and side views of the PBE-D3(BJ)-optimized geometries for the adsorption of N on the dH and dO sites. Bond distances are in Å

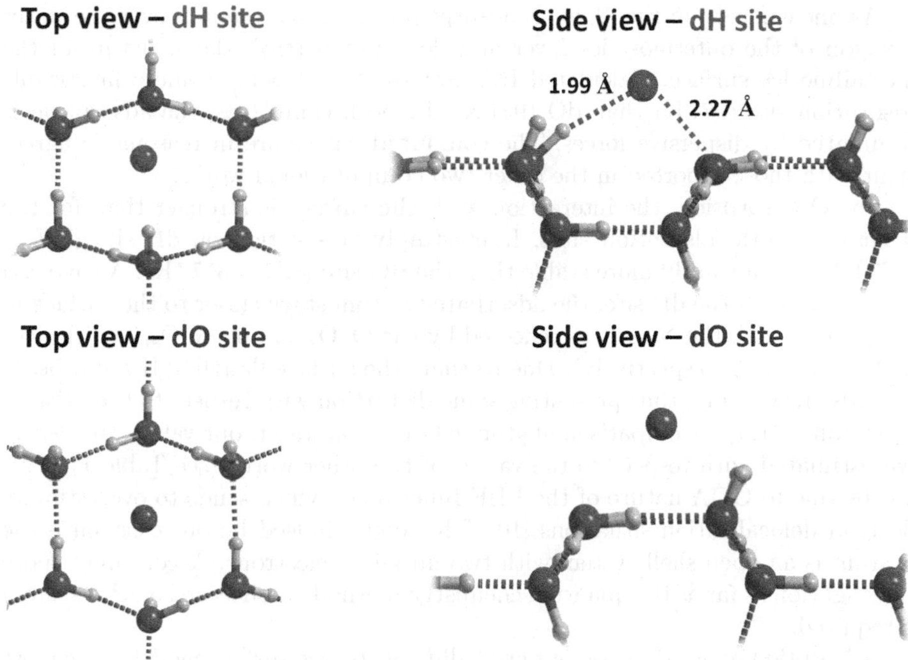

Fig. 3. Top and side views of the PBE-D3(BJ)-optimized geometries for the adsorption of O on the dH and dO sites. Bond distances are in Å

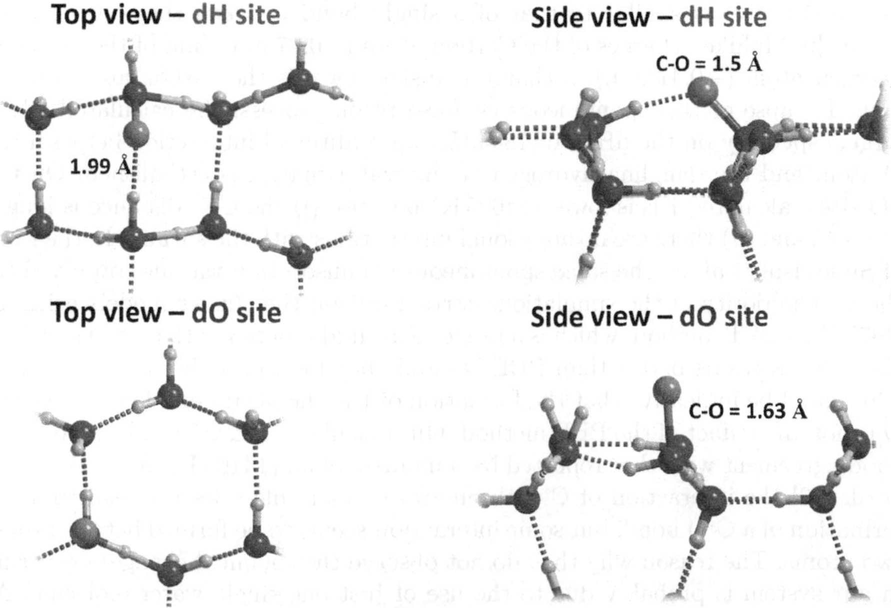

Fig. 4. Top and side views of the PBE-D3(BJ)-optimized geometries for the adsorption of C on the dH and dO sites. Bond distances are in Å

As one can seen in Fig. 2, for N adsorption, the atom remains over the water hexagon of the outermost ice layer and does not perturb the structure of the crystalline ice surface. Calculated BEs are small, dH being a more favourable adsorption site (977 K) than dO (937 K). In both complexes, the adsorption is dominated by dispersive forces. The computed values are in reasonable agreement with those reported in the other two computational works.

For O adsorption, the interaction with the surface is stronger than for the N case on both adsorption sites. Interestingly, adsorption on dH site (BE = 4673 K) is significantly more stable than the dO site (BE = 3177 K). As one can see in Fig. 3, on the dH site, the adsorbate O atom stays closer to the surface in comparison with the N case, as reflected by the O–O_{surf} and N–O_{surf} distances (2.27 and 2.85 Å, respectively). Due to that, the surface dangling H atom bents towards the O atom, thus presenting some distortion with respect to the pristine crystalline surface. Comparison of atomic O BEs on water, our values are clearly overestimated with respect to the values of the other works (see Table 1). This can be due to GGA nature of the PBE functional, which tends to overestimate electron delocalization situations [10]. This could indeed be our case since the O atom is an open-shell system with two unpaired electrons. Accordingly, more investigation as far as the quantum chemistry method is concerned on this system is required.

Adsorption of atomic C on our crystalline water ice surface model is the most peculiar case because it reacts spontaneously with an oxygen atom of the surface forming a •COH radical (see Fig. 4). This event triggers a chain displacement of a hydrogen atom to a nearby water molecule. The C-O distance (about 1.5 Å in the dH site) is similar to that of a single bond between these two atoms. From the Mulliken charges of the Carbon atom (−0.27 a.u.) and of the attached Oxygen atom (−0.41 a.u.), a charge transfer towards the carbon atom can be seen. Because of this spontaneous chemisorption process, the calculated BE is large, especially on the dH site (18449 K) an additional interaction between the C atom and the dangling hydrogen of the water matrix is estbalished. On the dO site, calculated BE is lower (14605 K) because (i) the C-O distance is longer (1.63 Å) and (ii) there are no additional interactions with the surface. In the work of Simonishi et al. [9] the same spontaneous chemisorption was also observed for the vast majority of the simulations carried out on the cluster models using ω-B97XD as DFT method, which is a range separated functional that can treat long range interactions better than PBE-D3 and therefore, probably more accurate. This could be indicative that the formation of the chemical bond between C and O is not an artifact of the PBE method. Our calculated BE value, moreover, is in good agreement with that reported by Simonishi et al. (14100 K) [9]. In Wakalem et al. [13] the interaction of C with one water molecule does not lead to a full formation of a C-O bond, but some interaction seems to be formed between these two atoms. The reason why they do not observe the chemical changes occurring in our system is probably due to the use of just one single water molecule. As mentioned above, the chemisorption brings associated with a H transfer from the reacting water to a nearby water molecule, which favors the formation of the

C-O chemical bond. This H transfer is not possible in the Wakelam's model and accordingly, the system does not evolve to fully form •COH. Because of that, the Wakelam's BE value is lower (10000 K) than the computed by us and by Shimonishi et al.

5 Conclusions and Perspective

The adsorption of atomic $C(^3P)$, $N(^4S)$ and $O(^3P)$ on a crystalline water ice surface model based on the P-ice system has been investigated by means of DFT PBE-D3(BJ). Our results are in general in good agreement with those reported in the literature using smaller, non periodic water ice models and different DFT methods, although some differences have been detected. The physisorption of N and O and the chemisorption of C are qualitatively similar. Calculated BE values for N are in good agreement with the other computational data. For C adsorption, in which spontaneous formation of •COH takes place, results indicate the importance of using relatively large water ice surfaces, otherwise the chemisorption is not properly described (i.e., full formation of •COH does not occur). The major drawback of the present work is the overestimated BE value for atomic O, which is over stabilized with respect to the reported values, probably due to the GGA nature of the PBE functional. Further investigations in that aspect (e.g., to refinement of the BE values using highly accurate quantum chemical methods) are mandatory. As a perspective, the next step will be to simulate the same adsorption processes on an amorphous ice surface, which will resemble more closely astrochemical ices, to assess the changes that a disordered surface can bring to the BE values of these atomic species.

Acknowledgements. This project has received funding from the European Union's Horizon 2020 research and innovation programme under the Marie Skłodowska-Curie grant agreement No 811312 for the project "Astro-Chemical Origins" (ACO). AR is indebted to the "Ramón y Cajal" program. MINECO (project CTQ2017-89132-P) and DIUE (project 2017SGR1323) are acknowledged. BSC-MN is kindly acknowledged for the generous allowance of supercomputing time through the QS-2020-1-0009 project.

References

1. Casassa, S., Ugliengo, P., Pisani, C.: Proton-ordered models of ordinary ice for quantum-mechanical studies. J. Chem. Phys. **106**(19), 8030–8040 (1997)
2. Cuppen, H., et al.: Grain surface models and data for astrochemistry. Space Sci. Rev. **212**(1–2), 1–58 (2017)
3. Goedecker, S., Teter, M., Hutter, J.: Separable dual-space Gaussian pseudopotentials. Phys. Rev. B **54**(3), 1703 (1996)
4. Grimme, S., Antony, J., Ehrlich, S., Krieg, H.: A consistent and accurate ab initio parametrization of density functional dispersion correction (DFT-D) for the 94 elements H-Pu. J. Chem. Phys. **132**(15), 154104 (2010)
5. Grimme, S., Ehrlich, S., Goerigk, L.: Effect of the damping function in dispersion corrected density functional theory. J. Comput. Chem. **32**(7), 1456–1465 (2011)

6. Hutter, J., Iannuzzi, M., Schiffmann, F., VandeVondele, J.: cp2k: atomistic simulations of condensed matter systems. Wiley Interdisc. Rev. Comput. Mol. Sci. **4**(1), 15–25 (2014)
7. Lippert, G., Hutter, J., Parrinello, M.: A hybrid Gaussian and plane wave density functional scheme. Mol. Phys. **92**(3), 477–488 (1997)
8. Perdew, J.P., Burke, K., Ernzerhof, M.: Generalized gradient approximation made simple. Phys. Rev. Lett. **77**(18), 3865 (1996)
9. Shimonishi, T., Nakatani, N., Furuya, K., Hama, T.: Adsorption energies of carbon, nitrogen, and oxygen atoms on the low-temperature amorphous water ice: a systematic estimation from quantum chemistry calculations. Astrophys. J. **855**(1), 27 (2018)
10. Sodupe, M., Bertran, J., Rodríguez-Santiago, L., Baerends, E.: Ground state of the $(h_2o)_2{}^+$ radical cation: DFT versus Post-Hartree-Fock methods. J. Phys. Chem. A **103**(1), 166–170 (1999)
11. Tasker, P.: The stability of ionic crystal surfaces. J. Phys. C Solid State Phys. **12**(22), 4977 (1979)
12. VandeVondele, J., Krack, M., Mohamed, F., Parrinello, M., Chassaing, T., Hutter, J.: Quickstep: fast and accurate density functional calculations using a mixed gaussian and plane waves approach. Comput. Phys. Commun. **167**(2), 103–128 (2005)
13. Wakelam, V., Loison, J.C., Mereau, R., Ruaud, M.: Binding energies: new values and impact on the efficiency of chemical desorption. Mol. Astrophys. **6**, 22–35 (2017)

A Combined DFT and RRKM-Based Study on the Reactivity of $HCO + NH_2$ on Amorphous Water Ice Surface

Joan Enrique-Romero[1,2(✉)], Albert Rimola[2], and Cecilia Ceccarelli[1]

[1] Univ. Grenoble Alpes, CNRS, Institut de Planétologie et d'Astrophysique de Grenoble (IPAG), 38000 Grenoble, France
juan.enrique-romero@univ-grenoble-alpes.fr

[2] Departament de Química, Universitat Autònoma de Barcelona, 08193 Bellaterra, Catalonia, Spain

Abstract. Formamide is observed in the interstellar medium and it is thought to play an important role as a precursor of prebiotic molecules. In this work we study the reactivity of NH_2 and HCO on the open surface of amorphous ice model, which can either lead to the formation of formamide (through radical-radical coupling) or $CO + NH_3$ (through direct H-abstraction) by means of DFT electronic structure calculations, and derive their unimolecular rate constants within the RRKM scheme. We found that radical-radical coupling is faster and hence there is no competition between the two processes in this particular case. Despite of this result, the radical-radical mechanism in dust grain ices is still to be validated.

Keywords: Interstellar medium · Astrochemistry · DFT simulations · Kinetic RRKM calculations · iCOMs · Grains

1 Introduction

From the more than 200 molecular species detected in space, a subset called *interstellar complex organic molecules* (iCOMs), loosely defined as C-bearing species constituted by at least 6 atoms [6], is of special interest given that (i) they lock ~20% of the interstellar carbon budget, (ii) they could be inherited from star-forming regions into planetary systems and (iii) they could be related to the origin of life on Earth and the possible presence of life elsewhere in the Universe as they are thought to be precursors of more complex prebiotic species [5,11,16].

Among all iCOMs, formamide (NH_2CHO) is a species of particular interest as (i) it contains the four most essential elements for biological systems (i.e., C, H, O and N) and (ii) it has been observed towards a variety of prestellar, protostellar sources (e.g. [12,13]) and in comets (e.g. [3,4]). The formation pathways of this species, through either gas-phase processes or reactions occurring on the

O. Gervasi et al. (Eds.): ICCSA 2020, LNCS 12253, pp. 561–566, 2020.
https://doi.org/10.1007/978-3-030-58814-4_42

surfaces of grains, have received much attention, specially from the computational chemistry community. This is because quantum computations are robust tools capable to provide unique atomic-scale pictures of the mechanistic steps of the reactions, alongside reliable structural and energetic information. For example, the gas phase route of NH_2 + H_2CO → NH_2CHO + H has been studied by means of quantum chemical and kinetic calculations [2,17,19], which has received support from observational studies such as [7]. On the other hand, the formation of formamide on ice-covered interstellar dust grains was initially thought to happen mainly through the hydrogenation of HNCO, which was experimentally ruled out [14] and theoretically predicted to be very slow [18]. A generally accepted pathway to form iCOMs like formamide is via radical-radical couplings (Rc) on or/and in ice mantles [10]. Recent works [8,15] investigated the formation of formamide adopting this mechanism (i.e. the radical-radical combination of NH_2 and HCO) by means of quantum chemistry calculations and using as amorphous solid water (ASW) a water cluster model of 33 water molecules. However, this route was not found as unique but it has a competitive channel: the direct H-abstraction (dHa) reaction NH_2 + HCO → NH_3 + CO. [8] found that the ice vicinity strongly affects the reactivity of radicals. Specifically, formamide has more chances to be formed in cavities than in open surfaces, but there is still competition between Rc and dHa. Interestingly, the work by [15] proposed as an alternative route towards formamide formation the reaction of CN with a water molecule of the ice, assuming that the nascent energy of the first reaction steps is not quickly dissipated. In this contribution, the reactivity between NH_2 and HCO (i.e, both Rc and dHa reactions) on the same 33 water cluster model used in [8] in the side surface site (where the reactions exhibited the largest energy barriers) is extended by studying also the kinetics of the processes adopting the Rice–Ramsperger–Kassel–Marcus (RRKM) theory, which were overlooked in the previous paper.

2 Computational Details

All the electronic-structure calculations were carried out using the GAUSSIAN16 suit of programs [9]. The hybrid DFT BHLYP method in combination with a Pople's double-ζ basis set 6-31+G(d,p) was used, adopting an unrestricted and broken (spin)-symmetry formalism. The description of the stationary points (Fig. 1) identified in Enrique-Romero et al. (2019) were improved by introducing the Grimme's D3(BJ) dispersion correction in *a posteriori* way. The distance between radicals in the reactant geometry is longer than 5 Å (Fig. 1), and accordingly there is not interaction between them, but rather with the surface only. This means that BSSE is almost negligible, without any influence neither in the geometries nor in the reaction energetics and, therefore, BSSE corrections have not been accounted for.

Unimolecular rate constants for both Rc and dHa reactions were computed using an in-house developed code (e.g. [1,15,17]) based on the Ramspberger-Rice-Kassel-Marcus (RRKM) scheme. Under this approximation,

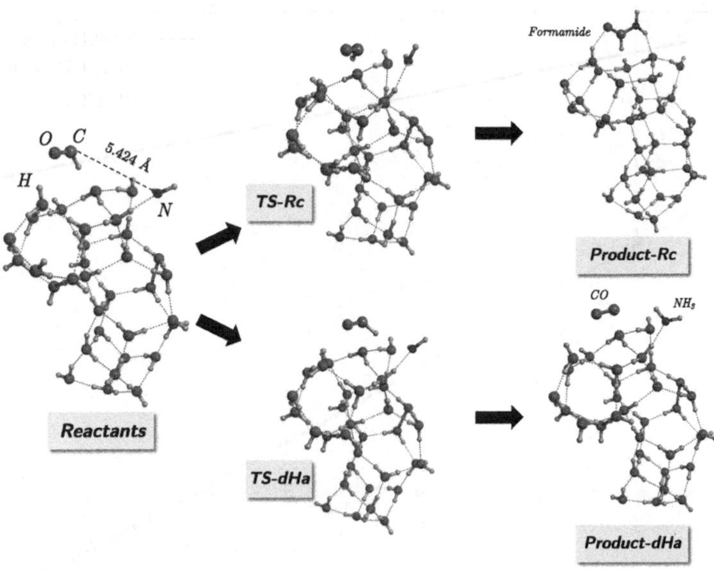

Fig. 1. Stationary points of the potential energy surfaces of the radical-radical coupling (Rc) and direct Hydrogen abstraction (dHa) reactions. Energetics can be found in the text (Sect. 3)

the ice + radicals system is considered to be a single supermolecule isolated from its surroundings, for which the fast intramolecular vibrational energy redistribution holds. The considered degrees of freedom include all the vibrational harmonic modes and the overall rotations of the cluster+radicals system. Under this circumstances, one computes the rates at a given total energy E by Eq. 1, where $N(E)$ is the sum of states of the transition state under the energy E, $\rho(E)$ is the reactant density of states and h is Planck's constant. This is followed by a Boltzmann averaging step in order to derive the temperature-dependent rate constant.

$$k(E) = \frac{N(E)}{h\rho(E)} \tag{1}$$

For the dHa case, tunnelling has been accounted for in an approximated way by means of the symmetric Eckart's barrier.

3 Results and Discussion: Arrhenius Plot

By adopting the BHLYP-D3(BJ)/6-31+G(d,p) theory level, the reaction and activation enthalpies at 0 K (i.e., the potential energy values including zero-point energy corrections) are: −390.1 and 2.3 kJ/mol for Rc, and −334.4 and 6.6 kJ/mol for dHa. Figure 2 shows the Arrhenius plots for both reactions.

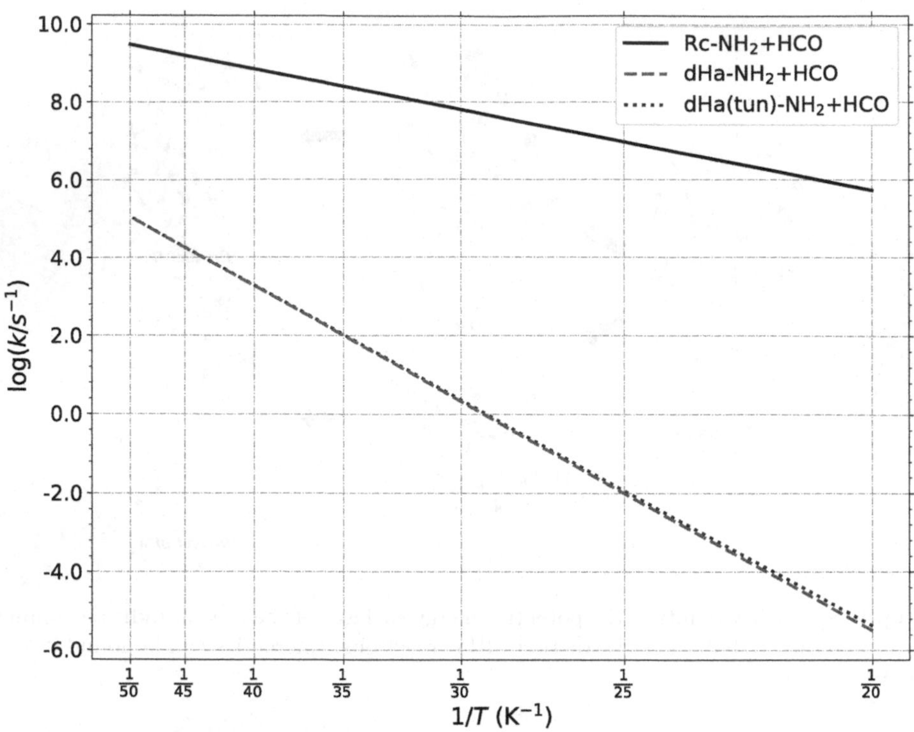

Fig. 2. Arrhenius plot for the radical-radical coupling (Rc) and direct H-abstraction (dHa) reactions between NH_2 and HCO on the side 33-water molecules cluster.

As a consequence of the lower energy barrier of Rc compared with dHa, calculated rate constants for the Rc reaction are larger than the dHa. That is, Rc rate constants stay over those for the dHa along the considered range of temperatures in the Arrhenius plot. It is worth mentioning that tunnelling does not exert any significant effect on the dHa rate constants. This is because the imaginary transition state frequency is very small ($\sim 43i$ cm^{-1}), and hence that the associated reduced mass is large, hindering tunneling to be dominant. In view of these kinetic results, therefore, the radical-radical coupling between NH_2 + HCO to form formamide actually dominates the chemistry on bare, open water ice surfaces (i.e. not taking into account pores nor cavities). We emphasis, though that, we are unable at this stage to say whether the radical-radical coupling reaction can actually occur on the grain surfaces. In order to verify it, the present rate coefficients should be incorporated into astrochemical models together with the other possible surface processes (such as diffusion and morphology effects, and their rates), which implies a change in the treatment of the grain surface chemistry of the current models.

4 Conclusions

DFT quantum chemistry computations alongside RRKM-based kinetic calculations indicate that formation of formamide on flat, compact water ice surfaces is actually a plausible channel by the coupling of the NH_2 + HCO radicals. It dominates over the direct H-abstraction reaction, which would lead to the formation of NH_3 and CO and that was previously postulated as a competitive channel to the radical-radical coupling. The dominance of the Rc over dHa is due to two factors: i) the Rc energy barrier is lower than the dHa one, hence giving rise to faster rate constants, and ii) tunnelling does not contribute to the rate constants of the dHa reaction, as a consequence of the associated low transition state frequency.

In order to validate whether radical-radical coupling mechanisms do actually take place in interstellar dust grains, the treatment of ice chemistry in astrochemical models should be modified incorporating kinetic data such as the one presented in this work, instead of assuming direct reaction upon encounter. Nevertheless, care must be taken given that the local surface properties may affect the potential energy surface and therefore the kinetics of any given radical-radical reaction, see for example [8].

Aknowledgement. We wish to thank Dimitrios Skouteris for his efforts in developing the RRKM code used in this work and making it available to us, and also to prof. Gretobape for exciting discussions. We acknowledge funding from the European Research Council (ERC) under the European Union's Horizon 2020 research and innovation program, for the Project "the Dawn of Organic Chemistry" (DOC), grant agreement No 741002. Some of the calculations presented in this paper were performed using the GRICAD infrastructure (https://gricad.univ-grenoble-alpes.fr), which is partly supported by the Equip@Meso project (reference ANR-10-EQPX-29-01) of the programme Investments d'Avenir supervised by the Agence Nationale pour la Recherche. Additionally this work was granted access to the HPC resources of IDRIS under the allocation 2019-A0060810797 attributed by GENCI (Grand Equipment National de Calcul Intensif).

References

1. Balucani, N., et al.: A Combined crossed molecular beam and theoretical studies of the $N(^2D)$ + CH_4 reaction and implications. J. Phys. Chem. **113**(42), 11138–11152 (2009). https://doi.org/10.1021/jp904302g
2. Barone, V., et al.: Gas-phase formation of the prebiotic molecule formamide: insights from new quantum computations. Mon. Not. R. Astron. Soc. Lett. **453**(1), L31–L35 (2015). https://doi.org/10.1093/mnrasl/slv094
3. Biver, N., et al.: Ethyl alcohol and sugar in comet C/2014 Q2 (Lovejoy). Sci. Adv. **1**(9), e1500863 (2015). https://doi.org/10.1126/sciadv.1500863
4. Bockelee-Morvan, D., et al.: New molecules found in comet C/1995 O1 (Hale-Bopp). Astron. Astrophys. **353**, 1101–1114 (2000)
5. Caselli, P., Ceccarelli, C.: Our astrochemical heritage. Astron. Astrophys. Rev. **20**(1), 56 (2012). https://doi.org/10.1007/s00159-012-0056-x

6. Ceccarelli, C., et al.: Seeds of life in space (SOLIS): the organic composition diversity at 300–1000 au scale in solar-type star-forming regions. Astrophys. J. **850**, 176 (2017). https://doi.org/10.3847/1538-4357/aa961d
7. Codella, C., et al.: Seeds of life in space (SOLIS) II. Formamide in protostellar shocks: Evidence for gas-phase formation. Astron. Astrophys. **605**, L3 (2017). https://doi.org/10.1051/0004-6361/201731249
8. Enrique-Romero, J., Rimola, A., Ceccarelli, C., Ugliengo, P., Balucani, N., Skouteris, D.: Reactivity of HCO with CH_3 and NH_2 on water ice surfaces a comprehensive accurate quantum chemistry study. ACS Earth Space Chem. **3**(10), 2158–2170 (2019). https://doi.org/10.1021/acsearthspacechem.9b00156
9. Frisch, M.J., et al.: Gaussian16 Revision C.01 (2016), gaussian Inc., Wallingford CT
10. Garrod, R.T., Herbst, E.: Formation of methyl formate and other organic species in the warm-up phase of hot molecular cores. Astron. Astrophys. **457**(3), 927–936 (2006)
11. Herbst, E.: The synthesis of large interstellar molecules. Int. Rev. Phys. Chem. **36**(2), 287–331 (2017). https://doi.org/10.1080/0144235X.2017.1293974
12. Kahane, C., Ceccarelli, C., Faure, A., Caux, E.: Detection of formamide, the simplest but crucial amide, in a solar-type protostar. ApJ **763**(2), L38 (2013). https://doi.org/10.1088/2041-8205/763/2/L38
13. López-Sepulcre, A., Balucani, N., Ceccarelli, C., Codella, C., Dulieu, F., Theulé, P.: Interstellar formamide (NH_2CHO), a key prebiotic precursor. ACS Earth Space Chem. **3**(10), 2122–2137 (2019). https://doi.org/10.1021/acsearthspacechem.9b00154
14. Noble, J.A., et al.: Hydrogenation at low temperatures does not always lead to saturation: the case of HNCO. A&A **576**, A91 (2015). https://doi.org/10.1051/0004-6361/201425403
15. Rimola, A., et al.: Can formamide be formed on interstellar ice? An atomistic perspective. ACS Earth Space Chem. **2**(7), 720–734 (2018). https://doi.org/10.1021/acsearthspacechem.7b00156
16. Saladino, R., Botta, G., Pino, S., Costanzo, G., Di Mauro, E.: Genetics first or metabolism first? The formamide clue. Chem. Soc. Rev. **41**(16), 5526 (2012). https://doi.org/10.1039/c2cs35066a
17. Skouteris, D., Vazart, F., Ceccarelli, C., Balucani, N., Puzzarini, C., Barone, V.: New quantum chemical computations of formamide deuteration support a gas-phase formation of this prebiotic molecule. Mon. Not. R. Astron. Soc. Lett. slx012 (2017). https://doi.org/10.1093/mnrasl/slx012
18. Song, L., Kästner, J.: Formation of the prebiotic molecule NH_2CHO on astronomical amorphous solid water surfaces: accurate tunneling rate calculations. Phys. Chem. Chem. Phys. **18**(42), 29278–29285 (2016). https://doi.org/10.1039/C6CP05727F
19. Vazart, F., Calderini, D., Puzzarini, C., Skouteris, D., Barone, V.: State-of-the-art thermochemical and kinetic computations for astrochemical complex organic molecules: formamide formation in cold interstellar clouds as a case study. J. Chem. Theory Comput. **12**(11), 5385–5397 (2016). https://doi.org/10.1021/acs.jctc.6b00379

Spatio-Temporal Dynamics of Urban and Natural Areas in the Northern Littoral Zone of Rome

Land-Cover Change Analysis During the Last Thirty Years. Preliminary Results

Maurizio Pollino(✉), Francesco Lodato, and Nicola Colonna

ENEA - Italian National Agency for New Technologies, Energy and Sustainable Economic Development, Casaccia Research Centre, Via Anguillarese 301, 00123 Rome, Italy
{maurizio.pollino,nicola.colonna}@enea.it, francescolodato888@gmail.com

Abstract. The present study is focused on the littoral zone between Rome and Civitavecchia, where the spatio-temporal dynamics of the land cover has been analysed during the last thirty years, by means of Remote Sensing and GIS procedures. In a few decades, the coastal municipalities within the study area have considerably increased their inhabitants. Population and urban expansion have grown in parallel, at the expense of agricultural and natural areas, especially in the narrow coastal strip between the sea and the hills. Landsat satellite data from 1990 to 2019 have been processed and classified in order to describe and map the Land-Cover change (LCc). Maps have been suitable integrated with population data and other geospatial layers (transportation network). The results obtained allowed to understand the natural and rural land transformations, especially those related to the urban growth and expansion that are related to the proximity of Rome City.

Keywords: Remote sensing · Land-Cover change · GIS · Territorial planning · Rural areas · Land fragmentation

1 Introduction

Given their complexity, in order to be adequately studied, environmental issues and territorial dynamics need approaches based on specific geospatial information at different spatial and temporal scales. This set of various information, suitably processed and synthesized, can be very useful for understanding phenomena and processes, especially where urban and rural/natural areas are facing urbanization processes [1].

In this general context, the availability of detailed and updated information about Land Cover (LC) and the related spatio-temporal changes (LCc) is fundamental, to analyse and understand the mutual relationships between anthropic activities and the natural environment. Remote Sensing (RS) techniques and GIS methodologies were largely exploited and continue to be currently used in a multitude of similar studies and works [2]. By means of multi-temporal datasets of RS images, it is possible to identify

O. Gervasi et al. (Eds.): ICCSA 2020, LNCS 12253, pp. 567–575, 2020.
https://doi.org/10.1007/978-3-030-58814-4_43

and map changes in the landscape, providing a valid support to planning and monitoring activities.

In Italy, in the recent past, the problem of the identification between urban and rural space has always been solved with a clear distinction between the two contexts, with a prevalence of planning actions addressed to the urban development and to the related aspects [3]. On the other hand, as is well known, in the last 50 years widespread urbanization has interested many parts of the Country: such expansion in many cases was not adequately planned or regulated, resulting in a penetration of the urbanization in agricultural areas, with the consequence that many rural parts have been incorporated into the urban landscape [4]. This development is able to deeply influence the landscape, causing the transformation of rural areas into urbanized ones and producing substantial changes, both from a morphological-structural and functional point of view [3]. In particular, in Italy, we have observed an increase of urbanisation pressure towards rural areas over the years, due to lower estate costs and to the transfer towards peripheral and suburban areas of functions typical of urban centralities [5].

In order to study the LCc that have occurred over a period of thirty years in the area of interest, a multi-temporal dataset of Landsat satellite images has been selected, processed, and classified [6]. In this way, seven LC maps have been produced for the time interval from 1990 to 2019, with 5-years steps. These results have been integrated, in GIS environment, to analyse and understand the dynamics in LCc.

2 Study Area

The case study described in the present paper is focused on a specific area located in the littoral zone north of Rome, including the Municipalities of Civitavecchia, Santa Marinella, Cerveteri and Ladispoli (Fig. 1), and extending for approximately 280 km^2.

This territory develops along the North-South direction, between the Tyrrhenian coast and the slopes of the Tolfa Mountains, integrating into the geomorphological and landscape scenario of the northern Latium Region.

The inner zone of the study area (max 482 m a.s.l.) represents the foothills of the Tolfa Mountains, which from a geological point of view are characterised by an acid volcanism (dated back to the Pleistocene), with "domo" formations, rich of tracheitis [7]. These geological characteristics, jointly with the geomorphological ones (i.e. steep slopes) have made difficult the exploitation of such hilly areas, which are still largely covered with broadleaf trees, in particular oaks, along with other species typical of the Mediterranean maquis (laurel, *ruscus aculeatus*, lentisk, ivy). The wooded areas are also characterised by coppice with a twenty-year cycle [8, 9].

The plain, separating the hilly backcountry from the coast, is quite limited in the Municipalities of Civitavecchia and Santa Marinella (northern part of study area, Fig. 1), whilst is mainly stretched in the territory of Cerveteri and Ladispoli (southern part of study area, Fig. 1). This land, once converted to agricultural use, has been intensively exploited (mainly vineyards and orchards), after the economic expansion occurred in Italy during the '60s of the past century. This factor also represented a driving force of the demographic and urban growth in the area (as well as for the most part of our Country [5]), in parallel with the increase of the agricultural sector.

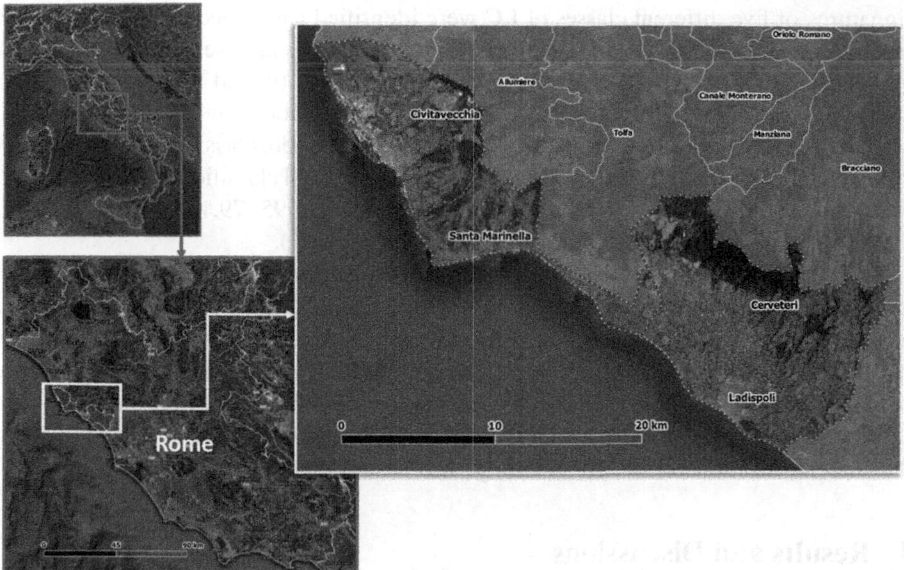

Fig. 1. The geographic location of the study area and municipalities administrative borders

3 Data and Materials

In order to classify and analyse the LCc in the study area over the thirty years (1990÷2019) a multi-temporal dataset was used consisting of seven Landsat satellite images [6]. Those multi-spectral images were downloaded from the NASA Earthdata portal [10], by means of the Semi-Automatic Classification (SCP) plugin [11] of QGIS. The same plugin was also exploited for the classification process of images, described in the following.

For the aims of the present study, five Landsat 5-TM scenes (06/26/1990–07/10/1995 – 06/05/2000–05/02/2005 – 07/14/2009), and two Landsat 8-OLI scenes (06/12/2014 – 06/26/2019) were downloaded and processed. The interval between two consecutive Landsat scenes was originally set of 5 years, but in some cases, such interval actually became of 4 years, due to a lack of useful images (e.g., 2009 and 2014 scenes were preferred respectively to 2010 and 2015 ones for cloud cover or missing data). In any case, the images have been selected in the same seasonal period, in order to account for the phenological phase of the vegetation, which - if not considered - could lead to errors in change detection. The images were co-registered, in order to avoid that spatial positioning errors of pixels can be interpreted as changes in land cover.

As stated before, SCP [11] is a free/open-source plugin for the semi-automatic classification (supervised and unsupervised) of remote sensing images, providing several tools both for downloading free images (Landsat, Sentinel-2, Sentinel-3, ASTER, MODIS), and for pre-processing, classification, post-processing, raster calculation procedures. Firstly, the images were converted to reflectance by applying DOS (dark object subtraction) atmospheric correction [12]. To perform the supervised classification, the spectral signatures of five different classes of LC were identified and collected: "Artificial Surfaces" (that includes urban areas, industrial settlements, greenhouses and other impervious surfaces), "Woodland", "Mixed Cultivated/Shrubland" (mixed areas, where moderately cultivated and uncultivated plots of land coexist), "Arable Land" (regularly worked or ploughed land) and "Water Bodies". The seven images were classified using the Spectral Angle Mapping (SAM) algorithm [13]. Then, the overall classification accuracy [14] was evaluated for each classified image (1990: 76.36%; 1995: 79.10%; 2000: 79.09%; 2005: 82.73%; 2009; 93.63%; 2014: 90.0%; 2019: 85.45%).

The seven different LC maps produced from the classified images, originally in raster format, were converted into the shapefile.*shp* vector format, in order to perform the LCc analysis by working directly on the attribute table [15]. For each classified map, the spatial information of LC classes (area, perimeter) has been available. By comparing each classified map with the successive, it has been possible to determine the changes in LC at different years for the time interval considered, and finally, the information about the amount, location, and nature of change was assessed [16].

4 Results and Discussions

Table 1 summarizes the LC area values (in hectares) obtained from the classified satellite images and reported at every ten-year interval.

Table 1. Total areas (values expressed in ha) for each LC type defined at every ten-year interval. The last column reports the percentage change in the overall time span 1990÷2019.

LC class	1990	2000	2009	2019	% 1990 ÷ 2019
Water bodies	49.68	43.92	32.94	53.46	+7%
Artificial surfaces	2143.98	2184.48	3794.94	3179.70	+33%
Woodland	3644.28	3580.47	4627.98	5191.47	+30%
Arable land	16435.80	15546.87	7621.38	8862.48	−85%
Mixed cultivated/shrubland	5947.20	6865.20	12143.70	10933.83	+46%
	28220.94	**28220.94**	**28220.94**	**28220.94**	

Table 2 reports the LC transition matrix [17] for the overall time interval analysed, in which the rows display the area values (in ha) for each LC class of 1990 and in columns the corresponding area values of 2019 are shown.

In Fig. 2 are mapped the LCc detected during the overall period considered (1990 ÷ 2019). Urban areas progressively grew-up over the last thirty years, with a particular intensification after 2000.

The turn of the millennium coincided with several urban transformations, such as the creation of the craft/industrial and shopping areas in the northern part of Ladispoli and the expansion of the Civitavecchia tourist harbour. Those changes were followed by

Table 2. LC areas (ha) transition matrix from 1990 to 2019

LC transitions 1990 ÷ 2019 *(Areas in ha)*	Artificial surfaces	Arable land	Cultivated/Shrubland	Woodland	Water Bodies
Artificial surfaces	–	134.00	280.40	18.17	–
Arable land	1320.74	–	7819.62	645.46	8.27
Cultivated/Shrubland	150.56	981.62	–	1335.97	–
Woodland	6.48	34.72	520.66	–	–
Water Bodies	–	–	1.26	–	–

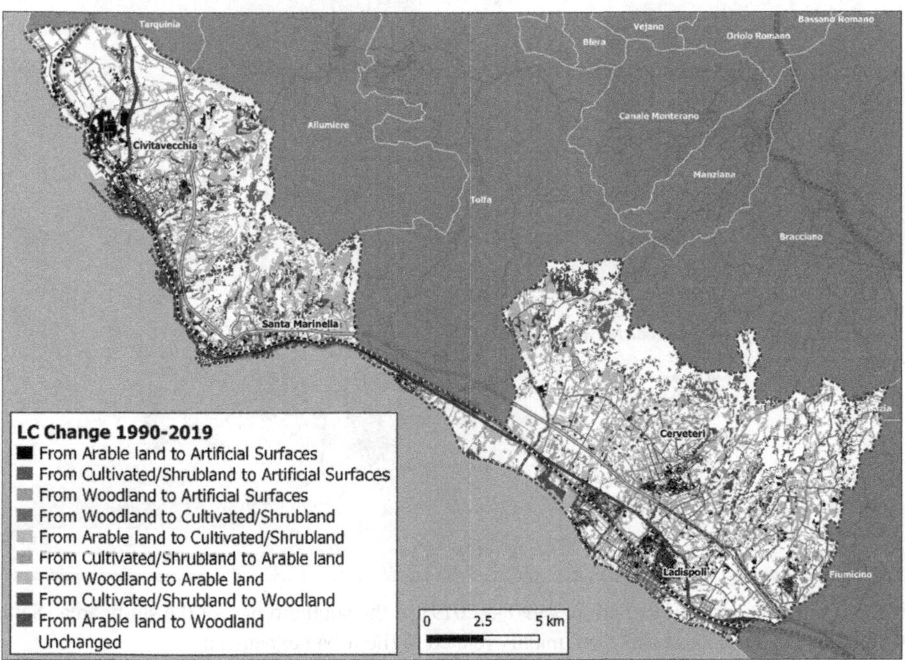

Fig. 2. LC changes and dynamics within the study area for the overall time span 1990 ÷ 2019

the construction or completion of important residential areas, such as Cerreto district in Ladispoli, Thyrsenia in Cerveteri. The development and subsequent densification of the built-up areas along the northern coast of Latium, clearly observed during the 30 years of the present study, has gradually changed the typically agricultural vocation of these Municipalities, relegating this activity to the adjacent peri-urban areas and increasing the impervious surface coverage.

A large littoralization process happened, linked to seasonal tourism pressure, due to the development of beach tourism, as in many other Mediterranean coastal areas [18]. In this sense, typical seaside districts, such as Marina di Cerveteri and Santa Severa, have changed their functionality: in the '70 and '80 they were characterised by floating population (temporary rents for summer vacations), whilst from the late '90 the commuters, benefiting of transportation connections, started to rent the dwellings here located, as typically has happened in many metropolitan areas [19]. In particular, focusing on the southern part of the study area, the analysis of RS data indicates a continuous expansion of the urbanized areas, especially along the major communication routes (Fig. 3), such as the Rome-Civitavecchia railway line (FL5), Via Aurelia (SS1) and the A-12 Motorway, which guarantee a fast connection with Rome and de facto make the four Municipalities as "residential" extensions of the Capital.

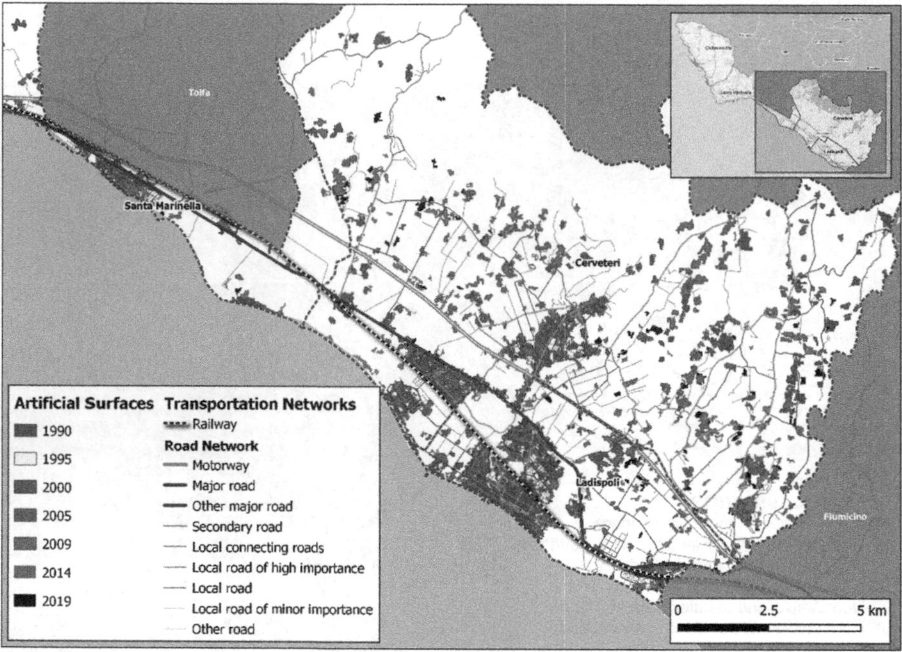

Fig. 3. Artificial surfaces evolution (1990 ÷ 2019) in the southern part of the study area (Santa Marinella, Cerveteri and Ladispoli), mainly related to the urban expansion

The population has almost doubled in just over 30 years, as confirmed by census data (Fig. 4), and the analyses carried out by exploiting satellite images have highlighted that urban areas increased according to the characteristic dynamics of such phenomenon: expansion, densification, and sprawl.

In Table 1 it is possible to observe the decrease of the areas covered by "Artificial Surfaces" during the last ten years (2009–2019). This can be related to the reduction of greenhouses (due to the economic crisis which has interested the agriculture sector in the recent years) and to the disappearance of tarp covers (largely used in the '90s, then fallen in disuse). Also considering Table 1, taking into account the seasonal conditions and the phenological phases of vegetation and crops, a considerable increase in the "Cultivated/Shrubland" LC class has been observed, especially in peri-urban areas, which at

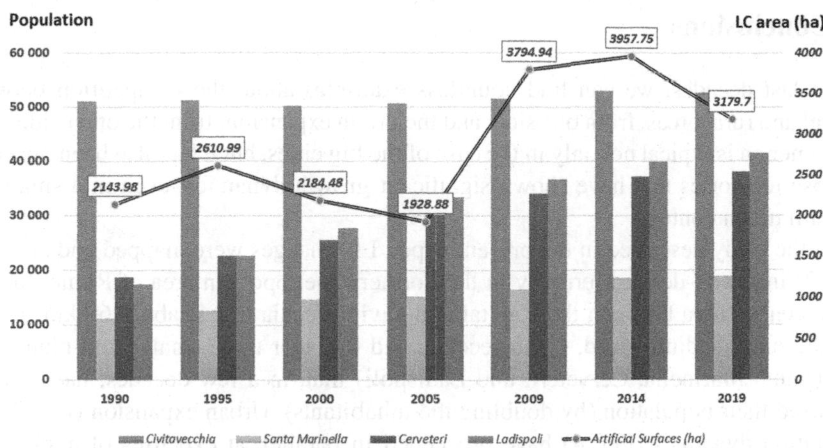

Fig. 4. Population growth in each municipality (source: ISTAT) and artificial surfaces dynamics within the study area during the time interval analysed (1990 ÷ 2019)

the beginning of the '90s were mainly covered by ploughed soil for arable crops. These areas have been progressively consumed as a consequence of urban sprawling. This border zone results in an LC mixture, where the gardens and the residual farmland areas are not clearly distinguishable, just as the pastures that are locally fragmented and often abandoned. In this latter case, it is also possible to observe a contained re-naturalisation process, especially in the most inaccessible areas.

The plain of Cerveteri and Ladispoli is mainly characterised by clay-rich soils, once covered by marshes and broadleaf forests. Then, after the hydraulic reclamation works (started during the '50s of the past century) this land was converted to agricultural uses. Here, the expansion of the "Cultivated/Shrubland" LC class can be related to the realisation of the "Consorzio di Bonifica Litorale Nord" aqueduct [20], which since 2002 serves the countryside areas of Cerveteri and Ladispoli, both for domestic (garden irrigation) and agricultural uses. This has favoured the exploitation of arable land with the introduction of water demanding crops, such as maize or cucurbitaceous, as well as guaranteeing an adequate water supply to orchards and vineyards. Fragmented residuals of those pre-existing natural areas [21] can be identified in some small oases (Macchiatonda, Palo, Torre Flavia), currently classified as EU Special Protection Areas (about 120 ha) under the regional legislation.

Concerning the wooded areas, no relevant variations over the last thirty years have been detected. They are mainly located in the innermost and hilly zones of the study area, where morphological or pedological conditions (but also environmental or archaeological constraints) have not allowed their rural exploitation or modification. Noteworthy is the forest expansion observed near the archaeological site of the Etruscan Necropolis of Banditaccia [22], especially after 2004 when it was inscribed in the UNESCO World Heritage List (WHL).

5 Conclusions

In the last decades, we can find countless examples about the competition between natural and rural areas, from one side, and the urban expansion, from the other side. This phenomenon is typical not only in the case of the big cities, but it has also been observed in those territories that have shown significant growth dynamics, even in a small and medium urban context.

In the study described in the present paper, LC changes were mapped and analysed (Fig. 2) in a well-defined territory in the northern metropolitan area of Rome, located in the coastal area between the Capital and Civitavecchia that is about 60 km far. We focused on a medium-sized, Civitavecchia, and on other three small-sized municipalities (Santa Marinella, Cerveteri, and Ladispoli) that, in a few decades, have largely increased their population (by doubling the inhabitants). Urban expansion (Fig. 3) and population dynamics (Fig. 4) have proceeded in parallel, at expenses of agricultural and natural areas. In particular, from the '80s (but with a remarkable increase since the year 2000) the population displacement from the nearby Capital (i.e. commuting), has favoured massive urbanization, deeply impacting the agricultural systems and the natural structures, especially in the coastal zone. In this sense, RS data and GIS approaches demonstrated to be very useful to describe dynamics that simple statistical data do not clearly reveal.

These areas have been progressively consumed as a consequence of urban sprawling. In particular, many detached houses and cottages with large private green spaces were built-up, although the spectral resolution of the images used in the present study was not suitable to classify such mixed areas as urban LC class: such aspect will be further investigated in the future developments of this study, by exploiting more effective approaches, based on RS data at an adequate spatial and spectral resolution [23, 24].

References

1. Di Fazio, S., Modica, G.: Historic rural landscapes: sustainable planning strategies and action criteria. the italian experience in the global and european context. Sustainability **10**(11), 3834 (2018)
2. Phiri, D., Morgenroth, J.: Developments in landsat land cover classification methods: a review. Remote Sens. **9**, 967 (2017)
3. Antrop, M.: Landscape change and the urbanization process in europe. Landscape Urban Plan. **67**, 9–26 (2004)
4. Modica, G., Praticò, S., Di Fazio, S.: Abandonment of traditional terraced landscape: a change detection approach (a case study in Costa Viola, Calabria, Italy). L. Degrad. Dev. **28**, 2608–2622 (2017)
5. Amato, F., Maimone, B., Martellozzo, F., Nolè, G., Murgante, B.: The effects of urban policies on the development of urban areas. Sustainability. **8**, 297 (2016)
6. Fichera, C.R., Modica, G., Pollino, M.: GIS and remote sensing to study urban-rural transformation during a fifty-year period. In: Murgante, B., et al. (eds.) ICCSA 2011, Part I. LNCS, vol. 6782, pp. 237–252. Springer, Heidelberg (2011)
7. Lombardi, G., Mattias, P.: Petrology and mineralogy of the kaolin and alunite mineralizations of Latium (Italy). Geologica Romana **18**, 157–214 (1979)
8. Blasi, C.: Fitoclimatologia del Lazio. Ed. Borgia, Roma (1994)

9. Pietro, R., Azzella, M., Facioni, L.: The forest vegetation of the tolfa-ceriti mountains (northern latium - central italy). Hacquetia **9**(1), 91–150 (2010)
10. Earthdata NASA, https://earthdata.nasa.gov/, Accessed 13 May 2020
11. Congedo, L.: QGIS Semi-Automatic Classification (SCP) Plugin Documentation: http://dx.doi.org/10.13140/RG.2.2.29474.02242/1 (2016)
12. Chavez, P.S.: Image-based atmospheric corrections - revisited and improved photogrammetric engineering and remote sensing. Am. Soc. Photogramm. **62**, 1025–1036 (1996)
13. Kruse, F.A., et al.: The spectral image processing system (SIPS) - interactive visualization and analysis of imaging spectrometer data. Remote Sensing of Environment, 44, 2–3 (1993)
14. Congalton, R.G., Green, K.: Assessing the Accuracy of Remotely Sensed Data: Principles and Practices. CRC Press Taylor & Francis Group, Boca Raton, FL (2009)
15. Petit, C.C., Lambin, E.F.: Integration of multi-source remote sensing data for land cover change detection. Int. J. Geogr. Inf. Sci. **15**(8), 785–803 (2001)
16. Fichera, C.R., Modica, G., Pollino, M.: Land Cover classification and change-detection analysis using multi-temporal remote sensed imagery and landscape metrics. Eur. J. Remote Sens. **45**(1), 1–18 (2012)
17. Modica, G., Vizzari, M., Pollino, M., Fichera, C.R., Zoccali, P., Di Fazio, S.: Spatio-temporal analysis of the urban-rural gradient structure: an application in a mediterranean mountainous landscape (Serra San Bruno, Italy). Earth Syst. Dyn. **3**, 263–279 (2012)
18. Fuerst-Bjeliš, B., Durbešić, A.: Littoralization and behind: environmental change in mediterranean croatia. In: The overarching issues of the European space - Strategies for Spatial (Re)planning based on Innovation, Sustainability and Change, pp. 136–147. Fundação Universidade do Porto (2013)
19. Manganelli, B., Murgante, B.: The dynamics of urban land rent in italian regional capital cities. Land. **6**, 54 (2017)
20. Consorzio di Bonifica Litorale Nord, https://www.consorziobonificalitoralenord.it, Accessed 13 May 2020
21. Modica, G., Merlino, A., Solano, F., Mercurio, R.: An index for the assessment of degraded Mediterranean forest ecosystems. For. Syst. **24**(3) (2015)
22. Caneva, G., Benelli, F., Bartoli, F., Cicinelli, E.: Safeguarding natural and cultural heritage on etruscan tombs (La Banditaccia, Cerveteri, Italy). Rendiconti Lincei. Scienze Fisiche e Naturali **29**(4), 891–907 (2018). https://doi.org/10.1007/s12210-018-0730-7
23. Modica, G., et al.: Using landsat 8 imagery in detecting cork oak (*Quercus suber L.*) woodlands: a case study in calabria (Italy). J. Agric. Eng. **47**(4), 205–215 (2016)
24. Solano, F., Di Fazio, S., Modica, G.: A methodology based on GEOBIA and WorldView-3 imagery to derive vegetation indices at tree crown detail in olive orchards. Int. J. Appl. Earth Obs. Geoinf. **83**, 101912 (2019)
25. Solano, F., Colonna, N., Marani, M., Pollino, M.: Geospatial analysis to assess natural park biomass resources for energy uses in the context of the rome metropolitan area. In: Calabrò, F., Della Spina, L., Bevilacqua, C. (eds.) ISHT 2018. SIST, vol. 100, pp. 173–181. Springer, Cham (2019). https://doi.org/10.1007/978-3-319-92099-3_21

Attractive Arcade-Based Platform Approach to Exam Preparation

Matheus Lorenzato Braga[1(✉)], Victor Martins de Sousa[1], Clara Scheffer Emerich[2], and Rafael Américo Führich[2]

[1] Instituto Federal Catarinense, Campus Sombrio, Santa Catarina, Brazil
{matheus.braga,victor.sousa}@ifc.edu.br

[2] Instituto Federal Catarinense, Campus Sombrio, Santa Catarina, Brazil
emerichclara@gmail.com, rafaelamericofuhrich@gmail.com
http://www.ifc.edu.br/

Abstract. This article describes the motivation, development and results obtained with the use of an arcade with a game designed to prepare for the selection process for admission to the Instituto Federal Catarinense. Realizing the importance of using technologies for educational purposes, combining the needs that schools have to prepare their students for academic life, FlipIFC presents itself as a possibility to make preparation attractive and stimulating. The platform developed with the Java programming language, the MySQL database and using the knowledge of the technical course for the development of the arcade machine, showed positive results, confirming the effectiveness of the proposal in attracting students and assisting them in the test preparation process.

Keywords: Arcade machine platform · Educational technology · Learning technologies

1 Introduction

During a student's school life, we noticed the presence of several exams and tests, for which the school must prepare its students. In Brazil, one of these exams is the Classification Examination for the Instituto Federal Catarinense (IFC), which seeks to assess students' knowledge and classify the best positioned to enter the institution. It is up to the school and the teachers to look for ways to prepare the student for these exams, creating and looking for didactic and methodological resources that promote better learning and lead to a good performance, such as the application of simulations and preparatory classes.

IFC aims to train professionals qualified to perform efficiently, functions in the various sectors of the Brazilian economy. IFC has 15 campuses spread across Santa Catarina's state, offering education in several areas from initial to post-graduation [6].

The use of technology as a tool that contributes to the contemporary educational process is the subject of several studies, which demonstrate, in its results,

O. Gervasi et al. (Eds.): ICCSA 2020, LNCS 12253, pp. 576–584, 2020.
https://doi.org/10.1007/978-3-030-58814-4_44

the success of this practice. Currently, there's no one educational technology designed to prepare for the classification exam. Bringing the idea out of the IFC - Campus Avançado Sombrio (IFC-CAS), the FlipIFC project arises, which aims to build an arcade machine platform with a game for solving questions of the IFC admission exam.

The games fit into an educational context aiming to stimulate and motivate individuals to perform tasks, behavior changes and learning. The use of that is a promising approach due to their abilities to teach and reinforce not only knowledge but skills such as problem solving. They utilize a number of mechanisms to encourage people to engage with them, often without any reward, just for the joy of playing and possibility to win [4]. This practice became known as gamification.

Therefore, bringing tools to the school environment that assist in the learning process can be considered an effective and efficient method of achieving the institution's objectives [5]. Gamification is a way of transforming school content into technology, with the aim of stimulating and motivating individuals.

Given this context, in this article, the focus is to discuss the use of FlipIFC and its evaluation. In particular, a gamified learning activity is presented in which FlipIFC is used and assesses its ability to influence students to improve. In addition, this proposal aims to collaborate with the divulgation of the institution, familiarizing students with exam model.

2 Related Work

The research in educational technology has grown from investigations attempting to apply that media and technology are effective tools for instruction, to investigations to examine the applications of processes and technologies to the improvement of learning [8]. Computer games and educational technology games have the potential to improve instruction. The idea among educational researchers is that computer games by themselves are not sufficient for learning to occur [13]. There are several proposals for educational and learning technologies, based on games, available for mobile devices or online access.

Gamification is an effective approach to make positive change in students' behavior and attitude towards learning, to improve their motivation and engagement [5,9]. A broad definition of gamification is "the use of game design elements in non-game contexts" [3]. With this, can affect students' results and understanding of the educational content and create conditions for a learning process. The gamification's use in order to make the content more attractive and engage users is a efficient approach [10] that combine intrinsic motivation with extrinsic one in order to raise motivation and engagement [15].

Quiz-based games are already known, used and analyzed to verify impact on students. A gamified quiz software tool was used in [2] as objective was to develop an approach in which gamification is used to motivate and enhance learning. The results showed that the proposed gamification implementation to improve learning has positive effects.

Previously, a survey based on an arcade platform showed that it is possible to integrate in an educational environment. In [1] a quiz game integrated into an arcade platform applied at an educational institution was proposed, which helps students to take an exam. It shows that structure was interesting and accepted by the users. The platform proposal was made available to students and there was a notable interest not only in using the game as a study. Being one of the goals of gamification, in addition to learning they also reported entertainment, exercising their knowledge without realizing it. This paper is based on this project. However, this being an initial survey, other forms of assessment can be done to measure the impact of different types of learning. Reference [14] suggests that quiz-based games there may be flaws that require further investigation to assess student learning.

The use of arcade in the educational area is already used in a version of Tux, of Math Command or TuxMath, an educational arcade game for learning mathematics [7]. It is an educational game in a space invasion where enemies are replaced by meteors accompanied by mathematical calculations. Besides, the study proposed in [7,12] shows that using TuxMath as an educational tool or teaching aid has a significant positive effect on students' learning.

Reference [11] reports that the use of arcade machines is old and as a form of entertainment, which can attract attention because of the distinguished structure. They lost space by computer games and consoles. Previously, games developed for arcade machines attracted attention, based that arcade developers focused on creating fast-moving, time-limited games that do not involve detailed story or character development [11]. In practice, it can be assumed that they often can and will give rise to playful behaviour.

3 Proposed Approach

This project started with an application of a questionnaire with 95 middle-level students from the Instituto Federal Catarinense - Campus Avançado Sombrio (IFC-CAS) in the first half of 2018. The questionnaire asked students about the period before joining at IFC-CAS. The objective was to analyze the efficiency of the institution's divulgation process and the students' interest in using games for admission to IFC. The divulgation process can be explained in the different ways that students knew IFC. Moreover, their interest based on using a platform like the one proposed in this article for the classification exam. The results of the questionnaire were 89.5% divulgation could be better, 72.6% and 24.2%, respectively, for yes and maybe would use.

Students use different ways of preparation for any exam. Confirming the current divulgation is not enough according to the data above, students were asked about the method for exam preparation: 71.6% by reviewing exams from previous years on their own, 3.2% by reviewing exams from previous years in the classroom, 13.7% by studying the exam's theme and 26.3% there was not exam preparation.

Based on this answers, the platform would be well received by students and through the positive results presented in the previous section, becomes a good educational technology to be applied as a proposal directed to federal institutions. In addition, as method applied by this project is in line with preparation method used by most students and the deficiency of divulgation of the institution inside schools of the city, there is a favorable field. The interest in using a game with questions from this classification exam being made available on school premises reinforced the proposal for a game with questions and answers applied on an arcade platform.

The game interface was developed in the Netbeans IDE environment using the JAVA programming language. For the storage of data of the questions and of the players was used the database manager MySQL Server. The integration between the interface and database has resulted in a set of questions from IFC's previous tests, following the same exam standards.

The last stage of the project was to install the game on a computer and adapt it to an arcade. The structure was made with wood material and has a joystick and buttons, both connected to the computer. Thus, the generated platform has a question game for the IFC, named FlipIFC.

This proposed approach was developed based on an arcade platform machine to serve and reach more students in the educational environment, in addition to presenting an attractive structure, which would increase the possibility of more students using it. In addition, it was developed to be applied on school premises, without the need for web or mobile applications.

4 Experiments and Results

This section presents details of the game and the results obtained after the use of FlipIFC, during the 30-day period, before the 2019 IFC-CAS's classification exam.

4.1 FlipIFC

The FlipIFC project is a technological and methodological resource platform capable of assisting the study of IFC's admission exam. It was developed as a game, to run on an arcade machine in a way that can be a attractive method.

Proposed Game. The purpose of this work was to create a game with questions and answers to be applied in a elementary school environment. It was produced through software development tools used in high school integrated computer science technical course at IFC-CAS.

The main screen of game has two rankings, the first one has a general ranking of the five best placed in the whole school and the other is a weekly ranking separated by knowledge area with five best players as shown in Fig. 1:

Fig. 1. Game's home screen.

The weekly ranking title changes according to the area of the week. By default, to exam of IFC, the knowledge areas are Portuguese Language, Mathematics, Human Sciences and Natural Sciences. Both rankings show the user's class, name, hits and misses. The weekly ranking contains only the hits and misses of the week, while the overall ranking contains all player's hits and misses. In addition the ranking, the home screen displays the project logo and instruction to start the game. As soon as any key is pressed, the login screen is displayed for player identification, which is to access and log in to the game.

The log in screen consists of a dialog box requesting the user code, one character icon on the left and one on the right. The user code is a number chosen by the players themselves. For users the number must contain six digits. Such a measure, as well as the request to avoid passwords composed of sequential or repetition numbers was taken to prevent the occurrence of repeated passwords. If the user attempts to enter the game without entering their code, an alert message prompts them to enter the number.

After identification, a screen with a countdown of five seconds appears to the player, as a way of preparation to receive the questions to be solved. So, the player is directed to the first question followed by alternatives. It is important to emphasize that knowledge area of the questions changes weekly. The player choose the alternative with the joystick and hit the enter key on the arcade machine. After that, the game checks if selected alternative is correct and shows the correct answer, like the Fig. 2.

This screen consists of the following items: name of the logged player (here omitted), time left to answer the question, area of knowledge question, statement of the question and five alternatives. In green, the correct alternative is identified. In red, the incorrectly chosen alternative. A character reacts according the result of the move, appears in the lower left corner. Both right and wrong question, the user is directed to the second question of the day, if not already answered. If the user doesn't answer the question within two minutes, the correct answer turns green and an error is counted. The questions are asked randomly according to the weekly knowledge area and it is not allowed to repeat questions for the same user.

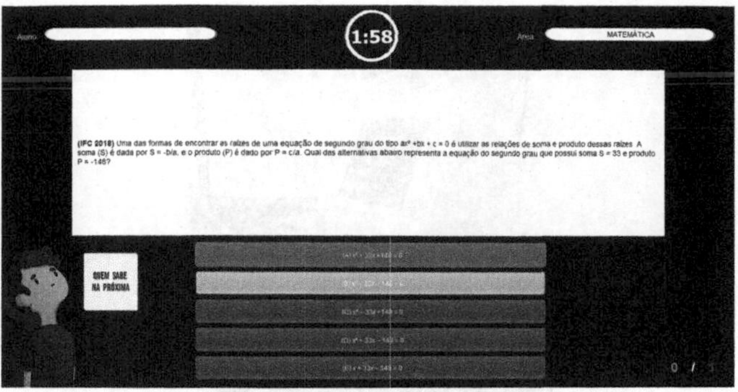

Fig. 2. Game's answer screen.

The many playful aspects included to the platform aim to make the experience more interesting, presenting a friendly environment and easy usability. Aspects worked in gamification and educational games was used, as appropriate to the context, based good results obtained as methodologies in education's field.

Arcade Platform. As described in Sect. 2, using an arcade game idea was tried already and achieved great results. This proposal tends to be a differential compared to other proposals, as it attracts the attention of the public, especially the younger ones. Therefore, to justify the idea of producing such a platform, it is because there's no platform with a software aimed at preparing admission to IFC. The intrinsic motivation generated through existing mechanics of this approach is represented maily engagement and competition.

Gamification implies an interaction with other participants, in this case with a ranking-based. Using an arcade platform at an educational environments can make an attractive possibility of fun and engaging, without undermining its credibility. Gamification helps students gain motivation towards studying, and because of the positive feedback they get pushed forwards and become more interested and stimulated to learn. In this case, it makes possible to increase exam divulgation of institution.

The arcade's assembly was performed using a desktop computer, an ordered wooden structure and a kit of buttons and joystick, which are responsible for all actions the game. Figure 3 shows the final format of the FlipIFC platform. Figure 3, positioned on the left, the joystick is shown. The center button represents an "OK" or "Enter" key, in which the player confirms the access or the alternative chosen in his attempt. The set of buttons on the right are positioned similar to a numeric keypad and with a "Clear" button, these are used to perform the individual code to access to the game.

Finally, the structure received stickers to make it even more attractive to users. The stickers also fulfill the function of informing the rule of daily moves: one move per day, two questions per move, two minutes per question.

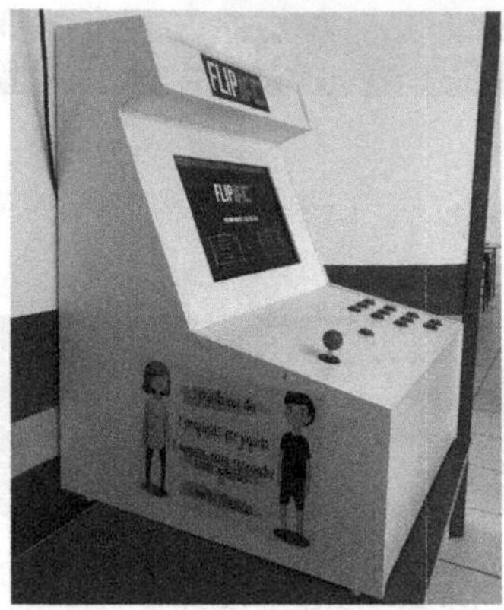

Fig. 3. Final structure of FlipIFC.eps

4.2 Analysis and Discussion of Experiments

Institution's divulgation objectives, scientific development and support for students' studies were achieved. The arcade machine platform was implanted in a municipal school at Sombrio (Santa Catarina - Brazil) for a period of 11 d for analyze and tests, being available to the registered users. It is important to note that students were not forced or encouraged to use the platform, they played for their own interest and will. In general, the results gained were very positives. After the platform's application in this period, these data could be analyzed based on the 47 registered players. Of these, 83% played at least once and, from these, 97.5% made more than one move.

FlipIFC reached 259 moves, obtaining 518 responses. This result stored were counted with an average of 23.55 plays per day, a standard deviation of 6.31. In relation to all participating students, the average of correct answers for the questions was 33.4%, which may present a lack of preparation by the students. The graph below shows the amount of students participating per day and amount of hits per class.

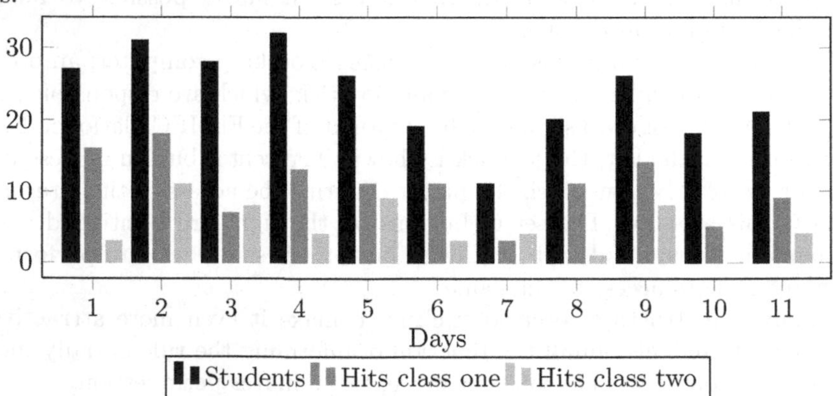

Based on these data, there was greater engagement and use in the first days, which can be considered by the novelty inserted in the school. The fall needs to be analyzed for what reason, which was not verified in this work. But, it can be something related to the school, since there was an increase in student participation in the last days of the project. A dedication was perceived by the students who are completing elementary school, who would be the initial target audience. The low rate of correct answers may have been due to the fact that students were not aware of the admission exam, a fact verified through the questionnaires. After this period, a questionnaire with closed questions was applied with the classes participating in the school and a total of 47 responses were obtained. The questions were intended to find out the students' opinions about the system and the experience they had using FlipIFC in addition to how it contributed, or not, in preparing for the IFC-CAS's admission exam. The three main questions asked are described below:

Question 1. What do you think about the appearance of the FlipIFC arcade machine platform?

Question 2. Do you think is FlipIFC a good educational technology for joining IFC?

Question 3. Have you ever had any contact with the admission exam or the exam questions before exam?

According to the responses of the participants 92% answered is atractive for question 1, 96.4% answered is a good educational technology for question 2 and 84.7% answered never had a contact for question 3. Analyzing these data, can be seen that few students had access to the IFC exam model. Therefore, they were asked whether it helped them to know the exam using FlipIFC, through the question 4.

Question 4. Did FlipIFC contribute in any way to the preparation of the exam or familiarization of the questions?

Based on the question 4 about how the game contributed to the preparation for the admission exam, 68.8% of the students answered that the platform had helped and gave them the opportunity to have contact with the exam questions template in addition to helping them prepare for it. Besides that, 13.8% responded that the game helped to train their knowledge for the exam. Which considers this approach as a possible tool to use, considering it as an additional tool in elementary education.

5 Conclusion

This work presented the development of a game as a way of preparing for the IFC classification exam. For those interested in the exam, the system provides prior contact with the test, seen by the result of the questionnaires. In addition, it allows the student on his own to check the effectiveness of his preparation and knowledge. Through the results it can also be seen that the platform was well accepted, based on the number of attempts made by the students. The amount of incorrect answers collected by the system can reflect on the students themselves, who, in turn, can spend more time preparing for the exam once the need is identified.

Educational games already used as strategies to help students' difficulties, improving performance and helping in the construction of knowledge, are also relevant for their playful potential, drawing attention to the theme worked on. Thus, FlipIFC proposes to evaluate the result of using this technology in municipal schools, as a tool for students to enter quality education.

References

1. Braga, M.L., De Sousa, V.M.: Arcade platform in education: analysis the impact of a preparation game for the enem. In: 2019 14th Iberian Conference on Information Systems and Technologies (CISTI). pp. 1–4. IEEE (2019)
2. Cheong, C., Cheong, F., Filippou, J.: Quick quiz: a gamified approach for enhancing learning. In: PACIS. p. 206 (2013)
3. Deterding, S., Dixon, D., Khaled, R., Nacke, L.: From game design elements to gamefulness: defining gamification. In: Proceedings of the 15th International Academic Mindtrek Conference: Envisioning Future Media Environments. pp. 9–15. ACM (2011)
4. Dicheva, D., Dichev, C., Agre, G., Angelova, G.: Gamification in education: A systematic mapping study. J. Educ. Technol. Soc. **18**(3), 75–88 (2015)
5. Erenli, K.: The impact of gamification-recommending education scenarios. International Journal of Emerging Technologies in Learning (iJET) 8(2013) (2013)
6. IFC: Sobre o ifc - instituto federal catarinense, Retrieved from http://ifc.edu.br/sobre-o-ifc/
7. Jagadesan, M.: Teaching basic mathematics by using tuxmath in primary education. Procedia Soc. Behav. Sci. **90**, 340–343 (2013)
8. Januszewski, A., Molenda, M.: Educational Technology: A Definition with Commentary. Routledge, Abingdon (2013)
9. Kiryakova, G., Angelova, N., Yordanova, L.: Gamification in education. In: Proceedings of 9th International Balkan Education and Science Conference (2014)
10. Muntean, C.I.: Raising engagement in e-learning through gamification. In: Proceedings of 6th International Conference on Virtual Learning ICVL. vol. 1, pp. 323–329 (2011)
11. Novak, J.: Game Development Essentials: An Introduction. Cengage Learning, Boston (2011)
12. Ntourlia, M., Gouscos, D., Meimaris, M.: Tuxmath: Is it possible for a game to enhance multiplication skills? In: Proceedings of the 4th European Conference on Games Based Learning. pp. 280–291 (2010)
13. O'Neil, H.F., Wainess, R., Baker, E.L.: Classification of learning outcomes: Evidence from the computer games literature. The Cirriculum Journal **16**(4), 455–474 (2005)
14. Tsai, F.H., Tsai, C.C., Lin, K.Y.: The evaluation of different gaming modes and feedback types on game-based formative assessment in an online learning environment. Comput. Educ. **81**, 259–269 (2015)
15. Viola, F.: Gamification-I Videogiochi nella Vita Quotidiana. Fabio Viola, Italy (2011)

The Cross Validation in Automated Valuation Models: A Proposal for Use

Agostino Valier(✉)

Università degli Studi di Padova, via Venezia 1, 35131 Padua, Italy
valier.agostino@gmail.com

Abstract. The appraisal of large amounts of properties is often entrusted to Automated Valuation Models (AVM). At one time, only econometric models were used for this purpose. More recently, also machine learning models are used in mass appraisal techniques.

The literature has devoted much attention to assessing the performance capabilities of these models. Verification tests first train a model on a training set, then measure the prediction error of the model on a set of data not met before: the testing set. The prediction error is measured with an accuracy indicator.

However, verification on the testing set alone may be insufficient to describe the model's performance. In addition, it may not detect the existence of model bias such as overfitting.

This research proposes the use of cross validation to provide a more complete and effective evaluation of models. Ten-fold cross validation is used within 5 models (linear regression, regression tree, random forest, nearest neighbors, multilayer perception) in the assessment of 1,400 properties in the city of Turin.

The results obtained during validation provide additional information for the evaluation of the models. This information cannot be provided by the accuracy measurement when considered alone.

Keywords: AVM · Cross validation · Real estate · Valuation

1 Introduction

Mass appraisal models are techniques for the evaluation of large sets of real estate assets, carried out using common real estate data, a unique evaluation protocol and performance verification tests [1]. Mass appraisal models are automatic calculation models, and therefore they are defined with the acronym AVM (Automated Valuation Models).

Each model expresses the function that links real estate characteristics to their prices. There are different ways in which a model can be defined. On the one hand, econometric models are based on hedonic price theory. On the other hand, machine learning models that learn directly from data [2].

Each model, once it has been defined, must be verified. The model verification phase consists of a test that provides an accuracy indicator which measures the model's error in price prediction. Accuracy tests have been very successful in scientific research. They

O. Gervasi et al. (Eds.): ICCSA 2020, LNCS 12253, pp. 585–596, 2020.
https://doi.org/10.1007/978-3-030-58814-4_45

have been used both for the evaluation of proposed models and for the comparison between various models.

The accuracy indicator is a quick indicator, easy to understand even for people who are not experts in writing algorithms. However, it is often insufficient to fully describe the nature and performance capabilities of the model. The accuracy indicator therefore needs to be implemented with other information that is equally capable of being understood by non-experts.

2 Framework

All tests that measure the predictive capacity of mass appraisal models adopt the same protocol. First, the real estate dataset containing the characteristics of the properties X and their prices Y-sales prices or asking prices- is divided into two sub-sets. On the one hand, the training set with which the model is trained. It tries to find the relationship between the variables X and Y. Next, the model is tested on the remaining part of the dataset (testing set). This subset contains data with which the model has not been trained, i.e. data so far unknown to the model. The actual prices (y) contained in the testing set are then compared with the predicted prices ($\hat{y}$) formulated by the model. The smaller the difference between $\hat{y}$ and y will be, the more the model can be defined as effective [3]. The accuracy measurements of mass appraisal models are widely used in the scientific literature. Many papers have as their main objective to compare different AVMs with each other based on accuracy parameters [4]. The introduction of machine learning models has increased the number and diffusion of these papers.

The first patented Automated valuation models employed regression analysis. Actually, this type of analysis is more effective in its inferential purposes than in its predictive ability. The inferential purpose is the ability to explain the role that individual regressors (property features) play in the final price [5, 6].

Machine learning models, on the other hand, are more skilled in predictive capacity. Their main weakness is their black box character: they are not able to explain the relationship between the price of the property and its characteristics. The comparison between regression analysis and machine learning models is not only a comparison between different techniques. Many authors understand it as the comparison between human intelligence and artificial intelligence in performing the same activity: evaluating [7–10].

In the field of mass appraisal the first machine learning models to be used were artificial neural networks. The first to propose accuracy tests was Borst [11]. Afterwards, Do and Grudnitiski [12] compared artificial neural networks with multiple regression by measuring their predictive capacity. These contributions triggered a debate in the scientific community, within which there were also those who refuted the superiority of machine learning models over traditional econometric models [13]. Nguyen and Cripps [14] were credited with studying the relationship between artificial neural networks and the size of their dataset. Still nowadays, artificial neural networks are successfully tested [15, 16].

Gradually, other types of machine learning models have been tested in mass appraisal techniques. Among them, the k-nearest neighbors. Such algorithms have rarely proved effective [17, 18]. In contrast, support vector machines have been shown to provide reliable estimates [19]. Even genetic algorithms have been successfully tested by researchers [20–22].

The ensemble learning models combine several individual models within a single metamodel, which offers better performance than those performed by each model considered alone. This is the case of random forests, which are the result of the aggregation of several regression trees. Their effectiveness in predicting real estate value is widely demonstrated [23–27].

The measurement of predictive effectiveness is in fact one of the main analysis tools with which to deal with the new models that have appeared more recently in the debate on real estate valuation. However, the excessive insistence that research exerts on the results of these tests risks making accuracy the only evaluation parameter of mass appraisal models [28].

This research methodology, although very widespread, has a statistical limit. The subdivision into only two subsets can create asymmetry in the data distribution. The split between training set and testing set takes place in a random way. The division into only two groups does not ensure a uniformity of the treated sub-samples. Sampling asymmetries often generate overfitting phenomena. Overfitting occurs when the model, over-trained on the training set data, is unable to predict effectively when it is provided with the testing set data. Some techniques can be used to prevent the phenomenon, the best known is cross-validation [29, 30].

3 Case Study

This study uses as data the offer prices of 1416 residential units for the year 2013. These prices have been collected from reading sales announcements.

To implement the information contained in the dataset, data from the Oict monitoring centre (Osservatorio Immobiliare Città di Torino) were used. This monitor is managed by the City of Turin, the University (Politecnico di Torino) and the local Chamber of Commerce. It is a tool that collects annually real estate prices since 2000. The Oict divides the city into 40 microzones. The microzone and its average sales value for the year 2013 have been added as variables to the dataset.

The dataset has 13 variables, described in the table below (Table 1 and Table 2).

Table 1. Description of the variables

Variable	Translation	Description
Locali	Rooms	Number of rooms
Bagni	Bathrooms	Number of bathrooms
Balconi	Terraces	Number of terraces
Box	Parking spaces	Number of private parking spaces
Affacci	Facades	Number of facades
Cantina	Cellars	Number of cellars
Ascensore	Lift	Has lift?

(continued)

Table 1. (*continued*)

Variable	Translation	Description
Piano	Floor level	Floor level
Piani edificio	Floors of the building	Number of floors of the building
Microzona	Microzone	Microzone in the real estate monitor
Mq	Squared meters	Seleable square meters
Prezzi medi	Mean value	Mean value (per square meter) in the microzone
Prezzo	Price	Total offer price in euros

Table 2. Description of the dataset

Variable	Type	Missing values	Range	Mean (St. Dev)	Most frequent value
Locali	Numerical	1	1–13	3,72 (1,53)	3
Bagni	Numerical	45	1–6	1,46 (0,69)	1
Balconi	Numerical	135	0–5	1,23 (0,86)	1
Box	Numerical	450	0–2	0,31 (0,49)	0
Affacci	Numerical	278	1–6	2,1 (0,75)	2
Cantina	Numerical	278	0–3	0,70 (0,54)	1
Ascensore	Dummy	0	0 (F)/1 (T)		
Piano	Numerical	53	0–13	2,90 (2,20)	1
Piani edificio	Numerical	92	0–14	5,01 (2,23)	5
Microzona	Categorical	0	Carlo Emanuele II/Vanchiglia/Rocca/San Salvario/Dante/San Secondo/De Gasperi/Duchessa Jolanda/San Donato/Palermo/Collina/Carducci/Unità d'Italia/Santa Rita/Mirafiori/San Paolo/Pozzo Strada/Parella		
Mq	Numerical	0	24-900	108,10 (70,34)	75

(*continued*)

Table 2. (*continued*)

Variable	Type	Missing values	Range	Mean (St. Dev)	Most frequent value
Prezzi medi	Numerical	0	1.523–4.242	2516,44 (759,53)	1.956
Prezzo	Numerical	0	23.000–2.500.000	297.786,01 (262.590,50)	195.000

The missing values of the variables 'Locali', 'Bagni', 'Balconi', 'Box', 'Affacci', 'Cantina', 'Piano', 'Piani edificio' have been replaced with the most frequent value of the corresponding variable. The replacement technique, called imputation, is frequently used to deal with missing values in large datasets. It consists of replacing each missing value with the average value or the most frequent value of the variable to which the missing value belongs. After the imputation process, the dataset consists of 1416 properties. Each of them is described by 13 variables. As can be seen from Fig. 1, the correlations between variables are very weak.

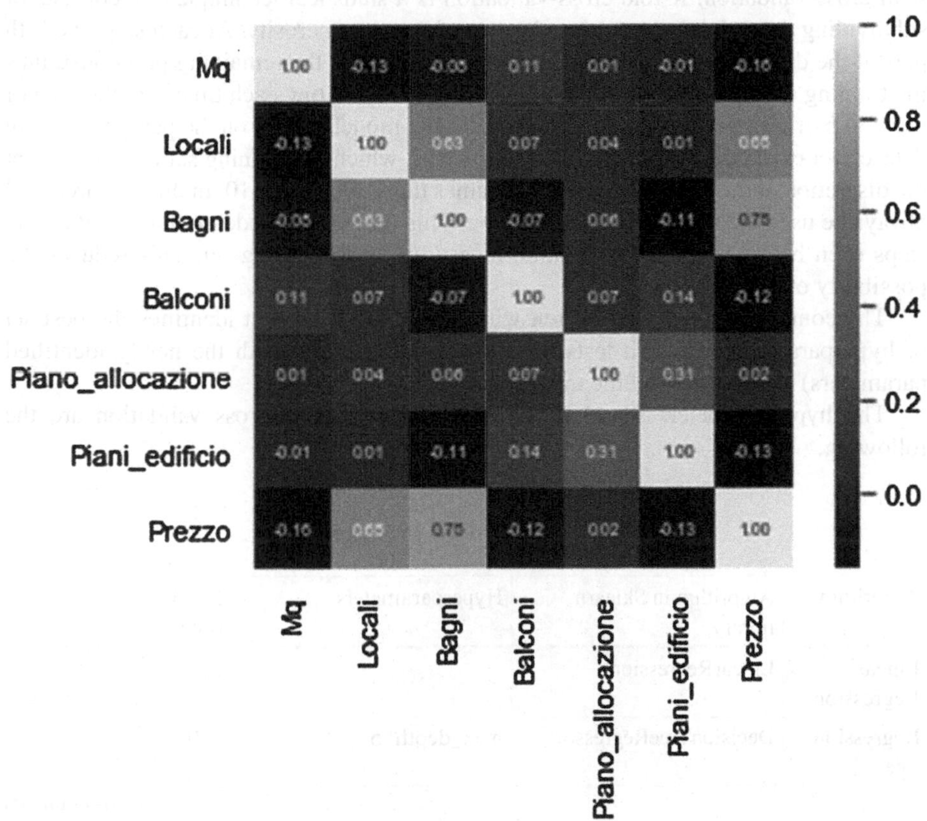

Fig. 1. Index of correlation between variables

4 Methodology and Results

The 1416 price dataset is divided into two sub-sets: the training set (75% of total data) and the testing set (25% of total data). Five models have been identified and trained. The first is a traditional econometric model, the remaining are more properly machine learning models. The models used in this research are the following:

- Linear regression
- Regression tree
- Random forest
- Nearest neighbors
- Multilayer perceptron

The models have been taken from the scikit-learn library. The GridSearchCV tool was used to detect the hyperparameters. It performs an exhaustive search by evaluating the model performance for each of the combinations in the list of values provided by the authors. It tests each combination until the optimal set is obtained.

Here the grid search has been further optimized through its use in combination with cross-validation. K-fold cross-validation is a statistical technique that consists of subdividing the training dataset into k parts of equal numerosity. At each step, the k-th part of the dataset becomes the validation dataset, while the remaining part constitutes the training dataset. Then k verifications are made by testing each time - on the data of the k-th part subtracted from the training set - the model trained on the parts of training dataset not excluded. The number k of parts with which the training set is divided is at the discretion of the authors, generally assumes the value of 5 or 10. In this research will always be used the ten-fold cross validation. This allows the model to have verification steps even before the final verification measured on the testing set. This reduces the possibility of overfitting.

The combined use of GridSearch with cross validation first identifies the best set of hyperparameters. Then it tests 10 times the algorithm (with the newly identified parameters) on the values of the training set (Table 3).

The hyperparameters found by GridSearch tool more Cross validation are the following:

Table 3. Definition of hyperparameters

Algorithm	Algorithm in Sklearn library	Hyperparameters	N° of combinations tested
Linear Regression	LinearRegression		
Regression tree	DecisionTreeRegressor	max_depth: 5	9

(*continued*)

Table 3. (*continued*)

Algorithm	Algorithm in Sklearn library	Hyperparameters	N° of combinations tested
Random forest	RandomForestRegressor	n_estimators: 9 max_depth: 8	54
Nearest Neighbors	KNeighborsRegressor	algorithm: 'brute' n_neighbors: 4	48
Multilayer Perceptron	MLPRegressor	Activation: 'identity' Alpha: 10000.0 Hidden_laye_sizes: (50,) Solver: lbfgs	960

The results are summarized in Table 4.

Table 4. Results of the cross validation (in R^2)

	Linear regression	Regression tree	Random forest	Nearest neighbors	Multilayer Perceptron
	0,693872	0,794822	0,794822	0,841647	0,905661
	0,735086	0,768665	0,684528	0,812143	0,531804
	0,679495	0,840759	0,800249	0,831772	0,879387
	0,685818	0,675845	0,628197	0,769928	0,907943
	0,628977	0,7728	0,7728	0,80649	0,79983
	0,725656	0,667922	0,70754	0,856838	0,730737
	0,734118	0,706022	0,865684	0,820216	0,914967
	0,719373	0,860305	0,865868	0,844873	0,873082
	0,713322	0,891006	0,734711	0,921169	0,450981
	0,752014	0,861159	0,860897	0,854688	0,473248
Mean	0,706773	0,78393	0,77153	0,835976	0,746764
Standard deviation	0,035833	0,0804	0,082114	0,03975	0,189925
Variance	0,00128	0,00646	0,00674	0,00158	0,03607

Then the models were tested on the testing set. They recorded the scores of Table 5.

Table 5. Results on testing set

Indicator	R^2	MAPE – Mean Average Percentage Error
Desirable outcome	Closer to 1	Minimum
Linear regression	0,638	37,70
Regression tree	0,828	24,31
Random forest	0,864	19,38
Nearest neighbors	0,820	22,15
Multilayer Perception	0,775	35,10

5 Analysis of the Results

Reading the results shows a clear superiority of machine learning models over linear regression analysis. The econometric model - here represented by linear regression analysis - records the lowest scores.

However, this research is not limited to the reading of the testing scores. The analysis of the results is divided into two parts. In the first part only the validation scores are analyzed, in the second part the validation scores are related to the testing scores.

5.1 Part I

The aim is to verify whether the models - beyond the differences in their internal structures - have a different behaviour in predicting results. For this purpose, an ANOVA single factor analysis was carried out of 50 results obtained during the cross-validation phase (Table 6).

The F value is greater than F critical value. The H_0 hypothesis, according to which the mean values recorded by all models are equal, is therefore rejected. Also the p-value, lower than the alpha value, confirms the rejection of the hypothesis H_0.

In Table 7 the ANOVA analysis is repeated, this time only on the 4 machine learning models (Regression tree, Random forest, Nearest neighbors and Multilayer Perceptron).

In this case F greatly exceeds F critical value, just as p-value exceeds alpha value. The hypothesis that the statistical behaviours of the various groups are similar to each other is therefore accepted.

These two ANOVA analyses show that the differences between traditional econometric models and machine learning models are not limited to the internal structures of the models. In fact, there are also differences in the results obtained and in their distribution.

Table 6. Anova of all five algorithms

SUMMARY

Groups	Count	Sum	Mean	Variance
Linear regression	10	7,067731	0,706773	0,001284
Regression tree	10	7,839305	0,78393	0,006464
Random forest	10	7,715297	0,77153	0,006743
Nearest neighbors	10	8,359763	0,835976	0,00158
Multilayer perception	10	7,46764	0,746764	0,036071

ANOVA

Source of variation	SS	df	MS	F	alpha	P - value	F crit
Between groups	0,090818	4	0,022704	2,177156	0,1	0,086813	2,074151
Within groups		45	0,010428				
total		49					

Table 7. Anova of only four machine learning algorithms

SUMMARY

Groups	Count	Sum	Mean	Variance
Regression tree	10	78,39,305	0,78393	0,006464
Random forest	10	77,15,297	0,77153	0,006743
Nearest neighbors	10	83,59,763	0,835976	0,00158
Multilayer perception	10	7,46,764	0,746764	0,036071

ANOVA

Source of variation	SS	df	MS	F	alpha	P - value	F crit
Between groups	0,042	3	0,014	1,112	0,1	0,356877	22,42,605
Within groups	0,457	36	0,012				
total	0,500	39					

5.2 Part II

The second part of the analysis correlates the results of cross-validation with the testing scores. The models that in the cross-validation phase recorded 10 similar values (and therefore, a low variance value) did not increase their performance once evaluated on the testing set. On the contrary, the scores decreased. The linear regression suffered a drastic drop in performance (from 0.70 to 0.63). The decrease of k nearest neighbors was more contained (from 0.83 to 0.82).

The multilayer perception algorithm records too high variance values, so it cannot be compared with the previous two. Very high values in the variation of the values indicate a random behavior of the model, so it is difficult to make predictions. Actually, on the testing set it has not suffered a drop-in performance but an increase.

The other two models (Regression tree and Random forest) have higher variance values. This means that the values obtained in the cross-validation phase are distributed over a wider range. These models experienced an increase in predictive performance once tested on the testing set. Their final accuracy results are higher than the average of the 10 cross validation values.

6 Conclusions

The research uses the cross-validation tool to provide additional information to forecasting accuracy tests, commonly summarized in the accuracy parameter alone.

Five models (one econometric, the remaining four machine learning) were used to predict value using 1416 properties in the city of Turin. The research came to two conclusions.

The first conclusion was obtained through the use of ANOVA analysis on the results of cross-validation. The analysis shows a different behaviour between the econometric model and the machine learning models. In fact, if all 5 models are considered together the hypothesis that the mean values are equal is denied. This hypothesis is confirmed if only the 4 machine learning models are considered. The cross-validation highlights - also from the statistical point of view - the different way in which traditional models act instead of artificial intelligence models do.

The second conclusion shows that models whose validation scores have a low variance lose their predictive efficacy once verified on the testing set. The average of the values obtained in the validation phase is in fact higher than the final accuracy output. Vicecersa, models with higher variance of the validation scores, during the testing phase can obtain higher scores than the average of the results obtained in the validation phase. This is not true for models that have such a high variance that their results have a semi-aleatory behavior.

The models tested in this research are not sufficient to give a general character to these conclusions, more studies will be needed to investigate the phenomenon.

References

1. IAAO: Standard on Mass Appraisal of Real Property. International Association of Assessing Officers (2013)
2. Athey, S.: The impact of machine learning on economics. In: Agrawal, A., Gans, J., Goldfarb, A. (eds.) The Economics of Artificial Intelligence: an Agenda, University Chicago Press, pp. 507–522 (2019)
3. McCluskey, W.J., McCord, M., Davis, P.T., Haran, M., McIlhatton, D.: Prediction accuracy in mass appraisal: a comparison of modern approaches. J. Prop. Res. **30**(4), 239–265 (2013)
4. Valier, A.: Who performs better? AVMs vs hedonic models. Journal of Property Investment and Finance, article in press (2020)
5. Mangialardo, A., Micelli, E., Saccani, F.: Does sustainability affect real estate market values? Empirical evidence from the office buildings market in Milan (Italy). Sustainability **11**(1), 12 (2018)

6. Mangialardo, A., Micelli, E.: New bottom-up approaches to enhance public real estate property. In: Stanghellini, S., Morano, P., Bottero, M., Oppio, A. (eds.) Appraisal: From Theory to Practice: Results of Siev 2015, pp. 53–62. Springer, Heidelberg (2017)
7. Rosen, S.: Hedonic prices and implicit markets: product differentiation in pure competition. J. Polit. Econ. **82**(1), 34–55 (1974)
8. D'Amato, M., Kauko, T.: Advances in Automated Valuation Modeling. SSDC, vol. 86. Springer, Cham (2017). https://doi.org/10.1007/978-3-319-49746-4_22
9. Kauko, T., D'Amato, M.: Mass appraisal methods: an international perspective for property valuers. Int. J. Strateg. Prop. Manag. **13**(4), 359–364 (2008)
10. Pérez-Rave, J.I., Correa-Morales, J.C., González-Echavarrìa, F.: A machine learning approach to big data regression analysis of real estate prices for inferential and predictive purposes of real estate prices for inferential and predictive purposes. J. Prop. Res. **36**(1), 59–96 (2019)
11. Borst, R.: Artificial neural networks: the next modelling/calibration technology for the assessment community. J. Prop. Tax **10**(1), 69–94 (1991)
12. Do, A.Q., Grudnitski, G.: A neural network approach to residential property appraisal. Real Estate Appraiser **58**, 38–45 (1992)
13. Worzala, E., Lenk, M., Silva, A.: An exploration of neural networks and its application to real estate valuation. J. Real Estate Res. **10**(2), 185–201 (1995)
14. Nguyen, N., Cripps, A.: Predicting housing value: a comparison of multiple regression analysis and artificial neural networks. J. Real Estate Res. **22**(3), 313–336 (2001)
15. Núñez Tabales, J.M., Caridad y Ocerin, J.M., Rey Carmona, F.J.: Artificial neural networks for predicting real estate prices. Cuantitativos para la Economia y la Empresa **15**(1), 29–44 (2013)
16. Yacim, J.A., Boshoff, D.G.B.: Impact of artificial neural networks training algorithms on accurate prediction of property values. J. Real Estate Res. **40**(3), 375–418 (2018)
17. Isakson, H.R.: Valuation analysis of commercial real estate using the nearest neighbors appraisal technique. Growth Change **19**(2), 11–24 (1988)
18. Borde, S., Rane, A., Shende, G., Shetty, G.: Real estate investment advising using machine learning. Int. Res. J. Eng. Technol. **4**(3), 1821–1825 (2017)
19. Kontrimas, V., Verikas, A.: The mass appraisal of the real estate by computational intelligence. Appl. Soft Comput. **11**(1), 443–448 (2011)
20. Del Giudice, V., De Paola, P., Forte, F.: Using genetic algorithms for real estate appraisals. Buildings **7**(2), 31 (2017)
21. Tajani, F., Morano, P., Locurcio, M., D'Addabbo, N.: Property valuations in times of crisis. artificial neural networks and evolutionary algorithms in comparison. In: Computational Science and Its Applications - ICCSA 2015, pp. 194–209 (2015)
22. Manganelli, B., De Mare, G., Nesticò, A.: Using genetic algorithms in the housing market analysis. In: Gervasi, O., Murgante, B., Misra, S., Gavrilova, M.L., Rocha, A.M.A.C., Torre, C., Taniar, D., Apduhan, B.O. (eds.) ICCSA 2015. LNCS, vol. 9157, pp. 36–45. Springer, Cham (2015). https://doi.org/10.1007/978-3-319-21470-2_3
23. Ceh, M., Kilibarda, M., Kilibarda, M., Bajat, B.: Estimating the performance of random forest versus multiple regression for predicting prices of the apartments. ISPRS Int. J. Geo-Inf. **7**(5), 168 (2018)
24. Mullainathan, S., Spiess, J.: Machine learning: an applied econometric approach. J. Econ. Perspect. **31**(2), 87–106 (2017)
25. Kok, N., Martínez-Barbosa, C.A., Koponen, E.L.: Big data in real estate? From manual appraisal to automated valuation. J. Portf. Manag. **43**(6), 202–211 (2017)
26. Antipov, E., Pokryshevskaya, E.: Mass appraisal of residential apartments: an application of random forest for valuation and a CART-based approach for model diagnostics. Expert Syst. Appl. **39**(2), 1772–1778 (2012)

27. Huang, Y.: Predicting home value in california, united states via machine learning modeling. Stat. Optim. Inf. Comput. **7**(1), 66–74 (2019)
28. Mooya, M.M.: Market value without a market: perspectives from transaction cost theory. Urban Stud. **46**(3), 687–701 (2009)
29. Baldominos, A., Blanco, I., Moreno, A., Iturrarte, R., Bernardez, O., Afonso, C.: Identifying real estate opportunities using machine learning. Appl. Sci. **8**(11), 2321 (2018)
30. Abidoye, R.B., Chan, A.P.C., Abidoye, F.A.: Predicting property price index using artificial intelligence techniques. Int. J. Hous. Market. Anal. **8**(11), 2321 (2018)

Neural Nets on FPGA a Machine Vision Algorithm Applied On MNIST Dataset Using Hls4ml Library

Fabrizio Alfonsi[1], Alessandro Gabrielli[1], and Elisabetta Ronchieri[2(✉)]

[1] Department of Physics, University of Bologna, Bologna, Italy
[2] INFN CNAF, Bologna, Italy
elisabetta.ronchieri@cnaf.infn.it

Abstract. In this paper we describe a machine vision Neural Net al.gorithm implemented in a FPGA. The algorithm is trained on a hand written digit MNIST dataset. For Neural Net Intellectual Property generation it is used the *hls4ml* library, which is a really powerful tool for fast implementation of Neural Net on FPGA.

Keywords: FPGA · Neural network · Machine learning

1 Introduction

The *hls4ml* [1,2] is a library that acts as a bridge between machine learning based on CPU/GPU (such as Keras, Tensorflow and PyTorch) [3], and VHSIC Hardware Description Language (VHDL) for designing FPGA's Neural Net Intellectual Property (NN IP) cores for fast inference. This library exploits High Level Synthesis (HLS), a way of synthesizing hardware from a pseudo-C++ code. *hls4ml* in fact automatically writes the HLS code that corresponds to the specified NN: it needs a json file for the architecture and a hdf5 file for weights.

Figure 1 shows the *hls4ml* workflow that is characterized by three phases. In the first phase, our workflow chooses a model and trains it on CPU by using Keras; it interactively, or just at the end, compresses the model by pruning weights; it exports and saves model's architecture in a json format and it weights in hdf5 format. In the second phase, our workflow generates a HLS project using *hls4ml*, it tunes the configuration of data type used by the model and it generates an IP core by using *hls4ml*. This task is carried out using the Vivado High-Level Synthesis (HLS) [4]. In the third phase, our workflow constructs a Vivado project [5] on the firmware design by importing the NN IP core.

In order to generate a HLS project, *hls4ml* needs to complete a yaml configuration file. The following *kindex_keras_config.yml* file is an example: XilinxPart contains FPGA's name [6], ClockPeriod sets the default clock period in ns, PrecisionL sets the default type and precision of numbers in NN processing and ReuseFactor represents the maximum number of times of reusing resources that increases the latency.

This work was supported by the University of Bologna and INFN.

O. Gervasi et al. (Eds.): ICCSA 2020, LNCS 12253, pp. 597–605, 2020.
https://doi.org/10.1007/978-3-030-58814-4_46

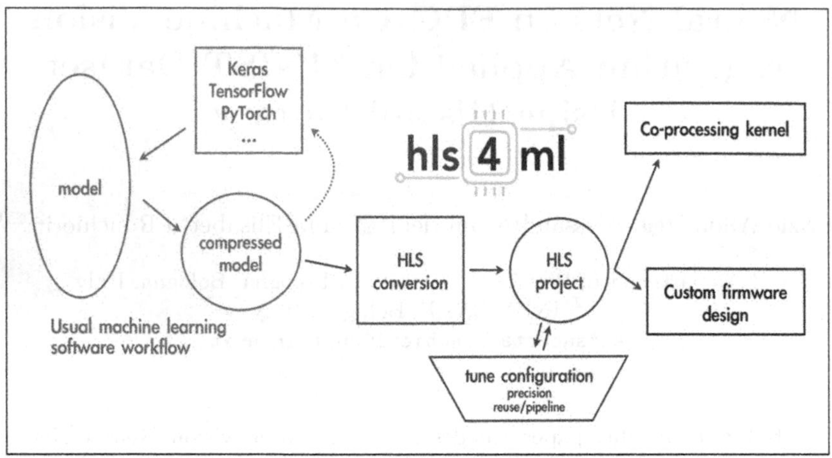

Fig. 1. hls4ml three-phase workflow

```
# Filename: kindex_keras_config.yml
KerasJson: My_NN/model_MNIST_flat8_5bit_pruned.json
KerasH5: My_NN/model_weights_MNIST_flat8_5bit_pruned.h5

OutputDir: Generated_NN/KINTEX/MNISTflat8_5bit_MinPrecision_v2
ProjectName: MNISTflat8_5bit_MinPrecision_v2

#kintex kc705
XilinxPart: xc7k325tffg900-2
ClockPeriod: 5

IOType: io_parallel #options: io_serial/io_parallel

HLSConfig:
  Model:
    PrecisionL ap_fixed<24,1>
    ReuseFactor: 1
```

2 Selected Model

The *hls4ml* library is an ongoing work in progress. Since updates with new capabilities and bug resolution are under development as require a long and detailed verification. This is why 2D convolutional NN is not supported. In order to work with images, one workaround is to flatten images into arrays and implement classical feed forward NN with dense layers.

By experiencing with capabilities of Vivado HLS to generate *hls4ml* cores, we have realized that nets with more than 100 nodes per layer cause a crash, because of several Vivado's critical warnings and excessive memory usage. We observed that the crash sometimes originated from a complete RAM saturation. In our experiments we used an 8 GB RAM PC and we used images of size 8×8 or 64 input nodes. MNIST dataset is a benchmark for machine vision tasks by ensembling single handwritten digits images in 8-bit gray scale of size 28×28 pixels. MNIST dataset is composed of 60'000 images for training and 10'000 for test/validation.

In order to satisfy the *hls4ml* limitations we decided to preprocess images by cropping the central portion of size 22 × 22 pixels and after that down sampling (e.g.. *scipy.ndimage.zoom()* in Python) to decrease the resolution to 8 × 8 pixels.

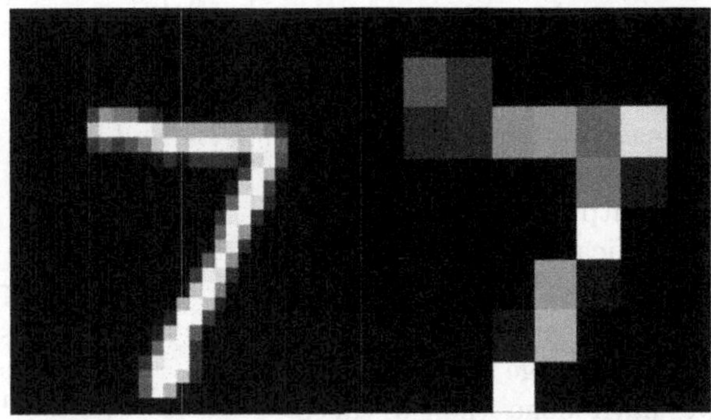

Fig. 2. Comparison between original images and processed images used to train the model: on the left there is the original image taken from the MNIST dataset (28 × 28 pixels, 8-bit color depth); on the right there is the processed image (8 × 8 pixels, 5-bit color depth).

The choice of transforming the color depth of pixels from 8-bit to 5-bit (see Fig. 2) has been made to reduce the PC resource consumption: on one hand for keeping the NN IP core as small as possible and on the other hand because these images were shown on a screen using the VGA port on the board featuring the FPGA implemented for the NN. This board used a 6-bit green and 5-bit red and blue colour coding. In this way we have reached a reasonable accuracy of image reconstruction. In other words, increasing in color depth at constant model causes on increase in test accuracy but with a 5-bit color depth we can reasonably say that we have almost reached the maximum possible accuracy.

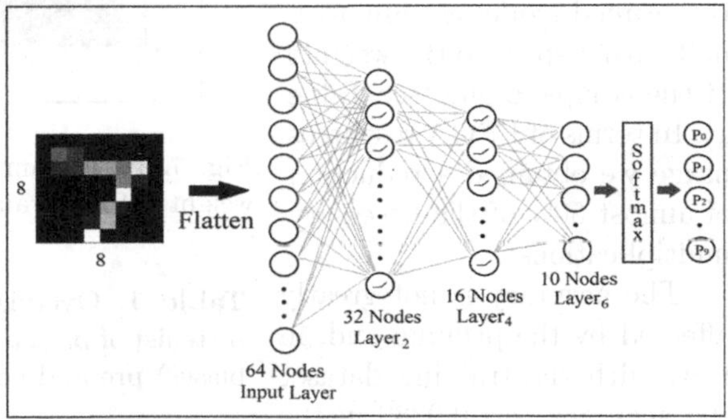

Fig. 3. Representation of model's architecture: symbols inside nodes are shown representing activation function (i.e. relu).

After some experimentation with different architectures we realized that the two hidden layers in Fig. 3 show an excellent accuracy on both training set and test set as shown in Fig. 4, proving its capabilities of generalizing well on new data. Figure 4 shows almost the same accuracy on both sets, which means that the net has learned the maximum amount of information without overfitting training data.

3 Training and Compression

After a training phase of 15 epochs the accuracy of the model respect to training data has already reached the maximum of almost 94%. One epoch occurs when all example of training set are presented at least one time to the net for training purpose.

When the model is trained we implement the compression. The *hls4ml* library is optimized for avoiding the implementation of unnecessary operations while writing the output HLS code, like multiplications per zero, with net effect of reducing model's hardware resource request. To take advantage of this feature we have done the so called pruning, i.e. artificially setting to zero weights smaller than, in absolute sense, a certain cutoff; of course this has been done after studying the resulting accuracy to avoid wrong outputs.

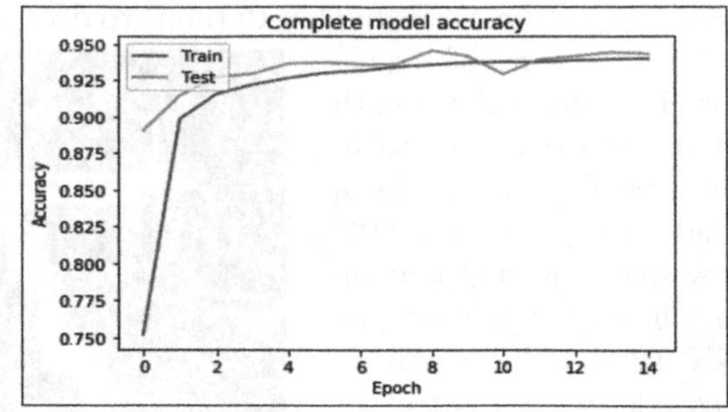

Fig. 4. Model accuracy obtained for the training and test samples.

Figure 5 shows that the cutoff used is equal to 2^{-5}. Furthermore we can notice that the shape of this histogram resembles an half Gaussian distribution and this is compatible with the fact that weights of the pruned model are almost a half with respect to the weights of the complete one (see Table 1). In terms of FPGA resources usage we obtained a reduction of almost 50% of the necessary multiplications.

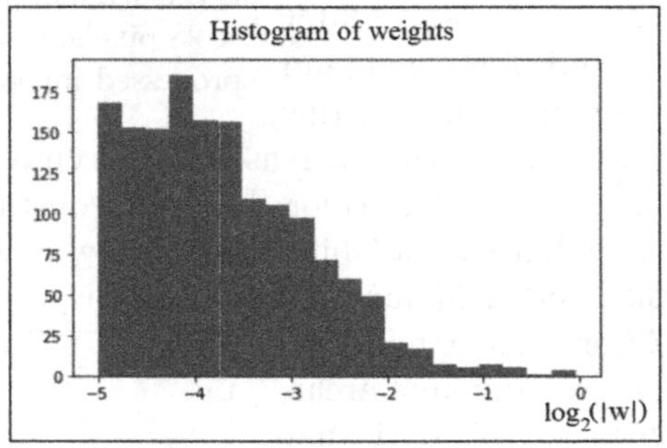

Fig. 5. Histogram of absolute values of non-null weights of the trained model after pruning.

The accuracy is not greatly affected by the pruning and, in fact, with the training dataset the accuracy was 0.9389 in the complete model, while it was 0.9392 in the pruned model. For the test dataset, accuracy was 0.9471 in the complete model, while it was 0.9423 in the pruned model. Eventually the model is saved and exported the model in order to generate the HLS project through *hls4ml*. The PrecisionL parameter in the configuration file (see the *kindex_keras_config.yml* file in Sect. 1) is tuned as described in Sect. 4.

Table 1. Overview table of compression. Complete list of parameter for every layer (weights plus biases) pre and post pruning.

	Parameters	
	Complete model	Pruned model
$Layer_2$	2'048 + 32	979 + 30
$Layer_4$	512 + 16	363 + 15
$Layer_6$	170 + 10	130 + 10
TOTAL	2'778	1'527

4 Implementation on FPGA

Once we have our NN HLS project, the fine tuning process on the data set takes place in order to fit our goal, consume less resource as possible and avoid overflow. The most widely used data type in HLS is an arbitrary precision fixed point numbers **ap_fixed<width, integer_size>** as shown in Fig. 6.

First of all, we focus our attention on weights (generically called w) and biases: $0.03125 = 2^{-5} \leq | w | \leq 0.97244$. Therefore, we need just 2 bits as integer size I_s (one for sign and one for 0) and at least 5 bits as fractional size $F_s = -log_2(min| w |max_1Delta_{rel}) = -log_2(2^{-5}2^{-3}) = 8$. If we choose 5 bits as fractional size we badly quantize our parameter's space, indeed we would than have a maximum relative error of 1.

In order to better represent our space of parameters we choose a maximum relative error $\max\{_1Delta_{ref}\}$ of $2^{-3} = 0.125$ or in other words 8 bits as fractional size. So for weights and biases should be enough **ap_fixed<10, 2>**.

Our NN returns probabilities due to the final Softmax operation (see Fig. 7). Predicted classes probabilities are, as always, less than or equal to 1. Therefore, 2 bits as I_s are enough and we choose for the last layer **ap_fixed<16, 2>**.

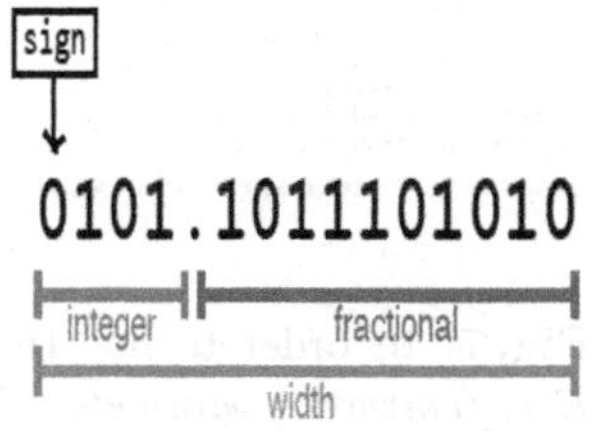

Fig. 6. **ap_fixed<14, 4>** with 14 as total data bits and 4 as the integer part of the number.

As input we choose the data type **ap_int<6>** and consider the sign. In order to fine tuning data types for hidden layers we have to calculate the maximum value that each node can take; this is necessary to prevent overflow. For this purpose we introduce a new quantity for the i-th layer A_i which is the maximum acceptable node numbers per layer. A_i is simply defined as the product of the maximum weight and the $A_j \cdot \#\text{node}_j$ of the incoming layer: because we are using relu as activation function, A_i for relu layers has the same value as the incoming layer.

- Layer_2

$$A_2 = max| w | \cdot A_{Inputs} \cdot \#node_{Inputs} < 1 \cdot 2^5 \cdot 2^6 = 2^{11} \quad (1)$$

$$\Rightarrow I_{s,2} = 1 + log_2(A_2) = 12 \quad (2)$$

- Relu_3

$$A_3 = A2 \Rightarrow I_{s,3} = I_{s,2} \quad (3)$$

- Layer_4

$$A_4 = max| w | \cdot A_3 \cdot \#node_3 < 1 \cdot 2^{11} \cdot 2^5 = 2^{16} \quad (4)$$

$$\Rightarrow I_{s,4} = 1 + log_2(A_4) = 17 \quad (5)$$

- Relu_5

$$A_5 = A_4 \Rightarrow I_{s,5} = I_{s,4} \quad (6)$$

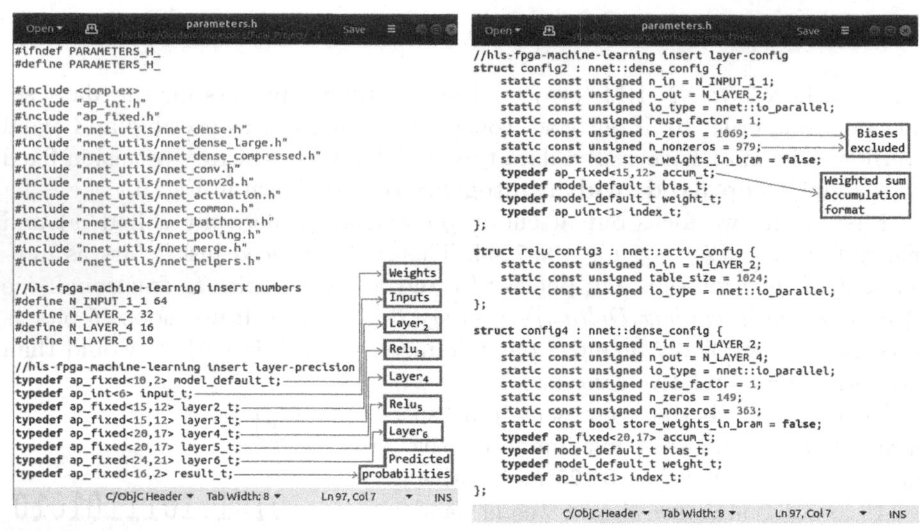

Fig. 7. In order to fine tuning the NN we have to actively modify the file *OutputDir//rmware//parameters.h.*

– Layer_6

$$A_6 = max| \, w \, | \cdot A_5 \cdot \#node_5 < 1 \cdot 2^{16} \cdot 2^4 = 2^{20} \tag{7}$$

$$\Rightarrow I_{s,4} = 1 + log_2(A_5) = 21 \tag{8}$$

We choose to assign as fractional size the value of 3 for all hidden layers: $F_{s,i} = 3$ for i = 2, 3, 4, 5, 6.

In the next Table 2 we show how data type fine tuning change demand for resources.

Table 2. Data type fine tuning.

NN IP core version	LUTs	FFs	BRAMs	DSPs
Not-tuned	58'109	58'628	25	512
Tuned	34'766	19'163	25	513

The not-tuned version is simply obtained setting, in the configuration file, the maximum required precision for weights and hidden layers: **ap_fixed<29, 21>**, which corresponds to $I_s = 21$ and $F_s = 8$. Data type of inputs and predicted probabilities are tuned as usual.

4.1 Lab Implementation

We use two FPGA boards (see Fig. 8): a *Kintex KC705* for NN IP core processing and a *Zybo Z701* to display input images on a screen through VGA port.

The second board is used to monitor the system. Indeed this board mounts a XILINX ZYNQ-7000 FPGA, a 28 nm device with available 17600 Look-Up-Tables and 36000 Flip Flops, which are not enough to apply high density computational systems. The ARM processor features with two cores at 800 MHz,

32 kB of Level-1 cache memory and 512 MB of RAM memory. The process can implement a custom Linux system to control all the mounted components on the board and any logic system implemented in the Programmable Logic FPGA, using only high level software. The XILINX Kintex-7 (always a 28 nm technology) works as computational station of the setup.

The 203800 Look-Up-Tables, the 407600 Flip Flops and the 840 Digital Signal Processors allow a complex algorithmic structure to be implemented, even at high speed due to the dense connections of all the logic components. The average frequency implementable in this kind of chips is up to 300 MHz. These two FPGAs are in the entry level of the 7 generation XILINX FPGAs. Today FPGAs have approximately 10 times higher numbers in terms of logic components, and many projects, including CERN ones, are planning to use them in the next years of High Energy Physics as real-time fast computational systems.

We designed the firmware of both FPGAs and 100 images were used from MNIST test set. The first 10 pictures correspond to digits 0,1,..., 9; while the others were randomly chosen. In this case the accuracy of our model, calculated with Keras and applied to this set of pixel numbers was as good as 97%. This result is very challenging for human capabilities, because it's really difficult to recognize these digits on some of these low-resolution images.

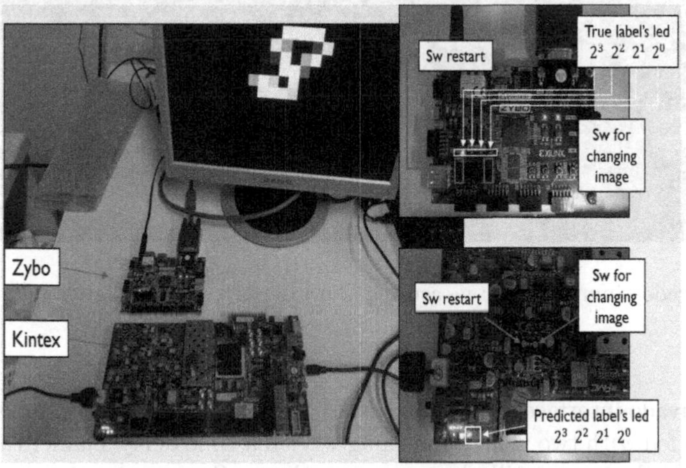

Fig. 8. Implementation settings in laboratory. Switches control the changing in input images. Leds on Zybo prints out true label and leds on Kintex the predicted ones.

4.2 Computation Time

We have evaluated the computational time needed by the NN to process an image. The inference time on FPGA, i.e. 125 ns, is relative to a Kintex kc705 FPGA, which has a 5 ns clock: in fact, this NN's elaboration takes 25 clock cycles. The inference time required on CPU, i.e. 1'982'269 ns is relative to a Intel(R) Core(TM) i7-8550U CPU @ 1.80 GHz 1.99 GHz, running Keras routines.

Figure 9 shows the Vivado tool interface which allows monitoring the behavior of the internal signals of the applied logic. The interface, called "waveforms table", has on the left column the name of the signal and on the right their behavior during the run time, with time going from left to right. In this implementation version (see Fig. 9) switches sw[:] controls the input image to the NN. sw = 0 gives an image of a zero, sw = 1 gives an image of a one and so on. The NN IP core is initially in idle mode. The inference process is triggered by **ap_start** signal in concurrence of the **input1_V_ap_vld** signal which is the signal that validates the input (**image_flat**). After 25 clock cycles the NN IP core returns a valid output in concurrence with the **ap_done** signal. The predicted class probabilities are than processed and the class label predicted is visible through led signal.

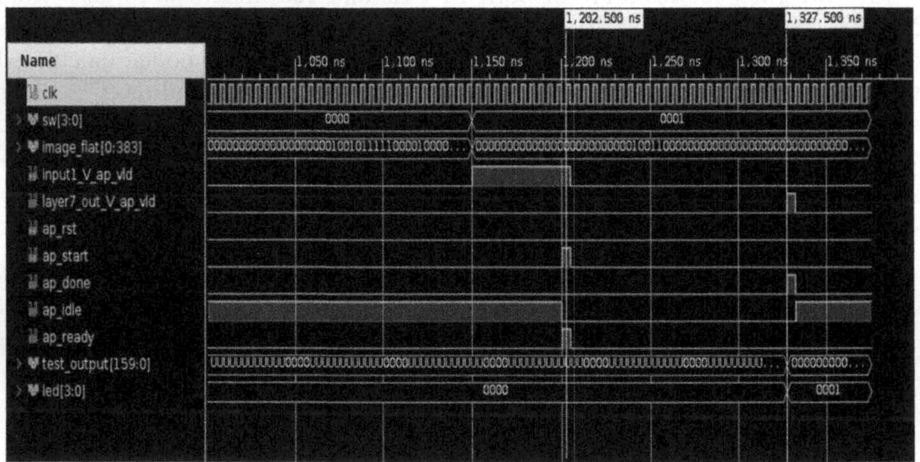

Fig. 9. Vivado simulation for measuring the inference time or latency of the NN IP core.

The Vivado interface proves the NN IP core capability of pipelining inference. The NN is fed with two valid input images with a time delay smaller than latency and the NN IP core is still able to process both. So, latency of the NN IP core is not a limiting speed factor and therefore this is a really interesting feature in order to apply this kind of hardware for triggering event mechanism such as pattern recognition in particle physics. We finally want to point out that the ReuseFactor parameter in the *hls4ml* configuration file has no effect, in term of resource usage, when applied to data type fine tuned NN IP cores. Benefits from this parameter instead can be seen when applied to not-tuned NN IP cores, but this will necessary cause an increase in latency.

5 Conclusion

The future challenges in terms of High-speed Data and Big Data are directing in the so called "hardware heterogeneity", which means the concurrent usage of several type of device genres as CPU, GPU, FPGA and custom ASIC(Application Specific Integrated Circuit), to solve data computing tasks. The implementation of "math" algorithms has almost always been implemented by using not-real-time devices as CPUs and GPUs, hardware architectures with great computational capability but with very low control in terms of latency. Future tasks as trigger structures of the biggest physics experiments at CERN [7] will require a latency control at ns level, not achievable by CPU or GPU. In the last years many groups and laboratories started to study FPGA and ASIC computational algorithm implementation [8], and the work shown in this paper wanted to demonstrate the general performance achieved with the implementation of a machine vision neural net on an FPGA. Other than the accuracy, the latency compared to the one reached by the used CPU demonstrates the capability of hardware implemented computational algorithm. The Bologna group is now working on exploiting our FPGA developing experience, acquired even with the type of task showed above, to study tracking algorithms for the ATLAS trigger, FPGA implemented.

Acknowledgment. The authors thank Giordano Calvanese for his collaboration in this work.

References

1. hls4ml: Software Open Access hls-fpga-machine-learning/hls4ml: v0.2.0 (2020). https://doi.org/10.5281/zenodo.3734261
2. hls4ml: hls4ml - GitBook. https://fastmachinelearning.org/hls4ml/
3. Duarte, J., Han, S., Harris, P., et al.: Fast inference of deep neural networks in FPGAs for particle physics. JINST 13 P07027 (2018). arXiv:1804.06913
4. HLS, V.: Vivado Design Suite User Guide - High-Level Synthesis. https://www.xilinx.com/support/documentation/sw_manuals/xilinx2017_4/ug902-vivado-high-level-synthesis.pdf (2018)
5. Vivado.: Vivado Design Suite User Guide - Getting Started. https://www.xilinx.com/support/documentation/sw_manuals/xilinx2018_2/ug910-vivado-getting-started.pdf (2018)
6. FPGA: KC705 Evaluation Board for the Kintex-7 FPGA - User Guide. https://www.xilinx.com/support/documentation/boards_and_kits/kc705/ug810_KC705_Eval_Bd.pdf (2019)
7. ATLAS collaboration. https://cds.cern.ch/record/2285584?ln=it (2017)
8. Shojaii, R.S.: An associative memory chip for the trigger system of the ATLAS experiment (2016). https://doi.org/10.22323/1.287.0058

Assessing the Impact of Land Use Changes on Ecosystem Services Value

Angela Pilogallo(✉), Lucia Saganeiti, Francesco Scorza, and Beniamino Murgante

University of Basilicata, Viale Dell'Ateneo Lucano 10, 85100 Potenza, Italy
angela.pilogallo@unibas.it

Abstract. Land use change significantly affects ecosystem services provision. This impact, however, is difficult to assess and thus often neglected in policy making. It is therefore the task of territorial planning discipline to explore methodological approaches capable of making explicit complex relationships in order to use them as tools for effectively designing the sustainable development.

In this paper, we report changes in land use over a 28-year period considering the territory of the Basilicata region. Our aim is to translate these changes in ecosystem services values, highlighting potentials of a framework able to integrate monetary figures into a larger approach based on the interactions between biomes and the meaning of human well-being more closely linked to the economics sector.

The results show that the greatest loss occurred at the detriment of wooded areas and agricultural mosaic while bare land and arable land increased. Several municipalities experienced significant changes involving above all the classes in the agricultural compartment. The growth of urban settlements took place everywhere affecting to a much greater extent the most important centers, the only ones not subject to depopulation.

Our estimate quantifies these changes in a total annual loss of ecosystem service delivery higher than €39 million with some municipalities where this loss corresponds to a significant part of GDP. Reversing the perspective, moreover, the internal areas emerge where, also due to depopulation, the monetization of ecosystem services leads to pro capita amounts equivalent to multiples of GDP per capita.

The study sets the basis for an approach oriented towards defining tangible criteria for assessing the sustainability of territorial transformations and land use change.

Keywords: Land use change · Ecosystem services values · Natural capital · Inner areas

1 Introduction

Providing a range of services essential for human survival, health and livelihood [1–3], ecosystems' contribution to human well-being has been widely deepened in science [4–7]. Although the relevance of this issue is also recognized by policy makers, there is

O. Gervasi et al. (Eds.): ICCSA 2020, LNCS 12253, pp. 606–616, 2020.
https://doi.org/10.1007/978-3-030-58814-4_47

still a need for full integration between the conceptual framework of ecosystem services (ES) and the effectiveness of decision-making processes.

Expressing the value of ES in monetary units can therefore be useful both because the decision-making process often uses a cost-benefit assessment to evaluate development strategies and planning alternatives [8], and because as also highlighted by Rodriguez-Loinaz et al. [9], most ES are outside the market system and this has often led to the degradation of non-marketed services as a result of measures implemented to increase the supply of ES marketed [10, 11].

The effort to monetize goods and both tangible and immaterial services is however all the more effective, the more appropriate the estimation method is in relation to the work scale [12, 13]: from the national scale to the local dimension, the contribution that the assessment of the ES value (ESV) can give, ranges from the estimation of the natural capital to the support in performing selections between project alternatives and transformation scenarios.

In this work, we estimate the ESV change in the Basilicata region following land use/land cover (LULC) modifications occurred over the period 1990-2018 derived from Corine Land Cover, and examine the comparison between these gain and loss and gross domestic product (GDP) at the municipal level. According to our assessment carried out using the values estimated by Costanza et al. [14], the changes over the 28 years considered resulted in an overall loss of capacity to generate ecosystem services of 39 million euros per year. At the municipal level, comparing these outcomes with the 2018 per capita gross domestic product highlights that the ESV is, in several inner municipalities, up to two times higher than the GDP.

A the regional level, this kind of outcomes could help to improve the territorial governance by measuring the performances of the transformation and to make decisions about allocating economic resources to promote sustainable development strategies capable to produce added value from natural capital while preserving the ESV for the future generations.

2 Materials and Method

2.1 Study Area and Land Use Changes

The Basilicata Region (Fig. 1) covers a total area of about 10,000 km^2 and is characterized by a prevalently mountainous territory. Only 8% of the total area is flat and it is mainly located along the Ionian coast.

Due to the presence of the Apennine chain that crosses it from north to south, two main sectors can be identified: a western one, characterized by higher altitudes and slopes and the eastern one where the hilly landscape prevails and slopes down to the low and sandy coasts of the Ionian Sea.

During the investigated time period ranging from 1990 to 2018 and according to Corine Land Cover, most of the changes in land use occurred in the semi-natural classes linked to agricultural use, although the loss of woodland is also significant.

As it can be seen from Fig. 2, the classes related to agricultural mosaic and pastures have decreased significantly while arable land, shrubs and bare land have expanded considerably.

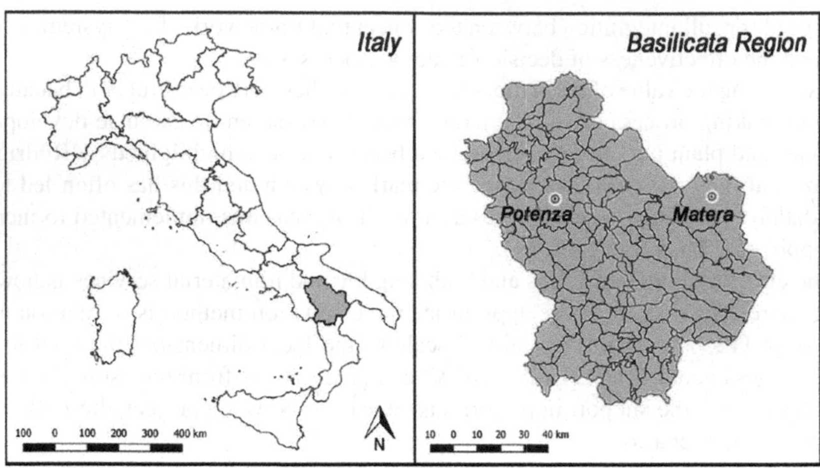

Fig. 1. Study area

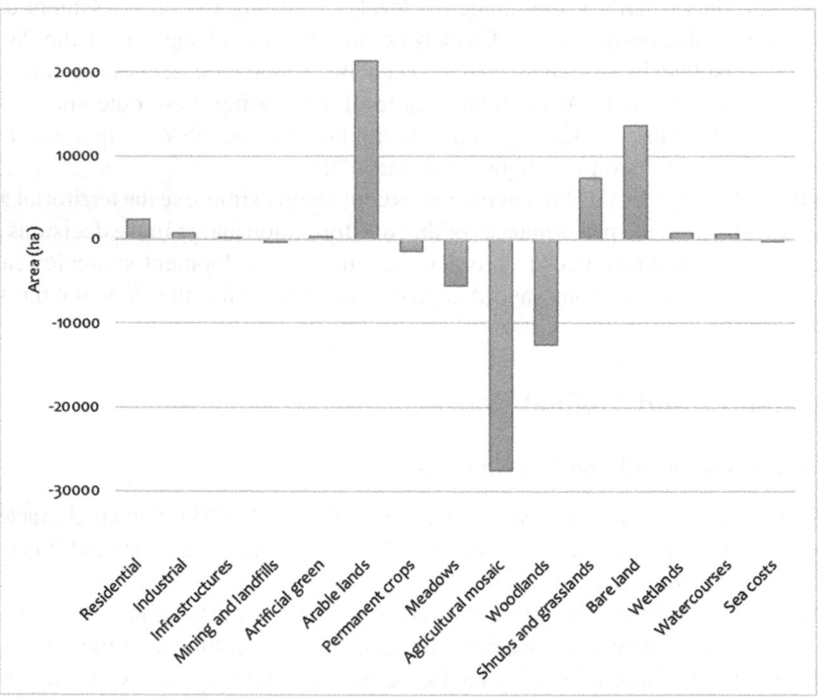

Fig. 2. Gain and loss for each LULC class resulting from changes occurred over the period 1990-2018.

Analyzing in detail the most significant transitions (Fig. 3), it emerges that most of the new arable land comes from the agricultural mosaic but also from previously wooded land. n a mirror-like way, the agricultural mosaic has given space mainly in favor of arable land but also of orchards and permanent crops, even if the area for new urbanization, which amounts to about 2480 hectares and equal to 4% of the total transformations suffered by the class, is not entirely negligible.

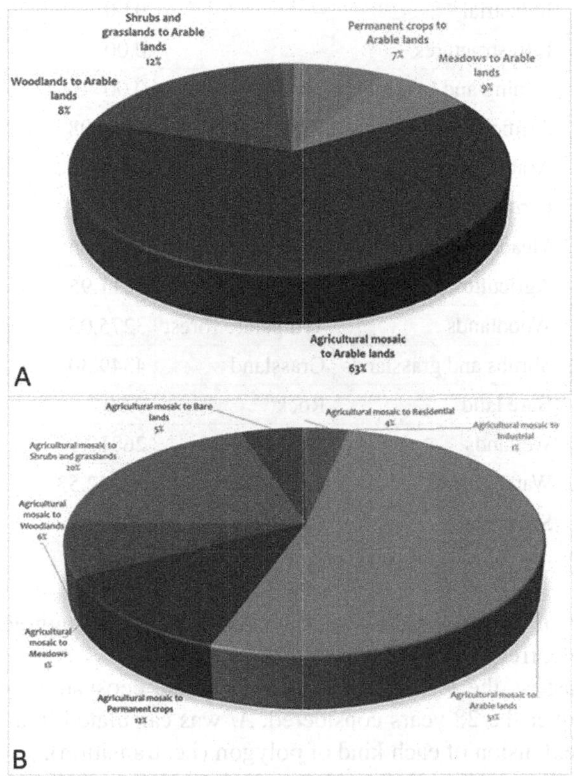

Fig. 3. Transitions from all LU classes to "Arable lands" (A) and from "Agricultural mosaic" to all LU classes (B).

2.2 Methods

The approach used to assess the ESV is shifted from the work developed [1] and carried out by Costanza et al. [14] which quantifies the economic value of the aggregated ecosystem services through the following formula:

$$ESV = \sum (VL_i \times A_i)$$

where A_i is the area (ha) of the biome i and VL_i represents the annual monetary unit value, in our case expressed in €/ha/yr.

This method assumes that every kind of biome produce a constant unit value per hectare, not considering any other features but the kind of the ecosystem. Starting with

Table 1. Unit value per hectare for each of the biomes

LULC class	Biome	VL_i (€/ha/yr)
Residential	Urban	6954.08
Industrial	–	0.00
Infrastructures	–	0.00
Mining and Landfills	–	0.00
Artificial green	Urban	6954.08
Arable lands	Cropland	5811.95
Permanent crops	Cropland	5811.95
Meadows	Cropland	5811.95
Agricultural mosaic	Cropland	5811.95
Woodlands	Temperate forest	3275.03
Shrubs and grasslands	Grassland	4349.30
Bare land	Rock	0.00
Wetlands	Wetlands	26810.96
Watercourses	Lakes/rivers	13062.53
Sea costs	Coastal	9337.54

the classification of Corine Land Cover, the classes were then aggregated into biomes and assigned the corresponding unit value (Table 1).

In order to assess the loss of capacity to generate ecosystem services following LULC changes over the 28 years considered, A_i was calculated in a GIS environment considering the extension of each kind of polygon (i.e. transition).

To deeply understand the relationship between ESV and socio-economic features of all the municipalities belonging to the study area, we considered the per capita GDP of the Basilicata region referred to 2018 and equal to 22,200 € [15] and population data provided by the Italian National Statistical Institute (ISTAT) [16].

3 Results and Discussion

According with this method, the LULC changes occurred in the last 28 years resulted in an overall loss of capacity to generate ecosystem services higher than 39 million euros per year. To this value conspicuously contribute both the artificialization of natural and semi-natural areas (e.g. the transition from agricultural to industrial land or the expansion of urban agglomerations [17] to the detriment of meadows or cultivated fields) and the processes of forest advancement in areas where pastures and agricultural land have been abandoned and renaturalisation has been allowed to proceed. This happens because, as can also be seen from the values shown in the table, the value of VL_i referred to temperate forests is lower than the biomes referring to cultivations and shrubs.

The most significant aspect of this approach lies in having an aggregate index (i.e. a significant number of different ecosystem services) which, however, maintains the spatial dimension, giving the possibility to identify the areas that have suffered the greatest loss due to the changes that have occurred but also to highlight hotspots at regional level, indicative of areas that are particularly functional from the perspective of ecosystem service provision [18].

The following Fig. 4 is a representation of land use changes expressed in monetary terms: areas in red correspond to a decrease in value (proportional to color gradation), areas in green indicate a gain in terms of capacity to provide ecosystem services.

Fig. 4. Representation of land use changes in monetary terms: red correspond to a decrease of ESV, green to a gain.

Knowing the GDP per capita and population resident in each municipality in 2018, the municipal GDP was calculated. Comparing the change in ESV compared to this value, a distribution of municipalities where land use changes have had a more or less significant impact emerges. In the following Fig. 5 there is a representation of municipalities made winners or looser by land use transition: in green are represented municipalities where transition and transformation implied a gain in ESV value; on the other side, municipalities with colors ranging from light yellow to red are those in which LULC transitions correspond to a decrease in ES overall value.

As can be seen from Fig. 5, the municipalities located along the internal areas of the Apennine chain are those that have on average been most affected by the changes in LULC. The highest value, equal to more than 30%, is recorded in a municipality where in recent years there has been a significant decrease in agricultural land [19–21] due both to renaturation processes that have favored the conversion into shrubland and

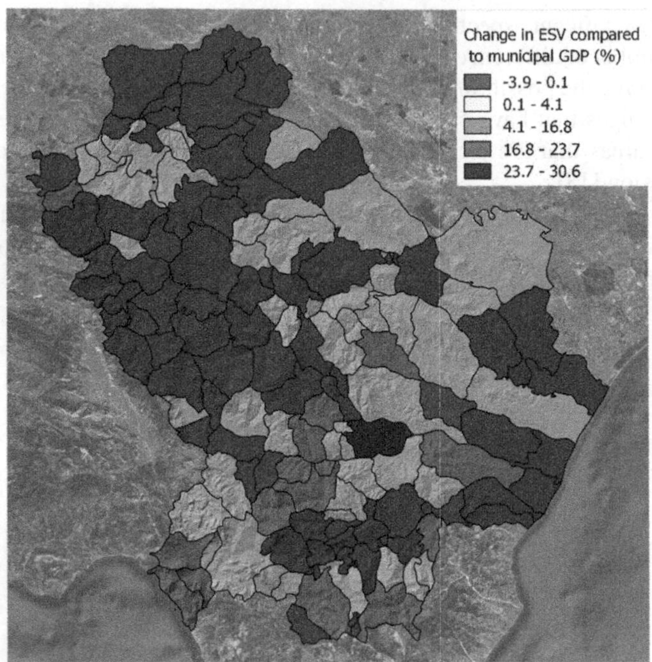

Fig. 5. Change in ESV expressed as a percentage of the GDP assessed at the municipal level (Color figure online)

to transformations in bare soil. It also emerges that, taking for granted the unit values assumed, there are quite a number of municipalities in which land use changes have had a positive impact, which, however, does not reach 4% of the municipal GDP.

Finally, the total value of ESV at 2018 was calculated for each municipality and then divided by the surface area of the territory and by the number of resident inhabitants (Fig. 6).

Analyzing the normalized data with respect to the extension (Fig. 6 – A), it emerges the role of municipalities with a significant percentage of territory dedicated to agricultural activity but also of those along the Ionian coast, with a high conservation value linked to the presence of habitats belonging to the dune and back dune environment. Equally significant is the representation of the ESV per inhabitant (Fig. 6 – B) which returns maximum values twice higher than the GDP per capita (€ 22,200). The municipalities where this value is higher correspond to the inner areas which, as shown in the figure above, are also those where land use changes lead to a significant decrease in ESV compared to GDP per capita. The reasons for this are related both to the scarce presence in these areas of industrial sites and artificial soils (which do not contribute to the ESV) but also to the small resident population, whose trend is considered, for some of those municipalities, irreversible.

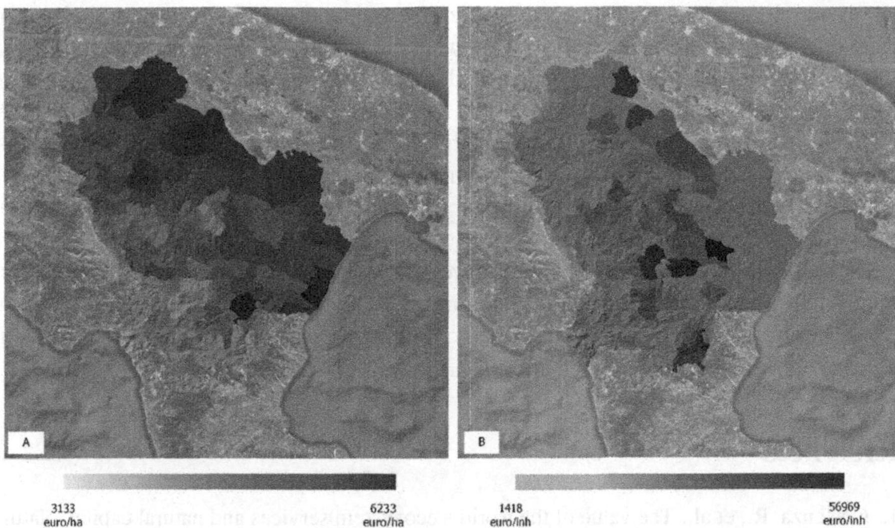

Fig. 6. 2018 ESV normalized with respect to surface area (A) and resident population (B)

4 Conclusions

The ES methodological framework represents a useful tool in interpreting changes in land use and in assessing the effects of territorial transformation. The aim of the paper was to show the potential of an aggregate index, representative of the capacity of a territory to provide simultaneously different ecosystem services. In this paper we used the ESV, calculated on the basis of the work done by Costanza et al. [1, 14] at the global scale. As also highlighted by Jiang [22], the accuracy of such kind of this assessment depends on the LULC data resolution and on the methodology applied for calculate the annual monetary unit value (VL_i) for each of the biomes present in the study area. This parameter is therefore very important because it derives from a market analysis characterized by dynamics and processes that certainly differ according to the working scale and, on an equal degree of detail, from the territorial components of the study area [23]. Therefore, replicating the ESV calculation methodology developed on a world scale, within a study area extending about 10,000 km^2, brings with it non-negligible margins of error. In addition to these are to be considered the simplifications deriving from the Corine Land Cover Map whose resolution fails to capture the detail of certain transformations which, however, even with the same surface area involved, have different impacts in terms of ecosystem services. This is the case, for example, of the phenomena of urban growth already studied by the authors [24–26] and that highlight the inefficiency of the sprinkling process with which urban settlements continue to grow despite the marked depopulation that characterizes the overwhelming majority of municipalities. However, as highlighted in previous works [22–24], the ecosystem services approach is particularly effective in interpreting territorial transformations by providing useful tools both in the ex-ante planning phase [27] and in the assessment of cumulative impacts [28, 29]. Although the strength of this approach lies in the possibility of expressing the values of individual territorial components at different scales, the use of aggregate indices of the overall capacity to provide ES is useful in identifying hotspots or, conversely, in defining regeneration priorities for particularly degraded areas. The use of synthetic indicators can certainly be included in that toolkit [30–32] useful for decision makers and policy designers to pursue sustainability objectives in the evaluation processes. The comparison with socio-economic parameters makes explicit the relationship of the population with ecosystems, thus allowing to assess the demand for ES and to orient regional programming more effectively.

Future developments will certainly have to remedy the weak points of this work, namely that a globally developed evaluation methodology is not scalable on a regional level. Therefore, further studies and research are needed for the evaluation of ES unit values according to a place-based approach.

References

1. Costanza, R., et al.: The value of the world's ecosystem services and natural capital. Nature **387**, 253–260 (1997). https://doi.org/10.1038/387253a0
2. Alcamo, J., Bennett, E.M.: Millennium Ecosystem Assessment (Program): Ecosystems and human well-being : a framework for assessment. Island Press (2003)
3. Ten Brink, P.: The economics of ecosystems and biodiversity in national and international policy making. (2012). https://doi.org/10.4324/9781849775496
4. Corbera, E.: Problematizing REDD + as an experiment in payments for ecosystem services. Curr. Opin. Env. Sust. **4**(6), 612–619 (2012). https://doi.org/10.1016/j.cosust.2012.09.010
5. Maes, J., et al.: Mapping ecosystem services for policy support and decision making in the european union. Ecosyst. Serv. **1**, 31–39 (2012). https://doi.org/10.1016/j.ecoser.2012.06.004
6. Burkhard, B., Kroll, F., Nedkov, S., Müller, F.: Mapping ecosystem service supply, demand and budgets. Ecol. Indic. **21**, 17–29 (2012). https://doi.org/10.1016/j.ecolind.2011.06.019
7. Schröter, M., Stumpf, K.H., Loos, J., van Oudenhoven, A.P.E., Böhnke-Henrichs, A., Abson, D.J.: Refocusing ecosystem services towards sustainability. Ecosyst. Serv. **25**, 35–43 (2017). https://doi.org/10.1016/j.ecoser.2017.03.019
8. Fisher, B., et al.: Ecosystem services and economic theory: integration for policy-relevant research. Ecol. Appl. **18**, 2050–2067 (2008). https://doi.org/10.1890/07-1537.1
9. Rodríguez-Loinaz, G., Alday, J.G., Onaindia, M.: Multiple ecosystem services landscape index: A tool for multifunctional landscapes conservation. J. Environ. Manage. **147**, 152–163 (2015). https://doi.org/10.1016/j.jenvman.2014.09.001
10. Gutman, P.: Ecosystem services: foundations for a new rural-urban compact. Ecol. Econ. **62**(3-4), 383–387 (2007). https://doi.org/10.1016/j.ecolecon.2007.02.027
11. Gómez-Baggethun, E., de Groot, R., Lomas, P.L., Montes, C.: The history of ecosystem services in economic theory and practice: from early notions to markets and payment schemes. Ecol. Econ. **69**, 1209–1218 (2010). https://doi.org/10.1016/j.ecolecon.2009.11.007
12. Pistorius, T., et al.: Lessons for REDDplus: a comparative analysis of the german discourse on forest functions and the global ecosystem services debate. For. Policy Econ. **18**, 4–12 (2012). https://doi.org/10.1016/j.forpol.2011.09.001
13. Roseland, M.: Sustainable community development: integrating environmental, economic, and social objectives. Prog. Plann. **54**, 73–132 (2000). https://doi.org/10.1016/S0305-9006(00)00003-9
14. Costanza, R., et al.: Changes in the global value of ecosystem services. Glob. Environ. Chang. **26**, 152–158 (2014)

15. Eurostat: GDP per capita in EU regions., Bruxelles (2020)
16. Istat.it Popolazione e famiglie, https://www.istat.it/it/popolazione-e-famiglie, Accessed 06 Dec 2019
17. Nolè, G., Lasaponara, R., Lanorte, A., Murgante, B.: Quantifying urban sprawl with spatial autocorrelation techniques using multi-temporal satellite data. Int. J. Agric. Environ. Inf. Syst. **5**, 20–38 (2014). https://doi.org/10.4018/IJAEIS.2014040102
18. Murgante, B., Borruso, G., Lapucci, A.: Sustainable development: concepts and methods for its application in urban and environmental planning. Stud. Comput. Intell. **348**, 1–15 (2011). https://doi.org/10.1007/978-3-642-19733-8_1
19. Murgante, B., Borruso, G., Balletto, G., Castiglia, P., Dettori, M.: Why italy first? health, geographical and planning aspects of the covid-19 outbreak. Sustainability. **12**, 5064 (2020). https://doi.org/10.3390/su12125064
20. Lasaponara, R., et al.: Spatial open data for monitoring risks and preserving archaeological areas and landscape: case studies at kom el shoqafa, egypt and shush. Iran. Sustainability. **9**, 572 (2017). https://doi.org/10.3390/su9040572
21. Las Casas, G., Murgante, B., Scorza, F.: Regional local development strategies benefiting from open data and open tools and an outlook on the renewable energy sources contribution. In: Papa, R., Fistola, R. (eds.) Smart Energy in the Smart City. GET, pp. 275–290. Springer, Cham (2016). https://doi.org/10.1007/978-3-319-31157-9_14
22. Jiang, W.: Mapping ecosystem service value in Germany. Int. J. Sustain. Dev. World Ecol. **25**, 518–534 (2018). https://doi.org/10.1080/13504509.2018.1430623
23. Elfadaly, A., Attia, W., Qelichi, M.M., Murgante, B., Lasaponara, R.: Management of cultural heritage sites using remote sensing indices and spatial analysis techniques. Surv. Geophys. **39**(6), 1347–1377 (2018). https://doi.org/10.1007/s10712-018-9489-8
24. Saganeiti, L., Pilogallo, A., Faruolo, G., Scorza, F., Murgante, B.: Territorial fragmentation and renewable energy source plants: Which relationship? Sustain. **12**, 1828 (2020). https://doi.org/10.3390/SU12051828
25. Scorza, F., Saganeiti, L., Pilogallo, A., Murgante, B.: Ghost Planning: the inefficiency of energy sector policies in a low population density region. Arch. DI Stud. URBANI E Reg. (2020, in Press)
26. Saganeiti, L., Pilogallo, A., Faruolo, G., Scorza, F., Murgante, B.: Energy landscape fragmentation: basilicata region (italy) study case. In: Misra, S., et al. (eds.) ICCSA 2019. LNCS, vol. 11621, pp. 692–700. Springer, Cham (2019). https://doi.org/10.1007/978-3-030-24302-9_50
27. Scorza, F., Pilogallo, A., Saganeiti, L., Murgante, B.: Natura 2000 areas and sites of national interest (sni): measuring (un)integration between naturalness preservation and environmental remediation policies. Sustainability. **12**, 2928 (2020). https://doi.org/10.3390/su12072928
28. Pilogallo, A., Saganeiti, L., Scorza, F., Murgante, B.: Ecosystem services approach to evaluate renewable energy plants effects. In: Misra, S., et al. (eds.) ICCSA 2019. LNCS, vol. 11624, pp. 281–290. Springer, Cham (2019). https://doi.org/10.1007/978-3-030-24311-1_20
29. Scorza, F., Pilogallo, A., Saganeiti, L., Murgante, B., Pontrandolfi, P.: Comparing the territorial performances of renewable energy sources' plants with an integrated ecosystem services loss assessment: a case study from the basilicata region (Italy). Sustain. Cities Soc. **56**, 102082 (2020). https://doi.org/10.1016/J.SCS.2020.102082
30. Casas, G.L., Scorza, F.: Sustainable planning: a methodological toolkit. In: Gervasi, O., et al. (eds.) ICCSA 2016. LNCS, vol. 9786, pp. 627–635. Springer, Cham (2016). https://doi.org/10.1007/978-3-319-42085-1_53

31. Dvarioniene, J., Grecu, V., Lai, S., Scorza, F.: Four perspectives of applied sustainability: research implications and possible integrations. In: Gervasi, O., et al. (eds.) ICCSA 2017. LNCS, vol. 10409, pp. 554–563. Springer, Cham (2017). https://doi.org/10.1007/978-3-319-62407-5_39
32. Scorza, F., Grecu, V.: Assessing sustainability: research directions and relevant issues. In: Gervasi, O., et al. (eds.) ICCSA 2016. LNCS, vol. 9786, pp. 642–647. Springer, Cham (2016). https://doi.org/10.1007/978-3-319-42085-1_55

Cyber-Physical Platform for Preeclampsia Detection

Iuliana Marin(✉), Maria Iuliana Bocicor, and Arthur-Jozsef Molnar

SC Info World SRL, Bucharest, Romania
{iuliana.marin,iuliana.bocicor,arthur.molnar}@infoworld.ro
http://www.infoworld.ro/home/

Abstract. Hypertension-related conditions are the most prevalent complications of pregnancy worldwide. They manifest in up to 8% of cases and if left untreated, can lead to serious detrimental effects. Early detection of their sudden onset can help physicians alleviate the condition and improve outcomes for both would-be mother and baby. Today's prevalence of smartphones and cost-effective wearable technology provide new opportunities for individualized medicine. Existing devices promote heart health, they monitor and encourage physical activity and measure sleep quality. This builds interest and encourages users to require more advanced features. We believe these aspects form suitable conditions to create and market specialized wearable devices. The present paper details a cyber-physical system built around an intelligent bracelet for monitoring hypertension-related conditions tailored to pregnant women. The bracelet uses a microfluidic layer that is compressed by the blood pressing against the arterial wall. Integrated sensors register the waveform and send it to the user's smartphone, where the systolic and diastolic values are determined. The system is currently developed under European Union research funding, and includes a software server where data is stored and further processing is carried out through machine learning.

Keywords: Cyber-physical system · Smart bracelet · Biosensors · Blood pressure · Hypertension

1 Introduction

Hypertensive disorders affect up to 8% of all pregnancies [13], with increased prevalence in women who already carried a preeclamptic pregnancy. In the United States, hypertension related conditions affect between 7 to 15% of pregnancies [15]. They are classified into chronic hypertension, gestational hypertension and preeclampsia [17,26], and represent the most common medical problem encountered during pregnancy. Chronic hypertension is present before 20 weeks of pregnancy, or in cases where the woman is already on anti-hypertensive medication. Gestational hypertension is diagnosed after 20 weeks of pregnancy. When combined with proteinuria (the presence of protein in urine), or organ dysfunction such as renal or liver involvement, it is diagnosed as preeclampsia. If left

O. Gervasi et al. (Eds.): ICCSA 2020, LNCS 12253, pp. 617–625, 2020.
https://doi.org/10.1007/978-3-030-58814-4_48

untreated, preeclampsia can lead to adverse effects for both the mother and baby, including restricted fetal growth, organ damage, and seizures (eclampsia), which necessitate delivering the baby to prevent further consequences [17].

Early detection allows medical intervention with the aim of maintaining blood pressure under a safe threshold, managing the time of delivery for minimal risk to both mother and baby as well as prophylactic use of magnesium sulphate during labor [8,24].

In the last decade, medicine is going through an important transformation fueled by the ubiquity of wearables, together with increased awareness and interest from the general public [14]. We believe this can be harnessed to improve the outcomes for conditions such as preeclampsia, which are well known, but under reported in many parts of the globe. In one region, 77% of pregnant women affected were unaware of the condition or its possible consequences [25].

In this paper we detail a cyber-physical system that targets early detection of preeclampsia and other hypertension conditions related with pregnancy [10]. The system is being developed under funding from the European Union. It integrates a custom developed wearable bracelet for real-time measurement of blood pressure with a smartphone application and a software server.

The system connects the would-be mother with her clinician and provides an integrated platform to alert clinicians at the onset of persistent hypertension [20]. As preeclampsia can have sudden onset and is difficult to manage, registering its early warning signs allows more flexibility in its diagnosis and management [24].

One of the principal innovations regards the sensor-driven bracelet used to monitor blood pressure. Current products are based on infrared or oximeter sensors that directly measure pulse and blood oxygen levels, which they then correlate with blood pressure [3,4,16]. They enable taking measurements at shorter intervals and without so much preparation [3]. However, these devices can require calibration and they use approximation to estimate blood pressure. The proposed solution increases accuracy by measuring blood pressure directly and eliminates calibration requirements.

The wrist-worn bracelet is built around a diminutive sensor comprised of a microfluidic layer located between two sensing membranes. External pressure of the blood pushing on the arterial wall is picked up by the microfluidic layer and results in a change of impedance which leads to the complete signal of the waveform being recorded. Readings are transmitted to the wearer's smartphone using an integrated wireless module with a BLE chip. The energy efficiency of BLE and the sensor allow the wrist bracelet to measure blood pressure several times during an hour and transmit data without requiring frequent charging. Reading history and trends can be consulted using the smartphone application. They are also forwarded to the software server, which clinicians and end-users can access over the web. When hypertension is detected, the associated clinician receives an application alert; this helps with continuously monitoring patients and lower the time to intervention.

2 Related Work

Hypertension is a major cause of premature death worldwide [27] and an important cause of complications during pregnancy [2]. The idea of continuous measurement of blood pressure outside of medical facilities has only recently been adopted and during the past years various applications and devices have been developed for this purpose. One such device is H2-BP, a wearable blood pressure monitor in the form of a light wrist band [9]. It measures blood pressure with an accuracy of 5 mmHg every 30–50 s, as well as heart rate with an accuracy of ±5%. While measuring, the indication is to hold a correct position, in which the device is at heart level, and not to move or speak [9]. An Android application is also available and communication between the device and smartphone is achieved via Bluetooth.

Omron's HeartGuide Blood Pressure Watch is an oscillometric wrist wearable blood pressure monitor composed of miniaturised components for traditional oscillometric measurement [22]. It includes an inflating cuff and can take a blood pressure reading in approximately 30 s. Reading is triggered by pressing a button and lifting the arm to heart level, where it must be kept still during the measurement. The company also offers the Heart Advisor smartphone application, which synchronises readings to a cloud service and optionally with Apple HealthKit. It provides features for monitoring blood pressure, activity and sleep quality and it allows for configuration of reminders and settings.

Unlike the devices presented above, the SeismoWatch introduced by Carek et al. [3] measures blood pressure via a novel technique which employs the theory of pulse transit time. The device they propose is a wrist watch that must be held against the sternum for less than 15 s to detect micro-vibrations of the chest wall associated with the heartbeat. Blood pressure is estimated by considering its inverse correlation with the time interval for a pulse wave to travel from a point close to the heart to a more distant location along the arterial tree (e.g. the wrist). An accelerometer and an optical sensor on the watch measure the pulse wave travel time and according to this the device estimates systolic and diastolic blood pressure. A similar idea is used by Hsu et al. [11], who propose a non-invasive method of measuring blood pressure: two pressure sensors simultaneously detecting blood pressure waveforms are placed on the person's neck and wrist and the delay time between them is used to determine the local pulse waveform. The skin-coupled wearable system can continuously capture blood pressure waveforms and the experiments showed that the prototype was capable of detecting high-fidelity blood pressure waveforms.

A solution specifically tailored for preeclampsia uses an F1 smart wristwatch which measures blood pressure and sends the triggered values via Bluetooth to a mobile application installed on the user's cell phone [21]. The bracelet model was selected after comparison with other wristwatch models where it was found that taking measurements from users with dark complexion was difficult, resulting in finger tip measurements to determine blood pressure [6]. The mobile application is intended to be helpful for the expectant mother and her caregiver.

This application includes a maintained database comprising gathered records. The caregiver is alerted if the expectant mother is in a critical circumstance.

A device utilized for dealing with the health and well-being during pregnancy is the Ava bracelet [1]. It determines cycle, fertility, sleep quality and pregnancy based on physiological signals which are collected automatically while asleep, at night time. At the point when the user awakens, the bracelet is synchronized to the mobile application and the algorithm of Ava shows the outcomes. Its mobile application displays the information about pulse and breathing rates, skin temperature, and heart rate variability ratio which determines physiological stress. Sleep is checked by the Ava bracelet and it calculates complete rest time, percentage of light contrasted with deep and REM sleep, including the rest patterns. At the point when the woman is pregnant, the mobile application can screen her weight and show the development on its graphical user interface. The mobile application monitors and informs its user about the baby's advancement during pregnancy.

When compared with existing solutions, our proposed wearable-based system has clear advantages: first, it automatically measures blood pressure without the need to maintain a certain position, it does not use inflatable cuffs, and it is comfortable and easy to wear continuously. Measurement accuracy is ensured by the design of the device, in which the sensor covers a large surface of the inner wrist. Furthermore, the software server employs machine learning techniques to detect potential signs of preeclampsia [20]. Considering the above, the system we propose is original, technologically advanced and accessible both with regard to cost and ease of use.

3 Technological Solution for Preeclampsia Prevention

The platform provides an end-to-end solution for monitoring the onset and progression of hypertension-related conditions tailored for pregnant women. In addition to the custom-developed smart bracelet, it incorporates one of the end-user's smart mobile devices. A custom developed application is installed on this device, which is usually an Android or iOS powered smartphone or tablet. It is used to communicate with the bracelet using the low power BLE standard, process raw readings and transmit them to the software server. This fills the gap between the power-constrained environment of the bracelet and the cloud-deployed software server. The clinician associated with the patient can consult her reading history through a web interface. Clinicians can sign up to receive real-time alerts in case the system detects the onset of hypertension. The present section presents the hardware and software components and details the design decisions behind the system architecture shown in Fig. 1.

3.1 Hardware Components

The wearable bracelet device is comprised of innovative biosensors that monitor the user's blood pressure. They measure the microfluidic channel deformation

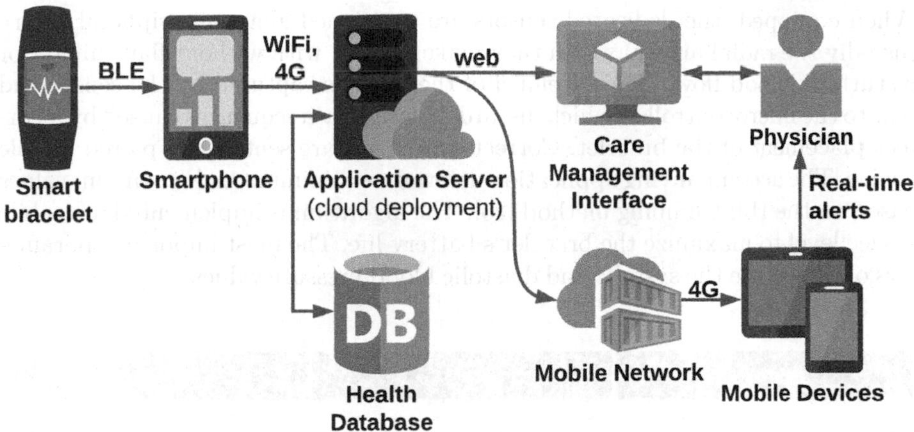

Fig. 1. High-level architecture of the platform

based on the impedance principle. Their large size covers a sufficient area of the wrist to detect the small changes in pressure as blood pushes against the wall of the radial artery. The sensor is connected to an electronic module comprised of a lock in amplifier, a microcontroller, a current generator, a screen, battery and a USB port.

The current generator is connected to the electrodes of the sensor used to measure the impedance of the deformable microfluidic channel. The lock in amplifier uses the sensor voltage signals from which noise is extracted. The signal is converted from analog to digital, after which it is forwarded to the microcontroller. The microcontroller is responsible for sensor data acquisition, data encryption and wireless transmission to the associated user device. The microcontroller encrypts the waveform information and transmits it to the paired device over Bluetooth. The bracelet includes a screen used to pair it with a mobile device. The power supply for the integrated electronic modules is provided through the use of a battery, which can be recharged using a USB port.

3.2 Software Components

The software components are spread across the bracelet, a mobile application with Android and iOS implementations and the software server. The bracelet includes the required software to record and carry out initial analysis on the pressure waveform [20], be paired with a mobile device and send encrypted reading data to it. The mobile application acts as the bridge between the bracelet and the software server. Its inclusion reduces the bracelet's weight, complexity and cost, as it only requires a BLE chip for communication. Furthermore, it keeps end users in control of the recorded data, which can be viewed and managed through the mobile application.

The bracelet's sensing layer is comprised of several dedicated sensors that use the arterial tonometry technique [12] to calculate hemodynamic parameters.

When equipped, the dedicated sensors are positioned along a peripheral artery (usually the radial artery) which they make contact with without flattening it or disturbing blood flow. The waveform of the pulse is captured by the sensor and sent to the microcontroller, which discards corrupt data sequences caused by incorrect placement of the bracelet. Correct waveforms are sent to the paired mobile device. The accompanying application determines minimum and maximum values based on the Hill Climbing method [23]. The algorithm is implemented at mobile device level to maximize the bracelet's battery life. The most important parameters obtained are the systolic and diastolic blood pressure values.

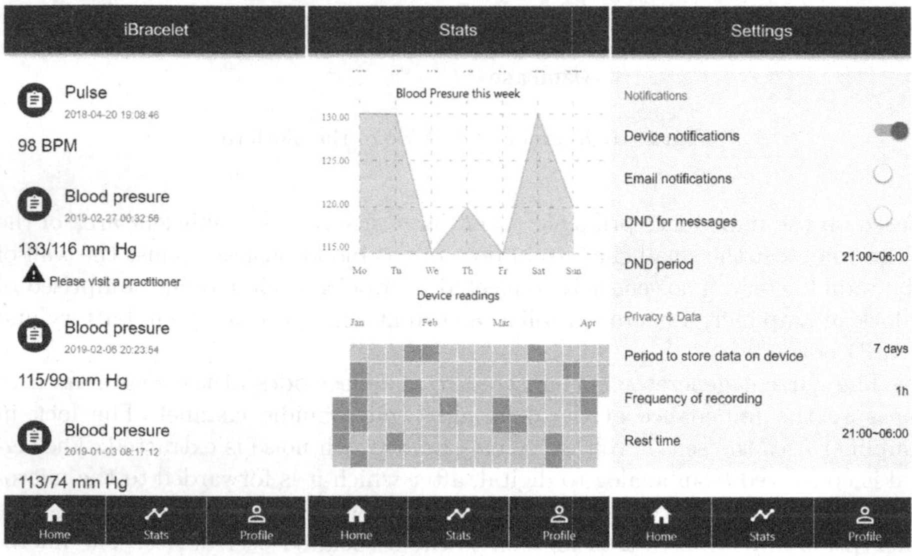

Fig. 2. Mobile application user interface screens

Users can monitor blood pressure values using the mobile application or through the software server's web interface. Both offer the possibility of registering family members or physicians, giving them access to data. Physicians have the possibility of receiving real-time alerts at the onset of persistent hypertension. As shown in Fig. 2, the application also records heart rate. The user can configure the measurement frequency, mark the period of time they reserve for resting and configure how they choose to be notified. The settings are designed to provide balance between the frequency of measurement, device battery life and avoiding the psychological observer effect. Furthermore, values recorded during the resting period are important, as they might signal increased risk [7].

The risk of preeclampsia is present when persistent hypertension is detected. This is defined as systolic values over 140 mmHg or diastolic values over 90 mmHg recorded over two measurements at least 6 h apart [5]. In this case, the mobile application can raise an alert to notify the end user to contact their physician. All recorded values are stored locally by the mobile application. Once an Internet connection is available, they are sent to the application server.

The server is the central repository where all recorded blood pressure values are stored. End-users and physicians access the server through a web application that enforces role-based access to ensure data privacy. The application allows all users to visualize recorded values, statistical data and alert history. The server also carries out the final, but most complex phase of data processing. Physicians can enter additional contextual and clinical information into the system such as patient age, weight, height, race, smoking status and cholesterol level. These values are fed to a machine learning classifier - one of the project's innovations on the software side. The classifier was trained using the open data set from the Massachusetts University Amherst and National Health and Nutrition Survey and is described in [20]. It provides a finely tuned risk profile for hypertensive conditions in pregnancy and identifies those cases that are most prone to preeclampsia, before physiological changes (e.g. proteinuria) can be detected.

3.3 Technical Challenges

The most important challenge regarded the accuracy of the waveform-based measurement in the context of a permanently-equipped bracelet. The research team considered placing the device both on the arm, like a regular blood pressure cuff and on the wrist, similar to a watch.

The main trade-off concerns the fact that the arm is closer to heart and at the same level, which increases the likelihood of accurate readings; since technical evaluation showed that a wrist-mounted bracelet produces accurate readings, it was preferred. This also has the added advantage of not looking out of place, as the device resembles a fitness tracker[1]. Additional optimizations were carried out to minimize battery consumption and ensure that normal wear and tear does not affect reading accuracy or result in leaks from the microfluidic layer. Dividing software components across the bracelet, mobile device and server complements hardware design choices, lowers entry cost and allows additional features related to disease identification and early warning to be evaluated and rolled out on the server side.

4 Conclusions

Hypertensive disorders can appear at any time during pregnancy, while preeclampsia is usually reported after 20 weeks. Early detection is paramount to give the mother the opportunity to receive proper treatment and minimise risks during pregnancy and delivery. The platform described is part of the *i-bracelet* project [10], which aims to contribute towards decreasing hypertension related risks in pregnant women. The current paper is focused on the software components, while hardware aspects are discussed in our previous work [18–20].

[1] Further details are subject to patent protection.

When compared with existing approaches, our proposal provides an end-to-end solution for continuous, real-time monitoring that combines an innovative, easy to use piece of hardware integrated with software services that enable data collection, advanced data analysis to predict future cases of persistent hypertension together with statistical reporting.

From the hardware side, we believe the greatest improvement will be to extend the project's scope in order to cover prevention and management of hypertension in the general population. The best way to achieve this is to integrate the bracelet's technology into well-known wearable devices. In the interim, we aim to integrate recordings with globally used platforms such as Apple HealthKit[2] and Google Fit[3]. On the server side, we have evaluated several machine learning algorithms and obtained promising results [19,20]. We intend to further improve classification and increase its predictive power, both in the particular case of pregnant women and within the general population.

Acknowledgement. This work was funded by a grant of the Romanian National Authority for Scientific Research and Innovation, CCCDI-UEFISCDI, project number 59/2017, Eurostars Project E10871, i-bracelet- *"Intelligent bracelet for blood pressure monitoring and detection of preeclampsia"*.

References

1. Ava: Ava Bracelet (2020). https://www.avawomen.com/. Accessed 10 Mar 2020
2. Braunthal, S., Brateanu, A.: Hypertension in pregnancy: pathophysiology and treatment. SAGE Open Med. **7**, 1–15 (2019)
3. Carek, A.M., Conant, J., Joshi, A., Kang, H., Inan, O.T.: SeismoWatch: wearable cuffless blood pressure monitoring using pulse transit time. Proc. ACM Interact. Mob. Wearable Ubiquitous Technol. **1**(3), 1–24 (2017)
4. Dias, D., Cunha, J.P.: Wearable health devices-vital sign monitoring, systems and technologies. Sensors **18**, 2414 (2018)
5. English, F.A., Kenny, L.C., McCarthy, F.P.: Risk factors and effective management of preeclampsia. Integr. Blood Pressure Control **8**, 7 (2015)
6. Faith Mueni Musyoka, M.M.T., Muketha, G.M.: An assessment of suitable and affordable smart armband for preeclampsia management in antenatal care. Int. J. Inf. Technol. **3**(6), 1–7 (2020). https://doi.org/10.5281/zenodo.3685168
7. Friedman, O., Logan, A.G.: Nocturnal blood pressure profiles among normotensive, controlled hypertensive and refractory hypertensive subjects. Can. J. Cardiol. **25**(9), S312–S316 (2009)
8. Goldenberg, R.L., McClure, E.M.: It takes a system: magnesium sulfate for prevention of eclampsia in a resource-limited community setting. Glob. Health Sci. Pract. **7**, 340–343 (2019)
9. H2Care: H2-BP (2018). https://h2care.com/18. Accessed 28 Jan 2020
10. Home of i-bracelet (2020). http://i-bracelet.eu/
11. Hsu, Y.P., Young, D.J.: Skin-coupled personal wearable ambulatory pulse wave velocity monitoring system using microelectromechanical sensors. IEEE Sens. J. **14**(10), 3490–3497 (2014)

[2] https://developer.apple.com/healthkit/.
[3] https://www.google.com/fit/.

12. Kemmotsu, O., Ueda, M., Otsuka, H., Yamamura, T., Winter, D.C., Eckerle, J.S.: Arterial tonometry for noninvasive, continuous blood pressure monitoring during anesthesia. Anesthesiology **75**(2), 333–340 (1991)
13. Kongwattanakul, K., Saksiriwuttho, P., Chaiyarach, S., Thepsuthammarat, K.: Incidence, characteristics, maternal complications, and perinatal outcomes associated with preeclampsia with severe features and HELLP syndrome. Int. J. Women's Health **10**, 371 (2018)
14. Kumar, S., et al.: Mobile health technology evaluation: the mhealth evidence workshop. Am. J. Prev. Med. **45**(2), 228–236 (2013)
15. Lo, J., Mission, J., Caughey, A.: Hypertensive disease of pregnancy and maternal mortality. Curr. Opin. Obstetr. Gynecol. **25**, 124–132 (2013)
16. Majumder, S., Mondal, T., Deen, M.: Wearable sensors for remote health monitoring. Sensors **17**, 130 (2017)
17. Mammaro, A., et al.: Hypertensive disorders of pregnancy. J. Prenatal Med. **3**(1), 1 (2009)
18. Marin, I., Goga, N.: Securing the network for a smart bracelet system. In: 2018 22nd International Conference on System Theory, Control and Computing (ICSTCC), pp. 255–260, October 2018
19. Marin, I., Pavaloiu, B., Marian, C., Racovita, V., Goga, N.: Early detection of preeclampsia based on a machine learning approach. In: 2019 E-Health and Bioengineering Conference (EHB), pp. 1–4, November 2019
20. Marin, I., Goga, N.: Hypertension detection based on machine learning. In: Proceedings of the 6th Conference on the Engineering of Computer Based Systems, ECBS 2019. Association for Computing Machinery, New York, NY, USA (2019)
21. Musyoka, F.M., Thiga, M.M., Muketha, G.M.: A 24-hour ambulatory blood pressure monitoring system for preeclampsia management in antenatal care. Inf. Med. Unlock. **16**, 100199 (2019)
22. Omron Healthcare: HeartGuide (2020). https://omronhealthcare.com/products/heartguide-wearable-blood-pressure-monitor-bp8000m/. Accessed 28 Jan 2020
23. Rawat, R., Chandel, S.: Hill climbing techniques for tracking maximum power point in solar photovoltaic systems - a review. J. Sustain. Dev. Green Econ. **2**, 90–95 (2013)
24. Sibai, B.: Diagnosis, prevention, and management of eclampsia. Obstetr. Gynecol. **105**, 402–10 (2005)
25. Vyata, P., Chauhan, N., Nallathambi, A., Hussein, F.: Assessment of prevalence of preeclampsia from Dilla region of Ethiopia. BMC Res. Notes **8**, 816 (2015)
26. Webster, K., Fishburn, S., Maresh, M., Findlay, S.C., Chappell, L.C.: Diagnosis and management of hypertension in pregnancy: summary of updated nice guidance. BMJ **366**, l5119 (2019). https://doi.org/10.1136/bmj.l5119
27. World Health Organization: Who recommendations for prevention and treatment of preeclampsia and eclampsia (2011). Accessed 24 Jan 2020

System Integration and Functional Priorities to Maximize Profit and Loss for Smart Factory

Jeong Seog Kho and Jongpil Jeong(✉)

Department of Smart Factory Convergence, Sungkyunkwan University, Suwon, Gyeonggi-do 16419, Republic of Korea
matt.js.kho@gmail.com, jpjeong@skku.edu

Abstract. Smart factories have already become a key theme in the manufacturing industry. Advanced IT technology, industrial engineering, and management know-how will be combined to improve all areas of manufacturing. Improving productivity is the most important goal for a factory. However, this is only part of the overall goal of corporate management. Corporate management pursues a greater goal of optimizing all of the company's resources to reduce losses, increase profits and achieve sustainable growth. All companies should achieve smart factories to prevent unnecessary waste of time and resources and maximize profits by increasing productivity. This paper deals with the integration effect of the major fundamental system, including the Manufacturing Execution System that operates production, and the method of measuring it. When integrating core systems to maximize successful inventory management and revenue, a method of assessing them is required. Here it would be appropriate to have an evaluation method in which scores are given and calculated differently depending on the results and functional priorities obtained by the system. This approach will help solve the problem of which systems each company will use and integrate when introducing smart factories.

Keywords: Smart factory · Manufacturing Execution System · Enterprise Resource Planning · System integration

1 Introduction

Smart factory is already being distributed as a global trend. The combination of cutting-edge IT technology, industrial engineering, and know-how in management has resulted in the improvement of the productivity of manufacturing companies. It is expected that Smart Factory will be able to efficiently and profitably produce customized small lot products since the setting for vertical integration as it means collecting data from factories and realizing manufacturing sites with high flexibility and reconfiguration [1]. The introduction of smart factories has already enabled companies to utilize accurate market information on consumers' tastes and demands and to fine-tune the purchase of raw materials and components needed for manufacturing. It is also operating all of the resources required for manufacturing rationally, reducing waste and reducing manufacturing lead time while increasing factory utilization. As a result, the ratio of compliance

O. Gervasi et al. (Eds.): ICCSA 2020, LNCS 12253, pp. 626–635, 2020.
https://doi.org/10.1007/978-3-030-58814-4_49

with customer delivery has also increased, greatly improving customer satisfaction and enjoying the effects of smart factories.

Although the manufacturing sector has set productivity gains as its most important goal, this is only part of its overall management. Corporate management must achieve a greater goal: how to optimize all the company's resources to reduce losses and increase profits, and how to achieve sustainable planning and implementation. Therefore, this paper deals with the establishment and operation of the Advanced Planning System (APS) [2] which is a system in which inventory management and production are planned from a profit-and-loss perspective so that all companies seeking to improve productivity through the achievement of smart factories can achieve another big management goal. In addition, Enterprise Resource Planning (ERP) [3] and Manufacturing Execution System (MES) [4] operate as basic systems, but many companies do not yet use a variety of systems, such as Supply Chain Management (SCM) [5], Product Lifecycle Management (PLM) [6] and Quality Management System (QMS) [7]. This paper would like to emphasize that when operating with ERP, MES, SCM and PLM, achieving the upgrading of plant operations at the enterprise level can bring about productivity maximization and loss minimization.

This paper consists of: Sect. 2 reviewed the production and operation factors of profit and loss perspective studied in the past as related tasks, and dealt with the non-production factors that should be added additionally. In addition, in terms of system operational efficiency to achieve that goal, proposals were added for the integration of ERP and MES currently being used by businesses. Section 3 numerically illustrates the conditions under which gains and losses are achieved under the assumption that all major systems are integrated and all of its core functions are used, and Sect. 4 compares the figures that can be achieved only by systems that are substantially insufficient compared to performing all four core systems integration and various functions. It is an effort to quantify reality on the premise that it can vary depending on industry, manpower and corporate financial conditions. The following study concludes that the conditions and results analysis of Artificial Intelligence (AI) based APS deployment will be faithfully performed, and that a review of the conditions and expected system environment for system integration of smart factories is proposed.

2 Related Work

The problem that manufacturers always worry about is the management of production and inventory. Inventory management is based on the premise that adequate quantities of safe stock must be secured in line with the sales schedule. Excessive inventory is also one of the major reasons for reducing profit margins and must be carefully managed. Products with large price variations or long production lead times depending on the operating level of the safe inventory often face a crisis of existence, as well as the benefits of the enterprise, depending on the success or failure of that operation. This is especially true for companies that involve huge Fabrication (FAB) facility [8] investments, such as the Dynamic Random Access Memory (DRAM) manufacturers. However, for industries like Fast-Moving Consumer Goods (FMCG) [9] that have a fast turnover and relatively low price fluctuation, the amount of safe stock holdings should be small and its impact on profit or loss is not so great [10] Fig. 1.

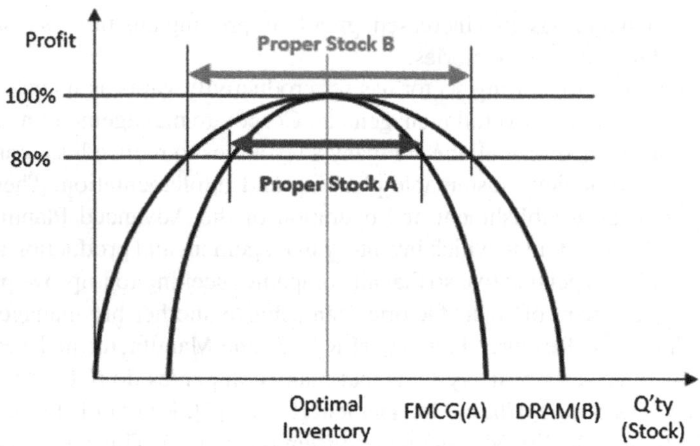

Fig. 1. Optimal inventory range

2.1 Inventory Management

In general, the inventory control curve is as follows and the operating level of the safe inventory is described as different for different types of products.

Determining output is the core of production management and manages all conditions for its implementation in the MES. The MES must meet the conditions of ISA-95 [11] and ensure that the production status is in real time how accurately it is planned beyond the basic requirements and executed in accordance with the work instructions without any abnormalities. And we need to accumulate and analyze that data to review how efficiently it was done and whether there was no abnormalities. It is the APS that is responsible for the key functions of this production management and it is a key function of the MES to build smart factories, which is a basic requirement for improving productivity. In past papers, the logic and additional considerations for the establishment of accurate production plans, including inventory operations, are as follows.

- Raw Material Supply Situation [Price and Period]
- Sales Price Fluctuation
- Cost and Average Sales Price
- Customer Service Experience
- New Product Development Period
- New Product Sample Supply and Qualification Progress
- Facility Operation Rate
- Capital Expenditures (CAPAX) and Operational Expense (OPEX)

2.2 Integration of ERP and MES

The direct impact on production plans is current inventory and sales plans and availability of available raw materials and production facilities. In addition, however, external factors that determine the implementation of the production plan are described in 2.1, in which business management only needs to consider these external environments first, then develop a sophisticated planned production plan and then implement the plan faithfully. If a faithfully executed plan is wrong, the effect of the outcome on the firm in the long term is critical and can affect the existence of the entity Fig. 2.

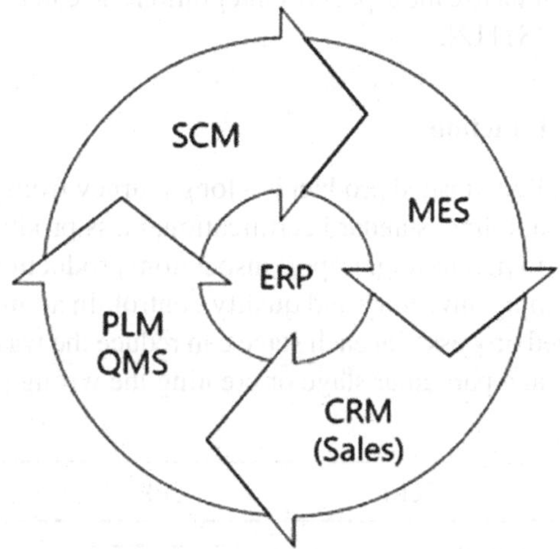

Fig. 2. System integration for smart factories

The direct element of the production plan is well-run within the MES. That is, materials required and retained, facility capacity, and basic information for operation. Other factors for production include inventory holding and demand for finished products, the schedule and type of products desired by the customer and most importantly, sales price information. Because companies must consider both profit margins and customer satisfaction, a simulated production plan must be established, both of the customer priorities determined by the sales department and the profit-to-market ratio calculated by the management. Large companies have nothing to worry about as they establish mid- and long-term production plans and repeat implementation and analysis through consultation of important departments such as sales and production and management. The problem, however, is that small and medium-sized enterprises that have failed to introduce smart factories or are currently under consideration do not precisely make comprehensive judgments on production by these external environments, as they have very small staff and their roles in sales, production and management.

Large companies are using ERP packages supplied by large companies such as SAP and Oracle well. In addition, SCM, PLM and MES are developing very well and working together smoothly. However, the problem again this time is small and medium-sized enterprises. Small businesses can hardly afford to introduce large packages for each sector. Given the small-scale operating workforce or simple processes, the fact that it is too many, complex and heavy a system is a major stumbling block for representatives of small and medium-sized enterprises to decide on investment in such smart factory systems.

Therefore, it is essential to have an integrated system of scale in order to build a smart factory that fits the reality. Thus, in recent years, frequently chosen MESs by small and medium enterprises include some of the ERP and SCM functions, which in fact demonstrate the need to establish and implement production plans, such as resources available and external environmental factors based on MES-specific capabilities. And there are attempts to emphasize the aspects of integration and call it the integrated Factory Information System (FIS) [12].

2.3 System-Specific Function

The process of making one finished product is a long journey from product planning and development, design, sampling, standard certification, mass production testing, marketing and sales activities to purchasing, import inspection, production planning, manufacturing, shipping and supply, inventory and quality control. In addition, smooth information sharing and detailed processes at each stage can reduce the waste of time and money generated by stopping at a particular stage or creating the wrong product Fig. 3.

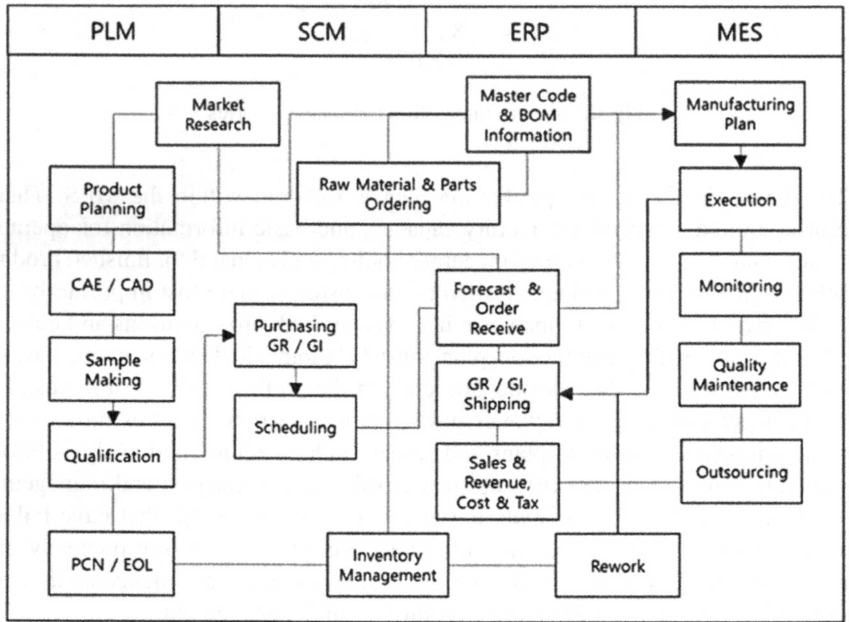

Fig. 3. Function diagrams

The purpose of standardization of each process, the establishment of an essential information sharing system at that stage, and the collection and storage of data are all aimed at improving productivity by managing factors that affect profit or loss As such, planning a single product and neglecting any of the cycles from manufacturing to sales has a significant impact on quality and is difficult to manage without integrating each process. Currently, small and medium-sized enterprises are not able to collect their respective data and are not equipped with such manpower and systems, and are experiencing numerous trial and error, overloading and inconvenience, and feeling the limits of productivity improvement. Therefore, listing all of these functions and defining each association will give you a clearer relationship and priority. The figure below represents the full function of the entire process, from planning to shipping, and market research, including simple manufacturing activities. From this we can see that all functions are connected and very few function independently. Of course, modules related to personnel management and training, and the use of expenses, such as overseas travel, among ERP functions do not seem to be able to establish direct links to manufacturing activities. Ultimately, however, we have to get a Forecast or Order to increase its hit rate, so we can only link it to the gross profit ratio, but we will skip it here.

3 Functional Priorities

Each of the system-specific functions discussed above will be able to establish a more accurate production plan from a profit-rate perspective, provided that all companies can use it. This is a step that is proposed as a model that can be implemented and applied at a corporate site and is not yet subject to practical verification. However, if there is any accumulated data in the system, it is quite a meaningful approach to actually calculate the difference in weight and then extract the priority of the production plan.

Table 1 shows the lists the items used as important system factors in a semiconductor production company and scores them in a meaningful order. The sum of each system is arranged so that the sum of values listed in order of importance within the system is 1 as well. Although there will be other items to be added by industry, we have first made efforts to add as much as possible what can be selected as an important factor in general manufactured goods manufacturing companies. Each of these data may exist, but if the data were difficult to collect or manage, the factors were all rated at 0.01 level, which did not mean much. However, all of the management items above 0.05 are important data management, and efforts to obtain each data must be made to take into account the priorities of the scores.

Table 2 is evaluated based on the priority and weight of the very basic core system in the smart factory. It is arranged randomly so that the total is all 1. All four key systems are designed to define companies that hold and operate with one point, or 100 percent gain or loss achievement, or to clearly show a reduction in other large and small gains and losses. The assessment is based on a detailed analysis and comparison of the results simulated in the next Section. The above model used the functions of the system-building model obtained through on-site surveys at the factory over about six months and the weights derived from numerous meetings with the company's management and working-level staff. Although the same application cannot be applied to all industries, commercialization can be considered because it reflects the opinions of a total of 20 executives and practitioners. This model used the functions of the system-building model obtained through on-site surveys at the factory over about six months and the weights derived from numerous meetings with the company's management and working-level staff. Although the same application cannot be applied to all industries, commercialization can be considered because it reflects the opinions of a total of 20 executives and practitioners.

Table 1. Scores of each system function

System	Function	Score	System	Function	Score
ERP ($w1$)	Profit Margin	0.250	**MES** ($w2$)	Manufacturing Plan	0.300
	Raw Material	0.200		Execution	0.300
	Order	0.150		Quality Maintenance	0.100
	Forecast	0.150		Yield Performance	0.100
	Customer Priority	0.100		Facility Matenance	0.050
	Sales Price	0.050		Monitoring	0.050
	Production Cost	0.030		KPI Management	0.050
	Goods Receive	0.025		Outsourcing	0.030
	Goods Issue	0.020		Others	0.020
	Shipping	0.010			
	Tax	0.005			
	BOM	0.003			
	HR Cost	0.002			
	Master Code	0.002			
	Part Number	0.002			
	Others	0.001			
	0.40	**1.000**		**0.50**	**1.000**

System	Function	Score	System	Function	Score
PLM ($w3$)	Product Planning	0.300	**SCM** ($w4$)	Purchase Price	0.300
	Qualification	0.150		Forecast Accuracy	0.200
	PCN	0.100		On Time Delivery	0.150
	Sample Making	0.100		Scheduling	0.100
	Market Reasearch	0.100		Goods Receive	0.100
	CAE / CAD	0.100		Goods Issue	0.100
	EOL	0.100		Others	0.050
	Others	0.050			
	0.03	**1.000**		**0.07**	**1.000**

4 Comparison of System Integration and Partial Operation

Of the configurations of smart factory basic systems presented in the previous Section, the priorities of each industry may differ from those presented. However, the general manufactured goods are presented here, and the graph presented in Sect. 1 compares the relatively short production lead time of the FMCG with the relatively short inventory turnover rate of the FMCG and the long production lead time of the semiconductor. First of all, if all four basic systems, including large companies, are in place and detailed menus of items are organized and managed by system, it will be very easy to maintain the peak in response to long production lead times or changes in the internal and external environment. This can be assumed to be one point, or 100%, and the formula is as follows.

$$\mathcal{W}1 * \sum \text{ERP (n)} + \mathcal{W}2 * \sum \text{MES (n)} + \mathcal{W}3 * \sum \text{PLM (n)} + \mathcal{W}4 * \sum \text{SCM (n)} \quad (1)$$

Table 2. Examples of scores for small and medium enterprises

System	Item	Score	System	Item	Score
ERP ($w1$)	Profit Margin	0.250	MES ($w2$)	Manufacturing Plan	0.300
	Raw Material	0.200		Execution	0.300
	Order	0.150		Quality Maintenance	0.100
	Forecast			Yield Performance	
	Customer Priority			Facility Matenance	
	Sales Price	0.050		Monitoring	
	Production Cost	0.030		KPI Management	
	Goods Receive			Outsourcing	
	Goods Issue			Others	
	Shipping				
	Tax				
	BOM				
	HR Cost				
	Master Code				
	Part Number				
	Others				
	0.40	**0.680**		**0.50**	**0.700**
PLM ($w3$)	Product Planning	0.300	SCM ($w4$)	Purchase Price	0.300
	Qualification	0.150		Forecast Accuracy	
	PCN			On Time Delivery	
	Sample Making			Scheduling	0.100
	Market Reasearch			Goods Receive	
	CAE / CAD			Goods Issue	
	EOL			Others	
	Others				
	0.03	**0.450**		**0.07**	**0.400**

The scores for each item in the Table 2 are calculated as follows.

$$0.40 * 1.0 + 0.50 * 1.0 + 0.03 * 1.0 + 0.07 * 1.0 = 1 \quad (2)$$

However, most small and medium-sized enterprises or basic plants without smart factories do not have all the above four systems. That is, either MES or ERP will be selected and used. Thus, the table below can be filled with scores and calculations based on the random assumption of this situation.

$$0.40 * 0.680 + 0.50 * 0.700 + 0.03 * 0.450 + 0.07 * 0.400 = 0.664 \quad (3)$$

Comparing (2) and (3) may be an intuitive explanation that while all conditions are met, they can be optimized for 100% profit or loss, it is difficult to reach 100% profit or loss if the system is not equipped at all or only some functions are used.

This shows that if the production process, such as semiconductors, is complex and the production lead time is long, it is imperative to utilize many systems to increase productivity and maximize profits through organic information sharing between processes.

Products with fast inventory turnover, such as the FMCG, need not be as complex as semiconductors because even if the amount of safety inventory they have is small, it affects profit or loss.

5 Conclusion

Existing APS is a high-tech planning system that focuses only on production parts themselves and establishes production plans based on priority of delivery dates considering inventory. Of course, this is because production, including the limitations of accumulated data volumes, is divided into unique tasks for the production department, and there are many difficulties in planning beyond the production elements.

But the introduction of smart factory now, as mentioned earlier, should not only be an area of manufacturing itself, but also a plan that includes a variety of factors beyond manufacturing as demand and its attributes, price and delivery, and the need for multi-species small production or mass customization increase. Each company will have a different system and different menu configurations that it considers important for each industry it produces. In addition, the KPIs (Key Performance Index) [13] that are managed intensively may vary. However, ultimately, the nature of the manufacturing industry, which processes and assembles raw materials and materials to produce finished products, remains unchanged in that purchasing and inventory management are the biggest factors that determine gains and losses, and the importance of SCM linking sales to purchases cannot be overemphasized. The reality is that ERP and MES are considered the most important component systems. APS is a key feature of MES that needs to be organically connected to the SCM, which also comprises SCM and MES as a single system, depending on the enterprise. What it seeks to achieve through system integration is to establish a more efficient production plan and ensure appropriate inventory operation standards. And it is a meaningful study that more objective and systematic evaluation criteria have been presented to achieve the goal of integration.

Next, more advanced system configurations than conventional APS can be assisted by machine learning using AI, and the importance order for angles is re-determined by organizing the above system functional elements and multiplying weights. Of course, each company will have to decide and implement whether to re-calibrate after the final judgment or to a level that can automatically control production based on AI's judgment.

References

1. Wang, S., et al.: Implementing smart factory of industrie 4.0: an outlook. Int. J. Distrib. Sensor Networks **12**(1), 3159805 (2016)
2. Meyr, H., Wagner, M., Rohde, J.: Structure of advanced planning systems. In: Supply Chain Management and Advanced Planning, pp. 99–106. Springer, Berlin, Heidelberg (2015). https://doi.org/10.1007/978-3-642-55309-7_5
3. Rashid, M.A., Riaz, Z., Turan, E., Haskilic, V., Sunje, A., Khan, N.: Smart factory: E-business perspective of enhanced ERP in aircraft manufacturing industry. In: 2012 Proceedings of PICMET 2012: Technology Management for Emerging Technologies, pp. 3262–3275. IEEE, July 2012

4. Zhong, R.Y., et al.: RFID-enabled real-time manufacturing execution system for mass-customization production. Robot. Comput.-Integr. Manuf. **29**(2), 283–292 (2013)
5. Liboni, L.B., Cezarino, L.O., Jabbour, C.J.C., Oliveira, B.G., Stefanelli, N.O.: Smart industry and the pathways to HRM 4.0: implications for SCM. Supply Chain Manage. Int. J. **24**(1), 124–146 (2019)
6. Stark, J.: Product Lifecycle Management, vol. 1, pp. 1–29. Springer, Cham (2015). https://doi.org/10.1007/978-3-319-24436-5_1
7. Lech, M.M., et al.: Quality management system with human-machine interface for industrial automation. U.S. Patent No. 6,539,271, 25 Mar 2003
8. Schulze, B.D.: System and method for automated monitoring and assessment of fabrication facility. U.S. Patent No. 6,671,570. 30 Dec 2003
9. Kerry, J., Butler, P. (eds.): Smart Packaging Technologies for Fast Moving Consumer Goods. John Wiley & Sons, New York (2008)
10. Kho, J.S., Jeong, J.: On reflecting optimal inventory of profit and loss perspective for production planning. Procedia Comput. Sci. **155**, 722–727 (2019)
11. Unver, H.O.: An ISA-95-based manufacturing intelligence system in support of lean initiatives. Int. J. Adv. Manuf. Technol. **65**(5–8), 853–866 (2013)
12. Hao, Y., et al.: Designing of cloud-based virtual factory information system. In: Advances in Sustainable and Competitive Manufacturing Systems, pp. 415–426. Springer, Heidelberg (2013). https://doi.org/10.1007/978-3-319-00557-7_34
13. Ge, Z.: Distributed predictive modeling framework for prediction and diagnosis of key performance index in plant-wide processes. J. Process Control **65**, 107–117 (2018)

Impact of Renewable Energy Installations on Habitat Quality

Valeria Muzzillo, Angela Pilogallo, Lucia Saganeiti(✉), Valentina Santarsiero, Francesco Scorza, and Beniamino Murgante

School of Engineering, University of Basilicata, 85100 Potenza, Italy
valeria.muzzillo@studenti.unibas.it,
{angela.pilogallo,lucia.saganeiti,valentina.santarsiero,
francesco.scorza,beniamino.murgante}@unibas.it

Abstract. In all the disciplines referring to environmental protection, the reference to ecosystem services (ES) is widely increasing. The growing awareness of climate change and the recognized need to secure energy production has been a driving force behind the expansion of the Renewable Energy Sources (RES) and their technologies.

However, RES has a spatial impact on the landscape and consequently on ES. This paper analyzes some critical aspects of their spatial mutual relationship considering an area of the Basilicata region including 5 municipalities (Cancellara, Pietragalla, San Chirico Nuovo, Tolve and Vaglio Basilicata) with particular reference to the impact that coming from not-regulated wind farms installation. For this approach it's fundamental integrate the concept of ecosystem services into land management and planning decisions for control the pressures that threaten the ecosystem and their functionality, and "build" a model of governance that preserve their biodiversity and sustainability.

Keywords: Ecosystem services · Habitat quality · Renewable energy sources

1 Introduction

The Millennium Ecosystem Assessment [1] defines Ecosystem services (ES) as goods and benefits humans derive from nature, identified as provisioning (e.g. food), regulating (e.g. carbon sequestration), cultural (e.g. tourism and recreation) and supporting (e.g. nutrient cycling). Since ES have both direct and indirect effects on human well-being, it is useful for territorial planning discipline to deeply understand how land use changes affect ES provision and, above all, how to integrate the concept of ES in decision making and policies design processes. The energy transition underway in favor of the use of renewable energy sources affected the Basilicata region where the forecast of in-stalled power and energy produced for wind farm installation has been saturated since the end of 2017. The exploitation of wind natural resource to produce energy represents an essential way to tackle climate changes and to ensure energy security. Several factors have contributed to the diffusion of wind energy at local level, in particular mini wind tur-bines

O. Gervasi et al. (Eds.): ICCSA 2020, LNCS 12253, pp. 636–644, 2020.
https://doi.org/10.1007/978-3-030-58814-4_50

[2, 3] for self-production and self-consumption needs: increasingly efficient technology, low construction and maintenance costs of a plant, the possibility of financing and the simplification of authorization processes. However, their strong diffusion is accompanied by an absence or inadequate planning of guidelines for the proper inclusion of plants in the territory [4, 5]. Since the landscape is considered as the result of interactions over the centuries between natural and anthropic activities, it is recognized that the inclusion in a landscape context of a wind farm, be it industrial, mini or micro wind, certainly determines a more or less significant impact on the territory and on the ecosystem services [6]. This work is aimed in spatially representing some critical issue of the relationship between RES and ES, analyzing a case study from the Basilicata region.

2 The Territorial Assessment Methodology

2.1 Study Area

The study area extends for a total area of about 304 km^2 and includes five municipalities belonging to the province of Potenza: Cancellara (680 m above s.l, 1256 residents), Pietragalla (834 m above s.l, 4025 residents), San Chirico Nuovo (745 m above s.l., 1294 residents), Tolve (568 m above s.l, 3160 residents) and Vaglio Basilicata (954 m above sea level, 1964 residents). It is characterized by a settlement system traditionally arranged on peaks with an average density of about 44 inhabitants per sq. kilometer (source ISTAT, 2018 [7]).

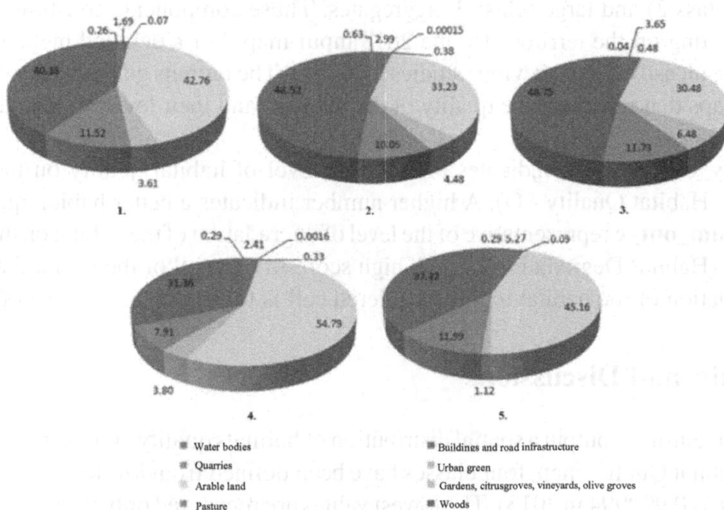

Fig. 1. Classification of land use: 1. Cancellara, 2. Pietragalla, 3. San Chirico Nuovo, 4. Tolve, 5. Vaglio Basilicata

The whole territory has a high naturalistic value and does not have areas subject to naturalistic constraints. The graphs in Fig. 1 represents the distribution of land use classes on the five municipalities.

2.2 Methodology

A spatial approach has been used for the evaluation of territorial transformations through the toolbox provided by InVEST (Integrated Valuation of ES and Tradeoffs) developed by Stanford University within the "Natural Capital Project" [8].

The "Habitat Quality" module is instead the model associated with the ecosystem service as a proxy for the assessment of the level of biodiversity and the associated risks of degradation. The concept of habitat referred to in this work is considered in a general sense as an environment suitable for the presence of different plant and animal organisms.

Inputs for InVEST models were obtained mainly by collecting soil data from GeoTopographic DataBase made available by the RSDI Basilicata geoportal in the "DGBT & CTR" section. A spatial and temporal comparison was made considering an interval of time from 2013 to 2018 to appreciate the territorial transformations following the installation of RES. The first land use map refers to 2013; in the second, related to 2018, the classes of wind aggregates were added. In the study area, wind power plants have been mapped and classified according to their power (P) in 4 typologies: micro ($P < 1$ kW), mini (1 kW $< P <$ 100 kW), medium (100 kW $< P <$ 1000 kW) and big ($P >$ 1000 kW).

Each turbine was represented by a polygon obtained by buffering with a radius proportional to their power output. The polygons thus obtained were then aggregated using the threshold distance of 250 m as a criterion to consider the loss of ecosystem functionality. Aggregates were then classified according to footprint in: small (class 1), medium (class 2) and large (class 3) aggregates. These components constitute a source of threat acting on the territory for the 2018 input map. For a detailed methodological description please refer to previous studies [6, 9–14]. The outputs generated by the model are two maps that represent the quality of the habitats and their level of degradation for a current scenario:

quality_out_c which indicates the relative level of habitat quality on the current landscape (Habitat Quality - Q). A higher number indicates a better habitat quality;

deg_sum_out_c representative of the level of degradation of the habitat on the current landscape (Habitat Degradation - D). A high score in one cell of the grid indicates that the degradation of the habitat in the considered cell is high compared to the others.

3 Results and Discussions

The model returns as output a spatial distribution of habitats quality and their degradation. For the Habitat Quality map, four classes have been defined from *low* to *very high* values (max value is 0.999994 in 2013). The lowest values are registered only in correspondence to the most populated centers and areas. Consistent with the values assigned in the habitat definition, the quality is higher in wooded areas and along watercourses (Fig. 2 and 4).

Following the installation of wind turbines, there is a decrease in habitat quality (max value is 0.999993 in 2018) in the areas immediately surrounding the wind turbines.

Figure 6 shows that in 2013, more than 37% of the total surface has very high quality, 10,15% has high quality, 49,68% has medium quality and just 2,52% has low quality value.

Fig. 2. Habitat quality 2013

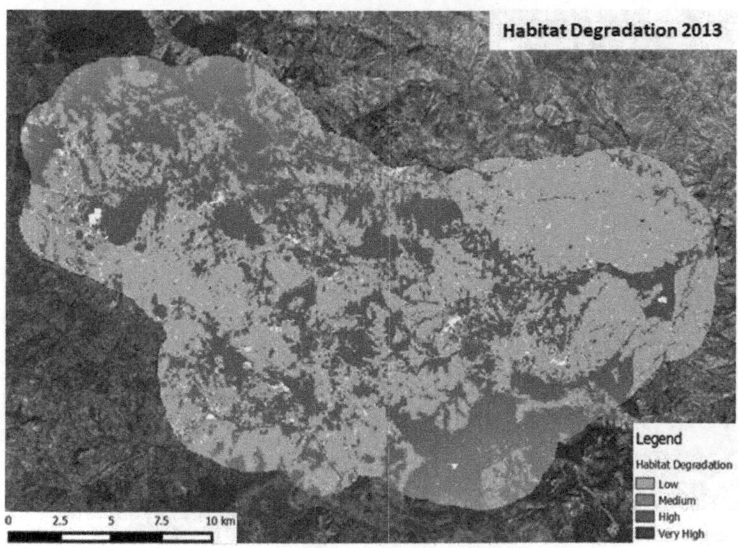

Fig. 3. Habitat degradation 2013.

Note that the areas characterized by low quality values increased by +16,23% (about 2 km^2) from 2013 to 2018.

In the Figs. 1 and 3 is shown the comparison between the habitat quality distribution histograms related to 2013 and 2018.

The decrease in habitat quality is particularly evident in the areas were from 2013 to 2018 wind turbines were installed. In particular there is a greater reduction in quality

Fig. 4. Habitat quality 2018

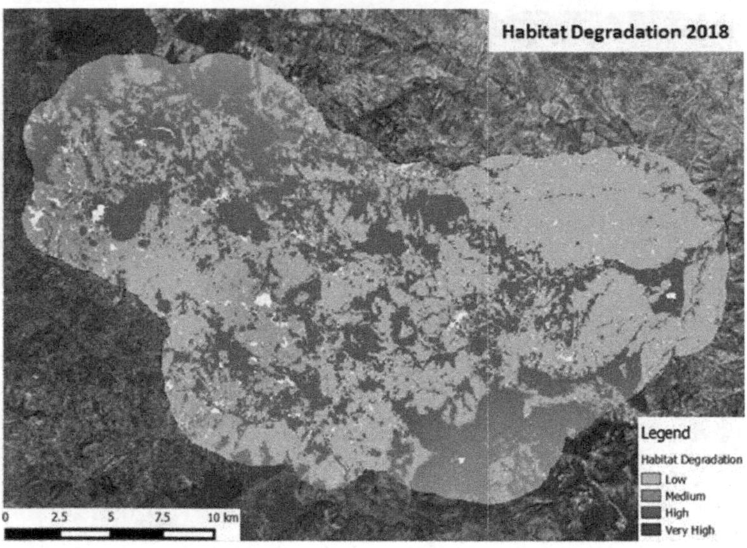

Fig. 5. Habitat degradation 2018.

for medium (−0,61%), high (−0,44%) and very high (−0,16%) classes from 2013 to 2018.

The variation in the degradation degree over the entire period was analyzed in the same way, identifying four degradation classes: low, moderate, high, very high.

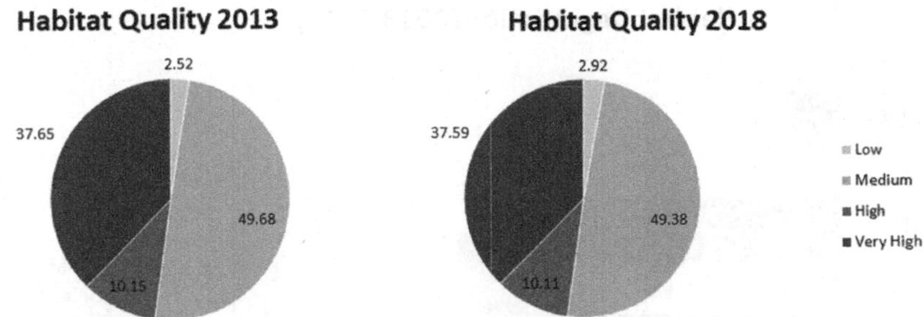

Fig. 6. Habitat quality 2013–2018.

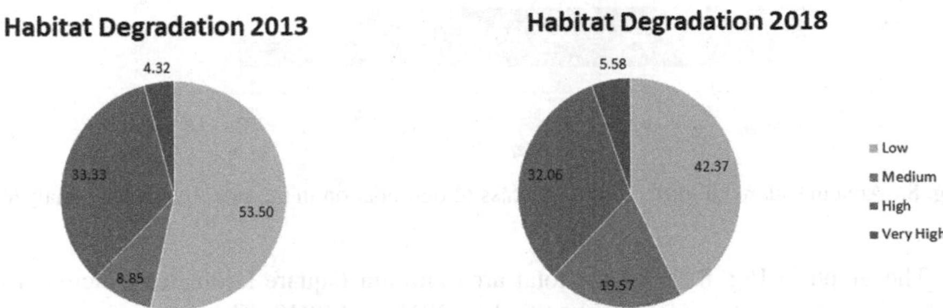

Fig. 7. Habitat degradation 2013–2018.

Figure 7 shows that in 2013, more than 4% of the total surface has *very high* degradation, 33,33% has *high* degradation, 8,85% has *medium* degradation and more than 53% has *low* degradation value.

The classification of the level of degradation is shown in the maps of the Habitat Degradation of 2013 Fig. 3 and 2018 Fig. 5. The areas characterized by medium and very high degradation values increased from 2013 to 2018. In particular there is a greater increase in degradation for medium (+54,78%) and very high (+22,63%) classes. The alteration occurs mainly near areas that from 2013 to 2018 change their intended use of the land and are classified as "Wind turbine use" in the map of land use and coverage 2018. An increase in degradation is visible especially where there is a greater density of class 2 and 3 wind aggregates, therefore those of larger size and power White areas represent wind energy aggregates and other threats which, have a null degradation value.

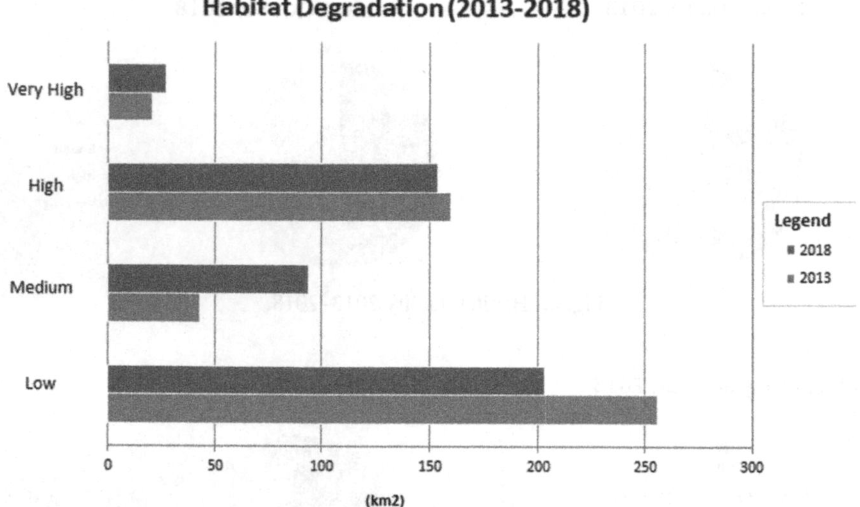

Fig. 8. Area in square kilometers for each class of degradation in the two-time phases analyzed

The graph in Fig. 8 shows the total area amount (square kilometers) included in each of the degradation classes identified in 2013 and 2018. The areas with average degradation have increased by about 50 km^2 from 2013 to 2018. Also, the area classified as very high Degradation has grown in the time interval. Additionally, the areas classified as low and high Degradation have decreased between the two temporal phases.

4 Conclusions

The increase in the number of plants for the production of energy from renewable sources in the last decade has changed the rural landscape of Basilicata in a marked way. These transformations have occurred in most cases in the absence of proper installation planning [15, 16] which has also affected real estate values [17–20]. Moreover, the lack of the Regional Landscape Plan and of sectorial rules aimed at limiting pollution by noise emissions and electromagnetic fields led to an uncontrolled increase of RES installations at local level. The proposed method can represent a concrete support for a land management process. It provides a spatial monitoring system that takes into account the quality of the habitat and its degradation status. It is suitable for the assessment of land use projects (ex-post) and allows the construction of scenarios (ex-ante) [21] for the assessment of impacts on the territory due to human transformations.

References

1. Millennium Ecosystem Assessment. Ecosystems and Human Well-being: Synthesis. Island Press, Washington, DC (2005). https://doi.org/10.5822/978-1-61091-484-0_1
2. Saganeiti, L., Pilogallo, A., Faruolo, G., Scorza, F., Murgante, B.: Territorial fragmentation and renewable energy source plants: which relationship? Sustainability **12**, 1828 (2010). https://doi.org/10.3390/SU12051828

3. Las Casas, G., Murgante, B., Scorza, F.: Regional local development strategies benefiting from open data and open tools and an outlook on the renewable energy sources contribution. In: Papa, R., Fistola, R. (eds.) Smart Energy in the Smart City. GET, pp. 275–290. Springer, Cham (2016). https://doi.org/10.1007/978-3-319-31157-9_14
4. Saganeiti, L., Pilogallo, A., Faruolo, G., Scorza, F., Murgante, B.: Energy landscape fragmentation: Basilicata Region (Italy) study case. In: Misra, S., et al. (eds.) ICCSA 2019. LNCS, vol. 11621, pp. 692–700. Springer, Cham (2019). https://doi.org/10.1007/978-3-030-24302-9_50
5. Santarsiero, V., Nolè, G., Lanorte, A., Tucci, B., Baldantoni, P., Murgante, B.: Evolution of soil consumption in the municipality of Melfi (Southern Italy) in relation to renewable energy. In: Misra, S., et al. (eds.) ICCSA 2019. LNCS, vol. 11621, pp. 675–682. Springer, Cham (2019). https://doi.org/10.1007/978-3-030-24302-9_48
6. Scorza, F., Pilogallo, A., Saganeiti, L., Murgante, B., Pontrandolfi, P.: Comparing the territorial performances of renewable energy sources' plants with an integrated ecosystem services loss assessment: a case study from the Basilicata region (Italy). Sustain. Cities Soc. **56**, 102082 (2020). https://doi.org/10.1016/J.SCS.2020.102082
7. Istat.it. https://www.istat.it/. Accessed 01 July 2019
8. The Natural Capital Project: Habitat Quality - InVEST 3.6.0 documentation. http://data.naturalcapitalproject.org/nightly-build/invest-users-guide/html/habitat_quality.html. Accessed 13 Nov 2019
9. Pilogallo, A., Saganeiti, L., Scorza, F., Las Casas, G.: Tourism attractiveness: main components for a spacial appraisal of major destinations according with ecosystem services approach. In: Gervasi, O., et al. (eds.) ICCSA 2018. LNCS, vol. 10964, pp. 712–724. Springer, Cham (2018). https://doi.org/10.1007/978-3-319-95174-4_54
10. Saganeiti, L., Favale, A., Pilogallo, A., Scorza, F., Murgante, B.: Assessing urban fragmentation at regional scale using sprinkling indexes. Sustainability **10** (2018). https://doi.org/10.3390/su10093274
11. Cannas, I., Zoppi, C.: Ecosystem services and the natura 2000 network: a study concerning a green infrastructure based on ecological corridors in the metropolitan city of Cagliari. In: Gervasi, O., et al. (eds.) ICCSA 2017. LNCS, vol. 10409, pp. 379–400. Springer, Cham (2017). https://doi.org/10.1007/978-3-319-62407-5_27
12. Lai, S., Leone, F., Zoppi, C.: Assessment of municipal masterplans aimed at identifying and fostering green infrastructure: a study concerning three towns of the metropolitan area of Cagliari, Italy. Sustainability. **11**, 1470 (2019). https://doi.org/10.3390/su11051470
13. Pilogallo, A., Saganeiti, L., Scorza, F., Murgante, B.: Ecosystem services' based impact assessment for low carbon transition processes. TeMA - J. L. Use Mobil. Environ. **12**, 127–138 (2019). https://doi.org/10.6092/1970-9870/6117
14. Scorza, F., Pilogallo, A., Saganeiti, L., Murgante, B.: Natura 2000 areas and sites of national interest (SNI): measuring (un)integration between naturalness preservation and environmental remediation policies. Sustainability. **12**, 2928 (2020). https://doi.org/10.3390/su12072928
15. Scorza, F., Grecu, V.: Assessing sustainability: research directions and relevant issues. In: Gervasi, O., et al. (eds.) ICCSA 2016. LNCS, vol. 9786, pp. 642–647. Springer, Cham (2016). https://doi.org/10.1007/978-3-319-42085-1_55
16. Attolico, A., et al.: Engaged communities for low carbon development process. In: Gervasi, O., et al. (eds.) ICCSA 2017. LNCS, vol. 10409, pp. 573–584. Springer, Cham (2017). https://doi.org/10.1007/978-3-319-62407-5_41
17. Morano, P., Tajani, F., Locurcio, M.: GIS application and econometric analysis for the verification of the financial feasibility of roof-top wind turbines in the city of Bari (Italy) (2017). https://doi.org/10.1016/j.rser.2016.12.005

18. Morano, P., Locurcio, M., Tajani, F., Guarini, M.R.: Fuzzy logic and coherence control in multi-criteria evaluation of urban redevelopment projects. Int. J. Bus. Intell. Data Min. **10**, 73–93 (2015). https://doi.org/10.1504/IJBIDM.2015.069041
19. Tajani, F., Morano, P.: Concession and lease or sale? A model for the enhancement of public properties in disuse or underutilized. WSEAS Trans. Bus. Econ. **11**, 18 (2014)
20. Torre, C., Morano, P., Tajani, F.: Saving Soil for Sustainable Land Use. Sustainability. **9**, 350 (2017). https://doi.org/10.3390/su9030350
21. Las Casas, G., Scorza, F., Murgante, B.: Razionalità a-priori: una proposta verso una pianificazione antifragile. Ital. J. Reg. Sci. **2**, 329–338 (2019). https://doi.org/10.14650/93656

Habitat Degradation: A Comparative Study Between Tomar (PT) and Potenza (IT)

Luciana Nolè[1], Angela Pilogallo[1(✉)], Lucia Saganeiti[1(✉)], Francesco Scorza[1], Luis Santos[2], and Beniamino Murgante[1]

[1] University of Basilicata, viale dell'Ateneo Lucano 10, 85100 Potenza, Italy
angela.pilogallo@unibas.it

[2] Polytechnic Institute of Tomar, Quinta Do Contador, Estrada Da Serra, 2300-313 Tomar, Portugal

Abstract. The increasing impacts of climate and land use change directly impact habitat quality and biodiversity. Monitoring the habitats quality can be a valuable tool for the conservation of biodiversity, as it is an indicator of biodiversity. This research work aims to ap-ply the InVEST Habitat Quality model to compare two different cases study from Portugal (Tomar) and Southern Italy (Potenza). Threats to biodiversity were considered taking into account the substantial territorial differences of the two areas considered: Tomar, an area particularly affected by forest fires-driven degradation phenomena; Potenza is, instead, an area particularly affected by the installation of wind farms. Results highlight how these tools can be considered a valuable support tool for spatial planning decisions for biodiversity conservation.

Keywords: Habitat quality · Tomar (Portugal) · Potenza (Italy)

1 Introduction

Intensive human activities can lead to a widespread loss of species, habitat fragmentation and habitat degradation [1, 2]. Habitat loss and degradation is a key cause of declining biodiversity [3, 4]. Biodiversity means biological wealth and therefore environmental quality: decision-makers and conservation organizations should learn about spatial changes in biodiversity and habitat and identify potential impact factors [5]. Consequently, the greater the diversity of the system, the less its vulnerability. Sometimes biodiversity is closely related to human activities. Therefore its quantification can be useful in order to better guide the decisions in territorial planning and in order to better understand the interaction and the consequent effect between territorial components and anthropogenic activities [6]. This new approach allows to better design sustainable and environmental policies and deeply understand the interaction among territorial components and relative processes and dynamics [7, 8].

The purpose of this work is to test InVEST-Habitat Quality (Integrated Valuation of Ecosystem Services and Tradeoffs) model [9] in order to compare the spatial distribution of biodiversity threats between Tomar (Portugal) and Potenza (Italy). As highlighted from many authors [10–12], this tool reveals to be useful in assessing the impact

O. Gervasi et al. (Eds.): ICCSA 2020, LNCS 12253, pp. 645–654, 2020.
https://doi.org/10.1007/978-3-030-58814-4_51

of changing in land use/land cover (LULC) or, equally, in appreciating benefits from conservation policies [13, 14]. As a result, we aimed to (1) identify habitat suitability and threats to biodiversity for different land uses; (2) apply the InVEST-Habitat Quality model to assess and map habitat quality from 2007 to 2015 for Tomar and from 2014 to 2018 for Potenza; and (3) to analyze and compare the potential impact factors of habitat quality.

2 Study Area

The study areas both belong to Southern Europe (Portugal and Southern Italy) and have similar characteristics: both areas are characterized by a low density of settlement and a high landscape value of the territory [15–17], articulated in a high naturalness environment (woods and forests) and valuable agroforestry mosaics (see Fig. 1 and Fig. 2). Although the important similarities, they have a fundamental difference: the main threat to biodiversity is represented for Tomar by the forest fires [18, 19] and for Potenza, as the rest of the Basilicata region [20–23], by the transformations due to the installation of wind farms [24].

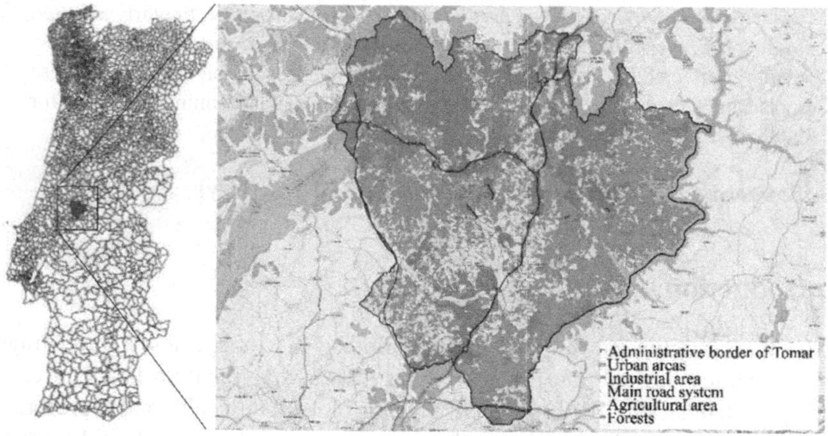

Fig. 1. Municipality of Tomar

Tomar. Tomar is a Portuguese municipality, located in the district of Santarém, in the Centro region, subregion Medio Tejo. It has an extension of 352 km^2 and has slightly more than 40,000 inhabitants. The municipal territory is mainly wooded. Forests are largely the result of policies from the 20th century [25], which have characterized changes in land use/land cover across the country. Nowadays, 97% of Portuguese woodland is privately owned, the result of this choice is that one of the most widespread tree species in Portugal is eucalyptus [18], one of the most easily flammable and fire-spreading species. The eucalyptus is a species not autochthonous but imported from Australia, starting from the 1970s to support the paper industry that began to grow in those years [26]. The eucalyptus plantations are intended solely for the cellulose industry and to

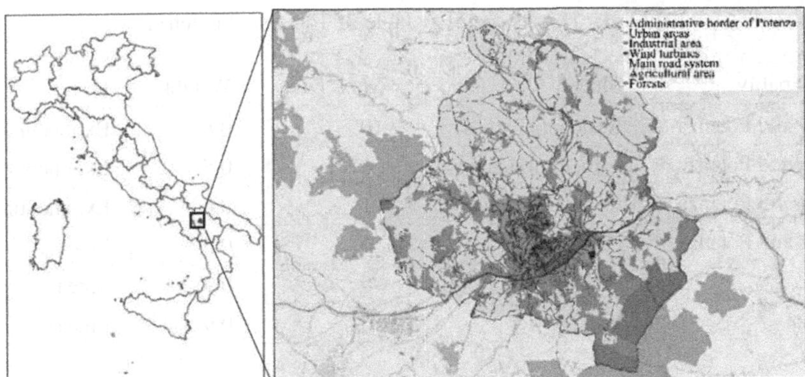

Fig. 2. Municipality of Potenza

ensure a faster financial return for the owners, as they are a rapidly growing species. The monoculture of eucalyptus, besides being highly flammable [27], also causes nutrient loss [28, 29] and other negative impacts [30], because it needs more water to grow and its structure does not allow the growth of other species in the surrounding area [31].

Potenza. Potenza is an Italian city, capital of the Basilicata region, with an extension of about 170 km^2 and counts, according to the National Institute of Statistics (ISTAT) [32], 66,391 inhabitants. It is a mostly rural environment characterized by very low population and building density [33, 34]. As the rest of the region, a significant part of the soil development process, during the last decade, is due to the expansion of urban areas, the transformation of rural areas, and the use of agricultural land for renewable energy production through the construction of ground-mounted photovoltaic systems and numerous installations of wind turbines [35]. Indeed, since 2010, a large part of the territory has been affected by the installation of RES plants, most of them with a total power output less than 1 MW which implied a relevant territorial impact not balanced by the low power output [21].

3 Methods and Materials

In order to evaluate the Habitat Quality of the two areas chosen for the comparison we applied the Habitat Quality module of InVEST (InVEST-HQ) [36]; this model generates a map of habitat quality, linking the land use maps and the threats to biodiversity considered. This approach evaluates habitat quality based on suitability and threats to biodiversity, and the hypothesis of the model is that areas with higher habitat quality support higher native species richness [37, 38]. In the model, habitat degradation by threat factors is indicated by declining habitat quality score. We have therefore selected buildings, road infrastructure, agricultural areas and quarries as the main threat factors for the habitat. The fifth source of threat to biodiversity was, instead, differentiated according to the characteristics of the two areas, considering the fires for Tomar and wind turbines

Table 1. Threats summary table of Tomar and Potenza.

Municipality	Threat	Max_Dist	Weight	Decay
Tomar and Potenza	Residential areas	10	0.8	Exponential
Tomar and Potenza	Agricultural areas	8	0.5	Exponential
Tomar and Potenza	Roads and railways	1	0.6	Exponential
Tomar and Potenza	Pollution	4	0.5	Linear
Tomar	Fire	6	0.9	Linear
Potenza	Wind power	6	0.9	Linear

Table 2. Habitat and sensitivity summary table.

LULC	Habitat	Residential areas	Agricultural areas	Fire	Pollution	Roads, railways
Water bodies	1	0.8	0.4	0	0.8	0.7
Residential areas	0	0	0	0	0	0
Industrial areas	0	0	0	0	0	0
Roads and railways	0	0	0	0	0	0
Quarries	0	0	0	0	0	0
Urban green and gardens	0	0	0	0	0	0
Wind power	0	0	0	0	0	0
Vineyards and olive groves	1	0.6	0	0.8	0.8	0.7
Landfill sites	0	0	0	0	0	0
Orchards and citrus groves	1	0.6	0	0.8	0.8	0.7
Deciduous forest	1	1	0.6	0.9	0.9	0.9
Coniferous forest	1	1	0.6	0.9	0.9	0.9
Fallow field	1	0.6	0	0.8	0.8	0.7
Forest	1	1	0.6	0.9	0.9	0.9
Vegetable gardens	1	0.6	0	0.8	0.8	0.7
Arable land	1	0.6	0	0.8	0.8	0.7

for Potenza. Each threat considered has been constructed from land use maps, and the information for each threat considered is listed in Table 1.

To compute on-board effects, an area with a greater extent was considered by a buffer operation equal to 10 km, the maximum distance from the threat i-th considered. In order to assign suitability, it was necessary to reclassify the land use classes to make them as homogeneous as possible, assigning to each class a value, 0 or 1, to de-scribe the propensity to perform a habitat function. A land use type could be considered as habitat in relation to the level of biodiversity present and the intensity of human activities [39]. The threat parameters were determined by an expert survey and are summarized in Table 2.

4 Discussion and Conclusion

The model returns in output a spatial distribution of habitats degradation, relative to the years considered, assuming a more intense coloration in the areas more degraded (see Fig. 3 (A) and (B)). The first difference is that Tomar degradation level achieved is fairly homogeneous and widespread over the whole area of study, because, as highlighted in the context analyses, major territorial transformations are not of anthropic origin but linked to the phenomenon of forest fires; instead, in Potenza it is evidenced a negative impact mainly in correspondence of inhabited centers and more anthropized areas.

By comparisons over time we have a second difference that emerges: in Tomar there is a decrease of habitat quality in wooded areas facing residential settlements, highlighting as most vulnerable areas the transition zones from woodland to residential; in Potenza there is a decrease of habitat quality in the area located to the North-West of the compact town, following the installation of wind generators, as from 2014 to 2018 the number of wind turbines has considerably increased. Therefore, the main threat to Tomar is represented by the forest fires, this source of impact is not negligible if we consider that the tree species are the more easily flammable ones and that propagate the fire, and furthermore this source of impact is believed to be potentially increasing because it is indirectly linked to climate change; in Potenza the main source of degradation is represented by the wind farms installation, these changes are justified by the common need to fight climate change, but they have taken place in a regulatory framework that is not adequate to balance this with all territorial values, preventing adequate control and the consequent impact on the territory. In conclusion, the most degraded area between the two ones is Tomar, as result of the threat sources considered. As regards the interpretation of final results, it should be noted that the linear overlap of the effects related to different threats has the disadvantage of neglecting a certainly non-linear interaction between different sources of impact which, acting simultaneously, can amplify the effects of the other. The proposed method, applicable to the different planning scales [40, 41], provides a low-precision biodiversity indicator, but may provide a synthetic support for land-use assessment in terms of reducing the habitats quality [42]and may provide appropriate information on a land-use planning [43] and management system that ensures [44], among other quality objectives, the reduction of soil consumption, taking into account territorial characteristics and their ecosystem functionality, with a view to the conservation of biodiversity not considering natural processes as, for example, landslides [45]. As highlighted in previous works [46–49], the ecosystem services approach reveal

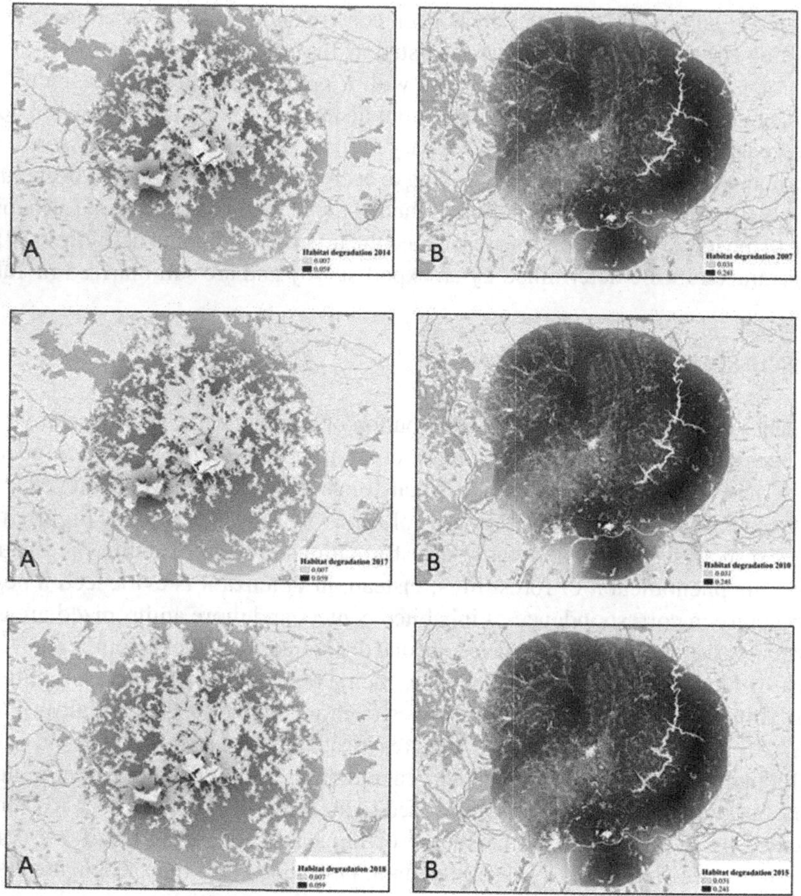

Fig. 3. Degradation maps for Potenza (A) and Tomar (B) study areas

to be particularly useful in supporting decision making and in designing conservation policies, but also in offering the possibility to use an effective monitoring tool of territorial transformation [35] and in overcoming a piecemeal structure of the normative framework [50].

References

1. Baral, H., Keenan, R.J., Sharma, S.K., Stork, N.E., Kasel, S.: Spatial assessment and mapping of biodiversity and conservation priorities in a heavily modified and fragmented production landscape in north-central Victoria, Australia. Ecol. Indic. **36**, 552–562 (2014). https://doi.org/10.1016/J.ECOLIND.2013.09.022
2. Hooper, D.U., Adair, E.C., Cardinale, B.J., Byrnes, J.E.K., Hungate, B.A., Matulich, K.L., Gonzalez, A., Duffy, J.E., Gamfeldt, L., O'Connor, M.I.: A global synthesis reveals biodiversity loss as a major driver of ecosystem change. Nature **486**, 105–108 (2012). https://doi.org/10.1038/nature11118

3. Duarte, G.T., Ribeiro, M.C., Paglia, A.P.: Ecosystem services modeling as a tool for defining priority areas for conservation. PLoS ONE **11**, e0154573 (2016). https://doi.org/10.1371/journal.pone.0154573
4. Polasky, S., Nelson, E., Pennington, D., Johnson, K.A.: The impact of land-use change on ecosystem services, biodiversity and returns to landowners: a case study in the state of minnesota. Environ. Resour. Econ. **48**, 219–242 (2011). https://doi.org/10.1007/s10640-010-9407-0
5. Costanza, R., Daly, H.E.: Natural capital and sustainable development. Conserv. Biol. **6**, 37–46 (1992). https://doi.org/10.1046/j.1523-1739.1992.610037.x
6. Liotta, P.H.: Development, O. of R.: the use of scenario analysis to assess water ecosystem services in response to future land use change in the Willamette river basin, oregon, achieving environmental security. Ecosyst. Serv. Hum. Welfare **69**, 97 (2010)
7. Bai, Y., Wong, C.P., Jiang, B., Hughes, A.C., Wang, M., Wang, Q.: Developing China's ecological redline policy using ecosystem services assessments for land use planning. Nat. Commun. **9**, 3034 (2018). https://doi.org/10.1038/s41467-018-05306-1
8. Ahern, J., Cilliers, S., Niemelä, J.: The concept of ecosystem services in adaptive urban planning and design: a framework for supporting innovation. Landsc. Urban Plan. **125**, 254–259 (2014). https://doi.org/10.1016/j.landurbplan.2014.01.020
9. The Natural Capital Project: Habitat Quality-InVEST 3.6.0 documentation. http://data.naturalcapitalproject.org/nightly-build/invest-users-guide/html/habitat_quality.html, Accessed 13 Nov 2019
10. Sharma, R., Nehren, U., Rahman, S.A., Meyer, M., Rimal, B., Aria Seta, G., Baral, H., Sharma, R., Nehren, U., Rahman, S.A., Meyer, M., Rimal, B., Aria Seta, G., Baral, H.: Modeling land use and land cover changes and their effects on biodiversity in central Kalimantan, Indonesia. Land **7**, 57 (2018). https://doi.org/10.3390/land7020057
11. Kim, T., Song, C., Lee, W.-K., Kim, M., Lim, C.-H., Jeon, S.W., Kim, J.: Habitat quality valuation using InVEST model in Jeju island. J. Korea Soc. Environ. Restor. Technol. **18**, 1–11 (2015). https://doi.org/10.13087/kosert.2015.18.5.1
12. Lai, S., Leone, F., Zoppi, C.: Assessment of municipal masterplans aimed at identifying and fostering green infrastructure: a study concerning three towns of the metropolitan area of Cagliari, Italy. Sustainability **11**, 1470 (2019). https://doi.org/10.3390/su11051470
13. Leone, F., Zoppi, C., Leone, F., Zoppi, C.: Conservation measures and loss of ecosystem services: a study concerning the sardinian natura 2000 network. Sustainability **8**, 1061 (2016). https://doi.org/10.3390/su8101061
14. Zoppi, C.: Integration of conservation measures concerning natura 2000 sites into marine protected areas regulations: a study related to sardinia. Sustainability **10**, 3460 (2018). https://doi.org/10.3390/su10103460
15. Lasaponara, R., Murgante, B., Elfadaly, A., Qelichi, M., Shahraki, S., Wafa, O., Attia, W.: Spatial open data for monitoring risks and preserving archaeological areas and landscape: case studies at kom el shoqafa, Egypt and Shush, Iran. Sustainability **9**, 572 (2017). https://doi.org/10.3390/su9040572
16. Murgante, B., Borruso, G., Lapucci, A.: Sustainable development: concepts and methods for its application in urban and environmental planning. Stud. Comput. Intell. **348**, 1–15 (2011). https://doi.org/10.1007/978-3-642-19733-8_1
17. Las Casas, G., Murgante, B., Scorza, F.: Regional local development strategies benefiting from open data and open tools and an outlook on the renewable energy sources contribution. In: Papa, R., Fistola, R. (eds.) Smart Energy in the Smart City. GET, pp. 275–290. Springer, Cham (2016). https://doi.org/10.1007/978-3-319-31157-9_14
18. Nunes, M.C.S., Vasconcelos, M.J., Pereira, J.M.C., Dasgupta, N., Alldredge, R.J., Rego, F.C.: Land cover type and fire in Portugal: do fires burn land cover selectively? Landsc. Ecol. **20**, 661–673 (2005). https://doi.org/10.1007/s10980-005-0070-8

19. Tedim, F., Remelgado, R., Borges, C., Carvalho, S., Martins, J.: Exploring the occurrence of mega-fires in Portugal. For. Ecol. Manage. **294**, 86–96 (2013). https://doi.org/10.1016/j.foreco.2012.07.031
20. Saganeiti, L., Pilogallo, A., Faruolo, G., Scorza, F., Murgante, B.: Energy landscape fragmentation: basilicata region (Italy) study case. In: Misra, S., Gervasi, O., Murgante, B., Stankova, E., Korkhov, V., Torre, C., Rocha, A.M.A.C., Taniar, D., Apduhan, B.O., Tarantino, E. (eds.) ICCSA 2019. LNCS, vol. 11621, pp. 692–700. Springer, Cham (2019). https://doi.org/10.1007/978-3-030-24302-9_50
21. Saganeiti, L., Pilogallo, A., Faruolo, G., Scorza, F., Murgante, B.: Territorial fragmentation and renewable energy source plants: which relationship? Sustainability **12**, 1828 (2020). https://doi.org/10.3390/SU12051828
22. Pilogallo, A., Saganeiti, L., Scorza, F., Murgante, B.: Ecosystem services approach to evaluate renewable energy plants effects. In: Misra, S., Gervasi, O., Murgante, B., Stankova, E., Korkhov, V., Torre, C., Rocha, A.M.A.C., Taniar, D., Apduhan, B.O., Tarantino, E. (eds.) ICCSA 2019. LNCS, vol. 11624, pp. 281–290. Springer, Cham (2019). https://doi.org/10.1007/978-3-030-24311-1_20
23. Scorza, F., Saganeiti, L., Pilogallo, A., Murgante, B.: Ghost Planning: the inefficiency of energy sector policies in a low population density region. Arch. DI Stud. URBANI E Reg. In press (2020)
24. Nolè, G., Lasaponara, R., Lanorte, A., Murgante, B.: Quantifying urban sprawl with spatial autocorrelation techniques using multi-temporal satellite data. Int. J. Agric. Environ. Inf. Syst. **5**, 20–38 (2014). https://doi.org/10.4018/IJAEIS.2014040102
25. Pereira, M.G., Trigo, R.M., Da Camara, C.C., Pereira, J.M.C., Leite, S.M.: Synoptic patterns associated with large summer forest fires in Portugal. Agric. For. Meteorol. **129**, 11–25 (2005). https://doi.org/10.1016/j.agrformet.2004.12.007
26. Da Silva Vieira, R., Canaveira, P., Da Simões, A., Domingos, T.: Industrial hemp or eucalyptus paper?: An environmental comparison using life cycle assessment. Int. J. Life Cycle Assess. **15**, 368–375 (2010). https://doi.org/10.1007/s11367-010-0152-y
27. Khanna, P.K., Raison, R.J.: Effect of fire intensity on solution chemistry of surface soil under a eucalyptus pauciflora forest. Aust. J. Soil Res. **24**, 423–434 (1986). https://doi.org/10.1071/SR9860423
28. Thomas, A.D., Walsh, R.P.D., Shakesby, R.A.: Nutrient losses in eroded sediment after fire in eucalyptus and pine forests in the wet Mediterranean environment of northern Portugal. Catena **36**, 283–302 (1999). https://doi.org/10.1016/S0341-8162(99)00051-X
29. Thomas, A.D., Walsh, R.P.D., Shakesby, R.A.: Solutes in overland flow following fire in eucalyptus and pine forests, northern Portugal. Hydrol. Process. **14**, 971–985 (2000). https://doi.org/10.1002/(SICI)1099-1085(20000415)14:5%3c971:AID-HYP4%3e3.0.CO;2-J
30. Shakesby, R.A., Coelho, C.D.O.A., Ferreira, A.D., Terry, J.P., Walsh, R.P.D.: Wildfire impacts on soil erosion and hydrology in wet mediterranean forest, Portugal. Int. J. Wildl. Fire. **3**, 95–110 (1993). https://doi.org/10.1071/WF9930095
31. Correia, A., Santos, L.A., Carvalho, P., Martinho, J.: The use of unmanned aerial vehicles in the monitoring of forest fires. In: Fernandes, F., Malheiro, A., Chaminé, H.I. (eds.) Advances in Natural Hazards and Hydrological Risks: Meeting the Challenge. ASTI, pp. 75–79. Springer, Cham (2020). https://doi.org/10.1007/978-3-030-34397-2_15
32. Istat.it. https://www.istat.it/, Accessed 01 Jul 2019
33. Saganeiti, L., Pilogallo, A., Scorza, F., Mussuto, G., Murgante, B.: Spatial indicators to evaluate urban fragmentation in basilicata region. In: Gervasi, O., Murgante, B., Misra, S., Stankova, E., Torre, C.M., Rocha, A.M.A.C., Taniar, D., Apduhan, B.O., Tarantino, E., Ryu, Y. (eds.) ICCSA 2018. LNCS, vol. 10964, pp. 100–112. Springer, Cham (2018). https://doi.org/10.1007/978-3-319-95174-4_8

34. Saganeiti, L., Favale, A., Pilogallo, A., Scorza, F., Murgante, B.: Assessing urban fragmentation at regional scale using sprinkling indexes. Sustainability **10**, 3274 (2018). https://doi.org/10.3390/su10093274
35. Scorza, F., Pilogallo, A., Saganeiti, L., Murgante, B., Pontrandolfi, P.: Comparing the territorial performances of Renewable Energy Sources' plants with an integrated Ecosystem Services loss assessment: a case study from the Basilicata region (Italy). Sustain. Cities Soc. **56**, 102082 (2020). https://doi.org/10.1016/J.SCS.2020.102082
36. Terrado, M., Sabater, S., Chaplin-Kramer, B., Mandle, L., Ziv, G., Acuña, V.: Model development for the assessment of terrestrial and aquatic habitat quality in conservation planning. Sci. Total Environ. **540**, 63–70 (2016). https://doi.org/10.1016/j.scitotenv.2015.03.064
37. Querner, P., et al.: Habitat structure, quality and landscape predict species richness and communities of Collembola in dry grasslands in Austria. Insects **9**, 81 (2018). https://doi.org/10.3390/insects9030081
38. Rondinini, C., et al.: Global habitat suitability models of terrestrial mammals. Philos. Trans. R. Soc. B Biol. Sci. **366**, 2633–2641 (2011). https://doi.org/10.1098/rstb.2011.0113
39. Elfadaly, A., Attia, W., Qelichi, M.M., Murgante, B., Lasaponara, R.: Management of cultural heritage sites using remote sensing indices and spatial analysis techniques (2018). https://doi.org/10.1007/s10712-018-9489-8
40. Bolund, P., Hunhammar, S.: Ecosystem services in urban areas. Ecol. Econ. **29**, 293–301 (1999). https://doi.org/10.1016/S0921-8009(99)00013-0
41. Aneseyee, A.B., Noszczyk, T., Soromessa, T., Elias, E.: The InVEST habitat quality model associated with land use/cover changes: a qualitative case study of the winike watershed in the omo-gibe basin. Southwest Ethiopia. Remote Sens. **12**, 1103 (2020). https://doi.org/10.3390/rs12071103
42. Murgante, B., Borruso, G., Balletto, G., Castiglia, P., Dettori, M.: Why Italy first? health, geographical and planning aspects of the COVID-19 outbreak. Sustainability **12**, 5064 (2020). https://doi.org/10.3390/su12125064
43. Geneletti, D.: Assessing the impact of alternative land-use zoning policies on future ecosystem services. Environ. Impact Assess. Rev. **40**, 25–35 (2013). https://doi.org/10.1016/j.eiar.2012.12.003
44. de Groot, R.S., Alkemade, R., Braat, L., Hein, L., Willemen, L.: Challenges in integrating the concept of ecosystem services and values in landscape planning, management and decision making. Ecol. Complex. **7**, 260–272 (2010). https://doi.org/10.1016/J.ECOCOM.2009.10.006
45. Pascale, S., Parisi, S., Mancini, A., Schiattarella, M., Conforti, M., Sole, A., Murgante, B., Sdao, F.: Landslide susceptibility mapping using artificial neural network in the urban area of Senise and San Costantino Albanese (Basilicata, Southern Italy). In: Murgante, B., Misra, S., Carlini, M., Torre, C.M., Nguyen, H.-Q., Taniar, D., Apduhan, B.O., Gervasi, O. (eds.) ICCSA 2013. LNCS, vol. 7974, pp. 473–488. Springer, Heidelberg (2013). https://doi.org/10.1007/978-3-642-39649-6_34
46. Scorza, F., Pilogallo, A., Las Casas, G.: Investigating tourism attractiveness in inland areas: ecosystem services, open data and smart specializations. In: Calabrò, F., Della Spina, L., Bevilacqua, C. (eds.) ISHT 2018. SIST, vol. 100, pp. 30–38. Springer, Cham (2019). https://doi.org/10.1007/978-3-319-92099-3_4
47. Pilogallo, A., Saganeiti, L., Scorza, F., Las Casas, G.: Tourism attractiveness: main components for a spacial appraisal of major destinations according with ecosystem services approach. In: Gervasi, O., Murgante, B., Misra, S., Stankova, E., Torre, C.M., Rocha, A.M.A.C., Taniar, D., Apduhan, B.O., Tarantino, E., Ryu, Y. (eds.) ICCSA 2018. LNCS, vol. 10964, pp. 712–724. Springer, Cham (2018). https://doi.org/10.1007/978-3-319-95174-4_54

48. Pilogallo, A., Saganeiti, L., Scorza, F., Murgante, B.: Ecosystem services' based impact assessment for low carbon transition processes TeMA-J. L. Use. Mobil. Environ. **12**, 127–138 (2019). https://doi.org/10.6092/1970-9870/6117
49. Attolico, A., Smaldone, R., Scorza, F., De Marco, E., Pilogallo, A.: Investigating good practices for low carbon development perspectives in basilicata. In: Gervasi, O., Murgante, B., Misra, S., Stankova, E., Torre, C.M., Rocha, A.M.A.C., Taniar, D., Apduhan, B.O., Tarantino, E., Ryu, Y. (eds.) ICCSA 2018. LNCS, vol. 10964, pp. 763–775. Springer, Cham (2018). https://doi.org/10.1007/978-3-319-95174-4_58
50. Scorza, F., Pilogallo, A., Saganeiti, L., Murgante, B.: Natura 2000 areas and sites of national interest (SNI): measuring (un)integration between naturalness preservation and environmental remediation policies. Sustainability **12**, 2928 (2020). https://doi.org/10.3390/su12072928

Fast Multiple Montgomery Multiplications Using Intel AVX-512IFMA Instructions

Daisuke Takahashi(✉)

Center for Computational Sciences, University of Tsukuba, 1-1-1 Tennodai, Tsukuba, Ibaraki 305-8577, Japan
daisuke@cs.tsukuba.ac.jp

Abstract. In this paper, we propose a fast implementation of multiple Montgomery multiplications using Intel AVX-512IFMA (Integer Fused Multiply-Add) instructions. The proposed implementation is based on a modified Montgomery multiplication. For Montgomery multiplication operands with 52 bits or fewer, the proposed implementation using Intel AVX-512IFMA instructions is up to approximately 12.22 and 4.30 times faster than the implementations using Intel 64 and Intel AVX-512F (Foundation) instructions on an Intel Core i3-8121U processor, respectively.

Keywords: Modular multiplication · Montgomery multiplication · Intel AVX-512IFMA instructions

1 Introduction

Modular multiplication, widely used in fields such as computer algebra and cryptography, includes modulo operations, which are slow because they involve an integer division process. Montgomery multiplication [1] avoids this drawback. Modern processors support single-instruction multiple-data (SIMD) vector instructions. The Intel Advanced Vector Extensions 512 (Intel AVX-512) [2] is a 512-bit vector instruction set. Montgomery multiplication algorithms that use vector instructions have been proposed [3,4], as has fast modular squaring with Intel AVX-512IFMA (Integer Fused Multiply-Add) [5]. Vector instructions have also been used to compute multiple Montgomery multiplications in parallel [4]. For multiple Montgomery multiplications, implementations based on Intel Streaming SIMD Extensions 2 (Intel SSE2) instructions [6] and the Cell processor [7] have been proposed.

Montgomery multiplication is usually performed on integers of several hundred bits or more; however, this paper considers the case of 52 bits or fewer. Multiple Montgomery multiplications with such numbers of bits are used in the modular fast Fourier transform (FFT) algorithm [8]. To the best of our knowledge, there are no existing implementations of multiple Montgomery multiplications using Intel AVX-512IFMA instructions. Here, we propose such an implementation and evaluate its performance.

O. Gervasi et al. (Eds.): ICCSA 2020, LNCS 12253, pp. 655–663, 2020.
https://doi.org/10.1007/978-3-030-58814-4_52

Algorithm 1. Montgomery multiplication algorithm [1]

Input: A, B, N such that $0 \le A, B < N$, $\beta > N$, $\gcd(\beta, N) = 1$, $\mu = -N^{-1} \bmod \beta$
Output: $C = AB\beta^{-1} \bmod N$ such that $0 \le C < N$
1: $C \leftarrow AB$
2: $q \leftarrow \mu C \bmod \beta$
3: $C \leftarrow (C + qN)/\beta$
4: **if** $C \ge N$ **then**
5: $\quad C \leftarrow C - N$
6: **return** C.

```
uint64_t mulmod63(uint64_t a, uint64_t b, uint64_t N, uint64_t mu)
/*  Compute mulmod63 = (a * b * 2^-63) mod N.
    We need mu = -N^-1 mod 2^63. */
{
  __uint128_t t;
  uint64_t c, q;

  t = (__uint128_t) a * b;
  q = ((uint64_t) t * mu) & 0x7FFFFFFFFFFFFFFF;
  c = (t + (__uint128_t) q * N) >> 63;
  if (c >= N)
    c -= N;

  return c;
}
```

Fig. 1. Montgomery multiplication of 63-bit integers

The remainder of this paper is organized as follows. Section 2 describes the vectorization of multiple Montgomery multiplications. Section 3 presents the proposed implementation of multiple Montgomery multiplications using Intel AVX-512IFMA instructions. Section 4 presents the performance results. Finally, Sect. 5 gives the concluding remarks.

2 Vectorization of Multiple Montgomery Multiplications

Montgomery multiplication [1] is shown in Algorithm 1. Figure 1 shows the Montgomery multiplication of 63-bit integers, which corresponds to $\beta = 2^{63}$ in Algorithm 1. This program uses the `__uint128_t` extension for 128-bit unsigned integer arithmetic supported by the GCC, Clang, and Intel C compilers. Because this program computes a single Montgomery multiplication, vectorization, which requires multiple Montgomery multiplications to be performed simultaneously, cannot be applied.

The Intel 64 instruction set supports `mulq` and `mulx` instructions, which perform 64-bit $\times$ 64-bit $\rightarrow$ 128-bit unsigned integer multiplication. In contrast, the Intel AVX-512F (Foundation) instruction set supports only the `vpmuludq`

Algorithm 2. Radix-β interleaved Montgomery multiplication algorithm [1, 4]

Input: A, B, N, μ such that $A = \sum_{i=0}^{n-1} a_i\beta^i$, $0 \le a_i < \beta$, $0 \le A, B < N$,
$\beta^{n-1} \le N < \beta^n$, $\gcd(\beta, N) = 1$, $\mu = -N^{-1} \bmod \beta$
Output: $C = AB\beta^{-n} \bmod N$ such that $0 \le C < N$
1: $C \leftarrow 0$
2: **for** i **from** 0 **to** $n-1$ **do**
3: $\quad C \leftarrow C + a_iB$
4: $\quad q \leftarrow \mu C \bmod \beta$
5: $\quad C \leftarrow (C + qN)/\beta$
6: **if** $C \ge N$ **then**
7: $\quad C \leftarrow C - N$
8: **return** C.

instruction, which performs 32-bit $\times$ 32-bit $\rightarrow$ 64-bit unsigned integer multiplication. Furthermore, a statement that contains `__uint128_t` variables cannot be automatically vectorized by the Intel C compiler. The radix-β interleaved Montgomery multiplication algorithm [1,4], shown in Algorithm 2, can be used to vectorize multiple Montgomery multiplications. In radix-2^{32} interleaved Montgomery multiplication, there is some overflow in 64-bit unsigned integer addition. A vectorized multiple Montgomery squaring operation of 62-bit integers with $\beta = 2^{31}$ and $n = 2$ has been proposed to avoid this overflow [9].

We modified the vectorized multiple Montgomery squaring operation to achieve vectorized multiple Montgomery multiplications. For multiple Montgomery multiplications, performance is degraded by the conditional subtraction $C - N$ when $C \ge N$ on lines 6 and 7 of Algorithm 2. The conditional subtraction can be replaced by the minimum operation $\min(C, C - N)$ for unsigned integer values C and N with wrap-around two's complement arithmetic [9]. The Intel AVX-512F instruction set supports the `vpminuq` instruction for the 64-bit unsigned integer minimum operation.

Figure 2 shows the vectorized multiple Montgomery multiplications of 62-bit integers, which correspond to $\beta = 2^{31}$ and $n = 2$ in Algorithm 2. In Fig. 2, `#pragma ivdep` instructs the compiler to ignore assumed vector dependencies and `#pragma vector aligned` instructs the compiler to use aligned data movement instructions for all array references during vectorization. The vectorized multiple Montgomery multiplications can be further optimized using the Intel AVX-512 intrinsics [10], as shown in Fig. 3. In this program, the Intel AVX-512 intrinsics `_mm512_mul_epu32()` and `_mm512_min_epu64()` correspond to the `vpmuludq` and `vpminuq` instructions, respectively. This program assumes that the vector length `VLEN` is divisible by 8. If `VLEN` is not divisible by 8, a remainder loop needs to be executed.

```
void vmulmod62(uint64_t *c, uint64_t *a, uint64_t *b, uint64_t *N,
               uint32_t *mu)
/*  Compute c[:] = (a[:] * b[:] * 2^-62) mod N[:].
    We need mu[:] = -N[:]^-1 mod 2^31. */
{
  uint64_t t0, t1, t2, t3;
  uint32_t a0, a1, b0, b1, N0, N1, q;
  int i;

#pragma ivdep
#pragma vector aligned
  for (i = 0; i < VLEN; i++) {
    a0 = a[i] & 0x7FFFFFFF;
    a1 = a[i] >> 31;
    b0 = b[i] & 0x7FFFFFFF;
    b1 = b[i] >> 31;
    N0 = N[i] & 0x7FFFFFFF;
    N1 = N[i] >> 31;
    t0 = (uint64_t) a0 * b0;
    t1 = (uint64_t) a0 * b1;
    t2 = (uint64_t) a1 * b0;
    t3 = (uint64_t) a1 * b1;
    q = ((uint32_t) t0 * mu[i]) & 0x7FFFFFFF;
    t0 = ((t0 + (uint64_t) q * N0) >> 31) + (t1 + (uint64_t) q * N1);
    t2 += t0 & 0x7FFFFFFF;
    t3 += t0 >> 31;
    q = ((uint32_t) t2 * mu[i]) & 0x7FFFFFFF;
    t2 = ((t2 + (uint64_t) q * N0) >> 31) + (t3 + (uint64_t) q * N1);
    c[i] = min(t2, t2 - N[i]);
  }
}
```

Fig. 2. Vectorized multiple Montgomery multiplications of 62-bit integers

3 Implementation of Multiple Montgomery Multiplications Using Intel AVX-512IFMA Instructions

Intel AVX-512IFMA instructions [2] are supported by the Cannon Lake and Ice Lake microarchitectures, and will be supported by the Tiger Lake microarchitecture. The Intel AVX-512IFMA instruction set supports the `vpmadd52luq` and `vpmadd52huq` instructions, which multiply 52-bit unsigned integers and produce the low and high halves, respectively, of a 104-bit intermediate result. These halves are added to 64-bit accumulators.

Algorithm 3 shows a modified Montgomery multiplication algorithm. $C+qN$ on line 3 of Algorithm 1 is divisible by β. That is, the lower-half bits of $C+qN$ are 0, and thus do not need to be computed. In this case, if q on line 2 of Algorithm 1 is 0, the carry added to the sum of the upper-half bits of C and the upper-half

```
void vmulmod62(uint64_t *c, uint64_t *a, uint64_t *b, uint64_t *N,
               uint64_t *mu)
/*  Compute c[:] = (a[:] * b[:] * 2^-62) mod N[:].
    We need mu[:] = -N[:]^-1 mod 2^31. */
{
  __m512i a0, a1, b0, b1, N0, N1, q, t0, t1, t2, t3;
  int i;

  for (i = 0; i < VLEN; i += 8) {
    a0 = _mm512_and_epi64(_mm512_load_epi64(&a[i]),
                          _mm512_set1_epi64(0x7FFFFFFF));
    a1 = _mm512_srli_epi64(_mm512_load_epi64(&a[i]), 31);
    b0 = _mm512_and_epi64(_mm512_load_epi64(&b[i]),
                          _mm512_set1_epi64(0x7FFFFFFF));
    b1 = _mm512_srli_epi64(_mm512_load_epi64(&b[i]), 31);
    N0 = _mm512_and_epi64(_mm512_load_epi64(&N[i]),
                          _mm512_set1_epi64(0x7FFFFFFF));
    N1 = _mm512_srli_epi64(_mm512_load_epi64(&N[i]), 31);
    t0 = _mm512_mul_epu32(a0, b0);
    t1 = _mm512_mul_epu32(a0, b1);
    t2 = _mm512_mul_epu32(a1, b0);
    t3 = _mm512_mul_epu32(a1, b1);
    q = _mm512_and_epi64(_mm512_mul_epu32(t0, _mm512_load_epi64(&mu[i])),
                         _mm512_set1_epi64(0x7FFFFFFF));
    t0 = _mm512_add_epi64(_mm512_srli_epi64(_mm512_add_epi64(t0,
                          _mm512_mul_epu32(q, N0)), 31),
                          _mm512_add_epi64(t1, _mm512_mul_epu32(q, N1)));
    t2 = _mm512_add_epi64(t2, _mm512_and_epi64(t0,
                              _mm512_set1_epi64(0x7FFFFFFF)));
    t3 = _mm512_add_epi64(t3, _mm512_srli_epi64(t0, 31));
    q = _mm512_and_epi64(_mm512_mul_epu32(t2, _mm512_load_epi64(&mu[i])),
                         _mm512_set1_epi64(0x7FFFFFFF));
    t2 = _mm512_add_epi64(_mm512_srli_epi64(_mm512_add_epi64(t2,
                          _mm512_mul_epu32(q, N0)), 31),
                          _mm512_add_epi64(t3, _mm512_mul_epu32(q, N1)));
    _mm512_store_epi64(&c[i], _mm512_min_epu64(t2, _mm512_sub_epi64(t2,
                              _mm512_load_epi64(&N[i]))));
  }
}
```

Fig. 3. Vectorized multiple Montgomery multiplications of 62-bit integers using Intel AVX-512 intrinsics

bits of qN is 0; otherwise, it is 1. We note that the lower-half bits of qN need not be calculated in Algorithm 3.

If the Montgomery multiplication operand is 52 bits or fewer, $\beta = 2^{52}$ can be set in Algorithm 3 by using the Intel AVX-512IFMA instructions. Line 1 of Algorithm 3 calculates the remainder of dividing AB by β, and thus only the low 52 bits of AB need to be calculated. We can use the vpmadd52luq instruction for this calculation. Line 2 of Algorithm 3 calculates the remainder of dividing

Algorithm 3. Modified Montgomery multiplication algorithm

Input: A, B, N such that $0 \le A, B < N$, $\beta > N$, $\gcd(\beta, N) = 1$, $\mu = -N^{-1} \bmod \beta$
Output: $C = AB\beta^{-1} \bmod N$ such that $0 \le C < N$
1: $C \leftarrow AB \bmod \beta$
2: $q \leftarrow \mu C \bmod \beta$
3: $C \leftarrow \lfloor AB/\beta \rfloor + \lfloor qN/\beta \rfloor$
4: **if** $q \ne 0$ **then**
5: $\quad C \leftarrow C + 1$
6: **if** $C \ge N$ **then**
7: $\quad C \leftarrow C - N$
8: **return** C.

```
void vmulmod52(uint64_t *c, uint64_t *a, uint64_t *b, uint64_t *N,
               uint64_t *mu)
/*  c[:] = (a[:] * b[:] * 2^-52) mod N[:]. */
    We need mu[:] = -N[:]^-1 mod 2^52. */
{
  __m512i q, t;
  int i;

  for (i = 0; i < VLEN; i += 8) {
    t = _mm512_madd52lo_epu64(_mm512_set1_epi64(0),
        _mm512_load_epi64(&a[i]), _mm512_load_epi64(&b[i]));
    q = _mm512_madd52lo_epu64(_mm512_set1_epi64(0), t,
                              _mm512_load_epi64(&mu[i]));
    t = _mm512_madd52hi_epu64(_mm512_min_epu64(q, _mm512_set1_epi64(1)),
                              q, _mm512_load_epi64(&N[i]));
    t = _mm512_madd52hi_epu64(t, _mm512_load_epi64(&a[i]),
                              _mm512_load_epi64(&b[i]));
    _mm512_store_epi64(&c[i], _mm512_min_epu64(t, _mm512_sub_epi64(t,
                       _mm512_load_epi64(&N[i]))));
  }
}
```

Fig. 4. Vectorized multiple Montgomery multiplications of 52-bit integers using Intel AVX-512 intrinsics

μC by β, and thus only the low 52 bits of μC need to be calculated. We can use the `vpmadd52luq` instruction for this calculation. On line 3 of Algorithm 3, the high 52 bits of AB and qN can be calculated using the `vpmadd52huq` instruction. The conditional increment $C + 1$ when $q \ne 0$ on lines 4 and 5 of Algorithm 3 can be replaced by the minimum operation and the addition $C + \min(q, 1)$ for unsigned integer values q and C. The minimum operation $\min(q, 1)$ is performed using the `vpminuq` instruction. The conditional subtraction on lines 6 and 7 of Algorithm 3 is also performed using the `vpminuq` instruction, as described in Sect. 2.

Table 1. Specifications of the test platform

Platform	Intel NUC 8 Home, a Mini PC
Number of cores	2
Number of threads	4
CPU Type	Intel Core i3-8121U Cannon Lake-U 2.2 GHz
L1 Cache (per core)	I-Cache: 32 KB D-Cache: 32 KB
L2 Cache (per core)	256 KB
L3 Cache	4 MB
Main Memory	LPDDR4-2666 4 GB
OS	Linux 4.15.0-74-generic

Figure 4 shows the vectorized multiple Montgomery multiplications of 52-bit integers using Intel AVX-512 intrinsics. In this program, the Intel AVX-512 intrinsics `_mm512_madd52lo_epu64()`, `_mm512_madd52hi_epu64()`, and `_mm512_min_epu64()` correspond to the `vpmadd52luq`, `vpmadd52huq`, and `vpminuq` instructions, respectively. This program assumes that the vector length `VLEN` is divisible by 8. If `VLEN` is not divisible by 8, a remainder loop needs to be executed.

4 Performance Results

For performance evaluation, a comparison among multiple 52-bit Montgomery multiplications using Intel AVX-512IFMA instructions, multiple 62-bit Montgomery multiplications using Intel AVX-512F instructions, and multiple 63-bit Montgomery multiplications using Intel 64 instructions was performed.

Since a processor based on the Ice Lake microarchitecture was not available at the time of writing this paper, the performance was measured on an Intel Core i3-8121U processor, which is the only processor based on the Cannon Lake microarchitecture.

In the computation of the Montgomery multiplication $C = AB\beta^{-1} \bmod N$, N is an odd random number in the range of 1–$2^{52} - 1$, and A and B are random numbers in the range of $0 \le A, B < N$. The modular multiplicative inverses μ in Algorithms 1, 2, and 3 were prepared in advance.

The batch size of Montgomery multiplications was varied from 64 to 1024. Each batch of Montgomery multiplications was executed one million times. The number of Montgomery multiplications per second (Mulmod$\times 10^9$/s) was calculated based on the average elapsed time.

The specifications of the test platform are shown in Table 1. The Intel Core i3-8121U processor has two cores. However, we evaluated the performance on a single core and a single thread to focus on vectorization. The Intel C compiler (version 19.0.5.281) was used. The compiler options were `icc -O3 -xCANNONLAKE`. The compiler option `-O3` enables the most aggressive optimizations for maximum speed. The compiler option `-xCANNONLAKE` generates instructions for the Cannon Lake microarchitecture.

Table 2. Performance of multiple Montgomery multiplications using various instruction sets (Mulmod $\times 10^9$/s)

Batch size	Intel 64	AVX-512F	AVX-512IFMA
	63-bit	62-bit	52-bit
64	0.45860	1.32821	5.57394
128	0.46901	1.33310	5.72937
256	0.47624	1.33138	4.90638
512	0.47970	1.34336	5.28162
1024	0.47235	1.32351	4.14454

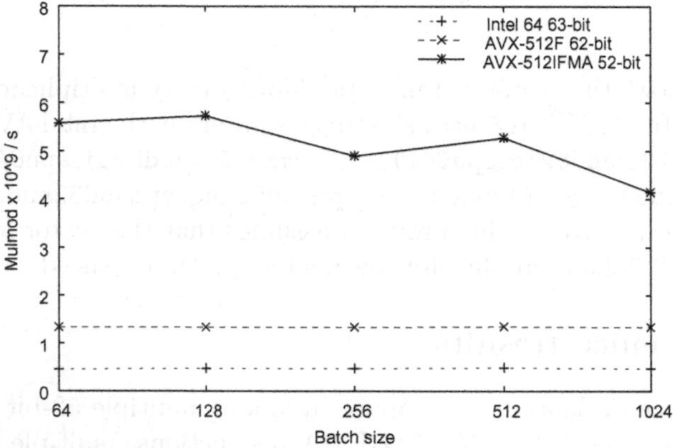

Fig. 5. Performance of multiple Montgomery multiplications using various instruction sets

Table 2 and Fig. 5 show the performance of multiple Montgomery multiplications using Intel 64, Intel AVX-512F, and Intel AVX-512IFMA instructions. When the batch size was 128, the proposed implementation using Intel AVX-512IFMA instructions was approximately 12.22 and 4.30 times faster than the implementations using Intel 64 and Intel AVX-512F instructions on the Intel Core i3-8121U processor, respectively.

The reason for this is that while the implementation using Intel 64 instructions calculates one integer at a time, the implementation using Intel AVX-512IFMA instructions calculates eight integers simultaneously. Furthermore, the number of instructions is smaller in the implementation using Intel AVX-512IFMA instructions than in the implementation using Intel AVX-512F instructions.

5 Conclusion

In this paper, we proposed a fast implementation of multiple Montgomery multiplications using Intel AVX-512IFMA instructions. The proposed implementation is based on a modified Montgomery multiplication algorithm. For Montgomery multiplication operands with 52 bits or fewer, the proposed implementation using Intel AVX-512IFMA instructions outperforms implementations using Intel 64 and Intel AVX-512F instructions on the Intel Core i3-8121U processor.

Our future work is to demonstrate the effectiveness of the proposed implementation on other processors that support the Intel AVX-512IFMA instructions.

Acknowledgments. This research was partially supported by JSPS KAKENHI Grant Number JP19K11989.

References

1. Montgomery, P.L.: Modular multiplication without trial division. Math. Comput. **44**, 519–521 (1985)
2. Intel Corporation: Intel 64 and IA-32 architectures software developer's manual, volume 1: Basic architecture (2019). https://software.intel.com/sites/default/files/managed/a4/60/253665-sdm-vol-1.pdf
3. Gueron, S., Krasnov, V.: Software implementation of modular exponentiation, using advanced vector instructions architectures. In: Özbudak, F., Rodríguez-Henríquez, F. (eds.) WAIFI 2012. LNCS, vol. 7369, pp. 119–135. Springer, Heidelberg (2012). https://doi.org/10.1007/978-3-642-31662-3_9
4. Bos, J.W., Montgomery, P.L., Shumow, D., Zaverucha, G.M.: Montgomery multiplication using vector instructions. In: Lange, T., Lauter, K., Lisoněk, P. (eds.) SAC 2013. LNCS, vol. 8282, pp. 471–489. Springer, Heidelberg (2014). https://doi.org/10.1007/978-3-662-43414-7_24
5. Drucker, N., Gueron, S.: Fast modular squaring with AVX512IFMA. In: Latifi, S. (ed.) 16th International Conference on Information Technology-New Generations (ITNG 2019). AISC, vol. 800, pp. 3–8. Springer, Cham (2019)
6. Page, D., Smart, N.P.: Parallel cryptographic arithmetic using a redundant Montgomery representation. IEEE Trans. Comput. **53**, 1474–1482 (2004)
7. Bos, J.W.: High-performance modular multiplication on the Cell processor. In: Hasan, M.A., Helleseth, T. (eds.) WAIFI 2010. LNCS, vol. 6087, pp. 7–24. Springer, Heidelberg (2010). https://doi.org/10.1007/978-3-642-13797-6_2
8. Meng, L., Johnson, J.R., Franchetti, F., et al.: Spiral-generated modular FFT algorithms. In: Proceedings of 4th International Workshop on Parallel and Symbolic Computation (PASCO 2010), pp. 169–170 (2010)
9. Takahashi, D.: Computation of the 100 quadrillionth hexadecimal digit of π on a cluster of Intel Xeon Phi processors. Parallel Comput. **75**, 1–10 (2018)
10. Intel Corporation: Intel C++ compiler 19.0 developer guide and reference (2019). https://software.intel.com/sites/default/files/cpp_dev_guide_190_u5_1.pdf

Algorithms for Enhancing Satellite Imagery to Discover Archaeological Finds Covered by Shadow

Stefano Chiappini(✉), Francesco Di Stefano, Eva Savina Malinverni, and Roberto Pierdicca

Dipartimento d'Ingegneria Civile, Edile e Architettura (DICEA), Università Politecnica delle Marche, Via Brecce Bianche 12, 60131 Ancona, Italy
{s.chiappini,f.distefano}@pm.univpm.it, {e.s.malinverni,r.pierdicca}@univpm.it

Abstract. Very high-resolution (VHR) images proved to be an invaluable source of information even in the archaeological domain, but sometimes shadows hinder their full exploitation. To overcome such limitation, this research proposes a workflow able to analyze shadowed zones, by processing Pléiades and World-View 2 images. The case study is the archaeological site of Maltai, in the Iraqi Kurdistan Region, which presents shadowed areas to be detected. Applying de-shadowing workflow has been tested over multispectral and panchromatic images, with different invariant color spaces. The proposed methods exploit the techniques of automatic thresholding and spectral ratio in the detection of shadow regions. This approach shows a clustering of shadow pixels for an enhanced images visualization and proves its suitability for archaeological settings.

Keywords: VHR imagery · Pléiades · World-View 2 · Multispectral images · Panchromatic images · Shadow algorithms · Archaeological area

1 Introduction

Remote sensing (RS) represents a useful tool for the analysis and evaluation of changes in environmental and urban processes, and not only. In fact, RS becomes a useful approach for investigation, documentation and planning also in the archaeological field. The new possibility offered by the processing of data collected remotely allows to analyze sites of particular interest and to discover the signs of ancient population activities on the land surface [1]. In particular, satellite imagery provides a high detailed resolution of land cover mapping [2]. The technological evolution of acquisition devices and the continuous refinement of data processing algorithms offer new possibilities for classification and extraction of information on the ground. For these reasons, RS is an effective technique to monitor the dynamics due to anthropogenic and natural actions [3], thanks to the processing of high or very-high resolution (VHR) multitemporal and multispectral satellite images [4]. The use of the VHR satellite systems represents an

O. Gervasi et al. (Eds.): ICCSA 2020, LNCS 12253, pp. 664–673, 2020.
https://doi.org/10.1007/978-3-030-58814-4_53

extremely valid tool for the monitoring of change detection of the terrestrial surface with a sub-millimetric accuracy, based on the definition of time series (TS) of satellite radar images [5]. However, thanks to the recent technological progress, different satellites have been launched such as IKONOS, QuickBird, Pléiades, GeoEye, RapidEye, Skysat-1, WorldView-2, WorldView-3, Jilin-1 and Kompsat [6]. The abovementioned satellites are able to acquire different images by several multispectral and panchromatic VHR sensors are used. In the use of satellite RS, a challenge is to detect and/or classify shadowed targets, where shading results in the decrease or total loss of spectral information [7], such as in mountain areas covered by vegetation [8]. The problem arises when the presence of shadowed areas in such archaeological sites may prevent their correct view and identification of the area that will be the subject of the archaeological expedition. In order to overcome this problem, various algorithms have been implemented to reduce or remove shadow pixel imagery [9].

The research work presented in this paper aims to exploit VHR images for the recognition of objects in hard-to-reach areas and to allow an accurate mapping of the archaeological area. After an initial analysis about related works, the article is setup as follows. The paragraph on the methodology of work starts with a brief description of the archaeological case study. Then the work performed to test the de-shadowing technique according to the type of image used is illustrated: first on multispectral images and then on panchromatic ones. This is followed by a summary of the results obtained and, in conclusion, comments on these approaches are discussed.

2 Related Works

In literature there are not many applications of satellite remote sensing for the identification and monitoring of archaeological areas [10]. Using multispectral and/or panchromatic satellite imagery, the monitoring process of archaeological sites can be effectively supported in a reliable, repetitive, non-invasive, fast and cost-effective manner [11]. The satellite sensors offer more advantages with spectral imagery in comparison with aerial photogrammetry [12]. Nowadays, the employment of multispectral sensors allows measuring each pixel imagery carried out usually derived between 3 and 10 different bands [13]. In addition, in areas where the work of archaeologists has been blocked, due to, for example, the outbreak of civil war or the occupation by militias [14], the inaccessibility of the sites is overcome by the use of satellite RS. In fact, with RS it is possible to acquire a time series of images to monitor and map all the archaeological sites and artistic heritage.

The problem arises when the presence of shadowed areas in such archaeological sites may prevent their correct view and identification of the area that will be the subject of the archaeological expedition. The presence of the shadow in images may have a dual effect. The first one shadow is considered as a support of information through a semantic process, while secondly it can cause distortions to return of the shape of objects in the image, for their recognition [15]. In order to overcome this problem, it has been used correction and analysis methodologies applied in contexts differing from the one under examination, such as urban and natural environments [16–18]. During the recent decades, different algorithms has been developed in order to improve the identification and detection of shadow pixels in color aerial images. Among these we can find Tsai [19], considering the multispectral images, describes the relationship between hue and intensity in order to identify the difference between shadow and non-shadow pixels, separating the shadow masks from the map with an Otsu threshold (1979) [20].

The set of de-shadowing processes allow the creation of raster images, being used by archaeologists for the generation of a basic map in GIS (Geographic Information System). This enables a thematization and the development of a predictive model that bases its roots both on the geometries of the non-shadowed entities present in the study area and on other types of data such as topographical, historical, geological, etc. [21].

3 Materials and Methods

3.1 Description of the Study Area

Traces of the Assyrian empire, which dominated ancient Mesopotamia in the first millennium B.C., were found in northern Iraq (Iraqi Kurdistan Region), thanks to an archaeological expedition led by the University of Udine. After research campaigns, almost 500 archaeological sites have been discovered, of which about 200 from the Neo-Assyrian period, consisting of ancient towns and rural villages, caves and wells, quarries, canals and ancient roadways. These sites are located in the "Land of Nineveh" (http://www.terradininive.com), an area straddling the provinces of Mosul (the ancient land of the Nineveh) and Dohuk. In these sites, bas-reliefs carved into the rock have been found, including the Maltai rock reliefs (Fig. 1), selected as a case study for this work. In this area these bas-reliefs were observed for the first time in the 70's and investigations on the site began in 2012. But the archaeological work was abandoned and hidden when ISIS became active in the region in 2014. In 2018, during the archaeological expedition led by Prof. Morandi Bonaccorsi, in collaboration with the archaeologists of the Duhok Antiquites Directorate, they discovered ancient rock carving dating almost 3000 years [22].

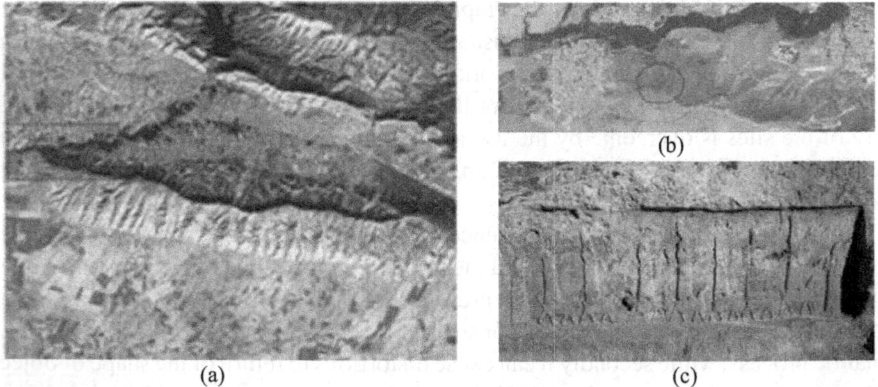

Fig. 1. (a) Individuation of the archeological area of Maltai (satellite image). (b) Core and buffer zone of Maltai. (c) One of the panels of Assyrian carvings unearthed.

3.2 Methodology Workflow

The methodology of research is based on the analysis of VHR satellite images, which can provide useful data about the archaeological area located along the rocky slope of the mountain. The satellite images examined are those given by the Pléiades and World-View 2 satellites, which include both multispectral and panchromatic images. The satellite imagery has been acquired in two different time. World View 2 imagery have been collected in four color scales each for band (R, G, B and NIR) and the panchromatic image have been captured on 7th September 2014. Pleiades imagery have been surveyed four in multispectral images (R, G, B and NIR) and the panchromatic one has been acquired on 18th November 2014. For this purpose, it has been used several algorithms, already known by literature, reporting in this paper the best results obtained compared to ground truth, also shown by processed images, as shown below.

Panchromatic images provide only intensity information. To avoid difficulties in recognizing shadow and non-shadow zones, the algorithm adopted is the one presented by Liu et al. [4]. This operation consists of two phases. In the first phase the sampling operation is limited to shadow regions, while in the second phase the selected pixel values of the previous sampling are processed with the algorithms. After the sampling phase, the image normalization was carried out in the range [0, 1] by 255 (for 8-b quantization) and the optimal automatic Otsu threshold [20] was applied as no further investigation is required (Fig. 2, Fig. 3).

Multispectral images were first analyzed, adopting the same approach for both Pléiades and World-View2. Basing on the characteristics of VHR satellite imagery and using multispectral bands, shadow regions are distinguished from non-shadowed ones [23]. For multispectral images, the parameters of chromaticity (hue component) and luminance (intensity component) in the invariant color space were considered, as well as the reflectivity of the bands themselves to highlight the shadow zones. For these reasons, it has been started with the application of Mixed Property-Based Automatic Shadow (MSPI) [24]. The processed image will then have higher values in shadow pixels than in non-shadow ones and the vegetation cover in non-shadow areas, applying the optimal shadow index threshold recommended by Otsu [20]. The subsequent algorithms used are functions already implemented in Matlab (R2019b version), which include: hue-intensity-saturation (HSI) [25], hue-saturation-value (HSV) [26], hue chroma value (HCV) [27], Luma-in phase-quadrature (YIQ) [28], Luma Chroma Blue Chroma Red (YCbCr) [29]. The choice fell on them, as the de-shadowing approach [19] was adopted, which exploits the properties of shadows in luminance and chromaticity applied in different invariant color spaces. This operation consists of four phases: color transformation, shadow segmentation, shape preservation and shadow compensation. Results of these processes highlight the distinction between shadow and non-shadow regions (Fig. 4, Fig. 5).

The application of these models aims to divide the pixels of an image into categories based on spectral properties. The ground truth has been defined manually, identifying parts of shadow zone from non-shadow ones, that is a time consuming. The confusion matrix, obtained by comparing each pixel of the ground truth and the images generated by the de-shadowing operations, is used as objective evaluation of the accuracy of the shadow images and is based on values of different metrics [24].These metrics are: the producer accuracy (PA), omitted error (EO), specificity (SP), error committed (EC), and overall accuracy (OA). They are calculated as follow:

$$PA = \frac{TP}{(TP + FN)}; EO = \frac{FN}{(TP + FN)}; SP = \frac{TN}{(TN + FP)}; EC = \frac{FP}{(TN + FP)};$$

$$OA = \frac{TP + TN}{(TP + TN + FP + FN)}$$

they are based on the confusion matrix calculating pixel by pixel. Thus, it has been obtained a set of indexes (TP, TN, FP, FN) with the purpose to estimate the output of methods applied to satellite imagery of this case study.

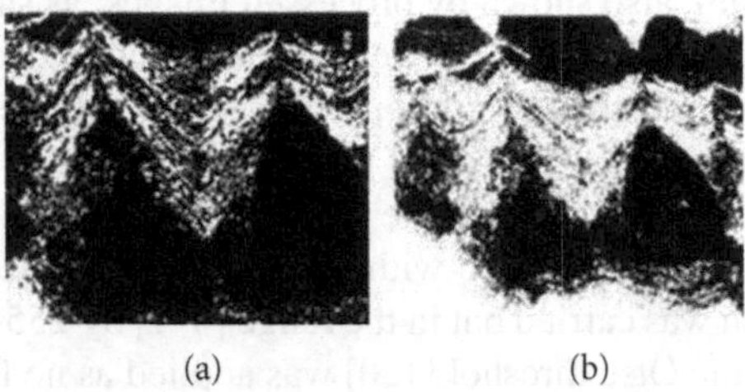

(a) (b)

Fig. 2. Panchromatic Pléiades images. (a) The original image. (b) The de-shadowing result by Liu et al. (2011) [4]

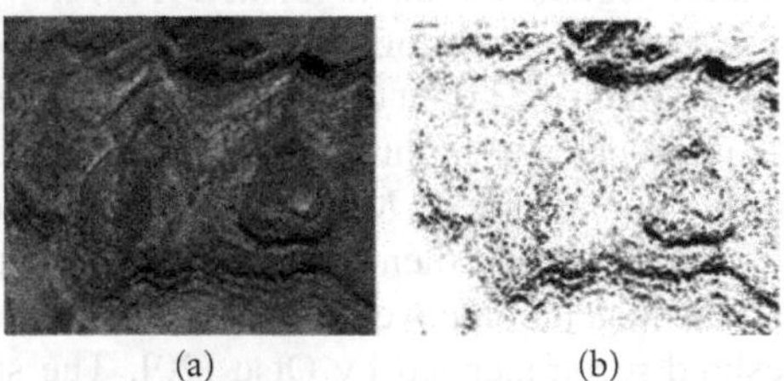

(a) (b)

Fig. 3. Panchromatic World-View 2 images. (a) The original image. (b) The de-shadowing result by Liu et al. (2011) [4]

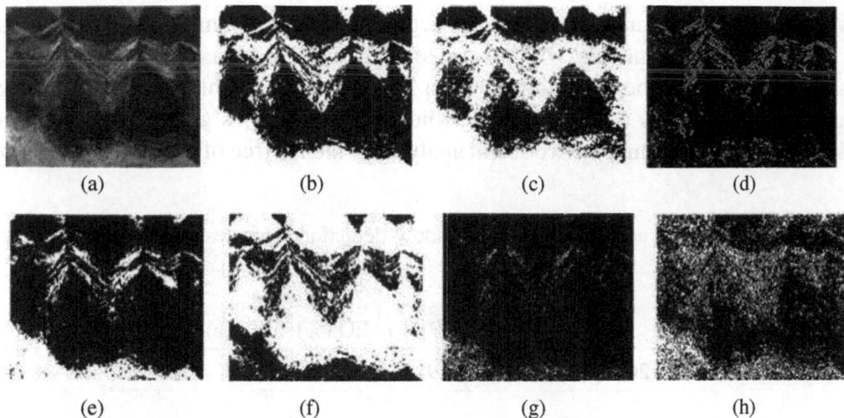

Fig. 4. Multispectral Pléiades test images. (a) The original image. (b) The reference shadow image. (c) Shadow image by MSPI based approach [24]. (d) Shadow image by HSI model [25]. (e) Shad-ow image by HSV model [26]. (f) Shadow image by HCV model [27]. (g) Shadow image by YIQ model [28]. (h) Shadow image by YCbCr model [29]

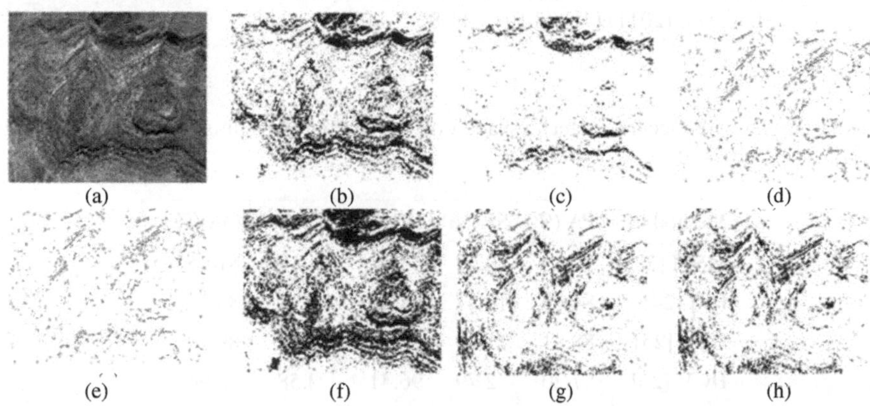

Fig. 5. Multispectral World-View 2 test images. (a) The original image. (b) The reference shadow image. (c) Shadow image by MSPI based approach [24]. (d) Shadow image by HSI model [25]. (e) Shadow image by HSV model [26]. (f) Shadow image by HCV model [27]. (g) Shadow image by YIQ model [28]. (h) Shadow image by YCbCr model [29]

4 Result Assessment

In the tables below, are listed the results of the workflow explained above, where the values of the evaluation metrics are reported. The accuracy data for shadow de-tection of the methods applied both to multispectral Plèiades images (Table 1) and for panchromatic ones (Table 2) is tested. Same operations for the results obtained on World View 2 multispectral (Table 3) and panchromatic (Table 4) images. The effectiveness of the various models for shadow detection has been evaluated. Among the methods applied to multispectral images, with pixel size 2.0 m, the optimal values of OA for HCV and PA for MSPI have been obtained. But a better accuracy has been achieved with the method used for panchromatic models, with pixel size 0.5 m, both in terms of OA and PA. On the basis of these results, the algorithms are applied very well for high resolution images, recognizing small areas of shadow and avoiding distortions as geometrical distortion, thanks to the type of natural environment analyzed which is free of vegetation and ponds.

Table 1. Display of the accuracy data for shadow detection from test panchromatic Pleiàdes images (Fig. 2).

Method	PA (%)	SP (%)	EO (%)	EC (%)	OA (%)
Liu *et al.* (2011) [4]	99.09	0.91	64.12	35.88	82.46

Table 2. Display of the accuracy data for shadow detection from for test panchromatic WorldView 2 images (Fig. 3)

Method	PA (%)	SP (%)	EO (%)	EC (%)	OA (%)
Liu *et al.* (2011) [4]	88.19	11.82	90.32	9.68	90.01

Table 3. Display of the accuracy data for shadow detection from test multispectral Pleiàdes images (Fig. 4)

Method	PA (%)	SP (%)	EO (%)	EC (%)	OA (%)
MSPI [23]	99.33	0.67	63.90	36.10	81.05
HSI [24]	84.13	15.87	78.09	21.91	83.95
HSV [25]	88.81	11.20	99.85	0.14	89.59
HCV [26]	97.20	2.79	96.41	3.58	96.94
YIQ [27]	82.89	17.11	97.56	2.43	83.01
YCbCr [28]	66.45	33.55	76.42	23.59	74.16

Table 4. Display of the accuracy data for shadow detection from shadow detection from test multispectral World-View 2 images (Fig. 5)

Method	PA (%)	SP (%)	EO (%)	EC (%)	OA (%)
MSPI [23]	98.41	1.59	83.96	16.03	84.93
HSI [24]	23.99	76.01	78.55	21.45	76.83
HSV [25]	23.86	76.10	78.55	21.45	76.89
HCV [26]	60.13	39.87	99.18	0.82	85.55
YIQ [27]	82.90	17.11	97.57	2.43	83.01
YCbCr [28]	0.00	100.00	78.13	21.87	76.87

5 Conclusion

In this paper, different approaches to shadow detection based on the properties of shadows (luminance, chromaticity and spectral reflectivity) have been applied to obtain a set of images separated from shadows. The proposed methods exploit the techniques of automatic thresholding and spectral ratio in the detection of shadow regions. For the objective evaluation, Pléiades and World-View 2 satellite imageries are used. Analyzing the results, best data were obtained from the World-View 2 images, where the geometric shape of the shadows and the surface area of the rock profile are better defined. The same cannot be said from the Pléiades ones, because the shadow zone is too wide and covers almost the entire site under study. The set of operations carries out false pixels deleting that are associated with non-shadow regions and allow users to have a greater understanding of the territory, seen from above. The basis of this study will serve to evaluate the advantages and disadvantages of the results in the use of de-shadowing algorithms. As future work, a geo-referenced database will be created, where all the information related to the rock finds of the Assyrians will be stored, integrating the data acquired during the different expeditions and surveys and ensuring their interchange between the several archaeological institutes.

Acknowledgements. The authors thank Prof. Daniele Morandi Bonaccorsi of University of Udine and the archaeologists Arch. Roberto Orazi and Dott. Francesca Colosi of ISPC-CNR for the opportunity to give us the input data on which to perform the research tests.

References

1. Malinverni, E., Pierdicca, R., Bozzi, C., Colosi, F., Orazi, R.: Analysis and Processing of nadir and stereo VHR pleiadés images for 3D mapping and planning the land of nineveh. Iraqi Kurdistan. Geosciences. **7**, 80 (2017). https://doi.org/10.3390/geosciences7030080
2. Tolt, G., Shimoni, M., Ahlberg, J.: A shadow detection method for remote sensing images using VHR hyperspectral and LIDAR data. In: International Geoscience and Remote Sensing Symposium (IGARSS), pp. 4423–4426 (2011). https://doi.org/10.1109/igarss.2011.6050213
3. Aplin, P.: Remote sensing: ecology. Prog. Phys. Geogr. **29**, 104–113 (2005)

4. Liu, J., Fang, T., Li, D.: Shadow detection in remotely sensed images based on self-adaptive feature selection. IEEE Trans. Geosci. Remote Sens. **49**, 5092–5103 (2011). https://doi.org/10.1109/TGRS.2011.2158221
5. Solano Correa, Y., Bovolo, F., Bruzzone, L.: An approach for unsupervised change detection in multitemporal VHR images acquired by different multispectral sensors. Remote Sens. (2018). https://doi.org/10.3390/rs10040533
6. Deilami, K., Hashim, M.: Very high resolution optical satellites for DEM generation: a review. Eur. J. Sci. Res. ISSN **49**, 542–554 (2011). ISSN 1450-216
7. Reiche, J., Verhoeven, R., Verbesselt, J., Hamunyela, E., Wielaard, N., Herold, M.: Characterizing tropical forest cover loss using dense sentinel-1 data and active fire alerts. Remote Sensing. **10**, 777 (2018). https://doi.org/10.3390/rs10050777
8. Shahtahmassebi, A., Yang, N., Wang, K., Moore, N., Shen, Z.: Review of shadow detection and de-shadowing methods in remote sensing. Chin. Geogra. Sci. **23**, 403–420 (2013). https://doi.org/10.1007/s11769-013-0613-x
9. Arellano, P.: Missing information in remote sensing: wave-let approach to detect and remove clouds and their shadows. Enshede, the Netherlands: International Institute Geo-Information. Science and Earth Observation (2003)
10. Malinverni, E.S., Fangi, G.: Comparative cluster analysis to localize emergencies in archaeology. J. Cult. Heritage **10**, e10–e19 (2009)
11. Parcak, S.H.: Satellite Remote Sensing for Archaeology. Routledge, London (2009)
12. Alexakis, D., Agapiou, A., Hadjimitsis, D., Sarris, A.: Remote sensing applications in archaeological research. Remote Sens.-Appl. 435–462 (2012)
13. Pavlidis, L.: High resolution satellite imagery for archaeological application (2005)
14. Casana, J., Laugier, E.J.: Satellite imagery-based monitoring of archaeological site damage in the Syrian civil war. PloS One **12**(11), e0188589 (2017)
15. Jin, X., Davis, C.H.: Automated building extraction from high resolution satellite imagery in urban areas using structural, contextual, and spectral information. EURASIP J. Appl. Sig. Process. **14**, 2196–2206 (2005)
16. Polodorio, A.M., Flores, F.C., Imai, N.N., Tommaselli, A.M.G., Franco, C.: Automatic shadow segmentation in aerial color images. In: Proceedings of XVI Brazilian Symposium on Computer Graphics and Image Processing, pp. 270–277 (2003)
17. Abraham, L., Sasikumar, M.: An efficient shadow detection method for high resolution satellite images. In: 2012 Third International Conference on Computing, Communication and Networking Technologies (ICCCNT 2012), pp. 1–5. IEEE (2012)
18. Zhang, H., Sun, K., Li, W.: Object-oriented shadow detection and removal from urban high-resolution remote sensing images. IEEE Trans. Geosci. Remote Sens. **52**(11), 6972–6982 (2014)
19. Tsai, V.: A comparative study on shadow compensation of color aerial images in invariant color models. IEEE Trans. Geosci. Remote Sens. **44**, 1661–1671 (2006). https://doi.org/10.1109/TGRS.2006.869980
20. Otsu, N.: A threshold selection method from gray level histograms. IEEE Trans. Syst. Man Cybern. **SMC-9**(1), 62–69 (1979)
21. Orlando, P., de Villa, B.: Remote sensing applications in archaeology. Archeol. Calcolatori **22**, 147–168 (2011)
22. Orazi, R.: The archaeological environmental park of sennacherib's irrigation network. Recording, Conservation and Management of the Cultural Heritage of the Northern Region of Iraqi Kurdistan. Italian Archaeological Mission to the Kurdistan Region of Iraq. Monographs 1, Forum, Udine (2019)
23. Kadhim, N.: Building assessment using shadow analysis for the architectural documentation. Int. Arch. Photogr. Remote Sens. Spat. Inf. Sci. (2019)

24. Han, H., et al.: A mixed property-based automatic shadow detection approach for VHR multispectral remote sensing images. Appl. Sci. **8**, 1883 (2018). https://doi.org/10.3390/app8101883
25. Pratt, W.K.: Digital Image Processing, 2nd edn. Wiley, New York (1991)
26. Smith, A.R.: Color gamut transform pairs. In: Proceedings of SIGRAPH, Atlanta, GAvol. 3, pp. 12–19. ACM (1978)
27. Smith, H.J.: Putting colors in order. Dr. Dobb's J. **1993**, 40 (1993)
28. Xiao, F., Miao, S., Guo, L.: Color image enhancement on YIQ color space. Appl. Mech. Mater. **631–632**, 478–481 (2014). https://doi.org/10.4028/www.scientific.net/AMM.631-632.478
29. Basilio, J., Torres, G., Sanchez-Perez, G., Medina, L., Perez-Meana, H.: Explicit image detection using YCbCr space color model as skin detection, pp. 123–128 (2011)

Test Case Generation Framework for Client-Server Apps: Reverse Engineering Approach

Emine Dumlu Demircioğlu[1(✉)] and Oya Kalıpsız[2]

[1] Yıldız Technical University-Borsa Istanbul, 34467 Istanbul, Turkey
eminedumlu@gmail.com
[2] Yıldız Technical University, 34220 Istanbul, Turkey
oyakalipsiz@gmail.com

Abstract. In this paper, the message-driven test case generation framework is proposed for client-server architecture systems which are communicated with each other by using API messages. Basically proposed framework automatically generates test cases, which are extracted with reverse engineering mechanism from captured network packets between client-server communications over networks. We propose a novel approach to record packets for regression testing. The studying is motivated due to the fact that there is a lack of regression test automation framework in a specific domain: client-server apps which uses API messages for the communication, such as financial applications, banking applications, trading systems, real-time apps. Our approach supports the reuse of test cases and will ensure 100% automation from test case generation to execution in API regression testing for client-server applications. Our work reports the significant reuse capability and reduction of effort on a real-word financial system example.

Keywords: Software testing frameworks · Automation testing · API testing

1 Introduction

Software failures may cause havoc at banks, airlines, trading systems in the stock exchange and resulting in billions of pounds of damage. To avoid this and to develop reliable and high- quality software products, software testing is a major step within the software development process. Testing can be implemented either manually or automatically. Especially in companies using incremental development process model, the software should be developed incrementally. New requirements at each increment or changes necessitate changes in the software. Thus, testers should verify the new function as soon as possible; and before going live, effective regression tests must be applied [7]. Regression testing is selective re-testing of a system to verify that changes in the software systems have not caused side effect [10]. Accomplishing this manually is very difficult and laborious particularly in medium-size or large-size business software systems, since such systems contain hundreds of business functions and there is a need to consider a huge amount of test scenarios. So the manual creation and execution of

O. Gervasi et al. (Eds.): ICCSA 2020, LNCS 12253, pp. 674–683, 2020.
https://doi.org/10.1007/978-3-030-58814-4_54

these test scenarios would necessitate an enormous investment in human resources [5, 12]. It is also difficult to do manual API tests repeatedly because manual API testing is very time-consuming, error-prone and tedious [3, 13, 14]. Moreover, based on common experience, it is known that the success of manual testing can be affected by the personal problems or the mood of the tester on any given day. These can affect the productivity and can harm the whole project; the effects are from delay, lack of attention, decreased focus [15, 16].Therefore, we want to eliminate the human impact from repetitive testing for the systems based on client-server architecture and to speed up the release cycle. Our aim is to improve the efficiency of software testing and shorten the test cycle.

Test automation should be considered as end to end automation from test case generation to execution and defect reporting [2]. Studying on how to automatically generate test cases is a key problem in automatic software testing [11, 17]. In this study, we decided to automate the manual API regression testing process for the systems based on client-server architecture. To be able to do this, we have divided our studying into the three parts: The first part is test case generation automatically, the second one is test execution of created test cases automatically, and the last part is validation and defect reporting. Our approach supports the reuse of test cases and will ensure 100% automation in API regression testing for client-server applications. Such automation takes the cumbersome of doing manual tests from testers. In this paper, how test cases are generated automatically will be shown.

In Sect. 2, we continue by providing necessary background information for understanding the proposed systems and discuss the related work. Next, Sect. 3 describes the proposed framework, Sect. 4 describes the empirical studies, and Sect. 5 presents concluding remarks and future work.

2 Background and Related Work

Figure 1 shows the targeting system architecture. There can be many client applications connecting to server app on the predefined ports. There is no GUI for the targeting server app. An established connection from client to server is uniquely identified by the combination of client-side and server-side IP/Port pairs. The server and clients talk over TCP or UDP using a well-defined messaging format. TCP is a reliable connection-oriented protocol designed to send data packets over the Internet. UDP is an unreliable connectionless protocol that run on top of IP. Communication between client and server is established by using TCP or UDP data packets. Each data packet has header and payload sections. The header section contains Source/Destination Port information. In addition, the TCP header also has sequence numbers to keep track of how much data has been sent. The payload section contains data (API messages) carried for the application [11].

The approach uses information at the packet level and produces test cases. So, we will use the Wireshark tool to obtain communication data packets between client-server applications. This tool is a free and open source packet analyzer tool.

Packets between client and server are captured in a PCAPs (Packet Captures) file by using Wireshark. The PCAPs file is a data file composed of packet data of network traffic and captures client's profile (actual usage data produced by the client). Each packets in the

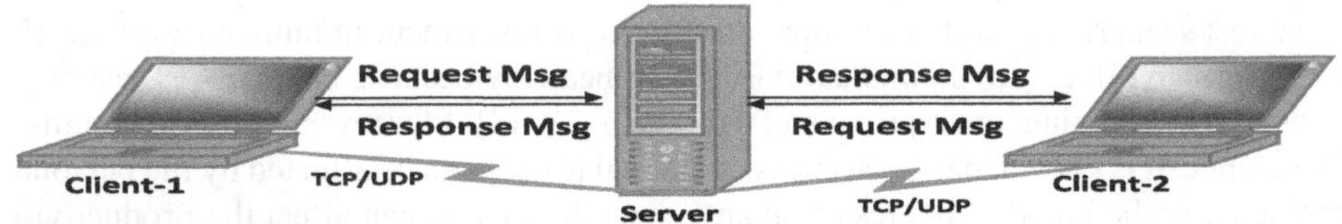

Fig. 1. Client-server architecture

PCAPs file displays the communication data packets including API messages between client and server applications.

A large number of large enterprises such as airlines (e.g. real-time flight updates), banks (e.g. mobile apps) or government apps have been using APIs to provide services such as data queries and functionalities [21]. However, dynamic characteristics of APIs raise new threats to the quality of systems. A defect in an open API may cause software failures in a large scale. API testing is thus becoming necessary to ensure the quality and reliability of APIs for individual services. API testing is a type of testing that involves testing Application Programming Interface and of great importance to ensure functionality, reliability and delivery of business logic. API testing is performed at the message layer because APIs lack a graphical user interface. The existing API testing tools are mostly for Web APIs which can be accessed using HTTP protocol; especially REST (Representational State Transfer) API are most widely employed APIs [4, 6, 14]. REST-based web applications basically use JSON or XML formats to deliver REST API responses [14]. These are not suitable for our proposed targeting systems and its message structure in terms of usability. The proposed system is not a Web Server and does not support JSON or XML formats. It can have its own message structure and can have its own application layer protocols instead of HTTP protocol. In many cases, the input messages to an API call depends on the response messages obtained from other API call. Existing API testing tools does not support extracting input from response [14], hence not provide 100% automation. In proposed framework, we will parse response message coming from server and use it for the next input message when specifying input data. So we will increase the automation.

According to the purpose of testing, there are different types of test automation tools. For example, if there is a web application and functional tests are conducted to validate the application, the Selenium tool can be selected. To do a functional test, the tester writes test scripts code using Selenium IDE and performs automation testing or JMeter IDE can be selected to conduct load testing. These are mostly for web, mobile and desktop applications. In order to implement third-party testing tools, the tester should develop test script code to adapt the existing test automation to the desired system. Test script code requires a maintenance process which is a costly one [3] and is very difficult for the tester. The tester needs to update the test script code when there are changes in any requirement. We would like to eliminate test script code development and the maintenance process.

In addition, existing API tools have some shortcomings like high overhead, long test data preparation and difficulty in reuse [18–20]. Creation of test cases is done manually by existing API tools. TCP packets which payload section contains API messages are send to the targeting systems. But the API messages in the test cases can have volatile values. So these values should be extracted and changed not to face assertion failures when executing test cases by using such tools. Our approach solves this problem.

In this endeavor, we have proposed a regression testing framework for large-scale client-server applications based on a capturing packet at the network level, followed with the analysis and re-constructing of the information in the messages. Thus, this paper suggests a reverse engineering approach for information at the packet level to create regression testing test cases. The idea here is to capture the usage data at packet level to ensure they are more application independent. Actually, this process is the easiest method to obtain different requests from various clients.

3 Message-Driven Regression Test Case Generation Framework

In this section, we have described the main workflow of proposed framework. It is developed in Java by using pkts.io open source library in [1] to read the PCAPs file. The input file to the framework is a PCAPs file in which data packets between client-server apps are captured. This file is then analyzed, and reverse engineering is used to determine values sent back and forth between the server and the client. Basically, the framework reads the PCAPs file and produces test suite, which is a collection of test cases, to replay PCAPs file through the targeting test system. Each test case in the test suite contains both messages sent by the client and the responding messages sent by the server to the client. The framework does this mapping according to the Source IP/Port, Destination IP/Port information to create test suite.

When the time data packet in the PCAPs file is read, the framework starts to analyze the packet. Initially, it detects which transport layer protocols (TCP or UDP) were used in the communication. If TCP is used, the framework analyses the packet to determine whether the packet is retransmitted. Each packet has sequence number and payload section which stores the data carried for the packet. To be able to detect whether or not the packet is retransmitted, sequence numbers on the packet and payload section length are used. The sequence number of the next package is calculated by summing the sequence number of the current packet and the length of the payload section. If the sequence number of the next packet is less than calculated sequence number, this packet is marked as a retransmitted packet and retransmitted data portion is calculated. This means that the original version of the retransmitted data portion is already stored in the memory. Hence, we ignored retransmitted packets when creating the list of test cases. Since UDP is a connectionless protocol, retransmissions are not handled. After detecting communication protocol, heuristic search techniques are applied to detect which application layer protocols for the targeting systems are used. The determined message patterns according to the targeting systems are searched in the payload section of the packet. For example, according to the FIX protocol [8], each protocol message starts with "8 = FIXT" and ends with "10 = XYZ". When determining the used protocol (for example FIX), below search pattern in java can be applied:

Pattern.compile("8 = FIXT.*?\\x0110 = .{3}\\x01")

Other search patterns can be specified for the targeting systems. After detecting used application layer protocols, the payload section which contains data in the packet is extracted and parsed according to the predefined messaging format of the software system in question. When composing a message, we took into consideration the fact that the payload section may have been fragmented, because the payload section has the maximum size of data payload. If the fragmentation is detected in the packet, the payload section will first be stored in the memory and then reassembled with the next packet's payload section. After reassembly, data in the payload section is parsed according to the predefined messaging format of the software system in question. Finally, information such as arrival time, Src/Dst IP/Port of the packet, and messages in that packet will be included within the packet. Consequently, the final obtained packet is mapped to understand whether the packet is a client message which is a request message sent by the client to the server, or a server message which is a response message sent by the server to the client. Given the previous discussion our basic algorithm should now be easy to follow. Algorithm 1 describes the main createTestSuite routine that loops until the end of PCAPs file, making a call to getNextPacket to get a packet in the file once per iteration. After extracting packet details like Arrival Time, Src/Dst IP/Port and used protocol (TCP or UDP) by calling extractPacketDetail (packet), it makes a call to constructMessagesInThePacket to create messages in the packet according to the pre-defined messaging format of the targeting software system. Finally, we add the created messages to the test suite by mapping as request or response messages making a call to addToTestSuite (messages). These approach can be applied to different business domains by implementing only constructMessagesInThePacket (packet) method for the targeting system's message structure. With this approach, test cases can be generated at packet level automatically. This was the first motivation of our study.

Algorithm 1 – createTestSuite
Input: pcapFile: Pcap File **1.** **repeat** **2.** packet ← getNextPacket(); **3.** extractPacketDetail(packet); **4.** messages ← constructMessagesInThePacket(packet); **5.** addToTestSuite(messages); **6.** **until** end of pcapFile

Some protocol contains various packets which are related to an environment thus they cannot be reused. For example, HTTP response contains last-modified time of target page, response date, or session information which are volatile. Saving whole packets without any analysis may cause assertion failures because of these volatile values. To realize record and replay automation, it is required to extracting these kinds of environment related values. Therefore, the extraction of application layer packets is done instead of saving and resending whole TCP/UDP packets. Hence, in the second part of this studying which will be replaying part, volatile values will be identified and extracted for these test cases not to face assertion failures.

4 Case Study

We conducted a set of empirical studies to evaluate the usability of the proposed test automation framework and applied it to the trading system in the Borsa Istanbul Stock Exchange. FIX and OUCH Protocols are used as an API Protocols by trading system.

Table 1. Selected Sample Test Cases from Testsuite.pcap File for OUCH protocol

Test id	Send message from client to server	Receive messages from server
1	Soup packet type: login request [ABCEH4,XXXXXX,TR2602280,3]	Soup packet type: login accepted [TR2602280,0]
2	Soup packet type: client heartbeat	Soup packet type: server heartbeat
3	Soup packet type: unsequenced data [**O**, 253588, 70798, Buy, 10, 600,,NoChange, MRG, REF, 12345, 0, Client, Normalhours]	Soup packet type: sequence data [**A**, 253588, 70798, Buy, 7153059811473522662, NoChange, MRG, OnBook, REF, 12345, 10, 0, Client, Normalhours]
4	Soup packet type: client heartbeat	Soup packet type: server heartbeat
5	Soup packet type: unsequenced data [**U**, 253588, 253589, 100, 0, NoChange, 0, Empty]	Soup packet type: sequence data [**U**, 253589, 253588, 70798, Buy, 7153059811473522662, 100, 600, NoChange, MRG, OnBook, REF, 12345, 100, 0, Client]
6	Soup packet type: unsequenced data [**X**, 253588]	Soup packet type: sequence data [**C**, 253590, 70798, Buy, 7153059811473522662, Canceled]
7	Soup packet type: unsequenced data [**Y**, 70798, Buy, 7153059811473522662]	Soup packet type: sequence data [**J**, Rejected]
8	Soup packet type: logout request	Soup packet type: logout response

FIX is the standard protocol for exchanges within the finance world as it is considered the standard method to communicate trading information electronically between brokers, buy-side institutions, and markets. The FIX Protocol language is comprised of a series of messaging specifications used in trade communications [8]. OUCH is a simple protocol that allows trading users to enter orders, cancel and replace existing orders and receive executions. The OUCH protocol is composed of logical messages passed between the OUCH host and the client application [9]. There is a huge number of functionalities/scenarios in order to test systems which use the FIX and OUCH protocols as a message infrastructure. These two protocols have completely different message structures and these are application layer protocols.

Table 2. Selected Sample Test Cases from TestSuite.pcap File for FIX protocol

Test id	Send message from client to server	Receive messages from server
1	***8 = FIXT.1.1*** 9 = 160 **35 = D** 34 = 39 49 = BIABC 50 = F61 52 = 20190719-14:31:06.843 56 = TEST 1 = ACC 11 = 40359 38 = 20 40 = 2 44 = 11.000 54 = 1 55 = XXX.E 59 = 0 60 = 20190719-14:31:06.843 70 = AAA 528 = A ***10 = 044***	***8 = FIXT.1.1*** 9 = 264 35 = 8 34 = 45 49 = TEST 52 = 20190719-14:31:07.002 56 = BIABC 57 = F61 1 = ACC 6 = 0 11 = 40359 14 = 0 17 = 152 22 = M 37 = 6363BF0000008101 38 = 20.0000000 39 = 0 40 = 2 44 = 11.0000000 48 = 70616 54 = 1 55 = XXX.E 151 = 20.0000000 528 = A ***10 = 032***
2	**8 = FIXT.1.1** 9 = 160 **35 = D** 34 = 40 49 = BIABC 50 = F61 52 = 20190719-14:31:09.810 56 = TEST 1 = ACC 11 = 40360 38 = 20 40 = 2 44 = 11.000 54 = 1 55 = XXX.E 59 = 0 60 = 20190719-14:31:09.810 70 = AAA 528 = A **10 = 022**	**8 = FIXT.1.1** 9 = 264 35 = 8 34 = 48 49 = TEST 52 = 20190719-14:31:09.967 56 = BIABC 57 = F61 1 = ACC 6 = 0 11 = 40360 14 = 0 17 = 157 22 = M 37 = 6363BF0000008105 38 = 20.0000000 39 = 0 40 = 2 44 = 11.0000000 48 = 70616 54 = 1 55 = XXX.E 59 = 0 60 = 20190719-14:31:09.962 70 = AAA 119 = 220.0000000 150 = 0 151 = 20.0000000 528 = A **10 = 054**
3	**8 = FIXT.1.1** 9 = 188 **35 = G** 49 = BIABC 56 = TEST 50 = F61 34 = 42 52 = 20190719-14:31:16.492 43 = N 37 = 6363BF0000008105 41 = NONE 11 = 40362 55 = XXX.E 60 = 20190719-14:31:16.492 38 = 27 59 = 0 54 = 1 40 = 2 44 = 11.000 **10 = 035**	**8 = FIXT.1.1** 9 = 000302 35 = 8 49 = TEST 56 = BIABC 34 = 50 57 = F61 52 = 20190719-14:31:16.645 37 = 6363BF0000008105 11 = 40362 17 = 89485 150 = 5 39 = 0 1 = ACC 55 = XXX.E 48 = 423253 22 = M 54 = 1 38 = 27.0000000 40 = 2 44 = 11.000 59 = 0 151 = 27.0000000 14 = 0 6 = 0 60 = 20190719-14:31:16.492 **10 = 166**
4	**8 = FIXT.1.1** 9 = 149 **35 = F** 34 = 41 49 = BIABC 50 = F61 52 = 20190719-14:31:15.492 56 = TEST 11 = 40361 37 = 6363BF0000008105 38 = 20 41 = NONE 54 = 1 55 = XXX.E 60 = 20190719-14:31:15.492 **10 = 184**	**8 = FIXT.1.1** 9 = 224 35 = 8 34 = 49 49 = TEST 52 = 20190719-14:31:15.645 56 = BIABC 57 = F61 1 = ACC 6 = 0 11 = 40361 14 = 0 17 = 158 22 = M 37 = 6363BF0000008105 38 = 20.0000000 39 = 4 41 = 40360 48 = 70616 54 = 1 55 = XXX.E 60 = 20190719-14:31:15.644 70 = AAA 150 = 4 151 = 0 528 = A **10 = 252**

4.1 Preparation of Data

Market experts and testers in Borsa Istanbul designate a list of test cases via exploratory testing. Test case design conducted manually based on human knowledge is known as exploratory testing [2]. While testers execute prepared test cases manually towards to the system under test (SUT), the network packets are captured via the Wireshark tool. Thus, we obtained PCAPs files and introduced them to the proposed framework.

Another method of obtaining the PCAPs file is getting it from production environment instead of creating it manually. So real data is obtained and test cases are created from real data.

4.2 Analysis of Proposed Framework

In this study, we have one PCAPs file named TestSuite.pcap which contains both FIX and OUCH protocol messages. The proposed framework absorbs this file as input and produces separate test suites for each different protocols. Table 1 demonstrates the selected output of the test case generation framework for the OUCH protocol. 8 test cases are selected to show output of the framework. Each line shows the send message from client to server and received messages from server to client as a response. In other words, when a tester deals with test case 1, if a Login Request packet with the specified data within the table is sent to the server; the Login Accepted Packet is received as a response. In test case 3, when Unsequenced Data Packet with the specified data within the table is sent to the server, the server should send the Sequence Data Packet with the specified values in the table. The first value of the message data is "O". It shows message type of the OUCH message. According to the OUCH protocol specification, "O" means "Enter Order" message. The response to a successful Enter Order is an Order Accepted message. According to the table, the first value of the response message is "A" which means "Order Accepted Message". The list of OUCH protocol message structure is available in [9]. Table 2 also illustrates the selected test cases produced from TestSuite.pcap file for the FIX protocol.

5 Concluding Remarks and Future Work

Software testing is a means of detecting bugs within the process of evaluating whether the software product meets specified requirements to ensure that software products have no defects and high-quality software products can be produced. Repetitive manual testing is time consuming, tedious and error prone. Automation testing overcomes the difficulties of manual testing and is the best method to improve accuracy, test coverage, efficiency and speed up the testing process. Hence, we have aimed to automate the manual API regression tests for client-server applications. With this objective, the message-driven regression test case generation framework was developed. With this framework, test case generation has become automatically for the systems based on client server architecture such as trading systems in the stock exchange and banking applications. The rationale behind this message-driven test automation framework is the fact that test data is stored in the "PCAPs File. With this framework, we increase the automation in API testing by generating test cases automatically. We can replay whole PCAPs files to the system being tested and subsequently simulate and validate the client's behavior by using real data in production environment using production PCAPs file towards the system under test. Replaying and validating part will be next part of the study. We are planning to replay the whole PCAPs file to the SUT with validation by using the produced test case list from the proposed framework. In order to accomplish this, we intend to determine validation methods for the system.

Acknowledgments. This study was supported by Borsa Istanbul of Turkey.

References

1. Java Library for reading and writing PCAPs. https://github.com/aboutsip/pkts
2. Garousi, V., Elberzhager, F.: Test automation: not just for test execution. IEEE Softw. **34**(2), 90–96 (2017). https://doi.org/10.1109/ms.2017.34
3. Liu, Z., Chen, Q., Jiang, X.: A maintainability spreadsheet-driven regression test automation framework. In: IEEE 16th International Conference on Computational Science and Engineering, Sydney, NSW, pp. 1181–1184 (2013). https://doi.org/10.1109/cse.2013.175
4. Sneha, K., Malle, G.M.: Research on software testing techniques and software automation testing tools. In: 2017 International Conference on Energy, Communication, Data Analytics and Soft Computing (ICECDS), Chennai, pp. 77–81 (2017). https://doi.org/10.1109/icecds.2017.8389562
5. Sharma, R.M.: Quantitative analysis of automation and manual testing. Int. J. Eng. Innovative Technol. (IJEIT) **4**(1), 1–6 (2014)
6. Bhateja, N.: A study on various software automation testing tools. Int. J. Adv. Res. Comput. Sci. Softw. Eng. **5**(6), 1250–1252 (2015)
7. Sultanía, A.K.: Developing software product and test automation software using agile methodology. In: Proceedings of the 2015 Third International Conference on Computer, Communication, Control and Information Technology (C3IT), Hooghly, pp. 1–4 (2015)
8. FIX Protocol. https://www.borsaistanbul.com/docs/default-source/nasdaq-dokuman/genium-inet-fix-protocol-specification-.pdf?sfvrsn=46
9. OUCH Protocol. https://www.borsaistanbul.com/docs/default-source/nasdaq-dokuman/bistech-ouch-protocol-specification-va-2410.pdf?sfvrsn=8
10. Dalal, S., Solanki, K.: Challenges of regression testing: a pragmatic perspective. Int. J. Adv. Res. Comput. Sci. **9**(1), 499–503 (2018)
11. Itkonen, J., Mantyla, M.V.: Are test cases needed? Replicated comparison between exploratory and test-case based software testing. Empirical Softw. Eng. **19**(2), 303–342 (2014). https://doi.org/10.1007/s10664-013-9266-8
12. Han, X., Zhang, N., He, W., Zhang, K., Tang, L.: Automated warship software testing system based on loadrunner automation API. In: 2018 IEEE International Conference on Software Quality, Reliability and Security Companion (QRS-C), Lisbon, pp. 51–55 (2018)
13. Bangare, S., Bangare, S., Borse, S., Bangare, P., Nandedkar, S.: Automated API testing approach. Int. J. Eng. Sci. Technol. **4**, 1–4 (2012)
14. Isha, A.S., Revathi, M.: Automated API testing. In: 2018 3rd International Conference on Inventive Computation Technologies (ICICT), Coimbatore, India, pp. 788–791 (2018). https://doi.org/10.1109/icict43934.2018.9034254
15. Gonçalves, W., de Almeida, C.B., Araújo, L., Ferraz, M., Xandú, R., Junior, I.: The impact of human factors on the software testing process: the importance of these factors in a software testing environment. J. Inf. Syst. Eng. Manage. **2**, 24 (2017). https://doi.org/10.20897/jisem.201724
16. Engström, E., Runeson, P.: A qualitative survey of regression testing practices. In: Ali Babar, M., Vierimaa, M., Oivo, M. (eds.) PROFES 2010. LNCS, vol. 6156, pp. 3–16. Springer, Heidelberg (2010). https://doi.org/10.1007/978-3-642-13792-1_3
17. Fernandez-Sanz, L., Misra, S.: Practical application of UML activity diagrams for the generation of test cases. Proc. Romanian Acad. Ser. A **13**(3), 251–260 (2012)

18. Xu, D., Xu, W., Kent, M., Thomas, L., Wang, L.: An automated test generation technique for software quality assurance. IEEE Trans. Reliab. **64**(1), 247–268 (2015). https://doi.org/10.1109/tr.2014.2354172
19. Chen, Y., Gao, Y., Zhou, Y., Chen, M., Ma, X.: Design of an automated test tool based on interface protocol. In: 2019 IEEE 19th International Conference on Software Quality, Reliability and Security Companion (QRS-C), Sofia, Bulgaria, pp. 57–61 (2019). https://doi.org/10.1109/qrs-c.2019.00024
20. Aiya, K.V., Verma, H.: Keyword driven automated testing framework for web application. In: 2014 9th International Conference on Industrial and Information Systems (ICIIS), Gwalior, pp. 1–6 (2014). https://doi.org/10.1109/iciinfs.2014.7036478
21. Wang, J., Bai, X., Li, L., Ji, Z., Ma, H.: A model-based framework for cloud API testing. In: 2017 IEEE 41st Annual Computer Software and Applications Conference (COMPSAC), Turin, pp. 60–65 (2017). https://doi.org/10.1109/compsac.2017.24

A Novel Cleaning Method for Yield Data Collected by Sensors: A Case Study on Winter Cereals

Antonio Natale[1], Sara Antognelli[1(✉)], Emanuele Ranieri[1], Andrea Cruciani[1], and Antonio Boggia[2]

[1] Agricolus SRL, via Settevalli, 320, 06132 Perugia, Italy
discover@agricolus.com

[2] Department of Agricultural, Food and Environmental Sciences, University of Perugia, Borgo XX Giugno, 74, 06123 Perugia, Italy

Abstract. Winter cereals yield tracking is a common practice since decision support systems can greatly benefit from the integration of these data. However, scientific literature highlights that many systematic errors occur during yield data collection. An efficient and easy to automatize protocol to clean collected field data is still missing despite its development is essential to integrate this useful tool in a smart-farming platform.

This paper focuses on the development of a yield data cleaning procedure, easy to industrialize and performant in different contexts. This method is based on both empirical cleaning steps and statistical analysis on the "moving windows". The developed cleaning procedure enabled the mixing of data coming from different combine harvesters and considered yield data measurements from the farmers to strengthen the results. In order to create readable and complete maps, an interpolation method concludes the procedure. The developed method is applied on a case study on real farm data.

Keywords: Yield maps · Winter cereals · Smart farming · Harvest · Outlier

1 Introduction

Winter cereals are widespread cultivated and farmers often adopt smart farming solutions mainly to i) define field management strategies, ii) optimize the nitrogen fertilizations. In this context, yield maps of winter cereals are very powerful tools to reach both targets. Based on these maps, in fact, it is possible to diagnose field problems and plan new strategies. Most important, these maps could be an input of a machine-learning algorithm for the early-prediction of winter cereals yield [1].

The smart farming platform Agricolus® is integrating yield maps in its Decision Support System (DSS). Agricolus DSS collects and analyses data from different sources (field sensors, remote sensing, crop scouting) to allow farmers to take the best data-driven decision [2]. The addition of yield maps to the other information provided by the

O. Gervasi et al. (Eds.): ICCSA 2020, LNCS 12253, pp. 684–691, 2020.
https://doi.org/10.1007/978-3-030-58814-4_55

system will not just complement the data but it will be a key object in the field-specific activity planning.

However, it is known that different problems can occur in the creation of the yield map. The main one concerns the data-collection in field with yield tracking systems, since bias are very common, and they can easily lead to a dangerous misinterpretation of results. Scientific literature, in the last decades, was focused on analyzing the main causes of errors on the yield data collection [3–5]: i) *header cut-width*: errors affect the sensed area that may be generated from a) errors of the harvester in identifying "active" or "non active" cutting bar sections; b) too wide cutting bar sections for the definition of the local harvested area; ii) *header position*: errors due to the combine harvester sensor or by the driver can cause a misregistration of the header position. This determines recorded points with yield = 0; iii) *lag time (or flow delay)*: this parameter is fixed and it represent the time from the moment the cereal is cut to the moment the yield flow is measured. It is needed to associate the yield flow to the exact location. However, even if it is set accurately, it may vary depending on the field conditions, and this may cause errors in data georeferentiation. iv) *travel distance measurements*: when the combine speed is locally very irregular (stop and start) it may generate area with speed = 0 and high yield, followed by areas with high speed and low yield. This affects both the localization of yield and the sensed area; v) *GNSS Positioning errors*: yield data can have wrong coordinates due to technical errors.

Given that, an efficient protocol to clean collected field data is still missing, despite being recognized very important [4, 6–8]. The aim of this paper is to define a robust and easy to industrialize cleaning methodology for yield data collected by tracking systems. To do that, a literature review on the existing data cleaning methodologies was carried on. Then SWOT analysis was used to compare 5 papers. Then, different steps were extracted from the reviewed methods following a SWOT criterion (strength, weaknesses, opportunities and threats), and merged in a chain process. Finally, a case study was tested and evaluated.

2 Methodology

SWOT analysis was performed on 5 papers - [5, 9–12] - published from 2002 to 2019 on scientific journals (Table 1). The methodologies were analysed with the aim of understanding the robustness and the suitability of the suggested method to be automatized. In fact, the protocol should be feasible in different contexts, without recurring to local empirical knowledge. Plus, the process shouldn't require ancillary data (such as the machinery speed at harvest or the grain humidity), as they might not be always available. As the output would be provided to the final users, it should be also clearly explicable. The SWOT analysis for yield data cleaning methodologies is presented in Table 1. The definition of the cleaning protocol was based on the results of the SWOT analysis and it includes several steps.

The missing data resulted from the cleaning procedure were filled by interpolation through Inverse Distance Weighting method (IDW) [13]. The IDW parameters were: 1) Power = 2, as suggested by [13]; 2) research radius: 12 m to consider at least 3 parallel swaths, and a minimum number of points of 12, to clean properly the field borders. The spatial resolution of the final raster was set to 10 m. The resolution of the original data was reduced to create usable results, easy to manage and comparable with commonly used satellite data, like Sentinel 2, that would be used in further studies.

Table 1. SWOT analysis of selected methodologies for yield data cleaning

Reference	Strengths (S) and weaknesses (W)	Opportunities (O) and threats (T)
[5]	• Use of empirical criteria, easy to understand (S) • Calculations are easy (S) • Needs a lot of input data (W) • The user has to define many threshold values (W) • Not considering spatial relation between elements (W)	• It can be adapted to different contexts, as many criteria are user-defined (O) • Errors are easy to identify (O) • Need of local knowledge: difficult to industrialize (T) • Some criteria can be correlated, increasing the complexity of the model but not the efficacy (T)
[9]	• Use of empirical criteria, easy to understand (S) • Calculations are easy (S) • Needs a lot of input data (W) • The user has to define many threshold values (W) • Not considering spatial relation between elements (W).	• It can be adapted to different contexts, as many criteria are user-defined (O) • Errors are easy to identify (O) • Need of local knowledge: difficult to industrialize (T) • Some criteria can be correlated, increasing the complexity of the model but not the efficacy (T)
[10]	• Calculations are relatively simple, and can be made in a single step (S) • Considers spatial relations between elements (S) • Input-wise: the method only uses yield data as input (S) • Use of statistical criteria, not immediate to understand (W) • Need the definition of two thresholds by the data analyst (W)	• Easy to industrialize: no need of local knowledge (O) • The model is relatively efficient to calculate, as it only needs a single variable (O) • Statistical based: the process should be tested as the errors are not easily identifiable during the process (T)
[11]	• Considers spatial relations between elements (S) • Input-wise: the method only uses yield data as input (S) • Use of statistical criteria, not immediate to understand (W) • Calculations are relatively complex and made in many steps (W) • Need the definition of many thresholds by the data analyst (W)	• Easy to industrialize: no need of local knowledge (O) • The model is relatively efficient to calculate, as it only needs a single variable (O) • Statistical based: the process should be tested as the errors are not easily identifiable during the process (T)

(*continued*)

Table 1. *(continued)*

Reference	Strengths (S) and weaknesses (W)	Opportunities (O) and threats (T)
[12]	• Considers spatial relations between elements (S) • Input-wise: the method only uses yield data as input (S) • Use of statistical criteria, not immediate to understand (W) • Calculations are relatively complex and made in many steps (W) • Need the definition of many thresholds by the data analyst (W)	• Easy to industrialize: no need of local knowledge (O) • The model is relatively efficient to calculate, as it only needs a single variable (O) • Statistical based: the process should be tested as the errors are not easily identifiable during the process (T)

2.1 Case Study

The methodology was then tested on a case study. The experiment was conducted during 2017-2018 season, using 4 selected fields: B33 (3,45 ha), B34 (8,68 ha), B35 (6,58 ha), and B37 (7,73 ha). The fields are located nearby the Badiola farm centre, on a hilly area nearby Perugia, in the central Italy (geographic coordinates: 12,3034; 42,9986). They were all cultivated with durum wheat (Variety: Odisseo). The fields belong to the Fondazione per l'Istruzione Agraria (Perugia, Italy). They were harvested using two different models of combine harvester: CLAAS Lexion 750, and CLAAS Lexion 630 (Fig. 1).

Preliminary field exploration showed that in the north-western areas of fields B33 and B35 cereals were partially lodged. This usually represents a limit for the harvesters, as they usually encounter problems in localizing the yield correctly.

Yield data were collected through a Volume-flow sensor mounted on the harvest machines. Yield tracking was performed by YieldTrakk (YM-1) system. The resulting dataset had an irregular spatial resolution, depending on the harvester working width (varying from 1,5 and 7,7 m) and its local working speed, as the point were recorded at regular time intervals. Centimetre-level positional accuracy was ensured by the Real Time Kinematic (RTK) positioning system. Data cleaning procedure was implemented in ESRI ArcGIS Pro software. Finally yield maps were produced.

Assuming that a good cleaning methodology should increase the normality of the distribution of the yield data [10], skewness and kurtosis indices were calculated before and after the data cleaning procedure as a performance test of the procedure itself. The skewness and kurtosis indexes assume respectively value of 0 and 3 in case of normal distribution.

Fig. 1. Map of the case study fields. The field areas harvested with different machines are highlighted *(Blue: CLAAS Lexion 630; Green: CLAAS Lexion 750).* (Color figure online)

3 Results and Discussion

Based on the results of SWOT analysis, a data cleaning method based on 6 steps has been defined:

1. Removal of null points: points where yield = 0 were eliminated from the dataset [5, 9, 12];
2. Removal of overlapping points, with the same yield value
3. Application of the cleaning data method suggested by [10]. This method is based on the concept of "moving window": each point is classified as "outlier" or "non outlier" based on values related to the points included in a circular neighborhood, defined by radius = R. The method includes the following steps:

   a. Definition of coefficient of maximum variation (CVmax - threshold of acceptability of the coefficient of variation): 20% was used [10]
   b. Definition of R of neighborhood: [10] suggested to use 1,5 times the working width as a radius, to ensure that at least 3 working width are used. A 12 m radius have been used in the experiment.
   c. Calculation of the number of points included in the neighborhood (N)
   d. Calculation of coefficient of variation (CV) of the points included in the neighborhood.

Fig. 2. Yield data (t/ha) of the fields included in the case study. A: raw yield; B: clean yield data; C: interpolated yield.

   e. Calculation of the number of points with CV > CVmax within the neighborhood (NCVmax).
   f. Definition of the outlier: points where N = NCVmax are identified as outlier.

4. Removal of points not included in the numeric interval between ($\mu - 3\sigma$) and ($\mu + 3\sigma$) [12] where μ is the population mean and σ the standard deviation;
5. Co-registration between different combine harvesters. Yield values of one combine harvester were varied proportionally to the difference between the mean of the yield recorded by the two different combines working on the same field.
6. Post-calibration of the co-registered yield with the measured yield (at the mill), where values were varied proportionally to the difference between the two means

Cleaned yield maps show a clear visual improvement of the yield data collected (Fig. 2). The method eliminated most of the values located in the areas of the field where lodging occurred, where the data recorded by the harvester combine resulted very locally variable. However, the interpolation filled the missing data coherently with the spatial trends observed in the original data. The post-calibration step avoided the risk of overestimating or underestimating the average yield per field.

Data distribution started with a skewness index ranging from 0,79 and 20,61 and a kurtosis ranging from 1,60 and 860,86 in the different fields. After the data cleaning, skewness ranged between 0,20 and 0,53, while kurtosis ranged between 2,81 and 3,88 after the implementation of the 6 steps (Table 2).

Table 2. Skewness and kurtosis indices of the yield data distribution in each test field before and after the application of the data cleaning procedure (harvester combine model is reported in parentheses).

Field name	Skewness before data cleaning (L630)	Kurtosis before data cleaning (L630)	Skewness before data cleaning (L750)	Kurtosis before data cleaning (L750)	Skewness after data cleaning	Kurtosis after data cleaning
B33	9,03	142,85	1,16	3,06	0,53	3,88
B34	20,61	860,86	5,74	112,71	0,23	3,77
B35	5,94	52,69	0,79	1,67	0,24	2,81
B37	2,57	20,42	2,06	19,46	0,20	3,12

4 Conclusion

The critical review of literature allowed the definition of a complete and flexible novel methodology for yield data cleaning. The methodology proved to be effective in eliminating most of the yield data errors. Plus, it is easily automatable as it is mainly based on statistical calculation rather than local knowledge. The points identified as outliers were located nearby the field margin, in the manoeuvring area of the tractor, as well as in the centre of the field, especially in the north-western area, where the yield appeared lower and irregular. In this area, in fact, the crop was damaged during the season by wind and hail. This specific problem clearly influenced the results obtained in fields B33, B35 and B37. Field B34 was less influenced by atmospheric events. Consequently, the number of outliers was lower.

The methodology is being tested on a wider dataset, including yield data of around 400 ha of winter cereals, harvested in 2018, 2019 and 2020, giving promising results. Then, further studies will be needed to test and improve it. After this stage, the procedure would be implemented in the Agricolus platform, to give to the farmer a powerful tool to produce correct and easy to read yield maps from the different combine harvester they may use in their fields.

Acknowledgements. We acknowledge Mr. Mauro Brunetti of the Foundation for Agricultural Education of Perugia for his very helpful and valuable support and collaboration in the data collection activities, and the University of Perugia to have supported the research activities as part of the PhD programme.

Funding. This research was developed within the framework of the project "RTK 2.0—Prototipizzazione di una rete RTK e di applicazioni tecnologiche innovative per l'automazione dei processi colturali e la gestione delle informazioni per l'agricoltura di precisione"—RDP 2014–2020 of Umbria—Meas. 16.1—App. 84250020256.

References

1. Luque Reyes, J.R., et al.: Early prediction of winter cereals yield. In: Global IoT Summit (GIoTS). IEEE (2020)
2. Guidotti, D., Marchi, S., Antognelli, S., Cruciani, A.: Water management: agricolus tools integration. In: Global IoT Summit (GIoTS). IEEE (2019)
3. Luck, J.D., Fulton, J.D.: Best management practices for collecting accurate yield data and avoing errors during harvest. University of Nebraska Cooperative extension, Institute of Agriculture and Natural Resources (2004)
4. Adamchuck, V.I., Dobermann, A., Ping, J.: Listening to the story told by yield maps. University of Nebraska Cooperative extension, EC 04-704 (2004)
5. Sudduth, K.A., Drummond, S.T.: Yield editor: software for removing errors from crop yield maps. Agron. J. **99**, 1471–1482 (2007)
6. Arslan, S., Colvin, T.S.: Grain yield mapping: yield sensing, yield reconstruction, and errors. Precis. Agric. **3**, 135–154 (2002)
7. Kharel, T., et al.: Yield monitor data cleaning is essential for accurate corn grain/silage yield determination. Agron. J. **111**, 509–516 (2018)
8. Blackmore, S.: The interpretation of trends from multiple yield maps. Comput. Electron. Agric. **26**(1), 37–51 (2000)
9. Kleinjan, J., Clay, D.E., Carlson, C.G., Clay, S.A.: Developing productivity zones from multiple years of yield monitor data. Site-Specific Management Guidelines (SSMG) Series, International Plant Nutrition Institute (IPNI) (2002)
10. Spekken, M., Anselmi, A.A., Molin, J.P.: A simple method for filtering spatial data. In: 9th European Conference on Precision Agriculture, ECPA (2013)
11. Maldaner, L., Corrêdo, L., Rodrigues Tavares, T., Mendez, L.G., Duarte, C., Molin, J.: Identifying and filtering out outliers in spatial datasets. In: 14th International Conference on Precision Agriculture, Montreal, Quebec, Canada (2018)
12. Vega, A., Córdoba, M., Castro-Franco, M., Balzarini, M.: Protocol for automating error removal from yield maps. Precis. Agric. **20**(5), 1030–1044 (2019). https://doi.org/10.1007/s11119-018-09632-8
13. Souza, E., Bazzi, C., Khosla, R., Uribe, O.M., Reich, R.M.: Interpolation type and data computation of crop yield maps is important for precision crop production. J. Plant Nutr. **39**, 531–538 (2016)

Physical and Numerical Models of Atmospheric Urban Dispersion of Pollutants

D. Toscano[3](✉), M. Marro[1], B. Mele[2], F. Murena[3], and P. Salizzoni[1]

[1] Laboratoire de Mécanique des Fluides et d'Acoustique, University of Lyon, CNRS UMR 5509 Ecole Centrale de Lyon, INSA Lyon Ecully, Lyon, France

[2] Department of Industrial Engineering, University of Naples "Federico II", Naples, Italy

[3] Department of Chemical Material and Production Engineering, University of Naples "Federico II", Naples, Italy

domenico.toscano@unina.it

Abstract. In this paper the application of numerical and physical models for the simulation of airborne pollutants in urban areas are presented. The assessment of the impact of cruise ships during the hoteling phase in the port of Naples is considered as case study. A physical model of the urban area of Naples has been realized (scale 1:500) and tested in the wind tunnel facility of the Ecole Central de Lyon. Results of wind tunnel tests are compared with CALPUFF and CFD simulations with the aim to validate the performances of the models. The results obtained give useful information for an optimized use of dispersion models.

Keywords: Air pollution · Physical models · Numerical models

1 Introduction

Urban air pollution is still a challenging task for the scientific community even though it is studied since several decades. Moreover, it is ever more a topic of current interest mainly due to the implications with human health but also with the preservation of historical heritage and natural systems. Some relevant political and sanitary events but also break-through in the human life-style have also direct implications with air pollution in urban areas. Examples are the terrorist threat, in the last years, and the SARS-CoV-2 pandemic in these days. They are new challenges to scholars of air pollution broadening the issues to be faced. Other feature of air pollution in urban areas is often the immediate contact with policy-makers, media and public opinion who have typically different ways of thinking and scale of time of answer with respect to researchers.

The first task in modelling air pollution was represent the urban canopies are a network of interconnected cavities. The main phenomena occurring are: pollutant emission from local sources present in the cavity, turbulent dispersion inside the cavity with chemical and physical phenomena like chemical reactions, deposition, coagulation and evaporation and, finally, mass exchange with the surrounding atmosphere at roof top level and cross-roads.

O. Gervasi et al. (Eds.): ICCSA 2020, LNCS 12253, pp. 692–699, 2020.
https://doi.org/10.1007/978-3-030-58814-4_56

The first attempt to model urban canopies was the definition of the "ideal street canyon": a cavity between buildings shaped like two parallelepipeds of same and constant height and infinite length with perpendicular wind [1]. It enables to highlight a fundamental geometrical parameter, the aspect ratio (AR) H/W, where H is the building height and W the road width. Street canyon are classified as: low-rise street canyon when AR < 0.7; regular street canyon when AR is in the range 0.7–1.5; and deep (or narrow) street canyon if AR > 1.5.

The first fluid dynamics studies showed as, in function of the aspect ratio, different flow regimes occur in the ideal canyon: isolated roughness flow, wake interference flow and skimming flow [2]. The skimming flow regime takes place in deep street canyons.

The bulk of the above-roof flow does not penetrate the canyon and a single vortex forms when 0.7 < H/W < 1.6 – 2 while if H/W > 1.6, the street canyon is classified as deep [3] and two or more counter-rotating vortices may form [4], with the bottom vortex weaker than the upper one.

For real canyons a second aspect ratio was defined H/L where L is the length of the road between two consecutives crossroads. Real street canyons are then subdivided into: short L/H = 3; medium L/H = 5; and long canyons L/H = 7. If the buildings that line the road have approximately the same height, the urban streets are defined symmetrical canyons, otherwise asymmetrical [3].

More sophisticated representations of street canyon require the use of parameters like building frontal area density and planar area density or packing density [5].

In recent years, with the increased of computing power and of the development and availability of GIS technologies the urban areas are represented as they are without any idealization, apart from a schematization of the real shape of buildings. However, this approach is still not feasible for large areas and several emitting or meteorological scenarios.

First models developed to simulate dispersion of pollutants in urban areas were at street scale level and were box models or operational models: STREET [6], CPBM0 [7] and OSPM [8]. The key parameter of these models was the mass transfer rate between the street canyon and the above atmosphere. Many papers as Salizzoni et al. [9], Murena et al. [10], Chung and Liu [11], Yaghoobian et al. [12], have been dedicated to evaluate it as a function of external forcing like wind speed, wind angle with street axis and incoming turbulence In many cases mass transfer rate has been evaluated using a reference velocity. In the OSPM model [13], when H/W > 1, the concentration of pollutant in the street canyon is evaluated as:

$$c = \frac{Q}{W\sigma_{wt}}$$

where σ_{wt} is the canyon ventilation velocity equal to $0.1u_w$ where u_w is wind speed at the top of the canyon. In the model developed by Soulhac et al. [14] the mass transfer velocity is proportional to friction velocity u*. Soulhac et al. [14] observed that better results are obtained when an urban canopy, more similar to real conditions, is considered if the box model equation is modified as

$$c = \frac{Q + Q_{up}}{u_w WH + u_d WL}$$

where Q_{up} is the mass flux entering in the canyon from the upwind intersection and L is the street length.

Gaussian models, developed to simulate dispersion of point sources (chimney) in industrial areas (ISC, AERMOD, CALPUFF), find application also in urban areas. In this case, the urban canopy is described assuming a surface roughness depending on the building height and density. These models have the advantage of a simple use and low computing time. They are especially adopted to simulate dispersion from point source and to assess their impact inside the urban areas. Typical example are emissions from industrial activities, waste incinerators and more recently ship emissions in ports [15, 16].

To specifically deal with dispersion phenomena associated to the dispersion within urban areas other models have been developed. An example is ADMS [17] that is essentially a Gaussian like models as AERMOD, but integrating a module to take into account the 'street-canyon effect' [18], i.e. pollutant retention within a narrow street, induced by is reduced ventilation (the module is activated when the street aspect ratio H/W is larger than 0.5). Another example is SIRANE [19], which instead includes a specific dispersion model simulating the pollutant transport within the urban canopy.

Other than the 'street-canyon effect' SIRANE simulates the horizontal advective transfer along the street axes and the pollutant dispersion at street intersections.

In the development and verification of these urban operational pollutant dispersion models, wind tunnel experiments are an essential tool. On one side they allow for an investigation of the phenomena that are responsible of the pollutant transfer, depending on the geometrical characteristics of the domain [9, 20–22]. On the other, they provide data sets that can be subsequently used to evaluate the accuracy of the dispersion models in prediction time-averaged concentrations [23–25].

To simulate pollutant dispersion at local scale in both ideal and real cases, computational fluid dynamics (CFD) is extensively used. CFD results provide insight into the role played by several parameters: wind velocity; aspect ratio; different height of buildings. Murena and Mele [26] applied the incompressible formulation of the RANS–URANS equations adopting second–order central schemes in space and time and a k–ω SST turbulence model. 3D CFD simulations were performed by Murena and Mele [27] adopting the scale adaptive simulation (SAS) model that can be ascribed to the category of hybrid models. In recent years, the large eddy simulation (LES) approach has been frequently applied to this topic. Chung and Liu [11] in a LES study on a 2D idealized canyon evaluated ventilation and pollutant removal, determining the following parameters: air exchange rate (ACH) and pollutant exchange rate (PCH).

This paper presents first results of a comparison between the experiments performed in wind tunnel with the results obtained with CFD and CALPUFF simulations.

2 The Case Study

2.1 The Area

More than 4 million people live in the Metropolitan Area of Naples (Fig. 1) which has an extension of 171 km^2 and a density of 2,649 inhabitants/km^2. Often limit values established by the European Community for the protection of human health are exceeded by NO_2, PM10, Ozone and Benzene as reported by the Higher Institute for Environmental Protection and Research (ISPRA) in the Annual Report on the Quality of the Urban Environment [28].

The port of Naples with an annual traffic of 5×10^5 TEU, 6×10^6 millions of passengers and 48,000 vessels is one of main sources of some primary pollutants in the urban area of Naples. The assessment of the contribution of the ship emissions in the port of Naples is object of some published papers such as Prati et al. [15] and Murena et al. [16].

2.2 The Wind Tunnel Experiment

The experiments were performed in the atmospheric wind tunnel of the LMFA at the Ecole Centrale de Lyon. This is a recirculating wind tunnel with a working section measuring 14 m long, 3.7 m wide and about 2 m height. The air temperature in the wind tunnel is regulated so that its variations during a 1-day experiment can be maintained in the range ±0.5 °C. A neutrally-stratified boundary layer was generated by combining the effect of a grid turbulence and a row of spires, placed at the beginning of the test section, and roughness elements on the floor. The spires were of the Irwin [29] type with a height H = 0.5 m, spaced by a distance H/2. Hot-wire constant temperature anemometer and fast flame ionization detector were used as techniques to investigate respectively flow fields and concentration levels. Ethane was used as tracer since it has a density like air.

The modelled area extends for about 1.2 km^2 and scale model is 1:500. Receptor points are 37 (Fig. 1). Scenario tested is: wind direction blowing from South-East; velocity ratio $u_s/u_h = 1$ (u_s is funnel gas velocity and u_h is wind velocity at stack height); emissions by three cruise ships at hotelling.

The model of the urban area of Naples reproduced in the wind tunnel and a map with the position of sampling point in the wind tunnel experiments are reported in Fig. 1.

2.3 CALPUFF and CFD Simulations

The fluid dynamic experimental conditions realised in the wind tunnel were reproduced with CALMET. SO_2 emission rates were calculated as the product of the emission factors for the power applied in the hotelling phase by each ship. The S content in the fuel was assumed at 0.1% by weight following a resolution by the Port Authority of Naples.

CFD simulations have been performed adopting ANSYS fluent software. The computational domain is 7 $km^2 \times$ 1 km height, ships and buildings reproduce the wind tunnel model. A multiblock mapped mesh of about 10 million hexahedral cells with refinements at the walls has been generated. The incompressible formulation of the Reynolds Averaged Navier-Stokes (RANS) equations with k-ω SST turbulence model have been employed together with species transport equations (air-SO_2 mixture), neglecting chemical reactions and thermal effects. These settings well reproduce the wind tunnel configuration.

Fig. 1. Model of the urban area of Naples reproduced in wind tunnel experiments (up) and map of Naples with the locations of sampling points in the wind tunnel experiments (bottom)

3 Results

The main input data of CALPUFF simulations (Q_{SO_2}, H_f, D_f, WD) are reported in Table 1. H_f (funnel height from sea level) and D_f (funnel diameter) were scaled by a factor 1/500 to design the WT test. The flow field parameters measured during WT tests (WS_f wind speed at funnel height, u* and z_0) are also reported in Table 1. The non-dimensionalised vertical profiles of the average wind speed and the turbulence intensity measured in WT experiments are normalized with respect to the reference height δ (z/δ) and reported in Fig. 2. These profiles were used to define the input data (WS_f, σ_v and σ_w) of CALMET/CALPUFF modelling chain to ensure the similarity of the flow fields.

Table 1. Main parameters of the wind tunnel experiments and CALPUFF simulations

Source	Q_{SO2} (g/s)	H_f (m)	D_f (m)	WS_H (m/s)	WD (deg)	u* (m/s)	Z_0 (mm)
A	0.34	30	1.1 m	3.2	135	0.13	2
B	0.89	40	1.1 m	3.4	135	0.13	2
C	0.92	40	1.1 m	3.4	135	0.13	2

Vertical concentration profiles in correspondence of the sampling points (Fig. 1) are produced to compare results obtained by wind tunnel experiments with CALPUFF and

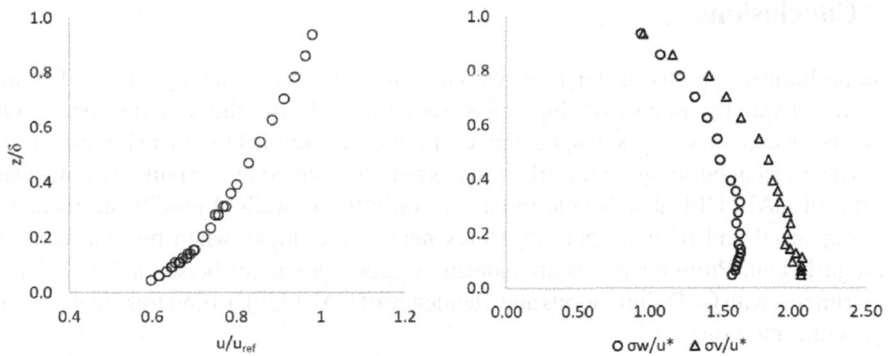

Fig. 2. Mean velocity and turbulence intensity profiles from WT experiments

CFD simulations. The ethane concentration measured in WT experiments were scaled to be compared with SO_2 concentration obtained by CALPUFF and CFD simulations. Comparison of WT experiments with CFD simulations are reported in Fig. 3 at receptor point: 1, 8, 10 and 28 sampling points (Fig. 1).

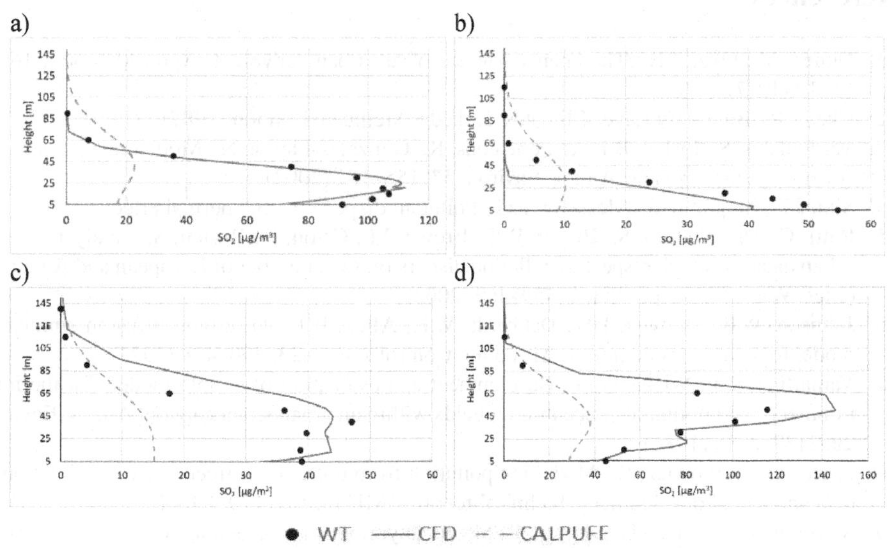

Fig. 3. Vertical Profiles of SO_2 concentration of Wind tunnel experiments, CFD and CALPUFF simulations at sampling points: a) 1; b) 8; c) 10; d) 28

As can be observed the agreement is in general quite good. The same agreement is not observed when results of wind tunnel experiments are compared with CALPUFF simulations. In fact, Fig. 3 shows how CALPUFF generally underestimates SO_2 concentrations (sampling points 1-8-10-28).

4 Conclusions

The preliminary results of our research show how the urban canopy can modify in a significant way the impact of ship emissions emitted during the hotelling phase. Our study is focused on cruise ships, but the results can be extended to other ship categories.

The effect of buildings in the urban area is not represented by the building downwash option of CALPUFF that is able to capture only the flow field modifications due to the ship itself and to some port structures near to the docks when present and if of enough height. Preliminary results indicate a good agreement between Wind Tunnel experiments with CFD simulations and a tendency of CALPUFF to underestimate ground level concentrations.

Port and port urban areas all over the world are quite different in dimensions, volume of ship traffic, meteorological conditions, orography, and relative distances. Therefore, a general rule cannot be established. However, in specific case the use of wind tunnel tests or CFD simulations can give important and quantitative information to validate dispersion models like CALPUFF increasing the precision of simulations. In this way more reliable results of studies of the assessment of the impact of ship emissions on port urban areas can be achieved.

References

1. Nunez, M., Oke, T.R.: The energy balance of an urban canyon. J. Appl. Meteorol. **16**(1), 11–19 (1977)
2. Oke, T.R.: Boundary Layer Climates, 2nd edn. Methuen, London (1987)
3. Vardoulakis, S., Fisher, B.E.A., Pericleous, K., Gonzalez-Flesca, N.: Modelling air quality in street canyons: a review. Atmos. Environ. **37**, 155–182 (2003)
4. Sini, J.F., Anquetin, S., Mestayer, P.G.: Pollutant dispersion and thermal effects (1996)
5. Ratti, C., Di Sabatino, S., Britter, R.E., Brown, M., Caton, F., Burian, S.: Analysis of 3-D urban databases with respect to pollution dispersion for a number of European and American cities. Water Air Soil Pollut. **2**, 459–469 (2002)
6. Johnson, W.B., Ludwig, F.L., Dabberdt, W.F., Allen, R.J.: An urban diffusion simulation model for carbon monoxide. J. Air Pollut. Control Assoc. **23**, 490–498 (1973)
7. Yamartino, R.J., Wiegand, G.: Development and evaluation of simple models for the flow, turbulence and pollutant concentration fields within an urban street canyon. Atmos. Environ. **20**, 2137–2156 (1986)
8. Hertel, O., Berkowicz, R.: Modelling pollution from traffic in a street canyon. evaluation of data and model development. Technical report, DMU Luft A–129, NERI (1989)
9. Salizzoni, P., Soulhac, L., Mejean, P.: Street canyon ventilation and atmospheric turbulence. Atmos. Environ. **43**, 5056–5067 (2009)
10. Murena, F., Di Benedetto, A., D'Onofrio, M., Vitiello, G.: Mass transfer velocity and momentum vertical exchange in simulated deep street canyons. Bound.-Layer Meteorol. **140**, 125–142 (2011)
11. Chung, T.N., Liu, C.H.: On the mechanism of air pollutant removal in two-dimensional idealized street canyons: a large-eddy simulation approach. Bound.-Layer Meteorol. **148**(1), 241–253 (2013)
12. Yaghoobian, N., Kleissl, J., Paw, U.K.T.: An improved three-dimensional simulation of the diurnally varying street-canyon flow. Bound.-Layer Meteorol. **153**, 251–276 (2014)

13. Berkowicz, R., Hertel, O., Larsen, S.E., Sorensen, N.N., Nielsen, M.: Modelling traffic pollution in streets. Ministry of Environment and Energy, National Environmental Research Institute, Roskilde, 55 p. (1997)
14. Soulhac, L., Salizzoni, P., Mejean, P., Perkins, R.J.: Parametric laws to model urban pollutant dispersion with a street network approach. Atmos. Environ. **67**, 229–241 (2013)
15. Prati, M.V., Costagliola, M.A., Quaranta, F., Murena, F.: Assessment of ambient air quality in the port of Naples. J. Air Waste Manage. Assoc. **65**(8), 970–979 (2015)
16. Murena, F., Mocerino, L., Quaranta, F., Toscano, D.: Impact on air quality of cruise ship emissions in Naples, Italy. Atmos. Environ. **187**, 70–83 (2018)
17. CERC: ADMS-Urban, USER Guide. Available from Cambridge Environmental Research Consultants, Cambridge, UK (2006)
18. McHugh, C.A., Carruthers, D.J., Edmunds, H.A.: Adms-urban: an air qualitymanagement system for traffic, domestic and industrial pollution. Int. J. Environ. Pollut. **8**, 666–674 (1997)
19. Soulhac, L., Salizzoni, P., Cierco, F.-X., Perkins, R.J.: The model SIRANE for atmospheric urban pollutant dispersion: part I, presentation of the model. Atmos. Environ. **45**, 7379–7395 (2011)
20. Gailis, R.M., Hill, A.: A wind tunnel simulation of plume dispersion within a large array of obstacles. Bound.-Layer Meteorol. **119**, 289–338 (2006)
21. Garbero, V., Salizzoni, P., Soulhac, L., Méjean, P.: Experimental study of pollutant dispersion within a network of streets. Bound.-Layer Meteorol. **136**(3), 457–487 (2010)
22. Marucci, D., Carpinteri, M.: Dispersion in an array of buildings in stable and convective atmospheric conditions. Atmos. Environ. **220**, 117100 (2020)
23. Carpentieri, M., Salizzoni, P., Robins, A., Soulhac, L.: Evaluation of a neigh-bourhood scale, street network dispersion model through comparison with wind tunnel data. Environ. Modell. Softw. **37**, 110–124 (2012)
24. Ben Salem, N., Garbero, V., Salizzoni, P., Lamaison, G., Soulhac, L.: Modelling pollutant dispersion in a street network. Bound.-Layer Meteorol. **155**(1), 157–187 (2015)
25. Soulhac, L., et al.: SIRANERISK: modelling dispersion of steady and unsteady pollutant releases in the urban canopy. Atmos. Environ. **140**, 242–260 (2016)
26. Murena, F., Mele, B.: Effect of balconies on air quality in deep street canyons. Atmos. Pollut. Res. **7**(6), 1004–1012 (2016)
27. Murena, F., Mele, B.: Effect of shortetime variations of wind velocity on mass transfer rate between street canyons and the atmospheric boundary layer. Atmos. Pollut. Res. **5**, 484–490 (2014)
28. Annual Report on the Quality of the Urban Environment. http://www.isprambiente.gov.it
29. Irwin, H.P.A.H.: The design of spires for wind simulation. J. Wind Eng. Ind. Aerodyn. **7**(3), 361–366 (1981)

Optimal Field Calibration of Multiple IoT Low Cost Air Quality Monitors: Setup and Results

E. Esposito[1(✉)], G. D'Elia[1,2], S. Ferlito[1], A. Del Giudice[1], G. Fattoruso[1], P. D'Auria[3], S. De Vito[1], and G. Di Francia[1]

[1] ENEA, DTE-FSD-SAFS, P. le E. Fermi, 1, 80055 Portici, NA, Italy
elena.esposito@enea.it

[2] Department of Industrial Engineering (DIIn), University of Salerno, via Giovanni Paolo II, 132, Fisciano, SA, Italy

[3] ARPAC, Campania Regional Agency for Environmental Protection, Torre 1, CDN, 80143 Naples, Italy

Abstract. The assessment of Low Cost Air Quality Multisensor Systems (LCAQMS) performance is a crucial issue in the Air Quality (AQ) monitoring framework. The devices calibration model is one of the most important drivers of the overall performances. As we know, on field calibration is increasingly considered as the best performing approach for air quality monitor devices. Field recorded sensor data together with co-located reference data allow to build suitable datasets that are more representative of the complexity of real world conditions. In this work a co-location experiment is presented, in which four multisensor devices are co-located with a mobile ARPAC (Campania Regional Agency for Environmental Protection) reference analyzer station. Two types of calibration models, linear and nonlinear have been tested on the recorded datasets, in order to determine the best calibration strategy to use to optimize the calibration procedure time in the real world operative phase. The results show that for pervasive AQ scenario, a reasonable choice is provided by a multilinear approach during one-week short co-location period.

Keywords: Air Quality Multisensor Systems · Sensor calibration · Backup reference data

1 Introduction

The next generation of air quality monitoring network will rely on the integration among regulatory grade analyzers and IoT based smart chemical/particulate multisensor devices [1]. The former will provide a backbone of sparse but high reliability, high quality, measurements at a significant procurement and operational costs. Smart multisensor devices will provide high resolution and possibly redundant measurements with affordable costs but with reduced precision and accuracy. Data assimilation models will be then capable to integrate the stream of incoming data with emissions or regression factors and weather data to produce high resolution air quality maps capable to produce informed remediation decisions. PM and NO_2 are foreseen to be the most problematic pollutants since

O. Gervasi et al. (Eds.): ICCSA 2020, LNCS 12253, pp. 700–708, 2020.
https://doi.org/10.1007/978-3-030-58814-4_57

most of urban chemical pollution is constantly decreasing, in high GDP countries, over the past 20 yrs. Smart air quality monitors, either developed for fixed or mobile deployment, suffer from intrinsic issues linked with their sensors transduction mechanism. Low cost gas sensors, whichever technology they rely on, are ultimately hampered by lack of sensitivity, selectivity and stability. Most of them have they response be significantly influenced by so called interferents being other pollutants or just environmental variables, specifically Temperature and Relative Humidity [2]. In the long term their response is influenced by slow poisoning or just ageing of their components, including the active surface. Nonlinear behaviour can be observed in some of the relevant technology family. Field calibration relying on statistical or, more generally, machine learning models seems the only viable and feasible method to guarantee the short term accuracy and precision of these systems [3, 4]. Although its robustness to long term deployment and so different environmental and pollution composition is criticized [5–7] it allows to rapidly and so cheaply expose the sensors grabbing their response to a variety of (uncontrollable) condition that are similar to the ones that will be encountered during operational life in opposition with lab based calibration that would need significant time and human efforts to achieve similar variability in controlled settings. As shown by several recent works, long term operational deployment may keep the accuracy level if enjoying a stream of high accuracy data by either *rendez-vous* with fellow nodes, periodic visit to regulatory grade analyzers in the mobile case or projected in their position through an adequate model by nearby stations [8–10]. One of the major challenges in field calibration is the optimal choice of the calibration model and the length for the colocation period [11]. Additionally, we still have no clue of the variability of the performance indices among different calibrated mobile analyzers that are known to exhibit significant fabrication variability. In this contribution, we analyse this issue by a field calibration experiment lasting two months using a mobile regulatory grade analyser deployed in the city of Portici located nearby Naples in the south of Italy during the first months of 2020. The experiment is part of the efforts of the AIR-Heritage project, an Urban Innovative Action EU funded project which foresee the deployment of tenths of mobile analyzers to be used by citizens [12] during their daily mobility routines so to contribute AQ ground data to high resolution mapping facilities.

2 Experimental Framework

2.1 IoT AQMS Station Architecture

In this study, we rely on the use of the ENEA MONICA AQMS, designed for cooperative mobile air quality quantitative sensing operations. MONICA device is based on electrochemical sensors array using Alphasense™ A4 class sensor units, respectively targeted to Carbon Monoxide (CO), Nitrogen Dioxide (NO_2) and Ozone (O_3). Relative Humidity (RH) and Temperature (T) sensors complete the sensing array. The sensors analog front-end is provided by the same company and allows to connect sensors to an ARM microcontroller based ST Microelectronic Nucleo board. The latter captures and digitalize the two relevant sensors terminal voltages of each sensor, namely Working Electrode (WE) and Auxiliary Electrode (AE), along with the temperature and RH readings from a SHT11 sensor device. In particular, AE readings may be used to partially correct for temperature interference affecting these sensors WE. The effect of temperature on the different electrodes readings are different and temperature still affect their difference (WE-AE), due to their particular geometry and manufacturing difficulties (see Sensors Datasheet in reference [13]). Raw sensors data are captured by a 10-bit ADC and transmitted via a Bluetooth serial interface to a Raspberry Pi Mod. 3 + based datasink with Raspbian OS providing for local storage and WAN connectivity services through a mobile router wi-fi tplink M7650. Data is captured at 15 samples/minute rate. At remote side, an ad-hoc IoT backend architecture relying on a contained NodeJs REST APIs server and MongoDB provides data inception, device management, storage, preprocessing and map based visualization functionalities (see Fig. 1).

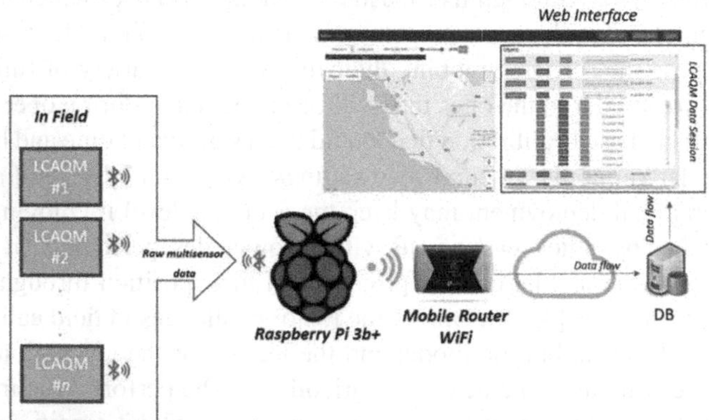

Fig. 1. Scheme of IoT AQMS architecture.

2.2 Recorded Datasets Description

Four MONICA devices (since now on identified as AQ6, AQ8, AQ11, AQ12) have been located on a mobile ARPAC station in a Portici city area, for two months (January 2 to March 2, 2020). In Fig. 2 the co-location architecture is shown.

The recorded datasets consist of 1440 h captured in a continuous sampling fashion. Specifically, for each node, two datasets, with samples averaged at minute and hourly rate, have been built. These datasets contain averaged data from each of sensors embedded into the device, i.e. WE and AE raw sensors readings (mV) for NO_2, CO, O_3 targeted sensors plus T (°C) and RH (%), joined to same time scale averaged data from a mobile ARPAC reference analyzer for NO_2 ($\mu g/m^3$), CO (mg/m^3), O_3 ($\mu g/m^3$). Table 1 resumes the acquired data from the 4 co-located nodes and data losses. Recorded data have been preprocessed, analyzing the missing values, detecting the possible outlier's carrying out a correlation analysis.

The analysis of the ARPAC validated data, collected during the co-location period shows a cyclical and long-term trend, according to the emission characteristics of the site. The significant decrease in average hourly NO_2 concentrations in the time series is due to the wind influence, with different intensity and direction (N-NW and N-NE). This allows

Fig. 2. MONICA AQMS network co-located with ARPAC mobile reference station in Portici city area.

Table 1. Recorded data and data losses.

Monica node	Acquired data (hours/minutes)
AQ6	1432 h/83990 min
AQ8	1392 h/81854 min
AQ11	1422 h/81460 min
AQ12	1268 h/73832 min

the dispersion of pollutants of emission origin. In Fig. 3, four similar meteorological conditions occurring during the co-location period are highlighted by ellipses (Fig. 4).

2.3 Sensor Calibration Models

It is now common knowledge that chemical sensors array raw data needs to be processed by a calibration function to accurately and precisely estimate target gases concentration taking care of nonlinearities and interferents. Several and extensive on-field experiments along with theoretical results led to select two main calibration approaches, each of which has shown to be suitable in specific conditions: Multiple Linear Regression model (MLR) and Shallow Neural Network model (SNN).

Assuming that X is the input features and *y* the predicted value, the MLR model is the classic linear regression with multiple input features, mathematically expressed by

$$y = X\beta + c \tag{1}$$

where *c* is the intercept. The selected nonlinear model is SNN, that has already proven very efficient for AQMS on field calibration. The analyzed SNN model is a three layers' architecture, empirically equipped with [3, 5, 7] standard sigmoidal tangent neurons units in the hidden layer and a linear output layer. Automatic Bayesian Regularization (ABS) was used as training algorithm. In this study, we focused on NO_2 hourly averaged concentration estimation problem using hourly averaged WE and AE sensors data of

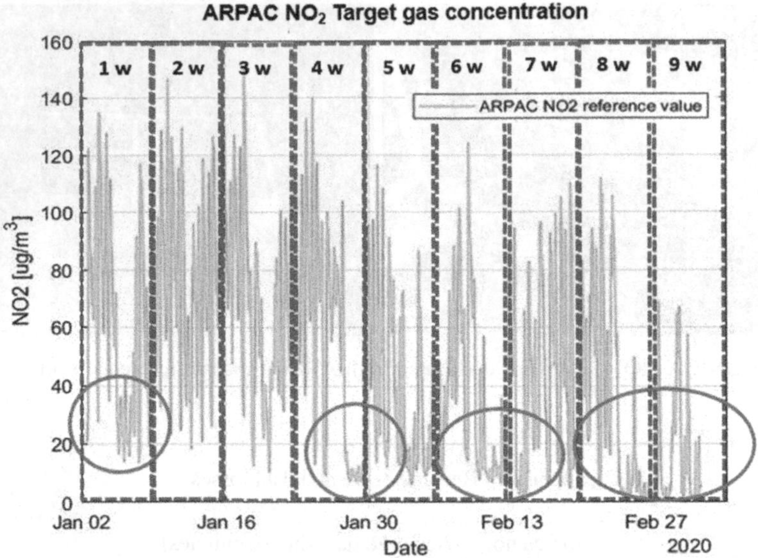

Fig. 3. NO_2 gas concentration provided by mobile ARPAC reference analyzer. It can be observed the gas behavior during the entire co-location period and also the daily trend, depending on the meteorological conditions.

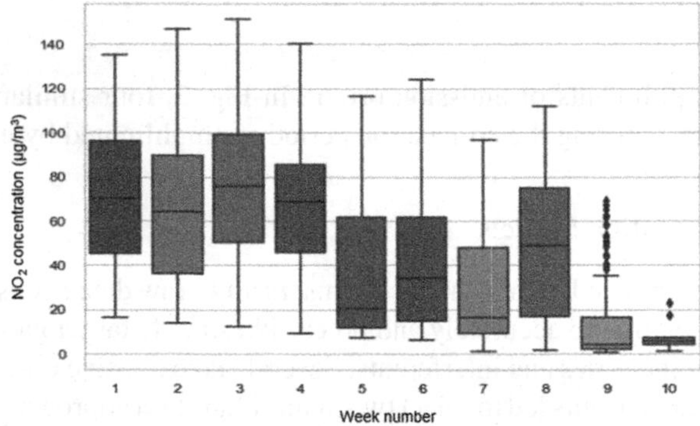

Fig. 4. Box-plot representation of NO_2 gas concentration distribution along the entire co-location period.

NO_2, O_3 sensors plus T and RH data as inputs for the two calibration algorithms. The input matrix X, thus, consists of 6 features vectors as columns (WE_NO_2, AE_NO_2, WE_O_3, AE_O_3, T, RH) and the rows number depends on the training set length. The two calibration algorithms have been tested using different choices of training/validation/test sets. In particular, calibration is performed in an ex-post fashion by selecting for testing purposes only those samples that are temporally located after all the data used for training and validation purposes. This setting is the most adequate to simulate real conditions where nodes will be operated after the calibration took place. Details and results are reported in Sect. 3.

3 Results

As previously mentioned, performance assessment experiments have been carried out using different training/validation/test sets combinations, aiming to the optimization of the involved parameters. Table 2 captures the preliminary results of our experimentation. At a glance, it is possible to spot the different performance obtained by the different analyzers. Irrespective of the calibration model and at each training/validation/test combination AQ8 node appear as the worst performing node. AQ12 node seems instead to express the best performance with respect to all the other nodes particularly when calibrated using an MLR approach. NN model performances are hampered when using data from second week; actually, without resorting to a validation set the learning process result in overtraining conditions that prevent the network to obtain good generalization capabilities. Generally, results obtained by MLR and NN models appear similar with MLR keeping a limited edge on the performance obtained by NN.

Table 2. Mean absolute errors obtained using two calibration procedures with different choices of operational and test sets for each AQMS node.

Training + Validation setting	Mean Absolute Error (MAE) [$\mu g/m^3$]							
	AQ6		AQ8		AQ11		AQ12	
	NN	MLR	NN	MLR	NN	MLR	NN	MLR
1st w + 0 w	11.70	7.94	17.42	23.36	8.20	7.78	11.45	**6.56**
1st w + 2nd w	7.15	7.70	24.04	16.79	10.69	9.51	8.27	**6.92**
2nd w + 0 w	***54.46***	***9.55***	***92.41***	***21.92***	***64.26***	***10.37***	***97.68***	***8.21***
1–2nd w + 3rd w	*8.65*	*7.73*	*17.63*	*13.30*	*11.17*	*8.86*	*8.29*	***6.50***
1–3rd w + 4th w	8.13	7.56	15.98	12.63	9.50	9.89	6.63	**6.31**
1–4th w + 5th w	7.44	7.63	15.57	11.37	10.38	9.66	6.53	**5.15**

The first two experiments have been performed using the first week for the training phase (1st and 2nd row in Table 2), while in the second experiment we use only the second week for the training (3rd row in Table 2). We can observe that the NN performances decrease when the meteorological conditions change in the operative phase wrt the training phase (result highlighted in blue in Table 2). Then, we compared these results with those obtained incrementally enlarging the training set up to one month (rows 4–6 of Table 2). The obtained results show that no significant improvements have been achieved extending the co-location period. Figure 5 depicts the behavior of NN model based estimations along with true concentrations for all the four nodes under calibration when using the first two weeks of data for training purposes and the third for validation (results highlighted in Italic in Table 2). It is easy to spot the sudden performance worsening attained at the end of the colocation period when concentration of the target pollutant is significantly lower than those encountered during training and validation period. Performance worsening are more evident for node AQ8 confirming its low capability to accurately estimate the target gas concentrations.

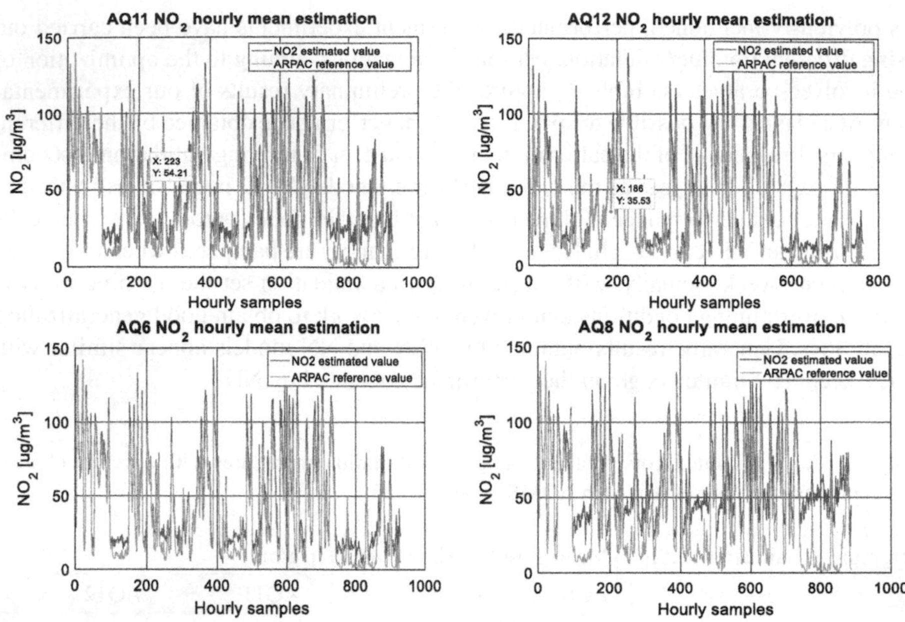

Fig. 5. NO_2 hourly concentration estimations versus target gas concentration starting from the 4th week of the co-location period.

By focusing on Fig. 6 the underlying drivers of the poor performance of AQ8 node become evident with a significant bias error found along all the target concentration range and dramatic lack of precision when dealing with low target gas concentrations. A careful and continuous estimation of performance of the nodes can be helpful to rapidly detect poorly performing node and freeing its calibration spot to accommodate a new node. When benefitting from a continuous access to ground truth data significant differences in the linear fit parameters between node estimations may establish a fast and robust way to determine anomalies in sensors operative performances (see Fig. 7).

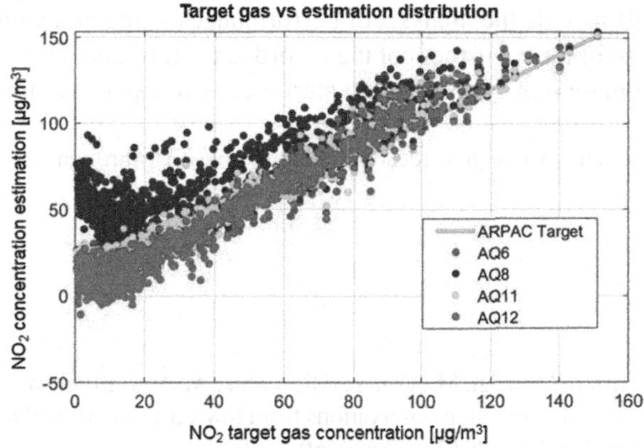

Fig. 6. NO_2 gas concentration estimation computed for each node, along the entire co-location period versus target gas concentration line. The differences among the four sensors performances become apparent when considering low true concentration of the target pollutant.

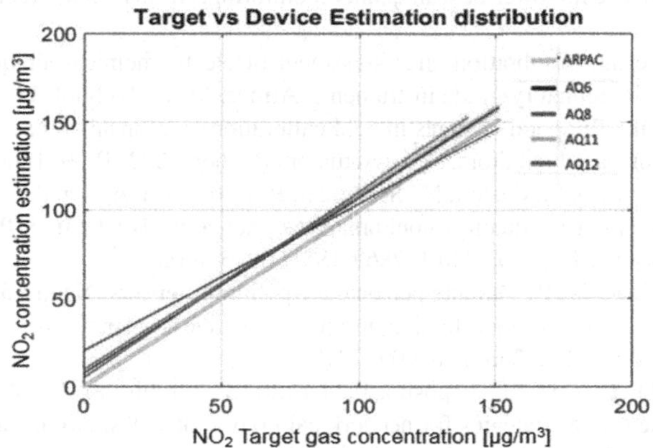

Fig. 7. Differences in linear fit parameters among the difference nodes highlight the malfunctioning node.

4 Conclusions

A mid-term colocation experiment has been carried out for the purpose of analyzing and comparing the performance of calibrated smart air quality monitoring nodes. The analysis of the dependence of performances from calibration extension did not highlighted a significant correlation among training duration and performances with good performances obtained by considered model starting as early as just one week of calibration data. Performance seems consistent among the two considered model while sustained performance variance has been recorded among a node and the majority of the others. In fact, while three of the node undergoing the calibration process expressed similar performances while the remaining one suffered both from high amount of bias and lack of precision and accuracy at lowest end of the target gas observed concentration range.

Further works will include the analysis of performances along an extended duration as well as the increase of the robustness of the recorded performance indexes by averaging on different combination of calibration set start, i.e. by adequate resampling process.

Acknowledgments. This work has received funding by EU through UIA 3rdcall Project "AirHeritage".

References

1. Schneider, P., Castell, N., Vogt, M., Dauge, F.R., Lahoz, W.A., Bartonova, A.: Mapping urban air quality in near real-time using observations from low-cost sensors and model information. Environ. Int. **106**, 234–247 (2017). ISSN 0160-4120
2. Cross, E.S., et al.: Use of electrochemical sensors for measurement of air pollution: correcting interference response and validating measurements Atmos. Meas. Technol. **10**, 3575–3588 (2017)
3. Zimmerman, N., et al.: A machine learning calibration model using random forests to improve sensor performance for lower-cost air quality monitoring. Atmos. Meas. Technol. **11**, 291–313 (2018)
4. Hagan, D.H., et al.: Calibration and assessment of electrochemical air quality sensors by co-location with regulatory-grade instruments. Atmos. Meas. Technol. **11**, 315–328 (2018)
5. Masey, N., et al.: Temporal changes in field calibration relationships for Aeroqual S500 O3 and NO2 sensor-based monitors. Sens. Actuators B Chem. **273**, 1800–1806 (2018)
6. De Vito, S., Esposito, E., Castell, N., Schneider, P., Bartonova, A.: On the robustness of field calibration for smart air quality monitors. Sens. Actuators B Chem. **310**, 127869 (2020). https://doi.org/10.1016/j.snb.2020.127869. ISSN 0925-4005
7. Lewis, A.C., Edwards, P.: Validate personal air-pollution sensors. Nature **535**, 29–31 (2016)
8. Kizel, F., et al.: Node-to-node field calibration of wireless distributed air pollution sensor network. Environ. Pollut. **233**, 900–909 (2018)
9. De Vito, S., Di Francia, G., Esposito, E., Ferlito, S., Formisano, F., Massera, E.: Adaptive machine learning strategies for network calibration of IoT smart air quality monitoring devices. arXiv preprint arXiv:2003.12011 (2020)
10. Miskell, G., et al.: Reliable data from low cost ozone sensors in a hierarchical network. Atmos. Environ. **214**, 116870 (2019). https://doi.org/10.1016/j.atmosenv.2019.116870. ISSN 1352-2310
11. Esposito, E., De Vito, S., Salvato, M., Bright, V., Jones, R.L., Popoola, O.: Dynamic neural network architectures for on field stochastic calibration of indicative low cost air quality sensing systems. Sens. Actuators B Chem. **231**, 701–713 (2016)
12. Castell, N., Liu, H.-Y., Schneider, P., Cole-Hunter, T., Lahoz, W., Bartonova, A.: Towards a personalized environmental health information service using low-cost sensors and crowdsourcing EGU general assembly (2015)
13. NO2-A4 datasheet downloaded in February 2020 from Alphasense ltd website. www.alphasense.com

An ADMM Approach for Constructing Abnormal Subspace of Sparse PCA

Wenmin Jiang[1], Ying Zhao[1(✉)], and Kazi Abir Adnan[2]

[1] Tsinghua University, Beijing, China
jwm17@mails.tsinghua.edu.cn, yingz@tsinghua.edu.cn
[2] University of Melbourne, Melbourne, Australia
kazi.adnan@unimelb.edu.au

Abstract. Despite the popularity of principal component analysis (PCA) as an anomaly detection technique, the main shortage of PCA-based anomaly detection models is their interpretability. Constructing the abnormal subspace of PCA (i.e., the subspace spanned by the least significant principal components (PCs)), with sparse and orthogonal loading vectors provides a means of anomaly interpretation. However, solving all abnormal sparse PCs one by one through semi-definite programming is time consuming. In this paper, we derive an adapted projection deflation method for extracting least significant PCs and propose an alternating direction method of multipliers (ADMM) solution for constructing the sparse abnormal subspace. Our experiments on two real world datasets showed that the proposed ADMM solution achieved comparable detection accuracy and sparsity as the SDP solution and is 10 times more efficient, which makes it more suitable for application domains with higher dimensions.

Keywords: Anomaly detection · Sparse PCA · ADMM

1 Introduction

Principal Component Analysis (PCA) is one of the best-known statistical analysis techniques for detecting anomalies and has been applied to many kinds of data, such as network intrusion detection, failure detection in production systems, and so on [1]. Although PCA and derived techniques are not the only solutions for unsupervised anomalies detection, they are among the most widely used ones. However, traditional PCA-based anomaly detection models are not suitable for anomaly interpretation (i.e., pinpointing the causes of detected anomalies) [2] and are treated as black-box techniques. Recently, detection models based on sparse PCA [3,4] were proposed to offer better interpretation since sparse PCA can improve the interpretability of PCA's dimensionality-reduced subspace.

This work is funded by the National Key Research and Development Program of China (Grant No. 2016YFB0200100).

O. Gervasi et al. (Eds.): ICCSA 2020, LNCS 12253, pp. 709–717, 2020.
https://doi.org/10.1007/978-3-030-58814-4_58

We have investigated the anomaly interpretation problem of PCA-based models in our previous publication [4]. In [4], we proposed an abnormal subspace sparse PCA (ASPCA) model that can find the abnormal subspace defined by sparse and orthogonal principal components (PCs). The proposed ASPCA model prioritizes the sparsity of the abnormal subspace by extracting PCs with least significant variances through a semi-definite programming (SDP) approach. We project each of the data record onto the abnormal subspace and calculate their projection lengths. For those detected anomalies that have higher projection lengths, the ASPCA model interprets its detection results by identifying the set of projections that contribute the most. Although this ASPCA model can provide desirable detection and interpretation to individual anomalies, it suffers from high computational costs due to the SDP optimization. In this paper, we adapt a projection deflation method to extract least significant principal components, and derive an alternating direction method of multipliers (ADMM) solution to improve the efficiency. We make the following contributions:

- Derive an ADMM solution for backward ASPCA that guarantees the orthogonality of extracted principal components through an adapted projection deflation method.
- Conduct experiments involving two real world datasets to show that the proposed ADMM solution can achieve comparable detection accuracy and sparsity as the SDP solution and is 10 times more efficient.

The rest of this paper is organized as follows. Section 2 discusses the related work. Section 3 introduces the ASPCA model and the proposed adapted projection deflation method. Section 4 describes an ADMM solution. Section 5 presents an experimental evaluation on the efficiency of the ADMM solution. Finally, Sect. 6 provides some concluding remarks.

2 Related Works

PCA is mostly known as a dimension reduction tool [5], but it is also widely used as an anomaly detection method thanks to its scalability and communication efficiency [1]. Recently, the sparse PCA introduced by Jolliffe *et al.* [6] showed plausible performance for anomaly detection. Luo *et al.* [7] used sparse PCA to monitor industrial processes and showed that the sparse PCA-based method had better monitoring performance than the PCA-based methods. Yu *et al.* [8] proposed a nonlinear and sparse PCA method (RNSPCA) for industrial as well. Sparse PCA also improves the interpretability of PCA's dimensionality-reduced subspace, which can be used to interpret detected anomalies. Jiang *et al.* [3] proposed a joint sparse PCA (JSPCA) model to achieve a sparse representation of the abnormal subspace and identify the set of features that distinguish anomalies. Bin *et al.* [4] proposed the ASPCA model to construct the abnormal principal components (PCs) with sparse and orthogonal loading vectors and interpret detected anomalies by identifying the set of such PCs on which they have large projection values.

Various methods solving the sparse PCA problem were proposed in the literature, for example [9] and [10]. Aspremont *et al.* [10] proposed a SDP relaxation to the sparse PCA optimization problem. Recently, the alternating direction method of multipliers [11] was used for solving the sparse PCA problem more efficiently [12] and extended by Vu *et al.* [13] by forming a novel convex relaxation of sparse principal subspace estimation based on the convex hull of rank-d projection matrices (i.e., Fantope). In this paper, we examine these techniques to improve the efficiency of the backward ASPCA model.

3 Sparse PCA for Anomaly Detection and Interpretation

We first introduce the notations used in this paper. Bold uppercase letters such as $\mathbf{X}$ denote a matrix and $\mathbf{X}_{ij}$ is the entry of $\mathbf{X}[i,j]$. Bold lowercase letters such as $\mathbf{v}$ denote a column vector. Greek letters such as λ, β are coefficients. $||\mathbf{X}||_{1,1}$ is the $L_{1,1}$ norm of $\mathbf{X}$ as $||\mathbf{X}||_{1,1} = \mathbf{1}^T|\mathbf{X}|\mathbf{1}$. $Tr(\mathbf{X})$ represents the trace of matrix $\mathbf{X}$. $<\mathbf{X},\mathbf{Y}>$ represents the matrix inner product defined as $<\mathbf{X},\mathbf{Y}> = Tr(\mathbf{X}^T Y)$. $Card(\mathbf{X})$ denotes the cardinality (number of non-zero elements) of matrix $\mathbf{X}$. $\mathbf{I}$ is the identity matrix. $\mathbb{S}_+^p$ is the set of all symmetric positive semi-definite matrices in $\mathbb{R}^{p \times p}$, where p is the number of dimensions.

Principal Component Analysis (PCA) captures the principal components of a multi-dimensional dataset defined by a set of orthogonal eigenvectors with the highest variance. Given a p-dimensional dataset, an anomaly detection model can be constructed by forming a normal subspace (defined by the first k principal components returned by PCA) and an abnormal subspace (defined by the remaining d principal components).

In [4], we proposed an interpretable PCA-based anomaly detection model, the Abnormal Subspace Sparse PCA (ASPCA) model, which can detect and interpret anomalies using the abnormal subspace directly. In particular, the ASPCA model tries to find the abnormal subspace defined by sparse and orthogonal principal components. Given a $n \times p$ data matrix $\mathbf{D}$, its covariance matrix $\mathbf{A} = \mathbf{D}^T\mathbf{D}$, and a sparsity constraint constant c, for each $i = p, ..., p-d+1$, the backward ASPCA (ASPCA-B) model tries to solve:

$$\begin{aligned} &\underset{\mathbf{v}_i}{\text{argmin}} \ \mathbf{v}_i^T \mathbf{A} \mathbf{v}_i \\ &s.t. \ \mathbf{v}_i^T \mathbf{v}_i = 1, \ \mathbf{v}_i^T \mathbf{v}_j = 0 \ \forall i < j \leq p, Card(\mathbf{v}_i) \leq c. \end{aligned} \tag{1}$$

When we extract d loading vectors $\mathbf{v}_{p-d+1}, ..., \mathbf{v}_p$ using Eq. 1 to span a subspace $\mathbf{V}$, we make sure that the orthogonal complement of $\mathbf{V}$ has major variance for describing the normal patterns in the dataset. Given a p-dimensional data record $\mathbf{y}$, the the squared prediction error (SPE) can be calculated as $||\hat{\mathbf{y}}||_2^2 = \hat{\mathbf{y}}^T\hat{\mathbf{y}} = \sum_{i=p-d+1}^{p}(\mathbf{v}_i^T\mathbf{y})^2$ for judging whether $\mathbf{y}$ is an anomaly or not. The loading vectors that contribute the most to the SPE score can be used to interpret the cause of the anomaly since they are sparse and understandable to users.

Instead of solving Eq. 1 with the orthogonality constraint, we can also adopt a deflation method [14] that ensures orthogonality to extract these components sequentially, in which case we drop the orthogonality constraint from Eq. 1 and the objective function of our ASPCA-B model becomes:

$$\begin{aligned} &\underset{\mathbf{v}}{\operatorname{argmin}}\ \mathbf{v}^T\mathbf{A}\mathbf{v} \\ &s.t.\ \mathbf{v}^T\mathbf{v}=1, Card(\mathbf{v}) \leq c. \end{aligned} \tag{2}$$

Here, we adapt the original deflation method proposed in [14] and make it usable for extracting the least significant components. By the symmetric Schur decomposition, we have $\mathbf{I}-\mathbf{v}_i\mathbf{v}_i^T=\mathbf{Q}^T\mathbf{\Lambda}\mathbf{Q}$, where $\mathbf{Q}$ is orthogonal and $\mathbf{\Lambda}$ is a $p\times p$ diagonal matrix with $\mathbf{\Lambda}_{ii}=0$ and $\mathbf{\Lambda}_{jj}=1$ for $j\neq i, 1\leq j\leq p$. By eliminating the ith column of $\mathbf{Q}$ we obtain a $p\times(p-1)$ matrix $\hat{\mathbf{Q}}$. Now we can use the deflation as $\hat{\mathbf{A}}=\hat{\mathbf{Q}}^T\mathbf{A}\hat{\mathbf{Q}}$, and the following proposition states its correctness.

Proposition 1. *If $\lambda_1\geq\lambda_2\geq\cdots\geq\lambda_p$ are the eigenvalues of $\mathbf{A}\in\mathbb{S}_+^p$, $\mathbf{v}_1,\mathbf{v}_2,\cdots,\mathbf{v}_p$ are the corresponding eigenvectors, and $\hat{\mathbf{A}}=\hat{\mathbf{Q}}^T\mathbf{A}\hat{\mathbf{Q}}$ for some $i\in 1,\cdots,p$, then $\hat{\mathbf{A}}$ has eigenvectors $\hat{\mathbf{v}}_1,\cdots,\hat{\mathbf{v}}_{i-1},\hat{\mathbf{v}}_{i+1},\cdots,\hat{\mathbf{v}}_p$ with corresponding eigenvalues $\lambda_1,\cdots,\lambda_{i-1},\lambda_{i+1},\cdots,\lambda_p$, where $\hat{\mathbf{v}}_j=\hat{\mathbf{Q}}^T\mathbf{v}_j$, for $j\neq i, 1\leq j\leq p$.*

Proof. $\forall j\neq i, \hat{\mathbf{A}}\hat{\mathbf{v}}_j=\hat{\mathbf{Q}}^T\mathbf{A}\hat{\mathbf{Q}}\hat{\mathbf{Q}}^T\mathbf{v}_j=\hat{\mathbf{Q}}^T\mathbf{A}(\mathbf{I}-\mathbf{v}_i\mathbf{v}_i^T)\mathbf{v}_j=\hat{\mathbf{Q}}^T\mathbf{A}\mathbf{v}_j=\hat{\mathbf{Q}}^T\lambda_j\mathbf{v}_j=\lambda_j\hat{\mathbf{v}}_j$.

4 Optimization Methods

4.1 Solving Backward ASPCA with SDP

We transform Eq. 1 without the orthogonality constraint $\mathbf{v}_j^T\mathbf{v}_i=0, \forall 1\leq j<i$ to Eq. 3 through a SDP relaxation.

$$\begin{aligned} &\underset{\mathbf{X}_i\in\mathbb{S}^p}{\operatorname{argmin}}\ Tr(\mathbf{A}\mathbf{X}_i) \\ &s.t.\ \mathbf{X}_i\succeq 0, rank(\mathbf{X}_i)=1,\ Tr(\mathbf{X}_i)=1, Card(\mathbf{X}_i)<k^2, \end{aligned} \tag{3}$$

where $\mathbf{X}_i$ is a positive semi-definitive matrix with the constraint $rank(\mathbf{X}_i)=1$, which can be uniquely decomposed as $\mathbf{X}_i=\mathbf{v}_i\mathbf{v}_i^T$. With $\mathbf{X}_i=\mathbf{v}_i\mathbf{v}_i^T$, $Tr(\mathbf{X}_i)=1$ is equivalent to $\mathbf{v}_i^T\mathbf{v}_i=1$, $Card(\mathbf{X}_i)\leq k^2$ is equivalent to $Card(\mathbf{v}_i)\leq k$, and we have $\mathbf{v}_i^T\mathbf{A}\mathbf{v}_i=Tr(\mathbf{A}(\mathbf{v}_i\mathbf{v}_i^T))=Tr(\mathbf{A}\mathbf{X}_i)$.

Now let $\mathbf{V}_i=(\mathbf{v}_1,\mathbf{v}_2,...,\mathbf{v}_i)$ and $\mathbf{R}_i=\mathbf{V}_i\mathbf{V}_i^T$, the orthogonality constraint $\mathbf{v}_j^T\mathbf{v}_i=0, \forall 1\leq j<i$ is equivalent to $||\mathbf{V}_{i-1}^T\mathbf{v}_i||_2^2=Tr(\mathbf{R}_{i-1}\mathbf{X}_i)=0$. After moving the sparsity constraint into the objective function and dropping the non-convex constraint $rank(\mathbf{X}_i)=1$, we have an objective function that can be solved by semidefinite programming (SDP) as in Eq. 4.

$$\begin{aligned} &\underset{\mathbf{X}_i\in\mathbb{S}^p}{\operatorname{argmin}}\ Tr(\mathbf{A}\mathbf{X}_i)+\lambda||\mathbf{X}_i||_{1,1} \\ &s.t.\ \mathbf{X}_i\succeq 0,\ Tr(\mathbf{X}_i)=1, Tr(\mathbf{R}_{i-1}\mathbf{X}_i)=0. \end{aligned} \tag{4}$$

We refer to this method as **backward SDP ASPCA (SDP-B)**.

4.2 Solving Backward ASPCA with ADMM

Following the SDP relaxation framework, Eq. 2 can be transferred to the following optimization problem,

$$\begin{aligned}&\underset{\mathbf{X}\in\mathbb{S}_+^p}{\operatorname{argmin}}\ Tr(\mathbf{AX})+\lambda||\mathbf{X}||_{1,1}\\&s.t.\ \mathbf{X}\succeq 0,\ Tr(\mathbf{X})=1.\end{aligned} \tag{5}$$

Let $\mathcal{C}$ denote the simplex of the cone of the semidefinite matrices, i.e., $\mathcal{C} = \{\mathbf{X} \in \mathbb{S}_+^p : \mathbf{X} \succeq 0,\ Tr(\mathbf{X}) = 1\}$, $I_{\mathcal{C}}(\mathbf{X})$ denote the indicator function of set $\mathcal{C}$, i.e., $I_{\mathcal{C}}(\mathbf{X}) = 0$ if $\mathbf{X} \in \mathcal{C}$, and ∞ otherwise. By introducing a new variable $\mathbf{Y}$ and following the augmented Lagrangian framework, we can solve Eq. 5 using the alternating direction method of multipliers (ADMM) as follows,

$$\begin{aligned}&\underset{\mathbf{X}}{\operatorname{argmin}}\ I_{\mathcal{C}}(\mathbf{X})+Tr(\mathbf{AX})+\lambda||\mathbf{Y}||_{1,1}\\&s.t.\ \mathbf{X}-\mathbf{Y}=0.\end{aligned} \tag{6}$$

The augmented Lagrangian associated with Eq. 6 has the form

$$\begin{aligned}\mathcal{L}_\rho(\mathbf{X},\mathbf{Y};\mathbf{U}) &= <\mathbf{A},\mathbf{X}> + I_{\mathcal{C}}(\mathbf{X}) + \lambda||\mathbf{Y}||_{1,1}\\&+\frac{\rho}{2}||\mathbf{X}-\mathbf{Y}||_F^2 - <\mathbf{U},\mathbf{X}-\mathbf{Y}>,\end{aligned} \tag{7}$$

where $\mathbf{U}$ is the Lagrange multiplier associated with the constraint $\mathbf{X} = \mathbf{Y}$ and $\rho > 0$ is a penalty parameter.

Now we minimize Eq. 7 with respect to $\mathbf{X}$ and $\mathbf{Y}$ alternatively and update $\mathbf{X}^{t+1}$ and $\mathbf{Y}^{t+1}$ iteratively by

$$\begin{aligned}\mathbf{X}^{t+1} &= \mathcal{P}_{\mathcal{C}}(\mathbf{Y}^t - \mathbf{U}^t/\rho - \mathbf{A}/\rho),\\ \mathbf{Y}^{t+1} &= Shrink(\mathbf{X}^{t+1} - \mathbf{U}^t/\rho, \frac{\lambda}{\rho}).\end{aligned} \tag{8}$$

where $\mathcal{P}_{\mathcal{C}}()$ calculates the projection on $\mathcal{C}$ that can be solved in $O(p\log p)$ [12] and $Shrink()$ is the shrinkage operator. Lastly, the Lagrange multiplier $\mathbf{U}^{t+1}$ is updated by $\mathbf{U}^t + (\mathbf{X}^t - \mathbf{Y}^t)/\rho$. We choose to terminate our ADMM when

$$max(||\mathbf{X}^t - \mathbf{Y}^t||_F^2, \rho^2||\mathbf{Y}^t - \mathbf{Y}^{t-1}||_F^2) \le d\epsilon^2, \tag{9}$$

where ϵ is a convergence parameter. As the resultant $rank(\mathbf{X})$ might not be 1, we use the dominant eigenvector of $\mathbf{X}$ as the approximate solution for $\mathbf{v}$. Finally, we use the proposed adapted projection deflation method to annihilate $\mathbf{v}$ to prepare for the next eigenvector. We refer to this method as **backward ADMM ASPCA (ADMM-B)**, and show its procedure in Algorithm 1.

Algorithm 1. Backward ADMM ASPCA (ADMM-B)

Input: $\mathbf{A}, d, \lambda, \rho, \epsilon$

d is the number of abnormal subspace PCs; λ is the sparsity penalty parameter; ρ is the Lagrangian penalty parameter; ϵ is the convergence parameter.

Output: $\mathbf{V}$

for $i = p$ to $p - d + 1$ **do**
  $\mathbf{V}_{i+1} \leftarrow (\mathbf{v}_{i+1}, \cdots, \mathbf{v}_p)$;
  Schur decomposition $\mathbf{Q}^T \mathbf{\Lambda} \mathbf{Q} = \mathbf{I} - \mathbf{V}_{i+1}\mathbf{V}_{i+1}^T$;
  $\hat{\mathbf{Q}} \leftarrow$ the first i columns of $\mathbf{Q}$;
  $\mathbf{A}_i \leftarrow \hat{\mathbf{Q}}^T \mathbf{A} \hat{\mathbf{Q}}$;
  $\mathbf{Y}_i^0 \leftarrow 0, \mathbf{U}_i^0 \leftarrow 0, t \leftarrow 0$;
  repeat
    $\mathbf{X}_i^{t+1} \leftarrow Pc(\mathbf{Y}_i^t - \mathbf{U}_i^t/\rho - \mathbf{A}_i/\rho)$;
    $\mathbf{Y}_i^{t+1} \leftarrow Shrink(\mathbf{X}_i^{t+1} - \mathbf{U}_i^t/\rho, \frac{\lambda}{\rho})$;
    $\mathbf{U}_i^{t+1} \leftarrow \mathbf{U}_i^t + (\mathbf{X}_i^{t+1} - \mathbf{Y}_i^{t+1})/\rho$;
    $t \leftarrow t + 1$;
  until $max(||\mathbf{X}_i^t - \mathbf{Y}_i^t||_F^2, \rho^2||\mathbf{Y}_i^t - \mathbf{Y}_i^{t-1}||_F^2) \leq d\epsilon^2$
  $\hat{\mathbf{v}}_i \leftarrow$ the dominant eigenvector of $\mathbf{X}_i$;
  $\mathbf{v}_i \leftarrow \hat{\mathbf{Q}}\hat{\mathbf{v}}_i$;
end for
$\mathbf{V} \leftarrow (\mathbf{v}_{p-d+1}, ..., \mathbf{v}_p)$;
return $\mathbf{V}$;

5 Experiments

The various ASPCA models were evaluated on their anomaly detection performance, sparsity of loading vectors of their abnormal PCs, and efficiency using two real-world datasets **Breast-Cancer** and **KDD99**.

Breast Cancer Wisconsin (Diagnostic) Dataset [15] provides features to distinguish malignant and benign tumors. Our dataset includes 357 benign records and 20 malignant records sampled randomly from the original dataset as anomalies. For each data record, there are 30 features describing characteristics of the cell nuclei present in a digitized image of a *fine needle aspirate* (FNA) of a breast mass. All 30 real-valued features were deducted by the mean values and linearly scaled to $[-1, 1]$. **KDD 99 Intrusion Dataset** [16] is widely used for anomaly and intrusion detection. Each instance is a connection record classified as normal or one of 22 classes of attacks. We kept all 97278 normal instances and sampled 5173 abnormal records. We followed a similar preprocessing procedure as in [3]. There are 41 features and all features were deducted by the mean values and linearly scaled to $[-1, 1]$.

We summarize the various evaluated models here:

- **PCA:** A standard PCA is our baseline model for anomaly detection performance and PCs sparsity.
- **SDP-B:** The backward ASPCA model optimized using SDP presented in [4] is another baseline model in our experiments.

- **ADMM-B:** The proposed ADMM solution can efficiently optimize the backward ASPCA objective function.
- **ADMM-A:** Another ADMM-based sparse PCA model presented in [13] was also considered in our comparison, which forms a convex relaxation of sparse principal subspace estimation based on the convex hull of rank-d projection matrices. The ADMM-A model extracts all d abnormal PCs simultaneously, but cannot guarantee the orthogonality of extracted PCs.

For all the models, the most important parameter is the number of abnormal subspace PCs d. We chose d such that the abnormal subspace PCs explain roughly 5% of the total variance [2] for all the models as shown in Table 1. For all the ASPCA models, we chose the PC sparsity penalty parameter λ as suggested in [4]. For ADMM models, the Lagrange penalty parameter ρ was set to be equal to λ as suggested in [11]. The convergence parameter ϵ was set to be 0.01. Finally, we implemented all methods with MATLAB and CVX, and performed all experiments on a laptop computer with 8 GB memory and a Intel Core i5 1.4 GHz CPU.

Table 1. Parameters for various models.

	d (PCA)	d (ASPCA models)	λ (sparsity penalty)
Breast-Cancer	19	15	0.5
KDD99	34	34	100

Anomaly Detection. We used the abnormal subspace PCs obtained by various models to predict all the anomalies in the dataset and generated ROC curves to evaluate the anomaly detection performance. The results are shown in Fig. 1. Recall that we chose d to make sure that the abnormal subspace PCs obtained by various models explain roughly 5% of the total variance. Under this condition, we can see that the various ASPCA models achieved similar anomaly detection performance as the standard PCA model indicated by the similarities of their ROC curves for both Breast-Cancer and KDD99 datasets.

Sparsity Evaluation. The next set of experiments were designed to compare the sparsity of the loading matrix generated by various ASPCA models and we used the result of PCA as our baseline. We used three metrics to evaluate the sparsity of the loading matrix of the abnormal PCs, namely, $||V||_{1,1}$, $Card_{0.1}$ (number of entries with absolute values bigger than 0.1), and $Card_{0.01}$ (number of entries with absolute values bigger than 0.01), and showed the results in Table 2. We can see that all ASPCA models improved the sparsity of the loading matrix greatly over the baseline. The ADMM-B model indeed achieved the same sparsity performance as SDP-B. The ADMM-A model achieved a worse sparsity performance, which suggests that it is not suitable for constructing the sparse abnormal subspace for anomaly interpretation.

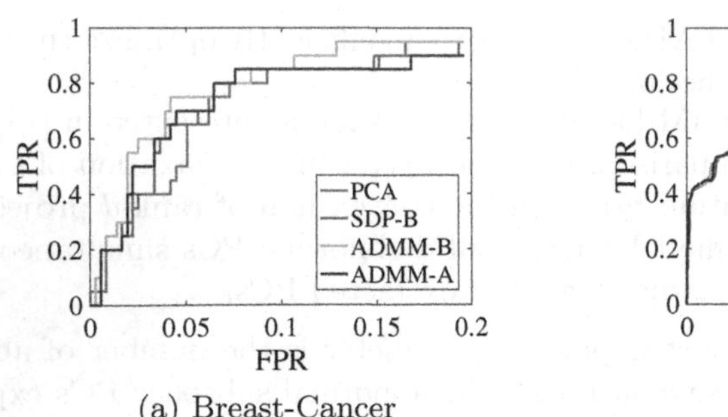

(a) Breast-Cancer

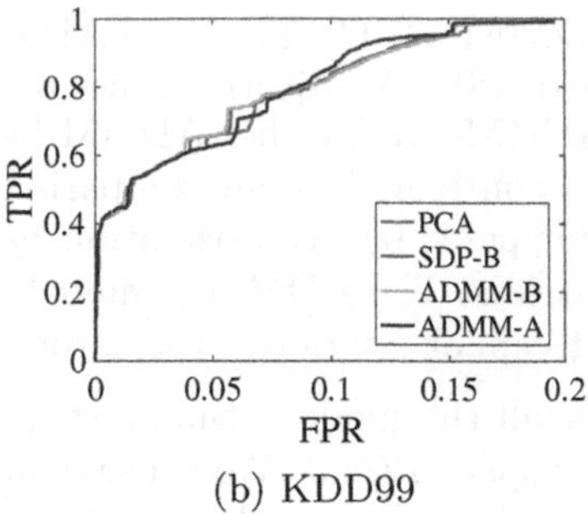

(b) KDD99

Fig. 1. ROC curve of PCs of Breast-Cancer and KDD99 obtained by various models.

Table 2. Sparsity on Breast-Cancer and KDD99.

Dataset	Method	$\|\|V\|\|_{1,1}$	$card_{0.1}$	$card_{0.01}$
Breast-Cancer	PCA	70.12	242	483
	SDP-B	26.77	59	80
	ADMM-B	27.37	52	112
	ADMM-A	49.05	149	329
KDD99	PCA	91.28	237	630
	SDP-B	52.08	95	194
	ADMM-B	52.07	93	192
	ADMM-A	76.03	203	421

Efficiency. We showed the runtime of various models on the two datasets in Table 3. We can see that all ASPCA models have higher time complexity than the standard PCA for computing sparse PCs. As expected, the ADMM-B model indeed improves efficiency over the SDP-B model. The ADMM-B model ran about 40 and 10 times faster than the SDP-B model on Breast-Cancer and KDD99, respectively. The ADMM-A model solves all the abnormal PCs simultaneously and is faster than the ADMM-B model, which solves the abnormal PCs one by one. However, the ADMM-A model cannot achieve the desirable sparsity performance.

Table 3. Runtime (in seconds).

Models	Breast-Cancer	KDD99
PCA	0.001	0.13
SDP-B	13.045	27.56
ADMM-B	0.335	2.60
ADMM-A	0.009	0.21

6 Conclusions

We proposed an ADMM solution to extract sparse abnormal subspace of PCA with sparse and orthogonal PCs for anomaly detection and interpretation. The proposed ADMM solution is much more efficient than a SDP solution, which makes it possible to apply to datasets with higher dimensions. In the further, we will study the efficiency and interpretability of this anomaly detection model on more application domains.

References

1. Chandola, V., Banerjee, A., Kumar, V.: Anomaly detection: a survey. ACM Comput. Surv. **41**(3), 1–58 (2009)
2. Ringberg, H., Soule, A., Rexford, J., Diot, C.: Sensitivity of PCA for traffic anomaly detection. In: The 2007 ACM SIGMETRICS International Conference on Measurement and Modeling of Computer Systems, pp. 109–120. ACM (2007)
3. Jiang, R., Fei, H., Huan, J.: A family of joint sparse PCA algorithms for anomaly localization in network data streams. IEEE Trans. Knowl. Data Eng. **25**(11), 2421–2433 (2013)
4. Bin, X., Zhao, Y., Shen, B.: Abnormal subspace sparse PCA for anomaly detection and intepretation. In: The ACM SIGKDD Workshop on Outlier Detection and Description, ODD 2015, pp. 1–10 (2015)
5. Jolliffe, I.: Principal Component Analysis. Wiley Online Library, Hoboken (2002)
6. Jolliffe, I.T., Trendafilov, N.T., Uddin, M.: A modified principal component technique based on the LASSO. J. Comput. Graph. Stat. **12**(3), 531–547 (2003)
7. Luo, L., Bao, S., Mao, J., Tang, D.: Fault detection and diagnosis based on sparse PCA and two-level contribution plots. Ind. Eng. Chem. Res. **56**(1), 225–240 (2017)
8. Yu, H., Khan, F., Garaniya, V.: A sparse PCA for nonlinear fault diagnosis and robust feature discovery of industrial processes. AIChE J. **62**(5), 1494–1513 (2016)
9. Zou, H., Hastie, T., Tibshirani, R.: Sparse principal component analysis. J. Comput. Graph. Stat. **15**(2), 265–286 (2006)
10. d'Aspremont, A., El Ghaoui, L., Jordan, M.I., Lanckriet, G.R.G.: A direct formulation for sparse PCA using semidefinite programming. SIAM Rev. **49**(3), 434–448 (2007)
11. Boyd, S., Parikh, N., Chu, E., Peleato, B., Eckstein, J.: Distributed optimization and statistical learning via the alternating direction method of multipliers. Found. Trends Mach. Learn. **3**, 1–122 (2011)
12. Ma, S.: Alternating direction method for multipliers for sparse principal component analysis. J. Oper. Res. Soc. China **1**, 253–274 (2013)
13. Vu, V.Q., Cho, J., Lei, J., Rohe, K.: Fantope projection and selection: a near-optimal convex relaxation of sparse PCA. In: Advances in Neural Information Processing Systems, vol. 26, pp. 2670–2678 (2013)
14. Mackey, L.: Deflation methods for sparse PCA. In: Advances in Neural Information Processing Systems, vol. 22, pp. 1017–1024 (2009)
15. Breast Cancer Wisconsin (Diagnostic) Data Set (1995)
16. KDD Cup 1999 Data (1999)

Prevalence of Calves' Cryptosporidiosis in Northern Kazakhstan

Altay Ussenbayev[1], Dariyash Kurenkeyeva[2(✉)], Christian Bauer[3], and Ablaikhan Kadyrov[4]

[1] S. Seifullin Kazakh Agro Technical University, Nur-Sultan 010011, Kazakhstan
[2] International University of Information Technologies, Almaty 050040, Kazakhstan
dariyash.kurenkeyeva@gmail.com
[3] Justus Liebig University Giessen, Giessen 35392, Germany
[4] L. N. Gumilyov Eurasian National University, Nur-Sultan 010008, Kazakhstan

Abstract. This work examines the prevalence of *Cryptosporidium* spp. infection of cattle in the Akmola region of Northern Kazakhstan. The research was carried out at 75 agricultural enterprises in 10 administrative districts where 894 calves aged from one month to 12 months were tested for cryptosporidiosis. The Bayesian inference method was used to predict the prevalence of cryptosporidiosis. The maximum likelihood estimate (MLE) of infestation of young animals in the region was 0.0391. To get a conjugate beta-posterior in Bayesian statistics, binomial and beta distributions were chosen for likelihood and prior respectively. A 95% credible interval for posterior prevalence was [0.0418, 0.0685]. Cryptosporidiosis was common in 22.7% of cattle farms in the Akmola region, mainly in large industrial enterprises, where there are more favourable conditions for maintaining the biotic potential of the disease pathogens. At the same time, calves up to one month of age are infested with cryptosporidia to a higher degree than animals of older age groups. The sex of animals had no correlation with the level of *Cryptosporidium* spp. invasion.

Keywords: Bayesian inference · *Cryptosporidium* · Prevalence

1 Introduction

Protozoa species of the *Cryptosporidium* Tyzzer, 1907 genus (Phylum Apicomplexa) are pathogens of many vertebrate animals, including humans [1]. The parasites have a global distribution and cause epidemiological outbreaks of the contagious disease – cryptosporidiosis – among people with symptoms of diarrhoea, abdominal pain, nausea, vomiting and fever [2]. It is an emergent zoonotic disease described in more than 90 countries and six continents. For those living in endemic areas, immunocompromised people such as infants, malnourished subjects or patients with T-cell immunodeficiency conditions (e.g. due to HIV infection), symptoms can be severe and even dangerous for life [3]. The recent occurrence of large outbreaks in several countries all over the world, as well as the results of many surveys of human and animal cryptosporidiosis, indicate that pathogens of this infection are widespread [4].

O. Gervasi et al. (Eds.): ICCSA 2020, LNCS 12253, pp. 718–726, 2020.
https://doi.org/10.1007/978-3-030-58814-4_59

Humans may acquire *Cryptosporidium* by direct con-tact with infected people or animals, and indirectly through contaminated water and food. Now, more than 20 species of *Crypt-osporidium* have been described [1, 2]. It was established that specific subtypes of the zoonotic *Cryptosporidium parvum* and the anthroponotic *C.hominis* are responsible for the majority of human cases. Furthermore, many surveys of cryptosporidiosis indicate that cattle may be the main source of *Cryptosporidium* infection of people, and transmission of *C.parvum* from calves is common in outbreaks in human populations [5]. The risk infection magnitude to camping in pastures people posed by contact with faeces, that produced by infected with *C.parvum* livestock, has been modelled. It was established that the time between grazing and camping is the most important control strategy, but increasing hand-washing frequency and the removal of cattle faeces before camping would also be beneficial [6]. However, in Central Asia there is only sporadic information about cases of human infection with cryptosporidiosis [7, 8], although prevalence of cattle's *Cryptosporidium* in northern regions of Kazakhstan is relatively high [9]. Therefore, studies of the epidemiology of the disease in the region in order to ensure the safety of livestock breeders and their families are considered relevant.

Because the calves in small and private farms are fed manually, it is important to study cattle infected with cryptosporidia, which can also infect people [10].

To date, cryptosporidiosis is an unexplored disease in Kazakhstan, and the risk it poses to the population is obvious. It is also known that modelling has become one of the main instruments of research in modern epidemiology. However, in Kazakhstan such study technology has only been used for limited zoonotic contagious diseases [11, 12].

This research, therefore, aimed to model the cryptosporidiosis distribution in calf populations in the farms of northern Kazakhstan using the Bayesian inference method.

2 Materials and Methods

Epidemiological data were collected in 2018–2019 in 10 districts of the Akmola region during expeditionary trips to 75 farms, including 16 dairy farms, 26 fattening farms and 33 small house-holding farms. In total, faeces were sampled from 894 calves of three age groups (257 animals were less than one month, 303 were one to three months and 344 were 4 to 12 months in age). Samples were examined microscopically for the presence of *Cryptosporidium* spp. oocysts after routine staining with carbolic fuchsin, according Heine (1982) [13].

The field data obtained on spontaneous infection of animals with *Cryptosporidium* spp. were processed by Bayesian statistics.

The observations followed binomial distribution:

$$f(y|\theta) = C_n^{\sum y_i}\theta^{\sum y_i}(1-\theta)^{n-\sum y_i},$$

$$0 \le \theta \le 1,$$

where n – total number of examined animals, $\sum y_i$ - number of infected animals.

The concept of starting with the beta-prior and getting the beta-posterior is used when a posterior is in the same distribution family as a prior. The conjugate prior for binomial likelihood is the beta-prior:

$$\theta \sim Beta(\alpha, \beta)$$

$$f(\theta|\alpha, \beta) = \frac{\Gamma(\alpha+\beta)}{\Gamma(\alpha)\Gamma(\beta)}\theta^{\alpha-1}(1-\theta)^{\beta-1}$$

where α, β – parameters of beta distribution.

It was assumed that each animal was independent and that the probability of being infected was the same for all animals.

The expected value of beta distribution is $\frac{\alpha}{\alpha+\beta}$. Thus the effective sample size of binomial likelihood is $\alpha + \beta$.

The posterior predictive mean is a weighted of the prior distribution mean and the data mean, with weights proportional to the sample size. The prior and the data contribute to the posterior distribution:

$$f(\theta|y) = \frac{f(y|\theta)\cdot f(\theta)}{\int_0^1 f(y|\theta)\cdot f(\theta)d\theta}$$

Rather than work out the integral in denominator we can use the Kernel of beta distribution. Then

$$\int_0^1 f(y|\theta)\cdot f(\theta)d\theta = C_n^{\sum y_i}\cdot\frac{\Gamma(\alpha+\beta)}{\Gamma(\alpha)\Gamma(\beta)}\cdot\frac{\Gamma\left(\alpha+\sum y_i\right)\cdot\Gamma\left(\beta+n-\sum y_i\right)}{\Gamma(\alpha+\beta+n)}$$

Thus

$$f(\theta|y) = \frac{\Gamma(\alpha+\beta+n)}{\Gamma\left(\alpha+\sum y_i\right)\Gamma\left(\beta+n-\sum y_i\right)}\theta^{\alpha+\sum y_i-1}\cdot(1-\theta)^{\beta+n-\sum y_i-1}$$

or $Beta\left(\alpha+\sum y_i, \beta+n-\sum y_i\right)$.

R package functions dbeta, pbeta, qbeta, rbeta were used to implement Bayesian inference and find values for the credible intervals.

3 Results and Discussion

Although cryptosporidiosis is a dangerous zoonotic disease, a few studies of the parasitosis have been carried out in Central Asia. Results of these studies have indicated that *Cryptosporidium* is widespread in northern Kazakhstan. Infection by *Cryptosporidium* spp. was observed in 80% of Akmola region districts. The study showed a problem with cryptosporidiosis in 22.7% of farms studied, including 75.0% of dairy farms, 15.4% of fattening farms and 3% of small house-holding farms. It was indicated that the parasites of this genus were more widespread in large agricultural enterprises specialising in dairy production, compared to small producers and private farms.

In this cross-sectional epidemiological surveillance we often have had small sample sizes of faeces, which were depended to seasonality of calving and limited possibilities to collect and investigate enough and equal samples in different types of livestock enterprises and house holding farms. Therefore we used the Bayesian inference which has an ability to do sequential updates. Using previous posterior as a prior to do another update makes straight forward a sequential analysis in Bayesian statistics. It is appealing and practical for predicting the prevalence and population dynamics of epidemically important diseases of people or animals [11].

As mentioned before, beta distribution is conjugate for the binomial distribution, and beta-prior will give beta-posterior. Parameters of beta-prior distribution were chosen according to a number of studies suggested that the mean of *Cryptosporidium* prevalence was between 0.05 and 0.28 [9]. Such practice is considered convenient for Bayesian modelling and used widely in mathematical epidemiology [11].

A total of 894 animals were tested, 35 of which were infected. The maximum likelihood (MLE) was 0.0391. The results of a numerical experiment showed that the posterior mean was 0.0543 (see Fig. 1).

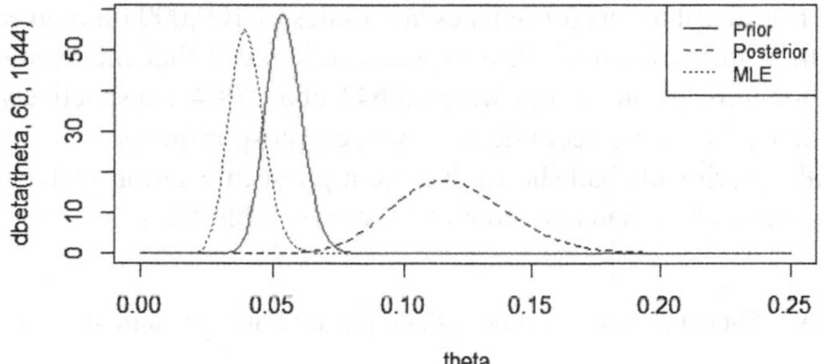

Fig. 1. Bayesian inference for total infection of animals.

In the tested animal population the 95% credible interval for θ was [0.0418, 0.0685].

473 of total examined animals were females, 19 of which were infected. For females, the corresponding MLE was 0.0402, the posterior mean was 0.0644 and 95% credible interval for θ was [0.0473, 0.0839] (see Fig. 2).

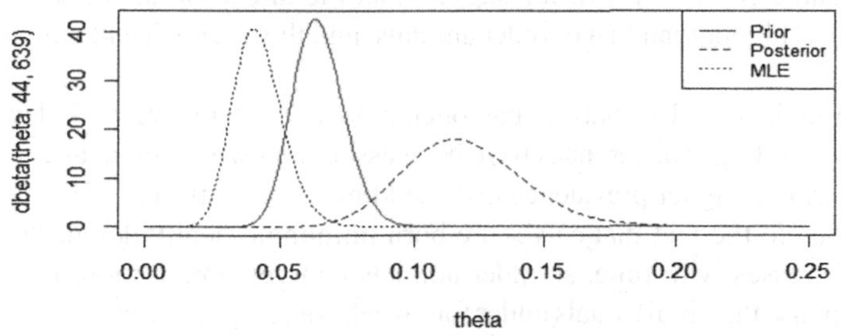

Fig. 2. Bayesian inference for infection of females.

16 of the 421 remaining males were infected. For males, the corresponding MLE was 0.0380, posterior mean was 0.0649, 95% credible interval for θ was [0.0471, 0.0855]

(see Fig. 3). The results showed that credible intervals for male and female animals were similar.

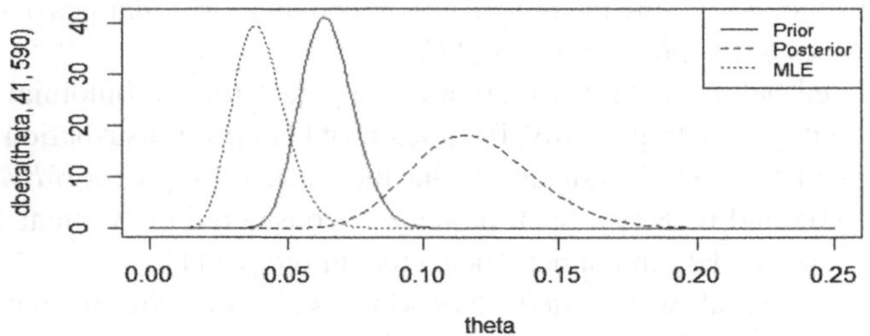

Fig. 3. Bayesian inference for infection of males.

The posterior distributions for females and males of 100,000 random samples were simulated. The results of a numerical experiment showed that the average empirical probabilities for females and males were 0.0644 and 0.0649, respectively. Therefore, the sex of animals does not affect infection with cryptosporidiosis.

Numerical experiments had shown that the highest infestation with cryptosporidia is observed in calves less than one month of age (see Table 1).

Table 1. Age fluctuations of infection with cryptosporidium of cattle in Akmola region

Age of calves	MLE	Posterior mean	95% CI for posterior mean	98% CI for posterior mean
Less than one month	0.0727	0.0953	[0.0695, 0.1248]	[0.0653, 0.1309]
One-three months	0.0293	0.0747	[0.0514, 0.1018]	[0.0478, 0.1076]
4–12 months	0.0244	0.0775	[0.0527, 0.1067]	[0.0488, 0.1129]

These characteristics of invasion suggest that the infection rate of calves at the first month of age is higher than that of older animals, and this is consistent with other studies [14–16].

It was established also that the pathogen's prevalence in livestock depended from season; however, larger differences have been associated with animal age, with younger animals showing a higher prevalence and shedding of oocysts [16, 17].

This is due to the fact that calves are born immunologically defenceless, and their immunity increases with time, so older animals can generate a more intense primary immune response than individuals under four weeks of age [18]. Apparently, the development of immunity leads to a relatively weak infection among animals of older age groups. However, the conditions for keeping and feeding animals of different ages maintain common sources and levels of infection in farms. In Kazakhstan, cow-calf-management in middle sized and small farms and large beef farms is described by the continuous contact between calves and dams that means also the development of natural colostral immunity in neonatal animals. Calves with dams appear to be protective, as they have the continuous and longer consumption of maternal antibodies with colostrum in the first days and with the mother milk before weaning. In support of this, it was found that using dehydrated milk can make calves more susceptible to infection [19].

Preliminary results of our study also indicated that such technology could be assessed as protective against *Cryptosporidium* infection. Analogical results were shown in the Czech Republic. Here the incidence level of *Cryptosporidium* invasion showed a greater increase in dairy farms where newborn animals were grown individually from birth, in comparison with beef farms, where neonatal calves were kept with their dams [16].

It is known that in the last decade, the number of reported human's cryptosporidiosis outbreaks has grown throughout the world [20]. The main source of the pathogen for people is water, and the huge amount of oocysts excreted by the infected host has defined the increasing of environmental contamination. Cattle have been involved in the epidemiological process as a source of *Cryptosporidium*, because cattle farms are located in watersheds [21]. Calves have the greatest prevalence and shedding intensity of *Cryptosporidium* at approximately first four weeks of age. In experiment, mean number of oocysts excreted by calves <30 days old was approximately 6×10^7 per g of faeces. These results indicated that one calf would excrete some 6×10^{11} oocysts in the first month after birth, taking both the quantity of faeces in a day and the period of excretion into consideration [22]. Thus, calving as the method of breeding management is important in relation to the peak numbers of pathogens released into the environment. It is known that calves produce less manure than adult animals, but the shedding intensity of pathogens by calves is greater and they realise more amount of cryptosporidia compared to the total cattle population.

In Kazakhstan, calving occurs mainly in the spring. Therefore, this period is potentially a critical time for contamination of water utilities.

Exposures to waterborne *Cryptosporidium* oocysts in recreational or drinking water are the global public health problem. Determining the sources of pathogens in the watershed and quantifying their environmental loading are very important from positions of biological safety for human and animals' populations. The natural variability of potentially pathogenic microorganisms in the environment from anthropogenic, natural, and livestock sources is large and difficult to quantify [23].

So, our research is the first step in characterizing the risk of contamination by non-point sources from pathogens of animal origin to determine the potential environmental impact based on the prevalence of animals in northern Kazakhstan.

Previously a probabilistic model was developed to evaluate the production of *Cryptosporidium* spp. from livestock sources within the watershed. For a real river watershed in a large geographic region, probability density functions were simulated, representing the daily rate of livestock pathogen production. The prevalence of cryptosporidia in cattle was modelled as a mixture of β-distributions. Analogically, Γ-distributions were obtained to describe the shedding intensity of animal pathogens. The methodology demonstrated possibilities to determine the initial terms for modelling the fate of pathogens and their transfer, as well as to identify and determine the regions that are most vulnerable to water pollution from pathogenic sources [23].

Results of our studies have shown that prevalence of *Cryptosporidium spp.* in calves of the studied region varies on different agricultural farms, in the range of 2.4 and 28.0% [9]. Average infection with cryptosporidia of calves in northern Kazakhstan was higher than in Canada [10], Mexico [24] and Spain [25], but lower than in Africa [14] and Germany [15]. This, apparently, reflects the influence of many factors, including the climate and the level of housing technologies used in farms (for example, individual boxes, hygienic conditions of calf housing places); physiological state of animals at the time of sampling (diarrhoeal and non-diarrhoeal); used research and coprological diagnostic methodologies. Furthermore, calves were more infected with *Cryptosporidium* on farms with large cow herds [25]. It was suggested that larger herds produce higher density of calf populations, which come to be infected *Cryptosporidium* and increased contamination of environment and risk infection to humans. It is also known that other numerous management characteristics (such as herd size, type of herd, water sources and weaning modality *etc.*) have been evaluated as potential risk factors for the transmission of these pathogens at farms, yet the results have been discordant [15, 26–28].

Therefore, further research would also be required to assess and modelling the risk factors in epidemiology of cattle's cryptosporidiosis for developing the optimal control management in farms of different types and preventing the environment contamination and infecting of people with the zoonosis in northern Kazakhstan.

4 Conclusions

Cryptosporidiosis is common in 22.7% of cattle farms in the Akmola region, mainly in large industrial enterprises, where there are more favourable conditions for maintaining the biotic potential of the disease pathogens. The maximum likelihood estimate (MLE) for the infestation of young animals in the region was 0.0391 and posterior mean was 0.0543. The credible interval for posterior prevalence was [0.0418, 0.0685]. At the same time, calves up to one month of age are infested with cryptosporidia to a higher degree than animals of older age groups. The sex of animals had no correlation with the level of *Cryptosporidium* spp. invasion.

The Bayesian inference technique allowed for predicting the prevalence of the disease and planning measures to control cattle cryptosporidiosis in the conditions of different types of enterprises in the Akmola region.

Acknowledgment. The research was supported by the grant of the Ministry of Education and Science of the Republic of Kazakhstan (Project APO5135550) in 2018–2020.

References

1. Fayer, R.: Taxonomy and species delimitation in cryptosporidium. Exp. Parasitol. **124**, 90–97 (2010)
2. Cacciò, S., Chalmers, R.: Human cryptosporidiosis in Europe. Clin. Microbiol. Infect. **22**(6), 471–480 (2016)

3. Insulander, M., Silverlas, C., Lebbad, M., Karlsson, L., Mattsson, G., Svenungsson, B.: Molecular epidemiology and clinical manifestations of human cryptosporidiosis in Sweden. Epidemiol. Infect. **141**(5), 1009–1020 (2013)
4. Xiao, L.: Molecular epidemiology of cryptosporidiosis: an up-date. Exp. Parasitol. **124**(1), 80–89 (2010)
5. Vieira, P., et al.: Molecular characterisation of Cryptosporidium (Apicomplexa) in children and cattle in Romania. Folia Parasitol. **62**(2), 1–4 (2015)
6. Hill, A., Nally, P., Chalmers, R., Pritchard, G., Giles, M.: Quantitative risk assessment for zoonotic transmission of *Cryptosporidium parvum* infection attributable to recreational use of farmland. Zoonoses Public Health **58**, 222–333 (2011)
7. Borodina, O., Zhukova, E., Kravets, Z.: The detection of the causative agent of cryptosporidiosis in man and animals in Turkmenistan. Med. Parazitol. **1**, 8–11 (1994)
8. Nurtaev, Kh., Badalova, N., Zalialieva, M., Osipova, S.: Intestinal parasitic diseases in HIV-infected patients in Uzbekistan. Med. Parazitol. **3**, 45–49 (2005)
9. Ussenbayev, A., Kurenkeyeva, D., Zhanabayev, A., Bauer, Ch., Leader, L.: Modelling the epidemiology of cryptosporidiosis in cattle in Central Kazakhstan. In: Digests 8th International Scientific Meeting "Days of Veterinary Medicine-2018, Ohrid, Macedonia, 23–27 September 2018, p. 49 (2018)
10. Gow, S., Waldner, C.: An examination of the prevalence of and risk factors for shedding of *Cryptosporidium* spp. and *Giardia* spp. in cows and calves from western Canadian cow-calf herds. Vet. Parasitol. **119**(1), 192–195 (2008)
11. Torgerson, P., Shaikenov, B., Rysmukhambetova, A., Ussenbayev, A., Abdybekova, A., Burtisurnov, K.: Modelling the transmission dynamics of *Echinococcus granulosus* in dogs in rural Kazakhstan. Parasitol. **126**, 417–424 (2003)
12. Abdrakhmanov, S., Mukhanbetkalyev, E., Ussenbayev, A., Satybaldina, D., Kadyrov, A., Tashatov, N.: Modeling the epidemiological processes of economically significant infections of animals. In: Misra, S., et al. (eds.) ICCSA 2019. LNCS, vol. 11621, pp. 551–560. Springer, Cham (2019). https://doi.org/10.1007/978-3-030-24302-9_39
13. Heine, J.: Eine einfache Nachweismethode für Kryptosporidien im Kot. Zbl. Vet. Med. **29**, 324–327 (1982)
14. Peter, G., et al.: Prevalence of Cryptosporidia, Eimeria, Giardia, and Strongyloides in preweaned calves on smallholder dairy farms in Mukurwe-ini district. Kenya. Vet. World **8**(9), 1118–1125 (2015)
15. Velez, J., Lange, M., Zieger, P., Yoon, I., Failing, K., Bauer, Ch.: Long-term use of yeast fermentation products in comparison to halofuginone for the control of cryptosporidiosis in neonatal calves. Vet. Parasitol. **269**, 57–64 (2019)
16. Kváč, M., Kouba, M., Vitovek, J.: Age related and housing-dependence of *Cryptosporidium* infection of calves from dairy and beef herds in South Bohemia. Czech Republic. Vet. Parasitol. **137**(3–4), 202–209 (2006)
17. Olson, M., Thorlakson, C., Deselliers, L., Morck, D., McAllister, T.: *Giardia* and *Cryptosporidium* in Canadian farm animals. Vet. Parasitol. **68**, 375–381 (1997)
18. Tizard, I.: In: Veterinary Immunology. An Introduction. 8th edn., pp. 224–238. Saunders Company, Philadelphia (2009)
19. Quigley, J., et al.: Effects of housing and colostrum feeding on the prevalence of selected infectious organisms in feces of Jersy calves. J. Dairy Sci. **77**, 3124–3131 (1994)
20. Smith, S., Elliot, A., Mallaghan, C., Modha, D., Hippisley-Cox, J., Large, S.: Value of syndromic surveillance in monitoring a focal waterborne outbreak due to an unusual *Cryptosporidium* genotype in Northamptonshire, United Kingdom, June–July 2008. Euro. Surveill. **15**, 19643 (2010)
21. Ramirez, N., Ward, L., Sreevatsan, S.: A review of the biology and epidemiology of cryptosporidiosis in humans and animals. Microbes Infect. **6**(8), 773–785 (2004)

22. Uga, S., et al.: Prevalence of *Cryptosporidium parvum* infection and pattern of oocyst shedding in calves in Japan. Vet. Parasitol. **94**, 27–32 (2000)
23. Dorner, S., Huck, P., Slawson, R.: Estimating potential environmental loadings of *Cryptosporidium* spp. and *Campylobacter* spp. from livestock in the Grand River Watershed, Ontario. Canada. Environ. Sci. Technol. **38**, 3370–3380 (2004)
24. Maldonago-Carmago, S., Atwill, E., Saltijeral-Oaxaca, J., Herrera-Alonso, L.: Prevalence of and risk factors for shedding of *Cryptosporidium parvum* in Holstein Freisian dairy calves in central Mexico. Prev. Vet. Med. **36**, 95–107 (1998)
25. de La Fuente, R., et al.: *Cryptosporidium* and concurrent infections with other major enterophatogens in 1 to 30-day-old diarrheic dairy calves in central Spain. Vet. Parasitol. **80**(3), 179–185 (1999)
26. Garber, L., Salman, M., Hurd, H., Keefe, T., Schlater, J.: Potential risk factors for *Cryptosporidium* infection in dairy calves. J. Am. Vet. Med. Assoc. **205**(1), 86–91 (1994)
27. Mohammed, H., Wade, S., Schaaf, S.: Risk factors associated with *Cryptosporidium parvum* infection in dairy cattle in southeastern New York State. Vet. Parasitol. **83**, 1–13 (1999)
28. Castro-Hermida, J., Gonzales-Losada, Y., Ares-Mazas, E.: Prevalence of and risk factors involved in the spread of neonatal bovine cryptosporidiosis in Galicia (NW Spain). Vet. Parasitol. **106**, 1–10 (2002)

Formal Language Model for Transcriptome and Proteome Data Integration

Reginaldo Inojosa da Silva Filho[1], Ricardo Luis de Azevedo da Rocha[2], and Claudio Santos Oliveira[1(✉)]

[1] Campus de Ponta Porã, Universidade Federal de Mato Grosso do Sul, Ponta Porã, Mato Grosso do Sul, Brazil
reginaldo.uspoli@gmail.com, claudio.santos@aluno.ufms.br
[2] Departamento de Engenharia da Computação, Escola Politécnica da Universidade de São Paulo, São Paulo, Brazil
rlarocha@usp.br

Abstract. We present in this article, for the area of structural and functional genetics, a preliminary theoretical model based on the representation of transcriptomes and proteomes as families of formal languages, in which the phenomenon of translation is described as a artificial language transduction process (present in programming languages compilers), making it possible to unify the transcriptomic and proteomic data.

Keywords: Calculi · Computational simulation · Transcriptome · Proteome · Formal languages

1 Introduction

Computer simulation is a fast and flexible virtual process that can significantly reduce the need for resources and time, which can make systems unfeasible [16]. It does not replace *in vivo* experimentation, but provides important information to achieve scientific and technological goals in critical areas of biology and health [5,13].

Our purpose, in this initial work, is to present a model (basis for the construction of a computational framework) for further simulation in the area of gene expression, more specifically, the mapping between the elements of the transcriptomes and the proteomes (apprehended by *omics*), in order to allow data integration between these two areas, and study their interactions.

Transcriptomic and proteomic are independent areas, however, there are efforts to integrate them [8,15,21]. Our objective is to create a model that integrates both under the same form of representation: **formal languages**. More specifically, we will represent the transcriptomes and the proteomes as families of formal languages, and model the phenomenon of translation as a transduction process of artificial languages.

O. Gervasi et al. (Eds.): ICCSA 2020, LNCS 12253, pp. 727–735, 2020.
https://doi.org/10.1007/978-3-030-58814-4_60

We seek the simplicity necessary to provide an immediate computational implementation, without however making it an *ad hoc* solution. We are inspired by a series of existing approaches that deal with the modeling of genetic processes [1], such as the π-*calculus* and the work of Searls [7,19]. In our model, we will present the biological substrate of the relationship between transcriptomes and the proteomes from the point of view of language processing [9]. Biological information processing is based on the DNA and RNA alphabets of 4 symbols each, and the protein alphabet containing 20 symbols. Biological translation mechanism is represented by the process of transduction between the *"strings of symbols"* [20] formed by such alphabets (RNAs and proteins). Thus, using an analogy with the activity of programming, we can say that a **"source code"** (**transcriptome**) is converted into an **"object code"** (**proteome**), which allows the **"computational architecture"** (**organism**) to execute the instructions contained therein (events that lead to the manifestation of **phenotypic characteristics**).

The work is organized as follows. Section 3 presents the definition both of formal proteome and transcriptome, as well as the main abstractions from biology such as the concept of organism and the establishment of a set of time intervals that serve as a basis for the construction of such definitions. Section 4 presents the different types of transformations that can be applied to the transcriptome. Such transformations take into account only the formal characteristics and, initially, we will not analyze their biological implications. Among these transformations, we highlight the modeling made of the translation phenomenon. Finally, Sect. 5 discusses the results and the next steps to be followed.

2 Background

In this section, we give several definitions and notations required for the adequate discussion of the present article. We assume that the reader has familiarity with basics genetic concepts and computational formal languages theory. The basic computational concepts used in this work (mostly concerning automata theory), as well the pertinent notation, are summarized in Table 1 of Annex; for more details see [11].

2.1 Biological Background

The first genome expression product is the **transcriptome** [6]. It is the complete set of coding transcripts that are active in a given cell organism, tissue, lineage or organelle in a given time interval; constituting the profile (or large-scale pattern) of all mRNAs present in the cell in a given period [12]. The second product of the organism's gene expression is its **proteome**, which is the complete set of all proteins, obtained by the process of **translation** in a given organ, tissue, lineage or cell organelle in a given period of time [4,12].

The Translation process involves ribosomes, mRNAs, tRNAs and amino acids. In the cytoplasm, amino acids must join with their respective tRNAs.

$\mathbb{N}$	**the set of natural numbers**
$card(\mathcal{Y})$	**the cardinality of** $\mathcal{Y}$, (number of elements in the set)
Σ	**an alphabet of symbols**
$\alpha \in \Sigma$	**a symbol of the alphabet**
$\Sigma^* = \bigcup_{k=0}^{\infty} \Sigma^k$	**the reflexive transitive closure over** Σ
$L \subseteq \Sigma^*$	**a language over** Σ
$w \in L$	**a word of** L
$\mathbf{L}$	**a language with repetition words**
$\|w\| = n$ with $n \in \mathbb{N}$	**the lenght of the word** w
$\Sigma^{\leqslant k}$	**the set of all words with lenght less than or equal to** k

Fig. 1. Notation for technical preliminaries related to computational theory.

During translation, the tRNA molecules bind to the ribosome. The ribosome, in turn, processes the entire coding sequence for the mRNA. As this reading takes place, a series of tRNA connections and disconnections are made with the ribosomes, which in concert bring the amino acids that will compose the resulting protein formed.

In the mRNA coding sequence, **each group of three nucleotides corresponds to a given amino acid**. Such a group is called **codon**, which is chemically recognized by the tRNA carrying the corresponding amino acid. Since there are four nucleotides that make up an RNA, there are 64 different codons (Table 1), where three of them do not encode amino acids, but serve as a stop sign for translation. Since there are only 20 amino acids (Table 1 of Annex, first column), **different codons can encode the same amino acid**. Because of this, it is said that the genetic code is **degenerate** [17].

The insertion and connection of amino acids occurs in the same order in which their respective codons are recognized, in a phenomenon known as **principle of collinearity** [14]. Thus, the linear sequence of the nucleotides determines the primary structure in a protein, forming, in parts, the resulting protein sequence, until it reaches the codon that serves as the termination signal.

2.2 Computational Background

Given two alphabets Σ_1 and Σ_2 distinct, the function $R : \Sigma_1^* \rightarrow \Sigma_2^*$ is **transduction** [2, p. 65], whose graph $\mathcal{R}$ is described as:

$$\mathcal{R} = \{(u, v) \in \Sigma_1^* \times \Sigma_2^* \quad | \quad R(u) = v\}$$

The function R can be performed by a machine called **transducer** [2, p. 77], defined as:

$$\mathfrak{R} = (\mathcal{Q}, \Sigma_1, \Sigma_2, q_0, \mathcal{F}, \partial)$$

Where $\mathcal{Q}$ is a set of states, Σ_1 is the constituent alphabet of the input strings, Σ_2 is the alphabet of the output strings, q_0 is the initial state, $\mathcal{F} \subseteq Q$ is the set

Table 1. Mapping between codons and amino acids [10]

Amino acid name	Codons
Alanine	GCA GCC GCG GCU
Arginine	AGA AGG CGA CGC CGG CGU
Aspartic acid	GAC GAU
Asparagine	AAC AAU
Cysteine	UGC UGU
Glutamic acid	GAA GAG
Glutamine	CAA CAG
Glycine	GGA GGC GGG GGU
Histidine	CAC CAU
Isoleucine	AUA AUC AUU
Leucine	UUA UUG CUA CUC CUG CUU
Lysine	AAA AAG
Methionine	AUG
Phenylalanine	UUC UUU
Proline	CCA CCC CCG CCU
Serine	AGC AGU UCA UCC UCG UCU
Threonine	ACA ACC ACG ACU
Tryptophan	UGG
Tyrosine	UAC UAU
Valine	GUA GUC GUG GUU
Stop	UAA UAG UGA

of final states and the transition relationship function ∂ is defined as:

$$\partial \subset \mathcal{Q} \times \Sigma_1 \times \Sigma_2 \times \mathcal{Q}$$

For a transducer $\mathfrak{R}$, a **computation** is a sequence of consecutive transitions

$$\Delta = (\delta_1, \delta_2, ..., \delta_n)$$

where:

$$\delta_i = (q', \alpha_i, \beta_i, q'') \text{ and } \delta_{i+1} = (q'', \alpha_{i+1}, \beta_{i+1}, q''')$$

with $\delta_i \in \partial$ and $1 \leq i \leq n$. Computation can also be represented by the notation:

$$\Delta^{(u,v)} = p \xrightarrow{\frac{u}{v}} s$$

where the word $u = \alpha_1\alpha_2 \dots \alpha_n \in \Sigma_1^*$ is the computing entry and $v = \beta_1\beta_2 \dots \beta_n \in \Sigma_2^*$ is the output word, for $p, s \in \mathcal{Q}$.

A computation is **successful** if $p = q_0$ and $s \in \mathcal{F}$ [3, p. 18]. Thus, for a computing entry u, the processing $\mathfrak{R}(u)$, calculated by the transducer, is the concatenation produced as a result of the computation. In this way, we have to:

$$\mathfrak{R}(u) = \{v \in \Sigma_2^* \mid \exists(\Delta^{(u,v)} \text{ is successful})\}$$

3 Transcriptome and Proteome as Formal Languages

Although formal (artificial) languages do not encompass the complexity of human language, they are useful not only for the study of linguistic themes, but also for several computational purposes [18]. In general, from a linguistic point of view, an occurrence experienced by someone (real or not) is expressed in a language (natural or artificial) and then transformed into a record, which can be passed on and transformed over time. Something similar is done to define the abstractions for transcriptomes and proteomes: we describe a biological phenomenon in terms of a (formal) language, establishing some assumptions and relaxing some restrictions in relation to the physical phenomenon, building an functional (in the mathematical sense) articulation of possible relationships, which can be "expressed" in the form of computer program and executed under different forms, circumstances and modes (based on experimental or hypothetical data). This abstract construction begins with the description of the prerequisites that serve as support for the model, described in the two items below:

1. (**First prerequisite**) We define the set, called $\mathcal{O}$, as the set of all organisms with transcriptomes and proteomes.
2. (**Second prerequisite**) Both, the RNA and the primary structure of proteins can be described as strings of characters.

Every element of $\mathcal{O}$ is represented by the ordered pair $o = (\mathcal{C}, \mathcal{I})$ where:

- $\mathcal{C} = \{c_1, c_2, \ldots, c_k\}$ (with $k \in \mathbb{N}$) is the **set of containers**. Each container is a set of a specific type of tissue, cell or cellular organelle, present in the organism $\mathcal{O}$, according to what the analysis at the moment requires. Such an abstraction gives the freedom to treat only the elements relevant to the analysis.
- $\mathcal{I} = \{i_1, i_2, \ldots, i_p\}$ (com $p \in \mathbb{N}$) is called **set of expressiveness intervals**, which consists of a **partition** of an interval Δt of the organism's lifetime.

Given the second prerequisite, we have the definition of the following two alphabets:

- $\Sigma_{\text{RNA}} = \{A, G, C, U\}$ composed of the symbols that represent the four ribonucleotides. A string $s \in \Sigma_{\text{RNA}}^{\leqslant n}$ represents the coding segment of an mRNA.
- $\Sigma_{\text{AM}} = \{A, R, D, N, C, E, Q, G, H, I, L, K, M, F, P, S, T, W, Y, V\}$, composed of letters that represent each of the 20 amino acids, according to Table 1 of Annex. A string $p \in \Sigma_{\text{AM}}^{\leqslant m}$, represents the primary structure of a protein.

The natural numbers m and n in $\Sigma_{\text{AM}}^{\leqslant m}$ and $\Sigma_{\text{RNA}}^{\leqslant n}$ are restrictions that prevent the occurrence of proteins or mRNA strings with infinite size.

Thus, the **Formal Transcriptome** (T) and the **Formal Proteome** (Π) can be defined by the functions:

$$T : \mathcal{C} \times \mathcal{I} \rightarrow \mathcal{L}_{\Sigma_{\text{RNA}}} \tag{1}$$

$$\Pi : \mathcal{C} \times \mathcal{I} \rightarrow \mathcal{L}_{\Sigma_{\text{AM}}} \tag{2}$$

Whose codomain $\mathcal{L}_{\Sigma_{\text{RNA}}}$ and $\mathcal{L}_{\Sigma_{\text{AM}}}$ are **families of indexed and non-empty languages**, so that for $\mathbf{max} = card(\mathcal{I}) \times card(\mathcal{C})$, they are specified as:

$$\mathcal{L}_{\Sigma_{\text{RNA}}} = \{\mathbf{L}_1, \mathbf{L}_2, \ldots, \mathbf{L}_j\} \text{ where } (j \leq \mathbf{max}) \text{ and } \forall(\mathbf{L}_i \in \mathcal{L}_{\Sigma_{\text{RNA}}})(\mathbf{L}_i \subset \Sigma_{\text{RNA}}^{\leqslant n})$$

$$\mathcal{L}_{\Sigma_{\text{AM}}} = \{\mathbf{L}_1, \mathbf{L}_2, \ldots, \mathbf{L}_z\} \text{ where } (z \leq \mathbf{max}) \text{ and } \forall(\mathbf{L}_k \in \mathcal{L}_{\Sigma_{\text{AM}}})(\mathbf{L}_k \subset \Sigma_{\text{AM}}^{\leqslant m})$$

where each member language, both in $\mathcal{L}_{\Sigma_{\text{RNA}}}$ and $\mathcal{L}_{\Sigma_{\text{AM}}}$, there may be repeated words.

The modeling presented in this section will allow the definition of a transformation on formal transcriptomes and proteomes.

4 Transformation over Formal Transcriptome

The transformation on formal transcriptomes is related to considerations about what the phenomenon of translation **computes**. First, we have to capture the main characteristics of the translation process in the form of **postulates**. They are:

Postulate 1. *From the Table 1 of Annex, the presence of* ***codons*** *(which we will call k_i) in the coding section of the mRNAs, allows to describe it as:*

$$t = k_1 k_2 \ldots k_l \text{ with } k_i \in \Sigma_{RNA}^3, \text{ where } l \text{ is the lenght of computation time.}$$

Postulate 2. *The fact that the genetic code is* ***degenerate*** *makes it possible to describe the equivalence table between codons and amino acids as being a total function D with 64 elements in the domain and 21 elements in the codomain (since stop codons are taken into account):*

$$D : \Sigma_{RNA}^3 \rightarrow \Sigma_{AM}$$

Postulate 3. *The principle of* ***collinearity*** *makes it possible to associate states to the processing steps of the codons by the ribosomes, so that we can represent function D through a set $\mathcal{D}$ of 64 computations:*

$$\mathcal{D} = \{\Delta^{(GCA,A)}, \Delta^{(GCC,A)}, \Delta^{(GCG,A)}, \Delta^{(GCU,A)}, \ldots, \Delta^{(UAA,\varepsilon)}, \Delta^{(UAG,\varepsilon)}, \Delta^{(UGA,\varepsilon)}\} \tag{3}$$

Postulate 4. *Reading the coding portion, done in a single direction, makes it possible to associate an initial state and stop codons (Table 1 of Annex, last line) and also makes it possible to establish a state q_f final. So for $q \in Q$, we have the following specifications for computations involving stop codons:*

$$\Delta^{(UAA,\varepsilon)} = q \xrightarrow[\varepsilon]{UAA} q_f$$
$$\Delta^{(UAG,\varepsilon)} = q \xrightarrow[\varepsilon]{UAG} q_f$$
$$\Delta^{(UGA,\varepsilon)} = q \xrightarrow[\varepsilon]{UGA} q_f$$

Now we can state the proposition that is the center of the modeling proposed in this article.

Proposition 1. *For each and every member of the set $\mathcal{O}$ of organisms that have a transcriptome T and a proteome Π formal, there is a transformation M for which:*

$$M(T) = \Pi \tag{4}$$

Proof. Let's build a transducer $\mathfrak{R}_{\text{RNA/AM}}$ to model the translation phenomenon, so that, for T and Π of a particular member body of $\mathcal{O}$, we have the graph:

$$\mathcal{R}_{\text{RNA/AM}} = \{(T(c,i), \Pi(c,i)) \mid \mathfrak{R}_{\text{RNA/AM}}(T(c,i)) = \Pi(c,i)\}$$

com $T(c,i) \in \Sigma^{\leqslant n}_{\text{RNA}}$ and $\Pi(c,i))\Sigma^{\leqslant m}_{\text{AM}}$

From the above postulates and using concatenation, union and Kleene's star operations, we built the $\mathfrak{R}_{\text{RNA/AM}}$ transducer shown in Fig. 2, for which:

$$\forall(c \in \mathcal{C})\forall(i \in \mathcal{I})\exists\Delta^{(T(c,i),\Pi(c,i))}\textbf{successful}.$$

Figure 2 presents the transducer for some codons. We have also suppressed the transitions and intermediate states related to the recognition of each of the nucleotides that make up the codons. Instead, the elements of the set were used $\mathcal{D}$, presented in the expression 3, through the use of a transition graphic with a differentiated arrow, as can be seen between the states q_0 and q_x, for example.

In possession of the transducer $\mathfrak{R}_{\text{RNA/AM}}$, we can develop a method to build Π from T for any $\mathcal{O}$.

$$\bigcup_{card(\mathcal{C})} \bigcup_{card(\mathcal{I})} \bigcup_{t \in T(c,i)} \mathfrak{R}_{\text{RNA/AM}}(t) = \Pi$$

However, we can use a more compact notation in place of expression

$$\bigcup_{card(\mathcal{C})} \bigcup_{card(\mathcal{I})} \bigcup_{t \in T(c,i)} \mathfrak{R}_{\text{RNA/AM}}(t)$$

replacing it with $M(T)$.

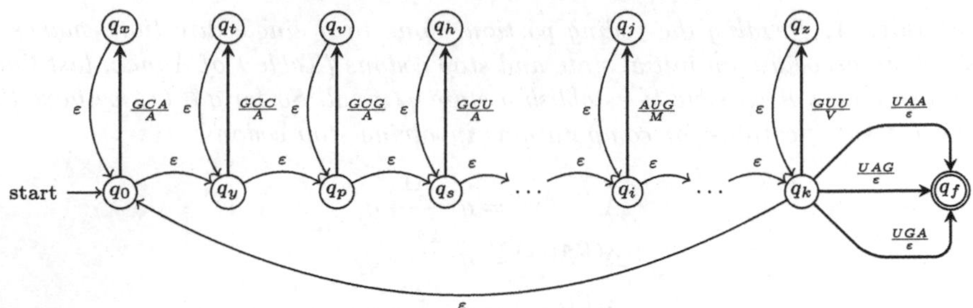

Fig. 2. The transducer $\mathfrak{R}_{\mathrm{RNA/AM}}$

5 Conclusion

When delimiting (by means of formal languages) the aspects of both transcriptomes and proteomes, we stipulate the criteria to show that, although they are heterogeneous in constitution, both are governed by an internal uniformity expressed by the formal structure that describes them, expressed through the developed model.

With absolutely reasonable considerations about the nature of the translation phenomenon, abstractly presented as a language processor, we arrive at the logical conclusion described by the equation $M(T) = \Pi$, which relates transcriptomics and proteomics information.

Thus, based on transcriptomics data, we can infer information about organism proteomics aspects, through *in silico* experiments, going beyond a simple database architecture, entering the field of inference and allowing the automatic generation of a **transcriptome - proteome mapping**, even in situations that have information gaps.

Throughout this preliminary article, we emphasize our approach to focus attention on formal linguistic aspects resulting from computational modeling, placing their biological meanings in the background and verifying the properties resulting from symbolic relations.

Continuing this idea, we can consider and imagine a mapping that is "inverse" to that resulting from the translation phenomenon, that is: morphism $M(\Pi) = T$, which, although not related to any biological phenomenon, could very well be useful in computationally simulated analyses. It would allow the application of **inverse problems** for questions of genetic expressiveness, that is, to answer the question *"given a desired phenotypic characteristic, which transcripts would produce it?"* It is important to note that in such a morphism M', for an input, there are two or more outputs. The implications of this fact and the resulting extensions in the model, as well the influence of other factors (as probability and heuristics, for example), are themes for future work.

References

1. Bartocci, E., Lió, P.: Computational modeling, formal analysis, and tools for systems biology. PLoS Comput. Biol. **12**(1), e1004591 (2016)
2. Berstel, J.: Transductions and Context-Free Languages. Springer, Heidelberg (2013)
3. Berstel, J., Perrin, D., Reutenauer, C.: Codes and Automata, vol. 129. Cambridge University Press, Cambridge (2010)
4. Bessant, C., et al.: Proteome informatics. Royal Society of Chemistry (2016)
5. Butcher, E.C., Berg, E.L., Kunkel, E.J.: Systems biology in drug discovery. Nat. Biotechnol. **22**(10), 1253–1259 (2004)
6. Cellerino, A., Sanguanini, M.: Transcriptome Analysis: Introduction and Examples from the Neurosciences, vol. 17. Springer, Heidelberg (2018). https://doi.org/10.1007/978-88-7642-642-1
7. Datta, S., Mukhopadhyay, S.: A grammar inference approach for predicting kinase specific phosphorylation sites. PLoS One **10**(4), e0122294 (2015)
8. Fan, M., et al.: Integration of deep transcriptome and proteome analyses of salicylic acid regulation high temperature stress in ulva prolifera. Sci. Rep. **7**(1), 1–19 (2017)
9. Gross, F.: The impact of formal reasoning in computational biology. In: Bertolaso, M., Sterpetti, F. (eds.) A Critical Reflection on Automated Science. HPHST, vol. 1, pp. 139–155. Springer, Cham (2020). https://doi.org/10.1007/978-3-030-25001-0_7
10. Hartwell, L., Goldberg, M.L., Fischer, J.A., Hood, L.E., Aquadro, C.F.: Genetics: from Genes to Genomes. McGraw-Hill, New York (2008)
11. Hopcroft, J.E.: Introduction to Automata Theory, Languages, and Computation. Pearson Addison Wesley, Boston (2007)
12. Kahl, G.: The Dictionary of Genomics, Transcriptomics and Proteomics. Wiley, Hoboken (2015)
13. Kitano, H.: Systems biology: a brief overview. Science **295**(5560), 1662–1664 (2002)
14. Klug, W.S., Cummings, M.R., Spencer, C.A., Palladino, M.A.: Concepts of Genetics. Benjamin Cummings, San Francisco (2014)
15. Kumar, D., Bansal, G., Narang, A., Basak, T., Abbas, T., Dash, D.: Integrating transcriptome and proteome profiling: strategies and applications. Proteomics **16**(19), 2533–2544 (2016)
16. Nutaro, J.J.: Building Software for Simulation: Theory and Algorithms, with Application in C++. Wiley Online Library, Hoboken (2011)
17. Pierce, B.A.: Genetics: A Conceptual Approach. Macmillan, New York (2012)
18. Rozenberg, G., Salomaa, A.: Handbook of Formal Languages: Volume 3 Beyond Words. Springer, Heidelberg (2012)
19. Searls, D.B.: The language of genes. Nature **420**(6912), 211–217 (2002)
20. Sempere, J.M.: On compensation loops in genomic duplications. Int. J. Found. Comput. Sci. **31**(01), 133–142 (2020)
21. Zhu, W., et al.: Integration of transcriptomics, proteomics and metabolomics data to reveal the biological mechanisms of abrin injury in human lung epithelial cells. Toxicol. Lett. **312**, 1–10 (2019)

Towards Integration of Containers into Scientific Workflows: A Preliminary Experience with Cached Dependencies

Bruno da Silva Alves(✉) and Andrea Schwertner Charão(✉)

Universidade Federal de Santa Maria, Santa Maria, Brazil
{bdalves,andrea}@inf.ufsm.br

Abstract. A scientific workflow consists of a large number of tasks that are typically performed on distributed systems. For each node in the distributed computing system, an entire environment must be configured to be able to run a set of tasks, which depend on libraries, binaries, etc. Containers can provide lightweight virtualization capable of isolating the application and its dependencies, ensuring flexibility to run the same environment on different hosts. In this work, we investigate the integration of containers into scientific workflows, by combining Docker and Makeflow technologies. We focus on performance issues and propose a cache system adapted to containers, considering that data transfers can represent a potential bottleneck on iterative executions typically found in scientific workflows. We use Docker Volumes to circumvent the volatility of containers, allowing files stored in the cache to be available when a new container is instantiated. Our experimental results from the execution of two real-world bioinformatics workflows (Blast and Hecil) show that using our cache system effectively decreases execution times. We also show that the number of workers per host impacts the workflow execution time in different ways.

Keywords: Scientific workflows · Containers · Distributed systems

1 Introduction

Research advances usually rely on experimentation, which allows scientists to support or refute previously formulated hypotheses. Scientists from various fields use software tools to process the data collected from experiments. Also, they usually establish a workflow in which tasks are performed over data. In general, a workflow describes how processes must be coordinated to achieve a common goal [3], and the development of a workflow can help scientists to automate the experimentation process.

Each task in a scientific workflow reads some input data, perform analyses and computations, then generates output data. The output generated by a task can be used as an input for another, generating a graph. However, workflow tasks not only depend on input data, they also require implicit dependencies such as

O. Gervasi et al. (Eds.): ICCSA 2020, LNCS 12253, pp. 736–744, 2020.
https://doi.org/10.1007/978-3-030-58814-4_61

source code files, binary files, and libraries [13]. Configuring an environment to carry out a workflow can be a challenging task involving specialized technical knowledge that many scientists do not have.

To provide preconfigured execution environments for scientific workflows, some authors explore the advantages of lightweight container technologies [13, 15]. Containers are an OS-level alternative to virtual machines, capable of isolating the execution of multiple processes in a single environment. Containers allow the same environment to be virtualized over different hardware, providing flexibility and scalability to the system. Once the entire environment is encapsulated by a container image, scientists can easily replicate experiments in the same environment. Despite its advantages, integrating containers into scientific workflows give rise to performance and design issues that must be carefully examined.

In this work, we explore the Docker container technology integrated to the Makeflow workflow system and its Work Queue component. We propose a cache system using Docker Volume, integrated to Work Queue, as a solution to circumvent the volatility of containers, so to avoid potential bottlenecks when new containers are instantiated. The rest of this paper is organized as follows: Section 2 describes the related work on integrating scientific workflows and containers; Section 3 provides a brief background on Makeflow and Docker container composition; Section 4 describes our integrated architecture, the cache problem and our proposed solution; Section 5 present our experiments and discusses the results, followed by the conclusion in Sect. 6.

2 Related Work

Previous research on containers has shown that they provide a low overhead solution for virtualized systems. Using containers, we may expect close to native CPU, memory, and disk performance [8,14]. While there are still concerns about container security [5], they proved to be a more flexible virtualization solution than virtual machines [7,12]. The virtualization offered by containers allows a container image to encapsulate all the necessary dependencies for the task to be run. Many authors choose Docker as the container engine as it comprises facilitating tools (Docker Swarm, Docker Volumes, overlay network tool) and a large container image repository, known as Docker Hub[1].

Some authors have already investigated the integration of containers and scientific workflows [13,15]. This integration must take into account aspects such as technologies for managing containers on the distributed system, overhead of transferring container images over the network, and the reuse of sent files (cache). Zheng and Thain [15] explore Docker along with Makeflow and Work Queue, in a set of experiments comparing methods of connecting containers to the infrastructure. They take into account the cost of creating and deleting containers, considering a real-world bioinformatics workflow named BWA [9]. Sweeney and Thai [13] focus on issues impacting execution times and network usage when incorporating containers into workflows. They explore strategies

[1] Docker Hub: https://hub.docker.com/.

for container composition, containerizing workflow tasks, and container image translation. To explore container composition, they identify different types of data and software dependencies that may be satisfied when building containers.

Our work goes further in the track open by these previous efforts. As in [15], we also explore Docker, Makeflow and Work Queue, but propose changes to the Work Queue communication protocol and explore deeply Docker and two of its facilities: Docker Swarm and Docker Volumes. We focus on the performance of each task and how different strategies can decrease execution time for another two real-world bioinformatics workflows. As in [13], we take into account dependencies for container composition, but we do not handle container translation as we only focus on Docker containers. On another hand, we analyze the impact of cached dependencies, which is not addressed in previous work.

3 Background

3.1 Makeflow: A Scientific Workflow Engine

Scientific workflow systems provide an environment for workflows to be described and subsequently run on distributed resources. Kepler [2], Taverna [11] and Triana [10] are among the main systems that emerged. However, we choose the Makeflow engine [1] for the following reasons: ability to execute large-scale distributed computations, fault tolerance, availability of a repository with examples of scientific workflows, ease of use and compatibility with a system to run on multiple hosts. Makeflow has a simple way of describing a scientific workflow: it uses a file with syntax similar to Unix Makefiles. A task is described using the following parameters: input files, command to perform the task and output files. In addition to these parameters, it is possible to add minimum requirements for each task: available disk space, RAM and processing cores. Only the workers with minimum resources will execute the workflow tasks.

Makeflow interoperates with another tool called Work Queue [1], which is responsible for reading the tasks defined by Makeflow, distributing (task scheduling) them among the workers, send the input files and finally retrieve the output files generated by the tasks. The order of execution is important, as there are tasks that depend on the output of others. The worker nodes must then connect to the Work Queue server informing that they are able to process tasks. When a worker start its communication, the number of available processing cores, the amount of available RAM and the available disk space is sent to the Work Queue server.

3.2 Task Dependencies and Container Composition

The process of analyzing and defining the dependencies of each task is important to determine the files, libraries and binaries that must be present in the container image that will be used to run these tasks. We classify dependencies into two broad types: **Input/Output Dependencies:** The set of input and output data files that each task receives and generates. This type of dependency must be addressed during the workflow execution, because new files are generated as tasks are completed. **Implicit Dependencies:** Scripts, binaries, configuration files and libraries that must be present in the OS. These files are more difficult to identify, as they are strongly related to the file system and can be placed at different locations. Implicit Dependencies are known before the execution and they are static (do not change at any phase). Those files must be present at the exactly same location on the file system to ensure the correct execution.

The first step to create Docker container images is to choose a base image. This image is a file that contains what is necessary for the execution of an operational environment. The Docker Hub provides several base images to choose from, such as Ubuntu, CentOS, Debian, etc. The base image must be chosen according to the compatibility of the packages, tools and software with the OS. From the base image, we must install all software dependencies for tasks to be performed.

The workflow execution is usually an iterative process, as scientists can add or remove tasks to the flow as the work evolves. When a new task is added to the flow, all the implicit dependencies also need to be present at the container image. As Docker images are organized by layers, so a new layer (with the new task and its dependencies) can be added on top of the previous image.

4 Integrated Architecture

4.1 System Components

Many workflows require a distributed system, so containers must be able to interconnect and communicate over the network. For this reason, we adopted Docker Swarm technology as a way to connect and manage the containers in each host. Figure 1 shows the system layout used in this work, where the Docker overlay network connects the containers that are running on hosts A and B. The manager node is located at host A, where there is also a local image repository, which is a container that acts as a local repository of all previously created images. Before the workflow execution, all hosts must download the base images from this repository. This procedure allows container images to be updated on worker nodes efficiently, as the hosts download only the layers that are not yet present in their file system.

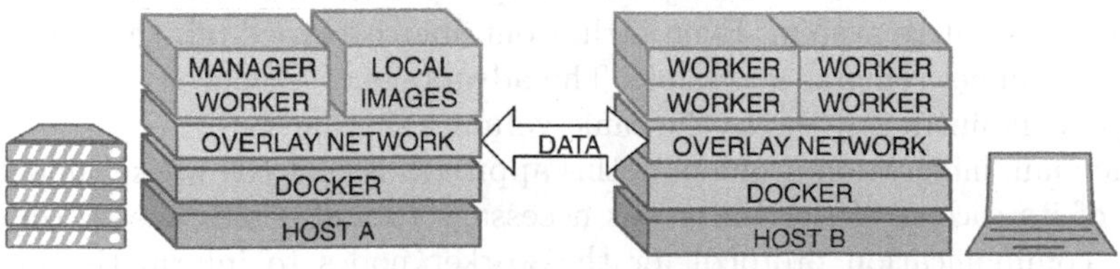

Fig. 1. System layout.

4.2 The Cache Problem

Each worker, before running, creates a sandbox (a directory on the file system) where the input and output are placed, the sandbox acts as a controlled environment where the worker can process the tasks, without worrying about changing or deleting important files from other areas. Then, when the workflow comes to an end and there are no more tasks to be processed, each worker erases its sandbox, leaving the file system unchanged. However, this approach is only valid when the worker nodes run directly on the host operating system, where changes to the file system can crash the entire machine and several processes can be stopped. When containers are used, they act as a large sandbox, where changes can be made without harming anything outside the container.

In addition to this, the entire flow must be performed several times with minor changes. In this way, when sending a file from one host to the other, it is advantageous that this file could be cached for the next iteration. Work Queue allows files to be cached using the following strategy: the manager node sends a file to the worker and records in a hash table that the node has received it. The worker node, in turn, stores this file inside its sandbox directory and keeps it until it is disconnected by the manager. When a new task uses the same previous file, the manager knows that this file has already been sent and does not sent it again. At the end of the workflow, the worker deletes all files in its sandbox, except those marked to be cached. However, this strategy cannot be applied over containers, because they are units made to be volatile and which can be replaced by other containers when an execution fails. Thus, at the end of the workflow, all the containers would be finished and the files marked to be in the cache would be lost.

4.3 Docker Volume as a Cache for Work Queue

To solve the cache problem, we analyzed the source code of Work Queue and Makeflow in order to determine how the cache process was done, and then modify it as follows, so the cache could work in the context of containers. The Work Queue cache system works in a way that the Work Queue server stores a list of all files that are being kept in cache by workers. The manager stores a hash table, which associates a worker identifier (key) with the files the worker has in cache (values). Each worker, when started, receives a unique identifier. To circumvent the problem of container volatility, we set up a persistent Docker Volume stored on the host's native system. Even if the container is turned off, the data stored on these volumes remains accessible. The advantage of a Docker Volume is that multiple containers can access the same volume, sharing data.

The main integration problem of this approach is that the worker node is not aware of its cached files, then it was necessary to add a message to the Work Queue communication protocol for the worker nodes to inform the manager that they already have files in their cache. Since the data in Docker Volume is shared between the containers on the same host, the file cannot be linked to the identifier of only one container, but it has to be linked to all containers ids that have access to the volume.

With this new approach, the worker node, encapsulated by a container, starts its execution and scans the files located at the Docker volume, transfer them to its sandbox directory, and then send a message to the manager containing all the hashes of the cached files. The manager node receives this information and stores the hashes of the files in the hash table, based on the identifier of each worker node. Therefore, when the workflow is re-executed, and all worker nodes (containers) are created again, the files present in the Docker volume will not be sent again, guaranteeing a cache system.

5 Experiments and Evaluation

The experiments described in this section aim to evaluate the impact of the proposed cache system on two real-world scientific workflows, with different number of tasks and dependencies. For each workflow, we also compare two strategies for mapping containers over the hosts: 1) one container per thread of the host; 2) one container per host, giving this container access to all the host's resources.

We selected two contrasting scientific workflows, Blast [6] and Hecil [4], from the Makeflow repository[2]. Blast has a set of 15 tasks: 3 of them run locally in the manager node and 12 tasks run distributed over the worker nodes. These tasks execute the same program (a binary named blastall) for several different entries, i.e., their software dependencies are the same. Hecil comprises 112 tasks that must be executed on the worker nodes. Hecil tasks are heterogeneous: they include Python scripts, Perl code and binary programs. Such heterogeneity characterizes an interesting scenario to stress the dependency management for executing the workflow over containers.

We set up our experimental infrastructure based on the architecture shown in Fig. 1. Host A has an Intel (R) Xeon (R) processor with 4 cores and 2 threads per core, 12 GB of RAM. Host B has an Intel (R) Core (TM) i53230M (Intel Core IvyBridge processor) with 2 cores and 2 threads per core, 8 GB of RAM. Using 11 workers, we can test the strategy 1, where 7 worker containers (plus one that should act as manager) run in Host A and another 4 workers in Host B. Using 2 workers on each host, we can test strategy 2. In total, we carried out the following set of test cases: Default Work Queue with 2 and 11 workers; modified Work Queue with 2 and 11 workers; modified Work Queue with 2 and 11 workers with clean cache.

Figure 2 shows the average execution times for Blast and Hecil workflows. Each reported execution time is the average of 10 executions. We can see that the longest execution time for Blast was obtained with 11 workers and the Default Work Queue. Despite having more workers, this case performed slowly because sending all the input files to all containers generates a bottleneck in which workers were delayed and parallel execution was hampered. The modified Work Queue leaded to the best execution times, because the files were already in the Docker Volume of each host. The cases that used the modified Work Queue and the

[2] Makeflow Repository: http://github.com/cooperative-computing-lab/makeflow-examples.

empty cache obtained better times than the executions with the Default Work Queue, since dependencies were transferred in parallel, once the data sent to the Docker Volume could be accessed by all running containers in its host.

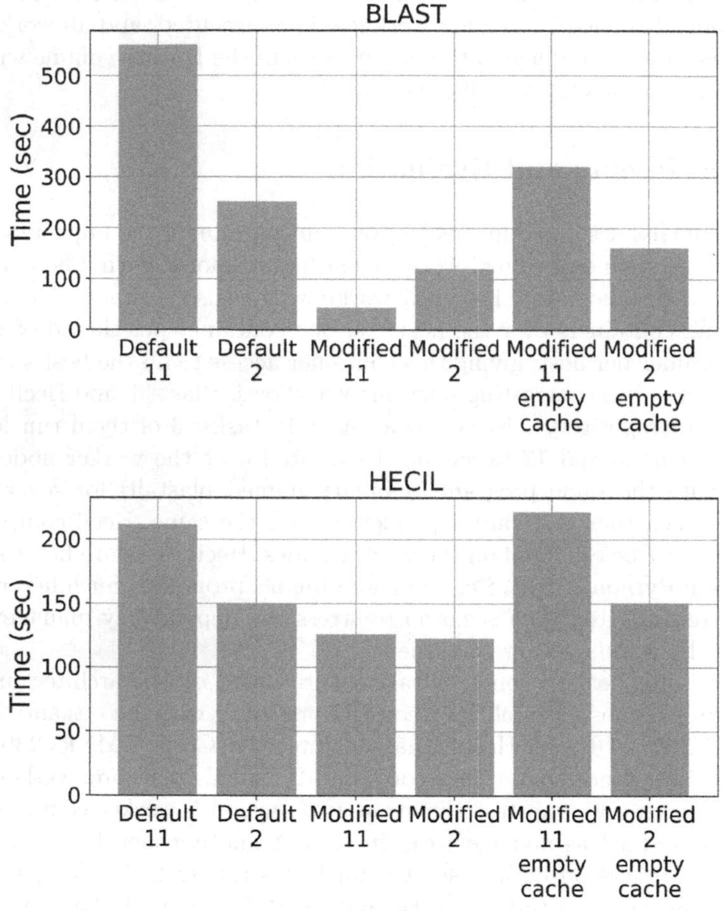

Fig. 2. Execution times for Blast and Hecil on multiple test cases.

In other hand, the Hecil workflow obtained the shorted times with 2 workers. This happens because this workflow comprises tasks where thread-level parallelism is better used than host-level parallelism. These results suggest that the mapping strategy should be chosen carefully. Choosing between container-per-host or container-per-threads is a decision that depends on each workflow and will impact its performance. However, we observed that using the cache was beneficial for both workflows and that using Docker Volumes decreases the network traffic, since the dependencies are sent to each host, and not to each container within the hosts.

6 Conclusion

Lightweight Docker containers are an effective solution to provide preconfigured execution environments for real-world workflows. In this work, we have explored Docker and Makeflow technologies to execute two bioinformatics workflows: Blast and Hecil. We have proposed a cache system leveraging Docker Volume and Makeflow's Work Queue. Our experiments have shown that using the cache was beneficial for both workflows. Also, we have shown the performance impact of container-per-host and container-per-threads strategies for mapping containers over the hosts dedicated to executing the workflows.

As future work, we intend to develop an adaptive system, where the strategies of instantiating one container per host or containers per threads could be evaluated as new rounds of the workflow are executed. We also intend to expand our experiments to other real-world workflows that may be described with the Makeflow language.

Acknowledgements. This research has been partially supported by the GREENCLOUD project (http://www.inf.ufrgs.br/greencloud/) (#16/2551-0000 488-9), from FAPERGS and CNPq Brazil, program PRONEX 12/2014.

References

1. Albrecht, M., Donnelly, P., Bui, P., Thain, D.: Makeflow: a portable abstraction for data intensive computing on clusters, clouds, and grids. In: Proceedings of the 1st ACM SIGMOD Workshop on Scalable Workflow Execution Engines and Technologies, SWEET 2012, New York, NY, USA, pp. 1–13. ACM (2012)
2. Altintas, I., Berkley, C., Jaeger, E., Jones, M., Ludascher, B., Mock, S.: Kepler: an extensible system for design and execution of scientific workflows. In: Proceedings of 2004 16th International Conference on Scientific and Statistical Database Management, pp. 423–424, June 2004
3. Barker, A., van Hemert, J.: Scientific workflow: a survey and research directions. In: Wyrzykowski, R., Dongarra, J., Karczewski, K., Wasniewski, J. (eds.) PPAM 2007. LNCS, vol. 4967, pp. 746–753. Springer, Heidelberg (2008). https://doi.org/10.1007/978-3-540-68111-3_78
4. Choudhury, O., Chakrabarty, A., Emrich, S.J.: HECIL: a hybrid error correction algorithm for long reads with iterative learning. Sci. Rep. **8**(9936), 1–9 (2018)
5. Combe, T., Martin, A., Di Pietro, R.: To Docker or not to Docker: a security perspective. IEEE Cloud Comput. **3**(5), 54–62 (2016)
6. Donkor, E.S., Dayie, N.T.K.D., Adiku, T.K.: Basic local alignment search tool. J. Mol. Biol. **3**(215), 403–410 (1990)
7. Dua, R., Raja, A.R., Kakadia, D.: Virtualization vs containerization to support PaaS. In: 2014 IEEE International Conference on Cloud Engineering, pp. 610–614, March 2014
8. Felter, W., Ferreira, A., Rajamony, R., Rubio, J.: An updated performance comparison of virtual machines and Linux containers. In: 2015 IEEE International Symposium on Performance Analysis of Systems and Software (ISPASS), pp. 171–172, March 2015

9. Li, H., Durbin, R.: Fast and accurate short read alignment with Burrows-Wheeler transform. Bioinformatics **25**(14), 1754–1760 (2009)
10. Majithia, S., Shields, M., Taylor, I., Wang, I.: Triana: a graphical web service composition and execution toolkit. In: Proceedings of 2004 IEEE International Conference on Web Services, pp. 514–521, July 2004
11. Oinn, T., et al.: Taverna: a tool for the composition and enactment of bioinformatics workflows. Bioinformatics **20**(17), 3045–3054 (2004)
12. Preeth, E.N., Mulerickal, F.J.P., Paul, B., Sastri, Y.: Evaluation of Docker containers based on hardware utilization. In: 2015 International Conference on Control Communication Computing India (ICCC), pp. 697–700, November 2015
13. Sweeney, K.M.D., Thain, D.: Efficient integration of containers into scientific workflows. In: Proceedings of the 9th Workshop on Scientific Cloud Computing, ScienceCloud 2018, New York, NY, USA pp. 7:1–7:6. ACM (2018)
14. Xavier, M.G., Neves, M.V., Rossi, F.D., Ferreto, T.C., Lange, T., De Rose, C.A.F.: Performance evaluation of container-based virtualization for high performance computing environments. In: 2013 21st Euromicro International Conference on Parallel, Distributed, and Network-Based Processing, pp. 233–240, February 2013
15. Zheng, C., Thain, D.: Integrating containers into workflows: A case study using Makeflow, Work Queue, and Docker. In: Proceedings of the 8th International Workshop on Virtualization Technologies in Distributed Computing, VTDC 2015, New York, NY, USA, pp. 31–38. ACM (2015)

Modeling Interstellar Amorphous Solid Water Grains by Tight-Binding Based Methods: Comparison Between GFN-XTB and CCSD(T) Results for Water Clusters

Aurèle Germain[1(✉)] and Piero Ugliengo[1,2]

[1] Dipartimento di Chimica, Università degli Studi di Torino, via P. Giuria 7, 10125 Turin, Italy
aureleroger.germain@unito.it

[2] Nanostructured Interfaces and Surfaces (NIS) Centre, Università degli Studi di Torino, via P. Giuria 7, 10125 Turin, Italy

Abstract. One believed path to Interstellar Complexes Organic Molecules (iCOMs) formation inside the Interstellar Medium (ISM) is through chemical recombination at the surface of amorphous solid water (ASW) mantle covering the silicate-based core of the interstellar grains. The study of these iCOMs formation and their binding energy to the ASW, using computational chemistry, depends strongly on the ASW models used, as different models may exhibit sites with different adsorbing features. ASW extended models are rare in the literature because large sizes require very large computational resources when quantum mechanical methods based on DFT are used. To circumvent this problem, we propose to use the newly developed GFN-xTB Semi-empirical Quantum Mechanical (SQM) methods from the Grimme's group. These methods are, at least, two orders of magnitude faster than conventional DFT, only require modest central memory, and in this paper we aim to benchmark their accuracy against rigorous and resource hungry quantum mechanical methods. We focused on 38 water structures studied by MP2 and CCSD(T) approaches comparing energetic and structures with three levels of GFN-xTB parametrization (GFN0, GFN1, GFN2) methods. The extremely good results obtained at the very cheap GFN-xTB level for both water cluster structures and energetic paved the way towards the modeling of very large AWS models of astrochemical interest.

Keywords: Interstellar medium · Complexes Organic Molecules · AWS water models · Tight binding

1 Introduction

The interstellar medium (ISM) contains a vast diversity of complex organic molecules (COMs) [1], but the formation of these interstellar COMs (iCOMs) is still a mystery for the most part. The chemical reactions producing iCOMs could be done in the gas phase of the ISM, but some observed chemical species were proven to be unstable when produced in the gas phase [2]. A way for them to be stabilized would be by the way of a third body

O. Gervasi et al. (Eds.): ICCSA 2020, LNCS 12253, pp. 745–753, 2020.
https://doi.org/10.1007/978-3-030-58814-4_62

in which the reaction energy can be injected [3]. This third body can be the silicate dust core grains in diffuse clouds or, in dense molecular clouds (MC), the multiple layers of amorphous water ice (AWS) covering dust core [4]. These water layers are not formed by direct adsorption of water molecules but by H and O recombination, first at the grain core surface, and then on top of the pre-formed water layers [5]. The molecules present in the gas phase of dense MC highly influence the composition of the layers, and so the ice water is "dirtied" by other molecular species like carbon monoxide, carbon dioxide, methanol, and ammonia to name a few [4]. It is assumed that these chemical species, after being adsorbed on the surface of these icy grains, will form iCOMs and desorb from the grains to return in the gas phase. A lot of unanswered questions arise, mainly involving the binding energies of these molecular species to the ice mantle, the way they diffuse from site to site, and by which mechanism they eventually desorb. Astronomical observations give us limited answers to these questions, and the extreme conditions of the ISM (low temperature and low densities of the species studied), coupled with the time frame in which these reactions are believed to occur, are nearly impossible to emulate in a laboratory. Computational chemistry gives us a way to circumvent these limitations and study what is impossible to observe or difficult to reproduce in terrestrial labs. Nonetheless, these studies are highly influenced by the way we model the AWS ice mantles.

Usually, in the literature, the AWS models are represented by water clusters envisaging very few molecules. Clearly, these models cannot represent neither the structural complexity nor the hydrogen bond cooperativity exhibited by the ice in large AWS grains. The paucity of the models is also due to our ignorance about how to model them within a physically sound approach, *i.e.* obeying the rules of their formation in the ISM. Therefore, the development of realistic AWS models is a key factor in astrochemistry, as they will be essential to compute accurate binding energies of the various iCOMs adsorbed on the grains. Unfortunately, the high computational power demanded to produce large enough AWS model grain can grow steeply with the cluster size, *de facto* preventing the application of current DFT methods to model large icy particles. The strategy adopted in our group is based on models defined within the periodic boundary conditions, either through crystalline ice unit cell or amorphous ones on which the results of the cheap HF-3c [11] method were compared with that of the more accurate B3LYP-D3 method [10]. The inclusion of the periodic boundary conditions mitigates the smallness of the unit cell size, better mimicking an extended AWS. On those models we have computed the binding energies of about 20 iCOMs, showing a relatively large dependence of these values on the adsorption site. The problem is that increasing the size of the unit cell to increase the variability of the surface sites is hampered by the cost of the calculation, even at the cheapest HF-3c level. Therefore, a different strategy is needed to really deal with large AWS models based on even cheaper methods than HF-3c to cope with larger sizes. However, cheaper methods may be inaccurate to the point in which the predictions become unreliable and, therefore, they should be carefully benchmarked against accurate quantum mechanical results.

In this paper, we benchmark the accuracy of a new family of semiempirical quantum mechanical (SQM) methods, the GFN-xTB methods (GFN-xTB stands for Geometry, Frequency, Noncovalent, eXtended Tight Binding) developed by Grimme and coworkers

[6–8]. GFN-xTB methods allow pushing the limit of the system size up to hundreds of molecules (or thousands atoms), and have been shown to be at least two order of magnitude faster than conventional DFT methods [6], while keeping a good level of accuracy for a variety of molecular properties, including intermolecular interactions, usually not well accounted for by SQM. The three different levels of GFN-xTB (GFN0, GFN1, GFN2) envisage different level of parametrization and treatment of dispersion interactions, providing different accuracy. In the following, we check for the accuracy of all of them using water clusters as a reference system as they exhibit similar features of larger ASW clusters.

2 Water Cluster Study

2.1 Energetic Features

We focused on a set of 38, already optimized, water clusters by the work of Temelso et al. [9]. These clusters are ranging from two to ten water molecules each. Geometries were optimized up to RI-MP2/aVDZ level and then, since the difference in geometry is minute between the two [9], a single-point calculation was performed using large basis-set and CCSD(T)/CBS/CBSnocp (Coupled Cluster Single Double Triple within the complete basis set extrapolation). We re-optimized these water clusters at GFN-xTB with the three levels of parametrization, by using a single laptop in less than half a day of computing time. On the optimized geometries, we computed the normalized binding energy (BE_N) of each water cluster as:

$$BE_N = \frac{\mathrm{BE}}{N_{H_2O}} = \frac{E_{H_2O} \times N_{H_2O} - E_{WC}}{N_{H_2O}}$$

Where BE is the non-normalized binding energy, E_{WC} is the total energy of a water cluster of N_{H_2O} water molecules and E_{H_2O} is the total energy of a fully optimized isolated water molecule. The BE value includes, therefore, the cost of geometry re-organization of water molecules caused by the building up of the cluster.

On Fig. 1 we contrasted the BE energies computed by GFN-xTB against the ones calculated by Temelso et al. CCSD(T)/CBS/CBSnocp level as a function of water cluster nuclearity. The black colored line of Fig. 1 is a best fit line through the 38 points while, the grey line is the "ideal" trendline that would represent the perfect agreement between GFN-xTB and CCSD(T) BE values.

Looking at Fig. 1, it is easy to notice that the first level of theory shown with GFN0 is not very accurate, while both GFN1 and GFN2 showed trendlines very close to the ideal one. Comparison between GFN1 and GFN2 also showed a better internal linear correlation coefficient R for GFN2 compared to GFN1.

The good accuracy of the results was expected from the general GFN-xTB benchmark work already conducted by Grimme [6–8], but it is impressive to see this level of agreement with CCSD(T) data, considering the negligible computer time requested for GFN-xTB compared to CCSD(T).

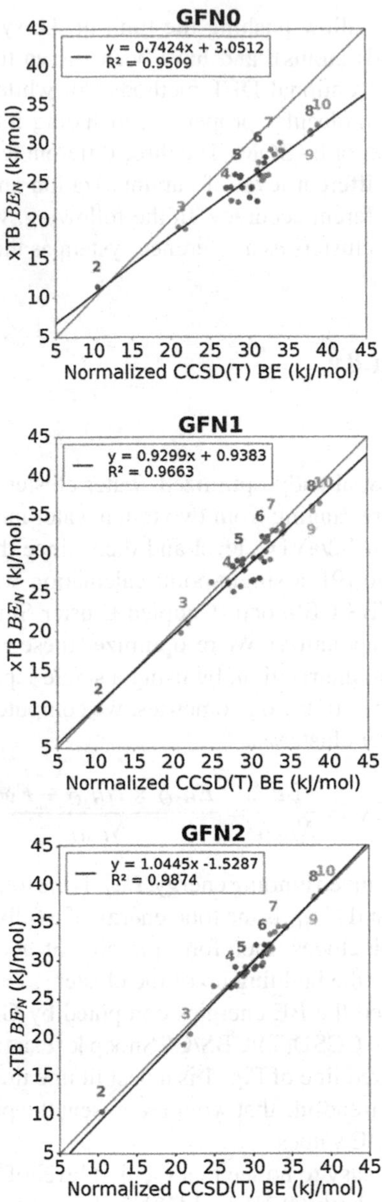

Fig. 1. Comparison between normalized BE values of the 38 water clusters computed by GFN-xTB and CCSD(T). GFN0, GFN1, GFN2, refer to the level of GFN-xTB parametrization (see text for details). Labels indicate the nuclearity of each water cluster.

Figure 2 shows the absolute percentage of the difference (APD) between the BE computed at CCSD(T) and those at GFN-xTB level, defined as:

$$APD = \left| \frac{BE(CCSD(T) - BE(GFN - xTB)}{BE(CCSD(T))} \right| \times 100$$

Results of Fig. 2, showed similar trend in the accuracy of the different GFN-xTB parametrization level, with errors of the GFN2 being almost half of those for GFN1 and GFN0, both providing exceedingly large deviations. An interesting point is that the APD decreases dramatically as the system size increases, a result extremely relevant for the forthcoming simulation of large AWS grains. We refrain from a too definitive conclusion about this matter, since we only have two water clusters envisaging 8, 9, and 10 water molecules, but it is very promising for our future research.

In conclusion, for the energetic part, we have showed GFN-xTB in its GFN2 incarnation to show a minimum/maximum/average APD values of about 1%/9%/3%, respectively. In the next paragraph we will discuss the structural features predicted by GFN-xTB against the accurate ones.

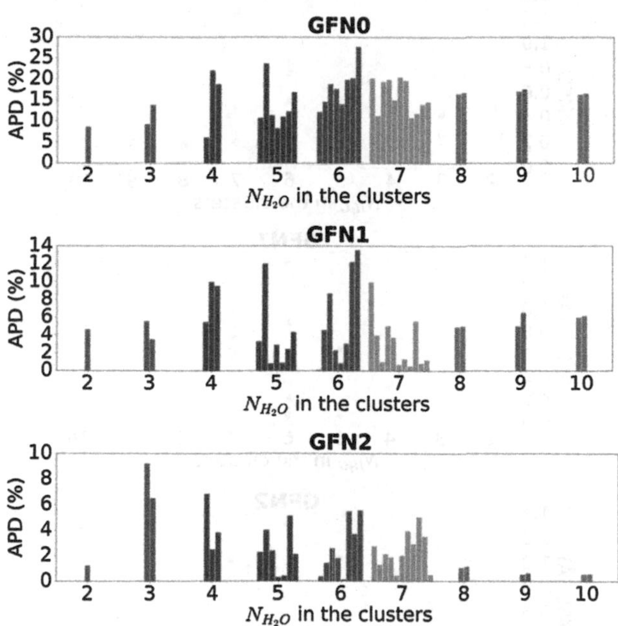

Fig. 2. APD between BE GFN-xTB and CCSD(T). Note that the boundaries of the y-axis change between the three plots.

2.2 Structural Features

As we are dealing with a large number of water cluster, a one by one comparison of their geometrical features will be too cumbersome. Therefore, we relied on a global indicator of geometrical similarity by adopting the root mean squared deviation (RMSD) as a figure of merit (the smaller the RMSD the better) between the GFN-xTB-optimized geometries and the reference ones. The RMSD are shown in Fig. 3, arranged by the number of water molecules of each cluster. The data shows, for a given cluster nuclearity, different RMSD values as a result of the different water organization of each cluster. For instance, clusters with N = 7 exhibit many different water configurations and, therefore, each of them shows a different RMSD value. We see here a slightly different behavior of the GFNx levels compared to the energetic results, as GFN0 provides RMSD values less spread than GFN1. GFN2 is, again, the most reliable method, while all of them give excellent results for clusters of nuclearity greater than 7. This is related to the much-reduced configuration space of water molecules for clusters at higher nuclearity compared to the smaller ones. A visual comparison limited to the water cluster with N = 7 is showed in Fig. 4. GFN2 provides almost a perfect match with the high-level structure, while GFN0 is giving a RMSD almost half than that of GFN1. This is confirmed by the average RMSD values of 0.30/0.38/0.36 Å for GFN2/GFN1/GFN0, respectively.

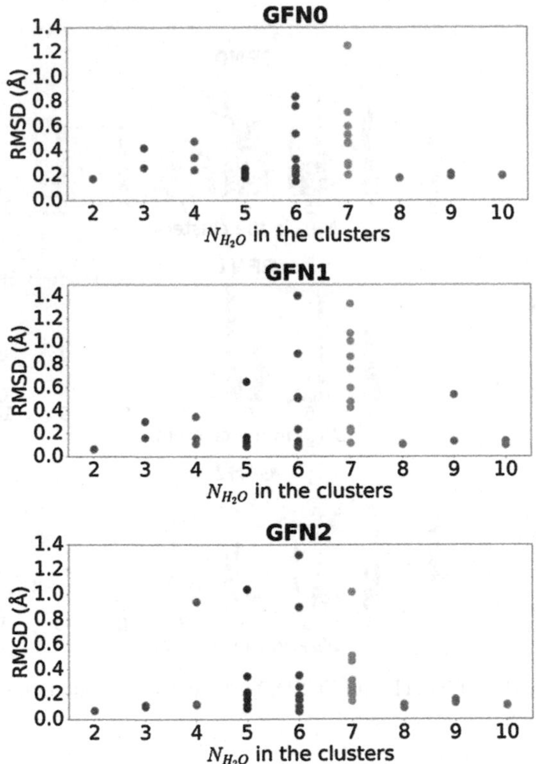

Fig. 3. RMSD for the water clusters. Different points for each cluster nuclearity represent different water organization within the cluster itself.

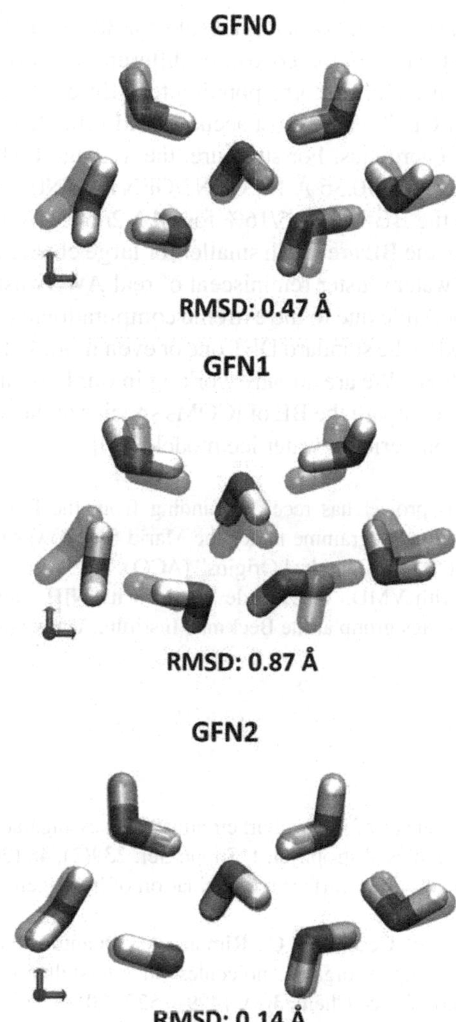

Fig. 4. Superposition of the GFN structures (full body) with the ones obtained at high level of theory (fade body) for one configuration of the water cluster exhibiting seven water molecules. RMSD values in unit of Å.

3 Conclusions

In this paper we have studied the accuracy of the new tight binding methods GFN-xTB recently proposed by Grimme and coworkers [6–8] to simulate the energetic and structures of water clusters. The reason for focusing on water clusters is that they are prototypes of AWS interstellar grains, as they share the same kind of intermolecular interactions (*i.e.* hydrogen-bond and dispersion interactions) and their size is limited enough to be treated at high level of theory to be served as a reference benchmark for the GFN-xTB methods.

Here we used the energetic and structural results for 38 water clusters already studied in the literature [9] which were compared to three different flavors of GFN-xTB methods, namely GFN0, GFN1, and GFN2, corresponding to different level of parametrization. Our results showed that GFN2 is the most accurate and reliable GFN-xTB incarnation, for both structures and energetics. For structure, the average RMSD for the whole set of water cluster was 0.30/0.38/0.36 Å for GFN2/GFN1/GFN0, respectively, while the whole average APD in the BE were 3/5/16% for GFN2/GFN1/GFN0. We observe that both RMSD and APD in the BE are much smaller for large cluster nuclearity, paving the way to treat very large water cluster reminiscent of real AWS dust with good accuracy. This will certainly be possible due to the extreme computational efficiency of the GFN-xTB approach compared to the standard DFT one or even more so for the most expensive post-Hartree-Fock methods. We are already working in our laboratory to extend the size of the cluster in order to compare the BE of iCOMs species at the ice grain surfaces with that of our recent work on periodic water ice models [10].

Acknowledgements. This project has received funding from the European Union's Horizon 2020 research and innovation programme under the Marie Skłodowska-Curie grant agreement No 811312 for the project "Astro-Chemical Origins" (ACO).

Figure 4 was made with VMD. VMD is developed with NIH support by the Theoretical and Computational Biophysics group at the Beckman Institute, University of Illinois at Urbana-Champaign.

References

1. McGuire, B.A.: 2018 census of interstellar, circumstellar, extragalactic, protoplanetary disk, and exoplanetary molecules. Astrophysi. J. Suppl. Ser. **239**(2), 48 (2018)
2. Hollenbach, D., Salpeter, E.E.: Surface recombination of hydrogen molecules. Astrophys. J. **163**, 155–164 (1971)
3. Zamirri, L., Ugliengo, P., Ceccarelli, C., Rimola, A.: Quantum mechanical investigations on the formation of complex organic molecules on interstellar ice mantles. Review and perspectives. ACS Earth Space Chem. **3**(8), 1499–1523 (2019)
4. Boogert, A., Gerakines, P., Whittet, D.: Observations of the icy universe. Ann. Rev. Astron. Astrophys. **53**, 541–581 (2015)
5. Dulieu, F., et al.: Experimental evidence for water formation on interstellar dust grains by hydrogen and oxygen atoms. A&A **512**, A30 (2010)
6. Grimme, S., Bannwarth, C., Shushkon, P.: A robust and accurate tight-binding quantum chemical method for structures, vibrational frequencies, and noncovalent interactions of large molecular systems parametrized for all spd-block elements ($Z = 1-86$). J. Chem. Theory Comput. **13**(5), 1989–2009 (2017)
7. Bannwarth, C., Ehlert, S., Grimme, S.: GFN2-xTB-an accurate and broadly parametrized self-consistent tight-binding quantum chemical method with multipole electrostatics and density-dependent dispersion contributions. J. Chem. Theory Comput. **15**(3), 1652–1671 (2019)
8. Pracht, P., Caldeweyher, E., Ehlert, S., Grimme, S.: A robust non-self-consistent tight-binding quantum chemistry method for large molecules. ChmRxiv (2019)
9. Temelso, B., Archer, K.A., Shields, G.C.: Benchmark structures and binding energies of small water clusters with anharmonicity corrections. J. Phys. Chem. A **115**(43), 12034–12046 (2011)

10. Ferrero, S., Zamirri, L., Ceccarelli, C., Witzel, A., Rimola, A., Ugliengo, P.: Binding energies of interstellar molecules on crystalline and amorphous models of water ice by ab-initio calculations, Submitted to ApJ, 25 August 2020
11. Sure, R., Grimme, S.: HF-3c – a corrected small basis set hartree-fock method. J. Comput. Chem. **34**, 1672–1685 (2013)

Error Correction in Nanopore Reads for *de novo* Genomic Assembly

Jacqueline Aldridge-Águila[1], Diego Álvarez-Saravia[2], Marcelo Navarrete[2], and Roberto Uribe-Paredes[1](✉)

[1] Computer Engineering Department, University of Magallanes, Punta Arenas, Chile
{jacqueline.aldridge,roberto.uribe}@umag.cl
[2] School of Medicine, University of Magallanes, Punta Arenas, Chile
{diego.alvarez,marcelo.navarrete}@umag.cl

Abstract. The purpose of genome sequencing is to determine the DNA sequence of a given organism. Current sequencing technologies can be classified by the type of output data. Whereas Nanopore technology generates long reads with high error rates, short read technologies - such as Illumina sequencing - generate shorter reads but with low error rate. Since *de novo* genome assembly of sequencing reads is defined as a NP-hard problem, it remains as one of the major challenges for defining reference genomes of different species. This paper aims to improve the quality of reads obtained through Oxford Nanopore Technologies (ONT). We developed an algorithm to associate the reads obtained from Illumina with the ones obtained with Nanopore. Low accuracy ONT reads were corrected with the high quality Illumina reads to achieve an improved sequencing data. The inclusion of this algorithm as a preprocessing step resulted in improved coverage, contig length, and mismatch rate when performing *de novo* genome assembly of a bacterial genome with well known tools.

Keywords: Oxford nanopore · Illumina · De novo assembly · Correction reads

1 Introduction

Genomics has advanced notoriously in recent years, currently there are several technologies allowing the DNA sequencing of different species in a simpler process at a tiny fraction of the cost of 20 years ago [6]. Thanks to these advances many species have been sequenced, but the vast majority still have not gone through the process of defining their reference genome, which empirically implies that their genetic maps remains unknown. In order to obtain biologically meaningful information from sequencing data, unreferenced species must still undergo through a process known as *de novo* assembly.

This work has been partially supported by the MINEDUC under the project MAG1895, and by Conicyt under the project Fondecyt 1180882.

O. Gervasi et al. (Eds.): ICCSA 2020, LNCS 12253, pp. 754–762, 2020.
https://doi.org/10.1007/978-3-030-58814-4_63

De novo assembly aims to reconstruct the genome from the reads obtained in the sequencing process, without having any information aside of the reads.

There is a wide range of technologies to perform DNA sequencing. In this work we selected two technologies based on their cost and the read length they can generate. The first is Illumina, a short reads technology, with reads of maximum 300 nucleotides and very low error rates but a high processing cost when assembling an entire genome. The second, Oxford Nanopore Technologies (ONT), technology of long reads, that provides reads of variable size (commonly 10,000 nucleotides), but with a higher percentage of error and a low cost of processing when assembling in time and resources.

1.1 DNA Sequencing

All living being have a unique and unrepeatable deoxyribonucleic acid (DNA) which contains all the genetic information of the individual.

The DNA consists of four nucleotides, adenine (A), thymine (T), guanine (G) and cytosine (C), which are intertwined forming DNA sequences that give rise to genes. The order of the nucleotides will determine the genes that the organism can express, that is, the biological instructions.

DNA sequencing is the process that aims to determine the order of nucleotides of a DNA molecule [18].

1.2 Next Generation Sequencing

Next generation sequencing technologies (NGS) allow sequencing of a species using new strategies that generate a very high number of genome reads with less effort, lower cost, and much less time per sequenced nucleotide [15]

Today there are different NGS platforms (IonTorrent, Illumina, PacBio, Oxford Nanopore) that differ in the used sequencing chemistry. An important difference between the sequencers is the quantity and quality of the data, some tools deliver sequences of very small fixed sizes while others deliver very long reads but of variable size, also each technology has different percentages of error [1].

Sequencing technologies deliver the raw data, that is, a file with the genetic information divided into disordered fragments. Each fragment is called read.

The size and accuracy of the reads will depend on the used technology. To obtain the final sequence in an orderly manner, some assembly method must be used to join the reads and reconstruct the genome.

This project will use a technology of long reads, Oxford Nanopore and Illumina, as a technology of short reads.

Oxford Nanopore. This technology through the use of electrical signals determines the nucleotide to be sequenced. Through this method very long reads of variable length can be obtained.

It is a technology of high portability and low cost. Its ability to determine DNA fragments of greater length is one of its advantages [3], But its high percentage of error compared to short read technologies remains its bigger drawback.

Illumina. This technology uses the method of "synthesis sequencing", where nucleotides are labeled with fluorescent colors that generate light signals that will determine the nucleotide to be sequenced [12].

Illumina has the advantage of providing a low cost per base pair and low error rates. However, one of its biggest disadvantages is the short length of this reads. Therefore, the processing to rebuild the genome is computationally expensive, and often unachievable when there is no reference genome to map the reads.

Reads assembly remains major challenge in DNA sequencing, whereas longer reads may help to facilitate this process, the read length is inversely proportional to read accuracy. Therefore, we aimed to improve the accuracy of long reads by the development of a preprocessing algorithm to facilitate genome assembly. This paper presents a preprocessing strategy for sequences obtained with Oxford Nanopore, with the aim to improve reads accuracy. For this, we start with a correction algorithm, which uses Illumina sequences, to then make an assembly of improved reads. With this strategy we achieve improvements in genome coverage and lower error rates.

2 Genome Assembly

The sequencing process delivers DNA information divided into fragments. In order to extract the relevant information, sequencing reads must be assembled, i.e. aligned and merged in order to reconstruct the original sequence. Genome assembly and can be of two types, comparative assembly and *de novo* assembly.

2.1 *de novo* assembly

De novo assembly is a process used to reconstruct genomes, without having prior knowledge of its genomic organization. In this type of assembly a reference genome is not used, but only the information contained in the sequenced reads. This type of assembly is generally used when sequencing the genome of a species that has not been previously referenced.

Error Correction Algorithms in Long Reads. Currently there are different ways to perform *de novo* assembly. In this work the strategy will be to make an error correction before making the assembly to identify and correct errors.

The error correction algorithms for long reads can be divided into three approaches [19]:

- Algorithms based on alignment of short reads: Short reads are aligned with long reads and these alignments are used to correct errors in long reads.

- Algorithms based on assemblies of short reads: The short reads are assembled. Long reads align with the assembly and are used to correct long reads.
- Algorithms using only long reads: The reads are self-corrected through consensus sequences obtained by overlays or alignments of the same reads.

There are several tools for the correction, in this work we selected Lordec [17].

The Fig. 1 presents a scheme used in this work to make *de novo* assembly with the steps previously described. In the second step (preprocessing) we include the algorithm explained in this work.

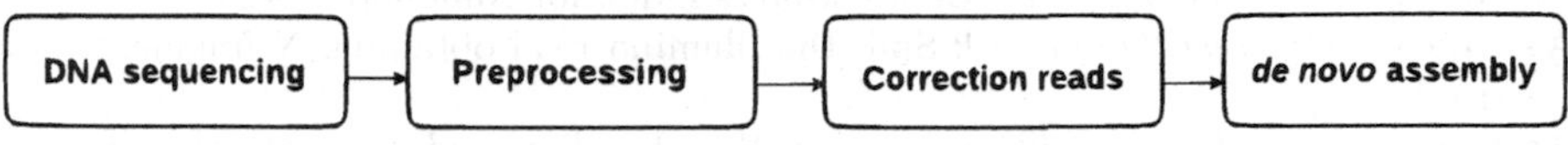

Fig. 1. Scheme of Pipeline used to *de novo* assembly.

3 Algorithm

In this work we developed an algorithm to associate the short reads obtained from Illumina with the ones obtained with Nanopore. We use a three step approach, starting with candidates selection, followed by filtering of short reads, and finally Nanopore read improvement through consensus.

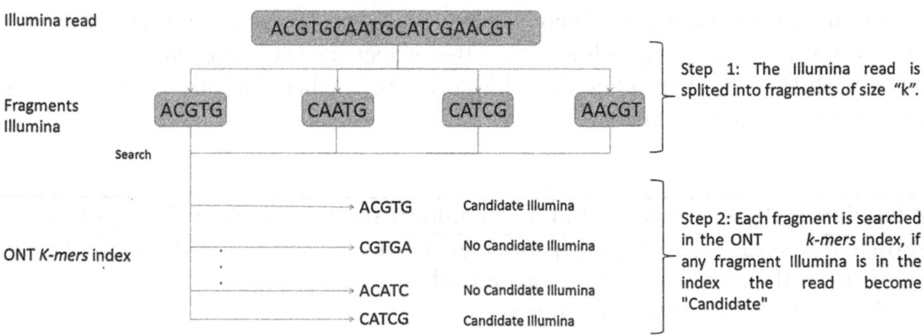

Fig. 2. First part of the algorithm: candidates selection

The first step is built upon the methodology presented by Kawulok J. [4]. This algorithm was adapted to perform a search for candidate reads within the Illumina library based on Levenshtein distance to Nanopore reads as presented in Algorithm 1. Given a Nanopore read, the Illumina reads that are similar are selected. First an index of *k-mers* is created, which stores all the sub-sequences of a defined size *k* along with their positions, then it is divide the Illumina read into N fragments of a size k. Each fragment is searched in the index and those that are found become Illumina candidates. This is explained graphically in the Fig. 2.

Algorithm 1. Candidates selection

Input: *ont*: Nanopore read to improve
Input: *ill_reads*: Illuminas reads
Input: *k*: Size of Illumina fragments to use
Output: *new_ont*: New improved Nanopore read through Illuminas reads
Assumes: *create_index(ont, k)*: Create *k-mers* index for Nanopore read
Assumes: *get_slices(illumina, k)*: Split the Illumina read obtaining N fragments of a size k
Assumes: *search(fragment_illumina, ont)*: Search, align and calculate the distance between the Illumina read and the ONT read based on the Illumina fragment.

```
index_ont ← create_index(ont, k)
for illumina in illumina_reads do
    slices_ill ← get_slices(ill, k)
    for fragment_illumina in slices_ill do
        if fragment_ill in index_ont then
            pos, dist ← search(ont, fragment_illumina)
            Appends illumina to candidatos
cands_m, pos_m ← define_cand(cands, pos)
new_ont ← consensus(cands_m, pos_m, seq_ont)
return new_ont
```

In the second step reads were filtered on basis of the estimated error rate of Nanopore sequencing technology. After selecting the candidates, were analyzed with the function *define_cand* (Algorithm 2) where Illumina reads serve to improve the Nanopore reads.

Algorithm 2. Selection of Illumina candidates apt to improve Nanopore read

Input: *dist_max*: User defined percentage to determine accepted range of error between Illumina read and Nanopore read

```
function DEFINE_CAND(cands, pos)
    dist_max ← (size_ill * (dist_max))
    for id_ill in cands do
        if cands[id_ill] ≤ dist_max then
            Appends id_ill to cands_mejora
            Appends pos[id_ill] to pos_mejora
    return cands_mejora, pos_mejora
```

Lastly, the Nanopore reads were improved with the information obtained in earlier steps (Algorithm 3).

Algorithm 3. Nanopore read improvement through consensus

Assumes: *get_max_nucleotide(cons, pos)*: Look at the position *pos* which nucleotide has greater distance weighting in the consensus array

```
function CONSENSUS(cands, pos, ont)
    for ill in cands do
        start ← pos
        end ← pos + size + 1
        p ← 0
        for x in start to end do
            for nucl in 'ACGT' do
                if ill[p] == nucl then
                    cons[nucl][x] ← cons[nucl][x] + 1/dist
                p++
    new_ont ← ''''
    for pos_ont in 0 to length(ont)-1 do
        max_nucl ← get_max_nucleotide(cons, pos_ont)
        Concatenates new_ont with max_nucl

    return new_ont
```

4 Results

4.1 Experimental Environment

Different tools were used during the development of this project:

- Sequence alignment: BWA [7], Minimap2 [9]
- Analysis and manipulation of sequences: Samtools [10], Tablet [11], Quast [2], Qualimap [13].
- Error correction: Lordec [17].
- *De novo* assembly: Miniasm [8], Smartdenovo [16], Flye [5].

The alignment, analysis and manipulation of sequences were used to validate data and sintonize the algorithm.

The Python programming language was used to develop the algorithm along with different libraries, including Biopython for the management of biological data. This work was implemented a multicore version of the algorithm proposed.

Data Set. It was decided to use bacterial sequencing libraries of *Escherichia coli.* The sequencing libraries used were obtained from the NCBI database.

Below are the libraries used along with their most important features.

Illumina Library Metrics:

- Amount of reads: 893,383
- Mapped reads with the reference: 85.31%
- Duplicate Reads: 26.34%
- Error percentage with reference: 3.14%

Oxford Nanopore Library Metrics

- Amount of reads: 15,911
- Mapped reads with the reference: 95.87%
- Duplicate Reads: 4.13%
- Error percentage with reference: 22.67%

4.2 Experimental Results

After performing different tuning experiments, we tested the potential benefit of the preprocessing algorithm proposed here with three different *de novo* assemblers: Miniasm, Smartdenovo and Flye. We performed *de novo* assembly of a testing data-set detailed in the 4.1 section under three different conditions:

- Basic assembly: Assembly made with the original Nanopore reads (without any preprocessing or correction step).
- Lordec Assembly: Assembly performed only with the error correction of the original reads with the Lordec tool.
- Improved Assembly: Assembly performed after preprocessing with our tool (step two of Fig. 1) and correction with Lordec tool.

The Table 1 presents the results obtained by using the three assemblers mentioned above. Under the analyzed conditions the inclusion of a preprocessing step as proposed here results in a significant increase of total aligned fraction, the size of largest contig and genome fraction coverage.

Table 1. Statistics of Miniasm, Smartdenovo and Flye assemblers

		Genome fraction (%)	Total aligned length	Largest contig	Mismatches per 100 kbp	Indels per 100 kbp
Miniasm	Basic assembly	2.5%	206	259,582	2,444.65	14.81
	Lordec assembly	66.463%	3,453,423	308,407	3,541.52	97.95
	Improved assembly	69.497%	3,609,974	434,975	2,967.11	133.01
Smartdenovo	Basic assembly	2.918%	149,865	619,175	2,305.21	6.01
	Lordec assembly	63.571%	3,273,485	1,605,886	3,829.54	187.43
	Improved assembly	67.073%	3,454,852	1,609,702	3,224.38	193.48
Flye	Basic assembly	71.002%	3,675,484	880,453	3,306.01	1171.86
	Lordec assembly	76.772%	3,958,214	1,259,122	2,436.21	319.19
	Improved assembly	76.774%	3,963,040	1,661,394	2,361.44	293.19

The basic assembly covers a very small fraction of the genome when using Miniasm and Smartdenovo assemblers, this is due to the low coverage of the Nanopore data set used, the inclusion of the Lordec error correction tool improves this results. The integration of our preprocessing algorithm further improves the assembly. The integration of our tool no only resulted in increased coverage but also in a lower number of mismatches per 100 Kb. The number of indels may be increased or decreased depending on the analyzed assembly tool.

5 Conclusions

Currently, the availability and accessibility to NGS technology has increased dramatically, and consequently the amount of sequencing data generated. However, the assembly of new genomes remains challenging and is defined as a NP-hard problem [14]. This paper presents an algorithm to associate high accuracy short reads with error prone long reads, that could add potential benefits when included as a preprocessing step during *de novo* assembly.

Our approach allows additional benefit in terms of genome coverage, contig length, and mismatch rate when performing genome assembly with Miniasm, Smartdenovo, and Flye. This improvement is also sizable when including error correction steps with tools such as Lordec.

The benefit of the here proposed approach in terms of coverage ranges from 5 Kb to 181 Kb in a small sized bacterial genome, indicating its potential for helping the advancement in *de novo* assembly strategies. These results warrant further research in computational optimization of the algorithm, analysis of its performance with larger genomes, and its integration into more complex pipelines.

References

1. Cadena-Zamudio, J., Martínez-Peña, M., Guzmán-Rodríguez, L., Arteaga-Garibay, R., De Morelos, T.: Aplicación de secuenciación masiva para el estudio y exploración de diversidad microbiana y su aprovechamiento biotecnológico. Agroproductividad **9**(2), 70–83 (2016)
2. Gurevich, A., Saveliev, V., Vyahhi, N., Tesler, G.: Quast: quality assessment tool for genome assemblies. Bioinformatics **29**(8), 1072–1075 (2013)
3. Jain, M., Olsen, H., Paten, B., Akeson, M.: The oxford nanopore minion: delivery of nanopore sequencing to the genomics community. Genome Biol. **17** (2016). https://doi.org/10.1186/s13059-016-1103-0
4. Kawulok, J.: Approximate string matching for searching DNA sequences. Int. J. Biosci. Biochem. Bioinform. **3**, 145–148 (2013). https://doi.org/10.7763/IJBBB.2013.V3.183
5. Kolmogorov, M., Yuan, J., Lin, Y., Pevzner, P.A.: Assembly of long, error-prone reads using repeat graphs. Nat. Biotechnol. **37**(5), 540–546 (2019)
6. Land, M., et al.: Insights from 20 years of bacterial genome sequencing. Functi. Integr. Genomics **15**(2), 141–161 (2015)

7. Li, H.: Aligning sequence reads, clone sequences and assembly contigs with BWA-MEM. arXiv preprint arXiv:1303.3997 (2013)
8. Li, H.: Minimap and miniasm: fast mapping and de novo assembly for noisy long sequences. Bioinformatics **32**(14), 2103–2110 (2016). https://doi.org/10.1093/bioinformatics/btw152
9. Li, H.: Minimap2: pairwise alignment for nucleotide sequences. Bioinformatics **34**(18), 3094–3100 (2018)
10. Li, H., et al.: The sequence alignment/map format and SAMtools. Bioinformatics **25**(16), 2078–2079 (2009)
11. Milne, I., et al.: Using tablet for visual exploration of second-generation sequencing data. Briefi. Bioinformatics **14**(2), 193–202 (2013)
12. Morozova, O., Marra, M.A.: Applications of next-generation sequencing technologies in functional genomics. Genomics **92**(5), 255–264 (2008)
13. Okonechnikov, K., Conesa, A., García-Alcalde, F.: Qualimap 2: advanced multi-sample quality control for high-throughput sequencing data. Bioinformatics **32**(2), 292–294 (2016)
14. Phillippy, A.M.: New advances in sequence assembly (2017)
15. Rodríguez-Santiago, B., Armengol, L.: Tecnologías de secuenciación de nueva generación en diagnóstico genético pre-y postnatal. Diagnóstico Prenatal **23**(2), 56–66 (2012)
16. Ruan, J.: SMARTdenovo: Ultra-fast de novo assembler using long noisy reads (2015)
17. Salmela, L., Rivals, E.: LoRDEC: accurate and efficient long read error correction. Bioinformatics **30**(24), 3506–3514 (2014)
18. Tubbs, R., Stoler, M.: Cell and Tissue Based Molecular Pathology. ClinicalKey 2012, Churchill Livingstone/Elsevier (2009)
19. Zhang, H., Jain, C., Aluru, S.: A comprehensive evaluation of long read error correction methods. BioRxiv p. 519330 (2019)

A Large-Scale Security Analysis of Web Vulnerability: Findings, Challenges and Remedies

Primož Cigoj[1,2(✉)], Živa Stepančič[2], and Borka Jerman Blažič[2]

[1] Jožef Stefan International Postgraduate School, Jamova cesta 39, 1000 Ljubljana, Slovenia
[2] Jozef Stefan Institute, Jamova cesta 39, 1000 Ljubljana, Slovenia
{primoz,ziva,borka}@e5.ijs.si

Abstract. This paper presents an analysis of the results obtained with an efficient and powerful tool developed to recognize the exploitable vulnerabilities of websites on the internet implemented with a web-content management system (WCMS). The key feature of this ethical tool is a dynamic, automated, and fast vulnerability scan of WCMS sites and the attached plug-ins for the live internet by obeying ethical requests. The collected scan results are impressive, and the presented analysis of these results provides an insight into the internet web system's health and the factors that influence the vulnerability levels of websites.

Keywords: Cyberspace · Databases · Software · Security · Search engines · Search methods · Metasearch · Web search · Websites · WCMS

1 Introduction

Web-content management systems (WCMSs) like WordPress are very popular because they are free of charge and simplify the creation of a website and the upgrading of its functionality with plug-ins. Currently, there are more than 54,000 free WordPress plug-ins available in the official directory of plug-ins and the total number of downloads to various websites is estimated to exceed 1 billion. WordPress runs Sweden's official website, Microsoft's news.microsoft.com website, as well as online stores such as that of Bata, a shoe company. Systems like WordPress manage and store valuable information, from banking to electronic prescriptions on medical websites, as well as an enormous amount of personal data, all of which are of interest to cybercriminals and cyber-attackers. Even websites that do not hold valuable data or sensitive information are often attacked by hackers or competitors to cause a reduction in sales or to prevent websites from spreading their messages. For this reason, knowing and being aware of web vulnerability has an important value and is a critical task.

Supported by organization J. Stefan Institute.

O. Gervasi et al. (Eds.): ICCSA 2020, LNCS 12253, pp. 763–771, 2020.
https://doi.org/10.1007/978-3-030-58814-4_64

The need to identify web vulnerability is vital, as it influences the whole of internet security. The most common threats to the internet data space were identified in a 2017 security survey carried out by the UK Government as part of the National Cyber Security Programme. The findings are as follows: fraudulent e-mails (72%), viruses, spyware and malware (33%), attacks based on online impersonation (27%), and ransomware [1].

2 Overview of the Area and the Problem

New web technologies are followed by W3Techs. According to their survey, about 41.1% of websites do not use any WCMS. WordPress is used by 37.5% of all websites, which is a 63.5% market share of the content-management systems [2]. Another survey conducted in 2020 by BuiltWith found that 36.51% of the Alexa database and the top ranked in terms of their market presence contain 1 million websites that use WordPress [3].

Due to a lack of security, WordPress was targeted by an exceptionally large Distributed Denial of Service (DDoS) attack in 2011 that in many cases affected website connectivity [5]. Besides a DDoS attack, the most common attacks on the WordPress platform were identified as SQL Injection, Remote File Inclusion, Directory Traversal, Cross-Site Scripting, Comment Spamming, Remote Command Execution and File Upload. Given that WordPress and its plug-ins are public, anyone can look at the source code and can look for the possibility of vulnerabilities. This situation makes web-page development easier and faster, but at the same time allows hackers to exploit security holes and vulnerabilities in the code and thus misuse websites.

3 Previous Work

The WordPress WCMS is very popular among internet users, but web servers and the associated applications were found [6] to be more vulnerable than those that do not use any form of CMS. There are two major types of web-vulnerability scanners. The first type consists of automatic scanning tools that inspect the security features of the ports within the IPv4 site and share the results publicly (Shodan and Censys). The best-known tools from this group are Mmap, Zmap and Masscan [10–12]. The port information collected with such tools does not provide details of the web-page content and the vulnerability of its plug-ins, as they do not inspect the content of the web pages. The second type is composed of personal, interaction-based scanning tools operated by the user, and their results are returned directly and only to the user. The main examples of such solutions are Nessus, skipfish, Acunetix, IVRE, Vulners, and Vega. The findings are not shared publicly and to obtain the results the user operator must be contacted for a presentation of the results. Several similar search engines [6–9] were created in the past by different researchers, who intended to provide an analysis of vulnerable WCMS websites. The major drawback of these applications is the time needed to inspect the large number of sites. The average scanner of this type needs a few days to explore a small data set, e.g., a group of 50,000 websites. So, success in identifying the vulnerability of a large internet web space depends on the speed of the crawling. Another drawback is the fact that they do not provide a complete image of a particular website, as some search features are not provided. An additional problem with some of the scanners is the approach used for inspecting the web servers, which is based on a simulated type of attack. In the case of success, the vulnerability is discovered. However, this is not a legal action. The use of this technique, known as the exploit technique, is forbidden in the case that the owner of the site does not allow the site to be inspected in this way. Another drawback of the existing scanners is that they access the websites using the IPv4 address and inspect only one website, thus neglecting the presence of many websites that are hosted on the same web server. The tool presented below overcomes these drawbacks and offers a more accurate vulnerability identification as well as a score for the insecurity level of the WCMS [4].

4 The VulNet Tool

The main objective that led to this tool's development was the intention to offer a solution that will improve web security by reducing the number of vulnerable websites with a fast, efficient and powerful method that can detect vulnerability and alert website owners immediately and worn them to improve their website's online hygiene. Another objective was to obtain a clearer picture of the web-security status within the internet space of the European registered domains. By identifying the status and the main characteristics of the vulnerable websites, the basic enablers that influence the level of insecurity in a particular European country can be identified and actions to improve the overall web security can be introduced. As there is no publicly available list of WordPress sites, it was necessary to review the entire web and to find out how many websites are powered by WordPress from the whole population of websites.

The designed methodology for data collection and scanning consists of five steps: 1) searching and collecting the URL queue of websites, where the initial list of websites is collected from the existing DNS domain zone files. A URL from the queue is visited and the links found there are added to the URL queue. The URLs that were not significant for our research were removed from the search (shortened URL providers, and large social sites), 2) accessing the website and asking for responses to the sent queries, 3) obtaining responses (metadata), 4) posting search queries for the application patterns, e.g., plug-ins, and collecting information from the CVE about the detected plug-ins, and 5) ad-hoc validating and storing of the results with the tool's in-built scoring mechanism. The scoring mechanism starts by identifying the vulnerability of the WCMS core in the predefined database identification of the vulnerabilities within the core WCMS pages and the plug-ins. A more detailed description of the search and scoring methodology, including a comparison of our search methodology with that of other researchers and tools, is presented in our published article [4].

5 Results and the Analysis

The scanning results provided by the VulNet tool are displayed with a web-based original interface developed with PHP. The interface displays the process of a live scanning and the obtained data. It also maps the path that the crawler has followed. VulNet provided information about the web space of 194 countries by establishing successfully 126,086,633 links. Among these websites there were 16,274,980 valid WordPress installations with 14,887,047 plug-in installations. In this web set, more than 5,018,262 were found to be vulnerable, representing 31% of all the WordPress installations on the internet. A total of 2,475,337 had a higher vulnerability, with a score of 5 or over. A total of 4,356,067 vulnerabilities were detected and among them 2,795,855 had an insecurity score that was higher than 5. The analysis of the results revealed that there are very vulnerable core versions of the WordPress website, especially the versions from series 4.0 (4.9.8, 4.9.3, 5.0.3, 4.9.6, 4.9.7, 4.9.4, 5.1, 4.9.5, 4.6.1).

Each plug-in or WP core version was assessed to be in one of three categories: secure, unknown, or insecure (with a score). Scores higher than 5 are considered critical and are reported separately (as a variable score). A website is considered secure if the core version and all (if any) plug-in versions are secure. As soon as one of the versions of the core and plug-in is unknown, the vulnerability status of the site is labelled as unknown. Otherwise, the site is considered as insecure. The main data set is composed (by domain) of the total WordPress sites (total WP), the number of insecure, secure, unknown sites, and insecure sites with a score of higher than 5 (variable score). The total number of plug-in versions, the total number of core versions, and their combinations were recorded as well.

A subset of the collected data was selected based on the fact that the parameters that can influence the increased appearance of insecure sites were available for these countries only. The following parameters were considered in the analysis: internet use (IU), frequency of internet use (FoIU), households with access to the internet (HH), and the digital skills (DS) index. The DS index was taken from an Information Society report from ITU [13] and the Eurostat portal [14]. Population-related data, such as the number of citizens (population), the gross net income (GNI), and the fixed cost of broadband access per GNI were analysed as well. These values were downloaded from the Eurostat portal [14].

The aim of the analysis was to explore the relationship between these indicators and the percentage of insecure websites found among the WP websites. Since we found that the internet-based indicators presented above correlate very highly among themselves, we decided to use only the DS index data, as it is considered to be the most indicative parameter in terms of web security for a general user. We hypothesized that the indicator of the DS index can show a statistically significant negative relationship with the degree of insecure sites, since better digital skills among the population implies better knowledge and an awareness regarding the use of cyber-security technology.

The final subset contained 31 different European countries: Germany (DE), Netherlands (NL), France (FR), Great Britain (GB), Italy (IT), Denmark (DK), Poland (PL), Spain (ES), Sweden (SE), Switzerland (CH), Czechia (CZ),

Ireland (IE), Finland (FI), Austria (AT), Romania (RO), Belgium (BE), Hungary (HU), Bulgaria (BG), Norway (NO), Slovakia (SK), Estonia (EE), Slovenia (SI), Portugal (PT), Croatia (HR), Lithuania (LV), Luxembourg (LU), Greece (GR), Iceland (IS), Latvia (LT), Cyprus (CY), and Malta (MT).

Summary statistics of the detected vulnerabilities are shown in Table 1. On average, we could not determine the vulnerability status for a third of the sites in a domain, due to unknown core or plug-in versions. The percentages of secure sites are between 21% and 40%, with an average of 28%. The percentage of insecure sites is in the range of 30% and 47%, with a mean of 38%, a median of 40%, and a standard deviation of 4.4%. There are no univariate outliers in either variable. In five cases, see Fig. 1, there is a higher percentage of secure sites than insecure: Germany, Denmark, the Netherlands, Switzerland and Norway. The first two are middle ranked in terms of digital skills, while the latter three show a very high DS index.

Table 1. Summary statistics of all the WP sites found, the vulnerability percentages, and the digital-skills (DS) index.

	Total WP	Unknown [%]	Secure [%]	Insecure [%]	Score [%]	DS
Count	31	31	31	31	31	31
Mean	120712.19	33.56	28	38.43	31.27	59.06
Std	182007.02	4.3	5.08	4.44	4.76	14.89
Min	10	20	21.22	30.31	22.13	29
25%	14715	31	24.28	35.5	27.27	49
50%	49345	33.57	26.12	39.65	32.24	57
75%	128049	36.86	31.4	41.59	34.9	71
Max	805361	40.15	40	46.96	40.83	85

The sites with very high insecurity scores are a subset of the all sites classified as insecure sites; therefore, the correlation between the variables score and insecure is very high ($r = .93$). There is also a high negative correlation ($r = -.6$) between the percentages of secure and insecure sites present in the whole set. For the validation of the hypothesis we used the percentage of insecure sites. The categorization of the DS index value was made in three groups, where we classified values below 50 as low skill, above 75 as high skill, and middle skill for the index values between 50 and 75. The descriptive statistics of the DS index are available in the last column of Table 1.

The dependencies among the variables are illustrated in Fig. 1. The countries with high digital skills, a high percentage of secure sites and a low percentage of insecure sites are grouped in the bottom-right corner of Fig. 1. In this group are the Scandinavian countries, Germany, the Netherlands, and Switzerland. In the group of countries with low digital skills and a high percentage of insecure sites are Lithuania, Poland, Bulgaria, Greece, Latvia, Ireland, Czechia, and Cyprus.

In the middle we can find Luxembourg, Belgium, Iceland, Great Britain, France, Austria, Estonia, and Italy. Malta is isolated, although not as a statistical outlier, but due to the small number of WP sites found.

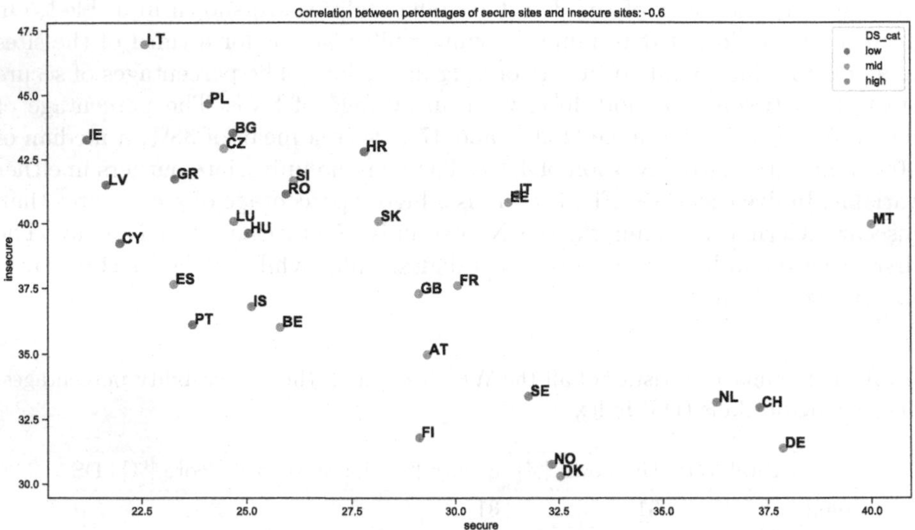

Fig. 1. Scatter plot of secure vs. insecure percentages per country with the digital-skill (DS) index categories.

A simple linear-regression analysis was made to predict the percentage of insecure WCMSs in the country based on the country's DS index. The data set was shown to be near-normally distributed and homoscedastic. A high correlation between the DS and the percentage of insecure sites (r $= -.65$) suggests a linear dependence. By modelling the regression on the whole data set, we obtained a regression equation as follows:

$$insecure = 50.41 - 0.20 * DS. \tag{1}$$

The first regression model with $R^2 = 0.462$ and RMSE $= 3.202$ was found to be significant, as $F(1, 29) = 24.94$ ($p < 0.001$) and both coefficients were significant at $\alpha = 0.001$ (the beta coefficient was $-.68$). TThe analysis of residuals, however, suggested improvements to the model, see Table 2. We used the Jarque-Bera (JB) test for normality [15], the Heteroscedasticity Test by Breusch-Pagan (LM-statistic) to test the homoscedasticity [16], the Harvey Collier Test for Linearity [17], and the Durbin-Watson (DW) test for first-order autocorrelation [18]. Improvements could be made upon JB and DW statistics. An analysis of the influential observations exposed three residual outliers (LT, DE, DK), three leverage points (IS, RO, BG), and one influential observation).

We removed the biggest outlier (LT), the influential observation (LU), and one leverage point (IS) from the data set to improve the model. These are also the same observations found to be significant in the bivariate outlier analysis using the Mahalanobis distance. The new model has the following regression equation:

$$insecure = 51.77 - 0.26 * DS, \tag{2}$$

which was again found to be significant with $F(1, 26) = 45.50$ ($p < 0.001$) and both coefficients significant at $p < 0.001$ (the beta coefficient was -0.81). The R^2 has increased to 0.665 and the RMSE dropped to 2.47. The residual analysis supports all four assumptions of linear regression, as shown in Table 2.

Table 2. Regression summary and residual analysis results for both models.

Model	Regression results summary							Residual analysis						
	Regressors	Coefficient	SE	CI 0.025	CI 0.095	AIC	BIC	JB	Prob (JB)	LM-statistic	p-value (LM)	HC-statistic	p-value (HC)	DW
1	const	50.41	2.47	45.355	55.457	164.1	167	1.096	0.578	2.495	0.114	1.649	0.111	1.507
	DS	−0.2027	0.041	−0.286	−0.12									
2	const	52.77	2.094	48.466	57.074	134.1	136.8	0.304	0.859	0.0948	0.758	0.713	0.483	1.917
	DS	−0.2553	0.036	−0.328	−0.182									

The regression analysis confirmed the hypothesis that the level of DS has a positive impact on the provision of security within the websites with WCMS applications.

6 Discussion

We can conclude that the scanning with VulNet gave us a thorough internal security view of popular websites across the internet. However, the dependencies between the number of insecure sites and the other potential influential parameters were investigated only for some European countries, because reliable data is only available for these countries on the Eurostat portal.

The analysis showed that all the parameters per country, like internet use, the cost per fixed broadband access, or the percentage of households with internet access correlate very closely and for that reason only digital skills was selected as an independent variable in the statistical research. The hypothesis that the percentage of insecure sites is lower, when the DS of the population in a particular country are higher, was confirmed to be valid. This finding holds for almost all the studied European countries. The other finding that resulted from the study is related to the source of the vulnerabilities. It was found that the major contributors to the website's high insecurity score are from installed plug-ins. Figure 2 presents the comparison between the percentages of insecure plug-ins and the core versions of Word Press against the percentage of all the insecure sites. It is clear that the plug-ins are those software applications that mostly influence the overall site insecurity of the website.

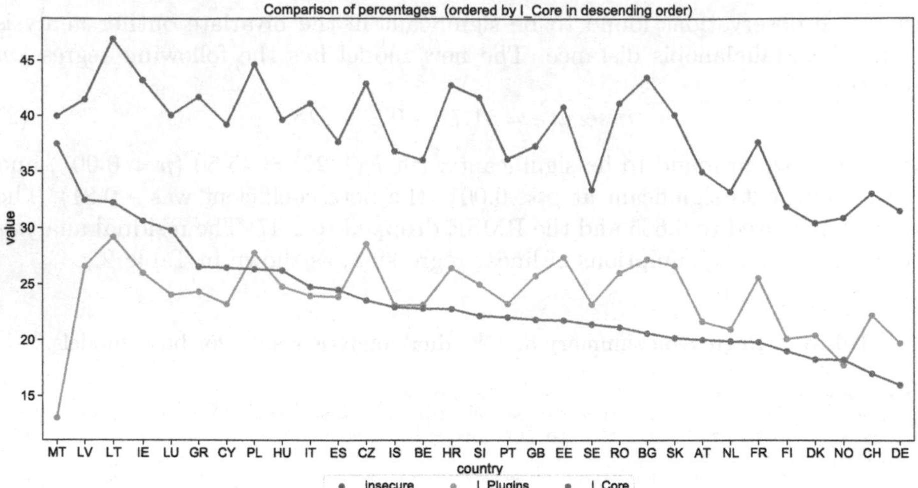

Fig. 2. Comparison of vulnerability percentages of core versions, plug-in versions, and overall insecure percentage.

7 Conclusions

The present paper provides a good insight into the security health of websites established with the Word Press core software for the whole internet. The major contributors to the insecurity of these sites are the used plug-ins. These are freely obtainable on the internet, with there being more than 54,000 available. This finding implies that the used plug-ins should be the major concern of the website owners when they decide to use them for improving the functionality and services offered by the website. However, an information service for providing awareness about the security health of the website for these types of website is still missing on the internet. Our investigation also found that there is a statistically significant relationship between a country's digital-skills index and the percentage of insecure web-content management systems: the higher the digital index of a country's population, the lower is the percentage of insecure sites in that country.

We can conclude that the security of websites is still a topic that needs further investigation and the provision of new remedies as the number of cyber-crime attacks are growing and the number of victims, although not known in detail, is growing as well.

References

1. Klahr, R., et al.: Cyber security breaches survey 2017: main report (2017)
2. W3Techs. https://w3techs.com. Accessed 5 May 2019
3. BuiltWith. https://builtwith.com. Accessed 5 May 2019

4. Cigoj, P., Blazic, B.J.: An intelligent and automated WCMS vulnerability-discovery tool: the current state of the web. IEEE Access **7**, 175466–175473 (2019)
5. Tsotsis, A.: WordPress.com suffers largest DDoS attack in its history (2011)
6. Vasek, M., Wadleigh, J., Moore, T.: Hacking is not random: a case-control study of webserver-compromise risk. IEEE Trans. Dependable Secure Comput. **13**, 206–219 (2015)
7. van Goethem, T., Chen, P., Nikiforakis, N., Desmet, L., Joosen, W.: Large-scale security analysis of the web: challenges and findings. In: Holz, T., Ioannidis, S. (eds.) Trust 2014. LNCS, vol. 8564, pp. 110–126. Springer, Cham (2014). https://doi.org/10.1007/978-3-319-08593-7_8
8. Stock, B., Pellegrino, G., Li, F., Backes, M., Rossow, C.: Didn't you hear me? – towards more successful web vulnerability notifications. In: Network and Distributed Systems Security (NDSS) Symposium (2018)
9. Schagen, N., Koning, K., Bos, H., Giuffrida, C.: Towards automated vulnerability scanning of network servers. In: Proceedings of the 11th European Workshop on Systems Security. ACM (2018)
10. Nappa, A., Rafique, Z.M., Caballero, J., Gu, G.: CyberProbe: towards internet-scale active detection of malicious servers. In: The Network and Distributed System Security Symposium (NDSS) (2014)
11. Kim, H., Kim, T., Jang, D.: An intelligent improvement of internet-wide scan engine for fast discovery of vulnerable IoT devices. Symmetry **10**, 151 (2018)
12. Li, F., et al.: You've got vulnerability: exploring effective vulnerability notifications. In: 25th USENIX Security Symposium (USENIX Security 16) (2016)
13. Digital Skills Insights 2019 - ITU. https://academy.itu.int/digital-skills-insights-2019. Accessed 15 Dec 2019
14. European Statistics - Eurostat. https://ec.europa.eu/eurostat. Accessed 15 Dec 2019
15. Jarque, C.M., Bera, A.K.: Efficient tests for normality, homoscedasticity and serial independence of regression residuals. Econ. Lett. **6**(3), 255–259 (1980)
16. Breusch, T., Pegan, A.: A simple test of heteroscedasticity and random coeffient variation. Econometrica **47**, 1287–1294 (1979)
17. Harvey, A., Collier, P.: Testing for functional misspecification in regression analysis. J. Econ. **6**, 103–119 (1977)
18. Durbin, J., Watson, G.S.: Testing for serial correlation in least squares regression III. Biometrika **58**(1), 1–19 (1971)

Embryo Spatial Model Reconstruction

Darius Dirvanauskas[1(✉)], Rytis Maskeliūnas[1], Vidas Raudonis[2], and Sanjay Misra[3]

[1] Department of Multimedia Engineering, Kaunas University of Technology, 51368 Kaunas, Lithuania
darius.dirvanauskas@ktu.edu

[2] Department of Control Systems, Kaunas University of Technology, 51367 Kaunas, Lithuania

[3] Computer Engineering Department, Atilim University, Ankara, Turkey

Abstract. Time lapse microscopy offered new solutions to study embryo development process. It allows embryologist to monitor embryo growth in real time and evaluate them without interfering into their growth environment. Embryo evaluation during growth process is one of the key criteria in embryo selection for fertilization. Live embryo monitoring is time consuming and new tools are offered to automate part of process. Our proposed algorithm gives new possibilities for embryo monitoring. It uses embryo images which are taken from different embryo layers, extracts embryo cell features and returns metrical evaluation to compare different embryos. High number of extracted features shows embryo fragmentation. Other tool which we present is spatial embryo model. Features extracted from embryo layers are combined together to spatial model. It allows embryologist to examine embryo model and compare different layers in one space. The obtained spatial embryo model will be later used to develop new algorithms for embryo analysis tasks.

Keywords: Image analysis · Spatial model · Feature extraction

1 Introduction

Different artificial fertilization methods, such as insemination or in vitro fertilization (IVF) are used by fertility doctors to reach successful pregnancies. If medicaments do not help IVF is used to treat infertility. Multiple embryos are grown in vitro at the same time. One of IVF success factors is selection of the most viable embryo [1]. Embryos for insemination are selected in visual inspection performed by embryologists. It is prone to error and requires time. In one cycle of IVF the pregnancy success rate can be as high as 60%. In some cases fertilization fails repeatedly and patients need multiple IVF cycles [2].

Time-lapse microscopy (TLM) has provided new tools for embryo image inspection. These machines are used to continuously monitor embryos and capture images in different layers. The aim is to inspect embryo's cell shape and measure development stage duration without removing from their growth environment. Embryo growth to 4-cell stage could last up to 48 h and 72 h to 8-cell stage. In most cases duration of 2-cell and

O. Gervasi et al. (Eds.): ICCSA 2020, LNCS 12253, pp. 772–780, 2020.
https://doi.org/10.1007/978-3-030-58814-4_65

4-cell stages defines quality of the embryo and could be used as one of the decision factors for embryo selection [3]. To decrease human error rate automated tools are required to accurately track duration of development stages for multiple embryos at the same time. In this study, we present a method for embryo's spatial model reconstruction. This spatial model will allow embryologist to analyze embryo features from different layer in one space.

2 Related Work

Different image analysis methods are already applied to embryo analysis. Real time embryo division monitoring techniques capture division time [4]. Different solutions using conditional random field [5] and VisSeg model [6] were proposed for cell counting. A. Khan applied deep learning techniques to estimate number of cells in embryo [7]. Other study applied deep learning to develop automated embryo grading system [8]. Fully convolutional neural network model was used for embryo inner mass segmentation [9]. Set of neural networks were trained to predict quality of embryos [10]. Embryo cell localization was achieved by using linear chain Markov model [11]. Three dimensional morphological segmentation using watershed based algorithm was presented [12]. Machine learning methods were used to develop model which helps to select potential embryo for implantation [13]. UNet architecture was proposed for blastomere centroids localization [14]. Dual ResUNet model which avoids loss of spatial and identity was proposed for zebrafish embryo segmentation [15]. High speed camera and deep learning model are used for real time cell population analysis [16]. Combination of Gaussian distribution and K-Means method was proposed for white blood cell segmentation [17]. Circular Hough transform was performed to count blood cells in microscopic images [18]. Different machine learning classifiers were used to classify blood cells for leukemia diagnosis [19]. Image based data analysis techniques for better results were presented in J. Caicedo and et al. study [20]. Deep learning architectures for medical image segmentation and classification were discussed in other study [21]. Machine learning algorithms were used to create image based cell sorting model [22].

There is lack of studies which proposes spatial embryo analyses algorithms. In this work, we aim to develop a method which would prepare embryo's spatial model and analyze its quality. Combination of image processing algorithm were used to extract embryo cell features. Images captured in different embryo layers were used to construct three dimensional model. This model will be a tool for embryologists to analyze spatial model and compare separate layers in one space.

3 Material

3.1 Dataset

Embryo images used in our study were taken with Esco Global incubator series, called Miri TL (timelapse) [23]. The embryo image sets were registered in the German, Chinese, and Singapore clinics. No identity data were ever provided to the authors of this paper. Embryo database consists of more than 26,000 image sets with a resolution of 600 × 600 pixels. One image set contains 7 photos taken from different embryo layers. Images are obtained from 24 different growing embryos in Esco Global incubator.

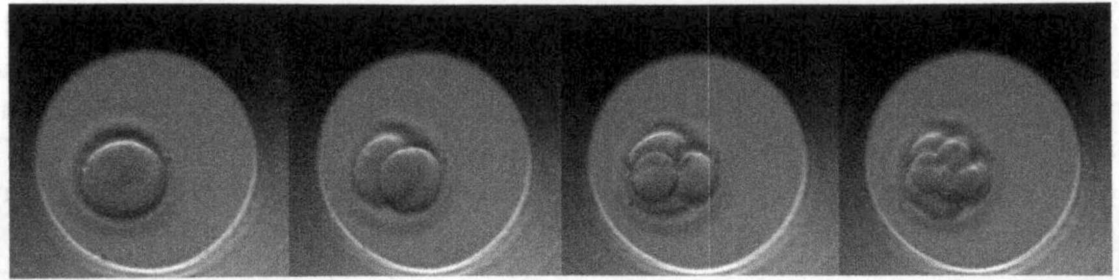

Fig. 1. Embryo development stages

3.2 Equipment

Esco incubator culturing conditions were: temperature of 37 °C, stable level of 5% CO2, and the controllable values of nitrogen and oxygen mixture. The embryos were photographed in a culture coin dish made from polypropylene with a neutral media pH = 7. The inverted microscopy principle was used, with 20x lenses, without zoom, with focusing and with field of view of 350 um. An example of embryo images in the Esco dataset is presented in Fig. 1. The embryo feature extraction and spatial model generation was done on an Intel i5-4570 CPU with a GeForce 1060 GPU and 8 GB of RAM.

4 Methods

Our proposed model process embryo images in multiple steps (see Fig. 2). User selects embryo sample for analysis and model loads images from seven embryo layers. Images are converted to grayscale format and smoothed to reduce noise level. After that, in vitro localization detects its contour in every layer's image to find most accurate contour for every layer. Background, which is outside in vitro contour, is removed. In embryo contour detection, cell edge and embryo fragmentation features are extracted. These features are used in next steps to compare embryos and prepare their spatial model.

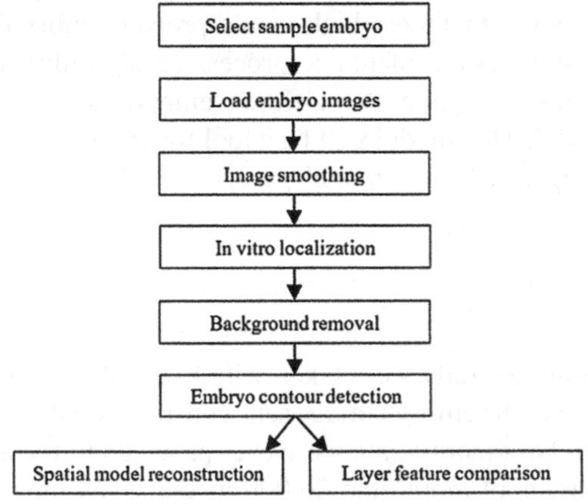

Fig. 2. A pipeline of spatial embryo model reconstruction

In spatial embryo model reconstruction our proposed method uses extracted features. It takes these features and plots them as 3D scatter model. Embryologist could use this model to evaluate and compare different embryo layers in one space. This comparison helps if cells grow equally in different layers. Spatial model have options to hide layers, change distance between layers and make X and Y axis cuts (see Fig. 3). Our tool gives new possibilities for embryo analysis. It transfers information from 2D images to 3D spatial plot.

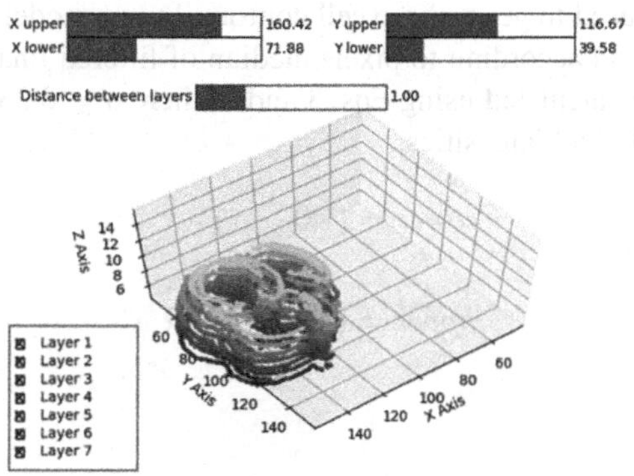

Fig. 3. Plot of embryo spatial model.

In layer feature comparison step embryo cell contour and fragmentations are counted as features. These features are added together and considered as base value for embryo evaluation. If test embryo feature number exceeds base value, it is considered that embryo's fragmentation rate is too high. This embryo comparison gives embryologists additional information for embryo evaluation.

For model evaluation extracted features are compared to base value. This comparison defines embryo fragmentation level. Embryo spatial model evaluation is done by embryologist visual inspection.

4.1 In Vitro Detection

At first in vitro localization part algorithm tries to find circle which define in vitro contour the best. Loaded seven embryo layer images are converted to grayscale format. To reduce noise, images are smoothed with 3 × 3 averaging filter. Filter takes average of pixels under kernel area and modifies central pixel value with the average. Circle Hough Transformation is used to find circle, which defines in vitro location [24]. A circle with radius R and center (a, b) can be described with the following parametric equations.

$$x = a + R\cos(\theta) \tag{1}$$

$$y = b + R\sin(\theta) \tag{2}$$

To reduce computation time we limit radius with lower and upper values. If multiple circles are detected, algorithm averages their radius and center. After circles are detected in every layer, algorithm averages their radius and centers to return parameters into one circle. If circle is not detected in layer, that layer is skipped and not used for circle parameter calculation. Background view which is outside detected circle is removed as not needed information.

4.2 Embryo Feature Extraction

View inside in vitro is used in next step to extract embryo features. Active Canny edge detection method is used to get embryo cell contour. In our model threshold values are calculated and adjusted according to pixels median of filtered image. Threshold lower and upper values are calculated using Eqs. 3 and 4, there $\sigma = 0.33$ and x is the median of the single channel pixel intensities.

$$lower = (1.0 - \sigma) * x \tag{3}$$

$$upper = (1.0 + \sigma) * x \tag{4}$$

5 Results

5.1 Feature Comparison

Our proposed model allows embryologists to evaluate embryo fragmentation number in different embryo layers. For our experiment we took 24 exemplary embryos while they evolved for 48 h. Average feature extraction duration 1.3 s. The following Table 1 gives average values, which could be used as a base value to evaluate embryo fragmentation. If test embryo feature value is significantly higher than base value in presented table we can predict that test embryo has higher number of fragmentation.

Table 1. Number of features extracted from images

	1 Cell	2 Cell	4 Cell
Layer 1	1306.5	1399.5	1535.1
Layer 2	1332.5	1455.9	1607.2
Layer 3	1392.7	1494.5	1598.1
Layer 4	1377.9	1485.9	1606.8
Layer 5	1349.0	1439.8	1589.3
Layer 6	1315.6	1376.2	1550.1
Layer 7	1226.7	1322.9	1422.2

After this evaluation we can see in Fig. 4 that embryos with bigger number of cells have higher feature number. This is caused, because of additional cell contour, which appears in two and four cell samples. From the graphic we can see that first layer feature number is 5–7% lower than feature number in third and fourth layer. It means that at lowest layer less features are detected and number increases till third layer. From fourth to seventh layer feature number decreases. This pattern allows to separate embryos which feature number is distributed differently compared to base values.

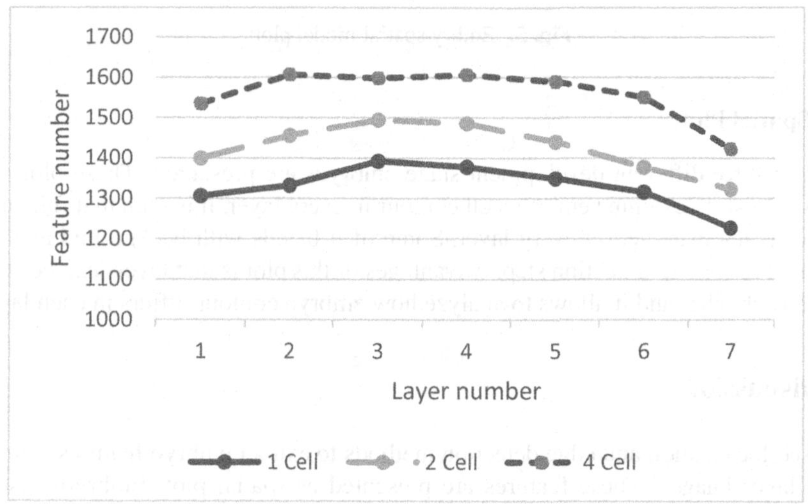

Fig. 4. Average feature number in layers

In our database we only had embryos which started to mutate at two cell stage. Therefore we were not able to compare one and four cell healthy embryo feature number to mutated ones.

We took test embryos which started to mutate in two cell stage to compare their feature level with base value. Results showed that average extracted feature number from these embryos there 1964. It is 37% higher compared to normal two cell embryo. We were not able to compare one and four cell mutated embryos, because our database did not had them.

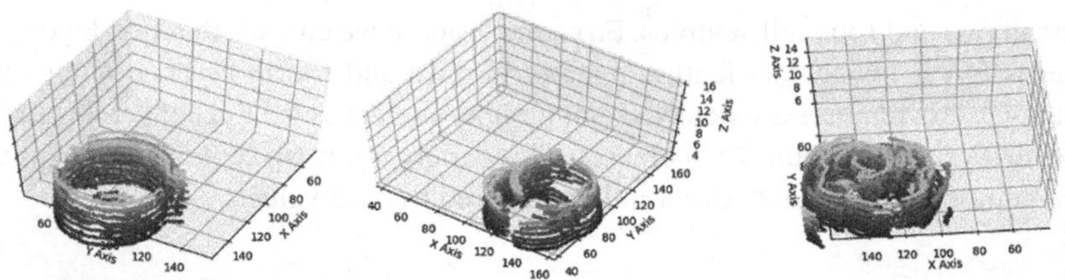

Fig. 5. Embry spatial model plots

5.2 Spatial Plot

In Fig. 5 three different development stage embryos are presented. These plots allow embryologists to examine embryo cell contour in every layer. It is seen that full embryo contour is not extracted in every layer. Some of it blends with background and is not separated in contour detection step. Advantages of this plot is that layers can be stacked one on each other and it allows to analyze how embryo contour differs in each layer.

6 Discussion

We used localization and edge detection methods to extract embryo features from their seven layer images. These features are presented as spatial plot. Embryologists can examine plot by rotating embryo 3D model. This model can be dynamically changed by making X and Y axis cuts and changing distance between layers or turning them off. Prepared spatial model could be utilized for embryo 3D model printing.

Features extracted from 24 sample embryos were averaged to make base values to which test embryo could be compared. If feature number in test embryo is higher than base value, we can predict higher fragmentation rate in that embryo. Feature numbers do not spread evenly in every layer. First layer has smaller number of features, which increases up to third layer. From third to seventh layer feature number decreases. This feature spread pattern could be used as template to which we can compare test embryo feature spread. Our database had only embryos which started to mutate in two cell stage. Therefore we were not able to carry out all three stages embryo base value comparison to mutated ones.

7 Conclusion

In our study we found embryo feature base value that increases while embryo grows. Average feature numbers in different stages are: 1 cell – 1328; 2 cell – 1423; 4 cell – 1558. Features extracted from mutated embryo which mutation started at two cell stage gave 37% higher feature number compared to healthy one.

Acknowledgments. The authors also would like to thank Esco Global for kindly provided embryo image dataset and Živilė Čerkienė for her expert opinion and helpful comments.

Conflicts of Interest. The authors declare no conflict of interest.

Ethics. The permit for ethical studies for using the human subject related materials was issued by the Ethics Committee of the Faculty of Informatics, in Kaunas University of Technology. The number of a permit is: IFEP201706-3.

References

1. Vaegter, K.K., et al.: Which factors are most predictive for live birth after in vitro fertilization and intracytoplasmic sperm injection (IVF/ICSI) treatments? Analysis of 100 prospectively recorded variables in 8,400 IVF/ICSI single-embryo transfers. Fertil. Steril. **107**(3), 641–648 (2017)
2. Margalioth, E.J., Ben-Chetrit, A., Gal, M., Eldar-Geva, T.: Investigation and treatment of repeated implantation failure following IVF-ET. Hum. Reprod. **21**(12), 3036–3043 (2006)
3. Lindner, G.M., Wright Jr., R.W.: Bovine embryo morphology and evaluation. Theriogenology **20**(4), 407–416 (1983)
4. Wang, Y., Moussavi, F., Lorenzen, P.: Automated embryo stage classification in time-lapse microscopy video of early human embryo development. In: Mori, K., Sakuma, I., Sato, Y., Barillot, C., Navab, N. (eds.) MICCAI 2013. LNCS, vol. 8150, pp. 460–467. Springer, Heidelberg (2013). https://doi.org/10.1007/978-3-642-40763-5_57
5. Khan, A., Gould, S., Salzmann, M.: Automated monitoring of human embryonic cells up to the 5-cell stage in time-lapse microscopy images. In: Proceedings of the 2015 IEEE 12th International Symposium on Biomedical Imaging (ISBI), New York, NY, USA, 16–19 April 2015, pp. 389–393 (2015)
6. Nandy, K., et al.: Segmentation and quantitative analysis of individual cells in developmental tissues. In: Lewandoski, M. (ed.) Mouse Molecular Embryology. MMB, vol. 1092, pp. 235–253. Springer, Boston (2014). https://doi.org/10.1007/978-1-60327-292-6_16
7. Khan, A., Gould, S., Salzmann, M.: Deep convolutional neural networks for human embryonic cell counting. In: Hua, G., Jégou, H. (eds.) ECCV 2016. LNCS, vol. 9913, pp. 339–348. Springer, Cham (2016). https://doi.org/10.1007/978-3-319-46604-0_25
8. Chen, T.-J., Zheng, W.-L., Liu, C.-H., Huang, I., Lai, H.-H., Liu, M.: Using deep learning with large dataset of microscope images to develop an automated embryo grading system. Fertil. Reprod. **01**, 1–6 (2019). https://doi.org/10.1142/s2661318219500051
9. Kheradmand, S., Singh, A., Saeedi, P., Au, J., Havelock, J.: Inner cell mass segmentation in human HMC embryo images using fully convolutional network. In: Proceedings of the 2017 IEEE International Conference on Image Processing (ICIP), Beijing, China, 17–20 September 2017, pp. 1752–1756 (2017)
10. Manna, C., Nanni, L., Lumini, A., Pappalardo, S.: Artificial intelligence techniques for embryo and oocyte classification. Reprod. Biomed. Online **26**, 42–49 (2013)
11. Khan, A., Gould, S., Salzmann, M.: A linear chain markov model for detection and localization of cells in early stage embryo development. In: Proceedings of the 2015 IEEE Winter Conference on Applications of Computer Vision, Waikoloa, HI, USA, 6–9 January 2015, pp. 526–533 (2015)
12. Cao, J., Wong, M., Zhao, Z., et al.: 3DMMS: robust 3D membrane morphological segmentation of C. elegans embryo. BMC Bioinf. **20**, 176 (2019). https://doi.org/10.1186/s12859-019-2720-x
13. Patil, S.N., Wali, U.V., Swamy, M.K.: Selection of single potential embryo to improve the success rate of implantation in IVF procedure using machine learning techniques. In: 2019 International Conference on Communication and Signal Processing (ICCSP), Chennai, India, pp. 0881–0886 (2019)

14. Rad, R.M., Saeedi, P., Au, J., Havelock, J.: Blastomere cell counting and centroid localization in microscopic images of human embryo. In: 2018 IEEE 20th International Workshop on Multimedia Signal Processing (MMSP), Vancouver, BC, pp. 1–6 (2018)
15. Zhang, K., et al.: Zebrafish embryo vessel segmentation using a novel dual ResUNet model. Comput. Intell. Neurosci. **2019**, 1–14 (2019). https://doi.org/10.1155/2019/8214975
16. Heo, Y.J., Lee, D., Kang, J., et al.: Real-time image processing for microscopy-based label-free imaging flow cytometry in a microfluidic chip. Sci Rep **7**, 11651 (2017)
17. Agrawal, R., Satapathy, S., Bagla, G., Rajakumar, K.: Detection of white blood cell cancer using image processing. In: 2019 International Conference on Vision Towards Emerging Trends in Communication and Networking (ViTECoN), Vellore, India, pp. 1–6 (2019)
18. Dvanesh, V.D., Lakshmi, P.S., Reddy, K., Vasavi, A.S.: Blood cell count using digital image processing. In: 2018 International Conference on Current Trends towards Converging Technologies (ICCTCT), Coimbatore, pp. 1–7 (2018)
19. Abdeldaim, A.M., Sahlol, A.T., Elhoseny, M., Hassanien, A.E.: Computer-aided acute lymphoblastic leukemia diagnosis system based on image analysis. In: Hassanien, A.E., Oliva, D.A. (eds.) Advances in Soft Computing and Machine Learning in Image Processing. SCI, vol. 730, pp. 131–147. Springer, Cham (2018). https://doi.org/10.1007/978-3-319-63754-9_7
20. Caicedo, J., Cooper, S., Heigwer, F., et al.: Data-analysis strategies for image-based cell profiling. Nat. Methods **14**, 849–863 (2017)
21. Razzak, M.I., Naz, S., Zaib, A.: Deep learning for medical image processing: overview, challenges and the future. In: Dey, N., Ashour, A.S., Borra, S. (eds.) Classification in BioApps. LNCVB, vol. 26, pp. 323–350. Springer, Cham (2018). https://doi.org/10.1007/978-3-319-65981-7_12
22. Nitta, N., et al.: Intelligent image-activated cell sorting. SSRN Electron. J. **175**, 266–276 (2018). https://doi.org/10.2139/ssrn.3204560
23. Esco Medical | Miri® Time-Lapse Incubator technical specification (2013). www.escoglobal.com/products/download/1381288481.pdf
24. Davies, E.R.: Machine Vision: Theory, Algorithms, Practicalities, 3rd edn. Morgan Kauffman Publishers, Burlington (2005). Chapter 10

Correction to: Evaluating the Urban Quality Through a Hybrid Approach: Application in the Milan (Italy) City Area

Alessandra Oppio, Marta Bottero, Federico Dell'Anna, Marta Dell'Ovo, and Laura Gabrielli

Correction to:
Chapter "Evaluating the Urban Quality Through a Hybrid Approach: Application in the Milan (Italy) City Area" in: O. Gervasi et al. (Eds.): *Computational Science and Its Applications – ICCSA 2020*, LNCS 12253, https://doi.org/10.1007/978-3-030-58814-4_21

In the version of this paper that was originally published the names and surnames of the authors have been inverted.These are now corrected as following:

Alessandra Oppio
Marta Bottero
Federico Dell'Anna
Marta Dell'Ovo
Laura Gabrielli

The updated version of this chapter can be found at
https://doi.org/10.1007/978-3-030-58814-4_21

O. Gervasi et al. (Eds.): ICCSA 2020, LNCS 12253, p. C1, 2020.
https://doi.org/10.1007/978-3-030-58814-4_66

Author Index

Printed in the United States
By Bookmasters